EUROPE
SINCE 1914
ENCYCLOPEDIA OF THE AGE OF WAR
AND RECONSTRUCTION

EDITORIAL BOARD

SCRIBNER LIBRARY OF MODERN EUROPE

EUROPE
SINCE 1914
ENCYCLOPEDIA OF THE AGE OF WAR AND RECONSTRUCTION

Volume 3

Gadamer to Myrdal

John Merriman and Jay Winter

EDITORS IN CHIEF

CHARLES SCRIBNER'S SONS

An imprint of Thomson Gale, a part of The Thomson Corporation

Detroit • New York • San Francisco • New Haven, Conn. • Waterville, Maine • London • Munich

THOMSON
GALE

Europe since 1914: Encyclopedia of the Age of War and Reconstruction

John Merriman
Jay Winter
Editors in Chief

For permission to use material from this product, submit your request via Web at http://www.gale-edit.com/permissions, or you may download our Permissions Request form and submit your request by fax or mail to:

Permissions Department
Thomson Gale
27500 Drake Road
Farmington Hills, MI 48331-3535
Permissions Hotline:
248-699-8006 or 800-877-4253 ext. 8006
Fax: 248-699-8074 or 800-762-4058

LIBRARY OF CONGRESS CATALOGING-IN-PUBLICATION DATA

Europe since 1914: encyclopedia of the age of war and reconstruction / edited by John Merriman and Jay Winter.
p. cm. — (Scribner library of modern Europe)
Includes bibliographical references and index.
ISBN 0-684-31365-0 (set : alk. paper) — ISBN 0-684-31366-9 (v. 1 : alk. paper) — ISBN 0-684-31367-7 (v. 2 : alk. paper) — ISBN 0-684-31368-5 (v. 3 : alk. paper) — ISBN 0-684-31369-3 (v. 4 : alk. paper) — ISBN 0-684-31370-7 (v. 5 : alk. paper) — ISBN 0-684-31497-5 (e-book)
1. Europe–History–20th century–Encyclopedias. 2. Europe–Civilization–20th century–Encyclopedias. I. Merriman, John M. II. Winter, J. M.
D424.E94 2006
940.503–dc22
2006014427

This title is also available as an e-book and as a ten-volume set with Europe 1789 to 1914:
Encyclopedia of the Age of Industry and Empire.
E-book ISBN 0-684-31497-5
Ten-volume set ISBN 0-684-31530-0
Contact your Gale sales representative for ordering information.

Printed in the United States of America
10 9 8 7 6 5 4 3 2 1

CONTENTS OF THIS VOLUME

CONTENTS OF OTHER VOLUMES

VOLUME 5

MAPS OF EUROPE SINCE 1914

The maps in this section illuminate some of the major events of European history in the twentieth and early twenty-first centuries, including World War I and World War II, the Holocaust, the breakup of Yugoslavia, and the formation of the European Union.

Versailles Settlement

- Newly-formed nations
- Boundaries, 1923

ICELAND

0   200   400 mi.
0   200   400 km

ATLANTIC
OCEAN

NORWAY

SWEDEN

FINLAND

Christiania
(Oslo)

Stockholm

Helsinki
Tallinn   Petrograd
ESTONIA

Riga
LATVIA   Moscow

North
Sea

DENMARK   Copenhagen

LITH.

Danzig   East
Prussia   Kaunas
(Ger.)

UNION OF SOVIET
SOCIALIST REPUBLICS

IRISH
FREE
STATE

UNITED
KINGDOM

London   Amsterdam
NETH.

Berlin

Warsaw

Brussels   GERMANY

POLAND

BELG.

LUX.

Prague

Krakow

Paris   Saar

CZECHOSLOVAKIA

FRANCE

Vienna
Bern   AUSTRIA   Budapest
SWITZ.   HUNGARY   ROMANIA

Venice

Belgrade   Bucharest

ITALY   YUGOSLAVIA

Black Sea

BULGARIA

ANDORRA   Sofia

Madrid   Rome   Tiranë   Constantinople

PORTUGAL   ALBANIA

Lisbon   SPAIN   GREECE   TURKEY

Athens

Tangier
(International   Gibraltar
Territory)

Spanish
Morocco   Mediterranean Sea

Tunisia
(Fr.)

Morocco (Fr.)   Algeria
(Fr.)

Baltic Sea

N

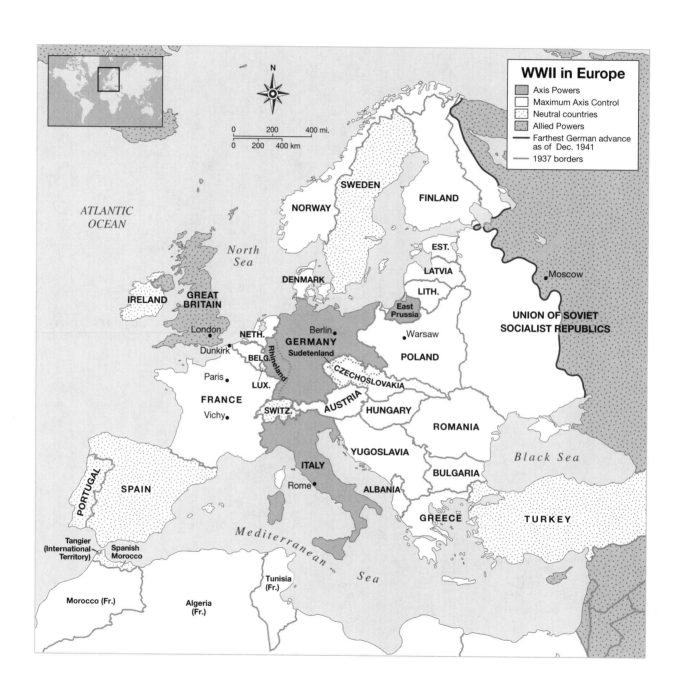

WWII in Europe

- Axis Powers
- Maximum Axis Control
- Neutral countries
- Allied Powers
- Farthest German advance as of Dec. 1941
- 1937 borders

0   200   400 mi.
0   200   400 km

ATLANTIC OCEAN

North Sea

SWEDEN

NORWAY

FINLAND

EST.

LATVIA

LITH.

Moscow

DENMARK

IRELAND

GREAT BRITAIN

London

Dunkirk

NETH.

BELG.

Rhineland

Berlin

GERMANY

Sudetenland

East Prussia

Warsaw

POLAND

UNION OF SOVIET SOCIALIST REPUBLICS

Paris

LUX.

CZECHOSLOVAKIA

FRANCE

Vichy

SWITZ.

AUSTRIA

HUNGARY

ROMANIA

Black Sea

PORTUGAL

SPAIN

ITALY

Rome

YUGOSLAVIA

BULGARIA

ALBANIA

GREECE

TURKEY

Tangier (International Territory)

Spanish Morocco

Mediterranean Sea

Tunisia (Fr.)

Morocco (Fr.)

Algeria (Fr.)

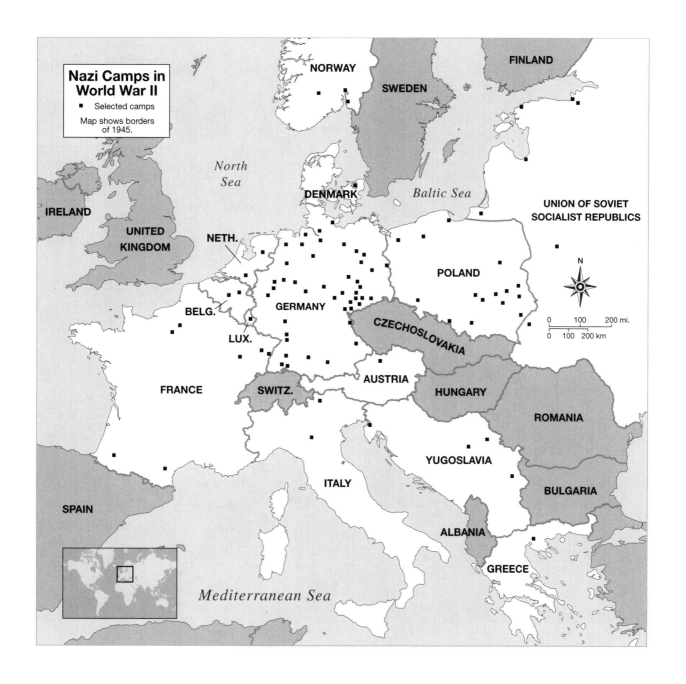

Nazi Camps in World War II
■ Selected camps
Map shows borders of 1945.

NORWAY

SWEDEN

FINLAND

North Sea

IRELAND

UNITED KINGDOM

NETH.

DENMARK

Baltic Sea

UNION OF SOVIET SOCIALIST REPUBLICS

BELG.

GERMANY

POLAND

LUX.

CZECHOSLOVAKIA

FRANCE

SWITZ.

AUSTRIA

HUNGARY

ROMANIA

YUGOSLAVIA

ITALY

BULGARIA

SPAIN

ALBANIA

GREECE

Mediterranean Sea

N

0   100   200 mi.
0 100 200 km

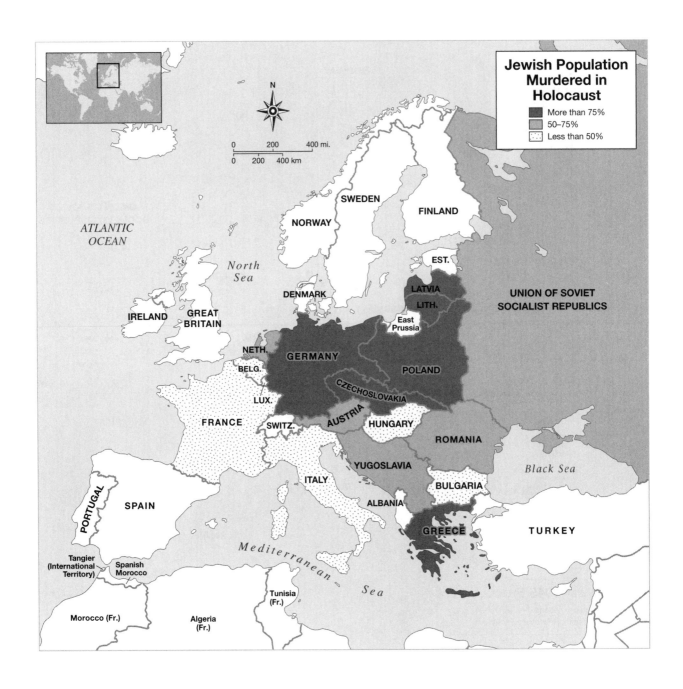

Jewish Population Murdered in Holocaust

- More than 75%
- 50–75%
- Less than 50%

Post 1945 Europe

Communist nations — Iron Curtain
Non-Communist nations ✪ Capital

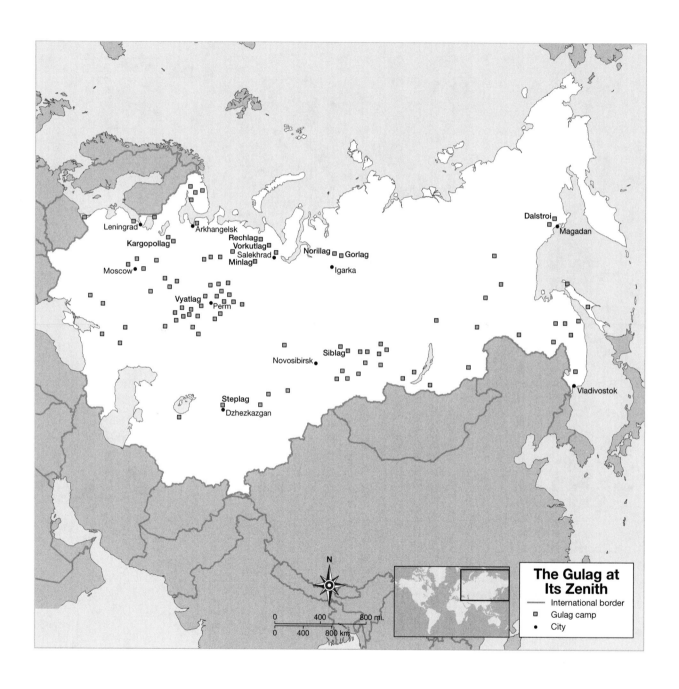

The Gulag at Its Zenith

International border
Gulag camp
City

Dalstroi
Magadan
Leningrad
Arkhangelsk
Rechlag
Vorkutlag
Kargopollag
Salekhrad
Norillag
Gorlag
Minlag
Moscow
Igarka
Vyatlag
Perm
Siblag
Novosibirsk
Steplag
Dzhezkazgan
Vladivostok

N

0   400   800 mi.
0   400   800 km

Yugoslavia Before the Breakup

— International border
–·–·– Republic border
– – – Autonomous area border
⊛ National capital
• Republic or autonomous area capital

AUSTRIA

HUNGARY

ITALY

•Ljubljana
Slovenia

•Zagreb
Croatia

ROMANIA

Vojvodina
•Novi Sad

⊛Belgrade

Bosnia and Herzegovina

•Sarajevo

Serbia

Adriatic Sea

Montenegro

Priština•
Titograd•

Kosovo

BULGARIA

ITALY

•Skopje

Macedonia

N

ALBANIA

0   40   80 mi.
0   40   80 km

GREECE

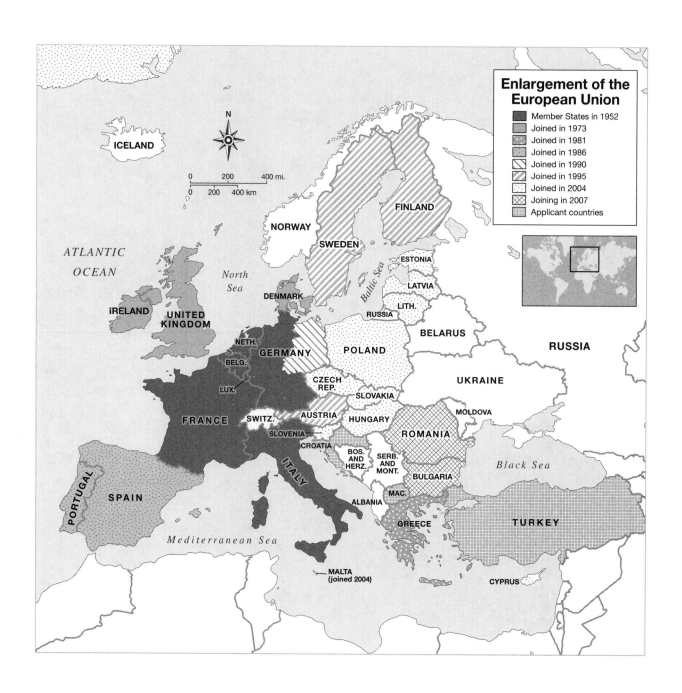

Enlargement of the European Union

- Member States in 1952
- Joined in 1973
- Joined in 1981
- Joined in 1986
- Joined in 1990
- Joined in 1995
- Joined in 2004
- Joining in 2007
- Applicant countries

GADAMER, HANS-GEORG (1900–2002), German philosopher influential in the development of twentieth-century philosophical hermeneutics.

Born in Marburg, Germany, Hans-Georg Gadamer studied philosophy in Breslau and Marburg, completing his dissertation in 1922. He was influenced by the poetry of Stefan George and other writers, thus balancing early tendencies toward philosophical abstraction through his engagement with the arts. He also had close contact with the Marburg School of Protestant theology. In 1923 he met Martin Heidegger and became his student and assistant in Freiburg. He studied classical philology and in 1928 completed his *Habilitation* under Heidegger. His academic career led him to teaching positions in Marburg (1928–1934), Kiel (1934–1935), Leipzig (1938–1947), Frankfurt/Main (1947–1948), and Heidelberg (1948–1968). After his retirement in 1968 he repeatedly taught in the United States.

Gadamer is best known for his pathbreaking work in philosophical hermeneutics, a field that he himself established. This new approach was first developed in *Truth and Method* (*Wahrheit und Methode*, 1960), although Gadamer revised and refined his thinking over the next four decades. Traditionally hermeneutics (from the Greek word *hermeneuein*, "to comprehend") refers to the correct interpretation and understanding of texts, first those of a religious nature and since the Renaissance also of ancient literary and philosophical texts.

Gadamer, by developing ideas introduced by Heidegger in lectures in the early 1920s, shifted hermeneutics from a technical skill that was meant to guarantee correct interpretations of texts to a characteristic of human existence that required philosophical interpretation. Hermeneutics was thus promoted from a theory of adequate textual understanding to the status of a fundamental philosophical discipline.

Understanding in Gadamer's reworking of hermeneutics no longer refers to a learned skill but rather to the fact that we are compelled to regard ourselves as always embedded in a tradition and in a community, both of which precede us. While we always find ourselves situated within already existing conditions, understanding does not so much refer to the act of catching up with the preexisting situation but rather to the act of communication with the conditions in which both we ourselves and the conditions are adjusted. Tradition is thus defined as linguistic to a great degree. Fundamentally, we take over preexisting conditions and traditions to a much larger extent than we challenge or alter them. Understanding is hence more an act of agreement with traditions than a critical distancing from them. Still, we are free to challenge traditions as well as continue them, yet both attitudes require a conscious decision. Keeping traditions alive is not automatism but requires our willing participation. This is why Gadamer wants to overcome the Enlightenment's negative valuation of prejudices. For him, it is not only impossible to move beyond all our inherited prejudices, it is also simply undesirable to attempt this as prejudices transmit to us the attitudes and values of the society in which we live. For Gadamer, the self is always secondary to the encompassing forces of history. But unlike the poststructuralist thinkers or his teacher Heidegger, he does not advocate the disappearance of the subject and instead holds fast to the humanist tradition.

At times the reception of his theories was rather controversial. Jürgen Habermas and Karl-Otto Apel of the second generation of the Frankfurt School attacked him for uncritically defending tradition and the status quo. The French deconstructionist Jacques Derrida declared that Gadamer's emphasis on understanding destroys the right of the interlocutor to remain different and unreconciled. With both camps Gadamer engaged in long debates in which he came to emphasize more the critical potential of his philosophical hermeneutics.

Apart from his writings on philosophical hermeneutics, Gadamer published extensively on the history of philosophy, especially ancient authors, German idealism, and phenomenology, as well as on art, literature, music, medicine, politics, ethics, anthropology, and so on. Art occupies a central place in Gadamer's philosophy because he claims that technologized science can only advance very limited truth claims whereas art is able to disclose to us much more fundamental truths of our existence. For him, technology and science depend in their work on a previous opening of a realm of inquiry that is achieved by art's truth. To understand a work of art means to engage in a dialogue with it that actualizes the work and simultaneously changes the recipient in the course of the encounter. Neither artwork nor viewer and reader have a predetermined essence. The meaning of the work and its relevance for our lives emerge from the dialogue between artwork and recipient.

Against technology's project to render the world both predictable and controllable Gadamer pits the wisdom of antiquity. Ancient philosophy can teach us that the Cartesian subject-object duality is nothing final; it can be corrected through an active and reflective embeddedness in the world, an attitude that characterized the *theoria* of the ancients. Greek philosophy can serve as a corrective to our thinking through three means. First, it brings to our attention the limits of all attempts to reify the world. Rather than seeing the world as an accumulation of objects waiting to be manipulated by us, Greek philosophy's concept of *pragma* reminds us of our connectedness with our surroundings. Second, ancient thought insists on the limits of the self by emphasizing our communal life, most dominantly in the institution of friendship that is of paramount importance for ancient thinkers. Third, we learn about the limits of self-comprehension in our encounters with Greek thinkers: self-consciousness is secondary to our interaction with the world.

Gadamer's hermeneutics greatly influenced the methodological self-reflection of a wide variety of disciplines like theology, jurisprudence, sociology, and literary studies. Outside of Germany, Gadamer's influence is particularly strong in Italy, France, Japan, and the United States. The publication of his *Collected Works* (1985–1995) brought a renewal of interest in Gadamer's philosophical writings, and the process of translation into English and many other languages is still ongoing.

See also **Habermas, Jürgen; Heidegger, Martin.**

BIBLIOGRAPHY

Primary Sources

Gadamer, Hans-Georg. *Gadamer in Conversation: Reflections and Commentary.* Translated by Richard E. Palmer. New Haven, Conn., 2001.

Gadamer, Hans-Georg, and Lewis Edwin Hahn. *The Philosophy of Hans-Georg Gadamer.* Chicago, 1996.

Secondary Sources

Hammermeister, Kai. *Hans-Georg Gadamer.* Munich, 1999.

How, Alan. *The Habermas-Gadamer Debate and the Nature of the Social: Back to Bedrock.* Bookfield, Vt., 1995.

Malpas, Jeff, Ulrich Arnswald, and Jens Kertscher, eds. *Gadamer's Century: Essays in Honor of Hans-Georg Gadamer.* Cambridge, Mass., 2002.

KAI HAMMERMEISTER

GAELIC REVIVALS (IRELAND AND SCOTLAND).

Although it is uncertain when speakers of the Gaelic language first came to Ireland, by the fifth century C.E. it was well established as the dominant language. By the end of the first millennium, it also became the main language spoken in Scotland. Thereafter, the Gaelic-speaking community was fragmented, initially by Norse incursions and later by the expansion northward and westward of English kingdoms. Differences subsequently developed between the language as spoken in Ireland (Irish) and the variant spoken in Scotland (Scots-Gaelic). There are still substantial similarities between the northern dialects of Irish and the southern dialects of Scots-Gaelic.

In demographic and spatial terms, the contraction of Scots-Gaelic in the face of the spread of English began in the eleventh century, and its retreat into the Highlands and Islands of Scotland was complete by the late fourteenth century. In Ireland, by contrast, Irish was still the dominant spoken language on the island until the end of the sixteenth century. But in the seventeenth century the Irish aristocratic families were overpowered and dispossessed by English forces and relatively large numbers of native-born English were introduced to form a new landlord class. Over the eighteenth century the shift to English spread through the urban network, diffusing into the rural hinterland along a general east-west axis. Census data would suggest that about 25 percent of the population, about 1.5 million people, were Irish-speaking by 1851. At this time, only about 11 percent of the population of Scotland (three hundred thousand people) spoke Gaelic.

LANGUAGE REVIVAL IN THE NINETEENTH CENTURY

Beginning in the late eighteenth century a succession of learned societies in Ireland showed an academic interest in the Irish language. The most influential language organization in the nineteenth century—Conradh na Gaeilge (The Gaelic League, established in 1893)—set itself objectives that far exceeded the limited ambitions of these earlier organizations. Its goals were the revival of Irish in areas where it had ceased to be spoken and the creation of a new modern literature in Irish. Within fifteen years after its foundation some 950 branches (with an estimated membership of one hundred thousand) had been established. Nonetheless, its political achievements before 1900 were limited.

In the same period, and for much the same reasons, there was a surge of interest and concern with the decline of Scots-Gaelic. An Comunn Gàidhealach (The Gaelic Society) was founded in 1891 to seek the preservation and development of the Scots-Gaelic language. Within the framework of the 1872 Education Act, it encouraged the teaching, learning, and use of the Gaelic language and the study and cultivation of Gaelic literature, history, music, and art. The Association also established an annual Gaelic Festival ("The Mod") modeled on the Welsh Eisteddfod.

LANGUAGE REVIVAL IN THE TWENTIETH CENTURY

In the early decades of the twentieth century, the political independence movement in Ireland incorporated the objectives of Conradh na Gaeilge into its program. However, only the southern part of the island became independent in 1922, first as the Irish Free State, later as the Republic of Ireland, but six counties in the northeast remained within the United Kingdom, forming the semiautonomous region of Northern Ireland. At that time, there were significant differences in the ethno-religious composition of the respective populations. The Republic of Ireland was predominantly (93 percent) Catholic and Nationalist, while Northern Ireland, by contrast was predominantly (62 percent) Protestant and unionist. As a result, the objectives and shape of language policy in subsequent years sharply diverged in the two jurisdictions.

In the Republic of Ireland the new native government adopted a broad strategy to enhance the social and legal status of Irish, to maintain its use in areas where it was still spoken, and to promote and revive its use elsewhere. A central element of the strategy was a new education policy designed to ensure, to the fullest extent possible, competence in Irish through appropriate school programs. For most of the twentieth century Irish was a compulsory subject on the curriculum in primary and secondary schools.

Traditional Irish-speaking areas were scattered along the western and southern coasts (in Ireland and Scotland, these areas were collectively referred to as the *Gaeltacht* and *Gaidhealtachd*). As these areas were among the most impoverished and remote areas in the state, this dimension of the strategy took on the character of a regional economic-development program.

A third element of the language strategy concerned the use of Irish within the public service.

Establishing the Irish language among state employees was considered critical, not only to ensure the provision of state services in Irish but also to create a section within middle-class occupations where Irish would be the norm. Finally, the language policy of the state required the use of Irish in public administration, in law, in education, and in the media. These were domains in which Irish had not been used for centuries. Therefore, a fourth element of the strategy focused on measures to standardize and modernize the language itself.

Although performance was by no means uniform either between or within different language-policy elements, this revival strategy was implemented with a good deal of determination and commitment and had some limited success between 1925 and about 1950. Since the mid-1960s, some key elements of the strategy have been scaled back, while at the same time the state has tried to develop other policy initiatives in, for example, television and radio services.

By contrast, throughout most of the twentieth century in Northern Ireland Irish had no official status, and it was a marginal and optional subject in the curriculum. With a permanent Protestant majority in the Northern Ireland parliament after 1922, unionist values dominated educational policy. While the teaching of Irish in the schools was not proscribed, its time in the schedule was restricted. Those wishing to learn Irish had to rely on the goodwill of some, but by no means all, Catholic schools and the informal educational activities of Conradh na Gaeilge. However, as the twentieth century moved into its closing decades, the political conflict in Northern Ireland generated a new impetus in the realm of language and cultural policy. In 1989 Irish was recognized as a second language in post-primary schools. There were also some advances in the provision of all-Irish or immersion education. The Good Friday Agreement between Northern Ireland politicians and the Irish and British governments (10 April 1998) consolidated and extended this development. The agreement included a separate and detailed section dealing expressly with Irish-language issues.

By comparison with Irish in the Republic of Ireland, Scots-Gaelic has no official status in Scotland and only very limited legal protection. The revival effort has been more low-key and more inclined to operate within existing frameworks than its Irish counterparts. Nonetheless, there are a number of acts of parliament that make provision for Gaelic in the domains of education, broadcasting, and the arts. At the local level, the Western Isles Council, which includes Gaelic-speaking districts in its area of responsibility, has been implementing a bilingual policy since its establishment in the 1970s. The position of Gaelic in the education system has improved over recent decades. In 1985 the government set up Comunn na Gàidhlig, a representative body to coordinate and promote public and private activities relating to Gaelic.

LANGUAGE REVIVAL: SUCCESS OR FAILURE?
At the end of the first millennium the Gaelic-speaking area encompassed all of Ireland and much of present-day Scotland. At the end of the second millennium, Irish-speaking communities survived only on the western and northern coasts of the original territories. Elsewhere, Irish and Scots-Gaelic are minority languages spoken among rather diffuse and dispersed networks of speakers in urban areas. Furthermore, these speakers are now located in three different political jurisdictions, and this has given a different character and focus to the language-revival effort in each case.

In census returns for 2001–2002, some 1.6 million persons were labeled as Irish speakers in the Republic of Ireland and 130,000 persons in Northern Ireland. This compares with a combined total of 650,000 Irish-speakers in both areas in the 1901 census. However, survey research suggests that census statistics overestimate the numbers fluent or nearly fluent in Irish—the surveys place this proportion at about 10 percent. They further indicate that less than 5 percent of the national population uses Irish as their first or main language, while a further 10 percent uses Irish regularly but less intensively.

Although the population of the Gaeltacht has declined in both absolute and relative terms, there has been a gradual, but continual, revival in the ratios of Irish speakers in other regions. Most Irish children learn Irish in both primary and secondary school as a subject. However, these improvements are mainly due to the capacity of the schools, rather than the home and community, to produce competent bilinguals.

In Scotland the statistical picture is less reassuring. In 2001 some 58,000 persons speak Scots-Gaelic, but this was down from 65,000 in 1991 and 210,000 in 1901 (5.2 percent). Nonetheless, even in Scotland there has been an increase in the numbers of people who learn Gaelic, and there was a slight increase between 1991 and 2001 in the proportion of Gaelic speakers between the ages of three and twenty-four.

Thus, while there has been no return to the Golden Age of Gaeldom, neither can the impact of the Irish and Scottish revivals be described as negligible. In Ireland, in particular, there was some real measure of maintenance and revival over the twentieth century. But the long-term future of the Irish language is not any more secure now than it was then, and the position of Scots-Gaelic looks quite precarious at the start of the twenty-first century.

See also **Education; Ireland; Scotland.**

BIBLIOGRAPHY

Hutchinson, John. *The Dynamics of Cultural Nationalism: The Gaelic Revival and the Creation of the Irish Nation State*. London and Boston, 1987.

Mac Póilin, Aodán, ed. *The Irish Language in Northern Ireland*. Belfast, 1997.

McCoy, Gordon, with Maolcholain Scott, eds. *Gaelic Identities: Aithne na nGael*. Belfast, 2000.

ó Cuív, Brian Póilin, ed. *A View of the Irish Language*. Dublin, 1969.

ó Riagáin, Pádraig. *Language Policy and Social Reproduction: Ireland 1893–1993*. Oxford, U.K., and New York, 1997.

Withers, Charles W. J. *Gaelic in Scotland 1698–1981: The Geographical History of a Language*. Edinburgh and Atlantic Highlands, N.J., 1984.

PÁDRAIG Ó RIAGÁIN

GAGARIN, YURI (1934–1968), Soviet cosmonaut and national hero.

On 12 April 1961 Yuri Alexeyevich Gagarin became the first human to leave Earth's atmosphere. While his feat triggered the most intense demonstrations of support for the regime since the end of World War II, it also transformed Gagarin into an iconic figure. Just twenty-seven years old when he made his historic flight, Gagarin was the "positive hero" of Soviet socialist realist fiction come to life: good looking, optimistic, and always able to flash his trademark smile. He was an uncomplicated man who believed the clichés and propagandistic claims of the regimes. Above all, he followed orders—even to his death in 1968, when his test flight of a new Soviet fighter jet ended in tragedy.

Gagarin's down-to-earth personality, combined with his above-earth heroics, made him ideal material for myth construction. Like the ideal new Soviet man he was a kind of palimpsest onto which a myriad of meanings and political agendas could be imprinted. "Gagarin was a servant of the cult," said one Russian journalist who covered his flight. "He was the guy who lived next door—but in reality he was one of the Gods. . . . [I]n the collective subconscious space was interpreted as a kind of replacement for the banned church" (*Izvestiya*, 3 March 2004).

Additionally, Gagarin's feat resonated with a population exhausted by the painful sacrifices of World War II and the ongoing burdens of socialist construction. Facing postwar reconstruction and global competition with a vastly richer enemy, Gagarin was seeming proof that Soviet culture could tackle the ideological and security challenges of the Cold War. Similar to John F. Kennedy in the United States, he suggested that Soviet society embodied youth, dynamism, technological progress, peaceful development, and the triumph of justice.

It was an image desperately sought by increasingly enfeebled Soviet leaders. The 1960s marked a kind of midlife crisis in the Soviet leadership, almost all of whom had begun their careers in the 1930s and 1940s. While Soviet leaders of the 1960s were tainted by their association with Joseph Stalin's terrifying purges, Gagarin had a morally unambiguous ascent into the rarified air of Soviet heroism. Through him leaders such as Nikita Khrushchev, as well as ordinary Soviet citizens, vicariously recaptured the romanticism and heroism of their revolutionary youth—minus the moral complexities brought about by Stalin's terror, since Gagarin was too young to be implicated in the purges of the 1930s.

Yuri Gagarin is given a bouquet of roses by a young English girl while visiting the Soviet Embassy in London, 1961. ©HULTON-DEUTSCH COLLECTION/CORBIS

Born on one of the new Soviet collective farms (in the village of Klushino, not far from the town of Gzhatsk, which was named after him following his death), Gagarin was the quintessential Soviet success story. He studied at a technical college, where he graduated with honors. Subsequently he enrolled in an aviation school in Orenburg, where he received a commission as a lieutenant in 1957. Noticed by Moscow higher-ups for his loyalty, common-man roots, and talents as a pilot, he was summoned to Moscow in 1959, and in March 1960 he was chosen as a member of the elite cosmonaut squad.

Gagarin's death continues to be shrouded in mystery. When the MiG-15 fighter jet he was testing flew too close to a nearby MiG-21 in March 1968, it went into a steep downward descent. Air traffic controllers then gave improper data to Gagarin, reporting that his altitude was higher than it actually was. When Gagarin pulled up the nose he was three seconds too late, and he crashed into the ground. The official investigation, unlike the Warren Commission report on Kennedy, was not released until 1988. But like John F. Kennedy's death, Gagarin's tragic flight spawned numerous conspiracy theories and dark rumors. They asserted that insiders jealous of his fame and concerned about his politics supposedly arranged it all and concealed the truth from the Soviet population. Even Gagarin's widow was skeptical. She refused to accept the official version, which is probably true, that his death was an accident. With Gagarin's tragic death at the age of thirty-four a symbol of youthful regeneration, idealism, and innocence also passed away.

Even though the Soviet Union has collapsed, the cult of Gagarin lives on. He continues to embody traits that many Russian citizens and leaders long to restore: optimism; an unflinching desire to serve the state and its cause; and an extreme tolerance for enduring trying situations with a sense of calm and good humor. A 2004 survey of Russians found that respondents ranked Gagarin's flight as the most significant event in Russia's modern history—second only to defeat of the Nazis in World War II. In 2001 the Russian Federation honored Gagarin's flight with a fortieth anniversary ten-ruble coin, making him the first Soviet figure to be officially celebrated on a post-Soviet coin.

See also Soviet Union; Space Programs; Sputnik.

BIBLIOGRAPHY

Doran, Jamie. *Starman: The Truth behind the Legend of Yuri Gagarin*. London, 1998.

Rossoshanskii, Vladimir Ivanovich. *Fenomen Gagarina*. Saratov, Russia, 2001.

Soviet Man in Space. London, 1961.

ANDREW L. JENKS

GANDHI, MAHATMA (Mohandas Karamchand Gandhi 1869–1948), Indian nationalist and spiritual leader.

Mohandas Karamchand Gandhi was born on 2 October 1869 in Porbandar (now part of Gujarat) into a merchant-caste family that had provided chief ministers and advisors to local rulers. In 1888 he trained as a barrister in England but faced professional failure in India. A reprieve came in 1893, when he was engaged by an Indian firm in South Africa, where he lived until 1914.

Gandhi's encounters with racial prejudice moved him to oppose discriminatory government policies on behalf of Indians in South Africa. In the process he acquired an arsenal of skills in political mobilization and publicity through papers, pamphlets, and correspondence. In 1909 Gandhi wrote *Hind Swaraj* (Indian Home Rule), a tract encapsulating much of his political philosophy. It embodies a powerful indictment of modern industrial civilization and the competitive materialism that produced imperial oppression. The British held India not by the sword but because Indians lured by English goods and institutions had given it to them. Therefore he emphasized the need to subvert British cultural and moral hegemony. The railways, the telegraph, hospitals, lawyers, machinery,

and other emblems of colonial modernity must be discarded. He idealized the simple village life as representing the "real" India of time immemorial. These views were to resonate among millions of India's peasants and artisans ruined by colonialism. Gandhi also insisted in *Hind Swaraj* that the ends of freedom could not justify the means of violence to achieve them. The "force of love or the soul," which would persuade the British of the error of their ways, was more powerful than any "force of arms."

When Gandhi returned to India in 1915, the Indian National Congress had returned to a quiescent political state. Although some congressmen had heard of his work in South Africa, his methods were deemed impracticable in India. In 1917 and 1918 Gandhi led three localized but successful movements of nonviolent resistance that demonstrated the effectiveness of his political strategy and leadership: in Champaran (Bihar) he won concessions for peasants forced to grow indigo; in Kheda district (Gujarat) he backed peasant protest against the state's high revenue demand; and in Ahmedabad (Gujarat) he negotiated a compromise between striking workers and mill-owners. By 1920, supported by Muslim leaders discontented with the postwar treatment of the Ottoman sultan and caliph, Gandhi captured strategic control of the Congress. The party endorsed his program for nonviolent noncooperation. Beginning with a boycott of British goods and institutions, resistance escalated to civil disobedience, with thousands defying laws and refusing to pay taxes.

While Gandhi undeniably revolutionized nationalist politics by shaping Congress into a potent mass-based tool of resistance, his achievement can be overestimated. Balancing conflicting interests to forge anticolonial unity also produced conservative compromises. Thus while sanctioning no-revenue campaigns he opposed peasant demands for no-rent drives that might alienate Indian landlords. Although condemning the practice of untouchability, he did not repudiate the upper-caste-dominated system that produced it. Moreover, peasant and worker radicalism owed as much to colonial economic policies and wartime dislocation as to Gandhi's influence. His skill lay in harnessing this popular tumult. Furthermore, Gandhi's prestige did not stem solely from the appeal of his ideas. Through rumors, peasants

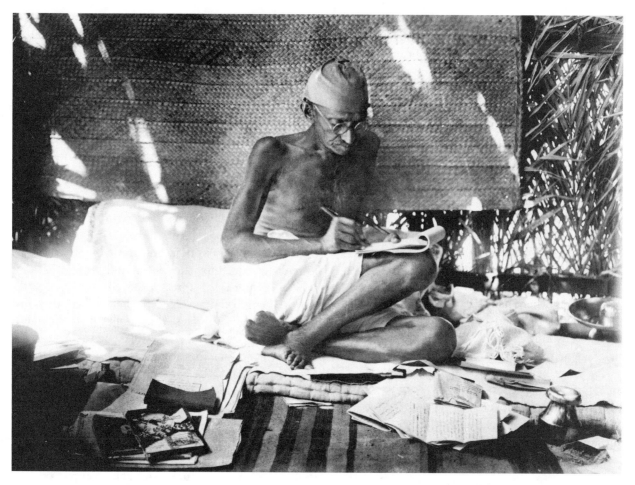

Mahatma Gandhi c. 1932. ©HULTON DEUTSCH COLLECTION/CORBIS

fashioned Gandhi to fit their millenarian hopes, reinterpreting his message to justify even violent acts that contravened his program. Aware of this volatile element in populist politics, Gandhi needed his masses fully disciplined. Therefore, when peasants killed twenty-two policemen in the northern town of Chauri Chauri in February 1922, he promptly suspended noncooperation.

Gandhi resumed civil disobedience in 1930 by marching to the sea to manufacture salt in violation of the government's monopoly. Depression had produced hardship and fresh grounds for political activism, rallying multitudes behind Gandhi until colonial suppression and 120,000 arrests ended the movement in 1934. With the Japanese advancing rapidly toward India during World War II, the British reopened discussions with Indian nationalists. But the meager concessions of the mission of Labour MP Richard Stafford Cripps in early 1942 prompted Gandhi to launch the "Quit India" movement on 8 August 1942. In this,

his last, nationwide campaign described by one historian as the "most un-Gandhian," the Mahatma appeared tacitly to accept the necessity of violence to free India. Although severe reprisals quickly snuffed out the agitation, it was the largest civilian uprising since the 1857 rebellion.

Although many factors combine to explain British decolonization in India, the cumulative effect of Gandhi's campaigns cannot be denied. While none had succeeded in driving out the British immediately, by provoking heavy-handed coercion they each eroded British moral authority and exposed colonialism's foundation not in consent but in brute force. But the India the British left in 1947 was not the nation whose freedom Gandhi had struggled so long for. Repeatedly declaring "the idea that Hinduism and Islam represent two antagonistic cultures" anathema to his soul, not only was he powerless to stop the partition of India amid a bloodbath, but he also saw it as his personal failure. In 1946 and 1947 he spent weeks, jeopardizing his own life, touring riot-torn areas to douse religious anger. Ironically, Nathuram Godse, a Hindu zealot with links to religious nationalists, assassinated Gandhi on 30 January 1948, holding him responsible for the humiliation of partition.

Dubbed the father of the Indian nation, Gandhi's ideas were embraced by leaders of protest movements across the globe. His principled abnegation of violence in politics inspired pacifists such as the American Richard Gregg in the 1920s and 1930s. Martin Luther King Jr. (1929–1968) found in Gandhi's movement a potent and Christian base for the mobilization of African Americans. Gandhi's nonviolent resistance in India showed that the "weak" everywhere had available a weapon effective against the best-armed tyrant. Even for individuals such as Nelson Mandela (b. 1918), who found nonviolence ineffectual against the South African apartheid regime, he symbolized the valiant stand of the oppressed. Perhaps Gandhi's most powerful contribution to political movements the world over was a moral activism that insistently refused to accept injustice.

See also **Colonialism; India; Pacifism.**

BIBLIOGRAPHY

Primary Sources

Gandhi, Mahatma. *Hind Swaraj, and Other Writings.* Edited by Anthony J. Parel. Cambridge, U.K, 1997.

Secondary Sources

Amin, Shahid. "Gandhi as Mahatma: Gorakhpur District, Eastern U.P., 1921–22." In *Selected Subaltern Studies,* edited by Ranajit Guha and Gayatri Chakravorty Spivak. New York, 1988.

Arnold, David. *Gandhi.* Harlow, U.K., 2001.

Brown, Judith M. *Gandhi's Rise to Power: Indian Politics, 1915–1922.* Cambridge, U.K., 1972.

———. *Gandhi and Civil Disobedience: The Mahatma in Indian Politics, 1928–1934.* Cambridge, U.K., 1977.

Dalton, Dennis. *Mahatma Gandhi: Nonviolent Power in Action.* New York, 1993.

Hardiman, David. *Gandhi in His Time and Ours.* Delhi and London, 2003.

Parekh, Bhikhu. *Gandhi's Political Philosophy: A Critical Examination.* Basingstoke, U.K., 1989.

MRIDU RAI

GARCÍA LORCA, FEDERICO (1898–1936), Spanish poet, playwright, musician, and artist.

Federico García Lorca is one of the great creative geniuses in the literary and cultural history of Spain, and, along with Miguel de Cervantes (1547–1616), his country's most celebrated and universal figure. One of the most striking characteristics of his creativity is his dazzling versatility. Primarily known for his poetry and theater, he was also an accomplished pianist, a composer of enduring popular songs, adept with the flamenco guitar and conversant with its culture, and a talented graphic artist, whose drawings and paintings have been increasingly recognized and acclaimed. This multifaceted talent gives a special vitality and richness to each of his creative dimensions. His drawings reflect and express the pain and private dilemma expressed in his poetry. His poetry skillfully exploits the lyric qualities of popular song and the dramatic possibilities of the folk ballad. And his theater enhances beautifully its dramatic portraits and representations with songs, lullabies, and lyric poetry.

Lorca's life and works must be understood against the background of an emerging modern Spain, undergoing a historical period of crisis and transition, from roughly the 1830s to the 1930s. The Carlist civil wars of the nineteenth century (1833–1839, 1872–1876) pitted the struggle of a "new" liberal Spain, embodying the democratic aspirations of middle class, and, toward the end of the century, working class peoples, against "old" Spain, traditional, monarchical, and oligarchical, embodying the power and privileges of the great landowners, a financial and industrial elite, the Catholic Church, and the army. This struggle of the "two Spains," left unresolved at the conclusion of the nineteenth century, reasserted itself again dramatically during the first four decades of the twentieth century. The triumph of the Second Spanish Republic (1931–1939), through democratic elections, augured well for the new Spain. But the oscillating fortunes of the new government, progressive for the first two years, regressive and repressive over the next two, led finally to the election on 16 February 1936 of the Popular Front government, the most advanced democracy in Spanish history. The radical measures of the new government provoked the insurrection by Francisco Franco (1892–1975) on 17 July 1936 and the explosion of yet another and more violent civil war (1936–1939), in which the nationalist forces of Franco were only able to prevail because of the decisive intervention and support of Nazi Germany and fascist Italy. Lorca, along with hundreds of citizens of his native Granada, was assassinated by a fascist squad on the outskirts of his city one month after the July uprising. The poet was a brilliant member of a resurgent new Spain, and one of the first victims of the treachery, terror, and cruelty of old Spain.

Lorca was born in Fuente Vaqueros, a small village a few miles west of Granada. His father was a prosperous farmer and his mother a dedicated schoolteacher, and he was always to enjoy the support and affection of a large and talented family. He was a precocious child and developed early into a gifted pianist and skillful mimic, who would delight family and friends at parties and social gatherings with improvised dramatizations. In 1915, he entered the University of Granada where he studied law and developed a serious interest at the same time in literature and folklore.

In 1919, he left Granada for Madrid, where he spent eight of the next ten years at the Residencia de Estudiantes (Residence of students), a kind of Spanish version of an Oxford College. Its liberal and progressive atmosphere and close friendships with the leading creative talents of his generation— Rafael Alberti (1902–1999), Luis Buñuel (1900–1983), and Salvador Dalí (1904–1989)—were to have an important influence on his intellectual and artistic development. In 1921, he published his first work, *Libro de poemas* (Book of poems). In 1927, he published what was almost immediately acknowledged as a major work of poetry, *Canciones* (Songs); scored his first dramatic success with a play, *Mariana Pineda,* based upon the Spanish liberal heroine of the early nineteenth century; and held a show of colored drawings in Barcelona. The appearance of his *Romancero Gitano* (Gypsy ballads) in 1928 was an immediate success, converted its author into a national celebrity within a few weeks, and became one of the most celebrated volumes of Hispanic poetry in the twentieth century.

The overwhelming success of this volume "for the wrong reasons," according to Lorca, and an emotional crisis caused by a failed personal relationship plunged the poet into a period of deep depression. On the advice of family and friends, he traveled abroad and took up residence at Columbia University for much of the nine months he spent in the United States. His experience of New York City was at once painful and liberating and inspired some of his most exciting and profound work. *Poeta en Nueva York* (Poet in New York, 1929–1930) is perhaps his supreme poetic masterpiece. Written during the Wall Street crash of 1929, it portrays a surrealistic vision of the megalopolitan jungle of the urban center, expresses compassion for the oppressed African American community of Harlem, horror at the impersonal, mechanistic forces of a cruel, inhuman system, and moral outrage at the betrayal of Christianity by Western civilization. The poetic personality lays bare the anguish of his tormented soul and makes explicit certain inner secrets of psyche—his condition of homosexuality, contained, but disguised, in the earlier poetry. Lorca began, though did not complete, two plays at this time, two masterpieces of experimental theater: *El público* (The public), and *Así que pasen cinco años* (Once five years pass). Dream autobiography, the themes of homosexual love and identity, the drama of a divided personality and the various masks it assumes, are the means by which Lorca introduces entirely new material to the Spanish stage and through which he proposes to create a revolutionary theater.

New York was followed by three months of a successful and joyful visit to Cuba. Liberated to an important degree and having a heightened awareness of himself and society, Lorca was ready to return to Spain and to participate with great energy and commitment in the cultural and educational programs of the Second Spanish Republic. He returned to Spain in June of 1930 and from this time until his assassination, he devoted himself primarily to the theater. Here, as nowhere else, did he passionately identify himself with the needs, interests, and education of the Spanish common people. He wrote *Bodas de sangre* (Blood wedding) and saw it play with great success throughout 1933 in Madrid, Barcelona, and Buenos Aires. He founded his own theater group, La Barraca (The hut or cabin), composed mostly of students playing during vacation time. With a government subsidy, he and his group traveled throughout Spain performing to rural audiences. The purpose was to bring the classics to the forgotten people, lost in the isolated and remote areas of rural Spain, and to put them in contact with the best tradition of Spanish art and theater.

In 1933–1934, Lorca again traveled overseas, to Buenos Aires and Montevideo, where he produced mainly Spanish classical plays. At this time, he met and formed a close friendship, a fraternal bond, with the great Chilean poet Pablo Neruda (1904–1973). Back in Spain, Lorca brought to a conclusion his tragic trilogy, *Bodas de sangre*, *Yerma* (the name of the female protagonist and a word meaning "barren"), and *La casa de Bernarda Alba* (The house of Bernarda Alba), completing this latter, his masterpiece, by mid-June 1936, just two months before his violent death. In these rural dramas, the playwright depicts with intensity and artistry the drama, the feuding, and the suffering of the Spanish people, with special sympathy for women, seen as victims of an inhuman social and moral code. Through his theater, Lorca believed he could raise the level of consciousness of his audience and develop the sensibility of his people to prepare them for social change, for movement into a more humane and liberated world. Indeed, throughout his work, in both poetry and theater, he was the champion of the marginalized and the dispossessed, the Andalusian gypsies of southern Spain, the black community of Harlem, the women of rural Spain, and homosexuals everywhere. It is clear that he was seen as a dangerous social force, as a threat to the old order, by the traditionalist, fascist, homophobic ruling authorities of Granada and Seville who ordered his execution.

The lyric cry of Federico García Lorca on behalf of the downtrodden, his dramatic protest against social injustice, and his redemptive vision of a liberated humanity speak to the twenty-first century with as much urgency as in his own day. He has left an enduring legacy of the very best poetry and theater written in the twentieth century.

See also **Spain; Theater.**

BIBLIOGRAPHY

Primary Sources

García Lorca, Federico. *Collected Plays.* Translated by James Graham-Luján and Richard L. O'Connell. London, 1976.

———. *Once Five Years Pass and Other Dramatic Works.* Translated by William Bryant Logan and Angel Gil Orrios. New York, 1989.

———. *Obras completas.* Edición de Miguel García-Posada. 4 vols. Barcelona, 1996–1997.

———. *Collected Poems.* Rev. ed. Translated by Catherine Brown et al. New York, 2002. The most complete collection of Lorca's poetry available in English.

Secondary Sources

Barea, Arturo. *Lorca: The Poet and His People.* London, 1944.

Edwards, Gwyne. *Lorca: The Theatre Beneath the Sand.* London, 1987.

García Lorca, Francisco. *Federico García Lorca y su mundo.* Edición y prólogo de Mario Hernández. Madrid, 1992.

Gibson, Ian. *Vida, pasión y muerte de Federico García Lorca.* Barcelona, 1992.

Morris, C. Brian. *Son of Andalusia. The Lyrical Landscapes of Federico García Lorca.* Liverpool, 1997.

Smith, Paul Julian. *The Theatre of García Lorca.* Cambridge, U.K., 1998.

Stainton, Leslie. *Lorca. A Dream of Life.* New York, 1999.

MICHAEL P. PREDMORE

GARZÓN, BALTASAR (b. 1955), Spanish investigative judge.

Baltasar Garzón worked to convert the cause of human rights into a matter of extraterritorial judicial action. He was born in the southern Spanish town of Villa de Torres and became a provincial judge at the age of twenty-three, three years after the death of the right-wing dictator Francisco Franco (1892–1975). Garzón was appointed a judge of the National Court in 1987 and served as one of six investigating judges.

In 1993 he stepped down from the judiciary and stood as a Socialist candidate for parliament, where he won a seat. A year later, he returned to the bench, where he felt he could make more of a difference. His work in this post was both high profile and politically explosive. He investigated the criminal activity of the Grupos Armados de Liberación (GAL), an assassination squad set up in the early 1980s by the Socialist government of Spain to eliminate Basque separatists. Indictments and convictions followed. Over the next decade, his investigative work expanded to include gathering evidence on drug trafficking, political corruption, and Islamic terrorism. All these criminal activities are transnational in character. In these inquiries, Garzón altered the field of international criminal law by insisting on his right to investigate crimes committed against Spanish nationals wherever those crimes took place. He also made it clear that prominent political figures were not immune from his investigation.

He became internationally prominent for an international arrest warrant he issued in October 1998 to detain the former Chilean head of state Augusto Pinochet (b. 1915). This warrant arose out of Garzón's investigation of Operation Condor, a coordinated operation among South American governments to assassinate opposition figures living outside their boundaries. The murder of Spanish nationals in Buenos Aires was traced to the Chilean secret police. The arrest warrant was served on Pinochet in London while he was receiving medical care. The resulting fifteen-month legal struggle produced a mixed outcome. On the one hand, the Law Lords of the House of Lords ruled that Pinochet's standing as a former head of state did not give him immunity from accusations that he ordered the torture and murder of Spanish nationals in Buenos Aires in the 1970s and 1980s. The duties of a head of state were never defined to include torture, and hence he was open to prosecution for such crimes. In addition, the International Convention against Torture had been interpolated into British law, and therefore the British courts had standing to hear the case. On the other hand, medical testimony persuaded the British Home Secretary that Pinochet was too infirm to face these charges; he returned to Chile, but Garzón had established the principle that human rights violations in one country could be subject to prosecution in a second country at the behest of a magistrate in a third. The enforcement of human rights conventions, such as those on torture, was now a matter of international law.

In this context, Garzón continued his investigation into Operation Condor, even seeking testimony about it from Henry Kissinger, the American secretary of state in the 1970s. In 2003 his request for the detention of an Argentine working in Mexico was honored by a Mexican judge; the result was the arrest of one of the torturers who had operated in Buenos Aires in the late 1970s. In 2001 he issued indictments of members of the Basque separatist movement suspected of involvement in criminal activities. In 2003 he investigated the international reach of Al Qaeda and other Islamic groups in Spain and North Africa. He collected evidence of corruption involving television companies owned by the Italian prime minister Silvio Berlusconi. Once again, the point was made: domestic courts may be subject to political pressure. Magistrates in other countries who, like Garzón, were dealing with criminal activity of a transnational nature had the right to seize documents and obtain testimony previously restricted to nationals alone. Thus his work helped erode state sovereignty at the very moment when the expansion and strengthening of the European Union was taking place.

Garzón came to represent the principle of universal justice at a time when the globalization of trade and migration was paralleled by the globalization of crime and conspiracy. He also embodies the principles enunciated in the Nuremberg trials in 1946, but rarely enforced thereafter, that crimes of state are crimes, and that, with respect to crimes against humanity, no head of state is untouchable.

See also **Al Qaeda; Basques; Globalization; Islamic Terrorism.**

BIBLIOGRAPHY

Broady, Reed, and Michael Ratner, eds. *The Pinochet Papers: The Case of Augusto Pinochet in Spain and Britain*. The Hague, 2000.

Burbach, Roger. *The Pinochet Affair: State Terrorism and Global Justice*. London, 2003.

Cruz, Miguel Ángel de la. *Garzón: La ambición de un juez*. Madrid, 2000.

Los documentos del juez Garzón y la Audiencia Nacional: El caso de España contra las dictaduras-Chilena y Argentina. Barcelona, 1998.

Rei, Pepe. *Garzón: La otra cara.* Tafalla, c. 1999.

Urbano, Pilar. *Garzón: El hombre que veía amanecer.* Barcelona, 2000.

JAY WINTER

GAUCK COMMISSION.

During the democratic revolution in the German Democratic Republic (GDR) in 1989 and 1990, civil rights activists stormed the regional and central headquarters of the Ministry for State Security, the GDR's omnipresent secret police (colloquially known as the Stasi), in order to halt the destruction of records and to press for an unsparing exposure of the abuses and crimes committed by this most important instrument of repression and surveillance of the communist government. In August 1990 the democratically elected People's Chamber voted to open the files and named a member, Joachim Gauck, a Protestant priest representing the civil rights movement, to head the parliamentary commission in charge of carrying out the work involved. Putting a federal commissioner in charge of preservation and reconstruction of and access to the files made this work part of the Unification Treaty between the Federal Republic and the GDR. Gauck acted as commissioner for the two terms that were allowed and in October 2000 was followed by Marianne Birthler, an economist, Green Party member, and former dissident who had held several parliamentary and regional government positions during the 1990s.

RESPONSIBILITIES OF THE COMMISSION

In December 1991 the Bundestag passed the Stasi records law, providing the legal basis for the commissioner's work, which involves: 1) making files accessible to the individuals who were spied on or otherwise affected by Stasi operations; 2) answering questions from public institutions and employers about their employees' involvement with the Stasi; and 3) assisting the public in uncovering the communist government's abuses of state power and in reconstructing the past by making records accessible to researchers and the media and by maintaining its own research and education department. In order to protect individual privacy, personal files are made available only to the individual victims of Stasi operations, and only through photocopies from which the identities of other individuals, with the exception of Stasi collaborators, are edited out. As a general rule, former full-time Stasi members and unofficial informants are denied access to personal files written by themselves. Only when Stasi victims are considered "important personalities of contemporary history" is anonymity not required. Access to information about full-time and unofficial Stasi collaborators and to the other nonpersonal files is unrestricted.

The sheer size of the Stasi's inventory (112 miles of files) made it difficult to put these rules into effect. Between 1991 and 2003, some two million individuals were given access to their files, three million inquiries from public institutions were answered, and fifteen thousand research applications were processed. Because according to the Stasi records law internal documentation of the archives (catalogs, card files, registries) is not accessible to the public, every query must be answered on the basis of a separate research process executed by one of the commissioner's employees. This is often time-consuming, because parts of the documentation as well as many of the files were destroyed during the last months of the Stasi's existence. During the 1990s, the commissioner employed some 2,650 people in several divisions and in regional outposts. The commission's own research unit, the Department for Education and Research, has some eighty historians and staff members and is responsible for procuring basic historical information on the structure and functions of the Stasi and developing educational programs for the public.

PRIVACY AND OPEN ACCESS

The legal principles informing the commissioner's work came under scrutiny in several court decisions when former Chancellor Helmut Kohl intervened against making accessible material from phone calls the Stasi had intercepted. Objecting, on the grounds of privacy, to the exceptions made for material gathered from individuals considered historically important, he insisted on the right to preclude any use of this material without his consent. On Commissioner Birthler's insistence, the matter was appealed to the Federal Administrative Court, which confirmed Kohl's position in the particular case but defined more precise standards for balancing the individual citizen's right to privacy and the public interest in an unrestrained approach to dealing with the communist past. Substantial discretion was accorded to the commissioner in weighing the rights of historical personalities against the public interest, and scholarly research was given more weight than media exploitation.

When the commission began its work, it was generally expected that open access to Stasi files would be socially disruptive. However, this has not turned out to be the case. In fact, the Stasi records law has contributed to an open debate on how to come to terms with the past, and the examination of individual cases has proved the Stasi records law to be an important instrument in helping redress past injustices. This is particularly true in the cases of individuals revealed as unofficial collaborators, whose eligibility for public service depends on the particulars of their involvement and their willingness to clear up their involvement in an honest way.

In 2005, the future of the commission became part of the public debates about historical commemoration. In particular, the commission's research department's privileged and uncensored access to Stasi files aroused the animosity of some historians, and some sectors of the public questioned the need to maintain such a large institution more than fifteen years after the collapse of communism. In 2005 responsibility for the commissioner was transferred from the Ministry of Interior to the Federal Commissioner for Culture and Media, placing it in the hands of an undersecretary within the federal chancellery, who is also in charge of the regular federal archives. The majority of experts agree that in the long term the Stasi records have to be integrated into the federal archives, even though they are not yet fully retrieved and physically restored, and legal restrictions continue to limit access to personal files. On the other hand, in its first fifteen years of existence, the Stasi record law set new standards in dealing with the dictatorial past of an open society, and that should not be given up hastily in the name of a return to "normality." The commission's innovative work is increasingly acknowledged in other countries of the former communist bloc, where the Gauck

Commission and its political independence are seen as a model democratic and pluralist way to deal with their own dark sides of recent history.

See also **Germany; Kohl, Helmut; Stasi.**

BIBLIOGRAPHY

Ash, Timothy Garton. *The File: A Personal History.* New York, 1997.

"Die Bundesbeauftragte für die Unterlagen des Staatssicherheitsdienstes der ehemaligen Deutschen Demokratischen Republik." Available at http://www.bstu.bund.de. Includes short versions in twelve languages.

Funder, Anna. *Stasiland.* London, 2003.

Suckut, Siegfried, and Jürgen Weber, eds. *Stasi-Akten Zwischen Politik und Zeitgeschichte: Eine Zwischenbilanz.* Munich, 2003.

THOMAS LINDENBERGER

GAULLE, CHARLES DE (1890–1970), French war hero and politician.

The right circumstances may not make men great; but it is rare to find a great man in the absence of the right circumstances. What would General Charles de Gaulle have become had circumstances not given him the chance to forge a destiny tied to the fate of France itself?

MILITARY TRAINING AND EARLY CAREER

De Gaulle, born in Lille, the son of a professor of philosophy and history, came from a devout Catholic family. At the time, that meant they were on the right, though his father, in not believing in Captain Alfred Dreyfus's guilt, displayed an original and open mind relatively rare for this milieu. After completing his secondary studies in Catholic schools, Charles was the only one of four brothers to choose a career in the army. He was accepted to Saint-Cyr in 1909 and graduated as a second lieutenant in 1912. He was assigned to the 33rd Infantry Regiment garrisoned at Arras, commanded by Philippe Pétain, then a fifty-six-year-old colonel nearing the end of his military career.

Even though Pétain had taught at the École de Guerre (War College), he had no hope of becoming a general, because he had voiced reservations about theories favoring offensive military strategies, which were then considered de rigueur. Although the war would allow Pétain to assume command of the entire French army in 1917 and to become its marshal in 1918, it was less favorable to the young de Gaulle. Wounded twice quite early on, first on 15 August 1914 and then again on 10 March 1915, he was wounded a third time, this time seriously, outside Douaumont during the battle of Verdun on 2 March 1916, and was taken prisoner by the Germans. Despite several escape attempts, he was not freed until the Armistice of 11 November 1918. He then returned to active service and took part in Maxime Weygand's military mission during the Russo-Polish War in 1920.

After becoming a major at thirty, he pursued a relatively atypical career. Part of a family of intellectuals, he began to reflect on World War I. He loved writing and wrote extensively on military questions, publishing in succession *La discorde chez l'ennemi* (Discord among enemy ranks) in 1924, *Le fil de l'épée* (The edge of the sword) in 1932, *Vers l'armée de métier* (Building a career army) in 1934, and *La France et son armée* (France and its army) in 1938. His reflections consisted largely of two facets: harsh judgments of how the French army had been commanded at the beginning of World War I, which led to phenomenal casualties; and speculations about what the war of the future would be like and what the army ought to become.

These reflections were particularly important because, though the nation's army had been the most modern in Europe in 1918, in the ensuing years France had allowed the programs for its tank and aviation equipment to fall into disarray. De Gaulle did not confine himself to writing but also took part in discussion groups, such as the one led by Colonel Émile Mayer, and made his way into political circles, where he met Paul Reynaud and managed to convince him of the desirability of armored combat. He also quit the infantry to assume command of the 507th Tank Regiment in Metz.

It is a testament to the brilliance of his career that de Gaulle attained the rank of colonel in 1937 at age forty-seven. He had been part of Marshal Pétain's cabinet, had taught at Saint-Cyr, was accepted to the War College, and was certified by the general staff college. He was also Middle East envoy for two years and was appointed to the General Secretariat for National Defense.

HEAD OF THE FREE FRENCH

But Charles de Gaulle's destiny was determined by France's defeat in 1940. This destiny lay not so much in the military sphere, though he did achieve some success in the Battle of Montcornet in the Aisne at the head of one of his vaunted armored divisions (without coordinated air support, the armored vehicles could not ultimately prevail, however). Nor was his success based on the fact that Paul Reynard, now appointed provisional brigadier general, had called upon him to join his government as undersecretary for war and national defense on 5 June 1940, which showed de Gaulle stood out from the rest of the officers. Instead, de Gaulle's fate was sealed by his apparently inescapable decision to reject France's capitulation and the resulting armistice, followed by his relocation to Great Britain and the launch of his 18 June appeal, which marked the starting point of the Gaullist saga and that of the Free French Forces.

De Gaulle was the sole senior officer, politician, or intellectual to possess the vision and audacity to make such a choice following the country's great debacle, though his initiative was made possible only by the authorization and support of the British prime minister, Winston Churchill, after 10 May. Lacking a better-known or higher-ranking interlocutor, the British government recognized General de Gaulle as the leader of the Free French Forces and gave him the financial and material means to carry on. Despite this, relations between Churchill and de Gaulle were strained, since de Gaulle sought to represent French legitimacy and therefore had to be particularly intransigent in defense of France's interests, given that he was now totally bereft. The situation did not improve when the United States entered the war. President Franklin D. Roosevelt saw de Gaulle as little more than an apprentice dictator, and in fact throughout his life de Gaulle never failed to inspire zealous devotees and consequently suspicions that he had dictatorial aims. Even more so than Churchill, who managed to feel some sympathy along with his irritation, Roosevelt endeavored to marginalize and ignore de Gaulle. Who can know the extent to which the general's sometimes deep-seated anti-Americanism, which appeared subsequently, was the result of this attitude during the war?

Charles de Gaulle delivers a radio address to the French people from his refuge in London during the Nazi occupation of France, June 1944. ©HULTON-DEUTSCH COLLECTION/CORBIS

When the Anglo-Americans landed in North Africa in November 1942 without alerting de Gaulle in advance, they tried to confer power on General Henri Giraud, whose positions were close to those of the Vichy government. De Gaulle managed to become the sole president of the French Committee of National Liberation created in Algiers in June 1943 only by ousting Giraud in November 1943. He then transformed the committee in June of the following year into the Provisional Government of the French Republic.

Before the landing at Normandy, which the general was not made aware of until the absolute last minute, the Allies had planned to govern France directly, and they only begrudgingly renounced this intention and allowed the Provisional Government to be transferred from Algiers to Paris. As for de Gaulle, he was in Paris on 25 August, Liberation Day. The aim of his speedy arrival was not only to reaffirm his power in opposition to the Allied Forces but to counter the Communists as well, whom he feared would take advantage of the situation to seize the reins. In August 1944 the unknown general became France's most preeminent personality and a man of international renown as well. Thus he began a second, essentially political, career, which entailed four phases.

POSTWAR POLITICAL CAREER

As president of the Provisional Government, he had three objectives. He wished to restore the French army at the end of the war (this was essentially the mission of General Leclerc's 2nd Armored Division and the French 1st Army of General Jean de Lattre de Tassigny) and return France to its former stature. Although de Gaulle was kept at bay at the Yalta Conference, French generals were present at the German surrender, and France obtained a seat on the security council of the United Nations. De Gaulle's second objective was to set in motion the major economic and social reforms laid out in the official program of the National Council of the Resistance formed during the Occupation: nationalization of mining, of gas and electricity production, of air transport, and of banking, as well as the creation of a social security system. Finally, de Gaulle's government sought to give the people back their voice (this included women, who were granted the right to vote), in order to reestablish democracy and create novel democratic institutions.

This last goal proved the most difficult. Although General de Gaulle was unanimously elected president of the Provisional Government, elected by the Constituent Assembly in October 1945, and even though an immense majority rejected the institutions of the Third Republic in a referendum, conflict erupted between the political parties, who believed the true reins of power should be returned to them, and the general, who sought to shield executive power from their incessant supervision. On 20 January 1946, de Gaulle resigned, with the reasonable expectation that he would soon be reinstated. This expectation proved unfounded, however, because in the meantime a Fourth Republic, whose organizational makeup he also opposed, was instituted.

After several months of silence, de Gaulle found it necessary to return to the political scene and to call for the creation of new governing institutions. Thus began the second phase of his political career. He was convinced France's defeat had been in large measure the consequence of the institutions that had produced a regime of the Assembly, and that those of the Fourth Republic only reinforced the already excessive powers of the deputies. This tendency was fueled even further by the change of name from the Chamber of Deputies to the National Assembly. In 1947 de Gaulle formed a political party called the Rassemblement du Peuple Français (RPF, Gathering of the French people). It elicited a tidal wave of support in municipal elections but was unable to bring about the National Assembly's dissolution, and its impact waned after four years. Its results in the 1951 legislative elections were mediocre, and the party was not able to return to power. In 1953 de Gaulle once again gave up politics, and for the second time it was believed his role was finished. Indeed he was the first to say so (if not to believe it), and during a long period of "wandering in the desert," he devoted himself to writing his memoirs.

Circumstances brought him back to political life for a third phase. The Fourth Republic was bogged down in various colonial wars, primarily the war in Indochina (for which, by the way, de Gaulle was largely responsible, having sought to reestablish French sovereignty there in 1945) but also in the Algerian War starting in 1954. The Cold War had also created a deep division within France between followers and enemies of the Soviet Union, and the country had been gripped for some time by enormous economic and social problems. In 1958 a major crisis following the rebellion of the army and of the French living in Algeria offered General de Gaulle the opportunity and the means to return to power. The National Assembly charged him with the mission of drafting a new constitution and, after 80 percent of the electorate voted to adopt it, he became the first president of the Fifth Republic.

During the fourth and final phase, de Gaulle's work was divided into three parts. His first task was to resolve the colonial issues. It may never be known whether General de Gaulle always believed Algerian independence was inevitable or whether he converted to this belief over time, but the fact remains that it was he who concluded the Évian Accords in March 1962 whereby Algeria became independent, though not without having to overcome several attempts at insurrection in Algeria, such as the so-called generals' coup of April 1961 and the numerous assassination attempts mounted by the Organisation de l'Armée Secrète (OAS; Secret army organization). At the same time, the colonies of sub-Saharan Africa and Madagascar became independent. For the most part, it was de Gaulle who ended the French colonial enterprise.

His second objective was to ensure the permanence of the new Republic's institutions. He proposed a referendum vote in October 1962, during which it was decided that the president of the Republic would be elected by popular vote, a change he had not thought possible in 1958.

Charles de Gaulle delivers a speech at Potopoto, near Brazzaville, French Equatorial Africa, in August 1958, during a tour of French African colonies. ©BETTMANN/CORBIS

His third goal was to restore France to its former stature by formulating a major strategic foreign policy, to which he devoted most of his energy. Because this policy required an economically strong country, de Gaulle spent much more time on this sector than he had in 1945. The replacement of the old franc by the new was the symbol of renewed stability, and France experienced one of the longest periods of growth in its history. Although the government's actions were not the sole cause of that prosperity, its role was obviously not negligible.

The leitmotif of General de Gaulle's foreign policy was national independence with respect to the two superpowers, the USSR and the United States. But since France was on the U.S. side in the Cold War, the brunt of this policy was essentially

directed at the United States. The hostility de Gaulle felt toward the United States was not the only reason for his choices, but it was never entirely absent from them either. This was the case for France's rapprochement with the Soviet Union and its recognition of Communist China; for the development of French nuclear capability, which had in fact begun during the Fourth Republic; for France's withdrawal from NATO; for de Gaulle's rejection of a supranational Europe and his opposition to British entry into the European Community because Britain was so closely allied to the United States; for his efforts to combat the dollar's supremacy by returning to the gold standard; for his speech in Pnompenh against U.S. policy in Asia; for his tour of South America; for his support for Quebec separatists; and finally for his condemnation of Israel in the Six-Day War. Despite de

Gaulle's enormous international prestige, the sheer dimensions of his foreign policy outstripped what France could realistically achieve.

THE RISING OPPOSITION

Those opposed to de Gaulle within France were increasing in number. His foreign policy provoked strong criticism and on the domestic front aroused hostility among social groups that considered themselves the injured parties, such as peasants, civil servants, and public sector employees, the growing ranks of the unemployed, and all those who rejected the new political culture, which they thought resembled a "republican-style monarchy" more than a traditional republic. The self-anointed leader of the opposition, François Mitterrand, condemned the government as a "permanent coup d'état." Among voters, de Gaulle encountered the undying opposition of a portion of the Right, which had never forgiven him for abandoning "French Algeria." He also increasingly began to lose the support of a sizable portion of voters on the left, who had supported him when he returned to power.

De Gaulle ran for a second term as president in 1965 (he was seventy-five) and was elected, but only in the second round of voting, and his party won the 1967 legislative elections by just one vote. These troubles were mere precursors to the great storm of protests that erupted in May 1968 and nearly toppled the entire government. It took General de Gaulle a great deal of time to grasp the importance of the movement in the short term (its deeper causes remain in dispute and were not confined to France alone). His words no longer seemed sufficient to guide the younger generations, whose background had nothing in common with his own, and it was only a powerful upswing in those who rejected the inescapable unrest of 1968 that allowed him to again win in the legislative elections that year. By then the damage was already done, however, and when he proposed a referendum to increase popular participation in public life, it was rejected on 27 April 1969. The following day, he stepped down, this time for good. He died on 9 November 1970, just a few days before his eightieth birthday. Gaullist politics, however, remains one of the most constant and important features of French political life.

See also **Algerian War; France; Indochina; World War II.**

BIBLIOGRAPHY

Primary Sources

Gaulle de, Charles. *Mémoires de guerre.* 3 vols. Paris, 1954–1969.

———. *Discours et messages.* 5 vols. Paris, 1970–1971.

———. *Mémoires d'espoir.* 2 vols. Paris, 1970–1971.

———. *Lettres, notes et carnets.* 13 vols. Paris, 1980–1997.

Secondary Sources

Azéma, Jean-Pierre. *De Munich à la Libération, 1938–1944.* Paris, 1979.

Berstein, Serge. *La République gaullienne.* Paris, 1989.

Gaulle, Philippe de. *De Gaulle mon père.* 2 vols. Paris, 2003–2004.

Lacouture, Jean. *Charles De Gaulle.* 3 vols. Paris, 1984–1986.

Peyrefitte, Alain. *C'était de Gaulle.* 3 vols. Paris, 1994–2000.

Rioux, Jean-Pierre. *La France de la IVe République (1944–1958).* 2 vols. Paris, 1980–1983.

JEAN-JACQUES BECKER

GDAŃSK/DANZIG. The city of Gdańsk (German: Danzig) is located at the outlet of the Vistula River to the Baltic Sea in Poland. By 1914 it was inhabited mainly by Germans; Poles and Jews were the two largest national and religious minorities. During World War I, Gdańsk was outside the main sphere of military operations. The rebirth of the Polish Republic and collapse of the German Empire in November 1918 opened the question of Gdańsk's future. Poland viewed Gdańsk as its main harbor on the Baltic Sea. Local Germans did not want to live in the Polish State. The participants of the Paris Peace Conference (1919) solved the problem by changing Gdańsk into the capital of the Free City of Danzig (FCD). This was an autonomous area governed by the local Germans under the supervision of the League of Nations, with Poland having limited rights.

In the years 1920–1933 Polish-Danzig relations were difficult. In order to become independent from the FCD, Poland set up a new harbor at Gdynia, 20 kilometers northwest of Gdańsk. Soon it became the main competitor of Gdańsk. Danzigers were severely effected by the great economic crisis of the interwar period. The existing social frustration helped the Nazis to win elections to the local parliament (Volkstag) on 28 May 1933. By October 1937 all political parties, except for the NSDAP, were dissolved. The local government (Senat) followed the orders of Hitler's representative, the gauleiter Albert Forster. On 24 October 1938, Berlin demanded that Poland return Gdańsk to Germany. Poland rejected the demand. The German attack on the Polish military depot at Westerplatte (part of Gdańsk) on 1 September 1939 marked the beginning of the World War II.

In the first days of the war Polish national activists were arrested. No fewer than 620 of them were murdered and their families deported to Poland. The Nazis had persecuted about six thousand Jews and forced them to emigrate. In August 1939 there were still some fifteen hundred Jews in Gdańsk. About half of them managed to leave for the free world, several hundred others perished in ghettos and Nazi camps. Only a few survived in place.

In Gdańsk there were 287,995 city dwellers in March 1944. During the war Gdańsk was an important center of the naval industry. The Allied air forces started to attack Gdańsk's factories in 1943 and went on bombing them for the next two years. The Red Army and auxiliary Polish troops eventually took control of Gdańsk on 30 March 1945. Until July 1945 Gdańsk was governed by the Red Army; later, a Polish administration was free to run public matters.

During the fierce fighting, 90 percent of the city center was destroyed. Civilians suffered miserably: they were robbed and raped, and their houses were burned down in the first weeks after the capitulation of the city's garrison. All Germans without Polish citizenship were to be removed from the country. Compared with 123,932 German and 8,525 Polish citizens in June 1945, there were only 13,380 Germans and 151,185 new Polish settlers one year later. From 1946 onward the local population was dominated by Roman Catholics.

Gdańsk became an important point on the map of Poland's economic and academic centers. Between 1945 and 1989 the majority of workers were employed in local shipyards, the most prominent being the Lenin Shipyard. The maritime industry benefited greatly from cooperation with the vast Soviet market. In 1945 technical and medical universities were founded, and in later years several other institutions of higher learning were started. The University of Gdańsk opened in 1970. Work and education made Gdańsk attractive for thousands of persons coming from all over the country. In two decades a new society was created.

SOCIAL UNREST

In the years 1946, 1956, and 1970, when workers went on strike, their demands focused on social issues. The most important was the December Revolt (14–16 December 1970), which began as a protest over sharp increases in food prices just before Christmas. Shipyard workers created a strike committee and soon left their factories. The situation went out of control. The crowd attacked the district police headquarters and prison, and the regional Communist Party headquarters was set on fire. To pacify the demonstration, the regime authorized the use of weapons. Several laborers were killed and many others were wounded.

During the 1970s large immigration and high birthrates exacerbated the city's housing shortage. Young laborers and university graduates were the two social groups most affected by the lack of accommodation and high cost of living. The situation worsened especially in the second half of the decade. In the years 1976–1979 young dissidents founded several opposition organizations. Some of them were close to the Warsaw Worker's Defense Committee (Komitet Obrony Robotników, or KOR). Among them was Bogdan Borusewicz (b. 1949. However, because of personal and ideological reasons, KOR was not accepted by all young people. Among KOR's members were some former communists who still hoped to reform socialism in Poland. An important part of the activists in Gdańsk did not want to reform communism but aimed at removing it from the country. They put the stress on the Catholic and national components of their ideology, criticizing ties that bound Poland with the USSR. In July 1979 the patriotic, antisoviet faction founded The Young Poland Movement (Ruch Młodej Polski, or RMP). Its members, led by Aleksander Hall, were mainly young intellectuals

Police use tear gas to disperse a crowd of Solidarity sympathizers who have gathered to protest the Soviet government, Gdańsk, Poland, May 1982. ©BETTMANN/CORBIS

who had already cooperated with members of the Free Trade Unions of the Coast (Wolne Związki Zawodowe Wybrzeża, or WZZ), an organization created in April 1978 by Andrzej Gwiazda, Błażej i Krzysztof Wyszkowski, Anna Walentynowicz, Borusewicz, and Lech Wałęsa. At that time the political opposition in Gdańsk was not very sizable. Nevertheless, it played an important role in the political education of workers. It disseminated illegal newspapers and books and organized patriotic demonstrations to celebrate national anniversaries.

The oppositionists became known when they took charge of the strikes in the summer of 1980, when social discontent grew high. On 14 August, Wałęsa became the leader of the strike committee in the Lenin Shipyard. The leaders of the strike movement were people in their twenties and thirties, backed by advisers from WZZ, KOR, RMP, and other opposition groups. To avoid repeating the experience of the December Revolt, strikers remained at their places of work and maintained strict discipline. Workers used nonviolent tactics of political struggle. The government accepted twenty-one demands prepared by the Interfactory Strike Committee. The most important political ones were those leading to the creation of self-governing labor unions and the liberation of political prisoners. On 31 August the Gdańsk Agreement was signed.

When the independent self-governing trade union "Solidarność" (Solidarity) was registered in October 1980, its headquarters were located in Gdańsk. During the first months of Solidarność, society became very active. Citizens believed that they could create the prosperity of the country and not merely obey arrogant communist officials. However, on 13 December 1981 the communist regime introduced martial law in order to retain power. The inhabitants of Gdańsk tried to protest, but their resistance was suppressed by the army and the antiriot police units. In the next few years there were many antigovernment demonstrations in the streets and in churches. The oppositionists continued their work toward the creation of a civil society. In May 1988 a new strike in the Lenin Shipyard broke out. Solidarity strikes began at the local institutions of higher learning. Some radical groups did not want any negotiations with the communists. But leaders on both sides concluded that the only solution was to start talking with each other in order to change the political and economic system while avoiding bloodshed.

POLITICAL AND ECONOMIC REFORM

After the fall of the communist regime, one of the most important changes in the city was the creation of a genuine local government. In the years 1990–2005 former communists were unable to gain political control over Gdańsk, although they were represented in the City Council (Rada Miasta). The anticommunist orientation of the majority of the population has been demonstrated in all elections since 1989.

Reform of the economy resulted in the dismantling of many state factories and enterprises. In 2004 the unemployment rate was 11 percent. Local enterprises lost much of the post-Soviet market and fought for new ones. The city ceased to be as economically attractive as it had been in the past. Thousands of young, well-educated people left for more economically developed cities. The combination of these factors, as well as a low birthrate, resulted in a decline in population. There were 468,400 city dwellers in the middle of the 1980s and only 453,719 in 1997. Yet Gdańsk continued to be an important academic center with about sixty thousand students in state or private universities. In 2004 Gdańsk, like the rest of Poland, was in the course of economic transformation.

See also **Germany; Poland; Solidarity; World War I; World War II.**

BIBLIOGRAPHY

Cenckiewicz, Slawomir. *Oczami bezpieki: Szkice i materialy z dziejów aparatu bezpieczestwa.* Kraków, 2004.

Cieślak, Edmund, and Czeslaw Biernat. *History of Gdańsk.* Translated by Bożenna Blaim and George M. Hyde. Gdańsk, Poland, 1988.

Karpinski, Jakub. *Countdown: The Polish Upheavals of 1956, 1968, 1970, 1976, 1980.* Translated by Olga Amsterdamska and Gene M. Moore. New York, 1982.

Levine, Herbert S. *Hitler's Free City: A History of the Nazi Party in Danzig, 1925–1939.* Chicago, 1973.

GRZEGORZ BERENDT

G-8 SUMMIT. Every year, leaders of the world's most powerful countries gather informally for three days to discuss international economic trends and monetary issues. The meeting of these world leaders, most commonly called the Group of Eight (G-8), is known as the G-8 summit. Unlike governments or international organizations such as the United Nations, the G-8 does not have an existing support bureaucracy and the decisions made at G-8 summits are not binding on the participating countries or leaders. The G-8 members are Canada, France, Germany, Italy, Japan, Russia, the United Kingdom, and the United States. The presidency of the G-8 rotates annually and the country that holds the presidency is expected to host the annual summit.

HISTORY

G-8 summits were initiated to support the declining economies of the industrial nations. As early as 1973, the United States had organized meetings with the top government finance officials from West Germany, France, Japan, and the United Kingdom; and because these meetings were held in the White House library, the group became known as the Library Group. In 1975, with growing economic and political crises in the west, including the first oil crisis, a recession, growing trade deficits, unemployment, unstable national currencies, and growing threats of war and the proliferation of weapons of mass destruction, the president of France called for informal annual meetings with the leaders of the major industrial nations. The meetings were designed to help overcome bureaucratic conflict and economic nationalism.

The first meeting of world leaders took place in Rambouillet, France, in November 1975. The meeting included the heads of government of France, Italy, Japan, the United Kingdom, the United States, and West Germany. The group became known as the Group of Six (G-6). This first meeting focused on economic and monetary concerns related to the oil crisis of the 1970s. Canada joined the group at the 1976 summit. A representative from the European Union (EU) has attended summits since 1977 but the EU does not participate in political and security discussions. Because it does have its own currency (the euro) and central bank, however, the EU participates in financial and economic discussions. The Soviet Union began attending the summits as an observer in 1984 and Russia finally became a member in 1997. The first G-8 summit took place in 1998. Since then, the G-8 summit has evolved from a forum focusing on macroeconomic issues to an annual meeting that addresses a wide range of international economic, political, and social issues, and more recently security and microeconomic issues such as employment and the information highway; transnational issues such as the environment, crime, and drugs; and other issues ranging from human rights and regional security to arms control.

FUNCTION

G-8 summits have proven valuable for policy coordination and face-to-face discussion on key issues, and these have encouraged agreement on some issues, although leaders disagree as often as they agree on economic and social policy. The summits are informal and operate with an understanding that agreements and decisions made there are guidelines for action and that there will be no penalties for failure to meet commitments made or adhere to policies arrived at during summits. However, these annual forums play a crucial role in the governance of the global economy. The G-8 members are industrial and market-orientated democracies and they are the world's most powerful economic and political countries. Although not representative of the world's population, these countries drive the policies and agendas found in formal international institutions. G-8 countries control nearly 50 percent of the vote in the World Bank and International Monetary Fund. They have enormous influence in the World Trade Organization and the United Nations Security Council. It is through these formal international institutions that many of the decisions made at the G-8 summits become reality. G-8 member countries often make deals and compromises with one another and then form power blocs to exert influence in world politics.

However, G-8 summits sometimes bring to the forefront the major points of disagreement between G-8 leaders. For example, at G-8 summits there has been little agreement between Europe and the United States, and therefore little coordinated action, on the issues of environmental pollution and global warming, military intervention, and debt relief for Africa and other Third World nations. In addition, other countries and groups of countries have power and a will to action in the world, and they sometimes vehemently disagree with G-8 policies and with actions agreed upon at G-8 summits. The G-8's critics argue that the ability of G-8 countries to dominate economic and military policies undermines the credibility of more representative institutions such as the United Nations, and that the world has enough resources to end poverty but that the market-orientated policies of the G-8 cannot solve the distribution problems that leave millions of people around the world living in poverty.

From a G-8 perspective, the macroeconomic policy coordination accomplished by G-8 summits has helped generate global growth and prevent a repetition of high rates of inflation and the worldwide recession of the 1970s. G-8 summits have helped deliver and manage a regime of flexible floating exchange rates that have enabled free-market practices to dominate the global economy. Since 1990 the G-8 has responded to numerous financial crises and attempted to reform the international financial system; the G-8 has protected the advanced industrial economies and encouraged the major multilateral institutions of global economic governance to respond more adequately to a rapidly globalizing world. In liberalizing trade, G-8 leaders have provided the critical political impetus to launch and successfully conclude every round of multilateral trade liberalization since 1975. In global development, the G-8 pioneered the process of debt relief for the world's poorest countries.

However, leaders of nations who are not invited to G-8 summits, along with civil society organizations and nongovernmental organizations, often claim that these same G-8 initiatives have failed abysmally or been misguided and that they have helped the G-8 nations but have failed the rest of the world. For example, the attempts to coordinate macroeconomic policies in the late 1970s and exchange rates in the 1980s failed to bring the development that was promised and actually devastated some economies. The critics agree that some initiatives have produced valuable changes, such as spurring multilateral trade negotiations, but only when more voices were allowed to participate and to affect decisions.

See also **European Union; United Nations and Europe.**

BIBLIOGRAPHY

Kirton, John J., Joseph P. Daniels, and Andreas Freytag, eds. *Guiding Global Order: G-8 Governance in the Twenty-First Century.* Burlington, Vt., 2001.

Kirton, John. "The Road from Rambouillet to the Sea Island Summit: Process, Accomplishments, and Challenges for the Corporate Community." Available at http://www.g7.utoronto.ca/scholar/kirton2004/kirton_atlanta_040507.pdf.

University of Toronto. "G8 Information Centre." Available at http://www.g8.utoronto.ca/.

LORNA LUEKER ZUKAS

GENDER. The term *gender* in its current usage challenges the idea of masculinity and femininity as fixed biological determinants. It suggests that there is a voluntaristic aspect to one's sexual role or nature, and especially that women can escape biological destiny to live an existence apart from the family. According to some anthropologists and sociologists, the term not only implies that the relationship between men and women is a social construction but also that this relationship is hierarchical and that sexual difference and the socially imposed division of the sexes are "imperative."

Gender is one of the most restless terms in the English language. It denotes a much-contested concept and a site of unease rather than agreement, drawing attention to the artificiality of what many perceive as "natural behavior." *Gender* continues to function as a grammatical term and as a euphemism for a person's sex but is now most widely used to refer to the social and cultural aspects of sexual difference. Because of the historical interdependency of theories of mind and body, it is hard to determine where sex ends and gender begins. The initial use of the late modern concept of gender cannot be traced precisely; it began to emerge in the United States during the post-1945 boom in sexology and psychoanalysis. In the 1960s sexologists, psychoanalysts, and anthropologists began to separate sex from gender analytically.

BINARIES AND CONFLICTING MEANINGS
Gender categorizations explore the binary division of people into male and female and the patterns of behavior that are associated with each group. A division into male and female bodies thus results in a masculine set of behavior appropriate for bodies classified as male and in a set of feminine traits considered appropriate for bodies defined as female. Sex differences have been explored for at least two hundred years. Even though shifts and changes occurred in the discussion about what constituted male and female identities, certain common themes emerged and are still evident. The most persistent dichotomy views males as rational and capable of universalist thought and females as emotional and bound to the particularities of their bodies. By the late nineteenth century, males and females were seen as opposites and biological facts were supposed to reveal underlying differences. Closer examination of evidence for masculine and feminine traits showed that it was unstable and that categories of distinction overlapped significantly. Strength, endurance, spatial and linguistic ability, and aggression can be weighted toward the male or the female, but there are always members of the other group who outperform members of the group to which the trait is supposedly attached. Apparently, John Stuart Mill's nineteenth-century dictum that we will not be able to discern the natural differences between men and women until we treat them the same socially still holds true to some extent.

SEX CHROMOSOME CHARACTERISTICS
The discovery of DNA in the late nineteenth century, the identification of the Y chromosome in 1905, the unveiling of the famous "double helix" or DNA structure in 1953, and, finally, the mapping of the human genome early in the twenty-first century have enhanced and challenged the notion that gender differences are based on natural divisions between male and female. The insight that biological sex results from a variation in just one chromosome made those categories appear a

matter of pure chance and fixed irreversibly by nature. By contrast, studies on the basis of genetic variation reveal a remarkable genetic similarity between males and females, since their genome sequences are about 99.9 percent identical. In the debate following the discovery of the double helix, the supposed objectivity of science itself was challenged and the fact that scientific theories—in all fields—reflect the culture from which they emerge was recognized. Consequently, the distinction between sex and gender based on "natural traits," be they chromosomes, hormones, or brain size, became problematic.

SHIFTS IN ELEMENTS OF THE GENDERED UNIVERSE

Following World War I, the first influential theories on gender were developed by anthropologists, notably the American Margaret Mead. Her descriptions of non-Western societies challenged Western gender roles and thus eventually led to a reappraisal of gender roles that had appeared to be fixed by "nature."

New philosophical approaches after 1945 combined Marxist, Freudian, literary, and anthropological theories. In her 1949 bestseller, *The Second Sex,* the French philosopher and novelist Simone de Beauvoir (1908–1986) drew on phenomenological and existential theories to claim that women, in contrast to men, acted in accordance with men's view of them, thus developing an inauthentic identity. In her view, femininity was not a natural condition but rather the result of a bad choice. For existentialists such as de Beauvoir, an authentic life entailed escaping the world of biology. Her suggestion that one's sexual role was a choice and her assertion that women's lives were not predetermined by their "nature" became one of the central foundations of gender theory and were highly influential throughout Western Europe and the United States, where Betty Friedan (1921–2006) spread them in the 1960s.

By 1980 the idea of the "social construction of gender" was widely accepted by sociologists, anthropologists, and some psychologists. At the same time, some scholars of gender theory took up the psychoanalytic insights of Sigmund Freud (1856–1939) and the somewhat nuanced Freudianism of Jacques Lacan (1901–1981). Scholars such as the American anthropologist Gayle Rubin criticized both Freud and Lacan for advocating sexism yet valued them for describing sexism as a pervasive psychosocial institution, for freeing men and women from biological determinism, and for establishing their psychosexual identity in relation to each other. Other feminist theorists have defended both the invention of psychoanalysis and its paradigms, finding them useful for understanding femininity. Proponents of "French feminism" such as Luce Irigaray (b. 1930) combined Lacanian, structuralist, and other approaches to further contribute to gender theory. Building on the concept of de Beauvoir's "other," these French feminists saw woman not only as one more version of masculinity but also as a fragmented self. In particular, they posed the question of how to write a history of fragmented, "decentered subjects" for whom conventions of historical interpretation did not exist.

Standard interpretations of social and political power were also challenged by the French philosopher Michel Foucault (1926–1984), who downplayed the traditional sense of human agency. Examining the mechanisms of surveillance and regulation in the activities of doctors, the clergy, and government officials, Foucault posited that power relations in the modern state operate primarily through the body.

Poststructuralist versions of gender theory, most notably the writings of the American historian Joan Wallach Scott, largely dismissed Marxist, anthropological, and psychoanalytical approaches because of their essentialist (or at least enduring) characteristics and advocated using Foucault's theories to introduce the concept of gender into political history, where it could serve as a category to analyze how power operates. Poststructuralist scholars such as Scott and the philosopher Judith Butler developed a critique of essentialism, arguing that it was impossible to legitimately claim a group identity based on one's own experience, and of universalism, which posited that women have a quality known as "womanhood" in common.

Scientific research underscored theories that emphasized the arbitrary and invented nature of gender. Scientists such as Ann Fausto-Sterling

(b. 1944) demonstrated that it is possible to distinguish five different sexes on the basis of physiological and chromosomal characteristics. Studies of the lives of those born with ambiguously sexed bodies reveal the inability of society to deal with more than two sexes, since parents, teachers, and doctors try to steer them toward identifying themselves as either male or female.

While postmodern theories have been praised for breaking down universalist assumptions, they have also been criticized for their fragmented and partial interpretations. Apparently, "sex" and "gender" cannot be neatly categorized as "natural" and "cultural" but are now seen as intimately related cultural categories used to describe and understand human bodies and human relationships. Sex and gender often overlap, sometimes confusingly so, and the concept of a male or female body in many contemporary societies has become increasingly open to reinvention, be it through drugs, dress, exercise, or surgery. This has resulted in widely different conceptions of masculinity and femininity, so much so that it makes sense to speak of "masculinities" and "femininities." In the last quarter of the twentieth century, however, opposing theoretical positions within Western feminism joined together in alliances around particular issues such as reproductive rights, the banning of nuclear power, and the outlawing of pornography.

NATIONAL AND REGIONAL VARIATIONS

In the twentieth century, gender relations underwent dramatic changes in some parts of Europe but remained more static in others. The factors contributing to or inhibiting these changes—notably religion, education, political structures, the gendered nature of work, and the availability of contraceptives—must be taken into account. Along with historical differences, class, race, marital status, and age must be considered.

Battles over the behavior and characteristics of women and men allowed European societies to address other painful issues. A prominent example is the debate about gender roles and "normalcy" that ensued in many European countries after both world wars. Thus, in the wake of World War I, many French perceived a loss of supposedly feminine traditions as a threat to civilization, and after World War II Germans were faced with the

everyday tasks of survival but quickly returned to the model of the traditional "breadwinner" family. It was permissible to speak about gender, whereas the question of Germany's responsibility for the war and genocide was unspeakable. In England and France, the percentage of female workers in industry and agriculture rose during World War II, and this phenomenon contributed to the postwar longing for a return to "normalcy."

Another issue that emerged in Europe after both world wars was how to reconstruct gender relationships after men had been away for four years killing, while women had led very different lives. While the experience on the battlefields was similar for the soldiers from different European countries, women's war experiences varied according to country and region—most British and German women, for example, watched the war from afar, whereas their Belgian and French peers were much closer to actually experiencing battle. This often resulted in differing views of soldiers and thus of gender relations in peacetime. Those who had remained at home implicitly or explicitly saw soldiers as killers, and the feminists among them espoused separate spheres after the war. Those few women who had actually seen maimed, hysterical, and infantilized soldiers had a more sympathetic view. European wars of the twentieth century thus complicated gender, with sexologists and other social experts playing a large role in "making peace."

Ideas about the "natural role" of women and men as "nurturers" and "providers" surfaced as well in the 1920s and 1930s, particularly in the gendered nature of work. The authoritarian regimes in Germany and Italy (and, initially, in the Soviet Union) transformed these ideas into government policy and celebrated work as inherently masculine.

Throughout much of the twentieth century, men's tasks were considered "work" and women's tasks "assistance," "housework" or "women's work." These gender hierarchies were temporarily challenged in times of crisis but generally survived massive economic changes. Elementary education, for example, was considered women's work (with the supervision of teachers reserved for men), except in Germany, where it was defined as a male profession. In Russia, the medical staff was predominantly female, which meant that medicine was low-status, poorly paid work.

Access to education itself was highly gendered. While literacy rates varied greatly across Europe, women's rates of literacy and of secondary schooling were consistently lower than men's at the beginning of the twentieth century, particularly in the Catholic and rural societies of southern Europe and in Eastern European countries, where the gender gap in literacy did not close until after World War II. While European universities had generally opened their doors to women by the 1920s, fascist regimes succeeded in driving women out of the universities (and the professions).

Social movements were often gendered as well. In the early twentieth century, women marched to demand the vote, access to birth control, legal abortions, and other social rights; food riots, a traditional form of protest among women, continued in times of crisis, most notably during both world wars but also during the Bolshevik Revolution. In some respects, gender tensions increased in the 1920s, and not only in Germany, where male workers were hardened by their military service, frustrated by the abortive revolution, and bitter about inflation and unemployment. In the Weimar Republic, fascists and communists alike organized militant and confrontational marches while women preferred to participate in peace parades, International Women's Day, or similar events.

IMAGERY AND DRESS

Changes in clothing, behavior, and imagery were among the most striking transformations in gender roles. When the twentieth century started out, women's skirts were ankle length, as they had been for over five hundred years. Hemlines started to rise with the beginning of World War I and, while fluctuating throughout the remainder of the century, never returned to ankle length again. Contemporaries were shocked. Not only could they now get a glimpse of the female ankle, but part of the leg, clad in transparent silk stockings, was also revealed. The ideal female figure also changed, from the "hourglass" silhouette produced by a tight corset to a more "boyish" shape. In addition, women started to cut off their hair, which had been considered "woman's

crowning glory" but was heavy, hot, difficult to wash, and potentially dangerous when working with machinery or open fire. During the 1920s the "Eton crop" or the *Bubikopf* (bob) became a fashion standard with young and middle-aged women of all classes, with the English "flapper" as well as with the French gamine. Fashionable women even donned pants for sports activities, and sport idols such as the French tennis player Suzanne Lenglen (1899–1938) and the Norwegian ice-skater (and subsequent Hollywood star) Sonja Henie (1912–1969) pioneered short sleeves and bare legs.

Women who demanded the masculine privileges of short hair, pants, and freedom of movement, and who used cosmetics—which had been associated with prostitutes until World War I—certainly irritated their contemporaries. The fashions of the "Golden Twenties" were short-lived for several reasons. First, the Great Depression impoverished the working class and large parts of the middle classes, and clothing became scarce during World War II, so many women made do with little. Second, the totalitarian regimes in Germany and the Soviet Union (as well as in Spain and Italy) developed distinct versions of masculinity and femininity, giving rise to more traditional clothing. In Germany, the National Socialists propagated an ideal of femininity that incorporated both traditional and modern elements. The party youth organization for girls stressed gymnastics as well as traditional household training. According to party ideology, "the German woman" was trim and fit (to ensure her reproductive capabilities) but did not smoke or drink, and she wore sensible shoes and clothing (the dirndl made a comeback) and her hair braided in a crown.

Notions of what constituted femininity and masculinity were increasingly polarized in the 1930s and ultimately served the all-out war effort, when soldier-husbands were defending wives and children against the Red Army, and soldier-wives, steadfast and never complaining, awaited their return while educating their children to be good soldiers or mothers. National Socialist doctrine and the speeches of Adolf Hitler sang the praises of brutal men and loving women. Hitler himself considered the masses passionate, weak, and "intrinsically feminine" and derived no small part of his success from styling himself as a swaggering, masculine master who dictated "like a man." This extreme masculinity was perpetrated throughout the party organizations in Germany as well as in other European countries under fascist rule.

Although gender images in Europe's authoritarian regimes displayed similarities, there were also significant differences. The "new Soviet man" of the Stalin era was portrayed first and foremost as the epitome of human capability in the workplace, whereas his female counterpart was expected to exceed expectations both at home and at work. While the "romantic" approach (as characterized by Barbara Ehrenreich and Deirdre English), which confined women to the home, remained dominant in western Europe, the Soviet rulers combined it with the "rationalist" approach, which saw women primarily as a vital economic resource. The ultimate "new Soviet woman" was thus both a mother of several children and a Stakhanovite, an industrial worker granted recognition and privileges for exceeding production standards. In the face of male workers' animosity, the regime celebrated women who had mastered technology, such as the tractor driver Praskovya Angelina ("Pasha") or the textile worker Mariya Vinogradova ("Marusya"), in countless newsreels and propaganda campaigns. Those heroines of the field and factory were portrayed as committed to the well-being of society and as dutiful daughters of their "dear father Stalin."

After a period of khaki jumpsuits and heavy work boots, propaganda posters in the 1930s showed women agricultural workers in wide skirts, peasant blouses, and head scarves, an image that in 1941 was transformed into an enormous "Mother Russia" who urged her children to fight the German invaders. This image of woman-as-mother was promoted even when war demanded that she turn into a fighter and killer, as many women did in the Red Army. There were attempts to revitalize the image of Pasha during a rural labor shortage in the 1970s; in the early 1990s, the demise of the woman tractor driver also signaled the end of the Soviet state and the new "chivalry" of emerging capitalism.

Throughout much of western Europe, the fashion immediately following World War II was dictated by scarcity. The abundance of fabric that characterized Christian Dior's "New Look" in the 1950s reflected a longing both for the end of rationing and for a return to traditional gender roles. For the woman who aspired to elegance, cosmetics and accessories such as hats and gloves were indispensable. By the end of the 1960s, the shift dress made its fashion debut and western European women copied the pillbox hats and pink costumes of the American First Lady Jacqueline Kennedy. In 1964 "Swinging London" took the place of Paris as the European fashion capital. The supershort hemlines of the miniskirt created by Mary Quant were revolutionary—made possible by the invention of pantyhose. The American hippie movement of the late 1960s also inspired new European fashions, especially male fashion, which had remained relatively unchanged for much of the century. Men and women alike now dressed "unisex"—in jeans and oriental-style shirts with colorful sunglasses and accessories bedecked with flowers and beads. The pantsuit became a socially acceptable alternative for women. Hemlines were much discussed in the 1970s, varied widely, and were often combined, as when a miniskirt was matched with a "maxi" coat. Fashion of the 1980s was influenced by the dark colors and ragged clothing of the "punk" subculture that had originated in England, and by the bold hues and luxury seen on the American TV series *Dallas* and *Dynasty*. The end of the 1980s saw a return to understated but elegant and refined clothing that fit the needs and the lifestyle of the new "young urban professionals." With the collapse of communism, Western styles spread more widely and more rapidly into Eastern Europe.

CONTRACEPTION

Throughout the twentieth century the advancement of contraceptive technologies and the increasing availability of this information had a significant impact on changing gender relations in Europe. During the nineteenth century, both middle- and working-class families in northern and western Europe had begun to see a large number of children as an economic liability and had realized that smaller families generally meant a higher standard of living. By the turn of the century, similar patterns were established in southern and eastern Europe. At the same time, according to some scholars, the rate of sexual activity increased, most notably among young people and the lower classes.

Until the advent of hormonal contraception in the 1960s, birth control methods in the twentieth century did not differ much from those of the nineteenth. Coitus interruptus and abstinence were widespread, especially in working-class families. The invention of the process for vulcanizing rubber in the 1840s increased the artificial means available, though knowledge of and about condoms spread only gradually. The use of "Parisian articles" was still considered something exotic until massive state information campaigns geared toward the soldiers on the battlefields of World War I. The use of the diaphragm spread among middle-class families.

While upper- and middle-class women seem to have had better information about and access to contraceptive devices (as well as to comparatively safe abortions), until the 1970s poor women had to rely on clinics operated by radical doctors or sex reformers. Facing almost universal hostility from the medical community, the Dutch physician and feminist Aletta Jacobs (1854–1929) opened the world's first birth control clinic in Amsterdam in 1882 and had become an internationally respected authority on contraception by the 1920s. A few northern European nations allowed birth control means to be dispensed in a limited manner during the interwar years. Jacobs's clinics were never legal, but there were only a few government attempts to close them. The situation was somewhat similar in Germany until 1933 and in Denmark, where the novelist Thit Jensen and the socialist Marie Nielsen advocated birth control and sex education in schools. Although sex education did not materialize in most European countries until well after World War II, increased literacy and better scientific knowledge about women's ovulatory cycles allowed more effective practice of the rhythm method. British feminists and sex reformers also battled over access to birth control. The government prevented them from distributing contraceptive information on grounds of obscenity until 1930. Even though contraceptives were nominally available in a few northern European cities, women had difficulties obtaining them in smaller towns well into the 1950s and 1960s.

The history of birth control is epitomized by a gap between policy and practice, which certainly widened in the twentieth century. Until the 1960s, governments throughout Europe—democratic, communist, and fascist alike—promoted population growth and restricted access to contraception. In 1920 France took the lead by outlawing abortions as well as information about and the sale of contraceptives; penalties for abortionists and their clients were increased in 1923 and 1939. In Germany, the National Socialists outlawed birth control immediately after they seized power and increased penalties for abortions among "Aryans" (while forcing the "racially unfit" to submit to sterilization). Throughout Eastern Europe, contraceptive devices were either unavailable or of poor quality well into the twentieth century, which at times forced Soviet women to rely on abortions as their chief method for avoiding childbirth. Even in the early twenty-first century, birth control techniques varied considerably, depending on custom and available options. Surgical sterilization, the birth control pill, IUDs, and the morning-after pill became available throughout Europe. Generally, Western European women seemed to prefer the birth control pill, while many Eastern Europeans distrusted it.

After an initial surge after World War II, birthrates continued to decline throughout Europe. Couples restricted their fertility even in Catholic societies, where contraception and abortion remained illegal. Only extreme policies were able to reverse this trend, as in Romania, where the birthrate nearly doubled between 1966 and 1967 because of stringent antiabortion laws. Nevertheless, faced with new levels of adolescent sexual activity, concerned about the spread of disease, and pressured by feminist movements, most European governments moved toward legalizing birth control in the 1960s. Change was most dramatic in Catholic countries such as France, where the sale of contraceptive devices and the dissemination of contraceptive information were legalized in 1968, and Spain, which followed suit in 1978. Yet contraceptives remain illegal in Ireland even in the early twenty-first century.

Reproduction rates in many European countries were near their all-time lows in the first years of the twenty-first century. Many marriages remained childless, some involuntarily, and the two-parent family was no longer the norm. Single parenthood (meaning chiefly single motherhood) was on the rise throughout Europe and was widely socially accepted. New contraceptive technologies not only altered motherhood but also the way it was represented. The spread of birth control and legalized abortions in the last third of the twentieth century resulted in more autonomy for many women in every aspect of their lives and not only with respect to reproduction and sexuality, as better availability of "choice" shifted gender relations in profound ways.

GAYS AND LESBIANS

In the twentieth century, Europeans started to reconsider homosexuality, which had been regarded as a disorder. As with the shifting senses of the term *gender,* the coining of new words and their changing usage offer important clues: the terms *drag* (to connote cross-dressing) and *lesbian* (to refer to female homosexuals), for instance, date back to the 1870s and thus predate Oscar Wilde's 1895 trial for homosexual acts, an event considered decisive in redefining the acceptable boundaries of gendered identity. The use of such terms as *homo* and *queer* (to refer to homosexuals) entered the English language in the 1920s. These linguistic shifts imply that modern gay and lesbian identities emerged from a complex interaction of subcultural values and practices on one hand and of attempts at control by the state and the professions on the other. Whereas *homosexual* was a term sometimes used by doctors and antivice campaigners, gay men commonly identified themselves as *queer* in the 1910s and 1920s. By the 1940s, when the cultural climate had turned more hostile, *queer* had acquired a different meaning, implying a passionate emotion, and homosexuals came to prefer *gay,* a word that was much more guarded: outsiders would not readily understand what "having a gay time" meant. The 1990s saw a strategic redeployment of the word *queer* to connote a form of political activism and to qualify a theory of literary and cultural criticism.

Gay men were persecuted in many European countries throughout the twentieth century, most severely under authoritarian regimes. Female homosexuality was generally ignored until the beginning of the century, when the writings of sexologists as well as popular discourse started to reflect a new weariness with lesbianism, which resulted in a curtailing of the range of behavior allowed to (privileged) women. Novels and films now emphasized the dangers of lesbian teachers in girls' schools and urged mothers to protect their daughters from female (and male) sexual aggression. Crushes on other women, a boyish or mannish style of dress, and even the ambition to pursue a career were seen as warning signs of "sexual inversion." In the 1920s lesbians appeared in western (and eastern) European medical and popular discourses. While the life of lesbians in Paris and Berlin has often been romanticized, limits were certainly placed on it. Although female homosexuality was not persecuted outright, lesbians in the cosmopolitan centers of Europe were still watched by the police and their clubs were periodically raided.

Lesbians had been active in European feminist movements throughout the twentieth century, but their sexual orientation had usually been ignored, sometimes denied. The British suffragist Christabel Pankhurst (1880–1958) was a lesbian who dressed mannishly and fell in love with the author Virginia Woolf. The German feminists Anita Augspurg (1857–1943) and Lida Gustava Heymann (1868–1943) lived in a lesbian relationship for decades. In the late 1960s the culture and society of male and female homosexuals increasingly came out into the open. Building on traditions of the first gay movement of the 1920s, a new gay liberation movement formed alongside the U.S. civil rights movement and the worldwide protest against the U.S. involvement in Vietnam. The women's liberation movement embraced the issue of open and legitimate lesbian relationships, and by the late 1970s society's general acceptance of male and female homosexuals had become a goal of both movements. In the 1980s and 1990s the politics of gay and lesbian groups shifted toward AIDS research and the right for homosexual couples to marry and adopt.

"Second wave" feminism also explored whether lesbians were "naturally" feminists (and vice versa), with some lesbians claiming that only lesbians were true feminists. Lesbian separatism demanded the demise of heterosexual relationships altogether, a demand that raised many perplexing questions. Ultimately, moderation replaced militancy and lesbian and heterosexual feminists found common ground. Second wave feminism must be credited with acknowledging the contributions of lesbian feminists, and specifically with a new perspective on society that eventually extended to the whole women's movement: their viewpoint took woman as the "center," not the "other," the standard, not the variant, and provided a crucial tool for analyzing all of European culture and society.

THE VEXED QUESTION OF MASCULINITY

The study of masculinity developed as a notable component of gender theory. Like femininity, masculinity was increasingly seen as a constructed, social, and not necessarily natural set of characteristics. Scholarship on men and masculinity in Europe was relatively scarce in the early twenty-first century, certainly lagging behind the developments in the United States, yet there were some partial and tentative results concerning such issues as boyhood, fatherhood, working-class masculinity, and crime.

Studies of masculinity and modernity traced the emergence of a masculine ideal to the growth of a commercial and industrial bourgeoisie in the nineteenth century. Masculinity essentially required an intense struggle of man against himself and his body, which was subject to self-discipline and restraint. Any emotion was to be held in check, and the differences between masculine and feminine traits were sharply emphasized and had to be kept firmly in their proper place. Although masculine ideals underwent many local modifications, some of the same features occurred throughout Europe and did not start to break down in western Europe until the 1950s.

In addition to on the warfront, questions of masculinity were also posed elsewhere. In the twentieth century, European men of all classes increasingly sought recreational outlets to display their masculinity. Sports provided not only a way for educating boys to be men but also an opportunity for adults to participate on the field and as spectators. Early in the century, youth movements such as scouting offered boys an opportunity to develop their masculinity outside the female-dominated school environment. Masculine aggressiveness was asserted much more explicitly in the emerging fascist movements, which combined the masculinity of party boots and uniforms with the promise to return women to their traditional roles and more traditional clothing.

Gender differentiations certainly became less pronounced in the second half of the twentieth century. With women's increasing participation in the workforce, the breadwinner justification for masculinity diminished, even though male superiority in the workplace was still widespread. Couples started to share consumer interests, family vacations, and sometimes housework. Male-female relationships became more informal and less committed, not the least because of the availability of birth control. A large family was no longer a sign of sexual prowess. It must be kept in mind, however, that not only was late-twentieth-century maleness defined by a complex interplay between recent changes and persevering traditions, but that these definitions varied greatly between Stockholm and Naples, Moscow and Paris.

See also **Beauvoir, Simone de; Feminism.**

BIBLIOGRAPHY

Abrams, Lynn, and Elizabeth Harvey, eds. *Gender Relations in German History: Power, Agency, and Experience from the Sixteenth to the Twentieth Century.* London, 1996.

Alsop, Rachel, Annette Fitzsimmons, and Kathleen Lennon. *Theorizing Gender.* Malden, Mass., 2002.

Barnes, Ruth, and Joanne B. Eicher, eds. *Dress and Gender: Making and Meaning in Cultural Contexts.* Oxford, U.K, 1992.

Beauvoir, Simone de. *The Second Sex.* Edited and translated by H. M. Parshley. New York, 1952.

Butler, Judith. *Gender Trouble: Feminism and the Subversion of Identity.* New York, 1990.

Duberman, Martin B., Martha Vicinus, and George Chauncey. *Hidden from History: Reclaiming the Gay and Lesbian Past.* New York, 1989.

Edmondson, Linda, ed. *Gender in Russian History and Culture.* New York, 2001.

Ehrenreich, Barbara, and Deirdre English. *For Her Own Good: 150 Years of Experts' Advice to Women.* Garden City, N.Y., 1978.

Foucault, Michel. *History of Sexuality.* Vol. 1: *An Introduction.* Translated by Robert Hurley. New York, 1978.

Frader, Laura L., and Sonya O. Rose, eds. *Gender and Class in Modern Europe.* London, 1996.

Hearn, Jeff, and David Morgan, eds. *Men, Masculinities, and Social Theory.* London, 1990.

Irigaray, Luce. *This Sex Which Is Not One*. Translated by Catherine Porter with Carolyn Burke. Ithaca, N.Y., 1985.

Kent, Susan Kingsley. *Gender and Power in Britain, 1640–1990*. London, 1999.

LeVay, Simon. *Queer Science: The Use and Abuse of Research into Homosexuality*. Cambridge, Mass., 1996.

Lévi-Strauss, Claude. *Elementary Structures of Kinship*. Rev. ed. Translated by James Harle Bell, John Richard von Sturmer, and Rodney Needham. Boston, 1969.

Mead, Margaret. *Coming of Age in Samoa: A Psychological Study of Primitive Youth for Western Civilization*. New York, 1928.

Merrick, Jeffrey, and Bryant T. Ragan, eds. *Homosexuality in Modern France*. New York, 1996.

Mosse, George. *The Image of Man: The Creation of Modern Masculinity*. Oxford, U.K., 1996.

Riddle, John M. *Eve's Herbs: A History of Contraception and Abortion in the West*. Cambridge, Mass., 1997.

Scott, Joan Wallach. *Gender and the Politics of History*. New York, 1988.

Stearns, Peter N. *Be a Man! Males in Modern Society*. 2nd ed. New York, 1990.

ANJA SCHÜLER

GENERAL STRIKE (BRITAIN).

The General Strike of May 1926 was the most important industrial conflict in British history and the only occasion on which representatives of the British trade union movement as a whole have struck for more than one day in support of fellow trade unionists. In fact, almost one and three-quarter million vital or front-line workers came out in support of about one million miners who had been locked out for rejecting reductions in pay and conditions. For nine days, from 3 to 12 May, Britain ground almost to a halt. A few trains and buses ran, but only when driven by volunteers from the anti-strike middle and upper classes. Yet despite this unity of the workers, fighting what seemed to be a class war, the General Council of the Trades Union Congress (TUC) called off the dispute amid controversy, was criticized by the Communist Party of Great Britain, and lost some prestige throughout the country for the rest of the interwar years.

The General Strike was the culmination of a number of events. Most obviously, the postwar coalition government led by David Lloyd George (1863–1945) wanted to return the coal industry, which had been taken over by the state in 1915, to the coal owners (rejecting the decision of the Sankey Commission of 1919 that the coal industry should remain under state control). Thereafter, the Conservative-dominated governments of the early 1920s resolved to bring down wages in mining and other industries. At the same time, the TUC formed a General Council in 1921, part of whose responsibility was the uniting of workers industrially in order to resist wage reductions. The volatile industrial relations in the coal industry operated within this context. The return of the mines to the coal owners in April 1921 provoked a mining dispute that the miners and the Miners' Federation of Great Britain lost. This defeat was due to the decision of the other unions in the Triple Alliance, the National Union of Railwaymen and the Transport Workers Federation, on 15 April 1925 (better known as "Black Friday") not to support the miners. There was a feeling that the miners had been let down, and when they were faced with further substantial wage reductions and longer hours again in 1925, the General Council of the TUC felt obliged to support them. That potential coal conflict was bought off at the last minute on 31 July 1925, known as "Red Friday," when the Conservative government of Stanley Baldwin (1867–1947) provided a nine-month subsidy for the coal owners. This action merely delayed the mining strike by nine months, during which period the Royal Commission on Coal, chaired by Sir Herbert Louis Samuel (1870–1963), deliberated and reported upon the need to nationalize the coal industry, to temporarily reduce wages and end the subsidy. These recommendations were unlikely to satisfy the miners or the mine owners, and it was no surprise that the coal owners announced wage reductions and the ending of national negotiations in coal from 1 May 1926, the day after the subsidy expired.

The miners refused to accept the cuts in wages and the worsening of conditions of employment, and were locked out of negotiations from May until November 1926. On the other hand, in a display of unusual unity, the affiliated unions of the TUC agreed on 1 May to call out some of the vital supply and transport workers, the "front-

Workers demonstrate in Crewe, Cheshire, England, during the General Strike, 1926. ©HULTON-DEUTSCH COLLECTION/CORBIS

line" workers, on strike from 11:59 P.M. on 3 May. A last-ditch attempt to avoid conflict failed when the Baldwin government refused to talk further with the TUC because the printers at the *Daily Mail* newspaper refused to print an editorial critical of the unions. Some "second-line" workers, such as engineers and shipbuilders, were called out on 12 May, the day the strike was terminated.

The General Strike was very effective in stopping the trains, urban traffic, and the movement of goods. There was violent conflict between the strikers and the authorities, although most of it was of a minor nature. The government had prepared for the dispute, producing the *British Gazette* under the editorship of Winston Churchill, gathering food at the Hyde Park food center, and ensuring the continued movement of vital supplies throughout the country. As a result, TUC leaders were convinced that they could not win and James Henry Thomas (1874–1949), the railwaymen's

leader, was put in charge of the TUC negotiation committee that sought a resolution to the conflict. Although it could not deal directly with the government, which refused to negotiate under the threat of a strike, it enlisted the good offices of Samuel, the Liberal who had chaired the Royal Commission on Coal in 1925–1926, to discuss possible solutions to the dispute, hoping that the Baldwin government would respond to his independent role. In fact, it was quite clear that the Samuel Memorandum that emerged and was presented to the miners' leaders on 11 May would not be accepted by anyone other than the TUC. The miners objected to the suggestion that wages should be reduced, and the government was not prepared to consider the Memorandum while in dispute. Therefore, in an act of capitulation, the representatives of the TUC met with Baldwin at 10 Downing Street and called off the dispute shortly after noon on 12 May. The miners, who stuck out the strike for another six months, were abandoned by the TUC, although trade unionists paid a financial levy to support them throughout their dispute. They were eventually forced to accept wage reductions, the lengthening of hours, and the end of national negotiations in November 1926.

The symbolic and political significance of the General Strike was immense. In an obvious way, the revolutionary potential of the British trade union movement was shown to be nonexistent. The role of the TUC thus caused prolonged bitterness among the more militant sections of the miners' unions and, in the *Workers' Weekly* newspaper of 13 May 1926, the Communist Party of Great Britain denounced the calling off of the General Strike as the greatest crime ever permitted in the history of the British working class and the working class of the world. Other, less militant forces agreed. The general strike was thus discredited as a political weapon, even though the TUC had at least demonstrated some potential for unity of action. The consequences of the strike were both positive and negative. There was anti-strike legislation, particularly the Trades Dispute Act (1927), which restricted general and sympathetic strikes. The Mond-Turner talks between the big employers and the TUC opened more channels of helpful communications between unions and business, which augured well for the industrial economy of the mid and late 1930s.

See also **Labor Movements; Strikes; United Kingdom.**

BIBLIOGRAPHY

Laybourn, Keith. *The General Strike of 1926.* Manchester, U.K., 1993.

Morris, Margaret. *The General Strike.* Harmondsworth, U.K., 1976.

Phillips, G. A. *The General Strike: The Politics of Industrial Conflict.* London, 1976.

Renshaw, Patrick. *The General Strike.* London, 1975.

KEITH LAYBOURN

GENEVA. In 1900 the capital of the Republic and Canton of Geneva, as it is officially known, was a modest city of 95,000 inhabitants. The entire canton had only 132,389 people. Located on the shore of Lake Geneva, its cosmopolitan character was known throughout Europe, and it became the seat of the International Committee of the Red Cross (ICRC), founded in 1863 to protect the wounded in war and legitimized by the Geneva Convention, ratified by twelve European states in 1864 to become a founding pillar of international human rights.

Protected by Switzerland's neutral status in the First World War, the Red Cross organized assistance to the wounded and, with the International Prisoners of War Agency, also located in Geneva, it provided relief to hundreds of thousands of POWs and their families, making no distinction between nationalities.

In 1919, once peace was reestablished, Geneva was designated as the site of the headquarters of the League of Nations, founded at the urging of the U.S. president Woodrow Wilson. Henceforth the city-state of Geneva would stand for international cooperation, peacekeeping, and disarmament. The International Labor Organization (ILO), founded at the same time as the League of Nations, began construction on its headquarters on the shores of Lake Geneva in 1922. The ILO began holding annual conferences that led to the establishment of the first international labor conventions and its building was completed in 1926, the year of the official inauguration. In the 1920s a myth developed around what the publicist Robert de Traz called "the spirit of Geneva," finding its sources in Calvinism, the social and political ideas of Jean-Jacques Rousseau, and the Red Cross founder Henry Dunant's humanitarian intuitions. According to de Traz, at each of these historical junctures, "Geneva overflowed on the world." Many were convinced, during the interwar years, that the canton had a universal mission. But it did not escape the consequences of the world crisis that began in 1929, in which the ideals of peace and justice were brought down by the rise of totalitarian movements.

The Second World War gave the International Red Cross another opportunity to act on behalf of prisoners of war and the wounded, while demanding observance of the international conventions ratified by the belligerents. But the League of Nations lost all credibility and eventually dissolved, while the ILO temporarily left Geneva for New York.

In the postwar period, the new centers of international relations were Washington, London, Moscow, and New York; the last became principal headquarters for the newly founded United Nations. However, Geneva was chosen as headquarters for the UN's European office in 1946. The city was then entering a dynamic period, economically and culturally, with a rapidly shifting demographic profile. Over the next twenty years, the population of the city and canton increased from 187,000 to 350,000, including more than 95,000 foreigners. Banking, luxury commerce, and high-tech industries prospered. Geneva continued to develop its international character. The return of the ILO in 1946 preceded the establishment of numerous large international organizations, including the International Telecommunication Union (ITU) in 1947 and the World Health Organization (WHO) and General Agreement on Tariffs and Trade (GATT) in 1948. The latter would be supplanted in 1995 by the World Trade Organization (WTO). In 1951 the headquarters of the United Nations high commissioner for refugees took up residence in Geneva; that year also saw publication of the first convention for the protection of refugees and displaced persons. A newly constructed European Community established the European Organization for Nuclear Research (CERN) and the European Free Trade Association (EFTA), both in Geneva, in 1960.

Many of the nongovernmental organizations (NGOs) that require contact with international organizations on a regular basis also located their headquarters in Geneva, or at least established a permanent representative. The World Council of Churches (WCW) was constituted in 1948, followed a year later by the International Confederation of Free Trade Unions (ICFTU). Amnesty International, founded in 1961, with headquarters in London, has an international outpost in Geneva. In addition, Geneva welcomes refugees. The period since the 1970s has brought victims of South American dictatorships, Vietnamese boat people, and victims of oppressive regimes and "ethnic cleansing" in Sri Lanka, Iraq, Rwanda, and Bosnia. The canton's work with refugees has led to concern in Bern, the capital of Switzerland, that in Geneva demand for asylum is too readily granted.

In the last fifteen years of the twentieth century, Genevans were compelled to confront certain questions, not pertinent to them alone, but which could not be ignored. They pertained to World War II and two major debates that issued from it. The first took place around the stance and role of the International Red Cross concerning the deportation of Jews who were exterminated in Nazi death camps. The Red Cross knew of the extermination program in 1942, but it chose not to exceed its traditional mission and spread word of the horror of the camps. The organization decided to act instead within its historic boundaries by helping and protecting only distressed prisoners and thereby "preserving its credibility." According to *The Red Cross and the Holocaust* by Jean-Claude Favez—written with the support of the Red Cross—this decision remains problematic. The second issue questions more generally Swiss policies regarding financial, economic, and humanitarian matters during the war. Had Switzerland taken advantage of its neutral status to do business with Nazi Germany by procuring for it capital funds that could weaken the Allied effort at economic blockade? Another question is whether Switzerland, a country that usually welcomed refugees, failed its historic mission by turning back Jews, particularly on the Franco-Swiss border. Finally, there is the question of whether or to what extent Swiss banks, especially in Geneva, had profited from deposits by Holocaust victims and later appropriated the unclaimed assets. These questions shocked public opinion and were serious enough that Swiss authorities established an Independent Commission of Experts, headed by Professor Jean-François Bergier. The Bergier Commission Report, published in 1999, after three years' work, confirmed the major charges against Switzerland, though it presented an image less somber than some had predicted.

Geneva did not lose prestige in the eyes of international organizations. Since the beginning of the twenty-first century, organizations based in Geneva have been awarded the Nobel Prize over forty times. This fact reinforces the city's international image—today more a site for meetings, exchanges, and humanitarian missions than for state or international decision making.

See also **Switzerland.**

BIBLIOGRAPHY

Favez, Jean-Claude. *The Red Cross and the Holocaust.* Edited and translated by John Fletcher and Beryl Fletcher. Cambridge, U.K., and New York, 1999.

Independent Commission of Experts Switzerland. *Switzerland, National Socialism, and the Second World War: Final Report.* Zurich, 2002.

Laederer, Benjamin, et al. *Geneva, Crossroad of the Nations.* Translated by T. J. Hamilton Black. Geneva, 1964.

Santschi, Catherine, et al., eds. *Encyclopédie de Genève.* Vol. 8: *Genève, ville internationale.* Geneva, 1990.

Traz, Robert de. *L'esprit de Genève.* Lausanne, 1995.

BERNARD DELPAL

GENOCIDE. The twentieth century has sometimes been labeled as the "century of genocide." In view of historical events, this description hardly amounts to an exaggeration: never before has violence, systematically aimed at exterminating ethnic, national, or religious groups, claimed more victims than over the course of the twentieth century. The extent of collective violence as the century came to a close—such as the massacres in disintegrating Yugoslavia or Rwanda during the 1990s—dampened the hopes cherished after World War II that crimes such as the mass murder of European Jews could be prevented in the future and thus fundamentally challenged the idea of a progressive historical process.

The term *genocide* was coined by the Polish-Jewish specialist in international law Raphael Lemkin (1900–1959). He had recognized that cases like the persecution of the Armenians by the Young Turks during World War I and, above all, the extermination policy of the Nazis throughout occupied eastern Europe differed qualitatively from other forms of violence such as war crimes and thus required a specific term of their own. Lemkin's concept of genocide formed a basis for the Convention on the Prevention and Punishment of the Crime of Genocide of the United Nations adopted by the UN General Assembly in 1948. However, not only specialists in international law grappled with the phenomenon of genocide. Since the 1980s, interdisciplinary research on genocide has also begun to establish itself, initially in the United States and Canada and more recently in Europe as well.

Genocide as first defined by Raphael Lemkin in 1944:

By "genocide" we mean the destruction of a nation or of an ethnic group. . . . Generally speaking, genocide does not necessarily mean the immediate destruction of a nation, except when accomplished by mass killings of all members of a nation. It is intended rather to signify a coordinated plan of different actions aiming at the destruction of essential foundations of the life of national groups, with the aim of annihilating the groups themselves. The objectives of such a plan would be disintegration of the political and social institutions, of culture, language, national feelings, religion, and the economic existence of national groups, and the destruction of the personal security, liberty, health, dignity, and even the lives of the individuals belonging to such groups. Genocide is directed against the national group as an entity, and the actions involved are directed against individuals, not in their individual capacity, but as members of the national group. . . . Genocide has two phases: one, destruction of the national pattern of the oppressed group; the other, the imposition of the national pattern of the oppressor. This imposition, in turn, may be made upon the oppressed population which is allowed to remain, or upon the territory alone, after removal of the population and the colonization of the area by the oppressor's own nationals.

Source: Raphael Lemkin, *Axis Rule in Occupied Europe: Laws of Occupation, Analysis of Government, Proposals for Redress.* Washington, D.C., 1944, p. 79.

RAPHAEL LEMKIN AND THE GENOCIDE CONVENTION OF THE UNITED NATIONS

The basic notion that minorities must be protected from persecution by international law dates back to the seventeenth century: the Peace of Westphalia concluded in 1648 already contained terms stipulating guarantees for religious minorities. Protection of Christian minorities in the Ottoman Empire was the express purpose of the treaties European Great Powers forced on the Ottoman government in the nineteenth century. However, this commitment to protecting minorities was not altogether selfless, because these provisions generally served the imperialistic powers as a welcome pretext for military intervention in the disintegrating Ottoman

Genocide as defined in Article 2 of the UN Convention on the Prevention and Punishment of the Crime of Genocide:

In the present Convention, genocide means any of the following acts committed with intent to destroy, in whole or in part, a national, ethnical, racial or religious group, as such: (a) Killing members of the group; (b) Causing serious bodily or mental harm to members of the group; (c) Deliberately inflicting on the group conditions of life calculated to bring about its physical destruction in whole or in part; (d) Imposing measures intended to prevent births within the group; (e) Forcibly transferring children of the group to another group.

Source: United Nations Treaty Series, no. 1021, vol. 78 (1951), p. 277.

Empire. Finally, at the turn of the century codification of the law of war contributed to the international protection of human rights, albeit to a limited extent. Among other things, the Hague Convention on land war of 1907 laid down the rules of conduct by a foreign occupying army toward the civilian population. However, massacres or atrocities committed by a government against a minority living within the national borders were not subject to these provisions and therefore did not constitute a statutory offense under international law.

The notion of an international law binding to all states, one that bans the persecution and murder of ethnic, national, or religious groups, only really began to take shape in the period between the world wars. The horrors of World War I and particularly the fate of the Ottoman Armenians quite drastically revealed to politicians and experts on international law the significance of such an international agreement. By issuing a joint declaration in March 1915 denouncing the massacre of the Armenians as a "crime against humanity," the governments of France, Great Britain, and Russia had already made it clear during the war that the murder of minorities by their own governments should not go unpunished. Following their victory over the Central Powers and their allies, at first the Entente Powers

indeed made efforts to open international criminal proceedings for war crimes and "crimes against humanity." Yet these endeavors came to nothing. Contributing to this failure at first was the fact that politicians and legal experts could not agree on which acts to subsume precisely under the category of "crimes against humanity" and on which existing legal grounds to base this offense. Moreover, the Young Turk politicians responsible for the massacre of the Armenians evaded prosecution before an international court of law, because the Treaty of Sèvres, whose provisions actually stipulated such legal action, was never ratified. The victory of the Turkish nationalist movement led by Mustafa Kemal Atatürk (1881–1938) and the founding of the Turkish nation-state resulted instead in an "amnesty declaration," internationally approved in the Treaty of Lausanne in 1923, which concerned any acts committed by the Ottoman Empire during World War I that may have been punishable.

Despite the lack of decisive and lasting success in these efforts to prosecute perpetrators of violations of human rights during the world war, in the interwar period experts on international law continued to work toward establishing a system protecting national and religious minorities. The so-called minority treaties under the League of Nations were one result of these endeavors. The parties to these treaties committed to guaranteeing the protection of minorities within their national borders. Raphael Lemkin began to make his mark in these debates on international law revolving around the protection of minorities.

Even as a youth, Lemkin, a native of Bezwodene in Poland, had already developed an interest in the prevention of state-organized persecution of minorities, especially since he also belonged to a minority that faced discrimination and persecution in eastern Europe. Moreover, the fate of the Anatolian Armenians had made a lasting impression on him. In particular, the sensational trial of Salomon Teilirian in June 1921 in Berlin had been a matter of concern to Lemkin. In March 1921 the Armenian Teilirian had shot and killed in broad daylight the former Turkish interior minister Talât Paşa (1872–1921), one of the men responsible for the Armenian genocide. As his unpublished autobiography reveals, this act of vigilantism led Lemkin to conclude that an international law had to be created

Genocide as defined by Helen Fein:

Genocide is a series of purposeful actions by a perpetrator(s) to destroy a collectivity through mass or selective murders of group members and suppressing the biological and social reproduction of the collectivity. This can be accomplished through the imposed proscription or restriction of group members, increasing infant mortality, and breaking the linkage between reproduction and socialization of children in the family or group of origin. The perpetrator may represent the state of a victim, another state or another collectivity.

Source: Quoted in Frank Chalk and Kurt Jonassohn, eds., *The History and Sociology of Genocide: Analyses and Case Studies.* New Haven, Conn., 1990, p. 16.

in order to make the deliberate annihilation of national and religious groups a punishable offense.

After obtaining his doctorate of philology from the University of Lvov in 1926, Lemkin rose to become a renowned expert in international law and a leading advocate of the protection of minorities. To him the protective provisions drawn up in the context of the minority treaties did not go far enough. For that reason he proposed, at the Fifth International Conference for the Unification of Penal Law in Madrid (1933), the establishment of two additional statutory offenses in international law: "vandalism" and "barbarism" were to be included in the domestic criminal law of the thirty-seven participant states. By "vandalism" Lemkin meant the deliberate destruction of the cultural heritage of a specific group; by "barbarism" the suppression and extermination of members of a racial, religious, or social group. However, the congress rejected Lemkin's proposals.

In 1939 Lemkin became a victim of persecution himself. He had to leave Poland and escaped to the United States via Sweden, initially teaching at Duke University and finally at Yale. The indifference the U.S. public displayed toward the extermination policy of the Nazis in eastern Europe was deeply troubling to Lemkin. He hoped that a treaty aimed at guaranteeing the protection of ethnic and religious minorities, signed by the Allies and the neutral countries, could deter the National Socialists from the annihilation of the European Jews. Yet his plans did not meet with any considerable echo among U.S. politicians.

In his book *Axis Rule in Occupied Europe,* which analyzed the brutal German occupation policy across conquered Europe, Lemkin made a powerful plea in 1944 for passing an international law outlawing and thus preventing the persecution and destruction of peoples and minorities. Since, according to the Hague Conventions on land war, the murder of a people by an occupying force during wartime was a punishable offense, now, Lemkin argued, a new international law would have to be in force during peacetime as well.

In *Axis Rule in Occupied Europe,* Lemkin introduced into international law the neologism he had coined: genocide. Lemkin compounded the word *genocide* from the Old Greek *genos* (race, people, or tribe) and the Latin verb *caedere* (to kill). The meaning of his definition of genocide was broad and narrow at the same time. Lemkin regarded as genocide solely the destruction of national groups. Yet he did not interpret "genocide" exclusively as the physical murder of all members of a nation but included all acts aimed at destroying their basis of life and culture. Moreover, in his work Lemkin explained the various "techniques of genocide" using the example of Nazi rule and exterminatory policy in Europe in political, social, cultural, economic, biological, physical, religious, and moral terms. The chapter on the concept of genocide in *Axis Rule in Occupied Europe* concludes with the demand that the crime of genocide must elicit universal jurisdiction and ought to belong to the *delicta juris gentium* (offenses of international law) just like slavery, child trafficking, and piracy.

Lemkin hoped that after the end of the war the statutory offense of genocide would be included in the charges brought by the International Military Tribunal (IMT) against the National Socialist war criminals, but this was not the case. In the so-called Nuremberg Trials lasting from 18 October 1945 until 1 October 1946 the twenty-two major German war criminals had to answer for, among other things, "crimes against humanity." The allegations included murder, extermination, enslavement or deportation, and persecution of the civilian population for racist as well as religious reasons. Consequently the indictment of the military tribunal charged the accused specifically with having systematically committed mass murders against racial and religious groups—above all, Jews, Poles, and Sinti and Roma—and to have annihilated them. The judges presiding over the court, however, linked the "crimes against humanity" to the war itself and thus differentiated between the persecution of the German Jews before the war and the German extermination policy during the war in the occupied territories. In order to include the persecution of the German Jews before the outbreak of war in 1939 in the charge nonetheless, the prosecutors and judges argued that these persecutions had served to prepare the German war of aggression, something even a representative of the French delegation deemed a threadbare line of argument. This linking of "crimes against humanity" with war soon posed an obstacle. Specialists in international law recognized that this new statutory offense was problematic for the future punishment of systematic persecution and massacres committed by a government during peacetime against an ethnic or religious group among its own national population. Therefore it would hardly be suitable as protection for minorities. New paradigms were called for in international law.

In April 1947, therefore, the secretary-general of the United Nations, Trygve Lie (1896–1968), commissioned Raphael Lemkin, the Romanian Vespasian V. Pella (1897–1952) who was president of the International Association of Penal Law, and Henri Donnedieu de Vabres (1880–1952), a French law professor and former judge at the IMT, to prepare a draft of an international criminal code against genocide.

Lemkin's concept of genocide constituted the basis of a possible draft, but the three experts on international law took differing views with respect to some crucial points. Lemkin deemed the deliberate destruction of a group's culture—for instance, by banning use of a language or destruction of religious and historical monuments—to be a form of genocide, something his two colleagues regarded as an inadmissible extension of the term. With the exception of the forced transfer of children into a different group, Pella and de Vabres did not consider forms of forced assimilation as being genocidal.

On 9 December 1948 the UN General Assembly meeting at the Palais de Chaillot in Paris eventually passed the final version of the Genocide Convention, which Lemkin, Pella, and de Vabres had agreed on, by a vote of 55–0–0. The convention came into effect on 12 January 1951, after being ratified by twenty countries as well. In arriving at the definition on which the convention was based the authors deliberately choose the formulation "in whole or in part," especially since the convention would otherwise only have taken effect if members of a certain group had already been murdered. By definition, political groups cannot be victims of genocide. The Soviet Union had opposed the inclusion of this group, fearing to come under suspicion of genocide itself because of the Stalinist terror.

Issues of the practical applicability and scope of the convention are detailed in the nineteen articles: Article 1 states expressly that genocide constitutes a crime according to international law, regardless of being committed during war or in peacetime. Furthermore, according to Article 3, even the attempt to commit genocide is punishable by law. Article 6 provides that persons accused of genocide will be brought before a court of competent jurisdiction in the country on whose territory the acts were carried out or before the International Criminal Court.

The actual innovation of the Genocide Convention consisted of the juridical abolition of the principle of sovereignty. Until the end of World War II, governments had been able, in principle, to destroy parts of their population unpunished. The Genocide Convention issued by the United Nations put an end to this deplorable state of affairs.

Nevertheless, the Genocide Convention had no effect for a long time following its adoption. The absence of international jurisdiction—the Rome Statute on the establishment of an International Criminal Court only came into force on 1 July 2002—and of an effective monitoring and control system made the convention appear as a mere statement of intent and thus actually as a superfluous provision. Contributing to this above all were the political constellations determined by the Cold War. The superpowers, which would have had the means at their disposal to punish the crime of genocide, did not wish to meddle in the domestic affairs of their respective allies. They merely denounced the offenses perpetrated by the opposing side. Although the Genocide Convention was not applied at first, it nevertheless represented a frame of reference to document the severity of state-organized crimes against minorities.

The end of the bipolar world order of the Cold War helped the convention achieve greater significance. In connection with the war in Bosnia (1992–1995) and the murder of 800,000 Tutsi and Hutu in Rwanda in 1994 its provisions were actually applied at last. In February 1993 the UN Security Council decided to set up an ad hoc tribunal for the punishment of the "serious violation of humanitarian international law" that had been committed on the territory of the former Yugoslavia, the International Criminal Tribunal for the Former Yugoslavia (ICTY). In November 1994 followed the resolution to entrust the International Criminal Tribunal for Rwanda (ICTR) with the legal prosecution of crimes committed in Central Africa. The statutes, very similar in both cases, included an assessment based on the Genocide Convention. On 2 September 1998, finally, the first verdict ever on the count of genocide was handed down, as the ICTR found Jean Paul Akayesu, the former mayor of the Rwandan town of Taba, guilty as charged.

These developments gave cause for optimism that in future the UN Genocide Convention would be able to contribute more substantially to the prevention and punishment of genocides. Chief among them was the breakthrough achieved at the 1998 international conference in Rome toward establishment of an International Criminal Court, intended to serve as an effective instrument to punish genocide, crimes against humanity, and war crimes. However, the helpless and largely indifferent reaction by the international community of states to the massacres of the minorities of the Fur, Zaghawa, and Masaalit initiated by the Sudanese government in 2003 in the province of West Darfur dampened this confidence. The example illustrates that the mere existence of provisions and instruments of international law alone does not suffice to prevent or punish genocides effectively.

Lemkin's role was second to none in the realization of an international law that makes systematic persecution of minorities a punishable offense. He not only provided the basis of the Genocide Convention in international law but also, as a lobbyist, fought untiringly for its realization. Lemkin, though, deserves credit not just because of his achievements in international law. He had also dealt in detail with the historical background to past genocides and was planning to publish a comprehensive work on forms of collective violence in human history. However, he was unable to find a publisher, as a result of which his manuscripts, for instance, on the murder of the Herero in German South-West Africa (1904–1908) and on the genocide of the Armenians remain filed among his unpublished papers. Only since the beginning of the twenty-first century have historians recognized the significance of Lemkin's historical works. Lemkin is now regarded as a pioneer of a new branch of research: genocide studies.

THE CONCEPT OF GENOCIDE IN THE SOCIAL SCIENCES

The interdisciplinary study of genocide started in earnest only in the 1980s, but by the early twenty-first century had managed to gain a firm foothold in the academic work at universities. Genocide studies comprise a broad field and are concerned, apart from questions of international law, with the social and individual psychological motivation of genocide perpetrators; they also deal with survival strategies as well as post-traumatic stress management for victims of persecution. Further, this research explores forms of remembrance and representation of genocide in literature and art and deals with the question of how this complex and straining topic ought to be conveyed in schools.

Transferring the concept of genocide as derived from international law into the social sciences has been rather difficult, posing a number of methodological problems. According to the definition of genocide by the United Nations, the express intention of perpetrators is to destroy a people partially or entirely, a constitutive feature of genocides. In international law, only proof of this subjective element of the offense can result in a conviction on the count of genocide. Such an intentionalist argument is difficult to reconcile with the insights of empirically oriented historical research, which contends that governmental extermination policies generally constitute complex processes that undergo various phases of radicalization and depend on a range of situational factors such as the course of a war. Studies on National Socialist population and extermination policy and on other mass murders have revealed that these cases were not murders exclusively organized by central authorities and carefully planned long before the actual crime. For instance, the mass deaths of Soviet prisoners of war during World War II, caused by hunger, disease, and exhaustion, or of the Herero and Nama in concentration camps during the colonial war from 1904 to 1908 in German South-West Africa were not brought about premeditatedly. If, therefore, one were to keep strictly to the definition of genocide by the United Nations, one could not call either of these two cases genocides. Yet causing the deaths of members of an ethnic or religious group by imposing unreasonable living and prison conditions nevertheless has to be characterized as being genocidal, because the prisoners' deaths were willingly accepted.

The UN definition of genocide excludes political groups and social classes as potential victims of genocide. The reasons for this restriction are political, certainly not scientific, and have their origins in the intervention of the Soviet Union. With respect to the murder of more than 1.5 million Cambodians between 1975 and 1979 by the Khmer Rouge, the strict interpretation of the United Nations' definition of genocide is highly unsatisfactory. To be sure, the murderous violence committed by Pol Pot (1928?–1998) and his followers was directed against ethnic and religious groups as well, thus constituting the offense of genocide. However, the majority of victims belonged to the ethnic group of the Khmer themselves. The Khmer Rouge strove to wipe out the bourgeois class comprising, in their view, city dwellers and merchants. According to the criteria and provisions of the UN Convention on Genocide, this crime strictly speaking does not constitute genocide, even though it involved the attempt by the ruling authorities to exterminate a defenseless group.

Due to these methodological problems and inadequacies inherent in the concept of genocide, a small number of scholars fundamentally reject its application outside the area of international law. The great majority of social scientists, though, who do not wish to do without the term, feel compelled to remedy shortcomings of definition and to redefine the term in part. As a result, by now a great variety of definitions of genocide exist.

The lack of a generally accepted definition as well as the use of numerous competing terms such as *ethnocide* and *politicide*, often used synonymously for genocide, is contributing to the vagueness attached to the concept in the social sciences. The large numbers of different definitions make broad agreement impossible with regard to which historical cases of mass murder should be classified unequivocally as genocide.

Nevertheless, a few definitions of genocide, useful for analyzing and categorizing mass murders, have gained acceptance among researchers. The definition provided by the sociologist Helen Fein (b. 1934) has provided a solid working basis. The great value of Fein's definition derives from the inclusion of political and social groups as possible victims. Moreover, she emphasizes that genocides are not only committed by states. Hence Fein also interprets the destruction of indigenous societies by settlers acting independent of state control as a form of genocide. The question of whether the expulsion or decimation of indigenous peoples by settlers in the age of European colonialism was actually genocidal is subject to controversial discussions among historians. As the following argument will show, the hypothesis often advocated in the scholarly literature—that genocides are only committed by modern state machineries—takes too narrow a view.

GENOCIDE AND THE MODERN AGE

Raphael Lemkin felt that genocide was "an old practice in its modern development." In fact, the annihilation of peoples by others is as old as history itself. Several examples have come down from ancient times, such as the devastating campaign by Athens against Melos (416 B.C.E.) and the destruction of Carthage by the Romans (146 B.C.E.). Most researchers on genocide, however, assume that the genocides of the twentieth century differ substantially from those of premodern times.

To begin with, the connection between genocide and the modern age was a matter of scholarly investigation for the two philosophers and cofounders of the Frankfurt school of social research, Theodor Adorno (1903–1969) and Max Horkheimer (1895–1973), in their work *Dialektik der Aufklärung* (1947; Dialectic of Enlightenment). Adorno and Horkheimer located the root causes of fascism in the

European Enlightenment. They ascertained that the rationalist disenchantment of the world, its turn away from magic, had changed into its opposite, creating a "modern mythology of science and technology." Ethics, they argued, had been sacrificed to the thirst for understanding inherent in the Enlightenment. In the end such fanaticism of knowledge had produced a favorable effect on the rise of fascism, considering after all that it had furnished the state with superior technology; at the same time, it had undermined moral scruples about the uninhibited exercise of an all-pervasive state power. This Enlightenment critique was taken up by the Polish-born British sociologist Zygmunt Bauman (b. 1925). He established that Enlightenment thought underlying the modern age favored forms of terror that strove to subjugate human societies to an ideological scheme by means of violence. To Bauman, rationality, bureaucracy, a cult of science, the idea of nation-states, and the ambitions and industriousness of political technocrats intending to create the perfect society (*societas perfecta*) were typical attributes of the modern age. Bauman compares the implementation of such utopian societal models to the work of a gardener, as human societies were, like ornamental gardens, slated to be redesigned according to clear organizing criteria. In Bauman's view, attempts to found nation-states or to establish "racially homogenous" societies were therefore bound to result in expulsion and genocide.

For historians working empirically, however, the distinction between modern and premodern genocides is rather difficult to prove. The genocide in Rwanda in 1994 saw the slaying of close to eight hundred thousand Tutsi within a matter of mere months by means of very simple weapons such as machetes. This seems to contradict the thesis that the genocides of the twentieth century were more devastating than premodern genocides only because of advanced technology and the greater destructive potential resulting from it. Advocates of the thesis about the different quality of modern genocides recognize modern, predominantly racist ideologies as the essential distinguishing feature. The French genocide scholar Yves Ternon (b. 1932) thinks that prior to the twentieth century the destruction of peoples had taken place because of vindictiveness, profit mongering, or thirst for conquest. The Armenians and the European Jews were murdered, however, because the Young Turk and National Socialist perpetrators, respectively, intended to put into effect their racist worldview. This conclusion is problematic. Neither the annihilation of the Armenians nor the murder of the Jews can be regarded simply as ideological genocides. Such a perspective involves the risk of monocausality. After all, empirically sound studies of both these genocides in the twentieth century have revealed that seemingly ordinary motives such as rapaciousness combined with racist and nationalist attitudes to contribute to the Turks' and Germans' readiness to use violence. As a rule, genocides are carried out for a variety of reasons. European settlers in Australia and America committed atrocities against the indigenous populations not solely because of their greed for land. At the same time, a religious sense of being chosen and of racial superiority was firmly embedded in the minds of the European conquerors, fostering their propensity for violence against the natives and simultaneously providing an ideological basis of justification.

COLONIAL GENOCIDES

Since the beginning of European overseas expansion in the fifteenth century, the indigenous population in the Americas had been decreasing drastically. In the period from 1500 to 1600 alone, the numbers of indigenous people diminished from approximately seventy million to about ten million. Even though the European conquerors treated the Native American inhabitants ruthlessly and contributed substantially to their weakening by subjecting them to forced labor, this decline in population cannot be viewed as the consequence of genocide. The occurrence of previously unknown infectious diseases, for instance smallpox and measles, proved decisive for the deaths of most people.

Nonetheless, the history of European colonialism is tied closely to the destruction of foreign peoples and civilizations. Victims of genocides were the indigenous populations in the Australian, North American, and African settlement colonies. Commonly extermination processes got under way when the natives were dispensable to the colonial economy and their lands earmarked for the settlement of European immigrants. The British colonialists in New England and later in Australia in any case believed the extinction of Native Americans and Aborigines to be part of a divine plan of salvation. The mass deaths of the natives due to newly introduced epidemics was interpreted by the Puritans as a result of divine providence. The demonization of the indigenous population and the firm belief in their own chosen status underpinned the settlers' ideological claim to land in the "New World." Armed confrontations with the natives such as the Pequot War (1637) and King Philip's War (1675) saw the line to genocide sometimes being overstepped. Thus the New England settlers declared the Pequot nation to be dissolved after they had massacred the majority of this people and sold the survivors into slavery. In 1763 Lord Jeffrey Amherst (1717–1797), the commander in chief of the British army in North America, ordered his subordinates to exterminate natives by distributing blankets contaminated with smallpox. In following the order, the British handed over blankets to chiefs of the Delaware Indian nation, who had arrived at Fort Pitt for negotiations. Indeed, shortly afterward a smallpox epidemic was raging among the Delaware natives. The European colonizers believed that by their murderous deeds they were doing God's bidding, feeling that the gradual extermination of pagan native inhabitants matched the divine will.

By the nineteenth century a social Darwinist justification was beginning to replace the religious one. European settlers in America and Australia now viewed confrontations with the indigenous population as "racial struggles." Consequently the fight for land and the right to exist in the New World became a zero-sum game, since the settlers believed that only the strongest would be able to triumph in the end. Now Europeans considered the destruction of the natives as an important step toward the conquest and cultivation of new living space. As a result, in Australia the racially justified violence against the Aborigines assumed devastating proportions. Settlers took the initiative and organized lethal campaigns against natives. In the second half of the nineteenth century, the degree to which extermination was organized also underwent change and assumed more modern features. Instead of settlers' associations acting independently, the period saw the establishment of special army and police units by the state that were entrusted with fighting the indigenous population. For instance, in November 1864 the Third Colorado Cavalry commanded by Colonel John Chivington committed a massacre against the Cheyenne on Sand Creek. And in Australia, the government's Native Police of Queensland, cynically made up of nonlocal Aborigines and European officers, was responsible for the expulsion and murder of natives on the "frontier" in Queensland, where land was required for settlers breeding livestock.

Cultural contact between European colonizers and the indigenous population was not solely characterized by massacres and displacement. Nevertheless, a genocidal quality seems to be fundamentally inherent in colonialism. Even colonialists' attempts to integrate native populations into their modern development projects were quite frequently carried out in a violent way. For instance, in order to force natives into the African settlement and plantation colonies as paid laborers, colonizers often felt they first had to destroy traditional socioeconomic and political structures, the essential elements of indigenous culture. The elimination of the economic basis for life of indigenous hunter-gatherer societies, for instance, by forced settlement of nomadic groups, runs throughout the history of European colonialism. According to the UN definition of genocide and consequently in the legal sense, this and other forms of forced assimilation, which could certainly also serve a supposedly humanitarian purpose in the Europeans' self-image as proponents of a "civilizing mission," do not, strictly speaking, constitute genocide. An exception is the forced transfer of children from one ethnic or religious group to another. Yet many forms of forced assimilation clearly correspond to Lemkin's concept of "cultural genocide," which he could not incorporate in the UN Genocide Convention.

In the final analysis, the distinction frequently encountered in the scholarly literature between modern and colonial genocide makes little sense. After all, in the context of European colonialism, racism and social Darwinism, which are fundamental ingredients of the exterminatory ideologies of the twentieth century such as National Socialism, have also served as an ideological basis contributing to the destruction of indigenous peoples overseas. One example underscoring this view is the genocide committed in South-West Africa in 1904–1908.

THE GENOCIDE OF THE HERERO AND NAMA IN GERMAN SOUTH-WEST AFRICA

"I believe that the nation as such must be destroyed." Those were the words the German general Lothar von Trotha (1848–1920) used to express his opinion about how the war on the Herero ought to be ended after they had been defeated militarily in the Battle of Waterberg on 11 August 1904. What had started on 12 January 1904 as a colonial war—not unusual in those days—developed into a real genocide against the South-West African native nations of the Herero and Nama, causing close to eighty thousand deaths and altering permanently the socioeconomic and political structures of the indigenous societies.

The German Empire became a colonial power in 1884, after Reich Chancellor Otto von Bismarck (1815–1898) had declared present-day Namibia a German sphere of influence and imperial protectorate. The start of colonization proved to be extremely difficult because Bismarck and his successors were not prepared to provide significant funds for the prestigious colonial project. In terms of implementing the German claim to power, therefore, the German governor Theodor Leutwein (1849–1921) had to rely on support from the chiefs of the local Herero and Nama, who primarily lived off raising livestock. Leutwein pursued a perfidious policy of "divide and conquer," thus gradually extending German influence.

The revolt of the Herero against German colonial rule broke out on 12 January 1904 in Okahandja. During the first months of the war the military initiative was with the Herero. Theodor Leutwein's inability to crush the rebellion quickly prompted Kaiser William II (1859–1941) and the German chief of general staff, Alfred, count von Schlieffen (1833–1913), to entrust General von Trotha with the military command in South-West Africa. This transfer of command led to a radicalization of the German conduct of war. Von Trotha was an experienced colonial warrior, who had already participated in suppressing the so-called Chinese Boxer Rebellion in 1900 and, prior to that, had waged an extremely ruthless war on the Wahehe nation in German East Africa. The German general made no secret of his aversion to Africans. He simply shrugged off the arguments put forth by members of the colonial administration in South-West Africa that the Herero were indispensable to the economic development of the colony as workers. Instead, he waged a war of extermination aimed above all at Herero women and children.

After the military defeat at the Battle of Waterberg, the Herero and their families fled into the Omaheke desert, the frontier to British Botswana. Von Trotha ordered pursuit of the fleeing survivors and had access to the watering places closed off. He deliberately accepted that thousands died an agonizing death of thirst. On 2 October 1904 the general issued his notorious genocide order, instructing his troops to shoot any Herero inside the German borders. He was absolutely determined to put an end to the Herero's existence in German South-West Africa. This intention was derived from the understanding, inspired by social Darwinism, that the war on the Herero was an inevitable "racial war."

The government in Berlin, however, feared that von Trotha's extermination policy might jeopardize Germany's reputation in the world and the very economic basis of the colony. Eventually he received orders to revoke his "shooting order" and to take the surviving Herero into concentration camps. Forced labor, inadequate nutrition, and poor hygienic conditions in these camps meant that half of the prisoners perished during this second phase of the genocide.

Following the bloody suppression of the Herero rebellion in 1904, the Nama rose up against the colonial rule. What ensued was a guerrilla war lasting several years, in the course of which German troops practiced a scorched earth policy in an attempt to destroy the basis for life of the Nama living in the south of Namibia. Captured Nama were also penned up in concentration camps.

Until 1908 the Herero were officially prisoners of war and hired out in exchange for a fee to private companies for work on the railways or on farms. According to the plans of the German colonial administration, any type of "tribal organization" in the colony was to cease to exist. Enactment of the so-called Native Peoples Act in 1907 aimed at permanently guaranteeing the power relationships in the colony, with the indigenous population to be transformed into a manipulable working class subjected to total control. Among these decrees was the obligation to carry a passport. All Herero were forced to wear a tin tag with a number around their necks. Nevertheless, the Herero found ways to circumvent the rigid German monitoring system and to reorganize over time. In historiography, the process of social reconstruction among the Herero has raised adequate interest only since the late twentieth century.

Forty years passed between the genocidal colonial war in Namibia and the murder of the Jews by the Nazis. Without any doubt, there are continuities between these two events that are rooted in intellectual history. Both the war on the Herero and the National Socialist genocide of the Jews in eastern Europe during World War II were viewed by the perpetrators in a characteristically social Darwinist manner as a struggle for living space. Moreover, even the type of violence used suggests continuities: just as the German colonial authorities approved of the mass deaths of their prisoners in the concentration camps, the Nazis readily accepted the deaths of Soviet prisoners of war and Jewish forced laborers due to exhaustion and hunger. Yet this constituted, of course, only a preliminary stage on the path toward systematic murder committed by using gas. To be sure, research into this and additional connecting links thus cannot aim at a monocausal argument tracing back the Holocaust to the first genocide committed by Germans in Africa. Nonetheless, the murder of the Herero and Nama has a significant place in the global history of genocide. As a colonial war waged by one state it represents, as it were, a connection between the destruction of indigenous populations in North America and Australia, which was largely carried out by settlers' associations, and the bureaucratically organized genocide by the Nazis. Certainly the genocide directed against the Armenians during World War I, eleven years after the murder of the Herero, did not reveal the same degree of bureaucratic organization as the National Socialist mass murder. Yet in terms of the historical evolution of genocidal violence, it nonetheless constitutes a further negative quantum leap, because in this case a government intended to exterminate a bothersome ethno-religious minority by using the state machinery at its disposal.

THE GENOCIDE OF THE ARMENIANS

The Armenians had been living in the region between the Caucasus and Taurus since about 1000 B.C.E. After their King Tiridates III (286–344) had been baptized in the year 301, the Armenians adopted Christianity. In the Ottoman Empire, they had been tolerated for centuries. As non-Muslims they did not suffer systematic persecution but faced permanent discrimination nevertheless. For instance, they were not allowed to bear arms, and before a court of law their word did not carry the same weight as a Muslim's testimony. Furthermore, they had to pay a special tax. Relations between Armenians and Muslims gradually deteriorated when the Ottoman Empire began to disintegrate in the second half of the nineteenth century.

Above all, it was the Armenians' "cultural renaissance" observed at this time by contact with Protestant missionaries from Europe and the United States that made their coexistence with Kurds and Turks more difficult. The Armenians now stressed their national identity and sometimes organized in small armed groups to defend themselves against attacks by Kurds. The fact that the Armenians had, in cooperation with U.S. missionaries, managed at the 1878 Congress of Berlin to make the "Armenian question"—the question concerning the Armenians' legal status and their safety in the eastern provinces of the Ottoman Empire—a subject of international diplomacy worsened mutual relations between Armenians and Muslims even further.

In the end, pressure exerted by the European Great Powers on the Ottoman Empire to improve the Armenians' status proved counterproductive. In the period from 1894 to 1896 serious anti-Armenian pogroms shook the multiethnic Ottoman Empire, with about 100,000 people falling victim to the violence. There is evidence that these violent clashes did not take place spontaneously but were encouraged by Sultan Abdul-Hamid II. These actions by no means aimed at the expulsion or murder of all Armenians. Rather, they represented an attempt to restore and cement the traditional order, in which Christians had been dominated by Muslims.

In 1908 the opposition Young Turks toppled the sultan and launched ambitious reform programs that were supposed to improve the status of ethno-religious minorities such as the Armenians.

However, severe military defeats during the Balkan Wars in 1912–1913 and the annexation of Libya by Italy in 1914 caused the Young Turks to abandon this course. Additionally, when in spring 1914 Russia planned to destabilize the Ottoman Empire even further, pushing for an international plan for reform that would have granted the Armenians greater autonomy, the Young Turks fully came to view their Armenian citizens as a "fifth column" threatening the survival of the empire. Immediately after the Ottoman Empire's entry into World War I on the side of the Central Powers, paramilitary units began carrying out systematic attacks on Armenian villages on the border with Russia. Yet it was not before February 1915 that the Young Turk policy toward the Armenians underwent a radicalization leading to genocide. Just prior to this, the Russians had inflicted a crushing defeat on the Ottoman army under the command of Enver Pasha (1881–1922) at Sarikamis. While the Russian army now advanced from the Caucasus, Allied forces were preparing a landing at Gallipoli. Increasingly, fears of complete collapse dominated the thoughts and actions of the Young Turk leadership. After substantial Turkish provocation, an Armenian uprising in the Anatolian city of Van in April 1915 confirmed the Young Turks in their view that the Armenians posed a significant military threat. But that was not all. An additional motive for the genocide of the Armenians had a material background: the Young Turks required the wealth of the murdered Armenians to ensure they could sustain the continued war effort financially. The Young Turk war administration intended to leave the lands expropriated from the Armenians to Muslims who had been expelled from lost territories in the Balkans and the Caucasus.

The detention and murder of Armenian intellectuals, artists, and politicians in Istanbul in April 1915 is considered the actual start of the genocide. In the eastern provinces, where most of the Armenians lived, the local authorities ordered Armenian men and older boys to be executed outside the villages and towns. Women and children were driven on foot to concentration camps in the Syrian desert. These were death marches and by no means militarily necessary resettlements, as the Turkish government maintains. Those in power in Ankara continue to deny the genocide. But overwhelming evidence shows that the deportees were poorly supplied and that the authorities deliberately took them on detours on their way to Syria. Repeatedly, Kurds and members of special military units attacked the deportees. Armenian women suffered not only from hunger, exhaustion, and from the heat but also became victims of sexual violence. Whenever the deportation marches passed through larger towns, local Turks and Kurds bought young women and children from the gendarmes and forced them into their households.

The authorities had made hardly any preparations for the arrival of the expellees in the Syrian desert. The Armenians were imprisoned in concentration camps, where hygienic conditions were atrocious. About 870,000 Armenians reached the final destination of the deportation in 1915. By early 1916 only around 500,000 of them were still alive, and from April to September 1916 another 200,000 became victims of systematic massacres. Overall, anywhere from 800,000 to 1.4 million Armenians were killed. For the time being, a more accurate count of the victims is impossible, as contemporary statistics are not reliable.

The murder of the Armenians during the world war was, like the expulsion of the Anatolian Greeks in the postwar period, an important prerequisite for the transformation of the multiethnic Ottoman Empire into a Turkish nation-state, which was initiated by the Young Turks and completed by Mustafa Kemal Atatürk. By accepting this fact at the Middle East conference at Lausanne in 1923 and refraining from punishment of the Young Turk perpetrators of the genocide, western diplomacy set a fatal precedent—for in Europe, revisionist and right-wing nationalist circles, including leading figures of the forming National Socialist Party in Germany, regarded the genocide of the Armenians as an admittedly unpleasant but all the more successful model for "solving" minority questions.

THE NATIONAL SOCIALISTS' POPULATION AND EXTERMINATION POLICY

The terms *Holocaust* and *Shoah* have become generally established as generic names for the National Socialist murder of the Jews during World War II. Both terms are problematic, however. The word *Holocaust* is derived from Greek, with the original meaning being "burnt offering or burnt sacrifice."

The Hebrew expression *Shoah* too originally has a religious connotation. In the Hebrew Bible, *Shoah* is used to denote a divine cloud, encompassing catastrophes and disasters threatening Israel, which have as a source God's anger. Such religious references are evidently out of place in this context. Another argument against the use of these terms is the fact that they leave out the overarching context of the National Socialist extermination policy, which also took the lives of Sinti and Roma, Russians, Poles, and patients of psychiatric hospitals. The Nazis were aiming not only at exterminating the Jews; they were rather pursuing visions of a gigantic pan-European displacement of peoples according to racial criteria. This scheme intended eastern Europe to be acquired as "lebensraum" and to be "Germanized." With respect to Poles and Russians, the German settlement plans such as the notorious General Plan East provided for partial extermination, deportation to Siberia, or transformation into a people of working slaves without any access to education.

The Jews had an essential position within the Nazi ideology. They were regarded as the dark force threatening to prevent the rise of the "Aryan race." Hitler very early on had expressed his intention to exterminate Jewry. Nevertheless, the genocide committed during World War II was not the outcome of years of careful planning. In the early twenty-first century historians generally view the anti-Jewish policies of the Nazis as a process, in which several bursts of radicalization led to genocide.

At the outset, Nazi policy toward the German Jews was aimless and marked by sporadic violent clashes. It attained a more systematic nature through the enactment of the so-called Nuremberg Laws in 1935. Henceforth the objective was to exclude the Jews socially and to classify them racially as well as to "Aryanize" their property. As well, the Nazis increasingly relied on radical terrorist measures, such as during the November Pogrom in 1938, in order to force Jews to emigrate. For a while the Nazis' calculation proved right. Between 1933 and 1937 more than 130,000 Jews left Germany. However, when the United States and neighboring European countries began regulating the admission of Jews, emigration was no longer an effective means to "solve the Jewish question."

Following the German military victory over Poland in 1939, the Germans had within their sphere of influence a population of 3.5 million Jews, whom they forced into ghettos. German population policy experts contemplated resettling the Jews to either Madagascar or Siberia. However, these utopian and rather crude plans proved impracticable not least for logistical reasons. Apparently the German authorities intended to make a final decision on a "solution of the Jewish question" only after the German military victory that was expected to materialize soon farther east.

After the German attack on the Soviet Union in June 1941 the line toward genocide was crossed. The planned murder of millions of Jews and Russians by mass shootings or due to hunger was part of the military strategy and matched a perfidious economic rationality, which ultimately corresponded with the racist worldview of the Nazis. The goal was to deprive the Jews and Slavs—racially inferior and "unworthy of life" according to the Nazis—of material goods and food in order to utilize these resources in the military effort that would bring "Aryan" victory in the "racial war." Above all, it was the so-called Einsatzgruppen (special task groups) that carried out massacres of the Jewish population, and they frequently operated behind the front, sometimes in tandem with the German Wehrmacht.

The definitive decision for the "Final Solution" came at some point after the initial invasion of the Soviet Union. On 20 January 1942 high-ranking officials meeting at the Berlin suburb of Wannsee discussed and coordinated the murder of all European Jews. The crucial element in this decision, which could hardly have been more radical, was not merely the Nazis' seemingly irrational racial hatred. In fact, expropriating European Jews made it possible to generate resources and funds essential for the conduct of war and to pass on the war-related social burdens faced by the populations in Germany and in the occupied territories.

About 6 million Jews became victims of the National Socialist extermination policy. Not only was the extent of the Nazi genocide inconceivable: in addition, the industrialized killing of 2.5 to 3 million people (90 percent of them Jews), carried out in a heinous division of labor at the extermination camps of Auschwitz-Birkenau, Chelmno, Majdanek, Treblinka, and elsewhere, stands out in the global history of collective violence and genocide, representing a staggering assembly line of death. Here genocide reached its culmination.

See also **Armenian Genocide; Concentration Camps; Convention on Genocide; Hague Convention; Holocaust; Wannsee Conference.**

BIBLIOGRAPHY

Aly, Götz. *"Final Solution": Nazi Population Policy and the Murder of the European Jews.* Translated by Belinda Cooper and Allison Brown. London, 1999.

Bartov, Omer, ed. *Studies on War and Genocide.* Vol. 8: *Genocide and Settler Society: Frontier Violence and Stolen Indigenous Children in Australian History,* edited by A. Dirk Moses. New York, 2004.

Bloxham, Donald. *The Great Game of Genocide: Imperialism, Nationalism and the Destruction of the Ottoman Armenians.* Oxford, U.K., 2005.

Chalk, Frank, and Kurt Jonassohn. *The History and Sociology of Genocide: Analyses and Case Studies.* New Haven, Conn., 1990.

Horkheimer, Max, and Theodor W. Adorno. *Dialectic of Enlightenment: Philosophical Fragments.* Edited by Gunzelin Schmid Noerr and translated by Edmund Jephcott. Stanford, Calif., 2002.

Kieser, Hans-Lukas, and Dominik J. Schaller, eds. *The Armenian Genocide and the Shoah.* Zurich, Switzerland, 2002.

Levene, Mark. *Genocide in the Age of the Nation State.* Vol. 1: *The Meaning of Genocide.* London, 2005.

———. *Genocide in the Age of the Nation State.* Vol. 2: *The Rise of the West and the Coming of Genocide.* London, 2005.

Mann, Michael. *The Dark Side of Democracy: Explaining Ethnic Cleansing.* Cambridge, U.K., 2005.

Stone, Dan, ed. *The Historiography of the Holocaust.* Basingstoke, U.K., 2004.

Weitz, Eric D. *A Century of Genocide: Utopias of Race and Nation.* Princeton, N.J., 2003.

Zimmerer, Jürgen. "The Birth of the *Ostland* out of the Spirit of Colonialism: A Postcolonial Perspective on the Nazi Policy of Conquest and Extermination." *Patterns of Prejudice* 39, no. 2 (2005): 197–219.

DOMINIK J. SCHALLER

GEORGE II

GEORGE II (1890–1947), king of Greece from 1922 to 1923 and from 1935 to 1947.

George II was the successor and eldest son of King Constantine I and Queen Sophia. After the defeat of the Greek army in the Asia Minor campaign (1922) and the expulsion of 1.5 million Greeks from Turkey, King Constantine was deposed and succeeded by his son George II. In 1923 King George was allegedly involved in an abortive military coup and was forced to leave the country. The parliament declared the country a republic, and in a plebiscite on 13 April 1924 Greeks voted for the abolition of the monarchy. The question of monarchy and the clash between republicans and royalists continued to dominate the political life of Greece in the interwar years. After the defeat of Elefterios Venizelos in the 1932 elections, the royalists came to power. After two abortive military coups organized by republicans, in 1935 the royalists organized a coup with the view to reinstate the king. General Kondylis seized dictatorial powers and abolished the republic. After a rigged plebiscite on 3 November 1935 King George was restored.

The elections in January 1936 did not give any party the majority and the small Communist Party held the balance of power in the parliament. In March 1936 King George appointed as new prime minister General Ioannis Metaxas, who was the leader of a minuscule party that had polled only 4 percent in the elections. The political deadlock and exaggerated fears of a communist danger drove King George to consent to the establishment of dictatorship by General Ioannis Metaxas on 4 August 1936, using as a pretext a general strike that was scheduled for the following day. The fact that King George consented to the abolishment of democracy and shared the power with a ruthless but weak dictator for more than four years marked his reign, questioned his legitimacy, and deepened the division between republicans and royalists.

King George was a loyal ally of Great Britain and the outbreak of the Second World War did not change that. Greece remained firmly on the side of the Allies and fought first against Italy (October 1940) and then Germany (April 1941). However, King George did not attempt to restore democracy in Greece, not even when Metaxas died in January 1941. He appointed Alexander Koryzis as prime minister, giving continuity to the dictatorial regime. After the capitulation of Greece to the Axis powers (23 April 1941), King George and the new prime minister Emmanuel Tsouderos

(Alexander Koryzis committed suicide on the day of capitulation) fled first to Alexandria, then to Cape Town, and from there to London. During the war King George stayed in London while the Greek government-in-exile moved to Cairo.

During the Second World War the constitutional question and the return of the king after the end of the war dominated political discussions in the government-in-exile in Egypt as well as in the resistance movement in occupied Greece. King George tried to dissociate himself from the General Metaxas dictatorship and declared that after the end of the war there would be a new government based on free elections. The political leaders believed that there should be a plebiscite on the question of the return of the king. In the discussions with the government-in-exile King George had the steady support of Great Britain, which saw in him a guarantor of British interests in the region and a bulwark against the powerful leftist resistance. However, there were strong objections to his return, and finally in the Lebanon conference (May 1944) between representatives of the Greek government-in-exile and the resistance organizations it was decided that after the liberation there would be a plebiscite on the question of the monarchy.

After the liberation and during the fighting between the communist resistance and government forces in Athens (December 1944) King George surrendered to British pressures and appointed Archbishop Damaskinos as regent with the view to unify the bourgeois parties against the communists. The Varkiza Agreement (12 February 1945) that concluded the defeat of the communists provided for a plebiscite on the question of monarchy. In the growing polarization that led to the outbreak of the Greek civil war (1946–1949) the most conservative and royalist forces prevailed in the bourgeois camp, and King George became their icon in the battle against communism. The royalist Populist Party won the elections of 31 March 1946 and swiftly moved to reinstate monarchy in Greece. The plebiscite was held on 1 September 1946 and 69 percent voted for the return of King George. The landslide victory of the royalists was a result of the polarization between nationalists and communists, terror, and several falsifications. King George returned to Greece on 28 September 1946. He died a few months later, on 1 April 1947, and was succeeded by his brother Paul.

See also **Greece; Turkey; Venizelos, Eleutherios; World War I; World War II.**

BIBLIOGRAPHY

Hondros, John L. *Occupation and Resistance: The Greek Agony, 1941–44.* New York, 1983.

Iatrides, John O., ed. *Greece in the 1940s: A Nation in Crisis.* Hanover, N.H., and London, 1981.

Papastratis, Procopis. *British Policy towards Greece during the Second World War, 1941–1947.* Cambridge, U.K., and New York, 1984.

POLYMERIS VOGLIS

GEORGE, STEFAN (1868–1933), German poet and intellectual.

The life and career of Stefan George are an especially acute example of the fickleness of fame. At his death on 4 December 1933 he was not only the most famous poet in Germany, but he was also revered as the leader of a cultural and quasi-political movement—what he called his "Secret Germany"—that, some believed, had presaged and even prepared the way for the regime that had come into power ten months earlier. Indeed, the minister for propaganda, Josef Goebbels, inaugurated that year the Stefan George Prize to be awarded annually to the best book by a German author. After the end of World War II, George's star had dimmed so low that it seemed all but extinguished. Even in the early twenty-first century, although there has been a resurgence of scholarly interest in George since the 1990s, Stefan George and the "Secret Germany" he created have been largely forgotten.

George began as a gifted, but fairly typical representative of European symbolism. Born in 1868 to a Catholic Rhineland family with close ties to France, he quickly assimilated the poetic ambition and gestures of Charles Baudelaire and particularly Stéphane Mallarmé, whom George met on his first trip to Paris in 1889. Unsure at first whether he would return to a Prussian-led, belligerently Protestant imperial Germany that he detested—he even considered emigrating to Mexico—George eventually made the compromise of staying in Germany but leading an itinerant life, constantly moving from city to town, staying with friends, lovers, benefactors. In this way he could—almost—deny the reality of the actual Germany while setting about the task constructing his own alternative.

This he did in a number of ways. First, there was his poetry. His first published volumes, the *Hymnen* (1890; Hymns), *Pilgerfahrten* (1891; Pilgrimages), and *Algabal* (1892) were all privately published in editions numbering only one or two hundred, and all evoked an alternative world of exquisite artifice and high gloss, all conveyed in a language of equally choice fabrication. In 1892 George also founded a journal, *Blätter für die Kunst* (Pages for art), that continued to appear until 1919 and formed the center of his activities during most of that period. The journal was not only a showcase for his own poetry and that of his friends, but it was also a place where his artistic, and increasingly his cultural, goals were articulated. As time went on, George's personal antipathy toward Wilhelminian Germany—with its glorification of material success and bourgeois comfort—turned into the official and explicit creed of the *Blätter für die Kunst* and thus of the group of people associated with it, and thus with George. This was the origin of George's "circle," which soon grew to include some extraordinary minds, including the literary critics Friedrich Gundolf and Max Kommerell, the historian Ernst Kantorowicz, the Nietzsche scholar Ernst Bertram, and many others who promulgated his vision in works of their own.

George published three more volumes of poetry in the 1890s, each one lavishly illustrated by the graphic designer Melchior Lechter, including *Das Jahr der Seele* (1897; The year of the soul), which contains some of George's best known poems. But it was his seventh book, called *Der siebente Ring* (1907; The seventh ring), that marks the turning point in his understanding of himself as not only a poet but also as a prophet and spiritual leader of his people. Corresponding to this shift in his self-perception is a change in the way those closest to him perceive him as well: they are no longer equal collaborators but rather disciples who refer to George as their "Master." In 1910

George initiated a new journal, called *Jahrbuch für die geistige Bewegung* (The yearbook for the spiritual movement), which published essays codifying and amplifying on these ideas, providing among other things one of the earliest and most compelling descriptions of the principle of the "Führer." Several of the contributions are likewise filled with contempt for the modern, democratic, bourgeois world and call for a holy war to end it.

In early 1914, a few months before the outbreak of the First World War, George published *Der Stern des Bundes* (The star of the covenant), which includes poems that seem prescient in their depictions of mass death and destruction. Indeed, one of his closest collaborators and followers wrote in the *Frankfurter Zeitung* that September that "our poet ... saw and predicted this war and its necessity and its virtues."

While George was gratified that the war caused the downfall of the German Empire, he hated the Weimar Republic no less and eagerly greeted its disintegration. His last book, *Das neue Reich* (1928; The new reich), seemed in its very title no less clairvoyant than the previous one. Although he refused to accept honors offered to him when the National Socialists assumed control, he did so by saying that he had already done all he could do. He died, unexpectedly, while spending the winter on Lake Maggiore in southern Switzerland. Contrary to a persistent myth, however, George had not gone there in exile: he regarded Switzerland as part of the larger, "secret" Germany, that had been his true home all along.

See also **Goebbels, Josef; Nazism.**

BIBLIOGRAPHY

Boehringer, Robert. *Mein Bild von Stefan George.* 2nd expanded ed. Düsseldorf and Munich, 1967.

Norton, Robert E. *Secret Germany: Stefan George and His Circle.* Ithaca, N.Y., 2002.

ROBERT NORTON

GERMAN COLONIAL EMPIRE.

On the eve of World War I, the German colonial empire consisted of a population of roughly fifteen million people spread over approximately one million square miles of territory. The principal German colonial possessions were its African holdings (German East Africa, Togoland, German Southwest Africa, and Cameroons) and its Far East territories (German New Guinea, Samoa, the Chinese leasehold of Kiaochow, and a number of small island groups). Defended in most cases only by a very small number of mercenary "protective forces," trained more for maintaining order than for actual combat, Germany's colonies lay largely exposed to the superior colonial forces of powers such as Great Britain and France.

GERMANY'S AFRICAN COLONIES

Following the outbreak of hostilities in August 1914, Germany's enemies moved quickly against its colonies. On 6 August, French forces invaded Togoland from French West Africa, and were joined one week later by British forces. After two small engagements, the acting governor Major H. G. von Doering capitulated to the French *tirailleurs sénégalais* and the British West African Rifles on 26 August 1914. Although also outnumbered, German forces in nearby Cameroons were initially more successful in resisting the British and French troops; many German soldiers fought on for more than a year in the colony's interior before fleeing in February 1916 to neutral Spanish Guinea. The remaining troops in Cameroons surrendered on 18 February 1916 from inside the Mora mountain fort to a combined British and French force of more than twenty-five thousand troops.

Events followed a similar course in German Southwest Africa. After invading in September 1914, the South African troops made little progress at first as a result of a Boer rebellion within South Africa, and it was only in January 1915 that the South African leaders Louis Botha and Jan Christian Smuts were able to start prosecuting the war fully. Germany's five thousand men were no match for South Africa's forty-three thousand soldiers; by mid-May 1915, the South Africans had captured the colony's capital, Windhoek, and driven the Germans to the northeast. There the remnants of the "protective force" held out for more than two additional months. Nevertheless, on 9 July 1915, Governor Theodor Seitz surrendered unconditionally to the South Africans.

The fighting in German East Africa differed from the other colonial campaigns in its duration and scope. Led by the experienced colonial soldier Colonel Paul von Lettow-Vorbeck, German forces began the war by invading Rhodesia, Uganda, and the Belgian Congo. Although Lettow-Vorbeck assembled the largest German colonial force, numbering at its peak more than twenty thousand men, the British and the Belgians fielded approximately 160,000 soldiers. Aware that they could not defeat such a larger army in open battle, Lettow-Vorbeck and his men retreated to the colony's interior and waged a guerrilla war. The combined strength of the British and the Belgians eventually forced the Germans to flee in November 1917 first to Mozambique and then to Northern Rhodesia, where they continued their guerrilla campaign. Lettow-Vorbeck finally surrendered on 25 November 1918, two weeks after the armistice ending World War I had been signed.

GERMANY'S PACIFIC COLONIES

In the case of the Germany's Far East colonies, the threat came not from the European powers directly but from their allies and dominions. Long resenting Germany's presence in the South Pacific, New Zealand and Australia immediately set about occupying Germany's colonies according to a prewar arrangement that awarded German Samoa to New Zealand and western New Guinea to Australia. On 29 August 1914, New Zealand forces took control of German Samoa. Australia's conquest of western New Guinea proved more difficult. Although Australia sent its entire fleet and an expeditionary force of more than fifteen hundred troops, unexpectedly strong German resistance convinced Australian commanders to negotiate a treaty of surrender that allowed, among other things, Germans to retain their property and to continue to participate in the colony's administration, though under Australian supervision. In return, Australia assumed control over not only western New Guinea but also the Bismarck Archipelago and the Solomon Islands.

Seizing the opportunity to build its own empire, the Japanese on 15 August 1914 issued an ultimatum to Berlin demanding that Germany remove its warships from the Chinese area of Shantung and hand over the leasehold of

Kiaochow. When Germany failed to agree to these terms by the deadline of 23 August, Japan declared war. Aware that its Chinese territories could not be defended, Germany unsuccessfully sought to convince the Chinese to allow Berlin, in accordance with terms of the original Kiaochow Treaty, to sell back the colony to China. The Germans also moved all available troops in China, about thirty-five hundred marines, to Kiaochow and put into uniform approximately two thousand German civilian army reservists. Such preparations, however, were no match for the Japanese forces. The Japanese quickly took control of the islands that made up German Micronesia and by October more than sixty thousand Japanese troops, as well as two British battalions, were amassed around the city of Tsingtao. On 31 October the final assault on Tsingtao began; eight days later, on 7 November, the Germans surrendered to the Japanese.

POSTWAR SETTLEMENT

By the time the diplomats assembled at Versailles in 1919 to negotiate the peace settlement, Germany had lost all of its colonies. The Japanese controlled its Chinese and Micronesian possessions, the British Dominion powers administered the rest of the Far East territories as well as Germany's African holdings, and Belgium had taken possession of part of German East Africa. In an effort to balance the annexationist demands of Great Britain and, more importantly, its Dominions with the wishes of the United States that the postwar settlement prohibit imperialist seizures of territory, diplomats at the Paris peace conference devised the mandate system for the former German and Ottoman colonies. Individual countries that were mandataries of the League of Nations were given the right to govern the colonies with the task of preparing them for eventual independence. Because the territories differed greatly in terms of political, economic, and social levels of development, the diplomats divided the colonies into A-, B-, and C-mandates: A-mandates were considered almost ready for independence and thus needed only minimal guidance and support from the mandatory power; B-mandates, which included all of the German colonies with the exception of German Southwest Africa, were seen as far less developed and thus requiring greater control by the mandataries, and C-mandates were viewed as the most primitive and were thus to be administered as de facto colonial possessions. Although some territories' borders were redrawn, the League of Nations' mandate system allowed Great Britain, France, Belgium, South Africa, Australia, New Zealand, and Japan to extend their wartime control over the former German colonies into the postwar era.

See also **Colonialism; Germany; World War II.**

BIBLIOGRAPHY

Gifford, Prosser, and William Rogers Louis, eds. *Britain and Germany in Africa: Imperial Rivalry and Colonial Rule.* New Haven, Conn., 1967.

Hiery, Hermann. *The Neglected War: The German South Pacific and the Influence of World War I.* Honolulu, 1995.

Keylor, William R., ed. *The Legacy of the Great War: Peacemaking, 1919.* Boston, 1998.

Schrecker, John E. *Imperialism and Chinese Nationalism: Germany in Shantung.* Cambridge, Mass., 1971.

Stoecker, Helmuth, ed. *German Imperialism in Africa: From the Beginnings until the Second World War.* Translated by Bernd Zöllner. London, 1986.

Strachan, Hew. *The First World War.* New York, 2004.

Wesseling, H. L. *The European Colonial Empires, 1815–1919.* Translated by Diane Webb. New York: Longman, 2004.

CHARLES LANSING

GERMANY. The course of German history in the twentieth century was anything but smooth and predictable. For some decades the national state ceased to exist altogether so that the country was reduced to a geographical expression. Five times the regime changed fundamentally, oscillating between dictatorship and democracy. The territory also fluctuated widely, expanding to an area from the Alsace to Poznań and contracting to a remnant between the Rhine and Oder rivers. Moreover time did not seem to progress in linear fashion, because traumatic memories of mass death and mass murder continued to intrude into the present. As a result, identities of belonging to or being excluded from Germanness varied greatly throughout the period. Because war and occupation involved many other countries, this history no longer concerned the Germans alone, but assumed a wider significance. Such turbulence makes it rather difficult to retell and interpret its trajectory.

Neither a purely positive nor an entirely negative rendition of the German story can do justice to the extremes of the last century. A Whiggish narrative, stressing the ineluctable progress of material prosperity and political liberty, runs head on into the National Socialist atrocities, which reveal the dark underside of modernity. Nationalist apologias that the Third Reich was merely an accident have been discredited by a broader understanding of the intellectual and structural roots of the Holocaust. But a strictly condemnatory account, favored by Western war propaganda that drew a straight line from Martin Luther to Adolf Hitler, also seems unable to deal with the more positive developments in the second half of the century. The interpretative challenge therefore consists of drawing a more complex picture, encompassing both unspeakable horrors and the recovery of civility.

One effort to deal with such contradictions is the notion of a German deviation from a common pattern of Western civilization. During the 1940s émigrés created this interpretation by inverting arrogant claims of German superiority in World War I and asserting that the country had fallen prey to a new kind of barbarism that rejected civilized norms. In the 1960s a younger generation of critical German historians picked up this notion in order to unearth the underlying reasons for the Nazi dictatorship and developed it into the theory that Germany had taken a "special path" to modernity, a *Sonderweg* that set it apart from its Western neighbors. But more recent comparative studies have shown that referring to British or French development as normative might be problematic, because each country's transition to modernity was different and fraught with its own pathologies. Especially when looking from Eastern Europe, the German example seems not especially backward, but instead rather progressive.

The erosion of the nationalist, Marxist, and modernist "master narratives" suggests a more modest approach to German history. Rather than pretending to present a coherent picture, it would be better to reassemble the fragments of a "shattered past" in the form of a kaleidoscope that offers a different pattern, depending upon the respective perspective. In unraveling this tangled story, it is particularly important to pay attention to the tension between the frequent ruptures and the underlying continuities. This requires organizing the narrative in the categories of the dominant political regimes, but also discussing the longer-term developments that cut across them. Moreover, it is equally necessary to be sensitive to the discrepancy between individual memories and the collective-memory culture that determines their meaning. This calls for not just discussing selected events themselves, but also commenting briefly on their interpretation in scholarship.

THE SECOND REICH

The starting point for any reconstruction of twentieth-century development must be imperial Germany, the famous *Kaiserreich*. After the subsequent catastrophes, many contemporaries remembered it positively as *die gute alte Zeit* (the good old days), an era of stability, order, and predictability in their personal lives. This somewhat nostalgic recollection, of course, elided its many conflicts and unresolved problems, but did correctly emphasize the contemporary feeling of confidence and progress. Searching for the short-term causes of World War I as well as long-term antecedents of the Nazi debacle, critical historians have instead stressed the authoritarian and aggressive features of imperial Germany. But more discerning scholars have also pointed to the Second Reich's considerable achievements in urban reform or higher education, which made the German example a positive point of reference in international debates.

In spite of its neofeudal style, the Second Reich was a rather new state, because it was founded only in 1871 as a result of the German victory in the Franco-Prussian War. The accession of the southern German states to the North German Confederation made it the first German national state, which, however, excluded Austrians and other German-speaking minorities in east-central Europe. The success of unification from above rather than from below, attempted in the revolution of 1848, meant that the political system was a tenuous compromise between remnants of Hohenzollern autocracy and aspects of popular sovereignty. It might be called "semiconstitutional," because its parliament, the Reichstag, was elected by universal male suffrage, while the Crown retained command over the army and foreign affairs. The crucial office, invented by the empire's creator, Prince Otto von Bismarck, was therefore the chancellorship, which mediated between the Reichstag and the Crown.

One source of pride was the rapid growth of the economy, which made Germany into a leading industrial power around the turn of the twentieth century. Prefigured by the Prussian-led customs union of the Zollverein, the unification of weights and measures, the introduction of a common currency, and the establishment of a national railroad and postal service created a larger domestic market. Moreover, the technical universities and Kaiser Wilhelm institutes contributed scientific discoveries to propel the development of steel, chemical, and electrical industries. At the same time the improvement in products turned the label "made in Germany," which the British had imposed as discrimination, into a guarantor of quality. The involvement of the banks in financing new ventures as well as favorable governmental policies fostered so rapid an increase in trade that Germany began to outstrip the home of industrialization, Great Britain. No wonder that by 1913 leading financiers were able to point to a general rise in prosperity.

Ironically this material progress aggravated social tensions, because it widened the gap between an ostentatious upper class and a still suffering proletariat. Around 1900 parts of the nobility, nouveau-riche entrepreneurs, and leading members of the educated middle class coalesced into a Wilhelmian elite that built impressive mansions to show off its success. In spite of government efforts to provide some insurance and pensions through social policy, the lot of the working class improved only slowly, failing to keep up with people's rising expectations. Based on Karl Marx's inspiration, a strong trade union movement coalesced that used the weapon of strikes to wrest concessions from a paternalist management. But the Social Democratic Party, the largest labor party in the world, remained caught between its revolutionary rhetoric and its reformist practice. The Second Reich therefore witnessed a stark discrepancy between new wealth and abject poverty in the urban tenements.

As the contrasting novels of Thomas and Heinrich Mann suggest, Wilhelmine culture was a perplexing compound of traditionalist impulses and modernist experimentation. On the one hand, the newness of the state and the rapidity of industrialization produced a longing for historical reassurance through neo-medievalist forms in public buildings, constructed in a mélange of neo-Romanesque, neo-Gothic, or neo-Renaissance styles. On the other hand, the sterility of the academic canon stimulated an artistic avant-garde to revolt with new styles of impressionist or expressionist painting and to secede from the official salon. These contradictions also mark the post-Romantic speculations of the philosopher Friedrich Nietzsche, whose texts show a restless search for creative genius. Because of their development of the research imperative, the German universities became the leading institutions in the world, producing such innovators as the playful physicist Albert Einstein and the rationalist founder of sociology Max Weber.

German foreign policy also vacillated unsteadily between expansionism and defensiveness, thereby confusing not just foreign observers. Confident of its growing power, Berlin tore Bismarck's web of alliances by letting the Reinsurance Treaty with Russia lapse. Rising aspirations also fostered the imperial dream of a "place in the sun," which propelled the turn away from continental policy toward *Weltpolitik*. In contrast, the effort to court England and to mediate in the Balkan conflicts derived from a defensive sense of limited resources in contrast to the British Empire and rising powers such as Russia or the United States. But an aggressive style, for instance in the Moroccan Crises, tended to overshadow the more cautious substance, making the kaiser appear as a troublemaker. These conflicting impulses led to a policy of increasing risks, which backed Austrian retaliation in the July crisis and thereby helped precipitate World War I.

In the gigantic military struggle ultimate victory continued to escape the Second Reich, though it appeared tantalizingly within reach. The initial western advance of the Schlieffen Plan was halted by the "miracle at the Marne," but not before the Germans had conquered most of Belgium and parts of northeastern France. After the defection of Italy from the Triple Alliance, the search for allies drew Berlin into the Balkans where the support of Turkey and Bulgaria facilitated the defeat of Serbia and Romania. In the west, the stalemate in the trenches produced a war of attrition,

Socialists rally in Berlin during the German Revolution of 1918. ©HULTON-DEUTSCH COLLECTION/CORBIS

symbolized by Verdun. In the east, the battle of the Masurian Lakes turned the tide in a war of intermittent movement that resulted in victory over Russia, forced to abandon large territories in the Treaty of Brest-Litovsk. But the kaiser's navy lost the struggle on the sea, the total mobilization of efforts led to a military quasi-dictatorship, and the escalation of the fighting through unrestricted submarine warfare precipitated the fatal entry of the United States.

The test of war proved to be the undoing of the Second Reich, because its authoritarianism lost the competition with democracy. In spite of the advantage of interior lines, in a war of attrition the Dual Alliance proved inferior to the Entente in manpower and natural resources. In the spring of 1918, the offensive launched by Erich Ludendorff gambled away the last reserves on a decisive victory, thereby hastening final defeat. In the contest for international opinion, German propaganda lacked a

universally appealing idea, because *Mitteleuropa* failed to inspire most neutrals. In domestic politics, the vaunted unity of the "truce within the castle" shattered on the clash between the war aims movement and the peace party. In spite of some social concessions many workers eventually wanted to end the fighting with a peace "without annexations and indemnities." When disgruntled sailors rebelled at last, belated political reforms could not prevent a popular uprising that forced the empire to collapse.

THE WEIMAR REPUBLIC

Born in defeat and revolution, the first German democracy has left an image of inevitable failure, sometimes expressed in the phrase "crippled at birth." In retrospect, the Weimar Republic appears as a fourteen-year period of endless crises, marked by civil war, hyperinflation, and international conflict that came to a disastrous end by allowing the Nazis to seize power. Left-wing historians accuse the Social Democratic and liberal leaders of the republic of timidity, because they did not go far enough to dismantle the imperial elites. In contrast, scholars interested in cultural innovation tend to celebrate "Weimar Culture" as the epitome of an experimental modernism that radiated abroad. Therefore interpretations face the challenge of balancing an appreciation for Weimar's creative potential with a more nuanced analysis of the reasons for its ultimate collapse.

In November 1918 Philipp Scheidemann's and Karl Liebknecht's competing proclamations of the republic announced a revolutionary contest for power between the provisional government and the council movement. Similar to the tsarist abdication in Russia, the last imperial cabinet handed the government over to the majority of the Social Democratic Party, led by Friedrich Ebert. At the same time, rebelling soldiers and workers followed the Soviet example by creating revolutionary councils that wanted to govern instead. But in Germany, the conflict had the opposite result, because army units and free corps suppressed the grassroots Räte (councils) of the left-socialists and communists in favor of a parliamentary republic. At the same time, the union leadership, to maintain production, struck an agreement with the leaders of business organizations. These initial decisions gave the discredited elites a chance to retain some of their power and to limit the changes to the political system.

The Treaty of Versailles (1919) did not exactly enhance the prospects for democracy, as it was at once too harsh to be freely accepted and too soft to be imposed against the will of the defeated. For the public, kept in the dark about the military situation by censorship, the extent of the defeat came as a profound shock. The ill-advised procedure of limiting negotiations to the "Allied and Associated Powers" without consulting the Germans also made it easy for opponents to denounce the settlement as dictated (a *Diktat*). The punitive provisions of extensive territorial losses (including Alsace-Lorraine, West Prussia, Poznań, and the colonies), the one-sided disarmament that limited German forces to one hundred thousand men, the imposition of a huge reparations bill, and the partial occupation did not make the treaty popular. Moreover, the attribution of "war guilt" to Germany alone seemed like a historical injustice.

Because the nationalist majority rejected the "shameful peace," the democratic minority was at a continual disadvantage in justifying its fulfillment.

The constitution, worked out in 1919 in Weimar, the city of the writers Johann Wolfgang von Goethe and Friedrich von Schiller, was nonetheless one of the most advanced democratic documents of its time. Its authors—Social Democrats, Catholics, and Liberals—drew on the heritage of local self-government and of the revolution of 1848 to constitute a parliamentary republic. Thus they insisted on a bill of rights, safeguarding the freedom of individual citizens. The constitution was also based on universal suffrage, granting women the vote, a generation before France. As in its imperial predecessor, the electoral procedure envisaged a combination of the single-member-district system and proportional representation, which gave both the big and small parties a chance. Though a powerful presidency was supposed to replace the dethroned kaiser, the actual government remained with the chancellor. A solid majority ratified the document, but sizable minorities remained opposed to its liberating thrust.

One impressive achievement of the Weimar Republic was the extension of the welfare state. In contrast to the paternalist beginnings in the empire, the first democracy based its legitimacy on guaranteeing "a comprehensive system of insurance." That meant not only compensating the victims of the war, such as mutilated veterans and widows, but also establishing an unemployment insurance against the vagaries of the economic cycles. The republic also launched a public health service that sought to prevent disease through social monitoring and improving the sanitary conditions of the poor. At the same time, the republic paid special attention to the needs of young people by trying to enlarge access to education for the underprivileged. This shift from charity to state provision also prompted the social work sector to professionalize. But at the same time, these initiatives required enormous financial expenditures that eventually outstripped the state's limited fiscal resources.

Another fascinating aspect of Weimar was its hothouse culture, which signaled the breakthrough of modernism. Emboldened by the lifting of Wilhelmian restrictions, avant-garde artists captured

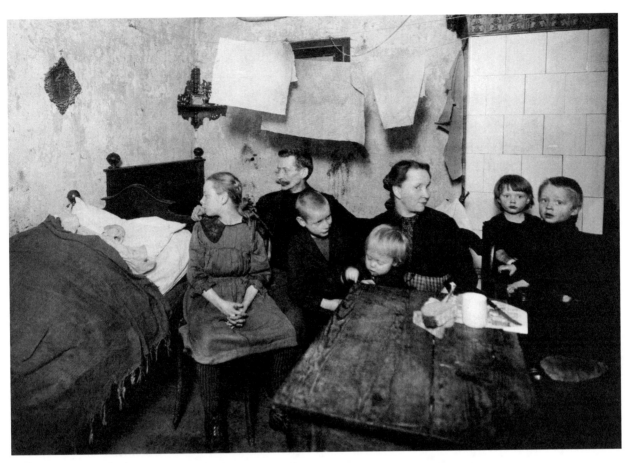

A poor German family in their apartment in Berlin, 1920s. ©Underwood & Underwood/Corbis

established cultural institutions, so that concert halls began to play Arnold Schoenberg's twelve-tone music, museums exhibited Wassily Kandinsky's abstract art, and theaters produced Bertolt Brecht's social-critical plays. This explosion of creativity drew artists from all over Europe to the capital, captured in Alfred Döblin's novel *Berlin Alexanderplatz* (1929). One center of experimentation was the Bauhaus, an art school in Dessau in which leading painters, architects, and furniture makers developed an international modernist style. At the same time an entertainment-centered mass culture coalesced that led German film to new artistic heights. But all this ferment produced an intense backlash against "Americanization," reinforcing Ernst Jünger's elitism and Oswald Spengler's "cultural pessimism."

Unfortunately, the Great Depression put an end to such progressive innovations. In the early 1920s the deficit financing of World War I had produced a hyperinflation that destroyed the savings of the middle class and reduced pensioners to poverty. The reparations struggle and the French occupation of the Ruhr further hindered recovery until the Dawes Plan produced an acceptable settlement in 1924. Thereafter the economy rebounded and optimism returned, only to be overshadowed by Fordist rationalization. Yet the withdrawal of U.S. loans after the stock market crash on Black Thursday in October 1929 triggered a massive industrial depression that reduced output to 53 percent of its previous level and swelled unemployment to more than six million, about one-quarter of the workforce. Because democratic cabinets found no convincing solution to this elemental crisis, many desperate citizens began to listen to the siren song of political extremists.

The republic's drawn-out agony failed, however, to prevent its ultimate collapse. From mid-1930 on, the disappearance of electoral support for democracy led to a series of minority governments, based only on presidential emergency decrees. While the Catholic Center Party leader Heinrich

A young man papers a wall with worthless German currency, 1923. ©Hulton-Deutsch Collection/Corbis

Brüning earned respect for his austerity program, his successors, the dilettante Franz von Papen and the intriguing Kurt von Schleicher, lacked any popular backing. Instead, on the extreme right an obscure Bavarian protest party named the National Socialist German Workers' Party (Nazi Party) gained a stunning 107 Reichstag seats in the 1930 election, then doubled its total to 230 seats two years later. Masterminded by Joseph Goebbels, its propaganda appealed especially to Protestant men in small towns who resented Versailles and hated the Jews. At the same time mass unemployment swelled the ranks of the Communists. Having run out of options, the conservative president Paul von Hindenburg turned the government over to the Nazi leader, the naturalized Austrian-born Adolf Hitler, in January 1933.

THE THIRD REICH

Why did a civilized country follow such a barbaric leader who would unleash war and genocide? This question has troubled historians ever since. According to personal preference, explanations have ranged from apologetic references to "mass politics" or Marxist claims of "monopoly capitalism" to critical indictments of "eliminationist anti-Semitism." Some scholars tend to stress that only the breakdown of the Weimar Republic gave the Nazis a chance, whereas others focus instead on the dynamics of an extra-parliamentary movement, which thrived on the resentments against the dislocations of modernity. One recent approach that seeks to reconcile the views of ideological intentionalists with the perspective of structural functionalists stresses the charismatic relationship between the leader (Führer) and his followers, a form of irrational bonding that created something like a "consensus dictatorship."

In contrast to the Beer Hall Putsch (1923), the Nazi seizure of power a decade later was formally legal and thus harder to resist. Although Hitler had viciously attacked the republic, he became chancellor as the head of the largest party in hopes of thereby restoring parliamentary government! The small conservative German National People's Party offered to enter a coalition with the rabble of the Nazi mass movement, because the traditional landed and administrative elites hoped to ride the populist tiger. Because the Nazi Party had lost some of its appeal in the second 1932 election, Hitler's initial cabinet represented only a minority—slightly more than two-fifths of the German electorate. But the liberal and democratic parties had already collapsed, and neither the Communists nor the Social Democrats dared unleash a general strike that might fail. Ironically, this initial legality was the springboard for subsequent illegality.

Hitler's first priority was therefore the transformation of his limited power into a full-blown dictatorship. While a victory parade of his followers in Berlin sought to impress the masses, the storm troopers of the SA (Sturmabteilung) brutally intimidated the critics. When the fortuitous Reichstag fire (February 1933) gave the Nazis a chance to throw most Communist and some Social Democratic leaders in jail, the no longer free elections produced a slim majority of popular votes for the government. Then Hitler coerced the Reichstag into passing the Enabling Law, which suspended civil rights and gave him dictatorial command. The partly voluntary, partly coerced "coordination" of organizations and interest groups put Nazis in control everywhere, while censorship silenced the independent voice of civil society. Finally, the civil service purge of presumed radicals and Jews created a pliable instrument for implementing Nazi policies. The speed and ruthlessness of the "national revolution" rendered its opponents helpless.

The growing popularity of the Nazi regime rested largely on the recovery of the economy and on the claim of a "national community" (*Volksgemeinschaft*). Borrowing massively, the Nazis reduced unemployment by instituting a national service year, restoring the draft, initiating public works such as superhighways (*Autobahnen*), and, most importantly, starting a clandestine rearmament program. Though wages remained frozen, the return of full employment did increase family incomes and restored hope. After breaking the power of the trade unions, the regime proclaimed an ideal *Volksgemeinschaft* in which all racial comrades would be equal, thereby leveling traditional social hierarchies. The Labor Front also offered new services, such as the vacation travel of the "Strength through Joy" program. While opponents derided these policies as "socialism of the fools," new consumption chances helped cement popular support for the Nazi regime.

Culturally speaking, the Third Reich was rather a desert, because the "flight of the muses" had robbed Germany of most of its creative talent. An artistic dilettante and lover of Wagnerian operas, Hitler loathed modernism and sought to purge culture of "degenerate art" or critical literature. Thus his ideology, presented in *Mein Kampf,* was a murky mélange of resentments against urban life, capitalism, Marxism, or the Jews. In painting, the Nazis returned to a pastoral realism with scenes of happy blue-eyed and blond-haired maidens, working in fields. Literature produced nothing better than the turgid novels of Hans Grimm, while theater was limited to presenting the expressionist plays of the aging Gerhart Hauptmann. In propaganda alone did the Nazis excel by staging the party rallies in Nuremberg and producing Leni Riefenstahl's films. Thus hopes for a more humane Germany could survive only in exile, the concentration camps, or the Resistance.

In foreign policy Nazi Germany followed a revisionist course so as to overthrow the restrictions of the Versailles treaty. To shield rearmament, Hitler initially pursued "bread, peace, and freedom," even reassuring Poland with a nonaggression treaty. But he also reintroduced the draft, remilitarized the Rhineland, and built a diplomatic "Axis" with Benito Mussolini's Italy and Tojo Hideki's Japan. His first success was the Anschluss of Austria in the spring of 1938, which incorporated the German-speaking remnant of the Habsburg Empire. Next he inflated the Sudeten German wish for autonomy into a demand for returning "home to the Reich," granted by a harassed Neville Chamberlain at the Munich conference (September 1938). But Hitler underestimated the moral outrage caused by his cynical annexation of the rest of Czechoslovakia and was surprised that the West thereafter resisted his demands for concessions in the Polish Corridor and the return of Danzig. In contrast to 1914, there was no doubt that it was the Nazis who unleashed war in September 1939.

In the first half of World War II the Germans won stunning victories, surpassing anything that they had achieved a quarter century before. Nazi military strategy rested on the concept of the blitzkrieg, a mechanized lightning strike of heavy armor with mobile artillery and tactical air support that slashed through enemy lines, surrounded entire armies of defenders, and forced their surrender by spreading confusion. Because of Hitler's personal fear of a two-front war, the Wehrmacht proceeded against one enemy at a time so as to achieve tactical superiority and use the resources of the defeated country to carry the war effort further. In this fashion he defeated Poland in September 1939, captured Scandinavia in the spring of 1940, beat France in the summer of that year, overran the Balkans in the spring of 1941, and invaded the Soviet Union thereafter. The only country able to repulse this massive onslaught was Great Britain.

Hitler's war aims envisaged a German hegemony over Europe beyond the wildest dreams of previous nationalists. First of all, the Nazis reannexed to the Reich disputed provinces such as Alsace-Lorraine in the west and West Prussia, Poznań, and other territories in the east. Second, they created a belt of occupied areas such as Bohemia and the Polish government general, run by military governors and mercilessly exploited for the war effort. Third, Hitler's power fantasies

Chancellor Adolf Hitler opens the German parliament c. 1940–1942. ©HULTON-DEUTSCH COLLECTION/CORBIS

focused on the conquest of German Lebensraum in the east in a primitive notion that national strength rested on living space for agrarian settlements. As the "general plan east" stipulated, his colonial territory could be found only in Poland and Ukraine—but it needed to be cleansed of its inhabitants so that ethnic Germans could be resettled there. Finally, in reconstructing Europe the Nazis were aided by allies such as Hungary, Slovakia, Croatia, and Romania and abetted by friendly neutrals such as Vichy France and Francisco Franco's Spain.

This expansionism was inspired by a biological racism that precipitated an unprecedented genocide, now called according to biblical references "the Holocaust." So as to reduce the local population to serfdom, the Slavic elite was sent to concentration camps and killed by slave labor. More radical yet was the murder of the Jews, because it sought to eradicate an entire people. In Vienna

Hitler had imbibed a deep-seated racial anti-Semitism that led him from discrimination of the German Jews in the Nuremberg Laws (1935) to their persecution in the pogrom of November 1938. But only eastern victories and dreams of Lebensraum made for the quantum leap to the complete annihilation of all European Jews. Pioneered through euthanasia on the handicapped, the mass killing first proceeded through mobile death squads but was subsequently perfected through the industrial method of gassing in concentration camps such as Auschwitz, where four million people died. Though communism might have claimed more deaths, this Nazi genocide is uniquely abhorrent because of its systematic and bureaucratic character that will darken the German name forever.

After six years of struggle, the Third Reich and its allies were finally defeated. In the long run the

Nazis had no way of countering the superior manpower and industrial strength of the grand alliance between Britain, the Soviet Union, and the United States. In the west, victory in the war at sea, the liberation of North Africa, and the landing in Italy were important, but not decisive. The brunt of the land fighting took place in the east, where "general winter" helped the Soviet Union to survive in 1941, the ferocious defense of Stalingrad in late 1942 turned the tide, and the tank battle of Kursk in the summer of 1943 established Soviet superiority. The Allied landing in Normandy (June 1944) and the air bombardment also contributed to weakening German defenses. Hitler's fabled "miracle weapons" such as jet fighters and rockets and his experiments with a small atomic bomb came too late. With Berlin surrounded, the Führer committed suicide, and the Reich surrendered in May 1945.

THE FEDERAL REPUBLIC

In contrast to the destructive drama of the Nazi regime, the postwar history of West Germany unfolded more peacefully and constructively. Five decades of democratic stability, economic prosperity, social concord, and cultural modernization made the Federal Republic of Germany seem like a success story. Only inveterate critics still bemoan "missed opportunities" for more radical changes, but most domestic observers and foreign commentators are impressed by the positive outcome. Instead, arguments tend to revolve around such issues as who should get the credit, the Allies or the Germans, or when things really improved, during the chancellorship of Konrad Adenauer or that of Willy Brandt. With so little to disagree about, it remains nonetheless necessary to explain why Germans were able to seize "their second chance."

Perhaps the new beginning after 1945 was more successful because conditions were much worse than in 1919, making it clear that a drastic change was necessary. This time the whole country was occupied by the victors, including the French, and eventually divided into two ideologically competing states by the Cold War. Moreover, the caretaker government of Admiral Karl Dönitz was dissolved and sovereignty assumed by the Allied Control Council. Also much more territory was lost by returning Nazi annexations to their previous owners and turning the entire eastern part of the country over to the Soviet Union (Kaliningrad Oblast) and Poland (East Prussia, Pomerania, Silesia, etc.). Moreover, the program agreed upon at the Potsdam Conference (July–August 1945) imposed a rigorous demilitarization, denazification, and decartelization on the defeated so as to prevent World War III. Finally, the Nuremberg trials (1945–1946) indicted the entire Nazi elite and Reich leadership for waging war of aggression as well as committing "crimes against humanity."

The minority of German democrats who drew up the Basic Law (1949) as a provisional constitution sought to learn from Weimar's fatal mistakes. Emerging out of the local and regional efforts to restore self-government, the leaders of the postwar parties tried to recover positive traditions from the Nazi rubble and find more stable institutional arrangements for a renewed attempt at democracy. Allied advisors also sought to share constructive precedents from their own traditions, but the Germans themselves made the ultimate decisions. The new constitution restored a bill of rights as well as federalism and a mixed electoral system, but weakened the presidency, instituted a 5 percent hurdle for representation, and abolished emergency decrees. The resulting representative system put its faith in parliament instead of direct participation. In time, the new system's success in solving problems overcame the widespread skepticism toward democracy.

The rapid revival of the West German economy, known as the "economic miracle," helped reinforce positive attitudes toward the new political system. Because the initial postwar controls produced stagnation, the Economic Council under the leadership of the neoliberal Ludwig Erhard was willing to gamble on restoring free competition. The success of the currency reform of 1948 has become legendary, because almost overnight shop windows began to fill with previously scarce goods, and the public, though losing its paper savings, found hard work once again worthwhile. Moreover, the credits of the Marshall Plan also helped revive production, because U.S. aid reintegrated German industry into a wider European context. This reliberalization of the economy led to annual growth rates of 5 to 7 percent over a couple of decades and dramatically improved living conditions by offering coveted consumer goods to

The German Reichstag building lies in ruins after the fall of Berlin, May 1945. ©Yevgeny Khaldei/Corbis

the masses. Thus the new deutsche mark (DM) quickly became the symbol of recovery and a source of German pride.

The acceptance of parliamentary government was also facilitated by the emergence of a "chancellor democracy" under Adenauer. Surviving the Third Reich in inner exile, the former mayor of Cologne helped create a new conservative party, the Christian Democratic Union, by appealing not only to Catholics but also to Protestants. As a septuagenarian, he represented continuity going back to the empire and used his seniority to cement his ascendancy within his party and parliament. In the first free postwar election in 1949, he barely managed to defeat the Social Democratic war veteran Kurt Schumacher and to assume the chancellorship of a coalition government with other middle-class parties. Once in power, he affected an authoritarian style that tried to control everything. While leftist critics sometimes ridiculed him as "*Ersatz* kaiser," his personal integrity and

competence won him great respect at home and abroad.

The establishment of the Federal Republic in 1949 with its capital in the Rhenish university town Bonn facilitated the westernization of German culture and society. The loss of the eastern territories and the separation of central Germany through the Iron Curtain shifted the center of gravity westward, rebuilding politics on more liberal foundations. Postwar encounters with the Western occupiers also tended to be more pleasant than dealings with the Stalinist Soviets. Because the Cold War rendered a neutralist course illusory, Adenauer committed himself to improving relations with France, fostering European integration (the European Coal and Steel Community and the Common Market), and participating in transatlantic defense (NATO membership). Aided by cultural exchanges, intellectuals rediscovered Western modernism, developing a critical stance toward their own society in the novels of Heinrich Böll and Günter Grass. Through the spread of Hollywood films and rock music, popular culture also Americanized, embracing U.S. models of consumption.

During the mid-1960s satisfied West Germans were nonetheless rocked by a generational revolt of unexpected scope and intensity. Young people found the bourgeois order and respectability, restored under Adenauer, too confining. They drew on the example of protests against rearmament and on the inspiration of a New Left, such as the Frankfurt school, which propagated an unorthodox Marxism. Spurred on by resentment against authoritarian structures in the university, worldwide demonstrations against the Vietnam War, and adult silence about participation in Nazi crimes, rebellious students such as Rudi Dutschke provoked the authorities with nonviolent sit-ins and teach-ins. In 1967 and 1968 police brutality and biased reporting by the Springer press created a mass movement, ready to launch a revolution. But Brandt's resolve "to dare more democracy" took the wind out of the protesters' sails. Their legacy was an impulse to grassroots democracy, a change in values and lifestyles, and a propensity for terrorist violence in the Red Army Faction.

In the early 1970s the social-liberal coalition attempted to remove the obstacles to reconciliation with the eastern neighbors by a more constructive *Ostpolitik*. Bonn's Hallstein Doctrine had refused to recognize the German Democratic Republic (GDR) as a separate state, because it did not rest on "free elections." Moreover the refugee organizations, formed by about ten million expellees from East Germany, had insisted on their "right to a homeland." Chancellor Brandt first tried to reassure the Soviet Union and its satellites that Germans harbored no revanchism by signing a series of nonaggression treaties. Then long negotiations with East Germany produced the Basic Treaty (1972), which recognized the GDR de facto so as to settle practical problems, but held out the possibility of later unity. Finally the four occupation powers agreed to a treaty concerning Berlin to clarify access rights. Instead of confrontation, this policy of "change through closeness" sought to overcome division by cooperation.

At the same time, the "German model" of the social market economy came under increasing pressure from global competition. Under Brandt expectations of continued growth had led to huge wage increases and a further extension of social benefits. But the oil shock of 1973 and the collapse of the Bretton Woods exchange rate system increased the costs of exports, because the country had few domestic energy sources and the deutsche mark was revalued upward. Chancellor Helmut Schmidt met this challenge with a combination of austerity and pump priming so that growth once again resumed. But the second oil crisis of 1979 triggered another recession, which was overcome only by his successor, Helmut Kohl. Accustomed to the superior performance of "Rhenish capitalism" during the past decades, German leaders failed to understand that they were facing a structural transition to postindustrialism and global competition that would overtax their welfare state by creating long-term unemployment and regional deindustrialization.

The transformation of political culture after 1945 was largely driven by an effort to distance Germany from the dark shadows of the Nazi past. During the occupation, the Allies forced a reluctant population to confront its crimes through reeducation. Although Adenauer did push through restitution to the state of Israel, the majority of the public would rather forget its complicity in Nazi crimes. Only in the 1960s did the voices of the minority become amplified through the trial of Adolf Eichmann in Jerusalem, the Auschwitz-*Prozess* in Frankfurt, critical television coverage, and changed teaching guidelines. While the antifascism of the student radicals oversimplified matters, scandalizing the Nazi past of public officials did have an effect. During subsequent decades local initiatives created memorials in former camps, and intellectuals embraced "a Holocaust identity." Hence public memory culture gradually assumed an astonishingly self-critical tone.

THE GERMAN DEMOCRATIC REPUBLIC

The collapse of communism in 1989 and 1990 has doubled the burden of dealing with the dictatorial past, because it created a similar need to confront GDR crimes. Through opening secret archives, instituting judicial proceedings, and holding parliamentary hearings with witnesses and experts, the German government sought to enlighten its citizens

A German man sits amid ruins following the Allied capture of the city of Cologne, March 1945. ©Bettmann/Corbis

about the misdeeds of the toppled communist regime. Eastern victims and western Cold Warriors thus denounced the GDR as an illegitimate system (*Unrechtstaat*) that rested on repression. In contrast, former regime members and some sympathizers in West Germany claimed that East Germany was "a noble experiment" that somehow failed to live up to its ideals. Between these extremes the intellectual task is instead to explore the contradictions between the dictatorial character of the regime and the relative normalcy of daily lives within it.

Undoubtedly the German Democratic Republic was a Soviet protectorate, because without Moscow's military support it simply ceased to exist. But the brutality of the so-called liberation in 1945 with its random killing, mass rape, and general pillaging also made "the Russians" unpopular in most circles, thereby handicapping their rule. For Joseph Stalin the conquered heart of Germany was the key prize of victory and the linchpin of his empire in Eastern Europe, secured by the stationing of about 450,000 soldiers there. Initially he wavered between using this area as a springboard for spreading communism to Western Europe or as a possible incentive for neutralizing a united German state. Eventually Walter Ulbricht persuaded him to opt for establishing an independent client state of his own in order to establish communism on German soil. But his radical measures remained so unpopular that the East German regime had to be rescued from the wrath of its own workers by Soviet tanks in June 1953.

The GDR was, nonetheless, also a product of indigenous traditions of Marxism and the labor movement. Because the Social Democrats had been the mainstay of Weimar, the Communists denounced them as "social fascists" and fought vigorously against the republic. But common suppression by the Nazis forced both rivals to understand that they needed to overcome their divisions in antifascist cooperation; therefore the Communist Party of Germany had to use only moderate force to compel the East German Social Democratic Party to join it in a Socialist Unity Party (SED) in the spring of 1946. West German Social Democrats denounced the move as "compulsory fusion," and East German moderates soon found out that they had been duped, because the Communists mercilessly purged the united party of all suspected deviants. Similarly, the SED captured the independent trade unions and turned them into transmission belts for its commands. Conscious of being a small minority, East German Communists increasingly relied on secret service surveillance and brute force.

To create a lasting basis for its rule the SED attempted to transform East Germany into a state of "workers and peasants," supported by a new socialist intelligentsia. This goal involved breaking the back of the bourgeois "class enemy" by confiscating all land of more than 100 hectares (250 acres) and redistributing it to landless laborers, as well as by nationalizing large industries and turning them into state-run enterprises. At the same time, it meant transforming the educational system, especially the universities, from training grounds for neutral experts into producers of loyal socialist cadres. The planned economy that resulted from subsequent collectivization and socialization of all businesses was run by these technical specialists, beholden to the party. On the one hand, this "real existing socialism" did subsidize food, housing, transportation, and health care. But on the other, its egalitarian aspirations were belied by the privileges of a new political "nomenklatura" elite.

Among many intellectuals, the radical distancing of the eastern leaders from the Nazi past fed the hope that the GDR would turn out to be the "better Germany." Strong antifascist rhetoric induced even the liberal Jewish survivor Victor Klemperer to join the SED. Such well-known émigrés as the playwright Bertolt Brecht, the novelist Stefan Heym, the composer Kurt Eisler, and the historian Jürgen Kuczynski were happy to return to the east. With reforms such as opening higher education to the workers, the party seemed to be fulfilling the hopes for a new beginning. But soon artists found themselves constrained by a primitive "socialist realism" whose pictures of blond tractor-drivers in wheat fields resembled Nazi examples. With the "Bitterfeld way," literature was dedicated to the class struggle, celebrating the advances of the proletariat. Creative writers such as Christa Wolf had a hard time reconciling their aversion to censorship with continued socialist loyalty.

The imprisonment of the East Germans by the Berlin Wall revealed the full repressiveness of the SED dictatorship. Before its construction about 3.5 million East Germans had gone to West Germany, but only half a million moved the other way. The exodus of farmers, managers, professionals and skilled workers created manpower shortages for the planned economy. Hence during the night preceding 13 August 1961 Ulbricht had barbed wire strung across the heart of Berlin and reinforced with concrete slabs in order to end the continual population drain. The elaborate system of electrified fences, minefields, trained dogs, jeep paths, guard towers, and cement barriers that is commonly known as the Berlin Wall sealed the western part of the former capital off from the eastern half of the city and from the surrounding countryside. Costing several hundred lives during desperate attempts at flight, the "antifascist protection wall" forced the public to come to terms with the system, but it thereby also became a central symbol of the inhumanity of the communist regime.

Ironically, the planned economy of the GDR lost the competition of living standards with the social market economy of the FRG. No doubt, its starting conditions for rebuilding were more difficult, because East Germany had to bear the brunt of industrial dismantling and pay a ten billion mark reparations bill to the Soviet Union. But central planning also contributed to the problem, because it succeeded only in organizing the rebuilding and in promoting smokestack industrialization with coal and steel, but not in providing sufficient consumer goods. Ulbricht's limited effort to restore competition with his "New Economic System"

Crowds gather at the German Reichstag building at midnight on the evening of 2 October 1990 to celebrate the official reunification of East and West Germany. ©Owen Franken/Corbis

was too timid to spur sustained growth. Erich Honecker's Keynesianism of "the unity of social and economic policy" seemed more promising, because it tried to motivate workers by raising living standards. But it used Western loans to satisfy consumer needs rather than to make investments. Though claiming to be the tenth-largest industrial power, the GDR economy stagnated in the 1980s and approached bankruptcy.

At the same time, the return of elements of civil society began to challenge the SED regime from within. The brutal repression of all anticommunist resistance allowed dissent only to emerge on the basis of socialism. During the 1970s the physicist Robert Havemann was the first to promote a more democratic form of Marxism, and his example was soon followed by the poet Wolf Biermann and others. During the early 1980s an independent peace movement emerged under the protection of the Protestant Church that called for turning "swords into plowshares." Secret police (Stasi)

persecution of pacifists, ecologists, and feminists led to the founding of a group dedicated to human rights (Initiative for Peace and Human Rights), which hed been written in the constitution but not observed in practice. Spreading its message through samizdat and Western journalists, an internal opposition, composed of a loose network of local groups, gradually began to form.

In the fall of 1989 the SED dictatorship crumbled as part of the general collapse of communism in the Soviet bloc. Among the long-term factors undermining its power were economic stagnation, erosion of faith in the socialist utopia, and the loss of Soviet support due to Mikhail Gorbachev's détente. The short-term causes involved the mass exodus of citizens who streamed across the Hungarian border and occupied the West German embassy in Prague, precipitating a reconsideration of travel policy that culminated in the breaching of the Berlin Wall on 9 November. Similarly important were the mass demonstrations that began with small

Monday eve vigils at the Nikolai Church in Leipzig and eventually mobilized more than half a million people on Berlin's Alexander Square. This dual pressure finally led to the overthrow of the aging Honecker, his replacement by the younger Egon Krenz, and the creation of a Round Table with dissident groups, dedicated to reforming the GDR.

Instead of fostering the renewal of socialism, the democratic awakening led to the self-dissolution of the GDR and its unification with the Federal Republic. East Germans turned to West Germany for help, because Bonn had appealed to the eastern "brothers and sisters" as the true representative of the nation during the division. Chancellor Kohl's ten-point plan ended the cooperation with the SED regime, demanded drastic reforms in exchange for aid, and proposed the restoration of unity. In the first free election in March 1990, about three-quarters of the East Germans voted for parties favoring quick unification. To stop mass migration, Kohl offered to create a "currency, economic, and social union" with East Germany, introducing the Western deutsche mark to the East. In complicated "two-plus-four" negotiations the German states and the victorious powers of World War II hammered out an international settlement that recognized the eastern frontiers. The domestic transition was regulated by a unification treaty so that the new states could join the Federal Republic on 3 October 1990.

INTERPRETING GERMAN HISTORY

How is anyone to make sense of this chaotic course of German history in the twentieth century? The return of a shrunken and chastened nation-state, the extension of its stable democracy to the eastern *Länder,* and the country's firm anchoring in European and transatlantic ties suggest a happy ending for the narrative. But ought this encouraging outcome erase the ruptures, the instability, or the suffering associated with prior Central European developments? The human cost was too high simply to forget the havoc wrought by the succession of one belligerent empire, one failed republic, two murderous dictatorships, and finally one successful democracy. Any reconsideration therefore has to begin by taking this turbulence seriously. Only then might one suggest that if there

is a pattern at all, it is a descent into catastrophe followed by gradual redemption.

For all those affected by it, this extraordinary history has left a trail of widely disparate, but generally troubling memories. Because perpetrators prefer to remain silent and collaborators tend to offer embarrassed rationalizations, it is the pained voices of the political and racial victims of the Nazis or Communists that clamor for sympathy. But some German authors are starting to ask: can maimed veterans, civilians terrorized by bombing, and refugees forced into flight not also claim some status of victimhood? The world wars and Hitler's genocide have connected countless lives in other countries with this murderous history, spreading its nightmares far and wide. In contrast, the more stable periods of "good times" that allowed recovery and reconciliation somehow seem less salient, although they are essential for going on living after mass murder and mass death. Because they contain so much suffering, these conflicting memories can hardly be brought into harmony—but they might be eased symbolically by accepting the pain of others.

In the popular imagination as well as in academic analysis, the catastrophic part of twentieth-century German history remains most prominent. Some of the attention is no doubt due to commercial catering to a voyeurism that exploits the fascination with the forbidden. More laudable is the construction of the Holocaust as ultimate evil, because it provides a telling example of the exact opposite of what a humane civilization ought to be. Racism, sexism, ethnic cleansing, unleashing of war, bureaucratic mass murder—the litany of Nazi crimes is as long as it is despicable. In reinforcing the identity of Western intellectuals, the Third Reich has come to serve as a metahistorical example of what can go wrong, whether it is considered an atavistic survival of primitivism or a consequence of the pathologies of modernity. But a ritualization of such a reading runs the risk of decontextualization, stylization, and moralization, which inhibit a rational analysis of the causes and consequences of genocide.

More neglected but equally important is the subsequent story of recovery, because it offers an encouraging example of rehabilitation from the worst of crimes. The administration of George W. Bush liked to cite the German success in recivilizing after 1945 as a justification for U.S. nation-building abroad. But it tended to forget that it took the military effort of a grand coalition to topple the Nazi dictatorship and the Germans' political distancing from Hitler to give the new beginning a chance. It required a fortuitous mixture of Allied compulsion and cooperation by a progressive minority of the defeated for democracy to have a second chance. It needed greater initial destruction and favorable conditions such as the Cold War and the postwar boom to rebuild the shattered society in a different image. Even if the reasons for success remain misunderstood, the second half of the century presents a more hopeful tale that suggests the possibility of learning from past mistakes.

See also **Adenauer, Konrad; Bretton Woods Agreement; Ebert, Friedrich; Economic Miracle; Hitler, Adolf; Holocaust; Nazism; Reparations; Versailles, Treaty of; World War I; World War II.**

BIBLIOGRAPHY

Bark, Dennis L., and David R. Gress. *A History of West Germany.* 2 vols. 2nd ed. Oxford, U.K., 1993.

Berghahn, Volker R. *Modern Germany: Society, Economy, and Politics in the Twentieth Century.* 2nd ed. Cambridge, U.K., 1987.

Browning, Christopher. *The Origins of the Final Solution: The Evolution of Nazi Jewish Policy, September 1939– March 1942.* Lincoln, Neb., 2004.

Chickering, Roger. *Imperial Germany and the Great War, 1914–1918.* 2nd ed. Cambridge, U.K., 2004.

Fulbrook, Mary. *The Divided Nation: A History of Germany, 1918–1990.* New York, 1992.

Jarausch, Konrad H. *After Hitler: Recivilizing Germans, 1945–1995.* Translated by Brandon Hunziker. New York, 2006.

Jarausch, Konrad H., and Michael Geyer. *Shattered Past: Reconstructing German Histories.* Princeton, N.J., 2003.

Kershaw, Ian. *Hitler.* 2 vols. New York, 1999–2000.

Maier, Charles S. *Dissolution: The Crisis of Communism and the End of East Germany.* Princeton, N.J., 1997.

Mommsen, Wolfgang J. *Imperial Germany, 1867–1918: Politics, Culture, and Society in an Authoritarian State.* Translated by Richard Deveson. London, 1995.

Peukert, Detlev J. K. *The Weimar Republic: The Crisis of Classical Modernity.* Translated by Richard Deveson. New York, 1992.

Ross, Corey. *The East German Dictatorship: Problems and Perspectives in the Interpretation of the GDR.* London, 2002.

Weinberg, Gerhard L. *A World at Arms: A Global History of World War II.* 2nd ed. Cambridge, U.K., 2005.

KONRAD H. JARAUSCH

GESTALT PSYCHOLOGY.

Gestalt psychology was an effort to reformulate the foundations of psychological thought and research that began in Prague, Frankfurt, and Berlin in the late nineteenth and early twentieth centuries. Its founders, Max Wertheimer (1880–1943), Wolfgang Köhler (1887–1967), and Kurt Koffka (1886–1941), did not claim that wholes are *more* than the sums of their parts. Rather, they maintained that experienced objects and relationships are *fundamentally different* from collections of sensations. The assumption that sensory "elements" are the basic constituents of mental life was widely accepted in the nineteenth century. Philosophers such as Wilhelm Dilthey (1833–1911) and Henri Bergson (1859–1941) argued that a psychology based on such assumptions contributed nothing to humanistic thought. The Gestalt theorists opposed atomistic conceptions of experience while remaining committed to natural science.

EMERGENCE

In 1890 Christian von Ehrenfels (1859–1932), one of Wertheimer's teachers, had introduced the notion of "Gestalt qualities" given alongside sensory "elements." Melodies, for example, sound the same in any key because they have such qualities. The Gestalt theorists asserted that dynamic structures in experience *determine* what will be wholes and parts, figure and background, in particular situations. In a 1912 paper on the seeing of motion, Wertheimer provided what he took to be experimental evidence for the existence of essentially dynamic mental realities that cannot be composed of or built up from elements, and conjectured that structured processes in the brain corresponded to these psychical events. In 1914 he introduced the principle of *Prägnanz* (good form), according to which experienced wholes and structured relationships spontaneously take on the simplest arrangement possible in the given conditions. He later elaborated this claim in work on perceptual grouping.

> I stand at the window and see a house, trees, sky. On theoretical grounds I could try to count and say there were 327 brightnesses and hues. Do I *have* 327? No, I see sky, house, and trees, and no one can really have these "327" as such.... The particular combination that I *see* is not simply up to my choice, but is a spontaneous, natural, normally expected combination and segregation that is given there before me.
>
> Max Wertheimer. "Untersuchungen zur Lehre von der Gestalt: II." *Psychologische Forschung* 4 (1923): 301. Translated by Mitchell Ash.

From 1914 to 1918 Köhler, while directing a research station of the Prussian Academy of Sciences on the island of Tenerife, demonstrated that nonhuman animals such as chickens or apes are also capable of perceiving wholes and structured relationships. He further showed that chimpanzees can solve problems in ways that appeared to result from insight into the solution required by a given situation—for example, by fitting two hollow sticks into one another in order to reach a distant banana.

Köhler then argued in a 1920 book entitled *Die physischen Gestalten* that there are Gestalten in the physical world. Examples include electromagnetic fields; a change in any part of such a system changes the arrangement of the whole. Köhler claimed further that the brain events underlying perception follow the same dynamic, self-organizing principle evident in the physical world. This postulate he later called psychophysical isomorphism. Since self-organizing processes occur in both inorganic and organic nature, he argued, they are not cognitive structures imposed on experience, but properties of both mind and nature.

ESTABLISHMENT IN GERMANY AND TRANSFER TO THE UNITED STATES

In 1922 Wolfgang Köhler was appointed to succeed his teacher, Carl Stumpf (1848–1936), as professor of philosophy and director of the psychological institute at the University of Berlin. In 1921 the Gestalt theorists established with colleagues a journal called *Psychologische Forschung* (now called *Psychological Research*), in which the results of their research program were published. These included studies of organization in visual perception, the influence of past experience on form perception, the minimal conditions for perceiving anything at all, and on problem solving and thinking. Also in Berlin, Kurt Lewin (1890–1947) developed an independent line of research on action and motivation, based in part on Gestalt psychology, with the aim of understanding and humanizing modern working conditions.

In the culture wars of Weimar Germany, the Gestalt theorists positioned themselves among the advocates of a "third way" between left and right by showing that holism need not be a monopoly of Romantic conservatives or folkish racists. In a 1925 article, "Über gestalttheorie" (translated as "On Gestalt Theory" in 1944), Wertheimer suggested that democracy, as a form of human self-organization, was more natural and meaningful than blind authoritarianism.

In the 1920s the Gestalt theorists were invited to lecture and teach in the United States, where their approach was perceived as an alternative to behaviorism. Koffka, then an associate professor in Giessen, accepted a professorship at Smith College in 1928. Wertheimer, who taught in Berlin during the 1920s, became a professor of philosophy in the natural sciences faculty at the University of Frankfurt in 1929. He was one of the first scholars and scientists to be dismissed by the Nazis for his Jewish descent and then accepted a professorship at the "University in Exile" at the New School for Social Research in New York. Köhler protested publicly in April 1933 against the Nazis' dismissals of Jewish scientists, one of the very few German academics to do so. He struggled to maintain control of his institute against denunciations from careerist colleagues and attacks by Nazi students and then accepted a professorship at Swarthmore College in 1935. Lewin resigned his position in Berlin in 1933 before he could be dismissed for his Jewish descent and leftist politics and reestablished himself in the United States at the University of Iowa before moving to MIT in 1944.

Other adherents of Gestalt theory tried to continue working under Nazism. Wolfgang Metzger (1899–1979), a student of Wertheimer's, joined the Nazi Party in 1937 and was appointed to a professorship in Münster in 1942. His two major works, *Gesetze des Sehens* (1936; *Laws of Seeing*) and *Psychologie* (1941; *Psychology*), were reissued after 1945 and became standard German-language accounts of Gestalt psychology.

IMPACT

In the United States, Gestalt theory was extended to social psychology by Solomon Asch (1907–1996), to the visual arts by Rudolf Arnheim (b. 1904), and to learning by George Katona (1901–1981); Wertheimer completed a major work on productive thinking. At Swarthmore College Köhler used electroencephalogram equipment to try to discover the brain events underlying perception. His work was initially received with interest, but then apparently refuted; however, interest in organized brain events extending beyond single firings of nerve cells in anatomically localized areas has recently revived.

Gestalt psychology has had a major impact on research in perception and the psychology of art and has also contributed significantly to studies on problem solving and thinking. Lewin is regarded as a founder of experimental social psychology. Köhler was one of the first to introduce, in the late 1920s, the distinction between "closed" and "open" systems into theoretical biology. Also fundamental were philosophical implications of Gestalt theory. The Gestalt theorists asserted the primacy of perception over sensations in the constitution of consciousness and advanced a conception of the subject as involved in, rather than separated from, the world. These ideas had an important impact on phenomenology and existentialism. Against the mode of thought still dominant in cognitive science, they claimed that form and order are not constructed on a foundation of sensory information according to fixed cognitive schemata or logical rules. Instead, they maintained that there is meaningful order that lies not behind, but *within* the flux of experience.

The popular psychotherapy called Gestalt was at best indirectly derived from Gestalt theory. Its founder, Fritz Perls (1893–1970), a nonorthodox psychoanalyst, acquired some Gestalt vocabulary during studies in Frankfurt, but the conceptual links end there. Students of Metzger developed a different approach to psychotherapy, which is still practiced in Germany.

See also **Academies of Science; Anti-Semitism; Existentialism; Germany; Phenomenology; Science.**

BIBLIOGRAPHY

Primary Sources

Arnheim, Rudolf. *Art and Visual Perception: A Psychology of the Creative Eye.* 1954. Rev. and exp. ed. Berkeley, Calif., 2004.

Asch, Solomon E. *Social Psychology.* 1952. Oxford, U.K., and New York, 1987.

Koffka, Kurt. *Principles of Gestalt Psychology.* London and New York, 1935.

Köhler, Wolfgang. *Gestalt Psychology: An Introduction to New Concepts in Modern Psychology.* 1929. Rev. ed., New York, 1947.

Lewin, Kurt. *A Dynamic Theory of Personality: Selected Papers.* Translated by Donald K. Adams and Karl E. Zener. New York and London, 1935.

Wertheimer, Max. *Productive Thinking.* 1945. Enl. ed. New York: Harper, 1959.

Secondary Sources

Asch, Solomon E. "Gestalt Theory." In *International Encyclopedia of the Social Sciences,* vol. 6. edited by David L. Sills, 157–175. New York, 1968.

Ash, Mitchell G. *Gestalt Psychology in German Culture 1890–1967: Holism and the Quest for Objectivity.* Cambridge, U.K., and New York, 1995.

King, D. Brett, and Michael Wertheimer. *Max Wertheimer and Gestalt Theory.* New Brunswick, N.J., 2005.

MITCHELL G. ASH

GESTAPO. The Gestapo (abbreviation for Geheime Staatspolizei; secret state police) was the political police force of the Third Reich and the major organ of persecution and mass murder under National Socialism.

ORIGINS AND DEVELOPMENT

The Gestapo was formed out of the political department of the Berlin police in April 1933 by the new Prussian prime minister, Hermann Goering. The personnel came from the Prussian criminal police, which during the Weimar Republic had also investigated political crimes, predominantly of communist origin. It took some time before the Gestapo became the unified political police of the German Reich. Already by 1933 a predecessor to the Gestapo, the Geheimes Staatspolizeiamt (Gestapa), had been established in Berlin, as had the Bavarian political police in Munich. All other German Laender formed similar Gestapo institutions by 1934. That year the SS (Schutzstaffel) leader, Heinrich Himmler, and Reinhard Heydrich, chief of the SS intelligence (Sicherheitsdienst) took over the police in Prussia, and in 1936 a unified SS and police system was installed. Hence, not only were the command of SS and police fully merged, but most Gestapo members were also incorporated into the SS.

The next year the Gestapo together with the criminal police formed the security police (Sicherheitspolizei). This buildup of new institutions culminated some weeks after the beginning of World War II with the creation of the Reichssicherheitshauptamt (Imperial Security Main Office; RSHA), the central persecution apparatus, which united the Gestapo, criminal police, and the security service of the SS (SD). The Gestapo now constituted Amt IV (Branch IV) of the RSHA. With the German territorial expansions from 1938 on, Gestapo members were integrated in the so-called Einsatzgruppen, which followed the German army. Gestapo offices were set up in all annexed territories as in the Protectorate of Bohemia and Moravia. In all other occupied territories it became part of the regional security police and SD structures, thus copying the RSHA on a small scale.

The Gestapo was headed from 1936 until the end of the war by Heinrich Müller, a functionary from the political police in Bavaria who never became a political-ideological planner but fully organized persecutions and mass murders all over occupied Europe. Until the mid-1930s the majority of the personnel consisted of career policemen, most of whom had worked there since the 1920s. From 1936 on, as the apparatus heavily expanded, it took over new personnel especially from the regular Schutzpolizei. Nevertheless, the Gestapo (including border police) never numbered more than thirty-two thousand functionaries, among them women, for the whole of Europe under Nazi rule. It took some time before most of the Gestapo men joined the SS, where they were

assigned ranks equal to their position in the criminal police. The SD, which in its beginnings had served as an internal intelligence for the Nazi Party, more and more developed into a parallel structure to the Gestapo, thus laying the ideological grounds for the persecution of all alleged enemies. Especially from 1937 on, this ideological merging of both institutions was visible. They gradually developed schemes not only for persecuting political enemies and Jews but also for "purifying the German social body." But the Gestapo still exclusively consisted of state officials and had executive power. This changed during the war. SD-functionaries such as Adolf Eichmann were integrated into the Gestapo structures. In the occupied territories, the SD took over more and more executive power, especially on a local level.

The main task of the Gestapo consisted in "combatting enemies" (Feindbekämpfung), first inside the Reich, then all over occupied Europe. Thus the Gestapo was internally structured according to "enemy categories"; especially important were the offices concerned with communism, Jews, and eastern Europeans. But there were also departments dealing with the churches and other religious institutions, Freemasons, right-wing opposition like monarchists, and so on. The persecution of Gypsies and homosexuals fell under the responsibility of the criminal police.

GESTAPO WORK

The Gestapo work at first glance resembled regular police work—investigating, keeping card indexes, and making arrests. But the Gestapo did not react to criminal activity; rather, it targeted "enemy groups" as a whole. Because of the lack of personnel, the Gestapo depended on informers, both official (V-Leute) and unofficial. In the Reich it profited heavily from individual denunciations, to a lesser extent in the occupied areas. Most important was information provided by low-level Nazi Party functionaries and by other police and SS branches. From 1933 on, the most important instrument of Gestapo executive work was the Schutzhaftbefehl (protective custody order), which was the pseudolegal basis for all preventive arrests. The arrested were imprisoned either in jails or in the new concentration camps. Their basic rights had been lifted in February 1933. The state

A crowd gathers to look at a Yugoslavian man hanging in the main square in Belgrade after having been executed by the Gestapo, 18 December 1941. ©BETTMANN/CORBIS

prosecutors, which traditionally controlled the police, were excluded from this procedure in 1934.

The Gestapo had at its disposal its own investigative prisons, where it interrogated and tortured prisoners—many were beaten to death. Inside each concentration camp the regional Gestapo had its own branch, the political department. Since 1939, Heydrich formally introduced the killing of Gestapo prisoners in concentration camps, officially called *Sonderbehandlung* (special treatment). With the beginning of the war, the Gestapo became involved in the forced population transfers, first in Poland, then in Yugoslavia. The same procedures applied to the deportation and killing of the Jews. During the war against the Soviet Union, the Gestapo constituted the central part of the Einsatzgruppen, which killed around six hundred thousand persons, most of them Jews. The stationary offices in the Soviet Union continued these

crimes, such as the murder of selected groups of Soviet prisoners of war (POWs) in Poland and in the Reich. In all areas except the General Government in Poland, the deportation of the Jews to the killing sites was organized by the Gestapo Department IV B4 under Eichmann and put into action by the local Gestapo (inside the Reich) or security police (outside the Reich) structures. By 1943 the main focus of Gestapo work turned to a violent fight against the resistance in occupied Europe and the surveillance of foreign forced workers inside the Reich. A new camp system, the *Arbeitserziehungslager* (work education camps) was installed under Gestapo control, where criminalized foreign workers were imprisoned.

In sum, the Gestapo was responsible for millions of murders. It was declared a criminal organization by the International Military Tribunal in 1946. Its members were interned under allied occupation, and comparatively many were tried and sentenced after the war. Nevertheless, during the 1950s a part of the personnel was able to return to the (West) German police apparatus.

See also **Concentration Camps; Eichmann, Adolf; Heydrich, Reinhard; Holocaust; Resistance; SS (Schutzstaffel).**

BIBLIOGRAPHY

Browder, George C. *Hitler's Enforcers: The Gestapo and the SS Security Service in the Nazi Revolution.* New York, 1996.

Gellately, Robert. *The Gestapo and German Society: Enforcing Racial Policy, 1933–1945.* Oxford, U.K., 1990.

Lozowick, Yaacov. *Hitler's Bureaucrats: The Nazi Security Police and the Banality of Evil.* London, 2002.

Paul, Gerhard, and Klaus-Michael Mallmann, eds. *Die Gestapo: Mythos und Realität.* Darmstadt, Germany, 1995.

———. *Die Gestapo im Zweiten Weltkrieg: "Heimatfront" und besetztes Europa.* Darmstadt, Germany, 2000.

DIETER POHL

GHETTO. The word *ghetto* originally denoted the traditional Jewish quarter of medieval Christian cities; the term evidently originated in a quarter of this kind that existed in Venice. From the early Middle Ages, Jews tended to live on separate streets or in separate neighborhoods, but they did so voluntarily to maintain their distinct way of life. The first ghettos imposed on Jews appeared in Spain and Portugal in the late fourteenth century.

From the end of the eighteenth century on, and especially after the political changes that the French Revolution brought about, the ghettos that had been established for Jews in Europe began to disappear. The ghetto of Rome was the last to be formally abolished—in 1883, after papal rule ended in Rome (it was thenceforth confined to the Vatican).

Although this type of ghetto existed mainly in Central and Western Europe, separate Jewish quarters also came into being in cities across the Muslim world. In the United States, during the struggle for equal rights by the African American population in the 1950s and 1960s, the term *ghetto* was widely used to denote the impoverished neighborhoods noted for rampant distress, crime, and violence that these citizens inhabited in major American cities. A diverse alternative culture, noted for its music and art and its sweeping social protest, evolved in the vicinity of the African American ghetto. To this day, the term *ghetto* is used for a neighborhood inhabited by an ethnic minority that is socially marginalized and suffers from inferior living conditions and fewer opportunities when compared to those of the established population.

THE NAZI GHETTO
The ghettos established by the Nazis for European Jews during World War II were totally different in structure and goals from those described above. The establishment of these ghettos, beginning in Poland shortly after the onset of the German occupation of that country in 1939, was a phase in the overall development of an anti-Jewish policy that aimed to find a comprehensive solution to the "problem" of the Jewish presence in Europe. The Nazi ghetto was not intended to be a permanent solution, a place where Jews would be strictly isolated from the surrounding society. Instead, it was something like a quarantine camp or at times a giant prison, where harsh and restrictive living conditions were imposed. The ghetto provided various German authorities with a reserve of available labor for various purposes and gave them an opportunity, unconstrained by laws and regulations, to oppress the Jewish inhabitants and dispossess them of money, valuables, and other goods according to Nazi officials' needs and caprices.

The first German directive regarding the concentration of Jews in separate urban quarters appeared in the *Schnellbrief* (quick brief) that the head of the Security Police, Reinhard Heydrich, sent to the commanders of the SS and the police special units (Einsatzgruppen) that followed the Wehrmacht into Poland in September 1939. According to the directive, within three or four weeks the Jews in the Polish areas were to be concentrated in special areas of the large cities so that they would be easier to control and eventually deport. Small Jewish communities were to be eradicated and their inhabitants removed to more central towns, preferably close to railroads. Several weeks later, Hans Frank, the governor-general of the General Government, issued a similar directive. Neither of these documents, however, speaks specifically about the establishment of a ghetto, that is, a closed and isolated area where the Jews would be concentrated under strict supervision.

In 1939–1940, it was the declared policy of Nazi Germany to resolve the Jewish issue in territorial ways. This goal, however, quickly proved unrealistic and unworkable. The absence of clear guidelines about what to do with the Jews, coupled with the abandonment of the total deportation policy, convinced the local authorities that they should deal on their own with the presence of Jews within their purviews. Consequently, the Nazi ghettos were established at different times and differed in their ways of life, in the type of official German control, and in the extent of freedom of movement allowed.

The first large ghetto, located in Lodz, was sealed on 1 May 1940, with 162,000 Jews packed into it. The Lodz model was closely studied and adopted by those who established ghettos in other Polish cities. The assumption behind the founding of the Lodz ghetto was that the Jews' continued presence in the city would be short-lived. Therefore, the Germans' main concern was how to exploit fully the Jews' property as the ghetto was being established. As it became increasingly evident that the Jews would not quickly disappear from Lodz, however, an economic structure was built in the ghetto, including a variety of workshops that exploited Jewish labor and funneled the profits into the pockets of the German ghetto administrators, merchants, and others.

The Warsaw ghetto was sealed in November 1940. It was the largest of all the ghettos, its population peaking at around 440,000 in mid-1941. The governor of Warsaw District, Ludwig Fischer, claimed that in the opinion of the German medical service in Warsaw, the Jews were spreading dangerous illnesses and therefore had to be isolated from the surrounding population. Allegations of Jewish involvement in the black market and in the corruption of the morals and culture of Polish society provided additional rationales for a sealed ghetto. The establishment of the ghetto also amounted to an admission by the local German authorities that they would not be able to deport the Jews of Warsaw rapidly. Since the plans for the ghetto did not include mechanisms that would keep the inhabitants fed and gainfully employed, however, the Warsaw ghetto became a focal point of distress, hunger, and severe epidemics. The situation did begin to improve slightly in mid-1941, when the Germans in charge of the ghetto decided to make the ghetto economically viable, to create jobs so that the Jews could support themselves and to increase food supplies. In March 1941, ghettos were established in Lublin and in Kraków, the seat of the governor-general and the administrative capital of the German occupation in Poland. The Kraków ghetto was established during a deportation action that had begun in the spring of 1940 with the aim of banishing some 50,000 Jews, leaving only 5,000 workers in high-demand trades. By economic necessity, however, the ghetto eventually held 18,000. In April 1941, ghettos were established in several other important cities in Poland: Kielce, Radom, and Częstochowa. By the spring and summer of 1942, when the deportations to the death camps began in Poland, hundreds of ghettos had been established across the country, including some in the Jewish communities of small towns.

The Germans' goal in establishing the ghettos remains unclear and various authorities who dealt with the Jewish question in Poland interpreted it in different ways. Obviously, the Nazis were not concerned about the high mortality rate that ghettoization and the living conditions in some of the ghettos caused among the imprisoned Jews. In 1941–1942, more than 112,000 Jews in the two most important ghettos in Poland, those of Warsaw and Lodz—20 percent of the Jewish population living there at the time—died of starvation and illness. In 1941 the deaths of thousands of Jews in the ghettos, especially in Warsaw, forced the leaders of the General Government to choose between allowing the starvation and slow extermination of the Jews to continue or transforming the ghettos to serve the Germans' economic interests. In mid-1941, those who favored the economic rationale won the day. Thus, German policy toward the ghettos in general favored economic considerations as long as a comprehensive territorial solution involving the deportation of the Jews had not been formulated.

A street in the Lublin ghetto, Poland. ©BETTMANN/CORBIS

Ironically, the Jewish labor force in the ghettos became more necessary than ever in early 1942, after the Final Solution was set in motion. As the war in the east expanded, the German war industry required more and more workers. Hundreds of thousands of Poles were sent to Germany as laborers, as were Soviet prisoners of war, who had survived a winter of catastrophic mortality in German prisoner of war camps. Demand for Jewish workers in the ghettos escalated so rapidly that in June 1942 Ludwig Fischer issued a directive to the effect that every effort must be made not to leave Jews idle. The fundamental goal of employing the ghettoized Jews changed at this time. The instrumental purpose—enabling the Jews to support themselves and absolving the German authorities of this concern—gave way to the needs of companies that urgently required a handy supply of labor. The decision about the Jews' ultimate fate, however, had already been made in Berlin and economic considerations were not central in its adoption. By then, local leaders no longer played a role in making decisions about the Jews.

The last phase in the establishment of ghettos began in 1941 in the newly occupied Soviet territories. Ghettos were established in various towns in Lithuania, Latvia, Byelorussia, and Ukraine. The formation of ghettos in cities in these areas— Vilna (Vilnius), Kovno (Kaunas), Riga, Minsk, Lwów (Lvov/Lviv), and so on—coincided with the mass murder of the Jewish populations there, beginning in the summer of 1941. Often the ghettos served as a mechanism for the selection of some Jews for immediate murder and others for continued survival based on their ability to contribute their labor to the cause of the war. Thus, the ghettos in the occupied Soviet areas were already part of the Final Solution that had been decided upon and that had begun to be implemented in autumn 1941. In some towns, fewer than 20 percent of the pre-Occupation Jewish populations were left in the ghettos. Some of these ghettos resembled huge labor camps in every respect.

Although almost all the ghettos were located in Eastern Europe, the Germans did establish

several ghettos for specific purposes elsewhere. The most notable of them was that in Theresienstadt, northwestern Czechoslovakia, to which in 1941–1945 some 140,000 Jews were deported from Germany, the Protectorate of Bohemia and Moravia, and Western European countries. Responsibility for this ghetto belonged to the SS Security Police (the RSHA), which transferred its guarding requirements to the Czech police. Theresienstadt had been established to concentrate selected groups of Jews—the elderly, the famous, or those who had special status in Germany and Western Europe. In this manner, the Nazis intended to disprove rumors about the fate of German Jews who were being deported to the east. The first groups of Jews from Prague reached this ghetto in November 1941, but by January 1942 extermination transports were already setting out from Theresienstadt to Riga, Latvia. Most Jews who were concentrated in Theresienstadt were sent in 1942–1944 to be killed at the Auschwitz and Treblinka death camps in Poland; by late 1944, only 11,000 remained there.

Another ghetto in Central Europe was that of Budapest, established in late November 1944. After approximately 70,000 Jews were led out of this city on a death march toward the Austrian border, members of the Hungarian Nazi Party, the Arrow Cross, which had seized power in Hungary, set up a ghetto in Budapest, where most remaining Jews were concentrated. In December 1944–January 1945, the Hungarian Fascists removed about 20,000 Jews from the ghetto and murdered them along the banks of the Danube.

JEWISH LIFE IN THE GHETTOS
The Germans left the Jews to their own devices in many respects. Even before the ghettos were established, Jewish councils—Judenräte—were set up in Polish towns. Their function, in addition to obeying the Germans' directives, was to oversee the Jews' lives. This created an impression of Jewish autonomy that was illusory, since the powers of the Judenräte were never entrusted to any Jewish leaders who had been active in the prewar Eastern European Jewish communities.

The Judenräte were composed of public figures who had remained in the Jewish communities after the Occupation began. Once ghettoization had occurred, the Judenräte had to cope with dire problems that they could rarely solve. They dealt with the allocation of apartments and other dwellings in the ghetto, the removal of waste, the distribution of food, the welfare and relief of the indigent and refugees, education, the operation of clinics and hospitals, and burial of the dead. In many ghettos, a Jewish police force was established to maintain public order, control the entrances to the ghetto, and escort groups of workers who set out from the ghetto to workplaces in town. In certain ghettos, the Germans even allowed the Judenräte to manage an independent branch of the postal service.

The Judenräte in the major ghettos, however, invested most of their effort toward creating an economic infrastructure that would provide the inhabitants with jobs. In ghettos such as those of Lodz, Białystok, and Vilnius, a systematic network of workplaces—ghetto workshops and employers outside the ghetto who hired Jewish workers—was built in cooperation with the Judenräte. Ghettos that had such systems were usually more orderly and stable than the others. Although chronic shortages of food, clothing, and other essentials persisted, mass mortality was not in evidence as in the Warsaw ghetto. Many Jews believed that a productive, well-kept, and functioning ghetto was the only instrument that might persuade the Germans to leave them unharmed and might increase their prospects of survival.

Community and cultural life continued in almost all ghettos that had been established in Eastern Europe. Even in small ghettos, Jews maintained their educational, cultural, and religious institutions as best they could, at the initiative of the Judenräte or of public activists and intellectuals. In Warsaw, Lodz, Vilnius, Kaunas, and other towns, drama groups put on Jewish and non-Jewish plays for the ghetto public. Public libraries collected thousands of books from Jewish libraries that had been shut down, including some that the Nazis had torched at the beginning of the Occupation.

Activists in Jewish youth movements were very important and had an impact on the lives of young people in the ghettos. In ghettos in the major cities—Warsaw, Lodz, Kraków, Vilnius, Kaunas, Białystok—these activists were the most dynamic group, secretly maintaining informal education and cultural and welfare endeavors. They organized social activity groups for children and young people, evening literary events, theater troupes, and choirs. The youth movements and underground activists of the former Jewish political parties also published dozens of underground newspapers in the Warsaw ghetto, which were disseminated to other ghettos in occupied Poland. In this way, the underground activists managed to break through the isolation that the Germans had imposed on the Jews in ghettoizing them. They also formed the core that established the resistance organizations in the ghettos in 1941–1942.

In early spring 1942, the Germans began to evacuate the ghettos in Poland as part of a comprehensive extermination scheme known as Operation Reinhardt. The operation started in Lublin District and culminated in the deportation of 350,000 Jews from the Warsaw ghetto to Treblinka for extermination in summer 1942. On 19 July 1942, Heinrich Himmler issued a directive for the final annihilation of the Jews in the General Government by the end of 1942, with the exception of selected groups that would be left behind for labor in several major cities. In another directive, on 21 July 1943, Himmler ordered the deportation of these remaining Jews to concentration camps in the Baltic countries and parts of Byelorussia. The last ghetto to be liquidated was that of Lodz, where the remaining Jews, some 70,000 in number, were sent in August 1944 to the Auschwitz death camp.

See also **Holocaust; Warsaw Ghetto.**

BIBLIOGRAPHY

Primary Sources

The Chronicle of the Łódź Ghetto, 1941–1944. Edited by Lucjan Dobroszycki. Translated by Richard Lourie, Joachim Neugroschel et al. New Haven, Conn., 1984.

Czerniaków, Adam. *The Warsaw Diary of Adam Czerniaków: Prelude to Doom.* Edited by Raul Hilberg, Stanislaw Staron, and Josef Kermisz. Translated by Stanislaw Staron and the staff of Yad Vashem. New York, 1979.

Kahane, David. *Lvov Ghetto Diary.* Translated by Jerzy Michalowicz. Amherst, Mass., 1990.

Kruk, Herman. *The Last Days of the Jerusalem of Lithuania: Chronicles from the Vilna Ghetto and the Camps, 1939–1944.* Edited by Benjamin Harshav. Translated by Barbara Harshav. New Haven, Conn., 2002.

Ringelblum, Emanuel. *Ksòvim fun Geto.* 2 vols. Tel Aviv, 1985.

Secondary Sources

Berkley, George E. *Hitler's Gift: The Story of Theresienstadt.* Boston, 1993.

Browning, Christopher R. "Nazi Ghettoization Policy in Poland, 1939–1941." In his *The Path to Genocide. Essays on Launching the Final Solution,* 28–56. Cambridge, U.K., 1992.

Gutman, Yisrael. *The Jews of Warsaw, 1939–1943: Ghetto, Underground, Revolt.* Translated by Ina Friedman. Bloomington, Ind., 1982.

DANIEL BLATMAN

GIDE, ANDRÉ (1869–1951), French writer awarded the Nobel Prize for Literature in 1947.

Called France's "leading contemporary" by André Rouveyre, André Gide indeed epitomizes not only the "great writer" but also, before Jean-Paul Sartre, the committed intellectual. Gide was never captive to his political commitments, however, and he always preserved his lucidity and independence of mind.

Born in Paris to a family of academics, André-Paul-Guillaume Gide was educated at the city's prestigious École Alsacienne, where he passed his baccalaureate examination in 1889. The following year he wrote his first book, *The Notebooks of André Walter* (*Les Cahiers d'André Walter,* 1891). From then on, literature—writing and incessant reading—would be Gide's world. During the years 1890–1896 he went in search of himself, traveling, discovering his homosexuality, writing *Fruits of the Earth* (*Les nourritures terrestres,* 1897) and *Marshlands* (*Paludes,* 1895), and making his first literary acquaintances, among them Oscar Wilde, Francis Jammes, and Paul Claudel. In 1895, he married his cousin Madeleine Rondeaux. A year later he was elected mayor of La Roque, a commune in Normandy. A supporter of Alfred Dreyfus, Gide took a great interest in the political problems of the time. During this period he also became friends with the Belgian painter Théo van Rysselberghe and his wife, Maria. Later nicknamed "la Petite Dame" (the Little Lady), Maria was to be the faithful chronicler of Gide's domestic life. In 1923 the van Rysselberghes' daughter Elisabeth gave birth to a baby girl, Catherine, whose father was André Gide.

After the turn of the century Gide published two major novels, *The Immoralist* (*L'immoraliste*) in 1902 and *Strait Is the* Gate (*La porte étroite*) in 1909. Thereafter his literary work would oscillate between two approaches, the one anchored in reality and involved with contemporary issues, the other more introspective, more concerned with formal experiment. At times the two were combined, as in *Corydon* (1924) or *If It Die* (*Si le grain ne meurt*, 1926), works in which Gide defended his homosexuality. Both approaches, moreover, were underpinned by the quest for an ethic lying beyond all traditional morality. Gide's public activities likewise had a dual aspect, at once literary and political.

In 1908 Gide helped found the influential *Nouvelle revue française* (*NRF*), and a year later the annual literary and socially progressive ten-day conferences, led by Paul Desjardins, known as the Décades de Pontigny. In 1914 Gide broke with the celebrated dramatist Paul Claudel over a passage in Gide's novel *The Vatican Cellars* (*Les caves du Vatican*) that Claudel deemed "pederastic." During World War I he did aid work with refugees, especially those arriving from Belgium, and flirted briefly with the right-wing organization Action Française. His friend Henri Ghéon converted to Catholicism, and Gide experienced a religious crisis of his own (he had himself converted in 1905, but this act was inconsequential).

After the war Gide resumed his international literary activism, seeking with Jacques Rivière to bring about a French-German intellectual rapprochement. In 1919 he published one of his most-read books, *The Pastoral Symphony* (*La symphonie pastorale*) and began work on *The Counterfeiters* (*Les faux-monnayeurs*, 1925), which would be another great triumph. The 1920s were also years of public political involvement for Gide, most especially with respect to the anticolonialist struggle, as witness *Voyage au Congo* (1927) and *Retour du Tchad* (1928), published as one volume in English translation as *Travels in the Congo* (1929). In the early 1930s Gide was attracted by communism. As the fascist threat grew ever more tangible (Hitler's coming to power, the burning of the Reichstag, the Stavisky

affair in France), Gide became a fellow traveler, a militant in the Vigilance Committee of Anti-Fascist Intellectuals, and a very active participant in the communists' great international congress "for the defense of culture" in 1935. The following year he was invited with a delegation of writers to visit the Soviet Union, where he even delivered an elegy for Maxim Gorky on Red Square in the presence of Stalin. On his return to France, however, he published *Return from the U.S.S.R.* (*Retour de l'U.R.S.S.*, 1936) and *Afterthoughts on the U.S.S.R.* (*Retouches à mon retour de l'U.R.S.S.*, 1937), expressing his disillusion with the Soviet regime and condemning the cult of personality. Targeted in consequence by the communist intellectuals, with Louis Aragon leading the pack, he broke with the party. He went so far as to lend his support to the Trotskyist POUM (Workers' Party of Marxist Unification) fighters under attack by the communists in Spain. Gide then gradually withdrew from political action, busied himself with the publication of his *Journal* in the prestigious Bibliothèque de la Pléiade, and resumed his traveling.

During the war and occupation, Gide went first into internal exile in Provence and later into an external one in Tunisia and Algeria. In 1941 he ceased all collaboration with the *Nouvelle revue français*, which was now under the control of the collaborationist Pierre Drieu la Rochelle.

The postwar years were a time of consecration for Gide. In 1947 he won the Nobel Prize. The film version of *La symphonie pastorale* (1946) was a great success, as was the staging of *Les caves du Vatican* at the Comédie-Française in 1950. The ultimate honor, perhaps, came after Gide's death, when in 1952 his complete works were added to the Vatican's Index of Prohibited Books.

See also **Action Française; Sartre, Jean-Paul.**

BIBLIOGRAPHY

Primary Sources

Gide, André. *Romans, récits et soties, oeuvres lyriques.* Paris, 1958.

———. *Journal.* 2 vols. Paris, 1996–1997.

———. *Essais critiques.* Paris, 1999.

———. *Souvenirs et voyages.* Paris, 2001.

Secondary Sources

Association des Amis d'André Gide. Available at http://www.gidiana.net. Official site.

Lepape, Pierre. *André Gide le messager. Biographie.* Paris, 1997.

Rysselberghe, Maria van. *Les Cahiers de la Petite Dame. Note pour l'histoire authentique d'André Gide.* 3 vols. Paris, 1973–1975.

NICOLAS BEAUPRÉ

GIEREK, EDWARD (1913–2001), Polish Communist leader.

Edward Gierek was born in 1913 in the village of Porąbka near Dąbrowa Górnicza, in the Russian part of Poland. His father, grandfather, and great-grandfather had been coal miners; all died in mining catastrophes. His widowed mother worked hard to raise him and his sister. In 1920 she remarried, and in 1923 the family migrated to France in search of job. Edward completed the French elementary school and, at the age of thirteen, started working as a miner. In 1931 he joined the French Communist Party, and after a strike in 1934, he was deported back to Poland. After two years of military service, having married and unsuccessfully sought a stable job, he left Poland again, this time for the coal mines in Belgium. There he joined the local Communist Party; during the German occupation he was involved in the Resistance. In 1945 he joined a pro-communist Polish association and was elected the chairman of an immigrant umbrella organization. A young worker and skillful organizer, who had not been involved in any of the prewar factions or stained by their ideological "deviations," he attracted the attention of the Polish Communist Party headquarters in Warsaw. In 1948 he was called back to Poland and assigned to the party provincial committee in Katowice.

In Upper Silesia his miner background helped him advance through the party ranks. He became a member of the Central Committee (CC) and director of the CC department for heavy industry beginning in 1954, a CC secretary in 1956 and, briefly, a Politburo member in 1956. In 1952 he became a deputy in the Sejm or Diet. To the career in Warsaw he preferred Upper Silesia, where he returned as the first secretary of the provincial party committee in the period 1957–1970. In this most industrialized region of Poland, with the largest party organization, Gierek built a solid power base. He earned a reputation as a pragmatic manager, keeping distance from intra-party factional struggles. He kept the CC secretary position, and in 1959 he regained his seat in the Politburo. During the student rebellion of 1968 he firmly supported Władysław Gomułka, as well as the "anti-Zionist campaign" and reprisals against the students.

When strikes and bloody riots followed an increase in food prices in December 1970, Gierek replaced Gomułka as the party's first secretary. He managed to calm the unrest, promising economic reforms, withdrawing from the price increases, and replacing Gomułka's men in the party leadership and government with younger technocrats. They launched ambitious plans of industrial expansion and technological modernization, combined with significant increases in individual consumption. Investments, wages, and consumption actually began to grow rapidly, thanks to the importation of Western technology, Western credits, and the Soviet blessing under the detente era. Gierek also improved relations with the Catholic Church, liberalized cultural policy, and allowed for more contacts with the West. He paid many visits to Western capitals and hosted many Western leaders, while enjoying very good relations with the Soviet leader Leonid Brezhnev.

Yet the economic miracle did not last long. Since the mid-1970s, the consequences of a lack of structural reforms combined with the economic downturn in the West put increasing strains on Poland. Attempts to remedy the situation through economic maneuvers (including price increases) did not improve matters but brought riots to Radom and Ursus (1976), which were violently suppressed. Through late 1970s, foreign debt, food shortages, and queues in shops grew. Gierek and the regime were losing authority, especially since the election of the Polish pope John Paul II in 1978. Now dependent on Western credit, the regime tolerated emerging opposition groups. Another price increase in summer 1980 set off protests across the country, which culminated in a massive strike in the coastal cities. To avoid the bloody scenario of 1970, the party leadership accepted strikers' demands, including the right to strike and the independent Solidarity trade unions, and removed Gierek from power a few days later. He and his friends were removed from the Politburo, the CC, and the party and were blamed for all the trouble and the various alleged abuses. When Poland's military leader Wojciech Jaruzelski introduced martial law the next year, he even interned Gierek and some of his collaborators for several months.

Through the 1980s Gierek remained politically marginalized. In the 1990s, when the social costs of economic transformation made many Poles nostalgic about the "old good days" of his rule, Gierek regained much popular sympathy, despite reminders from economists of the debt that Poland was continuing to pay back. Until his death in 2001 Gierek lived in his native region, where he published his memoirs *Przerwana dekada* (1990) and *Replika* (1990).

See also **Eastern Bloc; Gomułka, Władysław; Jaruzelski, Wojciech; Poland; Solidarity; Warsaw Pact.**

BIBLIOGRAPHY

Lepak, Keith John. *Prelude to Solidarity: Poland and the Politics of the Gierek Regime.* New York, 1988.

Rolicki, Janusz. *Edward Gierek. Życie i narodziny legendy.* Warsaw, 2002.

DARIUSZ STOLA

GIOLITTI, GIOVANNI (1842–1928), Italian politician.

Statesman Giovanni Giolitti embodied liberal Italy, its progress and its final failure when fascism came to power. He dominated two decades of Italian political history to the point that historians speak of an "età giolittiana" (age of Giolitti). The statesman from the Piedmont left a rather controversial image of himself that recent historiography has revisited in a more favorable light.

After studying law, Giolitti began his prefectorial (civil service) career in 1862 and was elected deputy in parliament in 1882. He served as prime minister in 1892–1893 and was minister of the interior in the Giuseppe Zanardelli government in 1901–1902.

He became prime minister once again in 1903, a post he would keep, with only a few brief interruptions, until World War I. He came back to power in the context of a postwar political and social crisis.

Giolitti encouraged the liberalization of Italian political life. He worked hard to consolidate the unitary state's social foundations by broadening the nation's political participation. This political modernization process would be accompanied by important economic and social transformations. Italy's industrial takeoff took place in the 1900s and gave birth to a bourgeois business class. Being pragmatic, not dogmatic, Giolitti wanted to be the man of "the fair middle." He invited leaders of the Socialist Party to enter the government on several occasions. Simultaneously, he wanted to encourage Catholics to participate in the nation's political life, as they had remained marginal since 1870 due to the conflict between the Vatican and the Italian state. Therefore the "Gentiloni Pact" was passed in 1913, after Count Vincenzo Gentiloni, leader of the Electoral Union, a Catholic lobby, proposed a pact with the moderate candidates of Giolitti's party, promising the support of Catholic votes to those who advocated Christian values in the Chamber of Deputies (with regard to divorce, family, education, and other issues). A new electoral law in 1912 established a system of universal suffrage for males aged twenty-one and older (thirty years for illiterates). The administration enjoyed tremendous growth under Giolitti, expanding the role of the state in the life of the country.

Giolitti's liberalism found its limits with the development of social movements, particularly in the south of Italy, where he justified police repression of strikers and protestors. Giolitti was also criticized by right-wing, nationalist Italians, whose organizations and ideas were flourishing at the beginning of the century. They denounced Giolitti's "Italietta" (little Italy), the lack of the ideal of national grandeur, and his "politician's" politics.

Giolitti's career was also stained by corruption. The Banca Romana (Rome Bank) case (in which he promoted the bank's allegedly corrupt director to senatorial rank) forced him to resign his position as prime minister in 1893, interrupting his career. But Giolitti was especially reproached for "giolittism," which consisted in governing with the support of parliamentary majorities where political differences and ideology mattered less than clienteles. The Italian historian Gaetano Salvemini stigmatized Giolitti's methods of governing, particularly in the south, labeling him the "ministro della malavita" (minister of the underworld). While his methods of governing brought about political stability, they also contributed to postponing in-depth social democratization, the differences between parties resting more on network and clientele rivalries rather than on opposing programs or ideas.

Giolitti's impact was also important in terms of foreign policy. He remained a partisan of Italy's loyalty to the "Triplice" (alliance with Germany and Austria-Hungary), regularly reaffirmed until 1912. Pressured by certain financial institutions, particularly the Banco di Roma, a group of moderate Catholics and Italian nationalists, he decided—with the king's assent, but without consulting parliament—to invade Libya, making it an Italian possession with the Treaty of Lausanne in October 1912. The conquest of Libya triggered a wave of nationalist sentiment and divided Italian socialists, some of whom were sensitive to the nationalist theme of "the proletarian nation" driven to find new territories to migrate to. Giolitti resigned in March of 1914 and failed to prevent Italy's participation in World War I, when it sided with the Allies in 1915.

Giolitti's last term in power (June 1920–June 1921) has become one of the most discussed periods of his career. Though he was firm in dealing with the seizure of Fiume by Gabriele D'Annunzio and his legionnaires, chasing them out of Trieste in December 1920, he let the social and political crisis that gripped Italy after the war deteriorate. In the same way that other politicians of the Liberal Party had, he underestimated the Fascist danger, supporting, for example, the Acerbo electoral law project when he was president of the parliamentary commission, which changed the law to favor the Fascist Party, dealing a decisive blow to democracy. After the Fascist March on Rome in 1922, Giolitti remained in Parliament, as part of the antifascist opposition after 1925, until his death in 1928.

See also **Fascism; Italy.**

BIBLIOGRAPHY

Gentile, Emilio, ed. *L'Italia giolittiana*. Rome, 1977.

Giolitti, Giovanni. *Memoirs of My Life*. Translated by Edward Storer. New York, 1973.

Preti, Luigi. *Giolitti, i riformisti e gli altri, 1900–1911*. Milan, 1985.

Salvemini, Gaetano. *Il ministro della mala vita e altri scritti sull'Italia giolittiana*. Edited by Elio Apih. Milan, 1962.

MARIE-ANNE MATARD-BONUCCI

GISCARD D'ESTAING, VALÉRY

(b. 1926), French politician.

Valéry Giscard d'Estaing became the third president of the French Fifth Republic after Charles de Gaulle (1890–1970) resigned in 1969 and Georges Pompidou (1911–1974) died in office in 1974. He was just fifty-five years old when his short but brilliant political career suddenly came to an end, when he lost reelection to a second term as president in 1981 to François Mitterrand (1916–1996).

Despite his aristocratic name (his father and uncle persuaded the authorities to add "d'Estaing" to Giscard), he in fact belonged to the upper-middle-class worlds of business, public administration, and politics, where he succeeded his paternal grandfather Jacques Bardoux (1874–1959) in 1956 in becoming the representative of Puy-de-Dôme in Auvergne.

Giscard d'Estaing was accepted into the École Polytechnique in 1946, then to the École National d'administration, from which he emerged a state finance inspector in 1954. He was not destined to spend much time in public administration and launched his political career almost immediately thereafter. He entered into his destiny when, after de Gaulle returned to power in the 1962 elections, his friends on the traditional right condemned the general's Algerian policy, whereas Giscard d'Estaing chose to remain loyal to him by forming the Groupe des Républicains Indépendants, which became the second largest pillar, although still a quite small one, in the Gaullist electoral "majority."

Financial management was to become Giscard d'Estaing's specialty. He quickly became finance minister on 19 January 1962 after having held several secretarial-level positions, where he remained until 1966 before returning in 1969 until 1974, through the successive governments of

Jacques Chaban-Delmas (1915–2000) and Pierre Messmer (b. 1916). Giscard d'Estaing's ambitions were not limited to financial planning. When he was forced to resign in 1966 following the mediocre results of an economic stabilization plan, he distanced himself from de Gaulle. Giscard d'Estaing sought to differentiate himself in the legislative campaign of 1967 by accompanying his "yes" to the Gaullist Majority with a "but" designed to preserve his capacity to form independent judgments. He criticized the "lone exercise of power" after de Gaulle made his famous declarations concerning a "self-assured and dominant Israel" and "Free Quebec." He even supported the "no" vote in the 1969 referendum that led to de Gaulle's final resignation.

His objective was clearly the presidency of the Republic, which he already had in mind during the elections of 1969 when, only forty-five years old, he chose the path of self-effacement behind the candidacy of Pompidou. But ambitions, to be realized, require favorable circumstances, and a two-term Pompidou presidency threatened to leave him in office until 1983. When Pompidou contracted a rare form of leukemia that led to his death in 1974, Giscard d'Estaing decided to seize the opportunity, especially in that he considered Gaullism to be at least in part finished. The "majority" had largely lost the support of the segment of the Left that had joined forces with de Gaulle in 1958. His electoral base regrouped on the right. In the first round of voting Giscard d'Estaing distanced himself completely from the Gaullist candidate Chaban-Delmas and was elected in the second round. The results were extremely close. With the support of the fast-growing Union of the Left, François Mitterrand closed the gap to within 2 percent of total votes cast.

As president of the Republic, Giscard d'Estaing fully intended to prove that a "new era" characterized by youthfulness and change had begun—he was just fifty years old—and an entire series of reforms were indeed enacted, including the legalization of no-fault divorce and abortion, the reduction of the voting age to eighteen, changes in the national television organization, and democratization of secondary education. In certain cases the Left appreciated these reforms more than did

Giscard d'Estaing's own right-wing majority. However the new president encountered at least two major obstacles: the economic recession that began in 1974 and lasted, with greater or lesser intensity, until the end of the decade, and his failure to gain the full loyalty of the Gaullist movement. Although he initially believed he would succeed by naming as prime minister a young Gaullist by the name of Jacques Chirac (b. 1932), the good relations were not to last and after two years a merciless war erupted within the confines of the majority between "Gaullistes" and "Giscardiens." A portion of the Gaullists had already refrained from voting for Giscard d'Estaing in 1974 and his contemptuous attitude toward them did little to smooth things over. At the same time left-wing forces continued to gather throughout the country. Although Giscard d'Estaing retained some small hope of winning the elections in 1981, the effects of the recession, the rise of the Left, the hostility harbored toward him by one segment of the Gaullist movement, and the "Diamond Affair" (he had been accused of receiving several diamonds as a gift from an African dictator) all combined in Mitterrand's favor, leading him to prevail over Giscard d'Estaing by 3 percent.

Although initially stunned by his defeat, Giscard d'Estaing would later seek to overcome it. However, even though he often had important political roles to play in the future, including a final act in 2002 as president of the convention to draft a new European Constitution—one that was turned down by French voters in May 2005—he never managed to regain the highest ranks. Despite his long life, his political career turned out to be short, not only because of changed circumstances but also because he never truly learned to be popular. General de Gaulle had already said it once before: "The *people* will be his difficulty."

See also **European Constitution 2004–2005; France.**

BIBLIOGRAPHY

Primary Sources

Giscard d'Estaing, Valéry. *Ses idées ont été exposées dans son ouvrage, Démocratie française.* Paris, 1976.

———. *Le pouvoir et la vie.* Paris, 1988

———. *L'Affrontement.* Paris 1992.

Secondary Sources

Becker, Jean-Jacques. "Les années Giscard (1974–1981)." *L'Histoire* (May 1990).

———. *Histoire politique de la France depuis 1945.* Paris, 2003.

Becker, Jean-Jacques, with Pascal Ory. *Crises et alternances, 1974–2000.* Paris, 2002.

Petitfils, Jean-Christian. *La démocratie giscardienne.* Paris, 1981.

Rémond, René. *Le siècle dernier (1918–2002).* Paris, 2003.

JEAN-JACQUES BECKER

GLASNOST. *See* **Gorbachev, Mikhail; Perestroika.**

GLEMP, JÓZEF (b. 1929), Polish cardinal and primate of Poland.

The son of a miner, Kazimierz, and his wife, Salomea, Józef Glemp was sent to forced labor in Germany during the Nazi occupation of Poland and did not complete high school until May 1950. Several months later he began training for the priesthood in Gniezno and Poznań, and was ordained on 25 May 1956. His first posts involved work with young people, including chaplaincy in homes for incurably ill children and youthful offenders, as well as a prefecture in a secondary school for girls.

In 1958 Glemp went to Rome for studies in canon and civil law at the Pontifical Lateran University, which he completed four years later. In 1964 he defended a doctorate on "The Evolution of the Concept of Legal Fiction." During these years he also witnessed firsthand the workings of the Second Vatican Council.

In 1964 Glemp returned to Gniezno, the seat of the primate of Poland, and worked in the education of priests but also as consultor to the primatial tribunal on ratified and nonconsummated marriage. He advanced to the secretariat of the primate in December 1967 and became a close collaborator and member of the household of Cardinal Stefan Wyszyński, accompanying the Polish primate on numerous meetings with Pope Paul VI and with functionaries of the Polish communist regime. He served as the cardinal's chaplain. Within the secretariat Glemp acted as specialist on legal issues, especially marriage cases, but also as press officer. Throughout this period he also found time to teach Roman law and matrimonial canon law at the Academy of Catholic Theology in Warsaw. This activity ceased in March 1979, when he became bishop of the northeastern diocese of Warmia.

On 7 July 1981, following the death of Cardinal Wyszyński two months earlier, Glemp became archbishop of Gniezno and Warsaw, and thus the primate of Poland (he was appointed cardinal in February 1983). Largely unknown to the Polish public and less charismatic than his predecessor, Glemp soon faced the challenges of mediation between the communist state and the trade union Solidarity in a deepening economic and political crisis. He warned both sides of their obligations to protect Poland from bloodshed.

After martial law was declared in December 1981, Glemp continued a low-key posture of mediation, failing to speak out in clearly critical terms against the state. This cost him sympathy among more radical members of clergy and laity but permitted real concessions, such as permission for the church to aid detainees and for a second visit to Poland of Pope John Paul II in the summer of 1983. He accompanied John Paul in subsequent pilgrimages to Poland in 1987, 1991, 1995, 1997, and 1999, as well as on trips to other countries.

Like the Polish pope, Glemp propounded a rigorously conservative Catholic morality, with high vigilance to banish all thought of homosexual unions and to keep the divorced away from the sacraments of the church. But politically his conservatism went a step further to the right than the pope's, into the realm of Polish National Democracy, which envisions Poland in ethnic terms. A reflection of this leaning was a particular insensitivity on the Jewish question, which surfaced repeatedly since the collapse of communism in 1989.

In the 1990s controversy centered on the construction of a convent and the planting of a multitude of crosses near the camp grounds of Auschwitz, things injurious to the sensitivities of many Jews. Glemp vacillated and failed to promote conciliatory positions, and at one point attacked critics for their "Jewish arrogance." In 2001 he rejected invitations to take part in a commemoration of the murder of Jews by Poles in the Polish town of Jedwabne sixty years earlier, and wondered whether "Jews should not recognize that they are guilty toward Poles, especially in their cooperation with the Bolsheviks and collusion in the deportations to Siberia" (*Rzeczpospolita*, 15 May 2001) Instead he held a mass of atonement in a Warsaw church that permitted a "patriotic" bookstore to operate in its basement, selling such works as the anti-Semitic *Protocols of the Elders of Zion*. Asked about his tolerance of this bookstore, or national chauvinist Catholic newspapers (*Nasz Dziennik*) and radio stations (Radio Maryja), Glemp or his representatives argued that they could not limit freedom of speech. Yet the church did act to censor one moderate priest, Stanisław Musiał, who had opposed the setting up of crosses at Auschwitz as an expression not of Christian love but of its opposite.

The 1990s witnessed vigorous forays of the institutional church into education and public morality, with at times successful efforts to roll back abortion rights. Critics maintain that such high political visibility has damaged the church, yet statistics show continued high Mass attendance among Poles, as well as the growth of certain devotions. As in Western countries, however, Poland too is experiencing a decline in religious vocations.

In March 2004 Cardinal Glemp stepped down as chair of the Episcopate of Poland and was replaced by the archbishop of Przemyśl, Józef Michalik.

See also **Catholicism; John Paul II; Poland.**

BIBLIOGRAPHY

"Biography of Cardinal Józef Glemp, Primate of Poland." Available at http://www.spp.episkopat.pl/bio/biography.htm.

Glemp, Józef. *Les Chemins des pèlerins: choix de sermons et d'allocutions.* Translated by T.-M. Sas. Paris, 1996.

Micewski, Andrzej. *Kościół-państwo: 1945–1989.* Warsaw, 1994.

Zieliński, Zygmunt. *Kościół w Polsce: 1944–2002.* Radom, Poland, 2003.

JOHN CONNELLY

GLOBALIZATION.

Globalization is an attractive analytic frame that frequently lacks empirical and historical specificity. In a review article on the concept, Mauro F. Guillen lists five questions that dominate the globalization literature and that typically yield competing and contradictory answers. First, is globalization happening? Second, does globalization produce convergence? Third, does globalization undermine the authority of the nation-state? Fourth, are globalization and modernity the same entity? And fifth, is there such a thing as a global culture? Each one of these questions addresses the situation in the early twenty-first century. In a 2005 article, Peer C. Fiss and Paul M. Hirsch map the emergence of the term *globalization* in the mass media and books in print. They demonstrate that a "discourse" around globalization began to appear in the mid-1980s and accelerated in the late 1990s as evidenced by an increase in the number of media mentions of the term.

GLOBALIZATION AS A HISTORICAL PHENOMENON

The discourse on globalization may be relatively new, but the process that the term describes began the first moment traders set sail in the 1300s in search of tea and spices. If we conceptualize globalization as the trans-border flow of capital, goods, persons, and, at a later stage, information, then we can properly date the beginning of a modern global universe in what Eric Hobsbawm calls the "Age of Capital"—the period between 1848 and 1875 when improvements in transportation and communications made global exchange possible and relatively efficient.

Historians generally date the first wave of global capitalism from around 1880 to World War I and the second wave during the years following World War II. (The interwar period does not figure prominently in discussions of globalization because these years were dominated by economic depression and protectionism.) Much of the discussion of the first period is focused upon Europe; the second period focuses on the United States. Only since the 1980s has the discussion of globalization incorporated what is in fact the globe.

1880 TO 1914: IMMIGRATION AND TECHNOLOGY

Most historical accounts identify the period between 1880 and 1914 as the takeoff years of globalization—years during which capital and people crossed borders at ever-accelerating rates. Sidney Pollard provides statistics that demonstrate an almost tenfold increase in exports between 1830 and 1910. As trade was increasing, information and standardization of temporal and spatial processes were evolving. Mass media, in the form of newspapers, became more salient as sources of information as literacy rates were inching up in Europe and America. Europe did not achieve universal literacy until after World War II, but language standardization and compulsory education were beginning to have their effects in the years before World War I. The early 1900s also saw the beginnings of radio and the cinema, both of which would play significant roles in the national and international politics of the 1920s and 1930s and come to full development after World War II. Standardization practices from passports to national currencies and international exchange rates flourished during this period; for example, in 1884 twenty-five nation-states agreed to divide the world into time zones.

The years between 1880 and 1914 were a breakthrough period in the realm of transportation. Shipping was modernized, national railway systems were developed, and the airplane emerged on the scene. Charles Lindbergh did not land at Le Bourget, France, until 1927, and it was not until 1958 that the first commercial jet crossed the Atlantic; however, the development in the late nineteenth century of a transportation infrastructure capable of taking people across oceans and continents with relative efficiency helped spur a wave of migration from Europe to the United States. Jeffrey G. Williamson accounts for some of the economic consequences of this migration. He marshals an array of economic data to show that immigration from the poorer countries of Europe—Italy, Sweden, and Ireland—depressed wages in the United States while it raised wages in the countries of out-migration. The combination of capital flows and immigration in the period leading up to World War I created a convergence that paradoxically disadvantaged the United States while advantaging the poorer countries of Europe. Given this fact, it is not surprising that U.S. immigration policy in the 1920s introduced quotas and that Americans were wary of such ventures as the League of Nations.

The first period of globalization, in which Britain and its colonies were the driving force, began with empire and ended with war. In the aftermath of the war, two events would have long-term consequences. First, the Treaty of Versailles and the carving up of what had been the Ottoman Empire set up a pattern of colonialism and resentment that dominates Middle Eastern politics to the present day. An innocuous development at the time, Britain seemed to be getting its due as a major imperial power as it carved up territories and displaced groups such as the Kurds and the Palestinians. The second outcome of the first period of globalization was the world depression that not only brought in Nazism and fascism but also ushered in a period of protectionism or autarky in all the major nation-states of Europe and in the United States.

1945 TO THE NEW MILLENNIUM: THE AMERICAN CENTURY

Whereas Britain had been the leader in globalization in the pre-1914 period, the United States became the leader after the Second World War. Henry Luce, founder of the *Time* magazine conglomerate, famously predicted that the post–World War II period would be the "American century." Despite the apparent national hubris of Luce's claim, the United States was the undisputed world leader arguably through the 1970s. The nation saw itself as a protector of democracy and freedom and an international bulwark against communism during the Cold War. But despite Korea and Vietnam and the presence of U.S. missiles on European soil, the United States was an empire of goods, not of guns.

Victoria De Grazia makes this point elegantly, arguing that the battle against communism would be won by socializing Europeans into the American "standard of living." Consumption was the linchpin of Americanization. As De Grazia reports, Woodrow Wilson had realized the connection between democracy and consumption in 1916 when he attempted to persuade a convention of salesmen that statecraft and salesmanship were linked. Wilson's success on this particular issue is unknown; however, the groundwork for the "Americanization" of Europe was laid in the 1920s and 1930s when U.S. advertising agencies and firms set up shop in Europe. The political turmoil in interwar Europe militated against a large-scale embrace of U.S. products and consumption regimes. It was during the post–World War II recovery, particularly with some of the cultural propaganda of the Marshall Plan, that the link between democracy and goods began to take hold on European soil, however tenuously. The idea was that American goods and American-style production practices would produce the standard of living that would fight off the advance of European communism.

Cultural globalization began to take hold as American movies that had been popular in Europe during the 1920s and 1930s asserted their presence in the 1950s and 1960s. American film was in the avant-garde of such global phenomena as rock music, which leveled cultural distinctions. Ironically, the big American success story was in the world of material consumption—food and drink. Coca-Cola reached its peak in the 1960s, with McDonald's superseding it beginning in the 1970s. McDonald's became such a symbol of Americanization and globalization that the French activist farmer José Bové could burn a McDonald's under construction in the north of France in 1999 and the media and the public would understand the significance of his target.

With viable communist parties in France and Italy, the threat of communism was not an American fantasy. However, there were several other forces at work that mitigated the effects of an American Empire of goods on European soil. Europe developed its own solutions to the problem of communism and markets. One solution was the Treaty of Rome in 1957 which ushered in the European Common Market. And when the French foreign minister Robert Schuman proposed the creation of the European Coal and Steel Community in 1950, he had peace as well as economics on his mind. Containing Germany, as well as the spread of communism, was a postwar priority. In contrast to U.S. citizens who experienced the Cold War through media propaganda, the Iron Curtain was real to those who lived in close proximity to Eastern Europe.

U.S. goods and free markets competed with European planned economies from the 1950s through the 1970s. The European postwar settlement aimed at growth, but it also aimed at containment of communism within Western Europe. Corporatist policies that brought business and labor together produced European welfare states as well as "thirty glorious years" of European prosperity. Europe and the United States were trading partners and the driving forces behind globalization, and with decolonization and the opening of markets in Latin America and Africa the character of trade gradually began to change.

The major continuity between early globalization and midcentury globalization was that Europe and the United States remained the key players. But a series of events beginning in the 1980s radically altered the economic landscape. First, a change in the character of immigration in both Europe and the United States altered the structure of labor markets and strategies of social and political incorporation. In postwar Europe migrants were guest workers from the poorer south—Italy, Spain, and Portugal—who migrated to the rich European core to fill temporary jobs in industry. This changed as the southern tier became richer and more immigrants flooded into France from former colonies and into Germany from Turkey. Suddenly there were migrants who would not return to their native lands and who by virtue of being Muslim were not considered properly European. The United States saw a parallel migration of persons from Mexico and Central America, many of whom entered the country illegally.

The second major change was that in 1989 the Iron Curtain fell, and suddenly Eastern Europe and Russia had to be factored into European and global markets. The third major change was the advance of technology. Until the early 1980s building a bigger and faster jet plane was considered the cutting edge of transportation and communications technology. Beginning in the 1980s a virtual revolution took place, bringing computers, the Internet, cell phones. The Internet made cybermarketing possible and detached markets from both time and space. Lastly, Asia became a major player in global capital markets beginning in the 1980s. The acceleration of what Europeans call neoliberalism and what Americans view as free-market capitalism is a response to these accumulated structural and political changes as well as an attempt to retain a position of dominance in the new global economy.

CONCLUSION: HISTORICAL LESSONS

The accelerated pace of European integration, known in Europe as Europeanization, is one sign that Europe and America no longer dominate global markets. Peter J. Katzenstein has argued that the locus of economic power has shifted to permeable regional alliances. Most social scientists agree that the world has entered a transterritorial or global age, although they are sometimes at a loss as to how to specify it. The lesson that might be taken from both early and post–World War II globalization is that expansion brings political costs. Nation-states do not give up economic dominance easily. In spring 2005 both France and the Netherlands rejected the proposed European Constitution—albeit for different reasons. In France the public widely viewed it as a blueprint for globalization; the French prime minister spoke of "economic patriotism." In the United States, immigration rules were being tightened and vigilantes patrolled the country's southern borders. A new age of protectionism and economic nationalism in a world of cybermarkets and Chinese advance was worrisome. The 1920s and 1930s, the period between the first and second waves of globalization, were not good years for economic growth and human rights—perhaps a lesson that twenty-first-century elites and citizens should heed.

See also Americanization; Anti-Americanism; European Constitution 2004–2005; European Union.

BIBLIOGRAPHY

De Grazia, Victoria. *Irresistible Empire: America's Advance through Twentieth-Century Europe*. Cambridge, Mass., 2005.

Fiss, Peer C., and Paul M. Hirsch. "The Discourse of Globalization: Framing and Sensemaking of an Emerging Concept." *American Sociological Review* 70, no. 1 (2005): 29–52.

Geyer, Martin H., and Johannes Paulmann, eds. *The Mechanics of Internationalism*. London, 2001.

Guillen, Mauro F. "Is Globalization Civilizing, Destructive or Feeble? A Critique of Five Key Debates in the Social Science Literature." *Annual Review of Sociology* 27 (2001): 235–260.

Hobsbawm, Eric J. *The Age of Capital 1848–1875*. London, 1975.

Katzenstein, Peter J. *A World of Regions: Asia and Europe in the American Imperium*. Ithaca, N.Y., 2005.

Maier, Charles S. *In Search of Stability*. New York, 1987.

Milward, Alan S. *The European Rescue of the Nation-State*. 2nd ed. London, 2000.

Moch, Leslie Page. *Moving Europeans: Migration in Western Europe since 1650*. 2nd ed. Bloomington, Ind., 2003.

Osterhammel, Jürgen, and Niels P. Petersson. *Globalization: A Short History*. Translated by Dona Geyer. Princeton, N.J., 2005.

Pollard, Sidney. "Free Trade, Protectionism, and the World Economy." In *The Mechanics of Internationalism*, edited by Martin H. Geyer and Johannes Paulmann. London, 2001.

Trumpbour, John. *Selling Hollywood to the World: U.S. and European Struggles for Mastery of the Global Film Industry, 1920–1950*. Cambridge, U.K., 2002.

Williamson, Jeffrey G. "Globalization, Convergence, and History." *Journal of Economic History* 56, no. 2 (1996): 1–30.

MABEL BEREZIN

GODARD, JEAN-LUC (b. 1930), French filmmaker.

Born in 1930 into a Protestant bourgeois family, from an early age Jean-Luc Godard frequented Henri Langlois's French Cinémathèque religiously. He met André Bazin, François Truffaut, Jacques Rivette, and Eric Rohmer there, and joined them as a writer for the *Cahiers du cinéma* (Cinema notebooks). In this journal, he criticized the established norms and defended the famous idea of "la politique des auteurs" (politics of the author), which stated that a filmmaker should only make his film according to his own personal preoccupations. It was with this in mind that, when he began filmmaking himself, he joined what was called the new wave.

This movement, which was developed between 1957 and 1962, was in utter conflict with the film production ideas of the time and was characterized by great creative freedom. The new wave movement includes a group of films that, whether explicitly or implicitly, dealt with existential, social, or political issues. Despite the great variety of personalities that made up the movement, it can be said that it was a school whose films were impertinent, playful, inventive, and whose aesthetic choices, while encouraging improvisation, had many things in common with modern art. At the same time, it was a kind of cinema that constantly referred to the history of cinema, which these young movie buffs usually knew well (they appreciated the classics of the silent era, but also American films, especially those of Alfred Hitchcock and Howard Hawks).

In 1959, after having made four short films, Godard used a script by Truffaut to make his landmark film *À bout de souffle* (1960; *Breathless*). The originality of the script, the "B" movie characters, the very modern acting method of the actors (the unforgettable Jean Seberg and Jean-Paul Belmondo), and the syncopated editing were striking to contemporary moviegoers. The producer, Georges de Beauregard, would go on to finance six more of the filmmaker's full-length films: *Le petit soldat* in 1960 (*The Little Soldier* was banned for three years by French censure because of its references to the war in Algeria), *Une femme est une femme* (*A Woman Is a Woman*) in 1961, *Les carabiniers* and *Le Mépris* (*The Riflemen* and *Contempt*) in 1963, and *Made in U.S.A.* in 1966.

From one film to the next, Godard explored every aspect of cinematographic expression and became a politically engaged artist. After having very subtly referenced Vietnam in *Pierrot le fou* (1965), *Masculin, féminin* (1966; *Masculine-Feminine*), *Made in U.S.A.*, and more directly in *La Chinoise* (1967; *The Chinese Woman*), he entered a period of activism with his collaboration in the group project film *Loin du Vietnam* (*Far from Vietnam*) in 1967. His contribution, the short film *Camera Eye*, was a brutal confrontation between political speech and its practice, a process that seeks to expose the mechanics of film to better denounce the illusion of an image's realistic objectivity. Very similar to the Brechtian method, this putting into perspective of the devices of cinema hinders any belief in what is shown to benefit critical judgment, changing the viewer's involvement from passivity to active comprehension. Filmed with a large Mitchell camera, the filmmaker began (the voiceover is the voice of Godard) by asking how the Vietnamese cause could be represented. To that end, he declared that if he had been a cameraman for American or Soviet news networks, he would have recorded the effects of the bombings on farmers. But he never received permission to go to Vietnam. According to Godard, this difficulty to endorse creative responsibility was even greater, as far as he was concerned, because his films primarily targeted intellectuals, a small community of cultured people, and not the masses. He focused on the gap that separated him from the working class who did not go see his films. Consequently, he deemed that the only solution was to let himself be completely absorbed by Vietnam. His film, he said, was not just a war film but a general symbol of resistance that would serve as a political framework to express any form of opposition.

After this film, Godard's approach to moviemaking rested primarily on questioning his own view of films, in which "the images serve not to see but to think," as he said. All of his following works (the most emblematic of which was *Passion*, made in 1982), beyond the constraints of reality, expressed this will to escape from dominant cultural models, in order to constantly question his own creative methods. From this point of view, his most ambitious enterprise was his *Histoire(s) du cinéma* (1989, 1997, 1998), an idea that dated back to 1975 but started off in 1980 with a book titled *Introduction à une véritable histoire du cinéma* (Introduction to a true history of film), which afterward became a film in eight parts, more than five hours long, about art history, humanity, and the shattering events of the twentieth century.

This tremendous work of collage and juxtaposition of images (his own and others') and sounds, interspersed with digressions and reflections (voiced by Godard himself), is a meditation on and retrospective vision of the place of film in human society that is simultaneously mournful and full of pertinence and beauty. In other words, it is film in the century, and the century in film. The result was dizzying but fascinating editing, lyrical as well as elliptical, saturated with aesthetic, philosophical, political, and religious references. Melancholy, poetry, light-heartedness, and humor melded together.

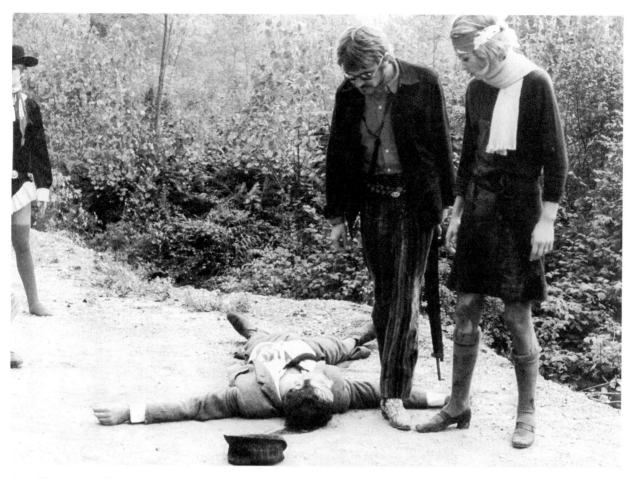

Jean Yanne and Mireille Darc in a scene from Jean-Luc Godard's *Weekend*, 1967. The story of a couple's weekend excursion to the countryside is told through a series of often-bizarre images satirizing modern life. COPERNIC/COMACICO/ASCOT/THE KOBAL COLLECTION

As a painter before his palette (which, in his case, would be graphic), Godard exposed the links, the relationships, and the similarities between painting and film, inspired by Élie Faure and André Malraux. From *For Ever Mozart* (1996) to *Notre musique* (2004; *Our Music*), most of Godard's films have been molded by the idea that film is not the witness but the analyst of history, far from the alleged duty of objectivity advocated by some audiovisual productions that are completely formatted for television (and, here, his films were also critical of the media). However, film is but one element in the great history of representation. It is an element, according to Godard's pessimism, that is in danger of disappearing, whose traces are perishable due to the very nature of the material that supports it. If the prophecy comes true, it is clear that his body of work, and his *Histoire(s) du cinéma* in particular, will serve as one of film's most beautiful graves.

See also **Cinema; French New Wave; Situationism.**

BIBLIOGRAPHY

Esquenazi, Jean-Pierre. *Godard et la société française des années 1960*. Paris, 2004.

Temple, Michael, Michael Witt, and James S. Williams. *For Ever Godard*. London, 2004.

LAURENT VERAY

GOEBBELS, JOSEF (1897–1945), Nazi minister for public enlightenment and propaganda.

Josef Goebbels was born in the Rhenish town of Rheydt, the pampered son of lower-middle-class Catholics. He was loved by his parents and four siblings but his childhood and adolescence were characterized by painful social marginalization that resulted from his physical shortcomings, most notably a clubfoot. Goebbels graduated from secondary school in 1917 and, having been exempted from service in the German military as a consequence of his disability, he matriculated that same year at the University of Bonn. In 1921 he was awarded a doctorate from the University of Heidelberg after completing a dissertation on a German Romantic playwright under the supervision of the Jewish Germanist Max von Waldberg. Goebbels spent the next several years in an unsuccessful effort to establish himself as a journalist and writer.

THE NAZI PARTY'S RISE TO POWER

In the summer of 1924, Goebbels attended a meeting of several *völkisch* (nationalist-racist) groups, including the still politically marginal National Socialist German Workers' (Nazi) Party. Convinced that he had found his calling in life, Goebbels began devoting his energies to Germany's political situation, writing and lecturing on behalf of National Socialism. Over the course of the next couple of years, Goebbels's success as a public speaker, as well as his intensive involvement in publications such as the *National Socialist Letters,* established him as an important representative of the north German, left-wing (i.e., pro-worker) branch of the Nazi movement around Gregor Strasser.

A series of meetings with Adolf Hitler in Munich in the spring of 1926 proved to be a turning point in Goebbels's life. Despite previous misgivings regarding Hitler and the south German branch of the Nazi movement, Goebbels returned to Berlin under Hitler's spell, convinced of his genius and leadership abilities. Hitler rewarded Goebbels's change of allegiances by appointing him head of the Nazi Party for the Berlin district. It was here that Goebbels developed the style and substance of his propaganda. As founder and editor of the Nazi newspaper *Der Angriff,* he liberally peppered his articles with slanderous statements and insults of city and state officials in an effort to mobilize, rather than simply inform, his readers. Slandering was a means, as he stated in an article in 1929, "to unleash volcanic passions, outbreaks of rage, to set masses of people on the march" (Fest, p. 92). Nor was mobilization to be accomplished solely by inflammatory articles and speeches; Goebbels regularly organized street and beer-hall

Josef Goebbels (left) and Hermann Goering confer in September 1936. LIBRARY OF CONGRESS

brawls between Nazi stormtroopers and political opponents such as communists and socialists. In 1930 Nazi thugs disguised as ordinary moviegoers disrupted the Berlin premiere of *All Quiet on the Western Front;* this was one of many episodes intended to demonstrate to Germans the dynamism and audacity of National Socialism.

GOEBBELS'S ROLE IN THE THIRD REICH

The creation of the Nazi dictatorship in 1933 provided Goebbels with the opportunity to apply his propaganda skills to the entire country. Appointed minister for public enlightenment and propaganda in March 1933, Goebbels sought to transform the German people into ardent National Socialists so that they would "think uniformly,...react uniformly, and...place themselves body and soul at the disposal of the government" (Reuth, p. 172). He subjected the country to a highly orchestrated program of suggestive National Socialist spectacles, slogans, and images intended to engage the German audience primarily on an emotional level. Goebbels's ministry organized public book burnings and festivals celebrating new National Socialist holidays, such Hitler's birthday, as well as special events, such as the Olympic Games in 1936. Popular media, including newspapers and the radio, were put under government control, and the ministry also supported the "Nazification" of German culture, including the purge of "un-German" and "degenerate" attitudes and individuals. The National Chamber of Culture, created by Goebbels in the fall of 1933, determined which authors, musicians, journalists, artists, and actors would be permitted to practice their professions, rewarding the regime's racial and political supporters and blacklisting its opponents. In 1937 Goebbels organized an exhibition of "degenerate" art by artists such as Ernst Barlach, Max Beckmann, and Oskar Kokoschka. Goebbels's direct involvement in cultural and artistic matters was especially strong in the film industry; he often involved himself at every stage of production, selecting the movies that were to be made, casting particular actresses and actors, and supervising the film's editing and distribution.

Goebbels's most important contribution to the Third Reich was his role in the development and dissemination of a pseudo-religious cult worshiping Hitler. According to this Hitler myth, Hitler—the personification of the German *Volk*, or people— was responsible for Germany's economic successes and its diplomatic and military victories during the 1930s and early 1940s. The Hitler myth played a crucial role in binding the German people to Hitler as well as holding together the disparate elements of the Nazi Party.

The German defeat at Stalingrad in 1943 signaled the beginning of the Third Reich's destruction but also provided Goebbels with the opportunity to reestablish himself as one of the most important men in the Nazi state after having been politically sidelined as Germany prepared for and fought the initial campaigns of the war. In response to the increasingly worsening military and economic situation, Goebbels used his propaganda skills to mobilize Germans to fight the "total war" until the absolute end. On 30 April 1945, following the suicides of Adolf Hitler and Eva Braun, Goebbels and his wife, Magda (who had earlier that day poisoned their six children), committed suicide.

Although historical scholarship since the 1980s has uncovered a high degree of contemporary popular German approval for the Nazi state and its policies and has thereby significantly changed historians' understanding of how the Third Reich functioned, it remains to be seen whether scholars will continue to see Goebbels as either a chameleon-like opportunist or a fanatical Nazi who used propaganda to brainwash a nation.

See also **Beckmann, Max; Hitler, Adolf; Nazism; Stalingrad, Battle of; World War II.**

BIBLIOGRAPHY

Crew, David F., ed. *Nazism and German Society, 1933–1945.* New York, 1994.

Fest, Joachim C. *The Face of the Third Reich: Portraits of the Nazi Leadership.* Translated by Michael Bullock. New York, 1970.

Low, Alfred D. *The Men around Hitler: The Nazi Elite and Its Collaborators.* Boulder, Colo., 1996.

Reuth, Ralf Georg. *Goebbels.* Translated by Krishna Winston. New York, 1993.

Smelser, Ronald, and Rainer Zitelmann, eds. *The Nazi Elite.* Translated by Mary Fischer. New York, 1993.

CHARLES LANSING

GOERING, HERMANN (1893–1946), one of the most important leaders of Nazi Germany.

Hermann Goering was born in Rosenheim, Bavaria, into a well-connected, Protestant, upper-middle-class family. His father, a lawyer and diplomat, served in the Reich Consular Service and was the first resident minister plenipotentiary in German Southwest Africa. After graduating with distinction from military cadet college in Berlin, Goering fought in the First World War, first in the German army as an infantry lieutenant and then in the air force, where he was the last commander, in 1918, of the famous Richthofen Fighter Squadron. His courageous exploits as a combat pilot earned him the Iron Cross (First Class) and the much coveted *Pour le Mérite.*

After Germany's defeat in 1918, Goering, the war hero, worked as a show flier at home and abroad and, as an avowed anti-Semite and anti-communist, became involved in right-wing nationalist political and paramilitary circles whose aim was to destroy the democratic Weimar Republic.

Having settled in Munich and married Baroness Karin von Fock-Kantzow in 1922, he joined the Nazi Party (NSDAP) the same year and assumed command of the party's paramilitary organization, the Storm Troopers (SA), until the abortive Beer Hall Putsch in November 1923. Seriously wounded during this escapade, he fled abroad, finally to Sweden, where he became a morphine addict during his medical recovery program. When a general amnesty by the German government allowed him to return to Germany in 1927, Goering rejoined the NSDAP, took a sales job with Bayerische Motoren Werke (BMW) in Berlin, and was elected one of the party's Reichstag deputies in 1928. Henceforth, his significance for the party grew substantially, for although he did not hold formal office, he became Adolf Hitler's roving ambassador in conservative, upper-class social, business, military, and political circles, soliciting financial support and sympathy for the Nazi cause. Goering became the respectable, almost debonair face of Nazism, an image boosted by his election as president of the Reichstag in late 1932. He emerged as an influential figure in the political intrigues that culminated in Hitler's appointment as Reich chancellor in January 1933.

Goering played a conspicuous role in consolidating the Third Reich. As Prussian minister of the interior and chief of police and of the Gestapo in Prussia, he attacked political rivals, especially those on the Left, consigning many of them to concentration camps. In June 1934 he was also the mastermind of the Roehm Purge, the murder of putative "socialist" elements in the SA and other suspected opponents. Thereafter, his power base extended rapidly. In 1935 he was appointed head of the Luftwaffe and in 1936 was given overall control of the Four-Year Economic Plan, which was designed to promote autarky and establish Nazi domination over the economy. The establishment in 1937 of the state-owned Hermann-Goering-Works, a huge industrial complex employing some 700,000 workers, allowed him to quickly amass a substantial personal fortune. His anti-Semitism was fully displayed during and after the infamous "Night of Broken Glass" (*Kristallnacht*) in November 1938, when the Nazis attacked Jews throughout Germany. It was Goering who fined the Jewish community a billion marks and who

Hermann Goering photographed during the trials at Nuremberg, May 1945. ©BETTMANN/CORBIS

confiscated and "Aryanized" their businesses and property. A determined supporter of the Third Reich's expansionist foreign policy, he continued to accumulate offices and titles, including chairman of the Reich Council for National Defense in August 1939, Hitler's heir apparent in September 1939, and field marshal in June 1940.

As the war progressed, however, his ostentatiously lavish lifestyle, which included ownership of a palace in Berlin, a country residence, and valuable (if often stolen) works of art, began to cloud his political and military judgment, while the failures of the Luftwaffe, in the Battle of Britain and on the eastern front, and of the war economy caused Hitler not only to sideline him from 1942 onward but also, shortly before the end of the war, to strip him of all offices and membership in the party. Despite a bravura performance before the Nuremberg Military Tribunal in 1946, Goering was condemned to death for crimes against peace and humanity, but before being hanged he committed suicide on 15 October 1946.

Goering played an integral role in the rise and development of the Nazi Party and the Third Reich. His ruthless ambition, militant nationalism, and loyalty to Nazism made him an invaluable ally of Hitler, until his personal and political weaknesses eventually caused his downfall. A multifaceted personality who enjoyed a public persona as the jovial, almost avuncular face of the Nazi regime, Goering was incontrovertibly, nonetheless, one of its most significant, amoral exponents.

See also **Anti-Semitism; Germany; Kristallnacht; Nazism.**

BIBLIOGRAPHY

Frischauer, Willi. *The Rise and Fall of Hermann Goering.* Boston, 1951.

Goering, Emmy. *My Life with Goering.* London, 1972.

Kershaw, Ian. *Hitler, 1889–1936: Hubris.* New York, 1999.

———. *Hitler, 1936–1945: Nemesis.* New York, 2000.

Manvell, Roger, and Heinrich Fraenkel. *Hermann Göring.* London, 1968.

Mosley, Leonard. *The Reich Marshal.* Garden City, N.Y., 1974.

Overy, R. J. *Goering: The "Iron Man."* London, 1984.

PETER D. STACHURA

GOMBRICH, ERNST HANS (1909–2001), art historian.

Ernst Hans Gombrich was probably the most famous and among the most original art historians of the second half of the twentieth century. His best-known book, *The Story of Art*, first published in 1950 and still in print, has sold more than six million copies in at least thirty languages. It is exceptional among art historical surveys in that it was little concerned with changes in style or in patterns of patronage but took as its theme the ways in which artists represented the visible world and how these changed over time. Gombrich's text, like all his writings, is notable for its unpretentious tone and clarity of expression.

Gombrich's studies at the University of Vienna gave him knowledge of a remarkably wide range of art, from ancient Egyptian onward, as well as a familiarity with the relevant written sources. His doctoral dissertation on the Palazzo del Te in Mantua, published in 1934, was an analysis of the style of that Renaissance building and its decoration. The thesis was influential in introducing the notion of mannerism into the history of architecture, but Gombrich himself soon became skeptical about the type of approach he had adopted, especially the assumption, then widely accepted, that artistic styles reflected in some direct way the spirit of the age in which they were created and that artistic change was governed by an inevitable process of historical development, a belief that he attributed especially to the influence of G. W. F. Hegel. Many of his publications, which often consisted of lectures and reviews, were devoted to challenging such ideas, suggesting instead that changes in artistic style, as in fashion, were often motivated by more readily analyzed factors such as technical innovations on the part of artists, a climate of artistic competition, or a desire for novelty on the part of patrons.

After completing his dissertation, Gombrich collaborated with the psychoanalyst and art historian Ernst Kris on a book on caricature. Although never completed, the project introduced him to problems of artistic representation and in particular to the question of how artists could use minimal and even highly distorted visual indications to create a likeness. In 1936, with Kris's help, he obtained a fellowship at the Warburg Institute in London, which was to remain his professional home for the rest of his life. His first task was to edit the unpublished works of the institute's founder, the German art historian Aby Warburg (1866–1929). This proved an unfeasible project, but soon afterward Gombrich wrote *Aby Warburg: An Intellectual Biography.* Largely completed by 1947 but not published until 1970, it remains the best and most accessible introduction to Warburg's ideas.

The two scholars could scarcely have been more different. Warburg, who always had great difficulty articulating his views in a definitive form, regarded works of art as powerful evidence of the mentality of the educated public of the period in which they were produced, whereas Gombrich was deeply skeptical about this attitude, which violated the approach he had learned from his great friend Karl Popper, namely, that the only hypotheses worth discussing are those that can be tested and refuted. In a sense, all his later writings can be read as challenges to the ideas and methods of Warburg.

This applies both to his articles on iconography, collected in *Symbolic Images* (1972), in which he revealed an increasing skepticism about the elaborate interpretations of paintings proposed by various scholars associated with the Warburg Institute in its early years (including himself), and also to his most important book, *Art and Illusion* (1960), in which he drew on recent developments in psychology to examine both the different conventions used by artists to represent the visible world and the ways in which these conventions are then interpreted by viewers. Gombrich's attempt to extend his analysis to decorative art in *The Sense of Order* (1979) was more controversial, but this book is also important for the extensive historical research on which the discussion is based.

Gombrich never concerned himself with the traditional art historical issues of connoisseurship and the dating of works of art, nor was he interested in challenging traditional ideas about the merits of individual artists. He preferred instead to explore the processes of change in artistic expression and in attitudes to art. Unrivaled in his ability to engage a nonspecialist audience, he was highly influential both in his attempts to apply the study of visual perception to the history of art and in his powerful criticisms of many of the assumptions that had dominated the study of the subject, especially in the first half of the twentieth century.

See also **Psychology.**

BIBLIOGRAPHY

Gombrich, E. H., and Didier Eribon. *A Lifelong Interest: Conversations on Art and Science with Didier Eribon.* London, 1993.

Trapp, J. B. *E. H. Gombrich: A Bibliography.* London, 2000.

CHARLES HOPE

GOMUŁKA, WŁADYSŁAW (1905–1982), Polish Communist leader.

Born on 6 February 1905 near Krosno, in the Austrian part of Poland, Władysław Gomułka was the son of an oil industry worker and socialist party member. At the age of fourteen he had to leave school and start working. He joined a socialist youth organization but tended toward more radical ideas, and in 1926 he joined the Communist Party of Poland (KPP). As he later wrote, his "faith in the party and in the socialist idea was most similar to the Roman Catholics' faith in God and the holy Church" (*Pamiętniki*, Vol. 1). This devotion encompassed his private life, which he shared with Zofia Szoken, a party member since 1921. His party activity focused on trade unions, he visited the Soviet Union for trade union congresses. Under police observation since 1927, he was arrested several times and eventually sentenced to prison in 1933. Temporarily released in 1934, he fled to the USSR, where he obtained political instruction and intelligence training in the Lenin International School. He returned illegally to Poland and resumed his party activity, which ended with a seven-year prison sentence in 1936.

Imprisonment likely saved his life (as he avoided the Soviet Great Purges), and the war brought him release from prison. In the 1939–1941 period he lived in the Soviet zone of occupation but did not play any political role there (albeit he joined the Soviet party). After the German invasion of the Soviet Union in 1941 he moved to his native Krosno, and in 1942 he was called to Warsaw to strengthen the leadership of the new Polish Workers Party (PPR). Following the mysterious murders of two consecutive party leaders in 1943 he became the PPR secretary general. As comrade "Wiesław" (his nom de guerre) he proved his skills as leader and as conspirator.

Beginning in late 1944 he combined the top position in the party with that of the first vice-premier and minister of the new, Soviet-backed government. He served alongside Bolesław Bierut, a key figure in the new regime. He supported the brutal crushing of the opposition but called for a "Polish path to socialism" rather than a crude imitation of Soviet patterns (collectivization in particular), and he tempered his comrades' revolutionary zeal. Fully loyal but not servile to Moscow, he attempted to restrain Soviet excesses in Poland and even dared to criticize Joseph Stalin for his policy on Yugoslavia in 1947. His fall came the following year with the noisy campaign against "right-wing nationalist deviation." He did not enter the Politburo of the now monopolist Polish United Workers Party (PZPR), was gradually

Władysław Gomułka addresses a crowd in Warsaw, 24 October 1956. ©Bettmann/Corbis

removed from his positions, and was eventually arrested (along with his wife) in 1951. Gomułka spent more than three years in isolation in a secret prison of the Ministry of Public Security, waiting for a planned show trial (similar to those of László Rajk or Rudolf Slánský). Yet, for reasons not clear, the trial did not come; he survived until the fall of 1954 when destalinization brought his release.

In 1956, with the rise of social unrest and intra-party factional struggles, Gomułka's restoration came. In October he returned to the political scene, elevated straight to the top position of the PZPR first secretary. His image as a "national communist" and as "Stalin's prisoner" gave him great popularity, a position further strengthened by his open critique of Stalinist "errors and deformations," the sending back of Soviet so-called advisors (who were actually supervisors of those advised), and the discontinuation of forced collectivization and the war against the Catholic Church. Decreases in military spending and some economic reforms resulted in an increase in real wages and the supply of consumer goods. However, when

the regime restabilized, Gomułka purged the party of "revisionists," tightened the grip on the media, returned to the old path in economic policies (except in agriculture), and renewed attacks on the church. He closed the period of brutal sovietization and quasi-revolutionary turmoil but did his best to keep Poland a one-party police state, a command economy, and a Soviet satellite.

Beginning in the mid-1960s, when stability turned into stagnation, popular frustration rose and his authority eroded. In spring 1968, to pacify student protests, Gomułka approved brutal police reprisals and the scapegoating of Jews in an anti-Zionist campaign; in the summer of that year he warmly supported the Warsaw Pact military intervention in Czechoslovakia. In December 1970, right after signing the treaty with the Federal Republic of Germany—his major success in foreign affairs—he sent troops to crush the wave of labor unrest in Gdańsk and Szczecin, a decision that resulted in more than forty people killed and one thousand wounded. The crisis raised serious concerns in Moscow, which allowed younger Politburo members to replace Gomułka with Gierek. Forced to retire, Gomułka lost all political influence, his popularity long gone. He died in 1982.

See also **Bierut, Bolesław; Eastern Bloc; Gierek, Edward; Poland; Slánský Trial; Warsaw Pact.**

BIBLIOGRAPHY

Primary Sources

Gomułka, Władisław. *Pamiętniki.* 2 vols. Warsaw, 1994.

Secondary Sources

Bethell, Nicholas. *Gomulka, His Poland and His Communism.* London, 1969.

———. *Le communisme polonaise 1918–1971. Gomulka et sa succession.* Paris, 1971.

Werblan, Andrzej. *Władysław Gomułka. Sekretarz Generalny PPR.* Warsaw, 1988.

DARIUSZ STOLA

GONZÁLEZ, FELIPE (b. 1942), Spanish political leader.

Felipe González was born and raised in Seville, Spain. He studied law at the university there and at the Catholic University of Louvain, in Belgium. González then went into private practice in Seville, specializing in labor law.

González became involved in politics quite early. He began in Catholic organizations, which were legal under the Franco regime, before joining the prohibited Socialist Youth in 1962 and the Spanish Socialist Workers' Party (Partido Socialista Obrero Español, or PSOE) in 1964. He quickly assumed leadership positions within the clandestine Party, first at the provincial level and then, after 1969, at the national level. González played a key role in the crucial XXVI PSOE Congress, held in Suresnes, France, in October 1974. Suresnes was the moment at which the leadership of the Socialist Party passed from the so-called historic group, which had been in exile since the end of the Spanish civil war (1936–1939), to younger militants inside Spain. González enjoyed the support of the leading figures of European social democracy, such as Olof Palme of Sweden and Willy Brandt of West Germany.

González thus found himself at the head of the PSOE when the death of Francisco Franco, in November 1975, began Spain's transition to democracy. His skill and sense of statesmanship, along with that of other key opposition leaders, were necessary elements in the rapid and peaceful transition the country made from the Franco dictatorship to a functioning constitutional democracy. González's tremendous charisma immediately became the Socialists' most valuable electoral asset, and helped the party establish itself as the second-largest political force in Spain's first two democratic elections (1977 and 1979).

At the same time, González worked hard within the PSOE to turn it into a broadly based party that could win democratic elections. Above all, this meant ending the definition of the PSOE as a Marxist party. When a party congress in May 1979 rejected González's proposal to remove the word *Marxism* from the program, he announced his resignation as party general secretary. This forced an extraordinary congress that took place in September 1979 at which the delegates overwhelmingly agreed to the changes he wanted. From this point on, González was the undisputed leader of the Socialists, and his authority was underlined by the rigid discipline imposed on the party by his longtime collaborator, Alfonso Guerra.

In the elections held in October 1982, the PSOE scored a victory of unprecedented proportions, receiving 48 percent of the vote and 202 of 350 seats in parliament. The Socialists had campaigned on the straightforward yet ambiguous slogan of "Change," and public expectations were tremendously high as they took office.

Almost inevitably, these expectations were disappointed. In fact, the Socialists governed in a much more moderate way than most people had anticipated. Economic policy was driven by the need to reduce inflation and promote growth. Public spending increased, although the autonomous regions were also given greater spending power. Limited wage increases produced growing alienation between the government and the Socialist trade union confederation, Unión General de Trabajadores, including a general strike in December 1988. González's greatest achievements lay in the field of international relations: on 1 January 1986 Spain realized its long-held goal of joining the European Community (forerunner of the European Union [EU]). At the same time, González reversed his own long-held opposition to Spanish membership in the North Atlantic Treaty Organization (NATO), organizing a referendum on the issue but making it clear that he favored remaining in the alliance.

González led the PSOE to three more election victories (1986, 1989, and 1993), although the margin of victory was smaller each time. After the 1993 election, the Socialists had only a minority government and depended on the Catalan nationalist Convergència i Unió to govern. The last years in power were also marked by a number of scandals. Some of these involved corruption by senior officials, such as the governor of the Bank of Spain, the director of the Civil Guard, and some cabinet ministers. The most damaging for González himself was the Ministry of the Interior's use of hit squads to kill suspected ETA (Basque separatist) terrorists.

In June 1997 González announced he was stepping down as general secretary of the PSOE, although he remained a member of the party's Federal Committee. Since then he has played a much smaller role in public life than many would have anticipated. Widely touted as a possible head of the European Commission, he refused to let his name go forward. He did serve as a special representative in Yugoslavia of both the EU and the Organization for Security and Cooperation in Europe, and has published three books.

See also **ETA; Franco, Francisco; Spain.**

BIBLIOGRAPHY

Juliá, Santos. "The Socialist Era, 1982–1996." In *Spanish History since 1808*, edited by José Alvarez Junco and Adrian Shubert, 331–343. London, 2000.

Preston, Paul. *The Triumph of Democracy in Spain.* London, 1986.

Share, Donald. *Dilemmas of Social Democracy: The Spanish Socialist Workers Party in the 1980s.* New York, 1989.

ADRIAN SHUBERT

GORBACHEV, MIKHAIL (b. 1931),
leader of the Soviet Union from 1985 to 1991.

Mikhail Gorbachev's leadership of the Union of Soviet Socialist Republics (USSR) between 1985 and 1991 was indeed "six years that changed the world." Elected general secretary of the Communist Party of the Soviet Union (CPSU) in March 1985, Gorbachev immediately signaled that a period of accelerated change would be launched, a process that he called "perestroika" (restructuring). Gorbachev represented the generation of politicians inspired by the spirit of post-Stalinist thaw in the 1950s, epitomized by the Twentieth Party Congress in February of that year at which Nikita Khrushchev delivered his "secret speech" condemning Joseph Stalin's destruction of the Communist Party and other crimes. The critical Soviet elite of the 1960s (known collectively as the *shestidesyatniki,* "the people of the [nineteen] sixties") sought to save Soviet-style socialism by giving it a more human face, a program implemented by Alexander Dubček in 1968 in Czechoslovakia. The attempt to create "socialism with a human face" was crushed by Soviet and allied tanks in August 1968, but now the Soviet system itself had come to the same point. On assuming the leadership Gorbachev and his colleagues agreed that the old system could not go on in the old way, mired in the "stagnation" of the Leonid Brezhnev years, and sought to implement the ideals of humanistic socialism. In the event, under Gorbachev's leadership the communist political system dissolved, the Soviet bloc of allied socialist countries in Eastern Europe fell apart, and ultimately the USSR disintegrated.

BIOGRAPHY
Gorbachev was born into a peasant family in the Stavropol region of southern Russia on 2 March 1931. This was a time of terrible privation as Stalin's policy of collectivization forced peasants off their own small plots and into giant collective farms (*kolkhozy*). This was the time of Stalin's terror, and both of Gorbachev's grandfathers suffered from repression, although his maternal grandfather went on to chair a collective farm. During the war Gorbachev's native village, Privolnoye, came under German occupation from August 1942 to January 1943. Living under the occupation usually had a devastating impact on people's career prospects, but for Gorbachev, being so young, it proved no obstacle to advancement. Gorbachev was a talented school pupil and at the same time a model agricultural worker, for which at age seventeen he was

awarded the Order of the Red Banner of Labor. This honor provided the impetus for Gorbachev to enter the highly prestigious Law Faculty of Moscow State University in 1950. Gorbachev's higher education and his legal knowledge would later distinguish him from his peers in the top Soviet leadership. His five years in Moscow University were a crucial formative period in his intellectual development, and many of the friends he made there were to remain close to him for the rest of his life.

This applies in particular to his fellow student Zdeněk Mlynář, who became one of the architects of the Prague Spring. Mlynář was the author of the Action Program of the Czechoslovak Communist Party that called for the transformation of the party into a genuinely accountable and democratic body at the head of a popular movement. Underlying this ideal was the view that Stalinism represented a shift toward an economic form of socialism that focused the relationship between things, whereas the proponents of socialism with a human face believed in a more democratic form of socialism that focused on relations between people. This was a view that lay at the heart of Gorbachev's reforms later.

It was while at university that Gorbachev married Raisa Maximovna Titorenko; they had two daughters. Raisa Maximovna was a notable sociologist in her own right, studying the condition of peasants in her native Stavropol region and honestly reflecting on the problems that faced them, despite the claims of "developed socialism" to have solved the social problems inherited from capitalism. She was to be Gorbachev's intellectual companion and source of moral support, and her death in 1999 was a devastating blow from which he never fully recovered. The couple lived in the Stavropol region from 1955 to 1978. Gorbachev soon realized that his talents lay in politics rather than in practicing law. He swiftly moved up the career ladder as a functionary, first in the regional Komsomol (Communist League of Youth) organization, which he came to head by 1958, and then in the Communist Party organization from 1962. By 1966, at the remarkably early age of thirty-five, he was first secretary of the Stavropol city organization of the CPSU, by 1968 the second secretary for the entire region, and in 1970 first secretary of the Obkom (Regional Party Committee). With the

latter post came membership in the national Central Committee in 1971. As head of the Stavropol region Gorbachev experimented with ways of achieving greater worker involvement, notably through the "link" system of granting greater autonomy to groups of workers, something he later sought to give to the whole country.

Although the hopes of the 1950s and early 1960s turned to disappointment and stagnation in the later years of Brezhnev's leadership (1964–1982), Gorbachev continued to thrive. Because Stavropol was located on the route to the top leadership's holiday destinations in south Russia, Gorbachev was host to many an important dignitary. In particular, the head of the KGB, Yuri Andropov, noted Gorbachev's ability and was later to favor Gorbachev once he became for a brief period leader of the country following Brezhnev's death.

In November 1978 Gorbachev was elected a secretary of the Central Committee, launching his rapid ascent in the national leadership. It soon became clear that Gorbachev was not only the youngest of the national leaders (only forty-seven years old compared to the average age of around seventy) but also had a spirit of resolution and political skills that would take him far. Granted candidate membership of the Politburo in 1979 and full membership in 1980, he was one of the nation's top figures when Brezhnev died in November 1982. Andropov assumed the leadership position but ill health prevented him doing much more than signaling that he sought to impose greater labor and political discipline balanced by some ideological flexibility. Gorbachev was shouldered aside in the leadership struggle following Andropov's death in March 1984, with the gerontocrats electing one of their own, the Brezhnevite Konstantin Chernenko. Gorbachev effectively acted as second-in-command, and Chernenko's death in March 1985 finally allowed a new generation to take over the reins of power.

POWER AND POLICIES

Gorbachev did not come to power with a clear set of policies, but he was convinced that change had to take place if the Soviet Union stood any chance of competing militarily and economically in the new international conditions. Gorbachev intended to oversee the modernization of the Soviet system. One of the characteristics of his leadership was the ability to discard old positions and to modify his thinking in the light of developments, but this flexibility came to be seen toward the end by many as unprincipled opportunism.

Gorbachev immediately turned his attention to the economy, where the high growth rates of the 1950s and 1960s had by the 1970s turned into stagnation and barely maintained standards of living. However, the attempt through the policy of acceleration (*uskorenie*) to achieve an intensification of economic output while launching structural reform was ill-advised. A spurt in economic growth was soon followed by a slump and by 1991 an economic meltdown. The anti-alcohol campaign of 1985–1986 was equally ill-advised, depriving the country of nearly one-third of tax revenues, and its implementation was crude and heavy-handed, alienating much of the population from the very first. The launching of glasnost (openness) in 1987 was intended at first only to expose corruption and to strengthen the Soviet system, but it soon became a devastating search for the truth about terror under Lenin and Stalin. Although a man of high intelligence, Gorbachev was unable to rid himself of an idealized vision of Leninism. His calls to return to some better version of the Revolution, epitomized by the works of the late Lenin stressing a gradual approach to building socialism, was anachronistic in the conditions of the 1980s.

By late 1987 the program of democratization (*demokratizatsiya*) came to the fore, in part to wrong-foot his opponents in the Communist leadership but also because Gorbachev had come to understand, like the Czechoslovak reformers before him, that socialism without democracy would inevitably give rise to Stalinist distortions. Experiments were conducted at the local level with multi-candidate elections. Gorbachev's own views at this time were eloquently developed in his book *Perestroika: New Thinking for Our Country and the World* (1987), in which he talked of perestroika as a revolution both from above and below. The country by now was swept by a wave of civic activity, with thousands of informal groups springing up. Many called for political pluralism, but at the same time, nationalist movements developed, in particular in the Baltic republics, the western part of the country, and the south Caucasus. The demands of popular movements began to outstrip Gorbachev's ability to respond to them.

The high point of Gorbachev's definition of perestroika was the Nineteenth Party Conference in June–July 1988, where he outlined a program of democratic political change and a new international role for the USSR. The conference was followed by measures to prevent the party apparatus from impeding change or challenging Gorbachev, and in November 1988 constitutional amendments created the rudiments of a parliamentary system. The elections to the new Congress of People's Deputies (CPD) in March 1989 saw many of the top party leaders lose, thus undermining the legitimacy of the old regime. The early debates of the parliament riveted the nation, as problems were openly discussed for the first time in decades. Mass demonstrations, echoing those that brought down the communist systems in Eastern Europe in the autumn of 1989, forced the Central Committee in February 1990 to relinquish its constitutionally entrenched "leading role," as embodied in article 6 of the 1977 Soviet constitution. On 14 March 1990 the CPD formally abolished the dominant role of the CPSU but on the very same day created a new executive presidency. The CPD elected Gorbachev to this post, and his failure to stand in a national ballot is often considered one of his major mistakes. Lacking a popular mandate, he was sidelined by those who did, notably Boris Yeltsin in the Russian republic.

National mobilization began to threaten the unity of the country. Gorbachev appeared to have a blind spot when it came to the sensitivities of the many nations making up the USSR, in particular the fifteen union republics that according to the 1977 constitution had the right to secede. Although Gorbachev was willing to grant greater autonomy to the union republics, he would have no truck with independence. The rise of Russia under Yeltsin came as a most unwelcome distraction for him, while the frustration of the Baltic states and Moldova about Gorbachev's failure at least to acknowledge the historical injustice meted out to them by Stalin finally provoked calls for independence. Gorbachev hoped to transform

Mikhail Gorbachev bows his head and grimaces in the Congress of People's Deputies shortly after Foreign Minister Edvard Shevardnadze has announced his resignation, December 1990. AP/WIDE WORLD PHOTOS

what was in effect a unitary state into a genuinely confederal community of nations by negotiating a new union treaty, but by the time that this seriously came on the agenda in 1991 many of the republics were ready for independence. Lithuania had already declared independence in 1990, followed by Georgia and other republics in 1991. Even though a large majority voted in favor of preserving a reconstituted USSR in the referendum of 17 March 1991, the boycott of the vote by six republics detracted from the victory.

Gorbachev had come to power when the second Cold War threatened to turn into a hot war, and it was his undoubted achievement not only to lift the threat of conflict with the West but also to provide the conditions for the overcoming of the Cold War in its entirety. Gorbachev proposed the idea of "new political thinking" based on the notion of interdependence and a new cooperative relationship with the West. Proof of this was the abolition of a whole class of intermediate nuclear

weapons in 1987. Withdrawal from Afghanistan in 1988 put an end to one of the Soviet Union's most futile military adventures. In Europe, Gorbachev talked of the establishment of a "common European home," but it was not clear what form this would take. Gorbachev looked on as one after another of the communist regimes in the Soviet bloc collapsed from 1989; although he would have preferred reform communism to have replaced neo-Stalinism, instead capitalism flooded in. Gorbachev facilitated the unification of Germany in 1990, although he is criticized for failing to guarantee in treaty form the demilitarized status of the eastern part of the new country.

Economic reform proved the stumbling block for his vision of perestroika. His inability to make up his mind in the early 1990s over a strategy for economic change encouraged Russia and the other republics to go it alone. Resistance to his aims and his policies grew to the point that a group prepared to seize power in a coup. The specific issue was the planned signing of the new Union Treaty on 20 August 1991, but the plotters were also concerned about economic disintegration and the loss of political control. For three days in August (19–21) Gorbachev was isolated in the Crimea, while Yeltsin faced down the plotters and emerged with renewed popularity. Gorbachev's hopes for a reformed democratic socialism lay in tatters. The pressure for increased sovereignty for republics grew into demands for independence, and despite Gorbachev's attempts to save the union, in December of that year the USSR was formally dissolved. Gorbachev resigned as president on 25 December 1991 and went on to head his Gorbachev Foundation dealing with historical and social science research.

Gorbachev proved a visionary transformative leader, but his attempt to reform the Soviet system provoked its demise. His reforms clearly showed that Soviet socialism had hidden potential, and it is not incredible to argue that a different set of policies might have allowed the Soviet system to emerge strengthened and renewed from the reform process. By 1991 the Soviet Union was in effect a functioning democracy, although it lacked a market system. Gorbachev achieved the relatively peaceful transcendence of the communist system, the ending of the Cold War, and the transformation of the USSR's fifteen republics into sovereign statehood. Gorbachev remained loyal to his vision of a humane democratic socialism, and for many in the chaotic transition to democratic capitalism that followed his humanism and intelligence remained a beacon of hope.

See also **Andropov, Yuri; Eastern Bloc; 1989; Perestroika; Soviet Union; Velvet Revolution.**

BIBLIOGRAPHY

Primary Sources

Gorbachev, Mikhail. *Perestroika: New Thinking for Our Country and the World.* London, 1987. Gives Gorbachev's own views at the time.

———. *Zhizn' i reformy.* 2 vols. Moscow, 1995. Gorbachev's full memoirs.

———. *On My Country and the World.* New York, 2000.

Gorbachev, Mikhail, and Zdeněk Mlynář. *Conversations with Gorbachev on Perestroika, the Prague Spring, and the Crossroads of Socialism.* New York, 2002. Vividly brings out the theoretical basis of Gorbachev's thinking.

Secondary Sources

Brown, Archie. *The Gorbachev Factor.* Oxford, U.K., 1996. One of the best political analyses of Gorbachev's leadership.

Hahn, Gordon M. *Russia's Revolution from Above, 1985–2000: Reform, Transition, and Revolution in the Fall of the Soviet Communist Regime.* New Brunswick, N.J., 2002. Reviews much of the memoir literature that has emerged since to give balanced analyses of the period.

Hough, Jerry F. *Democratization and Revolution in the USSR, 1985–1991.* Washington, D.C., 1997.

Sakwa, Richard. *Gorbachev and His Reforms, 1985–90.* Hemel Hempstead, U.K., 1990. Good coverage of the intellectual context of the time.

RICHARD SAKWA

GORKY, MAXIM (1868–1936), Russian writer.

Maxim Gorky (pseudonym of Alexei Maximovich Peshkov), a writer of fiction, poetry, plays, and criticism as well as an editor and activist journalist, was officially called the founder of socialist realism and of Soviet literature. But his record is actually contradictory and enigmatic. Born in Nizhny Novgorod (which for much of the Soviet period was renamed Gorky in his honor) into a family of artisans and entrepreneurs, Gorky's early years are chronicled in his autobiographical trilogy *Detstvo* (1913–1914; *My Childhood,* 1915), *V lyudakh* (1915–1916; *In the World,* 1918), and *Moi universitety* (1922; *My University Days,* 1923). The latter title is ironic because Gorky never received a university education but was an autodidact. He left school at eleven and led a peripatetic existence, going from place to place in the south of Russia and the Caucasus, and working at a variety of unskilled jobs ("universities"). During this period Gorky became involved with leftist groups, initially with a group of idealist socialists, the Populists (*narodniki*) and their efforts for the political and cultural education of the untutored masses. In this connection he was arrested in 1889, the first in a series of arrests and exiles. Later, especially during the 1905 revolution, he became involved with the Bolshevik faction of the Russian Social Democratic Labor Party (RSDLP). He joined the party in the summer of 1905 and his association with Vladimir Lenin (Vladimir Ilyich Ulyanov; 1870–1924) began shortly thereafter, but Gorky was never a party organization man, and his membership was not maintained.

Gorky began his literary career in 1892, publishing the story "Makar Chudra" in the Tbilisi newspaper *Kavkaz*. He initially wrote stories that romanticized the down-and-out, drifters, and loners (including a professional thief in "Chelkash"), moving on to longer works that provided critiques of the emerging entrepreneurial class and of the bourgeois intellectual who joins the proletarian revolutionary cause, such as *Foma Gordeyev* (1899), *Zhizn Matveya Kozhemyakina* (1910–1911; *The Life of Matvei Kozhemyakin*), and *Delo Artamonovykh* (1925; *The Artamonov Affair*).

Gorky's literary successes enabled him to become a prominent public intellectual in the service of leftist causes. But he was no radical in his literary orientation, favoring realism and periodically attacking "decadents" (modernist writers) and Fyodor Dostoyevsky. In the 1900s he wrote several plays that were performed at the Moscow Art Theatre of Konstantin Stanislavsky (1863–1938), such as *Dachniki* (1904; Summer Folk) and *Vragi* (1906; Enemies). The most famous of these, *Na dne* (1902; *A Night's Lodging*, 1905, better known as *The Lower Depths*, 1912) combines Chekhovian techniques and social critique with its portrayal of the down-and-outs in a flophouse.

In 1906 Gorky traveled to America to collect funds for the party and meet with intellectuals, publishing his impressions in *Moi intervyu* (1906; *My Interviews*) and *V Amerike* (1906; *In America*). At this time he also wrote the novel *Mat* (1907; *The Mother*), later to become a major model for socialist realist fiction. *Mat* tells the story of a simple, uneducated widow who is drawn to the revolutionary cause after her worker son is arrested for underground party work. She progressively acquires political consciousness until at the end she is killed as she bears the party banner aloft in a political demonstration. However, Gorky himself was soon drawn to "God-building" (*bogostroitelstvo*), an unorthodox form of Marxism—denounced by Lenin as a heresy—that he and several other party intellectuals, influenced by the writer Alexander Bogdanov, developed while in exile on the Italian island of Capri, and which is reflected in the short novel *Ispoved* (1908; A Confession).

In 1913 an amnesty allowed Gorky to return to Russia, where he became politically active. When the Bolshevik Revolution occurred on 7 November 1917, however, he became one of its most prominent critics, expressing dismay at the bloodshed and at the treatment of intellectuals. At the same time, Gorky worked indefatigably as a champion of intellectuals and of culture, editing a series of works in translation, *Vsemirnaya literatura* (World Literature). Though he became more reconciled to the Bolsheviks after an attempted assassination of Lenin in 1918, he left the country in 1921 (ostensibly because of his tuberculosis) and took up residence in Sorrento, Italy. From there he conducted a prolific correspondence with Soviet writers, advising them on their literary work. In 1928 and 1929 he made return visits to Soviet Russia, producing a volume of sketches in praise of the First Five-Year Plan *Po soyuzu sovetov* (1929; *Around the Land of the Soviets*). In 1931 he went back to stay. Gorky's record after his return, when he wrote several articles essentially endorsing the repressive measures of the Soviet state against "the enemies of the people," whom he characterized as "vermin," and his fulsome praise for Joseph Stalin (1879–1953), seem to contradict his earlier, more critical stance vis-à-vis Soviet power, but scholars can only speculate on his motives. Gorky also played a major role in the institutionalization of "socialist realism" after all independent writers' organizations were disbanded in April 1932 and a single Union of Soviet Writers formed. At the First Writers Congress in 1934 he gave one of the keynote addresses defining what the term meant. During the remaining years until his death from tuberculosis in 1936 Gorky worked indefatigably on bureaucratic and editing work. He initiated several series of publishing ventures such as *Istoriya fabrik i zavodov* (*The History of the Factories*) and *Istoriya grazhdanskoi voiny* (*The History of the Civil War*), both launched in 1931, in which ordinary Soviet citizens were to write their own life stories, a more politicized version of an activity he had fostered since the turn of the century. His literary output in these years was small, though he produced two plays, *Egor Bulychev i drugie* (1932; *Egor Bulychev and Others*) and *Dostigayev i drugie* (1933; *Dostigayev and Others*), and a reworked version of his earlier play *Vassa*

Zheleznova (1935), about a despotic merchant on the Volga. He also continued working on *Zhizn Klima Samgina* (*The Life of Klim Samgin*), an epic novel about a young intellectual, which he had begun in 1925 and which was intended to provide a canvas of the various intellectual groupings and political trends to be found in the first decades of the twentieth century. However, he was unable to finish the book before his death.

See also **Socialist Realism; Soviet Union.**

BIBLIOGRAPHY

Luker, Nicholas, ed. *Fifty Years On: Gorky and His Times.* Nottingham, U.K., 1987.

Scherr, Barry P. *Maxim Gorky.* Boston, 1988.

Yedlin, Tova. *Maxim Gorky: A Political Biography.* Westport, Conn., 1999.

KATERINA CLARK

GOTTWALD, KLEMENT (1896–1953), Czech politician and president of Czechoslovakia from 1945 to 1953.

Klement Gottwald was a prominent Czech politician, general secretary of the Communist Party of Czechoslovakia (CPCz) from 1929 to 1945 and its chairman from the inception of the post in 1945 until 1953, prime minister of Czechoslovakia from 1946 to 1948, and the country's president from 1948 until his death. Born into a poor rural family in 1896, Gottwald worked as a cabinetmaker and became active in left-wing politics as a youth. After serving in, and eventually deserting from, the Austro-Hungarian army in World War I, he participated in the founding of the CPCz in 1921. For the following five years he was a party functionary in Slovakia, where he also edited several party publications. As a member of the CPCz's Central Committee (from 1925) and its Politburo (1926–1929) he became a staunch advocate of the bolshevization of the party. With the victory of the left wing of the party in 1929, Gottwald became CPCz general secretary. Also in 1929, Gottwald became a member of the National Assembly, Czechoslovakia's parliament, a position he relinquished upon becoming president.

Beginning in 1928, he served as a member of the executive of the Communist International and deepened his work with that organization in Moscow after fleeing a Czechoslovak arrest warrant in 1934. While in the Soviet Union, he contributed to the creation of the "Popular Front" strategy and as a result of his labors was named secretary of the International's executive and editor-in-chief of its monthly journal. Upon returning to Czechoslovakia in 1936, he continued his advocacy of the Popular Front strategy. When Czechoslovakia became the target of Nazi German pressure in the late 1930s, Gottwald led his party in attempts to cooperate with all political currents committed to the defense of the republic. These culminated in the CPCz's opposition to the Czechoslovak government's acceptance of the Munich Accords of September 1938.

Six weeks after Munich, Gottwald again fled Czechoslovakia for Moscow, where he spent the war years coordinating CPCz activities in the domestic resistance and leading discussions with the official Czechoslovak government-in-exile in London. One turning point in these discussions came in December of 1943, when President Edvard Beneš (1884–1948) came to Moscow to discuss the future of a reconstituted Czechoslovak Republic. The agreement that was reached outlined wide-ranging changes in the postwar political structure of the state (including the truncation of the political spectrum through the banning of collaborationist parties), in its economic organization (including the nationalization of several sectors of the economy), and in its ethnic composition (including the expulsion of Czechoslovakia's German and Hungarian minorities). These principles were then enshrined in the first postwar government program announced in April 1945.

The Czechoslovakia to which Gottwald returned was remarkably open to radical change, and while serving as deputy prime minister and CPCz chairman he saw his party's membership rise from twenty-eight thousand in May 1945 to over one million by March of 1946. This support, encouraged by Gottwald's proclamation of a moderate, parliamentary program summed up as a "Czechoslovak road to socialism," was reflected in the CPCz's victory in the general elections of May 1946. The party won 40 percent of the Czech vote, and the strong showing catapulted Gottwald to the post of prime minister. While in office, he continued the nationalizations and social changes begun by the interim government, and promulgated and launched Czechoslovakia's first economic plan. As international and domestic tensions mounted in 1947, however, Gottwald, in line with Soviet desires, moved away from the conciliatory line of the first postwar years. Sharpening political antagonisms culminated in the resignation of many non-communist cabinet ministers in February 1948. When Gottwald received President Beneš's blessing to form a government based on the CPCz, the Communist Party of Slovakia, and fellow-travelers from the other parties, the communists' takeover of Czechoslovakia was complete. When Beneš, citing ill health, resigned from the presidency in June 1948, Gottwald became the first communist president of Czechoslovakia.

As president, Gottwald bears the responsibility for the Stalinization of the economy; the beginnings of collectivization; and the purges of political life, the army, the bureaucracy, and social life that took place in the first years of communist rule, as well as for the extra- and pseudo-judicial punishments of enemies real and imagined. These reached their apex in the show trial of Rudolf Slánský (until recently beforehand general secretary of the CPCz and Gottwald's longtime right hand man) and thirteen codefendants in late 1952, in a proceeding with markedly anti-Semitic overtones. Gottwald died on 14 March 1953, nine days after Joseph Stalin, at whose funeral Gottwald caught a cold that turned into pneumonia.

See also **Beneš, Eduard; Collectivization; Communism; Czechoslovakia; Popular Front; Slánský Trial.**

BIBLIOGRAPHY

Matějka, Jaroslav. *Gottwald*. Prague, 1971.

Suda, Zdenek. *Zealots and Rebels: A History of the Communist Party of Czechoslovakia*. Stanford, Calif., 1980.

BRADLEY ABRAMS

GRAMSCI, ANTONIO (1891–1937), Italian political theorist and activist.

Antonio Gramsci was one of twentieth-century Italy's most original political thinkers as well as a political activist who cofounded the Italian Communist Party (PCI) in 1921. Born in Ales, Sardinia, into a lower-middle-class family, he won a scholarship to the University of Turin in 1911, where he studied linguistics and philosophy. He was deeply engaged with prewar intellectual currents, including futurism and the Florentine circle around the journal *La voce* (The voice), particularly with the latter's efforts to bring southern peasants into closer economic and political alignment with the more industrial and prosperous north. He joined the Socialist Party (PSI) in 1914.

The Gramsci of 1916 and 1917 was strongly drawn to Giovanni Gentile's philosophy of the pure act, as well as to other voluntarist viewpoints such as those of Henri Bergson, Georges Sorel, Benedetto Croce, and even the interventionist Benito Mussolini. Although his Marxism, which he also came to early, made him appreciate objective conditions as a constraint upon action and as the context in which acts are historically framed, he rejected Marxist positivisms aiming at laws of social action. For him, theory was an account people used in understanding and acting; in this sense it was inherently unified with practice and immanent in a Gentilian way. In this period, he also devoted himself to political and cultural criticism (including extensive consideration of Luigi Pirandello's theater) for both the mainstream liberal and socialist press. He founded two reviews of his own, the short-lived *La città futura* (The future city) and *L'ordine nuovo* (The new order), which became the organ of the Turinese "factory council" movement and, later, of the early PCI.

Gramsci was awestruck by the Bolshevik victory in 1917, which he saw as a "revolution against capital," in the sense that it had obeyed the dictates of subjective will by reacting creatively to historical circumstances rather than reflexively following supposed historical laws. After Italy's "mutilated victory" in World War I reopened the revolutionary door, Gramsci sought to extend Vladimir Lenin's creativity to Italy by leading Turin's factory-council movement. The movement failed, and its quasi-syndicalist ideal of direct democracy through the workplace soon appeared to him naive, but it established his independence from any dogmatic Marxism or Leninism.

Within the PCI, Gramsci served as representative to the Comintern (the Third Communist International; 1922–1923) and as the party's general secretary (1924–1926), positioning himself between the ultraleftism of Amadeo Bordiga and those, such as Palmiro Togliatti, whom he viewed as too subservient to the Bolsheviks. With its original mix of idealist and Leninist themes, Gramsci's party politics emphasized the linkage between the working class, democratically organized from below, and a party leadership guiding it into creative alliances with other "subaltern classes," especially the peasantry. He believed that political leadership in Italy required an effective "Jacobin force," which, however, had been missing at every critical turn since the Risorgimento that culminated in 1860. Political change, including the advent of fascism, had always come as a "passive revolution" in which disconnected elites sought to move forward without engaging the masses.

For Gramsci, the rise of fascism was indicative of a crisis of political authority in Italy, one in which large sections of the bourgeoisie and petty bourgeoisie no longer believed in existing political parties and institutions. In this light, he also pondered parallels between the fascist and communist movements, both of which were attempting to amass a popular base in order to overcome the crisis of authority by transcending liberal ideas and institutions.

Gramsci worked tenaciously against fascism but became one of its most prominent victims. Ironically, however, his arrest in late 1926 and subsequent imprisonment by the fascist regime until his death of a cerebral hemorrhage in April 1937 gave him an opportunity for sustained theoretical and historical reflection that he would otherwise not have had. The twenty-nine notebooks he wrote in prison (roughly twenty-four hundred pages in the critical edition of 1975) ruminate upon an astonishingly wide range of subjects, from Dante's *Divine Comedy* to Japanese Shintō. Nonetheless, they do manifest a central preoccupation with the question of the nature and political significance of popular consciousness and the political means used to subject such consciousness to control. From a theoretical point of view, the problem for Gramsci was that the political consciousness necessary for revolutionary action always tended to arrive only after the economic conditions that also represented necessary conditions for change.

In connection with this theme, Gramsci's notebooks studied the role of intellectuals in politics, developing his well-known distinction between "organic" (consciously class-based) and "traditional" (ostensibly independent of class) intellectuals, and linking it to historical examinations of the Napoleonic era, the Risorgimento, the liberal Italy that followed it, and the rise of fascism. He also developed a broader analysis of "hegemony," the process by which ruling political forces attempt to shape and develop cultural traditions to gain the "consent" of the ruled for their ideals, goals, and policies. Through this and related concepts, he sought to explain how consent was possible even in opposition to the self-interest of the ruled, how "contradictory consciousness" (complex blends of "common sense" and semiconscious utopian strivings) developed in concrete historical settings, and how a genuinely "national-popular" political culture could be created.

After World War II, when his notebooks and prison letters were published in Italy, and especially after the European crises of 1968 and the rise of the New Left, Gramsci's Marxism came to be celebrated for his belief in creative human agency as a historical force, his appreciation of the many complex (structural and superstructural) factors that always appeared in concrete historical situations, his interest in popular culture and in the ways it could develop into politically critical consciousness, and his rejection of positivistic versions of Marxist theory as well as dogmatic political programs of all stripes. For the New Left, he was one of the few Marxists from earlier generations who had seriously grappled with the problems of revolutionary change in the economically and culturally complex societies of the modern West by thinking through how ideological-cultural forces could be mobilized by political movements opposing dominant bourgeois values. Even in the wake of the collapse of communism that began in Eastern Europe in 1989, Gramsci continues to be read for the conceptual nimbleness of his political theory and for the fertility of his theoretical and historical imagination.

See also **Bolshevism; Communism; Fascism; Italy; Socialism.**

BIBLIOGRAPHY

Adamson, Walter L. *Hegemony and Revolution: A Study of Antonio Gramsci's Political and Cultural Theory.* Berkeley, Calif., 1980.

Bellamy, Richard, and Darrow Schecter. *Gramsci and the Italian State.* Manchester, U.K., 1993.

Cammett, John M. *Antonio Gramsci and the Origins of Italian Communism.* Stanford, Calif., 1967. Classic study of the historical context and nature of Gramsci's preprison political activity.

Femia, Joseph V. *Gramsci's Political Thought: Hegemony, Consciousness, and the Revolutionary Process.* Oxford, U.K., 1981.

Fiori, Giuseppe. *Antonio Gramsci: Life of a Revolutionary.* Translated by Tom Nairn. New York, 1971. Vivid and reliable biography.

Holub, Renate. *Antonio Gramsci: Beyond Marxism and Postmodernism.* London, 1992. An important reevaluation of Gramsci's overall theoretical position.

WALTER L. ADAMSON

GRASS, GUNTER (b. 1927), German writer.

Disparaged by his critics but very quickly recognized abroad, Gunter Grass stands apart in the intellectual landscape of Germany because, as he said, "the subject of my books always seemed to me to be dictated by the history of Germany" (interview, 1995).

Grass was born in the Free City of Danzig. His father was a German Protestant and his mother was a Catholic from the Kashub region. He attended school from 1933 to 1944, and therefore experienced the full force of the National Socialist education system. He was sent to the battlefront but finished the war in a prisoner camp in Bavaria. It was in this landscape that he set his Danzig trilogy. *Die Blechtrommel* (1959; *The Tin Drum*) depicts the rise and establishment of Nazism, as well as the war, the fall of the Third Reich, and the beginnings of reconstruction through the eyes of a dwarf. *Katz und Maus* (1961; *Cat and Mouse*) opens with World War II and ends with the protagonist deserting to the Federal Republic of Germany. *Hundejahre* (1963; *Dog Years*) covers the period from 1925 to 1950, when communism, National Socialism, and antifascist ideologies followed each other in succession.

The end of the war and the ensuing displacements and ideological disillusionment gave Grass the freedom of the stateless. He entered the workforce, then studied at the Beaux-Arts Academy in Dusseldorf (1949–1952) and later in Berlin. Between 1965 and 1980, he lived first in Paris and then in West Berlin. As early as the 1950s, he established himself as the most peculiar author of the children-of-the-war generation. In 1955 he was a member of a group of young authors called Gruppe 47; another member, Heinrich Böll, would become a close friend. Feeling himself an exile, Grass sought to find a republic of letters within the writers' community. He also played a part in founding the Writers' Union and the review *L 76. Socialism and Democracy* (1976) with Böll and Carola Stern. Rejecting any literary break between the two Germanys, he found himself surrounded by writers not only from the Democratic Republic of Germany but also from countries of the Eastern bloc. In the following decade, Grass's works were devoted to what he called "a German past which does not pass." In *Ortlich Betaubt* (1969; *Local Anesthetic*), he criticized both the eclipsing of the past and the rejection of any kind of "petit-bourgeois" activism against the Vietnam War. This was also the time when he was a member of the Democratic Socialist Party (DSP)—an experience that inspired his *Aus dem Tagebuch einer Schnecke* (1972; *From the Diary of a Snail*).

From this point on, his writing and political commitment were intertwined. His "intentions were always to use literature as a means...to enlighten public opinion." He supported women's emancipation (*Der Butt* [*The Flounder*], 1977) and spoke out against the danger of nuclear disasters (*Die Rattin* [*The Rat*], 1986). He opposed the financial reconquest of the lost eastern territories (*Unkenrufe: Eine Erzahlung* [*The Call of the Toad*], 1992). In *Mein Jarhundert* (1999; *My Century*), he surveyed German history and described Germany's reunification from the standpoint of the Democratic Republic of Germany as sheer annexation. His 2002 book, *Im Krebsgang* (*Crabwalk*), traced the Germans' retreat before the Red Army in 1945. Grass also wrote five plays and many collections of poetry and produced a large number of artworks.

Grass stands out from other German intellectuals, who distanced themselves from politics (as under the Weimar Republic, when German intellectuals took the attitude that the status of a writer was incompatible with political engagement). In 1974 he left the Catholic Church because it condemned abortion. At the beginning of the 1980s he spoke out for peace and disarmament and against the Reagan administration in the United States. In an act of solidarity with the writer Salman Rushdie, whose life was threatened by a fatwa, he resigned from the Academy of Art of West Berlin in 1989 as a protest against colleagues who did not want to publicly express their support for the writer of the *Satanic Verses*. He created a foundation to provide assistance to the Roma and Sinti (Gypsies) who had been victims of the Nazis. In 1997 he accused the German government of supporting the Turkish repression of Kurds by means of weapons trafficking. The following year, he supported the Democratic Socialist Party–Green coalition but left the DSP in protest of its support for reforming the right of asylum. Grass has been a killjoy rather than the embodiment of Germany's good conscience. For some critics, the Nobel Prize he won in 1999 rewarded his literary work in the Republic of Bonn (that of Adenauer and Brand, who, without forgetting Germany's Nazi heritage, were students of democracy under the tutelage of the Western Allies), but also brought an end to Grass's polemics in the Republic of Berlin (capital of reunified Germany, clearly sovereign and ready to assume the responsibilities of a normal state).

Nevertheless, Grass remains a master of the German language, and his language stands in stark contrast to the German used for the Third Reich's lies and the postwar literature that called itself clear cut—a literary movement born out of the ruins of Nazism, which had reduced artistic production almost to the point of nonexistence. He knocked down the boundaries of literature. Using the spoken language to convey an abundance of disturbing images, he created a style that melded diary notes, poetry, realistic narratives, fables, and parody. Writing has been Grass's true home.

See also **Germany.**

BIBLIOGRAPHY

Everett, George A. *A Select Bibliography of Gunter Grass (from 1956–1973): Including the Works, Editions, Translations, and Critical Literature,* New York, 1974.

Görtz, Franz Josef. *Gunter Grass: Auskunft für Leser.* Darmstadt, Germany, 1984.

Joch, Oeter. *Zaubern auf weissem Papier: Das graphische Werk von Gunter Grass.* Gottingen, 2000.

O'Neill, Patrick. *Gunter Grass: A Bibliography, 1955–1975.* Toronto and Buffalo, N.Y., 1976.

Vormweg, Heinrich. *Gunter Grass.* Hamburg, 2002.

FABIEN THÉOFILAKIS

GRAVES, ROBERT (1895–1985), British poet, novelist, and classical scholar.

Robert von Ranke Graves, whose father was a school inspector and Gaelic scholar and whose mother was a great-niece of the German historian Leopold van Ranke, had a conventionally religious and sober London upbringing among nine other children, after which he was sent off to public school at Charterhouse, which he hated. He won a scholarship to St. John's College, Oxford, but did not take up his place. After the outbreak of war in 1914 he volunteered for military service with the Royal Welch Fusiliers, serving as a junior officer in the infantry. Graves fought at the Battle of Loos and was severely wounded on the Somme front, and while recuperating he managed to read his own obituary in *The Times* of London. During the war he befriended his fellow poet and officer Siegfried Sassoon and came to see these years both as entirely mad and as the forcing house of his career as a writer. Graves defended his friend when Sassoon decided in 1917 to protest publicly against the continuation of the war for no reason; facing a court-martial, Sassoon was persuaded by Graves to pretend to being temporarily insane and got off the charge. Graves's protest was more indirect and more bound up with his career as a writer. He published four volumes of poetry during the war and in the last months of the conflict was once more wounded. He survived the war as a twenty-three-year-old combatant, old before his time.

After returning to Oxford and completing his degree, he still showed lingering effects of his war service, encompassed by the generic term *shell shock*. A period of instability was followed by a decision to emigrate. Graves lived outside of Britain throughout the interwar years. He held a chair at the University of Cairo and then settled in Majorca. At the outbreak of the Spanish civil war he left the Balearic Islands for New York but returned to Majorca after World War II.

In 1929 he published *Good-bye to All That,* which has become a classic account of trench warfare in the 1914–1918 conflict. It is in the form of an autobiography, but much of it is fictional. As he later said, only by telling lies about the war can anyone tell the truth about it. This challenge to narrative, and particularly to heroic narrative, is one of the foundational texts of twentieth-century war writing. It encapsulates the bitterness of a generation of writers who felt betrayed by the older generation, who sent them off to a war their elders did not see and did not want to see. The theme of decency and youth thrown away by the blind prejudices of a handful of old men too stupid to understand what they were doing and totally blind to the suffering they set in motion has framed later fictional accounts of warfare in the twentieth century and beyond.

The Great War haunted Graves throughout his life. His book *Lawrence and the Arabs,* a sympathetic account of T. E. Lawrence, another troubled veteran, was published in 1927. In the 1930s Graves's poetic interests were inflected by his partnership with Laura Riding (1901–1991) as well as by a deepening passion for classical literature and for the narrative and aesthetic power of myths. Poetry for Graves was a cathartic force for writer and reader alike. His iconoclastic style and irreverent tone are evident in much of his later discursive work. He wrote a brilliant account of the interwar years in Britain, *The Long Weekend: A Social History of Great Britain, 1918–1939* (1940), a malicious but fair survey of a country in shock after one war and on the verge of another. He then turned to more learned themes, relating myth to religious belief and practice. His study *King Jesus* (1946) was followed by his two-volume synthesis of *Greek Myths* (1955). Both shared the deep scholarship and heterodox outlook that produced his two devastating accounts of Rome, *I, Claudius* and *Claudius the God,* both published in 1934. He was clearly influenced by Sir James George Frazer's *Golden Bough* but developed his own notion of myths, in particular those related to matriarchy.

In 1961 the prodigal son returned home, in a way, when he became professor of poetry at Oxford, where he taught until 1966. Never at ease in England, his poetry nonetheless retained its English cadences, echoing the rhythms of the landscape he saw blown to pieces in 1916. Never being able to say goodbye to all that, he was an artist whose lasting contribution as a poet was as a stubborn survivor from another world, the world before the Great War. He died in his beloved Majorca at the age of ninety.

See also **Sassoon, Siegfried; World War I.**

BIBLIOGRAPHY

Cohen, J. M. *Robert Graves.* New York, 1960.

Day, Douglas. *Swifter Than Reason: The Poetry and Criticism of Robert Graves.* Chapel Hill, N.C., 1963.

Graves, Richard Perceval. *Robert Graves.* 2 vols. London, 1986–1990.

Seymour-Smith, Martin. *Robert Graves, His Life and Work.* London, 1982; reprint 1995.

Stade, George. *Robert Graves.* New York, 1967.

JAY WINTER

GREAT WAR. *See* World War I.

GREECE.
Greece became independent from the Ottoman Empire by 1830, and during the nineteenth century the modern nation aimed at territorial expansion with the view to incorporating the Greek-speaking Christian Orthodox communities of the Ottoman Empire into the Greek kingdom. This project was known as the *Megáli Idéa* (Great Idea). The territorial expansion was nearly completed in the first two decades of the twentieth century. As a result of the Balkan Wars (1912–1913) Greece increased both its population and territory by 70 percent, and lands of the Ottoman Empire were incorporated into the Greek state,

notably Macedonia. The outbreak of World War I brought turmoil in Greek politics because of the dispute between the prime minister Eleutherios Venizelos (1864–1936) and King Constantine I (r. 1913–1917; 1920–1922) over the issue of Greece's participation in the war. The relations between Constantine and Venizelos deteriorated and the latter, who supported the entry of Greece in the war on the side of the Entente powers, resigned in 1915. It was the beginning of the conflict between republicans and royalists (known as the "national schism") that dominated Greek society and politics throughout the interwar period and reflected the conflict between the forces of capitalist modernization and social reform on the one hand and those of conservatism and small-holding peasants on the other. Venizelos abstained from the elections of 1915 and his supporters, backed by the Entente troops, led a coup and established a rival "government" in Salonika in August 1916 in opposition to the royalist government in Athens. The Entente powers repeatedly intervened in Greek politics in an attempt to obtain Greece's participation in the war, showing little concern about its sovereignty. In December 1916 British and French troops landed in Athens but retreated when skirmishes broke out. In June 1917 the Entente powers demanded that the Germanophile king leave the country. Constantine departed and Venizelos again became the prime minister of a deeply divided country.

THE ASIA MINOR DEBACLE

Greece finally entered World War I, in its very last phase, on the side of the Entente. Greece's territorial gains this time proved to be short-term. After the Treaty of Sèvres (1920) Greece took over the administration of the Smyrna region in Asia Minor, a former Ottoman land. Despite Venizelos's diplomatic triumph in the elections of 1920 he was defeated by the royalists, who took advantage of the war weariness of the population, and Constantine returned to the country. Greece sent troops to Asia Minor to defend its territorial gains against the rising tide of Turkish nationalism led by Mustafa Kemal. The Greek military campaign against the Turkish troops failed, and the Turkish counteroffensive resulted in the defeat of the Greek army and the expulsion of the entire Greek populations from Asia Minor in 1922. The flight of about 1.3 million

Greeks from Turkey was later ratified by the Treaty of Lausanne (1923), which also provided for the transfer of 380,000 Muslims to Turkey in the framework of the forced exchange of populations between Greece and Turkey. The defeat in Asia Minor caused a major political crisis. A Revolutionary Committee of officers forced Constantine to leave the country for a second time and a Commission of Inquiry put the blame for the Asia Minor debacle on leading royalist ministers and officers: six of them were sentenced to death and executed. Constantine abdicated and retired to Sicily, where he died soon after. After a plebiscite in April 1924 the monarchy was abolished and Greece was proclaimed a republic.

The defeat of Greece in Asia Minor (known to Greeks as the "Asia Minor catastrophe") marked the end of an era of territorial expansion and nationalism, while at the same time the arrival of destitute refugees represented an immense challenge that called for social reforms. The government with the aid of the Refugee Settlement Commission undertook a major program of settlement for the refugees. Half of the refugees (638,000) were settled in Macedonia, which thereafter became predominantly Greek. As part of the Ottoman Empire until 1912, Macedonia had been inhabited by an ethnically mixed population. Generally speaking, the exchange of populations and the arrival of refugees transformed Greece into an ethnically homogeneous country, even though there were small minorities of Jews, Muslims, Slav Macedonians, and Albanians. The influx of the refugees accelerated the process of land reform and large estates were broken up into smaller landholdings, which were distributed to the refugees. The refugees who settled in the cities (363,000 in Salonika, Athens, and Piraeus) provided abundant cheap labor and contributed greatly to the growth of Greek industry in the interwar era. The territorial and demographic changes had political repercussions as well. Greece was politically divided between the more conservative indigenous populations of "Old Greece" and the more liberal or radical refugees who inhabited the newly acquired lands.

After a period of political instability (1924–1928) Venizelos won the elections of 1928. One of his important achievements was the détente in Greek-Turkish relations, although he failed to respond to the new circumstances created by the world economic crisis. Venizelos lost the elections of 1932 and that defeat marked the end of republican hegemony and liberal economic policy and the beginning of a new period of political instability. Republican officers attempted twice (in 1933 and 1935) a coup against the royalist Populist Party, actions that fueled anti-Venizelist sentiments and led to a purge of the republicans from the state apparatus, which triggered a backlash by royalist conspirators. One of them, General Kondylis, staged a coup and organized a rigged plebiscite in November 1935 that restored the monarchy in Greece. In the beginning King George II followed a policy of reconciliation between republicans and royalists, forced dictator Kondylis to resign, and called for elections. The elections of 1936 produced a stalemate between the two major political parties and turned the Communist Party of Greece (KKE), which held the balance of power, into a significant political actor. In April 1936 the king appointed General Ioannis Metaxas, leader of a minuscule extreme rightist party, as the new prime minister. On 4 August 1936 Metaxas, having the consent of the king, proclaimed dictatorship using as a pretext the labor unrest (a general strike was organized for the next day) and the communist danger. The Metaxas dictatorship (1936–1941), lacking any political constituency, never became popular and was conditioned on the king's support.

WORLD WAR II AND OCCUPATION

When World War II broke out Metaxas worked hard to keep Greece out of the conflict without jeopardizing good relations with Great Britain. Benito Mussolini, however, wanted to demonstrate to Hitler that Italy was an equal and victorious Axis partner and picked Greece as an easy target. Italy attacked Greece in October 1940 but the Italian offensive was checked by the Greek army and the Italian troops retreated to Albania. In April 1941 Germany intervened and invaded Greece. The government and the king fled to the Middle East, and the country was ultimately divided by the three occupying forces (Germany, Italy, and Bulgaria), and a collaborationist government was installed in Athens. The economic dislocation of the country due to the war and the severity of the German occupation created serious food shortages in the urban centers. In the winter of 1941–1942 the

population of Athens faced a terrible famine that caused the death of more than thirty thousand people. The dire living conditions drove many people to form committees to address the food shortage problems, which often became the nuclei of the Resistance in the urban centers. In 1942 the Resistance spread to the countryside and grew to become one of the largest resistance movements in occupied Europe. The Communist Party together with other small socialist parties founded the National Liberation Front (EAM) and its military wing, the National People's Liberation Army (ELAS), which were by far the strongest resistance organizations in occupied Greece. The Resistance was, however, intertwined with a civil war between rival resistance organizations (leftist and rightist), but mostly between ELAS and the Security Battalions, Greek armed units that collaborated with the Germans in campaigns against the guerrillas. The brutality of the German occupation reached its climax in 1943–1944: sixty thousand Greek Jews (mostly from Salonika) were deported to be exterminated in concentration camps; hundreds of civilians were executed on the spot in mass executions in places such as Kalavryta, Kommeno, and Distomo; villages were razed to the ground in retaliation for guerrilla attacks; and hostages were taken and later executed after roundups in Athens neighborhoods.

LIBERATION AND CIVIL WAR

Greece was liberated in October 1944. When the government-in-exile and prime minister George Papandreou arrived in Athens the country was controlled by EAM. The civil war during the occupation had heightened political tensions. The government and the British feared that the communists might attempt a coup and sought to disarm ELAS. A new bloody conflict broke out in Athens in December 1944. The government with the support of British troops forced ELAS to evacuate the capital and after the Varkiza Agreement (February 1945) the guerrillas surrendered their arms. After the disarmament of the ELAS a period of "white terror" followed during which the ultra-royalist armed bands unleashed a campaign of violence against the leftists in the countryside. The Communist Party abstained from the elections of 1946 and in a climate of disorder and terror the royalists won the absolute majority. The polarization was further aggravated when the royalist government held a rigged plebiscite in September 1946, in which 68 percent voted for the return of the king to Greece.

The armed groups formed by leftists who took to the mountains to escape from right-wing violence began to swell in 1946 and a full-scale civil war between the army and the communist guerrillas of the Democratic Army of Greece (DSE) broke out (1946–1949). The failure of the army to defeat the guerrillas alarmed the United States, which viewed the Greek civil war as another instance of a Soviet-inspired communist expansionism. The declaration of the Truman Doctrine (March 1947) outlined the U.S. foreign policy of "containment" vis-à-vis the Soviet Union, and it was accompanied by generous economic aid to Greece and Turkey, which proved to be crucial for the military victory. On the other hand, the DSE, despite its initial success, faced insurmountable problems, such as few reserves, inferior weapons, and the limited support of the neighboring socialist countries, while the shift from partisan to regular army tactics increased its casualties. The Greek Civil War took a heavy toll: thirty-eight thousand soldiers and guerrillas were killed, seven hundred thousand peasants became war-stricken refugees, and twenty-five thousand boys and girls were evacuated by guerrillas from the war zones to the socialist countries, while in the final stages of the war about fifty-eight thousand people fled the country and became political refugees.

The civil war had a major impact on political developments in Greece. In the following decades political discrimination against the Left became an integral part of the state policy, a combination of anti-communism and nationalism characterized the official ideology, and the army gained considerable political power. Marshal Alexander Papagos, commander-in-chief of the army during the civil war, and Constantine Karamanlis were leaders from the Right who became prime ministers successively (1952–1955 and 1956–1963) and laid the foundations for the economic reconstruction and development. Greece became tied to U.S. security interests and to NATO while at the same time Karamanlis pursued closer relations with Western Europe and in 1961 signed the treaty of association with the European Economic Community (EEC). The elections of 1963 brought

to power the Centre Union and George Papandreou once again became prime minister. The center-left policy of Papandreou's government alarmed King Constantine II (r. 1964–1973) and the army and in July 1965 he was forced to resign when the king refused his request to take over the ministry of defense. Mass demonstrations followed for weeks against the "royal putsch" that ushered in a period of political instability. New elections were called for May 1967 but they never took place. On 21 April 1967 a group of officers organized a coup to preempt the forthcoming victory of the Centre Union in the elections.

THE JUNTA AND RESTORATION OF THE REPUBLIC

The military dictatorship or "colonel's junta" (1967–1974) was a violent reaction of the extreme right in the army against the drive for the democratization of the political structures and institutions that the Centre Union represented. After the abortive counter-coup of the king (December 1967), the dictator Colonel George Papadopoulos became the strong man of the regime. Despite his efforts to give a democratic facade to his regime, political protests against the dictatorship mushroomed in 1973 and culminated in the occupation of the Polytechnic School by students in November 1973, which was violently suppressed by the army. Papadopoulos was then overthrown by one of the hard-liners of the regime, Brigadier Demetrios Ioannidis, head of the military police. The fierce nationalism of the new dictator provoked a major debacle. The junta organized a coup in Cyprus (15 July 1974) and overthrew President Makarios, who fled the island. Turkey took advantage of the opportunity to invade Cyprus (20 July 1974) and has since occupied the northern part (40 percent) of the island. Within a few days the junta collapsed and Karamanlis, who returned from France, became the new prime minister (24 July 1974).

The fall of the dictatorship coincided with the end of Greece's "economic miracle." For twenty years (1953–1973) Greece had an unprecedented economic development as the GDP grew annually by 6.9 percent and the per capita GDP was quadrupled. Greece was no longer a predominantly agrarian country as the number of farmers were reduced (from 58 percent to 40 percent) and the contribution of agriculture to the national economy was halved (from 30 percent to 16 percent). The industrial sector grew, especially the chemical industry, metallurgy, and shipbuilding. During the same years the construction sector took off and became one of the main investments for the middle-classes. The boom of the construction sector was a direct outcome of the internal migration from rural areas to the cities. Athens attracted most of the internal migrants and its population nearly doubled between 1951 and 1971 (from 1.3 million to 2.5 million). During the same period there was also a significant wave of emigration abroad. Between 1951 and 1971, 758,000 Greeks emigrated to Western Europe, the vast majority to West Germany.

POLITICAL CHANGES AND SOCIAL TRANSFORMATIONS IN THE 1980S AND 1990S

The reestablishment of democracy in 1974 ushered in a new era of political stability and modernization. Karamanlis, founder of the New Democracy Party (ND) and prime minister between 1974 and 1980, took the necessary steps to consolidate democracy. After a referendum over the issue of monarchy Greece was proclaimed a republic, the Communist Party (after twenty-seven years of being banned) was legalized, the leading cadres of the dictatorship were prosecuted and received heavy sentences, and, in what represented a sharp symbolic break with the past, the vernacular (*demotiki*) instead of the formal (*katharevousa*) became the language of the state. The other objective that Karamanlis accomplished, despite the reservations of the European Commission because of the poor economic performance of the country, was Greece's entry into the European Economic Community (EEC) in 1981. With Greece's democracy consolidated, the next step was the introduction of social reforms. The Panhellenic Socialist Movement (PASOK), with a rhetoric that mixed nationalism, socialism, and populism and Andreas Papandreou's charisma, appealed broadly to the middle and lower classes and to leftists who had been persecuted for decades.

PASOK won the 1981 elections with the slogan "Change," which denoted both the need for reform in Greek society and for political change. With the exception of a brief period of Centre

Union rule, this was the first time in the postwar years that the power was not in the hands of the right wing. PASOK introduced reforms that were long overdue, such as the recognition of the leftist resistance to the Axis occupation, the right of the political refugees of the civil war to return, the institution of civil marriage, the democratization of the universities, the establishment of a national health service system, and so on. The Greek economy, however, continued to decline. The intensification of competition after the entry of Greece into the EEC and de-industrialization, the overextension of the public sector, and heavy borrowing brought the economy to a dead end in the mid-1980s. At the same time corruption scandals caused disillusionment with PASOK. In 1989 the ND, which won the elections but lacked the majority of the seats in the parliament, took the hitherto unprecedented step of forming a coalition government with the Left. In the elections of 1990 the ND won again and, now with a majority in the parliament, Constantine Mitsotakis became prime minister. The liberalization of the economy and austerity measures resulted in social unrest and union strikes, while the nationalist fervor over the name "Macedonia"— Greece's northern neighbor, the Former Yugoslav Republic of Macedonia (FYROM) sought to use the name, which most Greeks strenuously rejected—brought disarray in the party.

After the elections of 1993 Papandreou again became prime minister but due to failing health was succeeded in 1996 by Kostas Simitis. PASOK followed an economic policy similar to that of ND but sought the consensus of the trade unions. In the 1990s the economy recovered and Greece entered the Economic and Monetary Union (2000) thanks to a large extent to the EU funds, the increasing competitiveness of domestic businesses, the reduction of public expenditure, and the boost that came with winning the competition to host the summer Olympic Games in 2004. The downside of the economic recovery, however, was high unemployment (10 percent), especially among the young and women, the growth of poverty, and widening of economic inequalities. Social discontent with the economic policy of PASOK was expressed in the elections of 2004, in which ND won a clear majority and Kostas Karamanlis, a nephew of Constantine Karamanlis, became the new prime minister. The most significant social phenomenon in the 1990s was the arrival of about one million immigrants, mostly from Albania and the former Soviet Union, which constituted a new experience for a hitherto largely linguistically and religiously homogenous society. The transformation of Greece from a country of emigration into a country of immigration reflects the economic development and social and cultural changes that took place in the last decades of the twentieth century and will shape the Greek society in the future.

See also **Papandreou, Andreas; Venizelos, Eleutherios.**

BIBLIOGRAPHY

Clogg, Richard. *A Concise History of Greece.* Cambridge, U.K., and New York, 1992.

Close, David H. *Greece since 1945: Politics, Economy, and Society.* London and New York, 2002

Gallant, Thomas W. *Modern Greece.* London and New York, 2001.

POLYMERIS VOGLIS

GREENPEACE.

Greenpeace is an international nongovernmental organization that in 2005 had forty-one branches and 2.8 million supporters worldwide. It was founded in 1970 by Canadian and American antiwar activists in Vancouver, British Columbia, to promote a peaceful world based on ecologically sustainable principles. In 1979 it became Greenpeace International and moved its headquarters to Amsterdam.

Greenpeace activists are best known for embracing the Quaker philosophy of "bearing witness" and Mahatma Gandhi's strategy of "nonviolent direct action" to combat nuclear testing, commercial whaling and sealing, toxic-waste dumping, and the like. "We fire images rather than missiles," Robert Hunter, one of the group's founding members, once famously stated, "mind bombs delivered by the world media" (Dyson, p. 58). Since most of their campaigns involve protecting the world's oceans, they rely primarily on an "eco-navy" of small ships outfitted with cameras, satellite technology, and zodiacs (motorized inflatable rafts). They call themselves "Warriors of the Rainbow," a reference to a Cree legend, according to which the races of the world would one day band together under the symbol of the rainbow to restore the earth's biodiversity. Critics decry them as "peace pirates," "eco-guerrillas," and "antinuclear musketeers."

Greenpeace undertook its first major campaign in 1971, when a small group of founding activists steered an old halibut seiner (dubbed *Greenpeace*) and an aging minesweeper (*Greenpeace Too*) to the Aleutian waters of Alaska in a daring effort to stop the United States from detonating a five-megaton nuclear bomb below the surface of Amchitka Island. In 1972 and again in 1973, the group sent the yacht *Greenpeace III* in a similar attempt to deter France from detonating an aboveground nuclear device on Mururoa, an island near Tahiti in the Tuamotu Archipelago of French Polynesia. While these quixotic ventures failed to stop the detonations, they attracted world media attention and helped turn public opinion against the testing. In 1972 the U.S. Atomic Energy Commission announced that it would no longer conduct underground tests in the Aleutians. In 1975 France put a moratorium on all aboveground testing in the South Pacific.

For the next decade, Greenpeace engaged in a series of campaigns to end commercial whaling and sealing and to stop the dumping of toxic wastes in the world's oceans and rivers. In 1977 the group confronted a Soviet whaling flotilla—the factory ship *Dalniy Vostok* and nine whale catchers—off the coast of California. After trying unsuccessfully to position a zodiac in the line of fire between a catcher and a whale, the Greenpeace crew ran their cameras as a Soviet harpooner killed an immature sperm whale in flagrant violation of the 1946 International Convention for the Regulation of Whaling. These images, and many more broadcast around the world in subsequent years, eventually helped force the International Whaling Commission to declare a moratorium on commercial whaling in 1985. Greenpeace launched a similarly successful campaign to halt the killing of baby seals in Newfoundland in 1976. It used the same confrontational tactics to stop ships from dumping radioactive materials and chemical waste in the Atlantic Ocean and North Sea.

When France undertook a series of underground nuclear tests in Mururoa in 1985, Greenpeace sent its flagship, the *Rainbow Warrior,* to the South Pacific to disrupt the testing anew. On 10 July, however, the ship sank while in port in Auckland,

New Zealand, after two explosions blew its hull apart, killing the Greenpeace photographer Fernando Pereira. Suspecting sabotage, New Zealand police soon arrested two French commissioned officers, Major Alain Mafart and Captain Dominique Prieur, who were posing as a honeymoon couple using counterfeit Swiss passports. Further investigation by *Le Monde* and other French newspapers directly implicated the Direction Générale de la Sécurité Extérieure (DGSE), the foreign operations wing of the French secret service. In September, President François Mitterrand and Prime Minister Laurent Fabius admitted that high-ranking government officials had engineered the sabotage. Soon thereafter, Charles Hernu, the minister of defense, and Admiral Pierre Lacoste, the head of the DGSE, resigned their posts. France agreed to pay for the loss of the *Rainbow Warrior* and to compensate Pereira's family. A New Zealand court sentenced Mafart and Prieur to ten years in prison. Aside from tarnishing France's international reputation, there were no other negative consequences of the Greenpeace scandal. Mitterrand was reelected in 1988. France continued to use Mururoa as a nuclear test site (aside from a two-year moratorium) until 1996. Most of the remaining saboteurs, all presumably members of the DGSE, escaped conviction.

In the early twenty-first century Greenpeace remains one of the world's most active environmental organizations. It continues to apply its "bearing witness" and "direct action" strategies to the mining, transport, and disposal of nuclear and other hazardous materials, and to the maintenance of ocean wildlife and ecology.

See also **Environmentalism; Greens.**

BIBLIOGRAPHY

Brown, Michael, and John May. *The Greenpeace Story.* Rev ed. London, 1991.

Dyson, John, with Joseph Fitchett. *Sink the Rainbow!: An Enquiry into the "Greenpeace Affair."* London, 1986.

Hunter, Robert. *Warriors of the Rainbow: A Chronicle of the Greenpeace Movement.* New York, 1979.

Weyler, Rex. *Greenpeace: How a Group of Ecologists, Journalists, and Visionaries Changed the World.* Vancouver, B.C., 2004.

MARK CIOC

GREENS. The term *European Greens* refers to a federation of national political parties that place ecological sustainability and social justice at the forefront of their agendas. The first Green Party, initially called the Ecology Party, was founded by British environmentalists in 1973. The largest and most successful, Die Grünen (The Greens), was founded in West Germany in 1979; it changed its name to Bündnis 90/Die Grünen (Alliance 90/ The Greens) after reunification with East Germany. Similar parties were established elsewhere in Western and Central Europe—the Lista Verdi (Green List) in Italy, Vihreä Liitto (Green Alliance) in Finland, Die Grüne Alternative (The Green Alternative) in Austria, Miljöpartiet de Gröna (Green Ecology Party) in Sweden, Les Verts (The Greens) in France, among others—and by the end of the 1980s there were a small number of Green deputies in several national parliaments. After 1989 Green parties also began to emerge in the former Soviet bloc, most successfully in Latvia and Georgia. In 1984 Green leaders established the European Federation of Green Parties (also known as the European Greens), an umbrella organization headquartered in Brussels, to coordinate their national delegations in the European Parliament. As of 2005 it consisted of thirty-three Green parties from thirty European countries. The European Greens are also part of the Global Greens, a loose network of Green parties and movements from around the world.

FROM SOCIAL MOVEMENTS TO POLITICAL PARTIES

The European Greens began as an amalgam of extraparliamentary movements—led by radical students, feminists, ecologists, peace activists, and New Leftists—dedicated to a thorough transformation of modern industrial society. Over time they evolved into a pragmatic parliamentary force determined to reform the domestic and foreign policies of their governments from within. The transition from movement to party was by no means smooth. Many Green voters continue to think of their organization as an "anti-party party," and to prefer a "principled" (or "fundamentalist") oppositional stance to a "pragmatic" (or "realistic") coalition-building strategy.

The vast majority of Green voters identify with the political Left, and Europeans generally think of the Greens as "left," "center-left," "New Left," "ecosocialist," or (in countries with strong Communist parties) "libertarian left" or "ecoanarchist left." Nonetheless, the Greens defy easy categorization within the traditional European political spectrum. Prominent among West Germany's early members, for instance, were Herbert Gruhl, a disillusioned member of the right-leaning Christian Democratic Union, and Petra Kelly, an equally disillusioned member of the left-leaning Social Democratic Party. When Green deputies first entered the German Bundestag (parliament) in 1983, they insisted on sitting between these two parties on the grounds that they were neither "left nor right, but forward." Similarly, French Greens often refer to themselves as *ninistes*, short for *"ni droit, ni gauche"* (neither right nor left).

The Greens are also somewhat difficult to situate historically. Most of their ideas are firmly rooted in their experiences with the nuclear age, the population boom, mass consumerism, and urban congestion. However, some of their ideas—especially those concerned with natural-resource use and ecological sustainability—date back to the Romantic era and nature-protectionist movements of the nineteenth century. It is probably best to view the Greens primarily as heirs of the peace and ecological movements of the late 1960s and early 1970s and secondarily as neo-preservationists and latter-day Romantics.

Early publications, manifestos, and campaign platforms tended to critique capitalism, environmental degradation, female inequality, and the nuclear arms race while promoting grassroots democracy, nonviolence, and global responsibility—all familiar themes of the radical 1960s. Green writings were also deeply infused with the rhetoric of the 1970s, when issues of acid rain, the ozone layer, fisheries decline, global warming, species extinction, and "limits to growth" were front and center in the media. Since the collapse of the Soviet Union in the 1990s the Greens have placed more emphasis on the themes of cultural diversity, equal opportunity, indigenous rights, social justice, ecologically sustainable development, and global security. The commitment to a thorough rethinking of modern civilization has remained a constant theme, despite changes in tactics and slogans. The foreword to the Guiding Principles of the European Greens reads: "The so-called progress of the past centuries has brought us into a situation where the basis of life on Earth is seriously under threat. While technological development may delay the deterioration of the environment for a time, it cannot prevent the ecological and social collapse of civilization without a fundamental change in the ideology of unquestioned material growth which still prevails."

As a rule, Greens in northern (Protestant) Europe have fared better than those in southern (Catholic) Europe. This is partly because northern Europe is more heavily industrialized and possesses a more vibrant nature-protection tradition and partly because southern Europe has a number of well-entrenched Communist parties that absorb much of the protest vote that would otherwise go to the Greens. Western European Green parties are generally bigger and more influential than their Eastern European counterparts, no doubt because they are located in countries that already enjoy stable democracies and prosperous economies. The Greens do far better in countries that elect parliaments based on proportional representation than in those that do not. This is because the Greens typically receive only a small percentage of the national vote and therefore stand little chance in "winner-take-all" elections such as those in Britain and the United States. Internal dissension and factionalism has also undermined the electoral prospects of some Green parties.

GREENS IN GERMANY AND FRANCE

Germany's Alliance 90/The Greens has been Europe's most successful environmental party. It won twenty-seven parliamentary seats in 1983 with 5.6 percent of the vote and forty-two seats in 1987 with 8.3 percent. The party suffered a temporary reversal of fortunes in 1990 when it fell below the minimum threshold of 5 percent for representation in parliament, a setback that was largely a consequence of the party's inflexible opposition to the government's popular reunification policies. In 1991 the party embarked on a more realistic path to political power (the *Aufbruch*, or "new departure"), and enjoyed a string of electoral successes: 7.3 percent of the vote (forty-nine seats) in 1994,

6.7 percent (forty-seven seats) in 1998, and 8.6 percent (fifty-five seats) in 2002. The Greens became junior partners in a governing coalition for the first time in 1998 under Chancellor Gerhard Schröder (Social Democrat). The Greens have held three cabinet posts in each of Schröder's two administrations, including the Ministry of Foreign Affairs (held by Joschka Fischer since 1998); Ministry of Environment, Nature Conservation, and Reactor Safety (Jürgen Trittin since 1998); Ministry of Health (Andrea Fischer from 1998 to 2002); and Ministry of Consumer Protection, Food, and Agriculture (Renate Künast since 2002). No other Green Party in the world has enjoyed this level of influence and power.

France's Green Party (Les Verts) has struggled to find a niche for itself as a radical non-Marxist party capable of competing with the well-established Socialist and Communist parties. Initially dominated by New Left activists, Les Verts came under the control of the pragmatic Antoine Waechter from 1986 to 1993. Waechter's leadership netted the party some significant electoral successes, most notably in the 1989 European Parliament elections, when it captured 10.6 percent of the vote and received nine deputies. One of those deputies, Marie Anne Isler-Béguin, served as vice president of the European Parliament from 1991 to 1994. Dissension from within, however, led to the establishment of several rival parties, chief among them the Génération Ecologie. After several electoral defeats at the local and national levels, Les Verts came under the leadership of Dominique Voynet. As in Germany, Les Verts formed an alliance with the Socialist Party for the 1997 national elections and netted eight deputies to the National Assembly. It then joined the governing coalition of Prime Minister Lionel Jospin (Socialist) between 1997 and 2002, in return for which it received one cabinet position, the Ministry of Environment and Regional Planning (held by Dominique Voynet until 2001). In the 2004 European Parliament elections, Les Verts won 8.4 percent of the vote, giving it six deputies.

OTHER COUNTRIES

Other Green parties have also had a taste of power, if only fleetingly. Sweden's Green Ecology Party received 5.5 percent of the vote in the 1988 national elections, becoming the first new party to enter the Swedish parliament in seven decades. It dropped below the 4 percent threshold in the 1991 elections but rebounded with 5 percent of the vote in 1994 and 4.5 percent in 1998. It also won 17.2 percent of the vote in the 1995 European Parliament elections, a record high for an environmental party. It has maintained an informal alliance with the reigning Social Democratic government since 1998. Finland's Green Alliance won 7.3 percent of the vote and eleven seats in parliament in 1999. It was a junior partner in a broad governing coalition until 2002, when it quit in protest over the government's nuclear policies. Italy's Green List entered the legislature for the first time in 1987 with thirteen deputies and two senators and briefly became part of the governing coalition (with two ministerial portfolios) from 1998 to 1999. In 2004 Latvia elected the Green leader Indulis Emsis as its prime minister, marking the first time that a European Green has ever reached such a position.

Most Green parties had yet to move from being an opposition force to being part of a governing coalition as of 2004. Switzerland enjoys the distinction of being the first European country to elect a Green member to a national parliament, and the Swiss Greens typically capture 5 to 8 percent of the national vote, but the party has yet to join the circles of government. Austria's Green Alternative (or "Greens," as they came to be known in the 1990s) has had considerable success in local and regional elections and been represented in parliament since 1986. It allied itself with the Socialists in the 2002 elections and captured 9.5 percent of the vote, but that was still not enough to secure a Socialist-Green governing majority. Luxembourg's Greens have also been shut out of the corridors of power, despite winning 11.6 percent of the vote in the national elections of 2004, a record high for a Green Party in a European national election. Britain's Green Party has been hampered by internal divisions and by the "winner-take-all" voting system. It made a big splash in the European Parliament elections of 1989, when it garnered 14.9 percent of the vote, but it has never surpassed 2.9 percent of the vote in national elections and has never elected a member to Parliament.

In 2004 the European Greens collectively held 4 national ministerial posts, 169 legislative seats in 15 national parliaments, and 33 seats in the European Parliament. The German Greens alone accounted for 3 of those ministerial posts, 55 of the national seats, and 13 of the European Parliament seats. Many European voters continue to see Green parties as single-purpose environmentalists, despite the wide range of issues that they champion, and to view them with skepticism, despite their efforts to move from the extraparliamentary fringe to the parliamentary mainstream. The Greens have nonetheless managed to increase their share of the vote slowly but steadily since the 1980s, and they are likely to remain a vibrant force in European politics for the foreseeable future.

See also **Environmentalism.**

BIBLIOGRAPHY

Capra, Fritjof, and Charlene Spretnak. *Green Politics.* New York, 1984.

Dobson, Andrew. *Green Political Thought: An Introduction.* London, 1990.

Mayer, Margit, and John Ely, eds. *The German Greens: Paradox between Movement and Party.* Philadelphia, 1998.

O'Neill, Michael. *Green Parties and Political Change in Contemporary Europe: New Politics, Old Predicaments.* Aldershot, U.K., 1997.

Parkin, Sara. *Green Parties: An International Guide.* London, 1989.

Porritt, Jonathon, and David Winner. *The Coming of the Greens.* London, 1988.

Shull, Tad. *Redefining Red and Green: Ideology and Strategy in European Political Ecology.* Albany, N.Y., 1999.

Talshir, Gayil. *The Political Ideology of Green Parties: From the Politics of Nature to Redefining the Nature of Politics.* New York, 2002.

MARK CIOC

GROPIUS, WALTER (1883–1969), one of the most celebrated and influential architects of the twentieth century.

Walter Adolph Gropius enjoyed a lengthy and productive career in Germany, England, and the United States that spanned the years 1908 until his death in Cambridge, Massachusetts, in 1969. Descended from an established Berlin family that

included such successful architects as his great uncle, Martin Gropius of the nineteenth-century "Schinkel school," Walter Gropius experienced a meteoric rise to prominence through a combination of ambition, charisma, and organizational ability. His talent for attracting and collaborating with leading lights of the artistic and architectural world throughout his life helped him to realize a long line of significant projects. These, in turn, helped define the vocabulary and principles of twentieth-century architecture and design.

Gropius occupied a string of prominent leadership posts for most of his career. These included his founding and direction of the Bauhaus school in 1919; his catalytic presence as a faculty member and department head at the Harvard Graduate School of Design's department of architecture from 1937 to 1952; and his leadership of The Architects Collaborative (TAC) firm in Cambridge, Massachusetts, beginning in 1946. Frequent lectures and publications espousing Gropius's view that architecture should always take account of technical, economic, and social conditions kept him in the international public eye and at the center of the modern architectural profession for several decades.

Born in Berlin in 1883, Gropius completed studies in several Berlin Gymnasium schools. Following one semester at the Munich Technical University, he completed architectural studies at the Technical University of Berlin-Charlottenburg in 1907. After a year-long study tour in Spain, Gropius gained employment in the most prestigious and progressive architectural office of the day, the office of Peter Behrens in the Berlin suburb of Neubabelsberg. Assisting Behrens in work for the industrial giant AEG, Germany's General Electric Corporation, between 1908 and 1910, Gropius worked alongside Ludwig Mies van der Rohe and got to know his future design partner, Adolf Meyer, with whom he worked between 1910 and 1925.

Gropius and Meyer rose to prominence with their design of the pathbreaking Fagus Factory in Alfeld-an-der-Leine, Germany, in 1911, along with the equally provocative Model Factory at the Deutscher Werkbund Exhibition in Cologne in 1914. Both buildings are regarded to this day as among the earliest essays in an industrial, monumental architecture for twentieth-century secular, functional buildings. Each makes dramatic use of brick, steel, and wide expanses of glass in sober exteriors that owe something to the classicism of Behrens while exceeding the older master's work in their frank and expressive use of industrial materials.

Gropius's founding and directorship of the Bauhaus from 1919 through 1928 in Weimar and then Dessau secured him a leading role among the artistic and architectural avant-garde of the turbulent Weimar era. Assembling such artistic luminaries as Paul Klee, Wassily Kandinsky, Johannes Itten, Lyonel Feininger, and László Moholy-Nagy as faculty members for a small yet lively interdisciplinary school of fine art, applied art, architecture, and design, Gropius proudly polemicized in favor of a new German architecture and art that combined craftsmanship and industrial know-how with such international avant-garde artistic movements as expressionism, Dada, Dutch neoplasticism, and Russian constructivism. Gropius's Bauhaus building of 1926 in Dessau, completed in the same year that the school at last opened a department of architecture, again underscored Gropius's reputation as one of the most innovative and visionary architects of the industrial era. The building's expressive massing, ribbon windows and glass curtain walls, and functional differention all contributed to what in a few years would come to be known as the "International Style."

Emigrating to the United States in 1937 after a three-year stint in England, Gropius accepted dean Joseph Hudnut's invitation to join the architecture faculty of the Harvard Graduate School of Design. Partnering with former Bauhaus designer Marcel Breuer, and then founding a firm, The Architects Collaborative, in 1946, Gropius collaborated on a wide range of projects including modern suburban housing developments in Cambridge, Massachusetts; the U.S. Embassy in Athens, 1956–1961; the University of Baghdad, 1957–1960; and the Pan Am Building, a high-rise office building atop New York's Grand Central Station, completed with Pietro Belluschi (1899–1994) in 1957. Increasingly resented in his later years by a younger generation of architects who came to regard the German émigré architect as a dogmatic exponent for an intolerant, acontextual, and universalist modernist aesthetic, Gropius saw his popularity wane in the 1960s with the rise of new movements such as postmodernism, ecological design, and critical regionalism. Nevertheless, Gropius's insistence on humanistic design that took account of social, economic, and technical factors had a lasting impact on modern architecture in Germany, the United States, and throughout the industrialized world.

See also **Bauhaus; Kandinsky, Wassily; Klee, Paul; Mies van der Rohe, Ludwig; Moholy-Nagy, László.**

BIBLIOGRAPHY

Franciscono, Marcel. *Walter Gropius and the Creation of the Bauhaus in Weimar: The Ideals and Artistic Theories of its Founding Years.* Urbana, Ill., 1971.

Giedion, Siegfried. *Walter Gropius: Work and Teamwork.* New York, 1954. Reprint, New York, 1992.

Nerdinger, Winfried. *Walter Gropius.* Berlin, 1985.

Wilhelm, Karen. *Walter Gropius: Industriearchitekt.* Braunschweig, 1983.

Wingler, Hans Maria. *Das Bauhaus 1919–1933: Weimar, Dessau, Berlin.* Bramsche, 1962.

JOHN V. MACIUIKA

GROSSMAN, VASILY (1905–1964), writer.

Vasily Semyonovich Grossman was born on 12 December 1905 to cultured, assimilated Jewish parents in the town of Berdichev, in Ukraine. He graduated from Moscow State University in December 1929 as a chemical engineer but wanted to be a writer. A number of innovative but enthusiastically Soviet works gained him admission to the privileged Union of Soviet Writers in 1937. Grossman might have remained an ardent Soviet writer but for his experiences as a frontline correspondent during World War II. He spent more than a thousand days at the front, witnessing the street fighting at Stalingrad and accompanying the Red Army on its long drive from Ukraine to Berlin. He gained national fame for his lively, sensitive reporting and ended the war a decorated lieutenant colonel in the Red Army. After the war, his desire to tell the truth about the collaboration of some Soviet nationals in the murder of their Jewish neighbors during the German occupation put him at loggerheads with official government policy. Grossman had discovered that his mother was among the twenty thousand Jews murdered in Berdichev on 15 September 1941, and he would not give up trying to write that history. As a result, the Soviet authorities under both Joseph Stalin and

The Soviet Union's famous war memorial at Stalingrad (now Volgograd) quotes "In the Line of the Main Drive," Vasily Grossman's most celebrated war report, which appeared in *Red Star*, the Red Army newspaper, in 1942. In huge granite letters, a German soldier asks, "They are attacking us again; can they be mortal?" Inside the mausoleum, tooled in gold around the base of the giant dome, a Red Army soldier gives the answer: "Yes, we were mortal indeed, and few of us survived, but we all carried out our patriotic duty before holy Mother Russia." "In the Line of the Main Drive" was reprinted in *Pravda* during the war, but although Grossman finished the war as a decorated lieutenant colonel in the Red Army, he later became a critic of the regime and Soviet designers refused to speak his name at the memorial where he had witnessed and written about a soldier's courage under fire.

Nikita Khrushchev labeled him an enemy of the state. His manuscripts were suppressed and buried in archives; his published works were removed from libraries. When he died of stomach cancer on 14 September 1964 (the eve of the twenty-third anniversary of the murder of the Jews of Berdichev), he was officially a nonperson.

Grossman married twice. His first marriage ended in divorce but gave him his only child, Yekaterina, born in January 1930. In 1935 he married Olga Mikhailovna Guber, the former wife of the writer Boris Guber, who was arrested and executed in 1937 for "anti-Soviet activities." When Olga Mikhailovna was herself arrested by the NKVD (the Soviet secret police) in 1938, Grossman courageously wrote a letter to Nikolai Yezhov, the head of the NKVD, explaining that she was no longer the wife of an "enemy of the people" (Boris Guber) but his own spouse. Grossman obtained her release and adopted her two sons so they would not be sent to special camps for the children of those who had been arrested.

After the war, Grossman fell in love with Yekaterina Zabolotskaya, wife of the poet Nikolai

Zabolotsky, and they lived together for two years. Although both returned to their spouses, their love endured as deep friendship and trust until Grossman's death. Grossman secretly entrusted his final typescript of *Forever Flowing* to Zabolotskaya on his deathbed. She kept it safe for decades before giving it to John Garrard of the University of Arizona for transfer to the West, where it was deposited in the Andrei Sakharov Archive at Harvard University.

Grossman remained relatively unknown in the West until the posthumous publication of his major novel, *Life and Fate,* in Lausanne, Switzerland, in 1980, after friends smuggled a copy to the West. In 1962, after the KGB had seized the original manuscript of *Life and Fate,* Mikhail Suslov, the ideological boss of the Communist Party, told Grossman that the novel threatened harm to the Soviet people, the Soviet state, and "all those struggling to achieve communism beyond Soviet borders." The novel could be published inside the Soviet Union, he said, "in 250 years." What was so dangerous about a novel centered on the battle for Stalingrad written by the Red Army's premier war correspondent? This was the same Vasily Grossman whose pieces about the heroic Stalingrad garrison, such as "Stalingrad Hits Back" and "In the Line of the Main Drive," had been published in 1942 to universal acclaim in the Red Army's newspaper, *Red Star.* But *Life and Fate* struck at the heart of the Soviet assertion that Adolf Hitler's Germany was the diametrical opposite of Stalin's Soviet Union. Grossman showed two warring totalitarian regimes that were mirror images of each other. Grossman was the first Soviet writer or historian to perceive them this way but did not become the first to publish.

Grossman amplified this comparison in *Forever Flowing,* which after his death was also smuggled to the West for publication in Frankfurt, Germany, in 1970. In it, Grossman compared Hitler's hierarchy based on race to Vladimir Lenin's hierarchy based on class. Both grounded their appeals on the powerful nationalist extremism stirring in their populations, and both ideologies led to state chauvinism and state-sponsored anti-Semitism. In *Life and Fate,* Grossman spoke ostensibly about Nazi Germany, arguing that "in totalitarian countries, where society as such no longer exists, only State anti-Semitism

Vasily Grossman's "Trial of the Four Judases," in his novella *Forever Flowing,* is his strongest indictment of Soviet totalitarianism. Since the state's legal code punished not only the offender but also anyone who knew but did not report subversive behavior, the regime encouraged citizens to betray one another. Thus there were many Judases, for virtually no person—and Grossman included himself in this indictment—could survive and be totally innocent. In this page of the original typescript, Grossman added in his own handwriting "Iuda" (Judas), to emphasize that betrayal was at the heart of the Soviet state.

can arise. This is a sign that the State is looking for the support of fools, reactionaries and failures, that it is seeking to capitalize on the ignorance of the superstitious and the anger of the hungry." The criticism applied to Soviet Russia, as well.

See also **Anti-Semitism; Red Army; Samizdat; Soviet Union.**

BIBLIOGRAPHY

Primary Sources

Grossman, Vasily. *The Years of War (1941–1945).* Translated by Elizabeth Donnelly and Rose Prokofiev. Moscow, 1946. A collection of Grossman's articles and reports from Stalingrad to Berlin.

———. *Life and Fate: A Novel.* Translated by Robert Chandler. New York, 1986.

———. *Forever Flowing.* Evanston, Ill., 1997.

Ehrenburg, Ilya, and Vasily Grossman, eds. *The Black Book: The Ruthless Murder of the Jews by German-Fascist Invaders throughout the Temporarily-Occupied Regions of the Soviet Union and in the Death Camps of Poland during the War of 1941–1945.* Translated by John Glad and James Levine. New York, 1981.

Secondary Sources

Ellis, Frank. *Vasiliy Grossman: The Genesis and Evolution of a Russian Heretic.* Oxford, U.K., 1994.

Garrard, John. "The Original Manuscript of *Forever Flowing:* Grossman's Autopsy of the New Soviet Man." *Slavic and East European Journal* 38, no. 2 (1994): 271–289.

———. "Vasilii Grossman and the Holocaust on Soviet Soil." In *Jews and Jewish Life in Russia and the Soviet Union,* edited by Yaacov Ro'i, 212–225. Ilford, U.K., 1995.

Garrard, John, and Carol Garrard. *The Bones of Berdichev: The Life and Fate of Vasily Grossman.* New York, 1996.

JOHN GARRARD

GROSZ, GEORGE (1893–1959), German artist.

George Grosz, originally named Georg Ehrenfried Groß, was born in Berlin. After earning his diploma from the Royal Academy of Beaux-Arts in Dresden, he volunteered as a medical recruit in November 1914 in order to avoid the draft and was sent to the front. He received a medical discharge in 1915 and changed his name the following year as an act of protest against German nationalism and patriotism. He was joined in this by his artist friend Helmut Herzfelde, who renamed himself John Heartfield. He was called up again in 1917, became severely depressed, and was interned at the psychiatric hospital in Görden before being definitively discharged.

Grosz returned to a Berlin that seemed to him cold and gray. The pessimism he felt because of the war and his hospitalization among the maimed and wounded led him to produce oil paintings depicting apocalyptic end-of-war scenes. In his *Metropolis* (1916–1917), expressionist elements compete with futurist ones, with entangled lines, multiple planes, and sticklike, almost transparent figures suggesting the simultaneity of the various events being depicted. The predominance of orange-red speaks of fire, destruction, and the swirling abyss. The same spirit haunts *Widmung an Oskar Panizza* (1917–1918; Homage to Oskar Panizza), which expresses his disgust with war and his hatred of the Catholic Church and the political authorities. In this visionary representation of universal destruction, Grosz depicts half-human characters in ridiculous poses: "A diabolical procession of beings no longer at all human steals down a foreign street, with Alcohol, Syphilis and the Plague written on their faces. . . . I was protesting against a Humanity gone crazy, by painting it" (quoted in Kranzfelder, p. 23).

Gray Day. Painting by George Grosz, 1921. BILDARCHIV PREUSSICHER KULTURBESITZ/ART RESOURCE, NY. ART © ESTATE OF GEORGE GROSZ/LICENSED BY VAGA, NEW YORK, NY

In 1917 Grosz cofounded Berlin's Dada movement with Richard Huelsenbeck and Raoul Hausmann. Dada furnished a climate, philosophy, and method that permitted Grosz to unleash himself against the institutions of the young Weimar Republic. He mixed watercolor, collage, ink, and pencil. In oil paintings such as *Grauer Tag* (1921; Gray day), he caricatured what he called the Organizers, bourgeois war profiteers crushing their victims (workers or communists), who are compartmentalized by a stylized architecture averse to linear spaces.

After joining the Communist Party in 1918, "Marshal Dada" (as he nicknamed himself) rejected bourgeois traditions and engaged in a radical artistic political combat, in which the artist is dedicated to revolutionary change. In his drawing *Die Kommunisten Fallen und die Devisen Steigen*

(1919; The Communists fall and the foreign exchange rises), made in 1919, the same year Spartacus League founders Rosa Luxemburg and Karl Liebknecht were assassinated, Grosz denounced the crushing of the Spartacist revolution by Social Democratic leaders. His satirical drawings were characteristic of the revolutionary art and politics he had published in numerous journals since 1910, including *Ulk, Lustige Blätter*, and *Editions Malik*. To further the revolution he founded a satirical journal, *Die Pleite*, with the Herzfelde brothers, which later appeared under the name *Schutzhaft*, both of which were censored when they first appeared. Grosz defined himself as an "impartial and scientific observer" of German society. His rapid, uncorrected sketches from 1920 through 1923 focused on the situation immediately after the war and during the periods of runaway inflation; they depict cafés and street scenes filled with caricatured figures, including sinister-looking bourgeois humiliating maimed and dismembered veterans. His lines are blistering, deformed, and overlaid by watercolors. He made use of refined observation to denounce a bruised society: "In this way, bit by bit I developed the harsh and decisive style I needed to depict what was inspired in me by my absolute disgust with Men."

Grosz gave these remarks material content in his collection *Ecce Homo*, which was received with accusations that he was degrading public morals. In *Ecce Homo* (published in 1922–1923) and in *Das Neue Gesicht der Herrschenden Klasse: 55 Politische Zeichunungen* (The new face of the ruling class: 55 political drawings), published in 1922, he depicted bourgeois society at its most vulnerable point by exposing its private life, unveiling the obsessions and sexual excesses of a bourgeois hiding behind the mask of the upright man and defender of political morality.

As a friend of the painter Otto Dix, Grosz took part in the 1925 exposition *New Objectivity* at the Kuntshalle in Mannheim. Between 1925 and 1928 he returned to painting and the battle waged on: *Die Stützen der Gesellschaft* (1926; Pillars of society) and *The Agitator* (1928) denounced the enemies of democracy. As an artist he came to constitute a kind of memorial to the conscience of an entire nation. His status as a chronicler was transformed into that of clairvoyant witness to the rise of Nazism, and he became one of the most hated artists under the Third Reich, which labeled his works "degenerate" and subsequently destroyed them. He left for the United States in 1933 and in 1941 began to teach at Columbia University. As a distant observer of the political situation in Germany, he produced works that translated his personal dismay into visual form. Although his portraits and watercolors from this period appeared tranquil on the surface, they were still fueled by the underlying cynicism that marked his early work. He published his autobiography in 1946 before returning to Berlin, where he died in 1959.

See also Communism; Dada; Degenerate Art Exhibit; Dix, Otto; Liebknecht, Karl; Luxemburg, Rosa; Nazism; World War I.

BIBLIOGRAPHY

Primary Sources

Grosz, George. *Un petit oui et un grand non.* Translated by Christian Bounay. Paris, 1990.

Secondary Sources

Flavell, M. Kay. *George Grosz: A Biography.* New Haven, Conn., 1988.

Grosz/Heartfield: The Artist as Social Critic, October 1–November 8, 1980, University Gallery University of Minnesota. Minneapolis, Minn., 1980.

Hess, Hans. *George Grosz.* New Haven, Conn., 1985.

Kranzfelder, Ivo. *George Grosz.* Translated by Annie Berthold. Cologne, 2001.

CAROLINE TRON-CARROZ

GUERNICA. In 1937 Spain was in the midst of a civil war which had begun in 1936 between the left-wing government of the Second Republic (made up of a coalition of Socialists, Republicans, and reformists) and its supporters, and right-wing insurgents, known as Nationalists. With the active help of Fascist Italy and Nazi Germany, and aided by French and British indecisiveness, Spanish Nationalist generals, with their head, General Emilio Mola, mounted a new offensive, directed against civilian targets, on 31 March 1937. A German Luftwaffe squadron known as the Condor Legion, under the command of the future

Marshal Wolfram von Richthofen, carried out the attacks: one by one, the cities of Guernica, Bilbao, and Gijón were destroyed, leaving the Basque Country in ruins. The bombing of Guernica on 26 April 1937, which killed mostly women, children, and the elderly, stunned the world.

In response to a command issued by the Spanish Republican government, in June 1937 Pablo Picasso (1881–1973) presented, at the Spanish Pavilion of the Paris International Exposition, a painting laden with a mere three somber tones: black, gray, and white. Its title was *Guernica* (782 × 351 cm), a canvas unsigned, undated, and unframed, painted in Ripolin, an industrial paint. More than just a masterpiece, *Guernica* expresses the suffering and barbarity of war. *Guernica* has remained a tour de force because Picasso was so successful at signifying the meaning of a historical event by overlaying autobiographical elements onto allusions to the massacres and to death itself. However, in its depiction of the upheaval of an entire society, *Guernica* does more than merely mark an event. This canvas, completed just days after the bombardment of the Basque village Guernica by the Junker 52s and Heinkel 51s of the Condor Legion, gave Picasso the opportunity to pick up his brushes again in a way that synthesized his recent output with earlier exploratory works such as *La Corrida* (1933) and *Minotauromachy* (1935).

The point of departure for these pieces was Picasso's desire to construct a personalized mythological iconography that conveyed highly readable meanings through shapes that bordered on the irrational. *Guernica* was the result of a long process that transpired through numerous preparatory works, in particular the two series of etched engravings entitled *Dream and Lie of Franco, I and II* (1937). The detailing and positioning of the figures on the canvas is arranged into eight stages completed between 11 May and 4 June 1937, documented with the aid of photographs taken by Picasso's companion Dora Maar (1907–1997). Picasso chose not to literally retranscribe the massacre—there are no planes or bombs, but the name he chose belies any alternate interpretation of its subject. In this way he transferred the event into a more complex space insofar as its plot unfolds in the interval between inside (the light fixture, the

Guernica. Painting by Pablo Picasso, 1937. AP/WIDE WORLD PHOTOS

window, and the door) and outside. The tragedy occurs in an intermediary place where animals and women are icons of universal suffering. Picasso played with lighting in order to dramatize his composition, which was founded on nuances of gray that work together to forge a differentiation between planes and volumes. This is why the principal characters are bathed in bright light, including the bull, the horse, the warrior, and the four women: the woman with the child, the woman falling, the fleeing woman, and the woman by the lamp. These figures contrast with the remaining elements, which are darker, each assuming a place within a central triangle, on both sides of which two other triangles are drawn, encased within two white vertical stripes.

Guernica has elicited numerous interpretations, most notably concerning the symbolic significance of the characters and about the canvas's chromatic oppositions, which appear to be an attempt to re-create photographs that appeared in the press. Picasso avoided saying anything explicit in this regard in public, remaining content to reaffirm his support for the Spanish Republic. The author Michel Leiris, however, summed up the message and importance of *Guernica* in a few simple lines: "In a black and white rectangle like the appearance of a Greek Tragedy, Picasso is sending us our letter of mourning: Everything we love is

going to die, and this is why it was necessary that everything we love be encapsulated, like the effusion of some grand adieux, in something unforgettably beautiful" (Leiris, p. 128; translated from the French).

After World War II, Picasso produced numerous paintings, lithographs, posters, and ceramic sculptures, but created just one solitary work connected to the war. As he himself would say: "I did not paint the War because I do not belong to that class of painters who go out in search of a subject like a photographer does" (Daix, p. 280; translated from the French). He did nonetheless finish one painting entitled *Le Charnier* (Mass grave), dated 1945, following the discovery of the concentration camps, which utilizes the same underlying assumptions as those used to produce *Guernica. Le Charnier* is not about depicting the horror of the camps, but instead concerns transposing this reality into the iconography of a painter in search of the universal. The painting's expository context was also the focal point for numerous polemics. Many other of Picasso's works, such as *L'Aubade* (The dawn serenade) from 1942, contained underlying allusions to World War II. However, in 1951 Picasso produced a much more explicit painting based on the famous execution scenes by Francisco de Goya (1746–1928) and Edouard Manet (1832–1883) and titled *Massacre in Korea,* but it did not enjoy to the same success as *Guernica*.

Guernica's destiny echoed the political turmoil of the era—it was shown in Norway, then in London, after which it spent time in New York, before coming to rest in the Prado Museum, the venue Picasso himself had wished for it. *Guernica*'s travels were not limited by geography, however—its trek continued on film, when it became the primary object of an eponymous movie directed by Alain Resnais and Robert Hessens in 1950.

See also **Picasso, Pablo; Spain; Spanish Civil War; World War II.**

BIBLIOGRAPHY

Baer, Brigitte. *Picasso, peintre-graveur: Catalogue raisonné de l'œuvre gravé et des monotypes, 1899–1972.* Bern, Switzerland, 1993–1996.

Bernadac, Marie-Laure. *Faces of Picasso.* Translated by Jean-Marie Clarke. Paris, 1990.

Butor, Michel. *Picasso's Studios: The Alembic of Forms.* Paris, 2003.

Chipp, Herschel Browing, and Javier Tusell. *Picasso's Guernica: History, Transformations, Meanings.* Berkeley, Calif., 1988.

Cowling, Elisabeth. *Picasso: Sculptor/Painter.* London, 1994.

———. *Picasso: Style and Meaning.* London, 2002.

Daix. Pierre. *Picasso créateur.* Paris, 1987.

Daix, Pierre, and Georges Boudaille. *Picasso 1900–1906: Catalogue raisonné de l'œuvre peint.* Neuchâtel, 1966.

Florman, Lisa. *Myth and Metamorphosis: Picasso's Classical Prints of the 1930s.* Cambridge, Mass., 2000.

Leiris, Michel. *Haut Mal.* Paris, 1943.

McCully, Marylin. *A Picasso Anthology: Documents, Criticism, Reminiscences.* Princeton, N.J., 1981.

Nash, Steven A., and Robert Rosenblum, eds. *Picasso and the War Years, 1937–1945.* New York, 1998.

Opller, Ellen C. *Picasso's Guernica: Illustrations, Introductory Essay, Documents, Poetry, Criticism, Analysis.* New York, 1988.

Richardson, John, with Marilyn McCully. *A Life of Picasso.* New York, 1991.

Shapiro, Meyer. *The Unity of Picasso's Art.* New York, 2000.

Stein, Gertrude. *Picasso.* London, 1939. Reprint, New York, 1984.

CYRIL THOMAS

GUERRILLA WARFARE.

Carl von Clausewitz wrote in *On War* (1832) that a people's war (*Volkskrieg*) in "civilized Europe" was a phenomenon of the nineteenth century. He recognized that it was a function of the popular nationalism unleashed by the great French Revolution; it meant that war was no longer merely the business of generals and armies, limited by the rules, conventions, and laws of war. Instead ordinary people would fight with whatever weapons they had, however bad the military odds, to preserve the "soul" of their country. Clausewitz had seen this happen in Russia and in Spain, where the partisans, or *partidos,* had conducted protracted struggles against Napoleon's armies in what would become best known as guerrilla warfare, *la guerra de guerrillas* (literally, war of little wars). It would recur several times during the nineteenth century, notably during the American Civil War, the Franco-German War of 1870–1871, and the British invasion of the Boer republics (the so-called Second War of Independence) of 1899–1902. In all these cases, as in Spain and Russia, guerrilla warfare was a defensive reaction to foreign invasion, a product of international conflict; such reactions would recur in Europe in the twentieth century as well. But more striking still would be the proactive, insurgent form in which guerrilla warfare became the vehicle of internal revolution. This had been presaged by the Italian nationalist Giuseppe Mazzini, though his inspirational tracts on guerrilla fighting never succeeded in generating an effective guerrilla campaign—his dream of Italian national liberation was only realized by conventional military action.

The first modern European guerrilla insurgency in the cause of "national liberation" was launched in Macedonia at the beginning of the twentieth century. The Internal Macedonian Revolutionary Organization (IMRO) faced the task of building up a sense of nationality as well as conducting a military campaign and was strikingly successful in both enterprises until it took the premature decision to shift from guerrilla to conventional operations. This problem, of grasping the exact potential and limits of guerrilla methods, would recur in many subsequent attempts at insurgency. The technique became better understood at the end of World War I. The war in Europe was almost entirely "regular," though there was some guerrilla resistance in Serb territory occupied by the Habsburg army, and the German army used sporadic Belgian franc-tireur activity as the pretext for violent reprisals against civilians. In German East Africa, however, a remarkably successful guerrilla campaign was conducted by a regular German officer, Paul von Lettow-Vorbeck, with a small force of local *askaris*—the opposite, in fact, of a "national liberation" struggle. But Lettow's achievement in holding off a vastly larger (albeit very second-rate) British imperial army for the whole duration of the war demonstrated the potential of the strategy and may have added credibility to T. E. Lawrence's contention that the Arab revolt of 1916–1918 was a decisive guerrilla victory. The actual performance of the Arab forces that Lawrence and other British advisors helped to organize has been disputed, but the impact of Lawrence's writings about the campaign was indisputable.

Lawrence proposed a reversal of conventional military wisdom, contending that "granted mobility, security, time, and doctrine, victory will rest with the insurgents" (1920). Guerrilla forces that could hit and run, striking only in favorable situations, could outlast the power of regular armies. The key requirement was "doctrine," or ideology, and this might be either socialism or nationalism, or indeed both. The numbers of active insurgents might be very small—as few as 2 percent of the population, Lawrence suggested, provided 80 percent were sympathetic. This would ensure that the incumbent forces could not get the intelligence information they would need to locate the guerrilla forces. The theory was revolutionary, and if some people still questioned the relevance of the Arab campaign—"a sideshow of a sideshow"—from the European standpoint—its publication coincided with an Irish republican guerrilla campaign inside the United Kingdom in which a few hundred fighters defied the British army for long enough to bring about political concessions. The Irish Republican Army's (IRA) achievement was psychological as much as military; it convinced the British government that it had the backing of the Irish people and that purely military repression would be pointless. It never needed to develop the capacity to take on military units larger than a company fifty to one hundred strong. It demonstrated that survival was as important as the ability to inflict

damage. The question of whether a government less ready to compromise than the British could be defeated by guerrilla methods remained unanswered. The experience of the Russian civil war, however, in which a skillfully led anarchist guerrilla army was ultimately overwhelmed by the Red Army, indicated that Lawrence's claim might have been overstated.

Certainly the Bolshevik leadership seems to have drawn this conclusion. Leon Trotsky called guerrilla warfare "the truly peasant form of war," and in Marxist terms this was at best a limited endorsement. It was primitive, and though it might sometimes be necessary it was not inherently revolutionary. Joseph Stalin, originally a more enthusiastic "guerrillaist," soon lost his enthusiasm in the aftermath of the civil war. Its anarchic potential was increasingly unattractive, and in the Spanish civil war there was no Soviet support for a form of warfare that might have been expected to play a major if not decisive role in the struggle between nationalists and republicans. Despite the impression created by some visiting litterateurs, guerrilla activity was fleeting and disconnected. The overriding necessity of defending the main cities, and the fact that the Nationalist armies were less vulnerable to disruption, forced the republic's defenders—even the anarchists—into static trench warfare. It was left to Mao Zedong, in very different circumstances, to educate his fellow Marxists in the revolutionary potential of what he (who also warned against the propensity of "guerrillaism" to degenerate into banditry or anarchy) labeled "protracted war."

The Second World War, unlike the First, saw widespread guerrilla fighting. But it remained largely improvised and uninformed by theory. Stalin's army, in line with earlier priorities, had not drawn up any plans for partisan activity. It was only the staggering scale and speed of the German advance into the USSR in 1941, leaving thousands of Red Army troops cut off in a vast occupied zone, that made a revival of the partisan tradition almost unavoidable. On 3 July Stalin broadcast a call to all patriots to form partisan units and "make life intolerable for the invader," and formal orders were issued by the Central Committee a week later. The response was slow, with the number of partisans gradually increasing over a two-year period from perhaps 30,000 at the end of 1941 to some 250,000 in the summer of 1943. In the terms sketched by Lawrence, even the smaller of these numbers was enormous, but of course so was the expanse of territory involved. Much of the occupied zone was unsuitable for guerrilla operations, being flat and open, and most activity was concentrated in the (still huge) Bryansk forests and central marshlands of Byelorussia. From the start the main value of the partisan campaign seems to have been political as much as military, and it is clear from the tiny forces deployed on antipartisan operations by the German army that the threat was never vital. The German response was nonetheless extraordinarily violent. Antipartisan units repeatedly reported failing to find partisans, but nevertheless razing unfriendly villages to the ground and killing all their inhabitants, including women and children. Even before the invasion was launched, Wehrmacht forces were specifically exempted from the normal legal rules in using "collective measures of violence" against civilians, on the grounds of the large expanse of operational areas in the East, and, perhaps more significantly, the "special nature of the enemy" (Heer).

In the USSR guerrilla resistance remained auxiliary to regular military operations, but elsewhere, notably in the Balkans, it appeared independently and became the vehicle for a revolutionary transfer of power. In Yugoslavia, under an outstandingly determined and resourceful guerrilla leader, Josip Broz (Tito), the Communist Party was able to transform itself from a small underground opposition into the dominant political authority by the end of the war. From the summer of 1941 Tito assembled a formidable army, claiming a strength of 150,000 by late 1942, and 300,000 by the end of 1943, by which time a significant area of the country, some 50,000 square kilometers, had been liberated. Almost uniquely in modern history, this liberation was achieved with virtually no foreign support; by the time the Allies decided to supply Tito with arms, he was effectively self-sufficient. But he still insisted on the primacy of guerrilla methods and avoided a potentially terminal showdown with the occupying German forces. The Germans launched a series of large-scale antipartisan offensives, of which only the last and smallest—but most accurately

targeted—came close to capturing the partisan commanders.

The Greek Communist Party (KKE) also formed the backbone of the resistance movement that began in Greece in 1941, though in this case its potential was picked up more rapidly by outsiders. British aid, through the instrument of the Special Operations Executive (SOE), a bureau set up to support resistance movements, led to a significant sabotage operation, the destruction of the Gorgopotamos gorge viaduct (part of the supply line for Rommel's army in North Africa) in November 1942. The British chiefs of staff decided to "give all-out support to guerrilla warfare, even to the extent of prejudicing the activities of secret groups." But by contrast with Yugoslavia, there was a finer balance between the communist EAM (National Liberation Front) and the monarchist EDES (National Democratic Greek League). Both deployed substantial guerrilla forces, and though they cooperated in early operations like the Gorgopotamos viaduct, they were also fighting an internal struggle for power. ELAS (the National Popular Liberation Army, the military wing of EAM) had some capable commanders, but the party as a whole did not have the kind of charismatic leadership supplied by Tito in Yugoslavia. Its acceptance of Stalin's policy of detaching Macedonia from Greece was a serious handicap. But its resistance campaign had put it in a strong position by the end of the war, and its decision to launch an offensive early in 1946 seemed logical; by the end of that year ELAS, now known as the Democratic Army, had some 13,000 members operating inside Greece, with another 12,000 in cross-border sanctuaries in Yugoslavia and Bulgaria. Unusually, women formed a large proportion of these forces; equally unusually, a large proportion was conscripted by force. The National Army was weak and poorly organized when the civil war began and spent years in wasteful and ineffective attempts to round up the guerrillas. But the injection of American aid in 1948 tilted the balance decisively. The insurgents' premature transition to open military operations in 1947 speeded up the defeat of the KKE, though whether persistence in guerrilla action would have done more than perpetuate a bitter and destructive conflict is doubtful.

The defeat of the communist insurgency in Greece by 1949 indicated that what may be called "classical" rural guerrilla warfare in Europe was no longer viable. Terrorism, sometimes (misleadingly) labeled urban guerrilla war, would be employed by both nationalist organizations like the IRA and the ETA (Basque Homeland and Liberty) and revolutionary socialist groups like the Italian Brigate Rosse (Red Brigades) and the German Rote Armee Fraktion (Red Army Faction). But none of these approached the military dynamic laid out by Lawrence, or by Mao Zedong. The most effective integrated campaign appeared in one of Europe's smallest countries, Cyprus, where EOKA (National Organization of Cypriot Struggle, an offshoot of the Greek royalist *Khi* organization) fought for reunion of the island with Greece. Its leader, Colonel Georgios Grivas, was a regular soldier with a precise grasp of guerrilla techniques. To Archbishop Makarios III's objection that Cypriots were not brave enough to fight an insurgent campaign he replied, "No one is born brave; he becomes brave, given the right leadership." EOKA's part-rural, part-urban campaign (1955–1959) demonstrated that an irresolute imperial power could be persuaded by ruthless violence to abandon its colonies. Where the imperial power was more deeply entrenched, as in Algeria, which had been made a French *département,* guerrilla methods proved inadequate. The Front de Libération Nationale's (FLN) organization in Algiers itself was crushed by French military measures, and the key to the eventual achievement of Algerian independence (1962) was the reaction of French public opinion against those measures. The use of torture by a Western democratic state was, at that point in history, still felt to be deeply shocking.

See also **Counterinsurgency; Lawrence, T. E.; Partisan Warfare; Tito (Josip Broz).**

BIBLIOGRAPHY

Primary Sources

Lawrence, T. E. "The Evolution of a Revolt." *Army Quarterly* 1, no. 1 (1920): 55–69.

———. *Revolt in the Desert.* London, 1927.

Secondary Sources

Beckett, Ian. *Modern Insurgencies and Counter-Insurgencies: Guerrillas and Their Opponents since 1750.* London and New York, 2001.

Foot, M. R. D. *Resistance: An Analysis of European Resistance to Nazism, 1940–1945.* London, 1976.

Galula, David. *Counter-insurgency Warfare: Theory and Practice.* New York, 1964.

Greene, T. N., ed. *The Guerrilla, and How to Fight Him: Selections from the Marine Corps Gazette.* New York, 1962.

Heer, Hannes. "The Logic of the War of Extermination: The Wehrmacht and the Anti-Partisan War." In *War of Extermination: The German Military in World War II, 1941–1944,* edited by Hannes Heer and Klaus Naumann. New York, 2000.

Holland, Robert F. *Britain and the Revolt in Cyprus, 1954–1959.* Oxford, U.K., 1998.

Laqueur, Walter. *Guerrilla: A Historical and Critical Study.* Boston, 1976.

Talbott, John E. *The War without a Name: France in Algeria, 1954–1962.* New York, 1980.

Townshend, Charles. *The British Campaign in Ireland, 1919–1921: The Development of Political and Military Policies.* London, 1975.

CHARLES TOWNSHEND

GULAG. An acronym for the Soviet bureaucratic institution, *Glavnoe Upravlenie ispravitelno-trudovykh LAGerei* (Chief Administration of Corrective Labor Camps), tasked with oversight of the Soviet forced-labor concentration camp and internal exile system, the term *gulag* has come to represent the entire Soviet penal system. Often understood incorrectly as a system only for political prisoners, the gulag served more generally, holding millions of people convicted of various political and nonpolitical crimes in a myriad of different types of prisons, concentration camps, and internal exile.

THE INSTITUTIONS AND SCOPE OF THE GULAG

Gulag prisons primarily served as the place of detention for those under investigation. Prisons such as the Lubyanka, Butyrka, and Lefortovo along with countless lesser-known prisons in the regional cities of the Soviet Union were notorious as places of torturous interrogation and a rude introduction for the newly arrested to gulag life. Only a small portion of gulag inmates, usually those deemed too dangerous or too famous to be placed in regular forced-labor camps, actually served their sentences in prisons.

The gulag included a great variety of forced-labor concentration camps. This was the primary place of detention for nearly all who had been individually convicted of an alleged crime. Many prisoners lived in a camp zone surrounded by a fence or barbed wire, overlooked by manned watchtowers, and containing a number of overcrowded, poorly heated barracks. During nonworking hours, the prisoners were usually relatively free to move about the camp zone. Others lived in especially strict regime camps with locked barracks, barred windows, and heavily restricted and guarded movements within the camp zone. Not all forced-labor camp prisoners, however, lived in the typical camp zone. For many, a camp meant a relatively unguarded existence on the Kazakh steppe or in the frozen Siberian countryside. In whatever locale, life in a gulag camp was extremely harsh. Prisoners were poorly fed. Violence was endemic in the gulag. The largest Soviet concentration camps were located in the geographic extremes of the Soviet Union from the arctic north to the Siberian east to the Central Asian south, though camps existed in virtually every part of the Soviet Union. Some of the most famous gulag camp locales—Kolyma, Vorkuta, Norilsk, Solovki, and Karaganda—struck fear into prisoners much like the more famous place-names of the Nazi camp system.

The system of internal exile was used mostly for large groups of people condemned not for particular "crimes" but for membership in a suspect group sometimes defined by class—such as the so-called kulaks (rich peasants) deported during the early 1930s drive to collectivize agriculture—and sometimes including entire nationalities, such as the Soviet Germans, Chechens, and others deported en masse before and during the war. Exile typically required that a person live within a fixed region deep in Siberia or Central Asia. Exiles had a portion of their pay garnisheed in favor of the state and had to report periodically to the local secret police; leaving the region of exile without permission was treated as escape and subject to very stiff penalties. Otherwise, they lived remarkably similarly to other Soviet citizens.

The gulag was a mass, social institution. Before the opening of the archives in the late 1980s, historians speculated that the gulag's population was in the tens of millions. It is now known with a degree of accuracy that the total population of prisons, camps, and exile reached a maximum of some 5.2 million people in the early 1950s just before Joseph Stalin's death. With the exception of World War II, the gulag population grew almost without interruption throughout the Stalin era. Throughout its history, some 18 million people passed through the prisons and camps of the gulag, and perhaps another 6 or 7 million were subject to internal exile. An unknown number, well into the millions, died in gulag camps and in places of exile. At the same time, in one of the most important revelations of gulag archival studies, no less than 20 percent of the camp population was released every year from 1934 to 1953, with the number released in a given year never less than 150,000 and frequently topping 500,000. Though these gulag demographic figures are smaller than once thought, they still bespeak a massive institution that touched all parts of Soviet society.

Additionally, much more has been learned about the makeup of the prisoner population since the archives have opened. The near exclusive reliance on memoirs from political prisoners once gave the impression that they were the dominant gulag demographic. Political prisoners—a group not limited to real opponents of the Soviet regime but also including many caught up in the paranoid arms of the secret police—typically comprised no more than one-quarter of the gulag population. Many gulag prisoners were similar to detained criminals in any country. The gulag held the Soviet Union's robbers, rapists, murderers, and thieves. Nevertheless, the largest group was composed of the victims of arbitrary and draconian legal campaigns under which petty theft or unexcused absences from work were punished by many years in concentration camps. These "crimes" would likely have gone unpunished in most countries, but these prisoners made up the majority of the gulag population.

THE FUNCTIONS OF THE GULAG

The gulag served several functions; it was simultaneously a detention system, a forced-labor system, and a penal system participating in a radically utopian drive to end criminality and build a "socialist" society. These various functions sometimes competed with and sometimes complemented one another.

An abandoned prison in Pevek, Russia, photographed in 1992, demonstrates the desolation of gulag conditions. ©JACQUES LANGEVIN/CORBIS SYGMA

First, the gulag was a system of detention focused on isolating those deemed unfit for and/or dangerous to Soviet society. Soviet leaders frequently spoke of the gulag system as a prophylactic measure aimed at protecting society from criminals, class enemies, and enemies of the people. Gulag officials were constantly focused on battling with prisoner escapes, as they sought to complete their detention function. Often, however, this role as detention system was undercut by another function of the gulag—its role as a system of forced labor. For example, prisoners at Karlag, an agricultural camp in central Kazakhstan, simply could not all be kept in a camp zone, because they were constantly moving with herds of grazing animals about the steppe lands. This made prevention of escape very difficult.

In the gulag, all able-bodied inmates were required to work, and this massive system was an active participant in the Soviet economy. Gulag inmates opened remote regions to mine gold, copper, and coal; to build cities, railroads, canals, and highways; to fell trees; and to operate vast agricultural enterprises. Many historians have understood the gulag primarily as a slave labor system with the Soviet economy built on the backs of prisoner labor. In this view, the gulag arose and expanded primarily as a result of Stalin's crash industrialization policies, which created a need for a labor force in the geographic extremes of the Soviet Union. Scholarship, however, has revealed the extreme inefficiency of gulag labor and the tremendous expense of operating the camp system. The gulag was quite simply a financial burden, not a financial boon for the Soviet state. Further, convinced that they were using essentially "free" labor, Soviet economic planners utilized gulag laborers on a variety of projects that ultimately proved to have little or no economic value. Many of these projects were closed down immediately after the death of Stalin, as even gulag administrators had come to realize their pointlessness.

While the gulag's employees strove constantly to make their system more economically productive, new evidence suggests that economic motivation was not the primary explanation for the growth of the gulag. Arrests occurred chaotically and inefficiently, not at the urging of camp administrators, but as a result of various politicized legal campaigns. Camp administrators did not clamor for more prisoners, but were typically caught unaware and unprepared for massive influxes of prisoners, and they struggled to find shelter, food, and even work for new prisoners. Furthermore, arrests were not limited to the healthy working population, but included women, children, the ill, and the elderly.

Gulag prisoners were never treated in an undifferentiated fashion, and this in part served the gulag's third major function. It was an active participant in the utopian drive to build a new "socialist" society and a new "Soviet man." The most salient feature of the gulag was an apparent paradox: forced labor, high death rates, and an oppressive atmosphere of violence, cold, and constant hunger coexisted with camp newspapers and cultural activities, a constant propaganda barrage of correction and reeducation, and the steady release of a significant portion of the prisoner population. The gulag was more complex than a simple system of industrialized death such as the Nazi camp system. If more than 150,000 gulag prisoners were released every year, the question of how Soviet authorities determined who would be released and how they prepared them for reentry into Soviet society simply must be addressed. At the same time, each year thousands and sometimes even hundreds of thousands of gulag prisoners died. Their fate must also be considered in order to understand the function of the camp system.

The gulag upon closer reflection comes to appear as a "last chance" for prisoners to remake themselves into fit Soviet citizens. The Bolsheviks were engaged in a radical project to build a utopian socialist society. In accord with their Manichaean worldview, they fully expected opposition to building that perfect society. Many whom they understood as their most implacable enemies, they merely executed, but many others were kept alive (at least temporarily) in the gulag. The Bolsheviks could not escape their fundamental belief in the malleability of the human soul, and they believed that labor was the key to "reforging" criminals. The very harshness of the gulag was seen as necessary to break down a criminal's resistance in order to rebuild that person into a proper Soviet citizen. If a prisoner refused correction, the brutality of the gulag would lead to inevitable death. The Bolsheviks were no humanitarians. If mistakes were to be made, it was better to kill too many than too few.

Many gulag practices were designed based on a categorization matrix that placed prisoners into a hierarchy according to their perceived "redeemability" and level of reeducation. Complex hierarchies of living and working conditions, differentiation of food rations, and practices of early release tied survival directly to reeducation. The gulag served as a crossroads, constantly redefining the line between those who could be reclaimed for Soviet society and those who were destined to die in the camps.

THE CHRONOLOGY OF THE GULAG

The gulag was thoroughly integrated into the fabric of the Soviet Union. Major historical events and turning points greatly affected the lives and fates of gulag inmates and exiles. In many respects, the gulag was born with 1917's October Revolution itself. As early as 1918, Vladimir Lenin, Leon Trotsky, and other Bolshevik leaders spoke of putting class enemies in "concentration camps." Yet the origins of the gulag must be sought not only in these first Soviet concentration camps founded as part of the Leninist regime's extraordinarily violent reaction to its enemies after October. The gulag's origins are also found in the more utopian ideals that viewed inmate labor as the key to teaching the prisoner that under socialism work would no longer be a hateful, exploitive activity. Thus, corrective labor long preceded the arrival of crash industrialization and was filled with ideological and political content.

The explosion of the gulag population coincided with Stalin's great "revolution from above." This was not, however, a product merely of the economic demands of industrialization and collectivization. It was part of the all-encompassing social and cultural transformations accompanying the "building of socialism." Soviet authorities attempted with great haste to cleanse their newly emerging society of the criminals, class enemies, and political opponents who seemed to contaminate the new world.

The 1920s and the early 1930s represented the acme of Soviet belief in the capacity to rehabilitate prisoners by means of corrective labor. Corrective labor camps not only were openly discussed but were also in fact a source of pride. In the early 1930s, paeans to the building of the White Sea–Baltic Canal proudly announced the use of convict labor in their construction in the volume *Belomor*, which was published not only in the Soviet Union but also in the United States in an English translation. The Bolsheviks claimed to be transforming humans as proudly as they were transforming nature.

As the 1930s progressed, optimism and openness about penal practices gave way to skepticism and secrecy. Prisoner transports were hidden as "special equipment." Prisoner correspondence was severely restricted. Released prisoners signed secrecy agreements forbidding them to talk about the camps. Nobody could enter regions such as Kolyma without special entrance permits. With the adoption of the Stalin Constitution in 1936, the Soviet Union was officially declared a socialist state of workers and peasants. The class enemy had officially been destroyed; socialism had been achieved. The continued existence of criminality was an embarrassment for a polity that explained such problems in terms of the social milieu. Capitalism could no longer offer a legitimate excuse for crime, and the Soviet penal system became notably less compromising toward enemies and lawbreakers. In 1937 and 1938 the "Great Terror" saw a massive number of executions in and outside of the gulag, as many of those who failed to prove their rehabilitation during the transition period were annihilated. Nonetheless, the drive to reeducate prisoners never disappeared in internal gulag discussions. Not all prisoners were killed, and releases continued.

Socialism achieved did not end the gulag, but it did shift its understanding of its own population. With the class enemy defeated, the categorization of Soviet enemies increasingly turned from the terms of class toward the terms of nation. The class enemy became the enemy of the people. Although the focus on class never entirely disappeared, the path was cleared for a major wave of ethno-national group deportations that would continue right through the war. The 1937 exile of the Far Eastern Soviet Koreans, though not the first ethnic deportation, did offer the first instance in which an entire undifferentiated national group was deported from a particular territory. The deportation of the Soviet Koreans provided an example for the coming wartime exile of entire nationalities, when among others every last Soviet German, Chechen, Ingush, and Crimean Tatar was subject to internal exile regardless of their geographical location, class position, military service, or even Communist Party membership.

The 1939 and 1940 annexations of western Ukraine, western Byelorussia, and the Baltic changed the face of the gulag. These "westerners" had never been exposed to socialism in power and carried with them the living memory of different systems of government and different penal institutions. Many Poles arrested after 1939 but released after the June 1941 Nazi invasion of the Soviet Union would be the first major informants to the West about the gulag system.

The years 1941 and 1942 saw the largest prisoner releases at any time in the Stalin era, when some one million inmates sentenced for relatively minor crimes were released into the Red Army. Many went on to earn orders and medals for their deeds during the war. Not all inmates, however, could join the Red Army, as political prisoners were left behind in the camps. Further, a very small subsection of political prisoners, the so-called especially dangerous state criminals, were subjected to a new type of severe isolation in the harshest climatic conditions performing the most dangerous labor in so-called *katorga* (a tsarist-era term for forced labor) camp subdivisions.

Two new postwar prisoner contingents reshaped gulag society. First, the arrest of many thousands of Red Army veterans introduced a new and often prestigious element into camp society. Their firsthand experience with the standards of life outside Soviet borders combined with an assertiveness and sense of entitlement earned on the battlefield tended to render these postwar inmates less docile than their prewar predecessors. The second postwar contingent was even more assertive and combative. These prisoners from among the nationalist organizations and partisan armies of the western territories and the Baltic states brought to the gulag a strong sense of national identity, well-developed and explicitly anti-Soviet ideologies, and combat experience fighting Soviet power. Both Red Army veterans and the nationalist guerrillas played substantial leadership roles during the mass gulag strikes of the 1950s.

The late 1940s was the apogee of the gulag system, when the system became rigidified and the prisoner population reached historic maximums. In 1948 new "special camps" were created to hold a much-expanded group of so-called especially dangerous state criminals. For the first time, many political prisoners were largely isolated from the gulag's regular criminal population. Their isolation led to a new political consciousness that would be a strong contributing factor to the post-Stalin strikes. The postwar era also saw the application of permanent, lifelong exile to all those nationalities deported during the war and the permanent deportation of all those prisoners released from special camps.

Only Stalin's death in 1953 made the gulag's decline thinkable. Within three weeks of Stalin's death, the first major amnesty was declared, starting the gulag's population decline. The partial nature of the amnesty, especially its near total exclusion of political prisoners, touched off a wave of prisoner uprisings of a size and scope unprecedented in gulag history. Soon after the strikes, the gulag as the massive phenomenon containing millions of prisoners came to an end. Nikita Khrushchev's 1956 "secret speech" denouncing Stalin set in motion the final act of largely emptying the labor camps and the system of exile.

Forced-labor camps would continue to exist in the Soviet Union right up until the era of Mikhail Gorbachev, but they became much smaller and ever more focused on recidivists and serious criminals. Soviet dissidents made up an important but exceedingly small portion of the post-Stalin camp population. The last camp for political prisoners—located outside Perm, Russia—was closed in 1988 and was later turned into the Gulag Museum.

See also **Concentration Camps; Forced Labor; Soviet Union.**

BIBLIOGRAPHY

Primary Sources

Gorky, Maxim, L. Auerbach, and S. G. Firin, eds. *Belomor: An Account of the Construction of the New Canal between the White Sea and the Baltic Sea*. Translated by Amabel Williams-Ellis. New York, 1935. Reprint, Westport, Conn., 1977. The original ideologically correct presentation of Soviet corrective labor.

Khlevniuk, Oleg V. *The History of the Gulag: From Collectivization to the Great Terror*. Translated by Vadim A. Staklo with editorial assistance and commentary by David J. Nordlander. New Haven, Conn., 2004. A new English-language edition of documents from official Soviet archives.

Solzhenitsyn, Aleksandr I. *The Gulag Archipelago, 1918–1956: An Experiment in Literary Investigation*. 3 vols. Translated by Thomas P. Whitney. New York, 1991–1992. A combination primary source and secondary source. Still the best single study of the gulag.

Secondary Sources

Adler, Nanci. *The Gulag Survivor: Beyond the Soviet System*. New Brunswick, N.J., 2002.

Applebaum, Anne. *Gulag: A History*. New York, 2003. A recent—Pulitzer Prize–winning—popular history of the gulag.

Bacon, Edwin. *The Gulag at War: Stalin's Forced Labour System in the Light of the Archives*. Basingstoke, U.K., 1994. The first limited book-length English-language study to use select official archival sources.

Barnes, Steven A. "Soviet Society Confined: The Gulag in the Karaganda Region of Kazakhstan, 1930s–1950s." Ph.D. diss., Stanford University, 2003.

Courtois, Stéphane, Nicolas Werth, Jean-Louis Panne, et al. *The Black Book of Communism: Crimes, Terror, Repression*. Translated by Jonathan Murphy and Mark Kramer. Cambridge, Mass., 1999.

Dallin, David J., and Boris I. Nicolaevsky. *Forced Labor in Soviet Russia*. New Haven, Conn., 1947. Reprint, New York, 1974. The first scholarly study of the gulag.

Getty, J. Arch, Gábor T. Rittersporn, and Viktor N. Zemskov. "Victims of the Soviet Penal System in the Pre-War Years: A First Approach on the Basis of Archival Evidence." *American Historical Review* 98, no. 4 (1993): 1017–1049. The new demographic information on the gulag that is only now changing conceptions of the institution.

Gregory, Paul R., and Valery Lazarev, eds. *The Economics of Forced Labor: The Soviet Gulag*. Stanford, Calif., 2003. Groundbreaking study of gulag economy.

Ivanova, Galina Mikhailovna. *Labor Camp Socialism: The Gulag in the Soviet Totalitarian System*. Translated by

Carol Flath. Edited by Donald J. Raleigh. Armonk, N.Y., 2000.

Jakobson, Michael. *Origins of the Gulag: The Soviet Prison Camp System, 1917–1934.* Lexington, Ky., 1993.

STEVEN A. BARNES

GULF WARS. The two Gulf Wars, the latter often called the Iraq War, may be seen as a single conflict involving two periods of major combat, in January–February 1991 and March–April 2003, separated by a twelve-year strategic pause (which in turn was punctuated by several sharp air campaigns). The Gulf War resulted from the invasion (2 August 1990) of Kuwait by Iraq, which led to United Nations (UN) Security Council Resolutions 660, demanding immediate Iraqi withdrawal, and 678, authorizing member states to use "all necessary means" to force Iraqi compliance, both of which were rejected by the Iraqi leader Saddam Hussein.

Iraq had long had an irredentist claim on Kuwait stemming back to the days of the Ottoman Empire, at which time the southern region of Iraq around Basra and what is now Kuwait both belonged to the same province. The deep cause of the invasion, however, was the exhaustion of Iraq at the end of the Iran-Iraq War (1980–1988), which saddled it with a debt of $80 billion, at least $10 billion of which was owed to Kuwait. The only way for Iraq to pay its debt and rebuild its economic infrastructure was by exporting oil—of which Kuwait had a great deal. Kuwait consistently failed to observe OPEC's production quotas designed to restrict the supply of oil and thereby keep the price high, at a time when Iraq desperately needed to extract the highest price possible. This, combined with the refusal of the Gulf monarchies to cancel Iraq's debt, soured Iraq's relations with these states, particularly as Saddam earnestly felt that he had protected countries such as Kuwait and Saudi Arabia from revolutionary Iran under the Ayatollah Khomeini.

Iraq's invasion invoked a furious international response. It caused strategic alarm in the West, where it was feared that the Iraqi forces that swept through Kuwait in a few days might carry on into Saudi Arabia, leaving Saddam in control of much of the world's oil reserves. It was, moreover, such a blatant breach of the norm of state sovereignty that condemnation was general in the United Nations. President George H. W. Bush captured the spirit of the time in saying, in his 1991 State of the Union address, that what was at stake was "more than one small country: it is a New World Order—where diverse nations are drawn together in common cause to achieve the universal aspirations of mankind."

A U.S.-led coalition of thirty-four countries was formed between early September and 20 November 1990 when UN Resolution 678 was passed. Britain, which was traditionally prepared to meet challenges to international order with force, had a long imperial connection to the region, and saw an opportunity to reassert the Anglo-American "special relationship," strongly supported the war. As John Sullivan, writing in *The Independent* (2 September 1990) quipped, "For the British ... intervening east of Suez is like riding a bike: you never lose the knack." France's initial position was more equivocal, having been an ally of Iraq, around a quarter of whose military equipment it had supplied, and desirous of an approach to the region independent of the United States. As Saddam's intransigence grew, however, President François Mitterrand considerably stepped up France's military contribution. Within the Middle East all states supported the Coalition except Jordan, which sought a middle position. The stakes were highest for the Saudi monarchy, whose survival depended on a swift end to the war. Without Western help it could not resist invasion, but the deployment of non-Muslim troops in the heartland of Islam was domestically inflammatory. Iran put aside its hatred of the United States, portraying the war positively as an effort to "safeguard Arabia in the face of Iraqi threats" (Tehran Radio, 8 August 1990, quoted in Freedman and Karsh, 1993, p. 109).

Ultimately thirty-four states contributed about 700,000 troops to the Coalition, the largest being the 500,000-strong U.S. contingent supported by 45,000 British, 14,600 French, 100,000 Saudi, 33,000 Egyptian, and 15,000 Syrian troops. Iraq had roughly half this number of troops, the bulk of those being low-quality infantry divisions in static defensive positions on the Saudi border and a few armored divisions as a tactical reserve in central

Kuwait, while the better-trained and -equipped Republican Guard divisions were deployed mostly in southern Iraq.

Operation Desert Storm began on 17 January 1991 with a forty-three-day air campaign of almost 100,000 sorties targeting first the Iraqi air defense network, command and control network, and other infrastructure, and later concentrating on degrading Iraqi ground forces directly. Iraq had only one strategic response: attack the Coalition's weak point—the alignment of Islamic states with infidels against other Muslims—by attacking Israel with ballistic missiles with the aim of enticing it to retaliate and thereby fracture the Coalition. The plan failed as Israel was dissuaded from retaliating by U.S. political pressure and by a determined Coalition effort to destroy Iraq's missile launchers.

The ground campaign began on 24 February 1991 with attacks by U.S. Marines and Saudi forces directly into Kuwait in the south, which fixed the attention of the Iraqi command. Meanwhile, to the west the main Coalition forces consisting of U.S. Army units backed by British and French forces swung wide of Kuwait striking directly at the Republican Guard divisions in southern Iraq. The Iraqi collapse was swift. Conscript infantry surrendered in large numbers as Coalition forces overran their forward positions. Kuwait City was liberated on 26 February. By the morning of 27 February the Iraqi military had lost 3,700 tanks, 2,400 armored personnel carriers, and 2,700 artillery pieces. Estimates of Iraqi military dead range from 50,000 to 100,000. Coalition deaths amounted to less than five hundred—approximately half of those being noncombat deaths.

On 3 April 1991 the war's end was marked by the passing of UN Security Council Resolution 687 by which Iraq was obliged to accept not only the inviolability of its border with Kuwait but also, under international supervision, "the destruction, removal, or rendering harmless" of all weapons of mass destruction (WMD) and facilities. Compliance was to be enforced by sanctions and by the threat of renewed use of force. Overall, the strategy was to deal with Iraq by providing Saddam's subordinates incentives to depose him (it was assumed that many in his regime were eager to get rid of him) and if that could not be achieved then by containment. In actuality Saddam retained enough military power—

the Republican Guard divisions in southern Iraq had escaped destruction in the ground campaign—to crush the major uprisings against him.

Instead of acceding to Resolution 687, Iraq resisted all the way. Attempts by the UN Special Commission (UNSCOM) to root out and destroy Iraq's WMD were consistently obstructed (despite which UNSCOM made a good deal of progress, a fact conclusively revealed after the 2003 Iraq War). But questions remained, particularly about Iraq's chemical and biological weapons stockpile, which came to a head with Iraq's refusal to allow UNSCOM the right to inspect, at any time, any site where it suspected WMD facilities might be hidden. The crisis made apparent divisions within the Security Council: France, Russia, and China took a view, contrary to Britain and the United States, that inspections and sanctions had been taken as far as they could go and should be ended. The United States and Britain alone launched Operation Desert Fox in December 1998—air and missile strikes designed to "degrade" Iraq's WMD capabilities—but the inspections regime had effectively ended. Meanwhile the sanctions regime was subverted by smuggling and corruption, losing any coercive effect while simultaneously allowing Saddam the propaganda gift of blaming others for the steady impoverishment of Iraq's people.

The result was stalemate. Iraq could not be rehabilitated internationally while Saddam still ruled. Yet there was no will to take direct action against him. In 1991 when Saddam exclaimed, "O Iraqis, you triumphed when you stood with all this vigor against the armies of thirty countries…" the response was derision. In 2003 when he said, "In 1991 Iraq was not defeated. In fact, our army withdrew from Kuwait according to a decision taken by us," many people in the Middle East were inclined to agree.

Initially President George W. Bush looked set to continue the policies of his predecessor Bill Clinton. There was talk of reviving the sanctions regime—a policy on "smart" sanctions was agreed to by the Security Council in November 2000—but on regime change in Iraq the Bush administration was decidedly noncommittal. The turning point was the 11 September 2001 attacks on the United States, which prompted a reshaping of U.S. national security thinking. The United States' resolve to solve the problem of Saddam Hussein was undoubtedly animated by long-standing mutual antagonism, but underlying this was a genuine—albeit hypothetical—fear of the malign combination of weapons of mass destruction, terrorism, and rogue states. Since Saddam had never encouraged the idea that Iraq was in compliance with Resolution 687 (quite the opposite; the maintenance of the myth of him as a great leader depended on resolute defiance of any consequence of defeat in 1991), WMD provided the pretext for the Iraq War. The diplomatic brawl over this issue appeared to have been resolved with the passing of UN Security Council Resolution 1441 (8 November 2002), which found Iraq in "material breach" of its obligations under Resolution 687 and threatened "serious consequences" should that not be rectified. But it recommenced bitterly in January 2003 when it became clear that the quest for an even more explicit authorization for war was bound to fail. On the one side, Britain under Prime Minister Tony Blair—for whom WMD was not a pretext but the actual issue—strongly backed the threat of use of force (to his political detriment domestically). On the other side, France and Germany ferociously opposed it, accusing the United States of arrogant unilateralism. Undoubtedly their opposition was based in part on pecuniary commercial interests in Iraq, anti-Americanism, and, in the case of Germany especially, antimilitarism, but it also reflected the mood of much of the European public, including Britain's.

Although Iraq was on bad terms with all of its neighbors—Iran, Turkey, Syria, Jordan, Saudi Arabia, and Kuwait—none were really happy about the war. Iran under the rule of the ayatollahs remained implacably anti-Western. The Saudi monarchy feared it would provoke an anti-Western backlash domestically that could cause its downfall. Syria, accused by the United States of sponsoring terrorism, was hostile. Jordan, though its leadership was pro-Western, was popularly pro-Saddam. Turkey, officially secular and a member of NATO, was also captured by the mood of opposition to the Coalition that had swept the Islamic world. All except Kuwait rejected the use of their territory for staging facilities for the invasion.

The war began in the early hours of 20 March 2003 with a sharp air and missile attack on targets in Baghdad aimed at decapitating the regime, which failed. The next day ground forces comprising three groups launched attacks on Iraq northward from Kuwait. The U.S. Army V Corps advanced west of the Euphrates River before turning northeast to attack Baghdad. The U.S. First Marine Expeditionary Force advanced between the Euphrates and Tigris. The British First Armoured Division focused on Iraq's second city, the port city of Basra, and surrounding areas. Iraqi resistance was extremely weak, despite some pockets of hard fighting at An Nasiriyah (23–24 March), Najaf (25–28 March), around Basra until 6 April when it was captured, and in and around Baghdad from 1 to 9 April when the regime effectively ceased to exist. At a cost of fewer than one hundred Coalition casualties Iraq's army, numerically superior to the attacking force and entrenched in defensive positions on its own soil, was utterly routed in less than half the time and with less than a third of the troops it took to win the Gulf War in 1991—the previous historical benchmark of lopsided military victories. The Coalition forces were ably led, well trained, and for the most part superbly equipped professional soldiers with high morale. The Iraqi forces were poorly led, ill trained, and badly equipped; they could perhaps have exploited more of the advantages that naturally accrue to the defender in war, but that would not have changed the outcome significantly.

The aftermath of the conventional war was a far more significant challenge for the Coalition. The achievement of the March–April 2003 campaign to oust Saddam must be balanced against the feeble performance of the occupation. No weapons of mass destruction were found. Iraq became a magnet for Islamic militancy, which exacerbated the domestic insurgency. In 2005 it remained to be seen whether the slow and painful transition of Iraq to a stable democracy would catalyze democratic change elsewhere in the Middle East as the architects of the war hoped. The alternative—bloody civil war—could destabilize the entire region and the entire world. The Gulf Wars provided perhaps the greatest and most divisive international crises of the late twentieth and early twenty-first centuries.

See also **Al Qaeda; Anti-Americanism; Islamic Terrorism; United Nations and Europe.**

BIBLIOGRAPHY

Cornish, Paul, ed. *The Conflict in Iraq 2003.* Houndmills, U.K., 2004.

Freedman, Lawrence, and Efraim Karsh. *The Gulf Conflict 1990–1991: Diplomacy and War in the New World Order.* London, 1993.

Gordon, Michael R., and Bernard E. Trainor. *The Generals' War: The Inside Story of the Conflict in the Gulf.* Boston, 1995.

Williamson, Murray, and Robert H. Scales Jr. *The Iraq War: A Military History.* Cambridge, Mass., 2003.

DAVID J. BETZ

H

HABER, FRITZ (1868–1934), German chemist, winner of the Nobel Prize for Chemistry in 1918.

Fritz Haber is regarded as "the father of modern chemical warfare" (Lepick, p. 67). At the time he offered his services to the kaiser's army, he was already a famous scientist. From a wealthy Jewish family in Silesia—his father traded in chemical products and indigo—he studied at the Technische Hochschule in Berlin. He defended his thesis in organic chemistry there in 1891. The following year, he was baptized at the Protestant church in Jena. From 1894, after an unsuccessful spell in his father's business, he enrolled at the Institute of Technology in Karlsruhe, where he was made a freelance lecturer (*Privatdozent*) two years later, having qualified by defending a thesis on the combustion of hydrocarbons. He also obtained his first professorship there in 1906. Meanwhile, in 1901 he married Clara Immerwahr, who was also a chemist. The couple had a child, Hermann, in 1902, but relations between the spouses deteriorated.

In the years from 1904 to 1910, he developed, in collaboration with the firm BASF—and in particular its head engineer Carl Bosch (a Nobel Prize winner in 1931)—procedures for the fixation of nitrogen from the atmosphere and the catalytic synthesis of ammonia (the Haber-Bosch process), one of the first outcomes of which was the manufacture of industrial fertilizer. It was this discovery that won him the Nobel Prize and brought him substantial wealth as a result of the very rapid industrial applications of the procedure.

In 1911 he became director of the new Kaiser Wilhelm Institute for Physical Chemistry in Berlin. Just prior to this, while still in Karlsruhe, he had made the acquaintance of Albert Einstein (1879–1955) at a conference. A deep friendship developed between the two scientists, but they held radically opposing philosophical views during the First World War. Whereas Einstein had pacifist leanings from the outset of the war, Haber participated enthusiastically in the war effort—not without first having signed the "Appeal to the Civilized World" made in 1914 by ninety-three German intellectuals. The following year, by turning the faucets of chlorine cylinders under pressure, he opened the Pandora's box of modern chemical warfare at Langemarck. On 22 April 1915 Haber supervised the attack in person, and he had to overcome the misgivings even of certain officers. This attack unquestionably constituted a violation of the 1899 Hague Conventions.

In 1916 he ran the chemical warfare unit of the German army and had several hundred researchers working for him, including many brilliant young scientists. At that time there were very few like Max Born, who refused to work with him. His teams had already developed a gas mask and gas shells that were designed to replace the cylinders. In 1917 they developed yperite (or mustard gas), a highly corrosive gas for use in warfare. Haber remarried in 1917. Clara, who was opposed to his work, had committed suicide in May 1915, which had not deterred Haber from pursuing his chosen path.

The announcement in 1919 that the 1918 Nobel Prize was being awarded to Haber provoked an angry response in the former enemy countries. Haber subsequently featured on the first list of the people being pursued for war crimes in 1920, but his name was no longer included in a revised version of the list. In Germany, however, he renewed contact with those who had opposed him during the war, such as Einstein and Max Born, and assumed an increasingly important role in the nation's research. He thus devoted his efforts to reestablishing his country's scientific reputation and its international relations within the scientific field. Thanks to the spirit of the Locarno Pact (1925), he even became an honorary member of the French and English chemical societies and was elected to major science academies (in the United States and the USSR).

In 1933, after the Nazis took power, Haber resigned his post at the Institute in protest at the implementation of anti-Semitic laws. He then emigrated. On his way through Switzerland, Haber met the chemist and Zionist leader Chaim Azriel Weizmann (1874–1952), who had offered him a post in Palestine. After an initial rejection, Haber seemed to accept the post. However, at the invitation of William Jackson Pope (1870–1939), he then went to Cambridge but did not receive the friendliest of welcomes. In 1934, while on vacation in Switzerland and on the point of leaving for Palestine, Haber died of a heart attack on 29 January in Basel. The historian Fritz Stern discovered that a year after Haber's death, his son, who had settled in France in 1927, had made a request for naturalization, which met with constant rejection by the French authorities because of his father's activities during the First World War.

See also **Science; Technology; World War I.**

BIBLIOGRAPHY

Lepick, Olivier. *La Grande Guerre chimique, 1914–1918*. Paris, 1998.

Goran, Morris Herbert. *The Story of Fritz Haber*. Norman, Okla., 1967.

Stern, Fritz. *Einstein's German World*. Princeton, N.J., 1999.

Stolzenberg, Dietrich. *Fritz Haber: Chemiker, Nobelpreisträger, Deutscher, Jude; eine Biographie*. Weinheim, Germany, 1994.

NICOLAS BEAUPRÉ

HABERMAS, JÜRGEN (b. 1929), German philosopher.

At the turn of the millennium, Jürgen Habermas remained Germany's foremost philosopher, its internationally best-known and most cited thinker, and the archetype in his own country of the publicly engaged intellectual. He had attained this position early, and whether identified as the scion of the famous tradition of "critical theory," as the moral conscience of his nation in its relationship to its past, as a technical philosopher of collective language use, or as an interpreter of the foundations of democracy, he continued to occupy that central place for decades.

Raised in a small town, Habermas vividly recalled the formative experience of the Nazi years, including his military service as a young teenager as part of the last-ditch defense of his homeland in 1945. (His father was a Nazi Party member.) Having been trained in the traditions of German idealism and European phenomenology, however, Habermas quickly became a critic of the anti-Enlightenment tendencies of the recent German past. From very early on, Habermas mastered and joined the neo-Marxist tradition of the "Frankfurt School" and wrote in his most significant early work, *Structural Transformation of the Public Sphere* (1962), that transformations in capitalism and culture threatened to extinguish the originally liberatory thrust of modernity. Close to the Frankfurt philosophers Theodor Adorno (1903–1969) and Max Horkheimer (1895–1973) at the end of their lives (and for a long time the occupant of Horkheimer's Frankfurt philosophy chair), Habermas became their most recognizable successor, furthering their theoretical approach most notably in his *Knowledge and Human Interests* (1968).

But Habermas soon became best known and most important, in the years his thought assumed classic form, for his innovative fusion of the Continental social theory he inherited with the

Anglo-American "analytic" philosophy of language. Habermas's trademark remained the alchemical combination, carried out in forbiddingly dense prose, of diverse intellectual traditions (including linguistics, psychology, and sociology). His construction of systems provoked both awe for his synthetic abilities and worries about the eclecticism of the results. In the imposing tomes of his *Theory of Communicative Action* (1981), which served as the foundation for his later work, Habermas argued that modernity is best understood as a search for a society of uncoerced linguistic interaction. What he called "communicative reason" is perpetually threatened but never ruled out by the advances of instrumental, or means-ends, rationality. For Habermas, the nature of collective language use provides a discursive ground for intersubjective respect, which speakers, as well the states they form, violate only on pain of self-contradiction.

Habermas turned this social theory against postmodernism in a famous book, *The Philosophical Discourse of Modernity* (1985), in which he argued that modern philosophy has been continuously haunted by a theoretical solipsism that only his approach had the resources plausibly to overcome and charged that Friedrich Nietzsche and his French followers ignored the commitments to consensual truth and mutual understanding that speech by definition entails. In his later writings on legal and constitutional theory, Habermas extended his conclusions to contemporary democracy, notably arguing that democracy and rights, far from being in tension, are reciprocally necessary and implied.

Although internationally most prominent as a critical theorist, Habermas always counted in Germany as an engaged public intellectual who pondered the meaning and direction of his country's transit from Nazi barbarism through Cold War division to final reunification. Among his most significant contributions in this regard were in the mid-1980s *Historikerstreit* (Historians' debate), in which he confronted the conservative wish to "normalize" the Nazi past and escape the continuing burden—of which he perpetually reminded his countrymen—of atonement for the unique crimes they or their forebears had committed or allowed. For some, Habermas's restriction of the group identity to "constitutional patriotism," or an allegiance to democratic processes rather than inherited traditions or local specificity, went too far. At the time of German reunification, Habermas publicly worried about the risks of national fusion and expressed his doubts, but these were overtaken by events.

For decades Habermas often figured as a major foil of German conservatives, whether political, historiographical, or philosophical: aside from the *Historikerstreit*, Habermas also engaged, for example, in a celebrated polemic against the "traditionalism" of Hans-Georg Gadamer's hermeneutic philosophy. Later, along with the charge of eclecticism, Habermas more regularly faced withering skepticism from the Left. Taken to task by some for betraying the emancipatory criticism of society he inherited from the Frankfurt School—by the end of his evolution, his philosophy had come very close to the thought of the American liberal John Rawls in its emphasis on political rights and formal legitimacy—Habermas also found many critics for his stands in day-to-day politics (notably those in favor of America's successive Balkan interventions). The great thinker who achieved lasting renown thanks to his breathtaking range and multiple contributions disapproved of the U.S. invasion of Iraq and remained exploratory late in life, turning his attention to questions of bioethics and religion.

See also **Adorno, Theodor; Gadamer, Hans-Georg; Modernism.**

BIBLIOGRAPHY

Bernstein, J. M. *Recovering Ethical Life: Jürgen Habermas and the Future of Critical Theory.* New York, 1995.

Holub, Robert C. *Jürgen Habermas: Critic in the Public Sphere.* New York, 1991.

Ingram, David. *Habermas and the Dialectic of Reason.* New Haven, Conn., 1987.

McCarthy, Thomas. *The Critical Theory of Jürgen Habermas.* Cambridge, Mass., 1978.

Matuštík, Martin Joseph. *Jürgen Habermas: A Philosophical-Political Profile.* Lanham, Md., 2001.

Mueller, Jans-Werner. *Another Country: German Intellectuals, Unification, and National Identity.* New Haven, Conn., 2000.

White, Stephen K., ed. *The Cambridge Companion to Habermas.* Cambridge, U.K., 1995.

SAMUEL MOYN

HAGUE CONVENTION.

The two Peace Conferences of 1899 and 1907 (better known as the Hague Conferences) gave birth to many international protocols, called the Hague Conventions. These conferences are considered a turning point in the history of humanity because it was the first time that a major diplomatic assembly had been gathered outside a context of war or international crisis.

The first Hague Conference, in 1899, met at the initiative of Tsar Nicolas II of Russia (r. 1894–1917), and its objectives were to put an end to the progressive development of weapons and to seek out the most effective means to ensure lasting peace. The tsar had multiple reasons for doing this. He remembered his grandfather's success, at the Conference of Saint Petersburg of 1868, in banning explosive bullets or any bullet containing flammable materials. But the tsar was also intent on limiting weapons access in an attempt to counter the armament race. Finally, the Hague Conference of 1899 was inscribed in the wake of preceding international initiatives, supported by the pacifist movement, seeking to be rid of the threat of war, as had the Conference of Brussels of 1874, which dealt with the laws and customs of land wars.

The first Hague Conference took place from 18 May to 29 July 1899, at The Hague, Netherlands, and brought twenty-six states to the table. It consisted of a diplomatic forum divided into three commissions. The first was tasked with limiting levels of national armament, the second with codifying the laws and customs of war, and the third with finding peaceful solutions to disputes.

At the end of the meetings, the conference failed to adopt an agreement on how to limit armaments but won an undeniable victory in the development and codification of laws governing the peaceful resolution of disputes and those related to war. It adopted three conventions, the first of which—for the peaceful resolution of international conflicts—is regarded by scholars as the most important success of the conference, especially in light of the establishment of a Permanent Court of Arbitration. The second convention dealt with the laws and customs of land wars, and the third was concerned with the adaptation of the principles of the Geneva Convention of 22 August 1864, to naval warfare.

As far as the limiting of armaments was concerned, the conference adopted three declarations. The first outlawed the launching of projectiles or explosives from the tops of balloons or any other analogous new method; the second outlawed the use of projectiles whose only purpose is to diffuse asphyxiating or deleterious gases. And the third, following up on the work of the Declaration of Saint Petersburg (1868), prohibited the use of bullets that easily expand or flatten in the human body, such as the full metal-jacket bullets whose cases do not entirely cover the core or feature incisions (dum-dum bullets). Finally, steps were taken to call a second conference, as the participants recognized that the objectives of the conference of 1899 would only be met with time and the continuation of the process.

The second conference was delayed by the Russo-Japanese War (1904–1905). But once the conflict ended, Russia invited the governments of forty-four states to The Hague, from 15 June to 18 October 1907. The conference revised the three conventions of 1899 and adopted ten new ones. One dealt with the opening of hostilities, two with the rights and duties of the various powers and neutral countries, six with the various aspects of naval warfare, and one with limiting the use of force for the recovery of contractual debts. It also adopted a law extending that of 1899 prohibiting the launching of projectiles from balloons or any other analogous new technology. Finally, it recommended calling a third international conference, which never took place because of World War I.

The two Hague Conferences hold considerable importance in the history of international relations because they represent the first serious concrete efforts to solidify projects aiming to avoid but also to humanize war. They were also the starting point for the development of laws governing warfare. These laws developed throughout the twentieth century, leading up to what is presently referred to as laws of armed conflict (also known as international humanitarian law). The rules of law that were adopted at the Hague Conferences are considered today, for the most part, as international custom. They are often referred to within this law (as the Hague Law), specifically that part which regulates the means and methods used in armed conflict.

See also **International Law; War Crimes.**

BIBLIOGRAPHY

Primary Sources

Scott, James Brown. *The Hague Peace Conferences of 1899 and 1907: A Series of Lectures Delivered before the Johns Hopkins University in the Year 1908.* 2 vols. Baltimore, Md., 1909.

Schindler, Dietrich, and Jirí Toman, eds. *The Laws of Armed Conflicts: A Collection of Conventions, Resolutions, and Other Documents.* 3rd ed. Geneva and Dordrecht, 1988.

Secondary Sources

Aldrich, George H., and Christine M. Chinkin. "Symposium: The Hague Peace Conferences, Introduction and Concluding Comments." *American Journal of International Law* 94, no. 1 (2000): 1–98.

ISABELLE VONÈCHE CARDIA

HAIDER, JÖRG (b. 1950), Austrian politician.

An extreme right-wing populist, the charismatic leader of the Austrian Freedom Party (Freiheitliche Partei Österreichs, or FPÖ) Jörg Haider has had an uncommon political career. He led his party, which corralled only 5 percent of the votes in 1986, to become Austria's second most powerful political force, winning 27 percent of the votes in the 1999 general elections. This made him a figurehead of the European nationalist-populist movement.

Haider was born to a family that strongly supported pan-German nationalism and remained faithful to the Nazi regime. His father, a member of the Sturm Abteilung (SA), in 1937 joined the Nazi Party, becoming a permanent member after the Anschluss (German annexation of Austria in 1938). His mother, from a wealthy bourgeois family south of the Tyrol, was an active primary school teacher in the Bund deutscher Mädel (League of German Girls), Hitler's youth organization for girls. Haider has often thanked his parents for their sacrifices in enabling him to attend high school and later to study law in Vienna. His

gratitude also found expression in his defense of the Third Reich's "generation of soldiers" in search of postwar respectability. Inasmuch as many Austrians preferred to see themselves as victims with reference to World War II, eschewing the more painful work of remembrance and acknowledgment, Haider's sympathy for the Nazi legacy found a ready reception.

Haider's career as an activist began when he joined the Freedom Party's youth movement while still in high school. At age eighteen, thanks to his oratorical skills, he became the organization's leader. Then, even as he held that position from 1970 to 1974, in 1973 he obtained a university post. Decidedly attracted by a political career, as early as 1976 Haider served the Freedom Party in the state of Carinthia. His ascent was dazzling. He become the youngest deputy in the parliament in 1979, chief editor of the party's newspaper in 1983, and party chief for the state of Carinthia. In 1986 he bested Norbert Steger, a liberal, and took control of the Freedom Party. Elected governor of Carinthia in 1989, his cynical remarks on the "Third Reich's employment policy" subsequently forced him from office. Elected once again in 1996, he continued to hold that post in 2006.

Haider's success within the party and on the Austrian political scene more generally enabled him to transform the Freedom Party. He eliminated the party's liberal wing while bringing in the extreme Right; he then repositioned pan-German nationalist politics to reach younger voters for whom the older movement had little historical resonance. Haider reconstituted the leadership on an authoritarian basis with a single leader, replacing its parliamentary system by a *Bürgerdemokratie* (democracy of citizens) whose legitimacy would be determined by plebiscite, or popular vote. Finally, he created a right-wing rhetoric that was xenophobic; anti-Semitic; and hostile to immigrants, the Islamic religion, and the European community.

From 1945, Austrian politics was so constructed as to prevent emergence of a genuine alternative to middle-of-the-road politics. This undoubtedly worked in Haider's favor. In 1986 the Freedom Party's ever more effective attacks against the powers that be shattered what was known as the Small Coalition of the Social Democratic Party (Sozialdemokratische Partei

Österreichs, or SPÖ) and the Freedom Party; there ensued a coalition of the SPÖ and the Conservative Party (Österreichische Volkspartei, OVP) that lasted until 1999.

The charismatic Haider succeeded in uniting political currents with diverse ideologies. Making use of the media, he presented himself as defending those left behind in the course of Austria's postwar modernization and leading them in the struggles to treat the ills of Austrian society such as unemployment, corruption, and injustice.

In February 2000, after the stunning elections of 1999, the Freedom Party entered a power-sharing arrangement in coalition with the Conservative Party. Haider was obliged to renounce a cabinet post and to resign as party leader, but he installed his loyal follower Susanne Riess-Passer in his place and continued to wield power. His political objectives included developing a new neoliberal definition of the role of the state and the promotion of private initiative at the expense of the "social partnership" that had characterized the Austrian government's covenant with its people since the end of the Second World War. He also promoted what he considered empowerment and homogenization of the Austrian people, whose unity and identity, he maintained, were threatened by foreign "parasites" that must be excluded. Finally, he sought to monopolize public space so as to eliminate potentially divisive opposition and criticism. However, Haider remained aware of the gap between pragmatic government policy that obeyed European rules of conduct and the need to remain in step with radical populism, which brought the Freedom Party successive electoral debacles after the victories in 1999, as voters deserted it in large numbers. The crisis in the coalition that Haider created in September 2002 and his threat to withdraw from politics on a federal level were expedients designed to cast populists and their leader as providential saviors of unity.

In 2005, after a series of electoral defeats and much dissatisfaction within the FPO, Haider announced the formation of a new party, the Alliance for Austria's Future (AAF). This party, which included the current FPO ministers in the coalition government, offered a broadened populist appeal, diminished hard-right rhetoric, and was even favorable to antiglobalization initiatives and acceptance of Turkey as a member of the European Union.

See also **Anti-Semitism; Austria; Islam.**

BIBLIOGRAPHY

Primary Sources

Haider, Jörg. *Die Freiheit, die ich meine.* Frankfurt, 1994.

Secondary Sources

Betz, Hans-Georg. "Haider's Revolution; or, The Future Has Just Begun." In *Austria in the European Union.* Vol. 10 of *Contempory Austrian Studies,* edited by Günter Bischof, Anton Pelinka, and Michael Gehler. New Brunswick, N.J., 2002.

Livonius v. Eyb, Thilo v. *Die ideologische Entwicklung der FPÖ unter Jörg Haider.* Munich, 2002.

Zöchling, Christa. *Haider.* Osijek, Croatia, 2001.

FABIEN THÉOFILAKIS

HAIG, DOUGLAS

HAIG, DOUGLAS (1861–1928), commander of the British army that beat the Germans on the western front from 1916 to 1918.

Douglas Haig established a reputation as a competent staff officer in the small prewar British professional army. He served with some distinction in campaigns in the Sudan (1897–1898) and South Africa (1899–1902) before taking on a series of administrative, organizational, and training appointments in Britain and India. In these he played a major role in shaping the army that would take the field in 1914. Haig was studious and hard working, but he also fulfilled other requirements of the successful Edwardian officer, playing polo to a high level and engaging in the politics of a fiercely hierarchic organization that still placed a heavy emphasis on patronage.

At the outbreak of World War I, Haig went to France with the British Expeditionary Force (BEF). For the first two years of the war, he served as a subordinate to the British commander in chief on the western front, Sir John French, whom he replaced at the end of 1915. Under Haig's command over the next three years, the British army on the western front fought four great campaigns. In 1916 and 1917 it attacked the Germans on the

Somme and around Ypres. In both cases, the British suffered very heavy casualties while making only limited territorial gains. Neither campaign succeeded in breaking through the German lines in the way Haig hoped. Both succeeded, however, in killing large numbers of Germans as well as Britons—an attritional effect that was not Haig's primary aim but that did bring the end of the war closer. In spring 1918, the British faced a major German offensive for the first time since 1914. Unused to defensive operations, faced with new German tactics and with a recently extended front, parts of the British line rapidly collapsed. In the subsequent defensive battle, Haig acquitted himself well, keeping his head, not allowing the Germans to take the decisive objectives and maintaining the morale of his men with an "Order of the Day" on 11 April 1918 that was long remembered for its stirring words. With the German attack halted, the Allies moved to their own offensive in the summer of 1918. In the last months of World War I, Haig's forces performed very creditably, taking the main part in driving back the German army and forcing its commanders to ask their government to make peace.

In the years after the war, Haig achieved celebrity as a campaigner for British veterans. He became the figurehead of the newly formed British Legion, the most influential British veterans' group. On his death (29 January 1928) he was given a state funeral, and huge crowds lined the streets of London and Edinburgh to bid him farewell; towns across Britain held services of remembrance for him. It was only after his death, particularly in the 1960s, he became demonized in British popular culture.

Historical controversy over Haig centers on his personality, his strategy, and the losses suffered by his armies. The relevance of a critique based on modern historians' distaste for or incomprehension of Edwardian attitudes is not clear. Generalship is not a beauty contest. His strategic insight, that the British should concentrate their effort against their principal opponent—the German army on the western front—is hard to fault. If Britain wished to maintain its prewar existence, it had little choice except to commit to heavy fighting in France and Flanders. Haig is open to criticism for the length of time it took him to appreciate the implications of the tactical and technological context in which he fought. By aiming at decisive breakthroughs, rather than confining himself to the destruction of the enemy's forces, it could be argued that he inflicted unnecessary losses on his own men. Proper assessment of this criticism has been confused by an understandable horror at the sheer number of casualties and the absence of any comparable event in Britain's military history.

Haig's significance for Europe was that he helped to prevent the first German bid for hegemony in the twentieth century. This was also his key significance for Britain in geostrategic terms. In cultural and historical terms, it was perhaps more significant that he commanded the country's largest military force on the only occasion in which it confronted the main strength of a great-power opponent in a land war. In Britain in the early twenty-first century, Haig is remembered principally for the heavy casualties that were the inevitable result, rather than the victory he helped to achieve.

See also **Armies; Warfare; World War I.**

BIBLIOGRAPHY

Prior, Robin, and Trevor Wilson. *Passchendaele: The Untold Story.* New Haven, Conn., and London, 1996. A balanced assessment of British performance in the battle.

Sheffield, Gary. *Forgotten Victory: The First World War, Myths and Realities.* London, 2001. The most easily accessible history of Britain's part in World War I.

Travers, Tim. *The Killing Ground: The British Army, the Western Front, and the Emergence of Modern Warfare, 1900–1918.* London, 1987. A more critical view of Haig's performance.

Todman, Daniel. *The Great War: Myth and Memory.* London, 2005. An exploration of the development of British shared beliefs about World War I from 1918 to the early twenty-first century.

DANIEL TODMAN

HALBWACHS, MAURICE (1877–1945), French philosopher and sociologist.

Maurice Halbwachs studied with both the philosopher Henri-Louis Bergson (1859–1941) and the sociologist Émile Durkheim (1858–1917). His best-known work opened new perspectives on the concept of collective memory, understood as the social practices by which different groups of people recollect their common past.

Born on 11 March 1877, Halbwachs graduated from École Normale Supérieure, receiving his *agrégation* first in philosophy in 1901, later in sociology. He thus reached intellectual maturity about the time of the Dreyfus affair, which tore France in two. His outlook was cosmopolitan; Halbwachs was one of a number of French intellectuals who valued and absorbed German scholarship. His early work was on metropolitan life and living standards. In 1913 he published *La classe ouvrière et les niveaux de vie: Recherches sur la hiérarchie des besoins dans les sociétés industrielles contemporaines* (The working class and living standards: Research on the hierarchy of needs in contemporary industrial societies). Intellectual issues captivated Halbwachs, from the social sciences to mathematics, from philosophy to music, to such an extent that one might say he was a social scientific school unto himself. In 1914 the socialist Halbwachs, despite his usual lucidity, chose to support the French war effort and to work for social and political unity. Poor vision kept him from combat, and instead he served in the circle of civil servants surrounding the socialist minister of armaments and war, Albert Thomas.

After the war, he taught at Strasbourg University, which had been recaptured from the Germans, together with others among the French intellectual elite. Among them, the French historians Marc Bloch (1886–1944) and Lucien Febvre (1878–1956) invited him to join the editorial committee of the pathbreaking journal of economic and social history, *Annales*.

Halbwach's major works are his sociological analyses of memory and suicide: *Les cadres sociaux de la mémoire* (1925; Collective memory) and *Les causes du suicide* (1930; The causes of suicide). In the interwar years, he was developing a distinctive approach to sociology, halfway between Bergson and the late Durkheim. He did not share the political activism of his sister Jeanne Halbwachs, who with her husband was involved in the pacifist movement in France. Thus, Halbwachs's major work on the social construction of memory, written before World War II, makes virtually no reference to contemporary events. Despite the obsession with commemoration of World War I in interwar France,

Halbwachs never refers to war and remembrance in his sociological studies. Nevertheless, Halbwachs showed how individual memory cannot exist without a social framework, and that public events imprint themselves on the contemporary public, particularly the young, who are still developing an adult identity. We are never the first person who knows who we are: others tell us what we need to remember in order to be who we are. Memories are at once individual and private and, contrary to dreams, can be shared and are collectively defined. But "personal" memory also preserves traces, unique to each individual, that combine with communal and collective memories. We adjust our own memories to fit the social groups in which we live our lives. If individuals literally *remember*, it is the group to which they belong that determines what is memorable. Society's power is immense and serves above all as a powerful *constraint* in the sense that Halbwachs's teacher, Durkheim, understood it to be.

Yvonne Basch, Halbwach's wife, introduced him to the League for the Defence of Human Rights and its president, her father, the fiery Victor Basch. She also initiated him—he was an agnostic though born Catholic—into a world of assimilated French Jewish culture about which he knew little. Halbwachs refined his reflections on memory in what would be his last and most complete work to be published in his lifetime, *La topographie légendaire des Evangiles en Terre Sainte* (1941; The legendary topography of the Gospels in the Holy Land).

Halbwachs, who had early studied Gottfried Wilhelm Leibniz and German philosophy, was a pioneer of French and German cultural exchange, most particularly by introducing the work of the German sociologist Max Weber (1864–1920) into France. An early antifascist, he sheltered Italian and German refugees, including the German Jewish philosopher Walter Benjamin (1892–1940), joining the French Resistance together with his two sons in 1940. In 1944 a fascist militia murdered his wife's parents, Victor and Ilona Basch, and he was in ever greater danger. In the summer of 1944, with his younger son Pierre, he was deported to Buchenwald. He had just been admitted to the prestigious Collège de France but would not return for his inauguration speech. He died in Buchenwald. Although Halbwachs's contributions were largely forgotten over the next half century, they have since reentered American and European intellectual discourse. Restored to his proper place, the man who coined the term *collective memory* offers a variety of useful concepts toward an improved grasp of repression, forgetting, indeed amnesia—all at the heart of the processes of remembrance understood as a social phenomenon.

See also **Benjamin, Walter; Bloch, Marc; Holocaust; Resistance.**

BIBLIOGRAPHY

Primary Sources

Halbwachs, Maurice. *The Collective Memory.* Translated by Francis J. Ditter Jr. and Vida Yazdi Ditter. New York, 1980.

———. *On Collective Memory.* Edited, translated, and with an introduction by Lewis A. Coser. Chicago, 1992.

Secondary Sources

Becker, Annette. *Maurice Halbwachs: Un intellectuel en guerres mondiales, 1914–1945.* Paris, 2003.

Ricoeur, Paul. *La mémoire, l'histoire, l'oubli.* Paris, 2000.

ANNETTE BECKER

HAMILTON, RICHARD (b. 1922),

British painter, designer, and graphic artist.

Richard Hamilton studied at the Royal Academy Schools from 1938 until 1940, when the Second World War cut short his course. During the war he trained as a jig and tool draftsman, which gave him skills in precision drawing. He returned to the Royal Academy Schools but was expelled in 1946 and entered the Slade School of Art in 1948. He stayed there until 1951, his peers including William Turnbull, Eduardo Paolozzi, and Nigel Henderson. Hamilton and these men, together with the critics Lawrence Alloway and Reyner Banham, were the core members of the Independent Group, which met at the Institute of Contemporary Arts (ICA) between 1952 and 1955. This group shared strong enthusiasm for popular culture and a desire to widen the sources of contemporary art.

Hamilton taught design at the Central School of Art from 1952 to 1953 and from 1953 to 1966 at King's College, Durham University, at Newcastle-upon-Tyne. His gifts as an imaginative designer are evident in the exhibitions he designed and largely curated throughout the 1950s. The first, *On Growth and Form,* at the ICA in 1951, was based on D'Arcy Thompson's eponymous book. It was followed in 1955 by *Man, Machine, and Motion* at Newcastle, where Hamilton displayed photographs showing man's ambitious use of machines to extend the capacities of his body. Environmental exhibitions of mazelike spaces, devised with his colleague Victor Pasmore, followed in 1957 and 1959, and in the latter year they also mounted *The Developing Process* to explain their new teaching, based partly on Bauhaus methods.

The most famous of these exhibitions was *This Is Tomorrow* at the Whitechapel Gallery, London, in 1956. Though Hamilton did not originate this exhibition, in which teams of artists and architects worked together to create environments that were themselves works of art, he devised a section with John Voelcker and John McHale. Their section, a "fun house," had two themes—"imagery" and "perception." "Perception" involved optical illusions, such as Marcel Duchamp's *Rotoreliefs.* "Imagery" included material from popular culture, such as a blowup of Marilyn Monroe in *The Seven Year Itch.* Popular culture was the basis of a collage Hamilton made for the poster to his section. Entitled *"Just what is it that makes today's homes so different, so appealing?"* it was assembled from iconic images drawn from advertisements and popular magazines. This collage has been taken, with Paolozzi's collages of around 1950, which used similar imagery but in a less programmed manner, as the start of Pop Art in England.

Hamilton's earlier work is very different. His illustrations to James Joyce's *Ulysses,* begun in 1947, recall Pablo Picasso's neoclassical drawings of around 1919. Abstract paintings of around 1950 have systematically expanding linear compositions suggested by D'Arcy Thompson's explanations of natural growth. A series of figurative paintings of 1954–1955 recall Paul Cézanne, seen through the lenses of Eadweard Muybridge or Éttiene-Jules Marey. The suggestion of movement is important and was to remain so, although Hamilton's techniques were to change radically. Influences came from James Gibson's *The Perception of the Visual World,* Sigfried Giedion's *Mechanization Takes*

Just What Is It that Makes Today's Homes So Different, So Appealing? Collage by Richard Hamilton, 1959. BRIDGEMAN ART LIBRARY

Command, Amedée Ozenfant's *Foundations of Modern Art,* and, most importantly, Duchamp. In 1960 Hamilton produced a typographic version of Duchamp's *Green Box,* and in 1966 he curated a major Duchamp exhibition at the Tate Gallery. For this exhibition he painstakingly made a replica of Duchamp's *Large Glass.*

Duchamp's aim "to put thought back into art" and especially his invention of the "ready-made" were crucial for Hamilton. But where Duchamp chose his ready-mades with "aesthetic indifference," Hamilton was attracted by highly designed objects of two very different kinds. On the one hand, he admired the austere post-Bauhaus products of the Hochschule für Gestaltung at Ulm; on the other, he delighted in the glamorous advertising of rapidly obsolescent American consumer goods. In the early twenty-first century it is difficult not to see irony in his use of both these sources, but his enthusiasm was an antidote in the drab postwar years. Hamilton visited Ulm in 1958 and in 1963 made his first trip to the United States, where he was befriended by Duchamp. By then, Hamilton had made his first pop paintings, such as *Hommage à Chrysler Corp* (1957) and *$he* (1958–1961). His harnessing of the sexual glamour of advertisements predates that by the pop artists at the Royal College and by American artists such as Roy Lichtenstein and Andy Warhol. Hamilton himself has said that he has been engaged on "a search for what is epic in everyday objects and everyday attitudes" (1982, p. 37).

He has used photography extensively, translating images into his works with startling ingenuity. He will use photographic silkscreen, negative reversals, and soft and sharp focus, drawing his images from very diverse sources. He explores new techniques of reproduction as they become available. He has designed a hi-fi set and a computer for industrial production. In these ways he has broken down the division between design and fine art. Yet he thinks of himself primarily as a painter, and his genres are traditional—interiors, still life, figures, landscapes.

In much of his art there is a strong narrative content and, as Hamilton is left-wing, there is often sharp social comment. Examples are *Swingeing London '67,* based on a newspaper photograph of the handcuffed Mick Jagger and Robert Fraser after a drug raid, or the savagely satirical *Portrait of Hugh Gaitskell as a Famous Monster of Filmland* (1964). And since about 1973, Hamilton's view has darkened. *The Citizen* (1982–1983) and *The Subject* (1988–1990) use reportage photographs to present sectarian figures in the civil war in Northern Ireland. *Treatment Room* (1983–1984) and *Lobby* (1985–1987) convey the bleak alienation of modern corporate interiors. *War Games* (1991–1992), referring to the war in Kuwait, shows how war, as a news item, has become a spectator sport.

Hamilton had exhibitions at the Hanover Gallery in 1955 and 1964 and major retrospectives at the Tate Gallery in 1970 and 1992. An anthology of his writings was published in 1982.

See also **Pop Art; Popular Culture.**

BIBLIOGRAPHY

Hamilton, Richard. *Richard Hamilton.* Introduction by Richard Morphet. London, 1970. Catalog of an exhibition at the Tate Gallery, London, 12 March–19 April 1970.

———. *Collected Words.* London, 1982.

———. *Richard Hamilton.* London, 1992. Catalog of an exhibition at the Tate Gallery, London, 17 June–6 September 1992. Essays by Richard Morphet, David Mellor, Sarat Maharaj, and Stephen Snoddy.

ALASTAIR GRIEVE

HARRIS, ARTHUR (nicknamed "Bomber" Harris, 1892–1984), chief of the British Royal Air Force (RAF) Bomber Command from 1942 to 1945.

Born at Cheltenham in Gloucestershire, the son of an engineer-architect in the Indian civil service, Arthur Harris was educated at Gore Court, Sittingbourne, and Allhallows, Honiton. In 1914 Harris joined the first Rhodesian Regiment as a bugler and took part in the campaign against German South-West Africa. In 1915 he returned to Britain and was commissioned into the Royal Flying Corps. He participated in defensive night fighter operations against zeppelin raids and also served on the western front, where he earned enough victories to qualify as an air ace. After the war, he took a permanent commission in the RAF and was involved in air operations in northwest India, Iraq, and Palestine. In 1939 Harris was given command of No. 5 (Bomber) Group, which did valuable work against German shipping concentrations and airfields during the invasion threat in 1940. Later that year he became deputy chief of the Air Staff and in 1941 was appointed head of the RAF delegation to Washington, where he sought to speed up the delivery of aircraft and air supplies. In 1942 he was summoned back to Britain to become commander in chief of Bomber Command.

Under Harris, Bomber Command developed into a formidable weapon of war. His favored method of attack was the area bombing of German cities at night. He did not invent the policy—it was already in operation from 1941— but he pursued it with relentless zeal. He firmly believed that the destruction of German cities and the homes of the workers would bring the enemy to its knees and prevent a repetition of the bloody battles of attrition on the western front that he had witnessed during the previous war. While the United States Air Force concentrated on precision attacks during the day as part of a combined bomber offensive, Bomber Command unleashed a series of large-scale raids on such cities as Essen, Hamburg, and Berlin. The zenith of the area bombing campaign came at Dresden in February 1945, when the RAF started a massive firestorm that devastated the old city and killed between twenty-five and thirty-five thousand people.

Since the war the military and ethical justifications for Harris's area bombing policy have been called into question. The critics argue that the results of the bombing were not worth the heavy cost in RAF aircrew lives, that the extensive resources poured into Bomber Command could have been put to better use, and that the deliberate targeting of German civilians was an unacceptable means of waging war. Harris's defenders, however, contend that the bombing played a significant role in the Allied victory in Europe. Although the bombing did not prevent a sustained increase in German military production or fatally undermine civilian morale, the effects of the Anglo-American bombing offensive—and it is difficult to consider one in isolation from the other—were considerable. For example, a ceiling was placed on the growth of military output, and factories were diverted to producing items for home defense such as antiaircraft guns and ammunition, which deprived the German army of vital battlefield equipment. Many German troops were tied up in antiaircraft duties when they could have been more usefully employed on other fighting fronts, and German offensive airpower was restricted as the Luftwaffe was forced to defend the Reich against air attack. While the bombing of cities was undoubtedly a dreadful way to wage war, this was regarded at the time as little different from the policy of targeting civilians through blockade or siege in previous wars. The Allies were engaged in a war of survival against a brutal totalitarian regime, and civilian workers were at the heart of the enemy's war potential. Certainly Harris, who had watched London burn during the Blitz, had little sympathy for the Germans: they had sown the wind and would reap the whirlwind.

At the end of the war Harris was embittered by the seeming reluctance of the British government to acknowledge the role of Bomber Command in the defeat of Germany. He retired from the RAF and went to live in South Africa. In the 1950s he returned to Britain and spent his latter years quietly in rural Oxfordshire, with occasional forays onto the public stage. He died in 1984. In 1992 a statue of Harris was unveiled by the Queen Mother in London. The mayors of Dresden and other cities that had been heavily bombed expressed their disapproval. The Bomber Command veterans regarded it as a long overdue tribute to a much maligned commander.

See also **Armies; Warfare; World War II.**

BIBLIOGRAPHY

Harris, Sir Arthur. *Bomber Offensive*. London, 1947.

Overy, R. J. "Harris, Sir Arthur Travers, First Baronet (1892–1984)." In *Oxford Dictionary of National Biography,* edited by H. C. G. Matthew and Brian Harrison. Oxford, U.K., 2004.

Probert, Henry. *Bomber Harris: His Life and Times.* London, 2001.

JEREMY A. CRANG

HAVEL, VÁCLAV (b. 1936), Czech politician and writer.

In his life Václav Havel has been a child of privilege, a stagehand, a dramaturge, an author of absurdist plays, a brewery laborer, the founder of Charter 77, a prisoner of conscience, and—not long after—the president of his country. He was the mastermind behind the Velvet Revolution that overthrew communism in Czechoslovakia and the last president of his country, the man who managed the Velvet Divorce—the peaceful separation of Czechoslovakia into two nations. As the Czech Republic's first president, he helped reintegrate the country into Western Europe. He is a world-renowned author and statesmen. The playwright Arthur Miller (1915–2005) called him the first surrealist president. He is regularly on the short list to receive the Nobel Prize.

Havel's life has been full of contradictions, ironies, and strange twists. He was born into an affectionate, successful entrepreneurial family. He and his brother Ivan (b. 1938) were raised with a strong sense of discipline, independence, and responsibility inspired by Masarykian humanism, a highly cultured tradition of arts, philosophy, and literature (Tomáš Garrigue Masaryk [1850–1937] was Czechoslovakia's first president). But Havel was uncomfortable with the trappings of affluence, resulting in what he describes as a lifelong sense of unworthiness—which he credits with giving him a

Václav Havel flashes a victory sign during a trip to Canada, 19 February 1990.
©Reuters/Corbis

strong urge to succeed. When the communists seized power in 1948 the family fortune was confiscated; Havel became a "class enemy" and was denied admission to the Academy of Performing Arts. He claims that the discrimination he suffered—the sense of being an outsider—was the genesis of his attachment to the theater of the absurd. It was not until he started dating Olga Šplíchalová (1933–1996), whom he married in 1964, that he gained a sense of self-confidence.

Havel eventually enrolled at the Czech Technical University, where he was a lackluster student because the curriculum consisted primarily of Marxist economics. His greatest knack at that time was associating with talented people, including the writer Milan Kundera (b. 1929) and the future Academy Award–winning movie director Miloš Forman (b. 1932). Despite his shyness, during these years Havel had the temerity to introduce himself to Jaroslav Seifert (1901–1986), later winner of the Nobel Prize, and the Czech philosopher Jan Patočka (1907–1977).

Havel's predilection for telling the truth often landed him in trouble. While still a university student in 1956, he was invited to a Writers' Union conference for young artists. It was his first public address, and he found himself among writers of "socialist realism," the artificial and hagiographic style developed during Stalin's reign. Barely in his twenties and with no reputation to protect him, Havel promptly attacked socialist realism, the Writers' Union, the continued oppression of literature, and the blackballing of poets and artists who refused to copy accepted styles.

The future president began his professional life as a stagehand and eventually rose to dramaturge during the early 1960s. It was a hopeful time in Prague: the totalitarian Stalinist era had ended, and personal and artistic freedom flourished, although within some limits. That period was a particularly creative time in Havel's life: he wrote and directed *The Garden Party* (1963), *The Memorandum* in (1965), and *The Increased Difficulty of Concentration*, winner of an off-Broadway Obie Award in 1968.

Under the reform-minded Communist Party leader Alexander Dubček (1921–1992), Czechoslovakia became for a brief period in 1968 an open society, and Havel used the opportunity to call for a multiparty democracy. But communist authorities in Moscow feared that Dubček's brand of "socialism with a human face" threatened the Soviet Empire. In August, Soviet leaders sent the Warsaw Pact Army into Czechoslovakia to halt the reforms. In a desperate effort to rally his countrymen, the Charles University student Jan Palach (1948–1969) lit himself afire in Wenceslas Square as a symbolic protest. But the Soviets prevailed. The era of "Normalization" followed, a depressing period in which the communist government kept order and "calm" by quashing spontaneity and personal initiative—anything that deviated from the austere Soviet model. Havel's avant-garde plays were banned, and he was eventually barred from the theater altogether. But he proclaimed his defiance in an open letter to Gustav Husák (1913–1991), the secretary of the Czechoslovak Communist Party, a bitter indictment of the posttotalitarian system whose goal was to keep the nation as "calm as a morgue or a grave."

Charter 77 was a human-rights group that grew out of the trial and conviction of the Plastic People of the Universe, a rock band whose anti-establishment lyrics infuriated staid communist rulers. When Charter 77's activities drew Western attention, the government arrested leading Chartists, including Havel. During a weeklong StB (State Security Police) interrogation, Patočka, whom Havel had enlisted as spokesman for the group, died of a stroke. Havel dedicated his most famous dissident essay, "The Power of the Powerless," to Patočka. Widely distributed in samizdat, the underground publishing network often consisting of little more than a typewriter and carbon paper, the essay became the rallying point for dissidents throughout the communist world.

In 1979 Soviet authorities cracked down: Havel was convicted of subversion and sentenced to four and a half years at hard labor. But he turned this hardship into creativity, writing letters to his wife that became *Letters to Olga*—one of the strangest "philosophic" books ever published. Along with lengthy theoretical reflections, Havel used the letters to bare his soul. While exhibiting extraordinary courage and steadfastness, at times he showed himself to be frightened, self-absorbed, and demanding. When he became seriously ill after three years in prison, Olga raised such a stir that Havel was released.

In 1989, as European communism was collapsing, Czech students staged a demonstration that "happened" to deviate from its approved route to pass Havel's apartment. A melee ensued; people were arrested and some hurt. Havel quickly organized Civic Forum, a loose-knit opposition group of activists, writers, and theater people. Larger and larger demonstrations occurred, including a national strike that undermined the legitimacy of the government. The "Velvet Revolution," as the movement was called, culminated with Havel on a balcony in historic Wenceslas Square above a massive crowd of people jingling their keys. The sound was the death knell of communism.

Elected president of Czechoslovakia, the poet with a self-effacing wit who rode a scooter through the halls of the Czech Castle, loved Lou Reed's (b. 1942) music, and considered appointing the avant-garde musician Frank Zappa (1940–1993) to a government post was an international darling. And Havel's achievements were substantial, despite his limited constitutional powers. He negotiated the departure of Soviet troops from Czechoslovakia, dismantled the secret police (StB), helped reform the army, and oversaw the creation of democratic institutions with protection of citizen rights. Also—against his wishes—he guided the peaceful dissolution of the country into the Czech and Slovak Republics. He supported the difficult transition to a free-market economy and set the stage for the Czech Republic's entry into NATO and the European Union.

But no fairy tale lasts. Olga Havel succumbed to cancer in 1996. Long years of smoking and stress caught up with Havel, and he almost died of complications associated with the removal of a cancerous lung. On his sickbed, within a year of Olga's death, he married the Czech actress Dagmar Veskrnova (b. 1953)—to great public disapproval. At the same time, in 1996, the highly touted Czech economic miracle floundered, and Prime Minister Václav Klaus's (b. 1941) political party was implicated in an election scandal. Havel's popularity plummeted.

Against all odds, Havel survived, physically and politically. Thirteen years after he took office as leader of Czechoslovakia, he retired from the presidency of the Czech Republic. Although in 1993 Havel had been blamed for the breakup of the country, a week before the end of his term in 2003 Slovakia awarded him its highest civilian medal. Polls showed that he was the most respected public figure among Czechs—partly because a substantial portion of his wealth has been donated to the Olga Havel Foundation, established by his first wife.

Havel considers himself foremost a playwright, but his plays are difficult to categorize. He employs the absurdist genre to explore the loss of identity— the absence of belief in meaning beyond one's transitory existence. The plays raise the question of meaning by manifesting its absence. The works also point beyond that absurdity to the more "natural" view of life that includes transcendent principles such as love, hate, honor, justice, and friendship—virtues and vices that are never fully controlled or extirpated by those in power.

Havel is also an important social critic. He argues that the Enlightenment yearning to understand and control nature—a hope that has largely come to pass—has also resulted in the subjugation of people, whether by totalitarian communist governments that aimed to perfect human society but in fact oppressed millions in ideological straitjackets, or by Western economic entities and government bureaucracies that provide material well-being but rob people of autonomy. To counter this loss of control Havel proposes constructing and strengthening spaces in civil society where moral and responsible actions are possible. His long-term goal seems to be to restructure politics so that citizens can live in small, tightly knit communities and together create an integrated, peaceful, safe world.

See also Czech Republic; Czechoslovakia; Dubček, Alexander; Prague; Prague Spring; Velvet Revolution.

BIBLIOGRAPHY

Havel, Václav. *The Vaněk Plays: Four Authors, One Character.* Edited by Marketa Goetz-Stankiewicz. Vancouver, B.C., 1987.

———. *Letters to Olga: June 1979–September 1982.* Translated and Introduced by Paul Wilson. New York, 1988.

———. *Temptation: A Play in Ten Scenes.* Translated by Marie Winn. New York, 1989.

———. *Disturbing the Peace: A Conversation with Karel Hvížďala.* Translated and Introduced by Paul Wilson. New York, 1990.

———. *Open Letters: Selected Writings, 1965–1990.* Edited by Paul Wilson. New York, 1991.

———. *The Garden Party and Other Plays.* New York, 1993.

———. *Summer Meditations.* Translated by Paul Wilson. New York, 1993.

———. *Selected Plays: 1984–87.* London and Boston, 1994.

———. *The Art of the Impossible: Politics as Morality in Practice: Speeches and Writings, 1990–1996.* Translated by Paul Wilson et al. New York, 1997.

———. *The Beggar's Opera.* Translated by Paul Wilson and introduced by Peter Steiner. Ithaca, N.Y., 2001.

JAMES PONTUSO

HEATH, EDWARD

HEATH, EDWARD (1916–2005), British Conservative Party politician, member of Parliament, and prime minister (1970–1974).

Edward Richard George Heath, the son of a carpenter who won an organ scholarship to Balliol College at the University of Oxford, rose rapidly though the post–World War II Conservative Party. Elected to the House of Commons in 1950, he made his first speech advocating British involvement in European integration. This was to become the key theme of his political career and was crowned by Britain's admission to the European Economic Community (EEC) in 1973.

From 1952 Heath served in the Whips' Office, with a brief spell as minister of labour (1959–1960). As Lord Privy Seal (1960–1963), he had special responsibility for attempting to negotiate Britain's first application to join the EEC. This ended in failure when the French president, Charles de Gaulle (1890–1970), vetoed the application in 1963, but Heath emerged with his reputation enhanced. The Conservatives lost the 1964 general election and Sir Alexander Frederick Douglas-Home (1903–1995) agreed to resign as leader. Heath became the new leader in 1965 after becoming the first Conservative leader to be elected by a ballot of Conservative MPs. Aged forty-nine, Heath was the youngest leader of the party for over a century. During his period as leader of the opposition (1965–1970), he concentrated the party's energies on policy making, in preparation for a return to government. His leadership was tested in April 1968 by Enoch Powell (1912–1998). Powell made an anti-immigration speech in Birmingham that provoked outrage, and Heath fired him from the shadow cabinet.

Heath became prime minister in June 1970. After thirty-one days in office, the unexpected death of Ian Macleod (1913–1970), the chancellor of the exchequer, proved a massive blow. The policies of his replacement, Anthony Barber (b. 1920), proved controversial. Barber's "dash for growth" initially provoked economic prosperity, but rising inflation and record levels of unemployment soon followed. The government's rescue of the Upper Clyde Shipbuilders, previously perceived a "lame duck," was dubbed a U-turn by critics. Heath's imposition of an incomes policy in an attempt to deal with inflation led to a national coal strike in 1972. When Heath responded by declaring a state of emergency, waves of strikes broke out in the coal, power, and transport industries. The ensuing power shortages led to the imposition of a three-day week in December. During Heath's premiership, Northern Ireland reemerged as a major problem for the British. The first British solider was killed in Belfast in February 1971, obliging Heath to introduce internment (August 1971). Matters worsened when the army killed thirteen during the Londonderry "Bloody Sunday" riots in January 1972, and eventually in March the government was obliged to reimpose direct Westminster rule for the province. Heath's major accomplishment was to bring the United Kingdom into the European Community (later the European Union).

In February 1974, Heath called a general election to let the country decide "Who Governs Britain." His party lost, and he resigned as prime minister in March after failing to win the support of the Liberal Party to form a minority government. The Conservatives were defeated again in the October 1974 election. One year later Heath lost his post as party leader to Margaret Thatcher (b. 1925). Heath retained his seat in Parliament but held no posts in subsequent Conservative cabinets. He remained one of the chief spokespersons for the pro-Europeans within the Conservative Party. He stood down as a MP in 2001. Heath died on 17 July 2005.

Outside of politics, Heath pursued his passions for music and sailing. He led the British sailing team to victory in the 1971 Admiral's Cup and won the famous Sydney-Hobart race, aboard his yacht *Morning Cloud*, in January 1970. However, sailing was not without personal tragedy. In September 1974, *Morning Cloud III* sank with the loss of two lives, including Heath's twenty-two-year-old godson. It undoubtedly affected Heath's performance in the general election two weeks later.

Heath's premiership has been cast by Thatcherites as a disaster. His U-turns implied weakness, and ultimately failure. This analysis presumes that the January 1970 Selsdon Park shadow cabinet conference was a blueprint for monetarism and market economics. Heath never believed in laissez-faire, but was a traditional Tory who saw the state as an essential deliverer of economic and social policy and sensed the need for radical change. Much of Heath's post-1975 political life was motivated by personal antipathy toward Thatcherism.

See also **European Union; Northern Ireland; Thatcher, Margaret; United Kingdom.**

BIBLIOGRAPHY

Ball, Stuart, and Anthony Seldon, eds. *The Heath Government, 1970–1974: A Reappraisal.* London, 1996.

Campbell, John. *Edward Heath: A Biography.* London, 1993.

Heath, Edward. *The Course of My Life: My Autobiography.* London, 1998.

Holmes, Martin. *Failure of the Heath Government.* 2nd ed. Basingstoke, U.K., 1997.

Ramsden, John. *Winds of Change: Macmillan to Heath, 1957–1975.* London, 1996.

NICK CROWSON

HEIDEGGER, MARTIN (1889–1976),
German philosopher.

After enrolling at Freiburg University as a seminary student, in 1919 Martin Heidegger became Edmund Husserl's research assistant. Husserl (1859–1938) had made his name as the founder of the phenomenological movement. In works such as *Ideas toward a Transcendental Phenomenology* (1913), he attempted to place philosophical knowledge on a rigorous footing, free from unverifiable, metaphysical speculation and dogma. The epistemological linchpin of Husserl's efforts was the concept of "intentionality." Intentionality was Husserl's way of circumventing the problem of philosophical "dualism"—for example, the mind-body problem on which René Descartes's philosophy had foundered. The notion of intentionality suggested that "consciousness" was always *consciousness of* something, and that, consequently, the cognitive separation between "subject" and "object" was immaterial.

HEIDEGGER'S PHILOSOPHICAL INNOVATION

From the outset it was clear that Heidegger had a very different conception of phenomenology's mission. For Heidegger's generation, the project of "transcendental philosophy," as traditionally conceived, seemed sterile and feckless. As many scholars have pointed out, in central Europe the human and psychological toll taken by World War I resulted in the delegitimation of nearly all inherited intellectual paradigms. One of the main casualties was neo-Kantianism, which, prior to the war, had been the dominant philosophical methodology among German universities. Simply put, neo-Kantianism's arid rationalism, as practiced by the likes of Hermann Cohen, Emil Lask, and Wilhelm Windelband, seemed patently unable to address the vital, existential questions that had arisen in the war's wake.

It is clear that, from his very first Freiburg University lecture courses, Heidegger focused on existential problems and dilemmas that, as a rule, fell beneath phenomenology's radar scope. For Husserl, the classical dilemma of "certainty" remained central. For Heidegger, conversely, to inquire about the fundamental questions of human being-in-the-world made questions of certainty seem immaterial and tangential. In Heidegger's view, literary works by Søren Kierkegaard, Fyodor Dostoyevsky, and Vincent van Gogh (whose impassioned letters had recently been published) were as

important as—if not more so—the classic texts of transcendental philosophy.

As he began his academic career in the late 1910s and early 1920s, Heidegger's understanding of the history of philosophy was also influenced by an intensive reading of the classic works of Protestant theology: St. Augustine, Martin Luther, and Kierkegaard. Unlike the Scholastic tradition in which Heidegger had been schooled, in these texts questions of human self-realization or "selfhood" were paramount. Heidegger concluded that to dissolve such questions in abstract processes of transcendental-logical inquiry, as was characteristic of so much of the history of Western rationalism, was a testimony to academic philosophy's existential irrelevance. In this respect, he perceived Husserl's transcendental phenomenological inquiries as merely the last in a long list of offenders.

From this standpoint it is easy to see why, when it appeared in 1927, *Being and Time* was such an immense success. It offered a powerful and thoroughgoing response to the intellectual crisis of the 1920s. The book's ability to pose questions that were remarkably in tune with the zeitgeist left the various "school philosophies" of the day standing in the dust, as it were. Suddenly, with Heidegger's "existential ontology" there was talk of "care," "everydayness," "curiosity," "destiny," "authenticity," "choosing one's hero," and "being-toward-death." "Fundamental ontology" (as Heidegger described his project) boldly proceeded to "dismantle" (*abbauen*) the history of ontology, which, owing to its neglect of everyday human concerns, seemed entirely to deserve the fate that this upstart provincial philosopher had meted out to it.

HEIDEGGER AND THE NAZI PARTY

Yet, as a result of having imbibed the zeitgeist, Heidegger's philosophy was, in certain respects, very possibly *too* close to its time. Retrospectively, it seems that the basic categories of *Being and Time* bore eerie affinities with the "conservative revolutionary" critique of modernity. In this respect *Being and Time* is not only a work of "first philosophy." It is also a textbook example of interwar *Zivilisationskritik*—one that follows in the footsteps of Friedrich Nietzsche, Oswald Spengler, and Ernst Jünger. Hence, if one pays attention to the book's ideological traits—for example, the discussions of *Volk* (people) and *Gemeinschaft* (community) in paragraph 74—it is perhaps not so surprising that, come 1933, Heidegger leaped with alacrity into the brown uniform of the Nazi Party.

Heidegger, who had recently been named rector of Freiburg University, joined the Nazi Party on 1 May 1933 with great fanfare. Although his tenure in office was brief (he resigned a year later, upon realizing that Adolf Hitler and company had little interest in making the world safe for the "question of Being"), nevertheless, considerable damage had been done. In essence, Heidegger delivered the university, which possessed a long tradition of self-government, directly into the Nazi hands. In 1946 a favorably disposed denazification committee concluded that Heidegger, by virtue of his considerable international renown, played a key role in legitimating the Nazi seizure of power among Germany's educated elite.

As Heidegger would learn, it was impossible to emerge with clean hands from involvement with an inherently criminal entity like National Socialism. In his capacity as rector, Heidegger willingly enforced legislation ensuring that Jews and political undesirables were removed from positions of power and influence. One by one his talented Jewish students—Hannah Arendt, Karl Löwith, Hans Jonas, Herbert Marcuse, and Werner Brock—were forced to emigrate. Already during the late 1920s, Heidegger had openly lamented the "Jewification" (*Verjudung*) of the German university system. During the 1930s, he denounced colleagues to the Gestapo as insufficiently radical. He also proved a vigorous supporter of the November 1933 referendum called by Hitler on Germany's withdrawal from the League of Nations. He ended lectures and correspondence with the so-called *Hitler Grüss* ("Heil Hitler!") and remained a dues paying member of the party until the "collapse" of 1945.

AFTER THE WAR

As a result of these activities, Heidegger's *venia legendi*, or right to teach, was revoked after the war. Although he was permitted to write and publish, he was banned from university life for a period of five years. Former students implored him to publicly renounce his Nazi involvement, but their appeals fell on deaf ears. According to the writer Ernst Jünger, Heidegger felt that Hitler owed *him*—Heidegger—an apology insofar as the Nazi movement had failed to live up to its world historical potential. As late as 1953, the philosopher published texts that openly fantasized about the "inner truth and greatness of the Movement [i.e., National Socialism]."

Despite these setbacks, Heidegger's postwar career blossomed. He enjoyed a "second career" as lecturer among German neonationalist circles. He found a new audience in France owing to the patronage of the philosopher and former member of the French Resistance Jean Beaufret, the addressee of the 1946 "Letter on Humanism." (However, during the 1980s it was revealed that Beaufret was a covert supporter of the Holocaust denier Robert Faurisson.) In the United States, Hannah Arendt became his main patron, facilitating the translation and publication of his books and articles. Theologians readily embraced Heidegger's philosophy. His critique of the modern world as a "site of catastrophe" suited their misgivings about the displacement of religion and rise of secular humanism. They assumed that the "question of Being" (*Seinsfrage*) was merely an indirect way of talking about God. Curiously, the 1960s witnessed something of a Heidegger vogue. It was during this decade, marked by the American debacle in Vietnam, that his critique of technology—one of the major themes in his postwar writings—seemed to possess special clairvoyance. Whereas liberal political thought enthusiastically embraced the doctrines of atomistic individualism and technological progress, Heidegger's philosophy seemed to offer a powerful theoretical alternative. Paradoxically, Heidegger's resolute antimodernism had become au courant.

Whereas Heidegger's early philosophy focused on *Dasein,* or man's being-in-the-world, his later thought underwent a reversal: the emphasis now fell on *Sein* or Being. Critics took him to task for embracing a philosophy of heteronomy. For by harshly rejecting the ideals of subjectivity and will, Heidegger's later approach seemed to openly glorify human dependency. Increasingly, Being assumed the status of an autonomous and mysterious, otherworldly force. In Heidegger's view, it fell due to mankind to passively obey its cryptic "sendings." As he declared in one later text (*The*

End of Philosophy), "The history of Being is neither the history of man and of humanity, nor the history of the human relation to beings and to Being. The history of Being is *Being itself and only Being.*" It seemed that the more his later philosophy elevated Being, the more things human were diminished.

The contradictions and rigidities of his later doctrine of Being emerged unambiguously in the well-known 1966 *Der Spiegel* interview. Heidegger's despair about the modern age was in evidence when he proclaimed that modern art and literature were predominantly "destructive." In Heidegger's view, the history of metaphysics, beginning with Plato's theory of "Ideas," was essentially a history of error—a history that he alone had tried immodestly to set aright. Nor did Heidegger, when afforded the opportunity, choose to distance himself from Nazism. It, too, had been a product of the inscrutable "history of Being." When asked by his interlocutors what wisdom his philosophy might have for the historical present, his perplexity seemed complete: "Only a god can save us," he opined disconsolately.

See also **Arendt, Hannah; Jünger, Ernst; Marcuse, Herbert; Nazism.**

BIBLIOGRAPHY

Primary Sources

Heidegger, Martin. *Being and Time.* Translated by John Macquarrie and Edward Robinson. New York, 1962.

————. *Basic Writings.* Edited by David Farrell Krell. New York, 1993.

Secondary Sources

Pöggeler, Otto. *The Paths of Heidegger's Life and Thought.* Translated by John Bailiff. Atlantic Heights, N.J., 1996.

Safranski, Rüdiger. *Martin Heidegger: Between Good and Evil.* Translated by Ewald Osers. Cambridge, Mass., 1998.

Wolin, Richard, ed. *The Heidegger Controversy: A Critical Reader.* Cambridge, Mass., 1993.

RICHARD WOLIN

HELSINKI ACCORDS.

The Helsinki Accords (or as they are formally known, the Final Act of the Conference on Security and Cooperation in Europe) were signed on 1 August 1975. The Helsinki Accords were the culmination of a process that had its origins in the 1950s when the then Soviet Union began a campaign for the setting up of a European regional security conference. In May 1969 the government of Finland offered Helsinki as a venue for such a conference. In November 1972 the representatives of thirty-three European states together with the United States and Canada began talks about setting up the framework for such a pan-European security conference. On 1 August 1975 the leaders of these thirty-five states signed the Final Act of the Conference on Security and Cooperation in Europe.

The Final Act of the Conference on Security and Cooperation in Europe is a politically binding agreement that contains four sections or "baskets," as they are commonly known. The first basket includes a declaration of principles guiding relations between the participating states to the agreement. These include respect for human rights and fundamental freedoms. The second basket deals with economic, scientific, and environmental cooperation. Basket three deals with issues such as free movement of peoples and freedom of information. Taken together, basket three and principle 7 of basket one are known as the "Human Dimension" of the Helsinki Accords. The fourth basket deals with the follow-up process after the conference. The main tasks of the Conference on Security and Cooperation in Europe (CSCE) were the prevention of conflict, early warning, and post-conflict rehabilitation.

Following the Helsinki Conference a series of follow-up conferences were held in Belgrade (1977–1978), Madrid (1980–1983), Vienna (1986–1989), and Helsinki (1992). These conferences led to many amendments in the nature and scope of the CSCE. The CSCE as it was known in its opening phase from 1975 to 1994 was not a formal international institution. Its lack of formal structures proved an advantage in the Cold War period in its primary role as a conduit between the West and the Eastern bloc. Through its fluid diplomatic make-up it attempted in the period before the break-up of the Soviet Union to prevent conflict between the Western and Eastern bloc powers and tried to engage in narrowing the political gulf between both blocs. In the period after the 1975 Final Act many Helsinki-based human rights NGOs were set up in the Soviet bloc. Though persecuted in their home countries, these groups did help highlight human rights abuses in the Eastern bloc. The breakup of the Soviet Union together with the war in the former Yugoslavia forced the CSCE to rethink its role in the new world order. The reaction of the CSCE to the changed world situation would eventually lead to its transformation from diplomatic process to a formalized international organization.

In 1989 the concluding document of the Vienna follow-up meeting of the CSCE added a further dimension to human rights protection in the form of a four-stage monitoring process. This process, known informally as the "human dimension mechanism," considered questions in relation to the Human Dimension of the Helsinki Accords. In the first stage of this monitoring process information would be exchanged via diplomatic channels. The second stage would involve the holding of bilateral meetings with other participating states and would require them to exchange questions in relation to particular human rights issues. In the third stage any state would be able to bring relevant cases to the attention of other participating states. In the final stage participating states could broach relevant issues at the conference of the Human Dimension of the CSCE as well as at CSCE follow-up meetings. This mechanism was used seventy times in 1989 during the events that led to the breakup of the Soviet Union.

In 1990 the concluding document of the Copenhagen meeting of the Human Dimension of the CSCE brought further changes to the functioning of the CSCE in the post–Cold War era. In the Copenhagen document the participating states expressed their belief that in establishing a new democratic order in Eastern Europe, full regard was to be had for the values of pluralistic democracy, the rule of law, and human rights. Importantly it was noted that participating states would violate their commitments to the CSCE if they set up a nondemocratic political system. The Copenhagen document placed a particular emphasis on linguistic, cultural, and religious rights, noting that national minority questions could only be resolved within a democratic political framework based on the rule of law and with an independent judiciary. The document also contained recommendations for improving the implementation of the commitments set out in the Human Dimension of the Helsinki Accords. These included a recommendation to deploy independent experts to examine potential conflict situations on the ground.

On 21 November 1990 the heads of state and government of the CSCE participating states signed the Charter of Paris for a New Europe. The charter agreed that states would cooperate and support each other with the aim of making democratic gains in the former Soviet bloc "irreversible." The charter made institutional and structural changes to the CSCE and led ultimately to the creation of new structures and posts within the organization, namely the Secretary-General, the High Commissioner for National Minorities, a Parliamentary Assembly, a Ministerial Council (made up of the foreign ministers of participating states), the Permanent Council, the Chairman-in-Office (this is a revolving office held in turn by each participating state's foreign minister), and the initiation of regular summit meetings of heads of state or government of participating states.

At the Moscow meeting of the Human Dimension of the CSCE on 3 October 1991 the monitoring mechanism ("the human dimension mechanism") established in the concluding document of the Vienna follow-up conference of 1989 was amended to create a five-step mechanism for the sending of rapporteurs to investigate human rights abuses in participating states. The "Moscow mechanism" allowed for a group of participating states to send a mission to another participating state even if the latter did not agree to it. This principle is known as "consensus minus the party in question" or "consenus minus one." Rapporteurs sent on such missions are enabled to facilitate resolution of a particular problem relating to the Human Dimension of the CSCE. The "consensus minus one" principle was formally adopted in the Prague Document on Further Development of CSCE Institutions and Structures produced at the second meeting of the CSCE Council of Ministers in January 1992. This allowed the Council of Ministers to adopt formal sanctions against participating states that were deemed to be in breach of human rights commitments. This fact-finding procedure was used, for example, in relation to the investigation of attacks on unarmed civilians in Bosnia and Croatia. As a result of these interventions the CSCE decided to amend the practically cumbersome Moscow mechanism in favor of setting up ad hoc missions that were to be called "missions of long duration."

The fourth follow-up meeting of the CSCE was held in Helsinki in 1992 (known as Helsinki II). The question of the role of the CSCE in post-communist Europe was high on the agenda. The concluding document of the Helsinki II conference noted the dangers posed by aggressive nationalism, xenophobia, ethnic conflicts, and human rights violations in the new post-Soviet states and set up a number of conflict prevention mechanisms. The most significant of these was the formal establishment of the office of High Commissioner for National Minorities. This post was created with the objective of putting pressure on states to improve both their individual and collective rights records. The High Commissioner for National Minorities acts as a mediator in disputes between national minority groups that have the potential to develop into conflicts within the area covered by the CSCE. Helsinki II represented a major development in the history of the CSCE. It was now moving from being a diplomatic process to a formal international organization. In 1995 the CSCE was officially renamed the Organisation for Security and Cooperation in Europe (OSCE). It is now the largest regional security organization in the world, counting fifty-five states among its members.

See also **Bosnia-Herzegovina; Croatia; Soviet Union.**

BIBLIOGRAPHY

Bloed, Arie, ed. *From Helsinki to Vienna: Basic Documents of the Helsinki Process.* Dordrecht, Netherlands, and Boston, 1990.

———. *The Challenges of Change: The Helsinki Summit of the CSCE and Its Aftermath.* Dordrecht, Netherlands, and Boston, 1994.

Bloed, Arie, and Pieter Van Dijk, eds. *Essays on Human Rights in the Helsinki Process.* Dordrecht, Netherlands, and Boston, 1985.

Heraclides, Alexis. *Helsinki II and Its Aftermath: The Making of the CSCE into an International Organization.* New York, 1993.

———. *Security and Cooperation in Europe: The Human Dimension, 1972–1992.* London and Portland, Ore., 1993.

Kovacs, Laszlo. "The OSCE: Present and Future Challenges." *Helsinki Monitor* 6, no. 3 (1995): 7–10.

Maresca, John M. *To Helsinki: The Conference on Security and Cooperation in Europe, 1973–1975.* Durham, N.C., 1985.

Russell, Harold S. "The Helsinki Declaration: Brobdingnag or Lilliput?" *American Journal of International Law* 70, no. 2 (1976): 242–272.

Thomas, Daniel C. *The Helsinki Effect: International Norms, Human Rights, and the Demise of Communism.* Princeton, N.J., 2001.

PATRICK HANAFIN

HESS, RUDOLF (1894–1987), German Nazi leader.

Born on 26 April 1894 to a middle-class mercantile family living in Alexandria, Egypt, future Nazi Deputy Führer Rudolf Hess initially trained to follow his father into the world of commerce. World War I, however, derailed his career plans; Hess enlisted in 1914, saw combat on the western and eastern fronts, and ended the war as a lieutenant in the Air Force. For Hess, November 1918 and the subsequent Treaty of Versailles represented a national humiliation brought about by the actions of so-called traitors such as the Jews and the Marxists. Following demobilization, Hess enrolled at the University of Munich, where he came to know geography professor Karl Haushofer, who convinced him that Germany's survival depended on the acquisition of territory. Hess at this time also became active in Munich's Far Right political scene; he joined the anti-Semitic and anti-Marxist Thule Society and, as a member of the paramilitary *Freikorps*, participated in May 1919 in the bloody suppression of the Munich Soviet.

One year later, Hess attended a lecture given by the then-obscure Adolf Hitler (1889–1945), an experience that Hess later claimed transformed his life. Convinced of Hitler's prophetic powers and messianic significance, Hess threw his support behind him and his fledgling German Workers' Party, the predecessor of the Nazi Party. Imprisoned alongside Hitler in the Landsberg Castle as punishment for participating in the November 1923 Beer Hall Putsch, Hess cemented his position as a member of Hitler's inner circle. As Hitler's

Rudolf Hess (front row, left) sits with co-defendant Joachim von Ribbentrop during the Nuremberg trials. ©CORBIS

private secretary, Hess served as Hitler's mouthpiece and, more importantly, controlled access to Hitler. Hess also played the crucial role in developing the Hitler cult, establishing within the party the notion that the Führer "was always right and always would be."

HESS IN THE THIRD REICH

The early days of the Third Reich witnessed a proliferation of honors and an expansion of power for Hess. On 21 April 1933, Hitler made him deputy Führer within the Nazi Party, and Hess in December 1933 entered Hitler's cabinet as minister of state without portfolio. Over the course of the 1930s, however, Hess's relationship with Hitler deteriorated and, with no personal or territorial power base of his own, Hess became increasingly marginalized in the Darwinist Nazi political system as men like Martin Bormann outmaneuvered him. Hess's appointment on 1 September 1939 to the position of second in the line of succession after Hitler recognized Hess's enduring popularity with the German people but masked his deepening insignificance within the party and the government.

As most historians believe, this sense of political marginalization, combined with a misguided notion that Germany could appeal to a "peace party" within the British political establishment, convinced Hess to try to regain Hitler's favor by helping to end the war between Great Britain and Germany. In the summer of 1940, Hess unsuccessfully attempted to use an intermediary to arrange a meeting with a high-ranking British statesman on neutral soil. In desperation, Hess decided to fly to Great Britain in order to make the case for peace personally. After months of secret preparation and two abortive previous attempts, Hess flew a modified Messerschmidt Bf 110 fighter-bomber to Britain on the night of 10 May 1941 and landed by parachute on the Scottish estate of the Duke of Hamilton. Although there is still disagreement as to whether Hitler knew or approved of Hess's plans, news of the flight provoked official outrage in Nazi Germany and silence in Great Britain. The British interrogated Hess and then imprisoned him for the duration of the war.

THE NUREMBERG TRIAL AND HESS'S IMPRISONMENT

At the end of World War II, the British transferred Hess to Germany to stand trial as one of the twenty-two defendants at Nuremberg. Allied officials indicted him on four charges: conspiracy, war crimes, crimes against humanity, and crimes against peace. Hess considered the proceedings a farce, a case of victor's justice that he irrationally believed might nonetheless result in his being awarded control of the three Western occupation zones. In his closing remarks to the court, Hess stated, "It was granted to me for many years of my life to work under the greatest son that my people has ever produced in its thousand years of history. If I even could do so, I would not wish to erase this period from my life. I regret nothing." The court found Hess guilty of the crimes of conspiracy and crimes against peace; despite the demands of the Soviet prosecutor for the death penalty, the court sentenced Hess to life imprisonment. Hess served more than forty years in Berlin's special Spandau Prison, then hanged himself in a garden shed on 17 August 1987.

See also **Hitler, Adolf; Nazism; War Crimes.**

BIBLIOGRAPHY

Fest, Joachim. *The Face of the Third Reich: Portraits of the Nazi Leadership.* Translated by Michael Bullock. New York, 1970.

Knopp, Guido. *Hitler's Henchmen*. Translated by Angus McGeoch. Phoenix Mill, U.K., 2000.

Smelser, Ronald, and Rainer Zitelmann, eds. *The Nazi Elite*. Translated by Mary Fischer. New York, 1993.

Stafford, David, ed. *Flight from Reality: Rudolf Hess and His Mission to Scotland, 1941*. London, 2002.

CHARLES LANSING

HESSE, HERMANN (1877–1962), German author.

Both during and following their initial publication, the works of Hermann Hesse have been among the most widely read literary texts of German-speaking Europe; over twenty million copies of his texts also appeared in translation by the turn of the twenty-first century. Hesse's works have been particularly popular in the United States, where his fiction became a central focus of the hippie movement in the late 1960s and early 1970s, and where they continue to occupy a prominent position among canonical German texts.

The popularity of Hesse's works has no doubt been due in part to their hermetically open transparency, their accessibility, which offers the reader various possibilities for identification. Nearly all of Hesse's fiction concerns the alienation of the individual within modern society, as reflected in a host of characters who experience serious psychological trauma from which they only slowly emerge through a process of often painful inner reflection—universal themes that resonate with a wide and diversified audience.

While Hesse's production includes paintings, poetry, fairy tales, essays, a large correspondence with major figures of his time, and pedagogical and editorial projects, it is primarily his novels that have formed the basis of his popularity, especially *Unterm Rad* (1906; *Beneath the Wheel*, 1958), dealing with the oppressive forces of the German educational system at the turn of the century; *Demian* (1919; translation, 1923); *Siddhartha* (1922; translation, 1951); *Steppenwolf* (1927; translation, 1929); *Narziss und Goldmund* (1930; *Death and the Lover*, 1932), the story of two priests in the Middle Ages, one at peace with his religion, the other in search of a more meaningful, and

individual, religious system of thought; and *Das Glasperlenspiel* (1943; translated as *Magister Ludi*, 1949, as *The Glass Bead Game*, 1969), set in a futuristic, monk-like community devoted to the contemplative pursuit of mathematics and music. For *The Glass Bead Game*, Hesse received the Nobel Prize in Literature in 1946. All of these texts demonstrate the author's familiarity with such figures as the philosophers Baruch Spinoza, Arthur Schopenhauer, and Friedrich Nietzsche; the historians Jakob Christopher Burckhardt and Oswald Spengler; and the Swiss psychologist Carl Gustav Jung (in the 1910s Hesse underwent analysis with an assistant of Jung's, Joseph Bernhard Lang), as well as with Buddhism, and ancient Hindu and Chinese religious philosophy.

Demian, *Siddhartha*, and *Steppenwolf* remain Hesse's most popular novels. The central protagonist of *Demian*, a young student named Emil Sinclair (identical to the nom-de-plume under which Hesse originally published the novel), searches for an escape from the strictures of religious and moral traditions, and is aided therein by a new acquaintance named Demian, a dream-like figure who leads Sinclair on a quest to find a mythic god who unites the opposing forces of good and evil, male and female, and human and animal. This unification of opposing, universal forces constitutes a major theme in all of Hesse's fiction. It reemerges in *Siddhartha*, which tells the story of a young man who finds redemption through an increasingly contemplative approach to the vicissitudes and contrasting forces of the quotidian world. It also forms the center of *Steppenwolf*, in which the main figure is portrayed as an amalgamation of a man and a wolf, the latter constituting all that cannot be accommodated within the more traditional cultural traditions of Germany in the 1920s. The novel shows how diverse aesthetic signifiers appear to clash, not owing to any intrinsic qualities they may evince, but by virtue of the values with which they come to be associated; as the protagonist undergoes self-examination, the hallowed cultural icons of Germany come to function not in opposition to their modernist counterparts, but as their equals, and this reconfiguration suggests both a liberating transformation of the individual and, potentially, of the world in which he lives.

Throughout his life, Hesse was a pacifist, and therefore, unlike many contemporary authors such as Rainer Maria Rilke, Hugo von Hofmannsthal, and Thomas Mann, he vigorously opposed World War I, and in 1912 emigrated to Switzerland to join the French novelist and pacifist Romain Rolland in antiwar activities, deciding in 1923 to become a Swiss citizen. Hesse's multicultural interests continue to resonate with a worldwide audience. Indeed, some have gone so far as to suggest that Hesse's texts themselves even influenced some of the most important social concerns and movements of the later twentieth century: the ecology movement, the anti-authoritarian protests of the late 1960s, pedagogical reforms, the displacement of Eurocentrism in favor of globalization, the development of intercultural understanding through diplomatic relations that transcend the confines of individual nations and religions, and the widespread appearance of political platforms supporting nonviolence.

See also **Germany; Modernism; Rolland, Romain.**

BIBLIOGRAPHY

Hesse, Hermann. *Sämtliche Werke in 20 Bänden*. Edited by Volker Michels. Frankfurt am Main, 2002. The most complete edition of Hesse's works to date.

Pfeifer, Martin. *Hesse-Kommentar zu sämtlichen Werken*. Munich, 1980. A dated but still useful commentary, with bibliographic and biographical information.

Solbach, Andreas, ed. *Hermann Hesse und die literarische Moderne: Kulturwissenschaftliche Facetten einer literarischen Konstante im 20. Jahrhundert. Aufsätze*. Frankfurt am Main, 2004. A wide-ranging collection of essays intended as a corrective to the long-standing disinterest in Hesse's works within academia.

Weiner, Marc A. "Mozart, Jazz, and the Dissolution of the Bourgeois Personality: *Steppenwolf*." In *Undertones of Insurrection: Music, Politics, and the Social Sphere in the Modern German Narrative*, 101–149. Lincoln, Neb., 1993.

MARC A. WEINER

HEYDRICH, REINHARD (1904–1942),
chief of the German Security Police and the Security Service of the SS.

The son of an opera singer and music teacher, Reinhard Heydrich went to a gymnasium and developed into a talented musician and sportsman. He first joined a right-wing organization at the age of sixteen. After passing his Abitur exams in 1921, Heydrich entered the German navy (Reichsmarine) in Kiel in 1922, where he served on several ships and started a career as a radio communications officer, eventually reaching the rank of Oberleutnant (first lieutenant). In April 1931 a naval court dismissed him from the navy on the charge of a breach of promise to marry the daughter of a marine official. In July 1931 he joined the Nazi SS in Hamburg and was hired by the SS leader Heinrich Himmler to create an intelligence service inside the organization. Rumors concerning Heydrich's "non-Aryan ancestry" were proven wrong in an investigation. Heydrich built the so-called Ic Service of the SS, from July 1932 called Sicherheitsdienst der SS (SD; Security Service of the SS), which in the beginning served as a surveillance organ inside the Nazi Party.

After the Nazi seizure of power, Heydrich also served on Himmler's staff. As a member of the German delegation for the League of Nations, Heydrich caused a scandal in Geneva by raising the Nazi flag. In March–April 1933 he took over the political police in Munich and Bavaria, gaining control of the political police in all other German states in 1934, ending with the Geheime Staatspolizei Amt in Prussia (the Prussian Gestapo). Thus Heydrich obtained both party (SD) and state (Gestapo) functions at the same time. In 1934 the SD gained a monopoly in party intelligence work, and from the mid-1930s it extended its surveillance and racial planning to the whole German population and, from 1938, to annexed and occupied countries as well. Most of the civil foreign intelligence was also taken over by the SD. In 1936 Heydrich officially united the Gestapo and criminal police as Sicherheitspolizei. He held the high offices of both the SD and the Sicherheitspolizei. During the second half of the 1930s, the SD and Gestapo under his leadership developed new institutional and policing patterns, not only aiming at alleged resistance but also trying to intervene in all spheres of public life and keep the "racial body" of German society "clean" by combating all alleged racial enemies, such as Jews, Gypsies, and so-called asocials.

In September 1939 both the SD and Sicherheitspolizei were put under the direction of a new central institution, the Reichssicherheitshauptamt, under Heydrich's leadership. From the beginning of the war, Heydrich organized mass murder in the occupied countries, especially in Poland, and in concentration camps; his Sicherheitspolizei also organized the mass deportations in annexed territories until the spring of 1941. Despite the failure of his efforts to take over large parts of the occupation policy and even military intelligence, Heydrich became the central organizer of repression in Nazi-occupied Europe, especially against eastern European elites and alleged resisters, but from 1941 focusing on European Jewry. Heydrich instructed the Einsatzgruppen (mission groups) in the war against the Soviet Union and coordinated the deportation and mass murder of all European Jews. He organized the so-called Wannsee Conference in January 1942 in order to coordinate all institutions in regard to the "Final Solution," the program for exterminating all Jews in Europe. Named SS-Obergruppenführer und General der Polizei in September 1941, he also served as acting (officially deputy) Reichsprotektor in Bohemia and Moravia, where he pursued a policy of both compromising with the workforce and terrorizing the Czech population. He was wounded in an assassination attempt by the Czech exile resistance on 27 May 1942 in Prague and died a week later in a hospital. Following his death a foundation for SS racial research, the Reinhard Heydrich-Stiftung, was installed in Prague, and apparently the murder of most Polish Jews was named after him—"Aktion Reinhard."

Heydrich's career seems rather atypical: he was neither one of the old police officials from the Gestapo nor a young academician like in the SD elite. He was considered one of the few Nazi leaders who physically resembled the "Aryan ideal." But most important were his extreme National Socialist beliefs and his absolute ruthlessness, which was even feared among some Nazi functionaries. Heydrich was highly energetic in both conceptualizing and enforcing racist police policy. He created new party-state organizations, radicalized the whole Nazi regime, and organized mass murder on an unprecedented scale.

See also Gestapo; Holocaust; Nazism; SS (Schutzstaffel); Wannsee Conference.

BIBLIOGRAPHY

Calic, Edouard. *Reinhard Heydrich: The Chilling Story of a Man Who Masterminded the Nazi Death Camps.* New York, 1985.

Deschner, Günther. *Reinhard Heydrich: A Biography.* New York, 1981.

Herbert, Ulrich. *Best: Biographische Studien über Radikalismus, Weltanschauung und Vernunft, 1903–1989.* Bonn, Germany, 1996.

Wildt, Michael. *Generation des Unbedingten: Das Führungskorps des Reichssicherheitshauptamtes.* Hamburg, Germany, 2002.

DIETER POHL

HIMMLER, HEINRICH (1900–1945), leader of the SS and the German police during the Third Reich.

Born in Munich, Heinrich Himmler came from a Bavarian Catholic bourgeois family; his father was a schoolmaster, the director of a gymnasium. In 1917 Himmler was drafted into the Bavarian army but did not serve at the front. After the war he studied agricultural sciences at Munich Technical University, where he acquired a diploma. He worked from 1922 in a fertilizer company, until he became unemployed a year later. He came in contact early on with Bavarian right-wing extremism, especially the so-called Artamanen League, an agrarian youth group, which influenced his ideas on German agricultural settlement of the lands to the east. As a member of the extremist Reichskriegsflagge, he participated in Adolf Hitler's Beer Hall Putsch in Munich in November 1923. He joined the Nazi Party in 1925 and soon became deputy Gauleiter (regional leader), first in Lower Bavaria, then in Upper Bavaria. In 1926 he served as deputy propaganda chief (Reichspropagandaleiter) of the National Socialist German Workers Party (NSDAP; the Nazi Party). On 6 January 1929 he took over the small SS (Schutzstaffel der NSDAP), a kind of bodyguard group inside the Sturm Abteilung (SA; Storm Troopers), which had existed since 1925. From that date on he was a fully employed Nazi functionary; in 1930 he also became a member of the Reichstag.

With the Nazi rise to power in early 1933, Himmler immediately took over state functions. As police chief constable (Polizeipräsident) in Munich, he not only installed one of the first German concentration camps near Dachau but started to take over all branches of the political police in most of Germany, and in 1934 also the Gestapo in Prussia (formally as deputy chief). On 30 June 1934 Himmler actively took part in the action against the so-called Röhm Putsch (Night of Long Knives), which resulted in the killing of the SA leadership and the formal independence of the SS, which from now on was directly subordinate to Hitler. Finally in June 1936 Himmler formally united SS and police in his role as the new SS leader and chief of the German police in the Ministry of the Interior. He thereby centralized the police on the national level, taking over command of all branches of the police and accelerating the merging of the state police and the party SS.

During the second half of the 1930s Himmler constantly developed his empire of repression: from 1937 he greatly expanded the concentration camp system; at the beginning of the war he created the Reichssicherheitshauptamt (Imperial Main Security Office), the central institution of repression; and he developed the Waffen-SS, the military branch of the SS. In October 1939 Himmler received a specific authorization as Reichskommissar für die Festigung Deutschen Volkstums (imperial commissar for the strengthening of Germandom), thus becoming responsible for all deportations, settlement of ethnic Germans, and "racial screening" in German-occupied Europe. Himmler not only supervised demographic restructuring, especially in Eastern Europe, but also developed gigantic plans for deportations and mass murder (General Plan East, prepared in 1941–1942). These included the mass murder of all European Jews, the "Final Solution of the Jewish Question." The SS chief supervised the murder units that accompanied the army during Operation Barbarossa, the invasion of the Soviet Union in 1941, and oversaw the extension of the genocide over the whole of Europe at the end of the year. After the death of

Reinhard Heydrich in June 1942, he also took over the latter's position as head of the SS Security Police until January 1943 and organized mass murder in detail. By mid-1942 the SS also coordinated antipartisan warfare in most of Eastern Europe, which resulted in the murder of hundreds of thousands of civilians. In August 1943 Himmler took over the Ministry of Interior and tried to restructure the administration. He concentrated his military aspirations on the Waffen-SS, and after the plot against Hitler in July 1944 he additionally became Befehlshaber des Ersatzheeres of the Wehrmacht (commander of the replacement army), giving the SS control over the organization of the POW system.

Himmler was highly influenced by racist and agrarian ideologies. He represented a specific brand of National Socialism, focusing on settlement policy in the east, trying to integrate all groups that appeared to have "Germanic" or "Aryan" roots. He was able to monopolize the policies concerning ethnic Germans abroad. Himmler based his policies on a kind of feudalism, with feudal relationships between German settlers inside the SS leadership, especially the higher SS and police leaders—his personal representatives in the occupied territories—and the indigenous population. He aspired to develop the SS as the future elite of Germany, predominantly based on racist selection. The SS chief himself decided in most cases on individual SS entries and marriages of SS members. His elite was to provide personnel and intervene in all realms of political and social life. Due to his personal appearance and sometimes occult interests (like spice growing), he has often not been taken seriously by historians. But in reality Himmler was a restless manager of the SS, touring all territories where the SS was active and inspecting even extermination camps and mass executions. Inside the Nazi system he developed an enormous power base, yet he remained extremely loyal to Hitler and did not start his own political initiatives before the final period of the war. There are indications that Himmler tried to contact the western Allies from mid-1944, first to trade Jewish lives for money and, during the last months of the war, to negotiate a separate peace with the West in order to continue the war against the Soviet Union. Upon learning this, Hitler ousted the SS chief in April 1945.

Himmler tried to escape Allied arrest with false papers but was soon recognized and put in British custody, where he committed suicide.

See also **Heydrich, Reinhard; Nazism; SS (Schutzstaffel).**

BIBLIOGRAPHY

Breitman, Richard. *The Architect of Genocide: Himmler and the Final Solution.* New York, 1991.

Himmler, Heinrich. *Geheimreden 1933 bis 1945 und andere Ansprachen.* Edited by Bradley F. Smith and Agnes F. Peterson. Frankfurt/Main, 1974.

———. *Der Dienstkalender Heinrich Himmlers 1941/42.* Edited by Peter Witte et al. Hamburg, 1999.

Koehl, Robert Lewis. *The Black Corps: The Structure and Power Struggles of the Nazi SS.* Madison, Wis., 1983.

Padfield, Peter. *Himmler: Reichsführer-SS.* London, 1990.

Smith, Bradley F. *Heinrich Himmler: A Nazi in the Making, 1900–1926.* Stanford, Calif., 1971.

DIETER POHL

HINDENBURG, PAUL VON (1847–1934), German field marshal and president.

The career of Paul von Beneckendorff und von Hindenburg illustrates the difficulties and perhaps even the pointlessness of distinguishing between appearance and substance. Throughout a long public career, he projected an almost stereotypical image of German patriarchal authority—honest, unshakeable, aloof, intimidating. Not least, Hindenburg looked the part. Ample in personal appearance, he had disciplined, brushed-back hair and a formidable mustache, complimented by perfect posture and a stately walk.

To some extent, Hindenburg's image saved him from relative obscurity in 1914. Born to a Junker family of good pedigree but modest property, Hindenburg had worn a uniform since entering cadet school at age eleven. He enjoyed a successful military career, though lack of royal and imperial favor excluded him from the innermost circles. Hindenburg had actually retired in 1911, and was recalled to active duty in August 1914 as a consequence of the purge of the German command following the momentary Russian success invading East Prussia. The predictable and

aristocratic Hindenburg would be seconded by the talented but erratic and common-born Erich Ludendorff. Together, the pair would win the two greatest German victories of the war, the battles of Tannenburg (August 1914) and Masurian Lakes (September 1914).

These victories, carefully spun so as to divert attention from the stagnating western front, rendered Hindenburg the most formidable German military hero since Frederick the Great. Hindenburg managed to remain above politics and above reproach. Success accrued to him, while failure could be sloughed off on to subordinates, civilians, or later even Kaiser William, who had always feared Hindenburg's greater popularity. When Hindenburg and Ludendorff were called from the eastern front to head a reorganized supreme command in August 1916, they became leading political figures. The so-called Hindenburg Program (in which Ludendorff actually played a far greater role) sought to reorganize war production for greater efficiency in waging "total" war. It raised expectations more than production. Military results remained mixed, with success on the eastern front counterbalanced by costly and inconclusive battles at Verdun, the Somme, and the Chemin des Dames, as well as by the entry of the United States into the war in April 1917. Yet the cult of personality around Hindenburg seemed only to grow with Germany's difficulties. In one of the more peculiar cultural practices of the Great War, giant wooden statues of Hindenburg were erected in cities and towns across Germany. A contribution to the Red Cross gave the donor the right to drive a nail into the wooden titan.

The cult of Hindenburg survived the defeat of 1918 and the demise of the imperial regime. Hindenburg played a major role in the abdication of Kaiser William, the decision to sign the armistice, and the bloody establishment of the Weimar Republic, yet always managed to remain above the fray. He carefully timed his resignation as supreme commander to precede the signing of the Versailles Peace Treaty in June 1919. He claimed somewhat disingenuously that "I would rather perish in honor than sign a humiliating peace."

Following the unexpected death of Friederich Ebert in 1925, Hindenburg was persuaded to run for president of the republic as a national unity candidate. He won, though by a more narrow

Hindenburg shakes hands with Adolf Hitler after appointing him to the chancellorship, January 1933.
©HULTON-DEUTSCH COLLECTION/CORBIS

margin than expected in a polity experimenting with genuine democracy. Some, indeed, feared a return to military rule. Yet Hindenburg maintained a very Lutheran sense of loyalty to secular political power, though he remained frustrated and confused by tumultuous and poisoned party politics. He greatly disliked Adolf Hitler. According to legend, Hindenburg suggested Hitler be made a postal clerk, so that he could "lick my rear on a stamp."

Yet Hindenburg found himself increasingly adrift, politically and probably mentally, in the later years of his presidency. The last hero of imperial Germany proved ill-suited to the crises of the Weimar Republic. Above all, he wanted to avoid presiding over a civil war as violence became common political practice. Hindenburg finally acquiesced in the formation of a Hitler-led cabinet in January 1933. Hitler had little difficulty persuading him of the perils of communist revolution after the Reichstag fire of February 1933, and induced him to sign the emergency decrees paving the way for the consolidation of Nazi power. Hindenburg's death in the summer of 1934 removed the last

pretenses of restraint as the supreme symbol of the old regime gave way to the new.

See also **Germany; Hitler, Adolf; Ludendorff, Erich; World War I.**

BIBLIOGRAPHY

Craig, Gordon. *The Politics of the Prussian Army, 1640–1945.* Oxford, U.K., 1955.

Demeter, Karl. *The German Officer-Corps in Society and State, 1650–1945.* Translated by Angus Malcolm. London, 1965.

Dorpalen, Andreas. *Hindenburg and the Weimar Republic.* Princeton, N.J., 1964.

Herwig, Holger. *The First World War: Germany and Austria–Hungary, 1914–1918.* London and New York, 1996.

LEONARD V. SMITH

HITCHCOCK, ALFRED (1899–1980), English film director.

One of the most popular directors of motion pictures, Alfred Hitchcock always paid attention to the possible reactions of the audience and established a special and permanent relationship between him as a director, the actors, and the spectators. He personally supervised some of the trailers of his films in such a way that the truth of the story hung in the balance until the beginning of the screening. He often made a short appearance in his movies, driving the spectators to try to spot him. From 1955 to 1965, he was the host and producer of a television series entitled *Alfred Hitchcock Presents;* his voice, image, and figure thus became instantly recognizable. He directed some fifty films over the course of his career, with several of them becoming box office hits, which are still highly valued in the early twenty-first century.

Hitchcock worked first in England, his native country, where he got his start in film in 1920 in London, designing the titles for silent movies. He stayed for a while in Germany at the UFA, the major Berlin studio, where he supposedly discovered the work of Fritz Lang. He made a name for himself with *The Lodger* (1926) and *Blackmail* (1929), his first talkie, where he explored the dramatic and symbolic possibilities of sound. During

Desmond Tester (left) with Oscar Homolka in a scene from Hitchcock's *Sabotage*, 1937. Homolka portrays a European saboteur willing to use his young brother-in-law to deliver a bomb concealed in a package. GAUMONT-BRITISH/THE KOBAL COLLECTION

the 1930s most of his films were influenced by the prewar atmosphere of Europe (*The 39 Steps,* 1935; *Sabotage,* 1937; *The Lady Vanishes,* 1938). Asked by his friend Sidney Bernstein, head of the British Ministry of Information's film division, to make two shorts for supporting the French Resistance during World War II, he directed *Bon Voyage* and *Aventure malgache* (1944). If a political consciousness manifests itself here, it is mixed with a good deal of humor and suspense. However, he also contributed to the editing of a one-hour documentary on the story of Nazi concentration camps (*Memory of the Camps,* 1945).

By the end of the 1930s he came to the attention of Hollywood. The mogul David O. Selznick invited him to come to America to direct *Rebecca* (1940), an adaptation of the Daphne du Maurier's

best-selling novel. *Rebecca* had been a project initiated by Selznick, not Hitchcock. While the film won an Oscar, Hitchcock did not win for best director and never would, although he would receive honorary Oscars. It was a French director coming from the "Nouvelle Vague" (new wave), the former critic François Truffaut, who made possible the recognition of Hitchcock as an "auteur." Truffaut had a long interview with Hitchcock in August 1962, in Universal City, which became a book known as the "Hitchbook."

In Hollywood Hitchcock experimented with color films, widescreen formats, and even 3-D in *Dial "M" for Murder* (1954), working with stars like Cary Grant, James Stewart, Ingrid Bergman, and Janet Leigh. The common themes of his movies—fear, sex, evil, innocence or guilt—cannot be separated from their mise-en-scène. Hitchcock was not interested in the perpetrator of the action, or in the action itself, the famous "whodunit," but, as Gilles Deleuze emphasized, in "the set of relations in which the action and the characters are taken" (Deleuze, p. 270).

To take only one example, in *Vertigo* (1958) the titles (Saul Bass), the music (Bernard Herrmann), the projection technique (VistaVision, developed by Paramount to compete with Fox's Cinemascope), the "real" locations (San Francisco), all help to create very complex feelings. At one stage in the film, Madeleine/Judy (Kim Novak) and Scottie (James Stewart) are in a redwood forest. On an old sequoia, some landmark dates are inscribed from the center of the tree trunk to the edge. Madeleine thinks of her own lifetime and suddenly disappears behind the trees. The perception of time is rendered with a great intensity, and at that point Hitchcock creates some of the most haunting mental images he ever made. Suddenly we bump into the "portals of the past," and we try to take the plunge. It is not surprising to see how Hitchcock influenced a lot of filmmakers, the most talented being Brian de Palma (*Obsession*, 1976; *Body Double*, 1984), the most scrupulous, Chris Marker (*The Pier*, 1962)—both of whom were inspired by *Vertigo*—and the most unexpected being Gus Van Sant, whose exact, shot-by-shot re-creation of Hitchcock's *Psycho* (1960) was released in 1998.

See also **Cinema.**

BIBLIOGRAPHY

Allen, Richard, and Sam Ishii-Gonzáles, eds. *Hitchcock: Past and Future*. London and New York, 2004.

Auiler, Dan. *Hitchcock's Notebooks: An Authorized and Illustrated Look inside the Creative Mind of Alfred Hitchcock*. New York, 1999.

Deleuze, Gilles. *L'Image-mouvement*. Paris, 1983.

Hitchcock, Alfred. *Hitchcock on Hitchcock: Selected Writings and Interviews*. Edited by Sidney Gottlieb. Berkeley, Calif., 1995.

Krohn, Bill. *Hitchcock at Work*. London, 2000.

McGilligan, Patrick. *Alfred Hitchcock: A Life in Darkness and Light*. New York, 2003.

Rohmer, Eric, and, Claude Chabrol. *Hitchcock, the First Forty-four Films*. Translated by Stanley Hochman. New York, 1979.

Ryall, Tom. *Alfred Hitchcock and the British Cinema*. 2nd ed. London, 1996.

Spoto, Donald. *The Dark Side of Genius: The Life of Alfred Hitchcock*. Boston, 1983.

Truffaut, François. *Hitchcock*. Rev. ed. New York, 1984.

CHRISTIAN DELAGE

HITLER, ADOLF (1889–1945), German chancellor and Führer.

No single figure, except perhaps the Soviet dictator Joseph Stalin, had as great an impact on the history of the twentieth century as Adolf Hitler, the man who became Germany's chancellor in 1933, who led his country into history's largest war six years later, and whose defeat in 1945 ushered in a new age in European and world history.

EARLY LIFE

Hitler was born in the small Austrian town of Braunau am Inn on 20 April 1889. He was the second son of Alois Hitler, a small-time official in the Habsburg Empire, and his second wife, Klara. Little in his childhood indicated his later impact on history. He was a modest pupil at the local schools he attended near Linz, where his parents moved in 1898. He lost interest in schooling as he grew older. His early years were dominated by loss: four of his brothers and sisters died in childhood; his father, for whom he had scant affection, died in 1903; and his mother, to whom he was devoted, four years later in December 1907, when Hitler was eighteen. He left school at sixteen, and two years later moved from Linz to the capital, Vienna, where he hoped to enroll at the prestigious Academy of Fine Arts to pursue a career as an artist. His rejection by the academy left him embittered and rootless. In 1913, partly to avoid military conscription, he left Vienna for Munich. Though he was eventually forced to return briefly to Austria, where he was pronounced unfit for service in February 1914, he went back to Munich where his bohemian existence ended abruptly with the outbreak of World War I. He volunteered to fight for Germany and was accepted into the Bavarian army in August 1914.

Hitler's Austrian background was important in many ways in shaping his views about society and politics. He became interested in the parliamentary

An election poster urges citizens to vote for Hindenburg and Hitler, Berlin, 1933. ©BETTMANN/CORBIS

debates and listened to them from the gallery. He later claimed that his contempt for parliaments was formed watching the many small Austrian parties squabbling. He was attracted to the pan-German movement and saw the future of Austria in a larger "Greater German" state than the loose Habsburg confederation with its large non-German minorities. His profound sense of German identity became the core of his political being. Other influences were particularly Viennese. He developed his love of opera in Vienna, particularly, but not exclusively, Richard Wagner. His dislike of artistic modernism almost certainly dates from this period, as he struggled to sell neat and conventional landscapes in a city that hosted the artistic fin de siècle.

Myths abound from his time in Vienna. He was never the penniless artist and laborer in the self-constructed legend of his later years but was able to survive on several small legacies and the money he made from selling pictures. The claim that life in Vienna explains Hitler's anti-Semitism has little foundation in fact, though hostility to the Jews was all around him in the prewar capital. He sold his pictures to Jewish galleries and had a number of

Jewish friends. His favorite conductor at the Vienna Court Opera was the German-Jewish Gustav Mahler. Hitler would have witnessed the arrival of many eastern Jews in the capital before 1914, but prejudices against them were shared even by Vienna's own established Jewish community. The assumption that Hitler's hatred of the Jews stemmed from these early encounters has not been demonstrated with any certainty.

Hitler's anti-Semitism became an evidently central part of his worldview only at the end of World War I. He served throughout the war at the front, much of the time as a "runner" between the front line and headquarters. He was promoted to corporal and earned the Iron Cross, Second Class, in 1914, and First Class in 1918. Shortly before the end of the war he was in the hospital after being temporarily blinded in a gas attack. Here he heard about the Armistice, and it was from around this point that his hatred of Jews and Marxists, who it was widely alleged had "stabbed Germany in the back," became the keynotes of his worldview. Hitler was one of many veterans of the war whose own sense of personal loss was projected onto the fact of German defeat and dishonor, but with Hitler these hatreds and anxieties became psychological props of extraordinary power to the extent that he came to see himself as the personification of Germany's suffering and also the instrument of German salvation.

RISE TO POWER

Following the Armistice, Hitler was invited by one of his officers to become an army informer working among the many political splinter groups in Munich, which was in the throes of political crisis following a brief communist republic. During one of these visits, to a meeting of the German Workers' Party, Hitler was very impressed by that party's mixture of nationalism, anti-Semitism, and populist quasi-socialist politics. He joined the tiny party in September 1919 and was soon appointed to be its propaganda chief. He abandoned the army and devoted himself full time to radical nationalist politics. In 1920 he encouraged the party to change its name to the National Socialist German Workers' Party (the NSDAP, or the Nazi Party). A party program was drawn up, and, after a brief power struggle with the party's leader, Anton

Drexler, Hitler emerged as the party's undisputed master in July 1921. He set out to transform the party into a mass movement committed to the revolutionary transformation of Germany and the reassertion of German national power. When the young Weimar Republic was plunged into political chaos in 1923 during the hyperinflation, Hitler and the party leadership decided to collaborate with other extreme-right forces in Bavaria to stage a coup and a possible march on Berlin. The so-called Beer Hall Putsch took place on 8–9 November when the Bavarian government was taken hostage and Hitler and his allies marched through the streets of Munich to the town hall. Police and army units met the march and opened fire. Hitler narrowly avoided injury. The fiasco brought him to the edge of suicide, but when he was arrested and put on trial between February and April 1924 alongside his National Socialist colleagues and the nationalist general Erich Ludendorff, he used the trial as the opportunity to campaign for German national revival. He was sentenced to five years in Landsberg prison, but served fewer than nine months before he was amnestied. During his incarceration he dictated his autobiography and a summary of his worldview. The manuscript was published a year later under the title *Mein Kampf* (My struggle). The book became the bible of the National Socialist movement and by 1945 more than eight million had been sold.

Hitler emerged from prison to find his movement split and scattered. In 1925 and 1926 he struggled to reimpose his authority, but not until the party congress at Weimar in July 1926 did he finally unite the party factions and have himself declared party leader (Führer), the title by which he was generally known from then until his death in 1945. After the failure of the coup in 1923, Hitler determined to take the legal path to power by taking part in national and local elections. By the general election in 1928 the party had grown considerably in size but won only a tiny fraction of the vote and twelve seats in parliament. The economic slump that started in 1929 helped Hitler and the party to move to the political center-stage. Growing fear of German communism combined with exceptional levels of economic and social hardship to create a large constituency looking for some form of political salvation. Hitler used party propaganda remorselessly to promote the idea that he was the German messiah who would lead his adopted country into a future of social harmony, economic well-being, and national rebirth. The traditional right and center of German politics collapsed, and millions flooded to support National Socialism. In the election of 1930 the party became the second largest. After Hitler contested the presidential election against the aging field marshal Paul von Hindenburg in April 1932, which Hitler lost by a small margin, the Nazi Party won the largest share of the vote (37 percent) in the July 1932 election. This did not secure a majority in the German parliament, but it made stable government impossible for the loose coalitions that tried to govern. Hitler would not join forces with other parties unless he was made chancellor. Following new elections in November, Germany became almost ungovernable. Hindenburg was persuaded by a clique of nationalist aristocrats around Franz von Papen to appoint Hitler as part of a broad nationalist front. On 30 January 1933 he was summoned into office as German chancellor.

Though Hitler was soon to have an exceptional impact on German and European affairs, the man who assumed the chancellorship was little known outside Germany and even among the German people. Hitler was a private person, who relied largely on a constructed "cult of personality" to project his image and win mass support. The private Hitler was unassuming, socially awkward, capable of bursts of hysterical irritation, but otherwise colorless. He chose not to marry, modeling himself on Karl Lueger, mayor of Vienna from 1897 to 1910, who had deliberately avoided matrimony so that he could serve his political office. Hitler is said to have had an affair with his niece Geli Raubal, and her suicide in 1931 affected him profoundly. Later in the 1930s he took as his companion Eva Braun, a former photographic assistant, but she was forced to live in the shadows. Hitler's public persona was remarkably different. He was a violent and evangelical speaker who developed the capacity to sway a crowd (even if most of them were composed of the party faithful) with his messianic vision of a German future. He used the personality cult to create the legend of the humble German who had survived life in the trenches to save Germany from the Marxists, Jews, and international plutocrats who had stifled and subverted it since 1918. His ideology was a mix of pseudoscientific race theory, modern illiberalism, and ideals of community that he picked up from discourses that were European-wide. He gave the latter a particularly German gloss, presenting Germany as the nation destined to save and rebuild European culture and succeed the decadent empires of the West. This worldview was seldom articulated fully (he followed *Mein Kampf* with a second manuscript dictated in 1928, but this was not published until 1961, long after his death). During the life of his regime, which was soon described as the Third Reich or "empire," Hitler wrote very little. His ideas were worked out in great set-piece speeches delivered at party congresses and rallies.

HITLER IN POWER

Hitler's appointment in January 1933 opened the way for a nationalist revolution supported by more than those who had joined the party or voted for Hitler. At first the regime was a coalition of nationalist forces. Hitler was chancellor, but only three other party leaders were in the cabinet. Following an arson attack on the parliament building in Berlin on the night of 27 February 1933, Hitler got the president to approve emergency powers that became the basis for a regime of "legal" terror exercised principally against communist, social democratic, and Catholic opponents of the party. New elections were called in March, and Hitler and his nationalist allies won more than 50 percent of the vote. A few days later, on 24 March, an Enabling Bill was promulgated that allowed the cabinet to approve changes to the constitution and to draft legislation. Over the next nine months other political parties were banned, the trade unions were abolished and their assets seized, and the provincial governments were forced to accept rule directly from Berlin. The dictatorship was consolidated in 1934 following the murder on 30 June of leaders of the party's paramilitary wing, the SA (Sturmabteilung), who were accused of plotting against the party leadership. Hitler himself arrested the chief of the SA, Ernst Röhm, who was shot on his orders the following day. Parliament then approved Hitler's right to take the law into his own hands. In early August, President von Hindenburg died, and Hitler took the opportunity to fuse the function of president and chancellor together by creating a single office of Führer, which was formally approved by national plebiscite later that month. The office was a unique one; Hitler was effectively above the law, able to make and enforce it as he saw fit. This was the essence of his personal rule.

Hitler's style of ruling was deliberately unconventional. He saw himself as the country's messiah whose task was to guide the German people to its new destiny. He disliked committee meetings and his attendance at cabinet meetings declined rapidly after 1934, until the cabinet ceased meeting altogether in February 1938. He preferred more informal governance. He met party leaders in secret meetings; ministers and officials discussed issues with him face-to-face; he delegated a good deal of responsibility to special commissioners who enjoyed his powerful backing; decisions were taken over lunch, at dinner, or on walks around his villa in the small Bavarian town, Berchtesgaden, that he chose as his retreat from Berlin and as a second political center. He preferred the company of party friends and leaders, and it was they who came to play an increasingly important part in pushing policy through and in subverting the normative state, vying for Hitler's attention and basking in his reflected glory. He indulged technical experts as well. Throughout his period as dictator Hitler was fascinated by monumental architecture and advanced technology; in 1934 he launched the construction of a network of fast motorways and in 1937 decreed the rebuilding of Germany's major cities, both projects a monument to his self-image as an "artist-ruler" rather than a mere politician.

The absence of settled administrative routine and the habit of delegation has led some historians to the conclusion that Hitler was a "weak dictator," dominated by the power structures around him and unable to insist on his own political intentions. The reality was more complex. There were no power centers that could effectively challenge Hitler's position after 1934; no major decisions could be taken without his consent, and Hitler could overturn minor decisions, even of the courts, if he chose to intervene. The cult of personality secured popular endorsement, while governing

Adolf Hitler in the military parade at the 1938 Nuremberg Rally. UNITED STATES HOLOCAUST MEMORIAL MUSEUM

circles around Hitler understood that loyalty to the dictator was the central element in their survival. But Hitler was aware that he faced circumstances that were not always under his control, either at home or abroad, and he continuously engaged in political activity designed to remove barriers to the exercise of his power. He displayed moments of uncertainty or fear of risk, but once decisions were taken he regarded them as irreversible, the result of what he regarded as an act of dictatorial will. But on the principal issues of Germany's international revival, remilitarization, and biological purification Hitler played a more direct part as befitted, in his view, a leader destined to create a utopian "new order."

Foreign and military policy absorbed a large part of Hitler's energy throughout the whole history of the Third Reich. As early as February 1933 he announced to the cabinet that the chief priority of the new regime was to re-create Germany's

military power. In October 1933 he took Germany out of the Disarmament Conference that had been called the year before at Geneva, and withdrew Germany from the League of Nations. He moved cautiously at first to avoid fear of foreign intervention, but in March 1935 he publicly declared German rearmament, and a year later, in March 1936, he ordered German forces to reoccupy the demilitarized zone of the Rhineland, imposed on Germany under the terms of the Treaty of Versailles. In August 1936, at Berchtesgaden, he drafted a memorandum that laid out the future of German strategy. He saw Jewish bolshevism as the greatest threat Germany confronted and called for rearmament on a massive scale at the expense of every other priority. In October he appointed Hermann Goering (chief of the German air force) to head the creation of a four-year plan to prepare the German economy and the German armed forces for war in four years.

WORLD WAR II AND THE GENOCIDE OF THE JEWS

Hitler had no clear blueprint for war, but he saw conflict as inevitable if Germany were to claim its just position as a world imperial power. On 5 November 1937 he finally revealed to his commanders his resolve to absorb Austria into the German Reich and to attack Czechoslovakia at the first opportunity. His homeland was occupied by German troops on 12 March 1938, and a few days later Hitler rode in triumph into Vienna, where he announced Austria's union in a Greater Germany. He then informed the army of his intention to invade the Czech state in the autumn, but the diplomatic intervention of Britain and France delayed conquest. At the Munich conference on 29–30 September Hitler was granted the German-speaking areas of the Sudetenland, but on 15 March of the following year he ordered the occupation of the rump Czech state in defiance of the Western powers. Two weeks later he decided on war against Poland for refusing to return the "German" territories Poland had been granted in 1919. This time he ignored threats from Britain and France, assuming they were too decadent and militarily weak to interfere seriously, and, after approving an expedient nonaggression pact with the Soviet Union signed on 23 August, he ordered German forces to attack Poland on 1 September. Two days later Britain and France declared war.

Hitler made foreign policy his own preserve. His initiatives were often opposed by more prudent military leaders, even on occasion by his party colleagues, but he was determined that Germany should become the dominant power in Eurasia during his lifetime. His role in German race policy is less certain. Hitler made anti-Semitism a central part of his worldview in the 1920s. He saw the Jew as an eternal enemy of all higher forms of culture; he identified the Jew with bolshevism and "social decomposition"; and he adopted popular biological racism and applied it to the Jewish "bacillus," which he thought infected the purity of German blood. This mix of prejudices was used by Hitler to define the threat to Germany and German national identity, but there is little evidence before 1939 that he ever considered the genocide of the Jews as the solution to what was defined as "the Jewish question." The lack of a clear genocidal program has divided historians over the issue of Hitler's responsibility; so-called intentionalists assume that he must have played a central part, while "structuralist" historians argue that the system moved step-by-step toward more radical racist solutions.

There is no doubt that race policy was pushed along by enthusiasts in the party and a science establishment keen to pursue a policy of race hygiene. Hitler approved but did not initiate the sterilization law of January 1934, nor did he take the initiative in the Race Laws approved in September 1935 at the party rally in Nuremberg, which forbade marriage between Jews and ethnic Germans and turned Germany's Jews into second-class citizens. Hitler never obstructed the radicalization of anti-Semitic policy, but his exploitation of race prejudice was rhetorical as much as practical. Only in January 1939, in a speech to the German parliament, did Hitler confront the "Jewish question" directly when he announced that if Germany were to be dragged into a global war again, it would mean the annihilation (*Vernichtung*) of the Jewish people in Europe. Hitler linked war and racism together from 1939. The Jew was seen as a malign international force using the cover of world war to destroy Germany, and it was this warped perception that made Hitler's anti-Semitism so dangerous.

Hitler's popularity in Germany reached its highest point between 1939 and 1940. In two weeks German forces defeated Poland. Hitler wanted to attack French and British forces at once, but was persuaded by his generals to wait until the spring. In April he ordered the occupation of Denmark and Norway, to protect the northern flank, and on 10 May German armies launched a campaign that in six weeks defeated the Netherlands, Belgium, and France and drove British forces from mainland Europe. Hitler was hailed as the greatest German; his regime began to plan the building of a new European order. In late July 1940 he announced to his military commanders that, despite the nonaggression pact, he would order an attack on the Soviet Union to complete the establishment of a new German empire and destroy forever the threat of "Jewish bolshevism." When the German air force failed to defeat the Royal Air Force in the autumn of 1940 as a prelude to a quick invasion of southern Britain, Hitler turned to the east. On 18 December he issued the Barbarossa order for an assault on the

Soviet Union in the early summer. In the spring German forces were diverted to the conquest of Yugoslavia and Greece, but on 22 June 1941 the invasion of the Soviet Union began. In the months beforehand Hitler had approved special orders allowing German troops and security forces to murder communists and Jews in state service, and from the early weeks of the invasion Jewish communities were targeted for indiscriminate murder.

Historians argue over when or if Hitler ordered the genocide of the Jews at some point in the second half of 1941. No document has ever been found, but Hitler can be shown to have played a part in all the key decisions about the murder of Soviet Jews. As German forces pushed into the Soviet Union, Hitler was convinced that victory was assured. Orders were given to extend Jewish executions to women and children, German Jews were finally rounded up and deported east, and orders were given for the first purpose-built extermination centers to be set up. On 12 December, a day after Germany's declaration of war on the United States, Hitler gave a speech to party leaders in which he was reported to have announced a program for the physical annihilation of European Jews in line with the threat he had made in January 1939. Though there can be no certainty about the date, most historians agree that Hitler approved a policy of extensive mass murder at some point in the last weeks of 1941, and reconfirmed this in the course of 1942 as murder was applied to Jewish communities from other parts of occupied Europe. The genocide continued for the next three years, but Hitler seems to have taken only a limited interest once the program was under way. His decisive interventions came in 1941.

HITLER'S FALL

Hitler from the autumn of 1941 became absorbed in the details of the military campaigns. In February 1938 he had appointed himself supreme commander of the armed forces, and his headquarters became the center of the German war effort. In December 1941, disillusioned with the army leadership, he appointed himself commander-in-chief of the German army and conducted the day-to-day war effort himself. He had staff reports and discussions once or twice a day and spent most of his time at headquarters, his public appearances reduced almost to nothing, his life a tedious routine of military briefings, technical reports, and dinners in which he engaged in monologues about every aspect of world history and world affairs. In December 1942 he faced his greatest challenge with the encirclement and defeat of German armies at Stalingrad. His health and temper deteriorated, sustained by regular applications of drugs prescribed by his personal physician, Theodor Morell. As Germany faced defeat on all fronts, Hitler became ever more determined to hold out to the bitter end in the hope that destiny might in the end rescue Germany from collapse. In October 1943 he ordered a program of underground construction so that Germany could carry on with the war despite bombing; he personally ordered the development and production in the autumn of 1943 of "vengeance weapons" (the V1 flying bomb and V2 rocket) to turn the tide of the war, though he made little effort to support programs of nuclear research. In spring 1944 he insisted on dividing German forces along the French channel coast to meet the expected Anglo-American invasion, a decision that made it possible for the campaign in Normandy to succeed when it was launched on 6 June 1944. Throughout the period of German retreats Hitler refused to acknowledge reality. Though some of his entourage made tentative peace feelers, Hitler seems never to have entertained the idea of surrender.

On 20 July 1944 an attempt was made to assassinate Hitler at his headquarters, carried out by a coterie of disillusioned senior soldiers. This was one of at least forty-two known attempts on Hitler's life. The bomb left him injured but alive. In the aftermath hundreds of senior soldiers and officials, drawn mainly from Germany's upper classes, were arrested and executed. Hitler's personal rule remained unshaken and no further effort was made to stop him from dragging Germany down into a state of complete destruction. In March 1945 he ordered a policy of scorched earth inside Germany to deny the German people any chance of their survival. The policy was ignored by most local authorities as Allied armies approached. In his last recorded conversations Hitler blamed defeat not only on the Jews, but also on the Germans for failing the supreme test of racial superiority. On 30 April 1945 he shot himself in his command bunker in Berlin rather than risk capture by the encircling Red Army. Eva Braun, whom he had married the day before, took cyanide. Their bodies were incinerated; only their dental remains could be found and definitely identified. The Allies had intended to put Hitler on trial in 1945 for crimes against peace and crimes against humanity. Every effort was made to avoid making Hitler into a nationalist martyr.

Hitler's legacy has been a powerful one. He has continued to exert a fascination for historians and the wider public outside Germany. Inside Germany his legacy has provoked profound historical disagreements over how to come to terms with responsibility for war and genocide but has also encouraged a self-conscious democratic spirit and hostility toward populist nationalism and racism. Small groups of neo-Nazis have kept Hitler alive politically, but there has been no mainstream movement to revive National Socialism or to encourage a postwar cult of Hitler. His name has entered the language as the personification of modern evil.

See also **Germany; Holocaust; Nazism; Stalin, Joseph; World War II.**

BIBLIOGRAPHY

Primary Sources

Genoud, François, ed. *The Testament of Adolf Hitler: The Hitler-Bormann Documents, February–April 1945.* Translated by R. H. Stevens. London, 1961.

Heiber, Helmut, and David M. Glantz, eds. *Hitler and His Generals: Military Conferences, 1942–1945.* Translated by Roland Winter, Krista Smith, and Mary Beth Friedrich. London, 2002. The records of Hitler as warlord in the last four years of the war.

Hitler, Adolf. *Mein Kampf.* Edited by D. C. Watt. Translated by Ralph Manheim. London, 1969.

Maser, Werner, ed. *Hitler's Letters and Notes.* Translated by Arnold Pomerans. London, 1974.

Trevor-Roper, H. R, ed. *Hitler's War Directives, 1939–1945.* London, 1964.

———. *Hitler's Table Talk, 1941–1944.* 3rd ed. Translated by Norman Cameron and R. H. Stevens. New York, 2000. Records the evening monologues at Hitler's wartime headquarters.

Secondary Sources

Hamann, Brigitte. *Hitler's Vienna: A Dictator's Apprenticeship.* New York, 1999. The best account of Hitler's early years, debunking many accumulated myths.

Kershaw, Ian. *Hitler: Hubris, 1889–1936.* London, 1998.

———. *Hitler: Nemesis, 1936–1945.* London, 2000. These two volumes comprise the standard modern biography of Hitler.

Longerich, Peter. *The Unwritten Order: Hitler's Role in the Final Solution.* Stroud, U.K., 2001. The best account of Hitler's role in anti-Semitic policy.

Stern, J. P. *Hitler: The Führer and the People.* Rev. ed. London, 1990. One of the best short interpretative essays on Hitler.

Zitelmann, Rainer. *Hitler: The Policies of Seduction.* Translated by Helmut Bogler. London, 1999. The best account of Hitler's social, economic, and political thinking.

RICHARD OVERY

HLINKA, ANDREJ

HLINKA, ANDREJ (1864–1938), Roman Catholic priest and nationalist politician, journalist, and orator in interwar Slovakia.

Andrej Hlinka was the leader of the largest and most complex nationalist political movement in interwar Slovakia and an instigator of a unique brand of political Catholicism. He oversaw and directed the conversion of the Slovak People's Party (Slovenská ľudová Strana, or SĽS) from a confessional movement into a mass-based, modern national clerical party. Hlinka was a leading defender of Catholicism as an indispensable component of statehood and Slovak national identity. He was one of the few Czechoslovak politicians that achieved cultlike status in his lifetime—an opposition leader unafraid of political isolation, whose populist and conservative character informed his politics and shaped his party's appeal. He remained convinced that the solution to the "Slovak question" was to be found within the borders of Czechoslovakia, and that only political autonomy (albeit the precise nature of decentralization was not always clearly and consistently defined) would improve Czech-Slovak relations and strengthen the foundations of the state. He remains one of the most controversial figures of modern Slovak history.

Hlinka was born into a poor farming family in the Slovak village of Černová in Upper Hungary and was ordained as a Roman Catholic priest on 19

June 1889. Hlinka's political outlook was firmly rooted in the Christian socialism of the 1890s. In August 1895 he joined the Slovak National Party (SNS) and Ferdinand Zichy's (Hungarian) Catholic People's Party. Hlinka was unsuccessful as a candidate of Zichy's party in the elections to the Hungarian Diet in 1898 and left the party in 1901.

Hlinka became parish priest in Ružomberok in March 1905 and nine months later helped to establish a Slovak People's Party, the Catholic wing of the SNS. In May 1906 he was suspended from performing priestly duties for his support of a fellow SNS candidate in the run-up to the Hungarian parliamentary elections. On 6 December 1906 Hlinka was sentenced to two years' imprisonment for "political agitation." (This sentence was extended by eighteen months in a new legal case beginning in May 1908.) The shooting dead of locals by gendarmes in Černová on 27 October 1907 brought Hlinka's name to the attention of the European public for the first time. Before commencing his prison sentence at the end of November, he toured Bohemia and Moravia, lecturing about the cultural plight of the Slovaks in Upper Hungary. Following the intervention of the Vatican, Hlinka's suspension was lifted on 8 April 1909. His last day in prison was 22 February 1910.

Hlinka initiated the creation of an independent Slovak (Catholic) People's Party (SL'S) in Žilina on 29 July 1913. During World War I he remained in his parish. In August 1917 he embraced the "Czecho-Slovak" idea as a political concept. At a meeting of Slovak politicians in Turčiansky Sv. Martin in May 1918 Hlinka called for the severance of ties with the Hungarians and the creation of a common state of Czechs and Slovaks. On 30 October 1918 he joined other delegates in officially endorsing the existence of the new state (Martin Declaration). Hlinka assembled the first meeting of the Council of Slovak Priests on 10 November 1918. The council was the springboard for the re-formation of the SL'S on 19 December 1918, at which Hlinka was elected chairman of the party (a position he retained until his death). In November 1918 he became chairman of the Ružomberok National Council. A few months later he declined the position of head official for ecclesiastical matters in Slovakia. Hlinka's demand for Slovak political (legislative) autonomy dates from the spring of

1919 and was based on the so-called Pittsburgh Agreement (signed 30 May 1918). Eager to secure international recognition of the agreement, Hlinka traveled to the Paris Peace Conference in August 1919 under an assumed name. The trip was a failure and raised suspicion about his political intentions. He was arrested on 11 October and interned in Moravia. In April 1920 Hlinka was granted amnesty by Czechoslovak president T. G. Masaryk following his election to the National Assembly in Prague. (Hlinka retained his mandate at all successive parliamentary elections, 1925, 1929, and 1935). Following the elections Hlinka entered into a short-lived parliamentary bloc with the Czechoslovak People's Party. During the summer of 1921 he encouraged SL'S members to draw up plans for Slovak political autonomy (later declared an official party aim at a meeting of the SL'S in Žilina in August 1922). At the end of the summer Hlinka visited the Vatican and was received by Pope Benedict XV. The SL'S was renamed as Hlinka's Slovak People's Party (Hlinkova slovenská Pudová strana) on 17 October 1925.

Between June and September 1926 Hlinka attended the World Eucharist Congress in Chicago and lectured throughout Central America. In 1927 he was appointed apostolic protonotary by the Holy See. He negotiated his party's entry into government starting on 4 February of that year but never occupied a ministerial position himself. Hlinka remained above politics, which enabled him to unify radical, moderate, and clerical wings of the party. His support of the party ideologue and Magyarone Vojtech Tuka brought him into conflict with members of his own party and T. G. Masaryk, which resulted in the departure of the SLS from government. In the spring of 1929 and again in January 1930 Hlinka called, albeit with little success, for the cooperation of all Catholic parties in Czechoslovakia. He sporadically cooperated with the Czech radical Right between 1929 and 1934 but remained fiercely opposed to any form of Slovak-Hungarian alliance.

Hlinka and the SNS leader Martin Rázus created the short-lived "autonomist bloc" on 16 October 1932 (Zvolen Manifesto). In December 1932 at a joint SL'S–SNS congress in Trenčín, Hlinka made the most controversial speech of his political career, in which he placed the demands of the Slovak nation above the interests of the state. He publicly rejected Czechoslovak nationalism and demanded political autonomy in the Nitra Declaration speech delivered on 13 August 1933 at the Pribina celebrations (SLS demonstration). On 16 April 1935 Hlinka announced the formation of a new autonomist bloc composed of the SLS, SNS, and representatives of national minority parties (Ruthenians and Poles), and in December 1935 his backing proved crucial in securing the election of Edvard Beneš as Czechoslovak president.

On 19 September 1936 at the SLS congress in Piešťany, Hlinka insisted that active cooperation with the Prague government was conditional upon its honoring its promise of Slovak autonomy, and the following day he delivered the controversial "Piešťany Manifesto" drafted by party radicals. On 27 September 1937 the Polish government honored Hlinka with the order of Polonia Restituta. Representatives of the Sudeten German Party visited Hlinka in February 1938 to begin negotiations about the creation of a unitary opposition front of national minorities in the Republic. On 5 June 1938 Hlinka spoke for the last time in public at the jubilee celebrations of the signing of the Pittsburgh Agreement in Bratislava. He died on 16 August in Ružomberok.

See also **Masaryk, Tomáš Garrigue; Slovakia.**

BIBLIOGRAPHY

Bartlová, Alena. *Andrej Hlinka*. Bratislava, 1991.

Felak, James Ramon. *"At the Price of the Republic: Hlinka's Slovak People's Party, 1929–1938*. Pittsburgh, Pa., 1994.

Jelinek, Yeshayahu. "Storm Troopers in Slovakia: The Rodobrana and the Hlinka Guard." *Journal of Contemporary History,* no. 6 (July 1971): 97–119.

———. "The Slovak Right: Conservative or Radical? A Reappraisal." *East Central Europe* 4, no. 1 (1977): 20–34.

Kamenec, Ivan. "Metamorfózy výkladu Hlinkovej politickej osobnosti." In his *Hladanie a blúdenie v dejinách,* 48–55. Bratislava, 2000.

Kováč, Dušan. "Andrej Hlinka—bojovník za slovenský štát?" In *Mýty naše slovenské,* edited by Eduard Krekovič, Elena Mannová, and Eva Krekovičová, 174–180. Bratislava, 2005.

Krajčovičová, Natália. "Andrej Hlinka v slovenskej politike." *Historická revue* 15, no. 1 (2004): 22–24.

Lipták, Lubomír. "Andrej Hlinka." In *Muži deklarácie,* edited by Dušan Kováč et al., 56–75. Bratislava, 2000.

KATYA A. M. KOCOUREK

HÖCH, HANNAH (1889–1978), German Dada artist and pioneer in the use of photomontage.

Hannah Höch was the only female artist to exhibit substantially and regularly with Berlin Dada, a loosely federated group of artists who came together in 1917 during World War I out of a shared interest in pacifism, leftist protest in the streets and in art, and montage in a variety of media. Höch exhibited what is still her best-known work, *Cut with the Kitchen Knife through the Last Weimar Beer Belly Cultural Epoch of Germany* (1919–1920)—a photomontage caricaturing leaders of the Weimar government and military while lauding women, technology, dance, revolution, and Dada—as well as other works, in the dadaists' infamous 1920 Dada Fair, an exhibition closed by the police for including a hanging pig dummy dressed in a German military uniform.

Together with her then lover and fellow dadaist Raoul Hausmann (1886–1971), Höch is credited for pioneering the use of photomontage in avant-garde art. (It had been used previously in advertisements and popular postcards.) Her earliest photomontage works date from 1918. Montage can be defined as a representation or a process whose signification is dependent on the juxtaposition of parts, and Höch composed her photomontages of images cut from mainstream photo weeklies and magazines and juxtaposed them for wit, ambiguity, caricature, and sometimes beauty. She was particularly interested in mass-media images of the "new woman," the modern woman with bobbed hair and flapper-length dresses likely, as Höch was throughout her adult life, to be living and working in a city.

Höch was born and raised in the small town of Gotha. When she was fifteen, she was taken out of school to care for her youngest sister Marianne, and it was not until she was twenty-two that she was able to leave home, with her family's support, to pursue an artist's education. Arriving in Berlin in 1912, Höch studied applied arts, first at

Abduction (From an Ethnological Museum). Collage by Hannah Hoch, 1925. BILDARCHIV PREUSSICHER KULTURBESITZ/ART RESOURCE, NY

the Kunstgewerbeschule in Berlin for two years, until 1914. Then, after a brief interruption due to the outbreak of World War I, Höch enrolled with Emil Orlik (1870–1932) at the Staatliche Kunstgewerbemuseum in Berlin in 1915. While studying art, Höch supported herself by working part-time at Berlin's major newspaper and magazine publisher, Ullstein Verlag. From 1916 to 1926, Höch was employed as a pattern designer in the handicrafts department, which produced individual brochures for consumer purchase as well as patterns for the press's magazines.

Höch was affiliated with Berlin Dada from 1917 to 1922. In addition to her photomontages, during these years she also exhibited watercolors and other paintings and occasional three-dimensional works such as her *Dada Dolls,* 1916.

After 1922, she associated and at times worked with other internationally known avant-gardists who, like her, had been influenced by both Dada and constructivism, such as the German artist Kurt Schwitters (1887–1948) and the Dutch writer Til Brugman (1888–1958). In the mid-1920s Höch began her series *From an Ethnographic Museum,* photomontages in which she combined images of the "new woman" with others of objects from ethnographic museums, creating complex explorations of issues of race, femininity, and display—specifically of looking and being looked at—as in her 1929 montage *Strange Beauty.* Höch's mass-media scrapbook, assembled in the late Weimar years for private enjoyment, reveals her continuing preoccupations with images of women, cultures she found exotic, technology, and dance. In the late 1920s and early 1930s Höch exhibited frequently—

in solo and group exhibitions at art galleries and the Stedelijk Museum in the Netherlands, in international group exhibitions such as *Film und Foto* (1929–1931), and in a one-woman show in Brno, Czechoslovakia, in 1934. She also designed book jackets in this period.

In 1926 Höch began a lesbian relationship with Brugman, and the two lived together in the Hague from 1926 until 1929 and in Berlin from 1929 to 1935. Photomontages with erotic, same-sex themes, such as *Love* (1931) and *On the Way to Seventh Heaven* (1934), seem to refer to this relationship. In 1938 Höch married Kurt Matthies (1901–1984); they were separated in 1942 and divorced in 1944. In 1939 Höch moved to Heiligensee, a far, semirural suburb of Berlin, where she lived for the rest of her life. As a former member of Berlin Dada, she was unable to exhibit and lived in partial isolation during the National Socialist years. In 1945 she resumed exhibiting, and in 1976 was celebrated with a retrospective at the Musée d'Art Moderne de la Ville de Paris and the Nationalgalerie Berlin. Her archive, consisting largely of correspondence with other artists, resides at the Berlinische Galerie, Berlin.

See also **Avant-Garde; Constructivism; Dada.**

BIBLIOGRAPHY

Boswell, Peter, Maria Makela, and Carolyn Lanchner. *The Photomontages of Hannah Höch*. Minneapolis, Minn., 1997.

Höch, Hannah. *Hannah Höch: Album*. Edited by Gunda Luyken. Ostfildern, Germany, 2004.

Lavin, Maud. *Cut with the Kitchen Knife: The Weimar Photomontages of Hannah Höch*. New Haven, Conn., 1993.

Maurer, Ellen. *Hannah Höch: Jenseits fester Grenzen*. Berlin, 1995.

MAUD LAVIN

HOLOCAUST. The Holocaust (from the Greek *holokauton*, "burnt offering" or "sacrifice") is the term now most commonly used to describe the attempted Nazi genocide of European Jews. Between 1939 and 1945 mass shootings, gassings in specially constructed extermination camps, murderous labor, and other means resulted in the deaths of between 5.1 and 6.2 million Jews. The Nazis themselves referred to the extermination program as the "Final Solution of the Jewish Question." This portmanteau phrase began life before Hitler had definitively resolved on mass murder but soon became a euphemism for genocide. During World War II contemporary Jewish observers and scholars used the Hebrew terms *Churban* (traditionally denoting the destruction of the temple) or *Shoah* (meaning devastation) to describe the Nazi program, and the latter word is still commonly used, particularly by those who reject the "Holocaust's" connotation of sacrifice. In the immediate postwar period, murders of Jews were subsumed under the more general rubric of "War Crimes," the official terminology for Axis misdeeds deployed at the Nuremberg and Tokyo Trials. Historical literature in 1950s and 1960s, when it dealt with the subject at all, tended to refer to the "Final Solution."

Since the 1960s, the designation *Holocaust* has predominated. The term is normally reserved for the Jewish genocide, the most comprehensive, systematic, and unrelenting part of Nazi racially based extermination policies. Yet the Nazis targeted many other groups too, killing directly or through neglect many millions of Polish and Soviet civilians, Soviet prisoners of war (POWs), Roma, the mentally and physically handicapped, and homosexuals. Nazi policies adopted toward Jews often intersected and dovetailed with other racial and resettlement measures.

PRECEDENTS

The Holocaust has provoked deep disagreements among historians as to its causes and meaning. Many see in it the culmination of a long European tradition of Christian anti-Semitism, accompanied since the Middle Ages by intermittent savage violence. The Enlightenment introduced the idea of civil toleration of Jews but also gave rise to new secular critiques of Judaism. In an era of growing legal equality, nineteenth-century opposition to Jews aimed increasingly not to achieve their Christian conversion but to dissimilate them. From the 1870s on, particularly in German-speaking lands, racial anti-Semitism emerged (and with it the coining of the term anti-Semitism itself), condemning Jews for prescriptive biological flaws that had little to do with their failure to endorse Christianity. The most extreme late-nineteenth-century texts by writers such as Eugen Dühring talked of the need to exterminate Jewry, though it is not clear whether physical killing was meant. Anti-Semitism became a cultural code for a large part of the nationalist-minded community in Germany and Austria.

While there are clear similarities between Dühring's language and that of Hitler, the strength, homogeneity, or violent character of pre–World War I anti-Semitic traditions should not be over-emphasized. There was relatively little anti-Semitic violence in Germany before 1914, by which time Germany's few anti-Semitic political parties had dwindled to nothing. Contemporary observers around 1900, if they had predicted anti-Semitic atrocities in the future, would have anticipated them in the Russia of the pogroms, not in Germany.

Some scholars locate the Holocaust's roots less in anti-Semitism than in the modern world's search to control and order society. From the nineteenth century a growing cohort of medical and welfare professionals embarked on projects for improving the health of the population, which often involved controlling and segregating those seen as injurious to social peace. Social Darwinism and eugenics encouraged states to limit the reproduction of unhealthy elements while promoting the fertility of more valuable community members. In the early twentieth century, several world states carried out forced sterilizations of the mentally ill and others. Nazi sterilization, euthanasia, and exclusionary policies undoubtedly drew on these trends. There are parallels between these measures and the lethal modern rationality that can be seen in Germany's wartime plans for the racial resettlement and economic regeneration of eastern Europe, above all in Heinrich Himmler's notorious "Generalplan Ost." It is difficult, however, to see the single-minded and unrelenting commitment to eliminating Jewry as responding to any obvious societal logic.

The rise of modern nationalism was undoubtedly another important prerequisite, not just for the Holocaust but also for other twentieth-century genocides and ethnic cleansings. Modern nationalism, with its ethnic and populist conceptions of what it was that defined the people, created the logic for expunging from the nation those seen as alien. In the decades before World War I, the rise of nationalism in eastern Europe and the Balkan wars saw many acts of murderous ethnic cleansing, acts in turn eclipsed by the Turkish genocide of the

Armenians in World War I. One million Armenians were murdered as part of a gigantic and violent resettlement program involving more than five million people. What distinguishes the Nazi campaign from most ethnic-nationalist rivalries, however, is that the German Jews were not competing for power on any kind of ethnic basis; they were highly acculturated, regarded themselves as Germans, and were not seeking a collective position within the German state.

Beyond ethnic nationalism, the Holocaust drew also on the European powers' recent experience of imperialism. "What India was for England," Hitler said in August 1941, "the eastern territories will be for us" (Traveso, p. 71). Hitler's notion of "living space," which described the Russian and eastern European territory to be cleansed and prepared for German settlement, had its origins in pre–World War I writing about colonial settlement in Africa. Among nineteenth-century European anthropologists the view was widely shared that the extinction of inferior races as a result of contact with superior ones was a law of nature. In Algeria, the Congo, the Ivory Coast, the Sudan, and elsewhere colonialism led to reductions among indigenous populations of genocidal proportions. In South West Africa, the imperial German administration carried out a genocide of the Herero in 1904 that has been seen by some scholars as a direct antecedent of the Holocaust.

World War I was in many ways as significant an experience as all the above. It introduced European nations to technological mass slaughter, exercising a terrible hold on the European imagination. The image of men gassed at the front would reappear in Hitler's rhetoric against the Jews. At home, states became used to taking a direct interest in the nation's health and efficiency. In Germany, concern with "wastage" of scarce resources led to a starvation regime in many mental hospitals that anticipated later Nazi policies. Growing hardship and disillusionment on the German home front exacerbated internal divisions and led to a radicalization of anti-Semitism. The outbreak of revolution, first in Russia, then in Germany and eastern European countries, fomented widespread belief that Jewish circles were sowing discord in Europe's capitals. In this context, Germany's wartime social tensions and defeat could be blamed

Deported Jews under guard in the camp at Pithiviers, France, July 1942. More than 12,800 Jews, including 4,000 children, were arrested in Paris by French police and soldiers during the night of 15 July 1942. They were subsequently held in transit camps in the towns of Drancy, Pithiviers, or Beaune-la-Ronde before being sent to Auschwitz to be killed. ©ANTOINE GYORI/CORBIS SYGMA

by the Right on the Jews. It used to be thought that Adolf Hitler had learned his radical anti-Semitism in Vienna, where he spent his later youth, but it seems that it was in the atmosphere of Germany's defeat and in the fevered postwar political climate in Munich that Hitler fixed his hatred. All across Europe, the postwar era saw the spread of virulent anti-Semitism, particularly in states that had lost the war or felt mistreated by the postwar settlements.

In Germany, the 1918–1919 revolution and civil war carried the violence of war onto domestic streets and ushered in a new paramilitary style of politics. Radical splinter groups on the left and right sprang up out of nowhere; the early years of the new republic were dominated by fear and conflict. The respectable classes were open to violence,

if it assured stability. Virulent right-wing politics dominated the student unions, though until 1932 not the national polls.

PREPARATIONS

It has long been debated when and with what clarity Adolf Hitler formulated the idea of exterminating the Jews. By the mid-1920s he was virulently anti-Semitic. His two-volume autobiography *Mein Kampf,* dictated in prison in 1924, and his second unpublished book, written in 1928, were obsessed with Jewry. Other groups too fell foul of Hitler's racial vision, but only the Jews were seen as conspiring against the nation. Hitler's language is extraordinarily violent and bloodthirsty, redolent with metaphors of plague and parasite. The Jew was variously a maggot, a blood-sucking spider, a rat, a harmful bacillus, or a vampire. His followers expected a brutal reckoning with the Jews, but it seems that Hitler's main aim was to force German Jews to leave the country. The violent rhetoric may not have been a plan for genocide—nevertheless, the language of pests and parasites would give the later genocidal decisions a retrospective claim to consistency. Looking back in 1941 and again at the end of the war, Hitler would say that he had followed a straight path.

Hitler's racial anti-Semitism enjoyed wide resonance in Germany but was arguably not the reason millions of voters turned to the Nazis in Weimar's final crisis years. Indeed, from 1930 the party toned down the anti-Semitic content of its electoral materials in order to increase its appeal.

After Hitler's accession to power on 30 January 1933, Germany's Jews were targeted almost immediately. A government-sponsored boycott of Jewish businesses in April was followed by a purge of the civil service. Between 1933 and 1934 Jews were removed almost completely from German public life. After a brief lull, the period 1935–1937 saw a raft of further measures: in the so-called Nuremberg Laws of September 1935, Jews lost their citizenship and were forbidden to have sexual relations with Aryans. Toward the end of 1937, Jews were denied any possibility of earning an independent living. The regime massively increased the pressure to emigrate. After the Anschluss in March 1938, Austria with its particularly widespread anti-Semitism stepped into the vanguard for a while. But on *Kristallnacht* (Night of Broken Glass), 9–10 November 1938, Nazi brutality smashed through the doors and windows of almost every remaining Jewish home and business in Germany. By the outbreak of World War II, two-thirds of the Jews in Germany and Austria had managed to emigrate, while those left behind formed a huddled, terrified, and aging remnant.

As part of wider debates about the nature of the Nazi system, historians were long divided over the reasons for this rapid radicalization. While the "intentionalists" emphasized Hitler's purposeful drive to exclude the Jews, the "functionalists" believed that what took the regime into uncharted waters was competition between subordinates seeking to make their mark in an unregulated power jungle. It is now known that Hitler probably did

send the decisive signals, but the energy of the program depended on the willing compliance of a large number of players, who often shared the idea that Jewish influence should be removed from Germany. In the early years, state officials at national and local levels vied with Nazi Party members to be the torchbearers. When Jewish businesses and property were up for grabs, popular greed added further energy. Toward the end of the 1930s, the influence of the Heinrich Himmler's SS (Schutzstaffel) and police empire grew; during the war it would be the dominant force.

The tide of discriminatory measures was aimed toward the goal of a Jew-free society, not murder. In 1938 and 1939, special centers were established in Vienna and Berlin to "facilitate" Jewish emigration. As late as April 1940, the hardliners in the Reich Security Main Office (RSHA) laid down that Jewish emigration should be pursued with increased emphasis. Toward the end of the 1930s, however, the growing suspicion of Nazi expansionism by the rest of the world confirmed Hitler's view that an international Jewish conspiracy was manipulating world events. His pronouncements and warnings grew more threatening in an effort to intimidate the "Jewish-controlled" foreign powers from interfering with German ambitions. In a speech to the Reichstag on 30 January 1939, Hitler "wished to make a prophecy: if international Jewry in and outside Europe once again forced the nations into a world war the result would not be the Bolshevization of the earth and victory for the Jews but the annihilation of the Jewish race in Europe."

A sign of the relatively unplanned way in which the Nazis edged toward genocide of the Jews is that the drift toward using murder as a tool of racial policy began not with Jews and not as the result of anti-Semitism but out of the desire to remove the "burden" of the mentally and physically handicapped. Earlier in the 1930s the Nazis had implemented draconian measures of racial health, introducing compulsory sterilization for the mentally ill. By the outbreak of war 350,000 to 400,000 people, or more than 1 percent of the German childbearing population, would be forcibly sterilized. These measures did not initially target Jews and, indeed, much of the impetus came from medical and scientific proponents of eugenics, who until the early 1930s were not necessarily advocates of more *völkisch* racial thought. The enforced sterilization of the so-called Rhineland bastards in 1934 marked a first crossover toward combining eugenic and ethnic categories that, however, still did not target Jews.

In 1938 Hitler approved the killing of a handicapped child and in 1939 a nationwide program (dubbed "T4" after the Berlin address, Tiergarten 4, whence it was administered) for administering such killings. Hitler was acting in keeping with the attitude of an influential minority in the medical profession who regarded such "lives unworthy of living" as an exorbitant burden on the state. A program to eliminate mentally handicapped adults began in the same year. These operations claimed the lives of seventy thousand people over the following two years. The program also created precedent and expertise for the gassing of Jews. In summer 1940, a sign of the slippage, all mentally ill Jews in German psychiatric institutions were murdered.

In the longer view, the decisive event in unleashing the Nazis' full murderous potential was the outbreak of war. The war encouraged new radicalism and presented new challenges. Britain and its commonwealth were now closed as emigration destinations. The Nazis had acquired a huge Jewish population in occupied Poland. It was clear that for this group emigration was out of the question. The Nazis were stuck with millions of Jews.

Over the next eighteen months, the SS and other authorities would experiment with enforced resettlement of Jews onto a series of special reservations, first in eastern Poland, whither many thousands were dispatched under appalling conditions, then in Madagascar, though no Jews were ever sent there, and then in some distant part of Russia. These projects were much more lethal in intent than the drive to force emigration. The reservations would be policed and controlled—proposals included separating the sexes—and it was not assumed or desired that the deportees would thrive. Each of these projects failed to materialize, however. In the case of Madagascar and Russia implementation was predicated on military victories that did not transpire.

The problems in Poland revealed that Nazi attempts at Jewish resettlement were intersecting with far-reaching plans for the reorganization, ethnic cleansing, and partial Germanization of eastern Europe. It was Himmler's efforts to repatriate several hundred thousand ethnic Germans from the Soviet Union and elsewhere into German-held territory in western Poland that helped to stymie the Jewish reservation plan. To make way for the German settlers, western Polish farms were needed, and to clear the occupants, all available capacities were taken up bringing in ethnic Germans into western Poland and transferring almost half a million Poles (some Jewish, the majority not) out of that area and dumping them in the General Government, the rump Polish territory to the east. At this stage, then, Germanization and plans for Jews collided with each other. Later, they would reinforce each other in disastrous ways, as the Nazis own planning created problems and shortages that led them to look at the Jews as a surplus and unnecessary population.

In 1939–1940, the German authorities in Poland, anticipating the Jews' eventual removal to a reservation, acted with enormous brutality to isolate and concentrate Polish Jews and remove them from the economy. Several thousands of Jewish leaders were killed as part of a wider program of decimating the Polish intelligentsia to crush any national revival. Jews were forced to wear special armbands and were subject to confiscations and special taxes. Jews throughout Poland, except those performing protected tasks for the Wehrmacht, were pushed out of gainful employment. As hopes of speedy deportations crumbled, Nazi leaders sealed up Jewish ghettos. Horribly overcrowded and underresourced, the ghettos were at the whim of local officials' willingness to allow them to earn their keep. In Warsaw, the largest ghetto, presiding authorities systematically starved the occupants, sending death rates soaring in 1940 and 1941. According to official German figures, by the end of 1942 three quarters of a million Jews had died in the ghettos of "natural causes," quite apart from the killing programs that were by then well under way. In many parts of Poland, Jews were conscripted for forced labor under such unbearable conditions—as for example in building fortifications along the Bug River—that many died.

FROM MASS MURDER TO GENOCIDE

It was the war against the Soviet Union that sent the German authorities over the edge to mass murder. As in previous campaigns, special task squads (Einsatzgruppen) prepared to eliminate security threats behind the front lines. But because of the Nazi conception of the Bolshevik system, the scale and the character of the task was defined very differently. This was not an ordinary war, Hitler told his generals, but a fight to the death between two ideologies. The communist officials were all criminals and must be treated as such. Since Hitler believed Jews were at the heart of the communist system, his aim was the elimination of the "Judeo-Bolshevik intelligentsia." In Russia, therefore, the campaign against the elites was to be from the beginning also a campaign against the Jews, with the limits of the Jewish culpability and participation very poorly defined.

The climate for killing was further heated up by economics. Hitler's military strategy and longer-term plans depended on ruthless commandeering of Soviet resources, above all its foodstuffs. Civilian deaths in seven figures were a deliberate and integral part of the campaign. The German high command made no provision to feed the anticipated large numbers of Soviet prisoners. The result would be an astonishingly high death toll—two million by the end of 1941—making Soviet POWs the first group in German hands to die in the millions.

When the German troops swept in to the Soviet Union on 22 June 1941, four motorized Einsatzgruppen of six hundred to one thousand men each followed behind, with additional manpower supplied by police battalions and Waffen SS units. In close cooperation with the German army, these units carried out mass shootings of leading Bolsheviks, Soviet army political officers, state officials, intellectuals, and Jews. Very rapidly, the task squads moved to target all Jewish men of arms-bearing age, and in late summer extended their remit to women and children. The shootings took place at mass graves away from towns and cities, to which the Jews were marched or driven. In the Baby Yar valley in Ukraine, 33,771 Jews were murdered in just two days in September 1941. It is clear that the expansion of the scale of murder coincided with high level meetings between Hitler and Himmler in July. In August, Himmler

A Polish Jew sits at the edge of a mass grave as a German SS officer prepares to shoot him in the head. ©CORBIS

instituted experiments on the effectiveness of using gas as a means of killing, though shooting would remain the preferred option in the Soviet Union. Where demand for Jewish labor was low, and particularly where the male Jews had already been killed, the surviving Jewish populations were simply deemed "useless eaters." In this way the original racial-security concept shifted to a racial-economic one, with only a few skilled male workers enjoying temporary reprieve. By the end of the year more than three quarters of a million Soviet Jews had been killed, a number that eventually would reach two million.

The summer 1941 onslaught against Soviet Jews marked the single most significant step in the descent into genocide, yet it is not clear if the Nazis had yet resolved to murder all European Jews. Rather than a single moment of decision, a number of parallel developments took place in the months after July 1941 as the climate created by the Soviet killings progressively altered policy assumptions.

In September 1941, Hitler agreed that even before the end of the Soviet campaign German Jews could be deported to relieve pressure on housing stock depleted by bombing. By early fall the Nazis had clearly resolved that all Jews should be subject to some kind of territorial or more directly murderous solution. Emigration even of German Jews was now barred for all but a few exceptions. In readiness for deportations, all German Jews had to be clearly marked with the yellow star and were concentrated in special houses. Mass deportations from Germany to Lodz began in October and would be followed by transports to Minsk, Kovno, and Riga in November and December.

It is not clear that the deportees were slated for certain death, though Reinhard Heydrich's planning for the Lodz ghetto condemned nonworkers to overcrowding on a scale that suggested that death through disease would be most welcome. The knock-on effect of the planned deportations, however, was to incur the protest of the receiving authorities, particularly in Lodz. As a result Himmler and the local gauleiter, Artur Greiser, agreed on the construction of an extermination center at Chelmno to eliminate Polish Jews as a way of "making space" for the German deportees. The Chelmno gas camp would begin killing on 8 December 1941.

In September and October, it became clear to Nazi authorities in the General Government that the slow advance in the Soviet Union would not allow the Polish territories to off-load their Jews in the near future and thus that yet another reservation project had failed. Having excluded Jews from almost any way of earning a living, Nazi officials began discussing what to do with their "useless" subjects. The SS leader in the Lublin district, Odilo Globocnik, had been authorized to prepare his region for a German settlement program. In October, after a meeting with Himmler, he began preparations for the Belzec extermination facility, where killing would start in March 1942.

The available records do not allow historians to reconstruct Hitler's precise role in these developments, which seem to have arisen from regional initiatives, though always in coordination with Himmler. Hitler's own recorded pronouncements are seldom unambiguous. What is clear, however, is that by the end of 1941 Nazi leaders were assuming all Jews would be killed—and that such an assumption would have required Hitler's imprimatur. The infamous Wannsee Protocol reveals that by January 1942 at the latest Nazi leaders knew that all Jews would die through exhaustive labor or direct killing, though the final details of the program may not have been fully worked out even then.

The implementation of murder developed in stages in spring 1942, as Himmler and Heydrich progressively expanded the killing process. After Heydrich's assassination in June 1942, Himmler radically stepped up the pace of killings in Poland, in July calling for the entire General Government to be cleared of Jews by the end of the year. By December 1942 just over a quarter of a million Jews in the region remained alive. German Jews began to be killed in large numbers beginning in May 1942 and even those ostensibly reprieved to live out their days in the "old-age ghetto" of Theresienstadt would for the most part be sent on to Auschwitz. Large-scale transports of Jews from western Europe began to roll in June, most of them to Auschwitz. Though the Holocaust was a protracted affair, it is a macabre fact that more than half of all its Jewish victims were dispatched within eleven months. The period from mid-March 1942 to mid-February 1943 marks probably the most intensive period of murder in the history of mankind.

KILLING FIELDS

Half the Jews murdered in the Holocaust did not die in the gas chambers. The majority of these were shot on the plains of Russia. Others were worked or mistreated to death on labor sites throughout Europe. Tens of thousands more were shot near the end of the war. The view of the Holocaust as an almost automated affair, taking place with industrial precision in hidden death factories, is thus inaccurate. This was mass killing at close quarters and on open view, though much of it away from German soil.

But the Nazis' most radical innovation was indeed the creation of death factories in which the technology and efficiency of industrial production was transferred to the killing, processing, and destruction of human bodies. The camps themselves varied considerably in character. Because there were so few survivors, the Chelmno camp near Lodz, and the three extermination camps in the General Government—Belzec, Sobibor, and Treblinka—are less well known than Auschwitz, though together they accounted for twice as many deaths. Like the regular concentration camps they were ultimately under Himmler's control, but they stood outside the main camp system and were run locally, with the "Action Reinhardt" camps of Belzec, Sobibor, and Treblinka under the command of SS Major General Odilo Globocnik in Lublin. Within the camps, security police personnel and transferees from the euthanasia program were in charge while Ukrainian auxiliaries did much of the day-to-day guard duty. There were no selections at the camps: with the exception of the small Jewish labor force temporarily required to keep the machine running, all Jews brought there were murdered. The Chelmno camp near Lodz eliminated its inmates in specially constructed mobile gas vans, whose carbon monoxide fumes were pumped back into the sealed holds. The bulk of the camp's work was done between December 1941 and April 1943, but it was restarted in summer 1944 to eliminate the remnants of the Lodz ghetto. The Action Reinhardt camps used fixed installations into which motor engines pumped carbon monoxide. New arrivals were rushed into the extermination process. Under pretext of being prepared for delousing baths, they were made to undress, have their hair cut, and were sent into the gas chambers all within a couple of hours of exiting the often horrifically overcrowded trains. In the first five weeks of its operation, Treblinka, the most efficient of the three, "processed" three hundred thousand people, predominantly Jews from Warsaw. Overall, as many as nine hundred thousand Jews may have died there—almost as many as in Auschwitz. Between spring 1942 and fall 1943, the Chelmno and Action Reinhardt camps together were responsible for the deaths of perhaps two million Jews. Successful camp uprisings in 1943 allowed a few hundred inmates to escape Treblinka and Sobibor, but from Chelmno and Belzec together there were only three or four survivors.

For many of those Jews sent to Majdanek near Lublin and Auschwitz near Kraków, the experience was similar—death came a few hours after arrival and took place in camouflaged shower rooms, this time with prussic acid (Zyklon B). The corpses were searched for valuables and gold teeth before being cremated. These camps began their existence not as killing centers, however, but as part of the Nazi concentration camp empire, and even in their killing phase continued to hold a sizable working population—including many non-Jews. Jews arriving in these camps were subject to a selection, so that of the 1.3 million people taken to Auschwitz, four hundred thousand were initially selected for labor and given numbers. Because it was the largest complex, the size of a small town, and because it saw the most survivors, it is Auschwitz that has gripped our imagination. Whereas the pure extermination camps had all been shut down by the end of 1943 (though Chelmno would briefly be reopened), Auschwitz's peak murder period came in summer 1944, when 430,000 Hungarian Jews were dispatched in just seven weeks. By the time of its liberation, around 1 million Jews and perhaps 150,000 others had died there. Auschwitz is also noteworthy, though not unique, for the extensive and horrific medical experiments carried out on living patients there, causing many patients to die excruciating deaths in the name of dubious science.

Although a substantial minority of the concentration camp arrivals were selected for labor, the camp regime militated against their being deployed productively. The Nazi goal of "extermination through labor" was inherently contradictory, and the work remained senseless and brutal, designed to eliminate the worker as much as produce anything useful. An IG Farben plant attached to Auschwitz (Auschwitz III or Monowitz), and intended to manufacture artificial rubber, achieved no usable output throughout the war. Even Jews sent to concentration camps that were not formally extermination sites were often subject to such appalling working and living conditions that the camps were de facto killing centers. By 1944, however, German labor shortages were such that Jews began to be deployed more productively, including in factories on German soil. Auschwitz became a giant sieve, to which Jews from all over Europe were brought, subject to selection, and survivors sent on to subcamps in Germany and elsewhere to contribute to the German war effort. While conditions for many were appalling, being involved in useful factory work offered more chance of survival than remaining in the main camp.

Himmler forbade camp commanders from allowing inmates to fall into enemy hands. From January 1945, as foreign troops closed in on Auschwitz and other concentration camp sites, the prisoners were dispatched on senseless, grueling journeys inland, sometimes in open train cars in winter, often on foot, and often without food. Those who fell by the wayside were shot. Between one-third and one-half of all concentration camp inmates still alive in January 1945 perished in these so-called death marches (among Jewish prisoners the proportion was more like 50 percent).

JEWISH RESPONSES

For much of the postwar period, the picture painted of the Jewish response to the Holocaust was one of passivity. The oft-used phrase "like sheep to the slaughter" not only conveyed the similarity between abattoirs and death factories but also implied that Jewish communities put up no resistance to their fate. In the 1960s, Hannah Arendt and Raul Hilberg added to this general picture their influential and very critical judgment of the role played by the Judenräte or Jewish councils.

What is undoubtedly true is that only a small number of active Nazi personnel were required to achieve very large numbers of deaths. One of the Holocaust's most insidious features was that the Nazis incorporated Jewish involvement into the machinery of extermination. In the 1930s Jewish community leaders in Germany and Austria were made responsible for drawing up lists of names, passing on instructions, later even for assembling deportation lists. In September 1939 Heydrich ordered the creation for Poland of Jewish councils responsible for enforcing German orders. The ghettos were self-administered by these so-called Judenräte, who found themselves having to make ever more excruciating choices. In July 1942, for example, the Vilna ghetto leadership handed over the elderly and ill to the Nazis, and in September 1942 the Lodz ghetto council handed over all children under ten and elderly over sixty-five, in both cases to what they knew was certain death. It was the ghetto leaders, most notoriously Jacob

Gens of Vilna and Chaim Rumkowski of Lodz (both of whom were eventually murdered by the Nazis), of whom Hilberg and Arendt were particularly critical. Even in the extermination camps, much of the dirty work was done by Jewish prisoners themselves. In Auschwitz, so-called Jewish Sonderkommandos greeted the arriving prisoners, collected and sorted their belongings, ushered them into the fake showers, searched the corpses for valuables, and burned the corpses.

Research over the last several decades has placed many of the Jewish leaders in a more sympathetic light. For one thing, the genocidal character of Nazi policy was often not immediately visible. After the outbreak of war, Polish communities hoped that traditional responses to hostile authorities of paying fees, fines, and bribes could deflect the worst. Local Jewish leaders often stepped in of their own initiative to provide labor for Nazi conscription, hoping to avert the wild press-ganging of passers-by. In doing so, they found themselves caught up in a pattern of compliance to alleviate the worst, from which it was hard to withdraw. Nazi policy was initially inconsistent, giving hope of survival, particularly where communities could offer skilled labor to the German war effort. Even when evidence of Nazi murderousness was objectively overwhelming, it was understandable that Jewish leaders found it hard to believe the signs. Reprisals against refractory Jewish councils were utterly ruthless. In Stanislau in Ukraine, for example, the entire council was shot for failing to provide conscript labor. Confronted with such dilemmas, the head of the Warsaw ghetto, Adam Czerniakow, chose in July 1942 to commit suicide rather than superintend or actively resist imminent mass deportations to Treblinka.

The Jewish response was in any case far from passive. The most common and most successful stratagem was evasion—through emigration, escape, and hiding. As many as one million Jews survived by these means, including the majority of the Austrian and German Jewish communities, who managed to emigrate abroad, three hundred thousand Polish Jews who fled into the Soviet part of occupied Poland when the Nazis took over the western part, and some two hundred thousand

Jews across Europe who survived in hiding. In the ghettos, for the most part unable to escape, Jewish communities worked hard to maintain educational, spiritual, and cultural life. The early years of Nazi occupation in Warsaw, Lodz, and the Theresienstadt old-age ghetto in the Czech protectorate saw remarkable cultural activity. In Warsaw, Kovno, and other ghettos, organized groups made great efforts to record events for posterity, leaving behind rich and telling chronicles for the postwar world. The lack of arms and outside support made armed resistance extremely difficult—and Nazi reprisals against nonparticipants made it a morally agonizing choice. Full-scale uprisings, as in the Warsaw ghetto in April 1942 and in Bialystok in August of that year, took place only when it was clear that death was inevitable. Even so, there were many incidents of armed opposition. Perhaps as many as one hundred thousand Jews fought with partisans in Poland, Russia, and elsewhere. Ten percent of the French Maquis (resistance) were Jewish. There were armed uprisings in several camps, leading to successful breakouts in Sobibor and Treblinka in 1943 and the destruction of one of the crematoria in Auschwitz in 1944.

PERPETRATORS, COLLABORATORS, BYSTANDERS—AND RESCUERS

If historical research has in recent years been kinder to Jewish leaders and stressed the activism of Jewish responses, treatment of those not in the Holocaust's firing line has taken an opposite trend, widening the circle of those directly involved in the killing process, blurring the dividing line between bystanders and perpetrators, and drawing attention to the large number of European collaborators.

In the early postwar years, the extermination of the Jews was seen as the work of a small circle of SS men, conducted in secret in camps far away from public view. As scholars became aware of the huge bureaucratic apparatus required to identify the circle of victims, brand mark, expropriate, segregate, and transport them, the image of the perpetrator shifted from the secretive uniformed psychopath to the paper-pushing everyman with no vision beyond his or her immediate task. By the late twentieth century the diverse range of institutions and players involved actually in killing Jews became more clear. In the occupied territories in Russia and eastern

Europe, the killing was carried out by a heterogeneous array of German institutions—including the army, civilian administrations, and regular police forces as well as the SS. Even generals who would later join the plot against Hitler willingly cooperated with the extermination process. Postwar trials proved that participants had not acted under duress. The wide involvement was a sign that the war against the Jews proved surprisingly consensual. In both state and party institutions, and particularly in the RSHA, high-powered young men could be found who had already demonstrated strong commitment to *Völkisch* politics and right-wing activism in the 1920s. Anti-Semitism was far from the only motive—as the willing involvement of Nazi units in the mass murder of gypsies (of whom perhaps a quarter of a million were killed) of non-Jewish Poles and of Soviet POWs and conscripts revealed. Most participants, even those with strong ideological credentials or prehistories of violent activism, had been carried along by the regime's radicalization process to a point very far from what they would have regarded as thinkable and right just a few years earlier.

For the German population as a whole, concrete information about the killings in the Soviet Union was widely available in 1941, as soldiers on leave shared firsthand experiences from the front. Rumors of extermination camps circulated in 1942, though not with the same clarity or universality. The German public reacted with passivity and indifference, and with a certain degree of acceptance of the need for radical measures. In the course of the war, the German population grew increasingly frightened at the possibility of reprisals, and some interpreted the Allied air attacks as divine retribution for what was happening in the east.

Since the end of the Cold War there has been growing recognition of the extensive role of collaboration among foreign countries and nationals. In some cases, the collaboration took place at government level. In 1941–1942 Romania murdered or indirectly caused the death of more than a quarter of million Jews in territories it acquired from the Soviet Union. At different points in the war, Slovakia, Croatia, and Hungary all proved enthusiastic participants in the Final Solution, deporting

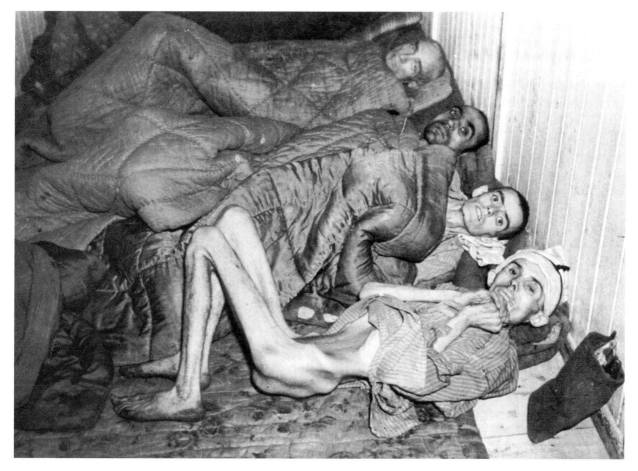

Emaciated men, too weak to stand, found during the liberation of the concentration camp at Buchenwald, May 1945. ©BETTMANN/CORBIS

all or most of their Jewish subjects. Of German allies, Italy and Bulgaria were the least willing to accede to anti-Semitic policies, and most of their Jewish populations survived. Some governments were happy to deport foreign Jews, but saw it as an infringement on their prestige to deport Jews with national citizenship; this was true of Bulgaria, which handed over Macedonian and Thracian Jews; of Romania, which, despite its earlier savagery, persecuted but did not deport most of its own Jews; and of Vichy France, which volunteered sending even children of stateless Jews to the death camps rather than include French citizens in the deportations.

National motives for collaboration varied. Anti-Semitism played a part, but so did the desire to gain German recognition or support. Targeting of foreign Jews was particularly attractive in newly acquired territories, where sharing out the vacated spoils and positions could be used to carve out jobs for the boys or win over local elites—a motive for Romania, Hungary, and Bulgaria. As the German star waned, some nations switched policies. Below government level, the Nazis were able to mobilize or foment local pogroms against Jews, as in Latvia, Ukraine, and briefly in parts of Poland in 1941. They also formed militias from indigenous elements, and most of the Action Reinhardt camp guards were so called "Trawniki" men, recruited in Ukraine. Material inducements were an important element in such recruitment. Some of the Ukrainians bought their way out of horrible conditions as POWs by serving in the camps.

For a long time, accounts of the Holocaust presented the Allies simply as liberators and read contemporary horror at the Holocaust on the faces of the Allied soldiers' and journalists who uncovered the nightmare of the camps. The critical mood occasioned by the Vietnam War and the resulting revisionist wave of American historiography, however, triggered a second look at Allied wartime policy, one that has been further refined as classified materials have become available. More evident now is the way government anti-Semitism, or government sensitivity to the limits of public tolerance of Jews, straitjacketed British and American efforts on behalf of refugees at a time when emigration was still possible. Franklin Delano Roosevelt's calling of the Evian conference in July 1938 to assist the refugees, a conference he did not himself attend, was as depressing as it was ineffectual. For the United States, the state department's assistant secretary in charge of the visa division, Breckinridge Long, has emerged as a particular villain, using administrative means in 1940–1941 to prevent even the modest immigration quotas from being fully exploited. Both British and U.S. governments and parliaments were, it must be said, understandably wary of admitting large numbers of foreigners at a time of continued mass unemployment. Once the Nazis moved to extermination, the Allies rapidly gained knowledge of the shootings through decoding German coded telegrams. Jewish and Polish sources gave them clear insight into genocide in summer 1942. Again, anti-Semitism in official circles or sensitivity to public opinion may have restrained Allied governments from mounting serious rescue operations. In 1943 they sought to limit domestic reporting on Nazi atrocities so as not to create pressure to act; the April 1943 Bermuda conference on the refugee problem was, according to the head of the British delegation, explicitly designed as a "façade for inaction." In 1944 the U.S. Air Force did not amend its bombing targets despite pressure from some quarters to destroy the railway lines to Auschwitz (the efficacy of so doing remains open to debate). There were, however, very obvious limits to what was achievable in wartime, other than defeating Germany as soon as possible. Moreover, behind the scenes in 1944 the U.S. War Refugee Board, acting in conjunction with American Jewish Joint Distribution Agency, did provide considerable financial and other relief where it could and even succeeded in negotiating for the release of a small number of Hungarian Jews.

The Holocaust thus found a great many people wanting, yet there were also rescue attempts to be found in every European country, again ranging from government measures to individual actions. The most spectacular was the Danish rescue of its Jews in October 1943, following a tip-off from German government circles that deportation was imminent. More than seven thousand Danish Jews were ferried to Sweden by boat. In many western European countries semiorganized religious and political networks provided hiding places for Jews. In Poland, despite the brutal German occupation, informal underground networks in "Aryan" Warsaw hid almost thirty thousand Jews, some twelve thousand of whom survived the war. Overall, somewhere between fifty thousand and five hundred thousand individuals risked their lives to provide assistance to Jews in danger. Rescue actions were prompted by a broad spectrum of motives from idealistic humanitarianism, to simple friendship, to material incentives, to crude calculation of the need to show the Allies that German measures had been resisted.

AFTERMATH

One third of world Jewry was eliminated by the Holocaust. Judaism's traditional spiritual centers in eastern Europe were almost completely destroyed, with 90 percent of Polish Jews murdered. The only other group targeted with anything like this comprehensiveness was the gypsies, perhaps one quarter of whose European population was killed. Almost 90 percent of German gypsies died.

At the end of the war between fifty thousand and ninety thousand Jews were on German soil along with seven to ten million other displaced persons (DPs), mostly conscript laborers from the German war machine. Whereas the non-Jews generally had homes to go to (though many Soviet citizens were sent home against their will), most Jews had nothing left behind them. Following the 1946 Kielce pogrom, Polish Jews who had survived the war in Russia and returned home to Poland in 1945 fled westward to the DP camps in Austria and Germany. By 1948 there were 250,000 Jewish DPs in Germany. Jewish leaders in Palestine with American support used the DP's plight effectively as an argument for the creation of an Israeli state, and by the early 1950s the DP problem had been solved through emigration to Israel, the United States, and other countries.

Allied discoveries of the horrors in the concentration camps added to the pressure for postwar trials, and the Holocaust was dealt with as part of the International War Crimes Tribunal at Nuremberg. Allied and former occupied countries also carried out their own trials in the postwar years. From the late 1950s the Federal Republic of Germany took up the issue with vigor and the 1963 Auschwitz trials in Frankfurt were the most high profile of a series of large legal cases that continued into the 1970s and 1980s. Of biggest international impact, however, was the Israeli trial of Adolf Eichmann in 1961–1962 following Eichmann's capture and abduction from Argentina. Though these diverse legal actions left many perpetrators without or with only light punishment, and showed how hard it was to target individuals when the whole system had been criminal, they nevertheless collected huge amounts of valuable records and testimony about the Holocaust. The Eichmann trial and Hannah Arendt's book about it created huge international awareness of the Holocaust for the first time.

As the Kielce pogroms and other postwar violence demonstrated, the Holocaust did not eliminate anti-Semitism from the world. In the 1950s, for example, U.S. holiday resorts were still more likely to be closed to Jews than German ones had been in the 1920s. But over time, the Holocaust impelled both Protestant and Catholic churches to rethink their historic attitudes and contributed more widely to greater Western sensitivity to the perils of racial hatred.

Indeed, it took time in general for the Holocaust's scale and implications to sink in. In the early years survivors found few listeners for their experiences and were themselves often keen to put the horrors behind them. In Israel, the United States, and elsewhere, however, the 1960s—with the Eichmann trial, a more confident Israeli state, and a greater tendency in general to celebrate one's ethnic differences and roots—was a watershed in public consciousness. In the work of writers such as Michel Foucault and postmodern theorists, the experience of the Holocaust seeped into the Western world's sense of the modern,

helping to create greater unease at the negative potentials of the enlightenment, rationality, and technical progress. The 1980s saw an explosion of fictional and nonfictional writing on the subject. Novelists, poets, and artists, many of them survivors, turned to the Holocaust as a theme, or found their earlier works now enjoying global recognition. Museums sprang up across the Western world, and a number of countries introduced Holocaust remembrance days. The subject of representing and remembering the Holocaust itself became a major academic field.

The result is that the Holocaust is the best documented act of violence in human history. Even so, since the 1970s a number of individuals have sought to deny that the Holocaust took place. The growth of the Internet has made it easier to disseminate such claims, despite a number of high-profile legal cases that have established their fraudulent character. In the Arab world, old forgeries, such as the Protocols of Zion, and new denial claims are widely disseminated.

Partly by dint of its special character, partly by dint of the enormous interest it has received, the Holocaust continues to pose particular challenges of understanding and representation. It is almost impossible for survivors to convey the reality of the experience, but by repeatedly emphasizing the Holocaust's unrepresentability, scholars have attached to the event a sacredness, which equally belies its reality. The Holocaust is without doubt one of the most momentous events of the twentieth century, yet the enormous and understandable focus on it is in danger of creating something too abstracted from other Nazi policies and other acts of genocide and violence in the world. The thrust of the most recent scholarship, therefore, has been to place the Holocaust within broader comparative contexts. Even within the broader framework of the bloody twentieth century, the Holocaust will always stand out for its bureaucratic thoroughness, its search for continent-wide comprehensiveness, and its industrialization of murder.

See also **Auschwitz-Birkenau; Concentration Camps; Germany; Israel; Jews; Wannsee Conference; World War II.**

BIBLIOGRAPHY

Aly, Götz. *"Final Solution": Nazi Population Policy and the Murder of the European Jews.* Translated from the German by Belinda Cooper and Allison Brown. London, 1999.

Arendt, Hannah. *The Origins of Totalitarianism.* New York, 1951.

———. *Eichmann in Jerusalem: A Report on the Banality of Evil.* New York, 1963.

Browning, Christopher. *Ordinary Men: Reserve Police Batallion 101 and the Final Solution in Poland.* New York, 1992.

Browning, Christopher, and Jürgen Matthäus. *The Origins of the Final Solution: The Evolution of Nazi Jewish Policy, September 1939–March 1942.* Lincoln, Neb., 2004.

Burleigh, Michael. *Death and Deliverance: Euthanasia in Germany, 1900–1945.* Cambridge, U.K., 1994.

Corni, Gustavo. *Hitler's Ghettos: Voices from a Beleaguered Society, 1939–1944.* Translated from the Italian by Nicola Rudge Iannelli. Oxford, U.K., 2002.

Delbo, Charlotte. *Auschwitz and After.* Translated from the French by Rosette C. Lamont. New Haven, Conn., 1995.

Friedländer, Saul, ed. *Probing the Limits of Representation: Nazism and the "Final Solution."* Cambridge, Mass., 1992.

———. *Nazi Germany and the Jews.* Vol. 1: *The Years of Persecution, 1933–1939.* New York, 1997.

Gerlach, Christian. "The Wannsee Conference, the Fate of German Jews, and Hitler's Decision in Principle to Eliminate All European Jews." In *The Holocaust: Origins, Implementation, Aftermath,* edited by Omer Bartov, 106–161. New York, 2000.

Gross, Jan T. *Neighbors: The Destruction of the Jewish Community in Jedwabne, Poland.* Princeton, N.J., 2001.

Herbert, Ulrich, ed. *National Socialist Extermination Policies: Contemporary German Perspectives and Controversies.* New York, 2000.

Hilberg, Raul. *The Destruction of the European Jews.* Chicago, 1961.

Ioanid, Radu. *The Holocaust in Romania: The Destruction of Jews and Gypsies under the Antonescu Regime, 1940–1944.* Chicago, 2000.

Kaplan, Marion. *Between Dignity and Despair: Jewish Life in Nazi Germany.* New York, 1998.

Kershaw, Ian. *Hitler.* Vol. 1: *1889–1936: Hubris.* Vol. 2.: *1936–1945: Nemesis.* London, 1999–2000.

Klee, Ernst, Willi Dressen, and Volker Riess, ed. *"The Good Old Days": The Holocaust As Seen by Its Perpetrators and Bystanders.* Foreword by Hugh Trevor-Roper. Translated by Deborah Burnstone. New York, 1991.

Klüger, Ruth. *Still Alive: A Holocaust Girlhood Remembered.* New York, 2001.

Levi, Primo. *The Drowned and the Saved.* Translated from the Italian by Raymond Rosenthal. New York, 1988.

Lewy, Guenter. *The Nazi Persecution of the Gypsies.* New York, 2000.

Longerich, Peter. *Politik der Vernichtung: Eine Gesamtdarstellung der nationalsozialistischen Judenverfolgung.* Munich, Germany, 1998.

Mann, Michael. *The Dark Side of Democracy: Explaining Ethnic Cleansing.* New York, 2005.

Mommsen, Hans. "The Realization of the Unthinkable: The Final Solution of the Jewish Question." In *From Weimar to Auschwitz: Essays on German History.* Translated by Philip O'Connor. Princeton, N.J., 2000.

Peukert, Detlev. *Inside Nazi Germany: Conformity, Opposition, and Racism in Everyday Life.* Translated by Richard Deveson. New Haven, Conn., 1987.

Roseman, Mark. *The Villa, the Lake, the Meeting: Wannsee and the Final Solution.* London, 2002.

Sereny, Gita. *Into That Darkness: From Mercy Killing to Mass Murder.* London, 1974.

Traverso, Enzo. *The Origins of Nazi Violence.* New York, 2003.

Trunk, Isaiah. *Judenrat: The Jewish Councils in Eastern Europe under Nazi Occupation.* New York, 1972.

Wildt, Michael. *Generation des Unbedingten: Das Führungskorps des Reichssicherheitshauptamtes.* Hamburg, Germany, 2002.

Zimmermann, Michael. *Rassenutopie und Genozid: Die Nationalsozialistische "Lösung der Zigeunerfrage."* Hamburg, Germany, 1996.

MARK ROSEMAN

HOMOSEXUALITY.

On the face of it, homosexual communities enjoy a position of relative acceptance and security in European culture after enduring the terrible persecutions of the twentieth century.

HISTORY

Homosexuality between men, and sometimes between women, was illegal in many European countries before the 1960s, and many gay men and women suffered far worse fates than mere harassment. The assaults on gay communities across Europe that characterized the twentieth century were carried out by political movements of all kinds, left and right, Nazi and communist, liberal and authoritarian. In spite of these attacks, gay communities have not only endured but have also succeeded in establishing their own forms of civil society, literature, and commerce, as well as political, cultural, and sporting organizations. In response to gay and lesbian protest movements that emerged in the 1960s, governments across Europe slowly began to liberalize nineteenth-century laws that outlawed homosexual acts. Since the 1970s, gay activism has made further gains in terms of recognition, political pressure, and civil rights. Discrimination on the grounds of sexuality—at least in theory—can now be challenged under the European Declaration of Human Rights, part of domestic law in all countries of the European Union.

However, this story of liberalization contains many false starts, gaps, and contradictions. In particular, this history applies mainly to the liberalization of law and culture seen in France, Germany, United Kingdom, the Netherlands, and Scandinavia since the 1970s. In this respect there has been a broad division between northwestern and Eastern/Southern Europe in attitudes to homosexuality. In the former states, homosexuality has become a matter for public policy and a site for debating civil rights more generally, whereas in the latter—notably Catholic countries such as Spain, Portugal, Italy, and Poland—homosexuality has tended to be strongly condemned or ignored by the political mainstream. In the early twenty-first century the illegal status of homosexuality remains in some countries. In Romania, for instance, *any* public expression of homosexuality by men or women is still outlawed, while public opinion in many Balkan countries continues to be largely hostile to gay relationships.

Another complicating factor in the story of liberalization is the fact that homosexual cultures are hardly a new invention. While the decade of the 1960s is generally seen as marking a turning point in Western European attitudes, the idea that homosexuality has only been visible in European culture since this liberalizing moment requires revision. It must be recognized that the flowering of gay culture that has characterized Western Europe since

the 1970s does not necessarily represent a historic reversal of centuries of persecution and invisibility, but is in many ways a return to the visible and vibrant same-sex culture that thrived in several European cities before the 1930s.

This prewar culture was characterized by the coexistence of two models of gay life. On the one hand, cultures of public sex existed in several cities in the 1910s and 1920s, mainly in Germany, France, Britain, Denmark, and Russia/the Soviet Union, while on the other a more intellectual, political, and cultural movement developed, especially in Germany. These urban cultures of public assignation and sex shared several characteristics. Although Paris and Berlin in the 1920s saw an efflorescence of lesbian culture, in other cities homosexual cultures tended to be overwhelmingly male and were marked by public sex, cruising, bar culture, and relationships structured around disparities of youth, age, and class. These street cultures also developed their own codes of behavior, and even their own extensive slang—the English version of which was known as Polari. Lesbian cultures tended to operate in more private spaces, and in both 1920s Paris and in tsarist Russia the salon became an important homosocial institution for women. In addition, Paris developed an extensive lesbian literary scene associated with writers Natalie Barney (1876–1972), Djuna Barnes (1892–1982), and Sidonie-Gabrielle Colette (1873–1954). Alongside these institutions of everyday gay life a growing interest in political advocacy and scientific inquiry into sexual behavior emerged. This "sex radicalism," as it was known in Britain, and which drew on the work of Sigmund Freud (1856–1939) and sexologists such as Karl Heinrich Ulrichs (1825–1895), Havelock Ellis (1859–1939), and others, argued for the legitimacy of homosexuality and sought to overturn nineteenth-century laws against it as part of a wider progressive assault on ignorance and inequality.

Gay politics and culture of this kind was strongest in Germany, where it took two main forms. Its scientific side was led by sexologists such as Magnus Hirschfeld (1868–1935), who was director of the Berlin-based Institut fur Sexualwissenschaft (Institute for Sexual Science, established in 1919). He was also the founder and leader of the Scientific-Humanitarian Committee, a body that campaigned for the repeal of anti-homosexual laws. Hirschfeld and his allies argued that punishment was pointless because homosexuality was congenital and could not be changed by punishment. This model of activism was imitated elsewhere, especially by the Netherlands Scientific-Humanitarian Committee (NWHK), which was established in 1911. On the other wing of gay culture were those writers and artists who disagreed with Hirschfeld's medical-scientific model of the self and tended to see homosexuality as an integral aspect of masculinity. They held that homoerotic desire arose naturally from the strong Germanic tradition of masculine sociability and association, or *Männerbund*. This view was particularly associated with intellectuals such as the poet Stefan George (1868–1933) and writer Adolph Brand (1874–?), editor of the homosexual journal *Der Eigene* (One's Own), established in 1897). Czech and Austrian homophiles influenced by George and associated with the *Wandervögel* (ramblers) youth movement developed arguments along similar lines. The association between the sexological and cultural sides of the Central European movement was reflected in other countries, notably Britain and France, where intellectuals adapted the work of Freud, Hirschfeld, and others.

This vibrant prewar homosexual culture was a target of both Nazi and Stalinist persecution. One of the first acts of the Nazis in power was to dismantle Hirschfeld's institute and burn his library, an event that was to prove a prelude to a much wider assault on homosexuality. Indeed, in 1933 a period of persecution began for gay men and women across Europe that was to continue into the Cold War and end only in the late 1960s. The Nazi assault on homosexuality began with "degenerates" in their own ranks when, during the Night of the Long Knives on 30 June 1934, Hitler's former trusted lieutenant Ernst Rohm (1887–1934), the leader of the paramilitary Sturmabteilung (SA) and an unapologetic homosexual, was killed. The following year male homosexuality was criminalized and a separate branch of the government established to deal with the "epidemic." Between 1937 and 1939, some ninety-five thousand men were arrested under this law. As many as sixty thousand men were interned in concentration camps between the mid-1930s and 1945, large numbers of whom were used as slave labor.

Others became the subject of medical experiments that involved castration and hormone treatment.

In the Soviet Union, 1933 also saw the recriminalization of male homosexuality as part of the purges of Joseph Stalin (1879–1953). Consenting sex between men was to be punished with five years hard labor, and thousands of men were sent to the Gulag. Soviet rhetoric echoed that of the Nazis in alleging that political opponents were tainted with homosexual "degeneracy." "Destroy the homosexuals," the Soviet author and propagandist Maxim Gorky, (1868–1936) declared, "[and] Fascism will disappear."

Many of the laws against homosexuality instituted by communist and fascist regimes in the 1930s survived the end of World War II. In West Germany and France, for instance, the respective Nazi and Vichy laws were incorporated into the criminal code of both new republics. East Germany also retained similar prewar laws, although these were amended in 1950. Suspicion of homosexuals as potential traitors, security risks, or threats to the family and the state was a feature of the Cold War on both sides, and across Western Europe and Scandinavia criminal codes were enforced with a new vigor in the 1950s. Signs of a thaw were visible, however. Alongside revisions to laws in East Germany, in Britain a commission was appointed to review the law against homosexuality and reported in 1957 that it should be repealed. In Eastern Europe, the post-Stalin relaxation of authority contributed to the repeal of anti-gay laws in Czechoslovakia and Hungary (1961) and Poland (1969).

In Western Europe, gay rights movements began tentatively to reassert themselves after 1945 and by the late 1960s had achieved some success as part of a wider movement for civil rights. These movements, which found strongest expression in Britain, Germany, the Netherlands, and Scandinavia, propounded a radical, often leftist agenda that sought to overturn the association of homosexuality with discretion and secrecy. Gay-rights advocates argued that homosexuals should set aside discretion and confront injustice wherever they found it. Homosexuality should mean publicity, "coming out," and affirming that "gay is good," as well as activism, marches, confrontation, and political organization devoted to securing equal rights with heterosexuals. Separate lesbian movements also emerged in the early 1970s as part

Pierre Garnier, right, manager of marketing and communications for Pink, the first gay television channel, discusses the station identification with members of the French band AIR. ©Tanguy Loysance/Corbis

of a feminist reaction against male-dominated leftist activism. Laws against sex between men were repealed in England (1967), East Germany (1968), West Germany (1969), the Netherlands (1971), Austria (1971), Norway (1972), Finland (1971), Spain (1976), and later France (1982) and Ireland (1993). By the 1980s, a backlash of sorts had set in, notably in Britain where homophobic legislation was passed that sought to prevent schools from teaching pupils about homosexuality, and where unequal age-of-consent boundaries were increasingly policed. In addition the emergence of AIDS in the early 1980s also marked gay life and politics. In Western Europe, groups such as ACT UP used tactics derived from an American model of confrontational "queer" activism to demand equal treatment and openness for those with the disease. In spite of these setbacks, earlier legal gains were followed in Scandinavia and the Netherlands by the equalization of ages of consent and antidiscrimination laws, the latter introduced in Denmark (1994), the Netherlands (1994), and Sweden (1999).

Registered partnership was introduced in 1989 in Denmark and in Sweden in 1994. In contrast, many former communist countries had to wait until the 1990s even for the establishment of small-scale gay advocacy groups.

IDENTITY

Throughout this period, gay identity has been understood in many different ways. In general, though, it has been influenced by three main strands of thought and life. Those influenced by interwar sexologists such as Hirschfeld preferred a medical-scientific model of the self, in which true homosexuality, as opposed to situational "perversion," was congenital, inborn, and ineradicable. In contrast, Central European writers of both sexes tended to see homosexuality as deriving naturally from homosocial association. However, many of the young men who participated in casual public sex in Moscow, London, Paris, or elsewhere would have rejected both models and instead seen this activity as a part of the life cycle. They did not necessarily define themselves as inherently homo-sexual or congenitally different from other men. Instead, sexual acts between men were seen in terms of gender roles and according to whether such acts were active or passive. This model has been strongest in the Mediterranean and in Balkan countries influenced by Ottoman conquest, but it also applied within working class communities in the West until the 1950s. In general a passive partner would be seen in the effeminate role. His ostensibly active partner, often younger and poorer and osten-sibly more masculine, would be his "trick" or "trade." This interpretation endured in Britain at least until the 1950s, where working class youth willing to be picked up in this way were described as "haveable."

A similar divergence between congenital and gender-based models of identity also influenced the terms in which lesbianism was understood. The fact that lesbianism was never illegal in most of Europe gave it a double character. On the one hand it was less visible culturally, but was as a result less liable to attack. Sexology also proved less useful for women as the basis of activism, since its view of lesbians tended to stress a supposed tendency toward mannishness and psychopathology. However, gen-der-based roles such as butch-fem (partnerships of masculine and feminine women) continued to be vibrant and were the principal models of identity used in the separate lesbian bar cultures that devel-oped in Western Europe after 1945.

The overall picture of homosexuality remains divided between northern and southern Europe. In the former, where specific laws against male homo-sexuality existed, most major cities have developed gay cultures and gay rights are well advanced. In the latter countries, with different legal tradi-tions, the model of Western identity and activism is still the best hope for local activists wishing to battle discrimination, although it is nevertheless seen as an Anglo-American import somewhat alien to local traditions. While in northwestern Europe acceptance of homosexuality has depoliticized gay life and encouraged its turn toward consumerism and domesticity, in many countries the fact that homosexuality has barely made it onto the public agenda means that it can pass without notice, thereby at least guaranteeing a degree of impunity.

See also **AIDS; Body Culture; Minority Rights; Sexuality.**

BIBLIOGRAPHY

Amnesty International. *Crimes of Hate, Conspiracy of Silence: Torture and Ill-Treatment Based on Sexual Identity.* London, 2001.

Healey, Dan. *Homosexual Desire in Revolutionary Russia.* Chicago, 2001.

Heger, Heinz. *The Men with the Pink Triangle.* Rev. ed. Translated by David Fernbach. London, 1994.

Merrick, Jeffrey, and Bryant T. Ragan, eds. *Homosexuality in Modern France.* New York, 1996.

Mosse, George L. *Nationalism and Sexuality: Respectability and Abnormal Sexuality in Modern Europe.* New York, 1985.

Steakley, James D. *The Homosexual Emancipation Movement in Germany.* New York, 1975.

Weeks, Jeffrey. *Coming Out: Homosexual Politics in Britain from the Nineteenth Century to the Present.* London, 1977.

H. G. COCKS

HONECKER, ERICH (1912–1994), East German politician.

Erich Honecker presided over both the flower-ing and the demise of the German Democratic Republic (GDR). His career was emblematic of the Communists who ruled the various states of the Soviet bloc after World War II.

Honecker was born into a politically active, working-class family in the Saar region of western Germany. His formative years transpired amid the turbulence of the Weimar Republic (1918–1933), which was marked by almost constant political and class conflict and large-scale unemployment. Honecker became active in the communist youth movement and in 1930 formally joined the Communist Party of Germany (KPD). The KPD gave young men like Honecker an identity and a purpose in life: to transform the difficult conditions around them through revolutionary activism. The party absorbed almost all their waking hours with an endless stream of meetings, rallies, demonstra-tions, leaflet distributions, and street fights. The promise of a prosperous and flourishing socialist future animated them, but they also came to sup-port an authoritarian and violent form of politics. The Soviet Union was their ideal model.

In 1933 the Nazis came to power. Honecker was involved in resistance activity, and in 1935 the Gestapo caught him. He spent the rest of the Third Reich in Nazi prisons until he was freed by Soviet troops in April 1945. The KPD leaders who returned from exile in the Soviet Union in the company of the Red Army quickly tapped Honecker as a valuable party worker. He became the KPD leader Walter Ulbricht's protégé and quickly acquired a reputation as a dedicated, determined, and authoritarian activist. Already in 1945 he was assigned to lead the communist youth movement, and in 1946, when the Soviet occupation forces and their German communist allies compelled the merger of the Social Democratic Party and the KPD in the Soviet zone, Honecker was elected to the executive of the new Socialist Unity Party (SED). After the German Democratic Republic was founded in 1949, Honecker retained the leadership of the youth movement and was given a series of other special assignments. He supervised the construction of the Berlin Wall in 1961 and in subsequent years led the campaign against dissident artists and writers.

In the 1960s Ulbricht began to stake out a more independent course from the Soviet Union. The Soviets threw their support behind Honecker, and in 1971 he became the first secretary of the Central Committee of the SED and in 1976 also the chairman of the State Council of the GDR, combining in his person the union of party and state typical of Soviet-style systems. Honecker sought to improve living standards and ease relations with the West. So long as the Soviets and the Western powers pursued détente, there was room for East and West Germany to follow similar policies. A series of agreements in the early 1970s eased Western access to the GDR and promoted trade and somewhat normal relations between the two states. The GDR won formal recognition from many countries, including the United States, and became a member of the United Nations. Domestically, Honecker announced the "unity of economic and social policies," a program that did greatly improve living standards and social services. The GDR had the highest formal labor participation rates of women anywhere in the world, and in the 1970s launched an extensive program of pre- and postnatal care, day care, and paid maternity leave for women.

In the early 1980s the GDR seemed like a successful communist society. But much of the material improvement was fueled by borrowing from Western banks. By the middle of the decade, the economy was faltering. Moreover, the state kept a rigid lock on politics. The realms of free expression were severely limited, East Germans were not free to travel, and the Ministry for State Security kept up an extensive net of informal operatives who spied on their fellow citizens.

In the 1980s Mikhail Gorbachev instituted major reforms in the Soviet Union. The reverberations came quickly to the GDR. Citizen groups formed and demanded democratization. In 1989, while thousands of East Germans gathered in demonstrations and fled to West German missions and embassies, Honecker maintained the rigid and repressive policies he had promoted for decades. Even Gorbachev made clear his discontent with the GDR leadership. Finally, a reform movement developed also within the SED and deposed Honecker in mid-October. But it was too little, too late. The GDR was swamped by a popular surge in favor of unification with West Germany and by West German political interests that also favored unification. After the absorption of East Germany in 1990, Honecker was criminally charged with complicity for murder in the shootings of East Germans who had attempted to flee to the West, but the charges were dropped because of his poor health. He went into exile to Chile, where he died in 1994. To the very end, he was a Communist formed by his experiences in Weimar and Nazi Germany, a world ever more removed from the concerns of GDR citizens of the late twentieth century.

See also **Cold War; Communism; Germany; Soviet Union.**

BIBLIOGRAPHY

Epstein, Catherine. *The Last Revolutionaries: German Communists and Their Century.* Cambridge, Mass., 2003.

Fulbrook, Mary. *Anatomy of a Dictatorship: Inside the GDR, 1949–1989.* Oxford, U.K., 1995.

Maier, Charles S. *Dissolution: The Crisis of Communism and the End of East Germany.* Princeton, N.J., 1997.

Naimark, Norman M. *The Russians in Germany: A History of the Soviet Zone of Occupation, 1945–1949.* Cambridge, Mass., 1995.

Weitz, Eric D. *Creating German Communism, 1890–1990: From Popular Protests to Socialist State.* Princeton, N.J., 1997.

ERIC D. WEITZ

HOOLIGANISM. Hooliganism at sporting events, especially at soccer matches, actually has a long history. As the world's first team sports began to professionalize in Britain from the late nineteenth century onward, young male "roughs" at soccer matches were regularly cited for their drunken misbehavior, gambling, and occasional violence. Local "derby" matches often provoked the worst incidents between fans, but home roughs also attacked and stoned match officials and visiting players, sometimes, literally, chasing them out of town. The British popular press, however, seemed measured in its reporting of sporting hooligan incidents, at least compared to the press coverage soccer violence began to attract from the 1980s onward.

Between the wars, British soccer generally became more "respectable" and crowd problems diminished, but they did not disappear. In Glasgow, Scotland, for example, sectarian overtones continued, routinely, to flavor violent sports clashes between soccer fans who followed ("Irish," Catholic) Celtic and (Scottish, Protestant) Rangers. But in the era of public welfarism and national renewal immediately after the Second World War, English soccer hooliganism declined. Indeed, in the early 1960s the nations of South America and southern Europe were more generally regarded as sources for hooligan soccer fan behavior. Barriers and stadium fences were a feature of soccer cultures in Italy and Argentina, for example, long before they became commonplace in Britain.

The modern variant of what became a new international strain of soccer hooliganism in Europe probably began in England from the mid-1950s, as national youth styles began to emerge: initially with the "Teddy boys" (1950s); then "mods and rockers" (early 1960s); and finally the so-called soccer skinheads (late 1960s). These developments were accentuated by a series of media moral panics about the behavior of young people, panics sparked by rising juvenile crime rates, uncertainty about the future, and growing racial tensions in British cities. In this climate, English soccer became increasingly identified as a stage for working-class masculine status contests, territorial fights, clashes with the police, and other kinds of disorder. Soccer hooliganism also began to take on the more cohesive and organized aspect more typically associated with the phenomenon today. Working-class skinhead fans in England, for example, seemed to see soccer grounds as an appropriate venue for a collective and excessively violent reassertion of the sort of place and community values they felt were now under threat from wider social and economic changes.

From the early 1970s the English also began to export hooliganism to parts of continental Europe. As English fans traveled abroad, often expressing violent nationalisms and forms of patriotism, for both club and country, so foreign hooligan gangs began to respond in kind. Many continental countries track the emergence of their own modern hooliganism problem to the violent English incursions from this period. By the late 1970s the soccer "casual" had also emerged in England and then Europe: a style-conscious and violent hooligan, drawn from a range of backgrounds, and for whom conspicuous consumption and street smartness were key identity struts.

By the 1980s racist political organizations of the Far Right in Britain had ditched their electoral ambitions and attempted instead to mobilize young men at soccer and music events. Racist political connections at soccer of this kind were—and are—also apparent at selected clubs in countries such as Spain, France, Italy, and Sweden. Sub-nationalisms and entrenched ethnic rivalries also routinely flavor violent soccer conflicts around the globe in areas as far apart as the Balkans and Australasia.

In 1985 thirty-nine, mainly Italian, soccer fans died, live on European television, at the Heysel stadium in Brussels, Belgium, following English hooliganism by Liverpool fans. A crowd panic and the subsequent collapse of a stadium wall before the European Cup final resulted in this loss of life. In 1989 ninety-six Liverpool fans were crushed to death after police crowd mismanagement at the Hillsborough stadium in England. Arguably, these two events proved something of a watershed in the history of hooliganism and its management in Europe.

Standing areas (the "terraces") were now outlawed at most major English soccer stadia and for major European soccer matches. In England, stadia were modernized and stadium space was now heavily surveilled, using closed-circuit television cameras. As ticket prices climbed and safety was highlighted in stadia, so the game in England itself was also marketed to a new, more bourgeois, fan base: to more female fans and more older, middle-class supporters. The most difficult days of soccer hooliganism, some twenty years before, were, perhaps, in abeyance. But in the age of the Internet and mobile phones, local and global hooligan gangs are also better able in the twenty-first century to set up their "honor contests" with young men who, like themselves, prefer direct combat to the symbolic contest played out on their behalf on the field of play.

See also **Football (Soccer).**

BIBLIOGRAPHY

Armstrong, Gary, and Richard Giulianotti. *Entering the Field: New Perspectives on World Football.* Oxford, U.K., and New York, 1997.

Dunning, Eric, Patrick Murphy, and John Williams. *The Roots of Football Hooliganism: An Historical and Sociological Study.* London, 1988.

Williams, John, Patrick Murphy, and Eric Dunning. *Hooligans Abroad: The Behavior and Control of English Fans in Continental Europe.* London and Boston, 1984.

J. M. WILLIAMS

HORTHY, MIKLÓS (1868–1957), Hungarian statesman.

Regent of Hungary during the turbulent period from 1920 until his arrest by the Nazis in 1944, Miklós Horthy de Nagybánya was born into a noble Protestant family in 1868. As a young man he served in the Austro-Hungarian navy, quickly ascending the ranks to become one of the navy's most valued officers. For most of World War I he served as captain of the *Novara* and the *Prinz Eugen,* and he was named vice admiral and made commander of the fleet in 1918.

When the postwar treaties left Hungary without access to the sea, Horthy retired to his family's estate in Kenderes, but in May 1919 he was drawn into the counterrevolutionary cabinet of Count Gyula Károlyi (1875–1955). The new government set out to replace the Republic of Soviets that had seized power a few months earlier, and as the only available high-ranking officer who had not taken an office during the revolution, Horthy was made Minister of War. As commander-in-chief of the minuscule National Army in Szeged, he—along with some of his fellow National Army officers— came to embody the so-called Szeged Idea, which was counterrevolutionary, right-leaning, and militant but also emphasized continuity and enjoyed the support of, among others, conservative aristocrats, the churches, and a part of the peasantry.

Despite their old-style conservative strain, the counterrevolutionary officers of the Szeged group were known for their arbitrary ruthlessness, particularly against Jews suspected of having collaborated with or participated in the revolution, or merely for the fact that they were Jews. The so-called White Terror initiated by the National Army was often shockingly violent, by the end claiming between one thousand and five thousand lives and resulting in tens of thousands of arrests.

After the Republic of Soviets had been crushed by the Romanian Army, Horthy had himself elected Regent of Hungary, weathering two attempts to restore the Habsburg King Charles (1887–1922) to the Hungarian throne. For much of the interwar period he remained under the influence of Count István Bethlen (1874–c. 1947), the conservative Prime Minister of Hungary from 1921 to 1931, who made every effort to steer him away from the Szeged right-wingers. But like all Hungarian statesmen of the time, Horthy was intent on reannexing at least some of the territory Hungary had lost to its neighbors as a result of the postwar treaties. This preoccupation brought him ever closer to the rising influence of Adolf Hitler (1889–1945), who was developing plans to redraw the map of Europe by harnessing the power of disgruntled, revisionist states such as Hungary.

In the wake of the 1938 Munich agreement, Hitler shared the territorial spoils of Czechoslovakia, returning parts of southern Slovakia to Hungary. Horthy later paraded into the reannexed territory on a white horse and was received with overwhelming enthusiasm. The scene was repeated in Subcarpathian Rus, Northern Transylvania, and parts of northern Yugoslavia when they were reannexed from Czechoslovakia, Romania, and Yugoslavia respectively over the course of the following two and a half years. Nevertheless, it soon became clear that by taking gifts from Hitler, Horthy had tied Hungary's fate to that of the Axis. In June 1941 Hungary entered the war against the Soviet Union, in part to compensate for the multiple territorial gains it had received with Axis help.

An anti-Semite in principle and practice, Horthy nevertheless had a soft spot for the more assimilated, urban, upper-middle-class Jews of Budapest. Miklós Kállay (1887–1967), the Hungarian prime minister from 1942, who enjoyed Horthy's trust and support, stubbornly resisted German pressure to deport the Jews of Hungary. But when, in 1944, Hitler demanded Kállay's removal and Horthy was forced to appoint a pro-Nazi government, he agreed to the deportation of most of Hungary's Jewish population. As a result, Hungarian Jews were ghettoized and deported to Auschwitz starting in the late spring of 1944. When it came to deporting the two hundred thousand Jews of Budapest, however, Horthy refused consent.

On 15 October, Horthy announced Hungary's withdrawal from the war. The Germans promptly arrested him and his family, installing the leader of the Hungarian fascist Arrow Cross party, Ferenc Szálasi (1897–1946), in his place. After the war, in which an estimated near-million Hungarians were killed and much of the country was left in ruins, the Western Allies and Soviets agreed that Horthy should not be tried as a war criminal. He spent most of the rest of his life in exile in Portugal, where he died in 1957. In 1993 his body was reburied in Kenderes. The controversial reinterment was aired on Hungarian national television and attended by fifty thousand people.

See also **Hungary; World War II.**

BIBLIOGRAPHY

Primary Sources

Horthy, Miklós, nagybányai. *Admiral Nicholas Horthy: Memoirs.* Annotated by Andrew L. Simon. Safety Harbor, Fla., 2000.

Secondary Sources

Braham, Randolph L. *The Politics of Genocide: The Holocaust in Hungary.* Rev. and enlarged edition. New York, 1994.

Sakmyster, Thomas. *Hungary's Admiral on Horseback: Miklós Horthy, 1918–1944.* Boulder, Colo., and New York, 1994.

HOLLY CASE

HOUSING. The development of European housing through the twentieth century was shaped by two major influences. First was the legacy of nineteenth-century industrialization, which brought in its wake urbanization on a scale unknown in history. Much of northern and central Europe witnessed unprecedented population growth, a huge scale of rural to urban migration, and major changes in patterns of social life based above all on the redivision of society into new social classes. The second seminal influence was the traumatic events of the two world wars (1914–1918 and 1939–1945) that shattered the European economy, destroyed millions of homes, and laid waste whole towns and cities. Civilian housing became a target for the war aims of both sides. Both of these issues, the nineteenth-century legacy and the wars, in their different ways created the problem that dominated housing policy in the twentieth century: how to provide enough dwellings at an affordable price for the growing number of households.

A key theme in pan-European housing throughout the era from 1914 to the early twenty-first century was the extent to which state-led solutions or the private market should spearhead the replacement of the nineteenth-century slums and/or repair the damage caused by the two world wars and build up housing stocks. Generally speaking the balance struck was different in different countries depending on political traditions and institutional arrangements.

THE NINETEENTH-CENTURY LEGACY

What happened to housing policy after 1914, like so much else in society, was largely an inheritance from the nineteenth century. Housing for the new industrial working classes was almost always provided in the privately rented sector either by factory owners who built and then rented at a profit housing for their workers or by rentier capitalists investing in housing as a business. Because wages were low and there was an expectation of profit, the rents that could be charged sustained only the most basic standards. As a result overcrowding was a common experience, with two or more families sharing small rooms or basements. Sanitation was primitive. Toilets, when they existed at all, were shared among dozens of families. For millions of working families water was bought from barrels and human excrement disposed of in so-called soil carts. For the better-off middle classes the coming of new forms of transport in the middle of the century offered the prospect of moving to the "suburbs," where housing was often detached with a garden, offering a much better environment, less prone to the diseases that were endemic in the inner cities.

Architectural forms varied from country to country. In central Europe rapidly growing cities such as Berlin and Budapest developed a tradition of tenement building with small flats facing onto a courtyard and with no outside windows. This was the same in Scotland but not in English cities, where terraces of so called back-to-back, two-story housing (houses facing away from each other and sharing a back wall) was the normal form. In France working-class housing was mainly of the tenement type in Paris but not in smaller towns and cities such as Bordeaux or Amiens. This diversity can be explained only by reference to local housing-market conditions and cultural and social histories; for example, a tradition of tenement building is sometimes associated with cities and towns that had medieval walls. The nineteenth-century legacy was thus one of rapid urbanization, the provision of large quantities of low-amenity housing by private landlords, and considerable diversity in built forms.

Because of the insanitary conditions of slum housing and the continuing shortages of affordable housing, the state became more involved in housing issues in the decades before 1914. What precisely happened varied according to political institutions and traditions. In countries such as Belgium, Germany, and Austria-Hungary, where landlords were an organized part of the political elite, demands by new working-class organizations for the state to be directly involved were resisted. Instead a variety of workers' cooperatives, trade unions, and specially created housing associations built their own housing using cheap loans subsidized by the government. By 1914 in Vienna, for example, 20 percent of residential building had been constructed using cheap government loans. In Berlin cooperative housing flourished, with nearly eleven thousand dwellings built by using government loans by the outbreak of World War I. In Britain private landlords were a disparate, politically unrepresented class, mainly amateurs owning only one or two properties. Here the new Labour Party embraced the state and looked to government to ameliorate the housing conditions of the workers. Beginning in 1919 it was local councils subsidized by central government that spearheaded the housing program for low-income families and went on to own and manage, at its peak in the mid-1970s, nearly one-third of the housing stock. In the mainstream of European housing the British case was unusual.

WORLD WAR I AND THE INTERWAR PERIOD

World War I had a traumatic impact on Europe. Old cultural certainties and social structures were literally shattered. For the first time in history war embraced the whole of society. In the combatant nations, the state conducted the war effort mobilizing and commanding the population of all classes. Revolutionary movements swept across Europe, culminating in the triumph of the Bolsheviks in 1917, leading to the establishment of the Union of Soviet Socialist Republics in 1922. Aware of the danger to their own nations, European governments initiated a period of social reconstruction in which nineteenth-century slums began to be cleared away and new visions of a fairer and more equal society emerged. Housing was at the center of this. In Britain the postwar Liberal government was elected on the slogan of building "homes fit for heroes." Drawing on Ebenezer Howard's idea of the "garden suburb" (combining the best of town and country in low-density developments

A low-income apartment building in Naples, Italy. ©KIDDER SMITH/CORBIS

away from the city) and the ideas of the Arts and Crafts estates of "council housing," low-rise, cottage-style terraces began to be built using generous central government subsidies. This was the first genuinely European housing form built on any scale in response to unregulated urbanization.

In the 1930s modernist architects and town planners began to believe it was possible to literally construct a new society. These radical ideas emanated mostly from Germany. From 1928 onward the Congrès International d'Architecture Moderne (CIAM) brought together leading modernist architects and had a massive impact on how housing was thought about and how it could shape society, particularly in its advocacy of high-rise building. At the second congress Victor Bourgeois proposed that housing should be a tool for living encompassing the revolutionary idea that every flat should have running water, indoor toilet, bathroom, fully equipped kitchen, and refuse disposal chute. At the

third congress in 1930 the Swiss architect Le Corbusier introduced his famous Ville Radieuse (Radiant City), at the center of which were blocks of high-rise flats, where most people would live. In the USSR a deformed variant of high-rise living was already being realized in the 1930s with the appearance of large-scale mass housing in many towns and cities. The "Stalin model" of housing involved the mass production of small, low-amenity flats (often unheated) in huge housing estates for very low rent, putting into practice Stalin's utopian dream of building a socialist society. In reality this dream became a nightmare of repression and appalling housing conditions. When the USSR collapsed in 1991 nearly half the population lived in flats with only two rooms.

THE SUBURBAN WAY OF LIFE

Less dramatic in its impact in the interwar period but significant nevertheless was the continued expansion elsewhere in Europe of middle-class sub-urbia. This phenomenon is best illustrated in the case of Britain, where millions of owner-occupied semidetached houses were built by thousands of small speculative building companies on estates on greenfield sites. These properties were heavily marketed to the new classes of white-collar workers and came with a distinctive lifestyle built around the nuclear family and a domestic culture that echoed Victorian values. Men went out to work while "housewives" stayed to create an "ideal home." The growing availability of electricity ended dependence on gas and open fires for lighting, heating, and cooking and enabled the mass production of household products such as electric cleaners made by Hoover. The Bendix "automated laundry" saved many hours of toil for women. Servants, who were common throughout the social spectrum before 1914, became too expensive and were replaced by these labor-saving devices. One of the major consequences of all this was that middle-class and upper-working-class standards of living began to converge, although the difference between working-class council estates (state housing) and middle-class estates (owner occupied) was still demarcated by housing design and location.

Suburbanization was a common feature of inter-war Europe and was based on the development of more stable salaried incomes. Easier transport (electric trams, the early metro systems, cars) and the availability of mortgage finance began to spread the idea of home ownership across Europe. Many rural communities were traditionally owner occupied—in low-amenity, often self-built dwellings—and the more peripheral and predominantly rural nations of Europe (Ireland, Spain, Greece, and southern Italy, including Sicily) have always had a strong tradition of owner occupation that has persisted up to the present.

Britain is an unusual case. In 1914 almost the entire nation was housed by private landlords, but by the outbreak of World War II, Britain was already becoming a modern home-owning society (more than 30 percent of households by then) with the unusual addition, as has been shown, of a large and expanding state housing program owned and managed almost exclusively by local councils. The private rental sector declined sharply, not least by

sales to sitting tenants as landlords quit the market for better investments.

This was not the case in the central Continental nations where private landlords were a much more politically powerful class than they were in Britain. Although wartime rent controls persisted in France and Germany after World War I, as they did in Britain (it was not politically feasible to allow sudden and sharp rent increases after the war), rental subsidies were still considered necessary for postwar economic recovery, and state involvement in housing was everywhere increasing. In Germany the collapse of the economy and hyperinflation under the Weimar Republic caused rents for newly built housing to soar. Without state intervention nothing would have been built under these circumstances. State subsidies to housing companies were paid for by a special tax on owners of housing whose mortgages had been wiped out due to inflation. As a result, house building slowed from prewar levels and the state assumed a very large role in funding the housing program, almost all of it for rent. In other countries, such as the Netherlands and Denmark, where the working-class movement was less organized and the political crisis was less severe, there was more pressure for a return to privately financed renting. New housing for better-off workers' families continued to be built until the early 1930s, when the global economic collapse swept through Europe.

There are thus very different stories to be told nation by nation and between town and countryside, though everywhere the state played a bigger role than before 1914. For the new middle classes—teachers, insurance salesmen, office workers, accountants, civil servants—unaffected by the economic catastrophes that devastated Germany and then the whole Continent in the 1930s, housing conditions and the "ideal home" vision began to take hold. Suburbanization brought with it a new way of life, of residential repose and respectability. But of course for the less well-off millions of working-class families, life continued to be a struggle for daily survival in small, aging, badly maintained flats and houses mostly without gas, electricity, hot water, indoor toilets, or bathrooms. The outbreak of war in Europe in 1939 heightened these problems and made the prospect of improvement even more distant.

WORLD WAR II AND THE POSTWAR PERIOD

The housing consequences of World War II were devastating. The war set back the advances that had been made before 1939 by a quarter-century. This was the result of the massive level of destruction suffered by the European mainland, with whole towns and cities reduced to rubble by tank battles and aerial bombardment. Equally as significant was large-scale population mobility due to refugees, the breakup of families, and new household formation. Moreover, there was no new building for the duration of the conflict. In Britain, for example, it is estimated on the basis of prewar rates of construction that some 1.75 million properties were lost. Added to the war damage, as a result of the Blitz and "doodlebug" attacks the losses to a stock of eleven million dwellings were very serious. New household formation (some two million during the war) worsened the deficit of dwellings to households, the problem that dominated housing policy for the next three decades. Similar and worse stories can be told for every European country directly involved in the war. As Europe approached midcentury the demand for housing had never been more urgent or the scale of the problem greater.

As was the case after World War I, the state played a major role in the reconstruction period. People expected benefits for the sacrifices of war, and housing was a key social policy objective all over war-torn Europe. Governments had led the war effort, and people expected their governments to lead the peace. Hence, for example, Britain's war leader, Winston Churchill, was swept from power by a landslide victory of the Labour Party in the postwar general election, committed to a state-led emergency house-building program (almost all of which was council housing) and the implementation of a welfare state.

The Communist bloc Crucially, of course, the political settlement after World War II caused the division of Europe for nearly half a century, from 1946 to 1990, into the Western capitalist nations and an Eastern bloc of socialist states dominated by the USSR. In the Communist bloc, state-led solutions to housing shortages predominated, although private self-help (and self-building) was not uncommon. To begin with, housing was a second priority after rapid industrialization. Until the housing program began, many people commuted long-distance from the countryside to the new factories. The Stalin model of state-built high-rise blocks eventually became a common feature of all these countries, although the timing, quality of the building, and degree of state control varied from country to country. For example, after the 1956 revolution against communism in Hungary the housing program was accelerated and incorporated a substantial number of state-built but privately owned flats. In Bulgaria high-rise building did not begin on a large scale until the 1980s, and here low-amenity state-built flats were sold rather than let.

In Eastern bloc nations new flats were often allocated to people favorably positioned in the Communist Party or as an inducement to key workers—teachers, engineers, and medics—to relocate to where they were needed. It was only toward the end of the communist era in the 1980s that waiting lists more generally catered to ordinary working families. The built environment was altered through the development of high-rise housing mainly in larger towns and cities, but low-rise properties continued to be built—mostly by self-building—although the extent of this varied considerably from country to country. In Hungary, where there was financial support for some forms of private self-build construction, 80 percent of new house building was of this type, whereas in Romania, under the bizarrely deformed Stalinist regime of President Nicolae Ceausescu, such activity was outlawed.

Western Europe In Western Europe new technologies involving the same prefabricated building techniques familiar in the USSR and emanating from the modernist prewar architectural movements quickly led to the large-scale industrialized building of high-rise blocks of flats. This was partly a response to slum clearance but mainly to the idea that bombed-out sites from the war could contain much higher densities of people if the housing was built vertically. Although built and managed by governments or social housing agencies with state subsidies, this new housing, unlike that of the Communist bloc states, was almost exclusively used to house low-income households, and despite attempts to engineer a social mix of population these huge estates often became sources of social tension. For two decades beginning at the end of the 1950s high-rise housing transformed the skylines of many northern and central European towns and cities. Almost all of this form of state-led construction was social housing, owned and managed by a variety of nonprofit companies, housing associations, and co-ops and overseen by local and federal governments. Only in the United Kingdom did local authorities exclusively manage social housing. Once the social defects of this form of housing became apparent its popularity and use declined sharply in the mid-1970s.

After the worst problems of postwar shortages and reconstruction were dealt with, private sector housing, especially home ownership, also made a major contribution to the housing recovery that dominated the two or three decades after 1945. This was clearly the case in some of the more peripheral, more agricultural countries such as Ireland, Spain, and Greece, where, despite rapid industrialization and postwar modernization, housing never encompassed strong state involvement apart from indirect support through their tax systems. Finland also had a long tradition of home ownership, and the share of owner-occupiers grew from 57 percent in the early 1960s to nearly 70 percent by 2004. Most other countries also saw some growth in home ownership in the later decades of the century, but the scale varied from country to country. Home ownership in Italy grew from 45 percent after the war to nearly 70 percent by 2004, whereas Germany only moved from 25 percent to 38 percent over the same period. The most unusual case here is Britain, which, as explained above, after 1914 began a long process of transition away from being a privately rented nation (90 percent of households), as the state sector of council housing was expanded and home ownership became more popular and widespread. These interwar trends simply carried on after the immediate postwar crisis abated, and by the early 1990s home ownership had grown to 70 percent of households, although council housing had declined significantly as a result of government policy.

It should also be noted that since the collapse of the Eastern European socialist states in 1989–1990 there has been a large-scale sale of state flats, usually to sitting tenants, because the economies of these countries were so damaged that they could not sustain even the most basic services and maintenance. In 2005 home ownership was in excess of 90 percent in almost all these nations and there was hardly any social housing provision. The creation of super-owner-occupied nations is one of the more perverse consequences of the collapse of state socialism.

In most of the major economies of Europe, however, the state continues to play a significant role in housing. This mainly operates through the mechanism of local authorities supervising rent levels so that the various public housing agencies and the private rented sector are treated as a common rental market in which the companies compete with each other on the basis of type of accommodation, location, and facilities.

It is possible, then, to identify two broad models of European housing in the early twenty-first century. In the social market economies of central Europe and Scandinavia, public and private renting are basically treated as a unified market, and while home ownership is available, it is not the dominant force. In the home-owning societies (Britain, Finland, Ireland, Spain, Greece, and the postcommunist nations) there is a clear separation between the three main housing tenures of home ownership, private renting, and social housing, and the public and private rental sectors are not connected. Thus, while the deficit between dwellings and households caused by two wars was a Europe-wide phenomenon, the ways in which that deficit has been addressed since 1945 have varied considerably, and in the early twenty-first century there is no one "European" housing system.

See also **Architecture; Reconstruction; Welfare State; Working Class.**

BIBLIOGRAPHY

Burnett, John. (1986) *A Social History of Housing.* 2nd ed. London, 1986. An account of the development of British housing from the Industrial Revolution to the 1980s, with a focus on architectural styles and social conditions.

Donner, Christian. *Housing Policies in the European Union: Theory and Practice.* Vienna, 2000. Incorporates short historical accounts and up-to-date statistics on all the European Union countries (not those later acceded from the former Communist bloc).

Lowe, Stuart, and Sasha Tsenkova, eds. *Housing Change in East and Central Europe: Integration or Fragmentation?* Aldershot, U.K., 2003. Collection of papers that give brief accounts of the communist era followed by research findings on the next fifteen years.

McCrone, Gavin, and Mark Stephens. *Housing Policy in Britain and Europe*. London, 1995. A mixture of one-country studies (includes the list in Power's book but includes Spain and the Netherlands) and chapters dealing with European integration, labor mobility, and mortgage finance.

Power, Anne. *Hovels to High Rise: State Housing in Europe since 1850*. London, 1993. Detailed accounts of housing policy in France, Germany, Britain, Denmark, and Ireland with an emphasis on the role played by the state.

STUART LOWE

HOXHA, ENVER (1908–1985), Albanian statesman.

Enver Hoxha, the undisputed leader of Albania until his death, headed the Party of Labor from its foundation as the Albanian Communist Party in 1941 until his death, and served as prime minister (1944–1954) and minister of foreign affairs (1946–1953). He can be described as an ardent nationalist and communist, whose legacy, autocratic and isolationist in the political sphere, effectuated the transformation of Albanian society from an agricultural backwater to a self-sufficient socialist industrial economy.

Born into the family of a Muslim Tosk, Hoxha was under the influence of his uncle, who participated in the national struggle for Albanian independence and later opposed the regime of King Zog (r. 1928–1939). He went to a French high school in Korçë and in 1930 won a state scholarship to study natural sciences in Montpellier, France. He moved to Paris to study philosophy but was mostly involved in reading Marxism and collaborating with the French communist newspaper *Humanité*. Between 1934 and 1936 he was secretary at the Albanian consulate in Brussels and studied law. Dismissed from his job for communist sympathies, Hoxha returned to Korçë, where his was employed as a teacher in the French lycée.

When Albania was occupied by Italy in 1939 and Hoxha refused to join the Fascist Party, he lost his job and relocated to Tiranë. He opened a small tobacco shop, which served as a cover for communist activities. With the help of Yugoslav communists, Hoxha founded the Albanian Communist Party (later Party of Labor) in 1941 and was the most influential of the seven-member Central Committee. In 1942 he became the political commissar of the communist-dominated Army of National Liberation, as well as First Secretary of the ACP in 1943.

With the resistance movement taking power in November 1944, Hoxha headed the provisional government and, after the elections of December 1945, became prime minister of the People's Republic of Albania. In the Paris Peace conference (August 1945) he dismissed Greece's territorial claims, and in the following years (1947–1948) opposed Josip Broz Tito's (1892–1980) intentions to annex Albania as a Yugoslav republic, claiming that Tito had promised Kosovo to Albania. He aligned himself with Joseph Stalin (1879–1953) and supported Moscow in the ideological breach with Yugoslavia (1948).

The 1950s saw the implementation of radical changes along Stalinist lines in all spheres of life: forceful nationalization of land and the creation of cooperatives; industrialization; and the development of education and culture. Aiming at complete economic autarky, by the end of Hoxha's rule, Albania had become virtually self-sufficient in food production; its industry, from practically nonexistent beginnings, made up half of the gross national product. Illiteracy was liquidated in a country that had been 80–85 percent illiterate, and epidemics were wiped out.

An admirer of Stalin, and himself notorious for his human-rights abuses, Hoxha repudiated Nikita Khrushchev's (1894–1971) denunciation of the cult of personality, as well as the USSR's hegemonic policies in the socialist bloc and its rapprochement with the United States. By 1961 Hoxha announced the "dual adversary theory" and rejected imperialism and revisionism as equal threats to Marxism-Leninism. In 1961 Albania broke off relations with the USSR and following the departure of Soviet advisors and aid Mao Zedong's China (1893–1976) stepped in, providing assistance and equipment for the Albanian army. In a 1967 attempt to promote national unity, Hoxha banned religion, destroyed mosques and churches, and proclaimed Albania the first atheist state. In 1968 he condemned the Soviet invasion of Czechoslovakia as an imperialistic move and also quit the World Trade Organization. His isolationism bordering on paranoia, he built six hundred thousand concrete bunkers as protection against foreign invasion.

The early 1970s saw temporary relaxations of his isolationist policies and domestic controls. Unhappy with the results, Hoxha cracked down and starting in 1973, purges of the party leadership, the officer corps, and the economic bureaucracy marked a reactionary backlash. The secret police—*Sigurimi*—was notorious for its brutality. Relations with China were soured over the latter's rapprochement with the United States, as well as its insistence that Albania seek closer links to Yugoslavia. After Mao's death in 1976, China suspended aid to Albania in 1978. Hoxha reverted to his complete autarky and announced that Albania was the only authentic socialist country left.

Having suffered a heart attack in 1973 and with deteriorating health, Hoxha finally retired from active political activities in 1981 but not before carrying out a final bloody purge at the highest party level, in which his longtime associate and prime minister Mehmet Shehu (1913–1981) allegedly committed suicide. Hoxha passed most state functions to his protégé Ramiz Alia (b. 1925), who succeeded Hoxha formally upon his death in 1985.

See also **Albania.**

BIBLIOGRAPHY

Primary Sources

Hoxha, Enver. *The Artful Albanian: Memoirs of Enver Hoxha.* Edited By Jon Halliday. London, 1986.

Secondary Sources

Biberaj, Elez. *Albania: A Socialist Maverick.* Boulder, Colo., 1990.

Crampton, R. J. *The Balkans since the Second World War.* New York, 2002.

O'Donnell, James S. *A Coming of Age: Albania under Enver Hoxha.* Boulder, Colo., 1999.

MARIA TODOROVA

HUMAN RIGHTS.

Human rights have triumphed in the world. They unite left and right, the pulpit and the state, the politician and the rebel, the north and the south. Human rights are the fate of our societies, the ideology after "the end of ideologies," the only values left in a valueless world after "the end of history." And yet many doubts about their effectiveness persist. Recent history has witnessed genocide, mass murder, ethnic cleansing, the Holocaust. Not one day passes without newspaper reports about the latest atrocity somewhere in the world. Triumph and disaster are never far apart. How did we reach this state?

A SHORT HISTORY OF HUMAN RIGHTS

The initial impetus for the age of rights was the adoption of the Charter of the United Nations in 1945, which made the protection of human rights one of the main aims of the organization. Three years later the UN General Assembly passed the Universal Declaration of Human Rights. The declaration was a nonbinding proclamation of minimum standards of treatment of citizens by their state authorities the world over. It paved the way for the drafting of two binding treaties, the International Covenant on Civil and Political Rights and that on Economic, Social, and Cultural Rights, which after long and difficult negotiations were adopted in 1966. The declaration and the two covenants are now considered as an International Bill of Rights and have created a model for regional and specialist standard setting.

The first reference to "human rights" is relatively recent. It appears in legal writings of the 1920s in relation to the position of minorities in the postimperial European states. But the intellectual pedigree of the concept of human rights is much older. It is associated with the idea of nature and natural law, which started in classical Greece and has occupied a prominent role in Western ethics, politics, and law ever since. In its original version, natural law is part of an archaic cosmology in which the universe (the cosmos) and every thing (and person) in it has its own unique nature that provides it with its purpose or aim in life. The nature and purpose of the acorn is to become a mature oak tree providing the best shade, that of a baby boy to grow and become a just man, that of a cobbler to produce the best possible sandals. A person is virtuous if he strives toward perfection according to his nature, and perfection can only be achieved politically, that is, in the city (*polis* in Greek) in collaboration with other citizens. A just city provides the conditions for people to develop fully according to their natures, and a city is just if people strive to act according to their natures. The order of the universe is a moral order, with every animate being and inanimate thing having a part to play in its own perfection and completion. Indeed the discovery of the idea of "nature" by early Greek philosophers was an attempt to use reason against received opinion, ancestral authority, and custom. Socrates and Plato, the Sophists, and the Stoics explored what is "right according to reason" in order to combat established powers and the common sense of their times.

It was this natural order of things that obliged Antigone, the loving sister of Polynices, to defy the order of her uncle, King Creon, and bury her brother. Polynices was killed while attacking his native Thebes and was left to be devoured by vultures, against religious law and family duty. As a punishment for her disobedience, Antigone herself was buried alive. But the divine order took revenge on the rationalist king. He was cursed for his arrogance and his family destroyed. In this early confrontation between state law and the order of things, between male reason and calculation and female emotion and devotion to sacred and familial duties, the first and still-greatest symbol of resistance against unjust law was born.

It is a short step from this natural cosmology to argue that generally shared moral principles exist. They depend on the nature of the cosmos and the interlocking purposes of beings and can be discovered by reason. In a legal dispute, the experienced judge, who knew through a long and prudent life the natural order of things, would redress the disturbed relationship and make it again harmonious. His judgment would be what was right according to the nature of things but also what the law requested. Indeed, for both the Greeks and Romans, the word for "right" or "lawful" (*dikaion* in Greek, *jus* in Latin) was also the word for "the just state of affairs."

The next step was taken by the School of Stoics around the third and second centuries B.C.E. The Stoics argued that all people share the ability to reason and that moral judgments have a rational foundation. Nature changed from a way of arguing to a source of rules and norms. The new natural law was universal and even divine and became the sole criterion of valid law. This God-given, eternal, and absolute natural law was the foundation of laws and institutions and was disclosed by reason. The Roman politician and philosopher Cicero expressed this change when he wrote that

> the true law is the law of reason, in accordance with nature known to all, unchangeable and imperishable; . . . nor will it be one law in Rome and a different one in Athens, nor otherwise tomorrow than it is today; but one and the same law, eternal and unchangeable will bind all people and all ages; and God, its designer, expounder and enacter, will be the sole and universal ruler and governor of all things.

Natural right used to be a matter of empirical observation, rational contemplation, and dialectical confrontation. Now it became a matter of introspection and revelation. The notion of universal humanity based on the rational essence of man and equal rights for all was a dramatic departure from the unequal and hierarchical Greek world.

But the main force moving the law toward a theory of natural rights was its gradual Christianization. Jewish cosmology believed that the universe is the creation of an omnipotent God, while Christianity placed the individual and his soul at the center of the universe. As a result, nature lost its normative character and became the inanimate natural world. Saint Paul's statement that God has placed a natural law in our hearts replaced classical natural law. And as the Judeo-Christian God is a severe legislator, the Roman idea of right, or *jus*, took the form of a set of commandments, or rules, found in the scriptures and ingrained in the conscience. By the Middle Ages a largely existential cosmology had been turned into a major weapon in the hands of the church. A crucial link in the Christianization of law must be sought in the theology of Augustine and Thomas Aquinas. Aquinas distinguished four types of law: the eternal, natural, divine, and human. The law lost the cosmic flexibility of the classical tradition and became definite, certain, and simple, its fundamental propositions formulated by God in the Decalogue.

The source of natural law moved from rational morality to divine commandment—a higher law that consists of a small number of abstract ideals and values. These principles were declared superior to state law, which should either follow them or forfeit its claim to the loyalty of the citizens. At the same time, the idea of equality entered the historical scene. It is exemplified in St. Paul's statement that in the eyes of Christ "there is no Greek or Jew, no freeman or slave." Initially this was a spiritual, not political, equality, created by the soul we all possess and our participation in Jesus' plan of salvation. These beliefs had revolutionary power. But when the church achieved its aim of superiority over secular authorities, it turned these beliefs into a doctrine of justification of state power and asked its members to respect and obey the secular princes.

The revolutionary potential of nature was realized after its next great mutation from natural law into natural rights. This sea change was prepared in the writings of the liberal political philosophers of the seventeenth and eighteenth centuries. Thomas Hobbes, John Locke, Jean-Jacques Rousseau, and Thomas Paine argued in different ways that natural law was no longer about abstract principles of state organization and state-church relations but rather a collection of individual rights that belong to the citizens because they pertain to their nature. The liberal philosophers argued that, before forming society, people lived in a state of nature where they enjoyed limitless freedom. However, the hazards and inconveniences of life led these noble savages to restrict their natural freedom by entering into a contract to establish society and political organization. This social contract transferred a large part of their natural freedoms to the government in return for protection and security. But a number of important rights, usually stated as those to life, liberty, and property, were retained by the contractors. The method used by the liberal philosophers was to observe people in their society, deduce their basic needs and desires, and then postulate the outcome of their observations as the basic characteristics of human nature, which must be protected by the institution of rights against state powers. For Hobbes, writing during the English civil war, human nature leads to conflict, and security, its greatest need, must be provided by an all-powerful state. For Locke, who lived in relative peace, man is naturally good, and the state must not interfere with his natural rights.

If state laws violate these natural rights they are invalid and could justify revolution against the unjust power. Rousseau was the favorite author of the French revolutionaries rebelling against the socially and economically static feudal ancien régime. The first act of the successful revolution was to pass a Declaration of the Rights of Man and of the Citizen. Similarly, Paine's *Common Sense* (1776) greatly influenced the American revolutionaries in their struggle against the colonial power. The American Declaration of Independence and the Bill of Rights were heavily influenced by natural rights theory.

The revolutionary potential of these principles did not escape the victorious revolutionaries. The centralized Western states, which developed out of the great bourgeois revolutions, soon abandoned and condemned the theory of natural rights and adopted the doctrine of legal positivism. For the positivists, the only law worthy of the name is the law posited by the state. A clear distinction separates law from morals, and appeals to a higher law, rights, or the dictates of conscience have no validity in the eyes of authority. The nineteenth century was the epoch of social engineering in the metropolitan states and of empire building and colonialism in the periphery. The law was seen as a tool in the hands of governments, institution builders, and reformers, and appeals to higher principles or individual rights were seen as reactionary hurdles to progress. As the utilitarian philosopher Jeremy Bentham put it, talk of natural rights is "nonsense, nonsense upon stilts, it is belief in witches and unicorns, for there is no right which when its abolition is advantageous to society, it should not be abolished."

The creation of large-scale theory in sociology, economics, and psychology and the rise of mass political parties accelerated the decline in the appeal of natural rights. The belief that political society was created by means of a social contract was seen as a myth while the claim that certain rights are eternal, inalienable, and absolute was exploded by Émile Durkheim and Max Weber, the founders of sociology, and Karl Marx, the founder of socialism.

By the first half of the twentieth century the theory of natural rights had been discredited. It was treated in academic writings as an outdated conservative tradition, part of the history of ideas.

The rehabilitation of natural rights under the new guise of human rights dates from the Nuremberg trials of Nazi war criminals after World War II. At a time when international law allowed states to treat their subjects as they liked, the Allied judges were faced with a legally compelling argument from the German defendants. From a positivist perspective, the only law that counts is the law of the state. The main defense argument was that in following the orders and applying the laws of the Nazi state, the defendants were acting within the limits of legality and should not be punished for carrying out their duty under the law. To answer this objection, the court ruled, however, that the systematized killing of Jews and others by the Nazis had been against the customary law of civilized nations and could not be overridden by national laws. In doing so, the tribunal rediscovered a main tenet of natural law. Certain acts are so heinous that they are banned by universal principles of humanity. These crimes against humanity have now become part of international law.

INSTITUTIONS AND IMPLEMENTATION

Since the creation of the United Nations in 1945, a major international process for the protection and promotion of human rights has been undertaken. Hundreds of human rights conventions, treaties, declarations, and agreements have been negotiated and adopted by the United Nations, by regional bodies like the Council of Europe and the Organization of African Unity, and by states. Human rights diversified from first-generation civil and political or "negative" rights, associated with liberalism, into second-generation economic, social, and cultural or "positive" rights, associated with the socialist tradition, and finally, into third-generation group and national sovereignty rights, associated with the decolonization process. The first-generation or "blue" rights are symbolized by individual freedom; the second or "red" rights by claims to equality and guarantees of a decent living standard; and the third or "green" rights by peoples' right to self-determination and, belatedly,

the protection of the environment. A second approach led to the creation of treaties with a more limited scope. Certain categories of persons may need special protection. Such specialist conventions have addressed the position of refugees and stateless persons, migrant workers, children, and women. Specific instruments were also drafted to eliminate particular forms of human rights violations such as genocide, torture, and racial and gender discrimination. But what lies behind this apparently unstoppable proliferation of human rights?

To paraphrase Friedrich Nietzsche, if God, the source of natural law, is dead, he has been replaced by international law. The horrors of World War II and the Holocaust made it clear that democracy and national legal and constitutional traditions cannot always prevent large-scale violations of rights. As Hannah Arendt put it, it is quite conceivable that one fine day a highly organized and mechanized humanity will conclude quite democratically—namely by majority decision—that for humanity as a whole it would be better to liquidate certain parts thereof. The Germans voted Adolf Hitler into power, and later Slobodan Milosevic was repeatedly elected president of Yugoslavia. International human rights were therefore conceived as a type of higher law that should prevail over national policies. They are supposed to impose restrictions upon governments to prevent them from being beastly to their own citizens. An endless process of international and humanitarian lawmaking has been put into operation, aimed at protecting people from the putative assertions of their sovereignty.

Lawmaking in the huge business of human rights has been undertaken by government representatives, diplomats, policy advisors, international civil servants, and human rights experts. Indeed the proliferation of treaties and codes has made human rights a new type of state law. Codification, from Justinian to the Napoleonic Code, has been the ultimate exercise of legislative sovereignty, the supreme expression of state power. Governments were the enemy against whom human rights were conceived as a defense. Undoubtedly the atrocities of the twentieth century shook and shocked some governments and politicians as much as they did ordinary people. But the business of government is to govern, not to follow moral principles.

Governmental actions in the international arena are dictated by national interest and political considerations, and morality enters the stage always late, when the principle invoked happens to condemn the actions of a political adversary. When human rights and national interest coincide, governments become their greatest champions. But this is the exception. In general, government-operated international human rights law is a good illustration of the poacher turned gamekeeper.

That human rights are superior to state law is seen as the result of their legal universalization. The law addresses all states and all persons as persons and declares their entitlements to be a part of the patrimony of humanity, which has replaced human nature as the rhetorical ground of rights. Every state and power comes under the mantle of the international law of human rights, every government becomes civilized as the "law of the princes" has finally become the "universal" law of human dignity. But this is an empirical universality, based on the competitive solidarity of sovereign governments and on the pragmatic concerns and calculations of international politics. A state that adopts the international treaties can claim to be a human rights state. Human rights become a tool for state legitimacy. Natural and human rights were conceived as a tool against the despotism of power and the arrogance of wealth. Their co-optation by governments means that they have lost some of their critical force and are often used to legitimize state practices.

Interestingly, national sovereignty and nonintervention in the domestic affairs of states were the foundation of the post–World War II international system. The contradictory principles of human rights and national sovereignty, schizophrenically both paramount in postwar international law, served two separate agendas of the great powers: the need to legitimize the new world order through its commitment to rights without exposing the victorious states to scrutiny and criticism about their own flagrant violations. While the major powers fought tooth and nail over the definitions and priorities of human rights, they unanimously agreed that these rights could not be used to pierce the shield of national sovereignty. This schizophrenia characterized human rights until the collapse of communism in 1989.

Problems in lawmaking are confounded by difficulties in interpretation and implementation. The international mechanisms are rudimentary and can scarcely improve, while national sovereignty remains the paramount principle in law. The main method is the drawing of periodic or ad hoc reports about human rights violations; the main weapon, adverse publicity and the doubtful force that shame carries in international relations. There are various types of reporting: monitoring, the most common, is carried out usually by volunteers and experts around the world under the auspices of the UN Human Rights Commission. "Special rapporteurs" appointed by the commission draw up reports about specific areas of concern, like torture, or about individual countries with poor human rights records. Under another model, states are invited to submit periodic reports about their compliance with certain treaty obligations to committees created for that purpose (the most famous being the Human Rights Committee under the International Covenant on Civil and Political Rights). Weak implementation mechanisms ensure that the shield of national sovereignty is not seriously pierced unless the interest of the great powers dictates otherwise, as events in the Balkans and Iraq since the late 1980s have shown. Finally, in a few instances international courts or commissions investigate complaints by victims of human rights abuses and conduct quasi-judicial proceedings against states. But the jurisprudence of human rights courts is extremely restricted and dubious, and its rapid changes in direction confirm some of the worst fears of legal realism: barristers appearing before international bodies such as the European Court of Human Rights quickly learn that it is better preparation to research the political affiliations of the government-appointed judges rather than to read the court's case law. It is well known that changes in the political orientation of the appointing governments are soon reflected in the personnel of international human rights courts and commissions.

The most effective international system of implementation has been that under the European Convention on Human Rights (ECHR). The convention protects the main civil and political rights, and no concession to the socialist tradition was made at its inception in 1950. But the convention introduced a radical innovation that has changed legal civilization. Traditional international law was the law of the "civilized princes," a states-based law with no place for individuals. But under the ECHR aggrieved Europeans (as well as residents in member states), after exhausting the remedies offered in their national legal systems, can submit an application to the European Court, based in Strasbourg, France, alleging that one of their rights has been violated by the actions of their state. The court conducts a full judicial investigation of the claim during which the citizen plaintiff is put on an equal footing with the defendant state. At the end of the process, the state is obliged to comply with any adverse findings of the court. Britain has changed its laws on telephone tapping, contempt of court, and the treatment of transsexuals; Germany gave non-German-speaking defendants the right to an interpreter; Austria abolished state monopoly on cable and satellite television; and Ireland decriminalized homosexuality. States can also bring applications alleging violations by their cosignatories against their citizens. When a number of governments brought an interstate application against the Greek dictatorship in 1968 they acted uniquely as their brothers' keepers. After it was found that every right in the convention had been violated by the military junta known as "the colonels," who were not prepared to end the emergency measures they had instituted, Greece had to withdraw from the organization on the eve of its expulsion. But that was the exception. Interstate cases are usually politically motivated. They have been brought by Ireland against the United Kingdom over British policies in Northern Ireland and by Cyprus against Turkey over the invasion and occupation of the island. This attitude represents the way that many governments approach human rights. They are happy to invoke them when their application happens to condemn an enemy.

But despite the various international agreements and mechanisms it must be emphasized that human rights are violated or protected at the local level. Human rights were created as a superior or additional protection from the state, its military and police, its political and public authorities, its judges, businesses, and media. These are still the culprits or—rarely—the angels. Irrespective of what international institutions say or how many treaties

foreign secretaries sign, human rights are violated or upheld in the street, the workplace, and the local police station. The relative weakness of international law means that local legal and political initiatives and campaigns may be more effective. Nongovernmental organizations (NGOs), such as the Red Cross, Amnesty International, and Oxfam have been the most important defenders of human rights and humanitarianism since the 1970s. They are able to mobilize international public opinion in the defense of rights more than governments because they cannot be accused of hypocrisy, double standards, and ulterior motives. Additionally NGOs rely on citizen initiatives and campaigns. This way they represent the radical potential of human rights and link to the spirit of popular organization and activism of the early modern natural rights tradition.

CATEGORIES OF RIGHTS

Human rights are the most striking institutional expression of the project of the Enlightenment, of the promise of emancipation through reason and law. The Americans rebelled against their colonial masters, the French against static and corrupt political and social power. That is why the early lists of human rights took a "negative" form and were predominantly defensive. They imposed restrictions upon state power, thus creating spheres of unregulated activity in which citizens can exercise their rights. The First Amendment of the U.S. Bill of Rights is a good example: "Congress shall make no law . . . abridging the freedom of speech, or of the press." By outlawing censorship, this article creates the conditions within which the right of free speech can be exercised.

This first generation of rights includes the protection of life, property, the liberty and security of the person, right to fair trial, prohibition on torture and slavery, and basic political rights such as the right to democratic elections. They are the civil and political rights of citizens, the backbone of the liberal state. Emerging out of the great upheavals of the eighteenth century, they aim at protecting the liberty, dignity, and integrity of the person and promote the ability of citizens to participate in public life.

The democratic and socialist struggles and traditions of the nineteenth century led to the development of the second generation—economic, social, and cultural rights. These rights aim to promote the well-being of people by guaranteeing a minimum standard of material life. They address groups of people, communities and classes rather than isolated individuals, and assume that social solidarity is a central characteristic of societies. The rights to work and decent conditions of work, to education, health care, social security benefits, an adequate standard of life, and participation in cultural life are central to this list. Their enforcement does not rely on legal and judicial procedures. Economic rights cannot be delivered if the state keeps out of society. On the contrary, economic rights are positive in outlook and request state intervention in economy and society in order to create the conditions necessary for their implementation. If civil and political rights underlie the values of liberty and dignity, economic and social rights promote equality, nondiscrimination, and a sense of community that cares for its members.

The differences between the two types of rights developed into a central aspect of the ideological Cold War conducted in various meetings of the United Nations, in legal journals, and in the world media. The West claimed that the communist gulags and lunatic asylums were logical extensions of Marxism's totalitarianism. The Soviets responded that social and economic rights are superior because material survival and decent conditions of life are more important than the right to vote. "The right to a free press is of no interest to a starving and illiterate peasant in an African village," ran the argument.

For liberals, civil and political rights have priority. Their aim is to place limits around state activities, and this negative conception of freedom as the absence of state imposition is the heart of human autonomy and rights. According to liberal theory, economic rights are not proper legal rights. They are claimed by groups, not individuals, and they are "positive" in their action—in other words, they call for state intervention in economy and society, for heavy taxation and central planning, in order to deliver the necessary levels of employment presupposed by the right to work or the revenues necessary for welfare provision and free health care or education. Finally, economic and social rights are not justiciable: they cannot be guaranteed by

legislation in a liberal state and, moreover, courts cannot enforce them. The appalling oppression of dissidents was seen as proof of the correctness of the Western arguments, and the assertion that the market is the superior, if not the only, mechanism of distribution was recited as a mantra in response to the communist claims about capitalist squalor and unemployment. These ideological conflicts made it impossible for the United Nations to draft a common international bill of rights. An indication of the liberal domination in the area is the fact that while the Covenant on Civil and Political Rights creates strong individual legal entitlements and state duties, that on Economic, Social, and Cultural rights requests only member states to take measures to implement these rights.

THEORIES OF RIGHTS

Human rights is a combined term. The *human* refers to certain standards of treatment to which people are entitled and that create a moral framework within which state policy, administration, and the law should operate. The reference to *rights* returns us to the discipline of law. Rights were the creation of early modern legal systems and constitute the basic building block of Western law. To have a legal right is (a) to have an entitlement, for example, a property right, which can (b) be realized through the respective action of one or many duty-bearers who must act or refrain from acting in certain ways (a property right creates a near-universal duty in people not to interfere with my property) and (c) can be legally enforced against duty-bearers who do not perform their obligations.

Human rights are a special category of right beset with a number of paradoxes. While they are legal rights, the main duty-bearer is the state. But it is state law that is called upon to enforce these rights, creating tensions within the legal system. Secondly, they combine morality and law, prescription and description, something that often leads to confusion and excessive rhetoric. In the expansive contemporary use of the term, human rights refer to moral or ideal rights that have no legal recognition. A South African during the apartheid regime or a political dissident in China could legitimately say that he or she has "the right not to be discriminated against." This is not a real, legally enforceable right, however, but rather the aim behind the struggle against the social and political system that does not recognize the right. A different form of confusion is evident in the use of the expression "I have a right to X" to mean "I desire X" or "X should be given to me." This linguistic inflation weakens the association of human rights claims with significant human goods and undermines their position as central principles of political and legal organization.

The confounding of the real with the ideal is characteristic of human rights discourse. Article 1 of the Universal Declaration of Human Rights states that "all human beings are born free and equal in dignity and rights." But as Jeremy Bentham commented about a similar article of the French Declaration of the Rights of Man and of the Citizen, infants are not free, as they are dependent for survival on their caregivers, while the idea that people are born or enjoy equality around the world flies in the face of the huge disparities between rich and poor or the north and the south. The descriptive statements of the declarations should be read as prescriptive: people are not, but ought to be, free and equal. Indeed the great power of human rights lies in their rhetorical character, which is strengthened by their ambiguity and openendedness.

But the rhetorical force of human rights is part of their weakness. Over the long history of natural and human rights, their source has moved from purposeful nature, to reason, to God and the scriptures, to human nature, and, in their final mutation, to human rights and to international law. What argumentation or procedure can be used today to attract wide agreement about their principles? As moral standards, human rights derive from a group of anthropological hypotheses and moral assertions about liberty, equality, and the well-being of individuals and their relationship to wider society. Indeed it would be comforting to say that human rights are recognized and given to people on account of their participation in the human race and not through any restricted or regional membership, such as citizenship, nationality, class, or group. Yet it is quite clear that the only real rights are those given by states to their citizens. Aliens and refugees, those who have no state or government to protect them and who could have been expected to be the main beneficiaries of the rights of humanity, have very limited if any rights.

Indeed, the change from natural to human rights marked a loss of faith in the ability to justify rights on the basis of generally acceptable truths about human nature. While arguments from human nature are still canvassed, the "human" of human rights refers mainly to their scope (they are rights that should be given to all human beings) rather than to their justification. Commonly accepted facts about human nature keep changing with scientific knowledge, and whatever they may be, they are not sufficient to generate moral commitments. The method used for justifying rights in the early twenty-first century is constructive. Starting from the basic assumptions of liberal democracy about individual dignity, equality, and tolerance, the moral philosopher builds a coherent system of rights and expectations. This approach has been criticized as excessively abstract and unrealistic. An alternative detects certain common value commitments in the social mores or "deep structure" of a society, which are then raised into principles worthy of legal protection. A problem with that approach is that it raises and enforces legally the values a society has already accepted, and to that extent it neglects the forward-looking and critical function of human rights in relation to power and to received opinion. In any case, human rights standards are set today in international organizations by government representatives, diplomats, and civil servants, and the work of moral philosophers often takes the form of *post facto* rationalizations.

UNIVERSALISM AND CULTURAL RELATIVISM

The debate about the meaning and scope of human rights has been dominated since the 1990s by the argument between the so-called universalists and cultural relativists. The universalist claim is that cultural values and moral norms should pass a test of universal applicability and logical consistency. Human rights have a necessary universalist aspect, partly legal and partly moral. Morally, the justifications behind human rights norms or standards claim universal validity and create a duty of compliance in all situations and irrespective of the state of national law. Human rights must be the same everywhere at least as to their essence, if not their actual formulation. Legally, the large number of human rights treaties and conventions accepted by almost every state in the world has formed a kind of universal law of nations and peoples.

Universalists believe that reason and law give the right answer to moral dilemmas. As a result, judgments that derive their legitimacy from local conditions are morally suspect. But because all life is situated, an "unencumbered" self and judgment based on the protocols of reason goes against the grain of human experience. The counterintuitive nature of universalism can lead its proponents to extreme arrogance: only we, as the real moral agents or as the ethical alliance or as the representatives of the universal, can understand what morality demands. If there is one moral truth but many errors, it is incumbent upon its agents to impose it on others. In such a case, human rights universalists can turn into imperialists, who promote the "civilizing" mission by the force of arms.

Cultural relativists start from the opposite and commonsensical observation that values are context-bound, that they develop within particular histories and traditions. Relativism challenges the presumed universality of normative standards and values. There are many competing views about what is right or wrong, and no transcultural values exist to allow the comparison of competing views and provide the basis of universal legislation. Normality and morality are culture-bound; human rights express the cultural assumptions of Western societies. Their cultural and historical provenance makes human rights European creations and universal declarations of rights a chapter of European idealism. International human rights law has taken little interest in the values, histories, and traditions of non-Western nations and societies. The African Charter on Human and Peoples' Rights (1981) includes an unprecedented part about the duties owed by individuals to African civilization, their states, communities, and families. This idea of a duty owed to one's community is largely unknown to the Western human rights tradition, for which the individual is the center of concern and rights are tools for his or her defense from the incursions of others.

But the relativists have to struggle with a metaethical contradiction. They must deny all absolute claims to truth except for that made for the principle of relativism. Furthermore, the relativist position has been often adopted by oppressive governments as a defense against criticisms of their highly inegalitarian and repressive activities. Indeed the cultural embedment of self and value is a sociological truism; the context, as history, tradition, and culture is malleable, is always under construction. History teaches nothing; it is historians and journalists, intellectuals and politicians, academics and ideologues who turn historical events into stories and myths and in so doing construct ways of seeing the present through the lens of the past. Often the relativist turns local norms and traditional values into absolute truths and imposes them on those who disagree with the oppressiveness of tradition.

In these extreme cases we can detect a certain similarity between universalists and relativists. The Kosovo war of 1998–1999 offers a good example. The Serbs massacred and ethnically cleansed the Albanians to protect the "threatened" community of the Serb nation. The Western allies, however, bombed the Serbs in the name of threatened humanity. Both principles, when they become absolute essences and define the meaning and value of humanity without remainder, can find everything that resists them expendable. Both positions exemplify, perhaps in different ways, the contemporary metaphysical urge: they have made an axiomatic decision as to what constitutes the essence of humanity and follow it with a stubborn disregard for opposing arguments and traditions. But humanity has no essence. The contribution of human rights lies precisely in the endless process of redefinition of humanity and its necessary but impossible attempt to escape external determination. Humanity has no foundation and no ends. Human rights, when not co-opted to the dubious cause of public and political power, are the definition of groundlessness.

See also **Convention on Genocide; International Law; Nuremberg Laws; United Nations; Universal Declaration of Human Rights.**

BIBLIOGRAPHY

Donnelly, Jack. *Universal Human Rights in Theory and Practice*. 2nd ed. Ithaca, N.Y., 2003.

Douzinas, Costas. *The End of Human Rights: Critical Legal Thought at the Turn of the Century.* Oxford, U.K., 2000.

Gibney, Matthew, ed. *Globalising Rights.* Oxford, U.K., 2003.

Ishay, Micheline. *The History of Human Rights: From Ancient Times to the Globalization Era.* Berkeley, Calif., 2004.

Kennedy, David. *The Dark Sides of Virtue: Reassessing International Humanitarianism.* Princeton, N.J., 2003.

Owen, Nicholas, ed. *Human Rights, Human Wrongs.* Oxford, U.K., 2002.

Steiner, Henry J., and Philip Alston. *International Human Rights in Context.* 2nd ed. Oxford, U.K., 2000.

COSTAS DOUZINAS

HUNGARY.

Hungarians—unlike Czechs, Romanians, and Serbs, for example—form a historical nation. For more than ten centuries, Hungary has had an almost continuous existence as a sovereign state. The upper classes, although ethnically mixed, proudly regarded themselves as Hungarians, possessed political rights, and exploited a multilingual peasantry. (In 1914, only about half of the population spoke Hungarian as a native language.) In the course of its thousand-year history, the country accumulated a rich and mixed tradition that included dark spots involving the repression of national minorities but also bright spots of liberalism and tolerance. Unlike Croatia and Slovakia, which before the 1990s had existed only as German satellites and were without democratic traditions, Hungary in the twentieth century could have built on a democratic heritage. Between 1867 and 1918, under the Habsburg Monarchy, the country enjoyed spectacular economic growth, although it remained primarily an agricultural nation. Advanced, industrial Budapest, then one of the fastest growing cities in the world, with its lively intellectual and artistic life, coexisted with a backward countryside where a multinational peasantry lived in material circumstances not much better than those of peasants the Russian Empire.

THE INTERWAR PERIOD

The years 1918 and 1919 were a great dividing line in Hungarian history. The Austro-Hungarian loss in World War I had more disastrous consequences for Hungary than for any other land. In October 1918 a revolution separated Hungary from the monarchy and created a republic, headed by Count Mihály Károlyi. This liberal government remained in office for less than five months. On 20 March 1919, the Entente made known its decision concerning the line of demarcation between the Hungarian and Romanian troops, implying a future territorial division. The next day, Károlyi was compelled to resign in favor of a Communist-Socialist coalition, in which the Communists played the dominant role. Károlyi's government could neither accept Allied demands nor successfully resist them. Ironically, it was only the nominally internationalist Communists who were willing to fight for the country's national interest, because they expected that Soviet Russia would come to their aid. The Hungarian Soviet Republic remained in existence for only 133 days, in the course of which it carried out a mindlessly radical policy with terror. By nationalizing rather than distributing land, it alienated the peasantry. Throughout its existence, the Soviet Republic fought Czechoslovak and Romanian armies. Ultimately it failed not because of domestic opposition, although a counterrevolution was gathering its strength, but because it was defeated militarily by armies supported by the Allies.

The treaty concluded with Hungary at Trianon in 1920 was part of the Versailles settlements. The country lost two-thirds of its territory and more than half of its population, leaving three million Hungarian speakers just beyond the newly drawn borders. It is indisputable that the terms of the treaty Hungary was forced to sign were not only unfair but also unwise. The desire to regain all or at least some of the lost territories came to dominate Hungarian politics. Ironically, Admiral Miklós Horthy, who became governor and regent in 1920 and pursued a nationalist policy, came to power with the aid of foreigners and was compelled to accept peace terms that the internationalist revolutionaries would not accept. The country remained a kingdom, but without a king. The surrounding countries, all of them beneficiaries of the Monarchy's collapse, would not accept a Habsburg restoration, and for the Hungarian political class a republic sounded too revolutionary.

Interwar Hungary was profoundly different from what it had been before 1914. As part of the Austro-Hungarian Monarchy, the Kingdom of Hungary, which had its government in Budapest, had administered a country of more than eighteen million people, a number that was now reduced to less than eight million. The multinational Austro-Hungarian Empire had ceased to exist and Hungary became the most ethnically homogeneous country in the area. The perceived injustice of the Treaty of Trianon determined the character of Hungarian politics in the interwar period. Revisionism alienated Hungary from its neighbors and justified a socially repressive policy in the name of national interest. A small landed aristocracy still possessed much of the land and controlled the government. After the war in eastern Europe, the new countries carried out meaningful land reform, but Hungary did not. Only about 8 percent of the land was distributed, and that in such small parcels that many of the new owners soon lost their land; consequently, in the 1920s and 1930s about a third of the peasantry was landless. The defeat of the Soviet Republic was followed by a White terror that claimed at least as many victims as the previous Red terror. In addition to Communists and left-wing Socialists, Jews in particular suffered in this second terror. Whereas prewar Hungary had made possible and even encouraged Jewish assimilation, in the changed circumstances a new Hungarian middle class resented Jewish domination in the nation's intellectual and economic lives. The disproportionate role that Jews had played in the Soviet Republic was used to justify a new wave of anti-Semitism.

During the interwar period, the left wing played only a small role in the nation's political life. The Social Democratic Party was allowed to organize workers but not landless peasants. The Communists had been compromised by the unhappy memory of the 1919 Soviet Republic and by association with the profoundly unpopular Soviet Union. Whatever opposition existed to the outdated social structure came from the ever-stronger radical right wing. The realistic choice for a politically minded Hungarian was between a government in the hands of conservatives, serving the interests of a landed aristocracy while retaining some of the restraints imposed by a certain type of liberalism, and a government of the extreme right, socially radical but very much attracted first to the example of Italian fascism and later to German National Socialism.

WORLD WAR II

That Hungary would end up on the German side in the developing international conflict was overdetermined. Nazi war plans promised to overthrow the Versailles settlement, something that Hungarians deeply desired. In addition, Hungary—like other countries in the region—was deeply hurt by the economic crisis and could be helped only by ties to the rapidly reviving German economy. Hungary needed the German market. Allied policies, as represented by the Munich agreement, made it clear to the people of Eastern Europe that they had no choice but to come to terms with a resurgent Germany. The Germans rewarded the Hungarians for their friendship, first by returning a part of Slovakia and in 1940 by giving back to Hungary the northern part of Transylvania.

Hungarian Prime Minister László Bárdossy declared war on the Soviet Union immediately after German troops crossed the Soviet border in June 1941. This war also turned out to be a disaster for the country. The 200,000-strong Second Hungarian Army was caught in the Stalingrad encirclement and destroyed in 1942. After it became clear that the Germans were unlikely to win, ruling circles under a new premier, Miklós Kállay, attempted by various means to contact the Allies in the hope that the country would be liberated by Anglo-American forces rather than by the Soviet Army. On 19 March 1944, the German army occupied Hungary, even though Hungary was an ally. The German High Command feared that Hungary might follow the Italian example and seek a separate peace, and such a development, if successful, would have had disastrous consequences for the German lines of communication. The occupiers forced Horthy to dismiss Kállay and replace him with the pro-Nazi Döme Sztojay. At this point, Hungarian Jews, who were the largest intact Jewish community in the German sphere of interest, began to be deported to Auschwitz.

As it became increasingly evident that the war was hopeless, Horthy made a clumsy last-minute effort to conclude a separate armistice with the

THE POSTWAR PERIOD

The period from 1945 to 1948 was at once hopeful and tragic. On the one hand, the semi-feudal socio-economic system was finally destroyed. The old ruling class had been discredited by its cooperation with the Nazis and Hungary finally experienced a radical land reform. Many believed that the creation of a democratic system would now commence. On the other hand, the terms of the armistice obligated the Hungarians to pay heavy reparations and that, combined with the wartime destruction, imposed great suffering on the people. Worst of all, the Allied Control Commission was a tool of Soviet policy. Although it seems that at the outset the Soviets did not plan to impose a communist system on the country, as the Cold War developed it became increasingly clear that the country would be reduced to the status of a satellite.

In the first free elections the country ever experienced, in November 1945, the nonsocialist Smallholders' Party received 58 percent of the vote and the Communists got only 17 percent. The Communists could come to power only with outside help. In February 1946, Hungary finally became a republic and the Smallholder leader, Zoltán Tildy, became the first president, and Ferenc Nagy, from the same party, became premier. If the Hungarians had been left to their own devices, they could have established a fairly well functioning democratic polity, but this was not to be. The Communists, with the aid of Soviet occupying forces, pressured their political opponents into one concession after another.

In 1947, as the Cold War grew bitterer, the Soviet leadership decided that it was no longer in its interest to maintain coalition regimes in Eastern Europe. In Hungary the noncommunist parties were gradually eliminated and prominent opponents of the communist takeover were arrested on trumped-up charges. Prime Minister Nagy was forced into exile and the Social Democratic Party was incorporated into the Communist Party. By the end of 1948, communist domination was complete. The Communist Party, headed by Mátyás Rákosi, introduced Soviet-style institutions and terror. The peasants were forced into collective farms; the state pursued a policy of forced industrialization, which called for high investment in heavy industry and resulted in a dreadfully low standard

A small crowd gathers to burn a picture of Soviet leader Joseph Stalin in Budapest, October 1956.
©HULTON-DEUTSCH COLLECTION/CORBIS

Soviets. The Germans learned of the plan and responded by carrying out a coup. On 15 October 1944, they arrested Horthy, together with his close associates, and installed the leader of the Nyilas (Hungarian Nazi, or Arrow Cross) Party, Ferenc Szálasi. Although in the first two years of the war, the country, as opposed to the army, had not suffered much, the last year of the war was different. Germany invested major forces in the defense of Budapest. It was in the interest of the German High Command to keep the fighting away from German territory as long as possible, and Hungary was a war zone for eight months. As a consequence of the intense fighting, the country, and especially the capital, suffered dreadfully. The task of reconstruction would be long and difficult.

of living; all independent voices were suppressed and hundreds of thousands of people arrested. The country experienced show trials that began in December 1948 with the trial of the most uncompromising enemy of the Communists, József Cardinal Mindszenty, who was charged with currency speculation. The next year it was the turn of Communist leaders, including László Rajk, the most prominent Communist who had not spent the war years in the Soviet Union.

The worst years of terror, from 1948 to 1953, coincided with Joseph Stalin's last years. After Stalin's death, in March 1953, the Soviet leaders introduced a "new course," which had immediate consequences in Hungarian politics. Under Soviet pressure, Rákosi, the most hated man in Hungary, gave up his job as head of the government, although he remained as leader of the party. The new premier was Imre Nagy, who had achieved a degree of popularity as the minister of agriculture and was responsible for the 1945 land reform. Also, unlike the other top leaders of the party, he was not Jewish. Nagy made attempts to raise the standard of living by paying more attention to the production of consumer goods and freed most of those who were in prison for political crimes. His tenure as premier, however, lasted for less then two years. He fell victim to the power struggle within the top leadership in the Soviet Union. When his mentor, Georgy Malenkov, was forced out as premier in Moscow, Rákosi was able to take advantage of the opportunity to have Nagy removed and replace him with his own man, András Hegedüs.

In retrospect, allowing Rákosi to become once again the dominant force in Hungary was a mistake on the Soviets' part. Nikita Khrushchev's attack on Stalin at the Twentieth Party Congress, held in February 1956, undermined Rákosi's hold on power. On the one hand, Rákosi could not prevent the news of Stalin's crimes from becoming public, and on the other his own record as the perfect Stalinist was evident to all. It was this contradiction at the top that allowed Rákosi's methods to be denounced increasingly explicitly, even while he remained in control of the party until June 1956. Even at that time, he was replaced as first secretary of the Party by Ernö Gerö, a man equally unpopular and almost as responsible for the Stalin-era crimes as Rákosi himself.

The spark for the Hungarian Revolution was the news from Poland, where the Soviet authorities had been compelled by popular pressure to make concessions. A demonstration on 23 October 1956 was originally meant to express solidarity with the Poles, but once tens of thousands came to the streets it quickly turned into an anti-Soviet and anticommunist movement. Fighting started that very evening. Although as the demonstrators demanded, Imre Nagy was named premier on 24 October, he could not take control of the popular movement. Under pressure, he allowed the re-formation of political parties and formed a coalition government. On 1 November, Nagy declared Hungary's neutrality and its exit from the Soviet-organized Warsaw military pact. The Soviet leadership, after some hesitation, on 31 October decided to suppress the revolution, and on 4 November Soviet troops, which had never left Hungary, reentered Budapest. Within a week, the fighting ended. Approximately 1,500 people died and 200,000 fled to the West. The people who left were, by and large, younger and better educated and consequently the loss for the country was disproportionate; however, the departure of the most bitterly anticommunist element made stabilization easier. The revolution was the only event in twentieth-century Hungarian history that had worldwide significance: it demonstrated that a communist regime outside of the Soviet Union itself could maintain itself only by the force of arms. Communism never fully recovered from this blow. The suppression of the revolution was followed by a bloody terror. Approximately 16,000 people received prison sentences and 361 were hanged, including Nagy and his closest collaborators. Nagy could have saved his life by supporting the government headed by János Kádár, but he refused.

In the early 1960s, a remarkable transformation occurred. Kádár made a successful effort to gain a degree of popularity. In 1963 his government introduced amnesty for those tried for their involvement in the 1956 revolution; after recollectivizing the land, it gave substantial material support to the farms and raised the peasantry's standard of living; it allowed increased intellectual freedom; and at the end of the decade it introduced economic reforms that raised the standard of living

Soviet tanks maneuver through the streets of Budapest during the crackdown of October 1956. ©HULTON-DEUTSCH COLLECTION/CORBIS

of the entire country. The consolidation occurred because people came to believe that this was the best situation they could achieve in the prevailing circumstances. Hungary, which in the first few years after the revolution was the most repressive among the communist states, within ten years had become the most liberal. Kádár was transformed from one of the most hated men in Hungarian history into a person who if he was not exactly loved was accepted.

THE POST-SOVIET PERIOD

The end of the communist regime came as a result of forces over which Hungarians had no control. The collapse of the Soviet Union, which allowed Hungary (and the other satellites) to regain its independence, was greeted with joy. However, within a short time it became clear that the transformation would be painful and that the burden would fall disproportionately on those who had no ties to the new business economy. The traditional markets for Hungarian agriculture and industry suddenly disappeared; switching to an economic system in which prices were determined by supply and demand resulted in a sudden burst of inflation. For a while, the gross national product declined, unprofitable factories were closed down, and most people's standard of living suffered. When the economy started to improve, at first only a minority benefited and the gap between the rich and the poor widened.

In spite of the difficulties, Hungary was more fortunate than other countries that went through the same process. The economic reforms introduced in the 1960s and 1970s made the shift to a capitalist system easier. For several years after 1991, Hungary received far more foreign investment per capita than any other country in the region, and this made economic recovery quicker there than elsewhere. Reform communists rather convincingly managed to turn themselves into social democrats. There was relatively little recrimination for the crimes of the communist regime and a reasonably mature political system emerged rather quickly. The moderate right won the first free elections, and after that in each election cycle the governing party was turned out of office. A multiparty system was quickly reduced to two major political forces: a moderate right-wing party (Fidesz) and a moderate left-wing Social Democratic Party. An extreme right-wing party does exist (MIEP) but in the elections of 2002 it failed to gain 5 percent of the vote and therefore did not achieve representation in the parliament.

Hungarians, with the exception of the extreme nationalist right, have been enthusiastic about joining a united Europe. Hungary's inclusion into NATO in 1999 had only symbolic significance, but the entrance into the European Union in May 2004 is expected to revitalize the economy and ultimately raise the standard of living.

See also **Budapest; Communism; Fascism; Károlyi, Mihály; Munich Agreement; Nazism; Trianon, Treaty of; Versailles, Treaty of.**

BIBLIOGRAPHY

Kontler, László. *A History of Hungary: Millennium in Central Europe.* New York, 2002.

Macartney, C. A. *October Fifteenth: A History of Modern Hungary, 1929–1945.* Edinburgh, 1957.

Molnár, Miklós. *A Concise History of Hungary.* New York, 2001.

Romsics, Ignác. *Magyarország Története a XX Században.* Budapest, 1999.

Sinor, Denis. *History of Hungary.* New York, 1959.

PETER KENEZ

HUXLEY, ALDOUS (1894–1963), English novelist and essayist.

Aldous Leonard Huxley was born in the last years of the nineteenth century, but his work constantly addresses itself to the present moment, forming a link between the world of the high Victorian liberal intellectual and the modern era. His paternal grandfather was the distinguished Darwinian scientist Thomas Henry Huxley (1825–1895) and his maternal great-uncle the equally famous poet and critic Matthew Arnold (1822–1888). His work, in its intelligence, its vivacity, and in the way it constantly pushes back the boundaries of thought, along with its assured grasp of the worlds of science and literature, placed him at the center of English writing in the twentieth century.

Welcomed into the Bloomsbury salon of Lady Ottoline Morrell (1873–1938) as a precociously brilliant undergraduate at Oxford during World War I, Aldous Huxley met in that milieu the writer D. H. Lawrence (1885–1930), who became a life-long friend. Despite poor sight resulting from an infection contracted on the playing fields of Eton and that caused temporary blindness, Huxley published his first collection of stories, *Limbo*, in 1920 and his bold and witty satirical first novel, *Crome Yellow*, in 1921; both made an immediate impact. Subsequent novels established him as a clever and provocative anatomist of the stuffy old-fashioned world of middle-class England. His writings were laced with the anger of a younger generation that had lost so many of its number in the war. This iconoclastic phase, during which Huxley supported himself with a flow of essays, articles, and travel books, culminated in his two most substantial novels, *Point Counter Point* (1928) and *Eyeless in Gaza* (1936).

Huxley spent much of the 1920s and the early 1930s living abroad, first in Italy, then in the south of France, where he was happiest at a house on the Côte d'Azur at Sanary-sur-Mer, in the company of other foreign writers such as Cyril Connolly (1903–1974) and Edith Wharton (1862–1937). The life at Sanary has been memorably captured in the writings of Sybille Bedford (b. 1911), who knew Huxley and his wife at this time and later became the writer's first authorized biographer.

In 1936, to the disappointment of some of his readers, the iconoclast was displaced by the moralist as Huxley, alarmed at the direction of world events in the 1930s, threw himself into the antiwar movement, publishing *An Encyclopaedia of Pacifism* in 1937. In 1932 he had already published what would prove to be his most famous novel, *Brave New World*, a dystopian portrait of a world where human beings are mass-produced in test tubes like cars on an assembly line. The novel expresses his lifelong distaste for "Fordism" and the manipulation of the individual by advertising and political propaganda. Now his nonpartisan political engagement became increasingly pronounced.

In 1937 Huxley and his wife, Maria Nys (1898–1955), left England on a lecture tour of the United States, which turned into a permanent residence after Huxley was offered work as a Hollywood screenwriter, though the work did not agree with him. While living mostly in California, where the light relieved his eyesight problems (about which he published a book called *The Art of Seeing* in 1942), Huxley became increasingly interested in the mystical tradition, Western and Eastern, and published an anthology of its key texts, *The Perennial Philosophy* (1946). But his most famous nonfictional work would prove to be *The Doors of Perception* (1954), an account of an experiment with mescaline, the result of his desire to explore the limits of human consciousness. Scientific in aspiration, the book, and its sequel, *Heaven and Hell* (1956), coming as they did at the start of the 1960s drug culture (which Huxley deplored), intensified his fame in the last years of his life when, as an honorary professor at the Massachusetts Institute of Technology in 1960, he drew record crowds attracted by his guru status. In his California years he continued to write fiction and essays and was a close friend of the writer Christopher Isherwood (1904–1986). His last novel, *Island* (1962), was an attempt to balance the dark dystopian premonitions of *Brave New World* with a bright vision of utopia drawing on all his beliefs of nonviolence, transcendence, and hope for human regeneration.

Aldous Huxley died of cancer at his home in Hollywood on 22 November 1963, the same day John F. Kennedy was assassinated. His second wife, Laura Archera Huxley, is said to have administered a dose of LSD to the writer at his request as he lay dying.

See also **Bloomsbury; Fordism; Lawrence, D. H.; Pacifism.**

BIBLIOGRAPHY

Primary Sources

Huxley, Aldous. Unpublished letters. A surprising number of letters can be found in manuscript collections at the Humanities Research Center at Austin, Texas, the Huntington Library in California, the British Library in London, the Royal Library in Brussels, Balliol College Oxford, the University of Reading (Chatto Archive), and elsewhere.

Huxley, Julian. *Memories.* Vol. 1. London, 1970. Recollections by Huxley's older brother.

Smith, Grover, ed. *Letters of Aldous Huxley.* London, 1969.

Secondary Sources

Bedford, Sybille. *Aldous Huxley: A Biography.* 2 vols. London, 1973–1974. Outstanding authorized biography by a writer who knew Huxley and his wife intimately.

Huxley, Julian, ed. *Aldous Huxley.* London, 1965.

Murray, Nicholas. *Aldous Huxley: An English Intellectual.* London, 2002. Now the standard biography.

Watt, Donald, ed. *Aldous Huxley: The Critical Heritage.* London, 1975. The major reviews of Huxley from 1918 to 1965.

NICHOLAS MURRAY

IBÁRRURI, DOLORES (LA PASIONARIA) (1895–1989), Spanish Communist leader.

Dolores Ibárruri was born in Gallarta, Vizcaya (Basque Country), on 9 December 1895. Her father was a Catholic, conservative miner, and she herself was a deeply religious woman until she married a Socialist. Later, her older brother would fight on Francisco Franco's side during the Spanish civil war (1936–1939). She took part in the general strike of 1917, and, like her husband, moved to the left wing of the Spanish Socialist Workers' Party, joining the Spanish Communist Party (Partido Comunista de España, or PCE) when it was founded in November 1921. She used the pseudonym La Pasionaria (the passionflower) for her writings, including her first article, published during Passion Week of the Lenten season of 1918.

Until the civil war, the PCE was a very small, sectarian organization, constantly riddled with infighting. Moreover, the local leaders often resented the tactics imposed by the Communist International. In 1931 the International decided that the PCE should not support the newly proclaimed, and still widely popular, Second Republic. This and other decisions were met with opposition by the then secretary general of the party, José Bullejos, a protector of Ibárruri who had promoted her to the Central Committee in 1930. He was purged and expelled from the organization in 1932, and she had to recant her initial support for Bullejos, whom she now publicly condemned. This was the first and last time she opposed the International, becoming a bulwark of the nascent Stalinist orthodoxy.

The PCE got a significant political boost first with the adoption of the Popular Front strategy by the International and then with its inclusion in the center-left electoral coalition that won the general election in Spain in February 1936. Ibárruri was one of the seventeen Communists elected to parliament, where she did not particularly shine. Her jump to political stardom came in July of that year with the outbreak of the civil war. The PCE grew enormously during the conflict mainly because only the Soviet Union provided the republic with the weapons it needed to survive. In reality, during the war the PCE was directed by the International delegates, the best known of them being the Italian Communist leader Palmiro Togliatti. The secretary general of the party, the former baker José Díaz, was not a particularly effective speaker. It would be in this context that Ibárruri became the most celebrated public symbol of the Republican determination to resist the advance of the Fascist forces.

In the figure of Ibárruri many saw both the new Spanish (and universal) progressive, antifascist woman, and the supposedly best traditions of Spain. Always dressed in black, like most mature women of the Mediterranean basin, she was the proud, mourning mother of democracy, the Republican soldiers, and her own children. At this point she had lost two girls (of the five she had) in their infancy; later during the battle of Stalingrad she would lose her son Rubén in combat, who

Delores Ibárruri at the first session of the Women's Internation Congress in Paris, December 1945.

of the party, a position she held until 1960, when she was replaced by Santiago Carrillo. A committed Stalinist, Ibárruri supported the Soviet repression of the successive popular risings in Germany, Poland, and Hungary and the purges the late 1940s and 1950s; only reluctantly and timidly did she condemn the invasion of Czechoslovakia in 1968. In fact, she never truly adapted herself to the increasing independence of her party from Moscow, which would lead to the adoption of the strategy of Eurocommunism. She returned to Spain after the death of Franco, and in June 1977, in the first democratic elections since February 1936, she was elected to parliament. She died in Madrid on 12 November 1989, just as the Berlin Wall was beginning to be dismantled, and although the circumstances that had made her a symbol of so many causes had by then long disappeared, her funeral was massively attended.

See also **Communism; Spanish Civil War.**

BIBLIOGRAPHY

Cruz, Rafael. *Pasionaria: Dolores Ibárruri, historia y símbolo.* Madrid, 1999.

Graham, Helen. *The Spanish Republic at War, 1936–1939.* Cambridge, U.K., 2002.

Low, Robert. *La Pasionaria: The Spanish Firebrand.* London, 1992.

ANTONIO CAZORLA-SANCHEZ

became the object of countless poems. But the suffering mother had another face, that of the wild courage of the aging communist Carmen confronting the horror of fascist aggression when so many men avoided doing so. Her bravery made her beautiful. Her eloquence seemed to open her bleeding heart to humanity in the sentences, discourses, and articles—for which she was credited authorship—that concentrated with precise, impacting words, this two-sided woman: "They shall not pass!" "Better to die standing than to live on our knees." Her constructed image, austere yet radiant, reproduced in posters and photographs, was widely circulated inside and outside Spain.

As the Republican resistance crumbled in the last days of the war, Ibárruri fled Spain for Moscow, where she would live in exile. After the death of Díaz in 1942, she became secretary general

---

ICELAND. The twentieth century in Iceland can be divided into two periods, before and after 1940. In the former, Iceland is best viewed as an essentially agricultural society that was undergoing a number of major changes, though without any fundamental disruption to people's cultural outlook. Society was grounded in the traditional "peasant" values of economic restraint and thrift. The turning point came with Iceland's forced entry into World War II in 1940, after which contact and commerce with the outside world came to have an ever greater influence on material and economic conditions within the country, although the traditional values of agricultural society continued to play a central part in the lives of the people until well on into the second half of the century.

In 1910 Iceland had a population of about 85,000 (the population in 2005 was 297,000). Of these, about 34 percent lived in centers of more than 200 people, with the rest scattered around the country (which covers 103,000 square kilometers) in isolated and sparsely populated pockets of farmland. Agriculture was based mainly on sheep and cattle raising, and most farms were single-family smallholdings isolated from each other by poor communications. The country's cultural heritage remained strong and unified in spite of the rudimentary infrastructure and the fragility of formal institutions. Literacy was all but universal, with almost all education taking the form of home instruction to the age of ten, followed by four years' compulsory schooling (from 1907). Confirmation at the age of thirteen or fourteen gave young people entry into virtually all aspects of the adult world.

Most Icelanders seem to have derived enormous benefits from their shared cultural background, which was centered on a common language (Icelandic), and a thousand years of recorded history going back to the first settlements in the second half of the ninth century. Icelandic literature and poetry proved exceptionally useful to many when faced with the new industrialized world of the twentieth century, for example on the first steam trawlers that arrived in Iceland in the early years of the century. The Icelandic people thus appear to have found the leap from the turf cottages of the nineteenth century to the mechanized technology of the modern age comparatively easy, without losing their links with the past. Expanding urban centers, for example, were a blend of town and country, exemplified by the widespread keeping of livestock. Yet change in general came slowly, with rural areas remaining sparsely populated and largely untouched by technological innovation.

Agriculture remained the main occupation in Iceland, but fishing grew steadily in importance after the mechanization of the fishing fleet in the early years of the twentieth century. This created a major new source of employment for working people, albeit casual and irregular, that accelerated urbanization. The conditions of the poor were frequently difficult, particularly during the Great Depression, when fish prices on European markets collapsed. However, one could argue that the structure of Icelandic society made it easier for people to feed themselves than was often the case in other countries, because agricultural production among urban dwellers remained considerable and there was always fish to be had from the shore.

In 1940, with the outbreak of World War II, British forces occupied Iceland. The British army had an immediate and enormous impact on all aspects of daily life, an impact that was to prove permanent. The population of Reykjavík, the capital, doubled almost overnight. Subsequently everyday life began to reflect trends in Europe and the United States. The U.S. army took over from the British in 1941, and an agreement was signed in 1946 between the government of the young republic, established in 1944, and the United States ratifying the U.S. military presence. This agreement divided the nation into opposing political camps, for and against the siting of U.S. troops on Icelandic soil. (In 2005 the United States still maintained a military base in Iceland, though of considerably reduced size and scope.) In 1949, shortly after the signing of the defense agreement with the United States, Iceland became one of the founding signatories of the NATO treaty, a move that also proved highly controversial within national politics.

The postwar years brought massive change to Iceland. Prices and inflation were high. The Icelanders received more than $38 million in aid under the Marshall Plan. This helped set up factories with the aim of strengthening their industrial base, which was still rudimentary, one-dimensional, and technologically backward. A part of the aid also went into developing hydroelectricity. Fishing became ever more important, and here, as in other areas of industry, human labor remained the main resource and motivating factor. The period after World War II was characterized by import and exchange controls. Policy was governed by traditional financial prudence, although waste and corruption were rife under cover of the state-operated rationing system in which party agents enjoyed favorable terms at the expense of the general public. In later years the impact of the Cold War on Iceland manifested itself in, among other things, fervent attempts on the part of the Icelanders to protect their country's culture and language against outside influences, with those in authority sometimes resorting to measures grounded in racial prejudice or similar narrow attitudes toward foreign influences.

Iceland did not fully succeed in extricating itself from its financial and commercial constraints until the mid-to-late 1950s. Until the late 1980s the Icelandic economy remained undiversified and subject to cyclical fluctuation, with business operations constantly at the mercy of inflation. However, in the 1990s Iceland's membership in the European Economic Area stabilized its links with its major trading partners and put its economy on a more structured footing. It was only at this point that Iceland embraced modernization fully and unconditionally.

Women had traditionally played an important part in Icelandic labor. In the years after 1930 a significant middle class began to develop and many women withdrew from the productive industries and retired into the home, their roles now being defined by the household purse and the upbringing of children. Working-class families, however, still had to rely on female labor. During the second half of the twentieth century women became an ever more important factor in all industrial and economic developments in the country and achieved a comparable level of formal education to men in the last decades of the century.

All this has had its effects on the country's culture and economy, and in the early twenty-first century Iceland occupies a position among the richest countries in the world. It is perhaps fair to say that Icelandic society has succeeded in combining innovation in the spheres of the economy, technology, and services with old traditions, and that this combination has bolstered Iceland's position in the community of nations.

See also **Agriculture; Marshall Plan.**

BIBLIOGRAPHY

Gunnlaugsson, Gísli Ágúst. *Family and Household in Iceland, 1801–1930: Studies in the Relationship between Demographic and Socio-economic Development, Social Legislation, and Family and Household Structures.* Uppsala, Sweden, 1988.

Jónsson, Guðmundur, and Magnús S. Magnússon, eds. *Hagskinna: Icelandic Historical Statistics.* Reykjavík, Iceland, 1997.

Karlsson, Gunnar. *Iceland's 1100 Years: The History of a Marginal Society.* London, 2000.

Magnússon, Sigurður Gylfi, and Davíð Ólafsson. "Barefoot Historians: Education in Iceland in the Modern Period." In *Writing Peasants: Studies on Peasant Literacy in Early Modern Northern Europe,* edited by Klaus-Joachim Lorenzen-Schmidt and Bjørn Poulsen, 175–209. Århus, Denmark, 2002.

SIGURÐUR GYLFI MAGNÚSSON

ILIESCU, ION (b. 1930), Romanian politician.

A founder and leader of the Romanian Social Democratic Party (PDSR, subsequently PSD) until 2004, Ion Iliescu has been one of a handful of politicians most influential in Romania's transition from its communist dictatorial past to a government prepared for membership in the European Union.

Iliescu, the son of a Communist Party member, became involved in the Union of Communist Youth when he was fourteen. He attended the Bucharest Polytechnic and later the Energy Institute in Moscow. After graduating from college in 1955 he returned to Romania as a researcher at the Institute for Energy Studies in Bucharest. His path through the party was more spectacular, as he moved very quickly to found first a Union of High School Students' Associations in 1948 and subsequently a Union of Students' Associations in 1956. It was in this position that he was able to show his full loyalty to the party and its harsh policies. Such actions catapulted him into the political center at a moment when the party was making a transition from the aging government of Gheorghe Gheorghiu-Dej (1901–1965) to the younger guard, whose leader became Nicolae Ceauşescu (1918–1989). In 1965, at the age of thirty-five, Iliescu became a candidate member of the party's Central Committee and three years later he received full membership in this body. By 1968, with the help of Ceauşescu, by then leader of Romania, Iliescu reached the highest position of power he was to hold in the Communist Party, as member of the Political Committee. Between 1967 and 1971 he served as Minister of Youth.

But in 1971 Iliescu was sidelined from the position of secretary of the Communist Party Central Committee. It will probably never be known whether the conflict with Ceaușescu was over ideology, whether it was over Iliescu's dislike of Ceaușescu's increasingly nepotistic bent, or whether it was over Ceaușescu's lack of trust toward this ambitious man. It was most likely a combination of these factors. Yet Iliescu's resulting marginalization, together with his frustrated ambitions as a politician, became important elements for his future political career. During the following decades Iliescu remained involved in party politics, as deputy chairman of the Iași County council (1974–1979), a regionally powerful position, then moved on to head the National Waters Council (1979–1984), and subsequently become director of the Technical Publishing House (1984–1989).

On 22 December 1989, as crowds were gathering in the Palace Square in Bucharest booing President Ceaușescu and his wife, Iliescu emerged suddenly as the leader of the "spontaneous" Revolution inside the Palace. Why Iliescu happened to be there is unclear and suggests that the Palace events were a coup masked by the street spontaneous rioting. Minutes after the Ceaușescus (later to be captured, summarily tried, and executed) fled in a helicopter, a National Salvation Front was created with Iliescu as its leader. This provisional government held power until 20 May 1990, when the first purportedly free elections since the 1930s were held. The brief period before this election was marred by instability, some of it real and some of it manufactured, which made it impossible for other political groups with a strong organization and platform to emerge, ensuring Iliescu's sweeping election as president. His party, now called the Democratic National Salvation Front, held a staunchly conservative line with regard to privatizing the economy, especially banks and large industries, and also liberalizing some of the important aspects of public life, and was dubbed "neo-communist" by most political observers. Yet Iliescu won another four-year term in 1992, with a platform emphasizing stability and national unity. In 1993 his party was renamed the Party of Social Democracy in Romania (PDSR), which was later combined with the Romanian Social Democratic Party (PSDR) and took the name Social Democratic Party (PSD).

After four years of economic stagnation and in the midst of rampant corruption Iliescu was defeated in 1996 by Emil Constantinescu (b. 1939), the leader of the Democratic Convention. Going into opposition was not an entirely new experience for Iliescu, but operating in a democratic system did transform Iliescu's approach to politics and the party he led. Together with Adrian Năstase (b. 1950), a younger ambitious prominent leader in his party, Iliescu rebuilt the regional branches of PDSR and invigorated the youth groups of the party. Maintaining a staunch stance on preserving the well-being of the workers employed in the increasingly bankrupt heavy industry, Iliescu also refashioned himself as a supporter of privatization and foreign investment.

In December 2000 Iliescu won elections again, the last mandate for which he was eligible. This time, his election was facilitated not so much by the platform of his party as by the opponent he faced in the runoff elections, the radical right-wing leader of the Greater Romania Party, Corneliu Vadim Tudor (b. 1949). During this last mandate Iliescu was more successful in transforming his party from neo-communist to social democrat, better equipped to encourage greater faith in Romania's democratic and economic potential in view of hopes for EU accession. Still, corruption in his party and Iliescu's own distasteful last measures while in power—giving the highest Romanian decoration to Vadim Tudor and trying to pardon one of the most disliked criminals of the 1990s, Miron Cosma (b. 1954)—played an important role in the demise of the Social Democrats from power in December 2004, and to their continued internal crisis in the aftermath. Since then, Iliescu has taken a secondary role in Romanian politics, as senator in the parliament.

See also **Romania.**

BIBLIOGRAPHY

Carey, Henry F., ed. *Romania since 1989: Politics, Economics, and Society.* Lanham, Md., 2004.

Light, Duncan, and David Phinnemore, eds. *Post-Communist Romania: Coming to Terms with Transition.* Houndmills, Basingstoke; Hampshire, U.K.; and New York, 2001.

Pasti, Vladimir. *The Challenges of Transition: Romania in Transition.* New York, 1997.

Siani-Davies, Peter. *The Romanian Revolution of December 1989.* Ithaca, N.Y., 2005.

Stan, Lavinia, ed. *Romania in Transition.* Aldershot, U.K., and Brookfield, Vt., 1997.

Tismaneanu, Vladimir. *Marele soc: din finalul unui secol scurt. Ion Iliescu in dialog cu Vladimir Tismaneanu: Despre comunism, postcomunism, democratie.* Bucharest, 2004.

MARIA BUCUR

IMMIGRATION AND INTERNAL MIGRATION.

The history of migration in twentieth-century Europe divides into three periods. During the first period, Europe became the world's major refugee-generating region during World Wars I and II, during the demise of the European empires and the Eastern European revolutionary changes of 1917, and during the rule of the fascist regimes in Italy and Germany. In addition, in the 1930s Germany and the Soviet Union instituted forced-labor migration systems.

In the second period, from the early 1950s, the division of Europe into a capitalist western and communist eastern half ended centuries-old patterns of east-west migrations. Migration in Eastern Europe was mainly internal, while in Western Europe the economic take-off of the 1950s resulted in a south-north labor migration system. Workers were expected to stay only for a limited period of time as "guest workers." Recruitment came to include West Asian men and women, especially from North Africa and Anatolia (western Turkey). In this period, Europe's colonizer countries lost their hold over dependent regions in Africa and Asia, and as a result three types of migration occurred: return of administrative, military, and commercial personnel; reverse migration of the descendants of nineteenth-century settler migrants; and in-migration of workers and refugees from the newly independent states.

In the third period, from the 1980s, Europe as a whole became an immigration region and, after the 1989 collapse of Eastern European communism, new east-west migrations commenced, if on a small scale. As regards migration and cultural contact, the borderlands of southeast Europe and West Asia became an area of contested belonging: Armenian refugees are usually considered European, as are Anatolian labor migrants and Jews in Israel. Other peoples of the same region, Palestinians and Ossetians, for example, are usually not considered European.

EUROPE AS A REFUGEE-GENERATING CONTINENT

In the decades before 1914 the nationalist impulses in Europe's empires imperiled the historic many-cultured coexistence of peoples, and at the beginning of World War I most of the five million intra-European migrants, who did not live in their state of birth, were suddenly labeled "enemy aliens." Then wartime displacement mobilized millions. Throughout history, Europe's peoples had migrated and established homes in culturally mixed rural and urban spaces, so that no political-national borderlines could neatly divide distinct ethno-cultural or "national" settlement areas. When the Versailles Treaty of 1919 moved borders over people, some twenty million Europeans found themselves living outside of the states they ethnically belonged to. The new nation-state governments, in an attempt to "unmix" peoples and to homogenize populations, expelled nonnational cultural groups and attracted conationals from outside the new borders. Population exchanges were imposed in the realm of the former Ottoman Empire on peoples of Bulgarian, Greek, and Turkish culture, and in the east central European region on German- and Slavic-language peoples. Millions migrated under duress.

In Russia, the Revolution of 1917 and the subsequent Russian civil war (1918–1920), resulted in several refugee movements. First, supporters of the old tsarist regime fled; then, political dissidents who differed with the Bolshevist regime left. So did members of the middle classes. Berlin and Paris became their centers. However, in the 1920s the expectation that the republic of the proletariat would become as dynamic a society as the middle-class republic of the United States had been, motivated some migration to the Soviet Union. Parallel, prewar migrants and emigrants returned to their newly independent countries of origin, especially the Polish and the Baltic states. Anti-Polish discrimination in Germany led tens of thousands of migrant worker families to move to jobs in Belgium and France.

Fascist rule in Italy after 1922, the accession to power of the Nazi Party in Germany in 1933, and the 1936 insurgency of General Francisco Franco (1892–1975) in republican Spain marked the beginning of flight from fascist persecution. Political dissidents and trade unionists migrated from Italy to France and from Germany to many states in Europe. The Spanish civil war (1936–1939), on the other hand, attracted political sympathizers who came in support of the Republican forces. Internally, millions fled the troops of the Falange (the fascist party in Spain), and after the collapse of the Republic in 1939 about 450,000 crossed the border to France. In Germany the Nazis' virulently anti-Semitic stance led to emigration and, soon, flight of Jewish Germans. By 1939 the Third Reich's policy and the beginning of World War II prevented escape. People fled as far as Latin America and China (Harbin and Shanghai in particular). Jewish flight to Palestine, later Israel, was to set in motion a vast refugee movement of Palestinian Arabs, the majority of which were of Islamic faith, in the late 1940s.

Throughout this period the traditional migration to North America stagnated. In 1914 the war had stopped migration to, as well as return migration from, the United States. The latter had amounted to about one third of the "immigrants," many of whom were and intended to be temporary workers. Migration resumed in the immediate postwar years but was countered by United States exclusion laws directed in particular against Eastern and southern Europeans, at the time identified as racially inferior because of the "dark" or "olive" color of their skin. The Great Depression after 1929 further reduced propensity to emigrate while increasing the numbers of earlier migrants who returned from the United States to reenter the supportive networks of their families in Europe. After 1933 only few of the refugees from fascism were accepted in the United States and Canada. Following the Evian Conference on the Question of Refugees of July 1938, one observer aptly noted that the refugee-generating fascist regimes were surrounded by refugee-refusing democracies. To negotiate an end to the chaos of expulsions as well as to ensure procedures of property transfer, U.S. diplomats insisted on establishing an Intergovernmental Committee on Refugees. Governments in the receiving societies wanted to ensure that refugees came with means and did not burden social

welfare services. Many of those excluded ended up in extermination camps.

In the 1930s, both the Soviet Union and Nazi Germany, for different reasons, established regimes of forced labor that mobilized many millions of men, women, and even children. In the Soviet Union, massive industrialization and mining projects required workers in regions with no native labor force. Collectivization of agriculture uprooted millions of peasant families and caused famine migrations. Rural-urban migrations in European Russia assumed unprecedented proportions, and the urban population more than doubled from 1921 to 1931. At the same time, skilled industrial workers had to migrate to the countryside to help mechanize agricultural production. The Stalinist government's system of forced labor was to involve, by 1941, more than twelve million people—but estimates vary widely. It lasted to the mid-1950s.

Parallel, the Nazi regime, at first hostile to non-Germanic working people, began to pursue its rearmament strategy and encouraged temporary in-migration of foreign workers. After the occupation of Eastern Europe in 1939, the Slavic populations, whom the Nazis considered racially inferior, were forced to labor for the Nazi war machine. By 1945 some seven million people had been deported to the Third Reich for forced labor. The Reich's troops also dislocated Polish and Ukrainian people en masse to make room for "Aryan"-German settlers. After the war, millions of these "displaced persons" (DPs) had to return home if coming from Western-occupied countries, or were left stranded if unwilling to return to the eastern countries under Soviet occupation. The United States, in a special program, admitted some 450,000 DPs, including survivors from the death camps. Others migrated to Australia and Canada.

The consequences of the war involved another unmixing of peoples. Some eleven to twelve million German-language people were expelled from Poland and regions farther east. The Polish state as a whole was moved west, and Poles expelled from the region coming under Russian Soviet control were forced to migrate to the western, formerly German, regions. In western Europe, refugees from occupation and war slowly made their way back to their homes if still existing. Because the

Polish emigrants wait to board a ship, 1927. ©BETTMANN/CORBIS

war-devastated economies seemed to provide no prospects for the future, transatlantic emigration resumed, but with the economic take-off in the 1950s this pattern of mass migration that had begun in the 1820s came to an end. Only from the surplus populations of Portugal and Italy did hundreds of thousands continue to migrate to Canada into the 1960s.

SOUTH-NORTH LABOR MIGRATIONS SINCE THE 1950S

Nineteenth-century labor migrations—from Europe's peripheral circle of Ireland, Scandinavia, Eastern Europe, and southern Europe to the highly industrialized core of Britain, France, Germany, Austria, and Switzerland—had continued on a far reduced scale during the 1920s and the 1930s. When, at the end of the 1940s, the United States' Marshall Plan encouraged reconstruction and economic growth in Western Europe, a shortage of workers in the core countries was felt as early as the 1950s. Britain integrated DPs; former German prisoners of war

stayed as workers in France; West Germany began to recruit laborers in Italy, and Irish still migrated to Britain, Italians to France, and Spanish to France and Germany. In northern Europe, Sweden began to attract labor, and Finns, especially Finnish citizens of Swedish ancestry, came. Eastern Europe was cut off by the Iron Curtain, and internal German east-west migrations ended with the construction of the Berlin Wall in 1961.

Though exit rules were liberalized in Poland and less so in Hungary, migration in the two Europes, with labor migration from Yugoslavia excepted, remained separate till 1989. In Eastern Europe, rural-urban and interregional migration systems operated, for example from Poland to Budapest, Hungary. Mediterranean Europe became the labor reservoir for the north. In the 1950s, Italy's conservative government initiated a labor migration program to rid itself of the unemployed (and the Socialist and Communist parties of potential voters). Men and women from the

Iberian Peninsula (Spain and Portugal), Italy, Yugoslavia, Greece, and finally from Turkey migrated to northwestern Europe. In France they mixed with migrants from the North African colonies. South-north mobility, encouraged and managed by intergovernmental agreements, followed the classic patterns of job availability, formation of cultural communities, and sequential moves. Historic links, whether cultural, economic, and/or political, and power relationships influenced decisions about destinations.

Receiving countries' recruitment policies to import temporary workers during labor shortages and return them during periods of recession were designed to "cushion" economic cycles by preventing wage increases in boom periods and high unemployment during economic downturns. Thus, no immigration policies were developed, rather the prewar concept of rotatory labor was continued. European attitudes toward temporary labor migrants remained diametrically opposed to North American concepts of immigration. To avoid the "foreign worker" label, used in Nazi Germany, as well as the rights-conferring term *immigrant*, the newcomers were colloquially called "guest workers." At first they filled shortages in skilled or semiskilled industrial sectors and subsequently in the service sector. Under continuous economic growth, and by taking jobs that native workers no longer accepted in view of wages and working conditions, migrants became structurally indispensable in the core countries. When the Italian and Iberian regions of recruitment no longer delivered workers, Yugoslav, Turkish, and North African workers began to be admitted.

Government-controlled labor recruitment ended after the oil-price increase of 1973. Contrary to administrators' projections of return, migrants initiated a family-reunion phase. To them, it made no sense to go back to unemployment-threatening societies of origin, and humanitarian concerns in receiving societies prevented involuntary repatriation. While not accepted to citizenship, labor migrants became "denizens" enrolled in social security systems. Thus, in the economic crisis of the late 1970s, they did not have to rely on family support at "home"—in fact, it had become unclear where home was. Transculturally competent migrants joined labor movements and participated in strikes; in some industries they had higher rates of unionization than native-born workers. Since the late 1970s, some fourteen to fifteen million "foreigners" resided in Western European countries, ranging from 3.3 percent of the population in Great Britain via a middle range of 6.5 to 9.0 percent in France, Germany, and Belgium, to 16 percent in Switzerland in 1989. In several states, even migrants' locally born children were forced to retain the status of "foreigners."

SOUTH-NORTH REVERSE MIGRATION AFTER DECOLONIZATION AND IMMIGRATION

In Asia and Africa, the European colonizers had set up regimes of bound labor and had relied on such workers to support their military campaigns. During World War I, some two hundred thousand men were brought to France and Britain; another million supported the British elsewhere. In the interwar period small settlements of African and Asian sailors and dockworkers emerged in many of Europe's port cities. Students from the colonies questioned their political and cultural position relative to the colonizing power: African students in France developed the concept of "negritude," Indian students in Great Britain the antecedents of "subaltern" and "postcolonial studies." Other migrants inserted themselves into the European labor movements and transferred practices of militancy back to their societies of origin. The number of these migrants was small, their stays temporary, their influence large.

After World War II, during which soldiers and workers from the colonies again supported the Allied war efforts, most of the colonies achieved independence through negotiation or wars of liberation. As a result, administrators, soldiers, and commercial personnel returned, and those descendants of former migrants to the colonies who would not or could not stay began a process of reverse migration. Some 5.5 to 8.5 million Italian, French, British, Belgian, Dutch, and other white colonials and nonwhite auxiliaries—colonials who had acted as local support staff for the colonizers—came before 1975. Mixed-origin families and their children faced racism; "colored" auxiliaries often ended up in camps or substandard housing.

"Home" governments assumed that nonwhite refugee auxiliaries would stay only temporarily, until conditions in their states of origin would permit return. However, in most cases, return never became an option, and European societies lost their white exclusiveness. "The empire strikes back," noted critics of colonialism.

During the postwar reconstruction and the 1950s mass production of consumer goods, former colonizing countries began to rely on labor from their (former) colonies in addition to the intra-European "guest workers." For example, demobilized and unemployed Jamaican soldiers came to the United Kingdom in 1948; uprooted Hindu, Sikh, and Muslim refugees from India and Pakistan arrived in the following years. By 1962, when the government tried to end immigration from nonwhite countries of the Commonwealth (a loose confederation of former members of the British Empire), some 430,000 nonwhite immigrants resided in the United Kingdom. In each of the next two decades about 450,000 arrived as families rather than as single male workers. In France a prewar North and West African community, numbering about 100,000 by 1939, provided supportive networks for those arriving since the 1950s. "Anticolored" exclusion bills remained ineffective. The former colonizer societies became multicolored against their will, but racism lost its hold only slowly. While France and Britain attempted to reduce migration by restrictive legislation and became multicultural against their will, the Dutch and Swedish societies began to reconstruct themselves in a conscious, but not unopposed, process of change.

Migration from the decolonizing Southern Hemisphere to socialist Eastern Europe remained small. Many of these migrants were connected to liberation movements or pro-Soviet governments, and their admission was categorized as "international solidarity." Migrants were positively segregated as political activists or negatively segregated as cheap labor and, thus, no everyday cultural exchange could develop. After 1989 these migrants found themselves in extremely precarious economic situations and faced further discrimination or expulsion.

CHANGES SINCE THE 1970S

Western Europe's overall migration balance in the 1950s was still negative, with a net loss of 2.7 million men, women, and children. It evened out during the 1960s and, from the 1970s, and clearly in the 1980s, Western Europe became an immigration region. The change was due first to demographic developments and their consequences: the aging of European populations and the resulting demand for service personnel, and high levels of training and educational achievement and the resulting reluctance of the younger generations to enter unskilled and low-income occupations. Second, it was an outcome of the previous guest-worker migrations: when recruitment ended in the mid-1970s, the workers did not return as postulated by population planners but engaged in strategies of family reunification. Third, in view of the imbalances of the global terms of trade and of the "gobal apartheid" between "white" high-standard-of-living and "colored" low-standard-of-living countries, Europe's economies attracted migrants from formerly colonized countries and from the Southern Hemisphere in general.

Compared to the south-north migrations and their potential in the future, post-1989 east-west migrations were limited. They included some 2.5 million, mostly temporary, refugees from the wars of dissolution of former Yugoslavia, who joined earlier migrating relatives; a few hundred thousand Polish and east central European seasonal workers; about 2.2 million "Aussiedler" (descendants of German emigrants to tsarist Russia) from the Commonwealth of Independent States in the decade after 1988; and several hundred thousand Russian Jews. In contrast, migration in post-1989 Eastern Europe, especially between Russia and the decolonizing newly independent states, involved an estimated twenty-five million migrants who regained the states of their particular ethnoculture. Since the mid-1990s, about half a million Chinese migrated seasonally or multiannually to the opportunities offered by the Russian economy.

Demography and statistical data notwithstanding, most Western European governments refused to develop immigration policies and concepts of multiculturalism. In the early 1990s the conservative German government categorically stated that the country—with about 10 percent of its population immigrants—was "not an immigration country." To prevent sizable east-west migrations from the ten new European Union (EU) member states of 2004, citizens of the latter have freedom to "circulate" to but not to migrate and take jobs in the "old" EU for a period of seven years—though some "old" EU countries permit admission under special regulations. Since the EU has no mandate to legislate in matters of immigration, intergovernmental agreements set policies: the Schengen Agreement (1985) created an internal zone of free mobility, while fortifying the barriers toward the outside ("fortress Europe"), and unified visa procedures for non-European entrants; the Dublin Convention (1990) changed policies and admission procedures as regards asylum seekers from protecting refugees to controlling in-migration; the Maastricht Treaty (1992) differentiated between EU- and non-EU Europeans; and in 1994 an "EU-citizens first" employment policy was announced.

In the mid-1990s, more than 60 percent of the "foreigners" in the EU had lived there for more than ten years and in North American terms of thinking would have been designated "immigrants." Many such "foreigners" are European-born children of immigrants who, under ius sanguinis (right of blood) provisions, remain foreigners by law. Of the 20 million interstate migrants in the "old" Europe (the original fifteen EU members) in 2000, 5 million were EU-internal migrants. The largest groups from neighboring regions came from Turkey (more than 3 million) and from the Maghreb (Morocco and Algeria, 2.3 million). Since the 1990s, the legal as well as undocumented migration from developing countries further away has increased, in particular from French- or English-language postcolonial states such as Pakistan, Sri Lanka, Senegal, and Ghana, but also from China. Figures amount to 1 million from sub-Saharan Africa and 2.2 million from Asia. Some 12 million Muslims live in Europe. Net immigration to Europe in 2000 amounted to 0.7 million, or 0.2 percent of the EU population. This compares to an annual immigration to Canada equal to about 1 percent of the population. Whatever the political declarations and the absence of immigration policies, since about 1980 Europe has been an immigration region.

See also **Displaced Persons; Refugees.**

BIBLIOGRAPHY

Bade, Klaus J. *Migration in European History.* Translated by Allison Brown. Malden, Mass., 2003.

Brass, Tom, and Marcel van der Linden, eds. *Free and Unfree Labour: The Debate Continues.* Bern, Switzerland, and New York, 1997.

Castles, Stephen, and Godula Kosack. *Immigrant Workers and Class Structure in Western Europe.* 2nd ed. Oxford, U.K., 1985.

Fassmann, Heinz, and Rainer Münz, eds. *European Migration in the Late Twentieth Century: Historical Patterns, Actual Trends, and Social Implications.* Aldershot, U.K., 1994.

Harzig, Christiane, and Danielle Juteau, with Irina Schmitt, eds. *The Social Construction of Diversity: Recasting the Master Narrative of Industrial Nations.* New York, 2003.

Hoerder, Dirk, with Christiane Harzig and Adrian Shubert, eds. *The Historical Practice of Diversity: Transcultural Interactions from the Early Modern Mediterranean to the Postcolonial World.* New York, 2003.

King, Russell, ed. *The New Geography of European Migrations.* London, 1993.

Kulischer, Eugene M. *Europe on the Move: War and Population Changes, 1917–47.* New York, 1948.

Marrus, Michael R. *The Unwanted: European Refugees in the Twentieth Century.* New York, 1985.

Moch, Leslie Page. *Moving Europeans: Migration in Western Europe since 1650.* 2nd ed. Bloomington, Ind., 2003.

Morokvasic, Mirjana, and Hedwig Rudolph, eds. *Migrants: Les nouvelles mobilités en Europe.* Paris, 1996.

DIRK HOERDER

IMPERIAL TROOPS. Imperial troops played a role in almost all the conflicts of the first half of the twentieth century. They fall into two distinct categories: the mainly white or mixed-race recruits who were citizens of the imperium, like the inhabitants of the British Dominions (Canada, Australia, New Zealand, and South Africa) or the French citizens with voting rights in Algeria and coastal Senegal, and those who were indigenous colonial subjects, the so-called native troops. The extensive use of native troops by the colonial powers became common with the rise of imperialism in the second half of the

Amadou Hampaté Bâ (1900–1991), a writer of Mali:

When the survivors returned home in 1918–19, they caused a new social phenomenon that would have long term consequences on the mentalities: I want to speak of the *collapse of the myth of the white man* as an invincible and exemplary human being.... Indeed, up to that moment, the white man had been considered a different being.... But, since then, the black soldiers had made war in the trenches alongside their white comrades. They had seen heroes, courageous men, but they had also seen the ones who were crying, who screamed and who were afraid. They had discovered crooks and depraved, and even, something unthinkable, almost unbelievable, they had seen in the cities white thieves, white poor people, and even white beggars!

When these *Tirailleurs* returned home, they told, during the long evenings, everything they had seen. No, the white man was not a superman ...

It's there, in 1919, that started to blow for the first time a spirit of emancipation and of claims, that would in the end develop in other layers of the population.

Source: Amadou Hampaté Bâ, *Sur les traces d'Amkoullel, l'enfant peul.* Paris, 1998. Author's translation.

---

modern war in Europe. Contemporary assessments referred to savage ferocity and low intelligence as the defining characteristics of nonwhite soldiery. During both world wars few belligerent powers employed colored or black troops in combat roles on European soil. This was partly due to racial prejudice but also because most colonial powers considered Europe's wars as exclusively white men's wars. They were afraid to put the white men's prestige at stake.

All the colonial powers possessed a hierarchy of perceived "martial races." The perfect "martial race" was an ethnic group that produced men who were both martial and loyal. Thus for example, Gurkhas, Hausa, Toucouleur, and Bambara were believed to be better warriors than others. Until the 1940s the martial races doctrine also provided the ideological foundation for the Indian army, where caste was played off against caste and weapons were restricted to those groups least likely to use them against their masters. The goal was to foster group spirit through rivalry and competition among units and to avoid the kind of cultural homogeneity that was seen as in part responsible for the mutinies of the past. Companies of a battalion in the Indian army might be divided by ethnicity, but they would all share the same regimental identity.

WORLD WAR I

World War I (1914–1918) brought changes. All the belligerent states suffered huge military manpower shortages. As a result more than 600,000 nonwhite soldiers from the French and British colonies were present in the European theater of war. Among them were 270,000 North Africans, 134,000 West Africans, and 153,000 Indians. Britain and France also recruited a large Asian and North African labor force for work in France. For almost the first time, the British employed Indian soldiers to fight a white enemy as regular troops under European command. Poorly motivated, ill-prepared, and suffering from the racist attitudes of their commanders, their small battalions were withdrawn in 1915, with a very high number of casualties. Despite growing pressure, the War Office refused to use black troops in combat roles because it was deemed undesirable to put them on a par with white men. To preserve established hierarchies of race and masculinity, black soldiers were mostly

---

nineteenth century. To guard and secure their new territories, the British made extensive use of their recruits from the North Indian plains, and the French of their *Tirailleurs* (riflemen) from North Africa and French West Africa. Enlistment in the armed forces was supposed to be voluntary, but a good deal of pressure was often exerted through local chiefs. The army offered paid employment, welfare services, regular food for the man and his family, clothing, status, and new loyalties not only to the army, but also an identification with the colonial authority. The vast majority of Asian and black imperial troops recruited in this way were illiterate, rural non-Christians, often with little idea of what their tasks might be. No longer the enemy of past colonial wars, they had become an arm of the imperium, loyally or pragmatically united in the great imperial cause. In fact it brought men into the army whose backgrounds made them a poor choice to fight a

From an official report (1918) of the French authorities:

Conditions of life in France will allow the native to develop an unaccustomed familiarity in his dealings with Whites. Having seen our weaknesses, he will seriously damage our prestige with the stories he tells when he gets home.

Source: Christopher M. Andrew and A. S. Kanya-Forstner, *France Overseas: The Great War and the Climax of French Imperial Expansion* (London, 1981), 141.

confined to labor battalions. From 1916 on, more colored recruits from British West Indies Regiments (BWIR) and South Africa (the Cape Coloured Labour Corps and the twenty-thousand-strong South African Native Labour Contingent) were sent to Europe, but they were used mainly in support roles and they were paid less than soldiers in British regiments. The South African authorities also feared arming black soldiers and allowing them to fight against Europeans. At the end of the war, mutinies occurred among colonial troops, occasioned by the slow process of demobilization resulting from shipping shortages and the priority given to white soldiers returning home.

Only the French used their North and West African soldiers as front-line troops in every corner of their empire, whether for the defense of the mother country, for conquest (Morocco and other African countries), for occupation (Rhineland, Middle East), or for counterinsurgency (North Africa, Vietnam). Unlike the British, the French saw their West African colonies as a vast reservoir of soldiers. In 1909 General Charles-Marie-Emmanuel Mangin (1866–1925) started the international discussion about the use of colored troops when he pleaded for the *Force noire* (black force) to help compensate for France's stagnant birthrate and the consequent military imbalance with Germany. He believed his *Tirailleurs Sénégalais* (soldiers from French sub-Saharan Africa) to be brave warriors for their strong physique and lack of a nervous system. Their first experiences on the front line in northern France were a disaster, but this did not result in their withdrawal. Statistics do not suggest

that their casualty rates were significantly higher than those of their white counterparts, but in certain localities such as Chemin des Dames (1917) and Reims (1918), they did sustain substantial losses. Whether they were used as cannon fodder because of the racist attitudes of their commanders remains difficult to ascertain. More than 20 percent of the approximately 134,000 *Tirailleurs Sénégalais* thrown into the murderous battles of the western front did not return home, not least because of the diseases they caught in the inhospitable European climate. Although their contribution to the French army's effectives had been largely symbolic (1.6 percent) and their combat effectiveness questionable, it nevertheless represented a heavy burden on sparsely populated African peasant societies. More important was the contribution of French North Africa, which provided 270,000 combatants who, like the British Dominion troops, had the reputation of being among the best in the field. These French colonial troops were completed with more than 43,000 soldiers from French Indochina, 41,000 from Madagascar, and 22,000 from the West Indies.

Throughout French West Africa, a system of general military conscription had been in place. Troops were recruited with the aid of the first African deputy, Blaise Diagne (1872–1934), who thought that the French would grant political rights in exchange. Similar expectations were held by other colonial soldiers, such as the British West Indian Regiments. The success of Diagne as high commissioner of recruitment of black troops contributed significantly to the government's decision to maintain colonial conscription after the war. The General Conscription Act of 1919 guaranteed a continuing supply of men. In the French colonial army, which was less color-conscious than the British, about one in ten officers was black, either African or Caribbean.

Spain also used recruits from its North African possessions in its armed forces. In 1934, on the advice of the then general Francisco Franco (1892–1975), the Spanish Republican government specifically employed Moroccan troops in the suppression of the Asturias rising. During the civil war, General Franco used between sixty and seventy thousand of these so-called Moors from North Africa as part of the nationalist army. As in the case of the French African soldiers, the much feared Moors were also used as a psychological weapon by their

French colonial troops from Africa fight in the trenches in France during World War I. Undated photograph.
©Bettmann/Corbis

commanders. Other European colonial states, such as Portugal, Belgium, Italy, and the Netherlands, also raised troops from indigenous populations before and after the First World War, but never used them in Europe.

In spite of the fact that the German armed forces had raised colonial troops in their African possessions, from the Second Moroccan Crisis (1911) onward, the German press had portrayed African soldiers as bloodthirsty barbarians. During the First World War, the novelist Thomas Mann (1875–1955) and the sociologist Max Weber (1864–1920) spoke for many Germans and non-Germans when they expressed indignation that Western civilization would be betrayed if the white civilized nations made use of the inferior races. The horror stories about charcoal-black Africans cutting off ears, noses, and heads of German soldiers found

a large German audience. After 1918 the propaganda campaign against what was called the "Black Shame" reached its climax when African soldiers, who were part of the French occupying forces in the Rhineland, were reported as roaming out of control across the Rhineland, raping German women at will, infecting the population with venereal diseases, and "polluting" German blood. During the overtly racist campaign against the "Black horror on the Rhine," the Germans not only mobilized world opinion against France but also shaped expectations of black troops' behavior. Colonial soldiers' alleged sexual attacks became the dominant subject of German propaganda; a propaganda war that was to be continued by the Nazis and that goes a long way to explaining the brutal way in which captured African soldiers were treated as prisoners of war.

As far as the white troops of the British Dominions are concerned, Australia, New Zealand, Canada, and South Africa all possessed armed forces of their own. The New Zealand and Australian imperial forces were both volunteer services that were sent overseas in both world wars. During the preparations for the landings at Gallipoli in 1915, the Australian and New Zealand Army Corps became known as the ANZACs. Gallipoli was to become a focal point of Australian life, and Anzac Day on 25 April became Australia's true (though unofficial) national day and served to define the identity of the young country. The ANZACs lost more than eleven thousand men at Gallipoli, and a further sixty thousand were to die on Flanders fields, at the Somme, and at Verdun. At the beginning of World War I, the use of Canadian forces on behalf of the British Empire was complicated by the French minorities hostile to the war, and individual Canadians thus enlisted in British units. From January 1916 onward, the Canadian Expeditionary Force (CEF) fought on the western front, suffering approximately 10 percent casualties.

WORLD WAR II

In World War II (1939–1945), Dominion forces played important roles in all theaters of war. South African, Canadian, and ANZAC troops were used in North Africa, Italy, and later in northwestern Europe. However, even more vigorously than in World War I, the nonwhite South African troops were restricted to noncombat roles. The Canadians lost about 14 percent of their troops in battle and through disease, the Australians 13 percent, and the New Zealanders 12.5 percent. ANZAC forces included some indigenous peoples. Maori participation was not accorded specific, separate, attention, unlike indigenous participation in Canada and Australia. These indigenous people had enlisted for various reasons, not the least being that their fathers and grandfathers had served in the First World War. The Australian Aborigines' enlistment was specifically linked to preexisting campaigns for citizenship rights.

In many ways this conflict mirrored that of World War I. Native troops fought again as well, in the Mediterranean, in Asia, and in Africa, releasing European forces for service in Europe. In World War II African troops constituted a much larger percentage of French total forces than in the First World War. Although the blacks were not excluded in the British services in either war, very few black men—or women—served in the British army, and none in the Royal Navy, although there were black and Indian seamen. In the United Kingdom, conscription was introduced in May 1939, and the globalization of war meant extensive use of non-European troops in other theaters like North Africa and Burma, where Indians and Africans made up over two-thirds of the "British" imperial forces. Most men in uniform had noncombatant roles as laborers, drivers, guards, and orderlies. Over two and a half million Indian citizens served during the war, most of them outside Europe, although the 8th and 10th Division participated in the taking of Monte Cassino. Italy became the most heterogeneous theater of war, and saw the contribution of many colonies and dominions: Canadians, West Indians, New Zealanders, Maoris, Indians, Gurkhas, Ceylonese, Seychellois, Mauritians, South Africans, Rhodesians, Basuto, Bechuana, and Swazi troops, *Tirailleurs Sénégalais*, North African goums, Zouaves, and Spahis fought side by side in the British and French armies. Not only in Italy but also during the second Rhineland occupation Moroccan soldiers were accused of sexual assaults.

LEGACIES

Never before had so many colored men stayed so long in Europe's cities and villages. Colonial soldiers and workers were left with experiences that changed their lives, particularly their perceptions of themselves and of the colonizers—precisely what the colonial authorities feared most. Until then, the Europeans were supposed to protect the "primitive races," but now this situation was reversed and the idea of inherent white supremacy seemed under siege. In the Second World War the imperial troops serving in the Far East witnessed the destruction of the myth of European invincibility as the Japanese overran South East Asia. The European powers therefore feared that demobilized soldiers might act as catalysts for resistance against white rule on their return. This "moral panic" about the impact that large numbers of men with experience of military service might have on the social and political order of the colonies was not to become a reality, as most demobilized colonial soldiers were reabsorbed into postwar society with relative ease. Most veterans appropriated the imagery of heroism and military sacrifice to convince the often skeptical members of their community back home. African veterans occasionally claimed that their wartime military experiences had inspired them to anticolonial activity, but the overwhelming majority were preoccupied with economic concerns. Returning native soldiers could be more assertive in their attitude but remained for the most part loyal to their motherland despite the fact that they had every reason to feel resentment. The payment of wartime bonuses, large sums in prewar terms, proved shockingly parsimonious in the light of inflation. Also, many soldiers had not been granted their full pensions, a recurring grievance of almost all imperial veterans. This occasionally caused revolts like the one in Thiaroye (Senegal), where thirty-five returning African former-POWs were killed during a mutiny by the French authorities in December 1944. (Thiaroye was to become the national shrine of the West African struggle for independence.) However, only in Algeria did war veterans play significant roles in the political movements that led to decolonization. More important was the psychological and sociological transformation of the soldiers and workers who had left their traditional values in Europe. They had developed an alternative masculinity that combined local ideas with those derived from other African or Asian cultures and the culture from the motherland. They had learned linguistic and technological skills that they hoped would enable them to earn a better living once they returned home. Not all their political and economic hopes and aspirations were to be met in the postwar years, but, paradoxically, for many Africans, African Americans, and Asians the army had been the "school of equality."

See also **Armies; British Empire; Colonialism; French Empire; Warfare.**

BIBLIOGRAPHY

Primary Sources

Diallo, Bakary. *ForceBonté.* Paris, 1985.

Omissi, David, ed. *Indian Voices of the Great War: Soldiers' Letters, 1914–18.* New York, 1999.

Secondary Sources

Clayton, Anthony. *France, Soldiers, and Africa.* London, 1988.

Echenberg, Myron. *Colonial Conscripts: The Tirailleurs Sénégalais in French West Africa, 1857–1960.* London, 1991.

Grundlingh, Albert. *Fighting Their Own War: South African Blacks in the First World War.* Johannesburg, 1986.

Killingray, David, and David Omissi, eds. *Guardians of Empire: The Armed Forces of Colonial Powers, c. 1700–1964.* Manchester, U.K., 1999.

Koller, Christian. *"Von Wilden aller Rassen niedergemetzelt": Die Diskussion um die Verwendung von Kolonialtruppen in Europa zwischen Rassismus, Kolonial- und Militärpolitik (1914–1930).* Stuttgart, 2001.

———. "Enemy Images: Race and Gender Stereotypes in the Discussion on Colonial Troops. A Franco-German Comparison, 1914–1923." In *Home/Front: The Military, War, and Gender in Twentieth-Century Germany,* edited by Karen Hagemann and Stefanie Schüler-Springorum, 139–157. Oxford, U.K., and New York, 2002.

Lunn, Joe. *Memoirs of Maelstrom: A Senegalese Oral History of the First World War.* Portsmouth, N.H., 1999.

Michel, Marc. *L'appel à l'Afrique: Contributions et réactions à l'effort de guerre en AOF (1914–1919).* Paris, 1982. Reprint, slightly renamed and modified as *Les Africains et la Grande Guerre: L'appel à l'Afrique (1914–1918).* Paris, 2003.

Perry, Frederick William. *Commonwealth Armies: Manpower and Organisation in Two World Wars.* Manchester, U.K., 1988.

Ruano, Francisco Sánchez. *Islam y Guerra civil española: Moros con Franco y con la República.* Madrid, 2004.

Smith, Richard. *Jamaican Volunteers in the First World War: Race, Masculinity, and the Development of National Consciousness.* Manchester, U.K., 2004.

DICK VAN GALEN LAST

INDIA. British colonial rule in India, established formally in 1757, lasted for almost two centuries. Ironically, however, it was when the territorial extension of the Indian Empire had reached its apogee with the final conquest of Burma in 1885 that the first stirrings of organized Indian nationalist opposition also began to manifest themselves.

EARLY NATIONALISM

The emergence of a structured movement of anti-colonial resistance in India is conventionally traced to the Indian National Congress established in December 1885. Its early membership was elite, urban, and Western-educated. Its methods and demands were moderate, petitioning for greater Indian participation in imperial governance and economic policies that would develop, not impoverish, India. Gradually a more militant strand emerged that declared self-rule a "birthright" and advocated assertive strategies of boycott to achieve it. These "extremists" also reached out to the masses but the symbols around which they mobilized—Hindu deities and historical figures—often alienated religious minorities.

Forming a quarter of India's population, most Muslims remained aloof from the Congress. Indeed, the reformer Syed Ahmed Khan (1817–1898) had warned that political activism by a community lagging educationally and economically behind the Hindu majority would mean its eventual obliteration. In December 1906, a few leading Muslims gathered in Dacca (eastern Bengal) to found the All India Muslim League. Earlier in October, a delegation of Muslim landlords had met with the viceroy to demand separate electorates and weighted representation for Muslims, a concession embodied in the Indian Councils Act of 1909. Elite Muslim and imperial interests dovetailed to represent Indians as divided into distinct communities requiring separate representation.

INDIA IN THE WORLD WARS

In August 1914, Britain unilaterally declared India a combatant in World War I. At first nationalists like Mohandas Karamchand Gandhi (1869–1948) supported the British in hopes of substantial political reward. Although Edwin Montagu (1879–1924), secretary of state for India, proclaimed on 20 August 1917 the new British policy of the "progressive realization of responsible government in India," reforms in 1919 disappointed even moderate nationalists, granting only less important provincial powers to Indians. Separate electorates were retained and the franchise restricted to propertied and educated men usually loyal to the Raj (imperial government). These meager concessions were offset by the Rowlatt Acts of 1919, which perpetuated draconian wartime measures such as the detention of Indians without trial. And on 13 April 1919, General Reginald Dyer (1864–1927) fired at an illegal but unarmed assembly that, unaware of the imposition of martial law, had gathered at the Jallianwallah park in Amritsar (Punjab), leaving 379 dead and over 1,200 injured. Becoming a symbol of colonial injustice, this act provoked widespread protest.

The deleterious economic impact of the war on India's poor, especially the shortage and high price of essential commodities, laid the groundwork for Gandhi's mass nationalism. Furthermore, the postwar dismemberment of the Ottoman Empire, whose sultan claimed to be the caliph of Sunni Muslims, provided an opportunity for a Congress alliance with Indian Muslims. Capturing the party's leadership in 1920, Gandhi launched a combined nonviolent noncooperation and pro-caliphate movement rallying Hindus and Muslims on parallel, though separate, platforms. Mohammed Ali Jinnah (1876–1948), until then a member both of Congress and the League, resigned from the former in protest against this welding of religion and politics. Gandhi's call to boycott British goods and institutions was heeded by large numbers of Indians. However, far from singlehandedly awakening popular ferment, Gandhi capitalized on already widespread labor and peasant unrest, channeling it along Congress's lines but never fully controlling it. Indeed, he was forced to call off noncooperation when in February 1922, breaching the dictate of nonviolence, angry peasants killed twenty-two policemen in the northern town of Chauri Chaura. In 1924, when Kemal Atatürk (1880–1938) abolished the office itself, the pro-caliphate movement also ended and earlier unity devolved into religious rioting in northern India.

Noncooperation remained dormant until the renewal of civil disobedience in the period from 1930 to 1934. Gandhi kicked off the movement in March 1930 with a 240-mile march to the sea to manufacture salt in violation of the government's monopoly. Thereafter, civil disobedience spread quickly, fanned by the economic dislocation of the Great Depression. The British replied with constitutional reform. The Government of India Act of 1935, while still maintaining firm colonial control at the center, enlarged the franchise to thirty-five million voters and provided fully elected Indian provincial governments. In the elections of 1937, the Congress benefited from its mass campaigns to win in eight of eleven provinces. The Muslim League, however, fared abysmally. In the two largest Muslim-majority provinces of Bengal and Punjab, cross-religious regional coalitions assumed power. Jinnah now revived the theory, first mooted by Syed Ahmed Khan in the 1880s, that Hindus and Muslims formed two equal nations as a way to trump the numerical minority of Muslims and to unite them across provinces.

Once again, in 1939, the viceroy announced India's entry into World War II without consulting Indians. This time Congress resigned its provincial ministries in protest. Now finding it convenient to endorse the League's claim that the Congress did not represent all Indians, the British pushed Jinnah to define his demands. Recent scholarship considers the League's Lahore Resolution of March 1940 an attempt to negotiate a power-sharing agreement for Muslims in India, not a call for partition. In formally asking for independent Muslim states in the northeast and northwest, Jinnah was pressing the more important stipulation that future constitutional arrangements be negotiated on the basis of a parity of "Hindustan" and "Pakistan" within India. Japan's bringing the war to Southeast Asia in 1942 produced fresh efforts to conciliate Indian opinion. On 8 August 1942, when negotiations had collapsed, Congress launched the Quit India movement, the largest civilian uprising since the rebellion of 1857. Far from leaving, however, the British responded with repression, using troops massed in India for the war.

BRITISH DECOLONIZATION IN INDIA

Domestic considerations combined with popular pressures in India pushed the eventual British offer of independence. For Britons emerging from the war, economic reconstruction at home took priority over diverting scarce human and material resources to reassert imperial control in India where political unrest had assumed worrisome proportions by 1945–1946. Apart from the growing nationalist orientation of the increasingly Indianized civil service, the vaunted "steel frame" of the Raj, British confidence in their Indian sword arms was also shaken. The Indian National Army,

formed from Indian POWs captured in Southeast Asia, had aligned with the Japanese in 1943–1945. The trial in late 1945 of three of its officers galvanized nationalist sympathy, turning these "deserters" into heroes, and spread to the Royal Indian Navy, whose ratings mutinied in Bombay from 18 to 23 February 1946.

In the elections of 1945–1946, while the Congress repeated its previous success, the League's performance improved spectacularly: it won all reserved central assembly seats and polled 75 percent of the provincial Muslim votes. With the League and Congress the only major parties left in the political fray, in March 1946 a high-powered British Cabinet Mission attempted to broker a constitutional arrangement for independent India. Their plan involved a three-tiered federation in which most powers would vest in three groupings of provinces—two comprising Muslim majority provinces in the east and west and the third the Hindu majority provinces. An arrangement that would have preserved Indian unity while satisfying the League demand for parity of representation through Muslim provinces that could influence the center, it was rejected by the Congress objecting precisely to the weak center. With this rebuff also went the last chance for an undivided India.

A frustrated League's call for "direct action" on 16 August 1946 to achieve Pakistan precipitated large-scale violence along the lines of religion in Bengal, Bihar and, later, Punjab. As northern India slid into chaos, on 20 February 1947 the prime minister Clement Attlee (1883–1967) announced a British departure by June 1948, moved up to August 1947 by the last viceroy Lord Louis Mountbatten (1900–1979). Upon Attlee's announcement, Hindu conservatives, followed by the Congress, called for a partition of Bengal and Punjab, separating Hindu from Muslim majority districts. Power was handed to Pakistan and India on 14–15 August 1947 in the midst of a bloodbath and the largest population transfer in South Asian history.

POSTCOLONIAL CONTINUITIES

While Jawaharlal Nehru (1889–1964), prime minister until his death in 1964, inaugurated a new era of nation-building and economic development in 1947, the colonial imprint on the postcolonial state

An Indian man blocks a cartload of British cloth during the boycott called by Mohandas Gandhi, September 1930. GETTY IMAGES

was striking. India was now a democratic, secular republic, but a remarkable 200 articles of its constitution were taken from the Government of India Act of 1935. Instituting a federal structure in which powers were shared between the union and the states, independent India retained provisions enabling the center to dismiss democratically elected but recalcitrant regional governments. Both Nehru and his daughter Indira Gandhi (1917–1984, prime minister in 1966–1977 and 1980–1984) perpetuated the colonial reliance on the nonelected administrative and police services to

shore up executive power. This top-heavy state, and sometimes vice-regal style of governance, was justified by the requirements of planned development in an impoverished country disrupted by the mayhem of partition. But one harmful result, particularly pronounced under and after Indira Gandhi, has been the decay of institutions that sustain democratic functioning from the grassroots up and a preference for personalized power. Postcolonial patterns of governance have veered between recourse to shortsighted populism and resort to authoritarianism to stem popular unrest (the most extreme example being the suspension of civil liberties during the Emergency in 1975–1977). In the 1980s these reflexes provoked secessionist movements in Punjab, the Northeast, and Kashmir.

HINDU NATIONALISM

Gandhi's assassination on 30 January 1948 by Nathuram Godse (1910–1949) was a dramatic reminder of the existence of a Hindu nationalism in place since the Hindu Mahasabha's (Greater Hindu Society) foundation in 1915. Though obscured by the Congress in the anticolonial movement, the two shared many members and ideals. Hindu nationalism, inspired by Vinayak Damodar Savarkar's idea of "Hindutva" (Hinduness) defining the core of the Indian nation, acquired a militant edge with the founding, in 1925, of the Rashtriya Swayamsevak Sangh, a formally apolitical paramilitary group propounding aggressively anti-Muslim ideas. Driven into the shadows after Gandhi's assassination, by the 1980s the Hindu Right reorganized itself sufficiently for the Bharatiya Janata Party (BJP)—evolved from the Mahasabha—to lead a national coalition government from 1998 to 2004. This recuperation was enabled partly by Congress's tendency, particularly in the 1980s, to buttress its weakening electoral and social bases of support by whipping up fears of a national unity threatened by religious minorities (the Sikhs in Punjab and Kashmiri Muslims). Such espousal of a majoritarian nationalism made ideological room for the BJP. To expand beyond its core base—upper caste, middle and lower class, urban and semi-urban, from the Hindi-speaking north—the BJP's rhetoric downplayed class and caste difference to emphasize religious unity. Muslims provided convenient targets against which to mobilize. With the insurgency in Kashmir "confirming" their "inherent disloyalty," since 1990 the BJP also made a sixteenth-century mosque in Ayodhya—allegedly built over a temple marking the birthplace of the deity Ram—symbolic of all the majority's woes. Though Hindu activists destroyed the mosque in December 1992, the campaign to build a temple on the site remains central to the BJP program, conveniently revived since their ouster from power in May 2004.

KASHMIR

While most of the 560-odd princely states of India were quietly absorbed by the country within whose territory they found themselves in 1947, the dispute over Kashmir brought India and Pakistan to war within two months of their independence. Physically wedged between the two, Muslim-majority Kashmir's integration touches vitally on the national ideals espoused by both. While on the one hand Pakistan's identity as a homeland for India's Muslims remains incomplete without Kashmir, on the other, the presence of Kashmir's Muslims in the union vindicates India's claim to being a religiously inclusive secular state. Following a cease-fire in 1949, two-thirds of the region has been under Indian and the remaining third under Pakistani control. Further bedeviling resolution of the Kashmir dilemma, a largely popular insurgency continuing since 1989—partly aided by Pakistan but mostly provoked by underdevelopment, corruption, and interference by the Indian center—has made clear that many Kashmiris themselves want independence from both postcolonial states. However, the Indian-administered portion includes, besides Kashmir, the sub-regions of Jammu and Ladakh, with large Hindu and Buddhist populations respectively, in favor of remaining with India. Despite periodic diplomatic parleys, the region remains a potential flashpoint between the now nuclear-armed countries and the dispute one of the most enduring, unresolved legacies of decolonization.

See also **British Empire; British Empire, End of; Colonialism; Gandhi, Mahatma; Pakistan.**

BIBLIOGRAPHY

Bose, Sumantra. *Kashmir: Roots of Conflict, Paths to Peace.* Cambridge, Mass., 2003.

Brass, Paul R. *The Politics of India since Independence.* Cambridge, U.K., 1990.

Guha, Ranajit, and Gayatri Chakravorty Spivak, eds. *Selected Subaltern Studies.* New York, 1988.

Jaffrelot, Christophe. *The Hindu Nationalist Movement in India.* New York, 1996.

Jalal, Ayesha. *The Sole Spokesman: Jinnah, the Muslim League, and the Demand for Pakistan.* Cambridge, U.K., 1985.

Khilnani, Sunil. *The Idea of India.* New York, 1998.

Sarkar, Sumit. *Modern India: 1885–1947.* New Delhi, 1983.

van der Veer, Peter. *Religious Nationalism: Hindus and Muslims in India.* Berkeley, Calif., 1994.

MRIDU RAI

INDOCHINA.

French colonial Indochina was a federation of protectorates, kingdoms, and colonies comprising Laos, Cambodia, Tonkin, Annam, and Cochinchina—the last three since subsumed into the borders of modern-day Vietnam. Named Indochina by the French because they situated it at the crossroads of Chinese and Indian influences, it was created by gradual accretion. It should not be confused with the more general term *Indochina*, designating a vast swath of Southeast Asia, often taken to include Thailand.

THE PROCESS OF COLONIZATION

Although the kingdom of Nam-Viet was established in 207 B.C.E., and Vietnamese independence from China was again achieved in the tenth century of the common era, neither the contours of Vietnam nor certainly the space known as Indochina came into focus until the French colonial era. Colonial conquest had been preceded by the influence of French missionaries, most notably members of the Société des Missions Étrangères, present in the region for centuries. In the second half of the nineteenth century, the French Second Empire undertook military conquest of the region. French forces radiated from Saigon into Cambodia (Kampuchea) between 1859 and 1867. A second wave of expansion in 1884 sealed the French conquest, in spite of military reverses at the hands of the Chinese at Lang Son. Treaties in 1884 granted France a protectorate over Tonkin in the north and French tutelage over the Vietnamese court in Hue (capital of Annam). That same year, the kingdom of Cambodia was officially transformed into a French protectorate. In 1893, under pressure from French gunboat diplomacy, neighboring Siam (later Thailand) recognized French rule over Laos, which France had claimed since 1887. The resulting federation of Indochinese regions known as the "Indochinese Union" constituted an ill-defined patchwork of languages and alphabets (Vietnamese, Laotian, Hmong, Khmer, among others), ethnic identities (highland minorities, ethnic Vietnamese, ethnic Khmer, ethnic Lao, ethnic Thai, etc.), religions (Confucianism, cult of ancestors, Theravada Buddhism, Catholicism), and government models (kingdoms, protectorates, and states).

INSTRUMENTS OF COLONIAL DOMINATION AND CONTROL

The French navy played a dominant role in both the conquest and administration of Indochina. While the French army was granted considerable control over Algeria, the navy was given carte blanche over Indochina for much of the colony's existence (1859–1954). Vietnam's last emperor, Bao Dai, quipped that in Indochina "the sovereign may rule, but the French Admiral governs."

The French practiced a policy of dividing and conquering in Indochina by playing upon old antagonisms (for example, northern and southern Vietnam had once been at war in the seventeenth century and much of southern Vietnam had been under Kampuchean, or Cambodian, control until the nineteenth century). In so doing, the French became not only the arbiters of Indochina but also the cement that held this heterogeneous federation together. The French administration dispatched many ethnic Vietnamese to manage Laos and Cambodia but not vice versa. They also placed ethnic Vietnamese in prisons located in highland minority areas and attempted to forge alliances with some ethnic minorities in view of checking a perceived Vietnamese dominance. In some cases, these triangular tensions shaped the actual contours of Indochina, as in Laos and Cambodia, where the French became extremely sensitive to Thai designs and intrigues with ethnic Thais living in French Indochina. Border skirmishes with Siam (later Thailand) occurred during much of the French colonial era. Siam itself served as a buffer zone between French and British agents of influence.

ECONOMICS

Indochina attracted considerable investment and speculation in France, from its rubber plantations and Michelin's stakes in them to the powerful Banque d'Indochine. By 1940 Indochina emerged as the third largest global exporter of rubber. Conditions were notoriously cruel on these rubber plantations, where some 133,000 laborers toiled by

1942. French Indochina also produced considerable quantities of minerals and rice. Liquor and opium monopolies played prominent roles in the colonial economy. France also introduced large-scale planning and public works to Indochina. The trans-Indochinese railroad, undertaken between 1905 and 1936, provided not only a motor and showcase of development and modernization but also, more ironically, a catalyst of Vietnamese national unity.

RESISTANCE AND REPRESSION

The very first French forays in Indochina met considerable resistance, although the shapes and degrees of resistance certainly shifted over time. They included an initial wave of monarchist, conservative resistance, a subsequent pro-Japanese streak, and the emergence of multiple Marxist opposition movements, out of which the Indochinese Communist Party eventually triumphed. Uprisings at Yen Bay and by the Nghe Tinh soviets in 1930 were met with brutal repression by a colonial administration increasingly reduced to a policing role. By 1936, when police repression was actually slightly relaxed under the Popular Front government in France, Indochina's detention ratios were 2.3 times higher than those in France, and roughly 1.5 times higher than those in the neighboring Dutch East Indies (later Indonesia). At the zenith of incarceration in 1942, some thirty thousand prisoners, many of them political, languished in the retrograde and brutal French penal system, emblematized by the penitentiary island of Poulo Condore.

Already in 1917 the Thai Nguyen prison revolt had featured some of the nationalist claims of future struggles. However, most historians identify the Nghe Tinh soviets of 1930 as initiating a significant escalation and militarization in the French response to Indochinese communism. The heavy-handed tactics used by the French army to quell these uprisings anticipated the large-scale violence that would break out again a decade later.

COLONIAL LIFE AND CULTURE

Indochina evoked more than a simple geographical area: it came to embody a set of fantasies in the colonial imagination. This mythical Indochina occupied a central place in French literature, from Roland Dorgelès to Marguerite Duras, but also in architecture, art, and film. Beyond the romantic vision of Indochina disseminated in these media, Indochina was in reality a colony marked by hierarchies: the French administration itself was more stratified than at home, and the chasm between colonizer and colonized was considerable in terms of access to employment or education. The settler's universe was far removed from life in the metropole. A metropolitan French visitor described the average settler's situation unkindly: "[they obtain] land from free concessions, employees through forced labor, and remuneration through bonuses" (Meyer, p. 234). Throughout the colonial period, with a handful of exceptions like the French novelist Marguerite Duras, the small European community in Indochina (some thirty-nine thousand in 1940) enjoyed a luxurious lifestyle in the opulent French quarters of cities like Hanoi and Saigon, at seaside resorts like the Cap Saint-Jacques, or at the hill stations at Tam-Dao, Dalat, and Bokor. In France, Indochina earned the reputation as a land in which the most humble European man—not to speak of high-ranking officials—could afford a coterie of servants and several *congai*, or mistresses. Many French colonial women, for their part, considered themselves more emancipated in Indochina than back home in France, although some, like a character in George Groslier's 1929 novel *Le retour à l'argile* (The return to clay), complained of ennui.

THE TWO WORLD WARS

In the First World War, some 48,922 Indochinese served in the French military. Of them 1,548 "died for France," according to inscriptions at the Temple du Souvenir Indochinois—a monument to Indochinese soldiers of the Great War located outside Paris. In the wake of the war, many Indochinese elites attempted, in vain, to translate this sacrifice into colonial reform.

The Second World War heralded far greater changes in Indochina. In September 1940, following France's defeat to Nazi Germany, Japanese forces launched assaults on French positions in Tonkin. That month, Japan and Vichy France reached agreements, one allowing Japanese troops to station in Indochina, another placing Indochina within the Japanese zone of economic influence. Although Japanese troops were present in

Indochina between 1940 and 1945, the Vichy French government of Admiral Jean Decoux remained in place until March 1945. Vichy reforms and ideology were introduced, and Vichy police forces forcefully suppressed rebel uprisings in both the north and south of Indochina. In fact, French Indochina was the only former Asian colony east of Bangladesh to remain in colonial hands in 1945, because in Hong Kong, Burma, the Philippines, the Dutch East Indies, Malaysia, and Singapore, the Japanese had simply toppled the colonial administration. However, while they did not actually remove the French administration until 1945, the Japanese nevertheless actively supported pan-Asian and anticolonial movements in Indochina. Among them was the religious sect Cao Daï, whose supporters were rounded up by the French in a move that typified the complexity of Vietnamese-French-Japanese relations in this era. Japan finally put an end to this uneasy working arrangement when on 9 March 1945 it orchestrated a coup that toppled French rule. In August–September 1945, after Japan's surrender to the Allies, Ho Chi Minh, who had slipped back into Indochina from exile in 1941 to found the Vietminh, declared Vietnam's independence. The removal of both the French and the Japanese in 1945 signaled a profound shift. The noncommunist nationalist resistance was largely compromised by its close ties with Japan. Only the Indochinese Communist Party emerged strengthened in August 1945, untarnished because of its reasoning that the French and Japanese had constituted a "double yoke of oppression."

Economic conditions were difficult in this period. Between 1940 and 1943, the price of rice in Tonkin rose eightfold. Poor food distribution, the confiscation of rice stocks by the Japanese army, and other factors, including a power vacuum, conspired to starve roughly one million Vietnamese in 1945.

A THIRTY-YEAR WAR

In August 1945 Indochina was occupied by Chinese troops in the north and British Commonwealth forces in the south. Ho Chi Minh's Vietminh and their sympathizers dominated large sections of Indochina. Within the Indochinese Communist Party, some advocated maintaining the unity of Indochina, although in the end the communist movements of Vietnam, Laos, and Cambodia ended up taking separate nationalist paths.

Starting in September 1945, the French government strove to retake Indochina, which it considered the keystone of its overseas empire. Vietnam would be at war almost continuously between 1945 and 1975. In late 1945 the French forces, led by Marshal Leclerc's (Philippe de Hauteclocque) armored division that had liberated Paris in 1944, made rapid headway in southern Vietnam but encountered stiff Vietminh resistance in the north. In March 1946 France recognized Vietnam as a "free state" within the French Union but retained control over former Cochinchina. In December 1946 war erupted again in the north. Although the French took and retook cities like Hanoi and Haiphong, they were unable to control rural areas—even near Saigon. From its bastion in the mountains of northern Vietnam, the Democratic Republic of Vietnam was able to direct a coordinated campaign featuring both guerrilla and regular Vietminh units, led by General Vo Nguyen Giap.

With the war's escalation came internationalization. France, still recovering from the ravages of World War II, was unable to bear the brunt of costs alone. The United States, once sympathetic to the cause of Vietnamese independence and even to the person of Ho Chi Minh, began around 1949 to consider Vietnam a theater of the Cold War. A now communist China (since 1949) was increasingly uneasy with this war at its doorstep. In 1950 both the Soviet Union and China recognized Ho Chi Minh's side as the only legal government of Vietnam. Increased American aid did not produce French victories. In 1950 French forces suffered a reverse at Cao Bang. In France, support for the war was waning. French forces, many of them hailing from colonies themselves, were drained by guerrilla warfare. In 1954 French troops were encircled in a valley at Dien Ben Phu near the border with Laos. General Giap laid siege to the French garrison, while at the same time diplomats attempted to reach a solution in Geneva. The diplomats were presented with a fait accompli when on 8 May 1954 Dien Ben Phu fell to the Vietminh. The Union indochinoise, and hence Indochine, technically ceased to exist in 1954. On 20 July 1954 in

Ho Chi Minh attending the annual congress of the French socialist party in Tours, France, December 1920. Ho later became the leader of the Communist Party in North Vietnam and led Vietnamese resistance to French and later U.S. intervention. BRIDGEMAN ART LIBRARY

Geneva, a cease-fire was signed, dividing Vietnam along the same seventeenth parallel that had separated British and Chinese forces in 1945.

This divide remained on the map until 1975. The years from 1955 to 1975 marked greater and greater American involvement in what was now a civil war between North and South Vietnam. In 1963 South Vietnam's Catholic president, Ngo Dinh Diem, was assassinated in a coup. That same year the Vietcong (communist guerrillas south of the seventeenth parallel) made major inroads. In 1965 Lyndon Johnson escalated the war on two fronts: trying to quell insurgency in the South, and bombing North Vietnam. The United States dropped some eight million tons of bombs on Vietnam, Laos, and Cambodia over the duration of the war. The Vietcong were supplied by the

Vietminh through a tortuous network of paths known as the Ho Chi Minh Trail, which ran largely through Laos. Near Saigon, in the so-called Iron Triangle (around Cu Chi), the Vietcong expanded by hundreds of miles underground galleries from which they had already fought the French. In 1968 the Vietcong launched the Têt offensive, which failed to hold its objectives but ultimately proved that the rebels could orchestrate large and coordinated attacks in the heart of the South. North Vietnam launched a final offensive against the South in 1975. The South fell in just over one month (10 March–30 April). Just over fifty-eight thousand U.S. troops died in combat, and approximately one million Vietnamese soldiers perished. Estimates of civilian casualties run in the millions. After 1975 a massive exodus of political and religious refugees took place, a diaspora composed of some 1.4 million people between 1975 and 1989.

CAMBODIA AND LAOS

In 1953 King Norodom Sihanouk of Cambodia declared independence from France. In 1975, five years after Sihanouk was deposed by a military coup, the Khmer Rouge took power. Under the murderous leadership of Pol Pot, they committed genocide against their perceived opponents, until the Vietnamese army invaded Cambodia in December 1978, in a move supported by Moscow but strongly opposed by Beijing. In retaliation, China invaded Vietnam in 1979, before being stymied by the Vietnamese army. Vietnamese troops remained in Cambodia for a decade.

Laos, like Vietnam, had become independent in 1945, only to see the French take over again a year later. Between 1953 and 1975 Laos was torn by civil war. Laos also became a major, though unofficial, theater of military operations during the U.S.-Vietnam war. In 1977, two years after a people's republic was established in Laos, the country signed a friendship treaty with Vietnam.

See also **Colonialism; Duras, Marguerite; French Empire; Vietnam War.**

BIBLIOGRAPHY

Brocheux, Pierre, and Daniel Hémery. *Indochine, la colonisation ambiguë, 1858–1954.* New ed. Paris, 2001.

Duiker, William J. *Ho Chi Minh.* New York, 2000.

Jennings, Eric T. *Vichy in the Tropics: Pétain's National Revolution in Madagascar, Guadaloupe, and Indochina, 1940–1944.* Stanford, Calif., 2001.

Marr, David. *Vietnam, 1945: The Quest for Power.* Berkeley, Calif., 1995.

Meyer, Charles. *Les Français en Indochine, 1860–1914.* Paris, 1996.

Norindr, Panivong. *Phantasmatic Indochina: French Colonial Ideology in Architecture, Film, and Literature.* Durham, N.C., 1996.

Tran, Tu Binh. *The Red Earth: A Vietnamese Memoir of Life on a Colonial Rubber Plantation.* Athens, Ohio, 1985.

Zinoman, Peter. *The Colonial Bastille: A History of Imprisonment in Vietnam, 1862–1940.* Berkeley, Calif., 2001.

ERIC T. JENNINGS

INDUSTRIAL CAPITALISM.

INDUSTRIAL CAPITALISM. The best way to approach the concept of industrial capitalism would seem to be through a definition of capitalism that existed prior to industrialization as well as through a debate that historians of industrialization have been having among themselves for many decades on whether and in what ways the appearance of industry on the historical stage amounted to a revolution.

According to the 1989 edition of the *Oxford English Dictionary*, capitalism is a "system which favours the existence of capitalists," and a capitalist is "one who has accumulated capital; one who has capital available for employment in financial or industrial enterprises." *Webster's Third New International Dictionary* describes capitalism as an "economic system characterized by private or corporation ownership of capital goods, by investments that are determined by private decision rather than by state control, and by prices, production, and the distribution of goods that are determined mainly by a free market."

These definitions indicate that capitalism existed before the arrival of industrial capitalism, primarily in the form of a commercial or merchant capitalism. Its foundations were in the trading links and routes that had been built up in different parts of the globe, often over thousands of years. With the proliferation of money as a means of exchange, this merchant capitalism became more and more sophisticated in its methods of handling payments for material goods that were increasingly transported over very long distances across Africa, Asia, and Europe and, after the discovery of the Americas, also across the Atlantic.

THEORIES OF INDUSTRIALIZATION

Once industrialization had emerged as a clearly discernible process, intellectuals and scholars came along to interpret its meaning and significance. Men like Claude-Henri de Saint-Simon felt that something remarkable was happening in their time in the early nineteenth century and turned their attention to what they perceived as a toiling and laboring industrial society. Subsequently, Karl Marx began to analyze the phenomenon more systematically, viewing it as a distinct stage in the long evolution of human society. To him industrial capitalism based on factory work and wage labor was preceded by feudalism—a system in which the owners of the large landed estates had established their domination over the mass of dependent peasants. According to Marx, this feudal system suffered increasingly from its inner contradictions and the conflicts it had been generating between the exploitative landlords and the exploited peasants. By the eighteenth century these contradictions had in Marx's view become so serious as to trigger a revolution from which a new socioeconomic system, industrial capitalism, was born. In it the bourgeois industrial entrepreneur had replaced the feudal lord and exploited proletarianized factory workers through wage labor. In the long run these proletarians were destined to challenge industrial capitalism and stage a further revolution that would abolish capitalist exploitation and lead to an egalitarian and democratic communist society characterized by perpetual peace and harmony.

While many of Marx's writings remained quite vague about the structures and shape of the communist utopia, he devoted most of his voluminous writings to an analysis of the "laws" and inner dynamic of industrial capitalism. Moving along the path that he had mapped out, his followers not only spoke and wrote about the evolution of industrial capitalism after Marx's death in 1883 but also looked more closely at its supposedly violent origins in the eighteenth century.

After World War II, Eric Hobsbawm became one of the most influential Marxist historians to examine this period, in his *Age of Revolution,* first published in 1962. In it he viewed the emergence of industrial capitalism as a convulsive phenomenon and a major divide in the history of humankind. Indeed, "by any reckoning," he wrote, "this was probably the most important event in world history, at any rate since the invention of agriculture and the cities" (p. 29).

Hobsbawm's study was in part a response to another interpretation to which he referred indirectly and which had been most powerfully presented two years earlier by the American economist Walt W. Rostow in his *Stages of Economic Growth.* Rostow saw the rise of industrial capitalism as an evolutionary process, perhaps best captured by the image of an airplane sitting at the end of a runway. If, according to Rostow, the socioeconomic and political conditions were right for the plane to start and accelerate down the metaphorical runway, it would reach a takeoff point and once airborne would eventually achieve a steady equilibrium in self-sustained growth and a mass consumption society.

Although Rostow's argument was essentially that of an economic historian who looked at the alleged experience of societies that had taken off into industrial affluence, its underlying assumptions were anti-Marxist and liberal-reformist. His subtitle was quite blunt about this: "A Non-Communist Manifesto." And indeed, there was also a contemporary significance to the debate on capitalist industrialization that revived after World War II. Both camps were implying, when writing in this Cold War period, that the competition of East and West was also a struggle for the hearts and minds of the still predominantly agricultural societies of the "Third World," of the millions in Asia, Latin America, and Africa who were wavering between the two systems.

Marxists argued on the one hand that industrialization could not be achieved without revolutionary upheavals of the kind that Europe had once seen; the Rostowians, on the other, held out the evolutionary solution that they believed had been experienced by the Europeans before the advent of prosperous mass consumer societies in Europe and North America.

While the argument over origins and fundamentals was going on, some scholars turned to more specific topics. There was the intriguing question of what had in fact triggered the shift from an agricultural-feudal to a capitalist-industrial society. Here the demographers asserted that it was changes in marriage patterns and birthrates that unleashed a population explosion. This in turn promoted a revolution in agricultural production in which the farming community, instead of merely growing enough food for its own subsistence, expanded the arable land and turned to more intensive agriculture that yielded a surplus for sale to a growing population in the towns and cities. Other scholars postulated a reverse chain of events where improvements in agriculture and a proliferating interest to produce for a larger market led to changes in marriage patterns and demographics. Yet another group of specialists focused on technological innovation, the decline in disease and infant mortality, or long-distance trade and Europe's expansion overseas as factors behind the socioeconomic changes that had so clearly taken place in Europe around the eighteenth century. If these controversies had subsided by the end of the twentieth century, it was perhaps also from a growing sense that a unique combination of factors had been at work and that it may never be possible to identify one as the *prima causa*.

The other controversy that occupied social and economic historians in the early postwar period, and in which Eric Hobsbawm was also engaged, concerned the question of whether standards of living rose or declined as industrial capitalism unfolded in the nineteenth century. The results of this debate are more clear-cut than those about the original trigger of industrialization. In the early twenty-first century it is generally agreed that the immediate impact in the eighteenth and early nineteenth centuries was quite disastrous for millions of Europeans who experienced the shift from agriculture to industry as an enormous upheaval, materially and psychologically. Impoverishment and starvation were widespread in those decades and contributed ultimately to the outbreak of the revolutions of 1848 in western and central Europe. However, if the standard-of-living problem is looked at over the longer term, a broadly based improvement of the situation of the mass of the population is discernible until the two world wars of the first half of the twentieth century destroyed most of these gains, and it took until the postwar decades before the upward trend in living standards was resumed.

PROTOINDUSTRIALIZATION

In the 1970s, then, there emerged a group of historians who had become skeptical of certain elements of the positions that Hobsbawm and Rostow had taken in the debate on the origins of industrial capitalism. They tended to agree with the liberals that industrial capitalism did not come as a sudden rupture. The transition from agriculture to industry was, they believed, gradual and indeed passed through an intermediate phase that they termed *protoindustrialization*. At the same time the group disagreed with the Rostowians that, once takeoff had been achieved, industrialization and the reaching of self-sustained growth were unstoppable.

The empirical base of the protoindustrial argument was provided by the methodological refinements that demography had meanwhile created. For a long time demographers had been struggling to develop at least some broad national data on population change in Europe in the early modern period. Along came Franklin Mendels and others in the 1970s, who began to evaluate local church records and birth registers in an effort to obtain more specific information on population size in certain localities. Focusing on Flanders in what is now southern Belgium and on northern France, Mendels found concentrations of families who were landless and, according to earlier theories, should have moved to the urban centers in search of jobs in the factory system. But Mendels's data showed that these families had stayed in their villages in the countryside and had become involved in extensive protoindustrial networks engaged in spinning and weaving. The raw materials and tools—as the "protoindustrializers" also discovered—were provided by merchant capitalists in the nearby towns who, motivated by the prospect of profit, were in search of cheap labor to escape the restrictions of the craft guilds in the towns and cities. They were also linked to a system of trade that enabled them to channel the finished products into transregional markets.

In this way a so-called putting-out system was forged, by which the landless cottagers collected the raw materials from the merchant capitalist and turned them into cloth and other textiles, which they returned to the putters-out for a cash payment to cover their daily subsistence. As research into the protoindustrialization phenomenon grew, other predominantly agricultural regions with similar employment structures were discovered. The northwest of England was one of the first regions of this type, where the factory system with its textile mills unfolded but slowly. Another protoindustrial region that attracted a good deal of attention was along the Belgian border with the German Rhineland south of Aachen and to the north around Krefeld. The Eichsfeld (southeast of Göttingen) and Thuringia also fell into this pattern, with the latter concentrating on cottage-industrial woodcrafts and toy making. The protoindustrial area of Upper Silesia farther east became famous in 1848 for the weavers' uprising on which

Gerhart Hauptmann based his drama *Die Weber*. Putting-out networks that often comprised thousands of households also emerged in northern Italy and in Sweden.

All these results of painstaking demographic research explain why these historians challenged not only the Marxists with their revolutionary perspective on the process of capitalist industrialization but also the Rostowians and their takeoff theory. For some of the regions that had once sustained flourishing putting-out networks lapsed back into a rural state, and factory systems arose elsewhere. In other words, protoindustries were always in a precarious balance, as was most strikingly demonstrated by the work of the British industrial archaeologist Robin Chaplin on Tern Hall in Shropshire, England. Going through the records of a legal dispute, Chaplin found that the estate had once housed one of the largest iron forges in Europe at the bottom of a hill on which the mansion had been built. Taking a spade, Chaplin did indeed find massive brick foundations on the banks of a lake and a creek that in the early eighteenth century had driven the forge's waterwheel. Today no traces can be seen of this development. It is covered up by grass, shrubs, and trees.

Thanks to the research by Mendels and others, it is now widely accepted that *Industrialization before Industrialization,* as Hans Medick, Jürgen Schlumbohm, and Peter Kriedte entitled their influential study of the subject, provides a more subtle interpretation of the genesis of industrial capitalism than Hobsbawm or Rostow. It is also agreed that protoindustries run by merchant capitalists were not simply displaced by the advent of the factory system. Rather there was a period of overlap, even if the cottage industries proved less efficient in the long run and disappeared. The reasons for this decline are not too difficult to discern. It was forever laborious, especially in the winter, to get the raw materials to the cottages and to return the finished products to the town. The decentralization of the system also hampered supervision and control. Here the factory that united all workers under one roof offered the entrepreneur considerable advantages. The surviving factory codes show how discipline was imposed and workers were held to a strict routine with fixed work hours, breaks, and penalties for "loafing," tardiness, and other infractions of the codes. Protoindustrial research also stimulated work on daily life within the cottages, on gender relations and child rearing within the families. This in turn influenced work that had begun earlier relating to the role of women in the emergent factory system, changing work patterns, and the structures of the industrial working-class family.

THE GROWTH AND EVOLUTION OF INDUSTRIAL CAPITALISM

Once industrial capitalism had firmly established itself, it experienced a rapid expansion. The principle of competition in the marketplace meant that many who had owned a small workshop went under or barely survived on the margins of the new factory system, while others were more successful, founding further factories, developing new product lines, and coming into wealth. Growth also confronted the successful enterprises with fresh problems. It became more and more difficult for the owner(s) to maintain an oversight over all parts of the operation from the acquisition of raw materials and the processes of manufacturing to sales and marketing and the keeping of the accounts. With the expansion of the workforce came the need for supervisors on the shop floor and for experts and managers securing production and a steady flow of orders, for shrewd accountants and circumspect dispatchers.

Expansion also required additional capital. Initially, many entrepreneurs relied on members of their family to provide capital. But with the growth of the banking system financial institutions also became involved in giving loans on a short-term and increasingly on a more long-term basis. Finally, there was the development of the joint-stock company designed to attract investors interested in buying shares that carried higher returns than could be achieved through a savings account. In tandem with financial institutions and manufacturing, industry workers also became more organized. In 1846 the ironworks of Friedrich Krupp in the industrial Ruhr region had some 140 workers; by 1913 there were 77,500. With the rallying of employers and workers came bureaucratization, as Jürgen Kocka has demonstrated in his study of the electrical engineering firm Siemens. Werner Siemens had been in charge of a small workshop producing railroad signals and other electrical equipment, where he himself worked as an inventor and innovator. By 1912 the firm had 44,400 blue-collar workers and some 12,500 engineers and other white-collar employees, and once quite personal relationships had inevitably become more distant and anonymous. Research and development had vastly expanded. The polytechnical schools and science departments of universities had been drawn into the training of specialists.

By the late nineteenth century technological innovation and the applied sciences had tangibly changed industrial capitalism. While the older branches of manufacturing (textiles, iron and steel making, coal mining) continued, the new and much more dynamic branches of electrical engineering, chemicals, and machine building had initiated a second phase in the industrialization process. These branches created much of the prosperity that Europe witnessed before 1914 and that was disrupted by two world wars before it resumed after 1945, until it was, from the 1980s, challenged by another shift into computers and the Internet.

However, it would be mistaken to see technology as the sole or even as the main driving force behind the transformations that industrial capitalism underwent from the late nineteenth century. Rather, technological change is inseparable from changes in the organization of capitalism. Whether technology is developed indigenously or imported from abroad, it is never adopted and adapted locally as such. What comes with it are ideas and processes of work that are compatible with the new machinery. During most of the nineteenth century, manufacturing practices tended to evolve from preexisting regional traditions of workshop organization or were adapted from those developed in Britain, "the first industrial nation" (as Peter Mathias called it, in his book of that title) and political hegemon of the age. Continental European businessmen traveled across the Channel to inspect the factories of the English Midlands and north, just as the American Samuel Slater did before he rebuilt the textile machinery he had seen there at his mill in Pawtucket, Rhode Island. Other entrepreneurs in the German Rhineland and elsewhere hired British engineers to help them with the organization of their shop floors.

The rise of electrical engineering, machine building, and chemicals by the late nineteenth century triggered further shifts in production methods and work organization. The need was now for highly skilled workers who were trained to deal with more complex processes of assembling automotive engines or testing dyestuffs and who were able to work with engineers and university-trained chemists. The working conditions became less disciplinarian and patriarchal and more rational-bureaucratic. Loyalty and expertise became important values that gave employees a voice within the enterprise. While heavy industry remained hostile to the idea of worker representation, the "new industries" began to negotiate with union representatives. It seemed better to secure cooperation in the interest of uninterrupted production than to have a disgruntled workforce that staged a sudden strike. Conversely, workers' associations, many of which could build on the experience of the guilds, were also interested in the company's prosperity offering opportunities to negotiate higher wages and job security. In short, a movement toward a more flexible handling of labor relations on the part of some employers coincided with a politically more conservative unionization that preferred gradual reform and an improvement of material conditions to the push of more radical Marxist politicians and intellectuals who wanted to prepare the overthrow of the existing capitalist system.

THE AMERICAN INDUSTRIAL MODEL

By the turn of the century, interest in Britain as the role model of industrial capitalism began to give way to an interest in the United States, which in the meantime had changed from a country of rural settlers, trappers, and "Red Indians" to one in which a growing number of people lived in cities and were engaged in manufacturing. Instead of journeying to England, continental European entrepreneurs could now be seen to board one of the fast luxury liners to take them across the Atlantic so as to visit the centers of American manufacturing in Pennsylvania, New York, Ohio, and Michigan.

Overall, the connections that were forged must be seen as part of a slow globalization process that had been going on for several centuries and that the European "scramble for colonies" in the late nineteenth century had accelerated, in the course of which Africa and parts of Asia were carved up between the great powers. This is where many of the raw materials for European industry came from, extracted under exploitative and often brutal conditions and under very unfavorable terms of trade. But the most intensive exchange in semifinished and finished goods took place among the industrialized nations of Europe, many of whom were each other's best customers, and increasingly also across the Atlantic, where a new industrial power was emerging in the pre-1914 decades.

European interest in the United States was furthermore stimulated by the rise there of the scientific management movement and the fame of one of its apostles, Frederick Taylor. He had been in the forefront of developing time-and-motion studies and of thinking more systematically about factory rationalization. A tireless propagandist of his ideas, he was convinced that their adoption by industry would benefit both employers and workers. Increased productivity, he argued, brought higher profits as well as wages. Another American, Henry Ford, preached rationalization as a means of producing a benefit in addition to higher productivity, profits, and wages. Next to the entrepreneur and worker to whom Taylorism was appealing, he introduced a third beneficiary of Fordism: the consumer. By passing some of the gains from rationalized production on to the buyer of goods in the form of lower prices, Ford hitched mass production to the provision of cheap consumer durables for a mass market. Having inspected Ford's assembly lines in Michigan, it is typical that the electrical engineering firm of Robert Bosch in Stuttgart and the French carmaker Renault should experiment with Taylorist and Fordist methods. This interest in American ideas of industrial production and marketing continued and deepened in the 1920s, when major American corporations came to Europe as investors or to establish their own production facilities, which in turn put pressure on European entrepreneurs to rationalize.

However, especially during the interwar years, a number of institutional and mental obstacles prevented a more far-reaching "Americanization" of European industrial capitalism. To begin with, the ravages of World War I left too many ordinary people too close to the existential minimum to turn them into consumers who could afford a mass-produced automobile or household appliance. Even if cheaper goods became available, the resources of the average family were too limited to help create a mass production and mass consumption society. No less importantly, European industrial capitalism had from the late nineteenth century onward developed a structural peculiarity that delayed the advent of an American-style mass consumer society until after World War II: cartelization.

CARTELS

Cartels are horizontal agreements between independent firms within one branch of industry designed to foster cooperation instead of competition in key areas such as output and pricing policies. Members of a cartel divide the market among themselves by negotiating, for example, production quotas for each company and/or by fixing prices. Many cartels also founded syndicates—organizations that took complete care of the sale of the cartel's products. The origins of this system went back to the 1870s and 1880s, the years of what was then known as the "Great Depression," when European industry tried to protect itself against losses by stabilizing prices. It was also the period when cartels attempted to shield themselves against foreign competition by urging their governments to introduce higher protective tariffs.

When in the 1890s the European national economies came out of the "Great Depression" (which was in effect more a period of retarded growth) and enjoyed another boom that lasted more or less continuously until World War I, protective tariffs were reduced. But in many countries on the Continent, major branches of industry had become so used to the comforts of cartels that they continued to fix production quotas and prices among themselves. Full market competition was not restored. In Germany the system was even legalized by a decision of the Reich Court of 1897, which declared cartels to be binding agreements between individual firms. Leaving a cartel in order to compete independently and not to be bound by quotas and fixed prices exposed a company to lawsuits for breach of contract. Conversely, enterprises that for some reason were not admitted to a cartel found themselves discriminated against. The larger consequences of cartelization are not too difficult to pinpoint: the market was virtually monopolized by cartels. Prices tended to be fixed at a level that secured the survival of the commercially weakest and least efficient member. The more profitable companies could use their resources to rationalize without the threat of a competitor and hence without the pressure of passing productivity gains on to the consumers via lower prices.

World War I, with its increasing need to coordinate production and prices for the sake of national mobilization for total war, perpetuated the European cartel system, and the difficult years after 1918 merely reinforced the incentive for interfirm cooperation. After a brief hiatus during the more prosperous mid-1920s, when American business appeared on the scene, the Great Slump of 1929 induced another period of protection against competition at home and from foreign corporations. Not surprisingly, the authoritarian political systems that emerged in the 1930s favored cartels. When Hitler, for example, placed his arms orders, it was advantageous to have to deal with a cartel rather than a welter of manufacturers. Ultimately, Germany became totally cartelized. It was an industrial capitalism that was still based on the principle of private ownership of the means of production, but the marketplace was for all practical purposes abolished and the consumer had no voice. After 1939, the Nazis tried to impose this system on the national economies of the neighboring countries they had conquered. It was envisaged that European industry would become a *Grossraumkartell*—a closed space, an autarkic system geared to German interests and completely cartelized.

THE POSTWAR MARKET SYSTEMS

Given the negative effects that European cartelization had both economically and politically, the United States, as the unquestioned hegemon of the Western world after 1945, insisted on a strict ban on cartels and their replacement by a model that had evolved in the United States since the late nineteenth century. It began in 1890, when Congress ratified the so-called Sherman Act, which prohibited the formation of cartels and a monopolization of the marketplace. Only price competition and production without quotas were held to be in the interest of the consumer. As a result, American industrial capitalism moved in the direction of oligopolies, of big individual corporations that, under the pain of severe penalties, were not allowed to cooperate, only to compete. The system also promoted the survival of small- and medium-sized firms that were efficient enough to occupy the many niches of specialized production that technological and economic change continued to open up next to the oligopolies.

With the negative experiences of European market restrictions in the first half of the twentieth century before their eyes, the Americans began to pressure all European nations to break with their cartel tradition and to introduce anticartel and antimonopoly legislation. This pressure was applied most directly and strongly to occupied West Germany, with the explicit calculation that if the potentially largest economy in the postwar reconstruction effort developed a competitive market economy, it would spill over into the rest of Western Europe, where the Americans did not have the lever of an occupying power.

There was much initial resistance against the introduction of anticartel legislation everywhere, as many industrial associations mobilized to block it or water it down. But by the late 1950s the movement against restrictive practices had gained the upper hand throughout the emerging European economic community. The spreading of the principle of market competition paved the way for the breakthrough of Fordism in its dual meaning—rationalized mass production of civilian goods from which the consumer would benefit, as rising living standards put consumer durables into the range of the average family budget.

The destruction of the cartel system did not mean, though, that industrial capitalism in Western Europe after World War II was totally unrestrained and unregulated. While the type of socialist planning that the Soviet Union imposed on the East European satellites under Stalinism was anathema in the West, there was the realization that the complexities of industrial capitalism required some kind of management of the present and a projection of growth and performance into the future. It was a principle that any shrewd director would apply to his own company as a matter of course, and it was also one that had become more widely accepted in light of the lessons learned from the collapse of the international economy in 1929. Industrial capitalism could not do without some kind of constitutional framework, set of rules, and management of the future. By the 1960s, politicians, employers, trade unionists, and academic economists worked hard to generate as precise an estimate as possible of the present state of the economy and of its future trajectory. Keynesian demand management blended with other ideas about economic steering, with the aim of securing full employment, low inflation rates, expanded international trade, and monetary stability.

INDUSTRIAL CAPITALISM AND THE WELFARE STATE

A key concern in the relationship between government, employers, and organized workers—also known as tripartism—was the maintenance and cautious expansion of the welfare state. This system of social security had first emerged in Germany in the 1880s. Subsequently Britain and other European nations also installed increasingly universal benefits such as health insurance, pension schemes, and insurance against unemployment and work-related accidents. These benefits were originally conceived as an instrument of social appeasement to keep a restive working class away from radical leftist movements and in particular from the orthodox Marxists who were agitating for the overthrow of the bourgeois-capitalist order. After World War I there was a growing sense that social and economic security was a citizen's right— a sense that was reinforced by the need to support large numbers of disabled veterans, war widows, and orphans, many of whom had been thrown into destitution. After the Great Slump of 1929 and another devastating world war, what had once started as a limited coverage for selected groups of workers and white-collar employees saw a further expansion and consolidation to provide a safety net for all. Not surprisingly, industry was never particularly happy with the rise of the welfare state, to whose funding it was obliged by law to contribute. In the long run, however, many of its representatives came to accept that it was in their interest and that of the stability and viability of the parliamentary democratic systems that comprised the political framework for industrial capitalism's

continued prosperity, which made it imperative to maintain the safety net despite mounting costs.

However, throughout the postwar decades voices never subsided that warned of an overburdening of the national economy with welfare expenditures and entitlements. The countermovement began in the United States, where it was both the overburdening and the growth of public bureaucracies administering the welfare state that drew increasing criticism. As the advocates of a scaling back of entitlements and of more generally reducing the public sector through privatization gained ground under the administration of Ronald Reagan, their arguments were also taken up in Europe, first in Britain, where Prime Minister Margaret Thatcher turned them into a program for political action. It proved to be a contentious and agonizing process, and even more so when the objective and ideological pressures to contain the further growth of the welfare state reached the countries of the European continent. The trade unions were in the forefront of the resistance, but in the meantime they had lost many of their members and hence much of their early postwar clout. In an ironic way this decline was partly due to the success of Fordism, which had turned once class-conscious and combative workers, demanding social security and a better distribution of the national wealth, into price-conscious consumers looking for individual improvement and a reduction of their taxes.

At the end of the twentieth century, industrial capitalism in Europe faced major sociological and attitudinal shifts of this kind, which were reinforced by a major technological change with its own pressures of decentralization and individualization. No doubt it was no longer the same as during its origins over two hundred years ago. To be sure, manufacturing in large factories continues, but much of it has moved outside Europe. It is a curious reversal from the nineteenth century. At that time the rural protoindustrial putting-out system came to be challenged by the urban factory, and both continued side by side. At the beginning of the twenty-first century it appears as if industrial capitalism exists in parallel to a growing pattern in which the managers sit in the metropolitan centers of Europe and North America to initiate and supervise the outsourcing of manufacturing to non-

European countries around the globe. Like the merchant capitalists of the eighteenth century, they are linked to a global network of sales agencies, wholesalers, and retailers who distribute the mass-produced goods to a receptive mass consumer, aided by a proliferating tertiary sector whose specialists are keen to offer their services, be it in leisure and entertainment, financial advice and banking, or the food business.

Some have called this regime a postindustrial capitalism. But it is unlikely that the production of industrial goods will cease, and it therefore seems premature to proclaim the end of a system that proved innovative and dynamic since the emergence of the first factories in Britain and other parts of continental Europe. There will be regional shifts, as there have been in the past.

See also **Americanization; Capitalism; Labor Movements.**

BIBLIOGRAPHY

Chandler, Alfred D., Jr. *Scale and Scope: The Dynamics of Industrial Capitalism.* Cambridge, U.K., 1990.

Hobsbawm, Eric J. *The Age of Revolution, 1789–1848.* New York, 1962.

———. *The Age of Empire, 1875–1914.* London, 1987.

Kriedte, Peter, Hans Medick, and Jürgen Schlumbolm. *Industrialization before Industrialization.* Translated by Beate Schempp. Cambridge, U.K., 1981.

Milward, Alan S. *The Reconstruction of Western Europe, 1945–1951.* London, 1984.

Nolan, Mary. *Visions of Modernity.* New York, 1994.

Rifkin, Jeremy. *The European Dream.* New York, 2004.

Rostow, Walt W. *The Stages of Economic Growth: A Non-Communist Manifesto.* Cambridge, U.K., 1960.

Shonfield, Andrew. *Modern Capitalism.* London, 1965.

Zunz, Oliver, Leonard Schoppa, and Nobuhiro Hiwatari, eds. *Social Contracts under Stress.* New York, 2002.

VOLKER R. BERGHAHN

INFLATION. Inflation is best described as a sustained rise in the general price level. That is sometimes expressed as nominal income rising in excess of real income. It is a relatively recent phenomenon in world history, belonging mainly—but with exceptions in a few rare episodes—to the twentieth century. There can be many pressures that produce price changes in the short term, but there is no inflation without a corresponding growth in the stock of money. That growth was not easily achieved before technology allowed the production of a reliable paper currency, and that technology belongs to the twentieth century. This in itself is highly suggestive of the basic cause.

For most of the world's history, the time plot of the general price level was almost flat. Occasionally, the discovery of silver and gold or improved mining or production techniques would produce a period of rising prices, though these were generally modest—seldom much above 5 percent per annum. There were one or two episodes before the twentieth century, such as in Britain during the Napoleonic Wars, when metallic backing for the currency was abandoned. But even in that period, inflation rates were quite low, 2 or 3 percent at most over a twenty-five-year period. Some other more extreme cases, such as the French Revolution or the U.S. civil war, are good examples of the use of paper money and consequent rapid inflation. What changed after 1914 was that inflation became a common feature of economies. Certainly after the mid-1930s there was a relentless rise in the general price level for the rest of the century, and that continued into the twenty-first century.

A discussion of "world prices" can be useful for individual commodities, but for the general price level it can be tolerated only up to a point. It is difficult enough constructing an index of prices for one country without attempting it for the world. However, since many countries have similar price experience, one modern industrial country tends to look like another in that respect. There are also some interesting differences that help in an understanding of inflation.

OVERVIEW OF TWENTIETH CENTURY
The general pattern of inflation in the twentieth century was as follows. Prices rose sharply after 1914 until about 1920. There was then a decade or so of hesitancy when major countries were pursuing deflationary policies in order to restore and then adhere to the new gold standard. But after that attempt collapsed in the 1930s, the monetary discipline of a metallic base had largely disappeared

and prices rose almost without interruption. World War II gave a boost to inflation, despite all manner of attempts at containing it. After 1945, inflation appeared to become endemic and increasingly a problem. After 1971, when the world was for the first time ever exclusively reliant on paper money, inflation accelerated almost everywhere. That 1970s experience concentrated attention on the problem, and there developed a widespread desire to contain and even kill inflation. In the last twenty years of the twentieth century, inflation seemed to be completely under control in most developed countries. There was even some concern that the opposite—deflation, a sustained fall in prices—might be emerging. But that was never a serious prospect, and in the early years of the twenty-first century concern about deflation had already all but disappeared. As of 2005 most Organisation for Economic Cooperation and Development (OECD) countries live with inflation, albeit at low levels by twentieth-century standards.

SOME MORE EXTREME EPISODES

In the course of the twentieth century, there were some experiences of violent inflation and some others that were extremely serious. The most violent have been described as hyperinflations. That can be defined in different ways, but one of the most accepted definitions is that of economist Philip Cagan: prices rising at more than 50 percent per month and accelerating. And the period of hyperinflation was over by this definition when the rate fell below 50 percent per month. The other "extreme" cases can be thought of as rates in excess of 100 percent per annum. There were several episodes of hyperinflation in the 1920s, mostly between 1919 and 1924. In these years, Hungary, Poland, Russia, Austria, and Germany all experienced hyperinflation, in fact in the millions percent per annum. In Germany, the worst of these, prices were rising at a rate of 1,000 million percent per annum in 1923–1924.

There was another burst of violent inflation episodes in the 1940s, when Greece, Hungary again, and China all suffered hyperinflation as defined by Cagan. In the years after the 1950s, there have been scores of examples of countries where inflation has been in excess of 100 percent per annum but without taking off into hyperinflation.

These were usually for brief—though sometimes recurring—periods. Many Latin American countries, for example, suffered persistent bouts of very rapid inflation right up until the 1990s. The same is true for many countries in Africa and others, such as Indonesia in the mid-1960s, Serbia and some other Balkan countries in the 1980s and 1990s.

The striking feature about all these episodes of very rapid inflation or of hyperinflation is that of an unbacked paper currency. The growth in the money supply was enormous. Such a growth was impossible in the absence of paper currency. The velocity of circulation can always change, but with a metallic currency it cannot change fast enough to produce such high inflation: it is just not possible to move it around quickly enough. The other feature that stands out is that money growth was accompanied by huge and growing fiscal deficits.

Deficits cannot be sustained for very long, eventually requiring monetization. What were the circumstances that produced such deficits? It has frequently been asserted that it is war that forces expenditure rapidly above the ability to tax. Up to a point, that is true. But the history of the world is in large part the history of war, and yet there is little or no inflation before the twentieth century. A closer look at these episodes reveals that it is civil war or revolution, or at minimum serious social unrest, that is present in almost all cases: in Russia after 1917; in Hungary in 1919; in Poland in the early 1920s. In Germany, too, there were attempted communist coups (and in Bavaria, a Bolshevik government, so the threat was real). In 1922 and 1923, there were armed uprisings and major breakdowns in public order in Germany. Then in the 1940s, there was civil war in China and in Greece. Hungary in 1946 was the worst case of hyperinflation up to that date, but it was slightly different in the way in which it was subjected to Soviet pressure.

SOME EXPLANATION

Governments have always been keen to get hold of resources, and on occasions they simply confiscate resources. The simplest way of doing that is through the inflation tax. The authorities can maximize their revenue from this when inflation is in excess of 100 percent per annum. Of course, such levels of inflation would have potentially dire political consequences. When would it be worth pursuing such a course? The answer must be when the state is seriously threatened from within. An external threat is not critical, since that usually stimulates patriotism so that borrowing can be carried out more easily and tax can be raised without too much complaint. But with a major threat from within, a government may calculate that the risk attached is worth running. Thus civil war is a prime cause of inflation. Expenditure rises sharply as the established authority fights to resist the rebellion, but tax revenues fall since tax payments from the rebellious section disappear. Borrowing becomes equally difficult. A resort to the printing press is immediate.

Not all wars have produced inflation, nor have all civil wars produced great inflation. One line of explanation is that monetary growth does not of itself lead to inflation. The prevailing and anticipated fiscal positions have to be considered in conjunction with monetary policy. The argument is that in a fiat money (that is, command money, usually by decree of government) regime, an appropriate fiscal policy can back the money stock: the value of government liabilities is determined in the same way as a firm's liabilities. An issue of additional shares in the absence of prospective improvement in the future stream of income leads to a fall in the price of the shares. In the case of government, an increase in its liabilities (banknotes) without an increase in prospective tax receipts provides an expectation of a fall in the value of the liabilities; that is, in inflation. An illustration of this might be found in Britain during World War I. Not only did Britain borrow on a huge scale, but huge budget deficits also opened up as the enormous scale of spending went on. The deficits were in excess of 50 percent of gross domestic product (GDP). Yet comparatively low inflation was recorded. Why did it not burst into the extreme kind? The explanation outlined above seems to have some applicability. As soon as it came to be believed that victory was likely, so did the appreciation that there would be a return to Gladstonian principles of finance—balanced budgets. And that is what happened very soon after the war.

WORLDWIDE INFLATION AFTER WORLD WAR II

The general path of prices for the world in the second half of the twentieth century was of a relentless rise across the period. Translated into inflation rates, what shows up is how inflation accelerated in the 1970s and that the rate of inflation has moderated greatly since the beginning of the 1980s. The path for some countries varies a bit. While there was inflation in all countries, and that pattern was similar, in some cases it was significantly lower than in others. The principal reason for the similarity was that in the years up to the early 1970s, most countries were on a fixed (or more accurately, a pegged) exchange rate—essentially tied to the U.S. dollar through the 1944 Bretton Woods Agreement. Under such a system, the small countries import the monetary policy of the large country.

From the early 1970s, though, exchange rates have floated and countries then regained control of their money supply. Those who exercised appropriate control appear to have had greater success with inflation.

MORE GENERAL EXPLANATION

There have been two main competing views on the explanation for the accelerating inflation that began in the mid 1960s. One has been called "international monetarism," and the other wage-push or "sociological." The first regards inflation as a monetary phenomenon. The second denies this and sees it as non-economic, pointing to supposedly spontaneous wage explosions of the late 1960s and early 1970s. Thus for international monetarism, the explanation lies in the United States in the 1960s. The United States had embarked on a huge spending program: domestically on the Great Society and abroad on the Vietnam War. The latter was unpopular, so could not be financed from borrowing or from increased taxation without serious electoral damage. It therefore had to be done by printing money. The monetary expansion produced inflation, and that was transmitted to other countries through the exchange-rate system. Other countries therefore experienced similar inflation to the United States. There were occasions when some countries changed their parity with the dollar—some up, some down—and that reflected their relative individual success or failure in controlling inflation.

The great weight of the evidence suggests that inflation is a monetary phenomenon. But

Italian workers protest inflation and unemployment, Rome, February 1974. ©Bettmann/Corbis

outcomes depend on the relative strengths of the parties involved—the government on the one hand and the people, or powerful interest groups, on the other. If there is strong government that can be trusted to behave with prudence, there is unlikely to be inflation. If the opposition to the government is sufficient to get its way, there will be inflation. It always requires an expansion of the money supply at a rate greater than the growth of real income, and over the long run that rate will be the rate of inflation.

The sociological explanation for inflation is that the cause was trade unions. The argument was that they exerted monopoly power, and monopolies can change the price—in this case wages—of their product when they wish. However, what this does is change relative prices—the wages of one union (or perhaps more) and not the general price level. What if the majority of the labor force belonged to monopoly unions? That is unlikely,

but it takes us back to the relative strength of government in resisting the claims and not expanding the money supply. Further, monopolies are much less common than was once supposed, and are much less likely to appear in an open world economy.

Other explanations have focused on the price of a major commodity—in the 1970s, this commodity was oil. However, a price shock does not produce inflation. Where it is accommodated by the monetary authorities, it can shift the price level to a higher point. But that is not inflation; it is a once and for all change. Thereafter, the trend rate of inflation will carry on from where it was, unless the authorities persist in monetary ease after having accommodated the shock.

POLICIES TO COMBAT INFLATION
Throughout history there have been attempts at controlling prices directly. This practice was given

a great boost in the twentieth century during wartime. Price controls were imposed in many countries, including the United States and the United Kingdom. And in some respects they did seem to work. However, they were supported by other factors. In wartime, patriotism possibly plays some part and people are more prepared to play by the rules for the sake of the greater good. More than that, rationing often accompanied the price controls and it was difficult or impossible to make purchases without coupons. That certainly supported the price controls. Subsidies were used, as well. And there were severe penalties for breach of the controls.

But while price controls seem to have worked for a period, the common experience was that when they were removed, prices jumped up to where they would have been had the controls never existed. They may have served their purpose in wartime, but not beyond that. Price controls were tried in peacetime, too, but in the absence of these other factors, they invariably failed.

Another approach to the control of inflation was to attempt to control wages or incomes more generally. This followed from the belief that trade unions caused inflation. So there were attempts in the 1960s and 1970s to contain inflation by resorting to controls on incomes. This was tried in many countries without success. Apart from being incompatible with a free society, there were simply too many ways of circumventing the controls.

There was for a while the belief that the economy could be managed primarily by operating on demand through fiscal policy. When the economy was growing "too fast" and inflationary pressures developing, tightening fiscal policy would dampen activity down. This course also proved a failure.

It was only after there was a better appreciation of the role of money in causing inflation that there developed a desire to control the growth of money as the means of controlling inflation. This appreciation and desire began to emerge in the 1970s. There was much debate about whether this monetary control was best exerted by trying to operate directly on monetary aggregates or by using interest rates. But whatever the conclusion of this debate, it became clear that it was only central banks that could control monetary growth; and

increasingly it was seen that they should be given the independence to do this—to produce the particular kind of price stability that governments laid down.

SOME CONSEQUENCES

There are several reasons for regarding inflation as a bad thing. The first is that it has damaging effects on the distribution of wealth. It works to the advantage of debtors and to the disadvantage of creditors. Huge debts disappear over a period of inflation. While this might be thought a useful way of rearranging the distribution of wealth, the fact is that it is governments who were the largest debtors in the twentieth century. They were thus able to cheat their populations out of their savings in a number of ways. (This may also be seen as a contribution to the distrust of government, and of the lack of trust more generally, which has led to ever-increasing and costly regulation, regulation being a substitute for the trust that formerly obtained.) Creditors suffer and that in turn dissuades saving and ultimately damages investment and so probably economic growth.

Inflation acts adversely on production in another way. When producers detect an increase in demand for their product, they have difficulty in distinguishing between the demand for their product alone and what might be a general increase in demand from the extra money (excess balances) that consumers are spending. The producer might therefore expand plant to cope with the new demand and then later be left with unwanted plant when the temporary burst of general spending is over.

Inflation distorts prices and interest rates. As inflation rises it becomes more volatile, and this contributes to the difficulty in using prices as good signals—their key function. Different prices will be affected in different ways. Long-term contracts will suffer at the expense of short-term and of flexible arrangements. To that extent it will discourage long-term contracts, and therefore some activity will not be undertaken that otherwise would have been in conditions of less uncertainty.

All in all, inflation is bad for morale and the sum of the distortions it creates makes it bad not only for income and growth, but bad for democracy and for a free society.

See also **Bretton Woods Agreement; Germany; World War I.**

BIBLIOGRAPHY

Cagan, Philip. "The Monetary Dynamics of Hyperinflation." In *Studies in the Quantity Theory of Money*, edited by Milton Friedman, 25–117. Chicago, 1956.

Capie, Forrest. "Conditions in Which Very Rapid Inflation Has Appeared." *Carnegie-Rochester Conference Series on Public Policy* 24 (1986): 115–168.

Capie, Forrest, ed. *Major Inflations in History*. Aldershot, U.K., 1991.

Gordon, Robert. "Can the Inflation of the 1970s Be Explained?" *Brookings Papers on Economic Activity* 1 (1977): 253–277.

Hall, Robert, ed. *Inflation: Causes and Effects*. Chicago, 1982.

Sargent, Thomas J. "The End of Four Big Inflations." In *Inflation: Causes and Effects*, edited by Robert Hall, 41–97. Chicago, 1982.

Velde, Francois. "Poor Hand or Poor Play? The Rise and Fall of Inflation in the U.S." *Economic Perspectives* (spring 2004): 35–51.

FORREST CAPIE

INFLUENZA PANDEMIC.

The influenza pandemic of 1918–1919 killed more people than did World War I itself. Estimates of pandemic influenza deaths vary between thirty and forty million. No one knows why the mutant virus that caused the disease appeared, and no one knows why it disappeared.

In March 1918 and October 1918, when the first two waves of the disease hit Europe and North America, discussions of the origins of the epidemic mirrored the stereotypes that war propaganda had made available everywhere. It was said that the German Bayer company—which invented aspirin—cleverly put the agent causing the flu in aspirin tablets, thereby destroying the Allies literally from within. If that hoary tale faded, others were quick to fill the vacuum of ignorance and fear. The flu was transported, it was said, by ship, probably from China, via the Iberian Peninsula—thus the name the "Plague of the Spanish Lady" or the "Spanish flu." Then it was shipped everywhere, once again the paranoid claimed, in German ships, which released clouds of suspicious materials. Or perhaps it was the U-boats that surfaced near Allied ports, sneaking ashore vials of influenza-soaked liquids, dumped into the water supply or released into the air in movie theaters or at rallies for war loans and in the United States for Liberty Bonds. So said Lieutenant Colonel Philip Doane, head of the Health and Sanitation Section of the America's Emergency Fleet Corporation in 1918. Wildly unlikely stories proliferated, by and large because no one had the slightest idea of the source of the infection or the vectors of its transmission.

It is certain, though, that the Germans and Austrians suffered just as badly as the Allies. Indeed, if there was any direct effect of the Spanish flu on the war it was to decelerate military activity on all fronts and in all armies in the late spring of 1918 and in the fall of 1918, when the first two waves of the epidemic hit. There was a third wave after the Armistice (11 November 1918), which may have been the most lethal of all.

What made this visitation so peculiar is that it hit with particular ferocity young adults in the prime of their lives. Like other viral infections that are relatively harmless in childhood, influenza was a killer to those previously healthy adults who contracted it. The elderly and the very young were also victims of the Spanish flu, but because they were hit year in and year out by ordinary strains of influenza, which killed them through its sequelae, bronchitis and pneumonia, there was nothing abnormal in the age groups ten years and under or sixty years and over falling to respiratory infections. What made the Spanish flu so frightening was that its morbidity (sickness) and mortality (death) rates were highest at ages twenty to forty, the age group of the bulk of the forces in uniform during the war.

The speed of this disease was astonishing. Active people would notice a headache, perhaps a burning sensation in their eyes, then the shivers, then cold that no number of blankets could relieve. Then came the fever, dreams, and at times delirium. The lucky ones would then begin to recover; the unlucky ones developed brownish or purple spots on their faces, and as their breathing became more labored, their feet would turn black. Death came quickly, but not painlessly, as the victims of the Spanish flu suffocated on the fluids released by

A public health worker carries a spray pump filled with anti-flu compound for use on buses, England, March 1920. ©HULTON-DEUTSCH COLLECTION/CORBIS

the infection, fluids which took the form of a froth that completely filled their lungs and bronchial passages. The Spanish flu killed by drowning its victims in their own body chemistry. The French poet Guillaume Apollinaire died of the illness a mere week after contracting what seemed like an ordinary cold. His tongue and face, his friends said, had turned black.

The unprecedented character of the Spanish flu had important implications for the history of public health and medical care. First, it came at a time when the bulk of the combatant populations were not served by physicians. The pressure on states to provide medical care or clinical assistance during times of medical emergencies increased as a result of the pandemic. This linkage is direct in the British case, where there was no Ministry of Health before 1919. The idea of bringing together in one ministry those who would be able to help the population at times of medical emergency came directly out of the visitation of influenza.

The paradox of the Spanish flu was that just as it inflected the political and social support for extensions of provisions for public health, it undercut the claim of the medical profession to offer effective antidotes to disease. This was a killer that came "like a thief in the night" in the words of Sir George Newman, chief medical officer of the British Board of Education. This infection defied virtually every kind of treatment. Quarantine was the only effective answer: the Australian state of South Australia simply closed the borders and let no one in or out. But aside from complete and universal isolation, there were no measures that made the slightest difference in the way the disease spread or in the lethality of its hold on its victims.

Bus conductors wore masks. Streets were sprayed with disinfectant. Schoolchildren were given special inspections, as were soldiers. Nothing worked. And when millions of people got the illness, there was absolutely nothing the medical profession could do to diminish the risks of death from the disease. It was beyond their comprehension and beyond their therapeutic power. Medicine was both more important and more impotent. For in the case of this disease, unlike AIDS, no one could tell people how to avoid it or what they needed to do *not* to get it. And no one could tell people what to do when they did contract it. It destroyed the pretensions of scientists and physicians to control natural phenomena. Here was one visitation that came and went as it pleased and how it pleased. Nothing like it happened during or after World War II.

See also **AIDS; Public Health; World War I.**

BIBLIOGRAPHY

Barry, John M. *The Great Influenza: The Epic Story of the Deadliest Plague in History.* New York, 2004.

Burnet, F. M., and Ellen Clark. *Influenza: A Survey of the Last 50 Years in the Light of Modern Work on the Virus of Epidemic Influenza.* London, 1942.

Collier, Richard. *The Plague of the Spanish Lady.* New York, 1974.

Duncan, Kirsty. *Hunting the 1918 Flu: One Scientist's Search for a Killer Virus.* Toronto, 2003.

Kolata, Gina. *Flu: The Story of the Great Influenza Pandemic of 1918 and the Search for the Virus That Caused It.* New York, 1999.

Phillips, Howard, and David Killingray, eds. *The Spanish Influenza Pandemic of 1918–19: New Perspectives.* New York, 2003.

JAY WINTER

INTELLIGENCE. Intelligence has a long European pedigree. The term itself originates from the "intelligencers"—specially assigned individuals who, during the reign of England's King Charles I (r. 1625–1649), were tasked with spying on the enemy. In other European countries too there was a growing trend in surveillance of both internal and external threats. However, intelligence as it is now understood is a twentieth-century creation.

PRE-1914 ORIGINS
The contemporary British system can trace its origins to 1909, when the newly formed Secret Service Bureau split, creating the Security Service (MI5), and the Secret Intelligence Service (MI6), dealing with domestic and foreign targets respectively. In France, following the 1870–1871 Franco-Prussian War, an intelligence organization was founded, though it was disbanded in 1899. In its place an intelligence component was assigned to the Deuxième Bureau of the Army General Staff. This complemented other intelligence organizations, in particular the Foreign Ministry's Cabinet Noir.

In Germany, as part of its General Staff, the earlier Intelligence Bureau was reformed in 1912 into a specialized intelligence and counterespionage division known as Department IIIb. In Italy, the secret services established in the mid-nineteenth century were reorganized many times, and in 1900 the Office of Information was established. The Russian secret police was initially founded in the sixteenth century by Ivan the Terrible. In 1883 the Okhrana was founded, which remained intact until the Bolshevik Revolution of 1917.

WORLD WAR I
World War I was a momentous event that demonstrated for the first time how useful an effective intelligence organization could be. As would be the case with World War II, rapid technological advances were made, particularly in cryptography. In some instances intelligence proved to be decisive. One of the greatest successes for French intelligence was the discovery of the German plans to launch a gas attack on the Allied armies in 1915. Despite such information, some British and French commanders rejected the warning—with dire consequences, as the Battle of Ypres would show.

Examples of good, close intelligence collaboration included the Anglo-French base at Folkestone, in southeast England, set up to conduct agent-running operations into occupied parts of western Europe. Perhaps the greatest coup for the French was their spy situated within the German High Command, who provided a stream of valuable information.

The British intelligence effort was just as important during the war, especially in the field of code breaking. A good example of this was the interception of the Zimmermann telegram, which detailed advances made by the Germans in requesting Mexican involvement in the war. As a response to this, the United States entered the war in 1917.

In contrast to the Allied effort, German intelligence was less effective, suffering mixed fortunes. There were some successes, for instance predicting military developments in Russia, but there were also notable failures, notably the overreliance on open-source (i.e., freely available, such as radio broadcasts and published) information, which was susceptible to British deception efforts. At the same time, the Austro-Hungarian intelligence service did produce good results, especially in code breaking, and overall fared relatively well, particularly with regard to the Russian army, whose messages they could read.

Italy's introduction to the war in 1915 resulted in an increase in the size and scope of its intelligence effort, with collection stations opened in numerous European cities, including London, Paris, Madrid, Bern, and St. Petersburg. Russian intelligence though badly structured, was generally good, particularly in terms of espionage. This was no doubt assisted through collaborative relations with the French. However, the poor structure caused great problems, for unlike some of its allies, Russia had to fight on two fronts.

THE INTERWAR PERIOD

World War I cannot be considered an "intelligence war" as World War II would be. To be sure, intelligence provided an effective means of gathering information, but in a period when such information was often novel, it was generally believed only when it conformed to the existing preconceptions of military and civilian decision makers. At the same time, however, the success of intelligence during the war served to increase its stature and importance, both militarily and diplomatically.

As a result, intelligence efforts were enlarged in all the major European countries. This was especially true among the victorious powers. In Britain, MI5 grew from nineteen staff members before the war to 844 by war's end. The code-breaking effort was increased, and in 1919 the Government Code and Cipher School was created. It was not until the mid-1930s, however, that the Air Ministry set up an intelligence outfit, and this would prove to be

crucial a few years later when hostilities again broke out. Of perhaps greatest importance was the creation in 1936 of the Joint Intelligence Committee—a body composed of the various elements of the intelligence system, designed to produce all-source estimates for military and political decision makers.

France, the other major European victor, also increased its intelligence effort with the introduction of new intelligence organizations, each geared toward different objectives, including code breaking and combating foreign agents within France. Following Benito Mussolini's accession to power in 1922, Italian intelligence became a bureaucratically controlled yet loosely organized system. Mussolini, as would become the norm with other authoritarian dictators, considered himself the supreme intelligence analyst, and he alone was allowed to see the full range of information available.

Of the defeated powers the biggest changes occurred in Germany. The imperial police intelligence system had been dissolved by the Allies, and in its place a new organization was installed with the primary task of providing information on any political threats. In addition, the armed forces retained intelligence units, yet these were also directed toward providing information on internal, not external, threats.

With the Nazi Party's acquisition of power in the early 1930s, intelligence in Germany altered irrevocably. The Third Reich attached huge importance to the gathering of information on potential enemies, in many ways reflecting the insecurity that would dominate Soviet intelligence for so long. Intelligence was therefore omnipresent. Like other areas of the government, competing intelligence organizations strove to dominate Adolf Hitler's affection, concentrating on diplomatic, military, economic, and social-ideological targets.

In Soviet Russia intelligence had become an effective mode of governance with Vladimir Lenin's rise to power. The tsarist Okhrana was replaced by the Bolshevik Cheka, a ruthless organization designed to suppress internal opposition. By 1919 a covert foreign section had been set up to organize and spread the worldwide communist revolution. By the 1930s the Soviet intelligence system, now known as the NKVD (the acronym for Narodnyi Kommissariat Vnutrennyk Del, or

People's Commissariat for Internal Affairs), had become Joseph Stalin's omniscient tool of terror, which, while coercing the populace at home, was also remarkably successful at recruiting agents abroad.

WORLD WAR II

After 1918 intelligence had grown to become an integral component of government in all the major European countries. From the mid-1930s onward it became crucial, not least in monitoring the rising German aggression. Traditionally it has been assumed that the Anglo-French appeasement policies of the late 1930s were a characteristic of the intelligence failure to identify the Nazi threat. Yet intelligence records reveal this explanation to be far too simplistic: information had been gathered on the nature of Germany's diplomacy and its military capabilities, but intelligence was only one cog in policy makers' decisions. Indeed, the failure of German intelligence to gauge the British and French reactions to Germany's invasion of Poland in 1939 was far more disastrous than appeasement ever was.

From the outset, World War II rapidly became an intelligence war. In every major conflict intelligence played a role. Scholars have debated ever since the impact of intelligence. While there can be no definitive answer, one simple fact is clear: without intelligence the war would have been unrecognizably different.

One key area was intelligence liaison, which in general terms was effectively maintained in defiance of a common enemy. Polish intelligence and resistance proved to be crucial in this respect, for, by providing the first Enigma machine to British intelligence—enabling the Allies to intercept and decipher German Enigma codes—they achieved what many regard as the greatest intelligence coup of the war. Through Ultra—the code name given to the breaking of the German code—the Allies were able to discern enemy plans. Thus crucial tactical and strategic information was provided and turned out to be decisive in, for instance, the Battle of the Atlantic and the Battle of El Alamein. A corollary of this was the "XX System," or double-cross system. British intelligence managed to identify and intercept every single German spy within its shores. It also was able to "turn" many of them,

so that they began to send false information back to Germany. Through Ultra, the Allies were able to observe the German acceptance of and reaction to such information.

A related war effort was the Allied use of deception. In its simplest sense, this involved camouflaging truck and tank movements in the desert so that their tracks could not be observed from the air. At the other end of the scale were the hugely successful campaigns to mislead the Germans about where the invasion of France would occur in 1944, codenamed Operation Overlord. Through the double-cross system and the fabrication of dummy army bases on the southeast coast of England, the Germans were tricked into believing that the attack would take place at the Pas de Calais, when in fact it would take place farther along the French coast in Normandy.

With the German war machine rolling through Europe, British Prime Minister Winston Churchill set up the Special Operations Executive (SOE), whose task was to "set Europe ablaze." This was intelligence in its covert action sense, and it proved to be extremely useful. Through SOE, European resistance efforts to German occupation could be coordinated and extended. To take one example, Norwegian workers provided the Allies with information regarding German attempts to build an atomic bomb and the fact that a plant in Norway was being used to make heavy water, a crucial stage of the process. Liaising with British intelligence, SOE and the Norwegian resistance were able to severely disrupt these efforts, eventually sinking a ferry laden with all the German stocks in a Norwegian fjord.

Despite such efforts, however, intelligence was not always as effective. There is still debate as to the extent to which the Japanese attack on Pearl Harbor on 7 December 1941 could have been avoided, given the quantity and quality of Japanese messages intercepted. A similar yet more clear-cut case is that of the German invasion of the Soviet Union—Operation Barbarossa—in June 1941. Stalin, as the self-appointed supreme authority on intelligence, could not and would not believe that Hitler would dishonor the 1939 Nazi-Soviet Nonaggression Pact. As a result he chose to ignore the plethora of reliable intelligence that indicated this was precisely what Hitler intended to do. Such an error was only rectified by the German miscalculation of their pace of advance, culminating in their defeat in the 1942 Battle of Moscow.

As a whole, however, Allied intelligence was exceptionally good during World War II. With the exclusion of the Soviet Union there were efficient chains of command, and intelligence data could flow freely both nationally and internationally. In the Soviet Union this passage was not as simple and often depended on whether intelligence confirmed existing beliefs. Where the Soviet Union did excel, as indeed it did in the 1930s and would continue to do so postwar, was in the recruitment of agents.

On the Axis side, intelligence, and in particular intelligence exchange, was more limited, and this can perhaps be seen as an outcome of the relationship between the Axis Powers. German intelligence remained divided and beset by internal competition. Given the Nazis' ideological stance, far more people offered their services to the Allies than they did to the Axis Powers, yet there were some notable exceptions. In Britain, the American William Joyce, more commonly known as "Lord Haw-Haw," provided a stream of pro-German propaganda, for which he was eventually executed. An Abwehr officer, Major Nikolaus Ritter, recruited various agents in Britain, Belgium, and America. Despite being called the "rising star of the Abwehr" by its head, Admiral Wilhelm Canaris, Ritter was also its biggest failing, for he inadvertently revealed all of its agents to an American spy in 1941.

The Germans managed to break several of the Turkish codes, which revealed some brief details of British-U.S.-Soviet discussions. Other intercepted signals in 1943 revealed to the Nazi high command the attempts by the Spanish to distance themselves from Germany. Militarily, in general terms German intelligence was better at the tactical level—individual military situations—than it was on the larger strategic level, and this may have been a direct result of the German inability to penetrate the higher echelons of Allied decision making.

The Italians, before their surrender, also maintained a network of foreign agents, in particular in North Africa, undoubtedly a remnant of former colonial presence. By the middle part of the war the Italian Military Information Service had a large code-breaking section. Despite collecting a vast amount of information, often through theft as opposed to interception, the Italians appear to have succumbed to Allied deception efforts.

Intelligence during World War II was therefore tantamount to the day-to-day running of the war. The accuracy and importance of such intelligence can only effectively be considered in hindsight, yet what is crucial is how much importance was placed on such information. While it may be known in the early twenty-first century that some things were correct and others false, what is more relevant is whether or not such material was acted upon at the time.

A stark contrast exists between the relative intelligence successes on the Allied side and the intelligence failings on the Axis side. While it is extremely difficult to gauge this difference and impact qualitatively, it is possible to state, as does the official history of British intelligence in the war, that "but for intelligence the war would have taken a very different course."

THE COLD WAR

The postwar period saw a monumental increase in intelligence, and this in part was due to the introduction of the United States as a major intelligence force. Taking its lead from the British system, the Americans in 1941 instigated the Office of the Coordinator of Information, replaced the following year by the Office of Strategic Services, which in 1947 became the Central Intelligence Agency (CIA). If there had been a nylon curtain separating the powers during the interwar period an impenetrable iron curtain separated them after 1945, and this had a direct impact on the importance of intelligence liaison.

Before the end of hostilities the British and Americans had identified that the Soviet Union would become the "new Germany," and intelligence efforts were redirected accordingly. Through several formal and informal agreements, the Anglo-American intelligence partnership flourished, bringing into its coalition several other European nations.

To those countries in the West, considerable U.S. assistance was offered, and this ensured that friendly intelligence organizations could be created, particularly in West Germany. Initially a CIA-controlled intelligence network was created there called the Gehlen Organization. In 1956 this became the BND (Bundesnachrichtendienst, or Federal Intelligence Service), which lasted throughout the Cold War. The BND was crucial in the gathering of intelligence on East Germany, as for many it became a "window on the east." Within Berlin, various military missions were established to observe conventional Soviet forces.

Several European countries were important due to their geographical proximity to the Soviet Union: Norway became the ideal spot to monitor Soviet missile and nuclear tests from the 1950s onward, and Turkey likewise was a site for capturing Soviet missile telemetry. Italy, with its large contingent of communists in the postwar period, was a useful base from which to disseminate propaganda, mainly through the sponsorship of terrorist attacks that could be blamed on the communists. In Germany, radio stations were used to spread information, and in many countries large military bases were established.

In the Eastern bloc, with the vast and all-pervasive KGB (Komitet Gosudarstvennoy Bezopasnosti, or Committee for State Security) at its heart, intelligence became synonymous with internal policing. As had long been its stable tradecraft, the Soviet Union, along with its Eastern bloc satellites, excelled in the recruiting of Western agents, and this continued right up until the end of the Cold War. The Soviet signals-intelligence effort, about which very little is known, was vast in scale and scope and included among its triumphs the bugging of numerous foreign embassies in Moscow, including that of the United States.

Intelligence became the stable ingredient of the Cold War, with ever-increasing budgets and ever-advancing technological means. As with World War II, it is extremely difficult to measure the impact of intelligence. Once more, it is possible to identify the often decisive role that intelligence played in individual episodes. In general terms, while it is difficult to quantify, it is possible to state that intelligence was consistently a crucial ingredient in policy making.

SINCE 1991

Famously, Western intelligence failed to foresee the implosion of the Soviet Union in 1991, as did, it seems, Soviet intelligence. The initial post–Cold War environment was a strange one, since for the first time since 1900, there was no easily discernible enemy or threat. Growing throughout the Cold War but really only evident afterward was the rising threat of terrorism. This had moved from its Cold War state-sponsored form to a post–Cold War non-state-sponsored form. As it did so, the threat diversified, culminating in the attacks on the United States in September 2001.

A growing characteristic since 1991 has been the increasing importance of liaison with countries that previously had been considered hostile targets, in particular those in the Middle East. Internal policing and security also have increased in importance, as has the exchange of information. This has become especially crucial in Europe, as many of the terrorist targets travel through and frequent European cities. By 2004, and in the wake of new high-casualty, high-impact terrorist attacks, intelligence liaison had become the crux of European security policy.

Since World War I intelligence has grown to become the cornerstone of governmental decision making and policy. Whereas its initial goal had been military, this scope has diversified to reflect the nature of the international scene, for as the target changes, so too must the intelligence organization. It is safe to say that intelligence will go through further stages, yet it is by no means clear how, when, or why this will happen. In the meantime intelligence, battered as it may be by the 2003 scandals regarding weapons of mass destruction in Iraq, will remain a permanent fixture of governance.

See also **Enigma Machine; Espionage/Spies; Warfare.**

BIBLIOGRAPHY

Andrew, Christopher M. *Her Majesty's Secret Service: The Making of the British Intelligence Community.* London, 1985.

Bungert, Heike, et al., eds. *Secret Intelligence in the Twentieth Century.* London, 2003.

Haswell, Jock. *Spies and Spymasters: A Concise History of Intelligence.* London, 1977.

Hess, Sigurd. "Intelligence Cooperation in Europe, 1990 to the Present." *Journal of Intelligence History* 3, no. 1 (summer 2003), 61–68.

Hinsley, F. H. *British Intelligence in the Second World War.* Cambridge, U.K., 1993.

May, Ernest R., ed. *Knowing One's Enemies: Intelligence Assessment before the Two World Wars.* Princeton, N.J., 1984. Reprint, 1996.

Plougin, Vladimir. *Russian Intelligence Services.* Vol. 1, *The Early Years.* Translated by Gennady Bashkov and edited by Claudiu A. Secara. New York, 2000.

Porch, Douglas. *The French Secret Services: From the Dreyfus Affair to the Gulf War.* New York, 1995.

Richelson, Jeffrey T. *Foreign Intelligence Organizations.* Cambridge, Mass., 1988.

MICHAEL S. GOODMAN

INTELLIGENTSIA.

INTELLIGENTSIA. Coined a century and a half ago in Russia, the term *intelligentsia* has known both a subjective and an objective meaning. Broadly speaking the word was originally conceived in terms of principle. It referred to a group characterized by a critical attitude toward social reality and an oppositional political stance. Later the term became defined as a matter of profession, encompassing those with a higher education. *Intelligentsia* as a concept thus bears some relation to the later and more familiar term *intellectuals,* but the two notions overlap only partially. The line of division between the subjective and the objective usage of the term runs approximately between the imperial and the Soviet period. As for the post-Soviet intelligentsia, it is still a phenomenon in search of self-definition.

Peter Boborykin, a Russian novelist of the 1860s, claimed authorship of the term *intelligentsia,* although there have been competing claims of earlier usage in Polish, German, and even in Russian. The word was immediately applied retroactively. Borrowing from Ivan Turgenev's novel *Otsi i Deti* (1862; *Fathers and Children,* sometimes incorrectly translated as *Fathers and Sons*), historians identified a first generation of intelligentsia "fathers," the "superfluous men" of the 1830s and 1840s, members of the gentry raised on German idealist philosophy and desirous of social reform but timorous and impotent in an era of harsh political reaction. The

"fathers" have been counterposed to the "sons," meaning both men and women of the 1860s, who were more diverse in their social origins, positivists intellectually, drawn to the natural sciences, more radical politically than their elders, and frustrated by the inadequate reforms that followed Russia's defeat in the Crimean War (1856).

By the turn of the twentieth century, the generation of intelligentsia "grandchildren" was already shifting from a self-understanding founded on opposition to the autocratic tsarist regime toward one based on professional occupation in a rapidly modernizing country. This redefinition was related to the explosion in the number of putative or potential members of the intelligentsia. Whereas in the 1840s the whole Russian Empire contained no more than a few thousand students, by the time of its first reliable census in 1897 Russia counted nearly a million educated individuals. Historians have invoked this transformation, as well as the admittedly timid liberalization of Russian society after 1905, to explain the decline in the critical posture of the intelligentsia. A marker of this reorientation is the collection of essays entitled *Vekhi* (1909; Landmarks), a self-critical repudiation of the revolutionary tradition by some of Russia's leading formerly radical Marxist intellectuals, such as Nikolai Berdyayev and Peter Struve.

According to a dominant narrative of Russian history, the year 1917 represented a historic test for the classic intelligentsia, entrusted with the task of creating a progressive order in Russia. Its failure to do so in the few months between the fall of tsarism and the Bolshevik seizure of power discredited the entire intelligentsia tradition along with its politicians of the time, such as the liberal conservative Prince Lvov, first prime minister of the provisional government; the foreign minister, Pavel Milyukov, eminent liberal intellectual and member of the Constitutional Democratic Party; and the last pre-Bolshevik prime minister, the Socialist Revolutionary lawyer Alexander Kerensky. The outcome of events in 1917 opened a debate that still continues over the responsibility of the classic intelligentsia, with its aversion to state power and high-minded ineffectiveness, for Bolshevik success and for the ensuing Soviet regime.

Soviet Russia could also be considered a creation of the classic revolutionary intelligentsia. In spite of their workers' ideology and their appeal to the peasantry, early Bolshevik leaders have been depicted by their critics as simply successors to the most extreme or "nihilistic" earlier trends in the intelligentsia. Most Bolshevik leaders were indeed educated individuals thoroughly imbued with the intelligentsia ethos of uncompromising, principled opposition to the ancien régime and a utopian vision for the future. Vladimir Lenin himself, though scornful of intelligentsia fecklessness, valued professional skills, considering these to be the essential material basis of socialism. Many members of the prerevolutionary intelligentsia emigrated from Russia or withdrew from professional and political activity after 1917. Some, however, particularly those with technical competencies, entered Soviet service, willingly or reluctantly. By April 1919 almost five thousand doctors were serving in the Red Army. A year later the army included some fifty thousand former generals and other higher-level tsarist officers. This alliance between the old intelligentsia and the new state lasted until the end of the 1920s. Passage from the moderate NEP (New Economic Policy) to a policy of intensive industrialization and collectivization brought the prominent role of the old intelligentsia to an end. The 1928 show trial of fifty-three engineers and miners announced its imminent disappearance. By 1933 only 17 percent of the Soviet intelligentsia consisted of former bourgeois specialists. Their ranks had been depleted by further emigration, natural attrition, and purges. Above all, they had been flooded by the emergence of a new socialist intelligentsia.

From the very outset, the Soviet regime was determined to create its own intelligentsia. By 1919 it had opened rabfaks (rabochiye fakultety, or "workers faculties") at every institution of higher education. Here, workers and peasants with only basic schooling received an accelerated higher education. By 1933 half of the students in universities were of worker or peasant background, though this figure fell later. The proletarianization or, as some have called it, the plebianization of the intelligentsia had been successfully carried out.

Soviet ideology soon formulated a new conception of the intelligentsia: "a social stratum consisting of people professionally occupied with mental work.... Being a stratum and not a class the intelligentsia is incapable of playing an independent political role in social life" (*Bolshaya sovetskaya entsiklopedia*, 2nd ed., 1953, vol. 18, p. 270). Article 1 of the 1977 Soviet constitution proclaimed "a socialist state of the whole people, expressing the will and interests of the workers, peasants and intelligentsia...." At this time the intelligentsia, in the Soviet sense, numbered more than thirty million individuals. Overall it was almost evenly divided between men and women; two-thirds of engineers, the numerically most important profession, were men whereas a similar proportion of doctors were women. Russians and Jews who numbered, respectively, 53 percent and 0.9 percent of the population accounted for 67 percent and 7.1 percent of scientific workers. Mathematicians and physicists enjoyed the highest professional prestige.

What became of the oppositional ethos of the classic intelligentsia? Stirrings in Russian culture after the death of Joseph Stalin in 1953 and hopes raised by Nikita Khrushchev's destalinization between 1956 and 1964 gave rise to a dissident movement founded on liberal, Christian, or socialist values. Regardless of the attention and support afforded the movement in the West, dissidents represented an infinitesimally small group. Unlike their nineteenth-century predecessors, there is no evidence that they enjoyed sympathy throughout society. Dissidents, or *inakomysliashchie* (those who think otherwise), did however represent the tip of a much wider phenomenon, the *shestidesyatniki*, (the people of the [nineteen] sixties). This was the generation whose hopes had been raised under Khrushchev only to be frustrated for two decades during the era of Brezhnevite *zastoi* (stagnation). In a sense Mikhail Gorbachev, who came to power in 1985, bore the aspirations of the *shestidesyatniki*. Though the Soviet intelligentsia never succumbed to Western-style "Gorbymania," it initially offered him its support. Disappointed with Gorbachev's halfhearted and unsuccessful measures, by 1991 the intelligentsia had transferred its allegiance to the new president of the soon-to-be independent Russian Federation, Boris Yeltsin.

Disorientation best characterizes the situation of the post-Soviet intelligentsia, even though *intelligentovedenie* (the study of the intelligentsia) has become a thriving academic subfield with its own institute and innumerable publications. Russia's integration into the world economy guarantees the continued growth and importance of the educated population. Debate continues, however, over the role of the intelligentsia, its critical function, and its social mission. Critics argue that wholesale privatization has also meant the privatization of knowledge and therefore the disappearance of a classic intelligentsia. Alexander Solzhenitsyn emphasizes the abyss between the *narod* (people) and the intelligentsia, attributing it to betrayal by a self-infatuated, opportunistic, and impious intelligentsia that possesses only *obrazovshchina* (book knowledge) rather than moral values. *Yabloko* (Apple), the party of the post-Soviet liberal and westernized intelligentsia, has done so poorly that it does not count on the political map.

Through its management of public opinion, its manipulation of the media and of national values, the Vladimir Putin regime has succeeded in co-opting a good part of the independent-minded intelligentsia. Already discredited by its identification with Yeltsin's disastrous economic reforms and his political misbehavior, that part of the intelligentsia that might play a critical role has largely withdrawn to nonpolitical and often lucrative activities. In the atmosphere of early-twenty-first-century Russia, even *kulturnost* (the quality of being cultivated or well-mannered and educated), recognized by Soviet sociologists as an intelligentsia trait, has retreated into the background. Is this the end of the intelligentsia, in its classic subjective meaning, as a group founded on moral principle and a critical sense? The question is widely debated in early-twenty-first-century Russia, suggesting that something of the ethos of the original intelligentsia persists.

See also **Gorbachev, Mikhail; Khrushchev, Nikita; New Economic Policy (NEP); Putin, Vladimir; Soviet Union; Yeltsin, Boris.**

BIBLIOGRAPHY

Churchward, Lloyd G. *The Soviet Intelligentsia: An Essay on the Social Structure and Roles of Soviet Intellectuals during the 1960s.* London, 1973.

Markiewicz-Lagneau, Janina. "La fin de l'intelligentsia? Formation et différenciation de l'intelligentsia soviétique." *Revue d'études comparative est/ouest* 7, no. 4 (December 1976): 7–72.

Pipes, Richard, ed. *The Russian Intelligentsia.* New York, 1961.

Sinyavsky, Andrei. *The Russian Intelligentsia.* New York, 1997.

ANDRE LIEBICH

INTERNATIONAL BRIGADES. On 17 and 18 July 1936 Spanish generals, soon to be under the command of General Francisco Franco (1892–1975), staged a coup against the Republican government, which had become strongly left wing after the Popular Front's legitimate electoral victory the previous February. The Soviet Union quickly decided to help the Spanish Republicans do battle against Francoism, which was widely viewed as a Spanish brand of fascism; but it acted cautiously, in consideration of English neutrality and French hesitation. Joseph Stalin (1879–1953) decided to supply the Spanish government with limited military aid—weapons, pilots, tank drivers, and military advisors (to total two thousand men for the entire war)—while entrusting to the Communist International (Comintern) the task of forming an international volunteer army. On 18 September 1936 the Communist International's executive committee met and decided, according to terms in the transcript, "to proceed with the recruitment, among workers of all countries, of volunteers with military experience, in preparation for their deployment in Spain." But the Comintern did not wish to be recognized as initiating the formation of foreign brigades, which only became official on 22 October 1936 by decree of the Spanish government.

A total of almost 32,000 foreigners from nearly fifty countries enrolled in the brigades. Among them were nearly 9,000 French; 3,000 Poles; 3,000 Italians; 2,300 Americans; 2,200 Germans; and 2,100 citizens from the various Balkan countries. There were 1,800 British; 1,700 Belgians; 1,000 Czechoslovakians; 900 from the Baltic region; and 900 from Austria. Scandinavian countries accounted for 800; 600 came from the Netherlands, 500 from Hungary, 500 from Canada, 400 from Switzerland, and 100 from Portugal. Jewish volunteers had a special presence. They numbered some 5,000, many of them Polish volunteers with the Botwin Company of the 13th Dombrowsky brigade, which published its own Yiddish newspaper.

Members of an International Brigade in formation during the Spanish civil war. ©Hulton-Deutsch Collection/Corbis

Generally, the term *International Brigades* designated all the anti-Francoist foreign fighters, and it should be noted that other foreign units, and Spanish units that included foreigners, participated outside the international brigades formation. About two thousand such foreigners enrolled in the regular Spanish army. In addition, about one thousand non-Spanish fighters fought with various militias, whether anarchist, anarchist-syndicalist, or part of the POUM (Workers Party of Marxist Unification). This brought the total number of foreign fighters to thirty-five thousand or about one-third of the foreign contingent (composed of Portugese, Italian, and Germans) enlisted by the pro-Franco nationalists. Of those thirty-five thousand, about five thousand were killed. Finally, the International Brigades were not limited to foreigners; from December 1936, they were open to Spanish volunteers and draftees, and by the autumn of 1937 they represented the bulk of brigade combatants.

Essentially, although modifications of the scheme were numerous, there were five International Brigades.

Each brigade was divided into four to six battalions and each of these, usually into five companies. None was homogenous in national or linguistic composition. German was the prevailing language spoken in Thaelmann Brigade; Italian predominated in the Garibaldi Brigade. The Dombrwoski Brigade was largely Polish; the Marseillaise Brigade, French; the Abraham Lincoln Brigade was predominantly English, even though its commanders were in succession Yugoslavian, German, Spanish, and Brazilian.

A sociological profile of recruits can be sketched from the largest contingent, from France. The average age of a volunteer was twenty-nine years, nine months; the modal age was thirty. More than half the combatants were young men between twenty-six and thirty-four years old. Unmarried men were overrepresented, but the most striking statistic concerned the overwhelming participation of the working class. They represented 65 percent of the French volunteers, to which can be added some 17 percent manual and unskilled laborers. Politically, two-thirds of the French volunteers were communists or declared fellow-travelers, the proportion was even higher in the other national contingents. In addition, proportionally more communists filled positions in the higher ranks of command. Some 52 percent of French combatants were card-carrying members of the Communist Party; that figure jumped to 68 percent for lower-grade officers, 79 percent of junior officers, and virtually all of the commanders and political commissars. In Spain, the French-Belgian communist André Marty (1886–1956) was appointed organizational leader of the International Brigades, assisted by Palmiro Togliatti (1893–1964), a member, like Marty, of the executive of the Comintern.

In the end, although communist participation in the Brigades was essential, the Comintern's appeal had reached beyond the communist sphere to touch a highly popular antifascist sensibility. In the 1920s Italian fascism could seem to be an historical exception. But this view changed during the 1930s with the rise of authoritarian regimes in Western and Central Europe, and with the development of protofascist movements in the European democracies. Most important, of course, were Adolf Hitler (1889–1945) and Franco. Carlo Rosselli, fighting in Spain in a unit independent of the International Brigades, encapsulated the antifascist sentiment with his slogan: "Today in Spain, tomorrow in Italy." Posterity offers the best evidence of the success of the International Brigades on a symbolic level. While their existence was proof of the success of the communist strategy, their archetypical antifascism was sustained by literary and cinematic creations not strictly communist, such as André Malraux's novel *L'espoir* (1937; *Man's Hope*), Joris Ivens's film *Terre d'Espagne* (1937; *Spanish Earth*), Ernest Hemingway's novel *For Whom the Bell Tolls* (1940), and George Orwell's *Homage to Catalonia* (1938).

But neither political nor symbolic successes were sufficient on the battlefield. While acquitting themselves well despite high casualties, in Madrid in November 1936 and on the Ebre River in July 1938, the International Brigades were, like the regular Spanish army, eventually defeated. On 25 September 1938 they were withdrawn from the front, then dissolved. Brigadists gradually left the country, but more than five thousand former volunteers from countries with authoritarian or fascist regimes were incarcerated by the French government. Several years later, a considerable number of these fighters would enter the anti-Nazi Resistance.

See also **Antifascism; Communism; Spanish Civil War.**

BIBLIOGRAPHY

Castells, Andreu. *Las brigadas internacionales de la guerra de España.* Barcelona, 1974.

Ranzato, Gabriele. "Brigate internazionali." In *Dizionario del fascismo*, edited by Victoria De Grazia and Sergio Luzzatto, vol. 1, 198–199. Turin, Italy, 2002.

Skoutelsky, Rémi. *L'espoir guidait leurs pas: Les volontaires français dans les Brigades internationales, 1936–1939.* Paris, 1998.

Zaagsma, Gerben. "'Red Devils': The Botwin Company in the Spanish Civil War." *East European Jewish Affairs* 33, no. 1 (2003): 83–99.

PHILIPPE BUTON

INTERNATIONAL CRIMINAL COURT.

After initial experiments in international criminal justice for perpetrators of atrocities, at Nuremberg and Tokyo (1945–1948) in the aftermath of the Second World War, proposals for a permanent institution stagnated. The tensions of the Cold War (1945–1989) made progress on international criminal law difficult, and only in late 1989, as the Berlin Wall was crumbling, did the United Nations General Assembly revive efforts to create an international criminal court. On 17 July 1998, at the conclusion of a diplomatic conference held in Rome, the Rome Statute of the International Criminal Court was adopted. The statute entered into force on 1 July 2002, following deposit of the sixtieth ratification of the statute. By late 1994 judges and a prosecutor had been elected, and the court was fully operational. By early 2005 major investigations were under way with respect to atrocities committed in northern Uganda and eastern Congo. The first arrest warrants were made public in October 2005, targeted at rebel leaders in northern Uganda.

Establishment of the International Criminal Court is part of a broader story, whereby international institutions such as the United Nations, inspired by the growth of human rights law and policy, have focused on the need for accountability in the face of serious violations of human dignity. In 1990 the U.S. president George H. W. Bush and the British prime minister Margaret Thatcher had called for an international tribunal to prosecute Saddam Hussein following Iraq's invasion of

Kuwait. The proposal never came to fruition, but the idea generated greater momentum two years later, as war raged in the former Yugoslavia. Two United Nations international tribunals were eventually created by the Security Council, for the former Yugoslavia and Rwanda. Elsewhere, amnesties have been withdrawn as part of a renewed insistence on addressing impunity. Various justice initiatives and related endeavors, such as truth commissions, have featured as measures in countries emerging from periods of conflict.

The International Criminal Court is an international institution independent of the United Nations and run by its member states, who numbered one hundred by October 1995; the number remained unchanged ten years later. Many of the world's major powers chose to stay outside the organization (China, Russia, India), although only the United States of America took a position of outright opposition. The popularity of the court among small and medium powers has revealed their frustration with existing institutions, such as the Security Council, which have been dominated by the great powers.

JURISDICTION OF THE INTERNATIONAL CRIMINAL COURT

As a treaty-based institution, in contrast with the tribunals for the former Yugoslavia and Rwanda, that were created by the Security Council and apply to all countries, in principle the International Criminal Court can only operate with respect to those states that have actually ratified or acceded to the statute. By joining the court, states agree that the court can prosecute their own citizens and that it can also prosecute any crimes committed on their territory. There is nothing exceptional here because international law has always acknowledged the right of states to prosecute crimes committed on their territory or by their nationals. What states party to the Rome Statute have done, then, is delegate their own criminal jurisdiction with respect to certain crimes to the International Criminal Court.

The Rome Statute also allows the Security Council to send a case to the International Criminal Court even with respect to a state that has not accepted the statute. Functioning in this mode, it is basically treating the court as if it were a permanent version of the Yugoslavia and Rwanda tribunals established in the early 1990s. In the first years of operation of the court, there were doubts that it would ever exercise this power, given the United States' hostility to the court and the likelihood that it would block such referral with its veto power in the Security Council. But in March 2005 the Security Council referred the situation in the Darfur region of western Sudan to the court, acting on the recommendation of an international commission of inquiry.

At the center of the court's operations stands the prosecutor, who has the authority to decide which cases will proceed. He can also decide which situations will not proceed, when cases are referred to him by the Security Council or by member states. When the Rome Statute was being drafted, the concept of an independent prosecutor was bold and controversial, with many states fearing it might lead to politically motivated charges following the prosecutor's ideological whims. To answer such concerns, the statute imposes a rule of "complementarity." The prosecutor must be in a position to demonstrate that the state that would ordinarily be responsible for prosecuting the case is either unwilling or unable to proceed. In this sense, the court is viewed as an adjunct to national justice systems rather than as their replacement. The preamble to the statute recalls that "it is the duty of every state to exercise its criminal jurisdiction over those responsible for international crimes" (*Rome Statute of the International Criminal Court*, UN DOC. A/CONF.183/9). By joining the court, many states have also adopted robust new legislation so that they can prosecute atrocities more effectively before their own courts.

According to the statute, the court is to prosecute what are called the "most serious crimes of concern to the international community as a whole." Four such crimes are listed in the Rome Statute: genocide, crimes against humanity, war crimes, and aggression. The first three are defined in some detail. As for aggression, the statute specifies that the court may not exercise jurisdiction over that crime until a definition and the conditions of prosecution have been agreed to. The plan was for the statute to be amended at the first review conference, in 2009, so as to enable the court to actually exercise jurisdiction over the crime of

Slobodan Milošević appears before the International War Crimes Tribunal in the Hague, Netherlands, December 2001. He was charged with genocide, war crimes, and crimes against humanity for his role in the conflict between Serbian forces and ethnic Albanians in Kosovo. AP/WIDE WORLD PHOTOS

aggression. Other serious crimes with an international dimension, including terrorism and drug trafficking, were also on the waiting list, possibly to be added to the court's jurisdiction at the 2009 conference.

PUNISHABLE CRIMES

Genocide, crimes against humanity, and war crimes together cover a wide range of serious atrocities that have figured in most of the grave humanitarian crises of recent times. Genocide was first defined in the 1948 Genocide Convention. It is relatively narrow in scope, confined essentially to acts involving the physical destruction of an ethnic group. Crimes against humanity comprise a much broader category. They encompass most serious human rights violations, such as disappearance, sexual violence, apartheid, and torture. In order to ensure a seamless coverage, the definition of crimes against humanity

also includes a broad act known as "persecutions." So as to distinguish them from ordinary violent crimes such as murder, crimes against humanity must be committed as part of a "widespread or systematic attack on a civilian population." Crimes against humanity had been prosecuted at Nuremberg and Tokyo but only to the extent that they were committed as part of aggressive war. The Rome Statute confirms an evolution in international criminal law, recognizing that crimes against humanity are now punishable even when committed in peacetime.

The most detailed list of offenses in the Rome Statute appears in the war crimes provision. Reflecting historic distinctions made by the international law of armed conflict, war crimes are divided according to whether they are committed in international or internal armed conflict. There are some gaps here, however. The court's jurisdiction over prohibited weapons is quite limited, reflecting concerns at the Rome Conference of nuclear powers who were afraid of the consequences of a broad general provision on inhumane weapons.

PROCEDURE BEFORE THE COURT

The court's eighteen judges are drawn from diverse legal systems around the world. This makes them well suited for the procedural system, which is a hybrid of various national systems. The court adopts a largely adversarial system, and in that sense follows the general scheme of common law courts, such as those in the United States, the United Kingdom, and countries of the Commonwealth. However, both the prosecutor and the judges are given significant duties with respect to protecting the rights of suspects and the accused. To this extent, the models are the inquisitorial criminal procedure systems that characterize continental Europe and many other parts of the world.

Upon conviction, the court may impose a maximum sentence of life imprisonment, although in such cases there is a mandatory review for purposes of release on parole after twenty-five years. The penalty regime of the court was a delicate compromise. At the extremes were some states favoring capital punishment and others opposed even to life imprisonment, which they viewed as inhumane. The Nuremberg and Tokyo tribunals imposed execution by hanging on several of the convicted offenders. Rejection of the death penalty by the International Criminal Court manifests an evolving consensus in international law that is also reflected in growing rates of abolition within national justice systems.

UNITED STATES OPPOSITION

One of the great enigmas surrounding the establishment of the court is the position taken by the United States of America. No country has been more enthusiastic about international criminal justice than the United States. It played a central role in the Nuremberg and Tokyo trials and was the driving force behind establishment of the Yugoslavia and Rwanda tribunals half a century later. Moreover, the United States was deeply involved in the establishment of the International Criminal Court and made many important and constructive contributions to the final draft of the Rome Statute.

U.S. opposition to the court is therefore not the result of any general diffidence concerning the idea of such an international institution but rather with dissatisfaction concerning the form that the body has actually taken. Specifically, in the course of negotiations over the years 1994 to 1998, an alliance of small and middle powers had diluted the role the Security Council might play in directing prosecutions and especially in blocking them altogether. This proved to be anathema for the United States, which has not been able to accept an institution that it cannot control through its dominance of the United Nations Security Council.

At Rome, the United States voted against the final draft statute, which was nonetheless adopted by 120 votes to 7, with 21 abstentions. For some years subsequently, the United States took a relatively benign approach of constructive engagement and actually signed the statute (a preliminary to ratification) on 31 December 2000. But by early 2002, when it seemed inevitable that the statute would enter into force and that the court would become operational, United States policy shifted toward active hostility. At the request of the United States, many states entered into agreements by which they refused to transfer American nationals suspected of crimes to the court. In 2002 and 2003 the United States also pushed through damaging resolutions in the Security Council, aimed at blocking the court's operations in specific cases. But in 2004, with the United States on the defensive in the context of shocking reports of prisoner abuses by its forces in Iraq, the resolutions were withdrawn. Then, in 2005, the United States abstained in a resolution referring the Sudan crisis to the International Criminal Court, in effect conceding the body's authority. This signaled the defeat of its policy of opposition and, at the same time, confirmed the viability of the International Criminal Court as one of the great institutions of the international legal order.

See also **Campaign against Torture; Convention on Genocide; European Court of Justice; Human Rights; International Law; Milošević, Slobodan; Nuremberg War Crimes Trials; Universal Declaration of Human Rights; Yugoslavia.**

BIBLIOGRAPHY

Bassiouni, M. Cherif, ed. *The Legislative History of the International Criminal Court: Introduction, Analysis, and Integrated Text.* Ardsley, N.Y., 2005. Documentary history of the court.

Cassese, Antonio, Paola Gaeta, and John R. W. D. Jones, eds. *The Rome Statute of the International Criminal Court: A Commentary.* Oxford, U.K., 2002. Detailed commentary on specific provisions of the statute, prepared by leading authorities in the field.

Sadat, Leila Nadya. *The International Criminal Court and the Transformation of International Law: Justice for the New Millennium.* Ardsley, N.Y., 2002.

Schabas, William A. *An Introduction to the International Criminal Court.* 2nd ed. Cambridge, U.K., 2004. Concise, accessible introduction to the court, with relevant documents.

Triffterer, Otto, ed. *Commentary on the Rome Statute of the International Criminal Court, Observers' Notes, Article by Article.* Baden-Baden, Germany, 1999. Each of the 128 articles in the statute is provided with a specific chapter.

WILLIAM A. SCHABAS

INTERNATIONAL LABOUR ORGANIZATION.

Universal peace "can be established only if it is based upon social justice." This was the principle, found in the preamble of Part XIII of the Versailles Peace Treaty, signed on 28 June 1919, upon which was established the International Labour Organization (ILO). The ILO, at first an independent body associated with the League of Nations, has been since the end of World War II a specialized agency within the United Nations.

Recognition of the necessity of international rules to govern labor practices gestated slowly over the course of the nineteenth century, mainly within the social reform and socialist movements. Social reformers in the early nineteenth century favored some form of regulation, but the first international labor congress took place in Berlin only in 1890 at the invitation of Kaiser William II (r. 1888–1918). The aim was to preserve social peace by improving conditions for workers without changing the rules of the international competition. The International Association for the Legal Protection of Workers, founded in 1901, pursued and institutionalized these goals; from its works arose the International Labour Office in Basel in 1901. This agency published the first compilations of pertinent social laws, a mission that the ILO pursues today.

Two conferences in Bern in 1905 and 1906 adopted the first two international labor conventions. These conventions, ratified by national parliaments, prohibited employers from hiring women for night work in industrial settings and forbade the use of white phosphorus in the manufacture of matches. In addition to this direct antecedent of the ILO, a permanent committee in charge of accidents at work and social insurances was founded in 1898, and an international association to fight unemployment was established in 1910. These groups attracted the first civil servants engaged in international social policy, including Arthur Fontaine (1860–1931), the first president of ILO's Governing Body; a Belgian lawyer, Louis Varlez (1868–1930), who served as a policy-making advisor at the Bureau International du Travail (BIT) from 1919 to 1928; and the English civil servant Malcolm Delevingne (1868–1950), a member of the committee that wrote the ILO statutes. These associations pursued three objectives: peace, social justice, and respect for fair competition. These represent the ILO's basic mission to the present day. Since the Declaration of Philadelphia in 1944 social activism has been viewed not only as a remedy to injustice or a means of keeping peace but as a fundamental human right.

The birth of the ILO was also a response to the increasingly reformist aspirations of workers' movements represented by the International Federation of Trade Unions (IFTU), which was formed in 1901. War World I reinforced these ambitions by bringing together representatives of workers' movement in the major belligerent nations in spite of the conflict. At international conferences they also demanded social rights be incorporated in future peace treaties. The sudden division of the workers' movement caused by the Russian Revolution in 1917 seemed to reinforce the urgent nature of these demands.

THE ILO IN ACTION

Only the victorious countries in World War I were invited to participate when the Commission on International Labor Legislation met in January 1919. Neither Germany, which in the 1880s had developed a distinctly progressive social policy, nor Switzerland, which had long made efforts in favor of international legislation, were invited. Representatives of the victorious countries, particularly the French and English, were in charge of the establishment of the new organization. Edward Phelan (1888–1967), a civil servant at the English ministry of labor, provided key inspiration for the ILO constitution. Albert Thomas (1878–1932), a French politician and socialist, was named first secretary of the ILO. From the beginning, the positions and roles assigned member countries would be a dominant problem. Tripartism, still in force in the early twenty-first century, favors national governments; each state sends to the ILO two representatives together with a representative of an employers' organization and a representative of a workers' organization. The Governing Body makes proposals that are submitted to these representatives for a vote during the annual ILO conferences. A proposal that obtains a two-thirds or better majority becomes a convention to be submitted for ratification by national parliaments. In the 1920s numerous international conventions were adopted concerning women and children, working conditions, length of workday, health and accident protection, and compensation. Ratification was often difficult. The refusal by France and Britain to ratify the first convention regarding the eight-hour day, which was a major issue for the new organization, questioned the ILO's very raison d'être.

However, the ILO functioned in a way that distinguished it from the usual intergovernmental bodies and created a new model of operation. In addition to requiring a two-thirds majority for ratification, the administrative tools to ensure that the conventions were respected were set up as early as 1919 and attended to from 1926 by a committee of experts. This approach, innovative at the time, continues to operate in the early 2000s and has been a factor in preserving the ILO's autonomy. Albert Thomas, the first president of the International Labour bureau, helped establish the stand-alone character of the ILO, traveling widely to open branches in many countries, appointing numerous permanent functionaries, and tirelessly promoting ratifications. Thomas nurtured a genuine European culture within the ILO, and his colleagues and successors extended his influence, among them

the English president of the organization, Harold Butler (1932–1938), and the Irish president, Edward Phelan (1941–1948). Finally and above all, from the beginning the two autonomous groups in the organization, employers and organized workers in unions from around the world, effectively and efficiently counterbalanced national interests.

This bipartisanship, however, also raised considerable difficulties of its own that have persisted to the present. The 1919 text specified that delegates and their advisors must be chosen with the consent of the most representative professional organizations. This arrangement was anchored in a liberal vision by which society hoped to encourage the organization of economic and social interests in order to favor dialogue. But the limits of this approach soon became clear. In countries with a pluralistic political system, when union organizations are divided, the choice of the "representative organization" in fact was decided upon according to the power dynamics within the directive bodies of the ILO. Favored were the best-represented factions in the international organizations, not necessarily the most representative of the country in question. In the case of dictatorships, the very notion of representation is problematic. In 1923 the Italian Fascist government sent a workers' delegate chosen by the national confederation of corporations, which led to protests by the workers' representatives; a similar situation occurred in 1937 with a delegate from Spain. Still more difficulties arose after the Soviet Union was readmitted to the ILO in 1954. Alongside the thorny question of the freedom of workers to choose a union, an issue raised with dictatorships, the employers' group objected to the representative character of the designated employer delegate when chosen directly by the government. The admission into the ILO of countries with planned economies put into question the liberal rules upon which the organization was based. An investigation in 1955 advised revision of the initial conventions, even a new definition of union freedom to save the principle of universality.

GLOBALIZATION OF A EUROPEAN ORGANIZATION

From the beginning, universality has been an important element undergirding the legitimacy of the ILO. In 1919 the organization included forty-five members, among them Germany and Austria, even though both were excluded from the League of Nations. Although twenty-seven member countries were non-European, western Europe played a dominant role in terms of the ILO's management, personnel, and overall conception as to role and operations. The organization's objective, influenced by nineteenth-century social reformers, was to prevent the exploitation and abuse of workers and to fight both material poverty and moral corruption. European domination was explained by the special status accorded "members whose industrial importance is more considerable" on the ILO's governing body and also by the fact that colonialism had not yet been put into question.

European supremacy diminished in the years after World War II, with more members—178 in 2005—including the former colonies that were agitating for and achieving independence. In the 1960s developing countries founded the Group of 77 and, with the support of socialist governments, began objecting to the way in which the ILO favored industrialized nations. Revision of the statutes in 1986 allowed a more equitable representation on the governing body of the ILO. In 1998 a Chilean, Juan Somavia (b. 1941), became the first director of the ILO from the southern hemisphere.

Overall, recent developments have led the organization to reconsider the rules that provided its foundation when it was formed in 1919, with a series of declarations and actions that, in addition to traditional efforts in the direction of social melioration, take a clear position in favor of development for all countries. This major orientation on behalf of norms has been modified. Apart from traditional efforts to improve work conditions, the conventions and directives aim to secure human rights in work: freedom to join a union, equal pay for men and women, and elimination of forced labor—the latter a central objective of the organization beginning in the mid-1960s. Due to increasing diversity among member nations, normative action tends toward regionalization, occasionally expressed through arguments that manifest hostility toward the economic and intellectual domination of Western countries. Consequently, the ILO has developed other modes of action aiming to reach not only specific groups but also entire countries. Technical aid and assistance missions

have increased in number. Already employed between the two world wars to meet the legal needs of European governments, such missions became part policies intended to provide aid to developing countries. At the start of the twenty-first century, the ILO, as an international agency of expertise about social affairs, is thus particularly well placed to chart and to help determine the effects of economic globalization. The ILO responds to the threat of war by appealing to economic development and to the threat of economic conflict by developing consultation and cooperation together with norms that favor a socially equitable globalization and "decent work."

See also **Labor Movements; League of Nations; Nobel Prize; United Nations; Versailles, Treaty of.**

BIBLIOGRAPHY

Primary Sources

International Labour Organisation. *Dix ans d'organisation internationale du travail.* Geneva, 1931.

Morse, David A. "ILO and the Social Infrastructure of Peace." Nobel lecture, Oslo, December 1969. Stockholm, 1970.

Organisation internationale du travail. *1919–1969, 50 années au service du progrés social.* Geneva, 1969.

Secondary Sources

Alcock, Anthony Evelyn. *History of the International Labour Organisation.* London and Basingstoke, U.K., 1971.

Bonvin, Jean-Michel. *L'Organisation internationale du Travail: Étude sur une agence productrice de normes.* Paris, 1998.

Follows, John W. *Antecedents of the International Labour Organization.* Oxford, U.K., 1951.

Ghebali, Victor Yves. *L'Organisation internationale du travail (OIT).* Geneva, 1987.

Guérin, Denis. *Albert Thomas au BIT 1920–1932: De l'Internationalisme a l'Europe.* Geneva, 1996.

SANDRINE KOTT

INTERNATIONAL LAW. International law comprises those rules and processes that are produced by states to regulate their mutual behavior, or that have arisen to regulate international transactions by states, private organizations, and individuals. Persons used to the certainties of

The "Martens Declaration" in the preamble to the Hague Regulations (1899)

[I]n cases not included in the Regulations . . . populations and belligerents remain under the protection and empire of the principles of international law, as they result from the usages established between civilized nations, from the laws of humanity, and the requirements of the public conscience.

municipal (that is, national or domestic) law are puzzled by several features characteristic of international law. No single authority acts as legislator or interpreter of the law. No court exercises compulsory jurisdiction over breaches in the law; sanctions are more often applied by the offended states, sometimes in the form of reprisal. And the sources of international law are not restricted to easily identifiable legislation issuing from an agreed-upon political process. Further, international law seems often ineffective, and surely some of the most catastrophic and murderous transgressions against it occurred during the bloody twentieth century. But Immanuel Kant (1724–1804) recognized that conflict and strife not only challenge the law, they also create it, as states attempt to solve the problems they have caused. And so the twentieth century saw not only the greatest crimes against, but also the greatest extensions of, international law in the areas most troubling to its success: the (as yet) incomplete creation of international cooperative authority in the League of Nations (1919), the United Nations (1945), and the European Union (1993); the establishment of a permanent Court of Arbitration (1899), which developed into the permanent International Court of Justice (ICJ, 1945), and a permanent International Court of Criminal Justice (ICC, 2003); the writing down (codification) of legal custom and the specification of the law's sources; and finally the expansion of the laws of war, which restricted the permitted methods of fighting as they widened the scope of recognized human rights.

SOURCES OF INTERNATIONAL LAW

The sources of international law are enumerated in Article 38 of the Statute of the International Court of Justice

1. Treaties between states are by far the most unambiguous and numerous sources. The League of Nations began the requirement of publicly registering treaties, and its successor the United Nations has recorded more than twenty-five thousand.

2. Custom, that is, the actual practices of states or collective actors, is the original form of international law, before it was written down. Custom is wider than treaties, because it applies to all actors in the international community, not just to those who have explicitly agreed to a written rule, for example, by ratifying a treaty. And custom changes over time, so it is naturally controversial. Some rules, such as the Geneva Conventions of 1949, which originally applied only to signatories, have since been accepted as customary and are taken to apply to everyone.

3. "The general principles of law recognized by civilized nations" is the third source. In the seventeenth century, the Dutch jurist Hugo Grotius (1583–1645) laid the foundations of international law in his *De Jure Belli Ac Pacis* (1625; The rights of war and peace), and through the eighteenth century these principles were known as natural law. In the first international codification of the laws of war at the First Hague Convention (1899), the Russian jurist Fyodor F. Martens called them "the laws of humanity." In the early twenty-first century they are known as *jus cogens* (compelling law). By any name they refer to principles basic to all law and human action and that are thus prior to and superior to positive, written law.

4. Judicial decisions also make international law. These may be judgments by the permanent courts (ICJ, ICC), by special tribunals such as the International Military Tribunals after World War II or by national courts, since most international law cases are tried in national venues.

5. "The most highly qualified publicists of the various nations" also help determine law by

discovering the patterns of custom or interpreting law, practices, and public opinion.

6. Equity, that is, basic principles of fairness, may also play a role in deciding cases in international law.

INSTITUTIONALIZATION, EXTENSION, AND CODIFICATION

The world wars before 1945, the civil wars thereafter, and the mass death caused by them all have driven international law to change in broadly three ways: it has become institutionalized, extended, and codified.

Institutionalization has occurred on several levels. International cooperative institutions such as the League of Nations and the United Nations simultaneously uphold and limit the sovereignty of their members, for example, by subjecting them to the human rights provisions of the UN Charter as a condition of joining. Regional security or economic organizations, such as the North Atlantic Treaty Organization or the Western European Union, have also burgeoned since 1945. The European Union, developing from the Organization of European Economic Cooperation (1948), has become so strongly integrated in economic, political, security, citizenship, and legal terms that it constitutes a new kind of federated state. Its various organs, including the European Parliament, European Court of Human Rights, and the European Court of Justice have produced abundant "European law," a subset of international law. Finally, international law is practiced and formed by nonstate institutions. The oldest is the International Committee of the Red Cross (ICRC), a private Swiss organization founded in 1874 to aid wounded soldiers. In order to gain the acceptance and cooperation of suspicious belligerent states, the ICRC had to assume a stance of neutrality and public discretion unique among nongovernmental organizations (NGOs). Its diplomatic savvy and expertise have allowed it to play a leading role in expanding the scope of the laws of war. Since the 1960s other, more partisan NGOs, such as Human Rights Watch or Doctors without Borders, have driven international law forward by providing information on current breaches of the law and by arousing public opinion to demand international intervention and sanctions.

Institutions do not work magic. The Hague Conventions (1899, 1907) did not achieve the disarmament for which they aimed, and the League of Nations and the United Nations have not provided universal security or peace. States have jealously guarded their sovereignty against legal limitations and have been reluctant to risk money or blood to uphold law; the League was famously undercut by the unparalleled, ideologically motivated lawlessness of Italian fascism, German National Socialism, and Soviet communism. But these institutions have all been successful in incrementally expanding the breadth and depth of international law.

The League did so, for example, by anchoring the sanctity of treaties (*pacta sunt servanda*) in its founding articles, protecting national minorities in treaties with the successor nations in eastern Europe, fostering arbitration of disputes, and creating subsidiary organizations (such as the International Labor Organization and the High Commissioner for refugees) to supervise areas of potential conflict. The League's template was then improved upon by the much more active United Nations. It established the first International Military Tribunal to try war crimes (1945–1946). Its subsidiary organizations create international regulations on everything from children (UN International Children's Emergency Fund, UNICEF) to culture (UN Educational, Scientific and Cultural Organization, UNESCO). The United Nations actively promotes the codification of international law in all areas. It does so partly in response to the huge growth of trade, commerce, communications, and transportation that are now labeled "globalization." Human activity is less constrained by national borders than ever before, and as international commerce, in every sense, grows, so will international law.

One might imagine the enormous spread of international law, especially since 1945, as occurring in three dimensions: spatially, thematically (that is, what sorts of areas are now regulated), and in terms of the subjects of law (that is, states, private organizations, and/or individuals).

As one can see from the ICJ's phrase "principles of law recognized by civilized nations," statesmen and lawyers originally thought of international law as limited to the West. But the law typically tends to expand by analogy. The British, for example, decided in 1900 that the Boer War, which they were fighting in South Africa, should fall under its sway. Whether the limits and protections of international law should apply to colonies was always controversial, but by the 1960s decolonization had solved the problem, as colonies became nation-states, members of the United Nations, and incontrovertibly part of the international community.

Increasingly, international law reached into the uninhabited areas of the earth and beyond. International treaties regulated the Arctic (1933), the Antarctic (1959), the sea floor (1982), and outer space (1976). True to Kant's principle, it was conflicts among nations newly active in these areas that produced the international law to govern them.

The same principle applies to the expansion of international law into new thematic fields. In 1900, international law concerned war, the sea, treaties, diplomacy, merchants, and the recognition and succession of states. By 2000 it focused also on international arbitration, refugees and immigration, trade, organized crime, international organizations, international financial law and taxation, state responsibility, the environment, and human rights.

In the nineteenth century international law was taken to be a law of states; states and their representatives (ambassadors, soldiers) were the only ones who had duties and rights under it. That has now radically changed. Individuals and their welfare are now an important focus of international law. Especially since 1945, the protection of civilians has promoted an astonishing catalog of human rights, most notably in the UN General Assembly's 1948 passage of the Universal Declaration of Human Rights. These go far beyond the minimal right to "life, liberty and security." They include the full panoply of liberal civil-political rights and also the socioeconomic and cultural rights ("to social security," work, a living wage, leisure time, and education) that socialists had put on the human agenda in the mid-nineteenth century. Human rights law is currently one of the most active sectors of international law.

If at the beginning of the twentieth century international law suffered from undercodification, some observers fear that it has become overcodified. They foresee three dangers. Committing the law to writing tends to freeze it, making it less able to respond to changing conditions. One of the advantages to (unwritten) custom was precisely its adaptability. A second problem lies in normativity. International law strives to reflect reality, including real force relations and actual practices. Some legal experts think that since the 1970s, codification has rushed ahead of practice and therefore contains too much "soft" law, that is, injunctions or "oughts" that make the law unlikely to be followed. That produces the third problem: it encourages scofflaws and undermines respect for law in general. This debate has nowhere been stronger than regarding the laws of war.

THE LAWS OF WAR (INTERNATIONAL HUMANITARIAN LAW)

The Laws of War, now called International Humanitarian Law (IHL), are in many respects the oldest and best-developed part of general international law. IHL has two parts: the law governing when it is permissible to engage in warfare (*jus ad bellum*), and the law regulating how to fight war (*jus in bello*). The purpose of *jus in bello* is "to alleviate, as much as possible, the calamities of war" and to prohibit practices that "uselessly aggravate the sufferings" of soldiers or civilians (Declaration of St. Petersburg, 1868). IHL is not designed to prevent war, to change power relations, or to make fighting war impossible. It must therefore be realistic in its assessment of weaponry and military requirements. Its codification in the nineteenth and twentieth centuries has always involved not just statesmen and lawyers but also military officers. During its centuries-long history IHL has developed principles that are then extended analogously to fit new situations and technologies. Three of the most important are: proportionality (destruction must be proportionate to the military gain), absolute prohibition (not everything goes in war, even in extremis), and discrimination (between soldiers, who are a legitimate target for killing, and civilians, who are not). In the twentieth century the protections of IHL have been extended from an almost exclusive focus on combatants to include civilians, whose increasing rights under international human rights law have steadily narrowed the permitted scope of military action. However, supervision and enforcement remain major problems.

By the time World War I broke out in 1914, IHL consisted of two domains of positive (written) law. The "Geneva" side protected soldiers no longer capable of fighting (the wounded, sick, or captured) and those who ministered to them, including the civilians of the Red Cross. These rules were set down in the Geneva Convention of 1864 and revised in 1906, 1929, and 1949. The "Hague" side regulated armed conflict itself. Since 1945 the tendency has been for Hague and Geneva law to fuse together.

The Hague Regulations Concerning the Laws and Customs of War (1899, 1907) were the first codification of the customs governing warfare, worked out by mostly Western states. Disagreements between large and small, and land and naval, powers restricted the rules' scope. They recognized, some would say too much, the legitimacy of military necessity in annulling legal curbs to destruction, but they limited recourse to that excuse to a few specific circumstances. The rules protected civilians by limiting bombardment and draconian occupation techniques but were silent on reprisals, concentration camps, forced labor, and deportations. The debate about the right of enemy civilians to resist occupation produced a wider definition of a combatant, who could now be a militiaman or civilian volunteer, so long as he or she was part of an organized force, recognizable as an enemy, carrying arms openly, and obeying the laws of war. The preamble underscored the important principle that international law has force even beyond written treaties.

World War I shocked contemporaries by the endless casualties, the terrific mistreatment of occupied civilians, and the use of horrifying new weapons (gas, tanks, submarines, airplanes). Allied propaganda sensationalized the (many) German violations, but the Allied blockade, which broke provisions of the Declaration Concerning the Laws of Naval Warfare (London, 1909), which many observers took to be customary law, starved hundreds of thousands of enemy civilians. The

postwar attempt to try war criminals ("Hang the Kaiser") was thwarted by considerations of political expediency and state sovereignty, except in Turkey, where some officials responsible for the Armenian Genocide of 1915–1918 were tried and even executed before the regime of Kemal Atatürk stopped the trials.

Disappointment with the efficacy of international law may have led to a concentration in the interwar years on preventing war rather than refining *jus in bello*. Both the League of Nations' founding articles and the Kellogg-Briand Pact (1928) reflect that sentiment. Nevertheless, Hague law was extended to cover aerial warfare (1923), prohibit poison gas (1925), and regulate submarines (1936). Attempts were under way to give occupied civilians greater protection under "Geneva" law when World War II began in 1939.

World War II appeared to obliterate IHL. The relatively humane treatment of most prisoners of war on the western European front and the avoidance of gas warfare were two of the few areas in which law appeared to work. Many factors canceled it altogether. National Socialist racial ideology launched a war of extermination in which millions of civilians and Soviet prisoners of war died. The Soviet Union responded with terrific ferocity. The Western Allies' area bombardment of cities was the complex result of an early inability to strike the enemy directly in any other way, retaliation, the desire to protect their own soldiers, and the air forces' military culture reaching back to World War I.

The seeming nadir of IHL led to systematic attempts after 1945 to make it stronger and more effective. Those attempts began immediately with the International Military Tribunals at Nuremberg and Tokyo, which inaugurated the legal concept of "crimes against humanity" and institutionalized the principle of individual responsibility, both for soldiers following illegal orders and for heads of state pursuing murderous policies. The Geneva Conventions of 1949 went further by giving national courts universal jurisdiction and responsibility to pursue and try war criminals regardless of where or against whom the crime was committed.

IHL, responding to the catastrophes of the past and to the interests of the victors, develops unevenly. Nuremberg ignored Allied bombardment and Soviet rapes and massacres. But civilian suffering obviously demanded protection. Immediately after the war the ICRC and then the United Nations pushed to revise the Geneva Convention. In 1949 their efforts produced international consensus extending protections listed in 417 articles to the classic "Geneva" groups: the wounded, sick, and captured combatants, at sea as well as on land. The fourth convention now also covered civilians in enemy hands. Besides universal jurisdiction, the Geneva Conventions contained two other novelties. They required signers to uphold its terms even if their foes violated them, thus rejecting the ancient principle of reciprocity. And the provisions cover not just international, but also domestic "armed conflict" (Common Article 3).

The extension of IHL to noninternational conflict was especially important because the nature of warfare changed after 1945 from predominantly interstate to anticolonial, civil, and guerrilla wars in which civilians were proportionately more victimized than ever before. Because IHL is supposed to apply to real practice, the ICRC proposed further changes and codification to reflect the new kinds of conflict. For the first time Third World nations played an active part in codification. The result was Additional Protocols (AP) 1 and 2 (1977) which nominally modified the Geneva Convention but which actually revised the Hague Regulations. AP 1 broke new ground in three areas. It protected even the enemy's civilians at home by narrowly defining permissible military targets and outlawing indiscriminate attacks (such as area bombing), methods of terror, starvation, and reprisals. It forbade "widespread, long-term and severe damage" to the environment. And it recognized guerrilla fighters as legitimate combatants, dropping the requirement that they always carry arms openly and be uniformed. Especially this last change was controversial and led many Western nations to withhold ratification. Opponents claim the APs make war impossible to fight and give unfair advantages to guerrillas; proponents reply that they simply recognize how wars are fought at the turn of the twenty-first century and that they protect vulnerable civilians. It was easier to reach consensus on the prohibition of land mines, booby traps, some incendiary devices, and fragmentation weapons invisible to X-rays (1981 UN Weapons Convention). However, neither napalm nor atomic weapons have been outlawed. These controversies and the continuing lack of adequate supervision and enforcement mechanisms (despite the establishment of the International Criminal Court) remain challenges to the operation of international law.

See also **Human Rights; League of Nations; Nuremberg Laws; Prisoners of War; United Nations.**

BIBLIOGRAPHY

Primary Sources

Grotius, Hugo. *The Rights of War and Peace: Including the Law of Nature and of Nations.* Translated by A. C. Campbell. New York, 1901.

Kant, Immanuel. *Perpetual Peace.* In *Kant's Political Writings,* edited by Hans S. Reiss. Cambridge, U.K., 1970.

Roberts, Adam, and Richard Guelff, eds. *Documents on the Laws of War.* 2nd ed. Oxford, U.K., 1989.

Scott, James Brown, ed. *The Hague Peace Conferences of 1899 and 1907.* 2 vols. Baltimore, Md., 1909.

Secondary Sources

Best, Geoffrey. *Humanity in Warfare.* New York, 1980.

———. *War and Law since 1945.* Oxford, U.K., 1994.

Brownlie, Ian. *Principles of Public International Law.* Oxford, U.K., 1966.

Draper, G. I. A. D. *The Red Cross Conventions.* London, 1958.

Hart, H. L. A. "International Law." In his *The Concept of Law,* 208–231. 2nd ed. Cambridge, 1972.

Marrus, Michael R., comp. *The Nuremberg War Crimes Trial 1945–46: A Documentary History.* Boston, 1997.

Meyer, Michael A., ed. *Armed Conflict and the New Law: Aspects of 1977 Geneva Protocols and the 1981 Weapons Convention.* London, 1989.

Oppenheim, Lassa. *International Law: A Treatise.* 8th ed. Edited by Hersh Lauterpacht. London, 1955.

Schwarzenberger, Georg. *International Law as Applied by International Courts and Tribunals.* 2 vols. London, 1968.

ISABEL V. HULL

IRA. Probably the longest-lived insurgent organization in Europe (and perhaps the world), the Irish Republican Army (IRA) has been in continuous existence since the Declaration of Independence by the first Irish separatist parliament, Dáil Éireann, in January 1919. In the Irish language, its title is Oglaigh na hEireann, or Irish Volunteers, and the title of its individual members is "Volunteer." This reflects the fact that the IRA grew out of the Irish Volunteer movement originally founded in November 1913. The aim of this first movement, to put pressure on the British government during the crisis over the proposed Home Rule legislation, was not necessarily a warlike one. The Volunteers could be seen as a pressure group in the form of a citizen militia. But from the start, they were closely connected with a still older organization, dedicated to removing British rule by armed action. This was the Irish Republican Brotherhood (IRB), founded in 1858 in the wake of the great Irish famine of the late 1840s and the failed Young Ireland rebellion of 1848. These "Fenians," or "physical force men," as they often were called, were dedicated to the simple proposition that Britain could not be influenced by the force of argument, but only by the argument of force. Their deep aversion to politics and politicians, whom they always suspected of readiness to compromise or sell out the cause of independence, was to be directly transmitted to the IRA in succeeding generations.

But although the republican objective—to "break the connection" with Britain—remained unambiguous and unchanging, the physical force method had to be adapted to the situation in the twentieth century. The key moment was the Easter Rising of 1916, when a minority of the Irish Volunteers, led by a secret IRB group, seized and defended positions in Ireland's capital, Dublin. The IRB had always been committed to open insurrection rather than terrorist violence, but to have any prospect of success it needed to choose a strategic moment. World War I seemed to offer such a moment of British weakness. In fact, the insurrection was crushed within a week. But its leaders, executed by the British government, became republican martyrs, and, just as importantly, their successors—most notably Michael Collins and Richard Mulcahy—abandoned the insurrectionist strategy when they set about rebuilding the Volunteer organization in the aftermath of the rebellion. The violence that began in 1919 was on a smaller scale, with local forces choosing their own targets and timing: guerrilla warfare, in other words. The most active IRA units, those in the southwest, built up their stock of weapons by stealth, and only began to try attacks on significant targets, such as Royal Irish Constabulary (RIC) posts, after at least a year of preparation. Attacks were preceded by a public boycott of the RIC, an armed semi-military police force portrayed by nationalists as a British "army of occupation" (though its rank and file were entirely Irish). At the same time a republican "counter-state" was established, with a parliament—the Dáil Éireann, elected at the British general election of 1918 on an abstentionist ticket—which issued a unilateral declaration of Independence in January 1919, and set up shadow ministries and judicial agencies.

This political-military guerrilla insurgency conferred a high degree of legitimacy on the IRA, which by 1921 was in a position to negotiate a formal truce with the British authorities (11 July 1921) as a prelude to extended political negotiations for an Anglo-Irish Treaty (6 December). The reception of this treaty, however, shattered the unity of the republican forces, and defined the political stance of the IRA thereafter. The 26-county Irish Free State created by the treaty was denounced as a British puppet state, largely because of the oath of allegiance to the British Crown that had to be taken by its ministers and members of Parliament. The treaty also accepted that the unity of Ireland, which had been taken by all nationalists as natural, if not God-given, could not be maintained in face of Ulster resistance. "Partition" gave the other six counties in the northeast their own devolved government, as Northern Ireland. On these two key issues, sovereignty and unity, a large part of the IRA rejected the Dáil's formal approval of the treaty (January 1922) and returned to armed action (June 1922). The year of civil war that followed was more destructive in life and property than the five years of Anglo-Irish war that preceded it. The anti-treaty IRA lacked sufficient popular support to wage a guerrilla campaign, and eventually conceded defeat in May 1923. There was no truce or surrender; instead there

Irish Republican Army forces entrenched in County Leitrim during the Irish civil war, 1922. GETTY IMAGES

was a "simple quit" as the "irregulars" (as the Free State government called them) simply halted operations and dumped their arms.

THE WILDERNESS YEARS

For the next thirty years, the irreconcilable republicans became increasingly marginalized. Sinn Féin/IRA candidates fought the 1923 election on an abstentionist ticket, but in 1926 the most substantial politician on the anti-treaty side, Eamon de Valera, decided to set up a political party—Fianna Fáil—that would be prepared to enter parliament. Since this would involve taking the oath of allegiance, his move split the republican movement. While Fianna Fáil quickly became a party of government, and de Valera was in power from 1933 to 1948, the IRA continued to give allegiance to the

few surviving members of the "Second Dáil," elected in 1921. Its only intervention in domestic politics was the assassination of the minister for justice in 1927. In the early 1930s, under the inspiration of Peadar O'Donnell, it experimented with socialism, but at the end of the decade it returned to violence. Under the leadership of Sean Russell it launched, for the first time, an avowedly terrorist campaign in Britain. In 1939 a bomb explosion in Coventry, and the discovery of the IRA target list (the so-called S Plan), led to draconian antiterrorist legislation by both the London and Dublin governments. Many IRA men spent the duration of World War II (called "the Emergency" in Ireland) in internment.

The final throw of the traditional physical-force strategy was the "border campaign" launched in

December 1956. Attacks on targets such as the BBC transmitter in Londonderry were intended to undermine partition, and trigger the collapse of the six-county state. Hundreds of IRA men were involved in sporadic operations, but there was little public support for them among northern nationalists. (Though the IRA gained two new martyrs when Fearghal O'Hanlon and Sean South were killed in an attack on a police station.) The campaign was eventually abandoned in 1962. In an atmosphere of détente between northern and southern governments, the IRA appeared to be an irrelevant relic of past obsessions. It was taken over by modernizers who tried to remodel its thinking from simple armed action to a more progressive, Marxist conception of revolutionary struggle. Ironically, perhaps, after half a century of unavailing effort, it was caught out by the sudden upsurge of popular agitation in the late 1960s. The Northern Ireland civil rights movement was much more than another IRA front organization, but it was the fact that Loyalists saw it as such that sparked a growing sequence of communal riots and street clashes through 1968 and 1969, eventually provoking British military intervention.

THE NORTHERN IRELAND CRISIS

The return of the British army restored the IRA's primary target and vindicated its long-standing critique of the 1921 settlement, but the IRA was in no state to take advantage of this, either ideologically or organizationally. Not until a group of traditional physical-force men, including Billy McKee, Joe Cahill, Seamus Twomey, and Daithi O Conaill, once again split the movement by creating the "Provisional" IRA (PIRA) in January 1970 did it return to armed action. Once it did so, the effects were spectacular. Through 1970, and especially in 1971, the PIRA—the "Provos" or "the Ra"—intensified its attacks on British troops as well as on the police. The first British soldier was killed in 1971, triggering a sequence of provocation and vengeance culminating in the clash in Derry city on 30 January 1972, "Bloody Sunday," when an ill-controlled military response to a riot killed fourteen civilians. The pressure on the Northern Ireland police, the Royal Ulster Constabulary and its auxiliary force, the "B" Specials, drove the British government to reform the security forces. Finally in March 1972 the Northern Ireland

Parliament was prorogued, and direct British rule restored. The clock had been forced back to 1919; this looked like the most dramatic republican success since 1921.

In military terms the PIRA made significant advances at this time, with the introduction by its Belfast Brigade of the Armalite rifle (which would become its trademark weapon) and the discovery of the "car bomb" (produced by the use of fertilizer-based explosives, which were so heavy that they could only be taken to their target by motor vehicle). These two developments pointed in different strategic directions, one to an engagement with the British army, and the other to indiscriminate terrorism. In 1972 and 1973 both were pursued, but the most destructive results followed the planting of car bombs, notably on "Bloody Friday" (21 July 1972). Here the intention was to give warnings, but so many bombs were planted that the security forces were overwhelmed. The hostile public reaction showed that "terrorist" attacks had to be carefully calibrated if they were not to be counterproductive. More impressive perhaps was the effective creation of IRA liberated areas like the Bogside ("Free Derry"), where the security forces could not operate and the republicans operated as a kind of rival governing authority.

In 1972 the PIRA also embarked on the first of several attempts at negotiation with the British government. The breakdown of this was followed by a major British military operation to reoccupy the so-called no go areas in July 1973, and new legislation to create juryless courts (the so-called Diplock courts) that would convict republicans on the basis of evidence from informers. Despite this, another and more lengthy cease-fire was arranged in 1975. When this in turn broke down, it was followed in 1976 by a more aggressive British policy of "criminalizing" IRA prisoners. The withdrawal of their political status provoked increasingly intense protests by IRA internees in the Maze prison (formerly called Long Kesh internment camp). At the same time the PIRA was reorganized on the basis of small cells, like urban guerrilla or terrorist groups, rather than the IRA's traditional quasi-military units. This cellular structure was more resistant to penetration by British agents, and it also tightened the control of the PIRA's central authority, the Army Council. The PIRA announced its

Two boys pose in front of a wall bearing pro-IRA graffiti, Belfast 1972. ©Bettmann/Corbis

determination to intensify the armed struggle by its simultaneous assassination of Lord Louis Mountbatten and killing of eighteen paratroopers in an ambush on 27 August 1979.

For the future, the key development of this period was the contest for control of the republican movement between the established leadership group of Ruairi O Bradaigh and Daithi O Conaill, and a group of challengers led by Gerry Adams and Martin McGuinness. The former committed themselves to a radical political program, Eire Nua (new Ireland), advocating a federal structure in which Ulster would have its own parliament, Dáil Uladh. This was aimed at reassuring Northern Unionists that they would be able to defend their interests (though, as critics of the plan pointed out, no such guarantees had ever looked like overcoming unionist fears in the past). The program also embraced a mild agrarian socialism, echoing the IRA's Saor Eire (Free Ireland) project of the early 1930s, which appealed to the rural communities over the border that provided the PIRA with

sanctuary and assistance. Possibly the Eire Nua program was too sophisticated and imaginative for an organization with the uncomplicated ideology of the Provisionals. In any case it was opposed by O Bradaigh's emerging rival Adams, who had the prestige of a decade as commander of the Belfast Brigade and latterly as head of the Army Council to back up his remarkable talents and ruthless determination. In 1982, the program was decisively rejected by Provisional Sinn Féin.

NEW STRATEGIES IN THE 1980S

The IRA now embarked on a new political-military course signaled in 1981 by the formula "the ballot box and the Armalite." The long struggle between the prisoners and the government reached a climax that year with the hunger strike led by Bobby Sands. The failure of the hunger strike was a heavy blow to traditional republican morale, and its eventual effects were to accelerate the move toward politics. Shortly before his death in 1981, Sands stood for election in the Fermanagh–North Tyrone constituency. Some republicans may have believed

Masked members of the IRA escort the coffin of Bobby Sands, June 1981. Sands died staging a hunger strike in prison to protest the incarceration of IRA members. ©BETTMANN/CORBIS

that if he became an MP he would have to be released from prison, but even though he was not, Adams was able to pursue the parliamentary strategy, and was himself elected MP for West Belfast in 1983. He also finally replaced O Bradaigh as president of Sinn Féin. The effect of the Sinn Féin political strategy on the British and Irish governments was noticeable: in 1985 even the staunchly unionist Margaret Thatcher was persuaded of the need for a formal Anglo-Irish Agreement, probably the most significant political development since 1921. The PIRA went on to plan a large-scale military offensive (modeled on the Tet offensive of the Viet Cong), involving the acquisition of big arms shipments from Libya, but at the same time Adams launched an attempt to construct a common nationalist front with the Social Democratic and Labour Party (SDLP) under John Hume.

The capture of a significant Libyan arms shipment—150 tons of munitions, including mortars and 106 mm cannon—at sea in November 1987 was a significant blow to the plan for a large-scale offensive. But the Hume-Adams talks that began in 1988 were an interesting alternative—a clear recognition that the IRA had little prospect of driving the "Brits out" by force alone. For the new leadership, if not yet for the rank and file Volunteers, the question of the validity of the traditional strategy clearly reasserted itself after two decades of armed struggle. The Provos' original raison d'être, "defending" Catholic communities against loyalist and police assault, was no longer convincing: IRA actions tended to endanger rather than protect them. Their larger strategy had always been problematical. Military victory had never been on the cards, and the hope that the IRA could raise the cost of British "occupation" high enough to persuade British public opinion to demand a "withdrawal" was based on a deep-rooted misreading of British motives. A tendency for the Sinn Féin leadership to distance itself from "botched" IRA operations now became more noticeable than before, and the announcement by the British minister for Northern Ireland in 1990 that Britain had "no selfish strategic or economic interest" in holding on to Northern Ireland was received as being more significant than the platitude it was. The equally platitudinous Downing Street Declaration of 1993, in which the British and Irish prime ministers announced that if terrorists abandoned violence they would be admitted to the political process (a proposition that had always been self-evident, in fact), was also greeted as momentous. Sinn Féin was animated by a sense that some real political reconstruction was possible.

THE PEACE PROCESS

The next five years saw Sinn Féin move an unprecedented distance toward both political participation and a modification of the republican demand for Irish "reunification." The acceptance that Northern Ireland might remain as a political unit (as McGuinness put it in 1994, unity might be compromised by the will of the Irish people) paved the way for participation in all-party talks in 1997. Sinn Féin accepted the 1996 Mitchell Principles, drawn up by U.S. President Bill Clinton's special envoy, Senator George Mitchell, including the commitment to decommission IRA weapons in some unspecified manner. After the signing of the 1998 Belfast Agreement (also called the Good Friday Agreement), the IRA eventually agreed in principle to put its weapons "beyond use," and accepted international inspection of some of its arms dumps. In July 2002 it even issued a guarded apology for the killing of "noncombatants" over the previous thirty years.

Such concessions, however, were asking a lot of a body that had never admitted any ambiguity in its fundamental beliefs or contemplated the possibility that its armed campaign might be unjustifiable. The dispute over the abandonment of abstentionism had already provoked one split, leading to the creation of the "Continuity IRA." And now in 1997 came the breakaway of the "Real IRA" under the leadership of a former chief of staff, Micky

McKevitt. But whereas former breakaway groups had been able to outflank the existing leadership (as the Provos themselves had), this time the Adams-McGuinness leadership proved able to maintain its position. It was helped by the Real IRA's disastrous debut operation, the Omagh bombing (15 August 1998), in which twenty-nine people and two unborn babies were killed, producing the fiercest public condemnation since the 1970s. This kind of terrorism seemed a barbaric throwback to a country that had at last, after a quarter century of virtual civil war, sensed a return to normality. The 11 September 2001 attacks on the United States would further reinforce this pressure to keep the peace process going. When Martin McGuinness joined the new Northern Ireland executive as minister of education in 1999—a development that would have seemed incredible on both sides of the unionist-republican divide only a few years earlier—it looked as though the momentum of the peace process was unstoppable.

But the issue of arms decommissioning remained intractable. The IRA rejected demands for public scrutiny that it saw as equivalent to surrender (and indeed the unionist leader Ian Paisley demanded that the IRA "wear sackcloth and ashes"), though it did accept an international commission headed by a Canadian general, John De Chastelain. The organization was still carrying a load of historical baggage that could not easily be discarded. For thirty years the IRA had acted as a semiformal police agency in its communities, and a tradition of "punishment beatings" went on (and still goes on) long after the cessation of "military" operations. More perniciously, the organization had financed itself by becoming a kind of criminal mafia, and extortion and robbery also went on at the same time as the republican movement negotiated to reenter power-sharing governments. At Christmas 2004, insiders and the police attributed the biggest bank robbery ever carried out in Northern Ireland to the IRA, and a major IRA money-laundering operation was also uncovered. Shortly afterward, a particularly gruesome murder outside a Belfast bar provoked a major public protest led by the victim's sisters. The IRA took the unprecedented step of expelling the killers, but its offer to shoot them deepened the sense of a new crisis in the republican movement.

Exterior of the Grand Hotel, Brighton, England, showing damage done by a bomb planted by IRA, 12 October 1984. The bomb was intended to kill prime minister Margaret Thatcher and her cabinet. ©BETTMANN/CORBIS

though, that it would take some time to convince unionists of this.

See also **Adams, Gerry; British Empire; British Empire, End of; Easter Rising; Ireland; Northern Ireland; Sinn Féin; Terrorism; United Kingdom.**

BIBLIOGRAPHY

Bell, J. Bowyer. *The Secret Army: The IRA, 1916–1970.* New York, 1970.

English, Richard. *Armed Struggle: The History of the IRA.* Oxford, U.K., 2003.

Hanley, Brian. *The IRA, 1926–1936.* Dublin, 2002.

Hart, Peter. *The IRA at War, 1916–1923.* Oxford, U.K., 2003.

Moloney, Ed. *A Secret History of the IRA.* London, 2002.

O'Doherty, Malachi. *The Trouble with Guns: Republican Strategy and the Provisional IRA.* Belfast, 1998.

O'Malley, Padraig. *Biting at the Grave: The Irish Hunger Strikes and the Politics of Despair.* Boston, 1990.

Smith, M. L. R. *Fighting for Ireland? The Military Strategy of the Republican Movement.* London, 1995.

Taylor, Peter. *Provos: The IRA and Sinn Fein.* Rev. ed. London, 1998.

Townshend, Charles. "The Irish Republican Army and the Development of Guerrilla Warfare, 1916–1921." *English Historical Review* 94 (1979): 318–345.

CHARLES TOWNSHEND

Nevertheless, the summer of 2005 witnessed what republicans saw as an epochal moment, the IRA's announcement on 28 July that it had formally ordered the termination of the armed campaign. This was followed two months later by a statement from the independent arms decommissioning body that the IRA had put its weapons beyond use. However impressive it was to republicans, however, Paisley's DUP held that this step had been far too long delayed to create confidence and that the alleged decommissioning (though witnessed by two churchmen, one Catholic and one Methodist) would not be believed unless it could be seen on film. Prime Minister Tony Blair accepted that the failure to deliver decommissioning had "become a major impediment to moving forward the peace process," but argued that there was no longer any barrier to peace. It remained clear,

IRELAND. In January 1914 Ireland was part of the United Kingdom; Irish members of Parliament (MPs) sat at Westminster, legislative and administrative control rested in Whitehall. By the end of that year, it was expected that responsibility for most domestic policy would have passed to a Home Rule parliament and government in Dublin, though this was strongly resisted by Irish unionist politicians and by Britain's Conservative Party to the point where by the summer of 1914 Ireland appeared on the brink of civil war, and discussions were underway to exclude the predominantly Protestant and unionist population of the northeast from the Home Rule settlement. When World War I began in August 1914, Home Rule was placed on the statute book, but its introduction was postponed until the war ended. By then, Home Rule no longer met the aspirations of nationalist Ireland.

A short-lived rebellion at Easter 1916 proclaimed an Irish Republic. At the general election of November 1918, a majority of Irish seats went (many uncontested) to the Sinn Féin Party, which was controlled by veterans of the 1916 Easter Rising and was committed to securing an Irish republic. The Sinn Féin MPs boycotted Westminster, establishing a parliament and administration in Dublin—Dáil Éireann. Simultaneously the Irish Volunteers (later renamed the Irish Republican Army [IRA]), launched a campaign to undermine British rule in Ireland, targeting policemen, local government, and tax offices; their goal was not to defeat the British forces, but to persuade Britain to concede an Irish republic. On the international front Dáil Éireann waged an unsuccessful campaign to secure recognition of an Irish republic at the Versailles Conference; they proved more effective at publicizing atrocities committed by British forces in Ireland in the international press.

The Government of Ireland Act, which became law in December 1920, established two Home Rule–style governments in Ireland—one in Belfast with responsibility for six northeastern counties, and one in Dublin, and a Council of Ireland with equal membership from north and south. The Northern Ireland parliament opened in June 1921; in July a truce was called between British forces and the IRA, opening the way for negotiations for a constitutional settlement. A treaty signed in December 1921 granted Ireland dominion status—considerably greater autonomy than Home Rule—with opt-out rights for the northern government; if they did so, a commission would determine the boundaries between the two states. Dáil Éireann accepted the treaty by 64 votes to 57; opponents claimed that it betrayed the commitment to a republic; the fact that it conceded partition was not a major issue.

THE IRISH FREE STATE, 1922–1937

The Irish Free State came into existence in December 1922 in the midst of a bitter civil war. Although 78 percent of voters in the June 1922 general election supported pro-treaty candidates, the disaffected minority refused to accept this verdict, and within two weeks of the election, the

The post office in Dublin burns during the Easter Uprising of 1916. BRIDGEMAN ART LIBRARY

standoff between government and anti-treaty forces flared into civil war. The war ended in May 1923 in victory for the government, achieved through draconian summary justice and the loss of 1,500 lives, including Michael Collins (1890–1922), commander in chief of the Irish army and the dominant figure in the provisional government. The new state got off to an inauspicious start; opponents of the treaty refused to take their seats in Dáil Éireann because this involved an oath of allegiance to the British monarch—a condition of the 1921 treaty; public finances were in a precarious state because of the civil war, and the militarization of Irish society over the previous ten years posed a serious threat to democracy. Between 1914 and 1926, the Protestant population of the Irish Free State fell by one-third; although some of this loss can be explained by the 1914–1918 war and the departure of British troops and officials, others left because they felt insecure and unwanted. Despite these unpromising beginnings, constitutional politics overcame the physical force tradition.

In 1926, Eamon de Valera (1882–1975), leader of the anti-treaty Sinn Féin, broke with that party and founded Fianna Fáil; in 1927 he led them into Dáil Éireann, and in 1932 they took office having won a near-majority in the general election. The transition was uneventful; there was no purge of senior army officers and civil servants. By 1932 Irish politics had taken on the shape that it still bears today: two major political parties—Fianna Fáil and Cumann na nGaedheal, later Fine Gael, divided primarily by their attitude toward the 1921 treaty, plus a smaller Labour Party, and some minor short-lived parties.

The Cumann na nGaedheal government that held office until 1932 had worked consistently to expand Irish sovereignty within the British Empire; Fianna Fáil came to office determined to remove the remaining limitations on Irish sovereignty imposed under the 1921 treaty. Relations between Dublin and London were rocky during the early years of de Valera's rule, as Britain resisted any erosion of its residual jurisdiction over Ireland; a trade war—the so-called Economic War—erupted when Ireland ceased making repayments on loans that enabled tenant farmers to buy out their landlords, but in 1938 both sides reached an amicable agreement, and with war looming in Europe, Neville Chamberlain (1869–1940) handed over Britain's three remaining naval bases in Ireland, believing that a friendly neutral Ireland would be a more valuable ally.

In 1937 de Valera replaced the hastily written 1922 Constitution, which reflected the limitations of the 1921 treaty, with the constitution that remains operative in the twenty-first century. The name of the state was given as Ireland (Éire in the Irish language); the territory of the state consisted of all of Ireland, but "pending the reintegration of the national territory," the laws enacted by the Irish parliament would only have jurisdiction over twenty-six counties. Partition was a low priority for the newly independent Irish state; in 1926 when it emerged that the boundary commission would recommend only marginal changes in the borders between the two Irelands, including some loss of territory by the Irish Free State, the Dublin government agreed that the report of the commission would be suppressed; it was only when the

constraints on Irish sovereignty had been resolved that Dublin turned its attention to partition.

A GAELIC AND CATHOLIC STATE

In cultural terms, the first twenty years of the new state were marked by introversion and cultural protection. Pro- and anti-treaty nationalists were equally committed to a state that embodied a Catholic and Gaelic ethos, and these causes served to unite and to heal political divisions, though at the expense of alienating the 5 percent of the population who were Protestant. However, the parties were divided on economic matters, with Fianna Fáil espousing self-sufficiency—tillage farming, small farms, heavily protected industries, whereas Fine Gael favored cattle farming and closer economic links with Britain. Self-sufficiency and a more generous attitude toward public spending helped Ireland to weather the economic crisis of the 1930s; although times were tough, few farms went bankrupt, and despite the cessation of emigration there was no mass unemployment, and the quasi-fascistic Blueshirt movement did not present a serious threat to democracy. By the late 1930s, the economic and social policies of the two major parties had converged, as had their positions on Anglo-Irish relations, so that changes in government in independent Ireland have rarely brought dramatic shifts in policy.

NORTHERN IRELAND, 1920–1939

Northern Ireland too had a violent birth; between June 1920 and June 1922, 428 people were killed and 1,766 injured; many houses and businesses were destroyed and Catholic workers were forced to abandon jobs in the shipyards. Most Catholics, who constituted one-third of the population, opted out of the new state, hoping that the boundary commission would resolve their position—such expectations were especially strong in western and southern areas, which had a Catholic majority. When the boundary commission dashed these hopes in 1926, the key structures of the Northern Ireland state were already in place, including a school system that favored the Protestant communities and a security service dominated by former Protestant paramilitaries. While the electoral arithmetic in a state polarized by religion made a change of government highly unlikely, the removal of proportional representation (imposed by Britain in

Eamon de Valera, president of Sinn Féin, is arrested in 1916. Tried and convicted for his participation in the Easter Uprising, De Valera escaped execution due to his American citizenship. He later served in various positions in the Irish government.

1918 in order to safeguard Ireland's Protestants) in parliamentary and local elections, and some very distorted electoral boundaries, reduced nationalist political representation and denied them control of some local authorities. Catholics were also seriously underrepresented among senior civil servants, because of concerns about their loyalty. In hindsight, unionist fears of an imminent takeover by Dublin were excessive; it was only in 1938 when the final trappings of British control had been removed that de Valera turned his attention to partition, but the political rhetoric emanating from independent Ireland reinforced the beleaguered attitude of Ulster unionism and served to consolidate Northern Ireland as a one-party state.

WARTIME IRELAND, 1939–1945

The war years exposed major shortcomings in the Northern Ireland government; at least 1,100 civilians died in air raids during 1941 because of inadequate air defenses, and an estimated 220,000 fled Belfast in panic; industrial unrest was three to four times greater than in Britain. However, the fact that Northern Ireland participated on the Allied side, whereas independent Ireland remained neutral, undoubtedly strengthened Northern Ireland's links with the rest of the United Kingdom, particularly in the face of Dublin's postwar campaign against partition. The postwar introduction of comprehensive state health welfare services, comparable with the rest of the United Kingdom, and the 1944 Butler Act granting entitlement to secondary schooling, were initially regarded with suspicion by the frugal, self-sufficient Ulster unionists, but they soon realized that these measures provided tangible evidence of the benefits of the United Kingdom, and a means of differentiating Northern Ireland from independent Ireland.

In many respects, World War II was de Valera's finest hour. He preserved Ireland's neutrality despite the threats posed by IRA collusion with Germany, and pressure from Winston Churchill (1874–1965) and to a lesser extent the United States; he gave considerable but discreet assistance to the Allies, and the country came through the war unscathed despite severe shortages of supplies. However, as in the north, the war exposed serious political limitations. Mass emigration had been a feature of Irish life since the early nineteenth century, but until the 1940s the Irish government had been able to convince itself that emigration was declining. During the war years, however, a growing number of Irish men and women emigrated to Britain, attracted by full employment and wartime earnings.

ISOLATION AND ECONOMIC DECLINE, 1945–1960

The ten to fifteen years immediately after the end of the war were a missed opportunity for independent Ireland. The country was denied membership in the United Nations until 1956 because of wartime neutrality, which enhanced an already strong tendency toward introversion. Ending partition became the primary focus of Irish foreign policy; they refused to join NATO because it would involve recognizing U.K. boundaries. The coalition government that took office in 1948 proclaimed a republic (which came into effect in 1949) in order to remove the gun from Irish politics. In order to ease Northern Ireland fears over the declaration of a republic, Westminster passed the 1949 Ireland Act, which stated that any decision over the future status of Northern Ireland was a matter for the Northern Parliament. In 1956 the IRA launched "Operation Harvest," a series of raids mounted

from the south, in order to end partition. IRA men were interned by both the Dublin and Belfast governments; the campaign ended in 1962.

During the 1950s, the Irish Republic and East Germany were the only two European countries with a declining population. The population of independent Ireland fell by almost 5 percent and over 400,000 men and women emigrated; they were part of the European-wide migration of workers from less developed rural and agrarian economies to more developed industrial economies. Economic failure challenged Ireland's claim to independence; Britain absorbed over 80 percent of merchandise exports and most Irish emigrants. By the late 1950s, the depressed state of the economy and proposals to create a European free trade area prompted a redirection of economic policy from self-sufficiency toward free trade and attracting foreign direct investment. In 1959, de Valera became president of Ireland, and the office of Taoiseach (prime minister) passed to Sean Lemass (1899–1971).

LEMASS AND O'NEILL: THE 1960S

Although Lemass, like de Valera, was a veteran of the 1916 Rising, his pragmatism, his focus on economic growth and industrial development, attracting foreign industrial investment, building closer economic and political links with Britain, and bringing Ireland into the European Economic Community (EEC), marked a major change from the previous focus on small farms and protected Irish-owned industries. Emigration fell sharply during the 1960s; living standards rose, and for the first time in the history of the state more people were employed in manufacturing industry than in agriculture. Economic prosperity coincided with a rise in Ireland's traditionally low marriage rate, a fall in the age of marriage, and clear evidence that Irish couples were controlling fertility. The 1960s also brought an easing in the stringent censorship of publications, and the first signs of a public debate over issues on which Irish legislation continued to reflect the teaching of the Catholic Church, such as divorce and contraception.

There are strong similarities between Lemass and Terence O'Neill (1914–1990), who became prime minister of Northern Ireland in 1963. Both

The Custom House in Dublin burns after being bombed in May 1921. The bomb was planted by insurgents fighting for Irish independence from the United Kingdom. ©HULTON-DEUTSCH COLLECTION/CORBIS

men focused on economic development and attracting foreign industrial investment—and in this respect Northern Ireland was much more successful; both were of the opinion that economic prosperity could overcome deep-seated political divisions. The O'Neill-Lemass meeting in January 1965, the first meeting between leaders of the two governments since 1922, was seen as inaugurating a new relationship between the two Irelands. Lemass believed that a prosperous independent Ireland offered a better way of promoting a united Ireland than a militant anti-partition campaign, and O'Neill once remarked that if Catholics were given good jobs and better housing conditions then they would behave like Protestants. Both were proved wrong. O'Neill's liberal rhetoric and public gestures such as a visit to a Catholic school (the first by a prime minister of Northern Ireland) served to raise expectations among Catholics and atavistic fears among unionists, but he proved slow to

remedy major grievances such as the partisan allocation of local authority housing and the lack of universal adult suffrage in local elections. In 1967 the Northern Ireland Civil Rights Association (NICRA), which took its name and its methods from the U.S. civil rights movement of that decade, began a series of marches to highlight discrimination in Northern Ireland, which provoked sometimes violent responses from militant unionists and the Royal Irish Constabulary. In November 1968 when O'Neill, under pressure from the British government, announced a program of reform that fell short of NICRA demands, many Ulster unionists were outraged by this apparent capitulation to British pressure. O'Neill resigned as prime minister in April 1969, having failed to secure sufficient support from moderate Catholics in a general election. By then Northern Ireland was increasingly polarized between intransigent unionist and rising Catholic militancy.

VIOLENCE IN NORTHERN IRELAND, 1969–1973

August 1969 is commonly seen as the beginning of "the Troubles." A traditional Protestant march in Derry ended in a riot; violence spread to Belfast, resulting in 7 deaths and the destruction of 179 properties, of which 83 percent were occupied by Catholics. Britain sent troops to the province, initially to protect the nationalist population, but within months they were coming under attack from the Provisional IRA, which was formed early in 1970. What began as an effort to redress Catholic grievances within a framework of the United Kingdom and civil rights had reverted to a more traditional struggle between British forces and the IRA.

Events in Northern Ireland caught the Dublin government unprepared. No government minister or department was responsible for Northern Ireland, and they had no contingency plans. The government came under pressure to invade Northern Ireland to protect the Catholic population; a speech by the Taoiseach Jack Lynch (1917–1999) stating that the "Irish government can no longer stand by and see innocent people injured and perhaps worse" heightened expectations. Although wiser counsels prevailed, in May 1970, in events that remain obscure, Lynch dismissed two cabinet ministers—Charles Haughey and Niall Blaney—on suspicion of involvement in a conspiracy to import arms for the IRA, but they were acquitted of these charges in court. Sympathies for Northern Ireland nationalists continued to rise in the south following the introduction of internment (which was directed exclusively against Catholics) in Northern Ireland in August 1971; they peaked in late January 1972 (Bloody Sunday) when British forces shot dead thirteen unarmed men during an illegal civil rights march in Derry. Britain put pressure on the Northern Ireland government to transfer control of security services to Westminster; when they resigned rather than accede, the Northern Ireland parliament was prorogued, and direct rule was introduced on 24 March 1972.

FROM SUNNINGDALE (1973) TO THE BELFAST AGREEMENT (1998)

When violence erupted in Northern Ireland in August 1969, the British government refused to concede that Dublin might have a role in finding a solution; however, this had changed by the early 1970s. The Sunningdale Agreement of December 1973, signed by politicians from both communities in Northern Ireland and by the British and Irish governments, set out a framework for the future government of Northern Ireland based on two principles: devolved government where power would be shared between politicians of different political traditions, and an all-Ireland dimension. The agreement collapsed within months when the newly elected minority Labour government in Britain capitulated to Protestant paramilitary protests and direct rule was restored. Although this was expected to be a temporary arrangement, the devolved government was not restored until 1998. The intervening years were punctuated by cycles of violence: the IRA's attempt to drive Britain from Northern Ireland through bombings and shootings in Northern Ireland and in Britain, Protestant paramilitary violence against the Catholic community, and deaths of some innocent civilians and terrorists at the hands of the security forces. IRA prisoners kept up pressure to be treated as political prisoners, ultimately embarking on a series of hunger strikes that resulted in ten deaths. Sinn Féin, the political wing of the IRA, mobilized sympathy for hunger strikers to capture electoral support in Northern Ireland and the Republic; their success (13.4 percent of the vote in the 1983 Westminster election) strengthened the hand of those who wished to employ a dual political and military strategy, described by one member as a ballot paper in one hand and an Armalite rifle in the other. However, the process of achieving an IRA ceasefire and Sinn Féin's inclusion in what came to be known as the "peace process" proved extremely tortuous, involving lengthy and initially secret talks between the Sinn Féin leadership; John Hume (b. 1937), leader of the moderate nationalist Social Democratic and Labour Party (SDLP) party; and British and Irish ministers and representatives and U.S. politicians. It was frequently derailed by some violent atrocity. A joint declaration by British Prime Minister John Major (b. 1943) and Taoiseach Albert Reynolds (b. 1932) in December 1993, the Downing Street Declaration, invited all who had permanently rejected armed force to take part in talks on the future of Northern Ireland. The declaration set out the broad parameters for a settlement: a statement that Britain had no selfish strategic or economic interest in Northern Ireland; recognition and respect for all traditions in Northern Ireland; an acknowledgement that any change in the status of Northern Ireland would only come with the consent of the majority of the people. This opened the way for an IRA ceasefire on 31 August 1994 that broke down in February 1996 and was not reinstated until July 1997. The Belfast (Good Friday) Agreement of April 1998 restored devolved government to Northern Ireland with an executive drawn from all the major parties, together with cross-border institutions and a British-Irish Council. The Dublin government undertook to amend Articles 2 and 3 of its constitution, which could be interpreted as laying claim to Northern Ireland. Since 1998 IRA activity has been much reduced; however, the failure to secure the decommissioning of IRA weapons has resulted in the collapse of the power-sharing executive and the restoration of direct rule. At the beginning of the twenty-first century, Northern Ireland provided guarantees of equality in employment, housing, and cultural recognition for both Catholic and Protestant communities; however, the "Troubles" inflicted severe damage on the economy. Although the number of children attending multidenominational schools is rising, housing is more segregated by religion than in 1911. In politics the communities are more divided than ever, with support increasing for the more extremist parties, the Democratic Unionist Party and Sinn Féin, at the expense of more moderate nationalist and unionist parties.

FROM CRISIS TO BOOM: THE IRISH ECONOMY AFTER 1973

Although Northern Ireland dominated television screens and the diaries of Dublin politicians since 1969, it had surprisingly little impact on domestic politics in the Irish Republic, except during periods of high emotion such as the hunger strikes. The key issues were the economy and pressures to change Irish social legislation in response to changes in Irish society. EEC membership in 1973 coincided with the oil crisis that brought a sharp downturn in economic growth in Western Europe. However, the initial impact was softened by the benefits of EEC membership, especially to the farming sector. By the early 1980s, the Irish economy was caught in a vicious cycle of double-digit unemployment

and inflation, heavy government borrowing, lack of economic growth, and rising emigration. This pattern was eventually broken in the late 1980s with the introduction of a more cautious approach to government spending that gave priority to productive investment, the drive to attract high-tech multinational companies to invest in Ireland with the promise of low tax rates and access to the European Union's single market, and lower personal tax rates. By the late 1990s, the Irish economy was the most dynamic in Europe with double-digit growth, and significant immigration.

A POST-CATHOLIC IRELAND?

The years from the 1970s to the 1990s saw a series of divisive political campaigns over access to contraception and divorce and securing a constitutional amendment prohibiting abortion (which was already outlawed), which reflected the tensions between those who were seeking to preserve a legislative system that reflected Catholic moral teaching, and those who believed that legislation should reflect the realities of contemporary Irish society. Contraceptives became freely available only in 1985; the constitutional ban on divorce was removed (by the narrowest of margins) in 1995; a constitutional "pro-life" (anti-abortion) amendment was passed in 1983 but was subsequently modified. Although church attendance remains high by European standards (63 percent of Catholics attend church every week), the authority of the Catholic Church has been seriously eroded, and declining numbers of religious have forced them to withdraw from schools and other institutions. Growing immigration from Eastern Europe, Africa, and Asia has strengthened the case for diluting Catholic influence in Irish society.

IRELAND IN THE TWENTY-FIRST CENTURY

There are several dimensions to Ireland's history over the past one hundred years: one is the retarded rate of economic development from 1914 to the 1990s—north and south—and the exceptionally rapid and belated catch-up in the decade around the turn of the twenty-first century in independent Ireland to become one of the wealthiest countries in Europe; the reversal of the population decline that began in the midnineteenth century, so that the population of all

Ireland in 2005 was at the level of the 1860s; the convergence in demographic and economic patterns with other Western states; the belated emergence of more multicultural and multi-ethnic states and the tensions that this brings. Another story concerns the birth of two states in the aftermath of World War I and their different trajectories. For many years, the Northern Ireland crisis was seen as a religious war that was an anachronism in twentieth-century Europe; at the beginning of the twenty-first century it looks like a precursor to the ethnic wars and terrorist threats that emerged at the end of the last millennium. While political leaders in Belfast, Dublin, London, and even Washington have devoted considerable attention to securing a long-term political settlement in Northern Ireland, this does not appear to be a major concern for most Irish people, provided that peace continues; a substantial majority of the population of Northern Ireland are happy with direct rule from London, and the majority of the population of independent Ireland have no wish or expectation of a united Ireland. It seems probable that the two Irish states born in the 1920s will continue to go their separate, but associated, ways.

See also **Adams, Gerry; British Empire; British Empire, End of; Easter Rising; IRA; Northern Ireland; Paisley, Ian; Sinn Féin; United Kingdom.**

BIBLIOGRAPHY

Arthur, Paul. *Special Relationships: Britain, Ireland, and the Northern Ireland Problem.* Belfast, 2000.

Brown, Terence. *Ireland: A Social and Cultural History, 1922–2001.* London, 2004.

Buckland, Patrick. *The Factory of Grievances: Devolved Government in Northern Ireland, 1921–1939.* Dublin, 1979.

Delaney, Enda. *Demography, State, and Society: Irish Migration to Great Britain, 1921–1971.* Liverpool, U.K., 2000.

Donnelly, James S., ed. *Encyclopedia of Irish History and Culture.* Detroit, Mich., 2004.

Fitzpatrick, David. *The Two Irelands: 1912–1939.* Oxford, U.K., 1998.

Goldthorpe, J. H., and C. T. Whelan, eds. *The Development of Industrial Society in Ireland.* Oxford, U.K., 1992.

Hennessy, Thomas. *A History of Northern Ireland, 1920–1996.* Dublin, 1997.

Hill, J. R., ed. *A New History of Ireland.* Vol. 7: *Ireland 1921–1984.* Oxford, U.K., 2003.

Jackson, Alvin. *Ireland, 1798–1998: Politics and War.* Oxford, U.K., 1999.

Kennedy, Kieran A., Thomas Giblin, and Deirdre McHugh. *The Economic Development of Ireland in the Twentieth Century.* London, 1988.

Kennedy, Liam. *The Modern Industrialisation of Ireland, 1940–1988.* Dublin, 1989.

———. *People and Population Change: A Comparative Study of Population Change in Northern Ireland and the Republic of Ireland.* Dublin, 1994.

Lee, J. J. *Ireland, 1912–1985: Politics and Society,* Cambridge, U.K., 1989.

MacMillan, Gretchen M. *State, Society, and Authority in Ireland: The Foundations of the Modern State.* Dublin, 1993.

Mulholland, Marc. *Northern Ireland at the Crossroads: Ulster Unionism in the O'Neill Years, 1960–69.* New York, 2000.

Nolan, Brian, Philip J. O'Connell, and C.T. Whelan, ed. *Bust to Boom? The Irish Experience of Growth and Inequality.* Dublin, 2000.

ó Gráda, Cormac. *A Rocky Road: The Irish Economy Since the 1920s.* Manchester, U.K., 1997.

Salmon, Trevor C. *Unneutral Ireland: An Ambivalent and Unique Security Policy.* Oxford, U.K., 1989.

Whyte, J. H. *Church and State in Modern Ireland, 1923–1979.* 2nd ed. Dublin, 1980.

MARY E. DALY

IRIGARAY, LUCE (b. 1932), French philosopher and a founding figure of contemporary Western feminist theory.

Born in Belgium, Luce Irigaray moved to France in the early 1960s to earn a master's degree in psychology and, in 1968, a doctorate in linguistics. During the 1960s she also trained as a psychoanalyst and participated in Jacques Lacan's psychoanalytic seminars, eventually becoming a member of the Freudian School of Paris, directed by Lacan. During the same period, Irigaray associated briefly with the Mouvement de Libération des Femmes (MLF), the most visible wing of the

French feminist movement, and in 1969 psycho-analyzed Antoinette Fouque, the MLF's founder and leader.

1974 Irigaray published her doctoral thesis, *Speculum of the Other Woman,* a work that set the stage for a mode of thinking that marks Irigaray's entire oeuvre. In *Speculum,* Irigaray demonstrated her claim that Western reason systematically suppresses sexual difference; she relentlessly critiques the patriarchal logic of the giants of Western thought, including Freud, Aristotle, Plotinus, Descartes, Kant, Hegel, and Plato. *Speculum* revealed the suppression of sexual difference by linking the philosophical quest for truth with the psychoanalytic quest for selfhood, a quest that requires the erasure of a maternal origin. For Irigaray, the suppressed maternal origin functions as the site of a true sexual difference denied by Western thought, where difference itself is subsumed into a logic that Irigaray calls "the same." Irigaray's scathing critique of both philosophy and psychoanalysis ironically led to the loss of her teaching post at the University of Vincennes and her expulsion from the Freudian School; for some, this attempt to silence Irigaray demonstrated the very logic of exclusion she had diagnosed in *Speculum.*

While *Speculum* remains, for many, Irigaray's most important philosophical work, others see her deconstruction of Western thought as the necessary precursor to the more important constructive work to follow. *Speculum*'s critical focus on the logic of the same in Western philosophy, for example, also introduced the more constructive Irigarayan concept of "mimesis," developed more fully in the 1977 volume *This Sex Which Is Not One.* Irigarayan mimesis describes a strategy of playful, even subversive repetition of the speech of the intellectual masters in order to redeploy the logic of the same against itself. Through parodic repetition, Irigaray argues, that which is suppressed becomes visible, opening up the possibility of different ways of speaking that would allow for the articulation of the "feminine" in language.

This concept of mimesis has significantly influenced postmodern thought, politics, and art, particularly in cultural venues where marginalized groups use parody and drag both as a critique of cultural norms and as a form of counterexpression that brings into being nonnormative experiences and identities. Articulated by some as "performativity," these mimetic strategies adopted by performance artists, theater troupes, photographers, and activist groups such as ACT UP parodically challenge the status quo and, by so doing, symbolically open up new avenues for political and cultural transformation.

Irigaray's work of the 1980s continued her early critique of Western philosophy and, at the same time, began to elaborate a constructive vision for the articulation of sexual difference. *Marine Lover of Friedrich Nietzsche* (1980), *The Forgetting of Air in Martin Heidegger* (1983), and *Ethics of Sexual Difference* (1984) all work to develop Irigaray's own philosophy of the radical alterity, or otherness, of "the feminine." Irigaray's work of the 1980s also put her in contact with other feminists, especially in Italy, interested in the practical application of her theoretical ideas about the transformation of the social and symbolic order. The work of the Milan Women's Bookstore Collective, in particular, gained notoriety for its application of Irigaray's work on female genealogies through the public, symbolic, and contractual affirmation of an ethical order among women.

Since the 1990s Irigaray's work increasingly turned toward the question of women and men together. In *Je, tu, nous: Toward a Culture of Difference* (1990), *I Love to You* (1992), and *To Be Two* (1997), Irigaray explores the possibility of a form that would allow for men and women together without the subsumption of difference into the "same." Imagining this "model of the two" as neither a replication of the same nor a hierarchical ordering, Irigaray argues that only in the "two-ness" of men and women as truly different can the singular subject of Western philosophy be radically transformed. This commitment to the radical possibility of true difference led Irigaray to attend to the rupture between Western civilization and its other in *Between East and West, From Singularity to Community* (1999) and in *The Way of Love* (2002), where she imagines new forms of love for a global democratic community.

See also Feminism; Lacan, Jacques.

BIBLIOGRAPHY

Burke, Carolyn, Naomi Schor, and Margaret Whitford, eds. *Engaging with Irigaray: Feminist Philosophy and Modern European Thought*. New York, 1994.

Chanter, Tina. *Ethics of Eros: Irigaray's Re-Writing of the Philosophers*. New York, 1995.

Deutscher, Penelope. *A Politics of Impossible Difference: The Later Work of Luce Irigaray*. Ithaca, N.Y., 2002.

Whitford, Margaret. *Luce Irigaray: Philosophy in the Feminine*. New York, 1991.

Whitford, Margaret, ed. *The Irigaray Reader*. Oxford, U.K., 1991.

LYNNE HUFFER

IRISH REPUBLICAN ARMY. *See* IRA.

IRON CURTAIN.

IRON CURTAIN. Popularized in a speech by Winston Churchill (1874–1965), the term *Iron Curtain* refers to the diminished contact and restricted travel imposed by the Soviet Union between the communist countries of Eastern Europe and the capitalist-democratic nations of Western Europe during the Cold War (1946–1989). A truly effective physical barrier between the two Germanys and Czechoslovakia and between Austria and Hungary did not exist until the early 1960s. For Western politicians and pundits, *Iron Curtain* dramatized the isolation of the police states forced upon the Eastern Europeans by the Soviet Union.

Forced from office in 1945, Winston Churchill, a leading voice against fascism and the wartime prime minister of Great Britain, returned to the cause of anticommunism, his personal crusade since the 1917 Bolshevik Revolution. The title of Churchill's speech, given at Westminster College in Fulton, Missouri, on 5 March 1946, was "The Sinews of Peace," and in it Churchill stressed that world peace required a continuation of the Anglo-American wartime alliance.

Churchill did not invent the term *iron curtain*, which had entered the discourse of European politics before World War I to describe territorial divisions created by the breakup of the Russian and Austro-Hungarian empires. Joseph Goebbels, head of Nazi propaganda, even used the term in *Das Reich* (1945), an attack on the Soviet Union.

Churchill's Iron Curtain speech was the brainchild of President Harry S. Truman and Secretary of State James F. Byrnes, who wanted to honor Churchill for his wartime leadership. They also wanted him to take the lead in criticizing Joseph Stalin's postwar uncooperativeness, which had been clear at the foreign ministers' conference held in Moscow in December 1945. Truman discussed the speech with Churchill, but neither he nor any U.S. foreign policy officer cleared the final draft. Truman cautioned Churchill not to attack the United Nations but approved of the concept of a continuing U.S.–Great Britain "special relationship" for military peacekeeping. For his part, Churchill needed no prompting to stress the enduring common interests of "the English-speaking world."

To Truman's dismay—he introduced Churchill at Westminster—Churchill used the speech as an all-out condemnation of the Soviet Union. Churchill stressed the growing danger of Soviet-backed subversion in Europe, especially in France, Italy, and Czechoslovakia. He predicted that the Soviet Union would never let occupied Germany reunite except as a Soviet satellite. He deplored the fact that the great cities of Eastern Europe now fell under the Soviets' "increasing measure of control." He introduced the theme of communist captivity: "From Stettin in the Baltic to Trieste in the Adriatic, an iron curtain has descended across the Continent." Predictably, Stalin condemned the speech as warmongering by the most notorious Western imperialist.

Churchill's call to arms against Soviet communism did not change America's reluctance to make a long-term commitment to the future of a free Western Europe. Subsequent Soviet actions moved the United States into a union with free Europe, characterized by the Marshall Plan for economic reconstruction and the NATO alliance for military defense after Stalin blockaded Berlin, pressured Greece and Turkey for political concessions, threatened to invade communist (but anti-Soviet) Yugoslavia, and backed a communist coup in Czechoslovakia. Churchill's call for "fraternal association" became the Truman Doctrine for the "containment" of communism in Europe, which continued until the Soviet Union collapsed in 1989–1991.

The "iron curtain" Churchill imagined in 1946 became a reality by the end of the 1950s. To prevent refugees from flooding into Western Europe, which had occurred twice in the decade as a result of revolts in East Germany and Hungary, the Soviets built a barrier of electric and barbed wire fences and minefields along the borders of East Germany, Czechoslovakia, and Hungary. This true iron curtain became a domain of border guards, watchtowers, guard dogs, and searchlights. The last addition to this system came in 1961, when the East German government, with Soviet help, built a wall from cinder blocks across the middle of Berlin to stop the flight of desperate Germans. When the Germans tore down the Berlin Wall on 9 November 1989 as part of a national revolt against their communist government and the Soviet armies that had occupied East Germany since 1945, the Iron Curtain, literally and figuratively, came tumbling down.

Churchill did not live to see his vision triumph. He returned as prime minister in 1951–1954 but found painting and the writing of history more congenial than parliamentary politics and the liquidation of the British Empire. He died, beloved for his wartime leadership, in 1965.

See also **Churchill, Winston; Cold War; Eastern Bloc.**

BIBLIOGRAPHY

Gerdes, Louise I., ed. *The Cold War*. Great Speeches in History. San Diego, Calif., 2003.

Gilbert, Martin. *Churchill: A Life*. London, 1991.

Harbutt, Fraser J. *The Iron Curtain: Churchill, America, and the Origins of the Cold War*. New York, 1986.

Leffler, Melvyn P. *A Preponderance of Power: National Security, the Truman Administration, and the Cold War*. Stanford, Calif., 1992.

Ryan, Henry B. "A New Look at Churchill's 'Iron Curtain' Speech." *Historical Journal* 22 (December 1979): 895–900.

ALLAN R. MILLETT

IRON GUARD. *See* **Romania.**

ISLAM. In 1913 the spiritual leader of Reformist Islam, Sheikh Muhammad Rashid Rida (1865–1935), a Syrian living in Egypt, wrote a rave review of an Arabic translation of a book by a French pamphleteer entitled *The Roots of Anglo-Saxon Superiority*. One should learn from the pace-setting civilization of our era, he wrote, and borrow as many of its ideas as possible, to the extent that they are compatible with Muslim identity. The fight against the British occupation of Egypt, to which he was committed, should by no means extend to its culture. Egyptians, said Rida, had a great deal to learn from the British, even though they had to flatly reject British political rule and claims about the "white man's burden."

A LOVE AFFAIR WITH EUROPE

This review nicely captures the mood on the eve of World War I, the high point of Islamic modernism's love affair with Europe. In a way, it marked the culmination of a process begun in the 1820s, when Muslim thinkers and decision makers in the Middle East drew the lessons of Napoleon's invasion, which had laid bare how far Muslims lagged behind Europeans. Travelers and students who flocked to Paris and London (some students were sent by modernizing rulers) confirmed the finding. Europe had developed a civilization that was not only dominant militarily but was also superior in science, organization, social etiquette, and government. A vast translation effort was undertaken, both by rulers, who issued fiats to that effect and by curious intellectuals eager to quench the thirst to discover and unlock the secrets of European superiority and to get to know its major exponents.

The impact on mainstream Islamists, not to speak of secularized intellectuals (many of them Christian) was enormous, despite the efforts of religious, dyed-in-the-wool conservatives to block any borrowing from the so-called Crusader West. The major outcome was the birth of the Salafi movement. It was headed by Sheikh al-Azhar, Muhammad Abduh of Egypt (1849–1905). In its glorious early age, Islam was able to progress and develop by rationally adapting to circumstances while preserving its essence. It had lost this ability, wrote Abduh, somewhere late in the third century of its existence. The aim of the Salafis was to regain this capacity.

Because Islam is an orthopraxis (a system in which behavior has precedence over belief) rather than an orthodoxy, the way to regain Islam's original flexibility, according to the Salafis, was to revitalize law and education rather than theology. The major tool was to be the *ijtihad*, the authority jurists possessed to amend, even change, the sharia (law) by applying personal legal reasoning in evaluating the urgent needs of the Muslim community. Innovation in such matters should not be considered evil, as most traditionalists held, but helpful. The innovative ideas to be absorbed could be indigenous or European. Had not Islam taken on the great ideas of Greek philosophy in the Middle Ages? As far as possible, said Abduh and Rida, such borrowing ought to be done under the norms of al-Salaf al-Salih, as expressed in the rich and pluralistic hadith (oral tradition) and legal literature.

The Salafi movement had a deep influence on the young high school–educated generation, especially in Egypt, Syria, Lebanon, and Tunisia. It had its Shiite analogues in Iran and Iraq.

THE DEFEAT OF THE OTTOMAN EMPIRE AND ITS AFTERMATH

World War I and its immediate aftermath abruptly changed all that. Rida and many of his disciples felt duty-bound to revise their ideas. The Ottoman Empire, a bulwark of Muslim identity, suffered a crushing defeat, lost most of its territory, and was soon abrogated by the secularist modernizer Kemal Ataturk. Large chunks of the Abode of Islam, including the Fertile Crescent (Rida's native region) fell under European domination. Egypt was no more the exception in the Middle East but the rule. Europe showed what Rida and his young, radical followers came to see as its real face—arrogant, domineering, and expansionist. For the radical wing of the Salafi movement, known as Al-Manar, which had grown apart from the older and more liberal wing, it was no longer possible to preserve the distinction between Europe's cultural and political facets, especially since the world war seemed to unveil underlying

irrational and destructive strains in European culture. Could it be that Europe itself was in decline and did not have much to offer anymore? This doubt was sustained by the translated writings of Oswald Spengler and the Nobel Prize–winning scientist Alexis Carrel. These prophets of doom, along with their British counterpart, Arnold Toynbee, headed the nonfiction best-seller list in Arab countries in the interwar years.

Yet the major preoccupation of the Al-Manar trend, named after the weekly newspaper edited by Rida, was not Europe but internal reexamination. The question the radicals asked was: Are we still Muslims? Could it be that, enfeebled by centuries of decline, Muslims had already surrendered to the temptations of European civilization? Unlike the liberal Salafis, who preserved the hope that Islam and modernity were reconcilable, Rida answered this last question in the affirmative. Most Muslims, especially those who were modernized, were no more than geographical, or nominal, Muslims, observing only the external rules of behavior, lacking belief and any understanding of the significance of those rules. They cut corners in ritual and, above all, did not apply the sharia either under foreign rule or even in regions that remained independent or autonomous. In such a state of affairs, *ijtihad* was still needed, but it should be more uniform, more controlled throughout the Muslim world. Because Islam's identity was weak during that period, it was incapable of assimilating a large number of innovations or any pluralistic practices. The radicals thus tried to build mental and behavioral walls to defend against the siege on a beleaguered faith.

The upshot was a split in the Salafi movement, which was completed by the 1930s. While the radicals grew in strength, thanks to the Muslim Brotherhood (founded in 1928), the liberals, who claimed loyalty to Abduh's legacy, moved to the left. They embraced world culture and progress. Some of them, like the Egyptian thinker Taha Hussein, put early Islam under scrutiny, following research methods learned from Western Orientalists. Rida as well as Hasan al-Banna, founder of the Muslim Brotherhood, saw such Westerners as enemies of the faith who were burrowing into and sabotaging Islam from within. But there was no doubt about who was winning this debate—the radicals with their broadening social base attracted great numbers of the young, the urban disenfranchised, and even the peasants, well beyond Egypt's borders.

JIHAD TURNED INWARD

If Islam in the first half of the twentieth century transformed *ijtihad,* in the second half it transformed jihad, or holy war. This was a much more politicized phase than the first. As Muslim countries achieved their independence, the attitudes that had given precedence to external enemies—the colonial powers—began to fade away, as did the tendency to externalize guilt, to blame others for all the problems of indigenous societies, to view them as the result of imperialist dominance. In other words, the jihad turned inward.

At that moment, the historical force that came to the fore was the populist state, which was able to mobilize the masses and was often controlled by military elites drawn from the lower middle class. This state, whether embodied in Gamal Abdel Nasser's Egypt (1952–1970), in Baath-led Syria (1970 on) or Iraq (1968–2003), or in Algeria under the Front de Libération Nationale, or FLN (1962–1988), was characterized by a sincere and combative anti-imperialism. The Muslim Brotherhood and its ilk could therefore not impugn the state as collaborationist or as besotted with the West, as they had the old upper-class rulers and their liberal Salafi allies. Besides, the elites in the new states were commoners and proponents of a new and galvanizing nativist ideology, namely, Pan-Arabism. These elites could thus reasonably aspire to gain cultural dominance and develop a modernizing civil religion with its own symbols and rituals, often using Islamic themes. And because the new elites were soldiers by profession, they possessed the advantages of the military: relative efficiency, order, ruthlessness, and disrespect for the legal process. They had at their service techniques to control the populace that they had learned from like-minded European regimes on both the Right and the Left, as their use of secret police, detention camps, and listening devices demonstrate.

Finally, the technological revolution in audiovisual communications (notably the transistor radio and television), which coincided with the advent of the nationalist state, favored the interventionist ambitions of the new masters. Initially these rulers exercised a virtual monopoly on the press and on book publishing. They saw the potential of the new audiovisual media, when buttressed by an ever-vigilant censorship. These media penetrated every corner of people's lives and reached the largely illiterate population of women, small children, and rural men. Social groups that had been beyond the reach of modernity, Europe's crowning achievement, were now drawn into the fold.

The social sphere was rapidly shrinking as the state's role increased. The fares the new media were selling were attractive in their substance and in their packaging: the nationalist gospel was a kind of ersatz religion. It focused on solidarity, deftly couched in Muslim terms, on the one hand, and on the promise of economic modernization as the avenue for the good life on the other. In this brand-new situation, the radical Salafis (notably the Muslim Brotherhood, first the allies of the military in power, then their victims) had to reassess their worldview.

WESTOXICATION AND ITS CURE

A number of thinkers in the late 1950s and throughout the 1960s (Sayyid Qutb in Egypt, Said Hawwa in Syria, Muhammad Baqr al-Sadr in Iraq, and, in a different setting, Ala Al Ahmad and Ruhollah Khomeini in Iran) pioneered the new thinking. This fell under three headings.

1. *The diagnosis:* Twentieth-century Islam faced a mortal danger, worse than anything it had ever known. The danger came this time from within, from leaders and movements that were technically Muslim, that were responsible both for enforcing the law and for persuading. In their manner, these rulers were sincerely devoted to the welfare of their people. And yet they were inadvertently bringing a calamity of spiritual extinction down upon these very masses. Indeed, the new masters, much more than the liberal Salafis, were deeply committed to "westoxication," a term coined both in Persian and in Arabic. They were intoxicated by Western, European ideas totally alien to Islam, such as nationalism, economic growth as an overriding goal, socialism, and the primacy of human-made over God-made laws. By manipulating the media and using the enticements and punishments at

their disposal, they inculcated these ideas into the subconscious of the masses. They thus fostered an addiction to modernity and to the "good life" it promised, here on earth and not in the hereafter. As a result, the Abode of Islam was in a state of virtual apostasy. It had abandoned its faith for faithlessness. This state of affairs was all the more deleterious for being subconscious. In Muslim terms, Islam was in a state of *jahiliyya*—a barbarity worse than that existing in Arabia before the appearance of the Prophet Muhammad.

2. *The cure:* True believers had to come back to the political arena, from which they had been absent for too long. For the archenemy was now the state, which was the agent of European thought, beliefs, and behavior. It behooved Believers to subject modernity to a rigorous and systematic critique in accordance with the norms of Islamic authenticity. Through such a critique they had to enhance religious awareness, especially among the brainwashed, westoxicated youth. High school- and university-educated youngsters were indeed the major target group and had to be immediately reclaimed and detoxified, liberated from their infatuation with pleasure-seeking, pseudoscientific modernity. It is likely that such a critique did not stand a real chance of bringing about a change from within, given the state monopoly on the means of compulsion and on education and the media. The Muslim radicals could not dodge the inescapable conclusion: the regimes in power had to be delegitimated.

3. *Administering the cure:* Delegitimation would inevitably lead to jihad, "by word [propaganda] or by sword [violence]," as the hadith had it, in a jihad against internal, not external enemies. Through the reeducation of society or through armed revolt, believers could eventually set up a state where religious law was applied. These ideas were developed in the heyday of the nationalist state but were given the chance to spread throughout society as a result of a series of defeats the nation-state had experienced from the late 1960s and to the 1990s. These included the 1967 defeat in the Arab-Israeli War, the failure of the Soviet-inspired command economy to truly take off, oil price slumps in 1979 and in 1985, and the decline of Pan-Arabism between Nasser's death in 1970 and the Iraqi invasion of Kuwait in 1990. The new Islamic radicals succeeded in taking power

only in Iran, and for a short time in Sudan and Afghanistan, but they became the major opposition force everywhere else. Their nongovernment organizations (NGOs) were active in civil society, which they managed to revive, and—despite harassment and persecution by the powers that be—they wielded enormous influence on mores, particularly among urbanized youth. It was indeed among such youth that suspicion of everything that Europe is supposed to stand for—enlightenment, progress, tolerance, and universal values—was evident.

ISLAM IN EUROPE

Another twist in this complex history came toward the end of the century. This was the fate of Islam *in* Europe. By the 1980s Europe had many more Muslims than ever before: 4.5 million in France, 3 million in Germany, 2 million in the U.K., 1 million in the Netherlands, and 1.5 million in the other countries of Europe, not including illegal aliens, who continued to arrive in waves. The most vulnerable group among them consisted of young males aged fifteen to twenty-four. They could be found at the bottom of the socio-occupational ladder, with an unemployment rate triple that of the same age group in the general population. They lived in overcrowded ghettos on the outskirts of large towns and were overrepresented among drug addicts, school dropouts, and prison inmates. This was the result in part of an inadequate investment by the states in housing, infrastructure, and medical services in these ghettos, either because of racial prejudice or because of the recent shrinking of the welfare state, which hit hardest the social strata lacking political clout. And the uneducated Muslims voted in lower proportions than the rest of the electorate. It was thus a vicious circle: lack of education brought about political underrepresentation and that in turn created further cuts in educational and other services.

Young Muslim men (women invested more in education to guarantee their freedom from dependence on the family) were victims of globalization. In the 1960s and 1970s the European economy needed the muscle power of the immigrants of their parents' generation, largely illiterate, to rebuild from the ruins of World War II and expand industry. By the 1980s it had started to transfer labor-intensive activities (cars, metalwork, mining,

Four veiled Muslim women sit on a bench in Kensington Gardens, London, August 1977. ©HULTON-DEUTSCH COLLECTION/CORBIS

textile, footwear) to central and eastern Europe and to Southeast Asia. Even the construction industry, which had employed so many of the parents, became mechanized. Young men with few technical skills and little education now had difficulty finding work in the new services and information economy. They were hence driven to the gray area of petty crime, drug peddling, and protection services. No wonder so many had brushes with the law, whose agencies were often permeated with racism. Alienation from mainstream society was growing. Besides, young Muslims rebelled against the compliant attitude of their fathers. Born in Europe, they sensed they had rights and insisted on respect.

That is why Muslim youth, restless and hopeless, were attracted by a new radical message coming from the fringe of the Islamic world—the message of Dr. Abdallah Azzam, leader of the jihad in Afghanistan against the Soviets (he was assassinated in 1988) and of his successor, Osama bin Laden. According to Azzam and bin Laden, the source of

all Muslim miseries was the United States and its lackey, Europe. These new crusaders, they argued, should become the target of a holy war directed at their economies. Collateral damage would also be inflicted upon apostate regimes in Islamic countries, which relied on the United States and Europe to ensure their survival. They would eventually totter as well. The new theory insisted on the essential hypocrisy of Christian civilization. In the twelfth and thirteenth centuries, what was supposedly a religion of peace produced the Crusades to subdue the Abode of Islam. Now its modern counterpart sought to maintain control of that Abode in order to ensure itself of oil supplies. These were vital to Western plenty, and without them the pleasure-seeking civilization could not survive. The West also found it vital to this end to exploit immigrants. Yet to cover up its immorality, it spoke of universal human rights, which gave it a justification for intervening everywhere in the Muslim world. And were these rights respected in the West itself? Ask unemployed Muslims harassed by racist police, said bin Laden, urging the young to stand up and fight.

Such a message provided young Muslim men with an outlet for frustration, a glimmer of hope, avenues for action and adventure. And as the differences between countries of origin blurred in the European diaspora, the emergent identity of the members of the second and third generations of Muslim immigrants was "Muslim"—in their own eyes and in the eyes of mainstream society. The stigma became a badge of honor and helped them accept an ideal and a form of organization (inspired by Al Qaeda but not necessarily beholden to it) predicated on the notion of an Islamic community, or *umma*. The clandestine or semiclandestine groups (*jamaat*) that the young joined provided them with a sense of belonging, of solidarity, and of empowerment, a warm home in a cold, individualistic, and often hostile European society. The young could make sense of their personal failures in finding employment, getting promotions, passing exams, and steering clear of the police. All these were the fault of an evil, immoral outside force, namely, Western civilization, as inimical to Islam in the twenty-first century as it had been in the Middle Ages.

If the youth were the victims of globalization, as new militants they also benefited from it. The message arrived in their ears though audiocassettes produced by preachers in Pakistan, Turkey, Egypt, the United Arab Emirates, Algeria, and Morocco. These cassettes were easy to smuggle and copy and also served as entertainment. Fledgling activists could get instructions from far away via cell phones, could get funds through telephonic bank transfers, and could receive instructions and educational material by means of the Internet. A new jihad was on.

See also **Algeria; Al Qaeda; Egypt; France; Globalization; Gulf Wars; Islamic Terrorism; Minority Rights; Morocco; Turkey.**

BIBLIOGRAPHY

Barbulescu, Luc, and Philippe Cardinal, eds. *L'Islam en questions: Vingt-quatre écrivains arabes répondent.* Paris, 1986.

Enayat, Hamid. *Modern Islamic Political Thought.* Austin, Tex., 1982.

Gibb, Hamilton. *Studies on the Civilization of Islam.* Edited by Stanford J. Shaw and William R. Polk. Boston, 1962.

Hourani, Albert. *Islam in European Thought.* Cambridge, U.K., 1991.

Labat, Séverine. *Les Islamistes algériens: Entre les urnes et le maquis.* Paris, 1995.

Rahman, Fazlur. *Islam and Modernity: Transformation of an Intellectual Tradition.* Chicago, 1982.

Rodinson, Maxime. *La fascination de l'Islam.* Paris, 1989.

Seurat, Michel. *L'État de Barbarie.* Paris, 1989.

Sivan, Emmanuel. *Radical Islam: Medieval Theology and Modern Politics.* 2nd enlarged ed. New Haven, Conn., 1990.

———. *Mythes politiques arabes.* Translated by Nicolas Weill. Paris, 1995.

EMMANUEL SIVAN

ISLAMIC TERRORISM.

Islamic terrorism is both a propaganda term and an analytical category to describe the work and beliefs of a loosely linked set of fundamentalist groups at war with westernized Arab regimes and the countries that support them. The term is both problematic and to many people offensive. It implies that as a religion Islam encourages violence and that Muslims may be especially susceptible to becoming terrorists. Critics correctly point out that although both Judaism and Christianity have motivated terrorist groups, these groups have seldom been labeled "Jewish terrorists" or "Christian terrorists." The 2006 controversy over cartoons published in a Danish newspaper and republished elsewhere in Europe underscores the sensitivity of this issue. The cartoons satirizing Islam included a sinister image of the Prophet Muhammad wearing a turban made to look like a bomb with a lit fuse. The drawings produced little response when they first appeared in Denmark in the fall of 2005 but unleashed a firestorm of protest when republished by papers in Muslim countries in February 2006. The cartoons reinforced the offensive stereotype that Islam is a violent religion that encourages terrorism. For these reasons many analysts prefer the terms *Islamist terrorism* or *fundamentalist terrorism*.

As a proselytizing religion, Islam (like Christianity) has historically permitted use of violence to spread the faith. However, the Prophet placed tight restrictions on any use of force. Following the battle of the Trenches before Medina, Muhammad articulated the concept of "lesser jihad," or defensive war, to protect the *uma* (community of believers). Contrary to popular belief, *jihad* does not mean "holy war." "Holy struggle" or "struggle for righteousness" better captures the meaning of the term. For this reason, the Prophet insisted that the "greater jihad" be the personal struggle to live as a good Muslim. Muhammad also outlined what Christians would call a just-war theory, laying down strict prohibitions against killing noncombatants, especially women and children.

While nothing in the core teachings of Islam justifies the abuses of contemporary terrorist groups, Islam, like any other religion, has been used by followers to justify a range of violent actions. Contemporary Islamic extremism has its roots in Wahhabism, an eighteenth-century revival movement that sought to restore the faith to its original, pristine form. This commitment to turning back the clock has led both followers and critics of the movement to refer to it as Salafism, from the Arabic word *salaf*, meaning "predecessors" or "ancestors." Although not inherently violent, Wahhabi theology rejected any "modern" additions to Islamic faith, practice, or even culture. Calls to purify Islam of these idolatrous trappings brought Wahhabis into violent conflict with Islamic regimes. Their founder, Ibn Abd al-Wahhab, declared a jihad against those who did not agree with his view of the faith. This mandate would find an echo in the radicalism of Osama bin Laden.

For most of its history Wahhabism remained isolated in Saudi Arabia. Despite its call for the restoration of an Islamic republic, the sect provided the theological underpinning and much of the muscle of the new kingdom of Saudi Arabia founded in 1932 by Abdul Aziz Ibn Saud. In the turmoil of the postcolonial world and especially following the Ayatollah Khomeini's Islamic revolution, Wahhabism spread farther afield and in its most militant form supported (or was appropriated by) the radical terrorist group Al Qaeda. In Egypt, Wahhabism took root in the Muslim Brotherhood, a largely nonviolent movement offering an alternative to the secular Arab nationalism of Gamal Abdel Nasser. The Brotherhood later spawned Egyptian Islamic Jihad, the terrorist organization responsible for the murder of Nasser's successor, Anwar Sadat, and linked to the 1993 bombings of the World Trade Center.

Until 1979 the Saudi Kingdom made little effort to encourage the spread of Wahhabism. The Iranian revolution, however, threatened Sunni Arab (and therefore Saudi) primacy in the Muslim world. To counter the spread of radical Shiite Islam, the Saudis funded the *madrassa* movement. The royal government and Wahhabi charities founded hundreds of free Koranic schools throughout the Muslim world. Although these schools did not necessarily espouse violence, their conservative theology would make them fertile recruiting grounds for extremist organizations in future years. Located in poor areas where families could not afford even modest fees at state schools, *madrassas* offered free education with an ideological bent appealing to socially and economically marginalized people.

Radical theology alone, even when coupled with economic and social disadvantage, did not produce "Islamic terrorism." A unique set of political circumstances caused these factors to coalesce around one of the deadliest terrorist organizations in history. The Soviet invasion of Afghanistan drew thousands of *mujahidin* (holy warriors) from around the Muslim world to help Afghans fight the infidels who had invaded their country. Among these warriors was a wealthy Saudi named Osama bin Laden. Although bin Laden played a relatively minor role in the ultimately successful war to expel the Soviets, he went on to organize Al Qaeda. Bin Laden offered his organization of *mujahidin* to the Saudi monarchy following the Iraqi invasion of Kuwait in the summer of 1990. The Saudis chose an American-led coalition instead, earning them and their allies the eternal enmity of Al Qaeda.

Al Qaeda and its affiliates, the organizations most people have in mind when they speak of "Islamic terrorism," espouse goals consistent with the principal tenets of Wahhabism. First and foremost, they seek to replace apostate regimes within the Muslim world. Any Muslim country not governed by strict sharia law (Islamic law based on the Koran and the Hadiths, or sayings of the Prophet) qualifies as apostate. Egypt, Pakistan, and Iraq (under Saddam Hussein and the subsequent government) lead the list of regimes needing to be replaced as does Saudi Arabia. Although it governs the kingdom according to sharia, the monarchy committed the unforgivable sin of inviting the "crusaders" (U.S. troops) onto the sacred soil of Saudi Arabia. Wahhabism also calls for the creation of an Islamic republic rather than a monarchy. Moving beyond the national level, bin Laden and his followers wish to create an Islamic caliphate of all Muslim people.

The anger of "Islamic terrorists" toward the West in general and the United States in particular is more complex. The United States became a target because of its support for the apostate regimes the extremists want to replace. Extremists also find the U.S. presence in the Persian Gulf unacceptable. U.S. support for Israel further angers Al Qaeda and its affiliates. Finally, Islamic extremists hate the secularism and what they see as the decadence of the West, corrupting influences brought daily into Muslim countries by the Internet and satellite television.

The invasion of Iraq has further angered Islamist terrorist groups and resulted in more attacks. On 11 March 2004, the Moroccan Combatant Group detonated 10 bombs, 8 on trains and 2 in a train station, during morning rush hour in Madrid, Spain, killing 192 people and injuring more than 2,000 others. On 3 April those suspected of carrying out the attacks blew themselves up in their Madrid apartment when cornered by Spanish security forces. The terrorist group formed in the late 1990s by former Afghan *muja-hidin* to promote Islamic revolution in Morocco launched the attacks to punish Spain for its support of the U.S.-led war in Iraq. A new government elected shortly after the attacks announced that it would be withdrawing Spanish troops from Iraq. The decision stemmed from complex domestic issues, but the terrorists claimed a victory and assured Spain the attacks would stop.

A year later Islamist terrorists struck again, hitting the London Underground with three near-simultaneous suicide bombs during morning rush hour on 7 July 2005. A fourth bomber detonated his device on a double-decker bus within an hour. The attacks killed 57 people, including the terrorists, and injured 700. Three of the four bombers were born in Britain and were of Pakistani descent; the fourth had emigrated from Jamaica. At least one of the men had ties to Pakistan that suggest

an Al Qaeda link. In a video statement recovered after the bombings, one of the bombers said attacks would continue so long as Muslims continued to suffer attacks, presumably from the West, although he made no specific reference to Iraq. Another group of suicide bombers attempted a follow-up attack on the London commuter system on 21 July, but their bombs failed to detonate. The terrorists were quickly apprehended.

Ironically, the religious nature of Islamic extremist terrorism makes it particularly deadly. Terrorists who believe their cause to be divinely inspired have little compunction about killing innocent civilians. One of the perpetrators of the 1998 embassy bombings in East Africa who later cooperated with the United States explained Al Qaeda's rationalization for the unavoidable deaths of Muslims who worked in the two buildings. If they are righteous in the eyes of Allah, he was told, they will go to paradise. If not, they deserve to die.

See also **Al Qaeda; Islam; Terrorism.**

BIBLIOGRAPHY

Esposito, John. *Unholy War: Terror in the Name of Islam.* Oxford, U.K., and New York, 2002.

Gunaratna, Rohan. *Inside Al Qae'da: Global Network of Terror.* New York, 2002.

Hoffman, Bruce. *Inside Terrorism.* London, 1998.

Kepel, Gilles. *Jihad: The Trail of Political Islam.* Cambridge, Mass., 2002.

Mockaitis, Thomas R., and Paul Rich, eds. *Grand Strategy in the War against Terrorism.* London, 2003.

TOM MOCKAITIS

ISRAEL. Relations between Israel and Europe are as much a product of the history of representations as they are of diplomatic history. These relations are permanently marked by the fact that Israel had its beginnings in Europe, both in the most profound cultural sense and in terms of the origins of a large part of its population. Relations between these two entities, in both their conflict-ridden history and their long-term affinities, cannot be understood without taking into account this fundamental fact: for Europe, Israel is not something external produced by a combination of geography and geopolitics. And conversely, Europe remains for Israel, beyond the conflicts, disagreements, and schisms between them, an indispensable matrix for understanding itself.

A EUROPEAN HISTORY, A RUPTURE WITH EUROPE

Israel's human, intellectual, and cultural origins must be sought in Europe. Born in Europe, the modern Zionist project grew out of the nation-building movements that multiplied in the wake of the "springtime of nations" in the second half of the nineteenth century. Inherent in it is the contradiction that continues to mark relations between Europe and Israel to this day: Jewish nationalism emanated from Europe, yet it manifested itself in a radical rupture separating it from the Old Continent. The liberal idea of the nation-state, applied to the Jews, provided the foundations of the Zionist project. But Israel's birth and genesis must also be understood in terms of a radical break between Judaism and Europe. The idea of Zionism, while it cannot be reduced to a simple reaction against anti-Semitism, is based on an interpretation of European history that sees Jewish emancipation as a resounding failure. Israel's national memory rests on a reading of European history wherein anti-Semitism, because it nullifies the goal of shared citizenship, definitively discredits the political ideal of the Enlightenment. This reading was confirmed after the fact by the Holocaust, a venture in which Nazi Germany was the mainspring, but which could not have been conceived without significant intermediaries across the Continent and without a certain complacent, or even consensual, passivity on the part of Europe's population.

In cultural terms, too, Europe's repudiation played a prominent role for Zionism. The history of Europe's Jews has been interpreted as a long litany of discrimination, humiliation, and vexation that culminated in the "degeneration" of the Jew, to use the term coined by Max Nordau (1849–1923), the counselor and close friend of the Zionist leader Theodor Herzl (1860–1904). The rupture with the Old Continent was intended to allow for "regeneration," the birth of a new Jew, freed at last from the stigmas of exile. From the Zionist perspective, the normalization of the Jew necessarily implied a break with Europe. Israel's mistrust of Europe, of which recurrent expressions may still be found at the beginning of the

twenty-first century, has its origins in this metahistorical narrative produced by Zionism.

ISRAEL AND EUROPE: A COLONIAL AND POSTCOLONIAL HISTORY, 1948–1967

The relationship between Israel and Europe must also be situated within the complex framework of colonial relations. Great Britain was the major tutelary power for Zionism. Beginning with the Balfour Declaration of 2 November 1917, in which Britain affirmed its support for the creation of a Jewish homeland in Palestine, British history and Israeli history have remained braided together. Britain became in 1921 the Mandatory power in Palestine, and therefore oversaw the early stages of what was to become the Arab-Israeli conflict. Great Britain played an ambivalent role in the region, defending its own interests above all, and not hesitating, in order to do so, to pit the Jewish and Arab communities against each other. By limiting Jewish immigration into Palestine, at a time when in Central Europe it was becoming urgent for Jews to find places of refuge, and by strongly suppressing Jewish attempts to establish means of self-defense in the face of the Arab revolts, Great Britain pursued a classic colonial policy that left a lasting and bitter residue. It was finally against British colonial power that Israel won its independence in 1948.

The regional role of the European powers did not end with decolonization. The first years of Israel's existence were marked by the establishment of privileged relations with France, its most important ally until the Six-Day War in 1967. This alliance was largely based on the fact that France, the colonial power in Algeria, saw Israel as a natural partner in the common fight against the Arab nationalism of the Gamal Abdel Nasser (1918–1970) era. The commonality of European and Israeli interests reached a climax during the joint military operations Mounted by the English, the French, and the Israelis against Egypt in the Suez Crisis of 1956. The end of France's presence in Algeria in 1962, and to an even greater extent, the economic pressure exerted by the oil-producing Arab countries during the consecutive oil crises and the Yom Kippur War of 1973, permanently called into question diplomatic relations between the European countries and Israel. After the Six-Day War the United States replaced France as Israel's foremost strategic partner.

Chaim Weizmann is sworn in as Israel's first president, 20 February 1949. ©HULTON-DEUTSCH COLLECTION/CORBIS

ISRAEL: EUROPE'S BAD CONSCIENCE

Relations between Israel and Europe were profoundly affected by the Holocaust. Europe after World War II felt a special responsibility toward the state into which a large share of the survivors were pouring. Israel became an acute reminder of the Old Continent's criminal past, transforming its bad conscience into an element that is crucial for understanding the dynamic of the relationship. Europe's position vis-à-vis Israel is by turns animated by great compassion for Israel's experience and by a severity of judgment in which can be discerned a desire, by designating Israel as guilty, to assuage a collective bad conscience that continues to be obsessed by the Shoah. It is certainly in terms of this characteristically European dynamic that Europe's stances toward Israel in the Arab-Israeli conflict must be reread. Thus, at the time when Europe's institutions were being put in place during the 1960s, privileged relations with Israel

formed immediately and naturally. In economic, commercial, scientific, and cultural agreements, an intense cooperation was established that resisted the various political crises. Acknowledged as a privileged partner, Israel was linked to the building of Europe. And yet, an integration of Israel into Europe was not seriously envisioned.

1967–2005: THE ENTRENCHMENT OF INCOMPREHENSION

The Six-Day War was a major dividing line in Israeli-European relations. After its conquest of new territories, Israel for the first time no longer appeared to be the victim of Arab hostility, but as a regional power that was responsible for blocking—or was even the main obstacle to—peace in the Middle East. From the time of the war with Lebanon in 1982, and to an even greater extent since the two Palestinian revolts against Israeli occupation in 1988 and 2000, relations between Israel and Europe have

Jewish women and children wait at the docks in Marseille, France, to board a ship bound for Israel, 15 September 1949. ©CORBIS

seemingly been characterized by a profound incomprehension. The European Union was built around a historic reconciliation between former belligerent parties and declared itself a haven of peace. This new reality resulted in an inability to understand Israel, a country determined to go it alone in the name of its extraordinary suffering and an ethnic and religious identity that is also difficult for most Europeans to understand.

Israel is engaged in a dynamic of insisting on the need for borders to guarantee Jewish continuity and survival, at a time when much of Europe is preoccupied with the disappearance of borders. The Jews, who were the precursors in the desire to transcend boundaries, now find themselves in the camp of those who stress their positive role. This contradiction cannot help but engender a strong incomprehension that is often tinged with hostility. Israel's identity, recognized as legitimate in the aftermath of the Holocaust, is out of synch with the postnational principles in vogue in early-twenty-first-century Europe. There is an erosion of the sympathetic capital that Europe and the Europeans once felt for the Jewish state. Brutality on the West Bank, and Israel's close alliance with the United States, put Israel squarely in the camp of George Bush and the set of advisors who led the invasion of Iraq. Anti-Americanism and anti-Israeli sentiment went hand in hand.

This critical reading of Israel by Europe is matched by an equally intense skepticism on the part of Israel. Many contemporary examples could be cited of mistrust in the face of what Israeli public opinion sees as the return of an old demon to European territory. The second *intifada*, and to an even greater extent the war in Iraq and its effects, have given Israel the sense of a return of anti-Semitic modes of reasoning. This negative vision of Europe, which in the early twenty-first century has spread in Israel, also reflects a profound demographic, sociological, and cultural shift within Israeli society. Public opinion in Israel is experiencing relations with Europe as a new betrayal. The comeback of a substantial level of anti-Semitic actions and discourse is convincing Israelis of the resurgence of old demons, and all of it contributes to an increase, among Israelis, in negative judgments about Europe. In Israel's eyes, Europe appears as a monster with multiple archaeological strata: a brutal, anti-Semitic past, a present that is indifferent or even hostile to Israel, and a new brand of anti-Semitism.

Relations between Israel and Europe in some respects recall recent difficulties in transatlantic relations. Similarly built on a community of values and interests, relations between Europe and the United States have been strongly shaken by Europe's rejection of the power politics unilaterally deployed by the United States.

The relationship between Europe and Israel is a magnifying mirror for twentieth-century history. This relationship brings to bear particularly painful episodes from the past that continue to have a decisive impact in the present. As is the case for transatlantic relations, however, the relationship between Israel and Europe is based on deep and shared beliefs, and this means that it is not optimistic to believe that it will transcend the repeated crises that have characterized it at the turn of the twenty-first century.

See also **Anti-Americanism; Anti-Semitism; British Empire, End of; Egypt; European Union; Holocaust; Jews; Suez Crisis; World War II; Zionism.**

BIBLIOGRAPHY

Aron, Raymond. *De Gaulle, Israel and the Jews.* Translated by John Sturoch. New York, 1969.

Avineri, Shlomo. *The Making of Modern Zionism: Intellectual Origins of the Jewish State.* New York, 1981.

Avineri, Shlomo, and Werner Weidenfeld, eds. *Integration and Identity: Challenges to Europe and Israel; A Project of the Bertelsmann Foundation.* Bonn, Germany, 1999.

Finkielkraut, Alain. *La réprobation d'Israël.* Paris, 1982.

Hertzberg, Arthur, ed. *The Zionist Idea: A Historical Analysis and Reader.* New York, 1972.

Sachar, Howard M. *Israel and Europe: An Appraisal in History.* New York, 1999.

JACQUES EHRENFREUND

ISTANBUL. Istanbul was founded in antiquity as the Greek city-state of Byzantium. It was the Byzantine imperial capital, known as Constantinople, from November of 324 C.E. until May of 1453, when it became the Ottoman imperial capital under Sultan Mehmed II. It remained the political, cultural, and economic center of the Ottoman Empire, often with the epithet "The Gate of Felicity" (Dersaadet), until that empire's demise and the establishment of the Turkish republic in 1923. After 1,600 years of political supremacy, the twentieth century saw Istanbul's political marginalization with the establishment of Ankara as the capital of the Turkish republic on 13 October 1923. Modernization and Turkification were two, often conflicting, processes in Istanbul's history between 1914 and 2004. While Istanbul was no longer the political capital of Turkey in the twentieth century, it remained the largest, the most economically and culturally vital, and the most demographically cosmopolitan of Turkey's cities.

TURN OF THE TWENTIETH CENTURY: POLITICAL AND CULTURAL MOVEMENTS

The political demise of the Ottoman Empire in the early twentieth century was accompanied, ironically, by the urban flowering of Istanbul; not only did the city's population expand drastically with the influx of non-Muslim groups from the countryside, but also its wealth as a commercial and port city attracted world, or at least European, attention. Fin de siècle architecture and fashion in Istanbul rivaled (and was derived from) that in Paris and Vienna, as many a European artist and intellectual, such as the Frenchman Pierre Loti, called Istanbul home.

But as culture and commerce flourished in port cities such as Istanbul and Izmir (Smyrna), the secret society born among Ottoman military officers, known as the Committee of Union and Progress, led to the Young Turk revolution in Istanbul and diverse provinces in 1908. Istanbul in the second constitutional period (1908–1918) was subject to intense campaigns of economic

ARCHITECTURE AND NATURAL DISASTERS

The imperial architecture of the turn of the twentieth century in Istanbul gave way to the modernism of Kemalist Turkey, typified by the new capital of Ankara and the Atatürk Cultural Center in Istanbul. In addition to these, by the second half of the twentieth century, modernist residential housing—apartment blocks—proliferated to house the populations arriving from the countryside. Finally, from the 1980s, illegal apartment blocks, often of dangerously low quality, known as *gecekondu* (meaning literally "built at night") have expanded Istanbul into a city of perhaps fifteen million people. While comparable to shantytowns for their dubious legal status, many *gecekondu* are now part of the electricity, water, and transportation systems of Istanbul proper, making it difficult to distinguish "illegal" from "legal" apartment developments. Earthquakes, such as the massive 1999 earthquake with its epicenter just to the east of Istanbul, are an ever present danger in Istanbul as in many other parts of Turkey and the Mediterranean, making the risk of living in *gecekondu* even greater.

modernization and political repression. Perhaps the most infamous event in the Young Turk period was the Armenian genocide, which occurred in 1915 at the terrible intersection between Ottoman imperial demise, civil unrest, and World War I.

1914–1922: WAR, OCCUPATION, AND THE BIRTH OF A NATIONAL RESISTANCE

The Ottoman Empire, under the rule of the Committee of Union and Progress (Young Turks), joined World War I on the side of Axis Germany and Austria (11 November 1914). After tremendously bloody battles that were won by Ottoman forces (such as the Battle of Gallipoli in spring 1915), Allied forces won the war and began negotiating an armistice. An armistice was reached on 30 October 1918 at Mudros on the island of Lemnos. Two weeks later an Allied fleet of sixty ships anchored in Istanbul's Bosphorus, and by 8 December an Allied military administration was set up in the Ottoman capital. As separate powers (France, Britain, Italy, Greece) occupied different Ottoman provinces, Istanbul became a truly international city, occupied as it was by several foreign powers at once. Istanbul, still nominally the Ottoman capital under Allied military administration, was not only the scene of many an international intrigue (one need only recall that the Orient Express left from Istanbul's Haydar Pasha train station to evoke such intrigues) but also the destination and refuge for Russian émigrés fleeing the Russian Revolution and civil war. Istanbul's days as political center were numbered, however; the last Ottoman parliament met there on 18 March 1920 and was dissolved by Sultan Mehmed VI on 11 April.

The occupation of the Ottoman capital by Allied forces and of the heartland of Anatolia (Asia Minor) by the Greek army sparked a nationalist insurgency led by Mustafa Kemal Pasha (1881–1938), later to be known as Atatürk (literally, "father of the Turks"). While Istanbul was the site of violent protests by the end of May 1919 (in Sultanahmet Square), at the same time Atatürk and his forces began to move westward from Samsun on the Black Sea, expelling the Greek occupying armies, lastly from Izmir in September 1922.

In the wake of the Turkish War of Independence (known as the "national catastrophe" in Greece), the Treaty of Lausanne, under the auspices of the League of Nations, was negotiated between Greece and Turkey, which featured two major changes: it established complete Turkish sovereignty and enacted the first internationally organized exchange of populations, which would forcibly remove about 800,000 Muslims from Greece and about 1.3 million Orthodox Christians from Turkey. With regard to Turkish sovereignty, Atatürk separated the Ottoman sultanate from the caliphate (or seat of the Muslim caliph), abolished first the sultanate and then the caliphate (an event of vast significance to Muslims as far away as Pakistan), and set up the National Assembly in Ankara, making that city the capital of the Turkish republic in October of 1923.

Regarding the exchange of populations between Greece and Turkey, Istanbul was again exceptional among Turkish cities in that its Greek Orthodox population of approximately 100,000, along with the institution of the Orthodox patriarchate, was

The waterfront in Istanbul, with the Sultan Ahmed mosque in the background, 1967. ©Bettmann/Corbis

allowed to remain and was ensured the right to education and religious worship under the international agreement. Thus, while Istanbul was no longer the imperial capital, it retained its sizable Greek Orthodox population as well as its Jewish and Armenian populations, making it the cosmopolitan holdover in a Turkish nation-state attempting to homogenize its population. Once again, Istanbul as a city seemed on a different trajectory from the polity to which it belonged; first it had thrived in an Ottoman Empire in collapse, then remained cosmopolitan in the homogenizing Republic of Turkey.

1922–1945: INVENTING TURKEY, TURKIFYING ISTANBUL

In Turkey as a whole, Atatürk's sweeping reforms were focused on bringing Turkey, as a secular, Turkish-speaking nation-state, in line with the expectations and conventions of "the West." This meant dramatic language reform that changed the Turkish writing system from Arabic-based characters to a Latin-based alphabet, a new legal code (based on the Swiss code rather than Islamic sharia law), a new parliamentary and voting structure, changing dress codes and the legal status of women, and education reforms, particularly in the large cities such as Istanbul and Ankara. To say that Atatürk played a crucial role in forming the Turkish republic would be an understatement; his mark on Istanbul and on the modern Turkish state is indelible. Aside from the countless images and statues of Atatürk, a common slogan inscribed in Turkish government buildings and private establishments in the twenty-first century is "We are in his [Atatürk's] shadow."

But what of the multiconfessional, multilingual Istanbul in a state whose motto was "How happy is he who calls himself a Turk"? The challenge for the next several decades of Istanbul's history was to modernize and "westernize" while minimizing the role of non-Turkish, non-Muslim groups in the city. This was a challenge because these very groups had spearheaded the modernization of the city from the turn of the twentieth century, working as bankers, doctors, lawyers, engineers, architects, and merchants, and receiving their education in Greece and in Europe. Their personal networks and technical expertise could not easily be replaced.

A new Turkish professional elite was educated and trained in the 1920s, 1930s, and 1940s, through measures such as state-backed industrialization programs. At the same time, non-Muslim groups, and particularly Greek Orthodox populations of Istanbul, were coerced or encouraged to leave the country through measures such as the Varlik Vergisi (capital tax) in 1942–1943, whereby property and wealth of non-Muslims were exorbitantly taxed (sometimes at a rate of several hundred percent). Those who could not pay the tax were interned in camps near Istanbul's Sirkeci train station or in eastern Anatolia and/or forced to leave the country. Another low point in Istanbul's modern history was on 6 September 1955, when, as a response to tensions between Greek and Turkish ambitions in recently decolonized Cyprus, there was a pogrom against mainly Greek shops, churches, and families in Istanbul, which sparked another wave of departures.

1945–1980: MODERNIZATION AND URBAN GROWTH

The one-party system established by Atatürk in 1923 lasted until 1946; from 1950 a multiparty system was in place, which itself was ended by a military coup and the new constitution of a second republic (1961–1980) in May 1960. Political and economic instability exacerbated each other in the 1960s and 1970s, leading to military coups every ten years (May 1960; March 1971; September 1980). Modernization was a process both guided and thwarted by the Turkish state in the post–World War II era.

That era was one of urban migration to Istanbul, and to a lesser extent to cities such as Ankara, Bursa, and Izmir. Thousands of Turks from the Black Sea coast and central Anatolia migrated to Istanbul and moved into the neighborhoods recently vacated by non-Muslim groups. Statistics show a doubling of the city's population, from 1,882,092 in 1960 to 3,904,588 in 1975. Since 1975 population growth has increased exponentially again; official statistics say around ten million reside in Istanbul, but other estimates put the population as high as sixteen million in 2004.

Social unrest was a hallmark of the 1970s, with leftist students and others engaging in violent conflict with police and paramilitary forces in the streets of the city. In 1978 Prime Minister Bülent Ecevit introduced martial law after scores had been killed over the preceding year and a half in sectarian violence. A combination of economic problems (International Monetary Fund austerity measures, reflationary economic policies, OPEC oil shock, sluggish exports), social tensions (urban students versus Muslim and nationalist groups), and geopolitical issues (Turkey's membership in NATO, its pact with the European Economic Community in 1963) were leading to an incipient civil war.

1980–2004: MODERNIZATION, PROVINCIALIZATION, AND ISLAMIZATION OF ISTANBUL

On 12 September 1980 the Turkish army staged another coup and ushered in the period of Turgut Özal's ascendancy. Özal (1927–1993; prime minister 1983–1989; president 1989–1993), whose economic policies are sometimes seen as modernization shortcuts that provoked the cycle of inflation and unemployment still going on in the early twenty-first century, was a proponent of opening Turkey toward the West and of membership in the European Union. The most overwhelming changes in Istanbul during his tenure were demographic, as rural populations flooded into the city in search of jobs and housing. By the time of Özal's death in 1993, several new trends had developed in Istanbul and in Turkish politics more generally: on the one hand, civil war between the Turkish military and Kurdish groups in the southeast of Turkey (PKK, or Kurdish Workers' Party) brought terrorism to Istanbul's prominent neighborhoods; on the other, Islamist populations and political movements arrived in Istanbul from the countryside. While the Kurdish conflict subsided somewhat with the

1999 capture of Abdullah Öcalan, a leader of the Kurdish separatist movement, the Islamization of Istanbul and of Turkish politics has proved a more durable feature of life and government. This is exemplified by the landslide 2002 victory of Recep Tayyip Erdoğan, former mayor of Istanbul and chief of the Islamist-based AK Party, as prime minister.

CULTURE, HIGH AND LOW

The late 1990s saw some fascinating, and often contradictory, cultural and social developments among Istanbul's middle and upper classes. Many of the quarters in the center and historic district of Istanbul, which were populated by non-Muslims in the middle years of the twentieth century, had been abandoned by the upper classes and left to Kurdish, Roma, and rural Turkish migrants. Wealthier Istanbulites chose the "Asian side" of the city, across the Bosphorus from the historic districts, as well as the more distant Bosphorus villages up the European coast toward the Black Sea. A recent reawakening to Istanbul's cosmopolitan past, particularly on the part of the Westward-looking intelligentsia, has spurred rapid gentrification and urban renewal in central areas such as Beyoğlu (formerly Pera), the old French quarter of Istanbul.

Beyond the fray of Istanbul's intelligentsia, the vast majority of Istanbul's population was born in the countryside and migrated to the city in the last decades of the twentieth century. Interestingly, the religious and ethnic cosmopolitanism of the turn of the twentieth century has given way to a different blend of languages and cultures in the onetime Byzantine and Ottoman capital; Greek, Armenian, and Ladino have been replaced by Kurdish, Arabic, Laz, Russian, Bosnian, and Central Asian Turkic languages on the streets and in the markets of Istanbul.

Istanbul opened the twentieth century as the "Gate of Felicity," the cosmopolitan capital of an Ottoman Empire in severe crisis. The city persisted as an Ottoman holdover, with its ethnic and confessional mosaic, under increasing pressure from the Turkish republic, centered in Ankara, that favored homogenization and Turkification. Istanbul opened the twenty-first century at the threshold of Europe, with some of its residents hoping to revive the city's cosmopolitan legacy and affinity to Europe and with others bringing a different set of Islam-focused values and cultures from the Turkish countryside. In 2005 it remains to be seen if the city of Istanbul, the Republic of Turkey, and the European Union will all join together to make one history.

See also **Atatürk, Mustafa Kemal; Turkey.**

BIBLIOGRAPHY

Alexandrēs, Alexēs. *The Greek Minority of Istanbul and Greek-Turkish Relations, 1918–1974.* Athens, Greece, 1983.

Bozdoğan, Sibel, and Reşat Kasaba, eds. *Rethinking Modernity and National Identity in Turkey.* Seattle, Wash., 1997.

Criss, Nur Bilge. *Istanbul under Allied Occupation, 1918–1923.* Leiden, Netherlands, 1999.

Frey, Frederick W. *The Turkish Political Elite.* Cambridge, Mass., 1965.

Lewis, Bernard. *The Emergence of Modern Turkey.* 3rd ed. New York, 2002.

Ökte, Faik. *The Tragedy of the Turkish Capital Tax.* London, 1987.

Mansel, Philip. *Constantinople: City of the World's Desire, 1453–1924.* London, 1995.

Mantran, Robert. *Histoire d'Istanbul.* Paris, 1996.

CHRISTINE PHILLIOU

ITALIAN CONCORDAT OF 1929.

Although tolerable working relations had been established between the church and liberal governments from the time of Italian unification, the "Roman question" still remained unresolved after World War I. The papacy (Holy See) wanted internationally valid recognition of its sovereignty within a defined territorial area, a recognition it did not enjoy under the Law of Guarantees of 1871. But in the early twentieth century the church had a powerful instrument of pressure in the form of the lay organization Popular Union, better known as Catholic Action. In addition, although in no way sponsored by the church, the Catholic political party, the Popular Party, was founded in 1919. This party was polarized between Christian democrats, with a progressive social program, and conservatives; its leaders, including its general secretary, Luigi Sturzo, were Christian democrats. Its members varied considerably in their commitment to the Vatican line on the Roman question.

THE FASCIST ERA

On 6 February 1922 Achille Ratti of Milan was elected pope as Pius XI, and in October the Fascists came to power. Ratti had been linked to Milanese Catholic conservative circles. He was strongly committed to Catholic Action and saw this, not the Popular Party, as the effective lay champion of the Catholic interest. He distanced the church from, and ultimately undermined, the Popular Party, whose independence and readiness to ally with the Socialists and other secular parties incurred his mistrust; banned by the Fascists, it disbanded in 1926. Benito Mussolini's government made friendly gestures toward the church from late 1922, starting with the restoration of the crucifix to schools. The early Fascist movement was strongly anticlerical, as Benito Mussolini had been himself. However, an opening toward the church was a way of out-maneuvering the Popular Party. Furthermore, Mussolini was sensitive to the positive evaluation of Catholicism, as cementing national values, that had spread among Italian nationalists from the beginning of the century. The absorption of the Italian Nationalist Association into the Fascist Party in 1923 brought in many men who had by now become religiously conservative. Conciliation with the church was part of a general Mussolinian policy of accommodation with the established forces in Italian society. Negotiations between the Vatican and the government to resolve the Roman question were pursued from 1923. A facilitating role was played by "clerico-fascists," socially eminent Catholic conservatives who had split from the Popular Party between 1922 and 1924. The pope was concerned not only to resolve the issue of the Holy See's status but also to secure a position of autonomy for the Italian church and security for Catholic Action. Fascist attacks on Catholic lay organizations made the latter issue one of urgency.

The *Patti lateranensi* (Lateran Accords), concluded between the Holy See and the Italian state on 11 February 1929, comprised a treaty regulating the relations between the two powers and a concordat regulating the position of the church in Italy. The treaty recognized the Holy See's independent territorial sovereignty in the area of the Vatican. Catholicism was now recognized as "the only state religion." An appended financial convention established compensation for the annexation of papal territories between 1860 and 1870. The concordat gave guarantees of the independence of the church in Italy. It recognized the pope's exclusive right to appoint bishops, while stipulating that the Holy See would consult the government. The state renounced exercise of the *exequatur,* the license releasing the revenues of newly appointed bishops and other major benefice holders, which governments had used in the past to deny revenues to papal appointees whom they had not approved. As previously, the state would subsidize the stipends of clergy. The legal personality of religious orders, abolished under legislation of 1866–1867, was now recognized. The civil validity of church marriages was also recognized for the first time since 1867. Furthermore, church courts were given exclusive jurisdiction over annulments of marriages; this was a highly contentious issue. The pope's special concerns regarding the organizations of Catholic Action were met by a clause permitting these, provided they remained nonpolitical. Under the Lateran Accords and in terms of general practice, the church was effectively given establishment status for the first time in united Italy.

The "Conciliation" reassured conservatives as to the character of the regime and doubtless contributed to the popular consensus for it in the 1930s, but the Lateran Accords were heavily criticized by hard-line Fascists, who were strongly irritated by the wave of militancy by the organizations of Catholic Action that was stimulated by the fortieth-anniversary celebrations of Leo XIII's encyclical on the "social question," *Rerum novarum,* in 1931. Attacks in the Fascist press on Catholic Action and the government's suspension of its youth organizations, which were seen as rivaling Fascist ones, led to a major church-state confrontation. This was resolved by the accords of September 1931, which reiterated the nonpolitical character of Catholic Action and prevented it from sponsoring trade union activities. But relations between the church and the regime became increasingly strained as Fascist hard-liners reasserted themselves in the 1930s and the regime became more totalitarian. In 1938 the regime set out to cripple Catholic Action, with some success in the short term. In other respects, however, the Italian church was able to build up its organization in the Fascist era so that it was able to play a crucial role in the chaotic period between the fall of the Fascist regime in 1943 and the peace.

THE POSTWAR ERA

After the fall of fascism, maintenance of the Lateran Accords was a priority both for the church and for the Christian Democrat Party. In March 1947 the Lateran Accords were inserted into the new constitution enacted by the Constituent Assembly; this insertion was secured by the votes not only of the powerful Christian Democrat Party but also of the Communists, who did not want to break the anti-fascist front.

The Lateran treaty governing the Vatican's status has never really been called into question. The concordat, however, appeared ever more anachronistic in an increasingly secularized society. The Christian Democrat Party, the dominant partner in the postwar government coalitions—which had disappointed the Vatican by its reluctance to push aggressively for the maintenance of Catholic values in society—became increasingly unable to defend the concordat, as its electoral position progressively weakened from 1952. The law of 1970 permitting divorce, supported by popular referendum in 1974, effectively breached the concordat. The referendum of 1978 in favor of a law permitting abortion was another step in the same direction. The Vatican and the Italian church, in any case, after the pontificate of John XXIII (1958–1963) and the Second Vatican Council (1962–1965), had now become more willing to accept a pluralist society.

The revision of the concordat was undertaken under center-left governments of the Pentapartito (party of five), in which the now much weakened Christian Democrats had been obliged to surrender more power to their coalition partners, the "lay parties" of the Liberals, Republicans, and Social Democrats, their old allies, now joined by the Socialists. The revision was amicably agreed to between the government and the church by the Palazzo Madama accords of 18 February 1984. The revised concordat effectively disestablished the church. It stated: "The principle of the Catholic religion as the only religion of the Italian state, originally indicated by the Lateran pacts, is no longer valid." Instead, "the state and the Catholic Church are each, within their own order, independent and sovereign." The obligation of the church authorities to consult with the state over appointments to bishoprics and other benefices was reduced to a simple obligation to inform. The state's positive commitment to support Catholic religious instruction in schools, under the terms of the Lateran treaty, was watered down: the principle of cooperation between the two powers in this area was balanced by a proclamation of the principle of religious freedom. Highly controversially, the cognizance of church courts of annulment of marriage remained. The prohibitions of political activities by clergy and of state employment of ex-clergy in the 1929 concordat disappeared. Provision was made for the phasing-out of state subsidies to the clergy; instead, tax rebates would be allowed on donations by the faithful. Significantly, a pointer to the more collegiate conception of the church that had emerged in the era of Vatican II, the Italian Episcopal Conference, rather than the papacy, was recognized as the supreme authority in the Italian church for normal purposes.

See also **Catholic Action; Fascism; John XXIII; Mussolini, Benito.**

BIBLIOGRAPHY

Coppa, Frank J. "Mussolini and the Concordat of 1929." In *Controversial Concordats*, edited by Frank J. Coppa, 120–181. Washington, D.C., 1999. Text of Lateran Accords in appendix.

Ferrari, Silvio. "The New Concordat between Church and State." In vol. 1 of *Italian Politics: A Review*, edited by Robert Leonardi and Raffaella Y. Nanetti, 134–145. London, 1986.

Pollard, John F. *The Vatican and Italian Fascism, 1929–1932: A Study in Conflict.* Cambridge, U.K., 1985. The best treatment in English. Texts of Law of Guarantees, Lateran Accords, and September Accords in appendix.

OLIVER LOGAN

ITALY. Italy is a major European country however measured. It is somewhat smaller in size than

France, Spain, or united Germany but larger than the United Kingdom, but its population in 2006, numbering slightly less than sixty million, was about the same as that of France or Britain. Economically, although the country's relative status in Europe was decidedly inferior for much of the twentieth century, the growth of Italian wealth since World War II has been spectacular, and while Italian gross domestic product (GDP) varied between 40 and 50 percent of British GDP over the period 1900–1950, by 2006 it was nearly equal to that of Britain (or France). Probably more than any other single factor, that rapid economic growth transformed Italy over the twentieth century. In quantitative terms, more than 40 percent of Italians still worked in a largely traditional agricultural sector following World War II; by 2006 that figure was 5 percent and much Italian farming was highly modernized.

In 1914, then, Italy was one of the poorer and less-developed countries of Europe (not helped by its lack of coal and iron). Most of the workforce was agricultural, and modern industry was largely confined to the recently developed industrial triangle in the northwest (Milan-Turin-Genoa). The division between a more advanced north and more primitive south was well established, and a majority of Italy's massive emigration at the time—it peaked in 1913 at about nine hundred thousand—came from the south. Politically, Italy's constitutional monarchy, inherited from Piedmont at the time of unification in 1860, relied on a small male electorate and remained in the hands of the liberal bourgeois elite, though a significant socialist opposition had developed over the previous two decades. Relations between the state and the Catholic Church (whose secular realm had been taken over by Italy during unification) remained strained though not so much as they had been in previous decades. In a move to assert its status as a great power, Italy had carved Tripolitania and Cyrenaica (later combined as Libya) off the faltering Ottoman Empire in 1911, adding to its earlier colonial holdings in Eritrea and Italian Somaliland (Somalia). Italy had been part of the Triple Alliance together with Germany and Austria-Hungary since 1882.

WORLD WAR I

Although a member of that defensive alliance, Italy was not officially informed about Austria's attack on Serbia and was unprepared for the outbreak of World War I in August 1914. Initially Italy opted for neutrality, and there followed a period of intense debate over whether or not to intervene and on which side. In favor of neutrality were Italy's dominant Liberal parliamentarian, Giovanni Giolitti, the Socialist Party (PSI, founded 1892), and the Catholic Church. Voices favoring intervention on the side of the empires (Germany and Austria-Hungary) were quickly drowned in a chorus calling for war on the side of the "democracies" England and France (and Russia). Liberals were divided over the issue, many rejecting Giolitti's position of neutrality. The Nationalists (founded as a political party in 1910) were strongly in favor of war, as was the erratic Benito Mussolini (1883–1945), who was expelled from the Socialist Party for his interventionism. Perhaps most prominent of all among the interventionists was the dashing literary figure Gabriele D'Annunzio, who (with the connivance of the French) returned to Italy in spite of financial difficulties that had forced his expatriation. In the so-called radiant days of May, D'Annunzio addressed huge crowds from his hotel in Rome, and the excitement he inspired helped to sway parliament in favor of war.

Italy declared war that same month and so opened up a southern front against its traditional enemy, Austria. Though the Central Powers saw this as a betrayal of the Triple Alliance, most historians agree that Italy was not bound to follow its allies into an aggressive war and that the choice to side with the Entente was legitimate. War on the southern front, though in mountainous terrain, resembled that in the west, namely trenches and stalemate. Stalemate until October 1917, anyway, when the Central Powers, thanks to the withdrawal of Russia from the war following the Bolshevik Revolution, were able to redirect some of their forces against Italy. The result was the devastating defeat at Caporetto, immortalized in Ernest Hemingway's *A Farewell to Arms* (1929). The Italians fell back more than one hundred kilometers and lost forty thousand lives (plus 275,000 prisoners) but ultimately held fast at the Piave River (hence the miracle of the Piave; the river reportedly ran red with blood). The Italian prime minister and chief of staff were both replaced, and still in the early twenty-first century Italians may describe a

Gabriele D'Annunzio speaks from the steps of the senate house in Rome, June 1915. The dashing and persuasive writer was instrumental in enlisting support for Italian involvement in World War I. ©BETTMANN/CORBIS

disastrous event or defeat as a *Caporetto*. The war of course dragged on for another year, until in October 1918 the Italian forces launched an attack against the already demoralized Austrian forces and scored a resounding victory in the battle of Vittorio Veneto, marking the end of the war and heralding the dissolution of the Austrian Empire. In three and a half years of war, Italy had suffered 650,000 deaths, nearly as many as the United Kingdom.

POSTWAR ITALY AND THE FASCIST SEIZURE OF POWER

Postwar Italy faced considerable economic and political challenges. Many soldiers from the middle-class were demobilized only to find that their sacrifices had left them worse off than before the war, largely because of inflation. Workers, however, both industrial and agricultural, found their position strengthened relative to capital and were able to push their advantage in what came to be known

as the red biennium (1919–1920). Meanwhile the liberal democratic program generally had been badly compromised by its failure to prevent the devastation of World War I, and the Bolshevik Revolution of 1917 offered a specter that might be either attractive or menacing depending on where one stood on the social question.

Italy's traditional leaders had no ready answers, and their credibility was further strained because of the failure to achieve Italian war aims at the Paris Peace Conference. By most measures, the settlement treated Italy well. It got Trentino-Alto Adige, Trieste, and Istria from the dismembered Austrian Empire but failed to get any colonial concessions and was denied the city of Fiume (Rijeka, Croatia), centerpiece of the so-called mutilated victory. It was once again D'Annunzio who grabbed the spotlight by leading a group of irregulars into Fiume and seizing it for Italy. In the face of this foreign-policy disaster, the government dithered and D'Annunzio ruled over the rogue city-state for a year at the end of which Giolitti, returned to the stage, sent in the troops to oust D'Annunzio and company in the so-called Christmas of Blood (1920), though in fact little was spilled.

It was a period rife with agitation. Nor did the changes in parliamentary politics point in any obvious direction. In 1919, after decades of Vatican-imposed boycott, the progressive Catholic political forces organized into a political party, the Popolari, and immediately captured 20 percent of the seats in the Chamber of Deputies. The Socialists had still more—nearly a third of the total—though in 1921 they would split into Communist and Socialist parties over the issue of adherence to the Third International organized by the Soviet Communist leader Vladimir Lenin (Vladimir Ilyich Ulyanov; 1870–1924). The Liberals only barely held on to power.

It was in this context that the former revolutionary Socialist Mussolini founded his Fascist movement, also in 1919. Reconstructing Mussolini's intellectual development is perilous, but it would seem that he became disillusioned with the workers as a revolutionary force following the various failures of the general strike before the war. Influenced by both French syndicalism (an antimaterialist revision of Marxism) and Italian futurism (an avant-garde art movement fascinated with speed and violence), he perceived of violence as a positive source of change—war as the world's hygiene—and moved in 1914 from Socialist opposition to the bourgeois war to strident interventionism. The enthusiasm of the European masses for the war seems also to have convinced him that the most dynamic political force of the day was not the working class but the nation. Initiating his "slide to the right," Mussolini found himself ever closer to the Nationalists (who would eventually be absorbed into the Fascist movement). The Fascists of the first hour were instead an eclectic group of veterans, syndicalists, and futurists, and for a time the movement was so marginal that Mussolini himself almost abandoned it. What fascism had going for it, however, was its antisocialism. In particular the rural *fasci* (as the Fascist groups were called) in the Po Valley began a systematic campaign of violence against Socialist strikers, chambers of labor, and politicians (to a lesser extent they also

targeted left-wing Christian Democratic organizers) that included beatings, forced drinking of castor oil, and the occasional murder. Not surprisingly these Fascist squads, largely made up of disgruntled petit bourgeois and veterans who saw in fascism a way to bring the war to the home front, quickly gained the sympathy of landowners and industrialists who provided support, while the police often turned a blind eye to their excesses. The movement-become-party grew rapidly and scored a significant triumph in capturing thirty-five seats in the 1921 election.

Mussolini saw his opportunity and organized the March on Rome in October 1922. Fascists seized local administration and infrastructure in the cities of the center-north and converged on the capital. As it turned out, no violent revolution or coup d'état occurred. Instead the king and Liberal political leaders agreed to Mussolini's demands and appointed him prime minister. He would remain in power for the next twenty-one years. Responsibility for the Fascist seizure of power has been variously assigned to the extreme Left that preached revolution, probably without conviction but sufficiently to terrorize sectors of public opinion; to the king, who decided against mobilizing the army against the Fascists (perhaps out of fear of a rebellion within the ranks); to Giolitti and the Liberals, who were willing to overlook Fascist illegalities and imagined they could manage Mussolini; to the church, which vetoed cooperation between the Popolari and the Socialists; and to the Popolari themselves, who refused to cooperate with Giolitti and so perhaps stabilize the political situation.

THE FASCIST PERIOD

Within a couple of years, Mussolini had established his dictatorship. Opposition parties were banned; the press was censored; and opponents of the regime were either jailed or went into exile (Paris became the center of the antifascist opposition). *Il duce* (the leader) sought to create a new Italy and a new Fascist man (and, to a lesser extent, woman). His was to be a third way between democracy and socialism. At its center was Fascist corporativism, according to which society (and government) were to be organized according to categories of production, and the state would mediate any conflicts between capital and labor. Little though was realized in this regard. Strikes were of course outlawed and wages controlled (in practice lowered on a couple of occasions). For the most part the regime sided with capital. Private property was never threatened, though Mussolini did at times assert his independence in the economic sphere, for example famously fixing the value of the lira at an exaggerated ninety to the pound sterling in 1927. Plans for the reorganization of Italy's parliamentary system along corporativist lines foundered, and while the Chamber and Senate continued to exist, their function was reduced to little more than approving Mussolini's policies. For a time the Fascist Grand Council served as something of a governing body but in later years it rarely met.

Mussolini had come to power thanks to the Fascist squads, and at times they and their leaders threatened to escape his control and even challenge his leadership. In order to bring them into line they were organized into a formal militia, the Milizia Volontaria per la Sicurezza Nazionale (MVSN), which would later participate in various of Italy's military adventures. Creation of the MVSN presaged the militarization of Italian society generally under fascism. Boys (the Balilla) and girls (the Daughters of the Wolf) from a tender age were organized into Fascist groups, where they donned uniforms, marched, sang Fascist hymns, and learned rifle practice (boys) or coordinated gymnastics (girls). These organizations continued right up through university students and were preparation for entering the Fascist Party as adults. Notably they coopted other youth groups such as the Catholic scouts.

Militarization was just one aspect of Fascist social control. Though only partially successful, fascism sought to penetrate all aspects of Italian life: school, the workplace, cultural production, academia, and even the home. In addition to participating in youth groups, then, school-age Italians read Fascist textbooks and, like Italians of all ages, participated in Fascist demonstrations that inevitably celebrated the regime and its *duce*. Workers were enrolled in Fascist unions (the Socialist, Catholic, and other ones having been eliminated) and were encouraged to participate in the *dopolavoro* (workingmen's recreation clubs) that organized leisure time activities outside of

work. Moreover, many occupations, especially public ones, came to require membership in the Fascist Party. Women meanwhile were organized into women's *fasci* (largely urban) and the *massaie rurali* ("rural housewives"; for peasant women).

Fascist cultural policy was relatively pluralist, encouraging both nostalgic and avant-garde literary and artistic movements (providing they were not antifascist). Important twentieth-century authors such as Alberto Moravia (1907–1990) and Elio Vittorini (1908–1966) and painters such as Giorgio Di Chirico (1888–1978) were active in the Fascist period, while even work that was frequently viewed as "fascist" in the immediate postwar period, such as the painting of Mario Sironi (1885–1961) and more generally Italian rationalist architectural production of the 1930s, has since been rehabilitated and its intrinsic worth recognized. University professors meanwhile were required to swear an oath of allegiance to fascism in 1931. The fact that only twelve refused can be taken as a sign either of widespread consensus or else general acquiescence in a climate of repression.

Convinced of the power of numbers, Mussolini also pursued a policy aimed at population increase. Indicative of fascism's failure to penetrate to the more intimate facets of Italian life, the policy sought to encourage marriage and large families, to little effect. Other aspects included severe restrictions on emigration and the encouragement of settlement on reclaimed lands and in new agricultural communities in the Italian colonies of Libya and later Ethiopia.

Probably the principal challenge to the fascistization of Italian society came from the church. Skeptical of democracy and avowedly opposed to socialism, the church had in some ways welcomed and facilitated the advent of Fascist rule. The regime, however, learned too well from Catholic practices and sought to emulate and co-opt the social program of the church on multiple levels. Initially it was Fascist-Catholic accord that dominated, culminating in the Lateran Treaty of 1929. That agreement ended nearly seventy years of conflict between the Italian state and the church. Roman Catholicism was recognized as Italy's official religion, religious teaching in the schools was guaranteed, and church jurisdiction over the Vatican City was recognized. It was one of

Benito Mussolini leads a parade of Fascist militia in Rome, 1928. ©HULTON-DEUTSCH COLLECTION/CORBIS

Mussolini's greatest foreign policy triumphs. The relationship continued to be a tense one, however; in proposing itself as a quasi-religion, fascism inevitably came into conflict with the older institution. Nonetheless, important strains of Italian Catholicism remained committed to fascism till the end.

In spite of its repressive nature, the Fascist regime had many admirers in the liberal democratic West. For while the Left was almost unanimously antifascist, important centrists and conservatives rationalized that while Fascist violence and the limitation of fundamental freedoms were unfortunate, Mussolini had managed to bring order to an unruly and potentially revolutionary place. Judging domestic attitudes about the regime is harder (and much debated). Whether one argues that a

majority of Italians supported the regime at some point or else simply silenced their dissent in a climate of dictatorship, it is likely that the regime enjoyed its most widespread acceptance in the period between the Lateran Treaty of 1929 and the Ethiopian conquest of 1936.

Both of those events played decisive roles in the international and domestic fortunes of Fascist Italy. Following on that earlier triumph and then on the Nazi seizure of power in Germany in 1933, Mussolini indeed appeared to some a force of moderation and order on the European scene. Most notably, following the assassination of the Austrian chancellor Engelbert Dollfuss (1892–1934) by Nazis in 1934 (his family was visiting with Mussolini's at the time), Italy sent troops to the Brenner Pass and so prevented the expected Anschluss, or annexation of Austria by Germany. Italy's role as a peacemaker was, however, to be short-lived, largely because of Fascist expansionist designs.

In 1935 Italy invaded Ethiopia in a move to round out its East African holdings and inevitably recalling the humiliating Italian defeat suffered there in 1896. Ethiopian resistance was fierce but ultimately no match for the massive effort of the Italians; infamously the Italian air force employed poison gas, contrary to international agreements. To cheering crowds in Piazza Venezia, Mussolini announced in May 1936 that empire had returned to the fatal hills of Rome. By some measures this moment marked his greatest triumph. By others it was the beginning of the end and of the spiral that led to World War II and disaster. By insisting on Italy's right to empire, Mussolini alienated most of the other great powers and earned both condemnation and sanctions from the League of Nations. The exceptions were the United States, which had never joined the League, and Nazi Germany, which had withdrawn in 1933. Mussolini's African adventure had the effect then of at once using up Italian military resources and pushing Italy into the Nazi camp. Later in 1936, *il duce* sent troops to fight alongside the nationalist rebels of Francisco Franco (1892–1975) in Spain (Franco also received support from Germany). The Spanish loyalists instead received some support from the Soviet Union and also from the volunteers of the international brigades. Notably, Italian antifascists fought alongside the loyalists, with the result that Italy was probably the only country with significant forces on both sides. Contemporary with the Spanish civil war Mussolini also declared formation of a Rome-Berlin Axis. When Adolf Hitler (1889–1945) again moved to absorb Austria into the Reich in 1938, Mussolini was neither capable nor inclined to resist the move. In 1939 the alliance between Italy and Germany was formalized in the so-called Pact of Steel.

NAZI ALLIANCE AND WORLD WAR II

By the time of the Pact of Steel, Fascist Italy had entered into its darkest and final chapter. Fascism, unlike Nazism, had not been based in a fundamental way on a racist vision, though its integral nationalism certainly held within it the seeds of racism. Those seeds bore fruit in the several African colonies where indigenous resistance to Italian rule was brutally repressed and the creation of the empire in 1936 was accompanied by the introduction of colonial apartheid legislation. Domestically there had not been much of a Jewish question in Italy prior to Hitler's seizure of power (except insofar as Italy was home to traditional Catholic anti-Semitism). Nonetheless, in 1938 Mussolini's scientists declared the existence of an Aryan Italian race to which Jews (as well as blacks and Arabs) did not belong. The laws passed in November of that year deprived Jews of various rights and in some cases their livelihood (though not, as in Germany, of their citizenship).

The laws were subsequently tightened and of course encouraged the emigration of a significant percentage of Italy's small Jewish population. Italy was certainly the poorer. To cite just one example, Enrico Fermi (1901–1954), who had discovered nuclear fission and had a Jewish wife, left for the United States, where he helped develop one of the atom bombs dropped on Japan. It is not clear precisely why Mussolini introduced the racial laws. There is, for example, no evidence that Hitler pressured him to do so. Yet the Italian dictator had become increasingly frustrated at the regime's failure to create the hoped-for heroic and new Fascist society. It may be that Mussolini's various and aggressive policies of the period—Ethiopia, Spain, the racial laws, alliance with Germany, and intervention in World War II—were a series of attempts to jostle Italians into taking up their appointed and historic role in world affairs.

The Pact of Steel stipulated that the two allies would come to the aid of one another should either become "engaged in war"—an offensive alliance—but also that they keep one another informed on "all questions of common interest and relative to the European situation" (author's translation). Hitler failed to inform Mussolini of his surprise attack of Poland in September 1939, and so Italy found itself in a situation analogous to that of 1914. Mussolini bought time by declaring a status of nonbelligerence (a Fascist could not really be neutral). In fact there were elements close to *il duce* sufficiently alarmed at the prospect of going to war alongside Germany that they urged continued neutrality. However, much as Mussolini had been determined to wipe out the humiliation of defeat in Ethiopia, so was he committed to erasing the "betrayal" of the Triple Alliance in 1915. As Germany was marching through France in June 1940, Italy declared war on the side of its Nazi ally.

The Italian entry into the war was little short of disastrous. Determined to act autonomously (as Hitler had), Mussolini opened up a new front by attacking Greece, but the combination of inadequate preparation, stiff resistance from the smaller opponent, and the Balkan winter bogged down the Italian forces. The stalemate continued until German forces launched an offensive that led to the conquest of both Yugoslavia and Greece in 1941. Certainly Italy bears as a result some responsibility for the suffering of the Yugoslav and Greek people during the occupation (including the deportation of Greek Jews to the death camps, perhaps the farthest-flung of the Holocaust's victims). At the same time, the Balkan distraction may have negatively affected the subsequent German campaign against the Soviet Union.

Italy's military debacles did not end with Greece. One month prior to the Greek invasion, the Italian military in Libya had attacked the British in Egypt only to suffer a withering counterattack and forced retreat. In this case too German troops (under Erwin Johannes Eugen Rommel; 1891–1944), came to the aid of the Italians. There ensued the back-and-forth battles of the North African campaign that culminated in the Allied occupation of Libya and defeat of the Axis forces in Africa by early 1943. Meanwhile similar hostilities between Britain (regularly referred to in the Italian press as "perfidious Albion" in the period) and Italy in the Horn of Africa led to the loss of Ethiopia (along with Somalia and Eritrea) in 1941, only five years after its capture.

Given Italy's limited industrial capacity and the military overextension related to Ethiopia and Spain, military experts were correct in deeming the country unprepared for a European war. Mussolini had gone ahead anyway. The combination of the setbacks described above (hard to disguise even in the heavily censored Italian media), material hardships suffered by the Italian people, and the bombing of Italian ports and cities by the Royal Navy meant that what little enthusiasm there had been for the war in Italy quickly waned. In July 1943, not long after Mussolini had

declared that foreign troops would never set foot in Italy, the Allies crossed over to Sicily from North Africa and took the island. In light of this crisis, Mussolini convened the long-inactive Fascist Grand Council. In a tense meeting that lasted until the early hours of 25 July—several members were armed—the Grand Council voted to return authority to the king. Mussolini, increasingly unrealistic at this time, fully imagined that he would be reappointed as head of state. Instead he was arrested and eventually held in a mountaintop retreat east of Rome.

Marshall Pietro Badoglio (1871–1956), who had fought in Libya, World War I, and Ethiopia, was appointed prime minister. Badoglio and the king at this point made a serious blunder. While initiating secret negotiations for a separate peace with the Allies, Badoglio announced that Italy would remain faithful to the Axis. Hitler had lost all confidence in the Italians and in order to counter an eventual betrayal he flooded Italy with German troops. By September, when Badoglio finally announced the armistice, the Nazis were able fairly easily to secure most of the peninsula and, in an embarrassing move, Badoglio and the king fled the capital, leaving most of the Italian population to its fate, and set up a new government in Brindisi, by then in the hands of the Allies. Had Badoglio moved immediately to end the alliance with Germany, he would have stranded the Italian troops fighting on the eastern front and the Italian workers in Germany—eventually they were stranded anyway—but might have saved a great deal of suffering in Italy.

September 1943 marked the beginning of the most difficult period of the war in Italy, effectively one of civil war. The Badoglio government operated in the South, where the Allies had secured a stronghold, and in October declared war on Germany. Most of the peninsula was instead in German hands. Contemporary with the armistice, Mussolini had been liberated from his prison by Nazi paratroopers and whisked off to Munich, from where he exhorted Italians to stand by their German allies. He subsequently returned to Italy at the head of a new Italian Social Republic (RSI), also known as the Republic of Salò (after the site of Mussolini's headquarters). Italy then had two governments at war against one another, though

Mussolini's administration was little more than a puppet of the Nazi occupation and Badoglio was largely subservient to the Allies. Contemporary with the arrival of the Nazi occupiers, groups of Italians began engaging in acts of armed resistance. In Naples, that resistance was seconded by the arrival of the Allies and the liberation of the city on 1 October 1943. In Rome, by contrast, armed resistance was suppressed and liberation delayed until June 1944, just two days before D-Day.

Between late 1943 and the end of the war in April 1945, the Allies slowly fought their way up the peninsula at considerable human cost. The Italian resistance meanwhile organized into the Committees of National Liberation (Comitati di Liberazione Nazionale, or CLN). The largest and best-organized of these committees was the Communists, who indeed had carried on their antifascist opposition since 1925. Also included were Christian Democrats, Socialists, and other smaller groups. The CLNs in fact laid the basis for Italy's postwar political landscape. In the south the CLNs were presided over by Ivanoe Bonomi, who in 1944 replaced Badoglio as head of the Italian government. In the center and north, the CLNs of course had to organize secretly. They and other linked organizations of partisans carried out armed actions against Nazi and Fascist forces. In one dramatic instance, a resistance group carried out an attack in the center of Rome in March 1944, killing thirty-three German soldiers. As on other similar occasions, the Germans responded by massacring ten Italians for every German killed. In all, 335 victims were shot and buried at the Ardeatine Caves, for the most part imprisoned antifascists and including a significant number of Jews.

The occupation had in fact sealed the fate of many of Italy's Jews. With the cooperation of Italian Fascist authorities, Nazis began systematic roundups of Jews in Italy and their deportation to the death camps. Best known of these was probably the chemist and writer Primo Levi (1919–1987), captured as part of a partisan band and sent to Auschwitz. He famously recounted those experiences in his *Se questo è un uomo* (1947; *If This Is a Man*, 1959, also published as *Survival in Auschwitz*). In all some eight thousand Italian Jews were killed (about 17 percent of the prewar Italian Jewish population). The racial laws had always been unpopular in Italy, and while many unrepentant Fascists (and opportunists) supported the RSI-Nazi alliance (including the organization of Black Brigades and an Italian SS), other Italians took great risks to hide both Jews and resistance fighters from the authorities. Monasteries, convents, and churches also played an important role in saving lives; the Vatican, however, did little.

The role of the Resistance in the conflict is debated. Allied officials generally maintained that while the partisans were not a deciding factor in the war, they did facilitate the taking of a number of cities. For postwar Italy, however, the significance of the Resistance was enormous. Not only was it the proving ground for most subsequent Italian political, social, and cultural leaders, it also allowed Italy to save face following the war (in a way that Germany never could) insofar as some Italians had taken up arms against Nazi-fascism and so implicitly the evils it had perpetrated. Significantly there was no Italian Nuremberg or postwar purge of the public bureaucracy. Since the end of the Cold War the antifascist legacy has been challenged, as revisionist interpretations have questioned the antifascist monopoly on virtue while arguing that both sides were guilty of excesses, that fascism had some real accomplishments, and that the alliance with Hitler was unfortunate and largely to blame for Fascist crimes.

That alliance of course finally ended with the victory of the Allies in April–May 1945. As American and British troops liberated the cities of northern Italy, Mussolini, disguised as a German soldier, sought to flee to Switzerland together with his mistress. Apprehended by a band of partisans, his party was summarily tried and shot. In a grisly finale, their bodies were driven back to Milan, kicked and spat on by the mob, and strung up by the heels in a gas station.

CREATION OF THE REPUBLIC AND THE ECONOMIC MIRACLE

Unlike Germany, Italy's status as a cobelligerent meant that it regained sovereignty fairly quickly (though it lost Fiume and Istria to Yugoslavia and some territory to France as well). The first postwar elections (also the first since 1924 and the first ever in which women voted) were held in June 1946.

The bodies of Italian Fascists hang from the roof of a gas station, April 1945. Mussolini and his mistress, Clara Petacci, are at center. GETTY IMAGES

That vote accomplished two things. It eliminated the monarchy, badly compromised by its association with fascism, and elected a Constituent Assembly in which most of the antifascist parties were represented. The two most significant of these were the Christian Democrats (Democrazia Cristiana, or DC) led by Alcide De Gasperi (1881–1954), who following a brief imprisonment had spent most of the interwar period working in the Vatican Library; and the Communists (PCI) led by Palmiro Togliatti (1893–1964), who had spent more or less that same period in Moscow. Initially the parties cooperated on drafting a new constitution. Notably, the Communist Togliatti had essentially renounced the path of revolutionary change and class warfare in favor of cooperation with the other political forces; he also accepted the Lateran Treaty and so recognition of Roman Catholicism as the official religion of Italy. Cooperation, however, was short-lived and at the urging of both the Vatican and the United States,

Prime Minister De Gasperi dropped the Left from his government before the first parliamentary elections of April 1948. In a passionately fought campaign, masses of Italians turned out for Communist and Socialist demonstrations. Meanwhile the church cast the vote as a choice between God and Stalin (Soviet dictator Joseph Stalin [1879–1953]), while U.S. officials openly supported the Christian Democrats and threatened to end financial aid under the Marshall Plan should the Left win. The DC in fact won a near majority, and so the stage was set for Italian politics of the next half century, namely Christian Democratic administrations (normally in coalition with other parties) and Communist opposition.

Italy had experienced limited economic growth during fascism. The regime had weathered the Depression fairly well and established the bases for public social services and state-owned industry and banks, but the war had left the country with a severe housing shortage, devastated infrastructure, and much reduced industrial capacity. Thanks in part to United States aid, however, recovery was remarkably rapid, and the traditional stereotype of a land of peasants, agriculture, and poverty gave way first to cinematic visions of *la dolce vita* (the sweet life)—in the cities of the center-north—against a background of relative misery, and then to a wealthy and largely American-inspired consumerist culture. The central years of what came to be known as the economic miracle were 1958–1963, during which period the Italian economy grew at incredible rates, more than 6 percent per year. Only Japan and Germany could match those rates at the time.

It was also a golden age for Italian cinema, and the flavor of the age is perhaps best captured in its movies. The neorealist movement of the 1940s and 1950s depicted most notably the war experience and resistance—for example, in Roberto Rossellini's (1906–1977) *Rome, Open City* (1945) and *Paisà* (1946)—and the crushing poverty under which most Italians still suffered, movingly depicted in Vittorio De Sica's (1901–1974) *The Bicycle Thief* (1948) and other films. Later the Christian Democratic politician (and seven-time prime minister) Giulio Andreotti (b. 1919) would famously criticize De Sica and other directors for washing Italy's dirty linen in public and casting the nation in such a negative light. Federico Fellini's (1920–1993) classics, *La dolce vita* (1960) and *8½* (1963), depict instead an exuberant Italy at once dedicated to the sorts of hedonistic pleasures made possible by the miracle and at the same time plunged into an existential crisis by those very opportunities.

And it was a time of great opportunity, change, and upheaval, all three perhaps best epitomized by the success of the Fiat automobile company in Turin. Fiat functioned as a major employer of labor and also manufactured a product, especially the small 500s and 600s, that represented an attainable though previously inconceivable luxury for working Italians. Moreover, the continued concentration of industries such as Fiat in the north combined with southern unemployment created intense internal migration in the period. The cities of the north exploded, resulting in overcrowding, the springing up of shanty towns, and severe taxing of infrastructure. And while southern workers were needed to fuel northern economic growth, there was considerable resentment on the part of local populations regarding the dark haired and poorly dressed immigrants who spoke strange and unintelligible dialects. This reality is again best captured in one of the film classics of the period, Luchino Visconti's (1906–1976) *Rocco and His Brothers* (1960). Emigration abroad also took off again following World War II. During 1946–1975, total Italian emigration exceeded seven million, about five million going to other European countries (Switzerland, Germany, France) and the rest overseas (Argentina, the United States, Canada, Venezuela). Well over half those emigrants came from the south (which accounted for only about a third of Italy's total population).

THE FIRST REPUBLIC AND ITS CHALLENGES

As mentioned above, the fundamental political division in Italy from 1948 to 1994 was between the Christian Democrats and the Communists. Indeed this was more than a political contest, as political affiliation came to inform the social and cultural lives of many Italians. In the workplace both parties had their own unions (which cooperated to a certain extent); outside the workplace both had their own after-work organizations. Both founded women's organizations. These were of course not the only political parties but they did

come to dominate much of Italian life. Italian cultural life—for example, publishing and literature, films, the university—was dominated by the PCI, while the business world tended to be strongly DC. As for parliamentary politics, never able to repeat the electoral success of 1948, the DC was constantly on the lookout for governing partners. Overtures to the neofascist Movimento Sociale Italiano (Italian Social Movement, or MSI) clashed with public opinion, so DC leaders looked to the left, in particular to the Socialists. Never terribly successful in advancing their own political agenda, the PSI did join a first center-left coalition in 1963 and would continue with some interruptions as a governing party for the next three decades. What can be said about the DC in the period through to the mid-1960s is that they did not prevent the miracle. The Communists might have, as evidence from Eastern Europe in the period suggests. The DC maintained Italy's adherence to the North Atlantic Treaty Organization (NATO) and the United States alliance as well as establishing Italy's charter memberships in the Coal and Steel Community (1951) and European Economic Community (by the 1957 Treaty of Rome). Yet the DC, at times complicit with the Mafia, permitted an unplanned and unregulated growth that scarred the Italian land and especially cityscapes forever.

The PCI meanwhile continued to garner the largest share of votes on the left and in the mid-1970s looked poised to surpass the DC. PCI secretary Enrico Berlinguer (1922–1984) had distanced the party from Moscow and proposed a democratic Eurocommunism. Notably, he reversed a previous PCI position and stated that the PCI in power would not pull Italy out of NATO. These positions attracted some DC politicians, most notably Aldo Moro (1916–1978), and raised the possibility of the so-called historic compromise, namely a DC-PCI coalition government. Others instead were alarmed by this possibility, in particular the Americans, who in the person of the U.S. secretary of state Henry Kissinger (b. 1923) warned against the communist threat.

The 1970s were a tumultuous period. As in France, the United States, and elsewhere, a series of dramatic but largely peaceful student and worker protests broke out in 1968–1969. Charting a new

Marxist-inspired political program, the students called for revolutionary change and collective action while challenging in a fundamental way the materialist individualism spawned by the miracle; the movement also took up related issues such as workers' and prisoners' rights and protested against the war in Vietnam and American imperialism generally. In terms of realizing their own goals, this revolutionary moment was a failure. But its impact was considerable, nonetheless, as a whole generation was indelibly marked by the experiences of the late 1960s and 1970s, and the movement may have forced Italy to become more self-critical and to question the American consumerist model it had adopted. That period also saw the birth of the Italian feminist movement and so an important challenge and revision of Italy's traditionally patriarchal society. And while little of the social legislation that had been demanded in the period was enacted, a couple of important laws, significantly championed by the feminist movement, undoubtedly owed something to the atmosphere of those times. One such law legalized divorce in 1970. Opposed by the church and the DC, this law was eventually upheld by popular referendum in 1974. Subsequently, there developed a grassroots movement to legalize abortion, which, also in spite of DC opposition, was successful in 1978.

It was also a decade of urban terror, the so-called years of lead. Probably in response to the perceived threat posed by this new Left, right-wing neofascist elements embarked on what came to be known as the strategy of tension, namely acts of terror intended at once to discredit the Left and encourage the introduction of more authoritarian policies. The first event in that sad history occurred when a bomb exploded in a Milanese bank in Piazza Fontana in December 1969, killing sixteen people. Following on the so-called hot autumn of worker and student protests, conservative and right-wing elements initially ascribed the bombing to anarchists. Several anarchists were in fact arrested, and one died suspiciously after falling from a police station window, an event made famous by Nobel Prize–winning Dario Fo's play, *Morte accidentale di un anarchico* (1970; *Accidental Death of an Anarchist,* 1979). These events were always cloaked in mystery, but the Piazza Fontana bombing did turn out to be organized by radical

neofascists. There followed a series of similar indiscriminate bombings culminating in the Bologna train station attack in summer 1980 that killed eighty-five people.

Contemporary with these bombings, frustrated elements of the new revolutionary Left also turned to violence, most notably those organized as the Red Brigades, whose first action dates from 1970. Left-wing terror tended to be more specific in its targets and included the knee-capping and assassination of policemen and political figures as well as a series of much-publicized kidnappings. The most famous was the dramatic kidnapping of the DC president Aldo Moro in Rome in 1978. Moro was held for almost two months during which the *brigatisti* demanded the release of their comrades from prison. Under Prime Minister Andreotti, the government refused to negotiate with the terrorists. In May, the kidnappers, who had already tried Moro and sentenced him to death, loaded him into the trunk of a Renault 4, shot him in the head, and abandoned the car in the center of Rome, tipping off authorities as to its whereabouts.

The motivations and forces behind the violence of the 1970s remain mysterious, and there exist both evidence for and much speculation about the involvement of political and secret service elements (perhaps with foreign, especially U.S., ties) seeking to achieve particular aims. The murder of Moro, for example, effectively torpedoed the historic compromise between DC and PCI. Yet while the perpetrators of neofascist violence were only sporadically identified, the Red Brigades were effectively dismantled by the police work of General Carlo Alberto Della Chiesa (1920–1982). And those convicted of the Moro kidnapping all denied that they had been in any way infiltrated by outside forces.

Della Chiesa's next assignment was to try his methods against a more deeply rooted challenge to law and order in Italy, namely the Sicilian Mafia. Complaining that he did not have adequate support from the state for the undertaking, Della Chiesa was in fact murdered within months of arriving in Palermo in 1982. In its more than century-long existence the Mafia had normally avoided this sort of high-profile killing; it signaled in fact a new phase in the relationship between the state and organized crime. Historically, claims about the

WORLD WAR II AND FASCISM

Nazi staff cars enter a village in the Sudetenland, October 1938. Following the annexation of Austria in March 1938, reclaiming control of the portion of Czechoslovakia inhabited by Germans was Adolf Hitler's next move in his plan for world domination by what he deemed the ethnically pure "Aryan race." Time Life Pictures/Getty Images

A rally at the Stadio dei Cipressi in honor of Adolf Hitler, Rome, May 1938. In October 1936, the fascist leaders of Germany and Italy, Hitler and Benito Mussolini, formalized their alliance as the Rome-Berlin Axis. In May 1938, Hitler made an official state visit to Italy, during which Mussolini mounted an impressive display of Axis solidarity. TIME LIFE PICTURES/GETTY IMAGES

BELOW: **Adolf Hitler delivers a speech to the German Reichstag, 28 April 1939.** It was during this speech that Hitler announced his intention to abrogate Germany's non-aggression agreement with Poland. He carried out this threat in September of that year, causing Great Britain, its dominions, and France to declare war. TIME LIFE PICTURES/GETTY IMAGES

LEFT: A building burns during the Battle of Britain, London, September 1940. The German defeat of France and the Low Countries in early 1940 was followed by an intensive period of aerial bombing of the British Isles. The bombing of cities, made possible by improvements in aircraft, became a common tactic for combatants during the war, causing enormous loss of life among civilian populations. WILLIAM VANDIVERT/TIME LIFE PICTURES/GETTY IMAGES

BELOW: World War II-era poster depicting British Commonwealth troops. As the German occupation of western Europe progressed, Britain relied heavily on the resources of Commonwealth nations — Australia, Canada, New Zealand, and South Africa — as well as its colonies in South Asia and West Africa. © SWIM INK 2, LLC/CORBIS

RIGHT: Women's Auxiliary Air Force members prepare a barrage balloon, London, c. 1941. Women played an unprecedented role in the Allied war effort, serving in a variety of roles from intelligence to aircraft maintenance. Although in most cases they served in support positions such as the ones depicted here, among resistance fighters and in the Soviet Union some women fought in combat along with men. © Hulton-Deutsch Collection/Corbis

BELOW: Royal Air Force command crew with their Avro Lancaster bomber c. 1941. Having thwarted Hitler's plan to destroy British air forces and launch an invasion across the English channel, the RAF stepped up bombing raids on Germany. The Avro Lancaster bomber was the most successful of the planes developed for this purpose. © Hulton-Deutsch Collection/Corbis

TOP: Allied troops arrive at the Piazza San Pietro in Rome, June 1944. After establishing a foothold in southern Italy in March 1943, Allied forces faced fierce resistance from Italian and German troops as they made their way north. They did not reach Rome until June 1944. © Bettmann/Corbis

MIDDLE: German artillery at Longues-sur-Mer, France, photographed c. 2003. Germany prepared for an Allied assault by creating what became known as the Atlantic Wall, a series of coastal fortifications stretching from Norway to southern France, including batteries of 150mm guns housed in concrete bunkers such as the one pictured here. This installation guarded one of the beaches used for the Allied D-Day landing and is one of the few that survived the pre-invasion bombardment. © Richard Klune/Corbis

BOTTOM: A memorial to the defenders of Stalingrad. In the summer of 1942, Germany launched a major offensive against the city of Stalingrad which lasted six months and ended in a major defeat for the Germans. The steadfast resistance of the residents of Stalingrad and the huge number of casualties on the Soviet side, numbering over one million, became a source of pride and solidarity. © Dean Conger /Corbis

OPPOSITE PAGE: French general Charles de Gaulle leads a parade in the Champs Elysées to celebrate the liberation of Paris, 26 August 1944. With help from French resistance fighters, Allied troops made their way eastward to Paris less than three months after the D-Day landing at Normandy. Time Life Pictures/Getty Images

RIGHT: The Nuremberg trials, 1946. After the war, Nazi leaders were tried in Nuremberg as war criminals. Pictured here are (front row, from left) Hermann Goering, Rudolf Hess, Joachim von Ribbentrop, Wilhelm Keitel, Ernst Kaltenbrunner, and (second row) Karl Dönitz, Erich Raeder, Baldur von Schirach, and Fritz Sauckel. Ribbentrop, Keitel, Kaltenbunner, and Sauckel were found guilty and executed. Goering too was sentenced to death but committed suicide before he could be executed. The rest were found guilty and received prison sentences. © Bettmann/Corbis

BELOW: The Small Camp at Buchenwald. Painting by Boris Taslitzky, 1945. Born in Paris to Russian parents, Taslitzky was a painter who was interned at Buchenwald as a result of his active resistance to the German occupation. He later attempted to capture the horror unleashed during the final stages of the war when German attempts to exterminate internees reached their frenzied peak. CNAC/MNAM/Dist. Réunion des Musées Nationaux/Art Resource, NY/© 2006 Artists Rights Society (ARS), New York/ADAGP, Pairs

Campaign posters for Silvio Berlusconi in Rome, March 1994. Berlusconi defeated the leftists in the 1994 election with his coalition of disparate political groups knit together to form the Forza Italia party. ©ORIGLIA FRANCO/CORBIS SYGMA

phenomenon had ranged from the simple denial of its existence to assertion of an articulated organization with links to politics and business. Mussolini's regime had undertaken a campaign to crush the Mafia, and while many arrests were made, they were primarily of petty criminals, and the Mafia bosses continued to operate undisturbed, generally supportive of fascism. Needless to say, organized crime took its share of postwar prosperity, and the continued failure of development in the south certainly owes something to its operation. Nonetheless, postwar governments and the Mafia generally maintained an uneasy coexistence until the 1980s.

Following the Della Chiesa murder, a new anti-Mafia "pool" of magistrates was created in Palermo, the best-known members of which were Giovanni Falcone (1939–1992) and Paolo Borsellino (1940–1992). Thanks largely to testimony from Tommaso Buscetta (1928–2000), an important Mafioso captured in Brazil and turned state's evidence, the pool pursued investigations

leading to the maxi-trial of 1986–1987. Held in a specially constructed bunker/courtroom, the maxi-trial resulted in convictions against 344 of 475 accused Mafiosi, easily the biggest blow the state had ever delivered against the organization. Subsequent disbanding of the pool of magistrates and reversal of some of these convictions lent credibility to the accusations of connections between the Mafia and government politicians. Falcone, however, with support in Rome, managed to uphold many of the convictions in early 1992, in part by blocking a chosen appointment of Salvatore "Salvo" Lima (1928–1992), a Sicilian Christian Democratic politician with close ties to Andreotti. Then in quick succession, Lima, Falcone, and Borsellino were all killed in Palermo.

As later came to light, the murders were ordered by Salvatore "Totò" Riina, a fugitive since 1969 (during which time he seems to have lived undisturbed in Palermo with his wife and children) and head of the Corleone Mafia family. Lima, the hinge between politics and crime in Sicily, had apparently outlived his usefulness (though his supporters continue to maintain his anti-Mafia credentials), while Falcone and Borsellino were a continuing threat for Riina. It was a dark moment, but the work of the pool had changed public attitudes in Sicily about the Mafia in a fundamental way. Countering the despair inspired by the deaths of Falcone and Borsellino was the arrest of Riina himself in January 1993; he was subsequently sentenced to multiple life sentences. On the political side, Andreotti (who was appointed senator for life in 1991 after forty-five years in the Chamber of Deputies) was formally accused of Mafia collusion; although initially convicted of ordering the murder of a journalist (in 1979), that conviction was overturned and the others failed to stick. As of 2006, he was still politically active.

TANGENTOPOLI AND THE SECOND REPUBLIC

The year 1992 also saw the beginning of the *tangentopoli* (bribe city) scandal that, like the Mafia investigation, marked the end of postwar Italian business as usual. In this case the pool of magistrates was centered in Milan, Italy's financial capital; its most notable exponent was the charismatic Antonio Di Pietro, a southerner who (like Falcone) rose from humble origins to near superstar status. Politically, Italy was governed throughout the 1980s by the *pentapartito*, a DC-led five-party coalition in which the significant junior partner was the Socialists, led from 1976 by the forceful figure of Bettino Craxi (1934–2000). Craxi gave new life to the PSI. He was Milanese and shaped the party in the image of that most dynamic of Italian cities. The PSI, in fact, from near extinction became under Craxi the party of Italy's new wealth, of which there was plenty in the boom years of that decade. A rare non-DC prime minister, Craxi held the post for an unprecedented three-and-a-half years (1983–1987). Among his accomplishments was the 1984 revision of the Lateran Treaty, which eliminated the privileged legal status of Catholicism in Italy and recognized the equality of all faiths. He also oversaw unprecedented levels of corruption as revealed by the Milan pool of magistrate's Clean Hands investigation. Starting with a retirement home in Milan, a vast world of kickbacks was revealed in which party representatives regularly received payments for the awarding of public contracts and other official favors. In the so-called maxibribe, one company apparently paid upward of $15 million (some claim much more) to ensure its purchase by the state. Revelations in that regard led to two (apparent) suicides. In all, by 1997 the pool had issued 2,575 accusations and won 577 convictions while uncovering about $3 billion in bribes.

The majority of those accusations targeted Christian Democrats and Socialists. Craxi, who would be convicted on several counts, claimed that all parties took bribes, as the Italian system provided no other way to finance political life. His apparent honesty earned him little sympathy. Given that the PCI was left virtually unscathed, he and others accused the Milan pool of carrying out a leftist political agenda, though subsequent scrutiny failed to reveal much Communist wrongdoing. The political fallout was enormous, so great that some have spoken of a Second Republic following the scandals. It was as if the end of the Cold War had unleashed Italy's demons, and the pro-U.S. DC was no longer unassailable. In fact, after performing poorly in the 1992 elections, the *pentapartito* essentially collapsed (Andreotti headed the last DC government). Both the DC and the PSI ceased to exist, while Craxi, for example, in 1994 fled to his villa in Tunisia (from which he would never return, dying in 2000). As elections in 1994 approached it seemed that the former Communists, renamed the Democratic Party of the Left (Partito Democratico della Sinistra, or PDS; later Democratici di Sinistra, or DS), were poised finally to take up the reins of power.

That, however, did not happen. At the eleventh hour a new political force emerged in the person of Silvio Berlusconi (b. 1936). The Milanese Berlusconi had erected a massive real estate and media empire in the boom years of the 1980s, often with Socialist patronage. Reportedly he is the wealthiest man in Italy. He also owns the A.C. Milan soccer team and structured his political organization, Forza Italia (Go Italy, a soccer cheer), like a series of sports clubs. Remarkably, in the few months leading up to the March 1994 elections, Berlusconi managed to counter the Communist threat by bringing together unlikely bedfellows, the National Alliance (Alleanza Nazionale, or AN) and Northern League (Lega

Nord, or Lega). The AN was the renamed neofascist, now postfascist, party led by the able Gianfranco Fini (b. 1952). A champion of the social state, its stronghold was in the center and south, especially among public employees. The Lega, instead, led by the gruff Umberto Bossi (b. 1941), was a northern secessionist party that protested against government corruption and the presumed siphoning off of northern wealth to fund the poor south. In spite of obvious differences, Berlusconi managed to join these three groups together and defeated the Left in the 1994 election. Appointed prime minister, Berlusconi's tenure was a brief one. Before the year was up, Bossi pulled out in protest and caused the government to fall. Following a couple of "technical" governments, elections were held again in 1996. By that time a clear center-left coalition, the Ulivo or Olive Tree, had emerged led by a respected economist with former DC connections, Romano Prodi (though the major partner remained the DS). The center-right coalition (Casa della Libertà, or House of Liberty) had repaired its differences. The Ulivo won, and Prodi was appointed prime minister. Fiscally responsible, Prodi's greatest triumph was putting Italy's financial house in order sufficiently so that it succeeded in joining the European and Monetary Union as a charter member in 1999 (the euro itself coming into circulation in 2002). Internal (and self-defeating) squabbles within the Ulivo led to Prodi's replacement in 1998 by Massimo D'Alema, Italy's first former-Communist prime minister.

Unable to capitalize on its achievements, however, the center-left was resoundingly defeated by Berlusconi's coalition in 2001. Such was his victory that Berlusconi was able to maintain the premiership for the entire five-year legislature. On the one hand, the 2001 victory signaled the introduction into Italy of healthy democratic alternation of power (as compared to the DC lock on power for over four decades). On the other hand, Berlusconi's near monopoly of Italian television has raised concern about his ability to manipulate public opinion, and various commentators claim that Berlusconi entered politics largely to protect his own financial interests. Officially accused numerous times of corruption, he has managed repeatedly to avoid conviction. Those accusations have even led foreign observers (most notably the *Economist*

magazine) to deem him unfit to rule. In foreign policy, his pro-U.S. stance—he once half-mockingly said "I am on whatever side America is on, even before I know what it is"—led him to support the U.S. invasion of Iraq in March 2003 and send troops to support the reconstruction effort in June of that year. Italian public opinion was however strongly opposed to the war, and in the run-up to the 2006 elections Berlusconi claimed—some thought cynically—that he had tried all along to convince U.S. President George W. Bush (b. 1946) not to go to war. Berlusconi was narrowly defeated in the April 2006 elections, losing to center-left candidate and former prime minister Romano Prodi.

Italy entered the twenty-first century a much different place than it had been one hundred years before. Economically it had moved from a minor European power to one of global importance, though politically it did not exert corresponding influence; in the context of European integration it probably never will. From an agricultural land of high fertility and emigration, it had become a service-dominated country with one of the lowest birthrates in the world (total fertility at or below 1.3 since the early 1990s) and the destination of large numbers of Third World immigrants (with all the problems of social dislocation and racism that the phenomenon brings). Italy had become a leader in design, fashion, and more prosaic small industries, and "made in Italy" had become a mark of quality and good taste. Its popularity as a tourist destination possibly unmatched (thanks to the art and architecture of earlier epochs and the cuisine and conviviality of the present one), Italy was still perceived as an enigmatic place maintaining signs of its past: pockets of traditional agriculture in the south, a tendency to autocracy in politics, corruption, and an easygoing approach to moral questions. In that, Italy fulfills each visitor's own expectations about the *bel paese* (beautiful country) and what it can offer.

See also **Axis; Berlusconi, Silvio; Craxi, Bettino; D'Annunzio, Gabriele; Economic Miracle; Fascism; Fellini, Federico; Lateran Pacts; Levi, Primo; Mafia; Mussolini, Benito; Red Brigades; World War II.**

BIBLIOGRAPHY

Ben-Ghiat, Ruth. *Fascist Modernities: Italy, 1922–1945*. Berkeley, Calif., 2001.

Ben-Ghiat, Ruth, and Mia Fuller, eds. *Italian Colonialism.* New York, 2005.

Bosworth, R. J. B. *Italy and the Wider World, 1860–1960.* London, 1996.

———. *Mussolini.* London, 2002.

———. *Mussolini's Italy: Life under the Dictatorship, 1915–1945.* London, 2005.

Cardoza, Anthony L. *Benito Mussolini: The First Fascist.* New York, 2006.

De Grand, Alexander. *Italian Fascism: Its Origins and Development.* Lincoln, Neb., 1982.

———. *The Hunchback's Tailor: Giovanni Giolitti and Liberal Italy from the Challenge of Mass Politics to the Rise of Fascism, 1882–1922.* Westport, Conn., 2001.

De Grazia, Victoria. *How Fascism Ruled Women: Italy, 1922–1945.* Berkeley, Calif., 1992.

Dickie, John. *Cosa Nostra: A History of the Sicilian Mafia.* New York, 2004.

Falasca-Zamponi, Simonetta. *Fascist Spectacle: The Aesthetics of Power in Mussolini's Italy.* Berkeley, Calif., 1997.

Gentile, Emilio. *The Sacralization of Politics in Fascist Italy.* Translated by Keith Botsford. Cambridge, Mass., 1996.

Ginsborg, Paul. *A History of Contemporary Italy: Society and Politics, 1943–1988.* New York, 1990.

———. *Italy and Its Discontents: 1980–2001.* London, 2003.

Ipsen, Carl. *Dictating Demography: The Problem of Population in Fascist Italy.* Cambridge, U.K., 1996.

Lyttelton, Adrian, ed. *Liberal and Fascist Italy, 1900–1945.* Oxford, U.K., 2002. Includes an extensive bibliography.

McCarthy, Patrick. *The Crisis of the Italian State: From the Origins of the Cold War to the Fall of Berlusconi.* New York, 1995.

McCarthy, Patrick, ed. *Italy since 1945.* Oxford, U.K., 2000. Includes an extensive bibliography.

Stille, Alexander. *Benevolence and Betrayal: Five Italian Jewish Families under Fascism.* New York, 1991.

———. *Excellent Cadavers: The Mafia and the Death of the First Italian Republic.* New York, 1995.

Willson, Perry R. *The Clockwork Factory: Women and Work in Fascist Italy.* Oxford, U.K., 1993.

———. *Peasant Women and Politics in Fascist Italy: The Massaie Rurali.* London, 2002.

Zamagni, Vera. *The Economic History of Italy, 1860–1990.* Oxford, U.K., 1993.

CARL IPSEN

IZETBEGOVIĆ, ALIJA (1925–2003), Bosnian Muslim activist, author, and politician.

Alija Izetbegović (8 August 1925–19 October 2003) was the leading Muslim political figure in Bosnia-Herzegovina in the twentieth century and was de facto president of Bosnia at the time it was recognized as an independent country in 1992. He had been imprisoned in socialist Yugoslavia from 1983 to 1988 for "counterrevolutionary acts derived from Muslim nationalism" based on his writings. While in no sense an Islamic extremist, he was a very strong advocate of Islam and of the rights of Muslims throughout the world and specifically in Bosnia and Herzegovina, where they comprise the largest single group.

Izetbegović was active in Muslim causes throughout his life. During World War II, when Germany and its allies occupied Yugoslavia, Izetbegović joined a group called "The Young Muslims," a nationalist organization promoting the interests of the Muslim community in Bosnia. This Muslim nationalist group was opposed to Josip Broz Tito's (1892–1980) Communists, and Alija Izetbegović was one of thousands imprisoned for anticommunist activities in 1946, as communist rule was consolidated. However, after three years in prison, Izetbegović was able to attend the University of Sarajevo, where he earned a law degree. He worked as a lawyer for the next thirty years.

Since at least the late nineteenth century, Bosnian politics have revolved around relations among the country's three largest communities: Muslims, Serbs, and Croats. Even during the regime of the officially atheist communists, great care was taken to ensure that none of these groups could dominate the others. Throughout his life, Alija Izetbegović argued for the need for Muslims throughout the world to unite and to strengthen their political power and religious identity. In communist Yugoslavia, claims that the Muslims should be more self-assertive were not only counter to communist atheism but also threatened to upset the political consensus that prohibited promoting the interests of any one of Bosnia's people over the others.

As communism failed in the late 1980s, however, Bosnia's people manifested once again the pre-communist political pattern in which Muslims voted overwhelmingly for one Muslim party, Serbs for one Serb party, and Croats for one Croat party. Izetbegović, newly freed from imprisonment for his pro-Muslim writings, founded what became the dominant Muslim political party in Bosnia-Herzegovina, the Party of Democratic Action (SDA from its Serb-Croatian initials), in March 1990. In the elections eight months later, the SDA won the great majority of votes from the 44 percent of Bosnia's population who were Muslim. Since no single group formed a majority of Bosnia's population, no single party received a majority of the vote, and the SDA ruled as part of a coalition with the leading Serb and Croat parties. Reflecting the complications of Bosnia's ethnic politics, the country had a collective presidency of seven members, two from each of the major groups and one additional member representing those not Muslim, Serb, or Croat. As leader of the largest party, Alija Izetbegović became president of this collective presidency. In theory he only represented decisions of the collective body, and the position of president of the presidency was to rotate to a Croat member. In practice, Izetbegović acted as sole president and did not rotate out of the presidency when his term should have expired.

Aware that most Serbs and many Croats did not favor Bosnian independence, Izetbegović sought to prevent Yugoslavia's collapse, but when that did happen he pursued independence even knowing that to do so risked war. The collective government also collapsed, with the elected Serb representatives and many of the Croats withdrawing. However, Izetbegović consistently favored a multiethnic government, at least publicly, and worked with other Serb and Croat representatives. He was a very effective representative of the Bosnian cause in international politics throughout the 1992–1995 war.

Following the war, in early 1996 Izetbegović became the first president of a new, smaller collective presidency of Bosnia-Herzegovina, but he finally retired in 2000 due to failing health. Until his death from heart failure in October 2003 he remained one of the most popular figures among Bosnian Muslims, but not among the Serbs and Croats.

See also **Bosnia-Herzegovina; Yugoslavia.**

BIBLIOGRAPHY

Primary Sources

Izetbegović, Alija. *Inescapable Questions: Autobiographical Notes.* 2nd ed. Translated by Saba Rissaluddin and Jasmina Izetbegović. Leicester, U.K., 2002.

Secondary Sources

Burg, Steven L., and Paul Shoup. *The War in Bosnia-Herzegovina: Ethnic Conflict and International Intervention.* Armonk, N.Y., and London, 1999.

Silber, Laura, and Allan Little. *Yugoslavia: Death of a Nation.* New York, 1996.

ROBERT M. HAYDEN

JAKOBSON, ROMAN (1896–1982), Russian-born American linguist.

The first son of an upper-middle-class Moscow family, Roman Jakobson showed extraordinary talent and interest in languages and literature from early on in his school years. Prior to 1914, the year he started his studies at Moscow University, he established contacts with the painter Kazimir Malevich (1878–1935), the poet Vladimir Mayakovsky (1893–1930), the painter and poet Alexei Kruchenykh (1886–1969), the poet Velemir Khlebnikov (1885–1922), and other authors and artists of the Russian avant-garde, and himself wrote radical "transrational" phonetic poetry (*zaum*) in the style of Russian futurism. At the same time, he pursued his interests in Russian dialectology and folklore and, increasingly, emerging structural linguistics. In 1915 he was a cofounder of the Moscow Linguistic Circle.

The change of regime in 1917 brought opportunities for Jakobson in the emerging Soviet foreign service. In 1920 he was assigned to a diplomatic outpost in Tallinn (Estonia) and, the same year, to the Soviet Red Cross Mission in Prague, where he went in July 1920, eventually living in Czechoslovakia until April 1939. His Czechoslovak years parallel his early years in Moscow. While closely allied with the Czech avant-garde, he intensively pursued academic interests, participating, among others, in founding the Prague Linguistic Circle in 1926, a group of linguists and literary theorists who made a major contribution to the foundations of European structuralism. A key area was the study of poetic language; another focus was on sound structure of languages. Together with another émigré Russian linguist, Nikolai Trubetskoy (1890–1938), who lived in Vienna, Jakobson worked on the development of phonology, a discipline concerned with the statement of laws governing the structure of sound systems across languages. In the 1920s Jakobson was active in Prague, pursuing his projects as an employee of the Soviet representation in Prague, but he moved to Brno in 1933 to become a professor at the new Masaryk University.

It was from Brno that Jakobson and his second wife fled to Scandinavia after the occupation of Czechoslovakia in March 1939. Jakobson first lived in Denmark, was then forced to flee further, to Norway, and eventually left for the United States from Sweden in the summer of 1941. Despite extreme circumstances, his Scandinavian years yielded the classic of European structural phonology, the monograph *Kindersprache, Aphasie, und allgemeine Lautgesetze* (1941; *Child Language, Aphasia, and Phonological Universals,* 1968). A substantial part of the study consists in working out a theory of markedness, rooted in the concept of a layered structure of systems. Echoing ideas of the founder of phenomenology, the German philosopher Edmund Husserl (1859–1938), laws of markedness are stated in the form of unilateral implications of the form *If A, then B.* Basing his reasoning on facts of language acquisition (child language) and language loss (aphasia), Jakobson generalized this approach to a panchronic analysis that later inspired the study of language universals.

Jakobson arrived in New York in June 1941 to first teach at the French émigré institution, École Libre des Hautes Études, where he met the French anthropologist Claude Lévi-Strauss (b. 1908); he later moved to Columbia University and, in 1950, to Harvard University. In 1957 he was also appointed a professor at the Massachusetts Institute of Technology in Cambridge, Massachusetts. Linguistics and poetics continued to be the foci of Jakobson's American years, while the development of United States Slavic studies was a distinct organizational project with a significant institutional impact. Together with his student and later collaborator Morris Halle, and initially in collaboration with the Swedish phonetician Gunnar Fant, he worked out the modern theory of phonological features, a cornerstone of phonological theory (*Preliminaries to Speech Analysis,* 1952).

At the same time, Jakobson continued to work on poetics and literary theory, extending the scope of his investigations well beyond the limits of Slavic studies and addressing authors as diverse as the French poet Charles Baudelaire (1821–1867), the German playwright and poet Bertolt Brecht (1898–1956), the German poet Friedrich Hölderlin (1770–1843), and the English playwright William Shakespeare (1564–1616). Likewise, *The Sound Shape of Language* (1979), written with Linda Waugh, aims at general properties of sound structure. Jakobson became increasingly interested in the structure of the brain as relevant for the study of language. Last but not least, in his numerous interviews and conversations he left invaluable testimony of the life of the Soviet avant-garde that he actively witnessed and shaped in his early years. His legacy forms a unique amalgam of a philological approach that sees language as embedded in culture and society, to an advocacy of formal approaches in linguistics, especially in phonology, to contributions to the philosophy of language, and, eventually, to forays into cognitive science.

See also **Brecht, Bertolt; Lévi-Strauss, Claude; Saussure, Ferdinand de.**

BIBLIOGRAPHY

Jakobson, Roman. *Selected Writings.* 8 vols. Places of publication vary, 1962–.

———. *Language in Literature.* Edited by Krystyna Pomorska and Stephen Rudy. Cambridge, Mass., 1987.

Rudy, Stephen, ed. *Roman Jakobson, 1896–1982: A Complete Bibliography of His Writings.* Berlin, 1990.

Toman, Jindrich. *The Magic of a Common Language: Jakobson, Mathesius, Trubetzkoy, and the Prague Linguistic Circle.* Cambridge, Mass., 1995.

JINDRICH TOMAN

JAPAN AND THE TWO WORLD WARS.

The history of Japan and the two world wars reveals that Europe was integral to the policy calculations of the Japanese government from 1914 to 1945. Although the United States became an increasingly important power in East Asia, especially after World War I, Britain, Germany, and the Soviet Union remained powerful players in the international relations of Japan.

WORLD WAR I

On 23 August 1914 Japan declared war on Germany as one of the Allied Powers. The Japanese reason for entering the war was to uphold Japan's obligations arising out of the Anglo-Japanese Alliance, which dated back to 1902. Ironically, however, the Japanese had failed to consult beforehand their alliance partner, Britain, and this fact tainted the relationship between the two allies during World War I. The signing of the Anglo-Japanese Alliance had been a coup for the Japanese, who rejoiced at concluding a military alliance with the world's foremost naval power. The primary objective of the alliance was to keep Russia at bay, as Russian encroachment into northeast China and Korea had been a grave security concern for Japan and Britain at the turn of the twentieth century. By the time of World War I, the Russian threat had become more manageable, as a result of the concerted efforts made by the Japanese government in the post-1905 period to conclude four agreements with Russia, in order to safeguard Japanese interests in northeast China, Korea, and Mongolia. As for Britain, the primary threat after the Japanese defeat of Russia in the Russo-Japanese War (1904–1905) became its alliance partner, Japan, itself. Foreign Secretary Arthur Balfour famously stated, "a paper alliance was crucially important where there was no natural alliance."

The key Japanese military leaders of the time, such as General Aritomo Yamagata, saw the preoccupation of European powers with the European theater of war as a "godsend" for Japan's expansion into China. Having first fought off the Germans effortlessly in the Shandong province of China, the Japanese followed with a swift campaign in the Pacific, capturing the German colonies in Micronesia. Throughout the war, however, the Japanese remained reluctant to assist militarily the Allied war effort in Europe because they perceived the war primarily as a "European war" in which Japan had a small role to play. As a result, Japan refused to send naval enforcements to the Mediterranean, or to send troops to the western front. The few instances in which they agreed were in response to requests to assist in nearby waters, such as in the Indian Ocean and the Strait of Malacca in February 1916, and in generally enlarged naval cooperation with the British in January 1917. Japan's limited wartime involvement, and transparently self-centered interests, meant that there existed among the Allied Powers the general view that Japan gained more than it gave in the war effort.

The Siberian intervention (1917–1918) was another sticking point in Japan's relationship with Europe during World War I. The British government's decision in January 1918 to ask the Japanese government to deploy troops to Vladivostok on behalf of the Allied Powers had caused a rift with the United States. This was one of a series of problems that the British had with the United States with regard to Japanese participation. On the whole, the United States remained highly suspicious of Japanese motives for expansion in China. The crisis within the Allied Powers was finally resolved when the United States agreed to a joint deployment of Japanese troops together with Czech forces in June 1918, to assist the White Russian forces against the Bolsheviks and the Germans. The Japanese deployed seventy-three thousand troops as opposed to the Allied request of seven thousand, and what was more, expanded the geographical scope of deployment from the Vladivostok area to a much larger one, reaching up to the east of Lake Baikal. The United States had correctly predicted that the Japanese were motivated principally by expansionist desires.

At the Paris Peace Conference of 1919, the Japanese were given the rank of one of the five Allied great powers. This was largely a result of the strength of the Anglo-Japanese Alliance. The Japanese made three demands at the peace conference: two were territorial in nature, involving the Shandong settlement and the Micronesian islands; and the third was a demand for racial equality. The series of secret agreements that the Japanese had signed with Britain, France, Russia, and Italy over the Micronesian islands was a reminder of how intimately entwined the Japanese had become in European great power politics. Like their European counterparts, the Japanese shared their skepticism of Wilsonian liberalism.

INTERWAR YEARS

The Anglo-Japanese Alliance, which had been the backbone of Japanese foreign policy since 1902, came to an end through the Washington Conference (1921–1922). The series of treaties leading to its abrogation in August 1923 were as follows: the Four Power Treaty (the United States, Britain, Japan, and France) instigated that powers should consult each other in order to avoid confrontation in the Pacific; the Five-Power Treaty (the United States, Britain, Japan, France, and Italy) was the most important, and established the naval ratio in the Pacific as 5:5:3:1.75:1.75, respectively, thereby demoting Japan to the position of secondary naval power; and finally, the Nine-Power Treaty, which included the five main powers plus Belgium, the Netherlands, Portugal, and China, promised to uphold the territorial integrity of China. Together, these treaties established the so-called Washington system as a new international order in East Asia. In Japanese historiography, the Washington system is usually used as a counterpoint to the so-called Versailles system, which was the new international order based on the League of Nations. Notably, the Soviet Union, which had been the most important European Pacific power until World War I, was not party to these treaties. Japan's diplomatic relations with the revolutionary Soviet regime started in January 1925. This belied, however, the substantial unofficial influence that the Comintern had on the left-wing movement in Japan (and China).

Elsewhere during the 1920s, Japan "worked" side by side as an imperial power with Britain, France, Italy, and the United States in China. One of the noteworthy events was the May 30th Movement in Shanghai in 1925, which began as an anti-Japanese boycott by the Chinese workers, but spread to become an anti-British, and more generally, anti-imperialist, movement. In spite of Japan's geographical advantage, Britain had an upper hand in the China trade until Japan turned northeast China (commonly known as Manchuria) into a Japanese puppet state in 1931. In fact, there was a principal difference between Japanese objectives, and Western (both European and U.S.) objectives in China: whereas the Japanese were keen to expand territorially to build a contiguous land empire, the Western powers were keen to hold onto their economic interests in China within the framework of an "informal" empire. The Manchurian Incident of September 1931 was, thus, a turning point in Japan's expansionist policy in China, as the Japanese began to show a clear preference for non-cooperation with the British, French, and Americans over the "China problem." International criticism from the Lytton Commission, which was set up to investigate the Manchurian Incident, pushed Japan to withdraw from the League of Nations on 27 March 1933. With the aforementioned Washington system now in tatters, Japan's withdrawal from the League was a signal to Britain, France, and other League powers that Japan no longer deemed cooperation with these powers as beneficial to its national interests, and instead, Japan turned its attention to Germany and Italy. Significantly, some Japanese historians date the incident as the beginning of Japan's "Fifteen-Year War."

Japanese domestic politics became increasingly marred by military coups and a culture of violence in the 1930s. On 25 November 1936, Japan signed a defense agreement with Germany that was ostensibly an anti-Comintern pact, but in reality was a containment policy to check Soviet advances. Apart from a brief period after the Russian Revolution of 1917, the Soviet Union took over Imperial Russia's mantle as the most threatening enemy of Japan in the "north." In November 1937 Italy joined Germany and Japan, forming the "have-not" nations, as opposed to the "have" nations led by the United States and Britain. Japan by this time had completely separated itself from the earlier alliance with the "have" nations, and was now forming the core of the Axis Powers.

THE ASIA-PACIFIC WAR, 1937–1945

The Japanese Army used the pretext of the Marco Polo Bridge Incident to expand territorially in China in July and August 1937. In September, China made an appeal to the 18th Plenary Session of the League of Nations to end Japanese hostilities, on the basis of their contravening the Nine-Power Treaty and the Kellogg-Briand Pact (1928). Even Germany attempted to mediate a peace because it considered the Japanese invasion as going against the primary German interest of having Japan act as a containing power against the Soviet Union, Britain, and France in Asia. The Germans, however, became more amenable to Japanese policy in China in 1938 when they began their preparations for war in Europe. Needless to say, Japanese relations with Britain and France deteriorated rapidly in this period as the Japanese held Britain responsible for keeping afloat the Chinese Nationalist regime under Chiang Kai-shek. As a result, anti-British sentiment was very high in Japan in 1939, with mass demonstrations in Tokyo's Hibiya Park.

Within the Japanese armed forces, views divided as to which side the Japanese should ally with. The army, which had been a traditionally pro-German institution, strongly advocated a tripartite agreement with Germany (and Italy), with a clause that did not limit its possible military engagement against the Soviet Union. On the other hand, the navy, a stalwart pro-Anglo-American institution, considered it suicidal to be drawn into a war against the two strongest naval powers in the world. In this period, the navy came under tremendous pressure from the ultraright-wingers, with assassination plots against the top brass, including Admiral Isoroku Yamamoto, the architect of Pearl Harbor. In the meantime, Japan's Kwantung Army clashed with Soviet forces on the border between northwestern Manchuria and Outer Mongolia in May 1939, an encounter known as the Nomonhan Incident. The army and its pro-Axis lobby, however, had to retrench temporarily with the shocking news of the German-Soviet Nonaggression Pact of

23 August 1939. But this setback was short-lived, as the pro-Axis lobby gained new ground with the news of successive German victories in Europe in 1940, and once again there surfaced the possibility of joining hands with Germany at this favorable juncture, and invading the British, French, and Dutch colonies in Southeast Asia.

The Tripartite Pact between Japan, Germany, and Italy was signed in Berlin on 27 September 1940. The basis of the "Matsuoka diplomacy" (named after Foreign Minister Yōsuke Matsuoka in the second cabinet of Prince Fumimaro Konoe), which led to the signing of the pact, was twofold. First, it was based on preventing U.S. entry into the war, by applying the united threat of the three Axis Powers. Second, it was to promote a rapprochement between Japan and the Soviet Union with the help of Germany. As mentioned before, the navy had agreed to the Tripartite Pact out of political expediency, though it remained convinced that Japan would never be able to win a war against the United States. In March and April 1941, Matsuoka made a last-minute attempt to persuade the Germans to work toward rapprochement between Japan and the Soviet Union. It was already too late, however, and Germany, instead, encouraged Japan to attack Singapore, in order to prevent America's entry into the war. Undeterred by the unhelpful response of the Germans, Matsuoka stopped over in Moscow on the way back from Germany and signed a Soviet-Japan neutrality pact with Joseph Stalin on 13 April 1941.

Meanwhile, to prosecute its war of attrition in China, Japan had to do two things urgently: first, to cut off the main supply routes buttressing the Chiang Kai-shek regime, the French route from Indochina and the British route from Burma; second, to secure alternative sources of raw materials from the Dutch East Indies. In July, Japan invaded southern Indochina. On the Pacific side, tension was fast rising, and the United States imposed a complete oil embargo against Japan on 1 August 1941. Japan was feeling the pinch of the so-called ABCD encirclement (Americans, British, Chinese, and Dutch). Within Japan, prowar sentiment against the United States was rising daily. The final blow to the antiwar lobby in the Japanese government came with the Hull Note, which reiterated the principles of U.S. foreign policy on China, and a Japanese imperial conference (*gozen kaigi*) was held on 1 December 1941, which concluded that Japan would go to war against the United States, Britain, and the Netherlands on 8 December (Japan time). The inability of the Japanese to resolve the war in China satisfactorily eventually pushed them to open two further fronts in the Pacific and Southeast Asia.

Immediately after the Japanese attack on Pearl Harbor, the Americans and the British declared war on Japan on 8 December. The Japanese tried to consolidate the Tripartite relationship with Germany and Italy by signing an agreement on 11 December that prohibited any one country from concluding a separate peace. Furthermore, the three countries signed a military agreement on 18 January 1942. From the Japanese perspective, however, the Axis alliance simply prevented Japan from becoming isolated in the war, but did not provide much practical military cooperation, as Japanese and German interests did not necessarily coincide.

The story of the rapid Japanese advance in Southeast Asia and the Pacific during the one hundred days after Pearl Harbor is well known. The Japanese conquered Guam on 10 December, Wake Island on 23 December, Hong Kong on Christmas Day, Manila on 2 January 1942, and Singapore and Sumatra on 15 February. On the same day as the fall of Rangoon on 8 March, the Dutch, British, Australian, and U.S. forces surrendered to the Japanese in the Dutch East Indies. The fall of the European colonies in Southeast Asia resulted in a sudden increase in the number of prisoners of war, whose maltreatment by their Japanese captors continues to be a source of contention in the postwar era. The Japanese experienced a rude awakening, however, when the American Doolittle raid successfully penetrated Japanese airspace, and bombed Tokyo, Nagoya, and Kobe, among other cities. As in the case of the rapid Japanese expansion in China, the Japanese then faced the problem of how to defend the huge defense perimeter that had now expanded to include East Asia, almost all of Southeast Asia, and the Pacific. Henceforth, Japan's wartime actions centered on defending and retrenching its vastly overstretched perimeter.

World War II in Asia was a colonial war, with the Japanese trying to expand their colonial empire, whereas the British, French, and Dutch were fighting to hold onto their colonial possessions. Not only were these possessions important for Japanese prestige, but they also secured for Japan the crucial supply of raw materials that it desperately needed to continue its war on now multifarious fronts. Japanese nationalists insisted all along that the war in Southeast Asia was a "war of liberation of Asia from the yoke of Western colonialism." The Japanese government paid lip service to its grandiose and ill-conceived plan of conquering Asia under Japanese domination through the Greater East Asia Co-prosperity Sphere. Under the elaborate facade of the Co-prosperity Sphere, Japan gave nominal independence to Burma on 1 August 1943, and also to the Philippines. Malaya and Indonesia were considered to be too important as suppliers of raw materials and were kept under the direct military occupation of the Japanese forces. On 5 November 1943 Japan convened the Greater East Asia Conference, at which the heads of all the Japanese-occupied territories gathered in Tokyo. Although the Japanese had effectively replaced themselves as masters of the former Western colonies in Southeast Asia, the Japanese "interregnum" nevertheless had an impact on national liberation movements in these territories.

As early as November 1944, Stalin mentioned to Winston Churchill that the Soviet Union could defeat the Japanese. In fact, Stalin formally stated at the Yalta Conference in February 1945 that the Soviet Union would invade Japan within three months of the German defeat. The Soviet Union took unilateral steps to abrogate the neutrality pact with Japan on 5 April 1945, coming into effect one year later. On 7 May, Germany surrendered and Soviet forces occupied Berlin. By this time, Japan was the only Axis power holding out, and was completely isolated in the war. The Potsdam Declaration, issued on 26 July, called for unconditional surrender by Japan. True to his words, Stalin declared war on Japan on 8 August 1945, two days after the first atomic bomb was dropped on Hiroshima. After the atomic bombing of Nagasaki on 9 August, the Japanese decision makers desperately sought to end the war, despite the indefatigable wish of the army to fight to the bitter end. The

Shōwa emperor (Hirohito) made the announcement of unconditional surrender on 15 August 1945, notwithstanding a last-minute, desperate coup attempt by the army to prevent the surrender from taking effect. With defeat, the wartime Japanese empire vanished overnight, and the colonial struggle in Southeast Asia resumed under the former European "masters" once they, in their turn, had taken up again the reins of power where the Japanese had been turned out.

See also **Warfare; World War I; World War II.**

BIBLIOGRAPHY

Barnhart, Michael A. *Japan Prepares for Total War: The Search for Economic Security, 1919–1941.* Ithaca, N.Y., 1987.

Calvocoressi, Peter, Guy Wint, and John Pritchard. *Total War: The Causes and Courses of the Second World War.* Vol. 2: *The Greater East Asia and Pacific Conflict.* 2nd ed. London, 1989.

Dickinson, Frederick R. *War and National Reinvention: Japan in the Great War, 1914–1919.* Cambridge, Mass., 1999.

Iriye, Akira. *The Origins of the Second World War in Asia and the Pacific.* London, 1987.

———. *Japan and the Wider World: From the Mid-Nineteenth Century to the Present.* London, 1997.

Nish, Ian H. *Alliance in Decline: A Study in Anglo-Japanese Relations, 1908–1923.* London, 1972.

Thorne, Christopher. *The Limits of Foreign Policy: The West, the League, and the Far Eastern Crisis of 1931–1933.* London, 1972.

———. *Allies of a Kind: The United States, Britain, and the War against Japan, 1941–1945.* London, 1978.

NAOKO SHIMAZU

JARUZELSKI, WOJCIECH (b. 1923), Polish general and head of state.

Wojciech Witold Jaruzelski was a most unlikely candidate for becoming the leader of the Polish Communist Party and state. Born in a noble, land-owning family, he was given the first name of his grandfather, a fighter in the anti-Russian uprising of 1863 who was deported to Siberia; his father had volunteered to fight Bolsheviks in 1920. Wojciech went to a private Catholic school and was an altar boy and a boy scout. In September 1939 his family found itself in the Soviet zone of occupation. In June 1941 the family was deported to Siberia, where Wojciech worked hard clearing forest and lost his father (he visited his grave forty-eight years later). In 1943 he joined communist-organized Polish troops and was assigned to officers' school in Ryazan. He went into combat in July 1944, and with the Second Infantry Division he reached the Elbe River in May 1945.

The war ended, he decided to stay in the army. An intelligent and diligent officer and a Communist Party member since 1947, he advanced swiftly through the ranks and in 1956 was the army's youngest general. The brilliance of his career led to increasingly political positions: head of the Main Political Authority (a body responsible for propaganda and indoctrination in the armed forces) in 1960, member of the party Central Committee in 1964, chief of the General Staff in 1965 (the first non-Soviet in this post), minister of defense in 1968, and Politburo member in 1970. This made him politically co-responsible for the Polish army's participation in such actions as repression against student rebellion and an anti-Jewish purge in spring 1968, the invasion of Czechoslovakia (July 1968), and the bloody crushing of labor protests in December 1970. During the latter he supported removing Władysław Gomułka and making Edward Gierek the party leader, but he usually refrained from intraparty struggles. In 1973 he was awarded the highest general's rank.

In 1980–1981, when a severe economic crisis and challenge from the Solidarity movement almost destroyed the party rule, both party leaders and Moscow saw the army as the last solid element of the regime. Jaruzelski became prime minister in February 1981 and the party's first secretary in October, thus occupying the top positions in the army, government, and party. He called for political dialogue while completing preparations for martial law, which he imposed as head of the Military Council of National Salvation (WRON) on the night of 13 December 1981. This massive military and police crackdown, including the arrests of five thousand opposition and trade union leaders (ten thousand through December 1982) and the brutal crushing of strikes and protests, proved effective in the short term; the Solidarity movement lost the battle, but it went underground and persisted. Martial law made it possible to drastically decrease real wages and stabilize the economy, but economic and political reforms that could reinvigorate the regime did not follow. Until the late 1980s, political repression, the expansion of secret police, and aggressive propaganda went along with repeated gestures toward the Catholic Church, amnesty for Solidarity activists, half-hearted economic reforms (including more opportunities for private small business), and the restraining of party hard-liners. Jaruzelski left the post of minister of defense in 1983 and exchanged the post of prime minister for that of chairman of the State Council in 1985, but he continued to control the party and government.

When Mikhail Gorbachev gave the green light for reforms in the Soviet bloc, Jaruzelski was the first to take the opportunity. Increasingly aware of Poland's stagnation and afraid of a possible explosion of unrest, he sought ways out of the drift. Realizing that for deep economic reforms the government needed stronger support in Poland and in the West (especially after a new wave of strikes in 1988), he decided upon negotiations with the opposition, despite resistance by some hard-liners. The round table talks of spring 1989 led in June to the first competitive parliamentary elections since World War II, which, by the almost complete victory of Solidarity, brought the regime to a bloodless end and greatly contributed to similar dismantling across central Europe. In July, under a compromise with opposition leaders, the National Assembly elected Jaruzelski (by a one-vote margin) as president; in September he in turn approved the new, Solidarity-led cabinet of Tadeusz Mazowiecki. He did not run in the presidential elections next year and in December 1990 was succeeded by Lech Wałęsa. Jaruzelski withdrew from active politics. A few years later a parliamentary commission investigated his responsibility for the imposition of martial law. He also has faced criminal charges for the massacre of 1970 and for destroying Politburo files in 1989, with no consequences. He has remained the authority for the postcommunist Left; Polish public opinion remains strongly divided on his past record.

See also **Gierek, Edward; Gomułka, Władysław; Poland; Solidarity; Wałęsa, Lech.**

BIBLIOGRAPHY

Berger, Manfred E. *Jaruzelski*. Düsseldorf, Germany, and New York, 1990.

Berry, Lynn. *Wojciech Jaruzelski*. New York, 1990.

Kowalski, Lech. *Generał ze skazą. Biografia wojskowa gen. armii Wojciecha Jaruzelskiego*. Warsaw, 2001.

DARIUSZ STOLA

JASPERS, KARL (1883–1969), German psychiatrist and philosopher.

Karl Theodor Jaspers began his academic career as a psychiatrist, specializing in psychotherapy. Influenced by the phenomenology of the Austrian philosopher Edmund Husserl (1859–1938), Jaspers soon gravitated toward philosophy, desiring as he wrote in his *Philosophical Autobiography* to "develop methods which would enable us to comprehend man as a whole," and "to order knowledge guided by the methods through which it is gained—to learn to know the process of knowing" (Schilpp, pp. 19–20). Jaspers was eventually granted a chair in philosophy at the University of Heidelberg in 1922, where he remained until 1948.

Early in his philosophical career, Jaspers was labeled an "existentialist." Like Husserl's student Martin Heidegger (1889–1976), Jaspers rejected the label, but he employed categories later adopted by other continental existentialists such as *existence* or human being and *essence* or pure being. Even in his great work on psychology, *Psychologie der Weltanschauungen*, the basic questions and themes of existentialist philosophy were present: "about the situation of man and about his ultimate situations from which there is no escape (death, suffering, chance, guilt, struggle); about time and the multi-dimensional nature of its meaning; about the movement of freedom in the process of creating one's self" (Schilpp, p. 29). He more systematically worked these themes out in his *Philosophy*. For Jaspers, existence was "the unreflecting experience of our life in the world. . . . the reality which everything must enter so as to be real for us." Jaspers also employed the German word *Existenz*, a related category, about which he made several key points: "*Existenz* is not a kind of being; it is potential being. That is to say, I am not *Existenz* but

possible *Existenz*. I do not have myself, but come to myself." *Existenz* and freedom are interchangeable: "*Existenz* is freedom . . . a freedom not of its own making [but] only as the gift of Transcendence, knowing its donor. . . . There is no *Existenz* without Transcendence." (1932, p. 446)

Freedom is also the term that connects Jaspers's philosophy to religious thought. Especially after 1945, he sought to create a post-theist, post-atheist religiosity, embodied in "philosophical faith." Jaspers rejected authority, mysticism, and revelation in traditional religious thought and practice. Because it offers a direct and immediate "vertical" communication between the individual and the deity, religion allows individuals to lose themselves in the deity and leave the world in which they have only the advice of their friends and the debates of "horizontal" communication to inform their choices; thus, it is ultimately incompatible with freedom. Philosophy renounces religious immediacy, confronts mysticism and revelation, and asserts itself as *ethics*, or a philosophy of human conduct in the world. Jaspers proposed a "philosophical faith" instead, a faith without revelation, Church, or objective Transcendence. The philosopher, he claimed, embraces freedom and lives without "religious certitude." Rather than direct communication with a deity, Jaspers preferred "ciphers," ideas by which we try to represent to ourselves realities that cannot be grasped by thought. Transcendent reality, to be experienced by human beings, is manifested in ciphers. Examples of ciphers are the personal God, the one God, and the incarnate God. All relate to Transcendence, but none conceptualizes or encapsulates it (Jaspers, 1932, pp. 529, 206).

Beyond their relationship as philosophers of existence, Jaspers and Heidegger formed a close personal bond, which was broken only during the Third Reich. Whereas Jaspers rejected Nazism, and, along with his Jewish wife, became a victim of its racial policies, Heidegger embraced it, even becoming Nazi Rector of Freiburg University. After the war Heidegger never accepted any personal moral responsibility for Nazism and its attendant atrocities. Jaspers not only accepted personal responsibility but also demanded that all Germans assume guilt. With *The Question of German Guilt* (1946), Jaspers sought to explain the German catastrophe and lay the basis for national renewal.

Although he argued that the catastrophe resulted, in some measure, from the overall cultural crisis affecting the entire West, he focused on German responsibility. Jaspers objected to the superficial talk of "collective" guilt and tried, instead, to distinguish between four levels of guilt: criminal, political, metaphysical, and moral. Although the first three were important, the crucial level was moral guilt. Coming to terms with it entailed admitting that each individual was morally responsible for his or her actions, "including the execution of political and military orders." Because the jurisdiction for moral guilt rested with the individual conscience, "and in communication with my friends and intimates who are lovingly concerned about my soul," each German had to examine his or her own responsibility for the German catastrophe (Jaspers, 1948, pp. 28–29, 52–53, 60–61, 71, 62).

It was on the moral level that renewal had to begin as individuals recognized their guilt, came to terms with it, and made radical moral change. Individual moral reversal would then lead to collective transformation:

> the future depends upon the responsibility of the decisions and deeds of men and, in the last analysis, of each individual among the billions of men.... By his way of life, by his daily small deeds, by his great decisions, the individual testifies to himself as to what is possible. By this, his present actuality, he contributes toward the future. (Schilpp, p. 69)

With *The Question of German Guilt,* Jaspers became the moral voice of postwar Germany. However, he did not succeed in creating a national reappraisal of the Nazi past and left Germany for Basel, Switzerland, in 1948, feeling that he had largely failed in his role as public intellectual. He had even failed to convince Heidegger, his former friend and philosophical comrade-in-arms, to assume personal responsibility. Partly for this reason, Jaspers played an important role in Heidegger's dismissal as a professor at Freiburg after the war. He tried unsuccessfully several times thereafter to renew dialogue with Heidegger and to convince him to come to terms with his Nazism.

Their strained friendship was complicated still further by their very different relationship with Hannah Arendt (1906–1975), Heidegger's student and lover and Jaspers's student. Although

Heidegger and Arendt broke off their relationship, which remained especially strained after 1933, Arendt and Jaspers became lifelong friends and engaged in a vigorous exchange of letters and ideas, even after Arendt's emigration to the United States. In the *Correspondence,* one finds not only their individual ideas in conversation with each other but also, as Steven Aschheim has pointed out, "their evolving attempts to grasp, at ever-deeper levels, the nature and consequences of Nazism and the interrelated political metamorphoses of their thought" (pp. 97–98).

Between 1948, when he left Germany, and his death in 1969, Jaspers continued to write about German affairs, but he dedicated the remainder of his life to working out various themes in his philosophy. Jaspers's reputation as a philosopher has suffered neglect in the years since his death. However, his influence is widespread even beyond the German orbit. In addition to Arendt, those influenced by Jaspers include Jürgen Habermas, Hans-Georg Gadamer, the French existentialists, Paul Ricoeur, and many others.

See also **Arendt, Hannah; Existentialism; Heidegger, Martin.**

BIBLIOGRAPHY

Primary Sources

Jaspers, Karl. *Psychologie der Weltanschauungen.* Berlin, 1919.

———. *Philosophie.* 3 vols. Berlin, 1932.

———. *Man in the Modern Age.* Translated by Eden and Cedar Paul. London, 1933.

———. *The Question of German Guilt.* Translated by E. B. Ashton. New York, 1948.

———. *Philosophical Faith and Revelation.* Translated by E.B. Ashton. New York, 1967.

Jaspers, Karl, and Hannah Arendt. *Hannah Arendt/Karl Jaspers Correspondence 1926–1969.* Edited by Lotte Kohler and Hans Saner, translated by Robert and Rita Kimber. New York, 1992.

Secondary Sources

Aschheim, Stephen. *Culture and Catastrophe: German and Jewish Confrontations with National Socialism and Other Crises.* New York, 1996.

Clark, Mark. "A Prophet without Honour: Karl Jaspers in Germany, 1945–1948." *Journal of Contemporary History* 27, no. 2 (April 2002): 197–222.

Rabinbach, Anson. *In the Shadow of Catastrophe: German Intellectuals Between Apocalypse and Enlightenment.* Berkeley, Calif., 1997.

Schilpp, Paul. *The Philosophy of Karl Jaspers.* New York, 1957.

Wolin, Richard, ed. *The Heidegger Controversy.* Cambridge, Mass., 1991.

MARK W. CLARK

JAZZ. The diffusion of jazz in Europe was a major musical phenomenon of the twentieth century that combined creativity with "Americanization" of the musical culture. Jazz brought European music a new kind of acoustical freedom. What follows briefly develops the phases of this history at the expense of portraits of individual artists.

Jazz, black American music with African roots, developed at the end of the nineteenth century, predominantly in the southern United States. Its two principal roots were vocal—the religious spirituals and the profane blues. However, when this music spread to Europe in the first decade of the twentieth century, it was first exposed in orchestral form while retaining, from its vocal origins, an original and highly expressive instrumental performing style modeled on the human voice.

Several other attributes characterize early jazz heard in Europe after World War I. First, jazz is a physical and sensual music. Rhythmic structure plays a key role both in composition of the orchestra and in the structure of the musical pieces themselves. Indeed, a jazz band typically included a tripartite rhythm section of bass, drums, and guitar or banjo (sometimes piano), and a melodic section of one or two cornets, trombone, clarinet, and at times a violin. Rhythm was essential to the music, and "swing" became a defining element. Second, jazz was partly "functional," and the early jazz bands played a good deal of European dance music. Third, jazz is a "living" music rather than formally composed, an art in which performance is more important than composition. With improvisations, solos, and variations, the role of interpretation is paramount. Finally, jazz was also a music of black people. Race prejudice in Europe was much different from that found in the United States. Coming to popularity during the era of European colonialism, jazz acquired special status as a "roots" music and enjoyed the appeal of authenticity.

Jazz became popular in Europe in several phases. The first black musicians in Europe were American soldiers during World War I, most memorably those with the 369th Regiment known as the Harlem Hellfighters, and with the 350th Artillery Corps, called the Seventy Black Devils. In February and March 1918, the Hellfighters toured for six weeks, visiting some twenty-five French cities, though not exclusively playing jazz. Other groups about the same time, predominantly composed of white musicians, performed in London and Paris. In 1919 in London, the Swiss orchestral conductor Ernest Ansermet (1883–1969) heard the Will Marion Cook band with Sidney Bechet (1897–1959) and upon returning to the Continent praised their performance in the review *Revue romande.*

In the 1920s jazz was in vogue in Europe. In 1925 the musical review, *La revue nègre,* was a huge and scandalous success. European dance orchestras began including drums, banjos, and saxophones. Jazz triumphed at the music hall and significantly influenced classical musicians. A market developed for records from the United States.

Enthusiasm for jazz continued to spread in the 1930s. Some of the American jazz stars toured in Europe, including Louis Armstrong in 1932 and Duke Ellington in 1933. In 1932 a small group of enthusiasts in Paris formed the Hot Club of France (HCF), led by Hugues Panassié, whose mission it became to educate the public about jazz. Beginning in 1933, the HCF organized concerts and the next year started to issue recordings, organizing the record company Swing in 1937. It published a review, *Jazz Hot,* beginning in 1935. The quintet of the Hot Club of France with Stéphane Grappelli and Django Reinhardt was the first European group genuinely able to compete with American groups. Others would follow.

In Britain as well, an indigenous brand of jazz appeared in the 1930s. Musicians with a background in brass fanfare, such as Tommy McQuater and George Chisholm, began to play jazz, and some went on to record in New York—Spike Hughes, in 1933 with the Benny Carter Orchestra, is a good example. Although Germany prohibited

The quintet of the Hot Club de France c. 1934. From left: Stephane Grapelli, Joseph Reinhardt, Django Reinhardt, Louis Vola, Pierre Ferret. ©Bettmann/Corbis

jazz after Adolf Hitler came to power in 1933, jazz spread to Sweden, Denmark, and the Netherlands. During War World II, jazz benefited from overseas appeal as a symbol of liberty. After the war, jazz was welcomed on European radio stations, such as the Jazz Club on the BBC, and could be heard on stage in prestigious theater venues, such as the Salle Pleyel. Bebop, which became highly popular in the United States, also won passionate fans in Europe. Jazz in its various styles in the 1950s became part of the new style of sociability at that time, symbolic of the postwar recovery of musical freedom.

In the 1960s jazz musicians began reorienting their work toward investigations of sound and rhythm, questioning the nature of composed music. Free jazz, rock jazz, jazz fusion, and neobop helped broaden the audience and led to diversification of styles. Finally, beginning in the 1970s, jazz won institutional legitimacy. European festivals became an important showcase for musicians. In France, in particular, conservatories began to teach jazz, and the

Orchestre National de Jazz was formed, a durable unit of about twenty musicians with a distinctive sound. One should also mention the Académie de Jazz, founded in 1955, which dispenses prizes and awards.

Since the 1930s jazz has exercised tremendous influence on entertainment generally and has become an integral part of the artistic landscape in the broad sense of the term. By the end of the twentieth century, jazz had become world music.

See also **Americanization; Baker, Josephine; Popular Culture.**

BIBLIOGRAPHY

Delaunay, Charles. *Django, mon frère*. Paris, 1968.

Hodeir, André. *Hommes et problèmes du jazz*. Paris, 1954. Rev. ed., Marseille, 1981.

Malson, Lucien. *Histoire du jazz et de la musique afro-américaine*. Paris, 1994.

Panassié, Hugues. *Le jazz hot*. Paris, 1934.

———. *La véritable musique de jazz.* Paris, 1938. Rev. ed., Paris, 1946.

Stearns, Marshall Winslow. *The Story of Jazz.* New York, 1956.

Tournès, Ludovic. *New Orleans sur Seine: Histoire du jazz en France.* Paris, 1999.

SOPHIE A. LETERRIER

JEDWABNE. Jedwabne, or Yedwabne, is situated in the Mazowsze region of Poland, twenty kilometers northeast of the city of Łomża. When it received its town charter in 1736, Jedwabne had already been settled for at least three hundred years. Jews had come to Jedwabne from Tykocin and were initially subject to the Tykocin Jewish communal authority. In 1770, when a beautiful wooden synagogue was built in Jedwabne, 387 Jews lived there, out of a total population of 450. In 1913 the synagogue burned down, and in 1916 most of the town was consumed by fire. At the end of World War I, as a result of devastation and the Russian Jewish resettlement policy, the town's population shrank to about 700. The 1931 census figures from Jedwabne (which had a total population of 2,167) do not make it possible to calculate accurately how many Jews lived there on the eve of the Second World War. Low estimates put the number at about 1,000, but according to Jewish sources close to 1,500 Jews resided in Jedwabne at the time. On the eve of World War II, the town's total population reached its all-time peak, approximating 3,000.

Jedwabne Jews made a modest living in the interwar period as craftsmen and merchants and the town was known for its shoemakers. The last rabbi of Jedwabne, Avigdor Bialostocki, was well respected by Jews and non-Jews alike. Even though the Łomża area and the local clergy were overwhelmingly sympathetic to the right-wing National Democratic Party and aggressively anti-Semitic, anti-Jewish episodes in Jedwabne were limited to the usual boycotts of Jewish businesses and the spreading of nationalistic propaganda. No pogroms were recorded in the interwar period.

During World War II Jedwabne was initially under Soviet rule and lay a dozen kilometers from the demarcation line separating the Soviet and the German occupation zones. As a result, the town was overrun by German troops immediately after the Nazi attack against the Soviet Union in the summer of 1941.

In June 1941, the first assaults occurred against local communist sympathizers, including Jews. Soon this entire area, known as Podlasie, was engulfed in anti-Jewish violence, in which the local Polish population, alongside German Einsatzgruppen (special detachments), took part. In some two dozen villages and small towns, Poles assaulted and killed scores of their local Jewish neighbors.

The mass murder of the Jedwabne Jews on 10 July 1941, however, stands out for its scope and brutality. The total number of victims is difficult to establish with exactitude. Witnesses and the accused at the trial of twenty-two perpetrators held in Łomża in 1949 spoke of 1,500 murdered on that day. An investigation by the Institute of National Memory carried out in Poland in 2000–2002 concluded that "at least 340" people were killed. All sources are in agreement that the entire Jewish population of Jedwabne (with the exception of 100–150 people who managed to escape), together with scores of Jews from surrounding towns who had sought refuge in Jedwabne over the preceding days, were murdered. They were axed, drowned, stoned, knifed, and finally burned to death in a large barn—by their Polish neighbors.

A small detachment of the German gendarmerie that was in town, and a mobile SS or Gestapo unit that may have passed through town earlier in the day, encouraged local Poles to proceed with the killing. But the actual murder was carried out by the inhabitants. The town's Polish self-styled mayor and other municipal authorities coordinated the action.

Even though the local population knew all the details of the mass murder and, as journalists were to find out, spoke about it freely, Polish historiography and a monument put up in the town in the 1980s to commemorate the event attributed the massacre to German occupiers. Only after the Polish publication in May 2000 of the book *Neighbors,* in which the 10 July 1941 killing in Jedwabne was reconstructed in detail, was the general public in Poland made aware of the truth about the murder. A few months after the publication of *Neighbors,* an all-encompassing discussion erupted in the Polish mass media. Countless press and magazine articles, as well as radio and television programs, discussed the issue and its implications for Poles' understanding of their collective wartime heritage. Many among the general public, as well as intellectuals, and politicians on the liberal end of the spectrum, recognized that a nonnegligible portion of Polish society (though as a whole severely victimized by the Nazis) was also complicitous in the persecution of Jews during the war. The Institute of National Memory in Warsaw conducted a thorough investigation of the matter and published a fifteen-hundred-page dossier fully documenting the circumstances of the crime.

On the sixtieth anniversary of the murder, on 10 July 2001, a new monument truthfully commemorating the deed was unveiled in Jedwabne. During a solemn nationally televised ceremony, the president of Poland, Aleksander Kwasniewski, offered an apology before the assembled mourners, who included numerous descendants of the Jedwabne Jews invited by the Polish government for the occasion from all over the world.

See also **Babi Yar; Genocide; Holocaust; Poland; War Crimes.**

BIBLIOGRAPHY

Baker, Julius L., and Jacob L. Baker, eds. *Yedwabne History and Memorial Book.* Jerusalem, 1980.

Gross, Jan T. *Neighbors: The Destruction of the Jewish Community in Jedwabne, Poland.* Princeton, N.J., 2001.

Machcewicz, Pewal, and Krzysztof Persak, eds. *Wokół Jedwabnego.* 2 vols. Warsaw, 2002.

Polonsky, Antony, and Joanna B. Michlic, eds. *The Neighbors Respond: The Controversy over the Jedwabne Massacre in Poland.* Princeton, N.J., 2004.

JAN T. GROSS

JEWS. The history of the Jews in Europe since 1914 is centrally dominated by the Nazi Holocaust of 1933 to 1945, and especially by the "Final Solution," Adolf Hitler's attempt, between 1941 and 1945, literally to exterminate all of the Jews of Nazi-occupied Europe. As well, the historical evolution of European Jewry was shaped in major ways by World War I and the Bolshevik Revolution in Russia of 1917, and by the establishment of the State of Israel in 1948 and the impact of this event on the self-perception and identity of Jews around the world. Many internal trends—religious, socioeconomic, and political—also figured strongly in the transformation of the Jewish people in Europe in this period.

A number of factors set the Jews apart from nearly all other peoples in Europe and, indeed, elsewhere. For nearly two millennia Jews lacked a homeland of their own, always living as a separate community among the nations where they lived. Religious Jews always looked to Palestine, their ancient homeland from which they had been driven into worldwide exile by the Romans; from the mid-nineteenth century, many secular and some religious Jews favored the re-creation of a Jewish state in Palestine, a movement known as "Zionism." Nearly everywhere they lived, Jews attracted a good deal of hostility, often expressed in violent fashion. Anti-Semitism—hostility to Jews—was traditionally based in religious prejudice but, from the mid-nineteenth century, was reoriented in the form of ethnic and racial hostility to Jews, who were increasingly seen by anti-Semites as a malign and hostile ethnic community in their host nation. Jews themselves were also deeply divided. Most Jews in eastern Europe still spoke Yiddish, a dialect of German written in Hebrew letters, although the Zionist movement was in the process of reviving Hebrew (a Semitic rather than an Indo-European language) as the "authentic" language of the Jews. Millions of Jews had, through immigration, become acculturated to their homelands, and regarded themselves as English, French, German, or some other nationality, and were, by 1914, often indistinguishable from any of their fellow citizens. Jews spanned the political spectrum, although they were often seen as typically on the left. In eastern Europe, many Jews practiced the strictly Orthodox form of Judaism, although many forms of "modern Orthodoxy" or non-Orthodoxy were also practiced, especially in western Europe.

INTERWAR EASTERN AND CENTRAL EUROPE, 1914–1939

On paper, World War I produced considerable gains for the large Jewish populations of eastern and central Europe. Tsarist Russia, the main oppressor of Jewry before 1914, was swept away during the war, as were the multinational empires of central Europe where considerable anti-Semitism existed. Officially, their successor states were all democracies, and were all committed in their constitutions to granting equality for their minorities, including the Jews. The communist ideology of the Soviet Union attacked organized religion and the traditional economic role of the Jews, but also outlawed anti-Semitism and regarded the Jews as a distinctive nationality.

The reality proved to be quite different. Interwar eastern and central Europe saw a continuing decline in the political and economic status of the Jews, especially after 1929, while in 1933 Germany gave supreme power to the most fanatical and murderous anti-Semite in history.

Throughout eastern and central Europe, most of the post-1918 successor regimes were impoverished and increasingly hallmarked by ultranationalistic hostility to their Jewish minority (and to other ethnic minorities). The dream presented in 1918 by Wilsonian liberal idealism soon proved utterly chimerical.

By far the largest Jewish population in interwar Europe was found in Poland, whose Jewish population numbered about 2.9 million in 1921, 3.1 million in 1931, and about 3.3 million in 1939. While most lived in cities, even the largest Jewish urban centers were surprisingly small—there were about 353,000 Jews in Warsaw, the largest center, in 1931, and about 202,000 in Lodz, the second largest. Many Jews continued to live in shtetls, small Jewish towns or villages. Most Jews were engaged in commerce as small tradespeople, or in manufacturing, especially in the clothing trade. There was only a tiny Jewish professional class but a very large, often impoverished, working class. Apart from Galicia (where many Jews spoke German), about 90 percent of Poland's Jews spoke Yiddish.

Initially, the new Polish government was fairly friendly to its Jews, but it became increasingly and openly anti-Semitic, especially after about 1929. Jews were almost entirely excluded from government employment, even in the school system. During the 1930s, a plethora of extreme right-wing movements, many openly anti-Semitic, arose, and there emerged an endemic problem of constant anti-Semitic violence by right-wing thugs. Jews at university lectures were often forced to sit in so-called ghetto benches, segregated from Gentiles. Nevertheless, face-to-face relations between Jews and Poles were often good, and Poland was virtually the only eastern European country in the 1930s not to enact legislation to reduce Jewish participation in the economy or the professions. To Polish nationalists, the problem was that there were simply too many Jews in Poland, an unassimilable mass with an entirely different language, religion, and culture from the Polish majority. Many Polish nationalists therefore supported the Zionist movement, the aims of which included the emigration of large numbers of Jews from Poland. Only the emergence of Nazi Germany—whose racial ideology saw Poles as scarcely better than the Jews—as the main threat to Polish independence in the late 1930s brought the two groups together, on the eve of the destruction of most of Polish Jewry.

The Polish Jewish community responded to its situation by producing a range of political parties with radically differing ideologies, and it must be stressed that Polish Jewry (and, indeed, world Jewry) was extraordinarily disunified during the interwar years and had no consensual view on its endemic problems. There were three main ideological groupings among interwar Polish Jewry, whose views were totally distinctive. Probably the largest of these groupings was the Bund, the Jewish socialist party founded in 1897. The Bund sought an alliance between the Jewish and Polish working classes and was committed to Marxism, although it opposed Soviet communism. It advocated a secular, Yiddish-based culture in Poland and strenuously opposed the Zionist solution of mass migration to Palestine. Second in size were probably the Zionists, themselves divided into many rival factions with differing ideologies. Zionism viewed anti-Semitism as a constant feature of European society, caused by the "abnormal" social structure of Jewry, and sought to create a "normal" Jewish society in Palestine, founded in a Hebrew-based culture. The moderate mainstream advocated the gradual growth of a viable Jewish community there, while a right-wing faction headed by Vladimir Jabotinsky, the Revisionists,

Jews in London protest pogroms in Poland, 7 July 1919. ©BETTMANN/CORBIS

sought immediate large-scale Jewish settlement and independence. Another major faction in Zionism, Mizrachi, sought to create a largely religiously based society in Jewish Palestine. The third major grouping in Polish Jewish life was Agudas Israel, the strictly Orthodox party, which represented Poland's traditionally Orthodox community. Socially conservative, it (unlike Mizrachi) was also opposed to the creation of an independent Jewish state in the Holy Land, viewing its creation by secular politicians as sacrilegious. Polish Jewry was often said to be divided between advocates of "hereness" (*doikeyt*) and "thereness," that is, between those wishing to oppose anti-Semitism and poverty in Poland, and those advocating emigration.

While not as large or ideologically fractured as Polish Jewry, nearly all the other Jewish communities of eastern and central Europe met very similar problems. Hungary's 450,000 Jews were relatively assimilated and westernized, especially in Budapest, and were often prosperous. In the 1930s their situation rapidly deteriorated, as Admiral Miklós Horthy's right-wing regime increasingly came under Nazi influence. A series of laws enacted in 1938 and 1939 sought to place severe limits on the participation of Jews in managerial positions and the professions. Many on the Hungarian right never forgave the Jews for forming so prominent a part of the Marxist regime of Béla Kun, which had briefly come to power in 1919. Similar attempts to limit Jewish economic power and Jews' role in the professions during the 1930s, in the context of a Europe-wide rise in anti-Semitism, occurred in Romania, where 750,000 Jews lived; in Lithuania, where there were 160,000 Jews; and elsewhere. In this region, perhaps only democratic Czechoslovakia (with 350,000 Jews) was largely immune from these trends, especially what is now the Czech Republic. The almost universal deterioration of the condition of Jews in interwar central and eastern Europe was caused by traditional anti-Semitism greatly enhanced by the Great Depression, which in turn was enormously magnified by the support given by local fascists to Nazi Germany and the apparent success of the Hitler regime. As well, the closing of immigration barriers, especially to the United States from 1921 to 1924, meant that impoverished Jews (and Gentiles) could seldom emigrate, greatly increasing tensions.

By 1939, virtually all of central and eastern Europe was in the hands of fascist regimes friendly to Nazi Germany and bitterly hostile to Jews. In addition, between mid-1939 and the invasion of the Soviet Union in June 1941, vast tracts of eastern Europe, including eastern Poland and the Baltic states, were forcibly incorporated into the Soviet Union as a consequence of the German-Soviet Nonaggression Pact (1939). There, the Jewish populations were compulsorily Stalinized, entailing a large measure of what would now be termed cultural genocide. Nevertheless, right-wing anti-Semitism was also outlawed, and full employment raised living standards for the poorest Jews. Overall, however, the highly unsatisfactory situation of eastern and central European Jewry showed no signs of being ameliorated when the Nazi conquest of most of Europe brought about the mass murder of Europe's Jews.

JEWS IN WESTERN EUROPE, 1914–1939

The situation of Jews in the democratic states of western Europe—Britain, France, the Netherlands, and Belgium—was obviously better than that of Jews elsewhere in Europe. Assimilationist trends had been greatly enhanced by the participation of hundreds of thousands of Jews in World War I (as had occurred throughout Europe) and by the lack of vast numbers of alien-seeming strictly Orthodox Jews or Jewish revolutionaries. Britain, with 300,000 Jews, victorious in the war and with a prosperous middle class, largely eschewed extremism. The local fascist movement, the British Union of Fascists, headed by Sir Oswald Mosley, enjoyed only limited popular support. There was, in fact, little overt anti-Semitism in interwar Britain, and newsreels of Hitler's demented rantings genuinely appalled the British "establishment." In 1917 the British Cabinet, motivated by philo-Semitic as well as strategic factors, issued the Balfour Declaration, promising the creation of a Jewish national home in Palestine, which it was in the process of conquering from the Turks. During the interwar period, many of the leaders of the international Zionist movement were located in Britain, especially Chaim Weizmann, the head of the mainstream World Zionist Organization, who was an academic in Manchester. Nevertheless, many aspects of British policy toward the Jews have been questioned by historians, especially the pro-Arab stance the British government increasingly assumed toward Jewish immigration to Palestine, and the much-debated issue of whether more could have been done to rescue Jews from the Nazis. Anglo-Jewry was also itself deeply divided, with many of its assimilated leaders opposing more than a token commitment to Zionism.

France, with about 280,000 Jews, was host to a largely assimilated community. Its most prominent Jewish politician, Léon Blum (1872–1950), was premier of France from 1936 to 1937 and in 1938 was head of the "Popular Front" socialist government, which introduced many social reforms. Nevertheless, France was still deeply divided between those who accepted the legacy of the 1789 Revolution and those who rejected it. It had many more anti-Semites than Britain, centered in Action Française, an extreme right-wing authoritarian movement. The Vichy regime, which ruled as a Nazi puppet government for four years after the fall of France in June 1940, was marked by extreme anti-Semitism, although most French Jews managed to survive the Holocaust. Other western European democracies also experienced rising anti-Semitism, although, paradoxically, the Netherlands, which had a long history of toleration for its Jews, saw 80 percent of its Jewish population deported and murdered by the Nazis during the war, a higher percentage than elsewhere in western Europe.

THE HOLOCAUST: NAZI GERMANY, 1933–1939

Hitler and his National Socialist German Workers' Party, the Nazis, came to power in January 1933 in coalition with other right-wing parties whose leaders wrongly assumed that they could keep the worst excesses of the Nazis under control. Within a year or so Hitler had made himself the absolute dictator of Germany, assuming the title of *Führer* (leader) on the death of President Paul von Hindenburg in August 1934. Hitler's rule brought about an anti-Semitism as thorough and, eventually, as murderous, as any in history. Nevertheless, it is important to keep in mind that there was (in Karl Schleunes's phrase) a "twisted road to Auschwitz," and that the actual genocide of the Jews did not begin for more than eight years after the Nazis came to power. While Germany had always had a potent element of anti-Semitism, its Jewish community of 500,000 certainly did not feel itself living in a nation of pervasive anti-Semitism. The constitution of the Weimar Republic, which existed from 1918 until 1933, had removed all barriers to the full participation of Jews in German life, and the Weimar period was something of a golden age of Jewish achievement in science and cultural life. Hitler's anti-Semitism, which eventually brought about the murder of millions of Jews not merely in Germany but throughout Europe, was also categorically more extreme than any form of anti-Semitism in modern history. Jews figured in Hitler's worldview as a demonic force, a vast, all-powerful international conspiracy everywhere working to control the world and undermine Germany and its "Aryans." Historians simply cannot fully explain insanity of this kind and have also been baffled as to how a civilized nation came to embrace a madman with a demented ideology, resulting in millions of ordinary Germans losing their lives in the war of conquest that Hitler unleashed.

It is customary to point to three major turning points in the deterioration of the Jewish position in Nazi Germany. First, shortly after Hitler came to power, most Jews were removed from the German civil service and from the universities. This began the exodus of Germany's renowned Jewish scholars and scientists such as Albert Einstein to the English-speaking world, to the immense advantage of the latter. Second, in September 1935 the so-called Nuremberg Laws were enacted. These defined who was legally considered to be a Jew (broadly, anyone with two or more Jewish grandparents), excluded Jews from German citizenship, and prohibited all extramarital relations between Jews and non-Jews. The process also began of systematically removing Jews from the German economy and the professions. The most decisive prewar turning point came in early November 1938 with the so-called *Kristallnacht* (Night of

Broken Glass). Following the shooting of a German official in Paris by a Jewish youth, the Nazis unleashed an orgy of anti-Semitic violence throughout Germany, in which nearly two hundred synagogues (previously untouched) were set on fire and hundreds of Jewish shops burned and looted. At least ninety Jews were killed and thousands taken to concentration camps (that is, to prison camps such as Dachau in Germany used by the Nazis to hold their political opponents; these were not the same as the wartime extermination camps such as Auschwitz, where millions were deliberately murdered, which were in Poland). Germany's Jews rightly took *Kristallnacht* as a signal that no future existed for them in Nazi Germany, and tens of thousands emigrated as quickly as they could. (Previously, emigration was surprisingly limited.) Probably no more than 185,000 Jews (out of the 500,000 there in 1933) remained in Germany in its 1933 boundaries by the outbreak of the war.

Between March 1938 and the outbreak of World War II in September 1939, Austria and the Sudetenland (comprising a large portion of what is now the Czech Republic) were annexed by Germany, adding about 320,000 additional Jews to Hitler's anti-Semitic realm. About two-thirds of Austrian Jewry managed to emigrate in the short period after March 1938 and the outbreak of the war, as well as about 26,000 Czech Jews.

THE HOLOCAUST: THE FINAL SOLUTION, 1939–1945

The period between September 1939 and the end of 1941 saw Nazi Germany secure hegemony throughout almost the whole of continental Europe, ruling directly, or through puppet or allied governments, virtually the entire continent from the Pyrenees to the gates of Moscow. As a result, millions of Jews fell into Hitler's hands or lived in regimes under his thumb, probably eight or nine million Jews in all. This situation was quite different from that of the 1930s, when the Nazis ruled only in Germany and had no direct control over Jews elsewhere. In contrast, by the end of 1941, nearly every center of Jewish life in Europe had become subject to the will of Hitler and the Nazis.

By May 1945, when Nazi Germany surrendered, at least five million Jews had died at the

A Jewish family in Amsterdam leave their house after being arrested and designated for deportation to a concentration camp in Poland, June 1943. ©BETTMANN/ CORBIS

hands of the Nazis, the greatest catastrophe in Jewish history and the defining event in European Jewish life in modern times. The Holocaust, as it is generally known (it is also widely known by the term the Nazis gave it, the "Final Solution," that is, of the "Jewish question in Europe," and it is also known as the *Shoah,* the Hebrew term for "catastrophe"), has become one of the best-known events in modern history and certainly the most infamous. Nevertheless, historians have endlessly debated almost all aspects of the Holocaust, many of which remain controversial and contested.

Because so much has been written on the Holocaust, only a brief summary of its main events will be given here. Between the start of the war and the invasion of the Soviet Union in June 1941, most Jews in Poland were herded into sealed ghettos, where tens of thousands died of disease and malnutrition. Almost everywhere else in Europe subject to Nazi influence, the situation of the

Jews also deteriorated still further, Jews becoming subject to an ever-increasing flood of anti-Semitic legislation in countries ranging from France to Romania. At this stage, it appears that the Nazis intended to deport all of Europe's Jews to Madagascar. With the invasion of the Soviet Union in June 1941, however, the Nazis, working through the SS and its accomplices, began a campaign of the mass murder of Jews (and other groups such as the Gypsies), initially restricting these killings to adult males but, by late 1941, encompassing all Jews who fell into Nazi hands in the USSR. The mass killings of Jews, generally in fields and pits at the edges of towns and cities, were carried out by the SS Einsatzgruppen, generally by machine-gunnings. The number of Jews who perished at the hands of the Einsatzgruppen has been estimated at between 600,000 and 1.3 million. From early 1942, Hitler and the Nazis embarked on a program of the total annihilation of Jewry in Europe, killing Jews in vast numbers by transporting them to gas chambers at six extermination camps in Poland, of which Treblinka, Belzec, and, above all, Auschwitz in southern Poland were the largest and most infamous. Certainly 2.5 million or more Jews—as well as tens of thousands of Gypsies, Poles, Russians, and others—were murdered in these six camps, among them an estimated 960,000 at Auschwitz. The Nazi SS, headed by Heinrich Himmler, was chiefly responsible for carrying out the Holocaust. Jews perished in other ways as well: in German concentration camps such as Buchenwald, in slave labor camps, and in pogroms carried out independently by regimes allied to Nazi Germany such as in Croatia and Romania.

As noted, many aspects of the Holocaust remain contentious. For instance, there is no consensus understanding of Hitler's role in directing the Holocaust, although he must certainly have instigated it and ordered the diversion of considerable resources necessary to carry it out in wartime. Nor is there an agreed understanding of when the decision to kill literally all of Europe's Jews was undertaken, although a consensus has emerged among historians writing since about 1990 that this decision was not made until some months after the invasion of the Soviet Union, or possibly later. (It was previously believed that the so-called

Wannsee Conference of January 1942, held by senior Nazis in suburban Berlin, was crucial to this decision, but most historians now discount its key importance.) Jews often resisted, and, in the Warsaw Ghetto Uprising of April to May 1943, put up a heroic struggle. Nevertheless, terrorized and lacking military leadership or armaments, successful resistance proved impossible.

As a general rule, the closer one comes to the Polish-Russian heartland of eastern European Jewry, the more comprehensive the slaughter became. In general the survival rate of Jews in western Europe (apart from the Netherlands) and the Balkans was higher. There, anti-Semitic fascist regimes often drew the line at genocide and offered some measure of protection to their Jews, although only the liberation of Europe in 1944 and 1945 allowed the survival of any Jews at all. That any Jews survived World War II in Nazi-occupied Europe was ultimately due to the success of the Allied armies at destroying the Nazi regime.

European Jewry was so decimated by the Holocaust that it has arguably never recovered and arguably never will. At the end of World War II, large Jewish communities remained only in the Soviet Union in areas not conquered by the Nazis; in Romania and Bulgaria; in Budapest; and in France and Belgium. Probably 80 to 90 percent of Polish Jewry, the largest in Europe, perished in the Holocaust, as well as the bulk of the Jewish population in most other continental European states. After 1945, European Jewry ceased to play a leadership role in the Jewish world, which was increasingly bifurcated between American Jewry and the State of Israel, founded in 1948, with an entirely new set of contexts and conflicts.

JEWS IN THE SOVIET UNION

Although much reduced in size by the granting of independence to Poland and other states, in the 1920s the Jewish population of the Soviet Union totaled about 2.6 million. Jews formed a disproportionate component of the leadership elite of the new Soviet regime, with figures such as Leon Trotsky (1879–1940) considered to be powerful and highly visible members of the new government. The large number of Jews in the Bolshevik government was seized upon by right-wingers and anti-Semites as evidence of a Jewish conspiracy, and

was one of the main factors in Hitler's ideology. Nevertheless, the new government showed itself to be anything but friendly to the interests of most Jews. It vigorously persecuted Orthodox Judaism, closed down most synagogues, confiscated Jewish property, and suppressed Zionists and Bundists. To be sure, the new regime also improved the situation of Jews in some ways. All forms of institutionalized anti-Semitism, ubiquitous under the tsars, now vanished, and many opportunities opened for Jews for the first time. To be "Jewish" was legally regarded as being a member of a distinctive nationality such as "Ukrainian," and some forms of Yiddish cultural life were allowed to continue. There was considerable growth in the Jewish populations of Moscow, Leningrad, and other large cities as Jews took advantage of opportunities in these locales. The negative trends in the Soviet treatment of Jews were greatly accentuated under the rule of Joseph Stalin (c. 1928–1953), who emerged as the Soviet Union's all-powerful ruler. Under Stalin, the Jewish proportion of the Soviet leadership elite declined sharply, although Jews continued to be overrepresented in managerial positions. Along with millions of others, tens of thousands of Soviet Jews certainly perished in Stalin's purges. By 1941, thanks to its annexation of large parts of eastern Europe as a result of the German-Soviet Nonaggression Pact, the Jewish population of the USSR had risen to over five million.

The Holocaust and the tremendous losses suffered by the Soviet army during World War II meant that, in its post-1945 boundaries, the Jewish population of the Soviet Union totaled about 2.3 million in the 1950s. In the last years of his rule, Stalin's paranoid anti-Semitism, always present, increased markedly, and there was severe repression of most remaining Jewish institutions and activists during the so-called Black Years, from 1946 to 1953. While the Soviet Union had supported the creation of the State of Israel in 1948, Stalin turned sharply against pro-Zionist Jews, considering them disloyal. There is some evidence that Stalin wished to deport large numbers of Jews from Moscow and Leningrad to Siberia when he suddenly died in March 1953.

The years after Stalin's death saw a softening of the condition of Jews under Nikita Khrushchev, but then another worsening of their condition under the rule of Leonid Brezhnev (1964–1982), a period that came to be marked by open anti-Semitism in such areas as the admission of Jews to universities. Many Soviet Jews rediscovered their roots and wished to emigrate to Israel or to the West. The USSR consistently favored the Arabs in the Middle Eastern conflict, especially after 1967, and most Jews who expressed a wish to emigrate to Israel lost their jobs. These "refuseniks" (as they were known in the West) attracted worldwide support during the 1970s and 1980s. The fight against Soviet anti-Semitism became a rallying point for Western Jews, liberals, and conservatives.

Although 250,000 Soviet Jews were allowed to emigrate in the early 1970s thanks to an agreement made by U.S. President Richard Nixon, real relief for Soviet Jewry had to await Mikhail Gorbachev's perestroika in the mid-1980s and the overthrow of the Soviet Union in 1991. The new Russian Federation and other successor states to the USSR adopted liberal constitutions and permitted unlimited emigration. In the decade or so after 1991, over one million Jews left the former Soviet Union, making for a much-reduced Jewish presence, although those remaining were now free to practice their religion and culture for the first time in generations.

The course of Jewish life in the Soviet Union's Eastern European satellites followed much the same course as in the USSR. The Communist regimes that seized power at the end of World War II often contained disproportionate numbers of Jewish Communists, who were almost all removed from power during the Black Years. Some, such as Rudolf Slánský, the former secretary general of the Czechoslovak Communist Party, were executed for being "Zionists." Most of the remaining Jewish populations of countries such as Romania fled to Israel in the years after 1948, or following the abortive revolutions such as in Hungary in 1956. Only tiny numbers of Jews remained when a free Jewish life became possible in the 1990s.

THE POST-1945 ERA IN EUROPE

The remnant of European Jewry that managed to survive the Holocaust was more numerous in some parts of Europe than in others. About 500,000

Jews survived in Romania and Bulgaria, 200,000 in Hungary, 200,000 in France, and up to 400,000 of Poland's 3.3 million Jews. In 1945 and 1946 many survivors, especially Poles, streamed into displaced persons camps in western Germany, temporarily increasing Germany's Jewish population to 250,000. The creation of the State of Israel altered the Jewish problematic in a fundamental way, giving the Jews an independent national existence they had lacked since Roman times. About 500,000 European Jews, chiefly from Poland and the Balkans, migrated to Israel during the first few years of its existence. Further waves followed, as well as considerable emigration to the English-speaking world. As a result, by 2004 Europe's Jewish population was only a fraction of what it had been even during the immediate postwar stage. The largest Jewish communities in Europe in 2004 were in France (700,000), the former states of the USSR (500,000), Britain (350,000), and Germany (120,000). In contrast to the general trend, considerable Jewish immigration to France from North Africa occurred during the late 1950s and early 1960s, as well as from Russia to Germany after 1990.

Knowledge of the unparalleled horrors of the Nazi period discredited old-style racist anti-Semitism in western Europe, and was increasingly made illegal. The period from about 1950 until the 1970s in fact saw something of the near-universal championing of the Jews in western Europe, which peaked at the time of the Six-Day War between Israel and the Arabs in 1967, when Israel's very existence appeared threatened.

The period since about 1970, however, has seen the growth of a new form of hostility to the Jews, virulent anti-Zionism that is intensely critical of Israel's actions toward the Palestinians and, in its extreme form, opposed to Israel's existence. This anti-Zionism has been strongly associated with the political far left, as well as with the ever-increasing Muslim presence in Europe. It is also closely associated with virulent anti-Americanism and was obviously linked with it during such events as the Iraq War launched in 2003.

On the other hand, life for individual Jews and for Europe's Jewish communities was not marked by endemic anti-Semitism. In 2004 the leader of the British Conservative Party and the premier of

Russia were Jews, as had been a recent premier of France and a head of the European Parliament. Paradoxically, while in some respects Jewish life in Europe had become freer than ever before in history, there were fewer Jews there to enjoy this freedom, and a pervasive sense that all was still not well.

See also **Anti-Semitism; Holocaust; Israel; Minority Rights; Nazism; Zionism.**

BIBLIOGRAPHY

Browning, Christopher R. *The Origins of the Final Solution.* Lincoln, Nebr., 2004. Authoritative account of the period from 1939 to 1942.

Friedländer, Saul. *Nazi Germany and the Jews.* Vol. 1: *The Years of Persecution, 1933–1939.* London, 1997. Much-praised account of what Nazi rule meant for Germany's Jews.

Hilberg, Raul. *The Destruction of the European Jews.* 3rd ed. 3 vols. New Haven, Conn., 2003. The most comprehensive account of the Holocaust.

Kochan, Lionel, ed. *The Jews in Soviet Russia since 1917.* 3rd ed. Oxford, U.K., 1978. A wide-ranging collection of essays by experts.

Levin, Nora. *The Jews in the Soviet Union since 1917: Paradox of Survival.* 2 vols. London, 1990. Comprehensive account of Soviet Jewish life.

Lindemann, Albert S. *Esau's Tears: Modern Anti-Semitism and the Rise of the Jews.* Cambridge, U.K., 1997. Very comprehensive, controversial history of modern anti-Semitism.

Marcus, Joseph. *Social and Political History of the Jews in Poland, 1919–1939.* Berlin, 1983. Sophisticated account of Polish Jewish life; very valuable.

Mendelsohn, Ezra. *The Jews of East Central Europe between the World Wars.* Bloomington, Ind., 1983. Truly outstanding account of interwar European Jewry.

Rubinstein, Hilary L., Dan Cohn-Sherbok, Abraham J. Edelheit, and W. D. Rubinstein. *The Jews in the Modern World.* London, 2002. Comprehensive textbook on Jewish history since 1750.

Rubinstein, W. D. *A History of the Jews in the English-Speaking World: Great Britain.* Basingstoke, U.K., 1996. Focuses on the post-1850 period and Britain's relative lack of anti-Semitism.

Ruppin, Arthur. *The Jewish Fate and Future.* Translated by E. W. Dickes. London, 1940. Immensely valuable demographic and socioeconomic account of world Jewry on the eve of the Holocaust.

Schechtman, Joseph B. *The Vladimir Jabotinsky Story.* 2 vols. New York, 1956–1961. Reprint, as *The Life and Times of Vladimar Jabotinsky,* with a foreword by Menachem

Begin. Silver Spring, Md., 1986. Excellent biography of Zionist leader; describes interwar Poland well.

Schleunes, Karl A. *The Twisted Road to Auschwitz: The Nazi Policy towards German Jews.* Urbana, Ill., 1970. Examines the many changes in Nazi policy toward the Jews.

Vital, David. *A People Apart: The Jews in Europe, 1789–1939.* Oxford, U.K., 1999. Lengthy general account covering all of Europe.

Webber, Jonathan, ed. *Jewish Identities in the New Europe.* London, 1994. Essays on contemporary European Jewry.

WILLIAM D. RUBINSTEIN

JOHN XXIII (1881–1963), pope from 1958 to 1963.

Pope John XXIII was born Angelo Guiseppe Roncalli in Sotto il Monte, Bergamo, on 25 November 1881 to a large family of poor peasants. After attending sseminaries in Bergamo (1892–1900) and Rome (1901–1905) he graduated as a doctor in theology. He was ordained a priest on 10 August 1904. From 1905 until 1914 he was secretary to the bishop of Bergamo, Giacomo Radini Tedeschi (1857–1914), who became his mentor in pastoral leadership. In those years he also lectured on church history in the priestly seminar of Bergamo and did historical research on the life of Carlo Borromeo (1538–1584), the sixteenth-century archbishop of Milan who played a model role in the implementation of the decrees of the Council of Trent. During World War I Roncalli served as a hospital orderly and as a military chaplain. In 1921 he went to Rome as director of the papal missionary works in Italy. In 1925 he was ordained a bishop and appointed (until 1952) to the diplomatic service of the pope. First he was apostolic visitor (later apostolic delegate) in Bulgaria, next from 1935 until 1944 apostolic delegate in Greece and Turkey. In 1944 he became papal nuncio in Paris. In 1953 he was created a cardinal and named as patriarch in Venice.

Following the death of Pius XII (r. 1939–1958), Roncalli was elected as pope on 28 October 1958 at the age of seventy-seven. He was expected to be a transitory pope with a short reign. His diplomatic experience and his moderate position within the conclave (he did not belong to the outspoken progressive or conservative wing) contributed to his election. Most of all however he was elected because of his contrast with the hieratic and rigid profile of his predecessor. Being a good pastor and a cordial and discreet personality, he was able to provide the church leadership with a new image. It was hoped that he would free the church from the stagnation that had characterized the last years of the pontificate of Pius XII, but at the same time it was generally expected that his church policy would mostly line up with that of Pius XII.

To some extent John XXIII met those moderate expectations. He normalized and reactivated the Curia by filling long-standing vacancies and reinstating regular audiences with the curial functionaries. Decentralization, deliberation, and shared responsibility were features of his governing style. By creating new cardinals (exceeding the traditional number of seventy) he rejuvenated and internationalized the consistory. But he entrusted key positions within the Curia to intimates of Pius XII. He appointed his former chief and opponent Domenico Tardini (1888–1961) as Secretary of State while Alfredo Ottaviani (1890–1979) retained his powerful position as head of the Holy Office. Mainly due to the initiative of the latter Roman congregation Pius XII's decisions and directions were reaffirmed, sometimes even strengthened: the condemnation of the worker-priests, the excommunication of communists, the warning against critical bible exegesis and against the evolutionary vision of Teilhard de Chardin (1881–1955). The apostolic constitution *Veterum Sapientiae* of 1962 underscored the importance of Latin as the language of the liturgy. The pope was a devout man, with a traditionally oriented spirituality.

From the onset of his pontificate, however, John XXIII showed a readiness to stress the character and goals of his pontificate. The choice of his name marked a break with the Pius tradition: since the fifteenth century no pope had been called John. More than his predecessors John XXIII regarded himself as Bishop of Rome and demonstrated this by solemnly taking hold of the Bishop's Church (St. John Lateran) and making visits to Roman hospitals and prisons. He kept a distance from the interference of the Vatican in Italian politics. On 25 January 1959 he astonished his church and the world with the announcement of an ambitious threefold program for his pontificate: the convening of an ecumenical council, the organization of a Roman synod, and the revision of canon law.

The convening of the Second Vatican Council was the most important achievement of the pontificate of John XXIII. Its goal, as put forward by the pope, was an *aggiornamento,* an adaptation of the church to "the signs of the time." After the announcement, the preparation was started in the summer of 1959. John XXIII solemnly opened the Council on 11 October 1962 and watched (with reserved distance and respect for the freedom of the Council fathers) the progress of its first session until 8 December 1962. The next three sessions (1963, 1964, and 1965) proceeded under the pontificate of his successor Paul VI (r. 1963–1978). The Council was one of the most outstanding events in the twentieth-century Catholic Church. It provoked not only a "new Pentecost" within the church itself, but also furthered its rapprochement to the other Christian churches and its openness to the world.

John XXIII devoted his pontificate to unity and peace. He proclaimed himself a shepherd of his flock but also of all humankind. In 1960 he established within the Curia the Secretariat for Christian Unity, in order to promote good relations with the Protestant, Anglican, and Orthodox churches. The pope contributed to the détente between East and West by intervening at crucial moments in the Cold War (the Berlin Crisis in 1961, the Cuban Missile Crisis in 1962). He improved relations between the Vatican and the Soviet Union. In spring 1963 the daughter and son-in-law of the Soviet leader Nikita Khrushchev (r. 1953–1964) were received in papal audience. Peace, social welfare, human rights, and just treatment of the developing countries were central themes in his most important encyclicals: *Mater et Magistra* (1961) and *Pacem in Terris* (1963). The pope opened the way for peaceful cooperation between Catholics and communists by making a distinction between a heretical philosophical system and its possible practical goals and between error and those who err. *Pacem in Terris* was the first papal encyclical directed not only to the Catholic believers, but to "all men of good will." It appeared a few weeks before the death of the pope on 11 April 1963. The pontificate of John XXIII left a deep impression on the Catholic

Church. He is remembered as "the pope of the council" and "the good pope." He was beatified in September 2000.

See also **Catholicism; Vatican II.**

BIBLIOGRAPHY

Primary Sources

Pope John XXIII. *Journal of a Soul.* Translated by Dorothy White. New York, 1965.

Secondary Sources

Alberigo, Giuseppe. *Johannes XXIII: Leben und wirken des Konzilspapstes.* Mainz, Germany, 2000.

Alberigo, Giuseppe, ed. *Jean XXIII devant l' histoire.* Paris, 1989.

Benigni, Mario, and Goffredo Zanchi. *John XXIII: The Official Biography.* Boston, Mass., 2002.

Cahill, Thomas. *Pope John XXIII.* New York, 2002.

Hales, E. E. Y. *Pope John and His Revolution.* London, 1965.

Hebblethwaite, Peter. *John XXIII: Pope of the Council.* London, 1984.

Trevor, Meriol. *Pope John.* London and New York, 1967.

Zizola, Giancarlo. *The Utopia of Pope John XXIII.* Maryknoll, N.Y., 1978.

LIEVE GEVERS

JOHN PAUL II (Karol Wojtyła; 1920–2005), pope from 1978 to 2005.

Karol Wojtyła was born on 18 May 1920 in Wadowice, Poland, a town near Kraków. A bright student, he studied philosophy before attending the underground seminary run by the archbishop of Kraków during World War II. A worker by day, he studied in the evenings. Ordained to the priesthood on 1 November 1946, he entered the Angelicum in Rome where he received a master's degree in theology, then a doctorate under the supervision of the Thomist priest Réginald Garrigou-Lagrange. Returning to Poland in 1948, he was active in the Kraków diocese and several years later continued his education; the bishop allowed him two years to prepare his aggregation in theology, opening up the possibility of a scholarly life within the church. He taught at the Catholic University of Lublin and at the Catholic seminary in Kraków from 1954, and held the chair of ethics at the Catholic University from 1956.

Appointed auxiliary bishop in Kraków on 4 July 1958, Wojtyła was consecrated archbishop on 13 January 1964. This appointment enabled him to take part in the final session of the Second Vatican Council, and in 1967 Pope Paul VI (r. 1963–1978) consecrated him cardinal. Wojtyła made common cause with the Polish primate in defying communist authorities. As cardinal, he also traveled abroad, developing solid contacts within the church.

When John Paul I died, and the college of cardinals needed to choose a successor, Wojtyła was not an obvious choice. He emerged on the eighth ballot. It could be speculated that Wojtyła's impressive education and linguistic facility—he could speak at least eight languages—and his natural charisma persuaded the conclave to elect him pope on 16 October 1978. He was the first non-Italian pontiff since Adrian VI (r. 1522–1523) and the first Polish pope in history.

John Paul II's first homily, in which he stated, "Do not be afraid! Open wide the doors for Christ," became emblematic of his pontificate. Clearly influenced by two conciliary popes, John XXIII (r. 1958–1963) and Paul VI, Wojtyła hoped to reinforce the volunteer and philanthropic aspects of the church as well as to make his mark with a balanced reading of the advances in church doctrine emerging from the Second Vatican Council.

Redemptoris Hominis, John Paul's programmatic first encyclical (published 15 March 1979), emphasized that the church's mission and human dignity are based on the mystery of Christ the redeemer. In thus proclaiming the integral notion of the human person, John Paul II presented himself as a defender of human dignity. He descried what he described as a "culture of death" in the *Evangelium Vitae* of 25 March 1995; he condemned euthanasia and abortion while promoting the value of conjugal love, inspired by the encyclical of his predecessor, Paul VI, *Humanae Vitae* (1968).

A force for unity, early in his pontificate John Paul II confronted the deep challenge of liberation theology. He denounced reinterpretation of scripture that cast Jesus as a political revolutionary, and

Pope John Paul II talks to reporters on a plane returning from a visit to the Philippines and Japan, 26 February 1981. ©HENRI BUREAU/CORBIS SYGMA

remained on guard against any such perspective, which he believed had the potential for creating divisions among Latin American Catholics.

Viewing himself as a pope of peace, John Paul II developed the Vatican's diplomatic initiatives and charitable activities. He spoke out "to defend human rights, in particular religious freedom," which he advocated as a universal human need. He spoke in defense of victims and refugees, and offered a reminder that principles of justice and equality must be the bases of international law and its application.

As the first pope from inside the Iron Curtain, John Paul was actively hostile to communism. Already engaged in political struggles against the Polish communist regime as priest and prelate, his activism only increased as pontiff. He supported Solidarity, the Polish independent labor union, and was a friend to the anticommunist movement

in the Soviet Union until its collapse and the fall of the Berlin Wall in 1989.

John Paul II was also a bridge-builder of sorts. He organized the first World Day of Prayer for Peace at Assisi, Italy, on 27 October 1986 and a second one on 24 January 2002, shortly after the terrorist attacks on the United States on 11 September 2001. Bringing together leaders of the major Christian and non-Christian religions, he promoted nonviolence and urged "a courageous choice of love, a choice that, implies effective protection of human rights and a firm commitment for justice and harmonious development." John Paul II thus became closely associated with ecumenicalism and interfaith dialogue. While working on a rapprochement with the Anglican and Orthodox churches, he also strengthened relations between the Catholic Church and non-Christian religions, particularly Judaism.

Less than a year after his election, the pope traveled to the former concentration camp of Auschwitz-Birkenau in Poland. This was a clear indication of the sovereign pontiff's interest in reaching out to the Jewish people. It was followed in April 1986 by John Paul II's visit to the Synagogue of Rome—the first official papal visit to a synagogue ever. These two occasions symbolized the Catholic Church's efforts to enhance its understanding of the Shoah and to express its love and respect for the Jewish people. They are harbingers of two later statements from the Vatican. The first, "We Remember: A Reflection on the Shoah" (1998), acknowledged the historical participation of Christians in the genocide and therefore called on each Christian to reflect on the significance of the Holocaust. The second, "The Jewish People and Their Sacred Scriptures in the Christian Bible" (2001), proposed a way of reading the Bible that, though Christian, implied no trace of contempt for the Jewish people. Taken together, these acts and texts depict a Catholic Church prepared to revise its relationship to the Jews in a way that includes esteem and dialogue.

John Paul traveled widely, and his various pilgrimages highlighted all the themes of his pontificate; he was above all evangelistic. He launched a "return to yourself" campaign in 1982 encouraging Europeans to recover their faith, to "discover their origins, revive their roots" and in 1985 inaugurated World Youth Day. His greatest effort to reach out to other faiths came in the Holy Land during the jubilee pilgrimage in 2000. In the Middle East, riven with conflict, he took considerable personal risks to meet with religious leaders from all corners of the earth, delivering his message of peace and hope, the leitmotiv of his pontificate.

Whether John Paul II should be considered a modern or conservative pope depends on where in the world the question is asked. The exceptional length of his pontificate—almost twenty-seven years—and the multiplicity of the issues he addressed during that time certainly make any simple answer impossible. In a world he viewed as contaminated by ethical relativism, John Paul II above all wanted to reassert clear principles, the signature of life and human dignity. He spoke out for a universal church clear about its beliefs and its

message. He symbolized the rejection of communism in Eastern Europe, which led to the end of the Cold War and to the Soviet system itself. (It is possible the Soviet secret services were behind a failed assassination attempt in 1981.) He was a statesman, but much more than that. He embodied the church at a moment when it returned to older values but reconfigured them in new forms. Whether John Paul II was indeed the conscience of humanity in an era of alienation and conflict, only time will tell.

See also **Catholicism; Poland; Solidarity.**

BIBLIOGRAPHY

Crosby, John F., and Gneuhs, Geoffrey. *The Legacy of John Paul II: His Contribution to Catholic Thought.* New York, 1999.

Gregg, Samuel. *Challenging the Modern World. Karol Wojtyla/John Paul II and the Development of Catholic Social Teaching.* Lanham, Md., 2002.

John Paul II. *In My Own Words.* New York, 2002.

Lecomte, Bernard. *Jean-Paul II.* Paris, 2003.

Les encycliques de Jean-Paul II. With a commentary by Joseph Ratzinger. Paris, 2003.

Vircondelet, Alain. *John-Paul II: The Life of Karol Wojtyla.* Paris, 2004.

OLIVIER ROTA

JOYCE, JAMES (1882–1941), Irish writer.

James Joyce was born in Dublin, Ireland, the first son of John Stanislaus Joyce. His father, having helped the Liberals to victory in the general elections of 1880, had been rewarded with the post of collector of rates, or taxes, for Dublin, earning the substantial salary of £500 per year. When the post was given to someone else in 1892, he was pensioned off with £132 per year, a sum further reduced in subsequent years. From birth to age ten, Joyce grew up in a comfortable middle-class environment; thereafter he lived in a world of sham gentility and genuine poverty, as his father's shrinking pension, improvidence, and alcoholism made life increasingly unstable for a family that now included ten children.

James Joyce c. 1938. ©Hulton-Deutsch Collection/Corbis

EDUCATION AND EARLY CAREER

After attending Clongowes Wood College (a distinguished Jesuit establishment) and Belvedere College (another Jesuit school), Joyce went to University College, a Catholic institution struggling for distinction. An admirer of the Norwegian dramatist Henrik Ibsen (1828–1906), Joyce was already writing poems, essays, and impressionistic sketches. After graduating, he went to Paris briefly to study medicine (1902), then returned to Dublin (1903). On 10 June 1904 he met Nora Barnacle, a young woman from Galway. They were still unmarried when the two left Ireland to move to the Continent (their marriage would take place only much later, in 1931). Their new home was Trieste, a city that, although part of the Austro-Hungarian Empire, was populated largely by Italians. Teaching English at the local Berlitz school, Joyce would reside there until 1915.

Almost immediately he began writing the short stories that would make up *Dubliners,* a milestone in short prose fiction. Its intensely accurate apprehension of the detail of Dublin life was brilliant and brutal, and Joyce also developed numerous devices for interweaving the stories to make them more than the sum of their parts. In 1907 he completed "The Dead," the last and longest of the stories. The book was accepted for publication by Grant Richards but was soon engulfed in interminable delays as first publishers and then printers demanded that Joyce delete or alter words, phrases, and proper names to accord with conventional decorum. While still engaged in protracted negotiations over *Dubliners,* Joyce began work on what would become his first novel, *A Portrait of the Artist As a Young Man,* a work that was far advanced by 1913, when *Dubliners* had still not appeared in print. *A Portrait* uses a highly developed symbolism to give ordinary incidents new resonance, layering associations around a scene or incident to make them evoke much deeper meanings, so that an ordinary pool of water, say, becomes suggestive of baptism.

Joyce's life changed irrevocably in late 1913, when he received a letter from the American poet, critic, and editor Ezra Pound (1885–1972), who had asked William Butler Yeats (1865–1939) to name younger writers who might have new materials to contribute to an anthology. Joyce sent him *Dubliners* and the first chapter of *Portrait.* As Joyce's great biographer Richard Ellmann wrote, "In Ezra Pound, as eager to discover as Joyce was to be discovered, the writings of Joyce found their missionary."

Pound arranged for serial publication of *Portrait* in the *Egoist,* a monthly journal devoted to the philosophical tenets of "egoism," a school of radical individualism derived from the writings of the German philosopher Max Stirner (1806–1856). The journal had some two hundred subscribers and was supported chiefly by subsidies from Harriet Shaw Weaver, an Englishwoman who had a deep sense of her duty to contribute to bettering the world. In 1915, after considerable prodding by Pound, *Dubliners* was at last published. In 1917 *A Portrait of the Artist* was issued by the Egoist Press, the book-publishing wing of Harriet Weaver's enterprise. By then Joyce was already at work on *Ulysses*—recognized today as one of the greatest novels of the twentieth century—and living in Zurich, where he had moved with his family a year after the outbreak of World War I.

ULYSSES: EXPERIMENTATION AND CONTROVERSY

Though he was paid for each installment of *Ulysses,* the sums were too little to make ends meet, and in 1916 Harriet Shaw Weaver began to act as Joyce's patron, sending him small but essential sums ever more frequently. Joyce never found the money to be enough, but it freed him to work with extraordinary energy on *Ulysses.* He had decided that each chapter would be written in a different style, but with episode 7, "Aeolus," this ambition became even more pronounced. Joyce was clearly fascinated by the idea of having an audience (he probably did not know just how small it was), and he was determined to dazzle. Each episode now became the occasion for a bravura performance, and Joyce became ever more determined to startle and provoke. The book, in effect, was becoming three books: a work of hyperbolic realism that minutely recounted the doings and thoughts of Leopold Bloom in the course of a single day in 1904; a work of richly textured symbolism, in which incidents in Bloom's day "correspond" with incidents recounted in Homer's *Odyssey,* or significant details became endowed with immense resonance; and a work that was increasingly preoccupied with the workings of language, chains of displacements, repetitions, and substitutions that go into fictional worldmaking. From the tenth to the eighteenth episodes, Joyce carried his experiments further and further, creating radically disparate styles and inventing new narrative conventions, or even departing entirely from storytelling in any ordinary sense.

In 1919 the *Egoist* ceased publication, but *Ulysses* continued to enjoy serial publication in the *Little Review,* an American journal with which Pound had also been involved. In early 1920 Joyce, now with two children (Lucia and Giorgio), moved to Paris, largely at Pound's urging, and he now contemplated the final episodes of his epic work. But because the *Little Review* was charged in October that year with publishing obscenity when it issued episode 13, "Nausicaa," the prospects for book publication grew clouded both in the United States and Britain. The *Little Review* editors were convicted in February 1921 and agreed not to publish further episodes of *Ulysses.* Two months later, Sylvia Beach, an American who owned an English-language bookshop in Paris, offered to take on the novel, promising to publish it as a limited and deluxe edition to be issued in one thousand copies.

Joyce, meanwhile, worked frantically on the book's final episodes, simultaneously writing these while he also revised all the earlier ones as they went through proof, a process that enabled him to layer in ever more detailed and subtle connections throughout the entire work. It has been estimated that as much as one third of *Ulysses* was written in the margins of the proofs. He completed the last writing on 30 October 1921, though proofs for the later episodes were still coming in and being revised as late as December. Finally, on 2 February 1922, the first copies of *Ulysses* arrived in Paris. Within eighteen weeks the edition was sold out, and in September 1922 copies that had originally sold at £3 3s (or $15), were selling in London and New York for as much as £40 (or $200). Beach published a second edition the next year and another each year until 1935, when a celebrated court ruling in the United States declared the book not indecent and hence publishable. Random House, under the guidance of Bennett Cerf, became the U.S. publisher of *Ulysses.*

Weaver, meanwhile, had settled £23,000 on Joyce, a sum that meant his annual income from it was £1,050 per year, then a sizable figure. Joyce now adopted the lifestyle of a middle-class family man, shunning the doings of expatriate and bohemian Paris and restricting himself to a small circle of admirers and collaborators. Meanwhile, he turned his attention to *Finnegans Wake,* a project that would consume the next seventeen years of his life. Published under the title *Work in Progress* in avant-garde journals such as *Transition,* which was edited by Eugene Jolas, the book became an unprecedented construction of a new language, one discernibly grounded in English but incorporating and punning on words from as many as seventeen other languages. Even when it was still incomplete and known only through the portions published serially, the work prompted extensive debate about Joyce's aims and procedures. Some charged that Joyce was becoming too obscure and losing all contact with reality and ordinary storytelling; others thought that he was charting the future of experimental writing. Even today there is sharp disagreement about the nature of *Finnegans Wake*: for some its obscurity conceals a hidden narrative or even a systematic mythology; for others its insistent punning entails forms of play inimical to the very ideas of character, plot, and story.

With the outbreak of World War II, Joyce and his family fled first to southern France, then to Zurich, where he had written so much of *Ulysses*. When he died a few months later in early 1941, all of Weaver's money had disappeared. Joyce had consumed not just the income but also the principal.

See also **Beach, Sylvia; Ireland; Pound, Ezra.**

BIBLIOGRAPHY

Primary Sources

Joyce, James. *Finnegans Wake.* New York, 1958.

———. *Ulysses.* Prepared by Hans Walter Gabler with Wolfhard Steppe and Claus Melchior. New York, 1984.

———. *Dubliners.* Edited by Jeri Johnson. Oxford, U.K., 2000.

Secondary Sources

Ellmann, Richard. *James Joyce.* New York, 1982.

Kenner, Hugh. *Joyce's Voices.* Berkeley, Calif., 1978.

Sherry, Vincent. *James Joyce: Ulysses.* Cambridge, U.K., 1994.

LAWRENCE RAINEY

JOYCE, WILLIAM (LORD HAW-HAW) (1906–1946), Nazi radio propagandist.

Known as "Lord Haw-Haw," William Joyce was the last man to be hanged for high treason in Britain, on 3 January 1946. His offense had been that he had given "aid and comfort to the King's enemies," and had assisted Germany "in her war against our country and our King."

Joyce had been a broadcaster for the Third Reich, and his radio commentaries had been disconcertingly successful: at one point, he attracted some sixteen million listeners in Britain and Ireland. His radio call signal "Germany Calling!" was used by stage comics to elicit hilarious laughter and instant recognition: for, although Joyce's propaganda broadcasts were odiously pro-Nazi, they nevertheless touched the British sense of humor.

Joyce's trial, in 1945, was a media sensation. The outcome was controversial, for William Joyce was not, technically, British. He had been born in America—the son of a naturalized American—and had grown up in Ireland. He had, in 1933, made an application for a British passport, in which he had mendaciously claimed to have been born in the United Kingdom. By this act, claimed the prosecuting attorney Sir Hartley Shawcross, Joyce had wrapped himself in the Union Jack: his value to the Reich was as a supposed Britisher.

Joyce was a difficult and aggressive individual, who grew up in Galway—his family origins were a troubled mixture of Irish and English—during the revolutionary early years of the twentieth century. From an early age he witnessed political street violence. He was a clever, precocious but rebellious boy, who was expelled from his Jesuit school, St. Ignatius College. He attached himself to the notorious Black and Tans and narrowly escaped being liquidated by the local branch of the Irish Republican Army. Aged fifteen, he fled to England where he enlisted in the Worcester Regiment, but was soon discharged for lying about his age. He attended Battersea Polytechnic to study medicine, but was also ejected from there for behavior problems.

At seventeen, he received a serious gash across his cheek after an encounter with a political opponent at an election meeting. The scar remained livid throughout his life and the significance of the wound went deep: he claimed that a "Jewish communist" had tried to kill him, and this theme became part of a lifelong and pathological anti-Semitism.

Subsequently, he attended Birkbeck College, London, where he gained a first class honors degree in English literature, and began to manifest a certain academic brilliance. He was a gifted philologist, a fine scholar in Anglo-Saxon and Old Norse. Politically, he was involved with the Chelsea Conservative Party.

Joyce was studying for a Ph.D. when he was smitten by Sir Oswald Mosley, leader of the British Union of Fascists. From 1933 until 1937, Joyce was a star speaker for Mosley; but in 1937, after the British Fascists began to lose ground, he was discharged from the organization, with whom he had a paid job. He and John Beckett formed their own group, the National Socialist League, but it failed hopelessly.

Increasingly, Joyce was living a hand-to-mouth existence as a private tutor, when, in 1939, he decided to live in Germany. He and his second wife, Margaret, took the boat to Ostend on 26 August 1939. He had probably been tipped off by the MI5 spymaster Charles Maxwell Knight that he would shortly be interned.

Through a series of flukes, Joyce was introduced to the Reich's propaganda broadcasting organization and in October 1939 found himself before a microphone. "Lord Haw-Haw" was born. The nickname came from a radio critic who described a broadcaster who "speaks English of the haw-haw, damn-it-get-out-of-my-way variety." Various broadcasters contributed to the Haw-Haw character, including Norman Baillie-Stewart, Wolf Mittler, and Eduard Dietze, but finally it was Joyce who took the role, with a particularly memorable rasping tone.

His broadcasts could be threatening, scoffing, sneering, comical, satirical, impertinent, and occasionally radical—he always criticized "the swells" and upheld "the workers." Josef Goebbels, the Nazi propaganda chief, issued the orders, but Joyce wrote the words. As he had an unrivaled topographical knowledge of Britain—and Ireland—he was able to mention specific places knowledgeably, and this developed into a myth of occult dimensions. It was believed that Lord Haw-Haw had said that one town would be bombed, another spared. There are still many anecdotes about Haw-Haw's prognostications, most unverifiable.

Joyce always feared the entry of the United States into the war, and after 1942, his star began to wane. His radio audience figures went as low as one and a half million. But he had made his commitment to Germany—he even became a German citizen—and he stuck with it. He and Margaret were captured in May 1945, near Flensburg in Schleswig-Holstein. He had been given the identity of "William Hansen," but when he spoke to two British soldiers, his voice instantly identified him.

In London, Parliament hurriedly revived a statute of 1351 to ensure that he could be charged with treason. The trial began in the Old Bailey on 17 September 1945 and was over in three days. An appeal followed on 30 October but failed, as did a final appeal to the House of Lords.

In prison, Joyce wrote many letters to Margaret, full of complex language and ironic puns. He was unrepentant about National Socialism.

The legend of Lord Haw-Haw lives on as a half-demonic, but half-comical character whose nickname crops up with British—and Irish—memories of World War II. Joyce's name has also endured as a byword for enemy propaganda, and during Britain's involvement in Iraq, there were many allusions to individuals who might prove to be "the Lord Haw-Haw of our time" (if they were to broadcast for Saddam Hussein or Osama bin Laden).

And among lawyers, there is a continuing forensic interest in Joyce's trial: contemporary legal opinion tends to the view that it was, technically, an erroneous verdict. But a view also prevails that it was, within the context of the time, morally justifiable.

Joyce had been married twice, first to Hazel Kathleen Barr, by whom he had two daughters, and then to Margaret Cairns White. His eldest daughter, Heather, remained attached to his memory while deploring his politics: in 1976 she had his remains transported to Bohermore Cemetery in Galway, where they were reburied near to the Atlantic Ocean where he had played as a boy.

See also **British Union of Fascists; Collaboration; World War II.**

BIBLIOGRAPHY

Kenny, Mary. *Germany Calling: A Personal Biography of William Joyce, "Lord Haw-Haw."* Dublin, 2003.

MARY KENNY

JUAN CARLOS I

JUAN CARLOS I (b. 1938), king of Spain since 1975.

Juan Carlos I succeeded the deceased dictator, Francisco Franco, as Spain's head of state in 1975. He is the grandson of King Alfonso XIII, who went into exile in Rome when the Second Republic was proclaimed in April 1931. Juan Carlos was born in Rome on 5 January 1938.

THE SUCCESSION ISSUE

Juan Carlos's father was Don Juan de Borbón, who although not the eldest child of the exiled king, became the legitimate heir to the throne. When civil war broke out in Spain in 1936, the monarchists supported the military rebellion against the republic, and Don Juan tried to join the rebel army. Franco, the emerging leader of the rebels, cunningly prevented this. Victory in the war consolidated Franco's political preeminence in the New State, while the monarchists became dependent on the dictator's will. As World War II loomed, Don Juan's family moved to Switzerland. From there, coinciding with the Allied defeat of the Axis Powers in 1945, he issued a manifesto requesting Franco's resignation and the restoration of both the monarchy and democracy in Spain. Because the Francoist regime did not collapse, the result of this manifesto was to expose Don Juan as a "liberal" thus making him an unacceptable choice for the restoration of the monarchy in Spain. In 1947 Franco made himself regent for life with the right to designate his successor. Don Juan was forced to reach an agreement with the dictator in 1947 and the following year sent his son Juan Carlos to Spain to study and, it was understood, to be prepared to succeed Franco. This arrangement created a contradiction between the continuity of the dynastic line in the person of Don Juan and the future of the monarchy in the person of his son. This situation created numerous tensions among the royal family, the monarchist sectors of society, and even the hard-core Francoists. The issue was not fully resolved until 1977, when Don Juan ceded all his dynastic rights to his son.

RELATIONSHIP WITH FRANCO

Franco supervised Juan Carlos's education, and the personal relationship between them was always good, albeit not exempt from moments of tension. Juan Carlos studied in the three military academies and took courses in the humanities, law, politics, and economics. The dictator's plan was to make him both a competent and politically reliable successor. In 1969 Franco made him his official successor but gave him the title of "Prince of Spain" instead of "Prince of Asturias," the traditional title of the

Spanish crown prince. Previously, in 1962, Juan Carlos had married Princess Sofia, daughter of Paul I, king of Greece. Juan Carlos and Sofia had two daughters, Elena (1963) and Cristina (1965), and a son, the future Crown Prince Felipe (1968). In political terms, Sophia was an excellent choice because she consistently proved to be a highly intelligent, skillful, and cultured partner, with a strong sense of duty.

In spite of the couple's credentials, as the dictator's health deteriorated rapidly in the early 1970s, many hard-core members of the regime still hoped that Franco would eventually reverse the designation of Juan Carlos as successor. Several other candidates from the different branches of the royal family were positioning themselves for this eventuality. Franco, however, stood firm in his decision. On 22 November 1975, two days after Franco's death, the Cortes, the dictatorship's rubber-stamp parliament, proclaimed Juan Carlos I, king of Spain.

PRESIDING OVER REFORMS AND TRANSITION TO DEMOCRACY

The new king's political plans were unknown, and many people, democrats and Francoists alike, distrusted him. His first signals were mixed. He declared his desire to be the "king of all the Spaniards," but he almost simultaneously confirmed Carlos Arias, Franco's last prime minister, in his post. Arias was no democrat, having had a prominent role in the extremely harsh political repression that took place in the country after the war. Consequently, political reform was stagnant, and Juan Carlos seemed bound to fail, with many predicting the king would not remain on the throne for long.

In July 1976, however, he surprised almost everybody by replacing Arias with the young Adolfo Suárez. This appointment was ill received by most democrats because Suárez until then had impeccable Francoist credentials and strong links to the dictatorship's single party (the Falange) and to the Catholic Right (Opus Dei). Working closely with Suárez and other lesser-known advisors, King Juan Carlos in the next months was able to dismantle the main obstacles to reform. In November 1976 Suárez used his knowledge of the inner workings of the system to cajole the

Cortes to pass a Law of Political Reform, which effected the dissolution of the very same Cortes and the legalizing of political parties. In early 1977 the king used his position as supreme commander of the armed forces to clamp down on growing military opposition to these reforms. The legalization of the Communist Party on Easter was a high point of tension. Eventually, in June 1977, the first fully democratic elections in Spain since 1936 took place. Suárez's own newly created, centrist party won, with the Socialists coming in a strong second. Both the far right and the far left were soundly defeated.

Political reform came at a time when other problems were mounting, such as increasing terrorist activity, mostly by the ETA (a Basque organization), economic decline, growing unemployment, and questioning of the national unity. The late 1970s were a period of tension, with frequent rumors of an impending military coup. Exhausted and probably with the intention of avoiding a coup, Suárez resigned in January 1981. On 23 February, during the debate to replace him, police units stormed parliament. This was the sign for unleashing the feared coup. In those crucial hours, with both parliament and government in the hands of the insurgents, the role of the king became crucial. His personal calls to the commanders of the major military units ensured that almost all of them abstained from participating in the coup. Juan Carlos appeared on television in the early hours of the next morning reassuring the population that he had the situation under control and that democracy was not at risk. These interventions not only doomed the coup but also radically transformed the public image of the king and the monarchy: both the person and the institution imposed by Franco were now seen as the main guarantors of the recently regained freedoms of ordinary Spaniards. By defending democracy in those crucial hours, Juan Carlos gained a political legitimacy and popular support that had been questioned until then. This phenomenon has been called "Juancarlism." Juan Carlos's popularity has remained consistently high ever since.

See also **Franco, Francisco; Spain.**

BIBLIOGRAPHY

Carr, Raymond, and Juan Pablo Fusi Aizpurúa. *Spain: Dictatorship to Democracy.* 2nd ed. London, 1981.

Pérez-Díaz, Víctor M. *The Return of Civil Society: The Emergence of Democratic Spain.* Cambridge, Mass., 1993.

Powell, Charles. *Juan Carlos of Spain: Self-Made Monarch.* New York, 1996.

Preston, Paul. *Juan Carlos: A People's King.* London, 2004.

ANTONIO CAZORLA-SANCHEZ

JULY 20TH PLOT. The plot to assassinate Adolf Hitler on 20 July 1944 was an attempt to overthrow his Nazi regime and end World War II. "Operation Valkyrie" was a plot to take power once the news of Hitler's assassination was confirmed. The bomb meant to kill Hitler was placed in his military headquarters in Rastenberg in East Prussia by a staff officer, Colonel Claus von Stauffenberg. It went off, but its force was muffled by a heavy wooden desk, which saved the Führer's life. Communications from Hitler's headquarters were not severed, and though Stauffenberg made it back to Berlin and tried to rally support, his efforts were doomed from the start. He and the other ringleaders of the plot were quickly caught and shot in the German Ministry of War. Thereafter hundreds of their associates were arrested; most were tortured or executed. For his own enjoyment, Hitler ordered films to be made of their slow deaths by strangulation with piano wire.

This one failed attempt on Hitler's life symbolized the elite character of this part of the German resistance. Most of the plotters were conservative men from prominent families. Many had religious origins and convictions, and they saw it as their mission not only to get rid of Hitler as an abomination but also to save some vestiges of honor for the German people as a whole. Carl-Friedrich Goerdeler was a conservative mayor of Leipzig, who resigned in protest over the Nazi decision in 1937 to remove a statue of the Jewish composer Felix Mendelssohn from the town square. Alfred Delp was a Jesuit priest. Count Helmuth James von Moltke, whose family included two German chiefs of staff, and Count Peter Yorck von Wartenburg organized a series of meetings in von Moltke's east German estate at Kreisau, in which like-minded men and women imagined a future Germany after the demise of the Nazi regime. One of the Kreisau circle was Adam von Trott, a lawyer and former Rhodes scholar, who used his international contacts to try to garner Allied support for the German resistance. Lutheran minister Dietrich Bonhoeffer tried to pass on word to the Allies of the plans of the resistance through his fellow clergyman Bishop G.K.A. Bell of Chichester, England. In every case the Allied response was hostile or indifferent. The German resistance could have gained popular support if it had been able to negotiate an armistice with the Allies. But the reply of Anthony Eden, British foreign secretary, was categorical. The only way to peace was through unconditional surrender. This left the resistance isolated and without a hope of ending the war before the total destruction of Germany.

This set of cultivated and well-placed individuals was in touch with, though separate from, a core of resistance to Hitler within the army. General Ludwig Beck had been chief of staff of the German army in the early days of the Nazi regime. Like Beck, General Erwin von Witzleben had served in World War I; as general he commanded the First Army in the campaign in France in 1940. He served on the eastern front as a field marshal but was dismissed for criticizing Hitler. General Günther von Kluge, another World War I veteran, commanded the German Fourth Army in Poland in 1939 and then in the breakthrough in the Ardennes forest in 1940 that led to the defeat of France. These three men were well aware of the plans to kill Hitler; all three were arrested and executed after the plot failed. Henning von Tresckow was chief of staff of German Army Group Center on the eastern front. He committed suicide when he learned that Hitler had survived.

A penumbra of military men surrounded these individuals and provided them with cover and indirect support. Admiral Franz von Canaris was head of the Abwehr, military intelligence. His movements and those of his circle were shielded by his role in German espionage. He provided fake passports to Adam von Trott and other conspirators. His role and that of other military figures was revealed only when the Gestapo found their secret papers in a safe in the Army High Command headquarters in Zossen.

There was a second facet of the military conspiracy to kill Hitler and overthrow the regime. On 20 July 1944 in Paris, General Karl Heinrich von Stülpnagel, the commander of occupied France, arrested all the Gestapo and SS men in the city and tried to persuade his superior General Hans Günther von Kluge to join the coup. Kluge refused to do so, since he knew that Hitler was still alive. Stülpnagel was arrested and sent back to Berlin. En route he asked to stop at Verdun, where he too had fought in World War I. He tried to commit suicide and succeeded only in injuring himself. He was tried in Berlin and shot. Kluge was implicated in the plot and took poison. The other major figure on the fringes of the plot was General Erwin Rommel. He was nearly killed in a car accident on 17 July and was hospitalized during the coup. When his name came out as one of the conspirators, he was given the option of suicide. He took it on 14 October 1944.

These two events—one in Prussia and one in Paris—represented the desperate gamble of a large group of German men and women to kill Hitler and overthrow the regime. The Allies treated their plans with suspicion. Was their plan simply a face-saving gesture on the part of people who had gone along with the regime when its military outlook was good? This is a view hard to support. The risks Stauffenberg and Stülpnagel took were enormous, and they paid for them with their lives. Their Germany had been turned into a slaughterhouse run by racists, sadists, and madmen. To strike, even when the chances of success were small, was simply a way of representing another Germany, one that people of goodwill could honor and rebuild.

See also **Hitler, Adolf; Resistance.**

BIBLIOGRAPHY

Fest, Joachim. *Plotting Hitler's Death: The Story of the German Resistance, 1933–1945.* Translated by Bruce Little. London, 1996.

Galante, Pierre, with Eugène Silianoff. *Operation Valkyrie: The German Generals' Plot against Hitler.* Translated by Mark Howson and Cary Ryan. New York, 1981.

Hamerow, Theodore S. *On the Road to the Wolf's Lair: German Resistance to Hitler.* Cambridge, Mass., 1997.

Heuss, Theodor, et al. *Reflections on July 20th 1944.* Translated by Larry Fischer. Mainz, Germany, 1984.

Hoffmann, Peter. *German Resistance to Hitler.* Cambridge, Mass., 1988.

Jacobsen, Hans-Adolf, ed. *July 20, 1944: The German Opposition to Hitler as Viewed by Foreign Historians, an Anthology*. Bonn, Germany, 1969.

Large, David Clay, ed. *Contending with Hitler: Varieties of German Resistance in the Third Reich*. Washington, D.C., 1991.

Manvell, Roger, and Heinrich Fraenkel. *The July Plot: The Attempt in 1944 on Hitler's Life and the Men behind It*. London, 1964.

Roon, Ger van, *German Resistance to Hitler: Count von Moltke and the Kreisau Circle*. Translated by Peter Ludlow. London, 1971.

Zeller, Eberhard. *The Flame of Freedom: The German Struggle against Hitler*. Translated by R. P. Heller and D. R. Masters. Coral Gables, Fla., 1969.

JAY WINTER

JUNG, CARL

JUNG, CARL (1875–1961), Swiss psychologist and psychiatrist, founder of analytical psychology.

Carl Gustav Jung was born on 26 July 1875 in Kesswil on Lake Constance, Switzerland. His family moved to Laufen by the Rhine Falls when he was six months old. He was the oldest child, and had one sister, Gertrud. His father, Paul Jung, was a pastor in the Swiss Reformed Church. His youth was marked by vivid dreams, intense religious questioning, and extensive reading. From 1895, he studied medicine at the University of Basel, where he engaged in extensive extracurricular reading—in philosophy, theology, spiritualism, and psychical research—and participated in séances.

After his medical studies, Jung took up a post as an assistant physician at the Burghölzli Asylum in Zurich at the end of 1900. In 1902 he became engaged to Emma Rauschenbach, whom he married and with whom he had five children.

His early experimental work on word associations established his reputation as one of the rising stars of European psychiatry, and together with Eugen Bleuler (1857–1939) he played an important role in establishing the modern diagnostic category of schizophrenia. Jung became a lecturer at the University of Zurich and in 1909 gained an honorary degree from Clark University. In 1906 he commenced a collaboration with Sigmund Freud (1856–1939) and played a critical role in launching the international psychoanalytic movement—organizing its first congress, editing its first journal, and becoming the first president of its international association. In 1909 he left the Burghölzli to devote himself to his burgeoning private practice and independent research. In 1914 he withdrew from the psychoanalytic movement and resigned from the University of Zurich.

By the outbreak of World War I, Jung had played a critical role in the institutional development of psychoanalysis and made critical interlinked contributions to the development of psychical research, dynamic psychiatry, psychological testing, psychotherapy, cultural psychology, and the psychology of personality. However, it was from that time onward that his most distinctive work took shape.

In 1913 Jung had a series of apocalyptic visions. Struck by the correspondence between these and the subsequent onset of the war, Jung engaged in a process of self-experimentation, which he termed his "confrontation with the unconscious." At the heart of this project was Jung's attempt to get to know his own "myth" as a solution to the mythless predicament of secular modernity. This took the form of provoking an extended series of waking fantasies in himself. He later called this the method of "active imagination." Jung elaborated, illustrated, and commented on these fantasies in a work that he called *The Red Book*, which was at the center of his later work and is only now in the course of publication. In his practice at this time, Jung encouraged his patients to undertake similar forms of self-investigation. His adoption of nonverbal techniques in psychotherapy was to play an important role in the rise of art therapies.

Jung maintained that his fantasies and those of his patients stemmed from the mythopoetic imagination, which was missing in the present rational age. Reconnecting with this could form the basis for cultural renewal. The task of moderns was one of establishing a dialogue with the contents of the collective unconscious and integrating them into consciousness. This was to play an important part in a popular "mythic revival." He maintained that cultural renewal could only come about through self-regeneration of the individual. He termed this the "individuation process," which was an account of the higher development of the personality. Consequently, for Jung, psychotherapy was no longer a process solely preoccupied with the treatment of psychopathology. It became a practice to enable the higher development of the individual through fostering the individuation process. This became the focus of Jung's later work. In his scholarly writings, he undertook a comparative historical study of the individuation process in various cultures and epochs. Conceived as the normative pattern of human development, it was to form the basis of a general scientific psychology.

From the 1920s onward, Jung embarked on the psychology of religion, taking his cue from the psychology of religions movement, and in particular, from the work of the American psychologist and philosopher William James (1842–1910) and the Swiss psychologist Théodore Flournoy (1854–1921). He attempted to develop a comparative psychology of the religious-making process. Rather than proclaiming a new prophetic revelation, his interest lay in the psychology of religious experiences. The task was one of studying the translation and transposition of the numinous experience of individuals into symbols, and eventually into the dogmas and creeds of organized religions, and finally, to study the psychological function of such symbols. Jung maintained that such a psychology of religion could in turn revivify Christianity, through explicating the living meaning of its symbolism and practices.

Jung engaged in the comparative study of, among others, Buddhist, Hindu, and Daoist practices of personality development. His studies of Eastern thought played an important role in mediating and introducing Eastern esoteric practices and conceptions to the West and bringing the work of contemporary Indologists and Sinologists to a wider audience. He devoted particular attention to the study of medieval alchemy. In the nineteenth century, figures such as Mary Atwood and Ethan Allen Hitchcock had argued that the chemical language and images of alchemy were simply an exoteric device covering the esoteric moral and spiritual purposes of alchemy. From around 1912 onward, Théodore Flournoy and the Viennese psychologist Herbert Silberer (1882–1922) developed this into a psychological interpretation of alchemy. From the

1930s, Jung embarked on an extensive study of alchemy. His understanding of it was based on two main theses: first, that in meditating on the texts and materials in their laboratories, the alchemists were actually practicing a form of active imagination. Second, that the symbolism in the alchemical texts corresponded to that of the individuation process that Jung and his patients had been engaged with. He maintained that the alchemical tradition had functioned as historical compensation for the one-sidedness of Christianity, and its study could provide what was lacking in the latter. As well as providing a psychological study of religious and cultural history, Jung's alchemical works functioned as an allegorical presentation of his own work. Rather than write directly of his experiences and those of his patients, he commented on analogous developments in esoteric practices.

From the 1920s onward a large international movement grew around Jung, and Jungian psychotherapy trainings began to be formalized in the 1940s, spreading throughout the world. Jung's readership was widespread and extensive, particularly in the English-speaking world, and his works played an important part in the rise of the new age and alternate religions movement. He died on 6 June 1961, leaving a vast corpus of manuscripts and correspondences, which is only partially published.

See also **Freud, Sigmund; Psychiatry; Psychoanalysis.**

BIBLIOGRAPHY

Primary Sources

Jung, C. G. *Analytical Psychology: Notes of the Seminar Given in 1925.* Edited by William McGuire. Princeton, N.J., 1989.

Secondary Sources

Ellenberger, Henri. *The Discovery of the Unconscious: The History and Evolution of Dynamic Psychiatry.* New York, 1970.

Hannah, Barbara. *Jung: His Life and Work: A Biographical Memoir.* New York, 1976.

Shamdasani, Sonu. *Jung and the Making of Modern Psychology: The Dream of a Science.* Cambridge, U.K., 2003.

SONU SHAMDASANI

JÜNGER, ERNST (1895–1998), German writer.

The German playwright Heiner Müller (1929–1995) wrote of Ernst Jünger: "The problem of Jünger is the problem of this century. Before he could experience women, there came the war." Although the multiform dimensions of modern violence in World War I certainly played an essential role in Jünger's life and work, his adventurous heart—*Das abenteuerliche Herz* (1929) was the title of one of his novels—made him throw fortune to the wind even earlier.

ADVENTURE, WARS, AND POLITICAL COMMITMENT

Born in Heidelberg on 29 March 1895, Jünger was brought up in a typical middle-class German family—his father was a pharmacist—and in 1913 he ran away from the home to enroll in the foreign legion, even shipping out to Africa. Shortly after his father succeeded in bringing him home, World War I broke out. Jünger immediately volunteered. He fought on the western front throughout the war, was wounded fourteen times, and was awarded a first class Iron Cross. He also returned home with about fifteen autobiographical notebooks. From these he composed *In Stahlgewittern* (1920), the war novel that made him famous. Initially self-published in 1920 with his father's financial help, the tone and style of the book, at once exalted and graphic, slowly found an audience, and in 1925 eighteen thousand copies were sold. The book was translated into French and, in 1929, into English as *Storm of Steel*.

Until 1923 Jünger remained an instructor in the army, for which he wrote articles and training manuals on modern warfare. He subsequently studied biology in Leipzig, furthering an interest in insects that dated to his childhood. Indeed, he would become a well-regarded entomologist and collector of insects; several species bear his name.

The 1920s may be considered Jünger's "fascist period." Through his articles—of which 144 from 1919 to 1939 were compiled for publication only in 2001—and autobiographical writings and publications of illustrated books on the war, Jünger became, with his brother, Friedrich Georg, also a

veteran and a writer, one of the major activists of the postwar conservative revolutionary movement in Germany. During this period, he was close to Ernst Niekisch and Carl Schmitt, publishing texts in *Standarte*, a publication of the right-wing veterans league, the Stahlhelm (the steel helmets). Jünger's work of this period glorified the soldier and the leader, and his attraction/repulsion for the prospect that advanced technology would create a new kind of human being was most completely developed in *Der Arbeiter* (The laborer) in 1934. His hatred for bourgeois society was suffused with anti-Semitism but, although Jünger's work undeniably contains racist elements, he did not hold to a fundamentally racist weltanschauung (worldview); he was, rather, an elitist. In this sense, he was more a fascist than a Nazi.

Indeed, Jünger's relationship to Nazism was ambiguous. He did not take direct part in the freikorps—the nub of Hitler's brownshirts movement—but he was close to some of its former members. In 1923 he wrote an article for the *Völkischer Beobachter*, the newspaper of the Nazi Party, then only a small group. Although admired by the Nazi leaders, he declined to enter the German Academy once it operated under National Socialist auspices. *Auf den Marmorklippen* (1939; *On the Marble Cliffs*, 1947) was a parable critical of Nazism, with its depiction of the cruel and bloodthirsty *Oberförster* (Grand forester). After the war, he presented himself as having lived through a kind of internal exile under Nazi rule. Nevertheless, once mobilized, he was a dutiful soldier. A diarist his whole life, his diaries from his time in occupied France, published as *Gärten und Strassen* (Gardens and roads) in 1942, offered a clinical description of a troubled period, introspection, and literary experimentation. One can certainly say that, little by little and more clearly after Adolf Hitler came to power, Jünger felt contempt and disdain for Nazism and Nazis.

EXPERIENCE AND EXPERIMENTATION

Experience and experimentation are in every sense key to Jünger's thought and work both in literature and in life. The war had already provided an "internal experience." Jünger was interested in suffering as an extreme and revelatory experience. He tested all available drugs and eventually became one of the first to try lysergic acid (LSD); his fascination with insects also involved experimentation. Finally, he experimented with various literary genres, such as utopian science-fiction (*Heliopolis,* 1949) and even invented a strange literary game (*Mantrana,* 1958).

After the war, Jünger refused to submit to denazification and came under suspicion because of his prewar politics. For several years under the Allied occupation he was not allowed to publish his work. In 1950 he returned to his Wilflingen estate in southwestern Germany, where he pursued his literary and entomological activities, continued to keep a diary, and welcomed friends and admirers. Jünger died in Wilflingen on 17 February 1998. Although he remained a controversial figure who was disliked, even despised by some both within and outside academia, he had a circle of devoted admirers. His conservatism, hieratic ideas, and aristocratic behavior, not to mention his ideas during the interwar years, meshed rather poorly with the pacifism adopted by Germany after 1945. But Germans were not his sole admirers. Jünger often enjoyed a better reputation abroad—as in France, where the Socialist president with a checkered political past, François Mitterrand (1916–1996), was one of Jünger's fervent admirers.

See also **Germany; World War II.**

BIBLIOGRAPHY

Primary Sources

Jünger, Ernst. *Sämtliche Werke.* 18 vols. Stuttgart, Germany, 1978– .

———. *Politische Publizistik, 1919 bis 1939.* Edited and presented by Sven Olaf Berggötz. Stuttgart, Germany, 2001.

Secondary Sources

Hagestedt, Lutz, ed. *Ernst Jünger: Politik—Mythos—Kunst.* Berlin, 2004.

King, John. "Writing and Rewriting the First World War: Ernst Jünger and the Crisis of the Conservative Imagination, 1914–1925." Ph.D. diss., University of Oxford, St. John's College, 1999. Also available at http://www.juenger.org.

Meyer, Martin. *Ernst Jünger.* Munich and Vienna, 1990.

Noack, Paul. *Ernst Jünger: Eine Biographie.* Berlin, 1998.

Palmier, Jean-Michel. *Ernst Jünger: Réveries sur un chasseur de cicindèles.* Paris, 1995.

NICOLAS BEAUPRÉ

KÁDÁR, JÁNOS (1912–1989), Hungarian communist politician.

János Kádár, the leader of Hungary between 1956 and 1988, was born in Fiume (now Rijeka, Croatia) in 1912. Because his father had left the family before his birth, he was brought up by his mother and given her last name, Csermanek. They moved in 1918 to Budapest, where after finishing the primary school he became a typewriter technician's apprentice.

EARLY POLITICAL CAREER

Kádár joined the illegal Communist Party of Hungary in 1931. In 1933 he was arrested and sentenced to two years in prison for illegal conspiracy. For acting in a cowardly manner during the police interrogations, the party excluded him. After release he was active in the social democratic movement for several years. In 1941 the communist movement re-embraced him and he got his new alias, Kádár. Soon afterward, he became the first secretary of the domestic party, which by that time had practically broken into fragments. In 1943, after Joseph Stalin (1879–1953) dissolved the Comintern, Kádár dissolved the domestic party and attempted to reorganize it as the Peace Party. In 1944 he was again arrested, but he managed to flee and went into hiding in Budapest till the end of World War II.

Between 1946 and 1951 Kádár held top positions in the party apparatus and in the government. Yet, he did not belong to the innermost power circles during the era of Mátyás Rákosi (1892–1971). His promotion was due to the fact that he was among those few cadres who had no Muscovite past and enjoyed some reputation among the public. He was not an independent policy maker but rather an obedient executor of Rákosi's orders. He was the deputy chief secretary of the ruling Hungarian Workers' Party between 1946 and 1951 and the minister of internal affairs between 1948 and 1950. In this capacity he played a prominent and cruel role in staging the show trial in 1949 of László Rajk, his former comrade in the domestic movement.

In 1951 he was arrested and charged with being a "secret agent" of the prewar political police and the "liquidator" of the party in 1943. He was sentenced to life inprisonment. After Stalin's death in 1953 mass rehabilitations were initiated during the first premiership of Imre Nagy. Kádár was released and rehabilitated in 1954.

As a former victim of the purges, he was regarded as one of the potential challengers of the Rákosi clique, especially by the mid-ranking party apparatus. In July 1956, when Rákosi was replaced, Kádár was elected as a member of the Politburo. On 25 October 1956, two days after the 1956 Hungarian Revolution broke out, he became the first secretary of the party. After the discredited Stalinist party was dissolved on 31 October he was nominated the first secretary of the newly established successor party, the Hungarian Socialist Workers' Party (HSWP). Kádár was also minister of state in Imre Nagy's brief revolutionary government in 1956. In a

Janos Kádár with Nikita Khrushchev, 1964. ©BETTMANN/
CORBIS

radio speech on 1 November he praised the people's "democratic socialist revolution." That same evening the Russians kidnapped him and took him to Moscow.

He was summoned before the Politburo of the Soviet Communist Party in Moscow on 2–3 November 1956. At the first hearing Kádár opposed military intervention, but the next day he capitulated and assumed the lead of the puppet government. On 4 November, when Soviet troops attacked Budapest, Kádár proclaimed the formation of the Revolutionary Worker-Peasant Government.

LEADER OF HUNGARY

In his first speeches he made conciliatory promises: amnesty and the restoration of national symbols. However, he was unable to convince the main actors of the domestic nonviolent resistance—Imre Nagy, the workers' councils, and the intelligentsia—that they should accept the "reality" of the Soviet occupation. In December 1956 Kádár opted to use mass violence to suppress resistance. Mass shootings took place in various cities against peaceful demonstrators; thousands were arrested

and hundreds were executed between 1957 and 1962. In June 1958 Imre Nagy and his supporters were also tried and hanged.

From 1956 until 1988 Kádár was the ultimate political authority in Hungary. He was prime minister (1956–1958 and 1961–1965), first secretary (1956–1985), chief secretary (1985–1988), and then president of the HSWP (1988–1989, already an honorary post). Kádár's policy was determined by the shocking experience of the revolution. After 1956 he faced an extremely hostile domestic and international environment. Although his power was based primarily on the party apparatus, the security forces, and the Soviet troops, he realized that a return to the power practices of the Rákosi era was impossible. After more than two decades of war and mass terror the people appreciated his offer for peace, relative autonomy in the private sphere, and modest economic progress. Despite its bloody beginnings, the Kádár regime turned out to be a "soft" dictatorship, as consolidation made considerable progress by the early 1960s. In a speech in December 1961 Kádár reversed the former Stalinist slogan, saying: Who is not against us, is with us! In 1963 he announced amnesty for the political prisoners, most of whom were later released.

Kádár's policy aimed at obtaining the support of the urban petty bourgeoisie, the workers, and the peasantry. The 1956 revolution, the one-party rule, and the country's adherence to the Soviet bloc remained taboos, but the relative freedom in culture and the reduction of the ideological pressure appeased the intelligentsia. The basis of the reconciliation was the guarantee of a perpetual improvement in living standards (goulash communism). Therefore, the regime had to revise the centrally planned economic system and launch cautious economic reforms in 1968. The reforms introduced some market elements aimed at increasing productivity and efficiency without endangering the hegemonic rule of the party. This contradictory claim, however, set forth the limits of the reform policy.

From the mid-1960s Kádár was able to develop a fairly good relationship with the Western democracies. He gained a remarkable reputation as a politician who was able to make peace and exert some independence from Moscow. His policy was widely regarded both at home and abroad as the best available option given the circumstances and as a partial fulfillment of the demands of the 1956 revolution.

In 1968 Kádár subscribed to Czechoslovak intervention in order to preserve his relative autonomy in domestic affairs. Yet in 1972 he was unable to resist the neo-Stalinist turn of the Soviet leader Leonid Brezhnev (1906–1982). The reform in the economy was halted and partly reversed. By the end of the decade the economy gradually sank into depression. The increase of the people's welfare could not be guaranteed any more. Throughout the 1980s the trends of foreign indebtedness and economic depression could not be stopped. Moreover, Kádár, who remained a true communist for all of his life, attempted to push through a conservative leftist turn in 1985 in order to reinforce the economic and ideological foundations of the regime. This only worsened the economic and political crisis. Within the rapidly changing international environment Kádár's "neoconservative" move was rejected even by the technocrats and pragmatists of his own party. In May 1988 he was forced to resign. In April 1989 Kádár gave a speech in front of the Central Committee of HSWP in which he tried to tackle the shadows of his past crimes. The speech indicated that he had been already suffering from a serious mental disorder. He died on 6 July 1989, the very same day that Imre Nagy was rehabilitated by the Hungarian Supreme Court.

See also **Eastern Bloc; Hungary; Nagy, Imre; Warsaw Pact.**

BIBLIOGRAPHY

Békés, Csaba, Malcolm Byrne, and János Rainer, eds. *The 1956 Hungarian Revolution: A History in Documents.* Budapest and New York, 2002.

Felkay, Andrew. *Hungary and the USSR, 1956–1988: Kádár's Political Leadership.* New York, 1989.

Gati, Charles. *Hungary and the Soviet Bloc.* Durham, N.C., 1986.

Huszár, Tibor. *Kádár János politikai életrajza, 1912–1956.* Budapest, 2001. The single full biography of Kádár published after 1989.

Kis, János. "The Restoration of 1956–1957 in a Thirty Years Pespective." In his *Politics in Hungary: For a Democratic Alternative,* translated by Gábor J. Follinus. Boulder, Colo., 1989.

Mink, András. "The Kádár of History." *Budapest Review of Books* 11, nos. 1–4 (2001).

Romsics, Ignác. *Hungary in the Twentieth Century.* Budapest, 1999.

Shawcross, William. *Crime and Compromise: Janos Kadar and the Politics of Hungary since the Revolution.* London, 1974.

Varga, László. *Kádár János bírái előtt: Egyszer fent, egyszer lent, 1945–1956.* Budapest, 2001. The volume contains an analysis and archival documents on Kádár's role in the Rajk trial in 1949 and of his own trial and rehabilitation from 1951 to 1956.

                                                    ANDRÁS MINK

KADARE, ISMAIL (b. 1936), Albanian writer.

Ismail Kadare is by far the best-known Albanian writer and the only one to have gained a broad international reputation. Kadare was born in the southern Albanian town of Gjirokastër near the Greek border and studied at the Faculty of History and Philology of the University of Tirana. He subsequently attended the Gorky Institute of World Literature in Moscow until 1960, when political relations between Albania and the Soviet Union became tense. On his return to Albania he worked as a journalist and became editor-in-chief of the French-language literary periodical *Les lettres albanaises* (Albanian literature). He carried out several formal political functions in the country, the most notable of which was as deputy head of the Democratic Front under Nexhmije Hoxha, the wife of the dictator Enver Hoxha. Kadare was not, however, politically active for or against the Stalinist regime. He simply did what was required of him or what was needed to survive in Albania and to promote what interested him most, his writing.

He began his literary career with poetry but turned increasingly to prose, of which he soon became the undisputed master and by far the most popular writer of the whole of Albanian literature. His works were extremely influential throughout the 1970s and 1980s and for many readers he was the only ray of hope in the chilly, dismal prison that was communist Albania. Ismail Kadare lived the next thirty years of his life in Tirana, constantly under the watchful eye of the Communist Party. At the end of October 1990, a mere two months before the final collapse of the dictatorship, Ismail Kadare left Tirana and applied for political asylum in France. His departure enabled him for the first time to exercise his profession with complete freedom. His years of Parisian exile were productive and accorded him further success and recognition, as a writer both in Albanian and in French.

Kadare became a member of the Académie des Sciences Morales et Politiques (Paris, 28 October 1996) and the French Legion of Honor. On 27 June 2005 he was awarded the first Man Booker International Prize in Edinburgh and was earlier nominated for the Nobel Prize for Literature. His first major prose work was the novel *Gjenerali i ushtrisë së vdekur* (1963; *The General of the Dead Army*, 1971). In view of the early publication date—the author was a mere twenty-seven years old at the time—*The General* could almost be viewed as a work of youth, and yet it is still one of Kadare's most effective novels, and one of his best known. It is the story of an Italian general in the company of a laconic priest on a mission to communist Albania to recover the remains of his soldiers who had fallen some twenty years earlier.

Of Kadare's other works translated into English, mention may be made of: *Kronikë në gur* (1971; *Chronicle in Stone*, 1987), set in the Second World War; *Kush e solli Doruntinën?* (1979; *Doruntine*, 1988), based on an Albanian legend; *Prilli i thyer* (1978; *Broken April*, 1990), which evokes the subject of blood-feuding in the northern Albanian mountains; *Nëpunësi i pallatit të ëndrrave* (1981; *The Palace of Dreams*, 1993), set in the Ottoman Empire; *Koncert në fund të dimrit* (1988; *The Concert*, 1994), a vast overview of communist Albania's alliance with Red China; *Piramida* (1993; *The Pyramid*, 1996), an allegory of absolute power set in ancient Egypt; *Dosja H* (1990; *The File on H*, 1997), a tale of two foreign ethnographers doing field research in Albania; *Ura me tri harqe* (1978; *The Three-Arched Bridge*, 1997), set in the late Middle Ages and based on Albanian legendry; *Krushqit janë të ngrirë* (1986; *The Wedding Procession Turned to Ice*, 1997), on the Kosovo uprising of 1981; *Tri këngë zie për Kosovën* (1998; *Three Elegies for Kosovo*, U.S. title,

Elegy for Kosovo, 2000), three short, historical tales of Kosovo set in different ages; *Lulet e ftohta të marsit* (2000; *Spring Flowers, Spring Frost*, 2002), once again on blood-feuding and its personal consequences; and *Pasardhësi* (2003; *The Successor*, 2005), based on the death of the communist leader Mehmet Shehu (1913–1981).

Kadare enthralled his readers at home and abroad with the magic realism of his historical novels, skillfully woven tales about various periods of Albanian history (Ottoman rule, the precommunist 1930s, and even the somber Stalinist era), in particular those novels first published during the dictatorship. His international success has been due in good part to the masterful French-language translations of his works—by the noted Albanian aristocrat Jusuf Vrioni (1916–2001)—that served as a basis for the English and other translations. In Albania itself, despite continued international recognition, there was a marked slump in readership for Kadare's works following the end of the dictatorship in 1991. Whether the author had lost contact with his Albanian public after years in Paris, or whether his readers, who now enjoyed unimpeded access to world literature, had simply moved on, remained unclear in the early twenty-first century.

See also **Albania.**

BIBLIOGRAPHY

Elsie, Robert. *History of Albanian Literature.* Boulder, Colo., 1995.

———. *Studies in Modern Albanian Literature and Culture.* Boulder, Colo., and New York, 1996.

———. *Albanian Literature: A Short History.* London, 2005.

Pipa, Arshi. *Contemporary Albanian Literature.* Boulder, Colo., and New York, 1991.

ROBERT ELSIE

KADETS (CONSTITUTIONAL DEMOCRATIC PARTY).

The Constitutional Democratic Party, nicknamed the Kadets, was Russia's most important liberal party during the revolutionary era of 1905 to 1921. Russian liberalism emerged in the latter part of the nineteenth century out of the changes occurring in society following the Great Reforms and the beginning of industrialization. It grew along with the new professional classes and the demand for rule of law, civil rights, and constitutionalism. The Revolution of 1905 provided the opportunity for formation of a liberal political party, the Constitutional Democratic Party. It was drawn overwhelmingly from the professions; few of its leaders came from the commercial classes. Among a constellation of talented figures, Professor Pavel (Paul) N. Milyukov, a historian at Moscow University, emerged as the party's generally recognized leader.

The Kadet party emphasized several principles, which remained largely consistent over its lifetime. It stressed that it was "above classes" and criticized other parties for their class orientations. Instead, it emphasized a broad nationalism, national unity, and "state consciousness." It emphasized the importance of rule of law, civil rights, constitutional government, and the "four-tail" suffrage—equal, direct, secret, and universal. It supported land reform and distribution among the peasants, but with compensation for landlords. It accepted the need to improve working conditions and wages for the new industrial working class, but within the existing framework of private property. It advocated full and equal rights for all ethnic and religious groups, but rejected the idea of federalism along nationality lines. How to achieve these and other objectives divided the party throughout its history. Some argued that it should seek alliances to the left and press ahead for rapid achievement of its goals, whereas others advocated a more gradualist approach and seeking allies among more conservative elements. This division on tactics became especially acute at the two times the Kadets were in a position to influence significantly the course of Russian affairs—during the First and Second Dumas (1906–1907) and during the Provisional Government formed after the February 1917 revolution.

The Kadets emerged from Russia's first national elections in 1906 as the largest party in the First State Duma. Their efforts to push further constitutional reform were blocked by the stubborn resistance of Nicholas II. The conservative counterrevolution of 1907 that severely restricted the franchise reduced them to a small minority in the restructured Third Duma. The remarkable abilities of their members, however, allowed the Kadets to play a prominent role in the conservative Dumas between 1907 and 1917, especially in the Progressive Bloc formed in 1915 to pressure Nicholas over failures in prosecuting World War I and in favor of renewed government reform.

When the Russian Revolution began in February 1917, Kadets played the leading role in the new Provisional Government. The Kadet-led government quickly expanded civil rights and aimed toward a new political era based on rule of law. They also worked to contain the radicalism and social-economic disruption of the revolution, and under Milyukov's leadership insisted on prosecuting the war to complete victory. Both of these policies put the Kadets on a collision course with popular opinion. The socialist leaders of the Petrograd Soviet pressured the government to seek a negotiated peace, and when Milyukov resisted, this sparked massive street demonstrations, the "April Crisis." Milyukov and some other Kadets resigned, and the Provisional Government was reconstructed on 4 May by the addition of socialist leaders from the Soviet. Although Kadets participated in this and all later reconstitutions of the Provisional Government, from May onward their influence declined.

The Kadets continued to be torn by their old division over tactics. A minority, led by Nikolai Nekrasov, advocated closer working relations with the moderate socialists and the Soviet, including adoption of some of their reform and peace policies. The majority, led by Milyukov, rejected this strategy. Indeed, with the virtual disappearance after February of truly conservative political parties the Kadets became the de facto right wing, the new "conservative" party, of Russian political life. As the revolution moved leftward in the summer, many Kadets joined the conservative reaction that sought a "restoration of order" through a military strongman. When General Lavr Kornilov emerged in the role in August, the Kadet party declined to support him officially, but many members did in fact or in spirit. After Kornilov's failure, many Kadets began to accept the inevitability of civil war. This was reinforced by their poor showing in the nationwide elections in November for the Constituent Assembly—they received only about

5 percent of the vote, although they fared better in major cities.

As civil war became a reality in early 1918, the Constitutional Democratic Party struggled to find a position consistent with its basic beliefs. Some Kadets supported efforts by moderate socialists to create an alternative to the Bolsheviks. More supported the military dictatorships of the various White movements. Within those, they tried to influence events while sustaining the party's traditional commitment to constitutionalism, rule of law, and a unified Russia. After the civil war, the party leadership tried to reconstitute a role for the party from émigrés in western Europe, but the old divisions over tactics quickly led to a formal split in July 1921 and the effective end of the party.

See also **Russian Revolutions of 1917.**

BIBLIOGRAPHY

Pearson, Raymond. *The Russian Moderates and the Crisis of Tsarism, 1914–1917.* London, 1977. Good account of the Kadets and the moderates during the war.

Rosenberg, William G. *Liberals in the Russian Revolution: The Constitutional Democratic Party, 1917–1921.* Princeton, N.J., 1974. The fullest and most authoritative account of the Constitutional Democratic Party.

———. "The Constitutional Democratic Party (Kadets)." In *Critical Companion to the Russian Revolution, 1914–1921,* edited by Edward Acton, Vladimir Iu. Cherniaev, and William G. Rosenberg, 256–266. Bloomington, Ind., 1997. A good short summary of the preceding.

Stockdale, Melissa Kirschke. *Pavel Miliukov and the Quest for a Liberal Russia, 1880–1918.* Ithaca, N.Y., 1996. The best biography of the Kadet leader.

REX A. WADE

KAFKA, FRANZ (1883–1924), German-Jewish writer.

Franz Kafka is widely considered one of the foremost European writers of the twentieth century, a visionary modernist whose dreamlike but precisely rendered narratives have been understood as allegories of existential homelessness, bureaucratization, and totalitarianism. A German-speaking Jew who was born and spent almost all of his life in Prague—until 1918 a regional capital of the Austro-Hungarian Monarchy—Kafka repeatedly experienced the clash of competing national, religious, ethnic, and linguistic identities, often from a minority perspective. Widespread anti-Semitism and anti-German sentiment from the Czech-speaking lower classes marked his entire life. He also suffered from a philistine family, tormented love relationships, and chronically poor health that led to a fatal form of laryngeal tuberculosis. Yet he was also the son of a successful businessman who studied law, occupied a managerial position in an insurance company, and had a devoted circle of friends and acquaintances, many of them artists and writers.

Like numerous Jews in his generation, Kafka rejected the assimilationist aspirations of his parents and became interested in new forms of political and cultural identity such as Zionism, cabalistic mysticism, and Yiddish theater, the latter providing major artistic inspiration. Starting with his breakthrough stories "The Judgment" and "The Metamorphosis" (both written in 1912), his works are characterized by dramatic plots, abstract or drab urban settings, a matter-of-fact narrative voice, and puzzlingly schematic characters who are befallen by unexplained disasters and punishments. These narrative predicaments—a salesman transformed overnight into a giant bug, a bank official arrested by an inscrutable Court for unknown reasons, a land surveyor who seeks unsuccessfully to find work in a mysterious Castle—gave rise in many languages to the adjective "kafkaesque," meaning an absurd, oppressive, hopeless situation. But Kafka's slim corpus of stories, aphorisms, unfinished novels (especially *The Trial* and *The Castle,* first published in 1925 and 1926) and remarkable diaries and personal correspondence (including his celebrated "Letter to His Father") have served as a source of visionary irony, dark humor, and compassion for generations of readers, including the first generation of Jews under Nazi rule; his three sisters all died in concentration camps. Nonetheless, Kafka eschewed overt political statements and dedicated himself to literature with almost religious zeal. A master stylist who schooled himself on German writers such as Johann Wolfgang von Goethe, Heinrich von Kleist, E. T. A. Hoffmann, and Franz Grillparzer, he also felt deeply related to Fyodor Dostoevsky, August Strindberg, and Gustave Flaubert, seeking in literature the moral, philosophical, and aesthetic meanings that traditional Christianity and Judaism seemed to him incapable of providing. "I am end or beginning," he wrote in a celebrated diary entry, adding that he was born too late for "fading" religions, but too early for the salvation promised by Zionism.

Despite promising success with his first publications, Kafka never became widely known during his lifetime and came to view his writing ambivalently, requesting his close friend Max Brod (1884–1968) to destroy all his papers after his death. But Brod chose to publish his work after Kafka's premature death, thus establishing the basis for his enduring reputation with writers, philosophers, theologians, and a remarkably broad international audience of general readers. During the Nazi period, Kafka's work was put on the list of forbidden Jewish authors; it first became known abroad through the efforts of German-Jewish exiles, and widespread recognition in Germany and Austria, where it is now regarded as a cornerstone of modern German literature, came after World War II. Hailed early on as an allegory of existential solitude and alienation (Albert Camus, Jean-Paul Sartre), social and political marginality (Hannah Arendt), or metaphysical uncertainty (Theodor Adorno, Walter Benjamin and, later, poststructuralist philosophers Michel Foucault and Jacques Derrida), his work has been increasingly interpreted in terms of his minority identity as a German-speaking Jew living in a Czech-speaking Catholic majority (Gilles Deleuze and Félix Guattari, Ritchie Robertson, Sander L. Gilman). Kafka himself, despite all his doubts about metaphor and the "business" of literature, held fast to his belief in the power of imaginative writing for its own sake, at once consolation for and a refuge from the absurd violence, misery, and confusion of everyday reality.

See also **Adorno, Theodor; Arendt, Hannah; Austria; Camus, Albert; Derrida, Jacques; Foucault, Michel; Sartre, Jean-Paul.**

BIBLIOGRAPHY

Primary Sources

Kafka, Franz. *The Castle.* Translated by Mark Harman. New York, 1998.

———. *The Trial.* Translated by Breon Mitchell. New York, 1998.

———. *The Metamorphosis and Other Stories.* Translated by Malcolm Pasley. London, 2000.

———. *Amerika: The Man Who Disappeared.* Translated by Michael Hoffman. New York, 2004.

Secondary Sources

Pawel, Ernst. *The Nightmare of Reason: A Life of Franz Kafka.* New York, 1984.

Robertson, Ritchie. *Kafka: Judaism, Politics and Literature.* Oxford, U.K., 1985.

MARK M. ANDERSON

KANDINSKY, WASSILY (1866–1944), Russian painter.

Born into a merchant family in Moscow on 4 December 1866, the painter, poet, playwright, and theorist Vasily Vasilyevich Kandinsky (commonly transliterated as Wassily Kandinsky) regarded Russia's ancient capital as his artistic departure-point. Graduating from Moscow University in 1892 with a degree in law, he explored many interests before deciding on the career of painter.

EARLY CAREER

Beginning in 1896, Kandinsky studied art in Munich, at first with Anton Azbè and then under Franz von Stuck at the Akademie der Künste, assimilating the principles of late realism and then jugendstil. Ever inquisitive, Kandinsky moved quickly toward a highly experimental palette after exposure to the bright colors and refractive light of North Africa in 1904 and then of the French impressionists in Paris in 1906–1907. These encounters coincided with his discovery and appreciation of indigenous art forms such as Bavarian glass painting and Russian icons with their simple forms and hieratic subjects. Seeking a more spontaneous and abstract style, Kandinsky arrived at his so-called *Compositions* and *Improvisations* and his first abstract paintings of 1911.

During the Munich years Kandinsky was part of a close-knit circle of German and Russian artists that included Alexei von Jawlensky, Franz Marc, Arnold Schoenberg, Marianna Werefkin, and his heartfelt companion, Gabriele Munter. Among his

Thirty. Painting by Wassily Kandinsky, 1937. CNAC/MNAM/DIST. RÉUNION DES MUSÉES NATIONAUX/ART RESOURCE, NY

German affiliations were the exhibition society Neue Künstlervereinigung (German New Artists' Association), of which he was elected president in 1909, and, more importantly, Der Blaue Reiter (The Blue Rider), a society and almanac that brought together talented painters, musicians, and writers, promoting an interdisciplinary and synthetic approach to questions of visual and material culture.

PHILOSOPHY

The desire to integrate the visual, the verbal, and the musical informed Kandinsky's major philosophical treatise, *Über das Geistige in der Kunst* (1912; *Concerning the Spiritual in Art*, 1914; later translated as *On the Spiritual in Art*), an abbreviated version of which was delivered on his behalf to the first All-Russian Congress of Artists in St. Petersburg in December 1911, before the entire text was published in Munich early the following year. Like many symbolists, Kandinsky, in *On the Spiritual in Art*, looked to music as the highest art, arguing that painting, too, should vibrate, emit an "inner sound," and function according to an intrinsic harmony. Kandinsky went on to identify certain parallels between the diatonic scale and the spectrum and to propose a consonance between colors and shapes, referring, for example, to the sharpness of a triangle and of the color yellow and to the high pitch of the flute or to the serenity of a circle, of the color blue and to the muted sound of the bassoon. Kandinsky welcomed the parallel quest for a new harmony in the work of the composers Arnold Schoenberg (1874–1951) and Alexander Scriabin (1872–1915).

In *On the Spiritual in Art* and elsewhere Kandinsky refers not only to established color theories—such as that of the German poet Johann Wolfgang von Goethe (1749–1832)—but also to more esoteric sources, especially theosophy with its emphasis on sensory totality and transubstantiation, extensions of which can be recognized in, for example, *Woman in Moscow* (1912).

However complex the sources, Kandinsky's elaboration of an abstract vocabulary—arhythmical and asymmetrical—depended on his fundamental recognition of the value of all modes of human perception. To this end he contemplated both the scientific and the cognitive and their combined relevance to the essential function of art—to summon the spiritual through the psyche of the artist. Although Kandinsky did not categorize himself as an expressionist, his notion of painting as the communication of an exalted vision left a deep imprint on succeeding generations, not least on the American abstract expressionists and action painters such as Jackson Pollock (1912–1956).

Overtaken in Germany by the First World War, Kandinsky returned to Moscow in 1915, where he continued to paint his abstract paintings and to develop his theories. But although he contributed after the October Revolution to various Bolshevik institutions, such as the Institute of Artistic Culture, Kandinsky found himself at loggerheads with other avant-gardists such as Kazimir Malevich and Vladimir Tatlin. In December 1921 he accepted an invitation to teach at the Bauhaus and, with his wife, Nina Andreyevskaya, left Russia forever.

Until the Nazis closed the Bauhaus in 1933, Kandinsky played an active role as teacher and researcher in Weimar and Dessau, moving closely with Walter Gropius, Johannes Itten, Paul Klee, and László Moholy-Nagy, in particular. He continued to concentrate on painting, at first supporting a geometric style informed by constructivism, and then entering a more biomorphic phase. He also gave attention to functional design, decorating porcelain and painting the sets for a 1928 production of *Kartinki s vystavki* (1874; *Pictures at an Exhibition*) by Modest Mussorgsky (1839–1881).

Moving to Paris, Kandinsky continued to paint and to write. He achieved wide acclaim through exhibitions in Europe and America and through important critical appreciations by Will Grohmann, Meyer Schapiro, and Christian Zervos, even if the Germany of Adolf Hitler (1889–1945) and Soviet Union of Joseph Stalin (1879–1953) rejected his art as pernicious—Kandinsky was represented at Hitler's "Entartete Kunst" (Degenerate Art) exhibition in Munich in 1937. His last paintings, such as *Twilight* (1943), carry references to both surrealism and zoomorphism, testifying to the inexorable curiosity and interpretive powers of their creator. Kandinsky died on 13 December 1944 in Neuilly-sur-Seine.

See also **Degenerate Art Exhibit; Expressionism; Modernism.**

BIBLIOGRAPHY

Barnett, Vivian Endicott. *Kandinsky Watercolours: Catalogue Raisonné.* 2 vols. London, 1992.

———. Introduction to "Vasilii Kandinsky and the Science of Art." Special issue, *Experiment* 8 (2002).

Boissel, Jessica, and Jean-Claude Marcadé, eds. *Wassily Kandinsky: Du théâtre—Über das Theater—O teatre.* Paris, 1998.

Grohmann, W. *Kandinsky.* New York, 1958.

Hahl-Koch, Jelena. *Kandinsky.* New York, 1993.

Kurchanova, N., ed. "Festschrift for Vivian Endicott Barnett." Special issue, *Experiment* 9 (2002).

Lindsay, Kenneth C., and Peter Vergo, eds. *Kandinsky: Complete Writings on Art.* 2nd ed. New York, 1994.

Poling, Clark. *Kandinsky-Unterricht am Bauhaus.* Weingarten, Germany, 1982.

Roethel, Hans K., and Jean K. Benjamin. *Kandinsky: Catalogue Raisonné of the Oil-Paintings.* 2 vols. Ithaca, N.Y., 1982–1984.

JOHN E. BOWLT

KAPP PUTSCH.

The Kapp Putsch of March 1920 involved an abortive attempt by disgruntled rightist politicians and military officers to overthrow the young Weimar Republic in Germany and replace it with a military dictatorship. The front man for the rebellion was a former Prussian civil servant named Wolfgang Kapp, but the real leader was General Walther von Lüttwitz, the commandant of Berlin. Muscle for the putsch came primarily from the Ehrhardt Marine Brigade, one of the right-wing Free Corps that cropped up in the immediate post–World War I period to fight against Polish encroachments in the Baltic region and communist insurgencies around Germany.

The immediate impetus for the Kapp Putsch was an order by the government of President Friedrich Ebert to disband the Free Corps, including the Ehrhardt Brigade. This decision was forced on the Ebert government by the Allied Powers, which saw the Free Corps as a violation of the military terms of the Treaty of Versailles. Convinced that the Ehrhardt Brigade was vital to the defense of Berlin, Lüttwitz ordered Captain Hermann Ehrhardt to march on the capital and take it over. On 13 March 1920, Ehrhardt's men, wearing helmets emblazoned with swastikas, set out from their base west of Berlin for the capital. They met no resistance from the regular army because Chief of Staff Hans von Seeckt, waiting to see how the rebels fared, refused an order from the Ebert government to repel the coup. Fearing capture by the rebels, the government fled to Dresden and then on to Stuttgart. Upon their arrival in the capital, Ehrhardt's men were met by Kapp and former General Erich Ludendorff, who was still a hero to the Right despite his central role in Germany's military defeat in World War I, which he and fellow rightists blamed on a "stab in the back" from leftists and Jews.

For the next few days Kapp and his men struggled to assert their control over Berlin and its environs, but their efforts were hampered by a general strike that shut down economic activity in parts of the city. The putschists were not equipped to deal with the strike, and their problems were compounded by their own ineptitude. It took them three days to find someone to type their manifesto announcing their seizure of power. Other paperwork was delayed because Ebert's government, in a brilliant act of preventative sabotage, had removed the rubber stamps necessary to the functioning of any German administration. Lacking money to pay the rebel troops, Kapp ordered Ehrhardt to take the necessary funds from the state treasury, but the latter refused on the grounds that he was an officer, not a bank robber. After just four days the putschists threw in the towel: Kapp flew to Sweden; Ludendorff decamped for Bavaria; and Lüttwitz resigned his command and fled to

Hungary. On their way back to their base, however, Ehrhardt's infuriated men took out their frustration on the Berliners. When a young boy mocked them, they clubbed him to death and then fired point-blank into a crowd of angry bystanders, killing twelve.

A persistent mythology credits Berlin's workers with single-handedly saving the republic, but opposition to the putsch from other elements was just as crucial. Many conservative bureaucrats refused to cooperate with the adventurers around Kapp, and the republic's central military officials, while not actively opposing the putsch, also refused to assist the operation.

Significantly, just as the coup was collapsing, Adolf Hitler flew up to Berlin from Munich to monitor the situation and possibly be of assistance to the rebels. Unable to be of any use in Berlin, he soon returned to Munich, where, some three and a half years later, he staged his own abortive grab for power, the so-called Beer Hall Putsch.

The comic-opera qualities of the Kapp-Lüttwitz fiasco should not mask the fact that this episode was a serious threat to the fledgling Weimar order. Although there is some disagreement among historians about whether, with better organization, the coup might have succeeded, virtually all scholars recognize that the behavior of the regular army at this moment revealed a grave weakness in the republican system. Scholars agree too that the putsch illustrated a deep loathing for democratic principles on the part of significant elements of the population, especially among the old elites. Moreover, it should be noted that while the putsch failed in Berlin, counterrevolutionaries in Munich used it as a pretext to stage a nonviolent coup in Bavaria that *did* succeed, thus creating a political environment in which Hitler's Nazi movement could take root and blossom.

See also **Germany; Hitler, Adolf; Nazism.**

BIBLIOGRAPHY

Erger, Johannes. *Der Kapp-Lüttwitz-Putsch.* Düsseldorf, 1967.

Feldman, Gerald D. *The Great Disorder: Politics, Economics, and Society in the German Inflation, 1914–1924.* New York, 1993.

Gordon, Harold J. *The Reichswehr and the German Republic, 1919–1926.* Princeton, N.J., 1957.

Large, David Clay. *Berlin.* New York, 2000.

Waite, Robert G. L. *Vanguard of Nazism: The Free Corps Movement in Postwar Germany, 1918–1923.* Cambridge, Mass., 1952.

DAVID CLAY LARGE

KARADŽIĆ, RADOVAN (b. 1945),
Serbian leader and accused war criminal.

In 2005 Radovan Karadžić was one of the two "most wanted" fugitives from justice at the International Criminal Tribunal for the Former Yugoslavia—the other was Ratko Mladić (b. 1943), with whom he stood indicted jointly on many counts. Karadžić is an ethnic Serb born in Montenegro in 1945. His early childhood was overshadowed by his father's imprisonment for his wartime service with the Chetniks, Serb guerrilla fighters who opposed the communist-led partisans. The Chetniks favored the restoration of the prewar Serbian monarchical dynasty and the authority of the Orthodox Church. The same allegiances clearly lodged deeply in Karadžić, but were necessarily concealed as he made his early career in communist Yugoslavia. In 1960 he moved to Sarajevo, where he graduated in medicine and later practiced as a consultant psychiatrist; he has also published poetry and is something of a musician.

As communist Yugoslavia began to break up, Karadžić and a group of nationalist intellectuals formed the Serb Democratic Party in Bosnia, which campaigned with the aim of creating a unified state for all Serbs—a Greater Serbia. They were backed by Slobodan Milošević (1941–2006), president of the Federal Republic of Yugoslavia (FRY), the successor state to Tito's (Josip Broz, 1892–1980) federation. Although reduced territorially to Serbia and Montenegro, the FRY controlled the Yugoslav army, by far the most powerful military force in the region. Anticipating international recognition of Bosnia-Herzegovina as a sovereign state (6 April 1992), the Bosnian Serbs rejected the authority of the Sarajevo government, and on March 27 proclaimed the breakaway Republika Srpska (Serb Republic), with its capital and assembly at Pale. The military arm of the new entity was the Bosnian Serb Army (BSA), fifty to eighty thousand regular troops of the Army of Yugoslavia, supposedly natives of Bosnia, assigned by Milošević to fight in what he presented as a civil war, not an invasion. At Milošević's insistence, General Ratko Mladić was appointed to command the Serb forces, although Karadžić was nominally Mladić's political superior.

Karadžić's brief moment in the international political limelight came in the context of a bigger game being played out by Milošević and Mladić. The BSA overran 70 percent of Bosnia within days, and (assisted by Serbian paramilitaries) carried out a campaign of ethnic cleansing, committing atrocities that drew mounting international condemnation. It seems clear that Karadžić had little influence over Mladić in deciding military strategy, which was coordinated through Belgrade in concert with the operations of the Yugoslav army in Croatia. Karadžić was politically secure only in his power base in Republika Srpska. As long as Milošević had a use for him, Karadžić was allowed to cut a genial and cultured figure in the media (he speaks good English) and at international peace negotiations. By the spring of 1993, however, Milošević was under enormous pressure from western sanctions, and he was forced to withdraw his support for the Serbs in Croatia and Bosnia. In May 1993 Karadžić was induced to agree to the Vance-Owen plan, which provided for the cantonization of Bosnia-Herzegovina, but stipulated that it must be ratified by the Pale Assembly. Two hardliners, Biljana Plavšić (b. 1930) and Momčilo Krajišnik (b. 1945), engineered a veto, egged on by Mladić. From then on, Karadžić increasingly faded from public view, but he did attempt a bold personal initiative in December 1994. Through a medical-school friend in the United States, he contrived to bring former U.S. president Jimmy Carter (b. 1924) to Sarajevo to negotiate an end to the war, and once more Karadžić's headquarters at Pale became the focus of intense media attention. Why the initiative failed is a matter of debate, but Karadžić emerges from the episode with unexpected credit, given the picture often painted of him as an intransigent nationalist and major war criminal. It is of interest to note that by this time his relations with Mladić, who was now entering a phase of wild defiance of international opinion in his brutal conduct of the war, had broken down completely.

The extent of Karadžić's culpability for genocide and war crimes remains to be decided at The Hague, where he is indicted on two counts of genocide and nine other grave charges of violations of human rights. Whatever the outcome, all the evidence is that Karadžić was, and remains, a charismatic and popular figure among the Bosnian Serbs. The Dayton Agreements left the Republika Srpska intact, and as of 2006 its people are probably hiding him still, after nine years on the run. Karadžić championed the right of the Serbs to self-determination in the face of what he saw as the breakup of Yugoslavia by outside powers, and they will not easily give him up.

See also **Bosnia-Herzegovina; Crime and Justice; Milošević, Slobodan; Mladić, Ratko; Montenegro; Sarajevo; Serbia; Yugoslavia.**

BIBLIOGRAPHY

Allcock, John B., Marko Milivojević, and John J. Horton, eds. *Conflict in the Former Yugoslavia: An Encyclopedia.* Denver, Colo., 1998.

Bulatović, Ljiljana. *Radovan.* Beograd, 2002.

Čavoški, Kosta. *The Hague against Justice Revisited: The Case of Dr. Radovan Karadžić.* Belgrade, 1997.

Moon, Paul. *The Shadow of Radovan Karadzic: An Investigation of a War Criminal.* Palmerston North, New Zealand, 1998.

O'Shea, Brendan. *Perception and Reality in the Modern Yugoslav Conflict: Myth, Falsehood, and Deceit 1991–1995.* New York, 2005. Has a great deal of interest to say about the character and conduct of Karadžić, in the context of a survey of the war in Bosnia written by someone close to events.

United Nations. International Criminal Tribunal for the Former Yugoslavia. Available at http://www.un.org/icty/.

LESLIE BENSON

KÁROLYI, MIHÁLY (1875–1955),
Hungarian democratic politician and president of the Hungarian Republic in January–March 1919.

Mihály, Count Károlyi von Nagykároli, was born in Budapest to one of the oldest and wealthiest of Hungarian aristocratic families. He started his political career in 1901 in the ruling Liberal Party but in 1905 broke off and became the member of parliament of the Independence Party. After the party was reorganized he became its president in 1913. Károlyi heavily criticized the conservatism of the old liberal elite and the selfishness of the Hungarian aristocracy. As he put it in his memoirs, he always felt ashamed of his own wealth in a country where the majority of the people lived in poverty and deprivation. His program urged the extension of democratic liberties, particularly universal suffrage. He opposed militarism and the German orientation of the Austro-Hungarian Monarchy's foreign policy. When World War I broke out in August 1914 he took a firm stand against it, notwithstanding public enthusiasm for war.

His political ideas allied him with the civil radicals and the social democrats. Károlyi believed that without democratic reforms and change in the policy of forced assimilation for national minorities—who actually made up the majority of the population—the growing social and national tensions would soon tear apart Hungary. His opponents, and their leading figure, Premier Count István Tisza, were convinced of just the opposite: that yielding to democratic and nationalistic demands would shake the social order and lead to the immediate collapse and disintegration of both the monarchy and Hungary.

As the public became weary of the war, Károlyi's peace agitation received increasing support. He established the leading opposition force, the Károlyi Party, which formed a political coalition, the Suffrage Bloc, with the civil radicals and social democrats. The bloc demanded universal suffrage and the federal reorganization of the monarchy. It also urged immediate peace talks with the Entente Powers. Károlyi, perhaps naively, believed that on the basis of Wilsonian principles fair peace conditions could be attained.

By late October 1918 the monarchy's military forces collapsed. On 31 October 1918 a civil democratic revolution broke out in Budapest. King Charles IV appointed Károlyi, leader of the National Council, as prime minister. The next day, under massive public pressure, the king abdicated and the independent Hungarian Republic

Mihály Károlyi, photographed in his office in Paris c. 1940. ©Hulton-Deutsch Collection/Corbis

was proclaimed. The Károlyi government faced an extremely difficult situation. The initial national and democratic enthusiasm was rapidly fading away. The government was unable to overcome the economic crisis and food shortages. The armies of neighboring states continued to march into and occupy former Hungarian territories with the tacit permission of the Entente. Apparently the government could not stop the disintegration of the country. The Entente Powers put off recognition of the new state and refused offers for negotiations with Károlyi, frustrating his hope that the Entente would appreciate the country's democratic transition.

On 11 January 1919 Károlyi was elected president. He introduced democratic political reforms and initiated modest land reform, which he started with his own lands near Kápolna. Yet he could not strengthen his position in the international field.

On 20 March 1919 the Entente resident colonel Ferdinand Vix submitted a memorandum that required Hungary's further retreat from its territories. Károlyi refused to concede the ultimatum and resigned. His resignation led to a takeover by Béla Kun and the Hungarian Bolsheviks.

In July 1919 he and his family emigrated to Paris. In 1921 he was tried in absentia for high treason and his lands and estates were confiscated. Károlyi was disappointed in the western democracies, which had come to terms with the "reactionary," "counterrevolutionary" regime of Governor Miklós Horthy. Károlyi sought partnership with the democratic leaders of neighboring countries, especially with the Czechoslovak president Tomáš Garrigue Masaryk. Meanwhile his political views became radicalized as he developed socialist and communist ideas. In 1931 he visited the Soviet Union. After Adolf Hitler took power in Germany in 1933, Károlyi's communist sympathies became even stronger. He even contemplated joining the Communist Party. His closest friend and political ally, the Hungarian civil radical politician and émigré Oszkár Jászi, heavily criticized him for his communist inclinations. Yet Károlyi, who had already given up his pacifist views, regarded communism as the single true force that could stop fascism and attain social progress.

During the war Károlyi lived in Great Britain. In 1944 he organized the Movement for the New Democratic Hungary. In May 1946 he returned to his home country and his name was mentioned as a potential candidate for president of the postwar Hungarian People's Republic. Eventually he was appointed Hungary's ambassador to Paris. In 1949 he resigned as an act of protest against the show trial of László Rajk. He lived in France for the rest of his life.

See also **Horthy, Miklós; Hungary.**

BIBLIOGRAPHY

Primary Sources

Károlyi, Mihály. *Memoirs of Michael Karolyi: Faith without Illusion.* Translated by Catherine Károlyi. New York, 1957.

Secondary Sources

Hajdu, Tibor. *Károlyi Mihály: Politikai életrajz.* Budapest, 1976.

Jemnitz, János, and Litván, György. *Szerette az igazságot: Károlyi Mihály élete.* Budapest, 1977.

Ormos, Mária. *From Padua to the Trianon, 1918–1920.* Boulder, Colo., 1990.

Romsics, Ignácz. *Hungary in the Twentieth Century.* Budapest, 1999.

Seaton-Watson, Hugh. *Eastern Europe between the Wars 1918–1941.* New York, 1945.

ANDRÁS MINK

KATYŃ FOREST MASSACRE.

On 23 August 1939 Adolf Hitler and Joseph Stalin signed the German-Soviet Nonaggression Pact. A secret protocol appended to the treaty divided up German and Russian spheres of influence in eastern Europe and opened the gates to war. Nazi Germany invaded Poland from the west on 1 September 1939, followed by the Soviet Union from the east on 17 September 1939. From September 1939 through June 1941, the Soviet Union occupied half of the territory of Poland. During a September 1939 campaign against the retreating Polish army, which had already been defeated by the Germans, the Red Army took approximately 250,000 Polish soldiers and officers as prisoners of war. The captive Polish officers, some ten thousand in all, did not represent a typical officer corps. Most of them were reservists mobilized at the time of the war, men with university education and advanced degrees, many prominent in their professions, including several hundred judges and university professors from legal, medical, and engineering faculties. Captured officers were put into three prison camps in the Soviet Union, in Kozelsk, Ostashkov, and Starobielsk, where they were interrogated by the NKVD, the Soviet secret police.

After Nazi Germany launched its assault on the Soviet Union in June of 1941, the USSR joined the Allied cause, and the Polish government in exile, which was based in London, renewed diplomatic relations with the Soviets. A treaty was signed between the two governments, and several hundred thousand Polish citizens who had been arrested and deported by the Soviet authorities during the previous twenty months were released in the Soviet Union. General Władysław Sikorski, prime minister of the Polish government in exile, signed the treaty with the Soviet Union in the face of vigorous protests from leading Polish politicians in London, who were disturbed by Stalin's refusal to renounce territorial acquisitions made by the Soviet Union in 1939 and guarantee postwar restoration of Poland within its prewar borders. Sikorski, nevertheless, decided that he must sign the treaty without delay since scores of Poles lingering in Soviet captivity were dying each day from mistreatment and destitution. As part of the treaty provisions, able-bodied men who were released by the Soviets could join units of a new Polish army in designated assembly points.

While the Polish army was being organized in the Soviet Union by the newly released General Władysław Anders, Polish authorities were unable to locate thousands of officers who had been taken prisoner in the eastern part of the country during the September 1939 campaign. Polish envoys repeatedly asked the Soviet authorities to find these men and release them promptly, both to fulfill the treaty obligation and because they were needed to staff the newly created military units. But to no avail. All trace of several thousand men, many identified by released colleagues or family members with whom they had corresponded briefly from captivity, vanished in the spring of 1940. In one of the most absurd and cynical dialogues of the war, Prime Minister Sikorski, most amicably received during his first visit to the Kremlin by Joseph Stalin, insisted that he had a list of several thousand officers who had been held in captivity by the Red Army and were not released. Stalin replied, "It is impossible. They must have escaped." "Where could they escape?" demanded a surprised General Anders. "Well, perhaps to Manchuria," retorted Stalin without missing a beat (Kot, p. 194).

Then, in April of 1943, inside a former Soviet secret police (NKVD) compound in the vicinity of a hamlet called Katyń, a German communications unit disinterred from a mass grave the remains of executed Polish officers. They were buried in uniform, many with bullet holes in the back of their skulls and personal documents and letters from home stuffed in their pockets. The Nazis immediately seized on the gruesome discovery to bolster their anti-Bolshevik propaganda. The Polish government in exile called on the International Red Cross to appoint a commission to carry out an exhumation and to issue an expert opinion about when, and therefore by whom, the crime had been committed. The Soviet government, which all along claimed that the German discovery was a hoax contrived by the Germans to mask their own war crimes, broke off diplomatic relations with Poland on 25 April 1943.

The truth about the mass grave of Polish officers in Katyń remained a closely held secret. A document preserved in the Soviet presidential archives, dated 5 March 1940, revealed that the Politburo of the Soviet Communist Party had issued the order to have Polish prisoners executed. Stalin's signature, together with those of Vyacheslav Molotov, Kliment Voroshilov, and Anastas Mikoyan, appear on the document. On the basis of this decision, 21,857 people (some

15,000 of them POWs; the rest were Polish policemen, civil servants, and other prisoners deemed politically dangerous) were put to death. Of this number, 4,421 were executed and buried in the mass graves at Katyń. For decades the USSR denied any complicity in the crime. After the Red Army reconquered the area near Smolensk that included the Katyń forest, a Soviet commission of inquiry (called the Burdenko Commission after its chairman) carried out some exhumations, interviewed local people, and declared as proven that the Germans had murdered Polish officers. Soviet prosecutors at the Nuremberg trials charged the Germans with the Katyń massacre, but the International Military Tribunal refused to accept the charge, and Katyń was not mentioned in the final verdict. Nevertheless, since all German war criminals were declared guilty as charged by the tribunal, the Soviet government, media, encyclopedias, and official history claimed that Germans were guilty of the crime. Finally, in April of 1990, President Mikhail Gorbachev made a tacit admission of Soviet responsibility, and on 14 October 1992 Russian president Boris Yeltsin gave copies of the 5 March 1940 Politburo decision ordering the massacre to Polish president Lech Wałęsa.

See also **Occupation, Military; Poland; Soviet Union; War Crimes; World War II.**

BIBLIOGRAPHY

Katyń Forest Massacre Hearings before the Select Committee. Eighty-Second Congress, First and Second Session. Washington, D.C., 1952.

Kot, Stanislaw. *Listy z Rosji do gen. Sikorskiego.* London, 1955.

Wosik, Ewa, ed. *Katyń: Dokumenty ludobójstwa: Dokumenty i materialy archiwalne przekazane Polsce 14 października 1992r.* Warsaw, 1992.

Zawodny, J. K. *Death in the Forest: The Story of the Katyń Forest Massacre.* Notre Dame, Ind., 1962.

JAN T. GROSS

KELLOGG-BRIAND PACT.

The Kellogg-Briand Pact marked the high point of the League of Nations and common security between the two world wars. Proposed by the head of the

U.S. State Department, Frank B. Kellogg, at the initiative of the French foreign affairs minister, Aristide Briand, this pact was signed in Paris on 27 August 1928 by fifteen countries. This was a declaration of the common renunciation of war, placing it "outside the law."

In 1927–1928 belief in common security was at its height. Economic conditions were satisfactory, and world public opinion believed in a lasting peace. The idea of incorporating in the common security system the two major powers that were not members of the League of Nations, the United States and the USSR, gained increasingly wide support. In France, Aristide Briand persevered with his policy of rapprochement with Germany. In fact, a few days after Germany was admitted to the League of Nations in September 1926, Aristide Briand met Gustav Stresemann, the German foreign affairs minister, in Thoiry. At this meeting, the two men reached agreement on the need to resolve the differences between their two countries. This project entailed some major political concessions for France: evacuation of the Rhineland, occupied since 1923; abolition of military control and restoration of the Saar region. In return, Stresemann accepted the principle of a capital payment to France from the interest on industrial and railway stock as reparations. While this proposal was well received in Berlin, it was rejected by the French president of the council, Raymond Poincaré. There was also a hostile reaction in parliamentary circles in Paris.

Confronted with this deadlock, from 1927 Briand turned his attention to the development of common security. In April 1927, on the tenth anniversary of the U.S. entry into the First World War, he addressed a communication to the American people, suggesting a joint Franco-American commitment to abjure war as a political method. This proposal emerged in a context in which Franco-American relations were strained by the question of war debts. In April 1926 an agreement had been signed between the two states to establish a reimbursement plan for French debts in sixty-two annuities (the Mellon-Béranger Agreement of 29 April 1926). One year later, France had still not ratified this agreement. Aristide Briand hoped that his proposal would bring the two states closer together.

Under the influence of Nicholas M. Butler (president of Columbia University), Senator William Borah (president of the Senate's foreign affairs committee), and the pacifist S. O. Levinson, Frank Kellogg—in his response to the Briand proposal on 27 December 1927—modified the project by transforming it into a multilateral pact to abjure war that would include all the states of the world. This new project far surpassed Briand's original intentions and led to discussions lasting several months. Some important questions then arose for the negotiators: would such a pact be compatible with the League of Nations pact that made provision for a member state having to take military sanctions against another in the event of an attack? Was it possible to agree to the American request for a reference to the right of peoples to legitimate defense? In the intervening period, on 6 February 1928, the anniversary of the first treaty of friendship concluded between the two states, France and the United States renewed their convention of arbitration for twenty years. It was finally in April 1928, after wide consultation with Germany, Great Britain, Italy, and Japan, that Frank Kellogg's proposal was accepted by France. The treaty stated in Article 1 that: "The high contracting parties solemnly declare in the names of their respective peoples that they condemn recourse to war for the solution of international controversies, and abjure it as an instrument of national policy in their relations with one another." Article 2 was formulated as follows: "The high contracting parties agree that the settlement or solution of all disputes or conflicts of whatever nature or of whatever origin they may be, which may arise among them, shall never be sought except by pacific means."

Accordingly, the Kellogg-Briand Pact was signed in Paris in August 1928 in an atmosphere of enthusiasm. The American president Calvin Coolidge telegraphed from Washington to say that "Briand's idea is as great as the world." Briand, who suggested dedicating the treaty to all the dead of the First World War, described this as a new date in the history of humanity. On 27 August 1928 the American government invited forty-nine states to sign the treaty. Fifty-nine states, including the USSR, finally subscribed to this. Nine of these were not then members of the League of Nations. A general mood of euphoria prevailed, despite the fact that this agreement was very general and only issued a moral condemnation of war, without envisaging either sanctions or any framework for specific action in the event of an act of aggression. It is true that international events in the following years showed that this agreement had had a huge symbolic impact but no practical effect other than reopening the Franco-German dialogue (evacuation of the Rhineland and establishment of the Young Plan). The criticism to which it has been open should not, however, be allowed to overshadow the innovative nature of the process in terms of both challenging the right to war and constructing a peaceful international society. In fact, until 1914 international law imposed no restriction on the use of force. In 1919 the League of Nations pact established a distinction between legitimate and illegitimate wars. In 1945 the UN Charter provided for the obligation to resolve conflicts by peaceful means (Article 33). The Kellogg-Briand Pact thus emerges as an intermediate stage in the development of the law relating to war in international relations. Furthermore, both Frank B. Kellogg in 1929 and Nicholas M. Butler in 1931 received the Nobel Peace Prize for their roles in the signing and promotion of the Kellogg-Briand Pact.

See also **Briand, Aristide; League of Nations; Reparations; Rhineland Occupation; Versailles, Treaty of; World War I.**

BIBLIOGRAPHY

Primary Sources

Butler, Nicholas M. *The Path to Peace: Essays and Addresses on Peace and Its Making.* New York, 1930.

Lysen, Arnoldus. *Le Pacte Kellogg: Documents concernant le traité multilatéral contre la guerre, signé à Paris le 27 août 1928, recueillis avec une préface, un tableau synoptique des projets américains et français, et une bibliographie.* Leiden, 1928.

Myers, Denys P. *Origin and Conclusion of the Paris Pact, and The Renunciation of War by Kirby Page.* 1929. Reprint, with a new introduction by Charles DeBenedetti. New York, 1972.

Wehberg, Hans W. *The Outlawry of War: A Series of Lectures Delivered before the Academy of International Law at the Hague and in the Institut Universitaire de Hautes Etudes Internationales at Geneva.* Washington, D.C., 1931.

Secondary Sources

Brownliei, Ian. *International Law and the Use of Force by States.* Oxford, U.K., 1963.

Buchheit, Eva. *Der Briand-Kellogg-Pact von 1928: Machtpolitik oder Friedensstreben?* Münster, 1998.

Elisha, Achille. *Aristide Briand: la paix mondiale et l'Union Européenne.* Louvain-la-Neuve, Belgium, 2000.

Ferrell, Robert H. *Peace in Their Time: The Origins of the Kellogg-Briand Pact.* New Haven, Conn., 1952. New edition 1968.

Ferrell, Robert H., ed. *The American Secretaries of States and Their Diplomacy.* Vol. 11. 1963.

DZOVINAR KEVONIAN

KELLY, PETRA (1947–1992), Green Party activist.

Petra K. Kelly was educated at American University (BA, 1970) and at the University of Amsterdam (MA, 1971). Her theoretical interest in international political affairs and European integration shaped Kelly's political activities throughout the 1970s and 1980s. Between 1972 and 1982, Kelly, as a member of the West German Social Democratic Party (SPD), held several administrative positions in the European parliament in Brussels, where she was involved in social, health, and environmental affairs. At the same time, she was also actively engaged in several West German social and humanitarian organizations, such as the Citizens' Organization for the Environment and the Society for Nonviolence

In 1979 Kelly left the SPD, became a founding member of the Greens, and was immediately elected one of the party's speakers. Much of the Greens' platform was derived from existing left liberal, antiauthoritarian, Marxist, feminist, gay, and nonviolent viewpoints, but only within the party did these positions become a serious alternative, an oppositional and anticapitalist program. Their demands included establishing a nuclear-free Central Europe, peace through disarmament, a decentralized economy, alternative energy sources, effective environmental protection, grassroots democracy, a reduction in noise pollution, equal rights for women, better health and social services for the elderly and the economically disadvantaged, an extension of basic rights to gays and foreign

German Green Party member Petra Kelly (right) and Gabrielle Gottwald hold a banner in the German parliament, May 1983. The bannner reads "Herr Kohl, support of the U.S.A. in Nicaragua means complicity in the death of Albrecht Pflaum." Pflaum was a German Peace Corps worker who was killed in Nicaragua. ©BETTMANN/CORBIS

workers, and the abolition of some authoritarian structures in society. In the following years, Kelly became known internationally as a courageous activist and spokesperson on these issues, and in 1982 she was awarded the so-called Alternative Nobel Prize by the Stockholm-based Livelihood Foundation. A year later, the Greens, then known as the "antiparty party," received worldwide attention when they were first elected to the West German parliament. In addition to her work as a member of parliament and of the Foreign Relations Committee, Kelly continued her worldwide political engagement, most notably through campaigns for the native peoples of Australia and North America.

Within West German society, the success of the Greens led to a public debate on reducing energy consumption, producing durable goods, and introducing mandatory recycling. Simultaneously, the Cold War, with its escalating arms race between the United States and the USSR, especially after NATO decided in 1979 to deploy more nuclear warheads and missiles in Central Europe, led to widespread fear of nuclear war. Disarmament, promoted by many European peace movements and by the Krefeld Appeal, which was signed by more than five million Germans and supported by churches, trade unions, and pacifists, seemed the only viable solution. Even large-scale political rallies between 1981 and 1983 could not prevent deployment, however. Throughout the 1980s, a period of constant economic growth and conservative politics, leftist and alternative attitudes and movements disappeared, and most members of the Greens chose to adapt to the changed political climate. Kelly remained true to her principles and as a result was not reelected to the first united German parliament in 1990.

In October 1992, Kelly and her companion Gert Bastian were discovered dead in their apartment. It remains unclear whether this was a double suicide and, if so, to what extent it was precipitated by Kelly's increasing disillusionment with ecological politics.

See also **Environmentalism; Feminism; Greens.**

BIBLIOGRAPHY

Primary Sources

Kelly, Petra K. *Fighting for Hope.* Translated by Marianne Howarth. Boston, 1984.

———. *Thinking Green! Essays on Environmentalism, Feminism, and Nonviolence.* Berkeley, Calif., 1994.

Kelly, Petra K., Glenn D. Paige, and Sarah Gilliatt. *Nonviolence Speaks to Power.* Honolulu, 1992.

Secondary Sources

Parkin, Sara. *The Life and Death of Petra Kelly.* London, 1994.

PETER MORRIS-KEITEL

KERENSKY, ALEXANDER (1881–1970),

leader during the February Revolution and prime minister of the Russian Provisional Government from July to October 1917.

Alexander Fyodorovich Kerensky was born in Simbirsk (later Ulyanovsk), Russia, where his father was a schoolteacher and administrator. Among his father's pupils, by a quirk of history, was Vladimir Ulyanov, the future Lenin. The two future rivals did not know each other in Simbirsk because of age differences. After spending his teen years in Tashkent in Central Asia, Kerensky studied history and law at St. Petersburg University. On graduation he became an attorney, joining a legal aid society that provided free legal assistance to the poor. Involvement in radical politics led to his temporary arrest in December 1905. In 1906 he became a defense lawyer in political cases and began to make a name for himself as a defender of popular causes and ordinary people against government or employer repression. In 1912 he was appointed to a special commission established by the Duma to investigate the Lena gold-field massacre, where about two hundred striking miners had been shot. In 1912 Kerensky was asked to stand for election to the Fourth Duma on the Trudovik ticket (variously translated as Toilers', Labor, or Workers' Party). The Trudoviks represented the moderate wing of the Socialist Revolutionary Party and of the nonparty populist movement. Kerensky's energy and untiring criticism of government abuses made him a leading spokesman of the radical wing in the Duma.

When the Russian Revolution began in February 1917 Kerensky plunged into the revolutionary thicket. During its earliest days he seemed to be everywhere—giving a speech here, haranguing soldiers there, scurrying in and out of meetings, issuing orders, dramatically arresting members of the old regime and equally dramatically rescuing others from mob violence. Still a young man of thirty-six, he was the popular hero of the February Revolution. He was variously dubbed the "people's tribune," the "people's minister," and "the symbol of democracy," among other sobriquets. When the Petrograd Soviet was formed on 27 February he was elected vice-chairman. He entered the Provisional Government when it was formed on 2 March, becoming the only person to be in both the Soviet and the government. This put him in a uniquely influential political position. His face adorned store windows and postcards, and a medallion bearing his likeness circulated.

Within the new government Kerensky, as minister of justice, quickly asserted himself in pushing a wide range of reforms and policies, and his popularity gave him tremendous authority. When the government divided between the more conservative government members around Pavel Milyukov and Alexander Guchkov—who attempted to assert government authority and to diminish the Soviet's role—and a group around Prince Lvov that felt it necessary to work closely with the Soviet because of its enormous popular support, Kerensky associated with the latter group. When the "April Crisis" over the question of Russia's continued participation in the war on the basis of "war to victory" led to Milyukov's resignation and the reorganization of the Provisional Government, Kerensky became minister of war and his influence grew. He became the embodiment of coalition government—one that included socialist leaders of the Soviet along with liberal political leaders—and the government's key figure.

Alexander Kerensky (in vehicle) inspects his troops, 1917. ©Hulton-Deutsch Collection/Corbis

In May and June he was the focal point for preparations for the June offensive, an undertaking the government hoped would both revitalize the army and relieve pressure on Russia's allies on the western front. Kerensky made long tours of the front to stimulate fighting enthusiasm among soldiers with his stirring oratory. The offensive was unpopular from the start and its outcome disastrous. Nonetheless Kerensky's personal reputation survived temporarily and he became minister-president of the new "second coalition" government. Moreover, as other prominent political figures left the government, Kerensky became increasingly dominant within it. Even as he achieved complete leadership of the government, however, both its and his own popularity eroded. The Provisional Government was failing to solve problems and to fulfill popular aspirations, and Kerensky's identity as its leader led to a rapid drop in his popularity.

The Kornilov affair in late August, a conflict growing out of the complex relationship between Kerensky and General Lavr Kornilov that many saw as an unsuccessful counterrevolutionary attempt, earned Kerensky the hostility of both left and right and completed the destruction of his reputation. Kerensky's government was now widely perceived as a stopgap until other leading political figures could decide on a new one. His decision to move against the Bolsheviks before the Second Congress of Soviets met sparked the October Revolution, which swept him from power.

Immediately after the Bolshevik seizure of power Kerensky attempted to regain power by leading a military assault against Petrograd but failed. He then spent several weeks underground, trying unsuccessfully to organize an anti-Bolshevik movement. In May 1918 he made his way out of the country. He played no significant role in the civil war and lived the rest of his life in foreign exile. During the 1920s and 1930s he was active in émigré politics in Germany and France, where he edited a newspaper, *Dni* (Days). In 1940 he fled the Nazis, coming to the United States, where he lectured and wrote. He died on 11 June 1970.

Kerensky was both the heroic and the tragic figure of the Russian Revolution of 1917. Thin, pale, with flashing eyes, theatrical gestures, and vivid verbal imagery, he was a dramatic and mesmerizing speaker with an incredible ability to move his listeners. Announcement of his appearance at the "concert meetings" that were so popular in 1917 drew huge crowds to hear him. The popular idol of the first weeks, he became the personification of the Provisional Government. Standing at the point where moderate socialism blended into the left wing of liberalism, he was the perfect political embodiment of the first six months of the revolution. As the year wore on, however, Kerensky's oratory could not compensate for the government's failures, and his weaknesses as a leader became more apparent. The new paper currencies issued by the Provisional Government under his leadership were popularly called *Kerenki,* and because inflation quickly made them worthless, his name thus took on something of that meaning as well. It was a tragic end for the hero of the February Revolution.

See also **Russian Revolutions of 1917.**

BIBLIOGRAPHY

Primary Sources

Browder, Robert Paul, and Alexander Kerensky, eds. *The Russian Provisional Government, 1917.* 3 vols. Stanford, Calif., 1961. Excellent collection of documents about the Provisional Government, in the process of which Kerensky's role is laid out.

Kerensky, Alexander. *The Catastrophe: Kerensky's Own Story of the Russian Revolution.* New York, 1927. An early memoir.

———. *Russia and History's Turning Point.* New York, 1965. His last and most extensive memoir, representing his final assessment of the revolution and his role.

Secondary Sources

Abraham, Richard. *Alexander Kerensky: The First Love of the Revolution.* New York, 1987. The only full-length scholarly biography.

Figes, Orlando, and Boris Kolonitskii. *Interpreting the Russian Revolution: The Language and Symbols of 1917.* New Haven, Conn., and London, 1999. Contains much information on Kerensky, including a chapter that focuses on his rise and fall as charismatic leader.

Kolonitskii, Boris I. "Kerensky." In *Critical Companion to the Russian Revolution, 1914–1921.* Edited by Edward Acton et al., 38–49. Bloomington, Ind., 1997. A good short account.

REX A. WADE

KEYNES, J. M. (1883–1946), economist.

With the publication of *The General Theory of Employment, Interest, and Money* in 1936, John Maynard Keynes (1883–1946) created a new paradigm for economic thought, establishing the basis for what would later be called macroeconomics. Keynes's academic base was at Cambridge University, where he was a Fellow of King's College, but he spent the years of both world wars working for the British government at the Treasury. In 1944 he played a major role at the Bretton Woods Conference, which led to the creation of the International Monetary Fund and the World Bank.

ECONOMICS AND WORLD WAR I

In *The Economic Consequences of the Peace,* written in 1919, after he had resigned from the British delegation at the Versailles Conference, Keynes denounced the punitive decision to make Germany pay for the war, arguing that the terms would prove impossible to fulfill. More important for his development as an economist, he also developed the thesis that the years of World War I had ended an epoch in human history and opened a new age. Prior to 1914, Keynes argued, "Europe was so organized socially and economically as to secure the maximum accumulation of capital" (Keynes, vol. 2, p. 11). The pre-1914 society had absorbed the lesson taught by Adam Smith (1723–1790): savings and investment had taken precedence over wasteful consumption. According to Keynes, however, the war had undermined the psychological basis of that society in two ways. First, it had changed the balance between classes. The high degree of inequality, previously justified in the name of future consumption, was not natural. The laboring classes had now paid for a new citizenship status by accepting mass conscription in the service of a nation whose people had common goals, and the war had shown that new levels of expenditure were possible. Second, the new circumstances of the postwar years were not propitious for the long view. What appeared, in retrospect at least, to have been a high degree of confidence about the continuity of the existing order had played a crucial role in capital accumulation, the distinguishing feature of industrial society. Inequality had made that accumulation possible, but capital accumulation was precisely what had justified the inequality.

In the postwar world a new political situation existed: the laboring classes would not be willing to live at such a low standard of living, and the capitalist classes, fearing for the future, might undermine their privileged role by indulging in high levels of consumption rather than investing. Adam Smith had held out a promise of well-being for all—cheapness and plenty, as he put it. John Stuart Mill (1806–1873) had worried that an eternally class-divided commercial society would not be politically viable. Karl Marx (1818–1883) had condemned the capitalist system, predicting that it was not economically viable. Keynes rejected Marx's analysis and his conclusions, but from 1919 onward his central concern was that liberalism would not survive unless capitalism delivered the goods.

SOCIAL AND ACADEMIC MILIEU

Keynes was born into the world of those who benefited from English liberalism. Both his parents were significant figures in Cambridge. He was educated at Eton, one of the most exclusive and well-connected schools in the country, and as a distinguished student in both classics and mathematics went from there to King's College at Cambridge, again a center of prestige and privilege. Before the appearance of the *Economic Consequences of the Peace,* Keynes had published *A Treatise on Probability* in 1921, but had yet to make his mark on economic thought. The younger Keynes's intellectual world was shaped by the philosophy of G. E. Moore (1873–1958), by his membership in the Apostles, a Cambridge club that was an elite within the elite, and by the "Bloomsbury" group, the non-Cambridge extension of the Apostles, a group that included Lytton Strachey and Virginia Stephen, who became better known later as Virginia Woolf. Keynes has been seen as the last of the great English liberals, but after 1914 certainly, he did not share the nineteenth-century belief in progress. He was a liberal who maintained Edmund Burke's conservative belief in civilization. Keynes did not see democracy as an end in itself. He was an elitist who continued to believe that the right solution to the economic questions of the day would "involve intellectual and scientific elements which must be above the heads of the vast mass of more or less illiterate voters" (quoted in Skidelsky, vol. 2, p. 224).

"Economics," Keynes once noted, "is a science of thinking in terms of models joined to the art of choosing models which are relevant to the contemporary world" (quoted in Skidelsky, vol. 2, p. 619). While finding his way to *The General Theory,* Keynes published a major study of money (*A Treatise on Money,* 1930), numerous essays, and lengthy newspaper articles. He also worked on or made appearances before committees, participated in workshops for the Liberal Party, and taught at Cambridge. He engaged in endless debate with colleagues, including his younger colleagues Richard Kahn and Joan Robinson, who, along with Piero Sraffa, Austin Robinson, and James Meade, formed the "circus," an ongoing seminar that served as a sounding board for Keynes's ideas and was the source of several significant contributions to the *General Theory.*

SAVINGS AND INVESTMENT

In *Wealth of Nations* (1776), Adam Smith had assumed that "what is annually saved is as regularly consumed as what is annually spent, and nearly in the same time too." That is, saving is turned into investment, understood as the purchase of raw materials, machinery, and labor for future production. Classical theory, as Keynes termed the prevalent economic assumptions that he had begun to question, relied on what is known as "Say's Law." In the formulation provided by Alfred Marshall (1842–1924), "a man purchases labour and commodities with that portion of his income which he saves just as much as he does with that which he is said to spend" (Keynes quoted in Skidelsky, vol. 2, p. 550). Recognizing that savers and investors are

John Maynard Keynes in his Bloomsbury study, March 1940. GETTY IMAGES

in practice frequently different people, the theory posited the rate of interest as the equilibrator between savings and investment. But as Keynes was ultimately to recognize, the rate of interest is merely the price for money itself. Furthermore, there is no market for savings and investment. Technically, after the fact, what is invested must be equal to what is saved, but the key issue is not what is actually saved and invested but what levels of savings and investment the community desires to achieve.

Keynes was particularly vexed by arguments that implied that a society with unemployed resources could not be more productive. To say, in a situation in which there were unemployed resources, that a society could not afford more consumption was "utterly imbecile": it is "with the unemployed men and the unemployed plant, and with nothing else" (quoted in Skidelsky, vol. 2, p. 298) that output is increased. In the *Treatise on Money*, Keynes underlines this point by making the crucial distinction between saving and investment: "mere abstinence is not enough. . . . It is enterprise which builds. . . . If enterprise is afoot, wealth

accumulates whatever may be happening to thrift; and if enterprise is asleep, wealth decays, whatever thrift may be doing" (Keynes, vol. 6, p. 132). The question, then, is what engine drives investment understood as enterprise. The answer, Keynes recognized, is not thrift but profit. This point was well understood by Smith but was obscured in the nineteenth century by the ideologically driven desire to equate profit with the natural and deserved return to abstinence or thrift.

To be successful, economic policy would have to create an adequate inducement to invest. Attempts to save for the future would be futile unless they were equivalent to investing for the future by actually producing something. Attempts to save without producing would generate unemployment. By 1932 Keynes had seen that a full employment equilibrium, where the desire for investment equaled the desire for savings, was in fact a special case. What was required was a general theory to explain the actual existing level of employment.

In the *General Theory*, Keynes developed a concept of aggregate demand, which includes both consumption demand and investment demand for past production. The key variable is investment demand. Investment demand ultimately determines the major variations in production and thus in income, and it is income levels that determine both consumption and savings. Thus savings are a consequence of investment, rather than the reverse. An attempt by the society to save more than entrepreneurs wish to invest will reduce income and eventually bring savings down to the same level as investment. The problem is that such an equilibrium might be achieved at a very low level of output and thus of employment. The point, as James Meade noted, was to get economic thinking to adapt the model in which "the dog called investment wagged the tail labeled savings" (Clarke, p. 245).

Put simply, the main argument of the *General Theory* was that entrepreneurs were failing to invest sufficiently. The main reason for this was uncertainty about the profitability of investment. Entrepreneurs wishing to borrow funds would need to pay interest rates that covered the lenders' anxieties about the future and would in addition face the risk of not meeting expected rates of returns. If such a chronic state of inadequate investment existed, governments would have to protect their societies, and their important values, by fostering investment. What was at stake, as Keynes concluded, was the maintenance of the general traditions of society. Those traditions included "a wide field for the exercise of private initiative and responsibility" (Keynes, vol. 7, p. 380). Individualism offered the efficiency of decentralization and the play of self-interest and "individualism, if it can be purged of its defects and its abuses, is the best safeguard of personal liberty...of personal choice...of the variety of life...the loss of which is the greatest of all the losses of the homogeneous or totalitarian state" (Keynes, vol. 7. p. 380).

THE PROSPECT OF WAR

Looking outward from Britain in the conclusion to the *General Theory,* Keynes touched on the growing threats to liberty and the prospect of war. As he notes, war has several causes, including economic causes. Even the idealized nineteenth-century international economy had produced a competitive struggle for markets because there were no other means to "mitigate economic distress at home" (Keynes, vol. 7, p. 382). A peaceful international division of labor might come into existence if nations could first provide for full employment by domestic policies. But by the time Keynes wrote these words, it was too late. Not many influential people were listening and the die had been cast long before. In the 1930s Keynes knew that the United States was the key to the survival of capitalism and of liberalism. Ironically, it required the outbreak of global war to engage the United States in the global defense of liberalism.

Robert Skidelsky, the author of a three-volume biography of Keynes, calls Keynes "the Churchill of war finance and post-war financial planning" (vol. 3, p. 1). He became the key figure, negotiating the complex issues of U.S. war loans to Britain, attempting to avoid British postwar financial weakness and dependency on the United States, working to institute a postwar international settlement that would avoid the punitive and politically disastrous perspective that had dominated at Versailles following World War I. In 1942, on the

recommendation of Prime Minister Winston Churchill, Keynes was made 1st Baron Keynes of Tilton.

Politically, in the 1930s Keynes was a voice in the wilderness, but the perspective of the *General Theory* swept the younger generation of economists. It was rapidly incorporated into mainstream academic thought in the versions developed by John Hicks and Paul Samuelson. Keynesianism focused on the concept of effective demand and the resulting equilibrium models of demand management. Roy Harrod extended the new concepts into a model of long-run growth. Joan Robinson attempted to maintain a more radical view of Keynes as a skeptic concerning the equilibrium between demand and supply and insisted that economists should continue the task of generalizing the *General Theory* to explain the more common world of nonequilibrium situations.

See also **Inflation.**

BIBLIOGRAPHY

Primary Sources

Keynes, John Maynard. *The Collected Writings of John Maynard Keynes.* 30 vols. Cambridge, U.K., 1971–1989.

Secondary Sources

Clarke, Peter. *The Keynesian Revolution in the Making, 1924–1936.* Oxford, U.K., 1988.

Krugman, Paul. *Development, Geography, and Economic Theory.* Cambridge, Mass., 1995.

Skidelsky, Robert. *John Maynard Keynes: A Biography.* 3 vols. Vol. 1: *Hopes Betrayed 1883–1920;* Vol. 2: *The Economist as Saviour 1920–1937;* Vol. 3: *Fighting for Britain, 1937–1946.* London, 1983–2000.

Solow, Robert. "Towards a Macroeconomics of the Medium Run." *Journal of Economic Perspectives* 14, no. 1 (winter 2000): 151–158.

Turner, Marjorie S. *Joan Robinson and the Americans.* Armonk, N.Y., 1989.

JOHN HUTCHESON

KHARKOV, BATTLES OF.

KHARKOV, BATTLES OF. There were two significant battles for Kharkov (now Kharkiv, Ukraine) in 1943, during which this Donets Basin (Donbas) city, the Soviet Union's fourth largest, was the scene of fierce urban combat. The first, 11–14 March, occurred during a successful German counteroffensive to regain ground lost to Soviet advances after the victory at Stalingrad, while the second, 21–23 August, occurred during a major Soviet counteroffensive following the Battle of Kursk. Each confrontation at Kharkov was nested in a larger set of operations, with each set tracing different trajectories and producing differing outcomes.

FIRST 1943 BATTLE

There had been two previous battles for Kharkov in 1941 and 1942, and that which the Germans called the "Third Battle of Kharkov" resulted from Soviet overreach on the southern flank of the eastern front during the winter of 1943. Various thrusts and counterthrusts by both the Red Army and the Wehrmacht before and after the capitulation of the German Sixth Army at Stalingrad on 2 February 1943 had left large gaps in the German lines between Voronezh and Rostov-na-Donu (Rostov-on-Don). In early February, as Field Marshal Erich von Manstein regrouped his scattered formations in the south to establish a coherent defense, Soviet Stavka, the Headquarters of the Supreme High Command, resolved to press the initiative. Accordingly, the armies of two Soviet fronts, Voronezh (General Filipp Golikov) and Southwest (General Nikolay Vatutin), knifed through the middle and lower Don Valley to envelop Kharkov, with the ultimate objective of pinning Manstein's forces against the Sea of Azov and the Dnieper River bend. Initially unable to stem the tide, the Germans gave ground nearly everywhere, including Kharkov, where on 15 February, I SS Panzer Corps—despite orders to stand fast—retired to the southwest after offering feeble resistance. Its commander, Obergruppenführer Paul Hausser, saw little purpose in making the city "a second Stalingrad."

Success, however, was to prove ephemeral for Stavka, at least for a time, with the result that Kharkov would not long remain in Soviet hands. Joseph Stalin and his generals had underestimated the resilience of the Wehrmacht and its associated SS formations and had overestimated the capacity of overtaxed Soviet logistics and depleted combat units to maintain offensive momentum. Worse, Soviet intelligence on German dispositions and intentions remained dangerously uncertain. Between 17 and 19 February, Soviet offensive operations culminated in the face of growing German resistance along a north-south line lying roughly 50 kilometers (30 miles) west of the Kursk-Kharkov meridian and cutting east in the extreme south to the Mius River. By now, Manstein had reorganized his troops into a resurrected version of Army Group South, and he was regrouping his armor and air assets to conduct a bold counterstroke spearheaded by the Fourth Panzer Army and Hausser's SS Panzer Corps. Manstein's intent was sequentially to smash leading elements of the two advancing Soviet fronts head-on and then to sink a deep thrust between them to bypass Kharkov on the way to seizing Belgorod and its crossings over the Donets River.

The result was mayhem for the overextended Soviets. From 19 to 21 February, XLVIII Panzer Corps and SS Panzer Corps overpowered and obliterated the forward formations of Vatutin's Sixth and First Guards armies. On 20 February, the First Panzer Army and XL Panzer Corps joined in the fray to begin destruction of another of Vatutin's advancing tentacles, Mobile Group Popov. With the German Fourth Air Fleet commanding the skies for the last time over German counteroffensive operations on the eastern front, the last week of February witnessed a merciless German pursuit of jumbled Soviet formations in full flight back to the Northern Donets River. Altogether the Soviets lost the bulk of two field armies, including 9,000 prisoners, an estimated 23,000 dead, 615 tanks, and 1,000 artillery pieces. After briefly pausing to regroup, Manstein's panzers turned northwest to confront Golikov's Third Tank and Sixty-Ninth armies on the southwest approaches to Kharkov. There, in an exercise of maneuver virtuosity between 1 and 5 March, German armored formations repeatedly outflanked and relentlessly pursued Golikov's defenders, levying the loss of an additional forty-five thousand troops on the Soviets.

As German exploitation continued, Hausser's SS Corps remained under orders to bypass Kharkov. However, the temptation for vindication proved too strong to resist. With rapid seizure of the city seemingly within easy grasp, Hausser allocated two SS divisions to the task. As a result, between 11 and 14 March, Kharkov was the scene of savage house-to-house fighting, during which Hausser's SS troops reclaimed their honor at the cost of 11,500 casualties. Meanwhile, Army Group South's remaining armored pincers lacked sufficient combat power to fully encircle and liquidate large Soviet troop pockets east and south of Kharkov. Although Manstein thereby probably lost an opportunity to produce a German equivalent of the Soviet victory at Stalingrad, momentum carried this last major successful German offensive on the eastern front to Belgorod. With this city in German hands on 25 March, the spring thaw halted operations for both sides. The line of farthest German advance became the southern shoulder of the Kursk salient that was to feature so prominently in Manstein's next offensive, Operation Citadel, resulting in the Battle of Kursk.

FINAL KHARKOV CONTEST

The final contest for Kharkov, known to the Germans as the "Fourth Battle of Kharkov" and to the Soviets and Russians as the Belgorod-Kharkov Operation, occurred during a series of battles and subsidiary operations, between 3 and 23 August 1943, growing out of the Battle of Kursk. With the Wehrmacht clearly now on the defensive, this major Soviet strategic counteroffensive, code-named Rumiantsev (for a Russian military hero of the eighteenth century), recaptured Belgorod and Kharkov, inflicted heavy losses on the Germans, and set the stage for the liberation of left-bank Ukraine.

Although Manstein had sought to renew German offensive operations after Kursk, Adolf Hitler had other ideas, including the redeployment of Hausser's now renamed II SS Panzer Corps to the west. After Citadel, consequently, the primary German strike forces in the south, including the Fourth Panzer Army and Detachment Kempf, conducted a fighting withdrawal to previously occupied and well-fortified positions north of Kharkov along an east-west line that stretched between Sumy and Belgorod, then dropped south.

Just as the case after Stalingrad, Stavka now sought a transition from the defensive at Kursk to a decisive counteroffensive that would produce significant gains, especially against German Army Group South. The main difference was that now the Soviets retained predictable command of the air and substantial reserves in manpower, armaments, and equipment. Stavka's primary objective was the encirclement and destruction of Manstein's groupings northwest of Kharkov. Meanwhile, other Soviet offensive operations targeted German Army Group Center, in part to disguise Stavka's intent and objectives in the south.

In consequence, on 3 August, when the Soviet Voronezh (Vatutin in place of Golikov) and Steppe (General Ivan Konev) fronts commenced offensive operations from the southern shoulder of the Kursk salient, Manstein was caught off guard. Elaborate local Soviet deception measures had enabled Marshal Georgy Zhukov, the coordinator of front operations from Stavka, to concentrate dense infantry formations and artillery fire power across a narrow frontage to facilitate penetration of the five successive German defensive belts protecting Kharkov. On 5 August, once having effected the breakthrough operation, Zhukov inserted his primary mobile groups, the First Tank Army (General Mikhail Katukov) and the Fifth Guards Tank Army (General Pavel Rotmistrov), into the resulting gap for deep exploitation. As they penetrated to depths of 60 kilometers (37 miles), Belgorod fell, while adjoining and supporting Soviet forces either widened the gap or made others to augment the advance.

While transiting and concentrating mobile counters from the north and from the Donbas, Manstein committed his local reserves piecemeal, but with little success. It was only on 11 August that Manstein had laboriously assembled four infantry and seven motorized or panzer divisions to halt the expanding Soviet torrent. But when Manstein reverted to the same sort of mobile maneuver scheme that earlier in the year had assured German success in the third battle of Kharkov, his troops encountered a different kind of opposition. Now commanding the air, the Red Air Force pummeled Manstein's counterattacking reserves, even as elements of both the Steppe and Voronezh fronts approached Kharkov. In anticipation of a German counterstroke from the southwest, Zhukov reinforced Voronezh Front with the Fifty-Seventh Army and the Fifth Guards Tank Army. Between 11 and 20 August, a series of vicious meeting engagements erupted between maneuvering heavy formations in the vicinity of Bogodukhov, some 30 kilometers (19 miles) northwest of Kharkov. With Zhukov feeding additional reinforcements into the fight, his right wing held its ground. Simultaneously, Konev's Steppe Front, reinforced by the adjacent Southwest Front (General Rodion Malinovsky), broke through Kharkov's outer defenses. The task of standing fast within the city now fell to the remnants of Detachment Kempf, but again the scent of Stalingrad was in the air, with the result that German troops quit the city after only two days' (21–23 August) hard street fighting. Unlike the earlier case with SS Obergruppenführer Hausser, Hitler removed General Werner Kempf from his command and renamed his detachment the Eighth Army.

OUTCOME

Over the course of Rumiantsev, the Soviets opened a 300-kilometer (185-mile) breach in German defenses and advanced to depths of 140 kilometers (85 miles). Zhukov's two fronts routed fifteen German divisions while losing nearly 250,000 troops, including 71,600 dead and invalided. Beyond the numbers and the reoccupation of Kharkov, Rumiantsev marked a maturing of the Soviet military art, in which Red commanders demonstrated a growing mastery of complex breakthrough and exploitation operations for encirclement and pursuit. They had conducted an echeloned attack against deep defenses, had held the shoulders of the penetration, and then had fed mobile forces through the gap for sustained and deep pursuit. Bogodukhov, meanwhile, revealed a newfound Soviet ability to beat the Germans at their own mobile maneuver game.

See also **Kursk, Battle of; Operation Barbarossa; Stalingrad, Battle of; World War II.**

BIBLIOGRAPHY

Chaney, Otto Preston. *Zhukov.* Rev. ed. Norman, Okla., 1996.

Erickson, John. *The Road to Berlin.* London, 1983. Reprint, London, 2003.

Glantz, David M., and Jonathan M. House. *When Titans Clashed: How the Red Army Stopped Hitler.* Lawrence, Kans., 1995.

Manstein, Erich von. *Lost Victories.* Edited and translated by Anthony G. Powell. Chicago, 1958.

Sydnor, Charles W., Jr. *Soldiers of Destruction: The SS Death's Head Division, 1933–1945.* Princeton, N.J., 1977.

BRUCE W. MENNING

KHRUSHCHEV, NIKITA (1894–1971), head of the Communist Party of the Soviet Union and leader of the Soviet Union from 1953 to 1964.

Like many Soviet leaders of his generation, Nikita Sergeyevich Khrushchev came from simple origins. He was born in a workers' family in the village of Kalinovka in southern Russia and spent his youth as a metalworker in the Donbas coal-mining region of eastern Ukraine. It was only the civil war that propelled him into a political career, when he became a political commissar in the Red Army. After the war he studied at the workers' education department of a technical college and advanced to prominent positions in the Ukrainian Communist Party bureaucracy, up to heading the organizational department of the Ukrainian Central Committee. In 1929 he enrolled in the Industrial Academy in Moscow and in 1930 became a party boss there. From then on Khrushchev began his swift and impressive move upward in the Communist Party bureaucracy. He consecutively headed the Bauman and Krasnaya Presnya District Party Committees in Moscow (1931), then (1932–1934) became the deputy head and later head of the Moscow City Party Committee and deputy head of the Moscow Regional Party Committee. In 1935–1938 he was simultaneously the head of the Moscow City and Region Party Committees, the top figure in the administration of the nation's capital. In this capacity he played an important role in the repression of thousands of innocent people during the Great Terror of 1937–1938—an act he remembered all his life and felt intensely guilty about even decades later.

From January 1938 through March 1947, and then again in December 1947–December 1949, Khrushchev headed the Ukrainian Communist Party. During the Great Patriotic War (1941–1945) he served as a top-rank political commissar in several important battle groups of the Red Army, participating, for example, in the Battle of Stalingrad in 1942–1943. Acknowledging his organizational energy, Khrushchev's biographers associate his name during the war with impressive victories but also a few defeats, for which he was partly responsible. After the war Khrushchev vigorously worked on the postwar rebuilding of Ukraine and proved a tough fighter against the nationalist guerrilla movement.

In 1949 he returned to Moscow as a secretary of the party's Central Committee and, again, the head of the Moscow regional party organization. Khrushchev's energy, combined with his simple ways and ostensible lack of claims for higher power, seems to have won him Stalin's trust, by no means a small accomplishment. Khrushchev was one of the very top leaders of the Soviet Union, and it was not accidental that after Stalin's death in March 1953 he was in a position to begin struggling for prominence in the country's leadership.

KHRUSHCHEV IN POWER

In September 1953 Khrushchev became the head of the Communist Party of the Soviet Union, the post Stalin had held during his successful bid for power in the 1920s. Just as it was with Stalin, leadership of the party proved to be a key weapon in power struggles. In June 1953, together with several other Politburo members, Khrushchev organized a plot that toppled one of his main rivals, Lavrenty Beria, the head and later patron of the special police under Stalin. After Beria was deposed and then shot (December 1953), Khrushchev successfully struggled against his other major rivals, Georgy Malenkov and Vyacheslav Molotov. By 1955 Khrushchev had won the fight for power, which enabled him to rule the country for the next decade.

Khrushchev's internal policies were marked, first of all, by a resolution to overcome the legacy of the Stalin terror. He promoted the dismantling of the repressive system and the release and rehabilitation (1953–1956) of the hundreds of thousands of concentration camp prisoners as well as the return of several deported nationalities to their original areas of residence. Proving bolder than his counterparts, Khrushchev was the first to attack Stalin openly. In February 1956, at the Twentieth Party Congress, he delivered a revolutionary speech, slamming the dead Stalin for having created a "cult of personality" around himself, for unleashing terror

against millions of innocent people, and for committing grave blunders in state leadership.

Khrushchev's "secret speech," called so because it remained unpublished in the Soviet Union at the time, was nonetheless read aloud to party members in local and institutional party organizations all across the country and thus became widely known. Although the dismantling of the repressive order and the homecoming of prisoners had started before the Twentieth Congress, Khrushchev's speech nonetheless shocked many Soviet people. For the first time they heard the country's top leader condemn Stalin, thus undermining the foundations of the worldview in which they had been raised during the previous quarter of a century. The attack on Stalin produced a major crisis of legitimacy of the Soviet order: since so much in the system had emerged under Stalin and was associated with his name, criticizing him could not but cast grave doubts about the validity of the entire Soviet project.

Khrushchev's anti-Stalin crusade had tremendous effects not only within the Soviet Union but also outside its borders, particularly in the communist bloc. In 1956, revelations about the terror brought about uprisings against Soviet power in Poland and particularly Hungary. The dethroning of Stalin also created a rift between the Soviet Union and Maoist China, which could never accept destalinization. After unsuccessful attempts to patch up Sino-Soviet relations in the late 1950s, Khrushchev abruptly withdrew Soviet specialists from China in 1960, and in the next decade the two countries occasionally found themselves on the brink of war.

All these complications of Khrushchev's attack on Stalin brought about a plot against him in the party leadership. In June 1957 his counterparts since Stalin's times, Vyacheslav Molotov, Georgy Malenkov, and Lazar Kaganovich, attempted to overthrow Khrushchev. However, the support of regional party secretaries, who were urgently flown to Moscow for an extraordinary plenum of the Central Committee, thwarted the coup.

Khrushchev took an active interest in trying to reform the Stalinist mechanism of economic administration. In 1957, within a project of decentralizing industrial management, many branch ministries in Moscow were liquidated and their powers

Nikita Khrushchev delivers his famous speech to the United Nations, 3 October 1960. AP/WIDE WORLD PHOTOS

were handed down to the newly created "councils of the economy" (*sovnarkhozy*) in the regions. Decentralization did not make industry much more efficient, though, because the producers still largely lacked market incentives to work.

Khrushchev took comparatively greater interest in agriculture, where he considered himself an expert. In 1953 taxes on agricultural produce were lowered, debts written off, procurement prices raised, and peasant private plots encouraged. Furthermore, it was now easier for peasants to travel or move to cities and thus the restrictions upon peasant mobility imposed during collectivization in the early 1930s became much less severe. In 1954, however, Khrushchev launched a campaign of growing grain in the Virgin Lands, uncultivated steppes in southwestern Siberia and northern Kazakhstan. Through a combination of draft and

propaganda, thousands of young men and women were mobilized for that purpose. Although the territory was indeed cultivated, the Virgin Lands campaign brought mixed results. Even less successful was Khrushchev's other agricultural project: the 1957 visionary plan to outstrip the United States in the production of meat, milk, butter, and other basic foods. He instigated a campaign of boosting agriculture by planting corn in various parts of the country often unsuitable for corn cultivation, which predictably failed.

Khrushchev's economic projects were not simply random disjointed initiatives but rather reflected his ideas of what socialism was to be. He seriously emphasized improving the quality of people's everyday lives, in the belief that the advantages of socialism as a world system could be demonstrated primarily through the well-being of Soviet citizens. Despite his many failures, Khrushchev was a vigorous, energetic administrator, and some of his projects were more successful than others. From the mid-1950s on, a massive program of affordable-housing construction was launched. In the course of a decade, millions of families moved from barracks, dugouts, and cramped communal premises to comparatively modern although cheap separate apartments with central heating, sewerage, and running water. Together with his dismantling of the Stalin terror regime, his housing reform was something for which Khrushchev was positively remembered in the Soviet Union during the decades to come.

Under Khrushchev the Soviet Union embarked on a rapprochement with the West. Cultural exchange started in 1954–1955, and trips abroad became easier for a (limited) number of Soviet citizens. One of such tourists was Khrushchev himself, who in 1956 traveled (together with Molotov) to Great Britain and in 1959 went on his famous trip to the United States, the first time a Soviet leader had ever visited the United States. Khrushchev's interest in the West brought quite a few Western artistic and economic exhibits to the Soviet Union, and Western books and films were imported in large numbers, influencing the ideas Soviet people held of their country and the world around. Above all, foreigners themselves began coming in increasing numbers to the Soviet Union, especially during the 1957 Moscow Festival of Youth and Students, one of the cultural landmarks of the Khrushchev years. Building ties with the West, however, did not go smoothly and was punctuated by numerous clashes between the two still-hostile sociopolitical systems. Khrushchev's relations with the intelligentsia were contradictory. The intelligentsia largely welcomed his denunciation of Stalin at the Twentieth and especially at the Twenty-Second Party Congress (1961), after which Stalin's monuments all over the country were destroyed, places named after him renamed, and his body taken out of the Lenin Mausoleum. The years 1962–1964 witnessed the peak of criticism against the Stalin terror in the Soviet press. A few powerful works of literature on the terror theme appeared in print, notably Alexander Solzhenitsyn's *One Day in the Life of Ivan Denisovich* (1962), the publication of which was sanctioned by Khrushchev himself. Yet, although the intelligentsia welcomed Khrushchev's efforts at dismantling the terror regime, it was alienated by his attempts to monitor intellectual life, such as the anti-Pasternak campaign (1958) and his censuring of artists and writers in 1962–1963.

While popular overall with the intelligentsia, Khrushchev ended up alienating much of the military establishment. His emphasis on peaceful coexistence with the West and on consumer-oriented economic production resulted in major cuts of the conventional armed forces, which was highly unpopular with many cadre officers.

DEMISE AND LAST YEARS

In 1963–1964 Khrushchev's situation became unstable as his popularity in the country ebbed. With the failure of his agricultural experiments and the corresponding crop failure, food supplies in the cities were dismal. Combined with rather tactlessly introduced pay cuts for workers, this brought about the riots of 1962, in which troops ended up firing at crowds in the city of Novocherkassk. But above all, what brought about Khrushchev's end was his policy toward the party apparatus. In 1962, in another act of administrative experimentation, he divided the regional party organs into industrial and agricultural committees—a reform that generated great resentment among the party bureaucracy. This time Khrushchev was deprived of the support of regional party leaders that had once saved him in 1957.

In October 1964 a well-prepared plot of the top party leaders, headed by his closest associates Leonid Brezhnev and Mikhail Suslov, deposed Khrushchev, stripped him of his rank of first secretary, and sent him into forced retirement. He spent the remaining seven years of his life in a country house near Moscow. There he managed to record on audiotapes his lengthy memoirs, which were published in the West while he was still alive—an act of unprecedented courage for the former leader of the Soviet Communist Party.

Khrushchev was a major political figure in twentieth-century history and a colorful, remarkable individual. A product of the Stalinist political and cultural order, he found strength and courage in himself to challenge, often successfully, many crucial aspects of that order and to begin its destruction. He also retained elements of utopian communist thinking of the 1920s—something that led him to numerous and frequently fatal blunders but also made his rule a dynamic, memorable time that, as research increasingly shows, proved highly significant for the historic fortunes of the Soviet Union.

See also **Brezhnev, Leonid; Destalinization; Soviet Union; Stalin, Joseph.**

BIBLIOGRAPHY

Primary Sources

Khrushchev, Nikita. *Khrushchev Remembers.* 2 vols. Translated and edited by Strobe Talbott. New York and Toronto, 1971–1976.

———. *Doklad N. S. Khrushcheva o kul'te lichnosti Stalina na XX s'ezde KPSS—dokumenty.* Edited by Karl Eimermacher and Vitalii IU. Afiani. Moscow, 2002.

Secondary Sources

Breslauer, George W. *Khrushchev and Brezhnev as Leaders: Building Authority in Soviet Politics.* London, 1982.

Jones, Polly, ed. *The Dilemmas of Destalinisation: A Social and Cultural History of Reform in the Khrushchev Era.* London, 2005.

Taubman, William. *Khrushchev: The Man and His Era.* New York and London, 2003.

Taubman, William, Sergei Khrushchev, and Abbott Gleason, eds. *Nikita Khrushchev.* New Haven, Conn., and London, 2000.

Tompson, William J. *Khrushchev: A Political Life.* New York, 1995.

Zubkova, Elena. *Russia after the War: Hopes, Illusions, and Disappointments, 1945–1957.* Armonk, N.Y., 1998.

DENIS KOZLOV

KIEFER, ANSELM (b. 1945), German painter, sculptor, engraver, and watercolorist.

Anselm Kiefer was born in 1945 in Donaueschingen, Germany. He first studied law but soon turned to the visual arts and attended the Art Academy of Karlsruhe and, from 1970 to 1972, the Academy of Düsseldorf, where he worked under Josef Beuys. His large-scale paintings develop historical themes and allude to the Kabbalah and Nordic mythology, including the Song of the Nibelungen and the legends of Edda, Kyffhäuser, and Alaric. His influences are as diverse as Richard Wagner—in his *Grane* (1980–1993), for example—the architect Albert Speer, the poet Paul Celan, the seventeenth-century alchemist Robert Fludd, the writer Jean Genet, the philosopher

Martin Heidegger, and the eighteenth-century poet Friedrich Hölderlin. Kiefer's paintings, sculptures, and installations are inseparable from his "books"—a form of freestanding sculpture—since Kiefer brings his subjects and representations to life by using one art form to expand on another. The repetition of themes and iconic motifs, the use of citations, and, in fact, any manner of varying or twisting the meaning, the medium, or the writing, are characteristic of Kiefer's heuristic method.

His first one-person show was at the Gallery am Kaiserplatz in Karlsruhe in 1969. The exhibition *Bilder und Bücher* (Pictures and books) at the Kunsthalle in Bern in 1978 and his participation in the Venice Bienniale two years later won Kiefer international renown. Alongside Georg Baselitz, he exhibited a collection of books at the German pavilion under the title *Verbrennen, Verholzen, Versenken, Versanden* (Burn, carbonize, dump, cover with sand), as well as *Deutschlands Geisteshelden* (1972; Germany's spiritual heroes), *Parsifal* (1973), and four versions of *Wege der Weltweisheit—die Hermannsschlacht* (1977–1978; Ways of worldly wisdom—Arminius's battle). These works were harshly criticized because of their overly Germanic character, but such attacks demonstrate only a superficial understanding. When in 1969 Kiefer presented the series *Besetzungen* (Occupations) and the book *Für Genet* (For Genet), in which he represents himself (in a photograph, a painting, and a watercolor) in civilian and military dress, standing at attention and giving the Hitler salute, his aim was to chastise the generation of postwar Germans that was struggling to forget the Nazi period. With this transgression Kiefer was not just reminding viewers of the past but was expressing a will to mourn as a means of self-reinvention. His works undeniably link art and politics.

Kiefer is neither a Romantic, nostalgic for Germany's glorious past, nor a mystic, as some of his creations, such as *Der Weltweisheit*, might suggest. In fact, that work is quite the opposite. In the very conception of the work and in its realization, he presents a geological vision of the past and an archaeological view of the present. His art operates on two levels, that of the perception of the canvas and that of its comprehension, moving from the macro to the micro level, from the representation to the message. In such landscapes as *Märkische Heide* (1974; March heath) and such architectural representations as *Dem Unbekannten Maler* (1982; To the unknown painter), he unravels historical events, and, by focusing on historical sites in *Nürnberg* (1982; Nuremburg) and *Jerusalem* (1986), he sutures Germany's wounds.

In 1975 Kiefer's work underwent a technical and iconographic upheaval. He produced eight works on painted canvas, which he burned and bound together under the title *Ausbrennen des landkreises Buchen* (Cauterization of the rural district of Buchen). Fire, a tool of destruction, generated to a new way of painting. In confronting German cultural traditions, Kiefer developed a singularly plastic means of expression in the art world of the 1970s to 1990s.

In 1980 his technique evolved still further. He began to create assemblages and collages, introducing various materials such as ashes, tar, seeds, toys, sand, sunflowers, and sheets of lead. Paul Celan's poems, for example, provided him with an opportunity to use straw on the canvas (*Margarethe*, 1981). Such materials began as iconographic motifs and then gradually became components of his work serving to call representation into question. According to Daniel Arasse, a change in iconography accounts for the transformations of his palette. Indeed, Kiefer created several works using lead—*Schwarze Galle* (Black bile) in 1989 and *Melancholia* in 1991 are two examples—at a time when he had decided to distance himself from German themes to focus on alchemy (*Athanor*, 1988–1991) and on the Old Testament, especially Exodus (*Auszug aus Ägypten;* 1984, Departure from Egypt). Lead became his preferred material for creating books and bookshelves such as *Zweistromland* (1990; The high priestess). In 1991 Kiefer finished his *20 Jahre Einsamkeit* (20 years of solitude), made up of white books and ledgers stained with sperm and etched with words written by the artist. This work looks like a summing up, with a series of reflections on the creative process inscribed on the white pages. Beginning in 1985, Kiefer produced a variety of subjects based on the Kabbalah, which find their apotheosis in the installation entitled *The Breaking of the Vessels* (2000), figuring a burnt library in opposition to the Kabbalistic approach to the problem of theodicy. This work represents a synthesis of the many themes and materials developed during the previous thirty years of his career.

See also **Celan, Paul; Germany; Heidegger, Martin; Speer, Albert.**

BIBLIOGRAPHY

Arasse, Daniel. *Anselm Kiefer.* Edited by Harry N. Abrams; translated by Mary Whittall. New York, 2001.

Beeren, Wim. *Anselm Kiefer: Bilder 1986–1980.* Exh. cat. Amsterdam, 1986.

Rosenthal, Mark. *Anselm Kiefer.* Exh. cat. Chicago, 1987.

Saltzman, Lisa. *Anselm Kiefer and Art after Auschwitz.* Cambridge, U.K., 1999.

Schütz, Sabine. *Anselm Kiefer: Geschichte als Material, Arbeiten 1969–1983.* Cologne, Germany, 1999.

Strasser, Catherine. *Chevirat Ha-Kelim, le bris des vases: Anselm Kiefer.* Paris, 2000.

CYRIL THOMAS

KIEV. Kiev (Kyiv in Ukrainian) was the ruling center of Kievan Rus, the largest political entity in medieval Europe. After Vladimir the Great, the grand prince of Kiev (980–1015), began to Christianize his realm in 988, Kiev became famous for its churches and monasteries. The Cave Monastery (Pecherska Lavra), founded in 1015, attracted thousands of pilgrims to the city each year until Soviet times. St. Sophia Cathedral, initially built between 1037 and 1100 and named for the Hagia Sophia in Constantinople, retains much of its original interior even in the early twenty-first century. By 1200, Kiev had become one of Europe's largest cities. Its estimated population of fifty thousand equaled that of Paris and exceeded that of London.

In 1240 the Mongols destroyed Kiev, and the city subsequently fell under Lithuanian, Polish, and ultimately Muscovite Russian control. Although it retained some importance as a religious, educational, and trade center, it had not recovered the size or significance it had enjoyed in medieval times even by the turn of the nineteenth century. Then, Kiev had only twenty thousand inhabitants and consisted of three barely connected settlements, each walled and villagelike in appearance: Podil, the trade district that lay along the Dniepr River; Pecherske, the site of the fortress and the Cave Monastery; and High City, sometimes called Old

Kiev, the location of many of the town's most majestic churches. Until the middle of the nineteenth century, Kiev's Contract Fair, held in January, brought together Polish landowners, Great Russian and Jewish merchants and traders, Ukrainian oxcarters and peasants, "itinerant dentists, Kazan soap boilers, Tula samovar smiths, Berdychiv booksellers, and hawkers of exotic delights from Persia, Bukhara, and the Caucasus," among others, and served as the city's most important social and commercial event.

Tsar Nicholas I (r. 1825–1855) Russified Kiev, establishing St. Vladimir University in 1834 partly for this purpose. Russian became the language of governance, education, and upward mobility. Most Kiev residents spoke Russian or a blend of Russian and Ukrainian called *surzhyk*. From the early 1870s, when railway lines to Moscow and the Black Sea port of Odessa (Odesa) were completed, Kiev grew very rapidly. Its three settlements fused into a modern city, and the Khreshchatyk, built along a wooded ravine, became its commercial center and one of imperial Russia's most famous main streets. Major employers included the rail yard and Greter & Krivanek, which manufactured machinery, much of it for Ukraine's sugar beet industry, but light industry dominated the city's economy. In 1870 Kiev had 70,000 residents; by 1914, 626,000. By then, of the cities in the Russian Empire, only St. Petersburg, Moscow, and Warsaw were larger.

REVOLUTION, CIVIL WAR, AND NEP

After the abdication of Tsar Nicholas II (r. 1894–1917) in March 1917 (February, Old Style), Ukrainian nationalists organized the Central Rada in Kiev, which called for a self-governing, free Ukraine linked with Russia in a democratic federation. After the Bolsheviks (Communists) seized power in Petrograd (St. Petersburg) in November 1917, the Rada refashioned itself into the Ukrainian National Republic, which promoted the nationalization of industry and the seizure and redistribution of land. Armed conflict over control of Kiev began in December 1917, as Vladimir Antonov-Ovseyenko's Soviet Russian army advanced on the city. The Bolsheviks held the city briefly in 1918, but for most of the year the hetman (cossack leader, or military commander) Pavlo Skoropadsky (1873–1945)

governed it in close alliance with occupying German forces. Referring to the city's relative peace and prosperity in 1918, the writer Konstantin Paustovsky (1892–1968) remarked that "Kiev was like a banquet in the middle of a plague."

However, from 14 December 1918, when the Directory, led by Volodymyr Vynnychenko (1880–1951), took the city, violence and repression returned to Kiev. The Bolsheviks reconquered the city in February 1919 and nationalized its services and larger enterprises. Various Ukrainian forces then held the city from the late summer until the Bolsheviks took it back on 16 December. In all, Kiev changed hands five times in 1919.

May 1920 brought a brief occupation by Polish and Ukrainian troops, but in June the Bolsheviks captured Kiev for good. By then, more than eight hundred buildings had been destroyed. Kiev's population, estimated at 467,000 in September 1917 and 544,000 in early 1919, fell to 367,000 in mid-1920, as residents fled into the countryside in search of food. By 1921–1922, industrial production had virtually shut down. Inflation soared. Adult workers were expected to live on two hundred grams of bread per day and six hundred grams of sugar per month. However, in 1921 the Soviet government announced the more relaxed New Economic Policy (NEP), which allowed for private entrepreneurial activity, and the economy began to rebound. By 1925, most Kiev enterprises were exceeding their prewar levels of output, and by 1926 Kiev's population had grown to five hundred thousand. The use of the Ukrainian language was encouraged during the NEP, and the number of Ukrainian speakers increased in Kiev, although Russian remained the primary language of the city. During this period of relative cultural freedom, Kiev remained an important center of artistic accomplishment, particularly for the Ukrainian and Russian avant-garde movements.

KIEV UNDER STALIN

Kiev was greatly transformed under Joseph Stalin (1879–1953) and the First Five Year Plan, which began in 1928. Property was seized by the state, economic decision-making was transferred to Moscow, and industrialization proceeded with reckless rapidity. By 1932, fifty-seven machine-building enterprises were operating in Kiev, compared with only three in 1928. Greter & Krivanek, now called "Bolshevik," became a leading supplier of equipment for the Soviet chemical industry. During the First Five-Year Plan, Kiev factories also turned out barges, river boats, steel cable, farm machinery, rubber goods, construction equipment, tram wagons, and about one-quarter of Ukraine's light industrial output. Unemployment, officially 35,900 in 1929, was eliminated by 1930. The state took over all educational and cultural facilities. School tuition was outlawed in 1927, and within a year, according to Soviet sources, the percentage of children enrolled in schools jumped from 65 to 92. Dozens of technical institutes were established, reinforcing Kiev's tradition as one of the country's most important centers of learning.

During the Second Five-Year Plan, which began in 1933, wages were said to double on average and the percentage of women in Kiev's workforce continued to climb, reaching 43 percent by 1938, compared with 33 percent in 1931. In 1936, Kiev shops were printing forty-one regional newspapers and twenty-six journals, making the city one of the Soviet Union's most important publishing centers. By 1939 Kiev's population reached 850,000. However, life in the 1930s was difficult and often brutal. The extraordinary pace of urbanization, and the ongoing emphasis on industrial production, kept housing and consumer goods and services in short supply, something that would characterize the Soviet economy until its collapse. Moreover, Russians or Russified Ukrainians had begun to replace Ukrainians in Communist Party posts in 1927, and by 1929 Ukrainian intellectuals began to be arrested and charged with "national deviation." Increasingly, terror stalked the city. Kievans were murdered in the basement of the NKVD (secret police) headquarters and in Lukianivka Prison. Burial sites located just outside the city are said to contain the corpses of tens of thousands of victims from Kiev and elsewhere in Ukraine.

Kiev also suffered massive physical destruction in the 1930s. Soviet planners sought to reshape it into a model proletarian city, and in 1934 the capital of Ukraine was moved to Kiev from Kharkov (Kharkiv). Beginning in 1935, under Stalin's Ukrainian deputy Pavel Postyshev, many of Kiev's ancient churches and other cultural landmarks were demolished, probably because they were viewed as symbols of Ukrainian national pride. This destruction is documented by Titus Hewryk in *The Lost Architecture of Kiev,* cited in the bibliography.

THE SECOND WORLD WAR

Aerial bombardment of Kiev began on 22 June 1941, the very first day of Adolf Hitler's monumental assault on the Soviet Union code-named Operation Barbarossa. The Nazi armies advanced quickly. In the first three weeks of fighting alone, the Soviet Army lost two million men, 3,500 tanks, and 6,000 aircraft. On June 27 machinery and inventories began to be evacuated from Kiev's arsenal, which required 1,100 railway cars. Over the next two months, 197 enterprises were dismantled and sent eastward. Kiev's "Bolshevik" plant, for example, was reassembled near Sverdlovsk, in the Urals. In early July, some two hundred thousand Kievans began to construct antitank and anti-infantry fortifications around the city.

Stalin had initially refused Ukrainian Communist Party boss Nikita Khrushchev's recommendation to abandon Kiev, but given the hopelessness of the military situation, relented on 17 September. On 21 September, the battle for Kiev ended. The Germans captured some 665,000 Soviet troops in the encirclement of Kiev, which Hitler called "the greatest battle in world history," but in reality the victory gave the Germans no strategic advantage. By October, half of Kiev's 850,000 residents had been evacuated, mobilized into the Red Army, or killed.

The German occupation of Kiev lasted for two years. Policies designed to starve the remaining population were put into place; already in November 1941 one onlooker described Kiev "as a city of beggars." Epidemics swept the city; murder for bread became an everyday occurrence. Kievans were not allowed to enter many shops, trams, and theaters, and curfew was set at 6:00 P.M. Streets and buildings were given German names, and at least twenty-three German industrial enterprises were established in the city. By mid-1943, however, about eighty partisan and sabotage units were operating in or near the city. Perhaps twenty thousand people were involved in the

Residents of Kiev welcome returning Soviet soldiers following the withdrawal of German troops, February 1944.
©BETTMANN/CORBIS

Resistance, which carried out some nine hundred operations, mostly against railway lines and roadways, supply depots, and police facilities.

Although Hitler's goal of reducing Kiev to rubble was averted because of a shortage of bombs, by the time the Nazi occupation was broken, on 6 November 1943, eight hundred industrial enterprises and six thousand buildings (about one-sixth of the total number of structures in Kiev) had been destroyed. Soviet sources estimate that two hundred thousand Kievans were killed during the war and another hundred thousand were sent into Germany as conscript laborers. Valuable books, archives, and records had been looted from libraries, museums, and various institutes. The Khreshchatyk and the central district lay in ruins, and an estimated two hundred thousand Kievans were left without housing. Rationing of basic

goods continued until December 1947. Kiev was declared a "Hero City" by the Soviet government, but the human tragedy of the battle for Kiev was not discussed openly until the Soviet political climate thawed briefly under Khrushchev (now Soviet premier) in 1962–1963. In January 1963, Leonid Volynsky published a short story in the journal *Novy Mir* (New World) about the battle, calling it "a vast and inexplicable tragedy."

THE FATE OF KIEV'S JEWS

With few exceptions, Jews had been forbidden to settle in Kiev until Tsar Alexander II (r. 1855–1881) liberalized residence restrictions. During the final decades of the nineteenth century Kiev's Jewish community grew rapidly, and by 1923 Kiev and Odessa, each with about 130,000 Jews, had the largest Jewish populations of any Soviet city.

Pogroms against Kiev Jews had occurred in 1881, 1905, and 1919, but under NEP, Jewish councils (soviets) and law courts were established, permitting limited jurisdiction over Jewish communal affairs, possibly in an effort to reduce rabbinical authority. The use of Yiddish was permitted in both institutions. However, under Stalin this limited autonomy disappeared. All of Kiev's synagogues were closed between 1929 and 1931, though one was reopened on appeal.

During the Second World War, the Soviet press began to publish stories about Nazi extermination policies only in June 1941. In occupied Kiev, on 29 September 1941, Jews assembled at a designated corner in Lukianivka district, apparently believing they would be evacuated to the east. Instead, on 29 and 30 September, 33,771 Jews were massacred in a ravine-filled area on the city's outskirts called Babi Yar (Babyn Yar). Many were women, children, and elderly people. Perhaps one hundred thousand Jews would ultimately die at Babi Yar, as well as tens of thousands of Russians, Ukrainians, and others. About 140,000 Jews had lived in Kiev on the eve of the war. On 8 November 1943, Moscow Radio reported that the Red Army had found only one remaining Jew when it liberated the city. Babi Yar remains one of the most notorious symbols of Nazi barbarity in the Second World War.

After the war, plans for a public memorial at Babi Yar were shelved, and the government decided to flood and fill in the ravines. In 1961 the poet Yevgeny Yevtushenko (b. 1933) was allowed to publish a poem indicting anti-Semitism that reminded his readers that "No monument stands over Babi Yar." The resulting furor forced Yevtushenko to rewrite his poem, adding the lines "Here together with Russians and Ukrainians lie Jews," and "I am proud of the Russia that stood in the path of the bandits." In 1966 a petition to restore Kiev's Jewish national theater was rejected, and its supporters were arrested. Ultimately, in 1976, a monument was built at Babi Yar. The inscription on the plaque notes only that some two hundred thousand Soviet citizens were killed on the site. It does not specifically mention Jews.

LATE SOVIET AND POST-SOVIET KIEV

After the war, Kiev rebuilt again. In the ensuing decade, natural gas replaced coal as the dominant energy source in the city. Trams remained the basic mode of transportation through the 1950s, but more and more buses and trolley-buses appeared each year. Planning for a subway system began in 1945, and with the opening of five stations in 1960, Kiev became the third Soviet city to operate an underground. From 1.1 million residents in 1959, Kiev grew to 1.4 million in 1967, and 2.6 million in 1989, the year of the last Soviet census. The city remained the third largest in the Soviet Union. However, Stalinist and Nazi destruction had destroyed much of the beauty of old Kiev, a city known for its churches, glittering onion-domed hilltop monasteries, wooded ravines, and spectacular vistas. The rebuilt Khreshchatyk, for example, featured dreary monolithic Stalinist architecture called "Mussolini modern" by one scholar.

By the 1970s, Kiev had joined Moscow and Leningrad (St. Petersburg) as one of the Soviet Union's showplace cities. Here the quality of life far surpassed that of virtually all other Soviet cities and even more so, that of the backward Soviet countryside. Nevertheless, the quality of life in Kiev remained well below that of comparable cities in the West. Most residents lived in large, uniform, prefabricated, and often poorly constructed apartment complexes, and shortages of consumer goods and services persisted. These problems reflected the inefficiencies of the Soviet economy and the continued emphasis on heavy industry and military-related production. Travel outside the country was virtually impossible. In 1959, only 2,200 Kievans were allowed such travel, almost all of it to other Soviet bloc countries. A small Ukrainian dissident movement surfaced in the 1960s. It was suppressed, and the KGB retained tight control over the city.

As the liberalizing reforms unleashed by Mikhail Gorbachev (b. 1931) in the late 1980s brought unprecedented freedom to Soviet citizens, Rukh, a Ukrainian organization that originally stressed the revival of the Ukrainian language, became increasingly influential in Kiev. In January 1990, following the tactics of popular front movements in the Baltic states, hundreds of thousands joined hands in a human chain that stretched for three hundred miles from Kiev to Lviv (Lvov) and Ivano-Frankivske, commemorating the proclamation of Ukrainian independence in 1918. Independence came in 1991, but Ukraine could not easily shed the institutional and cultural legacy of Soviet communism. Ukraine's GDP (gross domestic product) declined by 60 percent during the 1990s. Hyperinflation—said to be 10,000 percent in 1993—ruined many, and barter became a major means of economic transaction. The shadow economy, or black market, continued to grow, accounting for perhaps half of Ukraine's GDP by the mid-1990s. Despite its rich farmland, Ukraine became a net importer of food. An oligarchy of Soviet-era bureaucrats and managers, many of them racketeers and commodity traders, came to dominate the economy of Ukraine and Kiev, though none added value by actually producing goods. Corruption, complex tax laws and regulations, a lack of public confidence in the banking system, and the absence of enforcement of property rights discouraged foreign investment. Ukraine's per capita GDP in 2004, estimated at $1,160, was about one-fifth that of neighboring Poland. Income inequality increased; health care worsened for many; and life expectancy declined. Still, signs of progress could be found. By 1997 inflation had fallen to 10 percent. In 2000 the economy began to grow, and by then Ukraine had created a stable currency, the *hryvnia*.

Kiev fared considerably better than Ukraine as a whole in the post-Soviet period. Privatization of small enterprises such as taxi services, restaurants, and retail shops proceeded rapidly. Although Ukraine received less direct foreign investment than any other eastern or central European country after 1990, Kiev got about 40 percent of that investment. Censuses taken in 1994 and 2002 revealed a population of 2.6 million in Kiev. "Nontraditional" migrants—especially Afghans, Kurds, and Vietnamese—settled in the city, creating new sources of tension. In 1999, police officials maintained that foreigners committed one-quarter of the city's crimes.

In the late 1990s, under the leadership of the mayor Oleksandr Omelchenko, the Khreshchatyk and the area around the large Bessarabsky Covered Market underwent significant renovation. Many new buildings were provided with their own heating systems (Soviet planners had supplied heat and hot water by means of central plants). Shopping facilities were greatly expanded. In Soviet times, there had been few vehicles on the streets other than taxis and delivery trucks. By 2004, eight hundred thousand vehicles were plying Kiev streets each day, and traffic volume and flow had emerged as sources of concern.

Perhaps because Kiev had been heavily Russified, it was slow to remove the symbols of Soviet rule, and most Soviet statuary remains, including the enormous Mother of the Motherland, erected during the rule of Leonid Brezhnev, that towers over the city. However, the city has helped finance the rebuilding of some of the splendid structures that were destroyed in the Stalinist and Nazi years, for example the baroque St. Michael of the Golden Domes, originally built in 1108–1113 and destroyed in 1935–1936, and the Cathedral of the Assumption, demolished in 1941.

Although Ukrainian has become increasingly the language of choice, Kiev remains a bilingual city. About 40 percent of the city's native inhabitants cite Russian as their native language, as do more than half of those who have moved to Kiev from other cities. However, usage of Ukrainian is likely to continue to rise, as in the mid-2000s only ten of Kiev's four hundred public schools were teaching exclusively in Russian (with the exception of Ukrainian language classes). The privately run National University of Kiev Mohyla Academy, whose origins date to 1615, was revived in 1991. It has become an important center for liberal arts learning. Students are accepted on the basis of merit, and all study in English and Ukrainian. Russian is not taught.

In November–December 2004, Ukraine had a hotly contested presidential election that highlighted the corruption and ethnic divisions that continue to plague the country. The winner, Viktor Yushchenko, pledged to move Ukraine closer to the West, end corruption, and reverse the post-Soviet drift. The fate of Kiev and its residents will largely depend on the success of such efforts in Ukraine as a whole.

See also **Babi Yar; Russia; Soviet Union; Ukraine.**

BIBLIOGRAPHY

Berkhoff, Karel C. *Harvest of Despair: Life and Death in Ukraine under Nazi Rule*. Cambridge, Mass., 2004.

Gol'denveizer, A. A. "Iz Kievskikh vospominanii (1917–1921 gg.)." *Arhkiv Russkoi revoliutsii* 6 (1922): 161–303.

Hamm, Michael F. *Kiev: A Portrait, 1800–1917.* Princeton, N.J., 1993.

Hewryk, Titus D. *The Lost Architecture of Kiev.* New York, 1982.

Levin, Nora. *The Jews in the Soviet Union since 1917: Paradox of Survival.* 2 vols. New York, 1988.

Sarbei, V. G., ed. *Istoriia Kieva: Kiev perioda pozdnego feodalizma i kapitalizma.* Vol. 2. Kiev, 1983.

Suprunenko, N. I., ed. *Istoriia Kieva: Kiev sotsialicheskii.* Vol. 3. Kiev, 1986.

MICHAEL F. HAMM

KIROV, SERGEI (1886–1934), Soviet leader whose murder inaugurated the Stalinist purges of the 1930s.

On 1 December 1934, Leonid Nikolayev, a disgruntled former member of the Communist Party, shot and killed Sergei Kirov, head of the Leningrad Region Communist organization. Party workers apprehended Nikolayev immediately at the Leningrad party headquarters where the murder took place. In early interrogations Leningrad police sought evidence of a local conspiracy to kill Kirov, while Nikolayev initially claimed to have acted alone. However, Joseph Stalin intervened in the case within forty-eight hours and began concocting a narrative about a widespread plot to destroy the Soviet leadership. In the coming years of the Great Terror (1936–1938) Stalin and his subordinates used this story line to justify the arrest, torture, and execution of millions of Soviet subjects. At public show trials the Stalinist government convicted former rivals of Stalin in the Communist Party leadership (Nikolai Bukharin, Alexander Rykov, Lev Kamenev, Grigory Zinoviev, and others) on various charges, including plotting to murder Kirov and Stalin himself, working with foreign intelligence services, and sabotaging industrial production. Because of Stalin's political use of Kirov's murder, many scholars suspect that the dictator organized the assassination himself as an excuse to initiate the Terror.

Rumors of Stalin's involvement in Kirov's death began circulating in Leningrad well before the onset of the Terror, in fact within days of the assassination. Then, as the show trials developed in 1936–1938 a few Western journalists and socialist commentators speculated that Stalin might have ordered the killing in order to justify the Terror. In 1936 the Paris-based *Socialist Herald*, the organ of the Menshevik Party in exile, published a report purportedly from a senior Bolshevik leader that implied that Stalin *might* have organized the assassination. This "Letter of an Old Bolshevik" indicated that Kirov had been a "moderate" opposed to the excesses of Stalinist coercion.

From 1940 various journalists and scholars in the United States promulgated this narrative, in which Stalin had ordered Kirov's killing because the latter was a moderate and a serious threat to his power. In 1953 Alexander Orlov, a defector from the Soviet intelligence services, published memoirs in which he claimed to have heard from high-level NKVD sources that Stalin had most likely initiated the "hit" on Kirov. Three years after the publication of Orlov's memoirs, Nikita Khrushchev, Stalin's successor as head of the Soviet Communist Party, went public with his destalinization program. At the Twentieth Party Congress in February 1956 Khrushchev denounced Stalin's personal tyranny, his "cult of personality," and his persecution of innocent party members. As part of his attack on Stalin's former lieutenants still in the party leadership (Vyacheslav Molotov, Lazar Kaganovich), Khrushchev raised questions about Kirov's assassination and the death of Kirov's bodyguard in mysterious circumstances soon after. At a closed Central Committee session in 1957, Khrushchev supporters hinted broadly that Molotov had ordered Kirov's murder.

In 1968 the English poet and historian Robert Conquest made the claim that Stalin had ordered Kirov's murder a key element of his book *The Great Terror: Stalin's Purge of the Thirties.* Conquest based his account of the crime largely on Orlov's memoirs, the transcripts of Stalin's show trials, and Khrushchev's revelations. As a result of his writings, many well-read Americans came to assume that the case for Stalin's involvement in the assassination was ironclad.

Since the 1980s, however, several scholars have questioned Conquest's narrative of the assassination plot. In 1985 J. Arch Getty challenged Conquest's claim that Kirov's killing was part of a long-term plan by Stalin to initiate the Terror. Getty argued that the Soviet defector Orlov was an unreliable source, that Kirov was not a moderate but a loyal Stalinist, and that Stalin did not plan the Terror years beforehand. In the 1990s the Russian historian Oleg Khlevnyuk found no evidence in Central Committee documents that Kirov was a moderate. Another Russian scholar, Alla Kirilina, pointed out that in the weeks after the assassination Stalin was slow to settle on a single public version of the supposed plot. This was inconsistent with the claim that he himself had conspired to kill Kirov. Kirilina used documents on early interrogations of Nikolayev to argue that he was a lone gunman. She also noted that Khrushchev's investigation of the murder and his public comments on it had the political goal of discrediting Stalinists in the party leadership.

The question of Stalin's involvement in Kirov's murder remains open. There is no doubt, however, that Stalin used the killing to justify the Great Terror and the millions of arrests, deportations, and deaths associated with it.

See also **Purges; Soviet Union; Stalin, Joseph; Terror.**

BIBLIOGRAPHY

Conquest, Robert. *Stalin and the Kirov Murder.* New York, 1990.

Getty, J. Arch. *Origins of the Great Purges: The Soviet Communist Party Reconsidered, 1933–1938.* New York, 1985.

Khlevniuk, Oleg V. *Politbiuro: Mekhanizmy politicheskoi vlasti v 30-e gody.* Moscow, 1996.

Knight, Amy. *Who Killed Kirov? The Kremlin's Greatest Mystery.* New York, 1999.

Lenoe, Matthew. "Did Stalin Kill Kirov and Does It Matter?" *Journal of Modern History* 74, no. 2 (June 2002): 352–380.

MATTHEW LENOE

KIS, JÁNOS (b. 1943), Hungarian philosopher.

János Kis was the intellectual leader of the Hungarian democratic opposition of the 1980s. Born in Budapest, he has become one of the country's best-known philosophers, an important political commentator, and a senior professor at the Central European University in philosophy and political science.

Although less well known abroad than Jacek Kuron and Adam Michnik, Kis was a foremost theorist of the democratic transition in Soviet-type societies; he moved from critical Marxism to a conception of radical, structural reform from below, targeting an independent public sphere or civil society. Having been a student of the important neo-Marxist philosopher György Márkus, who brought him into the Budapest circle of George Lukács, Kis first worked on the problems and paradoxes of Marxian interpretations of Soviet-type societies. Two remarkable products of this enterprise, characteristic of the collective style of work of the period, were *How Is Critical Economics Possible?*, written in 1972 with György Bence and György Márkus but not published until 1992, and *Le marxisme face aux pays de l'Est* (*Towards an East European Marxism*), written with György Bence, published in Paris and London under the pseudonym Marc Rakovski in 1978. By the time of the publication of this last work, Kis had already come under the influence of the KOR of Michnik and Kuron, learned Polish, and proceeded to help import aspects of the new Polish strategy into reformist Hungary. Political conditions in Hungary being different from those in Poland, they placed more emphasis on creating an alternative public than on building an independent civil society, at least for a considerable period. The fruit of this effort was the samizdat journal *Beszélő*, of which Kis was the main theoretical and political editor. In early 1982, Kis and the other editors of *Beszélő* stood alone in interpreting the defeat of Solidarity in Poland as the beginning of the end of the Soviet imperium rather than as a defeat for attempts at democratization. Throughout the decade, in his many editorials Kis continued to refine the program of radical reform from below, drawing more and more intellectuals into the alternative public and by example into parallel endeavors. He concluded this period with an innovative radical reform proposal, *The Social Contract* (1987), and the formation of the liberal democratic Network of Free Initiatives (1988) and its successor, the Alliance of Free Democrats (SzDSz), the liberal party of which Kis became the first president. The party played a significant role in the National Round Table negotiations, and in the victorious referendum campaign of late 1989. However, after a close election in March of 1990 SzDSz was defeated, and in spite of a significant role in negotiating a constitutional pact with the victorious Hungarian Democratic Forum, Kis withdrew from the party leadership in favor of academic life, in which he had already been involved for some time.

In 1985 he published a Hungarian samizdat book, *Do We Have Human Rights?* (*L'Égale Dignité: essai sur les fondements des droits de l'homme*; Paris, 1989), which attempted to put the Dworkinian theory of fundamental rights on communicative theoretical foundations. This was his first effort at analytic philosophy, but after his withdrawal from active political leadership other works followed, of which *On Abortion: Arguments For and Against* (1992), *Political Neutrality* (1997), and *Politics as a Moral Problem* (2004) were the most substantial. He brought this new intellectual approach to bear on a series of old problems: the nature of the democratic transition and the construction of a constitutional democracy. The results were intellectually significant. A long article, "Between Reform and Revolution," was particularly innovative; it dealt with the nature of the new type of democratic transition and the ways it resembled a revolution in its effects but a reform in its legal continuity. In another work, *Constitutional Democracy* (2000), drawing on the Hungarian practice of constitutional jurisprudence from the post-transition period, he dealt with the supposed incompatibility between popular sovereignty and constitutionalism. That he was able to give an original solution to this problem testifies not only to his gifts as a philosopher but also the relevance of the experience of new democracies to the understanding of classical problems.

Kis's professional career is striking. He was not allowed to finish his doctorate in Hungary and was fired from his position at the Institute of Philosophy of the Academy of Sciences in 1973, during a major purge that included public attacks on *How Is Critical Economics Possible?* He survived during the next decade by translating Jean-Jacques Rousseau, Immanuel Kant, Johann Fichte, and Gehlen. After 1983 he was allowed to accept Western academic appointments, first at the École des Hautes Études en Sciences Sociales, then at the New School for Social Research. In 1992 he founded the Political Science Department at Central European University (CEU), and in 2001 he participated in launching CEU's Department of Philosophy. From 1996 to 2002 he was global professor of law at the New York University School of Law. During the fall of 2004 he was again at the New School in sociology and political science as Hans Speier Visiting Professor.

He remains influential in Hungary in spite of his withdrawal from active politics. He is a regular political commentator on issues of the day, from abortion to other rights-oriented issues, from the problems involved in referenda to those of the presidential types of government that various political forces would like to introduce. He has written major pieces on what he called conservative constitution-making and on almost all the major decisions of the Constitutional Court, to which he has submitted amicus curiae briefs of some importance.

See also **Human Rights; Hungary; Lukács, György; Michnik, Adam; Solidarity.**

BIBLIOGRAPHY

Primary Sources

Kis, János. *L'Égale Dignité: essai sur les fondements des droits de l'homme.* Paris, 1989.

———. *Politics in Hungary: For a Democratic Alternative.* Translated by Gábor Follinus. Highland Lakes, N.J., 1989.

———. *Constitutional Democracy.* Translated by Zoltán Miklósi. New York, 2003.

Kis, János, ed. *Contemporary Political Philosophy.* Budapest, 1997–2000.

Kis, János, and György Bence. *Towards an East European Marxism.* Published under the pseudonym Marc Rakovski. London, 1978.

Secondary Sources

Dworkin, Ronald, ed. *From Liberal Values to Democratic Transition: Essays in Honor of János Kis.* Budapest, 2004.

ANDREW ARATO

KITCHENER, HORATIO HERBERT

(1850–1916), British military leader.

At the outbreak of the First World War, Horatio Herbert Kitchener, Earl Kitchener of Khartoum, was Britain's most respected military figure. Yet by the time of his death two years later, his career was waning. He still stood high in the assessment of the general public but a good deal lower in the judgment of the political elite.

Kitchener was born in 1850, the son of a British colonel. After studying at the Royal Military Academy in 1868–1870, he qualified for a commission in the Royal Engineers. In 1871 he served with France's republican army in the attempt to rescue Paris from the Prussians. At the time, this action met with disapproval at home, but in 1914 it constituted a mark to his credit. Yet its real importance lay elsewhere. It was virtually the only time in a career of forty years that Kitchener saw battle in Europe. His huge reputation was gained in campaigns against the followers of Muhammad Ahmad (1844–1885) in the Sudan and against the Boers in South Africa, and his considerable administrative experience was secured in ruling foreign territories like Egypt and South Africa. By mid-1914 Kitchener was a field marshal, a founding member of the Order of Merit, and an earl.

On 3 August 1914, Kitchener, who was in Britain at the time, was summoned to London. The prime minister Herbert Henry Asquith (1852–1928) offered him the post of secretary of state for war—a key position in the civilian government. The appointment was wildly popular—Kitchener was known and highly regarded nationwide. He had already perceived, accurately if not quite as uniquely as is often claimed, that the war in which Britain was now involved would be a long struggle and that Britain would have to raise a major army and play a full part. That is, he recognized that Britain could not afford to limit its involvement to securing command of the seas and helping to meet the economic demands of a coalition war.

Yet his qualifications for this new task were less than total. His statement in 1915, in response to information about the impenetrable trench obstacles that British forces had attempted to assail, was simply one of bafflement: "This isn't war. I don't know what is to be done." Furthermore, he had little experience of military organization at home, or of the methods and machinery of the war office. And, having accepted a post in the civilian cabinet that was ultimately responsible for waging the war, he had little inclination to explain or justify his decisions to a gathering of individuals in whom he felt little confidence.

Yet it was hardly his fault if, along with himself, the cabinet, Parliament, and nation had eagerly adopted a widescale British involvement in a great international struggle. He set about providing the machinery, and the inspiration, for the creation of a mass volunteer army, stipulating early on its eventual expansion to seventy divisions—as against the six regular and fourteen territorial divisions then in existence. It has been argued—and probably with reason—that instead of creating his "New Army" (or "Kitchener's Army," as it was loudly proclaimed) from scratch, he would have done better to expand the existing territorial divisions and so avoided a military force in three distinct parts. But the fact remains that less than two years into the war the seventy divisions of British volunteers that Kitchener had summoned forth were trained and ready to take over the principal battle against the Germans.

Despite these accomplishments, the war was not a year old before Kitchener came under severe attacks from certain cabinet colleagues and sections of the press. He dealt expeditiously with a crisis early in the war, when the British Expeditionary Force was being driven steadily back toward Paris, and its commander, Sir John Denton Pinkstone French (1852–1925), proposed separating from the French and retreating to the coast. Kitchener, dressed perhaps inappropriately in the uniform of a field marshal, traveled to France to call Sir John to order. Thereby the military alliance with the French was preserved and the path set for an Allied victory at the Marne. So far Kitchener had done well. But the following April, when a British offensive suffered severe rebuff, he became the target of savage criticism, particularly by the Northcliffe press ("Lord Kitchener's Tragic Blunder"). The grounds of attack were provided by Sir John French and were of doubtful quality. But cabinet members had become tired of Kitchener's authoritarian manner, desperate overwork on less-than-important matters, and reluctance to recognize that munitions production was much more an industrial than a military matter. As part of the political upheaval in May, Asquith created under David Lloyd George (1863–1945) a ministry of munitions, which diminished much of Kitchener's power.

Munitions had been only one cause of political unrest. Another was dispute over the merits or folly of trying to capture Constantinople by forcing the Dardanelles. Initially Kitchener had endorsed this proposal as a purely naval activity, saying that if the fleet did not succeed the operation could be abandoned. But he then decided that the British Empire could not sustain a rebuff at the hands of the Turks and that an army must be sent to Gallipoli. For the rest of 1915 his actions were dogged by this alarming miscalculation, which culminated in November in his journeying to the Dardanelles and concluding that the endeavor must be abandoned.

On his return to Britain he offered the prime minister his resignation, which was declined. But his situation thereafter was much that of a figurehead, not least when Sir William Robert Robertson (1860–1933) was appointed chief of the imperial general staff with the sole authority to advise the cabinet on strategy. Yet, because of his reputation and personality, Kitchener remained an important public figure. His death on 5 June 1916 was an unprecedented calamity for the general public. And the great volunteer army of three million, raised at his call and about to take on the principal task of waging the war on the Somme, indicated the power of his endeavors.

See also **World War I.**

BIBLIOGRAPHY

Cassar, George H. *Kitchener: Architect of Victory.* London, 1977.

———. *Kitchener's War: British Strategy from 1914 to 1916.* Washington, D.C., 2004.

Magnus, Philip Montefiore. *Kitchener: Portrait of an Imperialist.* New York, 1959.

ROBIN PRIOR

KLAGES, LUDWIG (1872–1956), German philosopher.

Ludwig Klages was born on 10 December 1872 in Hanover, Germany, and studied chemistry, physics, philosophy, and psychology in Leipzig, Hanover, and finally Munich. In the turn-of-the-century cultural revival in the Schwabing district of the city, Klages formed part of the so-called cosmic circle (*Kosmikerkreis*), and the tone and content of his early work reflects his reading of Friedrich Nietzsche (1844–1900) as a philosopher of Dionysian ecstasy.

By this time Klages had become interested in graphology, the art of interpreting handwriting: in 1895 he had joined the Institute for Scientific Graphology; in 1896 he cofounded the German Graphological Society; and in 1905 he founded the Psychodiagnostic Seminar for Expressive Theory. His seminar lectures provided the basis for his first publications, *The Problems of Graphology* (1910) and *The Principles of Characterology* (1910). The broader cultural implications of these "new" disciplines, in their vitalist conception of the human individual, became clear in "Humankind and Earth," an address written for the Free German Youth Day held on the Hoher Meißner in October 1913, in its emphasis on the damage human beings do to themselves and their environment.

Following the outbreak of World War I, Klages moved in August 1915 to Switzerland, settling in 1919 in Kilchberg, just outside Zürich. There he began to address broader philosophical themes, producing between 1929 and 1932 his three-volume masterwork, *The Spirit as the Adversary of the Soul.* In 1932 he was awarded the Goethe-Medal for Art and Science, but in the late 1930s his ideas were attacked by the National Socialists, particularly the Nazi ideologist Alfred Rosenberg (1893–1946). Although a latent anti-Semitism in his writings has hindered their reception in recent times, Klages was never a Nazi.

In his final years, Klages produced an edition of his unpublished earlier, literary sketches (*Rhythms and Runes,* 1944) and an important study of language (*Language As the Source of Knowledge of the Soul,* 1948). He died on 29 July 1956 in Kilchberg.

In philosophical terms, Klages is best characterized as a vitalist, an exponent of *Lebensphilosophie* (philosophy of life), or, as he called it, "biocentric metaphysics." Klages considered his "science of expression" (*Ausdruckskunde*) to be a critical reaction and a corrective response to the eighteenth-century discipline of "physiognomy," while his "science of character" (*Charakterkunde*) was a criticism and a correction of psychology. Like Gestalt psychology, Klages was interested in perception; unlike Gestalt psychology, which drew on the phenomenology of the German philosopher Edmund Husserl (1859–1938), Klages's philosophical sources included the Greek philosopher Heraclitus (late 6th century B.C.E.), especially the idea that "what we see when awake is death, and what we see when asleep is life (reality)" (Diels-Kranz, 22 B 21), and Aristotle (384–322 B.C.E.), to whom he was indebted for his conception of "spirit" (*Geist*) as a *nous thurathen*, or "intellect from without" (*On the Generation of Animals*, Book 2, 736 b 27 and 744 b 22), and hence as something alien, and even hostile, to humankind. Whereas dreams reveal to us the "reality of the images" (*Wirklichkeit der Bilder*), the perception of the waking state is the province not of the soul (*Seele*) but of the mind, the intellect, the spirit—*Geist*. Within Klages's inherently conflictual system, "body and soul are the *poles* of the life-cell which belong inseparably together…into which from *outside* the spirit, like a wedge, inserts itself, in the endeavor to split them apart, to 'de-soul' the body, to disembody the soul, and in this way finally to kill all the life it can reach."

And nowhere could the deleterious influence of the spirit be more clearly seen, Klages argued, than in the modern world. In this respect Klages's thought anticipated the "dialectic of enlightenment," later advanced by Theodor Adorno (1903–1969) and Max Horkheimer (1895–1973). The parallel between Klages and the Frankfurt School lies in their view that the irrationality of instrumental reason is revealed in its turn against the very life whose interests it is meant to serve. Equally, the German literary critic and philosopher Walter Benjamin (1892–1940) took a particular and well-documented interest in Klages, even describing the coming to terms with the Swiss anthropologist Johann Jakob Bachofen (1815–1887) and Klages as "unavoidable," until he was instructed by Adorno to avoid both Klages and the Swiss psychologist and psychiatrist Carl Jung (1875–1961). Benjamin's concept of "aura" has parallels with Klages's, and Benjamin's "dialectical image" displays affinities with Klages's "archaic" version. So Klages may have been right when he described himself as "the most *plundered* author on the contemporary scene."

See also **Adorno, Theodor; Benjamin, Walter; Jung, Carl; Psychiatry; Psychoanalysis.**

BIBLIOGRAPHY

Primary Sources

Klages, Ludwig. *The Science of Character*. Translated by W. H. Johnston. London, 1929.

Secondary Sources

Block, Richard. "Selective Affinities: Walter Benjamin and Ludwig Klages." *Arcadia* 35 (2000): 117–136.

Furness, Raymond. "Ludwig Klages." In *Zarathustra's Children: A Study of a Lost Generation of German Writers*, 98–122. Rochester, N.Y., 2000.

Stauth, Georg. "Critical Theory and Pre-Fascist Social Thought." *History of European Ideas* 18 (1994): 711–727.

PAUL BISHOP

KLARSFELD, SERGE (b. 1935), French Jewish historian and Nazi hunter.

In the United States and Israel (where he is a citizen, as well as in France), Serge Klarsfeld is best known as a "Nazi hunter," and in France he is known as a historian of the deportation of French Jews and as the president and founder of the Association of Sons and Daughters of Deported Jews of France (Fils et Filles des Déportés Juifs de France). He is all of this at once, an activist grounded in his rigor as a historian and professional lawyer.

Born a Jew in Romania, Klarsfeld emigrated to France with his family. As a young boy he lived through the persecutions and the tragedy of the deportation of Jews from Nice and the murder of his father at Auschwitz-Birkenau.

It was probably when he met his wife, Beate Künzel, a German Protestant, at the beginning of the 1960s and told her of the horrors perpetrated by her country from 1933 to 1945 that the couple became "militants of memory." The Adolf Eichmann trial in Jerusalem in 1961 solidified their commitment. Many Jews, who had largely remained silent after the Holocaust, were beginning to make the voices of its victims heard. Beate and Serge Klarsfeld became known for their tenacity in exposing and bringing to justice Nazi criminals, sometimes by means of provocative symbolic gestures that led to their imprisonment. In 1968 Beate slapped the German chancellor Kurt Kiesinger; in 1971 they attempted to abduct Kurt Lischka to highlight the need to bring Lischka and two others, Ernst Heinrichsohn and Herbert Hagen, to trial for the deportations of Jews from France. They traveled to Iran, Syria (to hunt down Aloïs Brunner), and South America. Although Serge Klarsfeld and Regis Debray failed in their 1972 attempt to abduct Klaus Barbie in Bolivia, ten years later the head of the Lyon Gestapo was finally extradited and tried in France. His trial was followed by those of two Frenchmen—Paul Touvier, a former Lyon militia leader, in 1994, and the high-level state official Maurice Papon, in 1997–1999. The lawyer for the Jewish plaintiffs in this civil trial in Bordeaux was none other than Beate and Serge's son Arno Klarsfeld, named after his murdered grandfather.

At the same time as he was seeking out the executioners and their accomplices, Serge Klarsfeld published a major work of historical scholarship. This work describes the suffering of the Jews during the war, the crushing responsibility of the Vichy authorities in the deportations, especially of children, and also the not inconsiderable efforts of "ordinary" citizens that allowed many Jews on French soil to be saved. Klarsfeld is not a typical academic: above all, he assembled documents— documents from the convoys, letters, and photographs of eleven thousand children killed in the Holocaust. His historical work on deportation represents a standard of scholarship that many European countries are trying to equal.

Klarsfeld also personally established memorials to the Jews of Romania and Grodno; he later focused on Hungarian victims. His archival work aims above all to provide a "symbolic burial" of the victims. It also enables their descendants to assert their rights, which Klarsfeld, through the Association of Sons and Daughters of Deported Jews of France, is helping to defend. He participated in the Matteoli commission studying the confiscation of Jewish goods under the Vichy government and waged a successful campaign to secure indemnification for Holocaust orphans from Lionel Jospin's government in 1999.

Klarsfeld's initiatives continue to receive extensive media coverage. Personally close to Jacques Chirac, he helped to write the 1995 speech in which the president of the republic acknowledged France's culpability in the deportation of seventy-eight thousand Jews, of whom only twenty-five hundred returned. From 2002 to 2004 Klarsfeld invited survivors and descendants of the victims to come to the various points from which the convoys left, including Angers, Valenciennes, Compiègne, and above all Drancy, on the anniversary of the departures. Participants read the victims' names and sometimes spoke a few words. Klarsfeld restored to each of them a name, a life, and sometimes a face. He also gave their relatives a place to mourn: the wall engraved with names at the Shoah Memorial inaugurated in Paris in January 2005.

See also **Barbie, Klaus; Deportation; Holocaust; Wallenberg, Raoul.**

BIBLIOGRAPHY

Klarsfeld, Serge. *Le mémorial de la déportation des Juifs de France*. Paris, 1978.

———. *French Children of the Holocaust: A Memorial*. Translated by Glorianne Depont and M. Epstein. New York, 1997.

———. *La Shoah en France*. 4 vols. Paris, 2001.

Laqueur, Thomas. "Sound of Voices Intoning Names." *London Review of Books* 19, no. 1 (1997): 3–6.

Wieviorka, Annette. "Serge Klarsfeld, l'archive au cœur." *L'histoire* 261 (2002): 30–31.

ANNETTE BECKER

KLEE, PAUL (1879–1940), Swiss painter.

Color, composition, and line are perceptual elements in the construction of a work of art, either as means of representation, or as ends. However, to envisage Paul Klee's work according to these schemas, as either mimesis or pure abstraction, is to miss out on the process itself. Klee's painting eschews the principle of reflecting reality in favor of a return to the essence of painting itself: the sensation of a particular moment transposed through memory. Indeed what Klee sought, through a work of returning to memory and therefore beyond visible presence alone, was to restore this past moment in which there had been a fusion between man and nature. Like the mnemonic image, these elements then present themselves in a composition that only becomes coherent through progressive mental reconstruction. Although patterns are clearly identifiable, they are more like indicators than representations.

Reduced here to its essentials, this theory of painting governs the entirety of Klee's work, including the periods when it was yet to be formalized. Although his 1914 voyage to Tunisia is often associated with the moment when this theoretical approach revealed itself to him; it nonetheless underlies everything he painted from 1900 onward—years of exploration and relatively restrained productivity during which he was preoccupied with the education of his son, but which nevertheless constitute the indispensable groundwork for the production of works that principally question the relationship of fusion between man and world, and how not to betray it in images. This time was therefore a primordial and constitutive element in the foundation of Klee's theoretical approach, permitting him to engage and nourish his unique statement based on a training in a diverse array of artistic techniques including music, poetry and painting, as well as through the discovery of contemporary artistic techniques including postimpressionism, cubism, expressionism, and Blaue Reiter (a group of expressionist painters) especially.

EXPERIMENTATIONS

Born in Münchenbuchsee in 1879, Klee departed for Munich in 1898 and enrolled in Heinrich Knirr's Free Academy of Drawing. This, followed by Franz von Stuck's courses in painting in 1900, led Klee to make the most important choice of his life—to become a painter. Often interpreted as a means of escape from a preordained career as a violinist, Klee's choice also seems to have been his intuitive conception of what held true potential for him. Although he did not consider music capable

of expressing all the force of his connection to the world, the fact that he never ceased to play it reflected his continued belief that it was indispensable to his art. As such, an important part of his work was founded on his supple interpretation of musical scoring, which was not confined to the act of transposing musical notes but referred back to the principle of composition itself and induced a mode of reading through rhythm, harmony, and attunement. In short, before 1914, the year when his theoretical approach became enshrined, he continually felt the influence of music because of his intuitive predilection toward it.

Before this date, Paul Klee was in a phase of experimentation, during which he encountered a number of difficulties, primarily due to the fact that he was unable to go beyond the figurative. At the time, this made it impossible for him to represent nature according to his own self-conception. The persistence in his work of a pictorial story and the conditions this imposed on representation constituted the primary obstacle whose removal would be necessary in order to translate into images this man-nature intimacy. This difficult but ever-sought-after transgression of the rules of representation, however, tended also to entail challenges in the domain of technique, especially as concerns color. A series of works that is more or less exclusively black and white as well as certain statements he makes in his journal both speak of these troubles with color, a bitter marker during this so-called symbolist period of an impotence that assumed the attributes of an output saddled with irony, borrowing from the universes of the English poet and painter William Blake (1757–1827) and the Spanish painter Francisco José de Goya y Lucientes (1746–1828) their most grotesque and fantastic figures of disillusion. However, he was not to remain forever stymied in this impasse.

COLOR AND ITS CONSEQUENCES

It was between 1908 and 1914 that Klee discovered the force and expressiveness of postimpressionist color, particularly in the works of Vincent van Gogh (1853–1890) and Paul Cézanne (1839–1906). In 1911 he also met Wassily Kandinsky (1866–1944), August Macke (1887–1914), and Franz Marc (1880–1916), members of the Munich expressionist group Der Blaue Reiter (The blue

An Actor. Painting by Paul Klee, 1923. NIMATALLAH/ART RESOURCE, NY

works in color. His voyages to Tunis, Kairouan, and Hammamet set off the explosion. He wrote at the time in his journal, "color has taken hold of me, I no longer need to chase after it . . . color and I have become one. I am a painter." Composition, expressive color, pattern as a trigger of memory, the unreality of the image as expression of a shimmering instant in time—Klee's system was born, and he perfected it during his Bauhaus years, after Walter Gropius (1883–1969) contacted him in 1920 to propose he become one of the school's central teachers. Working within this framework of constant artistic and intellectual exchange for nearly ten years, Klee analyzed, nourished, and retouched his artistic procedures, making these teaching years particularly productive in creative terms. He also explored other functional modes, developing for example his series of magic squares that used mathematical schemas to combine color and composition.

But as time passed, teaching turned to constraint and hindered his creative activity, so he left the Bauhaus School on friendly terms in 1930 and joined the Düsseldorf Academy. Klee, ever unwilling to see things as they were, soon found himself caught up in the increasingly stultifying and repressive political context of his day. The Nazis stripped him of his post and quickly denounced his art as degenerate. Harsh years followed for Paul Klee. He left Germany for Switzerland but never found there the intellectual effervescence of the previous years. He felt increasingly isolated and was therefore all the more affected by the news of his illness in 1935. Knowing he had but a few years to live, he reduced his theoretical activities considerably, to the point that he abandoned them entirely, in order to consecrate himself to productive output exclusively. The knowledge of his impending death drove him to accelerate innovations in his creative procedures from 1938 onward. One last time therefore he won the day by extending the reach of his work.

See also **Bauhaus; Expressionism; Modernism; Painting, Avant-Garde.**

BIBLIOGRAPHY

Grohmann, Will. *Der Maler Paul Klee.* Paris, 1966.

Klee, Paul. *Journal.* Translated by Pierre Klossowski. Paris, 1959.

rider), in whose second exhibition he even participated. Klee's intuitions were reinforced by the principles the group espoused, including "to be inspired by neither the Past nor Nature, but from Oneself," an idea that he associated with his discovery in 1912 of the French painter Robert Delaunay's harmonious work with color, which he translated into his *Essay on Light.*

Doors began to open for him, and he prepared himself at last to formalize and put his theoretical approach to the test by extending its application to

Kudielka, Robert, ed., with an essay by Bridget Riley. *Paul Klee: The Nature of Creation Works, 1914–1940.* London, 2002. Exhibition catalog.

Lanchner, Carolyn, ed. *Paul Klee.* New York, 1987. Exhibition catalog.

Musée des Beaux-Arts (Bern). *Paul Klee, Catalogue Raisonné.* London, 1998–2004.

ALEXANDRA KOENIGUER

KLEMPERER, VICTOR (1881–1960), romance-language philologist of Jewish origin.

Victor Klemperer was born on 9 October 1881, in Landsberg an der Warthe (now Gorzów Wielkopolski). He was the eighth child of a reform rabbi but converted in 1912 to Protestantism. He attended a humanistic gymnasium in Berlin and served an apprenticeship at the same time. In 1906 he married the pianist Eva Schlemmer. While working as a freelance writer, he studied German language, romance languages, and philosophy at the universities of Berlin, Munich, Geneva, and Paris and earned his doctorate in 1912 and his habilitation (qualification to teach in a university) two years later, both in Munich. After a short employment in Italy he volunteered for the German army from 1915 to 1918, where he served in the artillery and later as a military censor in occupied Lithuania. In 1919 he obtained a position at the University of Munich, and in 1920 became professor of romance languages at the Technical University of Dresden. During the 1920s he published widely on French literature and philology. He died on 11 February 1960, in Dresden.

Because of his Jewish origins, the Saxonian government in Dresden fired Klemperer in 1935—the culmination of two years of discrimination he had experienced at the university. Restrictions against Jews gradually made it impossible for him to continue any kind of work; he was even not allowed to consult libraries. Instead, he studied Judaism. But he avoided severe persecution because of his marriage to an "Aryan"—what the authorities considered *Mischehe* (mixed marriage). Nevertheless, both he and his wife had to leave their house in 1940 and move into different, ghetto-like "Judenhäuser" in Dresden. From October 1941, Klemperer was obliged to wear a Star of David on his clothes; from 1943 he was periodically recruited to forced labor. After the heavy bombardment of Dresden in February 1945, both the Klemperers had to leave city. Hiding in Bavaria, Klemperer avoided deportation, as the "mixed marriages" partners of Jewish origin were scheduled to be deported during the last weeks of the war.

Klemperer's diaries extensively not only document but also analyze German anti-Semitism from 1918, especially at the universities, and the years of anti-Jewish persecution from 1933 on. They show the everyday consequences of administrative oppression, like loss of position and property, periodical police searches in his house, and the decline of health resulting from mental stress and disadvantaged supply. More depressing appears the gradual social isolation of persons of Jewish origin, even if they were Christians, in German society after 1933 and in Klemperer's bourgeois milieu. After some years, most of his friends had abandoned him. The diaries give detailed evidence on the knowledge of average Germans about the radicalization of the anti-Jewish policy, including mass murder and extermination camps in eastern Europe. Yet they also demonstrate that not all Germans condoned these policies.

After the war Klemperer returned to Dresden and joined the reestablished Communist Party in November 1945 because he regarded the communists as the only political force to prevent Nazism. He became leading council member of the Kulturbund (Cultural Union), an association concerned with cultural and educational affairs that was gradually taken over by the communist United Workers Party (SED). From 1950 to 1958, in his function as Kulturbund leader, he also became a member of the East German pseudoparliament Volkskammer. Klemperer returned to the University of Dresden but also taught in Greifswald (1947–1948) and from 1948 in both Halle and Berlin. After the death of his wife in 1951 he was remarried a year later, to Hadwig Kirchner. During the 1950s he became more and more critical of the repressive political development in the German Democratic Republic, but—as after 1933—did not intend to emigrate.

Klemperer became famous first by his early book on Nazi language, *LTI: Notizbuch eines Philologen* (*The Language of the Third Reich: LTI,*

Lingua Tertii Imperii: A Philologist's Notebook), which appeared in 1947. The posthumous publication of his 1933–1945 diaries in 1995 brought greater popularity, as the diaries were regarded as a literary sensation in Germany. His life under Nazism was even made the subject of a German television film. Klemperer had written diaries since he was seventeen years old, all of which were published subsequently after 1989. His notes from 1933–1945 became probably one of the most quoted diaries of Nazi victims because of their power of observation and distinguished style.

See also **Anti-Semitism; Nazism.**

BIBLIOGRAPHY

Aschheim, Steven E. *Scholem, Arendt, Klemperer: Intimate Chronicles in Turbulent Times.* Bloomington, Ind., 2001.

Heer, Hannes, ed. *Im Herzen der Finsternis: Victor Klemperer als Chronist der NS-Zeit.* Berlin, 1997.

Jacobs, Peter. *Victor Klemperer: Im Kern ein deutsches Gewächs: Eine Biographie.* Berlin, 2000.

Klemperer, Victor. *I Shall Bear Witness: The Diaries of Victor Klemperer, 1933–41.* Abridged and translated from the German edition by Martin Chalmers. London, 1998.

DIETER POHL

KOESTLER, ARTHUR (1905–1983),
political activist, anticommunist, Zionist, author of novels and popular science books.

Arthur Koestler was born in Budapest, Hungary, on 5 September 1905 to parents from the assimilated, prosperous Jewish bourgeoisie. He attended school in Budapest until 1919, when his family, fearing anti-Jewish disturbances, temporarily relocated to Vienna. He remained there, attending a private school and then studying engineering at the Vienna Technische Hochschule. He joined a Jewish student society and fell under the spell of Vladimir Jabotinsky, the founder of right-wing Revisionist Zionism. He left the university in April 1926, intending to settle in Palestine. Koestler failed as a pioneer, surviving only with the help of his Revisionist friends. After a spell in Berlin in mid-1927, he fortuitously obtained a post as Middle East correspondent for the Ullstein newspaper chain. He worked as a journalist in Palestine, Paris, and Berlin from October 1927 to December 1932.

As science correspondent for the Berlin *Vossische Zeitung,* Koestler joined a zeppelin expedition to the North Pole in 1931, a coup that made him famous. Responding to the rise of National Socialism in Germany, he joined the Communist Party in December 1931, largely as a means to combat fascism. Covert activities for the party cost him his job. After a period of political activism in Berlin, in July 1932 he traveled to the USSR to research a pro-Soviet book. He remained there until March 1933, when he moved to Paris and entered the world of antifascist exiles. From 1933 to 1938 he worked spasmodically for Willi Münzenberg, the Communist entrepreneur and propagandist.

Koestler briefly spied for the Communist Party in Fascist-held Spain in August 1936. While covering the fall of Malaga in February 1937 for British and French newspapers, he was seized by Francoist forces and held in prison under sentence of death. He was released in May 1937 after his wife led a campaign to save him. He then journeyed to England, where his account of his ordeal, *Spanish Testament,* brought him celebrity.

During 1937–1939, Koestler lived mainly in Paris and worked as a freelance journalist and writer. His first novel, *The Gladiators* (1939), reflected his disillusionment with the Communist Party. Nevertheless, in October 1939 he was arrested by the French authorities as a dangerous alien and interned in Le Vernet camp until January 1940. Koestler returned to Paris but in June fled to escape the German invasion. He went underground in unoccupied France and escaped to England via North Africa and Portugal. He reached England in November 1940, where he was temporarily imprisoned as an illegal alien.

In December 1940 influential political and literary friends rescued Koestler from prison. He was now lionized as the author of *Darkness at Noon,* a powerful attack on communist beliefs that was published while he was in custody. Despite his fame he joined the British Army, serving in the Pioneer Corps, until discharged on health grounds in

March 1942. During the next two years he worked for the Ministry of Information, writing scripts for propaganda films and radio. He completed another novel, *Arrival and Departure* (1943), and a collection of essays, *The Yogi and the Commissar* (1945), that included a potent critique of the Soviet Union. *Arrival and Departure* contained a sequence describing the mass murder of Jews in Nazi-occupied Europe. Koestler was unusual in comprehending the catastrophe, but his efforts to stir public opinion failed. After the Germans occupied Hungary in March 1944, he was involved in desperate rescue efforts. His widowed mother survived the war in Budapest, but many other family members were murdered in Auschwitz. In December 1944 Koestler traveled to Palestine, where he wrote *Thieves in the Night* (1945), a novel advocating Zionism.

Between 1945 and 1955 Koestler was torn between politics and science. He collaborated briefly with Bertrand Russell (1872–1970) and George Orwell (1903–1950) in an attempt to refound politics and morality on a scientific, value-free basis while avoiding the errors of discredited left- and right-wing ideologies. He frequently visited Paris to enlist French intellectuals, including André Malraux, Albert Camus, and Jean-Paul Sartre. He also traveled to the United States, where he rallied anticommunist intellectuals. In mid-1948 he spent several months covering Israel's war of independence and researching *Promise and Fulfillment* (1949), an account of how Israel had emerged. It concluded by admonishing Jews to choose between total assimilation or emigration to Israel.

In early 1949 Koestler purchased a home outside Paris. It became a hub for European anticommunist intellectuals such as Raymond Aron and Ignazio Silone. Koestler inspired *The God That Failed* (1950), an influential collection of confessional essays by former communists, and orchestrated the Congress for Cultural Freedom, which staged a major anticommunist rally in Berlin in 1950. Despairing of Europe, in October 1950 he moved to the United States. Meanwhile he wrote an outstanding volume of autobiography, *Arrow in the Blue* (1952). Disappointed by America, he returned to London in September 1952 and completed a second volume, *The*

Invisible Writing. In a collection of essays, *The Trail of the Dinosaur,* published in 1955, he renounced political activism in favor of scientific writing. But he devoted much energy to the campaign against capital punishment in England.

During the 1960s and 1970s, Koestler wrote popular science books, including *The Sleepwalkers* (1959), *The Act of Creation* (1964), and *The Ghost in the Machine* (1967), in which he inveighed against behaviorism. He published a travel book investigating India and Japan, *The Lotus and the Robot* (1960), and a fifth novel, *The Call-Girls* (1972), satirizing jet-set intellectuals. His last original work, *The Thirteenth Tribe* (1976), attempted to prove that European Jews were descended from the Khazars rather than the Semitic tribes that once inhabited the land of Israel.

Koestler had a tempestuous private life, married three times, and fathered an illegitimate daughter, whom he refused to acknowledge. He was made a Commander of the British Empire in 1971 and a Companion of the Royal Society of Literature in 1974. In his seventies he developed Parkinson's disease and cancer. Koestler was an advocate of voluntary euthanasia and took his own life on 1 March 1983. His third wife committed suicide with him under controversial circumstances.

See also **Anticommunism; Camus, Albert; Zionism.**

BIBLIOGRAPHY

Cesarani, David. *Arthur Koestler: The Homeless Mind.* New York, 1999.

DAVID CESARANI

KOHL, HELMUT (b. 1930), the longest-serving chancellor of the Federal Republic of Germany (1982–1998).

Born and raised in Ludwigshafen, Helmut Kohl joined the Christian Democratic Union (CDU) in his native Rhineland-Palatinate as a teenager. He received a doctorate in history from the University of Heidelberg, all the while continuing his rise through the party ranks during the chancellorships of the Christian Democrats Konrad Adenauer (1949–1963) and Ludwig Erhard (1963–

Helmut Kohl (right) and French president François Mitterrand join hands during a ceremony commemorating victims of World War II, 22 September 1984. ©BETTMANN/CORBIS

1966). Kohl was elected governor of Rhineland-Palatinate in 1969, the same year that the Social Democrat Willy Brandt became chancellor. In 1973 Kohl became chairman of the national CDU organization. In 1976 he narrowly lost a national election to Helmut Schmidt, Brandt's successor. Kohl became chancellor in October 1982 when the Free Democratic Party (FDP) abandoned its coalition with Schmidt and formed a government under CDU leadership.

The central event of Kohl's chancellorship was German reunification in 1989–1990. The democratic revolution in the German Democratic Republic took place suddenly and unexpectedly during the second half of 1989. Less than three weeks after the collapse of the Berlin Wall on 9 November 1989, Kohl put forward an ambitious ten-point plan for German unity. It was quickly overtaken by events. The East German revolution continued apace and, after its first democratic

elections produced a CDU majority in March 1990, Kohl and his foreign minister, Hans-Dietrich Genscher, pressed for all-German elections and rapid reunification. After several rounds of careful diplomacy with the four powers responsible for the question of German unity since the end of World War II—the United States, the Soviet Union, France, and the United Kingdom—the five states of the former GDR acceded to the Federal Republic on 3 October 1990. Kohl emerged victorious from the first all-German elections that December.

Before and after the pivotal events of 1989–1990, Kohl's chancellorship was marked by a series of difficult domestic and foreign policy challenges. The recession of the early 1980s that had precipitated the collapse of the Schmidt government left a legacy of high unemployment and stagnant growth. Kohl and the FDP sought, with mixed success, to trim the generous German welfare state over the objections of the labor movement and the Social Democratic Party (SPD), which retained control of several key state governments. On the foreign policy front, the 1980s saw a slow transition from East–West confrontation to renewed détente. In contrast to Schmidt, Kohl aligned himself unequivocally with the confrontational policies of U.S. president Ronald Reagan and carried through the controversial deployment of new U.S. intermediate-range nuclear forces on German soil in 1984. Initially skeptical of Mikhail Gorbachev's perestroika and diplomatic political opening to the West, Kohl emerged as one of his most vocal supporters by the late 1980s. The positive Kohl–Gorbachev relationship contributed to the successful transition from the GDR revolution to reunification in 1989–1990.

In the wake of reunification, domestic economic and political problems overshadowed foreign policy ones. Kohl, a longtime supporter of European integration, was one of the architects of the European Monetary Union and an influential backer of European Union membership for former members of the Warsaw Pact. But most of his political energies were spent trying to master the economic, social, and political integration of the new federal states of the former GDR. The weakness of the East German economy, exacerbated by the generous terms of monetary union, proved a steady drain on the overall German economy through the 1990s. Unemployment remained high, foreign investment stagnated, and powerful forces both within the CDU and the SPD blocked efforts at far-reaching reforms of the tax, pension, and health care systems. The CDU's popularity in the new states plummeted and the former Communist Party, the PDS, remained a fixture in its political landscape.

These accumulated problems contributed to Kohl's loss to Gerhard Schröder in the 1998 elections. An unprecedented career in postwar German politics came to an end. Kohl's domination of the CDU had been unrelenting. He served as its chairman for a quarter century and beat back several challenges to his leadership, most notably from Franz-Josef Strauss of the CDU's Bavarian sister party, the Christian Socialist Union. He won no fewer than four national elections—in 1983, 1987, 1990, and 1994. Dismissed early in his career by many as a provincial politician with little foreign policy experience, Kohl emerged as a major

international figure with proven political staying power. After he left office in 1998, Kohl's image was tarnished by evidence of involvement with a party financing scandal. But his legacy as the chancellor of German unity was assured.

See also **Germany; Perestroika; Schmidt, Helmut; Schröder, Gerhard.**

BIBLIOGRAPHY

Bering, Henrik. *Helmut Kohl: The Man Who Reunited Germany, Rebuilt Europe, and Thwarted the Soviet Empire.* Washington, D.C., 1999.

Clemens, Clay. *Reluctant Realists: The Christian Democrats and West German Ostpolitik.* Durham, N.C., 1989.

Clemens, Clay, and William E. Paterson, eds. *The Kohl Chancellorship.* London, 1998.

"The Kohl Chancellorship." *German Politics* 8, no. 1 (1998).

Livingston, Robert Gerald. "Life after Kohl? We'll Always Have Germany." *Foreign Affairs* 76, no. 6 (1997): 2–7.

THOMAS BANCHOFF

KOJÈVE, ALEXANDRE (1902–1968), Hegelian philosopher.

Alexandre Kojève is best known for a series of lectures he gave on *The Phenomenology of Spirit*, by G. W. F. Hegel (1770–1831), from 1933 to 1939 at the École Practique des Hautes Études. Kojève's auditors read like a who's who of future French intellectuals. Raymond Aron, Georges Bataille, André Breton, Jacques Lacan, Maurice Merleau-Ponty, Raymond Queneau, Eric Weil, and others attended Kojève's seminars at various times, and many of them testified to his acumen, rigor, and erudition. Kojève's lectures were published in 1947; and this, coupled with the publication of Jean Hyppolite's 1939 translation of the *Phenomenology of Spirit*, introduced Hegelianism to postwar France and set the stage for its subsequent sovereign reign there.

Kojève reads human history through the lens of Hegel's master-slave dialectic, and he sees the desire for recognition as the distinguishing characteristic of humanity. Human beings demand to be recognized and respected as free and equal individuals, and it is only when individuals are mutually recognized that they can lead fully satisfying lives. At the beginning of their historical development, however, human beings, while demanding that others recognize their individual particularity, refused to offer that recognition in return, and this led to a struggle for recognition or a battle for pure prestige. At some point in this struggle, one of the warrior's desire for self-preservation overcame his desire to risk his life for recognition, and he thereafter became the slave of the victorious master, recognizing his human dignity and working for him. But while the master may have won in the short run, over the long run the slave's recognition of the master is not satisfying precisely because the master does not recognize the slave's dignity. The slave, by contrast, was able to progress historically through the very activity that distinguished him as a slave, namely work or labor: the products of the slave's work became an objective confirmation of his own reality and worth. Kojève traces the development of slave consciousness through the historical stages of Christianity and capitalism, for example: in the former, God becomes a new and absolute master, but one who now recognizes the unique individuality and worth of all persons; in the latter, private property or capital becomes the new master, but one that aids and encourages the working slave's ongoing transformation and technological conquest of nature. According to Kojève, the end of history (understood as humanity's dialectical transformation and development) occurred during the French Revolution and the reign of Napoleon. The worker-warriors of Napoleon's army were willing to risk their lives for recognition, but only in order to create the egalitarian conditions whereby all individuals will recognize one another and be recognized as dignified and autonomous citizens. The only remaining task to accomplish historically is the worldwide propagation of the fundamental ideas of the Revolution, the achievement of which will result in what Kojève calls a universal and homogeneous state. This final or end state will be universal because it will encompass all of humanity; and it will be homogeneous because all citizens will enjoy equal rights and duties through the promulgation of a genuinely equitable system of justice.

Kojève exerted a broad influence over many segments of French intellectual life. For example, André Breton (1896–1966) and the surrealists discovered in Hegel's dialectic a demonstration of the inner harmony and unity of apparently opposite and irreconcilable concepts or forces. The psychoanalyst Jacques Lacan (1901–1981) borrowed a number of Kojèvean insights, including the desire for another desire, the struggle for recognition, and the master-slave dialectic. Lacan then incorporated these ideas into his interpretation of Sigmund Freud (1856–1939) to explain such phenomena as the origin of self-consciousness, the constitution of human subjectivity, and the socialization of children. In literature, many of the novels of Raymond Queneau (1903–1976) can be understood as depicting life at the end of history. Not without irony and humor, Queneau's characters are generally fully reconciled or satisfied with themselves and their surroundings. With little more to do or say in the modern world, they enjoy an essentially pacific and leisured existence in which the titanic, historical struggles between good and evil are gone forever. And lastly, Kojève laid the groundwork for the emergence of existential Marxism in such thinkers as Maurice Merleau-Ponty (1908–1961) and Jean-Paul Sartre (1905–1980). Abandoning Hegel's dialectical understanding of nature, Kojève maintained that human beings alone are defined by their radical freedom to negate or change or create themselves and the world around them. This existential ontology was then grafted onto Marx's historical materialism, resulting in a philosophical position that emphasizes the free creation of human essence, the inherently alienating structures of capitalistic society, and the struggle for a future free of exploitation. In sum, Kojève is often the hidden influence that stands behind much of postwar French intellectual life.

See also **Breton, André; Freud, Sigmund; Lacan, Jacques; Merleau-Ponty, Maurice; Phenomenology; Sartre, Jean-Paul.**

BIBLIOGRAPHY

Primary Sources

Kojève, Alexandre. *Introduction to the Reading of Hegel: Lectures on the Phenomenology of Spirit.* Assembled by Raymond Queneau. Edited by Allan Bloom. Translated by James H. Nichols Jr. Ithaca, N.Y., 1980.

———. *Outline of a Phenomenology of Right.* Translated, with notes and introductory essay by Bryan-Paul Frost and Robert Howse. Edited by Bryan-Paul Frost. Lanham, Md., 2000.

Strauss, Leo. *On Tyranny.* Revised and expanded edition, including the Strauss-Kojève correspondence. Edited by Victor Gourevitch and Michael S. Roth. New York, 1991.

Secondary Sources

Auffret, Dominique. *Alexandre Kojève: La philosophie, l'État, la fin de l'histoire.* Paris, 1990.

Butler, Judith. *Subjects of Desire: Hegelian Reflections in Twentieth-Century France.* New York, 1999.

Roth, Michael S. *Knowing and History: Appropriations of Hegel in Twentieth-Century France.* Ithaca, N.Y., 1988.

BRYAN-PAUL FROST

KOŁAKOWSKI, LESZEK (b. 1927), Polish philosopher.

Leszek Kołakowski figured in a sequential pair of movements of central importance to the story of twentieth-century intellectual life: the insider attempt to save Marxism from its communist perversion, and the outsider critique of Marxism as an unsalvageable messianism inseparable from its bloody and repressive "failures." Born in 1927 in Radom, Poland, and for a long time a professor at the University of Warsaw, Kołakowski's path also led geographically, and not just intellectually, away from the communist experiment, and his life neatly divides into periods before and after his 1968 migration. A wide-ranging intellectual historian important for studies of Christian as well as Marxist doctrine at different moments in time, Kołakowski's lasting significance likely resides, however, less in his specific arguments than in an ideological itinerary at once personal and typical.

At Warsaw, he led a fundamentally important cohort of philosopher-historians—the others included Bronisław Baczko, Krzysztof Pomian, and Andrzej Walicki—whose activities in their original home before 1968 and their various transits to and receptions in Western intellectual life after have not yet been collectively gauged. Deeply affected by Western European philosophy—he wrote influential studies of the phenomenologist Edmund Husserl and the overall movement known as positivism—Kołakowski's richest scholarly contributions were in his investigations throughout his life of early modern thought, beginning with what remains perhaps his most accomplished book, a treatment of seventeenth-century nonconformist theology. But also in the 1950s and especially after 1956, Kołakowski became one of the intellectual leaders in Poland of the "revisionist" attempt to imagine a socialism with a human face. The project intended to come to the rescue of the collectivist aspiration, redeeming the Eastern bloc whose properly emancipatory vocation had gone awry, and not simply to capitulate to Western capitalism, which was seen to have equal or worse flaws. Kołakowski's writings of this period, which earned him vilification from the Polish Communist leader Władysław Gomułka, were published in the West in the 1960s, for example in *Man without Alternatives* (1960) and *Towards a Marxist Humanism* (1968). Kołakowski remained an iconic figure in the Eastern bloc after his 1966 removal from his university position and expulsion from the party for a controversial speech. But his outlook both then and after his departure two years later differed in character from "antipolitics," the intellectual movement of dissident Eastern European thought in the 1970s. For in this period, Kołakowski became a famed apostate from the Marxist theory and practice he had once hoped to reform from within.

It was undoubtedly Kołakowski's three-volume *Main Currents of Marxism,* the fruit of his arrival at Oxford University after brief peregrinations elsewhere, that did most to establish his worldwide prominence and readership. Long after its publication in 1976–1978, it remains the most capacious study ever written of the history of Marxist doctrine. It is distinguished by its range and detail as well as by its positions. Though following the Hungarian philosopher Gyorgy Lukács in stressing the generally German and specifically Hegelian sources of Marx's own theory (it begins with the famous line "Karl Marx was a German philosopher"), *Main Currents* controversially located the "golden age" of Marxism in the late nineteenth and early twentieth centuries, normally dismissed as a period of scientistic decline for socialist philosophy. For Kołakowski, however, it was a period of fecund theoretical pluralization and enormous expansion, a process as much nipped in the bud as it was capped by Vladimir Lenin's theoretical and revolutionary accomplishment. After all, Kołakowski observed in the third and highly partisan volume of the trilogy, "The Breakdown," had not Lenin's achievement, as consummated by Joseph Stalin, finally revealed the bankruptcy of Marxism's original promise, leaving for the enlightened only the theoretically scholastic and politically juvenile alternative of "Western Marxism" as the expiring groan of a once heroic intellectual enterprise?

In the end, Kołakowski became one of the many who argued that socialism's disaster occurred because of its very "utopian" formulation, which foredoomed it to a violent outcome. His initial innovations in and final conversion away from Marxism made his emblematic trajectory a problem for those Western leftists who hoped to salvage the hope for a postcapitalist society from the wreckage of its betrayed communist incarnation. In a celebrated exchange in the *Socialist Register* in 1973–1974, the British Marxist historian E. P. Thompson castigated Kołakowski for abandoning his experimentation with doctrine while Kołakowski—in a response entitled "My Correct Views on Everything"—justified the remorselessness of his ultimate anti-Marxist conclusions. A figure most internationally prominent in 1970s intellectual life, Kołakowski, who in later years joined the University of Chicago's Committee on Social Thought, lived into the twenty-first century, publishing occasionally but slowly retreating from general consciousness, gradually leaving behind the ideological landscape whose overall mutations his personal adventure did something to cause and much more to capture in miniature.

See also **Communism; Eastern Bloc; Phenomenology; Poland.**

BIBLIOGRAPHY

Kołakowski, Leszek. *Toward a Marxist Humanism: Essays on the Left Today.* Translated by Jane Zielonko Peel. New York, 1968.

———. *Chrétiens sans église.* Translated by Anna Posner. Paris, 1969.

———. *Main Currents of Marxism: The Founders, The Golden Age, The Breakdown.* Translated by P.S. Falla. Oxford, U.K., 1978. Reprint, New York, 2005.

———. *The Two Eyes of Spinoza and Other Essays on Philosophers.* Translated by Agnieszka Kolakowska and others, edited by Zbigniew Janowski. South Bend, Ind., 2005.

SAMUEL MOYN

KONDRATIEV, NIKOLAI (1892–1938), Soviet economist.

Nikolai Dimitrievich Kondratiev studied at the University of St. Petersburg, where he took courses taught by Mikhail Tugan-Baranowsky and other economists. In October 1920 he founded the Institute of Business Cycle Analysis in Moscow, which by 1923 had become a large and respected center employing more than fifty researchers. Between 1923 and 1925 he worked on a five-year plan for Soviet agriculture. As a supporter of the New Economic Policy (NEP), he favored the primacy of agriculture and the production of consumer goods over the development of heavy manufacturing. On the scientific front, in the 1920s he published several books and articles on long wave cycles. He stated that the capitalist economy was characterized by a succession of long periods of expansion and decline, implicitly rejecting the Marxist notion of an imminent collapse of capitalism. These "unorthodox" ideas and Kondratiev's sympathy for NEP aroused Joseph Stalin's anger. In 1928 he was removed as director of the institute and two years later he was arrested, accused of being a member of an illegal party. Kondratiev was serving an eight-year prison term when in 1938, during Stalin's Great Terror, he was executed.

The most interesting feature of Kondratiev's work is his theory explaining the existence of long cycles of about fifty years (1790–1845, with a peak in 1815; 1845–1895, with a peak in 1875; 1895–?, with a peak in 1914). He introduced the concept of basic capital goods, large-scale investments in infrastructure (canals, railroads, etc.), and other important works (such as clearing of land). These investments are characterized by a long construction period and high costs. Kondratiev assumed that the production of basic capital goods initially took place in a particular period of time, so the replacement of these means of production is also concentrated in a relatively short time span, thereby giving investment a strong boost. This creates additional employment, new incomes, and a higher demand for consumer goods. Eventually all sectors participate in the economic expansion, which lasts for about two to three decades due to the long construction period of basic capital goods.

During the economic upswing investment is so high that more money is required than the financial sector can accumulate. Gradually the money reserves are exhausted, so that interest rates start to rise. At a certain moment the expected return on investment falls below the interest rate and capital formation collapses: the turning point in the long cycle is reached. Overcapacity in the basic capital goods sector gives rise to massive layoffs, which in turn reduces the demand for consumer goods. Unemployment increases rapidly and the whole economy is drowned in a long crisis period. Nevertheless, during the economic contraction the building blocks are put into place for a renewed period of expansion. Investment falls below the accumulation speed of financial resources, so that a new reservoir of money is formed. Consequently, there will be sufficient financial resources available when the replacement of basic capital goods takes off again. Moreover, the economic difficulties incite firms to look for cost savings, which usually generates inventions. Due to the low level of investment, however, these inventions often cannot be transformed into innovations. It is only when investment recovers again that the new technologies can be incorporated in the production process on a large scale.

Kondratiev's ideas provoked a lot of controversy. In the late 1920s the Soviet economist Alexander Oparin heavily criticized the empirical part of Kondratiev's work as statistical manipulation. But for obvious reasons the discussion in the Soviet Union soon came to a complete standstill. In the West Kondratiev touched more fertile ground. His seminal article of 1925 was quickly translated into German but only received real attention when the German version was translated, in abridged form, in *Review of Economic Statistics* (1935). After a brief vogue in the late 1930s, Kondratiev's ideas were swamped by the ideas of the English economist John Maynard Keynes. But in the 1970s Keynesianism proved unable to address the serious economic problems of the time, leading to the rediscovery of Kondratiev's work, which became more fashionable than ever before. In 1987 the Soviet Union officially rehabilitated Kondratiev, and in the 1990s high quality translations based on his original writings in Russian became available in English.

Nevertheless, the debate rages on. Many economists cannot accept, for instance, the periodical character of the replacement of basic capital goods. Because the depreciation rate of these investment goods ranges from ten to a hundred years, their replacement should be a continuous process and not concentrated in particular periods. The empirical part of Kondratiev's argument also has its weaknesses. The margin of error of the underlying historical series is sometimes very high. Moreover, the number of complete cycles is so small that coincidence can play an important role in identifying long waves.

See also **Five-Year Plan; New Economic Policy (NEP); Stalin, Joseph.**

BIBLIOGRAPHY

Kondratieff, Nikolai D. *The Long Wave Cycle.* Translated by Guy Daniels. New York, 1984.

Louçã, Francisco. "Nikolai Kondratiev and the Early Consensus and Dissensions about History and Statistics." *History of Political Economy* 31 (1999): 169–205.

Louçã, Francisco, and Jan Reijnders, eds. *The Foundations of Long Wave Theory: Models and Methodology.* Northampton, Mass., 1999.

Makasheva, Natalia, and Warren J. Samiels, eds. *The Works of Nikolai D. Kondratiev.* London, 1998.

Neumann, Manfred. *The Rise and Fall of the Wealth of Nations: Long Waves in Economics and International Politics.* Cheltenham, U.K., 1997.

ERIK BUYST

KOREAN WAR. Although the brutal conflict to reunify the Korean peninsula that broke out in June 1950 was rooted in civil war, it was provoked and sustained by superpower rivalry: Korea was where the Cold War turned hot. The belligerents agreed to an armistice in July 1953, but no peace treaty has been signed and the two Koreas remain, formally, in a state of war.

ORIGINS

Since the Russo-Japanese War of 1904–1905, Korea had been completely under Japanese control. When Japan collapsed in August 1945, the Americans arranged that their troops would take the surrender in the south and the Soviet army would do so in the north. A convenient demarcation line was the thirty-eighth parallel, which divided the peninsula almost equally and left the capital, Seoul, in American hands.

This was supposed to be an interim arrangement, until a democratic government could be formed for the whole country. But, as in Germany, the Soviets sealed off their zone and helped local communists to sovietize its institutions; in the south, the Americans fostered a rightist coalition of anticommunists. Following dubious elections in both Koreas in 1948, the superpowers withdrew most of their troops, hoping to sustain their client regimes by military aid.

But neither Kim Il Sung (1912–1994) in the north nor Syngman Rhee (1875–1965) in the south accepted partition as permanent. Each tried to reunify the country on his terms, and more than a hundred thousand people died in guerrilla operations and border clashes even before the formal war began. The critical step in escalation was Kim Il Sung's visit to Moscow in April 1950. There he persuaded Joseph Stalin (1879–1953) to back an all-out invasion of the south, arguing that the Americans were unlikely to intervene (having just done little to stop communist victory in China's civil war) and that, in any case, South Korea would be overrun in only a few days. Stalin provided arms, equipment, and advisors, and Soviet planners even drafted the operational plan. Kim also obtained the backing of the new Chinese communist government under Mao Zedong (1893–1976).

CRISIS, 1950–1951

North Korean troops crossed the thirty-eighth parallel on 25 June 1950 and drove rapidly southward. But Kim's predictions of American acquiescence proved fatally wrong. President Harry Truman (1884–1972) was under attack in Congress for "letting China fall"; he also believed that appeasement in the 1930s showed the dangers of not nipping aggression in the bud. Truman immediately ordered American troops into action and also secured the endorsement of the United Nations Security Council. This backing, immensely important for international credibility, was only possible

because the Soviet Union was boycotting the council in protest of communist China's exclusion. Otherwise Stalin would have imposed a veto on making Korea a UN operation. Eventually seventeen countries contributed troops to the UN command, though the bulk came from South Korea and America.

By late August 1950 only the southeast corner of Korea was not in communist hands. But on 15 September the American commander of the UN forces, General Douglas MacArthur (1880–1964), mounted a major amphibious landing behind enemy lines at the west coast port of Inchon. Now the North Koreans were in turmoil. On 28 September Seoul was retaken; two days later UN forces crossed the thirty-eighth parallel, seeking to implement the old policy of a unified, democratic Korea.

It was the American turn to miscalculate. Although unwilling to get directly involved, Stalin persuaded Mao to commit Chinese troops. The Americans were clearly warned through the Indian government that, if UN troops crossed the thirty-eighth parallel, they would provoke Chinese resistance, but this was dismissed as bluff. On 25 November MacArthur's final push to the Yalu River, North Korea's border with China, brought a major counterattack from three hundred thousand Chinese, and UN forces fell back in chaos.

On 30 November 1950 Truman told reporters that the United States would use "every weapon we have" to meet the crisis in Korea. Asked about the atomic bomb, he said there had "always been active consideration of its use." Alliance partners were shocked and the British prime minister, Clement Attlee (1883–1967), flew to Washington to urge restraint. The Republican Right and MacArthur himself now favored using the bomb against North Korea and China; there were real fears of a third world war.

STALEMATE, 1951–1954

By late January 1951 the northern quarter of South Korea was back in enemy hands. But then the UN line stabilized and its advance resumed. Seoul was recaptured on 14 March, changing hands for the fourth time since June 1950. Chastened, Truman was now ready for a peaceful settlement, but MacArthur undercut his efforts by calling publicly

A British officer (with field glasses) and South Korean soldiers in a trench overlooking the Naktong River during the Korean War, 1950. ©HULTON-DEUTSCH COLLECTION/CORBIS

for Chinese surrender. The president finally lost patience, and on 11 April MacArthur was relieved of his command. After an upsurge of fighting in the spring, the war settled into stalemate.

In July the belligerents began armistice negotiations. The biggest sticking point was the return of prisoners of war, which the Americans insisted should be voluntary—in other words, allowing North Korean and Chinese troops a choice about whether or not to go home. This impasse was not broken until 1953, mainly because of Stalin's death in March 1953 and the eagerness of the new Soviet leadership to extricate itself from Korea. Threats of escalation by the new Eisenhower administration may also have played a part. But although the armistice was finally signed on 27 July 1953, the international conference on Korea, held in Geneva the following spring, made no progress. Unable to unite the peninsula on its own terms, each superpower effectively agreed that a divided Korea was the best outcome for the foreseeable future.

LEGACIES

The human cost of the war was appalling: at least three million Koreans died, and probably a million Chinese were killed or wounded, including one of Mao's sons. The American death toll was thirty-three thousand. The United States and China were locked in bitter enmity for a generation. The war also had a profound effect on Europe. Fearful that the North Korean attack presaged a similar assault on Western Europe, the United States committed new combat divisions to Germany and turned the North Atlantic Treaty into a full-scale military alliance. And although other similarly partitioned countries such as Vietnam and Germany were eventually unified, albeit in very different ways, the two Koreas remained into the twenty-first century as grim relics of the Cold War.

See also Cold War; Vietnam War.

BIBLIOGRAPHY

Primary Sources

Cold War International History Project. Its Web site features research papers and translated primary source material on the Korean War. Available at http://wwics.si.edu.

Lee, Steven Hugh. *The Korean War.* Harlow, U.K., 2001. A good introduction, with documents.

Secondary Sources

Goncharov, S. N., John W. Lewis, and Xue Litai. *Uncertain Partners: Stalin, Mao, and the Korean War.* Stanford, Calif., 1993. Based on Soviet and Chinese sources.

Hastings, Max. *The Korean War.* London, 1987. Mostly a military history.

Stueck, William. *The Korean War: An International History.* Princeton, N.J., 1995.

DAVID REYNOLDS

KOSOVO. Kosovo lies between Albania, Macedonia, Serbia, and Montenegro. Its population of approximately two million people is estimated to be over 90 percent Albanian, with the remainder being Serbs, Montenegrins, Muslim Slavs, ethnic Turks, Roma, and others. While it remains a formal part of Serbia-Montenegro, it has been under the United Nations' international administration since 10 June 1999, when the UN Security Council passed Resolution 1244. This Resolution marked the end to NATO's military campaign, "Operation Allied Force," against the Federal Republic of Yugoslavia. The NATO campaign had begun on 23 March 1999 and was designed to compel the Yugoslav government to cease violating the human rights of Kosovar Albanians and to accept changes in Kosovo's political status.

Discord over Kosovo's legal and political status lay at the heart of the dissolution of the Socialist Federal Republic of Yugoslavia (SFRY) that began in the early 1980s and continues, as of 2006, to impede diplomatic efforts to end the fractious conflicts in this corner of southeastern Europe. Mediators from the United Nations, the European Union, and the United States have been addressing an issue that has defied resolution since the decline of Ottoman power in the Balkans just before World War I.

KOSOVO'S SIGNIFICANCE

Kosovo's deep emotional and symbolic significance to Serbs and Albanians has obstructed the search for a peaceful settlement of national differences. Albanians claim to have lived in Kosovo as Illyrians and Dardanians well in advance of the Slavic invasions of the Balkans in the sixth and seventh centuries. Kosovo was also the site of the Prizren League following the Berlin Congress in 1878 that gave birth to the modern Albanian national movement. On the other hand, Serbs claim Kosovo as "the cradle of Serbian civilization." It was the center of the medieval Serbian state and long the seat of the patriarchate of the Serbian Orthodox Church. The defeat of Serbian forces by the Ottoman Army on 28 June 1389 has forever anointed Kosovo as a symbol of the "new Jerusalem" that is central to the Serbians' sense of place in the Balkans. Over the centuries, a cycle of folk epics about Kosovo transformed these memories so that Serbs closely associated Albanians with the Ottoman Empire and saw them as incapable of governing their own state.

This history provides background to the formation of national states with the retreat of Ottoman power from the Balkans at the end of the Balkan Wars. This retreat led to the creation of an independent Albania that left up to 40 percent of ethnic Albanians outside its borders. The victorious Serbian and Montenegrin armies arrived in Kosovo in 1913 to find a land in which they were greatly outnumbered. The Yugoslav census of 1921 recorded that 280,440 of the 436,929 inhabitants, or 64.1 percent of the population, were Albanian speakers. After World War II Albanians comprised an absolute majority of Kosovo's population and grew from 498,242 people, or 68.5 percent of the population, in 1948 to 1,607,690 people, or 82.2 percent of the population, in 1991. In that same period, the Serbs' share of the population shrank from 23.6 percent in 1948 to 9.9 percent in 1991. Montenegrins' share of the population shrank from 3.9 percent in 1948 to 1 percent in 1991. The Serbian government's efforts to transform Kosovo back to the center of Serbian political and cultural life have been faced with these population trends.

WORLD WAR I

Albanian rebel bands known as Kaçaks resisted the advance of Serbian and Montenegrin forces into Kosovo. As many as twenty thousand Albanians in Kosovo were killed and tens of thousands fled the area during this initial Serb occupation in 1912–1913. With the Serbian defeat by German-Austrian forces in 1915 during World War I the situation was reversed. The Serbian Army, led by its government and royal family, was forced to retreat through Kosovo into Albania and as many as one hundred thousand people died in the trek. Kosovo's Albanian majority initially welcomed the partitioning Austrian, German, and Bulgarian powers. Local government in the Austrian sector employed the Albanian language and the Austrians set up three hundred Albanian-language schools and training academies. Conditions under Bulgarian occupation were significantly worse and were marked by compulsory labor service and forced requisitions of food. With the Austro-Hungarian forces' reversal of fortune in 1918 Serbian troops again brutally occupied Kosovo much as they had in 1913. According to agreements that were made during the fighting among the Allied powers, Kosovo was awarded to the Kingdom of Serbs, Croats, and Slovenes at the Paris Peace Conference and Kosovo was known as the "southern region" of Serbia and was part of "Old Serbia."

INTERWAR PERIOD

In the Kingdom of Serbs, Croats, and Slovenes that was proclaimed on 1 December 1918 Kosovo was part of southern Serbia. The establishment of Yugoslavia, ruled by a royal dictatorship, on 6 January 1929 led to an administrative reform in which the territory of Kosovo was split into three separate *banovinas* or regions. Albanians were considered a national minority but the government denied them important rights contained in the Treaty on the Protection of Minorities, which it had signed in 1919. Albanians could not legally attend schools taught in their own language, nor were any Albanian-language publications on sale. Only 2 percent of eligible Albanian students were enrolled in secondary schools. All leading administrative positions of authority were in the hands of ethnic Serbs.

Possibly in anticipation of this inequality, a Committee for the National Defense of Kosovo, or Kosovo Committee, was formed to encourage as many as ten thousand rebel Kaçaks to engage in an anti-Serbian insurgency throughout all Albanian areas in southern Serbia and Montenegro. This insurgency remained active until the end of 1924, when it was finally suppressed by the government in Belgrade with the cooperation of the Albanian government headed by Prime Minister Ahmet Zogu (1895–1961), who had been forcibly removed from this position a year earlier by a coalition that included the Kosovo Committee. The Serbian government assisted Zogu's return to power with this cooperation in mind.

Throughout the interwar period, the Serbian government focused on changing the ethnic composition of Kosovo and sponsored an agrarian reform that primarily featured a colonization program under which former Montenegrin and Serb soldiers were encouraged to emigrate in exchange for land. Under this program, just under two hundred thousand hectares of land—of 584,000 total hectares of land—were redistributed to as many as seventy thousand colonists. Between the two world wars, tens of thousands of Albanians emigrated to Greece, Albania, and Turkey. In 1938 the government signed a convention with the government in Turkey that foresaw the emigration of two hundred thousand people to Turkey over the next six years.

ITALIAN AND ALBANIAN OCCUPATION

These plans were interrupted by Nazi Germany's attack on Yugoslavia in April 1941 and the subsequent three-way partition of Kosovo. Bulgaria gained control of a small part of eastern Kosovo. The northern section that contained valuable zinc- and lead-producing mines in the city of Mitrovica was attached to the quisling regime in Serbia. The rest of Kosovo was joined with Albanian-inhabited regions of western Macedonia to Albania, which had been conquered by Mussolini's Italy in 1939. In a manner reminiscent of the pattern established during World War I the Italian region saw the establishment of Albanian-language elementary schools. The German military occupiers played a significant role in the occupation of the Serbian section. In the course of the war between thirty thousand and one hundred thousand Serbs fled from or were expelled from the region and between three thousand and ten thousand Serbs and Montenegrins were killed.

With the imposition of socialist power in 1944 and 1945 between three thousand and twenty-five thousand Albanians were killed.

Albanian collaboration with the Germans and Italians was driven more by their dislike of Serbs than for their fealty to the goals of the Axis powers. German efforts to develop a Kosovar division to fight against the Serbs were not very successful. Similarly, the antifascist partisans led by the Yugoslav communist leader Josip Broz Tito (1892–1980) failed to win significant Albanian support for their cause of establishing a government that gave every nation the right to self-determination. Even the communists' declaration at the beginning of 1944 that appealed to a desire for unity with Albania by working with the communist movement throughout Yugoslavia did not lead many Albanians to join the Communist Party. In July 1945 Kosovo was formally annexed to Serbia. In the period before Yugoslavia's expulsion from the Stalinist Cominform in 1948 there was hope that Kosovo could be reunited with Albania as part of a larger Balkan Federation.

THE ERA OF SOCIALISM

From 1945 until 1990 Kosovo enjoyed autonomous status within the Socialist Republic of Serbia. It was known officially as "Kosovo-Metohia" or "Kosmet" until 1968. (A *metoh* is an Orthodox Church holding and the title emphasizes Kosovo's Serbian character.) Kosovo was an "Autonomous Region" until the passage of a new Yugoslav constitution in 1963, when it became an "Autonomous Province." Under reforms that were promulgated in 1968 and strengthened in the 1974 constitution Kosovo's government gained a status equivalent in most respects to that of the six Yugoslav republics, with direct representation on Yugoslav federal bodies and the right to write its own constitution, but without the formal right of succession.

This constitutional evolution reflected the changing political circumstances in Kosovo and Yugoslavia more broadly. Yugoslavia's expulsion from the Cominform in 1948 raised fears in Belgrade that anti-Yugoslav propaganda emanating from Albania might have appeal among Kosovo's Albanians. The Serbian-dominated secret police subsequently imposed harsh rule over the region. In the 1950s Serbs and Montenegrins accounted for 50 percent of party membership and of industrial workers when they only made up 27 percent of the population. The regime held public show trials of Albanians accused of subversion and espionage. Thousands of Albanians declared themselves Turks and emigrated to Turkey. The pendulum swung back again with the reforms in the late 1960s, which gave Kosovo Albanians the right to fly a flag bearing the Albanian national emblem. The University of Pristina grew rapidly as an educational center and, under an agreement with the University of Tirana, Kosovo students used textbooks printed in Albania and were taught by visiting professors from Albania. The Albanian share of the industrial and professional workforce, management structures, League of Communists, and police force increased considerably in the period after 1974.

TOWARD DISSOLUTION

The improved position of Albanians in Kosovo led to increasingly strong demands for elevation of Kosovo's status to that of a republic within the Yugoslav Federation. The culmination of these demands came in massive student demonstrations less than one year after Tito's death in 1981. The strong suppression of these demonstrations and the efforts of Albanian communists to restore order quieted neither the demands of increasingly radical Albanians nor the province's Serbs, whose emigration from Kosovo had begun to increase still further. By the mid-1980s Serbs and Montenegrins in Kosovo began openly complaining that they were under a great deal of pressure and began to organize for defense of Serbs in Kosovo. The situation of Serbs in Kosovo became a national cause célèbre as the Serbian Academy of Arts and Sciences in 1986 drafted a memorandum that criticized Serbia's socialist politicians for allowing the genocide of Serbs in Kosovo and leading Serbia to its greatest defeat in history. Developments in Kosovo were also central in propelling the career of Slobodan Milošević (1941–2006), the first senior politician to acknowledge the validity of Serb anger toward Kosovo. Milošević manipulated Serb fears over Kosovo in support of his efforts to gain power throughout the Yugoslav federation and then to create the conditions for the wars that plagued Croatia, Bosnia, and Kosovo throughout the 1990s.

The Serbian constitution of 1990 eliminated Kosovo's autonomy and Kosovo began to be referred to again in official Serbian documents as Kosmet. The newly established administration systematically removed Albanians from the mass media, government and administration, business, and management, as well as from the health and educational systems. Albanian ceased to be a language of instruction in the university and in high schools. Legislation was passed forbidding the sale of property to Albanians. This repression increased still further as the Serbian government became involved in wars fought in Croatia and Bosnia.

TOWARD INTERNATIONAL ADMINISTRATION

This repression led many thousands of Albanians to emigrate from Kosovo and Albanians remaining in Kosovo to boycott participation in all aspects of official social and political life. They organized a nonviolent parallel political system that was led in the early years by the Democratic League of Kosovo or LDK. Its leader, Ibrahim Rugova (1944–2006), was overwhelmingly elected president in 1992. Contributions from Albanians employed at home and abroad provided the basis for the development of a parallel system of education and health care. By 1997 the failure of this movement to win independence or international recognition led to the emergence of the Kosovo Liberation Army (KLA), which engaged in guerrilla warfare in regions that were favored by the Kaçaks in the 1920s. Fighting escalated in 1998 and many thousands of Kosovar Albanians fled into the hills to continue the fighting. Threatened with NATO bombardment, Serbian president Milošević accepted an unarmed observer mission from the Organization for Security and Cooperation in Europe (OSCE) that would facilitate political negotiations between the Serbian government and the Albanian movement. The effort to build confidence between Serbs and Albanians on the ground failed with increasingly violent fighting between Serb and Albanian forces. Diplomatic efforts to hammer out a political settlement in February 1999 also failed when the Serbian government refused to sign an agreement that would give Albanians the widest possible autonomy within Serbia. This led to the seventy-eight-day NATO campaign, Operation Allied Force, which focused on Serbian military targets and civic infrastructure. During the fighting the Serbian forces killed an estimated eleven thousand Albanians and drove almost a million Albanians out of Kosovo.

The UN interim administration, which was charged with preparing Kosovo for self-government and for the settlement of Kosovo's future status, was bolstered by a NATO force of forty-two thousand troops to provide security. Hundreds of thousands of Albanian refugees quickly flooded back into Kosovo and have emerged as the predominant political force in Kosovo. These interim arrangements have succeeded neither in preventing thousands of Serbs from emigrating from Kosovo nor in providing a basis on which to build confidence between Albanians and Serbs who remain in Kosovo. There is hope among international negotiators that the negotiations over Kosovo's future status that began in 2005 will succeed at resolving the problems that remained unsolved throughout the twentieth century.

See also **Albania; Milošević, Slobodan; Serbia; World War I; World War II; Yugoslavia.**

BIBLIOGRAPHY

Banac, Ivo. *The National Question in Yugoslavia: Origins, History, Politics.* Ithaca, N.Y., 1984.

Cohen, Lenard J. *Socialist Pyramid: Elites and Power in Yugoslavia.* Oakville, Ont., New York, and Lanham, Md., 1989.

Horvat, Branko. *Kosovsko Pitanje.* Zagreb, 1989.

Janjić, Dušan, and Shkelzen Maliqi, eds. *Conflict or Dialogue: Serbian-Albanian Relations and the Integration of the Balkans.* Subotica, 1994.

Judah, Tim. *Kosovo: War and Revenge.* New Haven, Conn., 2000.

Malcolm, Noel. *Kosovo: A Short History.* New York, 1998.

Pipa, Arshi, and Sami Repishti, eds. *Studies on Kosova.* Boulder, Colo., and New York, 1984.

Vickers, Miranda. *Between Serb and Albanian: A History of Kosovo.* New York, 1998.

MARK BASKIN

KRACAUER, SIEGFRIED (1889–1966),

architect, cultural critic, philosopher, writer, sociologist, film scholar, theorist of history.

Siegfried Kracauer was one of the most significant and original thinkers of the first half of the twentieth century. A German-Jewish

> "The position that an epoch occupies in the historical process can be determined more strikingly from an analysis of its inconspicuous surface-level expressions than from that epoch's judgments about itself."
> Siegfried Kracauer, "The Mass Ornament," 1927

intellectual writing in the heady atmosphere of the Weimar Republic, Kracauer first gained prominence in the 1920s and 1930s, when he published influential essays on such topics as mass culture, photography, urban modernity, the cultural logic of visual surfaces, and even the philosophy of the hotel lobby. A selection of these essays was later published as *The Mass Ornament,* a book that, as a whole, devotes itself to a micrological analysis of modernity and the masses as they converge on a wide range of surface phenomena, the marginal and ephemeral experiences that structure modern life.

While Kracauer is best known for the works on film theory that he published in English after he was forced to emigrate to the United States to escape Hitler's regime—especially *From Caligari to Hitler: A Psychological History of German Film* (1947) and *Theory of Film: The Redemption of Physical Reality* (1960)—his significance for the development and structure of Weimar literature and cultural criticism cannot be overstated. He was known to a broadly educated audience as a leading contributor to the prestigious German newspaper *Frankfurter Zeitung* in the 1920s and also for such works as *Soziologie als Wissenschaft* (1922; Sociology as science). Devoting himself to the epistemological and political aspects of media aesthetics long before this practice became common in cultural theory, Kracauer pursued a kind of phenomenological reading that views culture as a complex text saturated with competing meanings, a method developed from that of his teacher the philosopher Georg Simmel, with whom he had an extensive correspondence and whose work he analyzed in a number of publications. Kracauer also crafted aesthetic complements to his own theoretical texts. Such works include the literary

documentary *The Salaried Masses* (1930) and the novels *Ginster* (1928) and *Georg* (1934).

Although Kracauer enjoyed personal relations with many of Weimar Germany's leading intellectuals, including Martin Buber, Ernst Bloch, Franz Rosenzweig, and Max Scheler, his thinking exerted the greatest impact on the work of those colleagues who collectively would come to be known as the Frankfurt School of Critical Theory, especially his close friends Theodor W. Adorno, Walter Benjamin, Max Horkheimer, and Leo Löwenthal. Adorno (1903–1969), who as a young man met with Kracauer for regular Saturday afternoon discussions of Immanuel Kant and later wrote that he had learned more from his older friend than from any academic teacher. Similarly, Benjamin's (1892–1940) well-known writings on media aesthetics, especially those devoted to photography and film, would hardly be thinkable without Kracauer's example and guidance. In fact, Kracauer even invented the term *illuminations* that later came to be synonymous with Benjamin's work. Lastly, as in the writings of his Frankfurt School colleagues, the project of a critical redemption of thinking suffuses Kracauer's final book, *History: Last Things before the Last,* which remained unfinished when he died of pneumonia in New York exile.

See also **Benjamin, Walter; Cinema; Frankfurt School.**

BIBLIOGRAPHY

Primary Sources

Kracauer, Siegfried. *The Mass Ornament: Weimar Essays.* Translated, edited, and with an introduction by Thomas Y. Levin. Cambridge, Mass., 1995. Translation of *Das Ornament der Masse* (1963).

———. *Theory of Film: The Redemption of Physical Reality.* With an introduction by Miriam Bratu Hansen. Reprint. Princeton, N.J., 1997.

Secondary Sources

Jay, Martin. "The Extraterritorial Life of Siegfried Kracauer." In his *Permanent Exiles: Essays on the Intellectual Migration from Germany to America,* 152–197. New York, 1986.

Koch, Gertrud. *Siegfried Kracauer: An Introduction.* Translated by Jeremy Gaines. Princeton, N.J., 2000.

Richter, Gerhard. "Siegfried Kracauer and the Folds of Friendship." *German Quarterly* 70, no. 3 (1997): 233–246.

GERHARD RICHTER

KRISTALLNACHT.

KRISTALLNACHT. On the night of 9–10 November 1938 Jews in Germany and Austria suffered an unprecedented assault. The "pogrom" was dubbed "the night of broken glass" by Germans because of the shattered windows that littered city streets. It was the culmination of exclusionary policies and sporadic violence directed against the Jews since the Nazis had come to power in 1933. The tempo of persecution had varied according to the priorities of domestic and foreign policy, but from late 1937 the pace accelerated as Hitler removed conservative elements from the regime and pursued an aggressive foreign policy. The annexation of Austria in March 1938 was accompanied by frenzied violence and looting, followed by sustained pressure on Jews to emigrate. By contrast, in Germany the slow pace of "Aryanization," the transfer of businesses from Jews to non-Jews, and low emigration was causing frustration to many Nazi leaders.

The radicalization of anti-Jewish policy led to the deportation of seventeen thousand Polish Jews from Germany to Poland on 27–28 October 1938. However, Poland refused to admit them, and they remained stranded in miserable refugee camps in the border zone. A young Polish Jew in Paris, Herschel Grynszpan (1921–?), was outraged at the treatment of the deportees, who included his parents. On 7 November 1938 he entered the German embassy in Paris and shot Ernst vom Rath, a minor official. Grynszpan was quickly apprehended.

Joseph Goebbels (1897–1945), the Nazi propaganda minister, seized on the shooting as the pretext for an "action" that he could lead against the Jews, with the partial aim of impressing Hitler. On 8–9 November he instructed the German press to highlight the shooting. Anti-Jewish disturbances followed in several German cities. On 9 November the Nazi leadership gathered in Munich to commemorate Hitler's attempted putsch in 1923. At 9 P.M. news arrived that vom Rath had died of his wounds. Hitler conferred with Goebbels and left the ceremony unexpectedly. Goebbels then made a speech stating that Hitler had agreed to "spontaneous" demonstrations against the Jews. The assembled leaders of the party and the SA (Sturmabteilung), the party militia, understood the signal and telephoned their local headquarters to instigate the assault. Heinrich Himmler (1900–

1945), leader of the SS (Schutzstaffel), was not consulted. However, he later ordered SS units and the police not to intervene. Subsequently, the head of the Gestapo issued instructions to arrest thirty thousand well-off Jews.

During the night of 9–10 November, more than nine hundred synagogues were vandalized and set alight and nearly eight thousand Jewish-owned businesses were wrecked. In a nationwide "degradation ritual," Jewish homes were invaded and smashed. Hundreds of Jews were beaten, and ninety-one were killed. Yet the erratic timing and intensity of the attacks revealed poor coordination and planning among different Nazi agencies. Popular participation was patchy. Many Germans were uneasy about the wanton destruction, but others welcomed the release of tension that had accumulated during the proceeding international crisis over the Sudetenland. Instructions to restore order were finally issued at midnight on 10 November. About thirty-six thousand Jewish men were taken to concentration camps, mainly Dachau, Sachsenhausen, and Buchenwald. Most were soon released in order to arrange for the transfer of their property and businesses or once their families had succeeded in obtaining visas to emigrate. But hundreds were killed or died before they could be extracted.

On 12 November, Hermann Goering (1893–1946), head of the economic Four Year Plan, convened a meeting of senior Nazi officials to deal with the aftermath. He was annoyed at the damage to the economy and used this to obtain from Hitler power to control anti-Jewish policy. The meeting agreed that German Jews would be fined one billion Reichmarks and cover all repair costs. Insurance payments would be confiscated. Goering used the pogrom to initiate the compulsory "Aryanization" of all remaining Jewish enterprises. Reinhard Heydrich, head of the SS security service, won approval for measures to accelerate Jewish emigration modeled on the centralized agency earlier established by Adolf Eichmann in Vienna. Other oppressive measures were discussed and later implemented. At the end of the meeting Goering said, "I would not like to be a Jew in Germany."

Consequently, Jewish flight from Germany increased massively. As many Jews left in 1938–1939 as had departed during 1933–1938. This

Broken shop windows in Berlin in the aftermath of Kristallnacht, 17 November 1938. ©BETTMANN/CORBIS

flood of largely impoverished refugees led many European countries to tighten immigration restrictions. Others, notably Britain, actually relaxed controls somewhat to allow entry to certain categories of refugee. World opinion was generally shocked by the November pogrom. The U.S. president Franklin Delano Roosevelt withdrew the U.S. ambassador from Berlin as a gesture of disapproval, but few other countries registered such serious concern.

See also **Anti-Semitism; Holocaust; Nuremberg Laws; Pogroms.**

BIBLIOGRAPHY

Friedänder, Saul. *Nazi Germany and the Jews: The Years of Persecution, 1933–39.* London, 1997.

Graml, Hermann. *Antisemitism in the Third Reich.* Oxford, U.K., 1992.

Kley, Stefan. "Hitler and the Pogrom of November 9–10, 1938." *Yad Vashem Studies* 28 (2000): 87–112.

Pehle, Walter H., ed. *November 1938: From Reichskristallnacht to Genocide.* Translated from the German by William Templer. New York, 1991.

Wildt, Michael. "Violence against Jews in Germany, 1933–1939." In *Probing the Depths of German Antisemitism,* edited by David Bankier, 181–209. Jerusalem, 2000.

DAVID CESARANI

KRISTEVA, JULIA (b. 1941), French linguist, psychoanalyst, literary theorist, and novelist.

Born in Sliven, Bulgaria, Julia Kristeva was educated by French nuns, studied linguistics, and worked as a journalist before going to Paris in 1966. While in Paris she finished her doctorate in linguistics at École des Hautes Études, where she worked with Lucien Goldmann, Roland Barthes, and Claude Lévi-Strauss. She also became involved in the influential journal *Tel quel* and began psychoanalytic training, which she finished in 1979. As of 2005, Kristeva is director of the Institute for the Study of Texts and Documents at the University of Paris VII. In 1997 she received one of France's highest honors, Chevalière de la légion d'honneur, for her thirty years of intellectual work, which has been translated into at least ten languages. In 2004 she received the prestigious Holberg Prize given by the Norwegian government. In addition to her work as a practicing psychoanalyst and her theoretical writings, Kristeva is a novelist.

Kristeva's writing is an intersection between philosophy, psychoanalysis, linguistics, and cultural and literary theory. She developed the science of what she calls "semanalysis," which is a combination of Sigmund Freud's psychoanalysis and Ferdinand de Saussure's and Charles Peirce's semiology. With this new science, Kristeva challenges traditional psychoanalytic theory, linguistic theory, and philosophy. Taking up the question of "Why do we speak?" in all of its ambiguities, Kristeva addresses the issues of the relationship of meaning to language, the relationship of meaning to life, and the relationship of language to life, in revolutionary ways. One of her most important contributions to the philosophy of language and linguistics is her theory that all signification is composed of two elements, the symbolic and the semiotic. She associates the symbolic element with referential meaning; that is, the element of signification that sets up the structures by which symbols operate, specifically grammar. She associates the semiotic element with rhythms and tones that are meaningful parts of language and yet do not represent or signify something. Although her critics sometimes make the mistake of identifying her position with one element over the other, Kristeva insists on the dialectical relationship between the semiotic and symbolic.

In what remains one of her most influential books, *La révolution du langage poétique* (1974; Revolution in poetic language), Kristeva maintains that bodily drives are discharged through rhythms and tones. She continues this analysis of the relation between drives and language two decades later in *Les nouvelles maladies de l'âme* (1993; New maladies of the soul), now illustrated by case studies from her analytic practice. Against philosophies of language that focus on the structure of language as a logical system that can be translated into computer code, Kristeva emphasizes the nonreferential or semiotic element of signification that cannot be symbolized. Her work suggests that while the symbolic element gives signification its meaning in the strict sense of reference, the semiotic element gives signification meaning in a broader sense.

In addition to her theory of meaning, particularly the symbolic-semiotic distinction, another of Kristeva's major contributions to contemporary theory is her notion of the abject. She introduces the theory of abjection in *Pouvoirs de l'horreur* (1980; Powers of horror), where she relies on anthropological research together with psychoanalysis. The abject is what is excluded in order to set up the clean and proper boundaries of the body, the subject, and society or nation; above all, it is ambiguity that must be excluded or prohibited so that identity can be stabilized. Bringing together Freud's analysis of the prohibition of incest with that of Lévi-Strauss, Kristeva suggests that ultimately the threatening ambiguity of the abject always comes back to the maternal body: the maternal body must be excluded in order to constitute and shore up both individual and social identity; but, like all repression, the abject maternal is bound to return. And its return can be transformative or even revolutionary. Kristeva's theory of the abject and abjection has had a significant impact on feminist theory across the disciplines, along with disciplines involving literature and art.

In the *Le génie féminin* trilogy (1999, 2000, 2002), Kristeva suggests that women, with their attention to the sensory realm, might provide an antidote for the meaninglessness that results from contemporary forms of nihilism. She argues that the genius of extraordinary women such as Hannah Arendt, Melanie Klein, and Colette help all women to see what is extraordinary in their own ordinary lives. Conversely, the genius of everyday life is women's genius, particularly the genius of mothers because in creating new human beings

Julia Kristeva, September 1983. ©SOPHIE BASSOULS/CORBIS SYGMA

they are singular innovators, reinventing the child anew all the time. The impact of this new work is just now being felt across the humanities.

See also **Feminism; Psychoanalysis; Semiotics.**

BIBLIOGRAPHY

Primary Sources

Kristeva, Julia. *Revolution in Poetic Language.* Translated by Margaret Waller. New York, 1984. Translation of *La révolution du langage poétique.*

———. *The Portable Kristeva.* Edited by Kelly Oliver. New York, 2002.

Secondary Sources

Beardsworth, Sara. *Julia Kristeva: Psychoanalysis and Modernity.* Albany, N.Y., 2004.

Oliver, Kelly. *Reading Kristeva: Unraveling the Double Bind.* Bloomington, Ind., 1993.

KELLY OLIVER

KRUPP. In May 1912 the large, tradition-rich, and powerful Fried. Krupp AG firm celebrated its one hundredth anniversary with a three-day long festival; in attendance were members of Germany's political, economic, and social elite, including Emperor William II and all of the princes of the German Empire. Years of remarkable prosperity and economic growth gave company officials and members of the Krupp family an additional reason to celebrate; sales increased more than fourfold in the period 1903 to 1913 and the size of the work-force approximately doubled in the same period. On the eve of World War I the Fried. Krupp AG consisted of a diverse array of enterprises, including iron and steelworks, rolling mills, shipyards, coal and ore mines, limestone quarries, and manufacturing plants that produced goods such as cast steel products and armaments.

World War I accelerated these growth patterns. The number of workers at Krupp increased from

The Krupp armaments factory at Essen, Germany, 1914. Getty Images

more than 80,000 in 1914 to 170,000 in 1918. Similarly the physical plant of the Fried. Krupp AG doubled in size in this period in order to meet the extraordinary demands of the war. Although armaments manufacturing accounted for no more than one-third of Fried. Krupp AG's total pre-1914 output, Krupp was devoting by 1916 ever more industrial resources to the production of armaments, including artillery pieces and shells, submarines, armor plate, explosives, and battleships. In the last years of the war more than 80 percent of Krupp's production capacity was used for the manufacturing of war-related goods.

Krupp weathered Germany's defeat in World War I remarkably well. The revolutionary disturbances that swept across Germany in 1918 and 1919 spared for the most part the various branches of the Krupp industrial empire. Although terms of the Treaty of Versailles, notably the prohibition of the manufacturing of many kinds of armaments and the compulsory dismantlement of certain industries, and the loss of traditional international market shares during the war directly impacted Krupp, the firm was not too adversely affected in the immediate postwar period. Krupp benefited

from the postwar inflation, allowing it to pay off debts at very advantageous rates, and modernized its production techniques and equipment, thereby offsetting some of the damage resulting from the postwar compulsory dismantling and destruction of much of its industrial plant. The firm also diversified its industrial and manufacturing activities. In place of large-scale armaments production, Krupp, for example, now built various kinds of locomotives and rail cars and machines for business and agriculture, as well as continuing its traditional activities in mining and steel production. Krupp, however, did not get out of the armaments business entirely, continuing to be involved in the designing and production of armaments despite its official prohibition from doing so; agreements with Swedish, Dutch, and Japanese firms ensured that Krupp cannons, submarines, and other arms continued to be manufactured during the Weimar Republic.

Following Adolf Hitler's ascension to power in 1933, the production of arms again became a central Krupp activity. As early as 1935, for instance, Krupp shipyards began to build submarines and destroyers; the Germania shipyard in Kiel alone built ninety Type VII submarines in the period from 1936 to 1944. Similarly Krupp factories soon began to produce great numbers of artillery pieces and cannons, massive quantities of armor plating, and "Tiger" tanks. A not insignificant cost of rearmament for Krupp was its rapidly diminishing loss of institutional independence vis-à-vis the Nazi state and party. The booming economy of the late 1930s also created labor shortages for the firm; Krupp eventually sought to overcome this problem during World War II by employing tens of thousands of forced laborers drawn from all over Europe, including inmates from concentration camps such as Buchenwald.

Germany's defeat in World War II again meant the substantial destruction and dismantling of the Krupp works. Compounding the damage inflicted by bombing raids on Krupp factories during the war was the postwar loss of machines and plants at the hands of the Allied forces' dismantling crews. Unlike after World War I, however, the victorious Allies held the head of Krupp, Alfried Krupp von Bohlen und Halbach, responsible for the firm's activities during the war. Tried at Nuremberg in 1947 for various war crimes, Alfried and ten Krupp directors were convicted of "spoliation of occupied territory and the employment of slave labor" and were sentenced to lengthy prison sentences as well as, in the case of Alfried, the complete loss of his Krupp family fortune. Also new were moves to break up the Krupp empire in accordance with the Allied policy of Germany's de-cartelization, intended to divide the Krupp group along horizontal and vertical lines.

The early release of Alfried Krupp from the notorious Landsberg prison in 1951, as well as the return of his confiscated property, signaled a new phase for the Krupp empire. Alfried and firm executives such as Berthold Beitz implemented a series of reforms that allowed the Krupp holdings to profit from the West German "economic miracle" taking place at the time. Sharp fluctuations in the price of steel beginning in the mid-1960s, combined with downturns in the German and global economies, the firm's overly aggressive expansion plans, its precarious credit-borrowing schemes, and its risky and not particularly profitable trade agreements with Eastern bloc countries created a series of crises for Krupp in the 1960s and

1970s. As a result, the structure of the Krupp empire underwent significant reorganization, including the creation of the "Alfried Krupp von Bohlen und Halbach Foundation" that, in addition to its financial support of educational, cultural, artistic, and public health ventures, had a controlling interest in the main Krupp holding, the Fried. Krupp GmbH. Another consequence of the crises was the selling on two occasions of large amounts of Krupp capital stock to the shah of Iran in exchange for much-needed cash infusions; by the late 1970s the Iranian government controlled a 25.01 percent interest in the Fried. Krupp GmbH.

Since 1990 Krupp has strengthened its global position through a series of mergers. In the early 1990s Krupp merged with the German firm Hoesch AG, forming Fried. Krupp AG Hoesch-Krupp. Shortly thereafter, merger negotiations began between Fried. Krupp AG Hoesch-Krupp and Thyssen Steel; the merger was finalized in 1999. In 2005 Thyssen-Krupp focused on steel and capital goods and services, employing more than 184,000 people worldwide.

See also **Forced Labor; Germany; Industrial Capitalism; War Crimes.**

BIBLIOGRAPHY

Bell, James. "The Comeback of Krupp." *Fortune* (February 1956): 101–108, 200–205.

Engelmann, Bernt. *Krupp. Die Geschichte eines Hauses—Legenden und Wirklichkeit.* 4th ed. Munich, 1986.

Friz, Diana Maria. *Die Stahlgiganten. Alfried Krupp und Berthold Beitz.* Frankfurt, 1988.

Gall, Lothar, ed. *Krupp im 20. Jahrhundert. Die Geschichte des Unternehmens von Ersten Weltkrieg bis zur Gründung der Stiftung.* Berlin, 2002.

CHARLES LANSING

KUN, BÉLA (1886–1938 or 1939), Hungarian communist politician and revolutionary.

Béla Kun, the leader of the Hungarian Soviet Republic, was born in Szilágycseh, Transylvania, into the family of a lower-ranking public clerk of Jewish origin. In 1902, at the age of sixteen, he joined the local branch of the Social Democratic

Party of Hungary in Kolozsvár (Cluj, Romania). In 1905 he broke off his studies in law and became a journalist. He was sentenced in 1907 to six months in jail for a radical leaflet he wrote in support of a construction workers' strike. After his release he worked for the Workers Indemnity Fund in Kolozsvár and became an influential figure of the leftist faction of the Social Democrats in Transylvania. In 1914 he was conscripted and dispatched with his regiment to the eastern (Russian) front. In summer 1916 Kun was captured and taken to a prisoner-of-war camp in Tomsk, Russia.

The Bolshevik Revolution of October 1917 reached Tomsk in December. Kun, who had already joined the Bolshevik faction, left for Petrograd. There he got involved in the activities of former Hungarian POWs. On 24 March 1918 Kun presided at the formation of the Hungarian Group of the Communist (Bolshevik) Party of Russia. In May 1918 he became president of the international federation of Socialist POWs. He also played a role in the suppression of the Social Revolutionaries' rebellion in Moscow in July 1918.

Kun returned to Hungary in November 1918 and became the unchallenged leader of the leftist radicals in Budapest. His pamphlet *What Do the Communists Want?* had been disseminated in Hungary months before his return. On 24 November 1918 he established the Communist Party of Hungary in a private apartment in Budapest.

The political situation in Hungary was chaotic. After the civil democratic revolution on 31 October 1918, the new government led by Count Mihály Károlyi could not control the situation and halt the disintegration of the country. Kun was an original theoretician who proved to be a genuine talent in revolutionary tactics. In Russia he had became a fanatic follower of Leninist ideas and the Bolshevik Revolution. Like the Soviet leaders at that time he believed that the worldwide proletarian revolution was under way and his mission was to facilitate this development in Hungary.

The Communists' tactic of "the worse the better" targeted the Social Democrats in particular. Their chief organ, *Vörös újság* (Red newspaper), tried to radicalize the discontented workers and launched harsh attacks on the Social Democratic leaders who "bent to the will of the bourgeoisie."

However, this tactic was largely unsuccessful until the end of February 1919. On 21 February, after a shooting, Kun was arrested and severely injured by some police officers. This incident raised sympathy for him. During the next three weeks, in the prison, Kun carried on negotiations with left-wing Social Democratic leaders. In the meantime the government found itself at a dead end after rejecting the Vix memorandum, in which the Allies demanded further retreat from Hungarian territories. President Károlyi resigned on 21 March. On the very same day, the Communists and Social Democrats declared unification as the Socialist Party of Hungary and proclaimed the Soviet Republic of Hungary. Kun, the leader of the new government, assumed the positions of both foreign minister and defense minister.

Kun was aware that chances were slight of his regime remaining in power. Yet initially, many intellectuals (prominent writers, artists, university professors, journalists) who believed that further social reforms were inevitable expressed modest loyalty toward the new regime. More importantly, a significant part of the public, including a great number of military officers of the former army, regarded his takeover as the last chance to halt the disintegration of the country and achieve fair peace conditions with the Entente, which, on the other hand, showed no inclination to treat the Hungarian Soviet government as a negotiating partner. Fearing that the "Bolshevik infection" might spread to other parts of the continent, the Entente encouraged the governments of neighboring countries to continue their military progress on Hungarian land. However, Kun was able to mobilize the Budapest workers by relying upon their national sentiments. The reorganized Hungarian Red Army launched a successful counterattack on the northern front line against the troops of the new Czechoslovak state in May. This success temporarily stabilized his government.

However, Kun's policy rapidly destroyed the initial hopes of the Hungarian public. Kun placed all his trust in the expected progress of the Bolshevik Revolution in Germany and in Europe. Therefore, instead of appeasing the public he opted for creating a proletarian dictatorship as radically as possible. The lands, factories, and banks were nationalized; the government refused to carry out land reform and it put the whole economy under strict central control. This intransigent policy quickly alienated both the urban and rural populations. The regime was unable to tackle the economic and military crisis. Forced requisitions in the rural areas provoked resistance. Harsh living conditions as well as forced recruitment for the Red Army led to strikes even among the working class in June and July. In order to suppress the resistance the regime set up special units such as the Cserny commando (called the "Lenin guys") and applied revolutionary "red" terror. These units committed mass murders in several areas of the country. Their actions provoked such outrage that in July, under pressure from the leaders of the Social Democrats, Kun dissolved the Cserny commando. Nevertheless, the Red Terror was the first occasion in the history of the modern Hungarian state when state authorities applied (unwarranted, illegal) violence against civilians. However, the counterrevolutionary regime that succeeded Kun's greatly exaggerated the scale of the Red Terror and the number of its victims. These leaders wanted to justify the horrendous crimes of their own so-called officer commandos, the Héjjas and Prónay units, during the White Terror in 1919 and 1920 against alleged Communists who were in fact mostly innocent bystanders (intellectuals, shopkeepers) of Jewish origin. The Jewish origin of Kun and many of his comrades would become the main topic of regime propaganda during the interwar period, which laid a new and long-lasting foundation for political anti-Semitism in Hungary. (The comparison of "red" and "white" terror and the suggested relationship between Jews and "liberalism/leftism/communism" that was responsible for the fall of royal Hungary is still a subject of pseudo-historical, ideological, and political debates.)

In order to save his regime and gain the recognition of the Entente powers, Kun on 30 June accepted the ultimatum of French premier Georges Clemenceau and withdrew his troops from those areas the Hungarian Red Army had occupied during its campaign in May. This move undermined his reputation as a leader capable of defending the country. Many believed that Kun subordinated the interests of the nation to the interests of his own increasingly unpopular regime. Discipline within the army quickly deteriorated, and by the end of July the Hungarian Red Army practically collapsed. Kun and his government resigned on 1 August 1919 and fled to Vienna, then to Moscow.

In the following years Kun held various positions in the Comintern and in the apparatus of the Soviet Communist Party. The émigré Hungarian party was severely split on the future prospects of a quick return to Hungary. Kun, still the leader of the party, miscalculated the potential domestic support of the Communists on Hungarian soil. His faulty decisions resulted in the collapse of the underground movement in Hungary, which also tarnished his reputation within the Comintern. In 1937 he fell victim to Joseph Stalin's Great Purges. After his former boss and friend Grigory Zinoviev was tried and executed, Kun was arrested. Sources are contradictory on his eventual fate: either he was shot to death in August 1938, or, as stated by the final order of his posthumous "rehabilitation" procedure in 1956, he died in prison on 30 November 1939.

See also **Communism; Hungary; Károlyi, Mihály; Purges.**

BIBLIOGRAPHY

Borsányi, György. *The Life of a Communist Revolutionary, Béla Kun.* Boulder, Colo., 1993.

Romsics, Ignác. *Hungary in the Twentieth Century.* Budapest, 1999.

Tőkés, Rudolf L. *Béla Kun and the Hungarian Soviet Republic: The Origins and Role of the Communist Party of Hungary in the Revolutions of 1918–1919.* New York, 1967.

ANDRÁS MINK

KUNDERA, MILAN (b. 1921), Czech writer and intellectual.

Milan Kundera is recognized internationally as one of the most eminent and influential of the twentieth-century Czech writers. Kundera rose to prominence both as an intellectual and a prose writer in Czechoslovakia during the harshest years of communism in the 1950s. As a leading intellectual he responded to political events with speeches and articles that initiated a number of important debates. In "Arguing about Our Inheritance"

(1955), he defended the influence of avant-garde poetry—censored at that time—on Czech letters. In 1967 a provocative speech delivered to the Fourth Congress of Czechoslovak Writers about the Czech national heritage and its future brought him to the forefront of the Prague Spring liberalization movement. And a year later, Kundera reacted to the Warsaw Pact invasion of Czechoslovakia with the article "Czech Destiny." His discussion of individual responsibility and the survival of a small nation subjugated by a great power provoked a critical response from Václav Havel.

During the 1950s Kundera also wrote poetry and drama, but he came into his own with the short story "I, the Mournful God" (1958). This story reappeared in his first prose collection, *Laughable Loves* (1963). Kundera kept reworking and republishing *Laughable Loves* throughout the politically more liberal and partially censorship-free 1960s, searching for themes and means of expression that would later be more fully developed in his novels. The result of this creative process is reflected in *The Joke* (1967), which became an enormous success both in Czechoslovakia and abroad. The French writer Louis Aragon praised the novel as "one of the greatest novels of the century." Although set in Czechoslovakia during the Stalinist 1950s, *The Joke* goes far beyond a critical reflection of politically difficult times. Employing a complex polyphonic structure, Kundera explores such timeless dilemmas as humankind's inability to control reality and its search for the meaning of existence. The director Jaromil Jires made a movie based on *The Joke* in 1968.

After 1970 renewed political oppression and censorship forced Kundera to write "for the desk drawer." Meanwhile, the author's novel *Life Is Elsewhere* (completed in 1970) marks a deliberate stylistic shift to a "clearer" language, caused by the realization that he would henceforth have to rely on translators. *The Farewell Party* (completed in 1972) is the last novel Kundera wrote in Czechoslovakia.

The opportunity to leave the oppressive political climate in the country and his status as a persona non grata presented itself in 1975 in the form of an invitation to teach at the University of Rennes in France. Accepting the position meant not only existence in exile but also the possibility of never seeing his homeland again.

Kundera adapted quickly to his new life in France, due to his excellent French and to his immediate participation in cultural events. He wrote for journals and newspapers and for fifteen years organized a seminar on the European novel at the École des Hautes Études in Paris. He also gained enormous popularity with his two novels *The Book of Laughter and Forgetting* (1981) and *The Unbearable Lightness of Being* (1985), written for both the small Czech émigré audience and Western readers. These novels were important not only for bringing attention to the complexities of exile but also in that they introduced Western readers to the historical plight of a small central European country. In 1988 Philip Kaufman directed the screen version of *The Unbearable Lightness of Being*.

However, in Czechoslovakia, where this novel was banned, it did not receive such a positive reception from certain dissidents. The Czech émigré journal *Svědectví* (1985–1988) documented a heated discussion that arose between the dissidents and émigrés over the novel's political and sexual themes. Almost simultaneously an international polemic erupted over Kundera's article "The Central European Tragedy" (1984), in which the writer accuses the Russians of destroying central European culture. The Russian émigré poet, Joseph Brodsky, ardently refuted Kundera's arguments.

Two highly respected collections of essays, *Art of the Novel* (1986) and *Testaments Betrayed* (1993), initiated the author's move into French. In prose this linguistic transition came about with the novel *Immortality* (1990). Likewise, *Slowness* (1995) and *Identity* (1998)—two playful short novels that explore the individual's search for meaning—were written in French.

What is interesting in Kundera's switch to French is his timing, for it occurred only after the fall of communism in Eastern Europe, when the author was once again free to go visit his homeland. He explores this new reality in *Ignorance* (2002), a novel that once again deals with the problems of exile and return, nostalgia and memory.

Paradoxically and sadly, Kundera's works have not "returned" to his homeland. As of 2005 *Life Is Elsewehere*, *The Book of Laughter and Forgetting*, and *The Unbearable Lightness of Being* have not been published there, nor have his French novels been translated into Czech.

See also **Czechoslovakia; Dissidence; Eastern Bloc; Havel, Václav.**

BIBLIOGRAPHY

Banerjee, Maria Němcová. *Terminal Paradox: The Novels of Milan Kundera.* New York, 1990.

Chvatík, Květoslav. *Svět románů Milana Kundery.* Brno, Czech Republic, 1994.

Dokoupil, Blahoslav, and Miroslav Zelinsky, eds. *Slovník české prozy 1945–1994.* Ostrava, Czech Republic, 1994.

Janoušek, Pavel, ed. *Slovník českých spisovatelů od roku 1945.* 2 vols. Prague, 1995.

Kosková, Helena. "Francouzské romány Milana Kundery." *Tvar* 7 (2004): 4–5.

Misurella, Fred. *Understanding Milan Kundera: Public Events, Private Affairs.* Columbia, S.C., 1993.

Petro, Peter. *Critical Essays on Milan Kundera.* New York, 1999.

HANA PÍCHOVÁ

KURSK, BATTLE OF. The Battle of Kursk comprised a failed German offensive operation and a successful Soviet defensive-offensive operation, 5 July to 23 August 1943, on the eastern front in World War II. One of the largest and most decisive confrontations of the war, Kursk marked Adolf Hitler's last serious attempt to regain the strategic initiative against Joseph Stalin's Red Army.

Soviet failures to crush German Army Group South after the victory at Stalingrad, along with the annual spring thaw, imposed an operational pause as both the Wehrmacht and the Red Army regrouped for the campaigns of 1943. To regain the initiative, Field Marshal Erich von Manstein successfully lobbied for an offensive against the Kursk salient, a prominent Soviet bulge in the German lines between Orel and Belgorod. However, Hitler delayed the offensive, code-named Citadel, until July to permit a buildup of German armor and assault guns. Thanks to this delay and also to good intelligence, possibly including information from Enigma intercepts passed to Stalin by the British, the Soviets were able to anticipate Manstein's attack. As the Germans built up their forces and

means, the Soviets reinforced their defense in depth with as many as six belts of field fortifications. Once the Germans had spent their offensive momentum, Stavka, the Soviet Headquarters of the Supreme High Command, planned to surprise them with an immediate and powerful counteroffensive. Accordingly, the Soviets concentrated about 1.3 million troops within the salient and on its shoulders. These troops were arrayed in five fronts (army groups) with 19,000 guns, 3,500 tanks and self-propelled guns, and about 2,000 aircraft. Another front lay in reserve, with the entire complex of multifront operations coordinated by two of Stavka's best commanders, Marshals Georgy Zhukov and Alexander Vasilevsky. Against these forces, Manstein marshaled the assets of Army Groups Center and South, with some 900,000 troops, 10,000 guns, 2,700 tanks and self-propelled assault guns, and 2,000 aircraft.

Manstein's offensive began on 5 July against the shoulders of the salient, with his primary assault groups making slow and painful headway as they fought their way through successive and well-defended Soviet defensive belts. The attack stalled almost immediately in the north with slight gains, while German offensive momentum culminated in the south on 11–12 July at the village of Prokhorovka, some 100 kilometers (60 miles) southeast of Kursk. There, a meeting between armored units flared into the largest tank battle of World War II, with more than twelve hundred tanks engaged. The Soviets fought the Germans to a bloody, flaming standstill. With losses of 400 tanks and more than 10,000 killed in this single encounter, Manstein withdrew to regroup and possibly renew the offensive. However, mindful of requirements to counter the growing allied threat in Sicily, Hitler ordered redeployment of II SS Panzer Corps to the west and bade Manstein to go over to the defensive.

It was at this point that Vasilevsky and Zhukov unleashed their counteroffensive operations, code-named after two imperial Russian great captains, Kutuzov (north) and Rumiantsev (south). Between 12 July and 18 August, the three Soviet fronts (Western, Bryansk, and Center) involved in Kutuzov assailed German Army Group Center in the north to liberate Orel and approach Bryansk. Between 3 and 23 August, the two Soviet fronts

(Voronezh and Steppe) involved in Rumiantsev inflicted severe losses on Manstein's Fourth Panzer Army, and, with the assistance of Southwest Front, enveloped and occupied Kharkov. Before these Soviet counteroffensive operations had spent their momentum, both opened wide breaches in the German lines, with penetrations of nearly 120 kilometers (75 miles) in the north and 160 kilometers (100 miles) in the south.

With Manstein's defeat at Kursk, the strategic initiative on the eastern front passed irrevocably into Soviet hands. Because the Red Air Force now possessed air superiority, German losses became ever more telling. Altogether, the operations at Kursk and its environs cost the Germans about a half million casualties and incurred losses of 1,500 tanks, 3,700 aircraft, and 3,000 guns. The Soviets counted about 850,000 casualties, including a quarter million dead and invalided.

For the Soviets, Kursk marked an important stage in the maturation of the conduct of operations. Representatives of Stavka gained additional experience with the coordination of multifront operations, while the entire Soviet strategic design reflected a calculated emphasis on serial defensive-offensive operations, initially to exact loss, then to harvest decisive gain. The Red Army had competently constructed and defended positions in depth, to include the development of effective counterattacks. On the offensive, Soviet operations demonstrated the ability to attain mass at decisive points, to accomplish breakthroughs and hold their shoulders, and to exploit those breakthroughs either for encirclement or for penetration into the German operational depths.

Because of its scale and implications for both positional and mobile warfare, Kursk has been the subject of numerous historical treatments, ranging from Manstein's memoirs to the ponderous and less-than-forthcoming Soviet-period official histories. Primarily because of accessibility, Western treatments relied heavily on German materials until the last several decades of the twentieth century, when the appearance of more complete Soviet and Russian materials gave rise to a more balanced perspective. The full intelligence story remains to be told.

See also **Kharkov, Battles of; Stalingrad, Battle of.**

BIBLIOGRAPHY

Erickson, John. *The Road to Berlin*. London, 1983. Reprint, London, 2003.

Glantz, David M., and Jonathan M. House. *When Titans Clashed: How the Red Army Stopped Hitler*. Lawrence, Kans., 1995.

Manstein, Erich von. *Lost Victories*. Edited and translated by Anthony G. Powell. Chicago, 1958.

Vasilevsky, A. M. *A Lifelong Cause*. Translated by Jim Riordan. Moscow, 1981.

BRUCE W. MENNING

LABOR MOVEMENTS. In Europe labor movements grew during good economic times and the two world wars but were weakened during economic recessions. Outside of Russia counter-revolution was usually more powerful than revolutionary socialism.

European labor often looked back to what it deemed to be a heroic past as a source of encouragement for future action. Across Europe men and women marched in May Day parades from 1890, sometimes paying homage to the memory of those who died in the attempts at revolution in 1848 or the Paris Commune of 1871, sometimes singing "La Marseillaise" or waving caps of liberty in memory of 1789. Cities such as Paris, Vienna, Berlin, Budapest, and, after 1905, St. Petersburg had their revolutionary traditions.

The red May Days and the Second International stemmed from meetings in Paris at the time of the centenary of the 1789 French Revolution. The first of May was chosen in honor of the Haymarket Martyrs (leading anarchists who were sentenced to death for the actions of others in the throwing of bombs at a public rally in Chicago in May 1886) in the United States, with the intention that the labor movements of each country would mark May Day in a way appropriate to the political conditions in their country. In many countries there were massive public demonstrations, with a range of socialist, anarchist, emigré, and trade union banners carried by the marchers. In Europe, and across the world, there were some common iconographical themes, such as the rising sun of socialism and the new growth of spring. In many countries work by the socialist artist Walter Crane (1845–1915) was reproduced on banners, leaflets, and posters.

Before 1914 May Day demonstrations focused on such issues as achieving the eight-hour workday and promoting international peace. After World War I the May Day demonstrations were especially successful when linked to major causes of the day, such as support for the Republican side in the Spanish Civil War, opposition to the Vietnam War, and hostility toward nuclear weapons. At times of political crisis in various countries, there were resurgences of support for May Day events. For example, during the Popular Front period, when various groups of the Left, including the Communists, united, the number of towns in France with May Day events rose from 235 in 1936 to 485 in 1938.

The Second International, which was set up in 1889, was dominated in 1914 by the mighty German Social Democrat Party (SPD). It met every three or four years and passed resolutions on industrial, international, and other matters, reliant on the socialist and labor bodies of the individual countries to take any action. With World War I, the revolutionary socialists in Russia gained immense prestige by taking power in October 1917. The international socialist body split three ways: the democratic socialists remained in the Second International; the revolutionaries, who followed Moscow's lead, supported the Third

Communist International, or Comintern, which was formed in March 1919; and a third group, known as the Vienna Union or "the two-and-a-half International," rejected both the anticommunism of the Second and the undemocratic policies of the Third International. In 1923 the Second International and the Vienna Union merged to form the Socialist International. The Third International was disbanded by Stalin in 1943 as a sign of goodwill to his American and British wartime allies.

On the eve of World War I the SPD was the largest socialist party in the world, with some one million fee-paying members and including 170,000 in its women's organization. It was powerful in the cities but much weaker in the countryside and small provincial towns; it was also underrepresented among women and Catholic workers. It had ideological divisions, between Marxists and revisionists, with some of the pre–World War I radical areas becoming later strongholds of the Independent Social Democrats (USPD) or the Communists (KPD).

The SPD's failure to secure as much support from women as men was common to European labor movements. The concern to protect workers' rights too often had an aspect of portraying women as a threat or hindrance to such aims. Workers' rights were also formulated in terms of the patterns of men's working lives, failing to engage with the different work patterns and concerns of women. Labor movement meetings were too often held in hostile environments for women, at unfriendly times, and conducted in insensitive manners. Gender awareness came slowly and most notably only in the last two decades of the twentieth century, when economic and political adversity forced changes in order to survive.

World War I shattered the unity of the SPD, with the majority of its representatives in the Reichstag voting for war credits (largely due to concern for a Russian invasion from the east) and becoming more integrated into the German state. While the German government needed to consult the SPD parliamentarians and trade union leaders during the war, the SPD only entered government as the imperial system was collapsing. The SPD split over the war, with a minority which no longer accepted that Germany had no annexationist war aims being expelled from the SPD and forming the USPD in April 1917. The USPD embraced a wide range of views, from the prewar revisionists to revolutionaries such as Karl Liebknecht (1871–1919) and Rosa Luxemburg (1871–1919).

In Britain before the outbreak of World War I the Labour Party was small and owed most of its 42 parliamentary seats in the December 1910 general election to pacts with the Liberal Party, which held office from 1905 to 1915 (and thereafter in coalitions until 1922). In Germany the SPD's political strength had been greater than that of the trade unions until the end of the nineteenth century. In contrast, in Britain there had been a substantial trade-union movement since the late eighteenth century but independent labor politics had been slow to develop, with the Labour Representation Committee (renamed Labour Party in 1906) formed in 1900, its main constituents being trade unionists and members of the Independent Labour Party (a democratic socialist party, founded in 1893). While socialist organizations were affiliated to it, the Labour Party did not have a socialist program until 1918.

World War I was decisive in ensuring that the British Labour movement became independent of other parties, becoming more like the continental European social democratic parties rather than following U.S. labor with its policies of seeking political influence with existing parties rather than creating its own party. The majority of Labour Party members of Parliament (MPs) supported the war, with Arthur Henderson (1863–1935), the leading trade unionist, joining coalition governments. The prewar Labour Party leader, Ramsay MacDonald (1866–1937), resigned as Labour's leader and led an antiwar minority (subsequently losing his parliamentary seat in the 1918 general election). However, Henderson resigned from government in August 1917 over his wish to attend an international socialist conference (which he hoped would strengthen anti-Bolshevik socialists in Russia) and the Labour Party reunited around a socialist peace and domestic reconstruction policies. It entered the 1918 general election with a socialist program and almost united (a few lesser figures staying in the Lloyd George [1863–1945] coalition government and for a few years there were a small number of breakaway "patriotic labor" members of Parliament). The war greatly strengthened British trade unions and led the cooperative movement to form the Cooperative Party in 1917, which soon acted in alliance with the Labour Party (an alliance that still continues). Ireland was similarly affected by food shortages and also saw a major expansion of the cooperative movement in 1915–1922.

While the German socialists feared the Russians invading, the French and Belgian socialists were faced with the Germans invading their countries. In both countries leading labor figures took office: in Belgium immediately and in France on 26 August 1914. In contrast, in Italy the labor movement was initially overwhelmingly hostile to the war. However, the moderate socialists adopted a patriotic stance when Central Powers' forces advanced into Italy in 1917. The General Confederation of Labour's journal bluntly observed, "When the enemy treads on our soil we have only one duty: to resist." Hence there were deep divisions between those who sought victory and a share of former Austrian Empire territory and the many who aspired to follow the Russian example.

In Russia, on the basis of his understanding of the 1905 revolutionary events, Vladimir Lenin (1870–1924) predicted revolution there would involve an alliance of the industrial workers with the peasantry. In the February 1917 revolution tsarism was weakening from military and economic failures and, unlike in the 1905 revolution, the army in Petrograd refused to shoot protesters and the High Command hoped for a more effective constitutional government. In the subsequent vacuum, moderate socialists supported the continuance of the war even if only as a matter of defending Russia from Germany. By the late summer economic, social, and military problems were more, not less, severe than in February, and in October the Provisional Government was easily overthrown in Petrograd by the Bolsheviks. As a result of the Bolsheviks' successful seizure of power and their ability to maintain it in the face of counterrevolutionary invading armies between 1917 and 1920, existing differences within European labor movements were deepened and exacerbated as some admired, while others abhorred, the Bolsheviks.

In the later years of World War I and in its aftermath there was widespread suffering in Germany and the countries of the Austro-Hungarian Empire. The Allied blockade was maintained, causing substantial food and other shortages, until the Versailles Peace Treaty was signed on 28 June 1919. Combined with the fall of discredited regimes and widespread desire for social change, these shortages fostered revolution in Germany, Austria, and Hungary. In Germany revolution in November–December 1918 led to a socialist government (SPD and USPD) and the democratic Weimar Republic, with the SPD winning some three-quarters of the votes in the January 1919 elections to the National Assembly. However, the divisions of opinion within the German labor movement were deepened and made permanent with the formation of the German Communist Party (KPD) at the end of 1918 and with the suppression of revolutionary socialist risings by the SPD government, acting with the army leaders and using Friekorps units.

Revolutionary socialism was thwarted outside of Russia by the threat of Allied military intervention, as well as by the continued blockade, or by external military intervention. In Hungary Béla Kun's (1886–c. 1939) Soviet-style government only lasted between March and July, being overthrown by Romanian and White (counterrevolutionary) Hungarian forces. While the revolutionary socialists in Hungary and Bavaria for a time secured some peasant support, in most of Europe the countryside was usually hostile to the red cities. In Western Europe in particular, there were strong middle classes willing and able to counter the labor movements' bids for power, whether revolutionary or democratic.

In Germany the labor movement was seriously damaged by ideological socialist divisions in addition to religious ones. While the SPD was a major defender of Weimar democracy, it only entered government as a coalition partner and provided prime ministers in only 1919–1920 and 1928–1930 (Philipp Scheidemann [1865–1939], Gustav Bauer [1870–1944], and Hermann Muller [1876–1931]). While the German labor movement could effectively undermine the Kapp Putsch, in 1920, in good economic times, it was seriously weakened by mass unemployment (as well as by its divisions) during the severe economic recession of 1931–1933. Adolf Hitler (1889–1945) in power smashed the German labor movement, with many of its activists being murdered or dying in concentration camps.

In Russia the Mensheviks and Socialist Revolutionaries were outmaneuvered by Lenin and the Bolsheviks. Although the Bolsheviks secured only 24 percent of the vote for the Constituent Assembly, which met in January 1918, they soon dissolved this democratic body. The Red Army and the Cheka (Soviet secret police) were created before the civil war but became key instruments of the Bolshevik regime in its use of "red terror" in its struggle with counterrevolutionary armies from 1918 to 1920. Bolshevik success in the Russian civil war enhanced their prestige and enabled Moscow thereafter to dictate to the Communist parties in other countries.

In Italy the Socialist Party was inspired by the Bolshevik revolution in Russia, joined the Communist International in October 1919, and adopted revolutionary rhetoric. In the 1919 elections it won 1,834,000 votes and secured 156 deputies, becoming the largest party in the 508-strong House of Deputies. During the "Biennio Rosso" (the red years, 1919–1920) there was much industrial militancy, with a factory-council movement spreading from Turin in August 1919, widespread strikes, and factory occupations. In late 1920 the Socialist Party made great gains in local elections, winning control of 2,162 out of 8,000 communes and twenty-six of the sixty-nine provincial councils. However, after 1920 the Socialist Party (PSI) was divided, losing many members from both its left and right wings. In January 1921 a large minority left to form the Italian Communist Party (PCI) and in 1922 the moderates were expelled (and formed the PSU). The Italian middle classes had been alarmed by the spread of revolution westward from Russia and by the events of 1919–1920. After a fascist campaign of violence, Benito Mussolini (1883–1945) took office in October 1922 and thereafter set about destroying the free trade unions and the parties opposed to him.

In Britain the Labour Party moved into being the second major political party between 1918 and 1924. In the 1918 general election it returned only fifty-seven MPs but secured some spectacular wins in local elections in 1919 and 1920. In the 1922 general election it secured 142 MPs, becoming the official opposition in Parliament. After the 1923 general election, with 191 MPs elected, it formed its first government, January–November 1924, with James Ramsay MacDonald as prime minister. Its status as a minority government limited its scope for radical legislation, but it also provided an excuse for its lack of achievement other than in housing and foreign policy. Defeated in the 1924 general election, partly because the Conservative Party benefited from a substantial collapse in votes for the Liberal Party, it recovered well in 1929. Then, for the first time, it became the largest party in Parliament, with 287 MPs, and formed a second government, June 1929–August 1931, with MacDonald again as prime minister. This government was overwhelmed by the world recession but had never appeared likely to deal innovatively with the rising volume of unemployment. MacDonald formed a National Government in August 1931 and in the ensuing general election defeated his recent colleagues, the Labour Party's representation in the House of Commons tumbling to 46.

While in Britain the Communist Party remained small and did not greatly undercut support for the Labour Party, in France in December 1920 Communist supporters took over the Socialist Party and renamed it the French Communist Party (PCF), keeping roughly three-quarters of the membership (some 109,000). However, membership dropped to 45,000 by early 1923 and until the mid-1930s its largest number of deputies was 26, elected in 1924. Both it and the reconstructed Socialist Party only flourished in 1936 when they united as the Popular Front coalition with the Radicals. In May 1936 the Socialist leader, Léon Blum (1872–1950), headed a Popular Front government that unsuccessfully tried to deal with an economic crisis, introduce reforms, and support the Spanish Republic.

The Swedish Social Democratic Party (SAP) was greatly influenced by the German SPD, especially its revisionist (less Marxist) wing. In the 1911 elections it gained 28.5 percent of the vote, winning sixty-four seats in the lower chamber. In 1917 there was a split with the newly formed Left Social

Democratic Party of Sweden, which won some seats in that year's elections. The SAP, however, became the largest party in the Riksdag that year, gaining 31.1 percent of the vote. Also from 1917 to 1920 it worked with the Liberals in a coalition government. It formed brief governments under Karl Hjalmar Branting (1860–1925) in 1920 and 1921–1923, Rickard Johannes Sandler (1884–1964) in 1925–1926, and then took office for most of the next decade under Per Albin Hansson (1885–1946) in 1932–1936 and 1936–1946, although in the later years with coalition partners. After the introduction of universal suffrage the SAP won 36.2 percent in 1921, 41.1 percent in 1924, 37.0 percent in 1928, 41.7 percent in 1932, 45.9 percent in 1936, and achieved 53.8 percent in 1940. In the 1930s Hansson's governments ran a controlled economy, limiting imports, assisting agriculture and providing unemployment insurance and higher old-age pensions. In the interwar years the Swedish Communist Party, founded in 1921, remained small, securing 5.1 percent of the vote in the 1924 election, but only secured much wider support during the hardships of 1944, when it gained 10.3 percent of the vote (while the SAP percentage dropped back to 46.7).

In Denmark the Social Democratic Movement was also greatly influenced by the German labor movement. It had secured the election of two members to the Lower Chamber (the Folketing) in 1884. In 1913 it had thirty-two members and took office in 1916 in a coalition government with the Radical liberals until 1920. After a political crisis in 1920, Socialist support grew while Radical Liberal support fell markedly. From 1924 to 1926 the Social Democrat Thorvald Stauning (1873–1942) was prime minister in a minority government, and he returned to office in 1929, forming a majority government with the Radical Liberals until World War II. Nevertheless, they were hampered by a lack of a majority in upper house until 1936. Then his government repealed legislation hostile to the trade unions and brought in legislation restricting overtime and ensuring workers had holidays with pay. Unlike Sweden the Social Democrats never secured over 50 percent of the vote, their highest level (46 percent) being achieved in 1935.

In Norway the Labor Party had achieved its first representation in the Storthing in 1903. From 1906 to 1918 its growth was impeded by a voting system that enabled its opponents to unite on a second ballot and so keep its candidates out. In 1918 eighteen candidates were returned whereas on the first ballot forty would have been elected. This electoral system and conditions during World War I made Norwegian labor more open to the influence of Russian Bolshevism in the post–World War I years. In 1919 the Labor Party joined the Comintern and accepted Moscow's Twenty-One Conditions. In February 1921 the moderate wing broke away to form the Social Democratic Labor Party. In the ensuing election twenty-nine of the Left were returned and eight Social Democrats. In 1923 the Labor Party left the Comintern but retained its very left-wing policies. A group broke away to form the Communist Party of Norway, which polled 6.1 percent of the vote in 1924 but thereafter faded. In 1927 the Labor Party polled 36.8 percent of the vote, and from 1933 onward it polled over 40 percent of the vote.

In several countries Hitler's securing of power in Germany in 1933 and the defeat of the Austrian socialists in 1934 encouraged popular-front politics in Spain, France, Belgium, and elsewhere. The growing threat of fascism also radicalized social democrat thought in the 1930s.

In Austria the Social Democrats (SDAP) had emerged from the postwar revolutionary unrest as the largest party, gaining almost 41 percent of the vote in 1919. Apart from 1920, the Left (the SDAP and Communists, KPO) continued to secure 40–42 percent of the votes in 1923–1930. The SDAP's membership was at its largest at 718,000 in 1929 while the KPO only reached 6,800 in 1931. The suspension of parliamentary government in 1933 by the anti-Marxist government, followed by strikes and armed resistance, led in 1934 to the crushing of the Austrian labor movement and the imprisonment of many of its leaders.

In Spain the Socialist Workers' Party (PSOE) had secured its first deputy in 1910 and been boosted by World War I. After the dictatorship of Primo de Rivera (1870–193) from 1923 to 1929 the socialists were the biggest party (116 seats) in the 1931 elections under the new Spanish Republic. After two years in a coalition government Francisco Largo Cabellero (1869–1946), the PSOE

French workers protest proposed limits on wage increases, Paris, October 1976. Provoked by prime minister Raymond Barré's plans to combat inflation, the protestors carry a banner reading "Let's fight and impose workers' control." ©RICHARD MELLOUL/CORBIS SYGMA

leader, broke away and in the ensuing 1933 elections his party and the Left generally did badly. The PSOE was part of the winning popular-front coalition in February 1936, although Cabellero and the PSOE did not join the Left Republicans in office. In September 1936 Cabellero became prime minister of a Popular Front government, but in May 1937 he was ousted in favor of Juan Negrín López (1894–1956), who was more acceptable to the powerful Spanish Communist Party (PCE). The Spanish Republic was defeated by March 1939 by the forces of General Francisco Franco (1892–1975), who suppressed the Spanish labor movement during his dictatorship (1939–1973).

The Nazi-Soviet Nonaggression Pact of 23 August 1939 divided Social Democrats, who were primarily antifascist, from Communists, who prioritized loyalty to Moscow, across Europe. With the German invasion of Russia on 22 June 1941

Communists concentrated on defeating fascism, becoming prominent in resistance movements. At the end of World War II Tito (Josip Broz; 1892–1980) and his partisans took over in Yugoslavia, as did Communist partisans in Albania. In Bulgaria and Romania the old elites were discredited because of their alliances with Germany and Italy. In Bulgaria Communist Party membership grew from 14,000 to 422,000 between September 1944 and 1946. It had worked with Socialists and other allies from August 1943 in the Fatherland Front. The Fatherland Front won 2,980,000 (69.6 percent) and 366 seats, against the United Opposition's 1,300,000 votes (30.4 percent) and ninety-nine seats in 1946. Thereafter, there was one-party rule until free elections were held in 1990. There was similar suppression of noncommunists in labor movements across Soviet-dominated Eastern Europe, the last broader-coalition government ending in Czechoslovakia in 1948.

In Greece Communist partisans were contained by Greek pro-monarchist forces backed by British and American military assistance. The Greek Communists (KKE) were crushed in 1948–1949 and were not legalized until the mid-1970s. The labor movement strengthened after the military dictatorship of 1967–1973. Andreas Papandreou (1919–1996) formed the Panhellenic Socialist Movement in 1974. The Panhellenic Socialist Movement won overall majorities in 1981 and 1985, stayed in office as a minority government for five months after the June 1989 election, and returned in the mid-1990s.

In Italy and France the Communists had gained prestige from their role in the Resistance. In both countries the Communist parties polled well in the elections after the end of the war, gaining 26.1 percent of the vote in France in 1945 (combined with the Progressives) and 19 percent in Italy in 1946. Elsewhere, Communist support faded after 1946, weakened by the Cold War and Soviet suppression of democratic dissent in Eastern European countries. In France the Socialist vote drifted down from 23.8 to 12.6 percent between 1945 and 1962, while the Communist and Progressive vote fell from 26.1 to 21.7 percent. The poor results resulted in a reorganization of the democratic Left under François Mitterrand (1916–1996) in 1971. Mitterrand succeeded in overshadowing the Communists, whose support crumbled in the 1980s, and was elected president, 1981–1995.

In Italy the Communist Party had nearly 2,500,000 members in 1948 and still had 1,600,000 members in 1965. In 1972 it polled over nine million votes, 27.2 percent of the vote, and secured 179 deputies. Under Enrico Berlinguer (1922–1984), general secretary from 1972 until 1984, the party adopted "Eurocommunism" as opposed to Moscow-dictated communism. Its support peaked in the 1976 and 1979 elections, gaining more than 30 percent of the vote and more than 200 deputies. After the collapse of the Soviet Union the party was relaunched as the Democratic Party of the Left (PDS). The Socialists were weakened by repeated splits, their voting dipping to under 10 percent in 1976. The party slowly recovered in the 1980s, with Bettino Craxi (1934–2000) as prime minister (1983–1987), but collapsed in 1994 amidst the corruption scandals of 1992–1994.

In much of Western Europe Social Democrat parties took office and carried out moderate social reform. In Britain Labour under Clement Attlee (1883–1967) formed a government (1945–1951), which managed postwar reconstruction, nationalized key industries, and brought in the welfare state. The Labour Party also held office in 1964–1970 and 1974–1979 and from 1997. After a long period in opposition, it dropped its socialist program and was notably electorally successful as "New Labour" under Tony Blair (b. 1953). In Sweden the Social Democratic Party governed on its own or in coalition from 1945 to 1976 and 1982 to 1990, with Olof Palme (1927–1986) as prime minister in 1969–1976 and 1982–1986 (when he was assassinated). In West Germany the SPD's vote slowly climbed from 29.2 percent in 1949 to 39.3 percent in 1965. It entered the Grand Coalition government (1966–1969) and thereafter governed in coalition with the Liberals (1969–1982). In 1998 the SPD returned to office, with Gerhard Schröder (b. 1944) as chancellor (1998–2005), in alliance with the Greens (the parties polling 40.9 and 6.7 percent of the vote). As in Britain, the SPD's socialism in the late 1990s was much diluted.

With the overthrow of the fascist regimes in Spain and Portugal in 1974 democratic socialists did well in elections. In Spain the socialists under Felipe González Marquez (b. 1942) came second in 1977 but won thereafter. In Portugal, after the "carnation revolution" of April 1974 and very radical provisional governments from 1974 to 1975, the social democrats ruled in coalition with their leader, Mario Soares, as prime minister (1976–1978 and 1983–1985) and president (1986–1996).

During the twentieth century the European labor movements were notably divided, not only between revolutionary and democratic socialists but also between these secular divisions and Catholic and Protestant movements. In Germany, for instance, the Catholic trade-union movement had over a million members in 1920 and 673,000 in 1930, but the separate religious grouping went with the reconstitution of the trade unions in 1945. In Italy, Belgium, and some other countries religious belief remained very powerful in determining association and politics. In all countries many trade unionists voted for parties other than those supported by their unions. In Britain, for example, in opinion polls in 1964, 24 percent of trade unionists favored the Conservative Party while in 1979, 30 percent did. The labor movements were also notably poor in taking up issues of concern to women or ensuring equitable female participation in their organizations or in government.

See also **Communism; Kapp Putsch; Socialism; World War I; World War II.**

BIBLIOGRAPHY

Alexander, Martin S., and Helen Graham, eds. *The French and Spanish Popular Fronts: Comparative Perspectives.* Cambridge, U.K., and New York, 1989.

Anderson, Perry, and Patrick Camiller, eds. *Mapping the West European Left.* London and New York, 1994.

Berger, Stefan. *Social Democracy and the Working Class in Nineteenth and Twentieth Century Germany.* New York, 1999.

Conway, Martin. *Catholic Politics in Europe. 1918–1945.* London, 1997.

Cook, Chris, and John Paxton. *European Political Fact 1918–1973.* London, 1975.

de Montgomery, Count B. G. *British and Continental Labour Policy.* London, 1922.

Geary, Dick. *European Labour Politics from 1900 to the Depression.* Basingstoke, U.K., 1991.

Hamilton, Malcolm B. *Democratic Socialism in Britain and Sweden.* Basingstoke, U.K., 1989.

Horn, Gerd-Rainer. *European Socialists Respond to Fascism: Ideology, Activism and Contingency in the 1930s.* Oxford, U.K., and New York, 1996.

Horne, John N. *Labour at War: France and Britain 1914–1918.* Oxford, U.K., 1991.

Horowitz, Daniel L. *The Italian Labor Movement.* Cambridge, Mass., 1963.

Lorwin, Val Rogin. *The French Labor Movement.* Cambridge, Mass., 1954.

Lyttelton, Adrian. *The Seizure of Power: Fascism in Italy, 1919–1929.* 2nd ed. London, 1987.

Magraw, Roger. *A History of the French Working Class.* Vol. 2: *Workers and the Bourgeois Republic.* Oxford, U.K., 1992.

Mazower, Mark. *The Balkans.* London, 2000.

Padgett, Stephen, and William E. Patterson. *A History of Social Democracy in Postwar Europe.* London, 1991.

Salter, Stephen, and John Stevenson, eds. *The Working Class and Politics in Europe and America, 1929–1945.* London, 1990.

Sassoon, Donald. *One Hundred Years of Socialism: The West European Left in the Twentieth Century.* London, 1996.

Sassoon, Donald, ed. *Looking Left: European Socialism after the Cold War.* London, 1997.

Tartakowsky, Danielle. *Les manifestations de rue en France, 1918–1968.* Paris, 1997.

———. *La part du rêve. Histoire du 1er mai en France.* Paris, 2005.

Thorpe, Andrew. *A History of the British Labour Party.* Basingstoke, U.K., 1997.

Weitz, Eric D. *Creating German Communism 1890–1990: From Popular Protests to Socialist State.* Princeton, N.J., 1997.

Wrigley, Chris, ed. *Challenges of Labour: Central and Western Europe, 1917–1920.* London, Routledge, 1993.

CHRIS WRIGLEY

LACAN, JACQUES

LACAN, JACQUES (1901–1981), French psychoanalyst and philosopher.

In 1932 Jacques Lacan defended his doctoral dissertation in psychiatry. In 1934 he became a member of the Société Psychanalytique de Paris, which certified him as a psychoanalyst in 1938. In 1953, refusing to submit to the time rule of a forty-five minute session with the patient, he resigned from the Société and joined the Société Française de Psychanalyse founded by Daniel Lagache. In so doing, he lost his membership in the International Psychoanalytical Association. In 1964 he left the new society and founded his own school of psychoanalysis, the École Freudienne de Paris (EFP), which lasted until 1980, when, sixteen months before his death, he established the École de la Cause Freudienne. This tormented relationship with institutionalized psychoanalysis testifies to Lacan's complicated personality but is also a symptom of the difficulty involved in including psychoanalysis as a formal discipline in an academic setting (a problem Sigmund Freud had already tackled).

CONTRIBUTIONS TO PSYCHOANALYSIS

Jacques Lacan redefined Freud's psychoanalysis in an oeuvre spanning fifty years and comprising the *Écrits* (1966), the *Autres écrits* (2001) and twenty-six *Seminars,* based on courses conducted between 1953 and 1979. From beginning to end, this immense body of work is characterized by its conceptual coherence and the vast knowledge put to the task: philosophy (Plato, Aristotle, René Descartes, Immanuel Kant, G. W. F. Hegel, Karl Marx, Søren Kierkegaard, Martin Heidegger, Ludwig Wittgenstein, Alexandre Koyré, Alexandre Kojève, Karl Popper), logic (Aristotle, George Boole, Jaakko Hintikka), mathematics and topology (Kurt Gödel, August Möbius, Georg Cantor), linguistics (Ferdinand de Saussure), game theory, literature (Sophocles, Jaufré Rudel, Arnaut Daniel, Shakespeare, the Marquis de Sade, Paul Claudel, André Gide, Marguerite Duras), religion, mythology, and art. No field of human endeavor is left untouched by Lacan.

Lacan's major contributions to psychoanalysis fall into three categories. First, he redefined the practice of psychoanalysis. The patient is called the analysand because he is doing the investigative work into his own mind. Sessions are ended when the analysand makes a discovery, not when the traditional forty-five minutes have elapsed. (Lacan took that practice to an unethical extreme when, at the end of his career, he limited the sessions to three minutes.) Second, he reemphasized the importance of the unconscious and the superego in Freud, unlike Freud's direct heirs, who worked mainly on the ego. Third, he displaced Freud's theories by submitting them to a logical and mathematical formalization in order to ensure their pertinence and transmissibility. Psychoanalysis was to operate as a reflective link repositioning the humanities and the hard sciences within a general epistemology.

AGENCIES OF THE PSYCHE

Lacan distinguishes three agencies in the psyche: the symbolic order, the imaginary order, and the real. The corresponding categories in Freud would be, respectively, the superego, the ego, and the id, though Lacan's renaming is a full remapping of Freud's work.

The *symbolic order* is the set of signifiers. For Lacan, signifiers are not just words: he gives the concept a tremendous extension, since any object in the human sphere is marked by language and thus functions as a signifying element. Also, he stresses the supremacy of the symbolic order: for him, it is the foundation and beginning of all psychic mechanisms. For example, the universal prohibition of incest (and hence the shift from animal instinct to human desire) depends on its formulation within the symbolic order. The symbolic order determines the human subject by its signifying chains, undermining the ego's autonomy. Indeed, the ego is submitted to a radical determinacy, which it chooses to largely ignore or repress.

The symbolic order is a universal characteristic of human societies; a group can be said to be human only if it is subordinated to a symbolic structure. At the same time, this mark of humanity differs by linguistic group: each existing language determines a symbolic order particular to the community that speaks it. The symbolic order is where societies hold their signifiers in common, and where the superego and cultural constraints operate.

The *imaginary order* replaces Freud's ego agency. Its contents are the signified, significations, and representations produced by the ego processes, namely, identification and projection on objects in the world. As such, it is always built between two poles, the ego itself and its mirror image, the other (written with a lowercase *o*). The imaginary order is in charge of actualizing repression; it is to be assimilated to what was known before psychoanalysis as "reality," which Lacan understands as an imaginary construct. Hence, imaginary reality has to be differentiated in principle from the Lacanian real, which is the locus of meaning and truth.

The imaginary order is completely subordinated to the symbolic order, also called "the Other" (capital *O*): the chain of signifiers is the determinant that organizes the signifieds and representations within the imaginary order. The imaginary order is the set comprising all the representations of an individual as he or she shares them with the group, community, ethnicity, nation, and so on. As such, the imaginary order defines a subject's particularity, through which he identifies himself as *part* of a group.

The *real* replaces Freud's unconscious. It is the locus of singularity, defined as an interdicted entity that is impossible to formalize or represent: as such, it cannot be called an *order*, unlike the symbolic and the imaginary. It overlaps with the real in science, which the incompleteness of our mathematical representations prevents us from knowing in its totality. Escaping any formalization, the real is where truth, meaning, and sense are to be. We have only partial access to the real, through lapses, dreams, and bungled actions: "The unconscious is to not remember what one knows" (Lacan 2001). Hence, "Truth can be told only in half, because, beyond this half said, there is nothing to say. . . . Here, in consequence, discourse disappears. We don't speak about what is unutterable" (Lacan 1991).

MATHEMATICAL FORMALIZATION

Lacan strove to transmit his theory unencumbered by the interferences that always appear in human linguistic communication. That is why he devoted himself to a mathematical formalization of his concepts, since, in an algorithm, everything is transmissible and not subject to the loss that occurs in ordinary language. At stake is a map of the psyche that connects the agencies (symbolic, imaginary, and real) and that dispenses with Freud's unusable diagram published in *The Ego and the Id* (1923). Lacan's first attempt, based on vector analysis, is *Schema L,* published in 1956. The last formalization is grounded in topology and knot theory; Lacan uses the Borromean knot and the Möbius strip as his models.

Lacan's theory belongs to the realist philosophical tradition, which holds that linguistic categories structure real, existing objects in the world. That is why he cannot be bundled with a nominalist "French philosophical school" represented by Jacques Derrida, Michel Foucault, and Gilles Deleuze, for example. In addition, Lacan belongs to a materialist tradition: matter, in his theory, is language, "the signifier transcended into language" (2001, p. 209). As such, language can be submitted to the procedures of modern (real) logic; it can also be submitted to mathematical formalization. This is his crowning, but not yet fully understood, contribution: the giant step taken by Lacan, and by no one else, was to mathematically formalize some parts of ordinary language while including in this formalization the unconscious "structured as a language." Of course, mathematicians and logicians (Gottlob Frege, Boole, Alfred Tarski, and Bertrand Russell, for example) have long been at work on this endeavor. But their goal is to refine the operation of language into an entirely consistent (that is, self-reflexive and conscious) set; their formalizations do not include the unconscious, which is inconsistency itself. Here lies Lacan's profound originality, which makes him one of the major thinkers of the twentieth century. Lacan created a new discipline that rigorously takes into account the symbolic effects of language on human beings.

Lacan's influence on psychoanalysis and other disciplines in the humanities has been enormous throughout the world. Lacanian schools have surfaced everywhere, especially in Latin countries with a Catholic tradition in Europe and South America. In the Protestant Anglo-Saxon world, his legacy has been more limited, restricted to literature departments and some scattered psychoanalytic societies. It has slowly faded as a theory and a practice to cure mental illnesses. The United States' rejection of Lacan can be explained by cultural differences: the American emphasis on clarity and pragmatism; the demonstrated efficiency of the imaginary order in the United States; the misinterpretation of Lacan's theory by feminist readers; Lacan's own anti-Americanism. All these factors work against an easy acceptance of his work in the United States.

Lacan predicted the demise of psychoanalysis as cure: "When psychoanalysis has been vanquished by the growing impasses of our civilization (a discontent that Freud foresaw), the *Écrits* indications will be taken up by somebody" (2001, p. 348). What will his legacy be when that moment arrives? It will consist in his breakthrough contribution to a general epistemology that combines and opposes the social sciences and the humanities on one side, and mathematics on the other. If psychoanalysis as a therapeutic practice dies, what will be left is Lacan's truly immense contribution to epistemology, a contribution that has not yet been fully mapped in English-speaking countries.

See also **Feminism; Postmodernism; Psychoanalysis.**

BIBLIOGRAPHY

Fink, Bruce. *The Lacanian Subject: Between Language and Jouissance.* Princeton, N.J., 1995. The structure of the subject.

Lacan, Jacques. *Le séminaire, Livre XVII: L'envers de la psychanalyse.* Edited by Jacques-Alain Miller. Paris, 1991.

———. *Autres écrits.* Paris, 2001.

Leupin, Alexandre. *Lacan Today: Psychoanalysis, Science, Religion.* New York, 2004. General introduction to his work.

Mitchell, Juliet, and Jaqueline Rose, eds. *Feminine Sexuality, Jacques Lacan, and the École Freudienne.* Translated by Jaqueline Rose. New York, 1985.

Rabaté, Jean-Michel, ed. *Lacan in America.* New York, 2000.

Vanier, Alain. *Lacan.* Translated by Susan Fairfield. New York, 2000. A general introduction.

ALEXANDRE LEUPIN

LAND REFORM. Land reform may be understood here as the transfer of land from one owner or group of owners to another for political, social, or ideological purposes. Throughout the nineteenth century and most of the twentieth it was thought that land reform would solve an array of political and social problems. The range of issues land reform was used to address included strengthening of political power, change of patterns of ethnicity, prevention of emigration from rural areas, economic support of poor people, and settlements for refugees or homecoming soldiers. Land reform always included other measures, such as the establishment of rural settlements and the extension of agricultural land, which generally meant forest clearances or other changes to the landscape. Sometimes the previous owners were compensated, but quite often they were simply dispossessed.

NINETEENTH-CENTURY BACKGROUND

An intense political discussion about land reform issues took place in the first half of the nineteenth century, most prominently in the reform movement of the Chartists in Great Britain. One of their speakers, James O'Brien (1805–1864), called for total socialization of private property. Their main argument was that the unequal distribution of land was the root of many social problems.

These claims became influential within the rising socialist movement in Europe. Authors, politicians, and philosophers such as Karl Marx (1818–1883), Karl Kautsky (1854–1938), and Eduard Bernstein (1850–1932) were critical of private landownership, and many called for the nationalization of land. An important book was *Progress and Poverty* (1877–1879) by the American economist Henry George (1839–1897), which was translated into a number of European languages. He argued not against the private ownership of land per se but that all landowners should pay taxes on the income they received from rents. In line with his thinking, numerous books and articles appeared in which the authors allowed private property but argued that the land should be seen as a finite resource that must be protected against misuse, speculation, and monopoly. For this purpose many different tax systems were devised. In 1890 the Austrian author Theodor Hertzka (1845–1927) published a utopian novel with the title *Freiland, ein soziales Zukunftsbild* (*Freiland: A Social Anticipation*). In this book he formulated the idea that land should be owned by rural cooperatives. The land and cooperatives should be accessible to everyone and serve as an economic foundation for egalitarian settlements. These settlements should be established in the European colonies abroad. This was tried; most attempts failed. In 1894 the German economist Franz Oppenheimer (1864–1943) published *Freiland in Deutschland*, in which he formulated a close relationship among collective ownership, rural cooperatives, and collective settlements. Oppenheimer's ideas strongly influenced the Zionist movement. Impressed with Oppenheimer's book, the Zionist leader Theodor Herzl (1860–1904) published *Altneuland* (Old new land) in 1902, and in 1911 the Zionist Congress assigned Oppenheimer to plan a settlement cooperative near Nazareth. Oppenheimer was one of the most prominent representatives of a third way between communism and capitalism. (One of his students, Ludwig Erhard, was a leading theorist of a social market economy after World War II and second chancellor of the Federal Republic of Germany.)

The year 1888 in Germany saw the founding of the Bund für Bodenbesitzreform, a powerful land reform organization that proposed a land reform without the abolition of private property. It was led first by the factory owner Michael Flürscheim (1844–1912) and later by the teacher Adolf Damaschke (1865–1935), who wrote a popular book about land reform entitled *Die Bodenreform* (Land reform). Published in 1902, it was reprinted many times through the 1920s.

LAND REFORM SINCE 1914

Twentieth-century Europe saw three periods in which the politics of land reform wrought vast changes on the Continent. All of these periods were times of economic crisis and political transformation. The first was the interwar period between World War I and World War II, especially in its early years. The second was the postwar period after World War II. The third was the period after the end of the Cold War, beginning in 1989.

The end of World War I was an era of social and political turmoil and radical change. In Russia, Germany, and the new countries within the territories of the old Austro-Hungarian Monarchy land reforms were a result of revolutions and newly established political systems.

The deepest change in rural society and land property rights took place in Russia and the later Soviet Union after the end of World War I. With land reform under the control of the tsarist prime minister and secretary of interior Peter Stolypin (1862–1911), the *mir* system, the collective ownership of land by all village inhabitants, was replaced by private landownership in 1905. Thus emerged a new type of farmer, the kulak, a wealthy middle-class farmer who now hired other village inhabitants as wage laborers. With the success of the Bolshevik Revolution, however, the new Soviet government in 1918 abolished private land property. The process of dispossessing the kulaks became increasingly radical after 1929 and was one of Joseph Stalin's core issues as he consolidated power as leader of the Soviet Union. The process was not finished until 1940, when more than 96 percent of the land was collectivized and cultivated in the form of huge farms. The result of this campaign was an economic and human catastrophe. Several million people in the rural areas died of hunger, and the level of agrarian production in 1940 was lower than in 1913. But this change enabled the Soviet government to obtain better control over the huge rural areas.

In the new Baltic countries, Lithuania, Estonia and Latvia, the old, partly German landed elite too was dispossessed; in this case the land was not collectivized but given to private farmers. Land reforms in many other European countries were organized at the same time.

In Germany, the German Reich Settlement Act (Reichssiedlungsgesetz) came into force in 1919. It was aimed at assisting returning war veterans and landless people as well as refugees from the eastern parts of Germany, which became Polish territory. The idea was to buy extensively cultivated land from big estates, to intensify cultivation efforts, and to reclaim wastelands. New settlement agencies, established in all the German territories, were in charge of parceling out the land, laying out new fields, and constructing farm buildings. In the 1930s some authoritarian regimes such as those of Germany, Italy, and Spain organized huge programs for rural reconstruction and reclamation of wastelands, such as the Bonifica Integrale in Italy under Benito Mussolini. But in most of these cases private property was not affected.

The most radical land reforms took place after 1945 in the countries of central and Eastern Europe that came under Soviet rule. At the end of World War II it was a common political opinion among the Allies that land reform needed to be carried out in Germany in order to break the political power of the Junker (a member of the Prussian landed aristocracy). The economic historian Alexander Gerschenkron (1904–1968) argued in his book *Bread and Democracy in Germany* (1943) that disempowerment of the landed elite was a crucial step in the process of democratization. But as tensions increased between the Western and the Soviet zones of occupation, ideas about land reform became an area of conflict in the emergent Cold War. In 1945 Stalin ordered the German Communist Party to organize land reform in the Soviet zone of occupation. All landowners with property of more than 100 hectares as well as all those who were considered Nazi activists were dispossessed. More than 3.3 million hectares of arable land were redistributed to refugees and small farmers and farmworkers. In this process more than 210,000 new farms were founded. The problem was that most of these new farmers had no machinery, seed, pesticides, or farm buildings and so were unable to produce enough food for the population of the Soviet zone. At the beginning of the 1950s the agricultural crisis became so severe that the Communist Party decided to collectivize all these farms. At the beginning of the 1960s, in a period that was called the "socialist spring," all private land was in the hands of the Landwirtschaftliche Produktionsgenossenschaften (LPG; agricultural production cooperatives). In the Western zones of occupation some early attempts at land reform were soon dropped after witnessing the results in the Soviet zone.

Similar processes took place in the other countries of Eastern Europe. A particularly radical program of land reform took place in Romania. Collectivization began in 1950 and was finished at the beginning of the 1960s. Subsequently Nicolae Ceauşescu, the general secretary of the Communist Party, initiated a "program for the systematization of the villages" (*sistematizarea satelor*), a plan wherein eight thousand small villages would be destroyed in favor of "agroindustrial centers" that would house the rural population in large tenement blocks with no infrastructure. This program was not yet finished by the time of Ceauşescu's death in 1989.

In Western Europe ideas of land reform essentially vanished in the 1950s and 1960s. With the development of the common market of the European Union, questions of land reform were superseded by issues such as overproduction, migration, and integrated management of rural areas.

After 1989 the land reform programs in all the former Warsaw Pact countries were more or less rescinded. The large state-owned farms and collectivized land were reprivatized. This process caused conflicts among the state, the new owners, and those who had owned the land before 1945. In Germany several organizations of landowners initiated a legal battle against the decision of the federal government not to give the land back to the old owners of the prewar period but instead sell it to new owners. Under this decision the only rights granted to the old owners were preferential terms if they were willing to buy back their estates and farms.

See also **Agriculture; Collectivization.**

BIBLIOGRAPHY

Bronstein, Jamie L. *Land Reform and Working-Class Experience in Britain and the United States, 1800–1862.* Stanford, Calif., 1999.

Christodoulou, Demetrios. *The Unpromised Land: Agrarian Reform and Conflict Worldwide.* London, 1990.

Davies, Robert W. *The Socialist Offensive. The Collectivisation of Soviet Agriculture, 1929–1930.* London, 1980.

———. *The Soviet Collective Farm, 1929–1930.* London, 1980.

Dovring, Folke. *Land and Labor in Europe in the Twentieth Century: A Comparative Survey of Recent Agrarian History.* 3rd rev. ed. The Hague, Netherlands, 1965.

Figes, Orlando. *A People's Tragedy: The Russian Revolution, 1891–1924.* London, 1996.

Laurent, John, ed. *Henry George's Legacy in Economic Thought.* Cheltenham, U.K., 2005.

Naimark, Norman M. *The Russians in Germany: A History of the Soviet Zone of Occupation, 1945–1949.* Cambridge, Mass., 1995.

Naimark, Norman M., ed. *The Establishment of Communist Regimes in Eastern Europe. 1944–1949.* Boulder, Colo., 1997.

Pallot, Judith. *Land Reform in Russia, 1906–1917: Peasant Responses to Stolypin's Project of Rural Transformation.* Oxford, U.K., and New York, 1998.

Repp, Kevin. *Reformers, Critics, and the Paths of German Modernity: Anti-Politics and the Search for Alternatives, 1890–1914.* Cambridge, Mass., 2000.

Rodgers, Daniel T. *Atlantic Crossings: Social Politics in a Progressive Age.* Cambridge, Mass., 1998.

Tuma, Elias H., *Twenty-six Centuries of Agrarian Reform: A Comparative Analysis.* Berkeley, Calif., 1965.

———. *European Economic History: Tenth Century to the Present.* New York, 1971.

———. "Agrarian Reform in Historical Perspective Revisited." *Comparative Studies in Society and History* 21 (January 1979): 3–29.

Turnock, David, ed. *Privatization in Rural Eastern Europe: The Process of Restitution and Restructuring.* Cheltenham, U.K., 1998.

Wegren, Stephen K., ed. *Land Reform in the Former Soviet Union and Eastern Europe.* London, 1998.

ANDREAS DIX

LANG, FRITZ (1890–1976), Austrian filmmaker.

Born in Vienna, Fritz Lang moved to Berlin in 1919 to begin a career that would define the emerging art of film. He created indelible images that epitomize Nordic myth (*Nibelungen*, 1924), the city of the future (*Metropolis*, 1927) and the psychotic criminal (*Dr. Mabuse*, 1922; *M*, 1931). All of his twenty German films are marked by an ambition to advance the possibilities of film as a *Gesamtkunstwerk*, a work amalgamating all traditional arts, including music and architecture. His

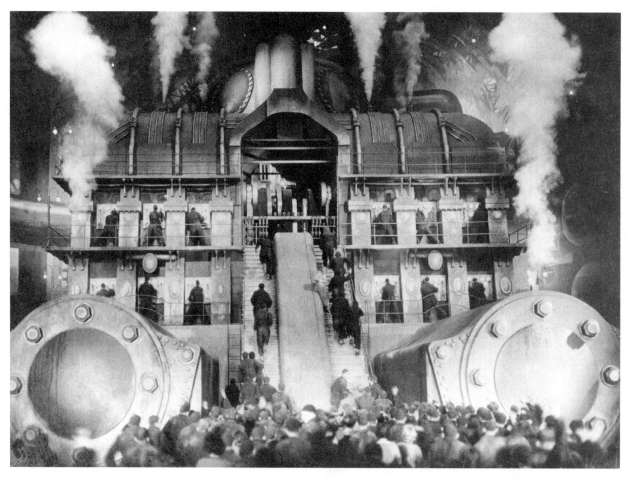

The teeming factory from Fritz Lang's *Metropolis*, 1927. UFA/THE KOBAL COLLECTION

American films, made in Hollywood during his exile from 1936 to 1956, are stylistically less daring because, unlike in Germany, none of the studios gave him complete autonomy. In addition, dialogue-driven sound films mostly steered clear of stunning visuals, and, in accordance with the strictly enforced production code, emphasized law, order, and morality. Lang never ceased battling the Hollywood production system, which in his view limited his artistic freedom, yet his return to Germany in 1956 was no solution either. He directed two German films in the tradition of his Weimar period, *The Tiger of Eschnapur* (1959) and *The 1000 Eyes of Dr. Mabuse* (1960), but the postwar German audience rejected both films. Deeply disappointed, Lang returned to Los Angeles. In 1963 Jean-Luc Godard asked Lang, by then a legendary auteur, to act in his film *Le mépris*. Lang played himself, a film director in exile, and took the opportunity to rant against the compromises and corruption of Hollywood.

Although Lang's work encompasses many genres and displays remarkable stylistic versatility, certain themes reappear with obsessive regularity in both his German and American films: the inevitability of destiny, fascination with crime and guilt, and the allure of total destruction. His German period falls into two categories: lavish fantasies with imaginary settings—for instance, the realm of death in *Destiny* (1921) or the lunar landscape in *The Woman in the Moon* (1929)—and the "realistic" but visibly stylized psychological studies of crime and urban life. In the latter, there is a progression from the expressionist detective film *Dr. Mabuse* in the early 1920s to the semidocumentary style of the New Sobriety in *M* ten years later. The power-obsessed psychoanalyst and master criminal Dr. Mabuse is replaced by M, a pathological child murderer who cannot control himself.

Lang's most ambitious film, *Metropolis,* may also be one of the most quoted films of all time.

A rebellious son challenges his industrialist father's world of machines after he falls in love with a worker's daughter. But it is not the story or the conciliatory ending, later dismissed by Lang as a fairy tale, that is remembered. Rather, it is the close-up shots of glistening pistons and moving cranks, the aerial shots of skyscrapers with airplanes flying between them, the special effects that capture explosions and biblical floods, and the creation of a female cyborg by a mad scientist. Endlessly recycled in visual cinematic culture (in *Blade Runner* of 1982 and *Terminator 3: Rise of the Machines* of 2003, among others), these images have indelibly etched themselves in popular memory.

Metropolis, the most expensive film ever made in the 1920s, bankrupted the UFA studio. Only a truncated version was released commercially and, even in the most recently reconstructed version, thirty minutes are still missing. In comparison to Lang's "monumental films" (a phrase of the time), a film such as *M* seems low budget. His favorite film, *M* is a documentary of the hunt for a serial killer in Düsseldorf in 1929–1930 but also a parable that demonstrates how fear can turn a collective into a fascist mob, a prescient motif two years prior to Hitler's rise to power. *M* was also Lang's first sound film. Always the innovator and modernist, he used sound as a new expressive tool and emphasized the tensions between sound and sight, seeing and hearing. For instance, the murderer betrays himself by the sound of his whistling (no silent film can show this), and it is a blind man who ultimately identifies him by aural clues, thus calling the act of seeing itself into question. Lang's exploration of crime, alienation, and the ambiguity of guilt makes *M* an influential forerunner of film noir. Lang himself reworked *M* in several films during his American period, relentlessly pitting, often with cruel irony, justice against the law, morality against fate, free will against social constraints, and desire for revenge against self-destruction. The Hollywood system required compromises, however. Lang's *Fury* (1936), *Ministry of Fear* (1944), *Secret beyond the Door* (1948), and *While the City Sleeps* (1956)—imply tragic double binds and deadly solutions, but end happily, as if to mock the studio.

See also **Cinema; Expressionism.**

BIBLIOGRAPHY

Gunning, Tom. *The Films of Fritz Lang: Allegories of Visions and Modernity.* London, 2000. A series of authoritative readings of Lang's major films.

Kaes, Anton. *M.* London, 2000. A paradigmatic study of Lang's pivotal film.

Kracauer, Siegfried. *From Caligari to Hitler: A Psychological History of the German Film.* Princeton, N.J., 1947. The classic study of Weimar cinema.

McGilligan, Patrick. *Fritz Lang: The Nature of the Beast.* New York, 1997. An exhaustive but controversial biography.

ANTON KAES

LA PASIONARIA. *See* Ibárruri, Dolores (La Pasionaria).

LATERAN PACTS. The signing of the Lateran Pacts, or Pacts of Conciliation, on 11 February 1929 was an important stage in the history of contemporary Italy and in the development of the Fascist regime.

CONTENT OF THE PACTS

The pacts, signed by the cardinal Pietro Gasparri (1852–1934), secretary of state for Pope Pius XI (r. 1922–1939), as representative of the Holy See and by Benito Mussolini (1883–1945), head of the Italian government, had three components: a treaty, a concordat, and a financial convention. The treaty resolved the "Roman question," or the long conflict that had pitted the Holy See against the Italian state since the unification of Italy (1871). The treaty guaranteed the independence of the Holy See: the Vatican City became a sovereign state under international law. The treaty reaffirmed Article 1 of the *Statuto* (the constitution of the Italian state), according to which Catholicism is considered the sole state religion. Under the financial convention (a separate document, but an integral part of the treaty), Italy agreed to pay a financial indemnity in compensation for the unification and the occupation of Rome in 1870: 750 million lire, and bonds at 5 percent interest per annum to yield an additional 1 billion lire. The concordat required the bishops to swear an oath of loyalty to the Italian state. Yet the positions of the Catholic Church were considerably strengthened within Italian society: religious marriages were valid under civil law, the ecclesiastical tribunals were empowered to grant annulments, and the teaching of the Catholic religion was made mandatory in elementary and secondary schools and was considered an essential component of public education. The Holy See obtained guarantees concerning the existence of Catholic Action, which thus remained the only mass organization not integrated into the structures of fascism. On the international level, the Vatican state declared itself neutral, prohibited from taking a position in conflicts.

NEGOTIATION OF THE PACTS

The signing of the pacts came after a year and a half of secret negotiations and several years of Fascist government policies that were very favorable to the church. After becoming the head of the government, Mussolini had quickly forgotten the anticlericalism of his youth and challenged the secularization of society under the governments of a liberal Italy. A number of measures were adopted in this direction: the reinstatement of crucifixes in public places, state financial aid for restoration of churches damaged in the war, recognition of the Catholic University of the Sacred Heart in Milan, and so forth. Although the suppression of all liberties and the *fascistissime* (ultrafascist) turn of the Fascist dictatorship in January 1925—after the assassination of the Socialist MP Giacomo Matteotti by Fascist hirelings—had provoked Pius XI to harden his positions, the tensions were quickly forgotten, each side seeing that rapprochement was in its interest.

Discussions aimed at reaching an agreement began in August 1926. The Vatican was represented by Francesco Pacelli, a lawyer and the brother of Eugenio Pacelli (the future Pope Pius XII). A senior member of the Council of State, Domenico Barone, represented the Italian government. At the end of the negotiations Mussolini took things in hand directly, assisted by Minister of Justice Alfredo Rocco.

Each side stood to benefit from the success of the negotiations. At the time, the Holy See took a fairly favorable view of an authoritarian state likely to restore the positions of Catholicism within society. Thus, the pro-family and pro-natalist policies of fascism, in particular, were perceived positively. For Mussolini, resolution of the "Roman question" was likely to strengthen his popularity and increase his prestige on the international scene. He would thus be able to present himself as the statesman who had been able to "finish" the work of Count Cavour (Camillo Benso; 1810–1861).

EFFECTS OF THE PACTS

The treaty was favorably received by the Italian people, the great majority of whom were Catholic. The national and international press gave major coverage to the event. In March 1929, a new Chamber of Deputies was elected; its members were to ratify the Lateran Pacts. Only one electoral list, *le listone* (the big list), was proposed for ratification by the deputies. Despite the antidemocratic nature of the election, the Catholic world supported the regime.

Only militant antifascist Catholics, such as Alcide De Gasperi (1881–1954), considered the pacts to be a political error, believing, correctly, that the Conciliation was a political success for fascism. The agreements were favorably received by the great majority of Catholics, who believed that Catholicism had reclaimed its traditional historical role in the peninsula. The Lateran Pacts allowed the Catholic Church to consolidate its positions and culminated in a "confessionalization" of Italian society. By contrast, the "minority" religions—Protestantism, Judaism—were signaled to the rest of the population as being "different."

After the signing of the Lateran Pacts, fascism continued to present itself as a new "faith" and to impose its own rites and civil liturgies. Although the church remained one of the pillars of the regime, grounds for tension between the regime and the Holy See continued to exist. The issue of Catholic youth organizations was one source of discord, because the Fascist government perceived them as structures that might impede the conversion of "hearts and minds" to fascism. In the summer of 1931, in the antifascist encyclical "Non abbiamo bisogno" ("We have no need"), Pope Pius XI proclaimed his refusal to entrust the state with full responsibility for educating the younger generations. In September 1931 an agreement was reached: the role of the youth organizations of Catholic Action, placed under the strict control of the bishops, was to be strictly limited to religious education. If, predictably, any interest in politics was excluded, athletic activities were also ruled out, sports being considered a particularly sensitive area of rivalry.

After the crisis of 1931, relations between the church and fascism were normalized. The war in Ethiopia and then the Spanish civil war helped to reestablish links between them. If the regime's adoption of racial laws in 1938 was a source of dissent between the regime and the church, this was less owing to the principle of state anti-Semitism per se than because of the prohibition of marriages between Jews and "Aryans," considered by the Holy See as a *vulnus* (literally, "wound"—figuratively, a sort of sin) against the Lateran Pacts.

See also **Catholicism; Italy; Rome.**

BIBLIOGRAPHY

Margiotta Broglio, Francesco. *Italia e Santa Sede dalla Grande guerra alla Conciliazion.* Bari, Italy, 1966.

Scoppola, Pietro. *La chiesa e il fascismo: Documenti e interpretazioni.* Bari, Italy, 1971.

Traniello, Franceso. "L'Italia cattolica nell'era fascist." In *Storia dell'Italia religiosa: III, L'età contemporanea,* edited by Gabriele De Rosa. Rome-Bari, Italy, 1995.

MARIE-ANNE MATARD-BONUCCI

LATVIA. For Latvia, the twentieth century was an era of revolution and war, independence and occupation. The achievements of its population both during independence and in the long decades of Soviet rule stand in contrast to periods of horrific suffering and loss of life, most notably during World War II and the early years within the USSR.

In the years immediately after the outbreak of World War I in August 1914, the fate of the territories in the Russian Empire that became Latvia, Lithuania, and Estonia was affected most by the struggle in eastern Europe between Russia and Germany. By the fall of 1915, German forces had occupied the Baltic littoral up to the Western Dvina (Daugava) River, which runs though the middle of the area of Latvian settlement. During the war, at least three quarters of a million fled as refugees, mainly to Russia.

With the Russian Empire increasingly unstable in 1917, nationalist and socialist visions for the future spread among Latvians. Under worsening wartime conditions, many in unoccupied Latvian areas turned to the political Left, and Latvian socialists, including Bolsheviks, grew in popularity. Bolsheviks controlled Riga from the spring of 1917 until its occupation by German forces in September, and Bolsheviks led the radicalized councils, or "soviets," in other cities and in the countryside. Latvian infantry regiments, which had sustained heavy losses in fighting German troops, joined the Bolshevik cause. Known as the "Latvian Riflemen," many of these troops later fought in the Russian civil war as Vladimir Lenin's most trusted forces. The weakening of the Germans' forward position on the eastern front encouraged supporters of Latvian autonomy to press for full independence. On 18 November 1918, a week after the general armistice, a self-appointed Latvian national council met secretly in German-occupied Riga, and proclaimed a provisional government and the independence of Latvia, consisting of Courland province, southern Livland province, and the Lettgallia region of Vitebsk province.

For yet another year, control over Latvia vacillated between competing groups, and violence continued. Latvian Bolshevik forces, accompanied by some Russian Bolsheviks, established a Soviet Latvian government in nonoccupied areas in late 1918 and then seized Riga in January 1919. The violence of their rule, including execution of opponents, weakened the support they had earlier enjoyed. Latvian national and German troops cooperated in driving them out of the main Latvian areas by May 1919. The prospects for the government of the Latvian prime minister Karlis Ulmanis (1877–1942) remained shaky as a result of ongoing intrigues by German military forces, whom the Western Allies were encouraging to leave. Ulmanis's national army defeated a combined army of Germans, White Russians, and Baltic Germans in the fall of 1919, and the remnants of the Bolshevik army were expelled from eastern Latvia by early 1920. A peace treaty with Soviet Russia was signed on 11 August 1920.

Latvians celebrate their independence, Riga, 1918. ©HULTON-DEUTSCH COLLECTION/CORBIS

INTERWAR INDEPENDENCE

In the nearly two decades of peace between the cessation of all hostilities in 1920 and the forced establishment of Soviet military bases in Latvia in 1939, Latvia achieved a number of successes, perhaps most notably in the development of effective national and local government and in the elaboration of a national Latvian culture and educational system. Ultimately, though, leaders failed to maintain a democratic political order.

Agrarian reform, ordered by the constitutional convention in 1920 that made Latvia a democratic republic, expropriated land from the tsarist-era privileged elite (primarily Baltic Germans). Land was distributed in stages to the landless and veterans of the national army. These beneficiaries were nearly exclusively Latvians, who now composed 73.4 percent of the country's 1.8 million inhabitants in 1925—a decline from the late tsarist era due to wartime deaths and the failure of some refugees to return.

The strongest political parties in the 1920s and early 1930s were the Social Democrats and the Agrarian Union, though because the socialists avoided coalitions, members of the Agrarian Union dominated high government office. The economic depression experienced elsewhere in the world affected Latvia as well in the 1930s. Increasingly unhappy with the political divisions inherent in a parliamentary democracy, Ulmanis and his supporters became convinced that parliament, called the *Saeima*, was not able to deal effectively with the country's political and economic difficulties. On 15 May 1934 Ulmanis carried out a bloodless coup, dismissing parliament. Political parties were forbidden, and several hundred political leaders were imprisoned. During the six years of Ulmanis's authoritarian rule, the government dominated public life, and it took steps to lessen the influence in society and the economy of non-Latvians.

END OF INDEPENDENCE AND WORLD WAR II

The nonaggression pact signed between the Soviet Union and Nazi Germany on 23 August 1939 contained a secret protocol dividing eastern Europe into Soviet and German spheres of interest. Latvia was included in the Soviet sphere, as was

Estonia, and in late September, Lithuania as well. Like its Baltic neighbors, Latvia was unable to oppose Soviet demands for military bases in the country, and by early 1940 several tens of thousands of Soviet troops had arrived. In June 1940 the Soviets gave Latvian leaders an ultimatum that a new government friendly to the USSR must be established (the Soviets labeled the Ulmanis government as unfriendly), and additional Soviet troops admitted, to ensure compliance of the agreement for the Soviet bases. Within days the number of troops increased dramatically, and with Soviet tanks rolling through the streets of Riga, the country was occupied. Sham elections were held in July for a new Saeima, which declared Latvia a Soviet republic and requested incorporation into the USSR.

The merging of Latvia's legal and economic systems with those of the Soviet Union and the broader Sovietization of society continued in the fall of 1940 and spring of 1941. This included arrests of over seven thousand persons accused of "political" crimes, of whom some fifteen hundred were executed; confiscation of private property over certain limits; broad dismissals of employees in state institutions; and forced changes in education. On 13–14 June, some fifteen thousand persons whom the Soviet authorities suspected as possible sources of resistance were arrested and deported eastward into the USSR; an additional twenty thousand met the same fate during this first year of Soviet occupation.

More deportations were halted by the invasion of the USSR by Adolf Hitler's forces on 22 June. The German occupation of Latvia was even bloodier than the Soviet one. By the end of the year, Nazi SS Einsatzgruppen (operational task forces) and Latvian collaborators murdered nearly all of the some sixty-six thousand Jews of Latvia who had not fled to the Soviet Union. No fewer than twenty thousand Jews brought from elsewhere in Europe were also exterminated in Latvia. Social and economic matters were directed by German civilian authorities, many of them Baltic Germans, who had left Latvia en masse before the Soviets' arrival in 1939. A Latvian self-administration was permitted to direct matters not seen as important to the German war effort, such as education and cultural policy, though within German-set

Soviet troops march near the Freedom Monument in Riga, 1940. The Freedon Monument was erected in 1935 as a tribute to Latvian independence. During the subsequent Soviet occupation, the monument served as a powerful symbol of Latvian nationalism. ©HULTON-DEUTSCH COLLECTION/CORBIS

guidelines. The statization of property carried out by the Soviets remained in place. The Nazis' expectation was that Latvia and the rest of the Baltic region would be colonized by Germans as part of a greater Germany. Some 146,000 Latvians were mobilized into Latvian legions within the Waffen SS through both voluntary enlistment and conscription; among these, fifty to sixty thousand were wounded in battle and four thousand killed. The largest population loss during the war occurred in the summer and fall of 1944 when, with the weakening of the German war effort and looming return of Soviet troops, some 120,000 Latvians fled westward as refugees. By 1945, Latvia had lost a third of its prewar population, and its cities and countryside were left devastated.

SOVIET LATVIA

Soviet troops recaptured most of the Baltic region in the summer and fall of 1944, and Latvia was again included in the USSR as the Latvian Soviet Socialist Republic. With all of Latvia, Lithuania, and Estonia back in Soviet hands by May 1945, the re-Sovietization of the Baltic began in earnest. In Latvia, some seventy thousand people were executed or deported as suspected German collaborators. Soviet-imposed press censorship and restrictions in education and the arts aimed at creating a society that condemned the interwar republic and praised Soviet Latvia. The small number of Latvian Communists assumed the leading positions in government.

In the economy, priorities set by Moscow were rapid industrialization and the collectivization of agriculture. To further the former, over half a million laborers arrived from elsewhere in the USSR during the first decade of Soviet rule. Because few of these were Latvians (mostly Russians, but also native-Russian-speaking Belorusians and Ukrainians), the ethnic makeup of Latvia was significantly changed, and by 1955, 38 percent of the population were Russians or native Russian speakers. In the countryside, initial resistance to conversion from private to collective farms ended after the deportation to Siberia of over forty thousand rural inhabitants in 1949. Soviet control of the countryside was challenged by upward of ten thousand Latvian anti-Soviet partisans, though this resistance ended by the mid-1950s.

With Joseph Stalin's death in 1953, the use of mass terror was halted. The relaxation of Soviet nationalities policy in the early years of the Khrushchev era (1953–1964) eased pressures on Latvian society. A thaw occurred in the arts and literature, allowing exploration and development of Latvian national culture. A degree of economic decentralization gave more autonomy in decision making to authorities in Latvia rather than Moscow. The percentage of Latvians rose in both administrative and Communist Party structures. Some leading Soviet Latvian officials in the late 1950s sought to limit in-migration of Russians and the broader russification of life. Khrushchev halted these efforts to create a Latvian "national communism," though he did so not with Stalinist arrests and executions, but by reassigning individual officials to lesser positions outside of Latvia.

During the Brezhnev era (1964–1982) no reform was contemplated within the Latvian Communist Party, and the portion of party members who were Latvians fell to one third. Russification continued in many areas of society, and freedom of expression was limited. In the economy the picture was brighter; Latvia became an urban industrial society in the 1960s and 1970s, with Riga as one of the more important industrial centers in the USSR. The state provided economic security, and the population saw a rise in living standard, which, however, remained well below that of Western European countries. By the end of the 1970s, however, shortages appeared for some goods, and industrial waste levels were rising. The population grew to 2,521,000 in 1979, an increase of over half a million since 1955. Underpinning this demographic expansion was increased migration of Slavic workers, especially to Riga; in 1970 Latvians made up only 40.9 percent of the city's population, and this figure fell to 36.5 percent by 1989.

THE DRIVE FOR INDEPENDENCE AND POST-SOVIET BEGINNINGS

The new openness in Soviet society introduced by the Soviet leader Mikhail Gorbachev (b. 1931), who took office in 1985, set in motion reform movements in Latvia, Estonia, and Lithuania that soon became massive in scope and national in tone. Large public demonstrations were held in Riga in 1987 protesting the harm Soviet industry was causing the environment in Latvia. Latvian intellectuals created in 1988 the Latvian Popular Front; this group, which soon had 250,000 members, pushed for a frank discussion of Latvia's historical experience within the USSR. The more radical Latvian National Independence Movement, also founded in 1988, called for an independent Latvia. The Latvian Communist Party split into reformist and pro-Moscow wings. The latter was supported by a group of mainly Slavic Communist loyalists within the Latvian population, known as the Interfront, but many non-Latvians threw their lot in with the Popular Front.

In elections held in March 1990, the Popular Front captured a majority of seats on the Soviet-era Supreme Council (Supreme Soviet of the Latvian SSR), which in May declared a "transition period" to full independence. Fears of a major crackdown by Moscow were raised in January 1991, when

Crowds watch as a statue of Lenin is brought down with a crane, Riga, Latvia, 25 August 1991. ©REUTERS/CORBIS

Soviet special troops were deployed in central Riga, killing five people. An estimated seven hundred thousand people—Latvians and non-Latvians alike—manned makeshift barricades before important public buildings in a show of support for the elected Latvian government. Full independence came suddenly; when Moscow hardliners staged a coup against Gorbachev in August 1991, the Supreme Council declared Latvia a sovereign republic, and with the coup's rapid collapse, the Russian Federation president Boris Yeltsin (b. 1931) recognized Latvia's independence.

Social integration of its large non-Latvian minority—mainly Russians and native-Russian speakers—has been newly independent Latvia's primary domestic challenge. In rebuilding the legal framework of their state, Latvians held to the guiding concept of continuity with interwar Latvia, not Soviet Latvia. The consequence of this for Latvia's citizenry was the effective disenfranchisement of most non-Latvians, who had no ties to prewar

Latvia; these could become citizens only through naturalization, which requires knowledge of Latvian. Liberalization of the citizenship law in 1998 has helped speed the pace of naturalization of noncitizens, but by 2006 a large number—18 percent of the entire population—were not citizens of Latvia. The state also took steps to strengthen the position of the Latvian language in public life and decided not to allow Russian to become a second official state language. Some non-Latvians, who tend to be monolingual, have opposed these measures as discriminatory.

Since the first post-Soviet elections to the Latvian parliament (now again called the Saeima) in 1993, Latvian politics have been dominated by parties on the right. Driving this tendency is a desire to distance Latvia from its Soviet past. Latvia's party system has been unstable as a result of weak party institutionalization and undeveloped party preferences among voters. Governments have changed frequently, with twelve formed between

1993 and 2006, all of them coalitions. The top foreign policy priority for Latvia's governments has been integration with pan-European political and security structures. In September 2003, 67 percent of voters approved Latvia's accession to the European Union, and in May 2004 Latvia became an EU member. In March 2004 Latvia became a member of NATO.

Newly independent Latvia quickly established a market economy and instituted tight control of monetary supply. Most of the economy has been privatized, and trade has been reoriented away from Russia and toward Western Europe, Scandinavia, and the two other Baltic countries. Primary economic products include timber and wood products, and machinery and equipment, though the service sector is much larger than either the industrial or agricultural economic sectors.

See also **Belarus; Estonia; Lithuania; Russia; Soviet Union; Ukraine.**

BIBLIOGRAPHY

Eksteins, Modris. *Walking since Daybreak: A Story of Eastern Europe, World War II, and the Heart of Our Century.* Boston, 1999.

Misiunas, Romuald J., and Rein Taagepera. *The Baltic States: Years of Dependence, 1940–1990.* Expanded and updated edition. Berkeley, Calif., 1993.

Pabriks, Artis, and Aldis Purs. *Latvia: The Challenges of Change.* London, 2001.

Plakans, Andrejs. *The Latvians: A Short History.* Stanford, Calif., 1995.

Rauch, Georg von. *The Baltic States: The Years of Independence: Estonia, Latvia, Lithuania, 1917–1940.* Translated from the German by Gerald Onn. Berkeley, Calif., 1974.

BRADLEY D. WOODWORTH

LAVAL, PIERRE (1883–1945), head of the Vichy government in France during World War II; considered by many to be the evil mastermind of collaboration.

Pierre Laval was born in Châteldon, in the Auvergne, to a family of shopkeepers. He did well in school, earning his Certificate of Primary Studies at twelve. In spite of his father's insistence that he work in the family business, Laval earned his baccalaureate in 1902. After a year of military service in the infantry in 1903, Laval was discharged as unfit for service owing to varicose veins.

EARLY CAREER

Laval eventually moved to Paris, completed a law degree in 1907, and began his law career, serving primarily a working-class, syndicalist clientele. In 1909 he married Jeanne Clausset, whose father had encouraged Laval's ambitions when he was a child, and in 1911 their only child, Josée, was born.

Laval won a seat in the Chamber of Deputies in 1914 as a Socialist, representing Aubervilliers, a heavily working-class suburb north of Paris. Unlike most Socialists, Laval refused to support World War I in August 1914, manifesting for the first time his rigid, antimilitarist pacifism. Laval never served in the war and lost his seat in the postwar conservative upsurge of 1919. Returning to his law career, he amassed a personal fortune and began shifting away from socialism.

Elected mayor of Aubervilliers in 1923, Laval built a strong public following as a hard-working pragmatist. His constant struggle with Aubervillier's powerful Communist Party gave rise to the second mainstay of Laval's political doctrine, fierce anticommunism. In his last run as a Socialist, Laval was elected to the Chamber in 1924.

Laval broke with the Socialists and in 1927 won a Senate seat as an independent. He served in various cabinets before becoming prime minister for the first time in January 1931. Laval dealt with the crisis sparked by U.S. president Herbert Hoover's call for a moratorium on German reparations for World War I, for which *Time* magazine designated him Man of the Year. By the time he fell in February 1932, Laval's three unwavering political beliefs—categorical pacifism, profound anticommunism, and an unshakable desire for rapprochement with Germany—had become entrenched. They drove his decisions to the end of his life.

Laval's appearance, personality, and style were all distinctive. His childhood left him with a driving ambition and a deep sense of being unloved. He was extremely hard-working, stubborn, and quick tempered. Laval always chafed at party discipline, preferring to deal with people one-on-one and negotiate his way through tough situations by bargaining and by wheeling and dealing his way to a solution. He attributed his reputation for being a horse trader to his Auvergnat origins. He saw himself as pragmatic. His stubbornness and sense of being unappreciated led him to dismiss outside advice and to develop a misplaced confidence in his diplomatic skills.

Laval again became prime minister on 7 June 1935. To deal with the Depression, Laval pursued a strictly deflationary fiscal policy. Prior to and during Laval's second ministry, he also served as foreign minister. Hoping to build an alliance, Laval made key colonial concessions to Italy that contributed to the Abyssinia crisis. After Italian forces invaded Ethiopia in October 1935, Laval and British foreign minister Samuel Hoare negotiated a secret plan to give Italy much of the territory it had conquered and permission to enlarge its colonial holdings in East Africa in exchange for ending the war. News of the secret plan leaked on 10 December 1935, resulting in public outrage over appeasement of Italian aggression. The scandal led to Laval's resignation on 22 January 1936.

Laval took this fall from power badly and began nurturing the illusion that he had a personal mission to preserve peace in this dangerous era and that he would someday be called on to fulfill it. Out of the limelight from January 1936 until war broke out in 1939, Laval returned to Châteldon, where he continued to amass wealth, building a media empire and ruminating on the idea that he alone knew what was right for France but that no one appreciated it. By the late 1930s, Laval's desire to reach an accord with Germany had become an obsession.

PEACE WITH GERMANY

By 1938 Laval led a right-wing, anticommunist, pacifist group of politicians who insisted on peace with Germany. He opposed the declaration of war in September 1939. During the Battle of France, which began 10 May 1940 and quickly became a military debacle, Laval worked to bring Philippe Pétain into the cabinet. On June 16, with German armies advancing across France, Prime Minister Pierre Reynaud stepped down and Pétain formed a cabinet. The next day, Pétain announced

that he would seek an armistice, which Laval strongly supported. Laval joined Pétain's cabinet on June 23. In spite of his years as a politician, Laval played a key role in the National Assembly's July 1940 decision to grant full powers to Pétain, destroy the Third Republic, and create an authoritarian government, simply called the French State, located in the spa town of Vichy. Pétain was chief of state, and on 12 July 1940 Laval became vice president of the Council of Ministers and Pétain's designated successor.

In 1940 Laval, sure of an imminent German victory against England, believed that France's empire and naval fleet gave it the leverage to bargain with Germany and calculated that to get concessions France had to offer solid proof of good will, even anticipating German demands. Collaboration thus was a choice Laval and other leaders at Vichy pursued. Laval met and developed a close working relationship with the German ambassador in Paris, Otto Abetz. Using that connection, Laval arranged the 22 through 24 October 1940 meeting in Montoire between Adolf Hitler and Pétain, which resulted in Pétain's announcement that France was ready to seek a policy of collaboration. Laval was abruptly fired on 13 December 1940 (only Abetz's intervention prevented Laval's arrest on 13 December), not because Pétain rejected Laval's pursuit of collaboration, which continued even without Laval, but because he hated Laval's secretive style.

Under the Armistice of June 1940 Germany directly occupied the northern two-thirds of France. It created a border, the demarcation line, between the occupied and the southern, or unoccupied, zone. This one-third of France, popularly called the *zone libre* or free zone, was not occupied by German troops after June 1940. The French state at Vichy (in the unoccupied zone) was the civil authority over all of France, but the German occupation authority had ultimate authority in the northern, occupied zone. However, in late 1942, with the Allied takeover of North Africa, German troops moved south and occupied all of France. Laval and others at Vichy considered the existence of "autonomous" unoccupied territory an important bargaining chip, but they did not resign when Germany occupied that zone.

Pierre Laval testifies at the trial of Marshall Henri Pétain (seated next to Laval), 21 August 1945. ©BETTMANN/CORBIS

On 27 August 1941, a student named Paul Collette tried to assassinate Laval as he reviewed French troops volunteering to serve with the German army in the Eastern campaign. Laval returned to power on 18 April 1942, never changing his assumptions in spite of the steady loss of all France's assets, its empire, its fleet, and its unoccupied territory. Laval met increasingly harsh German demands by continuing to anticipate them in hopes of gaining advantages. To avoid the imposition of forced labor, Laval negotiated an agreement in June 1942, called the Relève, whereby for every three skilled workers France sent to Germany, Germany would repatriate one French prisoner of war. In announcing the Relève to the public, Laval, sealing his doom, insisted, "I hope for a German victory." Otherwise, he said, bolshevism would spread across Europe. The Relève failed to satisfy

German labor demands and forced labor began in France in February 1943.

Shortly after Laval returned to power, Germany escalated its demands for the deportation of Jews from France, requiring fifty thousand Jews from the unoccupied zone. Laval's response provides another example of his style, its futility, and the way it implicated France in the worst aspects of the Nazi regime. Laval offered Germany stateless and foreign immigrant Jews in a vain attempt to spare French Jews. As a symbol of French sovereignty, Laval insisted that French police carry out raids to arrest Jews, something that aroused widespread public dismay. Although Germany had not asked for Jewish children, Laval insisted that Jewish children be deported with their parents because including them helped Laval fill his quotas.

FINAL DAYS

Still, Laval stayed on to the bitter end, insisting he would "make the French people happy in spite of themselves." In January 1943, he authorized the creation of the Milice française, an ultracollaborationist military force that waged war on the Resistance, communists, and Jews.

With the Allies advancing into France, the French government moved to Belfort in August 1944. In October the retreating German army ordered French authorities to leave, carting them to a castle in Sigmaringen, where they played out the last days of the war bickering over office space.

On 2 May 1945, Laval flew to Spain but on 31 July the Spanish dictator Francisco Franco turned him over to American forces in Austria, who extradited him to France on 1 August 1945. At his trial for treason, which lasted from 3 to 9 October 1945, members of the jury yelled insults at him. Convicted and sentenced to death, on the eve of his execution Laval attempted suicide with cyanide but his stomach was pumped and he was revived so that the execution could be carried out.

To the moment of his death, Laval expressed no remorse, only a sense that he had been unjustly accused by an ungrateful country that he had saved in spite of itself. His son-in-law, René de Chambrun, worked for years to rehabilitate his reputation. But in a 1980s poll taken in France, some 33 percent of those polled would have had him executed again.

See also **Collaboration; Fascism; France; Nazism; Pétain, Philippe; Reparations; Resistance; Socialism; World War II.**

BIBLIOGRAPHY

Cointet, Jean-Paul. *Pierre Laval*. Paris, 1993.

Kupferman, Fred. *1944–1945: le procès de Vichy: Pucheu, Pétain, Laval*. Brussels, 1980.

————. *Laval*. Paris, 1987.

Michel, Henri. *Pétain, Laval, Darlan, trois politiques?* Paris, 1972.

Paxton, Robert O. *Vichy France: Old Guard and New Order*. New York, 1982.

Warner, Geoffrey. *Pierre Laval and the Eclipse of France*. New York, 1969.

SARAH FISHMAN

LAWRENCE, D. H. (1885–1930), English writer.

David Herbert Lawrence was one of the greatest English writers of the first half of the twentieth century. Although preeminently a novelist, he was also an important and prolific poet, short story writer, travel writer, essayist, and even playwright. Lawrence is most commonly remembered for his frank depiction of sexual experience. This lent him notoriety during his lifetime and often embroiled him in censorship difficulties.

Lawrence's writings are characterized by spontaneity, vividness, and intensity of feeling. Like many other modernist writers, he sharply criticized industrial society while trying to imagine a new, more authentic basis for modern life. From World War I until his early death in 1930 he wrote out of a sense of cultural crisis. In his greatest, most innovative novels—*The Rainbow* and *Women in Love*—he aimed to reveal the elemental essences of his characters as well as their social selves. And, as he put it in an essay titled "Morality and the Novel," he believed that we moderns need to achieve "a pure relationship between ourselves and the living universe" in order to reenergize lives that have gone dead (*Study of Thomas Hardy and Other Essays*, 1985, p. 172).

LIFE

The son of a coal miner, Lawrence was born in 1885 in a mining village near Nottingham in the English Midlands. He attended Nottingham High School and later trained at Nottingham University College to become an elementary schoolteacher. In 1906 he began working on the book that would become *The White Peacock* (1911), his first novel. He taught elementary school in a south suburb of London from 1908 to 1911.

In the spring of 1912 he fell in love with Frieda von Richthofen Weekley, the wife of his language professor and a distant cousin of Manfred von Richthofen, the legendary German World War I flying ace known as the "Red Baron." Frieda left her three children when she and Lawrence traveled to Europe together. In 1913 Lawrence published his breakthrough novel, *Sons and Lovers*.

> Each thing, living or unliving, streams in its own odd, intertwining flux, and nothing, not even man nor the God of man, nor anything that man has thought or felt or known, is fixed or abiding. All moves. And nothing is true, or good, or right, except in its own living relatedness to its own circumambient universe; to the things that are in the stream with it. ("Art and Morality," 1925)

After two years in Italy, Lawrence and Frieda returned to England. They were married in July 1914, less than a month before the outbreak of World War I. Lawrence published *The Rainbow* in September 1915. The novel was prosecuted and banned for indecency in November 1915. No one in the literary establishment came to Lawrence's defense. The government viewed this outspoken critic of the war as subversive and refused to issue him and Frieda passports, thus barring them from leaving the country for the duration. Although Lawrence had completed *Women in Love* by 1917, no one would publish the book until 1920.

The Lawrences' second sojourn in Italy began in 1919. This marked the beginning of the self-exile that lasted until the end of Lawrence's life. Although he never again lived in England, he remained profoundly English, never assuming the cosmopolitanism of a writer like James Joyce (1882–1941). Lawrence's restless travels would take him and Frieda to Ceylon (now Sri Lanka) and Australia, and for two years in the first half of the 1920s they lived in Taos, New Mexico, and Oaxaca, Mexico. Their third stay in Italy lasted three years between 1925 and 1928. During this period he wrote *Lady Chatterley's Lover* (1928), his most controversial novel. The lung disease Lawrence suffered from most of his life was another reason he so often traveled in search of the sun.

D. H. Lawrence died of tuberculosis in Vence in southern France in 1930 at the age of forty-four. In recent years his literary reputation has declined, primarily because of feminist critiques of the sexual politics of some of his fiction. Lawrence, a passionate, provocative, sometimes disturbing writer, is not always politically correct. Nevertheless, he remains a major modern novelist, notable for his authenticity, his intensity, his range, and for his challenging assault on accepted ideas and modes of feeling.

WORKS

The semi-autobiographical *Sons and Lovers* is notable for its rich evocation of working-class life and its compelling depiction of the Oedipus complex. *The Rainbow*, Lawrence's boldly original family chronicle, traces three generations of the Brangwen family from 1840 to the turn of the twentieth century. The novel focuses primarily on the modern woman Ursula Brangwen's passionate quest for independence and self-fulfillment. *Women in Love* dramatizes Lawrence's turbulent vision of human relationship, in which love and elemental conflict are often difficult to distinguish. This masterpiece of literary modernism also offers a harsh critique of modern civilization.

In *Lady Chatterley's Lover* Lawrence confronts the "censor-morons" head-on, explicitly describing sexual intercourse and letting his gamekeeper-protagonist use four-letter words. The novel is also a tender fable of human renewal through touch and reciprocal love, but it presents no parallel vision of social regeneration. The court cases that legalized the publication of *Lady Chatterley's Lover* in the United States (1959) and the United Kingdom (1960) are landmarks in the history of freedom of expression. After the *Lady Chatterley's Lover* trials ruled that the novel was not obscene, no area of human experience and no language would be off-limits to American and English writers.

Lawrence's other greatest works include the stories of *The Prussian Officer* (1914) and *England, My England* (1922); the travel books *Sea and Sardinia* (1921) and *Etruscan Places* (1932); the novellas *The Fox* (1923), *The Captain's Doll* (1923), and *The Virgin and the Gipsy* (1930); the poems of *Birds, Beasts, and Flowers* (1923); and *Studies in Classic American Literature* (1923). The novella *St. Mawr* (1925) and the novel *The Plumed Serpent* (1926) grew out of Lawrence's experiences in the American Southwest and Mexico.

See also **Joyce, James; Modernism.**

BIBLIOGRAPHY

Daleski, H. M. *The Forked Flame: A Study of D. H. Lawrence.* Evanston, Ill., 1965.

Poplawski, Paul. *D. H. Lawrence: A Reference Companion.* Westport, Conn., 1996.

Siegel, Carol. *Lawrence among the Women: Wavering Boundaries in Women's Literary Traditions.* Charlottesville, Va., 1991.

Squires, Michael, and Lynn K. Talbot. *Living at the Edge: A Biography of D. H. Lawrence and Frieda von Richthofen.* Madison, Wis., 2002.

Squires, Michael, and Keith Cushman, eds. *The Challenge of D. H. Lawrence.* Madison, Wis., 1990.

KEITH CUSHMAN

LAWRENCE, T. E. (1888–1935), British soldier, archaeologist, and writer.

Thomas Edward (T. E.) Lawrence, known to posterity as Lawrence of Arabia, was the leader of the Arab revolt of 1916–1918 against the Ottoman Empire in World War I. Born in 1888, he learned as a teenager that he was illegitimate, as indeed was his mother. Having "no name" in the Victorian sense of the term, he would feel free to shed one name and choose another later in his life. He followed a brilliant Oxford degree with work on a British Museum excavation in Iraq. In 1914 he joined the British army and was posted to the Military Intelligence Department in Cairo. In November 1917 Lawrence was the British liaison officer between British forces in Egypt and Palestine and Arab tribes in revolt against Turkey. He was arrested while in disguise, scouting out the defenses of the Syrian town of Deraa. He was then severely beaten and raped. He carried on after being released and helped shape a partisan war that contributed to the defeat of the Turkish army. Lawrence became a legend.

After the Armistice (11 November 1918), Lawrence was demobilized but continued to work with his Arab allies and friends. He accompanied King Faisal of Saudi Arabia to France to take part in the Paris Peace Conference of 1919. From the beginning it was apparent that allies in war were now to be reordered as dominant and subordinate peoples. Lawrence had assured his Arab friends that Britain would live up to its word and give the Arabs their freedom. Nothing of the kind happened. He worked in 1921 and 1922 as advisor on Arab affairs to Winston Churchill, then colonial secretary, and tried to make up for the promises broken, the faith not kept. In these years he helped shape the future of modern Iraq.

After this highly public career Lawrence spent the rest of his life escaping from his celebrity status and his memories. In 1922 he took a new name and built a new life in the Royal Air Force (RAF) as Airman First Class John Hume Ross. It did not take long for the press to find out who he was, and Lawrence was discharged. The search for anonymity was far from over. This time he enlisted in the Tank Corps as a private soldier, under the name T. E. Shaw, found at random in the *Army List*. He was an aficionado of danger and sought it out in many ways. One was on his motorbike. He confided to a friend:

> When my mood gets too hot and I find myself wandering beyond control I pull out my motorbike and hurl it at top-speed through these unfit roads for hour after hour. My nerves are jaded and gone near dead, so that nothing less than hours of voluntary danger will prick them into life. (Wilson, p. 71)

This was written by the author of *The Seven Pillars of Wisdom*, the classic account of the revolt in the desert during World War I. The book was written during 1920–1922, then revised and published in 1926. It became a bestseller in America and in Britain.

The greater the celebrity status, the greater the wish to evade it, to fade into the background. "I know the reverse of that medal," he wrote, "and hate its false face so utterly that I struggle like a trapped rabbit to be it no longer," or at least to "shun pleasures," a partial "alleviation of the necessary penalty of living on" (Wilson, p. 714). After the Tank Corps came literary work, followed by reentry into the Royal Air Force. This time he tested speedboats and found some modicum of quiet in the service. He even went so far as to change his name by deed poll to Shaw. After twelve years in the RAF in Britain and India, hounded by the press to the end, he tried to find solace in Devon, in a country house built to his specifications. But journalists still dogged his steps and stripped him of the tranquility he so desperately

T. E. Lawrence, photographed in 1916. ©BETTMANN/CORBIS

sought. On 11 May 1935 he got on his motorbike to send a telegram to another World War I veteran and writer, Henry Williamson. He never sent it: he swerved off the road to avoid hitting two cyclists on a country road. They were uninjured. He crashed, suffered brain damage, went into a coma, and died on 19 May 1935, at age forty-six.

Lawrence was a writer and linguist of genius, a man who embodied the British fascination with Arabia. As such, he came to represent those whose dedication and decency were betrayed by the logic of imperialism in the period of World War I.

See also **Palestine; Turkey.**

BIBLIOGRAPHY

Aldington, Richard. *Lawrence of Arabia: A Biographical Enquiry.* London, 1957.

Graves, Richard Perceval. *Lawrence of Arabia and His World.* New York, 1976.

Liddell Hart, Basil H. *Colonel Lawrence: The Man behind the Legend.* New York, 1934.

Storrs, Ronald. *Lawrence of Arabia: Zionism and Palestine.* New York, 1940.

Wilson, Jeremy. *Lawrence of Arabia: The Authorized Biography of T. E. Lawrence.* London, 1989.

JAY WINTER

LEAGUE OF NATIONS. The League of Nations was established as part of the peace settlement of 1919, with the express aim of ensuring that no conflict on the scale of World War I would ever occur again. The United States president, Woodrow Wilson (1856–1924), took the lead in pressing for the immediate formation of a worldwide organization of states during the opening phase of the Paris Peace Conference. He insisted that the constitution of the new body—to be called the Covenant—should constitute the first twenty-six articles of each of the peace treaties concluded in 1919–1920. Ironically, Wilson's attempt to secure United States membership in the League by incorporating its constitution into the Treaty of Versailles failed when in November 1919 and again in March 1920, the United States Senate failed to ratify the treaty. Thus the United States never became a member of the League of Nations.

The major aims of the League were to prevent the outbreak of a major war, and to contain and resolve, by peaceful means as far as possible, any disputes that did break out between nations. In an attempt to maximize its effectiveness, the League was given a wide range of functions, all of which, separately or in combination, could provide "avenues of escape" from war. Thus the League was equipped to play many different roles: to act as a permanent interstate conference; as a disarmament agency; as the guarantor of the frontiers of its member states; as an agency for arbitration, conciliation, and the orderly settlement of disputes; as a body that could promote peaceful change and oversee mandates and minority provisions; and as an agency that could resolve wide-ranging international social and economic issues. It was also to oversee the International Labour Organization and other international bureaus. Geneva was chosen to be the headquarters for the new League.

The League of Nations came into existence in January 1920 and worked through two main decision-making bodies: an assembly that included

1628

delegates from all member states and met annually and the League Council, which comprised the major League powers and four representatives of smaller states, and met regularly during the year. There were four major powers who became founding members in 1920: Britain, France, Italy, and Japan. Germany and other former enemy powers were not invited to join the League in 1920 because the peacemakers at Paris agreed that they should have to demonstrate their fitness for inclusion by showing that they were carrying out the terms of the peace treaties. Nor was Bolshevik Russia—perceived as a hostile regime that aimed to undermine the peace settlement—regarded as an acceptable member. There were forty-three founding members of the League; sixteen from Europe; seventeen from Central and South America; five Dominions of the British Empire; China, Japan, and Siam from Asia; Persia (Iran); and Liberia. The League Assembly in 1920 voted for the inclusion of six more states, five from Europe and one from Central America.

FAILURES AND SUCCESSES

Any assessment of the League's effectiveness between 1920 and 1939 must take account of its many and complex functions. While it clearly failed to perform well in its most high profile roles, and failed abysmally to prevent the outbreak of World War II, it also recorded some modest successes and left an enduring legacy. As a permanent interstate conference that aimed to include all the peace-loving states of the world, it has already been noted that the League was severely weakened by the failure of the United States to join. Until the mid 1920s, the League Council contained as many minor powers as it did major ones, but in 1926 Germany joined the League and stayed until 1933. In that year, both Germany and Japan gave notice that they intended to leave the League, but in 1934 the USSR became a member, only for Italy to withdraw three years later.

Thus the League never contained all the world's major powers and it therefore failed in one of its major objectives. However, the members it did have met regularly, and the friendships forged among the delegates helped to oil the wheels of international diplomacy, especially between 1925 and 1933. More important, an influential

international secretariat was built up at Geneva of experts and civil servants from across the world, which administered League machinery and advised its member states. The wide-ranging expertise and specialist networks that developed at Geneva in the 1920s and 1930s exerted an influence on international affairs well beyond World War II.

As a disarmament agency, the League failed completely to persuade the great majority of its members to disarm to any great extent. It was the failure to achieve any lasting international arms limitation agreements that led people at the time and subsequently to dismiss the League as a totally ineffective body. However, in this role the League faced a number of severe obstacles that made success virtually unachievable from the start. In the face of a Germany that had been defeated but that was still territorially intact, and a hostile Bolshevik regime in Russia, mainland European powers demanded additional security from the League before they were prepared to reduce their armaments. With the United States out of the League, naval disarmament talks took place away from Geneva. Though representatives from both the United States and the USSR worked with League powers at Geneva from 1926 to draw up a disarmament convention, discussions were bedeviled by political and technical disagreements. The League Disarmament Conference that met in 1932 finally broke up in disarray after Adolf Hitler (1889–1945) led the German delegation out in October 1933.

League efforts to guarantee the political independence and territorial integrity of member states were also doomed to failure in the unstable aftermath of World War I. It proved impossible to preserve the postwar European and global territorial status quo, not least because leading League powers such as Japan and Italy had unsatisfied territorial ambitions that they were determined to pursue. And because neither Germany nor the USSR accepted the 1919 peace settlement as more than provisional, there was no way that the League would be able to prevent substantial territorial changes from occurring at some future point. The only issue was whether the changes would take place peacefully or through military challenge.

The League did have some success in resolving minor territorial disputes. A potential conflict over the Aland Islands between Sweden and Finland was peacefully settled in 1920, and the League also supervised the division of Upper Silesia between Poland and Germany in 1921. A dispute between Bulgaria and Greece was brought to an early end by firm League action in 1925. However, the seizure of Corfu by Italy in 1923 as retaliation for the murder of an Italian official, allegedly by Greek bandits, proved more difficult to resolve. Corfu was handed back to Greece, but only after the Italian dictator Benito Mussolini (1883–1945) had tried hard to cause divisions between League powers and to deny that the League should have any jurisdiction over the dispute. The Greeks had to pay Italy a large indemnity, and the crisis revealed how limited the League's power was in the face of strong divisions between its leading members.

The two major conflicts that fatally challenged the League's credibility and authority and as a peacekeeping agency were the Manchurian dispute between Japan and China in 1931–1933 and the invasion and occupation of Ethiopia—a League member since 1923—by Italian troops in 1935. The League failed to prevent Japan from establishing the Manchurian province in north China as a Japanese-controlled puppet state or to force Italy out of Ethiopia. Indeed, the effect of halfhearted League action to try to restrain Japan and then Italy helped to drive both powers into an alignment with Nazi Germany. And as substantial German rearmament got under way after 1933, east European League members came under threat. Austria was annexed to Germany in March 1938, and six months later the Sudeten part of Czechoslovakia was ceded to Hitler. In March 1939 German troops invaded and occupied the rest of Czechoslovakia. The League proved powerless to protect its members in the face of a resurgent German state, and in September 1939 World War II broke out when German troops invaded Poland. A last—and futile—League gesture in 1940 was to expel the USSR when it invaded Finland, the only time in its history that such action was taken.

As an administrative body, the League proved to be useful in supervising treaty agreements. It kept reasonable order in the Saar until 1935, and in Danzig, and it received annual reports from mandatory powers in respect of the mandates over German and Turkish colonies that had been established in the early 1920s. It also had responsibility for overseeing minority agreements entered into by a number of new central and east European states as part of the peace settlement, and it worked hard to try to resolve a range of potentially explosive ethnic tensions, though it lacked any means of enforcing its recommendations. And as Germany was not covered by any minority agreements, the League was unable to protect Jews from persecution after 1933.

The League also undertook a wide range of humanitarian activities such as assisting refugees, trying to prevent white slave trafficking and drug smuggling, and combating tropical diseases and the spread of infection. The International Labour Office was active in promoting labor agreements between employers and workers and improving working conditions. There was general agreement among member states that the League's social and economic activities had proved to be very effective, and in the late 1930s a League report called for an expansion of activities in these areas. While the League had failed in its major aims, its "nonpolitical" work was very successful and was continued and expanded upon by the United Nations.

LEGACY

Thus, the League did have some important successes, not least in providing the foundations for the United Nations after World War II. It is interesting that the United Nations has faced similar problems to the League, in particular the concern of member states to protect their own national interests and the difficulty of achieving any common agreement to pursue collective goals on a sustained basis. But globalization has resulted in increasing numbers of international bodies, and all of them have learned from the League's failures and are building on its foundations.

See also **Red Cross; United Nations; Versailles, Treaty of.**

BIBLIOGRAPHY

Bendiner, Elmer. *A Time for Angels: The Tragicomic History of the League of Nations.* New York, 1975.

Henig, Ruth, ed. *The League of Nations.* Edinburgh, 1973.

Northedge, F. S. *The League of Nations: Its Life and Times.* Leicester, U.K., 1986.

Scott, George. *The Rise and Fall of the League of Nations.* London, 1973.

Steiner, Zara. *The Lights That Failed: European International History 1919–1933.* Oxford, U.K., and New York, 2005.

Walters, Frank. *A History of the League of Nations.* London, 1952.

RUTH HENIG

LE CORBUSIER (1887–1965), Swiss-French architect, influential worldwide for both creating and subverting the ideas and forms of modernism.

Charles-Édouard Jeanneret-Gris, who adopted the pseudonym Le Corbusier in the 1920s, was born and brought up in La Chaux-de-Fonds, Switzerland, and attended the local arts school, where it was intended he learn the trade of his father, a watch engraver. Here he came under the strong influence of Charles L'Eplattenier, a passionate advocate of regionalist Arts and Crafts design. It was L'Eplattenier who encouraged Jeanneret to interest himself in architecture, and as early as 1905–1907 he designed his first house, for a jeweler, Louis Fallet, in an Arts and Crafts style. Jeanneret was to design five other houses in and around La Chaux-de-Fonds as well as a cinema and a number of unexecuted projects before he finally moved to Paris in 1917. In the ten years before his move Jeanneret spent much of his time traveling.

While in Paris in 1908–1909 Jeanneret worked in the office of Auguste Perret, where he acquired a fascination for reinforced concrete; the plan of his Schwob House in La Chaux-de-Fonds (1916–1917) was based on one of Perret's designs. In April 1910 Jeanneret left for a journey that would take him to Germany and eventually Athens and Italy. A highlight of this trip was his visit to the Acropolis, which Jeanneret considered to be a perfect building. Even more influential, however, was his second visit to the Carthusian monastery at Ema, near Florence, which not only convinced him finally to become an architect but provided the model for most of his housing projects.

In 1915, with the help of the engineer and entrepreneur Max Du Bois, Jeanneret submitted a patent for a housing prototype ("Domino"). Although impractical as a means of delivering cheap housing, this project contained in embryo many of the underlying ideas of modernism: use of reinforced concrete, separation of structure from enclosure, and the use of thin, round pilotis supporting thin floor slabs without visible horizontal beams. When Jeanneret moved to Paris in 1917 he embarked on a disastrous business career but was fortunate enough to meet Amédée Ozenfant and with him began the art movement called purism, exhibiting with him in 1918 and starting the art journal *L'esprit nouveau* (1920–1925). Purism was an offshoot of cubism, with a stress on geometry and the representation of heavily simplified objects of everyday use. For this journal Jeanneret wrote a series of articles under the pseudonym "Le Corbusier-Saugnier" (and later, "Le Corbusier") which were subsequently published as books. The most famous of these, *Vers une architecture* (1923; published in English as *Towards a New Architecture,* 1927), became one of the century's best-selling books on architecture. The basic idea was that architects should respond to the spirit of the age—a spirit redolent of industrialization and new forms of transportation—and rethink architectural form from scratch on the basis of rationalism and the search for harmonious forms based on geometrical relationships. In all his written work, however, Le Corbusier makes clear that he was opposed to functionalism and aspired to achieve the highest architectural qualities measured by those of the architecture of the past. Le Corbusier went on to write more than a hundred books and an endless stream of articles and lectures, which very effectively transmitted his ideas and buildings across the world. Le Corbusier continued to paint all his life, usually in the mornings.

Le Corbusier's architectural career in Paris picked up pace when he took on his younger cousin Pierre Jeanneret as a partner in 1922. Pierre worked closely with him until 1937, and again in India after the war, taking complete responsibility for running the office, carrying out the detailed design, and supervising construction. In a series of well-publicized buildings in the 1920s, the partners established their reputation as among the foremost modernist architects in Europe, publishing a first volume of their *Oeuvre complète* (Complete works)

La Cité radieuse, Marseille, France. Giraudon/Art Resource

in 1929. Unlike many of his modernist contemporaries, Le Corbusier very rarely benefited from state or municipal commissions. His main output in the 1920s was private houses for wealthy clients, studios for fellow artists and craftsmen, and a number of models and designs for public exhibition.

In 1927 Le Corbusier's profile was raised further on the international stage by his competition entry for the League of Nations building in Geneva, which was placed among nine equal first prizes. The scandal that blew up around the eventual allocation of the project to an eighty-year-old French beaux-arts architect, assisted by a number of the other prizewinning architects, helped mold modernists in different countries together into a group, leading to the formation of the CIAM (International Congresses on Modern Architecture) in 1928. This episode also helped Le Corbusier and Jeanneret obtain a number of prestigious commissions, including a ministry in Moscow (1928), the Salvation Army headquarters in Paris (1929), and the Swiss student hostel in the Cité Universitaire in Paris, completed in 1933. In 1930 he married and took French citizenship.

Around 1928 Le Corbusier had abandoned the purist style of painting for a richer idiom dominated by the forms of women, natural materials, and warm colors. In his architecture too he rediscovered natural materials and textures, stimulated by vernacular architecture. His villa for Hélène de Mandrot near Toulon marks a turning point in his work, as does the penthouse apartment he designed for himself in Paris in 1930. Here, reinforced concrete forms are juxtaposed with textured stone surfaces. During the 1930s Le Corbusier received very few commissions—he had the bailiffs in the office in 1935—as he concentrated on more and more ambitious urban projects in Algiers, Paris, and other cities. His book *La ville radieuse* (1935; *The Radiant City*) offers a rich and complex insight into his thinking. His political position, never very stable, veered in the 1930s between the left wing and sympathy for charismatic neofascist French nationalists, and Pierre Jeanneret, who was consistently on the left, began to practice separately after 1937.

After the French defeat in 1940, Le Corbusier joined a number of French architects (including Auguste Perret) in the collaborationist regime at Vichy, hoping to be asked to plan for the reconstruction of France. Finding that most of his enemies held the reins of power, he became disillusioned and eventually moved permanently back to Paris, where, in 1943, he founded a research group, ASCORAL (Association of Builders for an Architectural Renovation). When peace came, Le Corbusier's plans for rebuilding devastated cities were once again rejected, but he was given a special commission to build an eighteen-story "unit" of housing in Marseille (1945–1952) consisting of 337 maisonettes, two schools, a hotel, and a shopping street. He later built three more of these in other French cities and one in Berlin. The building made an impact for the sculptural treatment of the roof structures and for the rough concrete (*beton brut*), which led to the style known as "brutalism."

In the twenty years after the war Le Corbusier had an Indian summer in which building after building surprised and sometimes shocked his modernist contemporaries. Two important religious commissions, the pilgrimage chapel at Ronchamp (1950–1955) and the Dominican monastery of La Tourette (1956–1959) revealed Le Corbusier's astonishing formal and symbolic richness, and these qualities were also very much in evidence in the buildings he designed at Chandigarh, capital of the state of Punjab in India (begun in 1951). The Jaoul houses in Paris (1951–1955) and two houses in Ahmedabad (Villa Sarabhai, 1951–1956, and Villa Shodan, 1951–1956) also marked a complete break from the pristine but cold forms of the 1920s. The Carpenter Center for the Visual Arts in Cambridge, Massachusetts (1961–1964), offered Le Corbusier a unique opportunity to demonstrate his late style in America.

Le Corbusier was both a brilliant polemicist and a thoughtful and self-questioning artist, never satisfied with the solutions promoted by himself or others. He will be remembered as much as a humanist who stood against functionalism and social determinism as a purveyor of sometimes dogmatic and oversimplistic urban and architectural solutions.

See also **Architecture; Modernism.**

BIBLIOGRAPHY

Primary Sources

Le Corbusier. *Towards a New Architecture.* Translated by Frederick Etchells. New York, 1927.

Secondary Sources

Benton, Tim. *The Villas of Le Corbusier, 1920–1930.* New Haven, Conn., 1987.

Benton, Tim, et al. *Le Corbusier, Architect of the Century: A Centenary Exhibition Organized by the Arts Council of Great Britain.* London, 1987.

Brooks, H. Allen. *Le Corbusier's Formative Years: Charles-Edouard Jeanneret at La Chaux-de-Fonds.* Chicago, 1997.

Curtis, William J. R. *Le Corbusier: Ideas and Forms.* London, 1986.

Moos, Stanislaus von. *Le Corbusier: Elements of a Synthesis.* Cambridge, Mass., 1979.

Moos, Stanislaus von, and Arthur Ruegg, eds. *Le Corbusier before Le Corbusier: Applied Arts, Architecture, Painting, Photography, 1907–1922.* New Haven, Conn., 2002.

TIM BENTON

LÉGER, FERNAND (1881–1955), French painter.

Born in Argentan, Normandy, on 4 February 1881, Fernand Léger began painting at the age of twenty-five after starting out studying architecture. His first pictorial endeavors echoed the various phases of cubism. His palette was dull, while his entangled cones, cylinders, and cubes recalled the geometrism of Paul Cézanne (1839–1906) or the "Orphism" of Robert Delaunay (1885–1941). Léger described himself as a "tubist," and he followed his own path amid all the new experimentation then under way. Between 1912 and 1914, he painted a series of nonfigurative pictures known as *Contrast of Forms.* Short as it was, this period allowed him to articulate an aesthetic approach that he outlined in the review *Montjoie!* (June 1913). The canvas, he suggested, should be organized around a set of contrasts: contrasts between colors themselves (red/green), contrasts between primary colors on the one hand and black and white on the other, and contrasts between lines and forms. Together, these should set in motion a dynamic susceptible of evoking the modern world and its machines. This dynamic interplay of tubular forms was oriented directly toward the spectator, who was meant to perceive only the reality of the picture itself in its materiality. Thus both arrangement and combination were necessary. In *La partie de cartes* (1917; Soldiers playing at cards), human figures, now also contrasted, were transformed into a set of geometrical forms intermingled with the forms in the background.

During the First World War, Léger was mobilized, as were most of the cubist painters, first to the Argonne forest (1914–1917) and then as a stretcher bearer at Verdun for three months in 1917.) In letters Léger told his friend and future first wife, Jeanne Lohy (1895–1950) of the horrors of war. Many drawings he made in the trenches, on the pages of notebooks or the lids of boxes, served as studies for his oils on canvas and serve as a testimony, in a dull palette, of the activity of anonymous soldiers at the front, "his new comrades," such as *Le soldat à la pipe* (Soldier with a pipe) in 1916.

At the end of World War I, Léger delved into industrial reality. His practice centered on his *Disks* series, his *Éléments mécaniques,* or his *La ville* (City)—works that celebrate modern mechanics and the industrial object by filling the canvas with brightly colored stairs, façades, chimneys, robots, or mannequins. Human figures, reintroduced into urban settings or interiors, themselves operated as mechanical elements on a formal par with the machines. "It was not simply that I treated the human figure as an object, but that since I found machines to be so plastic I wanted the human figure to have that same plasticity" (quoted in Mathey, p. 31; translated from the French). In *Le mécanicien* (1920; The mechanic), a visionary worker in profile view stood for the beauty of a machine. Connecting rods, cogwheels, or gears

constituted sign-systems of elements transported from reality to the painting.

In 1920 Léger began working with the architect Le Corbusier (Charles-Édouard Jeanneret; 1887–1965), publishing articles in the purist review *L'esprit nouveau* (The new spirit). The machine, the basis of Léger's iconography, was simultaneously addressed in architectural terms by the theories of Le Corbusier. In Léger's easel paintings, as for example *La lecture* (1924; Reading), the background, which has its own spatiality, coexists with plastic-volumetric forms, squarely facing the viewer, that symbolize modern monumentality. Léger's interest in plasticity extended to the cinema. In the film *Le ballet mécanique* (1924), codirected with Dudley Murphy and accompanied (at least as intended) by George Antheil's "musical synchronism," the juxtaposition of diverse objects (hat, shoes, geometrical forms) is rhythmically associated with close-ups of machines in action. In the industrial society of the late 1920s machines were producing a multitude of manufactured objects, and Léger's purpose in his canvases or drawings was to transpose and study them (*The Siphon*; *Nature morte à la chope* [Still life with beer mug]). As early as 1926, he began to take inspiration from the graphic practices of advertising in contemporary life, experimenting with large surfaces reminiscent of the gigantic billboards of the time. "The modern street with its colorful elements, its lettering, has very often served me (for me, it is raw material)" (Léger, 1965, p. 26).

In 1931 Léger made his first visit to the United States, where his reputation as a modern painter had been established since the exhibition of works of his in the Armory Show in New York and Chicago in 1913. During a second stay (1935–1936), he realized that the Works Progress Administration (WPA), for which architects were being commissioned to design public housing and painters to decorate public buildings, was having a dynamic impact on artists, and that the murals of New Deal America embodied a vision at once social and artistic that resembled his own. The policies of Franklin Delano Roosevelt (1882–1945) corresponded to Léger's belief that art should have a social function and the artist a clear task, namely to intervene everywhere in the life of the city.

Leisure: Homage to Jacques-Louis David. Painting by Fernand Léger, 1949. CNAC/MNAM/Dist. Réunion des Musées Nationaux/Art Resource, NY

Léger was in the United States again in 1938–1939 and stayed there from 1940 to 1945. In the summer of 1941 he taught at Mills College in Oakland, California. His iconography changed at this time, as he introduced the idea of a "new realism" and incorporated typically American elements into the structure of his work. His American and New York landscape paintings treated colors, geometrical forms, and human figures in space with much greater freedom. His series of "Cyclists" and "Divers" suggested motion by means of elements at once static and dynamic. His women, now emphatically modern, wore shorts instead of skirts. Narrative returned, and henceforth Léger even referred to history painting (*Les loisirs—Hommage*

à Louis David, 1948–1949) as a symbol of modernity that exalted reality in its banality and functionalism. Finally, in the context of the 1950s, a work such as *Les constructeurs/Construction Workers* imposed the idea of a form of painting perpetually under construction and governed, still, by the concept of contrasts: "If I was able to get very close to realist representation here, it was because the violent contrast between my worker figures and the metal architecture into which they are inserted is AT A MAXIMUM.... Our modern life is made up of everyday contrasts" (quoted in Centre Georges Pompidou, p. 248). A prime commentator on his own work and on the machinist aesthetic, Léger contributed vigorously to the dissemination and clear explanation of his theoretical positions. He died in 1955 at Gif-sur-Yvette.

See also **Architecture; Cubism; Painting, Avant-Garde; Picasso, Pablo.**

BIBLIOGRAPHY

Primary Sources

Léger, Fernand. *Functions of Painting.* Preface by G. L. K. Morris, edited by E.-F. Fry, translated by A. Anderson. New York, 1965.

———. *Fernand Léger: Correspondances.* 3 vols. Paris, 1993–1996.

Secondary Sources

Centre Georges Pompidou. *Fernand Léger.* Paris, 1997.

Garaudy, Roger. *Pour un réalisme du XXe siècle: Dialogue posthume avec Fernand Léger.* Paris, 1968.

Kosinski, Dorothy, ed. *Fernand Léger, 1911–1924: The Rhythm of Modern Life.* Munich and New York, 1994.

Mathy, François. *Fernand Léger.* Paris, 1956.

CAROLINE TRON-CARROZ

LEIPZIG TRIALS. After World War I, the victorious Allies brought criminal proceedings for war crimes against a number of Germans. Allied bitterness over Germany's conduct of the war precluded the kind of amnesty typical of peace accords prior to 1919. But the trials, which began in Leipzig in 1921, failed to deliver either punishment or peace.

In Article 231 of the Treaty of Versailles, known as the War Guilt Clause, the victors of World War I (1914–1918) declared that Germany was solely responsible for the conflict: "The Allied and Associated Governments affirm and Germany accepts the responsibility of Germany and her allies for causing all the loss and damage to which the Allied and Associated Governments and their nationals have been subjected as a consequence of the war imposed upon them by the aggression of Germany and her allies." Total war, it was felt, called for total responsibility, and this must include punishment in the name of justice, democracy, and morality.

The treaty thus ordered "penalties" for and "reparations" from the main defeated party, Germany, starting with the German emperor, who had abdicated and taken refuge in the Netherlands: "The Allied and Associated Powers publicly arraign William II of Hohenzollern, formerly German Emperor, for a supreme offence against international morality and the sanctity of treaties. A special tribunal will be constituted to try the accused, thereby assuring him the guarantees essential to the right of defense.... In its decision the tribunal will be guided by the highest motives of international policy, with a view to vindicating the solemn obligations of international undertakings and the validity of international morality. It will be its duty to fix the punishment which it considers should be imposed" (Article 227). "The German Government recognizes the right of the Allied and Associated Powers to bring before military tribunals persons accused of having committed acts in violation of the laws and customs of war. Such persons shall, if found guilty, be sentenced to punishments laid down by law" (Article 28). "Persons guilty of criminal acts against the nationals of one of the Allied and Associated Powers will be brought before the military tribunals of that Power" (Article 229).

The treaty sought to supply a legal basis for Germany's responsibility, notably with respect to the violation of Belgian neutrality, and so justify the demand for full reparations for all damage inflicted. But the Germans were not mistaken in discerning moral condemnation in the treaty, hence their hatred of the articles quoted here in particular and of the Treaty of Versailles in general.

Of the four Allied leaders, it was British Prime Minister David Lloyd George who, unlike U.S. president Woodrow Wilson, pressed for these judgments; Georges Clemenceau of France and Vittorio Orlando of Italy went along, despite the difficulty of achieving consensus on an international law that did not in fact exist. As for the requested extradition of William II, the Dutch had no judicial basis for acceding to it. This caused many problems, summed up by a contemporary Frenchman as follows: "I see no need to turn the ex-Emperor into a martyr....I see any action that might tend to remove him from his present wretched and despised condition as nothing but a cause of difficulty." The Netherlands refused to extradite, and William II eventually died there in 1941, at a time when the country was once again occupied by Germany.

Dealing with other "war criminals" was far more difficult. Who was to be placed on the list? How could Germany be persuaded to arrest and try them? Even the Allies became concerned, fearing that the immense public hostility to such measures might overwhelm the young Weimar Republic if it complied with their most drastic requirements.

Nevertheless, by February 1920 lists had been drawn up naming 888 accused individuals. These included princes, officers charged with battlefield or prison camp atrocities, and submarine commanders who were held responsible for attacks on civilian and hospital ships. Fritz Haber, winner of the 1919 Nobel Prize in Chemistry, was among those indicted for his part in developing poison gas, as were former chancellor Theobald von Bethmann-Hollweg and the popular Marshal Paul von Hindenburg. Eventually this roster was winnowed down to forty-five individuals, who were to be tried by the German high court in Leipzig.

Proceedings began on 23 May 1921 and rapidly turned into a farce. The accused were treated like heroes by the German public, and all but seven were acquitted; these seven received light sentences, which were never served. The trial did much to boost nationalist and revanchist sentiments in Germany, further weakening an already fragile Weimar democracy, which was trapped between Allied demands and a public that damned the government for accepting Versailles's humiliating conditions, among which was the trial itself. The idea of German guilt, so dear to the Allies, was widely derided within Germany.

All the same, it was at the Leipzig trials that wartime acts were subjected to postwar legal judgment for the first time in history. For the first time the questions were raised: what was a war crime and how does it differ from other crimes? Thereafter, the idea that war crimes should not go unpunished took on increasing importance. It figured in the thinking of the United States in 1941, when it intervened in World War II, and it led to the war crimes trials at Nuremberg and Tokyo after 1945. What these proceedings also had in common with the Leipzig trials was that only the defeated were accused of war crimes.

See also **Haber, Fritz; Hindenburg, Paul von; Nuremberg War Crimes Trials; Versailles, Treaty of; World War I; World War II.**

BIBLIOGRAPHY

Becker, Jean-Jacques. "Les procès de Leipzig." In *Les procès de Nuremberg et de Tokyo*, edited by Annette Wieviorka. Brussels, 1996.

Hankel, Gerd. *Die Leipziger Prozesse: Deutsche Kriegsverbrechen und ihre strafrechtliche Verfolgung nach dem Ersten Weltkrieg.* Hamburg, Germany, 2003.

Schabas, William. *An Introduction to the International Criminal Court.* New York, 2004.

ANNETTE BECKER

LEISURE

LEISURE. Time free from work and other life- or family-sustaining activities changed dramatically across the twentieth century. Although regional and social distinctions, established long before this epoch, continued to shape leisure activities, a series of political, technological, and economic changes both expanded and transformed the use of leisure time.

VARIETIES OF LEISURE IN 1900 AND DEMANDS FOR CHANGE

Free time varied by class and occupation in 1900. While seasonal religious festivals had declined in the eighteenth and nineteenth centuries in rural areas, especially in southern Europe, leisure time depended on the weather, hours of daylight, and lulls in the agricultural work cycle and the saints' days that often coincided with such lulls. In areas in which industrial and modern commercial conditions predominated, leisure was fixed by the factory and shop hours (mostly set at ten hours per six-day week). In skilled, textile, and white-collar trades in Britain and more rarely on the Continent, a Saturday half-day prevailed, making possible an afternoon for club activities, shopping, and the development of the Saturday tradition of spectator sports (especially football, that is, soccer). Few hours free from work and, as important, slow and inadequate public transportation, limited leisure activities among wage earners. Drinking, games, and conversation at neighborhood bars dominated male leisure time, though in larger cities cheap

Skiers relax in St. Moritz, Switzerland, c. 1934. ©LUCIEN AIGNER/CORBIS

theater was available. Despite efforts of reformers (including trade unionists, socialists, and Catholics) to promote alternative leisure pursuits such as gardening and family outings, especially on Sunday, drink was often a refuge from the family hearth.

In 1900 few wage earners had the opportunity for annual vacations. While some trades (especially northern English textile and related workers) had established holiday savings clubs to facilitate treks to seaside resorts such as Blackpool during annual one-week factory shutdowns, this was rare even in Britain. Most seasonal factory or shop closures were simply times of unemployment or of seeking alternative work—for example, in harvesting or food processing. Professionals, business owners, and a few privileged white-collar workers had paid annual leaves. This assured that seaside resorts and holiday touring was predominantly bourgeois. By 1900, travel agencies such as Thomas Cook of England booked holiday packages for the English middle class to Switzerland, France, and northern Italy especially. Resorts for gambling and genteel

pursuits had long developed on the French and Italian Riviera and at San Sebastián on the Basque coast of Spain. Major cities were centers of middle-class shopping and entertainment (sometimes combined as when bourgeois women visited Paris to get measured for clothing and went to the theater while waiting for delivery).

Demand for increased leisure time had been central to European labor movements even before the Second (Socialist) International called for the eight-hour workday in 1889. This goal was supposed to stabilize employment (diminishing seasonal irregularities in work and forcing businesses to increase their staff to compensate for reduced work hours), but it also was intended to establish a human right to time free from labor. Leisure in this sense was the same as liberty. Labor and progressive politicians across Europe insisted not only that increased productivity made increased leisure time an economic possibility, but also that more free time compensated for the increased pace of modern industrial and commercial work. In the decade before World War I, shop clerks agitated in Britain and France for laws against Sunday commerce. Reformers also argued that Saturday afternoons free from wage work would provide fathers the opportunity to spend time with their children and that paid vacations would restore the spiritual unity of the family that had been undermined by the modern economy's division of the family unit during work (a view embraced also by the Right). Early in the twentieth century, organized workers resisted two- or three-shift systems, especially in textiles where women predominated. The ideal was not merely a short, but also a compressed, workday to free longer blocks of time for private life, especially for meeting the needs of coordinating family schedules.

The eight-hour day became a nearly universal concession only during the labor upsurge that accompanied the closing years of World War I and its unsettled aftermath (1917–1919), extending in principle from Bolshevik Russia to Britain. The two-day weekend (and forty-hour workweek) became a goal of labor movements in France and Britain in the 1930s. This standard became law in France in June 1936 during the strikes that accompanied the beginning of the leftist Popular Front government. Business, however, bitterly opposed this apparent unilateral disarmament of the French economy and military, and it was revoked in late 1938. Many wage earners in Europe won the weekend/forty-hour week only after World War II (for example, in 1958 in West Germany).

The movement for the paid annual holiday also intensified in the interwar period. Between 1919 and 1925, legislation provided paid vacations in six eastern and central European countries. The movement peaked in the mid-1930s with the widespread support for the two-week paid vacation in France in 1936 and a week's holiday in many British industries in 1938. In the generation after World War II, the vacation became the leisure concept of choice for most Europeans: The one- or two-week holiday expanded to three or more weeks in the prosperity of the 1950s and 1960s. By the 1980s, 80 percent of West Germans enjoyed six weeks of vacation.

Before 1945, the democratization of leisure threatened economic and social elites on multiple fronts. In the view of businesspeople, increased leisure would raise labor costs and reduce future economic expansion. Cultural conservatives were anxious that the masses would invade traditional bourgeois resorts (a fear raised during the French Popular Front period, for example) and worried that free time meant dissipation for a working class still unprepared for uplifting leisure. Intellectuals such as the French industrial sociologist Georges Friedmann argued that without meaningful work, leisure became mere escapism and passive excitement in pleasure. The so-called Frankfurt School, a group of neo-Marxist German sociologists in the interwar period, developed an even more pessimistic view of what they called the "culture industry." In pursuit of profit, the pleasure industry manufactured a leisure time of pseudochoice and illusory freedom. Sigmund Freud doubted that civilization could withstand any significant liberation from work. The growth of free time in the early twentieth century, however, produced more optimistic points of view. One largely British and French school of thought argued that increased leisure would produce a more egalitarian culture and even more sympathetic people. John C. Hammond, C. D. Burns, and Bertrand Russell advanced the idea of a progressive democratization of leisure.

USES OF LEISURE, 1900–1950

Between the wars, the pub or bar remained the center of male working-class leisure in Europe. At the heart of bar culture was the reciprocity of "treating" for drinks. A British study of pub life in the late 1930s likened the Saturday night pub habit to a Sabbath meeting—a liturgy of group drinking and "treating" and a litany of verbal exchanges. While "respectable" women increasingly appeared in pubs by the 1930s, the age of pubgoers also rose because the young were more attracted to the cinema or dance hall. The pub owner continued to perform the complex role of social mediator, banker, and participant in the nightly round of gossip, drinking, singing of familiar music hall numbers, and bar games. In addition to providing insurance benefits, clubs provided rooms for moderate drinking, darts, billiards, and singsongs, and occasionally fund-raising in card games. Boxing, prostitution, and other male pastimes were on the decline in the interwar years. But the male-oriented and casual leisure of the mechanical gaming arcade flourished in the cities. The most notable development in working-class leisure in the twentieth century was the growth of offsite gambling.

Women's daily leisure was considerably more constrained because of the demands of housework and child-tending as well as wage work. Socializing over the washing-line, at the corner shop, and with nearby relatives was supplemented by the occasional visit to the cinema or hour with her husband at his bar or club. By the 1910s, movie houses were accommodating women (62 percent of the audience in one British survey of the 1930s), often as part of regular shopping trips. By the 1930s, home-based work was eased by the radio. There were ten times more radios in Britain in 1931 than in France. By 1939, 71 percent of households in Britain held a radio license. But those women who held jobs outside the home had scarcely two hours of their own per day because of domestic chores waiting them.

In the wake of the eight-hour day, a wide range of movements for public recreation emerged across Europe. Government grants for adult education expanded in Britain and elsewhere in the 1920s, though these efforts were limited by budgetary constraints and then by cutbacks during the depression of the 1930s. British groups such as the Holiday Fellowship (founded in 1913) organized hiking and camping trips, while the Youth Hostel Association (1929) and what is now the Ramblers' Association (1931) promoted cheap, open-air holidays. Although these groups were mostly composed of clerical and skilled workers, some attracted manual laborers with their promise of relief from the bleakness of the industrial landscape. And, the nonprofit holiday camp, which had roots in the 1890s, grew especially in the 1920s.

The organized vacation was advanced by ideologues of the Right and Left. Both the Italian Fascist *dopolavoro* (recreational club) and the Nazi Kraft durch Freude (Strength through Joy) organized holiday tours, festivals, and tours to instill loyalty to the regime. The Left attempted to create alternatives to commercial spectator sports and to the sports press and clubs patronized by employers or the Catholic Church. Where possible, communists organized sports and cultural groups, hoping to appeal to members' families and to create a more

A couple dancing, London, 1956. ©Hulton-Deutsch Collection/Corbis

fun-loving image of the cause. The French Popular Front government of 1936–1937 opted for a less political form of mass tourism. Its minister for sports and leisure, Léo Lagrange, cajoled railway companies into accepting a program of inexpensive tickets for family excursions, built 653 sports arenas, introduced physical education in almost half the French schools, and advocated autonomous municipal leisure clubs, independent of political patronage. But Lagrange also believed that French visits to national historical sites and travels to meet fellow citizens in different regions and walks of life would lead to deeper patriotic sentiments.

Public recreation movements often failed to compete successfully against commercial leisure. British travel and holiday camp cooperatives lacked capital and managerial skill and were co-opted by commercial efforts such as Billy Butlin's holiday camps, which from 1937 offered much of the camaraderie of the Holiday Fellowship without the excessive seriousness and cliquishness that often bedeviled the nonprofit and volunteer holiday movement. It was easier and often more desirable to participate in a club organized by an outside commercial impresario than by a group of the participants themselves.

In 1900 commercialized entertainments were already well established in the form of traveling and annual fairs, music halls, spectator sports, and gambling. The amusement park dating from 1843 in Copenhagen was expanded to Vienna and elsewhere in the 1890s. The introduction of the cheap electric streetcar in the 1890s and subway slightly later made it possible for even wage earners to escape the neighborhood bar to traverse the city and its environs for the anonymous pleasures of mass entertainments. The seaside holiday was another commercial leisure. By the early twentieth century, Blackpool and its many imitators had become well-established sites for perfunctory seabathing and a vast range of amusements—from gypsy fortune-tellers, pinball boards, and roller coasters to music hall programs and rides up the Blackpool Tower (built in 1895).

Despite the European origins of the automobile (invented by the German Carl Benz in 1885 and manufactured soon thereafter by the French), the car played a relatively small role in European leisure before World War II. Europeans failed to develop low- and midpriced automobiles as did the American Henry Ford. The industry's concentration on the luxury vehicle and on military uses of internal combustion engines before World War I meant that in 1929, for example, there was one car for every 4.5 Americans but only one for every 42 British. In the interwar years, the auto brought picnicking, camping, and touring to the smart set with elite auto touring guides provided by the French tire company Michelin. The open-air bus, or charabanc, was available for pub crawling (the original "magical mystery tour"). But most wage earners were confined to the fixed routes of the rail.

POSTWAR LEISURE TRENDS

Following on the movements of the 1930s, postwar efforts to organize leisure increased dramatically in postwar France with the building of local youth and cultural centers, children's holiday camps, and sports facilities. Numbers of sports clubs rose 2.6 times in France in the 1960s and 1970s. By 1984, there were about 150,000 sports clubs in France enrolling some 12 million members. From 1960 to 1984, cultural clubs increased even more dramatically, from 600 to 4,116. French promoters of popular arts and recreation stressed wide participation, and many eventually lost their political or religious character to emphasize instead the democratization of culture. Government facilities and educators have contributed to the growth of amateurism in music and the other arts. In Britain, agencies such as the Arts Council (1946), national parks (1949), and the Ministry of Sport (1962) subsidized public recreational facilities of all kinds. Sociologists found in the mid-1980s that middle-class people in particular still readily joined groups around a wide variety of "enthusiasms" (caving, morris dancing, lace making, and lapidary, for example). Such organizations stressed group solidarity, and often did so with a militant opposition to commercialization as if in protest of the profit motive of sellers and passivity of buyers. In Germany, East and West, local sports, leisure, and arts facilities were built after the war, though in the East, the lack of opportunities for travel and access to new commercial forms of leisure probably contributed to the popular uprising of 1989 and decision to reunite with the Federal Republic in 1990.

Yet again commercialized leisure predominated. Following the austerity of postwar reconstruction, increased incomes allowed for new and expanded forms of leisure. Television was slower to enter the home than in the United States (in 1959, when over 90 percent of American households contained a TV, only 66 percent of British households did; in 1963, only 30 percent of French homes had TVs). This changed rapidly: TVs were in 90 percent of British homes by 1970 and 86 percent of French homes by 1976. A British study in 1974 found that half of leisure time was spent watching the screen; and by 1980 TVs were on 2.3 hours per day in French homes. Only 51 percent of French watched TV daily in 1967, but 82 percent admitted to doing so by 1987. Still, over the same period the percentage who read a book in the course of a month scarcely changed (going from 32 to 31 percent), and the rate of attending museums rose from 10 to 32 percent.

Increasingly, European families spend larger portions of their income on their homes and

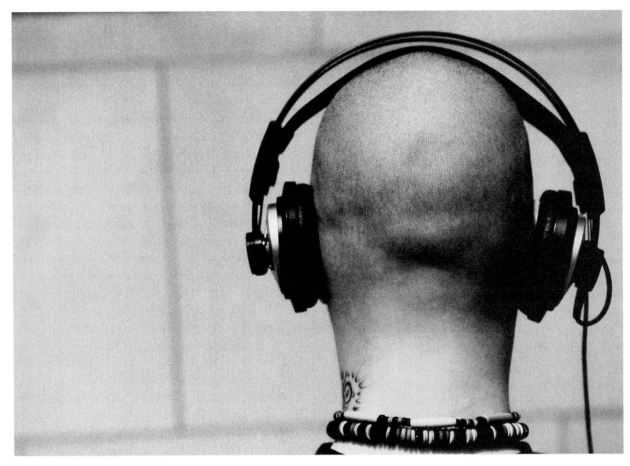

A young German man listens to music through headphones, Berlin, 2001. ©ROYALTY-FREE/CORBIS

furnishings, suggesting a domestication of leisure. While in 1950 food comprised 49 percent of the average French family budget and housing absorbed merely 14 percent, by 1985 food decreased to 19 percent and housing costs rose to 26 percent of family income. Suburbanization and detached houses gradually supplanted the traditional urban apartment living, and with these changes came new domestic leisure endeavors, especially the do-it-yourself movement. Automobile ownership also rose sharply, from 10 percent of French households in 1950 to 75 percent by 1980. The popularization of the family car transformed tourism. Blackpool's Central Station, the great railway hub of tourist arrivals as recently as the early 1950s, closed in 1964, reflecting the rising importance of the bus as well as the private car. Even more, the car facilitated holiday trips to quieter or sunnier climes in southwest England or on the European continent. It also increased the popularity of heritage tourism to ancient estates and castles.

Economic change after World War II broke up many old neighborhoods, especially in England, fostering new gang-based leisure styles among youth. For example, the amphetamine-driven and clothes-conscious "mods" of the early 1960s protested, through "rituals" of consumption, the dead-end jobs that they knew to be their collective fate. Groups such as the skinheads in the 1960s retained a tough macho image associated with the working class. Some protested their loss of territory by attacking immigrants and through gang violence at or near football (soccer) matches.

The most dramatic leisure trend in Europe is the growth of vacations and tourism. Whereas Americans tended to use their affluence to accumulate goods and activities around the home, Europeans spent much of it on holidays. In the 1990s, Americans had an average of only 13 days of vacation per year as compared to 35 in Germany and 42 in Italy. By the end of the century, tourism accounted for 5.5 percent of the European Union's economy, with twice that share for Spain and France. Especially enthusiastic tourists were the Germans, who in 1986 accounted for 20 percent of European recreational travelers (compared to the French, 11.8 percent, and the British, 9.9 percent). Moreover, the car became the vehicle of tourist choice: in 1985, 68 percent of European tourism was by automobile, compared to only 14 percent by train and 13 percent by plane. Despite resistance from cultural purists, even Euro Disneyland (1992) near Paris became successful with lowered prices and more thrill rides (along with a name change in 1994 to Disneyland Paris). Because of the advent of cheap air flights and packaged tours, northern Europeans shifted their tourism from nearby resorts (such as Blackpool in England) to the warmer climes of Spain, Greece, and elsewhere on the Mediterranean. While the Club Meds (self-contained resorts located in North Africa and elsewhere, originating in 1950) appealed primarily to a young and affluent population, especially from France, less elaborately themed resorts on the Mediterranean became very popular by the 1980s, making this broad region the destination of one-third of world tourism by the 1990s. The result was a rise in annual tourist visits to the Mediterranean region from 86 million in 1975 to 200 million in 1990.

Although economic downturns produce temporary declines in vacationing, leisure has become a central activity and perhaps life purpose of many Europeans. This is no surprise considering that the annual hours devoted to work dropped from about 3,000 in 1900 to 1,731 in the United Kingdom, 1,539 in France, and 1,397 in the Netherlands (compared to the 1,957 in the United States) in 1998.

See also Cinema; Football (Soccer); Television; Tourism.

BIBLIOGRAPHY

Bramham, Peter, Ian Henry, Hans Mommas, and Hugo van der Poel, eds. *Leisure Policies in Europe.* Wallingford, U.K., 1993.

Cross, Gary. *A Quest for Time: The Reduction of Work in Britain and France, 1840–1940.* Berkeley, Calif., 1989.

———. *Time and Money: The Making of Consumer Culture.* London, 1993.

Cross, Gary, ed. *Worktowners at Blackpool: Mass-Observation and Popular Leisure in the 1930s.* London, 1990.

de Grazia, Victoria. *The Culture of Consent: Mass Organization of Leisure in Fascist Italy.* Cambridge, U.K., 1981.

Hoggett, Paul, and Jeff Bishop. *Organising around Enthusiasms: Patterns of Mutual Aid in Leisure.* London, 1986.

International Monetary Fund. *France: Selected Issues.* Washington, D.C., 1998. Country Report 98/132.

Koshar, Rudy, ed. *Histories of Leisure.* Oxford, U.K., 2002.

LeMahieu, D. L. *A Culture for Democracy.* Oxford, U.K., 1988.

MacCannell, Dean. *The Tourist: A New Theory of the Leisure Class.* New York, 1976.

Mass-Observation. *The Pub and the People.* London, 1943.

Pimlott, J. A. R. *The Englishman's Holiday.* London, 1947. Reprint, New York, 1976.

Rabinbach, Anson. *The Human Motor: Energy, Fatigue, and the Origins of Modernity.* New York, 1990.

Rojek, Chris. *Capitalism and Leisure Theory.* London, 1985.

Walton, John K. *The British Seaside: Holidays and Resorts in the Twentieth Century.* Manchester, U.K., 2000.

GARY CROSS

LEMKIN, RAPHAEL (1900–1959), inventor of the term *genocide*.

Raphael Lemkin was born in tsarist Russia, in a village that became part of Poland in 1918 and of Belarus in 1945. In 1941 he emigrated to the United States, a typical itinerary for a "Polish" Jew and intellectual.

Lemkin had studied philology at the University of Lvov, becoming fluent in many languages. Then, after earning a doctorate in law, he became a public prosecutor for the District Court of Poland. In his unpublished autobiography, *Totally Unofficial Man* (1957), he said that he had long been interested in accounts of exterminations of national, racial, and religious minorities. Indeed, during World War I, he had witnessed the occupation of territories on the western and eastern fronts and the extermination of the Armenians. In 1921, during the trial of Soghomon Tehlirian, who had killed one of the perpetrators, the former Great Vizier Talât Paşa, in Berlin, Lemkin asked why the Germans had not arrested Talât: "It is a crime for Tehlirian to kill a man, but it is not a crime for his oppressor to kill more than a million men? This is most inconsistent" (quoted in Power, p. 17). He would spend the rest of his life devoted to eliminating this inconsistency, ensuring that these crimes were treated as crimes. In 1933 he presented a report to the Madrid International Conference for the Unification of Penal Law, arguing that actions taken with the purpose of elimination and oppression of populations ought to be penalized.

In 1939, while fighting the Germans during the invasion of Poland, Lemkin was wounded; he managed to escape to Sweden, where he began the work of compiling documents on Nazi rule in Europe. After making his way to the United States via Russia and Japan, he joined the law faculty at Duke University in 1941. He was then appointed chief consultant of the U.S. Board of Economic Warfare, Foreign Economic Administration.

In a speech on 24 August 1941 Winston Churchill called the slaughter of the Jews and other ethnic groups "a crime without a name" (British Library of Information transcription, Internet page). Raphael Lemkin gave that crime a name in 1943. He called it "genocide"—a compound made up of the Greek word *genos* (race) and the Latin *occidere* (killing)—in his seminal work, *Axis Rule in Occupied Europe* (1944). In his 1945 article "Genocide, a Modern Crime," Lemkin summarized his thinking. He quoted Marshal Karl Rudolf Gerd von Rundsted "aping the Führer" in 1943: "One of the great mistakes of 1918 was to spare the civil life of the enemy countries, for it is necessary for us Germans to always at least double the numbers of the peoples of the contiguous countries. We are therefore obliged to destroy at least a third of their inhabitants" (quoted in Lemkin, 1945, p. 39). Then Lemkin added: "Hitler was right. The crime of the Reich in wantonly and deliberately wiping out whole peoples is not utterly new. It is only new in the civilized world as we have come to think of it. It is so new in the traditions of civilized man that he has no name for it. It is for this reason that I took the liberty of inventing the word, 'genocide'" (Lemkin, 1945, p. 39).

He went beyond the invention of words. Material from *Axis Rule in Occupied Europe* was used in establishing a basis for the Nuremberg war trials, and Lemkin was appointed an advisor to the chief prosecutor of the Nuremberg trial, U.S. Supreme Court justice Robert Jackson. In 1946 the UN General Assembly approved a draft resolution naming genocide a crime under international law. With Lemkin as advisor, the draft was rewritten; in December 1948 in Paris, the UN General Assembly approved the first legally binding human rights international treaty by a vote of fifty-five to zero. Lemkin went on lobbying: by the time of his death in 1959, sixty countries had ratified the treaty, a majority of UN members at the time. Twice Raphael Lemkin was nominated for the Nobel Peace Prize. But his crucial invention was truly recognized only in the 1970s, when the Holocaust and other genocides began to be better understood in their complete horror.

See also **Armenian Genocide; Holocaust; Nuremberg War Crimes Trials.**

BIBLIOGRAPHY

British Library of Information. "Prime Minister Winston Churchill's Broadcast to the World about the Meeting with President Roosevelt." Available at http://www.ibiblio.org/pha/timeline/410824awp.html

Lemkin, Raphael. *Axis Rule in Occupied Europe: Laws of Occupation. Analysis of Government Proposals for Redress*. Washington, D.C., 1944.

———. "Genocide, a Modern Crime." *Free World* 9, no. 4 (1945): 39–43.

Power, Samantha. *A Problem from Hell: America and the Age of Genocide*. New York, 2002.

"Prevent Genocide International." Available at http://www.preventgenocide.org/

Totten, Samuel, and Steven Leonard Jacobs, eds. *Pioneers of Genocide Studies*. New Brunswick, N.J., 2002.

Totten, Samuel, William S. Parsons, and Israel W. Charny, eds. *Genocide in the Twentieth Century: Critical Essays and Eyewitness Accounts*. New York, 1995.

ANNETTE BECKER

LENIN, VLADIMIR (1870–1924), Russian revolutionary and founder of the USSR.

Vladimir Ilyich Ulyanov (Lenin) was born in the provincial capital of Simbirsk, located on the Volga River. His father, Ilya Ulyanov, worked for the tsarist government as a school inspector. The Ulyanov family was thus part of the professional middle class, although technically it was enrolled in the gentry or *dvorianstvo*. In 1887, after Ilya Ulyanov's death, there occurred an event that marked the Ulyanov family forever: Vladimir's older brother Alexander was executed for organizing an attempt to assassinate Tsar Alexander III (whose father had been assassinated by revolutionaries in 1881).

A few years later, around 1890, Vladimir adopted the political faith—"revolutionary Social Democracy"—to which he remained faithful for the rest of his life. Arrested in St. Petersburg in 1895, he was sent into internal exile in Siberia. While in Siberia, Lenin married his lifelong companion, Nadezhda Krupskaya, and developed his plan for a nationwide underground revolutionary newspaper.

As soon as he was released from exile, Lenin went abroad and carried out his newspaper plan with the help of distinguished Marxist revolutionaries from the older generation—particularly Georgy Plekhanov, the person most responsible for introducing Marx-based Social Democracy to Russia in the 1880s and 1890s—as well as revolutionaries from his own generation, such as Yuli Martov, later a leader of the Mensheviks, who opposed Lenin within Russian Social Democracy. The first issue of *Iskra* (The spark) appeared in late 1900 and owed much of its success to the growing revolutionary crisis in Russia that in a few years led to a cataclysmic explosion in the revolution of 1905. The pseudonym "N. Lenin" was first used during the *Iskra* period.

The *Iskra* group itself soon fell apart, with Lenin becoming the leader of the Bolshevik faction and the other members of the *Iskra* editorial board leading the Mensheviks. These two factions rapidly became separate political organizations uneasily coexisting within the framework of Russian Social Democracy.

The differences between Mensheviks and Bolsheviks were temporarily submerged during the 1905 revolution. The meager results of the revolution and the very limited opportunity for independent political activity again exacerbated those differences, and by the time of the outbreak of World War I in 1914, the two factions had

become separate parties. The years from 1906 to 1912 were depressing ones for Lenin, who spent them involved in various émigré squabbles and in trying to preserve a semblance of a viable, nationwide underground organization. Only in 1912 did a new wave of militancy among Russian workers provide support for Lenin's continued insistence that the Russian anti-tsarist revolution was not dead, but sleeping.

The outbreak of World War I in 1914 opened up a new chapter in Lenin's political career, shifting his focus from Russia alone to a Europe-wide and even worldwide revolution. Lenin was devastated by the support given by the major Social Democratic parties to the war effort of their respective governments. His political activity now concentrated on two goals: creating a new international organization of truly revolutionary socialist parties and "turning the world war into an international civil war"—that is, turning the clash between nation-states into a worker-led socialist revolution against capitalism.

For the first three years of the war, Lenin's position seemed hopelessly quixotic to most observers, but this perception rapidly changed when the tsarist system collapsed in early 1917. By the end of the year, the Bolsheviks had taken power in Russia at Lenin's insistence and surprised everybody (including themselves) by surviving a devastating civil war and foreign intervention, relying on ruthless repression, governmental improvisation, and passionate support from party members and sympathizers.

Russia's titanic civil war began to wind down only in 1920–1921. By this time, the country was prostrate and on the edge of total collapse. Lenin had realized one of his two goals of 1914. He had founded the Third or Communist International (the name "Social Democracy" was rejected as irrevocably tainted by the betrayal of 1914). But he was forced to admit that his other goal—Europe-wide socialist revolution—was not going to happen in the short term. He therefore instituted in 1921 the New Economic Policy, or NEP, under which capitalist forces (both small-scale domestic entrepreneurs and large-scale foreign entrepreneurs) were allowed to make economic gains while the new system consolidated itself.

Vladimir Lenin gives a speech at the unveiling of a monument to Karl Marx in Moscow, 6 December 1921.
©BETTMANN/CORBIS

NEP was only a stopgap measure that delayed the tough decisions about how to build socialism in a devastated, isolated Russia. Lenin did not live long enough to make any of these decisions. He suffered his first stroke in early 1922 and by the end of the year was no longer able to function as head of state or party. His last writings date from January 1923. Lenin died in January 1924. His body was embalmed and put on display in a mausoleum in Moscow, where it still resided as of 2006.

BASIC OUTLOOK

Lenin spent only the last six years of a thirty-year political career in power. Probably no earlier world leader came into office with a more elaborate political doctrine, defended with tenacity over decades.

When Lenin acquired his political identity as a "revolutionary Social Democrat" in the early 1890s, he was inspired not so much by a doctrine as by a movement—the European Social Democratic parties that seemed to combine a mass base with genuine revolutionary fervor. The flagship of international Social Democracy was the Social Democratic Party of Germany (SPD). The SPD strove to inculcate what its historian Vernon Lidtke has called an "alternative culture," using a vast array of agitation and propaganda devices, ranging from an extensive party press to choral societies and bicycle clubs.

The SPD derived its self-understanding from Marx's world-historical scenario, in which the proletariat took political power as a class in order to introduce socialism. The working class therefore had to be sufficiently enlightened about its true interest and sufficiently well organized to accomplish its assigned mission. This revolutionary payoff was the ultimate aim of the SPD's "alternative culture." The whole SPD strategy depended on the existence of a modicum of political freedom: freedom of speech, of assembly, of association. Karl Kautsky, the most authoritative theoretician of Social Democracy, wrote that anyone who downgraded the importance of political freedom for the proletariat was one of its worst enemies. Thus Russian Social Democracy, in contrast to earlier Russian revolutionaries, gave urgent priority to a nonsocialist democratic revolution that would replace tsarist absolutism with a constitutional system.

But the achievement of political freedom in Russia lay in the future, and for the present Social Democracy could only exist in Russia as an illegal underground organization. Was anything that remotely approached the SPD strategy of energetic mass agitation conceivable under these circumstances? An affirmative answer required some heroic assumptions about the Russian proletariat's receptivity to the Social Democratic message and about the ability of underground activists to create and sustain a viable nationwide organizational structure despite constant government repression. Among Russian Social Democrats, Lenin stood out for the fervor with which he defended the most optimistic assumptions about the validity of a mass underground movement.

In *What Is to Be Done?*, his famous book of 1902, Lenin asserted that the Social Democratic message had to be brought "from without" to the workers. According to a superficial reading, this assertion shows that Lenin was greatly worried about the revolutionary inclinations of the workers. In actuality, it was part of Lenin's highly optimistic argument that the message *could* be brought to the workers and that the workers *would* enthusiastically respond to the message, despite all the obstacles put up by tsarist absolutism.

Lenin's political program at this time can thus be summed up as: Let us build a party as much like the SPD as possible under underground conditions so that we can overthrow the tsar and become even more like the SPD. His political strategy for Russia

was based on the question: What nonsocialist forces in Russia will help us ensure that the upcoming revolution will result in the fullest possible establishment of political freedom? In Lenin's view, the elite middle class would be satisfied with a fairly meager set of freedoms that would allow elite groups room to maneuver but would severely hamper SPD-like activity by the Social Democrats. The peasants, on the other hand, due to their land hunger, would accept Social Democracy's campaign for a radically democratic republic. In doctrinal terms, this strategy was labeled "proletarian hegemony in the democratic revolution."

In the first two decades of his career, Lenin focused on importing Western models to Russia. In the last decade, after the traumatic betrayal by Western Social Democratic parties in 1914, he focused on importing Russian models to the West. This change of focus did not signify a rejection of his earlier beliefs. On the contrary, Lenin saw himself as the one who stayed faithful to what Social Democrats had always stood for, even when deserted by "renegades" such as Kautsky.

Four Russian experiences informed the model that Lenin now set up as authoritative on a world scale. The first was his decision in 1912 to create a party without "opportunists," that is, anyone who might be tempted to substitute reform for revolution (in practical terms, without Mensheviks, who certainly saw themselves as revolutionaries). After the betrayal of 1914, Lenin felt that such opportunist-free parties were necessary everywhere. The second Russian experience was the experiment with "soviet democracy" that first took place in the 1905 revolution and later in the 1917 revolution. The soviets were improvised elected councils that took on leadership functions during times of mass upheaval. Lenin argued that the soviets represented a new form of "proletarian democracy" that was higher than ordinary parliamentary democracy.

The third Russian experience was the nationwide process of social breakdown and political radicalization that brought the Bolsheviks to power in 1917. Lenin tended to define the situation faced by other Communist parties (for example, in Germany and Great Britain) in the same terms, resulting in some dubious tactical advice. The fourth Russian experience was the devastating civil war that followed the 1917 revolution, accompanied by openly dictatorial methods. Lenin and other Bolsheviks such as Nikolai Bukharin now generalized this experience and argued that any profound socialist revolution would lead to a similar episode of economic and political breakdown.

LENIN AS STATESMAN

From 1917 on, Lenin's biography is essentially a political history of Soviet Russia. Here we will list some of the major turning points for which Lenin was directly responsible. The first of these was the decision of the Bolshevik Party to take power in late 1917. The first Bolshevik government was authorized by a national congress of representatives from local soviets, but within a year the electoral soviet system had atrophied and all other parties were outlawed or barely tolerated, leaving the Bolsheviks with a permanent one-party dictatorship. This process is hardly conceivable without Lenin's driving participation, although it remains unclear to what extent Lenin's hand was forced by the profound tensions of civil war.

Another crucial decision was the signing of a separate peace with Germany, as ratified by the Brest-Litovsk treaty in early 1918. While this decision gave the new government some breathing space, it also profoundly alienated revolutionaries both at home and abroad, as well as Russia's former allies. The treaty also risked turning Soviet Russia into a satellite of imperial Germany, but this gamble paid off when the German state collapsed in late 1918. Despite the Brest-Litovsk treaty, Lenin did not lose faith in the short-term prospects of world revolution until mid-1919, particularly owing to the failure of the soviet-style revolution in Hungary. After mid-1919, Lenin's political calculations had to be made on the assumption of an isolated socialist Russia.

Another crucial decision in which Lenin played a central role was to establish an effective Red Army based on peasant recruits and tsarist officers, held together by committed party members who served as "political commissars." The same type of adoption and adaptation of "bourgeois" models occurred in the civilian state and the economy. Lenin and the Bolsheviks are sometimes said to have deceived themselves that Russia was about to take a "leap into communism" even amid the ruins of civil war Russia. Not only is this assertion without foundation but it distracts attention from the truly unexpected process of creative imitation that gave rise to many permanent features of the Soviet state.

Lenin was also responsible for the decision to adopt the New Economic Policy (NEP) in 1921. This decision was less of a profound turning point than it is often said to be. NEP was a pragmatic although risky relaxation of pressure on the economy in the aftermath of the economic and military emergency of the previous years. The risks inherent in this relaxation of pressure are often overlooked because the gamble paid off, but the threat of renewed military intervention or internal economic collapse remained real enough.

Looking back in 1921, Lenin felt that the basic cause of Bolshevik victory in the civil war was grudging but ultimately decisive support from peasants who saw the Bolsheviks as a bulwark against the armies mounted by dispossessed landowners. Looking ahead, Lenin sketched out yet another scenario in which the peasants would accept the leadership of the proletariat (as organized and represented by the Bolshevik Party). This time, proletarian leadership consisted in showing the economic superiority of socialism over the market. Lenin coined the phrase "who-whom" (*kto kovo*) to explain this strategy: Who would win out over whom in gaining the economic loyalty of the peasants—the socialist workers or the capitalists? (Ironically, the phrase *kto kovo*, coined to explain the logic of NEP, is often used as a symbol of the hard-line and repressive aspect of Lenin's outlook.)

IMPACT

In a book published in 1930, the American journalist W. H. Chamberlin wrote that "boundless hatred for the capitalist system and its upholders, boundless faith in the right and the ability of the working class to dominate a new social order—these were certainly the two dominant passions of Lenin's strong and simple character." This comment brings us closer to the truth than the commonly accepted version of Lenin as someone who profoundly mistrusted the revolutionary inclinations of the workers. Rather, both his successes and his failures were based on his bedrock assumption that the workers were rapidly moving toward

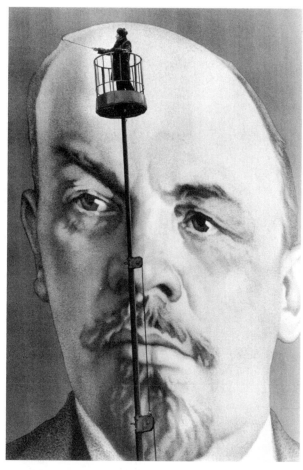

A painter touches up a mural of Lenin in preparation for the 60th anniversary of the Bolshevik Revolution, Moscow, November 1977. ©ALAIN NOGUES/CORBIS SYGMA

an acceptance of the world-historical mission assigned to them by the epic narrative of Marxism. Lenin's ultimate loyalty was to this doctrinal narrative.

Lenin is regarded as the founder of bolshevism, and this description can hardly be gainsaid. But even here we should not imagine Lenin creating a political faction ex nihilo. There existed currents among the Social Democratic *praktiki* (underground activists in Russia itself) who felt that Lenin was the voice among the émigrés that best expressed their problems and aspirations. As one of those young *praktiki*, Iosif Dzhugashvili (Stalin), wrote later, Lenin's writings in the 1902–1904 period "completely corresponded to Russian reality and generalized in masterly fashion the organizational experience of the best *praktiki*."

Neither Lenin nor the people around him (prior to his death and the beginnings of the Lenin

cult) believed in the existence of "Leninism," that is, profoundly new theoretical innovations. Rather they saw him as a great political tactician, someone who could give the party political and organizational orientation by applying the basic doctrine to concrete situations.

After the fall of the Soviet Union in 1991, archival documents were published that brought out the callous and ruthless side of Lenin, particularly during the civil war. In fact, this side of Lenin can be amply illustrated by material available many years earlier. But Lenin's willingness to countenance massive loss of life for political goals does not particularly distinguish him from other statesmen of the World War I period. The difference is rather that most other statesmen imposed sacrifices in the name of the nation-state, while Lenin did so in the name of class war and socialist revolution.

By the time of Lenin's death, the Soviet Union was a one-party dictatorship with a minimum of political freedom. To equate this system with the excesses of the Stalin era or even to draw a straight and unproblematic line of development from one to the other betrays a lack of understanding of what Stalin was all about. The key case is Stalin's violent campaign to impose collectivization on the peasants. For Lenin and for all other Marxists of his generation, the use of violence to impose new production relations was unthinkable. Lenin's most eloquent tirades on this theme come from the civil war period (many people believe that Lenin sanctioned such violence during so-called War Communism and only retreated from this hard line during NEP).

Lenin did employ violence to extract resources from the peasants during the civil war, as indeed did all the warring governments opposing the Bolsheviks. Precisely because of this pressure, he halted any effort to revolutionize production relations in agriculture. Both during the civil war and NEP, the basic strategy for changing production relations was demonstrating to the peasants the economic advantages of socialism, on the assumption that this process would span an entire historical era—and not, as in Stalin's collectivization campaign, a matter of months.

Early twenty-first-century efforts to portray the Lenin and Stalin eras as merely two phases in one "war against the peasants" fail in the light of these facts. Nevertheless there are other threads that do connect Lenin and Stalin. The Soviet system can be described as "the SPD model minus political freedom"—that is, reliance on an SPD-like campaign to inculcate an alternative culture, but now in the context of a state monopoly on all forms of expression. Paradoxically, the man who for many years fought for political freedom for Russia now ensured the entire absence of any social checks and balances that might have prevented the country's descent into state-induced hysteria.

Lenin's responsibility for Stalin resides less in any plans that he bequeathed than in the absence of any coherent strategy for responding to the inevitable dilemmas ahead. His gamble on world revolution had failed. His gamble on "the economic advantages of socialism" soon ran into serious trouble. His flailing attempts at the end of his life to address the problems created by political monopoly were superficial.

Lenin is perhaps the key figure in the transformation of nineteenth-century politics into twentieth-century politics. The Bolshevik Revolution of 1917 constituted a challenge to the "bourgeois" certainties of European civilization, thus providing the framework for the major conflicts of the ensuing decades. The new "Communist International" and its successors were responsible for some of the most powerful political institutions of the century (as well as for many botched and clumsy failures). The political system described earlier as "the SPD model minus political freedom" was influential far beyond the communist movement. No simple formula can do justice to Lenin's odyssey from provincial Russian Social Democrat to world leader and founder of communism.

See also **Bolshevism; Communism; Russian Revolutions of 1917; Stalin, Joseph; Trotsky, Leon.**

BIBLIOGRAPHY

Primary Sources

Fyson, George, ed. *Lenin's Final Fight: Speeches and Writings, 1922–23*. New York, 1995. Speeches and writings from Lenin's final period.

Krupskaya, Nadezhda. *Reminiscences of Lenin*. New York, 1960. Classic memoir account by Lenin's wife.

Lenin V. I. *Collected Works*. Moscow, 1960–1970. Lenin's complete works made available in English by the Soviet government.

———. *Neizvestnye dokumenty, 1891–1922*. Moscow, 1999. New documents from the archives. The English-language edition of some of these documents by Richard Pipes (*The Unknown Lenin*, New Haven, Conn., 1996) cannot be recommended due to manifold errors and strained interpretations.

Tucker, Robert C., ed. *The Lenin Anthology*. New York, 1975. A well-chosen selection of writings from Lenin's entire career.

Secondary Sources

Chamberlin, William Henry. *Soviet Russia*. Boston, 1930. A description of Soviet Russia just prior to Stalin's revolution by a veteran American journalist.

Donald, Moira. *Marxism and Revolution: Karl Kautsky and the Russian Marxists, 1900–1924*. London, 1993. Shows the intense interaction between German and Russian Social Democracy.

Lewin, Moshe. *Lenin's Last Struggle*. Translated by A. M. Sheridan Smith. New York, 1968. Argues that Lenin sketched out new perspectives in his final period.

Lidtke, Vernon L. *The Alternative Culture: Socialist Labor in Imperial Germany*. Oxford, U.K., 1985. A classic study of the SPD model.

Lih, Lars T. *Lenin Rediscovered: "What Is to Be Done?" in Context*. Leiden, Netherlands, 2005.

Tucker, Robert C. *Political Culture and Leadership in Soviet Russia: From Lenin to Gorbachev*. New York, 1987. See particularly the article "Lenin's Bolshevism as a Culture in the Making."

LARS T. LIH

LEOPOLD III (1901–1983), king of Belgium from 1934 to 1983.

Leopold III succeeded his father, Albert I, a hero of World War I, in 1934. In part under the leadership of Leopold, in 1936 Belgium decided to end its military alliance with France and to pursue an independent course instead. It was a move that foreshadowed Belgium's subsequent neutrality at the start of World War II in September 1939.

When Belgium was invaded by Germany on 10 May 1940, the government called for assistance from the Allies. A fortnight later, on 25 May 1940, a dramatic rift occurred between the king and his ministers. They all realized that the army would soon have to give up its resistance on Belgian territory. The ministers felt that the king should flee with them to France in order to continue the fight, if only symbolically, alongside the Allies. They believed that the allied front in France could be stabilized and they felt very strongly that Belgium should fight on as long as France did so. Belgium, they argued, should throw in its lot with the Allies.

The king, on the other hand, felt that he should stay in Belgium, alongside his people and his army. After all, the war seemed to be over for Belgium. Being a neutral state, it was allowed only to protect its own territory. Moreover, Leopold expected that France, too, would soon capitulate. That would mean the end of the war on the Continent. The king rested all his hope in a compromise peace between Germany and Great Britain, whereby the future of Belgium could also be safeguarded. While he feared that Adolf Hitler would rule over continental Europe, he also believed that the German army would dispose of the Nazis sooner or later.

Accordingly, the ministers fled to France, while Leopold stayed behind in Belgium. On 28 May, he and the surrounded Belgian army surrendered to the German forces. The French Prime Minister Paul Reynaud accused Leopold of having capitulated without consulting the Allies, which was clearly untrue. The Belgian ministers, too, accused the king of treason. After 17 June 1940, the day that France capitulated to the Germans, the Belgian government tried to reestablish contact with Leopold. However, the king refused to communicate with them and would continue to do so throughout the war.

As far as Leopold was concerned, Belgium's struggle had ended on 28 May 1940. He felt it to be the country's obligation henceforth to adopt a de facto neutral position vis-à-vis the conflict. He intended to remain politically passive until the war was over and he certainly did not wish to rule over a country under German occupation that was being used in a war with Britain, as that would have conflicted with Belgium's neutral status. On 29 June 1940, Leopold did ask Hitler to liberate part of Belgium under an arrangement similar to that agreed with Vichy France, but this request was rejected.

In part in response to the pro-British policy pursued by the Belgian government in exile, Leopold paid a visit to Hitler at his country retreat in Berchtesgaden on 19 November 1940. On that occasion, Leopold pleaded for a more lenient regime of occupation and, more importantly, asked for guarantees regarding Belgium's independent status in postwar Europe. He understood that full independence would be impossible in relation to foreign policy and defense, and stressed that what mattered "above all else" was the country's internal independence. Hitler expressed a favorable opinion on Belgium's retention of internal independence, but refused to confirm this in writing.

The king decided to play a waiting game and had preparations made for a future state, should the Germans win the war. At least up until 1942, his aides continued to work on an authoritarian constitution for a Belgium under the new order.

In 1941, Leopold III married his second wife, Lilian Baels (his immensely popular first wife died in a car accident in 1935). When news of the wartime wedding reached the Belgian public, the popularity of the "captive" king slumped to an all-time low. His passivity also gave rise to questions. Was it not his duty to protest openly in 1942 when Belgian workers were forcefully employed in Germany? The king felt it was not; he saw himself as *l'ultime réserve,* the trump card to be played during European-level peace negotiations.

In early 1944, realizing a peace of compromise was no longer in the cards, the king drew up a "political will," which was to be publicized upon the liberation of Belgium by the Allies. In it, he demanded that the government apologize to him for its position in 1940. Other than that, the document contained not a word about the Allies or the Resistance. The king did however also demand that Belgium should regain its fully independent status, which implied a rejection of the pro-Atlantic policy of the exiled Belgian government in London.

In June 1944, the Nazis deported Leopold to Germany, where he was liberated in May 1945. Meanwhile in Belgium, a debate had flared up over his position during the war. The king was unable to return home, so that his younger brother Charles served as Prince Regent. The country became polarized on what was known as the "Royal Issue" and which would eventually lead to King Leopold's abdication in 1950 in favor of his eldest son Baudouin. Leopold died in Woluwe-Saint-Lambert, Belgium, in 1983.

See also **Albert I; Belgium; Occupation, Military.**

BIBLIOGRAPHY

Höjer, C. H. *Le régime parlementaire belge de 1918 à 1940.* Brussels, 1969.

Stengers, J. *L'action du Roi en Belgique depuis 1831: Pouvoir et influence.* Paris, 1963.

Velaers, Jan, and Herman Van Goethem. *Leopold III. De Koning, het Land, de Oorlog.* Lannoo, Tielt, Belgium 1994.

———— "Léopold III en Belgique, sous l'occupation" In *Léopold III,* edited by M. Dumoulin et al., 141–170. Brussels, 2001.

Witte, E., J. Craeybeckx, and A. Meynen. *Politieke Geschiedenis van België van 1830 tot heden.* Antwerp, Belgium, 2005.

JAN VELAERS, HERMAN VAN GOETHEM

LE PEN, JEAN-MARIE (b. 1928), French politician.

While there are some politicians whose views change during their lifetime, Jean-Marie Le Pen, began at the extreme right of the political spectrum and remained there throughout his life.

Although ostensibly of humble origin—his father was a skipper who perished at sea in August 1942—as a war orphan, he pursued secondary-level studies privately in religious establishments and studied for a law degree in Paris, where in 1949 he became president of the Corpo of law students, a markedly right-wing organization. His various activities—his initiative among the royalist students, in particular, and his liking for violent confrontations—explain why, having obtained his baccalaureate in 1947, he did not graduate in law until 1952, although this is normally a three-year course of study. He then interrupted the deferment to which he was entitled as a student in order to carry out his military service. He volunteered for Indochina, but did not arrive there until 1954 after the battle of Dien Bien Phu, shortly before the Geneva Convention agreements put an end to the

French phase of the Vietnam War. He nevertheless remained for a time in Indochina, where he was employed in Saigon as the editor of the journal of the expeditionary forces, but he soon returned to France, having left the army.

A movement for the protection of traders and artisans against the tax system (Union de Défense des Commerçants et Artisans, or UDCA) was forming under the leadership of Pierre Poujade, a bookseller from Saint-Céré in Lot, a department of southern France that was particularly affected by economic modernization. But having started from corporate protests, "Poujadism" gravitated toward traditional far-right themes—antiparliamentarianism, condemnation of deputies as incompetents and swindlers, and nationalism with regard to those said to be "discarding" the colonies. The movement put forward candidates at the January 1956 elections; these were mainly traders, artisans, and small farmers, representatives of social categories that were in difficulties, but Jean-Marie Le Pen found some themes there that were dear to him and he achieved selection as the Poujadist candidate in the fifth arrondissement in Paris. The Poujadists obtained an unprecedented success that was facilitated by the elimination of Gaullism, which had freed up many electors. Through the proportional system then in force, Jean-Marie Le Pen was elected a deputy.

At twenty-eight years old, he was the youngest deputy in France. His relations with Pierre Poujade soon deteriorated, and he concerned himself primarily with Algeria, where the uprising for independence had started. He took parliamentary leave to rejoin the army for six months. He participated first in the Suez expedition in October 1956, then in the battle of Algiers, where he took part in what could mildly be termed "tough interrogations." He soon returned to Paris and resumed his parliamentary seat, just as power was collapsing. The question of Algeria undermined the Fourth Republic. During the crisis of 1958, which brought General Charles de Gaulle (1890–1970) to power, Jean-Marie Le Pen was one of the leaders of the activists, but disputes soon broke out between these extremist proponents of French Algeria and General de Gaulle. At the 1958 elections, Le Pen held his seat in the fifth arrondissement and, in the following years, he took part as far as possible in all the activities and all the plots in support of French

Algeria. Fiercely anti-Gaullist, he voted against the Évian agreements that granted independence to Algeria but at the 1962 elections he underwent the fate of most of the proponents of French Algeria and was roundly defeated by one of the Gaullist leading lights, René Capitant.

The last triumph of the extreme Right in this period was Jean-Louis Tixier-Vignancourt's presidential campaign in 1965, in which Le Pen played an active part, but for many years Gaullism reduced the extreme Right to nothing more than small factions. Lacking funds, Le Pen had to seek to provide for his family's needs through various businesses. He became rich only through a legacy from Hubert Lambert, the owner of Lambert cements, in circumstances that were in fact strongly debated at the time, in particular by one of his oldest friends, Jean-Maurice Demarquet, who had also been elected as a Poujadist deputy in 1956. At the same time, from 1972 he was nevertheless president of one of these small groups, the Front National, which was not to gain momentum until the 1980s. In fact, after a very early political youth, it was only around twenty years later that Jean-Marie Le Pen managed to reestablish himself in the French political landscape. At this point, his biography coincides with the progress of the National Front.

It is nevertheless highly unlikely that without Le Pen himself his far-right party would ever have achieved such great significance. Despite his verbal gaffes, such as the remark that "the gas chambers were a mere historical detail," Le Pen successfully retained an increasingly working-class following at presidential elections: in 1988 he garnered almost 15 percent of the votes cast, bettering this score in 1995 and creating a virtual panic in 2002 by cumulating nearly 17 percent in the first round, thereby eliminating the Socialists' candidate Lionel Jospin and getting through into the second round for the first time. In view of Le Pen's age—he was seventy-six in 2002—and his serious health problems, however, some asked whether he had not reached the high point of his political career, which may indeed have been close to its end.

See also **Immigration and Internal Migration; National Front; Riots in France.**

BIBLIOGRAPHY

Conan, E., and G. Gaetner. "Qui est vraiment Jean-Marie Le Pen?" *L'Express,* 12–18 March 1992.

Rollat, Alain. *Les hommes de l'extrême-droite.* Paris, 1985.

Sirinelli, Jean-François, ed. *Dictionnaire historique de la vie politique française au XXe siècle.* Paris, 1995.

JEAN-JACQUES BECKER

LEVI, PRIMO (1919–1987), writer.

Primo Levi is one of the great figures of postwar European literature. With his memoir *Survival in Auschwitz,* he also provided an indispensable description and analysis of the Nazi concentration camps.

Levi was born in Turin in 1919, into a non-observant Jewish family. Until 1938 his childhood and adolescence were little different from those of most young people in Italy under fascism, including membership in the youth organizations of the ruling party. In 1937 he began university studies in chemistry. The promulgation of anti-Semitic laws in 1938, however, changed the course of Levi's life. Initially he continued his education under trying conditions, and in July 1941 he received his doctorate in chemistry. Two years later, in September 1943, after the Nazi invasion of the north and center of the Italian peninsula and the establishment of the Italian Social Republic, Levi joined a group of resistance fighters close to the antifascist movement *Giustizia e libertà* (Justice and liberty). Arrested by the fascist militia on 13 December 1943, Levi chose to declare himself an "Italian citizen of the Jewish race" rather than a resistance fighter. He was sent to the internment camp at Fossoli di Carpi, then deported to Auschwitz, arriving on 26 February 1944 after a five-day journey by boxcar. He was set to work in the synthetic rubber factory at the Buna-Monowitz complex (sometimes called Auschwitz III).

Levi's *Se questo è un uomo (Survival in Auschwitz,* also published in English as *If This Is a Man*) describes in detail the operation of the camp: its regulations, the prisoners' understanding of how to negotiate the concentration-camp system, the language of the death camps, the wretched conditions of life and work, the petty theft and corruption, the camp hierarchies, and prisoners' survival strategies. Levi ascribed his survival to several factors, including his knowledge of enough German to understand orders and the wartime labor shortage that was used to justify the employment of Jews in the Buna-Monowitz complex.

Survival in Auschwitz also includes philosophical reflections on human behavior, on the nature of good and evil in extreme situations, and on God and religion. Levi equated Auschwitz with absolute evil, concluding that it was no longer possible to believe in God: "C'è Auschwitz, quindi non può esserci Dio. Non trovo una soluzione al dilemma. La cerco ma non la trovo." ("There is Auschwitz, and so there cannot be God. I don't find a solution to this dilemma. I keep looking, but I don't find it.") (Camon, p. 75).

When the Soviet Army arrived at Auschwitz on 27 January 1945, Levi was ill. In *The Reawakening,* also translated as *The Truce,* published in 1963, he recounted his return to Italy, a journey of several months through Eastern Europe. As the war wound down in the West, Levi discovered the dysfunctional nature of the occupying Soviet bureaucracy. Critical but not bitter, Levi described this transition as a "truce" or hiatus preceding his return to ordinary life. Although he was reunited with his family after arriving in Turin on 19 October 1945, he initially found no one waiting for him. Like many returning deportees, he was greeted with incredulity and indifference. He felt an urgent need to write about his experience and the result was *Survival in Auschwitz.* Although a major publisher, Einaudi, rejected the book in 1947, it was published by a smaller house in an edition of 2,500 copies. Levi started a family and worked in a chemical firm, where he eventually became a manager. An exhibition in Turin on the Jewish deportations boosted interest in *Survival in Auschwitz,* and Einaudi finally issued the book in 1956. After publication of *The Reawakening,* Levi began his career as a writer in earnest, while still pursuing his work in chemistry. He was awarded numerous literary prizes, and his books have been widely translated. *The Monkey's Wrench,* published in 1978, presented the stories of a construction worker from the Italian Piedmont; Claude Lévi-Strauss called it an important ethnographic work on labor. In 1982 his *If Not Now, When?* recounted the adventures of Russian and Polish Jewish resistance fighters during World War II. His meditative *Il sistema periodico* (1976), was well-received in the United States when translated into English as *The Periodic Table* in 1984.

Levi continued to be haunted by his concentration camp experiences, and in 1986 he published *The Drowned and the Saved.* Despite his success, his resumption of a normal life was more apparent than real, as is clear from the recurrent dream that he recounted in *The Reawakening:* "I am sitting at a table with my family, or with friends, or at work, or in the green countryside...yet I feel a deep and subtle anguish....I am in the Lager [concentration camp] once more, and nothing is true outside the Lager. All the rest was a brief pause, a deception of the senses, a dream; my family, nature in flower, my home" (p. 207).

In 1987, ill and depressed, Primo Levi committed suicide.

See also **Auschwitz-Birkenau; Concentration Camps; Fascism; Italy; Resistance.**

BIBLIOGRAPHY

Primary Sources

Levi, Primo. *Il sistema periodico.* Turin, 1975.

———. *The Reawakening.* New York, 1995.

———. *Se questo è un uomo.* Turin, 1995.

Secondary Sources

Angier, Carole. *The Double Bond: Primo Levi, a Biography.* New York, 2002.

Anissimov, Myriam. *Primo Levi: Tragedy of an Optimist.* Woodstock, N.Y., 1999.

Camon, Ferdinando. *Conversations with Primo Levi.* Translated by John Shepley. Marlboro, Vt., 1989.

Thomson, Ian. *Primo Levi.* London, 2002.

MARIE-MATARD-BONUCCI

LÉVINAS, EMMANUEL (1906–1995), French philosopher.

Born in Kaunas (Kovno), Lithuania, on 12 January 1906, the French philosopher Emmanuel Lévinas responded to the violence of the twentieth century by promoting ethics to the status of philosophy, in dynamic tension between the Jewish Bible and ancient Greek philosophy.

Lévinas enjoyed a happy childhood rudely interrupted by the First World War and revolution. His father's profession as a bookseller secured a comfortable existence for his family outside the old Jewish quarter. His mother tongue was Russian, but he learned Hebrew early. Lévinas grew up surrounded by books, including the Torah and the great classics of Russian literature. After he passed the entrance examination linked to the *numerus clausus* (a quota that limited the number of Jewish students), he attended the lyceum in Kharkiv (Kharkov), Ukraine, where the family moved during the war years.

In 1923 Lévinas registered as a philosophy student in Strasbourg, France, where he first met Maurice Blanchot (1907–2003), who would become a lifelong friend. His teachers at Strasbourg, notably Maurice Halbwachs, Charles Blondel, and Maurice Pradines, left a permanent mark on him. He proceeded to the University of Freiburg, Germany, to study phenomenology, then known as the "new thinking," and was present in 1929 at the celebrated "Davos encounter" in Switzerland, when Martin Heidegger (1889–1976) and Ernst Cassirer (1874–1945) clashed philosophically. In 1930, now in Paris, he defended a thesis published as *The Theory of Intuition in Husserl's Phenomenology* (English translation, 1973). He was a prime mover in the introduction of phenomenology into France, and important articles of his in this connection were collected in *En découvrant l'existence avec Husserl et Heidegger* (1949; Discovering existence with Husserl and Heidegger). He had close relationships with the French philosophers Léon Brunschvicg (1869–1944), Gabriel Marcel (1888–1973), and Jean Wahl (1888–1974). He joined the Alliance Israélite Universelle, a French international Jewish organization founded in Paris in 1860 to protect Jewish rights as citizens and to promote education and professional development among Jews around the world. Lévinas awoke very early to the threat of Nazism. Though he continued to admire Heidegger, he contested his thinking as early as 1935 in *De l'évasion* (*On Escape*, 2003). He was naturalized as French in 1931 and thanks to his classification as a prisoner of war escaped anti-Semitic persecution. His family, still in Lithuania, were murdered as early as 1941 by the Nazis and their allies. Thereafter Lévinas lived with what he called a "tumor on the memory."

After the war, Lévinas contributed much to the reconstruction of French Judaism, assuming the directorship of the École Normale Israélite Orientale (ENIO) of the Alliance Israélite Universelle. He welcomed the creation of the state of Israel. Beginning in 1947, he studied the Talmud under a somewhat enigmatic teacher known as "Monsieur Chouchani." He was inspired by such great Lithuanian figures as the Vilna Gaon (Rabbi Eliyahu of Vilna; 1720–1797) and Rabbi Chaim of Volozin (1759–1821), who worked out a "rational traditional system" in opposition to the Jewish enlightenment and to Hasidism. The Talmudic teaching Lévinas offered at gatherings of French-speaking Jewish intellectuals after 1957 constituted a major dimension of his work, in which he uncovered a forgotten tradition that had much light to shed on the modern world. In *Difficile liberté: Essais sur le judaisme* (1963; *Difficult Freedom: Essays on Judaism*, 1990), Lévinas described Judaism as a mature religion and argued that the fact of having been chosen merely added to the responsibility of the Jews. This ethical Judaism was directly inspired by the nineteenth-century philosopher Hermann Cohen (1842–1918).

Two years after defending a second thesis, *Totalité et infini* (1961; *Totality and Infinity: An Essay on Exteriority*, 1969), Lévinas took up university teaching, first in Poitiers, then at Nanterre, and finally at the Sorbonne. *Totalité et infini* was a kind of palimpsest of *Der Stern de Erlösung* (1921; *The Star of Redemption*, 1971), the main work of the German Jewish religious thinker Franz Rosenzweig (1886–1929), begun in the Balkan trenches in 1917. This time philosophy collides with the violence of the Second World War and the experience of Auschwitz. In *Totalité et infini* there is again a protest of a singularity against the totality, clearly expressing an ontology of war in which the other is reduced to the same, and an eschatology of messianic peace. Rosenzweig and Lévinas criticize the Hegelian philosophy of history. How is inhumanity to be averted? asks Lévinas. The "epiphany of the face" reveals at once the temptation to murder and its impossibility. But the relationship to the other man leads also to politics. A "third party" interposes itself between me and the other and demands justice and universality.

Autrement qu'être; ou au-delà de l'essence (1974; *Otherwise than Being; or, Beyond Essence,* 1998), dedicated to the victims of the Holocaust, represents a radicalization of Lévinas's philosophy. The subject now becomes hostage to the other. My neighbor "assigns" me; I am obliged to substitute myself for him and cannot escape. The interpersonal relationship is dissymmetrical. The face of the other embodies that trace of the infinite which Lévinas calls illeity. The parting words of this philosophy occur in *De Dieu qui vient à l'idée* (1982; *Of God Who Comes to Mind,* 1998): we must "hear a God uncontaminated by being." Lévinas died in Paris on 25 December 1995.

As heir of the Judeo-German philosophical synthesis effected by Hermann Cohen and Franz Rosenzweig, Lévinas supplied French philosophy with a grammar of ethics nourished by Talmudic teachings. As the exponent of a twentieth-century return to Judaism, he strove to reveal Judaism's universality. He was a profound influence on Maurice Blanchot, Paul Ricoeur (1913–2005), and Jacques Derrida (1930–2004).

See also **Derrida, Jacques; Holocaust; Phenomenology.**

BIBLIOGRAPHY

Chalier, Catherine, and Miguel Abensour, eds. *Emmanuel Lévinas.* Paris, 1991.

Poirié, François. *Emmanuel Lévinas.* Paris, 1987. Reprint, 1994.

MARGARET TEBOUL

LÉVI-STRAUSS, CLAUDE (b. 1908), French anthropologist.

Claude Lévi-Strauss was the key founder of the mid-twentieth-century movement called structuralism, which applied the linguistic theory of Ferdinand de Saussure (1857–1913) to anthropology and other fields. Born in Brussels, Lévi-Strauss moved with his family to France at age five. He studied philosophy and law at the University of Paris. In 1934 he became professor of sociology at the University of São Paolo. His interest shifted

to ethnology, and he did fieldwork among Brazilian tribes. He resigned from his post in 1937 and returned briefly to France. Fleeing the Vichy government, he went to the New School for Social Research in New York, where he attended the lectures of the linguist Roman Jakobson (1896–1982). He then served as French Cultural Attaché in Washington, D.C. In 1947 he returned permanently to France, received his doctorate, and in 1948 became adjunct director of the Musée de l'Homme in Paris. In 1952 he became Director of Studies of the École Pratique des Hautes Ètudes. In 1959 he became Professor of Anthropology at the Collège de France. In 1973 he was elected a member of the French Academy. He retired in 1982.

As important as Lévi-Strauss's analysis of kinship has been, his analysis of myth has been far more influential. At first glance his work seems to be a revival of the long-discredited intellectualist view of myth epitomized by the Victorian anthropologist Edward Burnett Tylor (1832–1917). Yet Lévi-Strauss is severely critical of Tylor, for whom nonliterate peoples concoct myth rather than science because they think less critically than moderns. For Lévi-Strauss, nonliterate peoples create myth because they think differently from moderns, but no less rigorously.

In Lévi-Strauss's view, myth expresses nonliterate, or "primitive," thinking. Primitive thinking deals with phenomena qualitatively rather than, like modern thinking, quantitatively. It focuses on the observable, sensory, concrete aspects of phenomena rather than, like modern thinking, on the unobservable, non-sensory, abstract ones. Yet antithetically to Tylor, Lévi-Strauss considers myth no less scientific than modern science. Myth is science, not the mere forerunner to science. Myth is primitive science, but not thereby inferior science.

If myth is an instance of primitive thinking because it deals with concrete phenomena, it is an instance of thinking itself because it classifies phenomena. Lévi-Strauss maintains that all humans think in the form of classifications, specifically pairs of oppositions, and project them onto the world. Among the many cultural phenomena that express these oppositions, myth is distinctive in resolving or, more accurately, tempering the oppositions it expresses. Those contradictions are to be found not at the level of the plot but at the deeper level that Lévi-Strauss famously calls the "structure."

All the contradictions expressed are apparently reducible to instances of the fundamental contradiction between "nature" and "culture." That contradiction stems from the conflict that humans experience between themselves as animals, and therefore a part of nature, and themselves as human beings, and therefore a part of culture. This conflict had long been noted by Jean-Jacques Rousseau (1712–1778), Sigmund Freud (1856–1939), and many others, but for Lévi-Strauss it originates in the mind, rather than in experience. The mind thinks "oppositionally" and projects oppositions onto the world, where they are experienced as if they were in the world itself.

Lévi-Strauss's clearest examples of the conflict between nature and culture are the oppositions in myths between raw and cooked food, wild and tame animals, and incest and exogamy. It is much less clear how other recurrent oppositions of his, such as those between sun and moon, hot and cold, high and low, male and female, and life and death, symbolize the split between nature and culture rather than a split within nature. Similarly, it is far from clear how oppositions such as those of sister versus wife and of matrilocal versus patrilocal kinship symbolize other than a split within culture.

Lévi-Strauss distinguishes his "structuralist" approach to myth from the "narrative" approaches of all other theories, which adhere to the plot of myth. The plot, or "diachronic dimension," of a myth is that, say, event A leads to event B, which leads to event C, which leads to event D. The structure, or "synchronic dimension," is either that events A and B constitute an opposition mediated by event C or, as in the Oedipus myth, that events A and B, which constitute the same opposition, are to each other as events C and D, an analogous opposition, are to each other. The structure is exactly the expression and tempering of contradictions.

Overall, Lévi-Strauss strives to decipher the unconscious grammar of myth. To demonstrate that myths, seemingly the most random of artifacts, actually adhere to a tight logic is for Lévi-Strauss to demonstrate that their creators do as well. While Lévi-Strauss writes about nonliterate peoples almost exclusively—his analysis of Oedipus is an exception—he really writes to show that all human beings are akin. "Savage" and modern thought are variant expressions of a common human mind.

Lévi-Strauss claims to have been much influenced by Karl Marx (1818–1883), whose concept of a dialectic purportedly underlies the structure of a myth. But Lévi-Strauss's focus on the unchanging nature of the mind, on the consummate rationality of the mind, on the mind as independent of society, and on myths as similar worldwide led to the association of structuralism with a reactionary ideology. Consequently structuralism was taken by some observers as typifying the modernity against which postmodernism positioned itself.

See also **France; Jakobson, Roman; Saussure, Ferdinand de.**

BIBLIOGRAPHY

Primary Sources

Lévi-Strauss, Claude. "The Structural Study of Myth." *Journal of American Folklore* 68 (1955): 428–444.

———. *Structural Anthropology*, vol. 1. Translated by. by Claire Jacobson and Brooke Grundfest Schoepf. New York, 1961.

———. *The Savage Mind*. Chicago, 1966.

———. *Introduction to a Science of Mythology*. 4 vols. Translated by John Weightman and Doreen Weightman. New York, 1969–1981.

———. *Tristes Tropiques*. Translated by John and Doreen Weightman. London, 1973.

———. *Myth and Meaning*. Toronto, 1978.

———. *Structural Anthropology*, vol. 2. Translated by Monique Layton. New York, 1976.

Secondary Sources

Hayes, E. Nelson, and Tanya Hayes, eds. *Claude Lévi-Strauss: The Anthropologst as Hero*. Cambridge, Mass., 1970

Hénoff, Marcel. *Claude Lévi-Strauss and the Making of Structural Anthropology*. Translated by Mary Baker. Minneapolis, Minn., 1998.

Segal, Robert A. *Theorizing about Myth*. Amherst, Mass., 1999.

ROBERT A. SEGAL

LEWIS, WYNDHAM (1882–1957), English writer and painter.

Percy Wyndham Lewis was born in Canada and moved to England with his family at age six.

Abandoned by his American father, he was raised by his English mother, who ran a laundering business in north London. At the age of sixteen he received a prestigious scholarship to the Slade School of Art but was later ejected for unruly behavior. For the next decade he lived a bohemian life supported by his mother, spending time in Madrid, Munich, and Paris. He published his first short story, "The Pole," in 1909 and by 1910 seemed poised to become a writer. But in 1911 he contributed to his first group exhibition: his paintings were immediately noticed by critics, who admired his taut, vigorous draftsmanship. Within a year he was producing major paintings that drew on the idiom of contemporary cubism yet elaborated a distinctly personal style: pictures of strange automatons, their faces locked in rigid grimaces, who stagger through desolate fields of piercing arcs and angles.

It was a propitious moment. Roger Fry's famous exhibition of postimpressionist artists had taken place in December 1910, followed by the first exhibition of futurist painting in early 1912, prompting unprecedented debate about contemporary art. Lewis admired the concerted polemical onslaught the futurists had mounted and resolved to shape a movement of his own. Teaming up with Ezra Pound, he launched vorticism with *Blast,* an avant-garde journal bristling with pugnacious manifestos and typography.

Lewis, briefly, became a celebrity. But he was also leading a double life. His illegitimate children, born in 1911 and 1913, were being cared for by his aging mother, and in 1919 and 1920 he had two more, these entrusted to a home for orphans. After serving as an artillery gunner during World War I, Lewis returned to face ever-mounting debts. He held major exhibitions in 1921 and 1937, but neither could rectify his indigence. He turned to portraiture, and while he produced modern masterpieces, including several of T. S. Eliot, he failed to earn a viable income. He also took up writing in earnest, issuing massive volumes of philosophical and cultural criticism such as *The Art of Being Ruled* (1926) and *Time and Western Man* (1927) and novels such as *The Apes of God* (1930), a mordant satire on wealthy bohemia, blemished by undercurrents of anti-Semitism.

In 1930 he married Gladys Anne Hoskins. That same year he cobbled together a biography of Adolf Hitler, the first in any language. The research was poor, the writing sloppy, and by 1933, when the climate of opinion had irrevocably altered, passersby would spit at shop windows displaying the book. Lewis's reputation was permanently damaged.

Undeterred, Lewis continued to produce travel books, novels, topical commentary, and occasional portraits. In 1937 he published *The Revenge for Love,* a novel of deceit and betrayal set against the background of the Spanish civil war. It brought no relief to his desperate financial straits. Lewis left for the United States and Canada in 1939, but commissions failed to materialize there.

When he returned to England in 1945, Lewis faced arrears of rent and unpaid taxes. He also learned that he was going blind. For some years a tumor had been growing in his brain, slowly crushing his optic nerves. Lewis completed his last portrait in 1949 and two years later publicly announced his blindness. His last years were spent writing the novels *Monstre Gai* and *Malign Fiesta* (both published in 1955). In 1956, only eight months before his death, his paintings were the subject of a major retrospective exhibition at the Tate Gallery.

See also **Cubism; Modernism; Pound, Ezra.**

BIBLIOGRAPHY

Edwards, Paul. *Wyndham Lewis: Painter and Writer.* New Haven, Conn., 2001.

O'Keefe, Paul. *Some Sort of Genius: A Life of Wyndham Lewis.* London, 2001.

LAWRENCE RAINEY

LIBERALISM. A European living in 1930, or even in 1970, would certainly have been astounded to learn that liberalism had outlived the twentieth century and even begun to dominate Europe at the beginning of the twenty-first. To understand this, one must remember that Europeans experienced the period between the outbreak of World War I in 1914 and the fall of the Berlin Wall in 1989 as *a continual and repeated crisis of liberalism.*

The history of liberalism between 1914 and the early twenty-first century is thus a rather curious one, for it is the history of a death followed by a resurrection. It is worth bearing in mind, however, that the definition of liberalism varies depending on which of its several aspects is under consideration. Even putting matters at their simplest, at least five dimensions must be taken into account: judicial liberalism, according to which rights protect all the freedoms required for the unfettered development of the individual; constitutional liberalism, or political arrangements designed to prevent or limit the concentration, concealment, or abuse of power; political liberalism, in which major political parties seek to promote their doctrine among the masses; economic liberalism, which assigns priority to free enterprise; and finally, too often overlooked, the moral and cultural liberalism that preaches tolerance for diverse opinions and behavior. These different facets together form the variegated picture offered by liberalism after 1914.

POST–WORLD WAR I: LIBERALISM IN CRISIS

One thing, though, can hardly be contested: liberalism as it came into being in the nineteenth century was the first victim of World War I. So great was the war's impact that *all* dimensions of liberalism may be said to have been thrown into question, including the moral one, whose retreat was clearly reflected by men's increased power over women, by the new tension between the generations, and by an increased repression of abortion in the context of policies designed to boost the birthrate.

The severest blow to liberalism was of an intellectual and philosophical order. Many thoughtful Europeans in the 1920s felt that their civilization was no longer liberal in its essence. The notion of moral progress had been shattered by the military exactions deliberately visited upon civilian populations (bombing, imprisonment, expulsions). Any notion of a law-governed community of nations (*droit des gens*) or of a peace founded on international law had been reduced to a mockery by the war aims of the various belligerents (including the annexation of foreign territories, the economic subjugation of conquered peoples, and the forced removal of populations). Neither the draconian economic measures decreed by the Treaty of Versailles (and denounced by John Maynard Keynes), nor the League of Nations, whose actions were for the most part ineffective, could restore the idea of a European civilization.

The mass slaughter of World War I was perceived as the destruction of the very principles in whose defense that war had been waged. The institution of press censorship, the opening of the mail, and restrictions on the freedom to buy and sell, and on travel and assembly, meant that all the liberties that had hitherto defined the individual's everyday relationship to a liberal order had been curtailed or suspended; what was more, they had been abridged by states, parties, or politicians who continued to call themselves liberal. It would be fair to say, however, albeit something of a generalization, that in the wake of the war European culture, as expressed through the arts, literature, and philosophy, became antiliberal, rejecting reason and individualism and embracing violence.

It was in the economic sphere that the crisis of liberalism was most acutely felt. The great crash of 1929 is often looked upon as the catalyst of the crisis of liberal capitalism, but so far as Europe was concerned, and in terms of public perceptions, economic liberalism had already been deeply wounded by the great financial and monetary upheavals of the 1920s. For the European middle class, liberalism as it existed prior to 1914 was founded not on credit and consumption but rather on the traditional forms of rent, thrift, and inheritance. The inflation, rising prices, and currency devaluation especially rampant in countries such as Germany ruined (in both senses of the term) the bourgeois forms of wealth, revenue from which depended on stable prices and the convertibility of national currencies into gold.

For the population at large, it was faith in the "laws" of the economy that was exploded by the developments of the 1920s and 1930s. How could one continue to believe in a liberal economy governed by an invisible hand, dispensing worldwide justice and prosperity, when one's own experience included multiple currency devaluations, mass unemployment (10 to 12 percent of the active population in Great Britain in the 1920s), rife stock-market speculation, and the manifest inability of liberal governments to introduce adequate policies in response? Economic liberalism as a set of social beliefs, including the possibility of steady self-enrichment, the prospect of passing on a significant inheritance, and the presumption that it was reasonable to plan for the future, was thus critically compromised as the century proceeded. Only a new liberalism founded on consumption, credit, immediate remuneration in the form of salaries, and massive social mobility—a kind of liberalism that most continental European countries would not experience until the 1960s—would restore a collective sense of confidence in liberal capitalism.

In Great Britain, the "fall" of the Liberal Party brought much grist to the mill for those who foretold the utter demise of liberalism. The party, which had still dominated British political life at the beginning of the war, emerged from the conflict deeply divided. The Liberals were at loggerheads on almost every major issue: the acceptability of economic intervention by the state; the partition of Ireland; the type of social reforms called for; the return to the gold standard (abandoned in 1931); free trade (abandoned in 1932); and the relationship between the nation and its colonial empire. In point of fact, the Liberal Party, divided as it was between David Lloyd George and Herbert Henry Asquith, was now the third political force in the country, behind the Conservative and Labour Parties; and, despite a certain revival in the 1970s, it remained in that position for the rest of the century. Liberals experienced a comparable collapse in numerous other European countries, and often for the same reasons (Norway, Sweden, Belgium, Denmark). Long in the majority, if not the parliamentary leadership, before 1914, liberal parties were relegated to the position of a structural minority everywhere in postwar Europe.

In France, the parties inspired by liberalism had always been split between moderate (Democratic Alliance Party) and radical republicans (Radical Party), but all tendencies had heretofore shared the same cultural attachment to economic liberalism and the same commitment to predominantly parliamentary institutions. In the course of the 1920s and 1930s, however, this common French liberal culture suffered a deep crisis: liberal politicians went so far as to criticize or reject the basic assumptions of liberalism, whether economic, as with the defense of a planned economy by the younger generation of radicals, or political, as with the call for a "strong" government overriding the parliamentary principle. By the mid-1930s, challenged on the one side by extreme right-wing leagues and on the other by powerful communist and socialist parties, French liberal republicanism had lost most of an influence that it was destined never to regain.

The Weimar Republic (1919–1933) is probably the most studied case of a general crisis of liberalism, one that combined not only a crisis of the liberal parties, a crisis in liberal institutions, and a crisis of liberal doctrine, but also arguably a crisis in liberal political mores, as moderation, the rule of law, and a public discourse governed by rational argument were challenged by rising violence, intimidation, sloganeering, and street propaganda. Both the right liberals of the Deutsche Volkspartei and the left liberals of the Deutsche Demokratische Partei were obliterated by the dual challenge of the nationalist and the Marxist parties. Though the liberals (specifically Hugo Preuss) had inspired the constitutional compromise of 1919, they drew no benefit from it; instead they were accused of treason for having accepted the Treaty of Versailles, of economic failure on account of inflation and of the currency crisis, and of political impotence as demonstrated by the instability of their ministerial cabinets. Liberalism had become the straw man of all political diatribes, be they driven by nationalist resentment or by the desire for radical social change. Cultural and artistic attitudes, themselves shot through by violence and radicalism, also hastened the crisis of liberal values. It is well worth recalling that Adolf Hitler's coming to power in January 1933 took place against the tripartite backdrop of the liberal parties' defeats, the crisis of liberal constitutionalism (as decrees and presidential ordinances replaced genuine parliamentary legislation), and the failure of intellectual and moral liberalism betokened by the triumph of violence and maximalism over rationality.

In not a few European countries that adopted neo-authoritarian regimes it was the weakness of liberalism—notably of liberal institutions, of judicial and constitutional liberalism—rather than the strength of authoritarian or fascist ideology that supplied the lever. Even the liberal democrats acknowledged this: liberalism was its own worst enemy. The image it presented in the face of a dysfunctional economy (whose crisis was only aggravated by the liberal policy of budgetary deflation), in the face of authoritarian governments, or in the face of international diplomatic crises, was one of impotence.

POST–WORLD WAR II: LIMITED APPEAL

The disfavor into which liberalism had fallen explained the ambiguous nature of the reconstruction of the so-called liberal democracies after 1945. Nazism and fascism were vanquished; the antiliberal Far Right was discredited; yet the disappearance of these rivals in no way heralded liberalism's return to grace. True, the shock caused by the revelation of Nazi crimes gave a significant fillip to liberalism as the guarantor of the basic rights of human beings. The idea that these rights must be protected by constitutions and declarations of first principles rather than abandoned to the vicissitudes of political majorities was decisively reaffirmed. Both international law (witness the Universal Declaration of Human Rights of 1948) and national constitutional law (for example, the Federal Constitutional Tribunal created in 1951 for West Germany or the French Constitutional Council of 1958) strove, in accordance with the intellectual legacy of the eminent jurist Hans Kelsen (1881–1973), to perpetuate the rule of law (in the European sense of an *État de droit* or *Rechtsstaat*). But, broadly speaking, in the Europe of 1945, liberalism had by no means retrieved its former status as the most popular political philosophy—and certainly not in the economic and social realms.

It is sometimes suggested that the economic and social system instituted in western Europe after 1945 had liberal roots. William Beveridge is usually cited in this connection for his contribution to the British welfare state, with its major public services providing protections against the ravages of illness, unemployment, old age, and poverty; and John Maynard Keynes is credited for his economic prescriptions justifying social spending and voluntary budgetary deficits. The contribution of liberalism here should not be overestimated, however. During these early postwar years, with their emphasis on the nationalization of big business

and often on economic planning, liberals, be they economists, politicians, or high civil servants, were largely relegated to the background. In fact the advent of the welfare state served only to divide European liberals once again: on the one hand were those (such as Friedrich Hayek) who were hostile to the very idea of economic and social intervention by the state, and on the other hand those who accepted a compromise with the social democrats in the shape of a "social market" economy. Where political parties calling themselves liberal still existed, they tended (except in Denmark, Sweden, and Norway, where they were more solid) to be small intermediate parties capable at most of adding their weight to coalitions of one kind or another, as in the cases of the German Free Democratic Party, the Italian Liberal Party, the French Centre National des Indépendants, or the Belgian Liberal Reform Party. These small liberal parties no longer represented anybody except particular minority sectors—liberal professions, artisans, small businessmen, or farmers—who had been forgotten or ignored by newly established social democratic regimes.

Liberalism did not disappear altogether between the 1940s and the 1970s, but this was due solely to its survival in an intellectual sense and to a continued niche existence within the other great political traditions. Thus liberal features were easier to recognize in the Christian social democratic movements of Alcide De Gasperi in Italy or Ludwig Erhard in Germany, with their attachment to the principles of competition and a stable currency, or even among some social democrats, than in liberal parties prone at times to drift into the politics of protest or populism, confining themselves to a critique of state bureaucracy and the social burdens imposed by fiscal inequities. Liberal attitudes on rational planning in a free market economy persisted too among high technocrats and functionaries, such as Jacques Rueff or Jean Monnet in France, or in the pressure groups of industrialists. It was as though liberalism had abandoned the political realm to other tendencies and no longer needed to engage in politics in the electoral sense.

LATE TWENTIETH CENTURY: RESURGENCE

Then came the last great surprise of the twentieth century: the almost triumphal "return" of liberalism. The economic crisis of the 1970s had the opposite effect to the antiliberal reaction of the 1930s. No longer a scapegoat, liberalism became a kind of miracle remedy.

In Great Britain, the political success of Margaret Thatcher, prime minister from 1979 to 1990, was based on a return to the social ethic of economic liberalism. Her policies, embracing anti-inflationary measures, privatization, reduced taxation, and the economic disengagement of the state, were underpinned not only by new economic theories (monetarism and the emphasis on supply rather than demand) but above all by an appeal to the values of hard work and individual merit as opposed to what she called a "culture of dependence" produced by the welfare-state era. Thatcherist neoliberalism has been adopted, though often in considerably modified form, as the political credo of many European governments since the 1980s, among them the administrations of Jacques Chirac, Édouard Balladur, and Alain Juppé in France, Helmut Kohl in Germany, José Maria Aznar in Spain, and Silvio Berlusconi in Italy. The only social features of the welfare state still defended everywhere are health services and unemployment protection—often in a reconceived version, as in Holland, Sweden, Finland, Norway, and Denmark.

There was more to liberalism's rebirth, however, than the fact that it effectively addressed economic crisis. The critique of European communism and its subsequent collapse brought a new intellectual and political generation into the liberal fold. Beginning in the 1970s, broad criticism of communist regimes put the defense of basic freedoms back on the order of the day, including freedom of information, freedom of expression, and freedom to practice one's religion. Once the communist regimes were gone, an economic liberalism holding out the prospect of rapid access to the consumer society, of free enterprise, and of geographical and social mobility, exercised a pronounced power of seduction over a portion of public opinion in formerly communist countries, most of all among young people.

The construction of the European Union (EU) also had an impact on the liberal renaissance. From the outset (the Treaty of Rome of 1957), liberal principles underlay a project driven by the wish to transcend international conflicts through peaceful cooperation among states. When the institutional process of European integration resumed with the Single European Act in 1986, the Maastricht Treaty in 1992, the formal completion of the single market in 1993, and the introduction of the single currency in 2002, these developments paralleled the successes of neoliberal policies within member nations. And indeed liberal conceptions of free trade, deregulation, and the disengagement of the state from economic management also informed (and still inform) the main decisions taken at the European level. The progression of EU membership from fifteen to twenty-five states, including the incorporation of former communist countries, has even further strengthened the influence of economic, judicial, and philosophical liberalism within pan-European institutions.

It is therefore tempting to conclude that liberalism has experienced a perfect resuscitation, as though the beneficiary of an egregious instance of the cunning of history after the successive disappearances of the great mass ideologies of the twentieth century—nationalism, fascism, Nazism, communism, and socialism. There can be no doubt that liberalism in its economic and judicial dimensions was far more solid in the first years of the twenty-first century than it was in either 1930 or 1950. Yet there is something ambiguous about this "victory" of liberalism.

EARLY TWENTY-FIRST CENTURY: DIVISIONS

In the first place, there has been no corresponding renaissance of the great liberal political parties of an earlier day, founded *exclusively* on the liberal credo. Strong in some senses but weak in others, liberalism is widely dispersed—discernible as easily in the British Conservative Party as among continental Social Democrats; it has no single incarnation. Precisely because of this broad, almost hegemonic presence, European liberalism is still the butt of sharp criticism from vast mass political movements. These may be of the Far Right, claiming that liberalism threatens the integrity of the nation, or of the Far Left, arguing that in its globalizing phase liberalism destroys social bonds.

Second, compared with nineteenth-century liberalism, neoliberalism seems seriously lopsided, being far more legal and economic in nature than political and constitutional. From the constitutional standpoint, in fact, liberalism is visibly in retreat: neoliberal experiments, notably in Great Britain and Italy, have been characterized by a personalized and media-driven exercise of power, a centralization of decision-making, and a marked decline in parliamentary process.

Finally, it should be pointed out that the aspect of liberalism that has perhaps made the most headway since the 1960s is the cultural and social emancipation implied by the progress of feminism, the extension of gay rights, and the transformation of the family and of mores. This kind of liberalism has nourished left-wing political culture but not that of the neoliberal Right. Left liberals are inclined to defend minority and women's rights and to embrace multiculturalism while frequently remaining opposed to economic liberalism, whereas neoliberals often ally themselves with such neoconservative demands as a return to the traditional family and the defense of moral and even religious values. Partisans of cultural liberalism are thus prone to find themselves in direct opposition to partisans of economic liberalism, so that the idea of a liberal movement that is fundamentally split is as pertinent in the early twenty-first century as it ever was.

See also **Asquith, Herbert Henry; Beveridge, William; Keynes, J. M.; Lloyd George, David; Monnet, Jean.**

BIBLIOGRAPHY

Aron, Raymond. *An Essay on Liberty.* Translated by Helen Weaver. New York, 1970. Originally published, 1965.

Burdeau, Georges. *Le libéralisme.* Paris, 1979.

Freeden, Michael. *Liberalism Divided: A Study in British Political Thought, 1914–1939.* Oxford, U.K., 1986.

Lippmann, Walter. *An Inquiry into the Principles of the Good Society.* Boston, 1937. Reprint, as *The Good Society,* with an introduction by Gary Dean Best, New Brunswick, N.J., 2005.

NICOLAS ROUSSELLIER

LIEBKNECHT, KARL (1871–1919), socialist agitator and a founder of the German Communist Party.

Karl Liebknecht was the son of Wilhelm Liebknecht (1826–1900), a prominent leader of the socialist movement from its beginnings in the 1860s. Karl Liebknecht studied jurisprudence at the universities of Leipzig and Berlin and completed his doctoral degree in 1897 (Würzburg). After qualifying as an attorney in private practice, Karl and his brother, Theodor, established their own law firm, and Karl earned renown as an able defender of political radicals in high-profile trials. His public role as a socialist politician began when he won a seat on the Berlin city council (November 1901), and subsequently he was elected to the Prussian state parliament (1908), a victory notable for the fact that it occurred while he was serving a prison sentence for high treason. In 1903 and 1907 he campaigned unsuccessfully for a Reichstag seat in the extremely conservative district of Potsdam-Spandau-Osthavelland but emerged victorious there in the election of January 1912.

Liebknecht sought to advance the cause of socialism by emphasizing particular issues—antimilitarism, the youth movement, anti-tsarism, and Prussian suffrage reform—and routinely promoted radical policies unacceptable to the Social Democratic leadership. In vain he urged Social Democrats to launch a vigorous fight against militarism, including the dissemination of propaganda in the army and navy. He addressed his antimilitarism directly to youth, especially as one of the founders of the Socialist Youth International (1907), and presented a comprehensive exposition of his arguments in *Militarism and Antimilitarism* (*Militarismus und Antimilitarismus,* 1907). Legal authorities used this publication as the basis for charging Liebknecht with high treason, for which he was tried (October 1907), convicted, and sentenced to eighteen months' fortress detention. Despite incarceration, Liebknecht continued his attacks on tsarism and his demands for Prussian suffrage reform, advocating the use of a general strike to effect changes in the electoral system. Regardless of Liebknecht's public prominence, his radical positions tended to isolate him from the other Social Democratic leaders.

The outbreak of World War I (1 August 1914) confronted international socialism with a major crisis. For years Liebknecht had demanded that socialists do everything possible to prevent and oppose war. However, when the German government immediately requested additional funds, the vast majority of the socialist deputies supported the credits. Liebknecht and thirteen other deputies argued unsuccessfully that the party should reject any action that implied support of the war. In the end, however, the radical minority also submitted to party discipline and the whole delegation voted for the war credits (4 August 1914). Nonetheless, as annexationists voiced their expansionist aims, Liebknecht and like-minded opponents of the war formed the International Group, which later evolved into the Spartacist League (Spartakusbund). Even then Liebknecht still stood alone, as he cast the only vote against the second war credits bill (2 December 1914), an act that, along with his inflammatory speeches, made him anathema to the great majority of Social Democratic deputies. Party leaders prohibited him from speaking in the name of Social Democracy and in effect expelled him from the delegation (February 1915). A few days later the government, wishing to silence him, drafted Liebknecht into the army, but he would not be silent and during the same year published *The Class Struggle in War* (1915; *Klassenkampf gegen den Krieg*), a telling exposure of militarism, capitalism, and the war. In February 1916 Liebknecht, Rosa Luxemburg, Franz Mehring, and others in the International Group founded the *Spartacus Letters* (*Spartakusbriefe*) to disseminate their critique of the war. At a huge antiwar demonstration in Potsdam Square in Berlin on the evening of 1 May 1916, Liebknecht, wearing his military uniform, spoke passionately against the war. Within hours he was arrested, tried for high treason, and sentenced to prison for a total of four years, six months. He did not serve the full term but was released from prison on 23 October 1918.

Liebknecht immediately threw himself into the revolutionary turmoil, and on 9 November 1918, impulsively but ineffectively, declared the birth of a German socialist republic. He refused in any way to collaborate with the provisional government led by the majority Social Democrats and turned his back on all parliamentary institutions. Instead he called for a government based on workers' and soldiers' councils—influenced by the Bolsheviks—and then played a leading role in transforming the Spartacist League into the German Communist Party (30 December 1918–1 January 1919). Consistent with his impetuous nature, he joined fully in the ill-advised call on 5 January 1919 for an insurrection to overthrow the government. Within days the infamous right-wing Freikorps brutally suppressed the uprising, and on 15 January Liebknecht and Luxemburg were captured, severely beaten, and murdered.

Liebknecht left essentially a one-dimensional legacy. The manner of his death raised him, along with Luxemburg, to the pantheon of Communist martyrs. Vladimir Lenin, Joseph Stalin, and the Russian communists embraced Liebknecht's heritage because it contained nothing, in contrast to that of Rosa Luxemburg, that in any way challenged their actions or ideology. The former German Democratic Republic (East Germany) celebrated Liebknecht's work as a foundation on which that state was built. Although Liebknecht wrote extensively, theory was not his strength. His chief contribution to the history of socialism lay in his unquestioned courage as an agitator and man of action, whether in the courtroom, in speaking fervently to crowds and demonstrators, or addressing parliament with provocative proposals.

See also **Luxemburg, Rosa; Spartacists; Zetkin, Clara.**

BIBLIOGRAPHY

Primary Sources

Liebknecht, Karl. *Gesammelte Reden und Schriften.* 9 vols. Berlin, 1958–1971.

Secondary Sources

Meyer, Karl. *Karl Liebknecht: Man without a Country.* Washington, D.C., 1957.

Trotnow, Helmut. *Karl Liebknecht: A Political Biography.* Hamden, Conn., 1984. Makes an argument, not entirely persuasive, that Liebknecht was motivated far more by ideals of humanity and justice than by Marxism.

Wohlgemuth, Heinz. *Karl Liebknecht: Eine Biographie.* Berlin, 1973. A work that reflects much of the official view of Liebknecht in the former German Democratic Republic and stresses his significance for that state.

VERNON L. LIDTKE

LISSITZKY, EL

LISSITZKY, EL (1890–1941), Russian painter, graphic artist, and designer.

During the 1920s and 1930s El Lissitzky did more than any other artist to define a practice of graphic design in the Soviet Union. Early in his career he collaborated actively with members of the European avant-garde, but after his return home in 1925 he worked almost exclusively for the Soviet regime.

Born in the town of Polshinok in the Pale of Settlement, a Jewish enclave in Russia, Lissitzky studied painting as a young man with the artist Yehuda Pen before going to Darmstadt, Germany, in 1909 to study architecture. Returning to Russia at the outbreak of World War I, he worked as an architect in Moscow, while exhibiting his paintings with avant-garde groups and collaborating with Marc Chagall and other artists interested in creating a modern Jewish art. He also began to illustrate Jewish children's books and to work actively with Jewish organizations, including the Kultur Lige in Kiev. Perhaps his best-known book illustrations in this genre were for *Chad gadya* (One billy goat), which he completed in 1917.

In 1919 Chagall, who became the commissioner for artistic affairs in the town of Vitebsk, invited Lissitzky to head an architecture and printing workshop at the local art school there. When the suprematist artist Kazimir Malevich joined the school's faculty, Lissitzky, with other professors and students, became a member of Malevich's UNOVIS group and adopted some of suprematism's visual language of geometric forms. But Lissitzky developed his own approach to painting, which he called the *Proun* (an acronym for Project for a New Art). Unlike Malevich, Lissitzky created canvases with architectonic structures, declaring that to fully understand his paintings, the viewer had to consider them from multiple perspectives. Lissitzky was later to call these pictures way stations between painting and architecture. While in Vitebsk, he also produced several propaganda posters for the Red Army, the best known of which is "Beat the Whites with the Red Wedge."

In 1921 Lissitzky left for Europe, where he spent four years. Initially he lived in Berlin, where he collaborated with the Scythians, a Russian émigré group, for whom he designed several issues of an avant-garde magazine, *Veshch* (Object). This publication was intended as a cultural bridge between Russians in Europe and in the Soviet Union. He also worked with a community of Jewish artists as well as with Theo van Doesburg,

the founder of the De Stijl movement, and Kurt Schwitters, the Dada artist who established his one-man Merz movement in Hanover. While in Europe, Lissitzky saw the publication of his children's book *Of Two Squares,* which he had designed in Vitebsk, as well as a book of poems by Vladimir Mayakovsky, *For the Voice.* The two books were among the first avant-garde publications to interest German graphic designers, including Jan Tschichold, who recognized Lissitzky as one of the forerunners of the "new typography" that he promoted in the 1920s.

After recuperating from tuberculosis in Switzerland for about two years, Lissitzky returned to the Soviet Union and began to take on commissions for the state. Among the first was the All-Union Printing Trades Exhibition. This was followed by a commission to design the mammoth exhibit on the Soviet press, which the Soviet government presented at the Pressa, an international survey of the world press that opened in Cologne in 1928. The Pressa design was the first of four state-sponsored displays that Lissitzky created for foreign exhibitions, the other three being the section on Soviet film and photography for the Werkbund exhibition *Film und Foto* of 1929 as well as displays for the International Fur Trade Exhibition and the International Hygiene Exhibition in 1930.

Following his return to Moscow, Lissitzky also joined the faculty of the Vhkutemas, the state design school, where he taught in the department of interior design. One of the major projects that he and his students worked on was the design for a small flat in a new communal building. Lissitzky continued as well to design books and periodicals for the government. His major work as a publication designer was for the propaganda journal *USSR in Construction,* which was published between 1930 and 1941. For this publication, Lissitzky designed almost twenty-five issues, some with his wife, Sophie. He developed a narrative style that combined photographs, drawings, text, and sometimes pictorial statistics in order to tell a story. In the early years of the journal's publication, Lissitzky's designs portrayed heroic feats such as the construction of the Dnieper dam and power station, but by the late 1930s, the journal served as

Beat the Whites with the Red Wedge. Poster by El Lissitzky, c. 1919. Snark/Art Resource, NY

a mask for the purges and harsh conditions of collective labor imposed by Joseph Stalin. In 1941, the year he died of tuberculosis, Lissitzky received his last commission—three posters to abet the Soviet war effort.

See also **Chagall, Marc; Malevich, Kazimir; Painting, Avant-Garde; Socialist Realism.**

BIBLIOGRAPHY

Lissitzky-Küppers, Sophie. *El Lissitzky: Life, Letters, Texts.* Translated by Helene Aldwinckle and Mary Whittall. London, 1968.

Margolin, Victor. *The Struggle for Utopia: Rodchenko, Lissitzky, Moholy-Nagy, 1917–1946.* Chicago and London, 1997.

Nisbet, Peter. *El Lissitzky, 1890–1941: Catalogue for an Exhibition.* Cambridge, Mass., 1987.

Perloff, Nancy, and Brian Reed, eds. *Situating El Lissitzky: Vitebsk, Berlin, Moscow.* Los Angeles, 2003.

Tupitsyn, Margarita. *El Lissitzky: Beyond the Abstract Cabinet.* New Haven, Conn., 1999.

VICTOR MARGOLIN

LITHUANIA. Lithuania's uneasy existence as a nation in the twentieth century was shaped by its location on the frontier between Eastern and Western Europe and the diversity of its inhabitants, a fate shared in large part with its Baltic neighbors,

Latvia and Estonia. Predominantly Roman Catholic, ethnic Lithuanians speak a Baltic language. This linguistic identity has served as a basis for nation building since the mid-nineteenth century.

Until the 1990s the writing of Lithuania's twentieth-century history was hampered in the West by limited access to archival material, and in Lithuania by the need to conform to the orthodoxies of Soviet historiography. Recently, historians have moved away from nationalist narratives, paying more attention to the ethnic groups that have been part of the Lithuanian state. Significant work has been done on Lithuanian Jews, though the Holocaust in Lithuania is only now undergoing closer study. Other ethnic minorities, such as the Poles, still await studies in English.

1914–1920

In 1914 most of the territory inhabited by ethnic Lithuanians was part of the Russian Empire, into which Lithuania had been incorporated at the end of the eighteenth century after two hundred years of a shared commonwealth with Poland. Of the approximately 2.7 million inhabitants most Lithuanians were peasants, while the major cities were populated by Jews, Russians, and Poles, with ethnic Lithuanians a minority. From the mid-nineteenth century a small educated elite had successfully developed a national consciousness among the Lithuanian-speaking population.

Having declared war on Russia, German forces occupied Lithuania in 1915. Taking advantage of the situation created by the Russian Revolution and Germany's eastern interests, the Lithuanian National Council issued a declaration of independence on 16 February 1918. It took two years, however, before the Republic of Lithuania was recognized internationally. During this time the Red Army invaded from the east, while White Russian forces entered from the north. The Lithuanians responded by hastily organizing a volunteer army. In 1920 Poland took Vilnius, which Lithuanians considered their historic capital, forcing the new republic's government to move to Kaunas.

1920–1939

The 1923 census revealed a population just over two million: 84.2 percent Lithuanians, 7.6 percent Jews, 3.2 percent Poles, 2.5 percent Russians, and smaller numbers of Germans, Latvians, Belorusians, Ukrainians, Tatars, Karaim, and Roma.

The first constitution, framed in 1922, established a liberal democracy with a parliament (Seimas) and a president at the republic's head. A new independent farming class emerged from the land reform, initiated in 1922, whereby land was confiscated from the larger landowners, usually local Polish-speaking gentry, and redistributed to veterans of the volunteer armies, landless peasants, and those with small landholdings. Consequently, interwar Lithuania's economy was dominated by agriculture, with exports of meat and dairy products to Germany and Great Britain. In 1922 the *litas* was established as the national currency. On 17 December 1926 an army-organized coup installed the right-wing Nationalist Union leader, Antanas Smetona (1874–1944), as president. By May of the following year, parliament was dissolved, with a new constitution, increasing the president's powers, instituted in 1928.

The interwar period witnessed a lively cultural life with advances in art, literature, and music. By 1932 the number of children attending schools had more than doubled. Illiteracy, which affected a third of the population in 1923, was significantly reduced. In 1922 a new university was established in Kaunas. Basketball was entrenched as a national sport when the Lithuanian team won the European championship in 1937 and 1939. The Catholic Church, to which about 80 percent of the population belonged, played a significant role in education. Clergy could also be found in parliament, especially in the ranks of the Christian Democrats.

The sizable ethnic minorities established their own schools. The Jews, comprising the largest minority, formed a Jewish National Council that operated in conjunction with the short-lived Ministry of Jewish Affairs. Lithuanian Poles made up the second largest ethnic minority. Their activity was often curtailed by the Lithuanian government as a reprisal against the treatment of Lithuanians in Poland.

The conflict with Poland over Vilnius was not resolved during the interwar period. Access to the Baltic, however, was established when, in 1923, Lithuania seized the port city of Klaipėda, which was former German territory. Otherwise, Lithuania maintained neutrality.

1939–1945

During the Second World War, Lithuania was occupied in turn by both the Soviets and Nazi Germany. On 23 August 1939, just a week before invading Poland, Germany signed the Molotov-Ribbentrop Pact with the USSR, establishing spheres of influence. The Baltic states fell to the Soviets. On 10 October 1939 Lithuania signed an agreement with the Soviets, in which the latter were given permission to create military bases on Lithuanian territory, in exchange for Vilnius. The following year the Soviets, accusing Lithuania of kidnapping several soldiers, issued an ultimatum that led to the Soviet invasion of Lithuania on 15 June 1940. A year later, in June 1941, the Soviets deported between 16,200 and 30,000 inhabitants to Siberia and the northern reaches of Russia. Shortly thereafter the Soviets themselves fled the advancing Germans. During the Nazi occupation, 220,000 Jews were murdered. The Soviets' return in the summer of 1944 caused 60,000 Lithuanians to flee to the West, thus adding to an already significant émigré community.

1945–1991

When the Second World War ended, Lithuania was a Soviet Socialist Republic (SSR), though the Soviet annexation was not recognized unanimously in the West. Lithuania now had Vilnius as its capital.

The government and Communist Party of the Lithuanian SSR, led for almost thirty years by Antanas Sniečkus (1903–1974), had a high proportion of ethnic Lithuanians, which helped to stem the russification of the new Soviet republic.

The years immediately after the war were marked by conflict between the occupying forces and the Lithuanian resistance movement. Guerrilla fighters impeded the collectivization of farms, curbed the numbers of Soviet settlers brought into the country, and slowed the development of heavy industry. Collectivization was, nevertheless, implemented between 1947 and 1952, facilitated in large part by the deportation of between 120,000 and 250,000 Lithuanian landowners and farmers.

The industrial sector was developed significantly, in line with Moscow's planning directives, creating

the opportunity of sending in ethnic Russians, who soon became the largest minority in the Lithuanian SSR. In the energy sector, the late 1970s and early 1980s saw the erection of an oil refinery in Mažeikiai and the Chernobyl-style nuclear reactor in Ignalina. Increasing industrialization spurred on urbanization, so that by 1975 over half of Lithuanians lived in towns, sharing with Estonia and Latvia the highest standards of living in the USSR.

Cultural life, which the government aimed to use for the inculcation of Soviet values, gained some reprieve after the death of the Soviet dictator Joseph Stalin (1879–1953). Art, music, and literature, particularly poetry and theater, came to play an important role in maintaining a national identity and were also often, though not always, avenues for dissent. Though the numbers of clergy and churches were reduced by almost half, the Catholic Church became the locus for long-standing and well-organized dissent. The *Chronicle of the Catholic Church in Lithuania* appeared in 1972, the same year that a student protesting Soviet occupation immolated himself in Kaunas, precipitating riots. This long-lived underground publication drew attention to violations of Catholic human rights. Meanwhile, broader concerns were championed by groups such as the Helsinki Human Rights watch group formed in 1976.

Lithuanians responded to the 1986 call of the new Soviet leader Mikhail Gorbachev (b. 1931) for glasnost and perestroika by forming Sajūdis (Movement) on 3 June 1988. Calling for national self-determination, Sajūdis's candidates won a majority in the 1990 elections to the Supreme Council of the Lithuanian SSR and went on to declare Lithuania's independence on 11 March 1990. They were soon followed by Latvia and Estonia, becoming the first three republics to break from the USSR. Moscow retaliated by implementing an economic blockade that culminated in an attempt to overthrow the Lithuanian government by force on 13 January 1991, to which citizens responded with peaceful resistance. Only after the failed coup in Moscow in August 1991 was Lithuania's independence recognized internationally. That September, Lithuania joined the United Nations.

1991–2004

The new republic had a population of close to 3.7 million (1989 census) and retained the boundaries of the Lithuanian SSR. Russians constituted the largest minority at 9.4 percent, with Poles at 7 percent. Over the next decade the population declined as a result of emigration. In the new democracy, voters have alternately elected free-market oriented conservative governments and ones dominated by former Communists. In 1993 the *litas* was reintroduced as the republic's currency. Transition to a capitalist economy was difficult with both the agricultural and industrial sectors experiencing decline in the early 1990s. Privatization of both housing and small- and medium-sized businesses was implemented, while numerous large state-owned industries were sold to private investors. A decisive turn westward is evident not only in cultural life but also in new alliances: Lithuania was received into the North Atlantic Treaty Organization (NATO) in 2002 and joined the European Union on 1 May 2004.

See also **Estonia; Latvia; Soviet Union.**

BIBLIOGRAPHY

Eidintas, Alfonsas, and Vytautas Zalys. *Lithuania in European Politics: The Years of the First Republic, 1918–1940.* Edited by Edvardas Tuskenis. New York, 1998.

Lane, Thomas. *Lithuania: Stepping Westward.* London, 2001.

Lieven, Anatol. *The Baltic Revolution: Estonia, Latvia, Lithuania, and the Path to Independence.* New Haven, Conn., 1993.

Misiunas, Romuald J., and Rein Taagepera. *The Baltic States: Years of Dependence, 1940–1990.* Rev. ed. Berkeley, Calif., 1993.

Nikžentaitis, Alvydas, Stefan Schreiner, and Darius Staliūnas, eds. *The Vanished World of Lithuanian Jews.* Amsterdam, 2004.

O'Connor, Kevin. *The History of the Baltic States.* Westport, Conn., 2003.

Snyder, Timothy. *The Reconstruction of Nations: Poland, Ukraine, Lithuania, Belarus, 1569–1999.* New Haven, Conn., 2003.

Sužiedėlis, Saulius. *Historical Dictionary of Lithuania.* Lanham, Md., 1997.

INDRĖ ČUPLINSKAS

LLOYD GEORGE, DAVID (1863–1945), British statesman.

In August 1914 David Lloyd George already occupied a secure and meritorious place in British affairs. Despite occasions when he had cast doubt on the solidity of his liberal principles, overall he had established himself as the principal "New Liberal" of his time, uplifting the doctrine of social welfare and leading the legislative battle against poverty, unemployment, illness, malnutrition, and the powers of the House of Lords.

The outbreak of war did not change this. He reacted to the threat of the European bully to "little" Belgium and liberal France, and proclaimed his views to a huge gathering of Nonconformists in London. Thereafter, his every action attracted public attention. As chancellor of the exchequer, his early financial arrangements tided the country over initial difficulties. His negotiations with trade unions reduced the numbers of strikes, opened the way to considerable "dilution" in the engineering industry, and facilitated widespread female employment in industry. Less effective were his condemnation of heavy drinking among munitions workers, of the dominant western strategy in the war (as against action in the Balkans), and of certain actions by Horatio Herbert Kitchener (1850–1916), the war secretary. (It is often claimed, in addition, that he favored naval and then military action at the Dardanelles. This ignores the fact that his then target was Austria-Hungary, not Turkey.)

MINISTER OF MUNITIONS

In May 1915 the Liberal government was rocked by a series of disagreements. Herbert Henry Asquith (1852–1928) promptly dissolved the Liberal government and formed a coalition ministry with Liberals and Conservatives in roughly equal numbers and a sprinkling of Labour members. Lloyd George accepted readily enough the high-profile position it thrust on him—that of the newly created minister of munitions. Thereby he seized control of weapons production out of Kitchener's hands, derived credit for some of Kitchener's accomplishments, and placed munitions production, appropriately, in devotedly civilian control. In consequence, by 1917 (although certainly not before) Britain was producing weaponry sufficient for its hugely increased army.

Life, meanwhile, was not easy for the new coalition government. It now included a considerable element disbelieving in voluntary military service.

Most of these were Conservatives, but the truly conspicuous member was Lloyd George. Having favored the idea of conscription in 1910—in conversation with the Conservatives if not publicly—he was not passionate in its cause. Steadily, during 1916 he drove Asquith and his onetime Liberal colleagues to capitulation.

This did him no harm with the general public and much good among right-wing imperialists. But it caused a potential rift with the more devoted Nonconformist Liberals, who hereafter viewed him with a measure of distrust. Whether he would find a new, equally secure political base elsewhere remained in question. In these circumstances, his position seemed less than secure. Yet the fact remained that, in the popular conception, the Allied cause appeared to be making no progress. Above all, the four-and-a-half-month saga during 1916 of the British army on the Somme yielded trivial progress and cost monstrous casualties. The British public did not suspect Lloyd George (who had failed to provide the vast supply of munitions required) or Douglas Haig (1861–1928) (who fought the campaign on the fanciful basis that the munitions were at his disposal) of responsibility. All they knew was that things were going severely wrong. A new, more authoritarian, prime minister might be a solution.

In November 1916 Lloyd George made his move. With the consent of the Conservative Party leader, Bonar Law (1858–1923), he demanded that direction of the war be placed in the hands of a committee of only three, of whom Asquith—although still remaining nominal prime minister—would not be one. Asquith, torn between becoming prime minister without power or not being prime minister at all, eventually rejected the scheme and resigned. His action made sense: he no longer possessed a majority in the House of Commons and stood no chance of winning one in a general election. That Lloyd George succeeded him, leading a government with solid Conservative support and also the endorsement of some less-distinguished Liberals (and, strictly for the duration, of the Labour Party) also made sense. If his standing among politicians raised questions, his standing in the country did not.

PRIME MINISTER

Almost immediately, Lloyd George as prime minister introduced changes. Some, regarding health and housing and education, were far removed from the war except as regards a changing (but not necessarily permanent) national mood. Others concerned shipping, transport, and the food supply and were a response to the German U-boat campaign against merchant ships. That these new arms of government were placed in the hands of independent businessmen revealed something of Lloyd George's novel approach to government.

In matters directly concerned with the war Lloyd George's premiership brought less dramatic consequences. At sea he was slow in responding to the menace of U-boats, and not much ahead of the admiralty in concluding that the only answer lay in convoys. Nevertheless, after a fraught couple of months the nation's resort to this instrument became highly effective, and by the end of 1917 the crisis was surmounted.

In military matters the war in 1917 presented no straightforward solution. Lloyd George was determined to assert his control over strategy. He first proposed to place the main burden of the offensive on the Italians, a predictably unacceptable maneuver. Then he set about taking control of the battle on the western front out of the hands of Haig and placing the British army under the direction of General Robert-Georges Nivelle (1856–1924), the French commander-in-chief. But Nivelle's planned war-winning offensive proved a calamity. It reduced the Gallic army to mutiny, caused Nivelle to be abruptly sacked by the French government, and "let down" (in Frances Stevenson's words) Lloyd George. For the moment he was in no position to remove Haig.

In any case, despite their differences and personal dislike, Lloyd George and Haig were more alike than either cared to admit. Each yearned for a campaign that would produce a great sweeping victory, rupturing the enemy line and putting its army to rout. As he could not produce a meaningful scheme of his own for this purpose, Lloyd George allowed Haig (whom he could easily have stopped) to launch the lamentable battle of Third Ypres (July–November 1917), which he would thereafter regard as Haig's supreme act of folly.

By the start of 1918 the prospect of early victory seemed remote. The United States had entered the war, but the western front appeared deadlocked, and Russia was firmly out of the war. Lloyd George, convinced (with some reason) that Haig was eager to go on attacking, failed to awake to the nature of the German threat and withheld from the western fronts the troops that were needed. The consequence, on 21 March, was a staggering early impact by the German offensive.

Lloyd George, to his credit, was not shattered. He summoned troops from the many distant fields to which he had sent them, appealed to the Americans to dispatch the forces that they were tardily assembling, provided the shipping by which U.S. forces might be transported, and sent to France large numbers of British youngsters and older men hitherto protected from active service. (His attempts to conscript Irishmen, by contrast, were a lamentable failure, and drove that country ever further into the arms of Sinn Féin.)

The Germans failed in their attempt to win a breakthrough victory. By mid-1918 the British army was secure and refreshed. It was still under Haig's direction but, with Lloyd George's enthusiastic support, all three Allied armies in the West were now subject to the overall command of Ferdinand Foch (1851–1929). And William Robert Robertson (1860–1933), the chief of the imperial general staff, had been replaced by Lloyd George's favorite Henry Maitland Wilson (1881–1964). This situation has been depicted as a triumph for Lloyd George. Yet it amounted to little. Henry Wilson, while abusing Haig privately, conformed more readily than Robertson to his demands. And Foch, to Lloyd George's fury, directed American troops to the French sector while delegating the main attacks to Haig and the British. This proceeding Lloyd George could not now forbid.

Yet the truth was more complex than even these remarks suggest. In fact the war was not proceeding in accordance with the dictates of either Lloyd George or Haig (or Foch). The British army attacked simply to clear the enemy from the sensitive districts to which the Germans had penetrated, called off these operations when resistance became too great, and then attacked elsewhere. This was the product not of Lloyd George but of civilian diligence and the direction of those further down the military scale. Yet its adoption produced a conflict proceeding irresistibly to Allied victory.

AFTER THE WAR

Already Lloyd George was planning an election. He was determined to remain prime minister of a government overwhelmingly Conservative but with a Liberal element. Thereby Lloyd George converted his differences with Asquith into a fundamental Liberal division. He chose 150 Liberal candidates (many of them ostentatious in his support in the old house) to be free of Conservative opponents, whereas all other Liberals were subject to Tory opposition. In the short term this maneuver succeeded utterly. In the 1918 general election the conservatives swept the field, securing 333 seats, and the Coalition Liberals (fighting without Conservative opponents) gained 136. Their opponents were all but annihilated. Labour secured 59 seats and became the official opposition. The Asquithian Liberals secured 29, of whom Asquith—even though his Conservative opponent was denied Lloyd George's "coupon"—was not one.

Lloyd George set the tone of the election, which as it happened was preceded by Germany's capitulation. At one moment he played up the brave new world he hoped to create, at another he indulged in unrestrained Hun-hating. This conduct remained henceforth a millstone round his neck. The collapse of the economy in 1920 brutally terminated the schemes in housing and education on which he had embarked. The persistence of Irish resistance led his government to resort to barbarities from which his subsequent success in negotiating a settlement never rescued him. And his attempts both to justify the peace settlement (for which there was much to be said) and to modify its extremities were submerged by recollections of the malevolent election campaign. When, after four years of peace, the Conservatives concluded that they did not need him any longer, he was simply ejected from power.

His fall was stunning and proved irreversible. Yet nothing about his career, and his many questionable actions, could obliterate his huge accomplishments. He played a great part in founding the welfare state in Britain. He espoused the validity of Britain's action in going to war in defense of liberal values. He organized much of the nation's male and female power for war purposes. And he led the nation to victory. It was not a small achievement.

See also **Haig, Douglas; Kitchener, Horatio Herbert; United Kingdom; World War I.**

BIBLIOGRAPHY

Grigg, John. *Lloyd George: War Leader, 1916–1918.* London and New York, 2002.

Lloyd George, Frances. *Lloyd George: A Diary.* By Frances Stevenson, edited by A. J. P. Taylor. London, 1971.

Rowland, Peter. *Lloyd George.* London, 1975.

ROBIN PRIOR

LOCARNO, TREATY OF. At the beginning of 1925 relations between Germany and its European neighbors, especially France, were beset by the troublesome issues of war reparations and compliance with the conditions of the Treaty of Versailles of 1919. On 9 February Gustav Stresemann (1878–1929), the German foreign minister, sent a note to the governments of the Allied Powers proposing that a security pact be concluded under which Germany, France, Great Britain, and Italy would undertake not to engage in war, with the United States serving as guarantor of the agreement. An annex to his note further proposed an arbitration treaty between France and Germany intended to ensure the peaceful resolution of bilateral conflicts between the two states. Stresemann's proposal also sought to secure Germany's western frontier but contained no German commitment regarding the eastern borders or its entry into the League of Nations, both decisive issues for France.

For several months neither Britain nor France responded to these proposals. It was Aristide Briand (1862–1932), the newly appointed French foreign minister, who in the spring of 1925 first urged that they be followed up. The French replied in July that they would consider the terms of the German note provided that Germany agreed to join the League of Nations unconditionally.

Over the summer of 1925 the issue was the subject of lively debate in Germany, because

Stresemann's proposal in effect ceded Alsace-Lorraine to France. The aim of the German minister was to internationalize the Rhineland question so as to avoid any future unilateral action by France comparable to its invasion of the Ruhr in 1923. Germany's agreement was further intended to avoid the signing of any Franco-British pact; to facilitate the anticipated withdrawal of the allies from the Rhineland; and ensure their departure from Cologne, which they still occupied even though they were in principle to have evacuated the city in January 1925. The French and the British insisted that Belgium should be involved in the negotiations and that its borders also be recognized by Germany. In France's eyes any pact would have to respect French undertakings with regard to its Czech and Polish allies, notably the promise of intervention in case of outside aggression (even though such a condition ran counter to Articles 15 and 16 of the Covenant of the League of Nations).

The Locarno Conference was held from 5 to 16 October 1925, assembling Briand for France, Austen Chamberlain (1863–1937) for Great Britain, Stresemann for Germany, Émile Vandervelde (1866–1938) for Belgium, and Benito Mussolini (1883–1945) for Italy. The negotiations were difficult, not only because of the narrow margin for political maneuver left to Stresemann and Briand by public opinion in their respective countries but also because they opened with a formal objection to the Treaty of Versailles by the German delegation.

The conference eventually resulted in a set of accords. The main treaty, known as the "Rhineland Pact," enshrined nonaggression undertakings concerning the German, French, and Belgian borders; Britain and Italy were guarantors. Germany thus gave sovereign acknowledgment to what the Treaty of Versailles had imposed: the definitive cession of Alsace-Lorraine and the demilitarization of the left bank of the Rhine. The treaty provided that in case of Germany's occupation of the demilitarized zone military action might be taken in response. Appended to this treaty were several arbitration conventions between Germany on the one hand, and France, Czechoslovakia, Belgium, and Poland on the other.

None of the agreements concluded at Locarno committed Germany in any way with respect to its eastern borders. Stresemann had no intention of recognizing frontiers that he considered unjust and contestable. France, for its part, on the basis of attached Franco-Polish and Franco-Czechoslovak agreements, hoped to open negotiations later concerning its own frontiers. The British representation at Locarno declared that Britain intended to keep its options open in case of conflict in central and eastern Europe. This explains the bitter disillusionment of the Polish delegate, Foreign Minister Alexander Skrzynski (1882–1931), who felt that the security of his country had been sacrificed at Locarno on the altar of Franco-German reconciliation. In Berlin the reaction to the Locarno agreements was fury: three nationalist government ministers, Martin Shield, Otto von Schlieben (1875–1932), and Albert Neuhaus (1873–1948), resigned in protest. In Paris, meanwhile, the right-wing view was that Briand had been duped by Stresemann. In 1932, after Briand's death, an even greater uproar occurred upon the publication of Stresemann's papers. These included a letter dating from September 1925 from the German foreign minister to Crown Prince William (1888–1951), the elder son of William II (r. 1888–1819), in which Stresemann indeed set forth his plans for dismantling the order laid down in the Treaty of Versailles. The French saw this as a German admission of bad faith in the Locarno negotiations. At the same time a parallel controversy was raging in Germany, with Stresemann accused of having been hoodwinked by Briand: had it not taken until 1930, it was asked, for the Allies to withdraw from the Rhineland? Chamberlain would later write in his memoirs that there were neither rogues nor dupes here—merely "a great German and a great Frenchman" striving amid the blood-soaked ruins of the past to erect a temple to peace.

The fact is that the Locarno agreements were less the outcome of either German or French deception than the reflection of profoundly differing visions of European security and peace. Both sides felt they had made the more significant concessions concerning their security or sovereignty, but results did not meet with expectations for either. Adolf Hitler's (1889–1945) remilitarization of the Rhineland in March 1936 doubtless constituted the definitive rejection of the Locarno Pact, but the "spirit of Locarno" was already long dead by that time. A considered view of the causes of this failure must surely lay as much blame on a France

immovable in its insistence on guarantees as on a nationalistic segment of German opinion that even in 1925 looked upon these agreements as just one more shameful capitulation.

See also **Belgium; Briand, Aristide; France; Germany; Italy; Mussolini, Benito; Stresemann, Gustav; United Kingdom.**

BIBLIOGRAPHY

Primary Sources

The Locarno Conference. (October 5–16, 1925). Boston, World Peace Foundation, 1926, pamphlets IX–1.

Foreign Policy Association. *The Significance of Locarno,* discussed by Mlle. Louise Weiss, Mr. James G. McDonald, and Dr. Paul Leverkuehn. Miss Christina Merriman, Chairman; 81st luncheon discussion, Hotel Astor, New York, November 21, 1925.

Secondary Sources

Gaynor, Johnson, ed. *Locarno Revisited: European Diplomacy, 1920–1929.* London and Portland, Ore., 2004.

Keeton, Edward David. *Briand's Locarno Policy: French Economics, Politics, and Diplomacy, 1925–1929.* New York, 1987.

Wright, Jonathan. *Gustav Stresemann: Weimar's Greatest Statesman.* Oxford, U.K., and New York, 2002.

DZOVINAR KÉVONIAN

LONDON. In the summer of 1914, as Europe prepared to tear itself apart, it was clear that the future of London was not the smallest stake at play in the struggle for continental and imperial supremacy. London was the largest city the world had ever seen: at 7.16 million people, its population outnumbered Berlin, Paris, St. Petersburg, and Moscow combined. It was the world's busiest port, one of its greatest manufacturing districts, and its richest consumer market. Most important of all, the square mile of the City of London was the world's banker, determining the price of international commodities, arranging credit for most of the world's merchants, and accommodating the debts—even printing the banknotes—of many governments across the globe. All that would change, should war rearrange the shape of empires and the power of nations to the detriment of Britain and its capital.

HYPERTROPHY AND STRANGULATION: 1914–1939

World War I did indeed change London. During the four years of war most alterations seemed for the worse. Pubs closed longer, beer was watered, the streets were blacked out, and nightlife shut down. Bombing by zeppelins and Gotha biplanes killed some six hundred Londoners from the summer of 1917 to November 1918. The return home of London's German minority, its largest, and of some French, Italians, and Russians narrowed the capital's cosmopolitan appeal. A virtual halt on slum clearance and nonmilitary construction meant that London's housing problem, the city's biggest social demerit, deteriorated even further. The deaths and maiming of tens of thousands of Londoners in battles in Flanders and elsewhere brought agony to every street.

But the hidden effects proved larger in the long run, and these were greatly more positive. A huge wartime rise in working-class incomes accompanied full employment, with masses of women brought into the workforce for the first time. This stoked demand for better housing and higher living standards. New industrial areas for war production, notably in west London at Park Royal, expanded the capital's manufacturing capacity to meet the demand for modern goods. And the dislocation of German and French banking in the turmoil of war provided further opportunities for the City, a big factor in the continuing prosperity of London's middle classes during the war and after.

This twin effect of pent-up demand in all classes, especially within a great sector of the population historically submerged in under-consumption, and enhanced industrial capacity on the edge of the metropolis fueled one of the great London phenomena of the twentieth century: its enormous suburban expansion between the two world wars. From 1924 to 1939, London doubled in size on the ground, covering a built-up area some thirty-four miles across. Around 860,000 houses were built in these years. In 1934, the most frantic of all, 1,500 were being run up every week. And, following the lead of Park Royal, by far the fastest growth was on London's western edge, where new semidetached suburbs at Wembley, Neasden, Hayes, and elsewhere were connected to London by improved rail links above and below ground, and by a spreading network of motor buses. This was the biggest land-grab in London's—indeed, Britain's—history.

With new houses came more and more Londoners. Not all these, though, were new to the city. Much of new London was occupied by middle-class movers from inner London, tempted out by electric railways and the tube (London's underground rail system), by mortgages as cheap as inner-city rents, and by the delights of suburban life with a garden, and neighbors just like themselves. Many others were of the upper working class, moving out to council estates (most noticeably, a new town of ninety thousand at Becontree in Essex) and to the cheaper zones of owner-occupation, such as Bexley in southeast London. But many suburbanites were newcomers to London. And other newcomers filled some of the spaces in inner London that older-established Londoners now found so irksome. London's outer ring housed almost 900,000 more people in 1939 than just eight years before, nearly as many as if the people of Birmingham, Britain's second-largest city, had marched lock and stock to the capital. In that year, London's population reached 8.62 million, a number unlikely ever to be surpassed. Londoners made up more than one in five of the people of England and Wales. And that was a proportion also never likely to be bettered.

This overwhelming expansion of London and Londoners was largely built on the ferocious enterprise of metropolitan manufacturing industry. London had been the original home of new industries even in 1914, especially electrical commodities, motorcars, and airplanes. The wartime industrial growth-points secured much of the new factory building of the interwar years for the capital. Between 1932 and 1937, 83 percent of the nation's net increase of new factories employing twenty-five or more persons were built in London. Many employed predominantly young women—fifteen thousand of them at the Gramophone Company (later EMI) at Hayes—revolutionizing the prospects and aspirations of the London working class in the process. Here the new world of radios, gramophone records, film, cosmetics, artificial fabrics, plastics, convenience foods, and everything to do with sport were not only made but found their readiest market.

A bustling London street in 1938. ©Hulton-Deutsch Collection/Corbis

Against the grain of catastrophic slump in most of the older industrial areas of Britain, London was the beacon leading the country out of depression. Metropolitan fortunes seemed to triumph independently of the nation's. Small wonder that most planners and politicians saw provincial decline and the hypergrowth of London as two sides of the same coin. By the end of the 1930s, there was a virtual consensus among those who thought about such matters. London was a "national menace." Its growth had not just to be stopped but put into reverse.

THE REMAKING OF LONDON: 1940–1989

Indeed London's growth was put into reverse. Not by planners or government, but by the second period of total war to descend on the city in a generation. This time the negative outcomes overwhelmed the positive, and not only in the short term. First were the casualties. No true figure can ever be known, but officials put the civilian death toll of all the various periods of "the Blitz" from September 1940 to March 1945—prolonged night bombing, daylight raids, V1 buzz bombs and the terrible V2 rockets—at 29,890. Second was the damage to London's fabric. This was immense. The City lost a third of its floor space in a single night, 29–30 December 1940. Some 166,000 London houses—containing probably three times as many dwellings—were utterly destroyed or damaged beyond repair. Whole districts in east London were razed to the ground. The port was so heavily damaged that some parts never worked again. But out of all this destruction, and despite some well-founded fears for morale, the spirit of the Londoners and their city proved a symbol of heroic resistance to Free Europe and the world.

Indomitable it may have been, but London would never be the same again. Industrially, the battering received by inner London cleared out many factories and workshops from districts already uncongenially crowded. The port recovered its prewar trade for a time, but wartime developments would eventually make goods handling on the upper Thames obsolete in a generation. Redevelopment of the City, its land values the highest in Europe, encouraged the revolution in tall buildings that interwar London, with the sole exception of London University's Senate House, had fought hard to avoid. It would be on architects' drawing boards of the late 1940s that London's lukewarm flirtation with skyscrapers would first find expression.

Even grander schemes were afoot. Prewar orthodoxy over the damaging hypergrowth of London dominated thinking about how the city should be reconstructed after the peace. In 1943–1944, visionary plans were produced by men such as Patrick Abercrombie who believed that emptying London of people and jobs would solve not just metropolitan problems but the nation's too. Once industry and population had been moved out to a ring of New Towns, what was left would be redeveloped where possible and "zoned" for specialist functions—residential here, commercial there, industrial somewhere else. And traffic, the second of London's great social and economic demerits, would be steered away from the center in a series of giant ring roads.

In the event the plans proved too visionary by far. Imposing order on London was not only impracticable and prohibitively expensive but also, finally, undesired by Londoners who valued the chaotic variety of their city. Comprehensive redevelopment of some parts of the East End was attempted, but in general rebuilding was piecemeal and the most destructive of the ring roads was never built. Some of the planners' objectives were achieved, but usually without their intervention. The 1940s and 1950s were bleak decades in London, its fabric war-scarred, its housing crisis worse than before the war, a juvenile crime wave made more dangerous by the ready availability of ex-service handguns. Londoners left when they could. And industry had moved out too, finding no niche in areas redeveloped predominantly for housing. By 1961 the population was below eight million, lower than it had been for more than thirty years.

There were two other key players in the momentous changes of the first two postwar decades. The destruction of the City had deprived London of much-needed office space. Although backstreet industry might be leaving the metropolis, office jobs were increasing daily. The City had more than maintained its share of European and some worldwide financial services, and international business increasingly sought London headquarters. Capitalizing on this demand, the developer of office towers would be one of the great hate-figures of the postwar metropolis. Towers were built all over central London, not just the City. The notorious Centre Point, designed by Sir Richard Seifert for developer Harry Hyams at the corner of Oxford Street and Tottenham Court Road, stayed empty for ten years after completion in 1967. It came to symbolize the quintessence of wasteful finance capitalism at Londoners' expense.

If the developers were one force, then a reinvigorated London government was the other. Remodeled in 1964 to cover virtually the whole of the built-up area, it comprised a strategic authority in the Greater London Council (GLC), and thirty-two new all-purpose London boroughs. The old City Corporation was left untouched. The changes went a long way to put right the fractured and outdated arrangements inherited from the Victorians. Reinvigorated government proved destructive for old London. The 1960s and 1970s saw widespread clearance of working-class areas for new housing in giant council estates. Much of the Victorian housing that was destroyed could have been saved, and much of the systems-built towerblocks and high-density estates that replaced it proved unfit for their purpose within a generation.

REMAKING THE LONDONER: 1948–1989

These were great changes in the fabric of London, and more were to come. But they were as nothing compared to the change wrought in the Londoner. Up to 1948, for 150 years or more, black people had been rarities in London. During the nineteenth century there had been a steady rise in European migration to London, especially among eastern European Jews, who represented one of the most vibrant and influential of London's minorities in the twentieth century. In 1914, around 4 percent of the population of inner London was foreign born, the vast majority Europeans by birth. In 1951, the figure had crept up to some one in twenty, many of them Poles dislocated from their homeland by war and repression. Few were warmly welcomed. Among many working-class Londoners and others, xenophobia and a mistrust of foreigners, especially those with black skins, were not often openly expressed but were deeply felt nonetheless.

So Londoners could not have been more ill-prepared for what began on 22 June 1948 with the docking at Tilbury, London's downriver port, of

The dome of St. Paul's Cathedral in London can be seen through smoke from buildings burning after the bombing of 29-30 December 1940. ©Bettmann/Corbis

the SS *Empire Windrush* carrying five hundred mainly Jamaican migrants. There had been harbingers of the West Indian diaspora—with London as a prime destination—both during the war and immediately after. But the huge publicity given to the *Windrush* brought the realities of postwar migration home to Londoners as nothing had before. As thousands followed—there were said to be 100,000 West Indians in London by 1961—resentment battled with notions of fair play. London's housing problem and a resurgence of marginal fascist movements in east London gave resentment something to bite on. In the summer of 1958, London's only genuine race riot of the century broke out in Notting Hill, a desperately rundown area of inner west London. There were some serious assaults and cries of "lynch him," but

it all petered out after a few days. And it was noticeable how some white Londoners of all classes had rallied to the cause of the black newcomers.

There were no further race riots, but dangerous times were to come. The free-and-easy camaraderie of the English-speaking West Indians generally made them more acceptable to indigenous Londoners than more "foreign" migrants from India and Pakistan who entered from the mid-1950s on. And the forced migration of Asians from East Africa after 1960, reaching crisis levels in 1967–1968, provoked demonstrations in favor of repatriation. From 1968 through the 1970s, racially motivated assaults—and a dozen or so murders—put the success or failure of multicultural London on a knife-edge. Or perhaps just appeared to do so, for in the end, weight of numbers and the diversity of communities made harmony, even at a respectful distance, a practical necessity. There was also, especially between Afro-Caribbeans and whites, a considerable amount of intermarriage. No one could conceivably have forecast that as a future for Londoners in 1948.

Perhaps the key decade in building toleration in London was the 1960s, despite the great difficulties experienced from 1968 and despite the bleak reaction of the decade that followed. A contributory factor was the rediscovery of inner London by the young aspiring middle classes, often sharing it with black migrants, in a reversal of the trend to suburbanization between the wars. The sociologist Ruth Glass called this phenomenon "gentrification" in 1964, and the name happily stuck. Areas of north London, especially Hampstead, Camden Town, and Islington—districts apparently marked only for the bulldozer—found champions in middle-class newcomers who saw much to be admired in Victorian streets and houses and much to be deplored in what was put up in their stead. There were some notable campaigns against council-led destruction spilling into the 1970s, most famously of all in Covent Garden, a district scheduled largely for total reconstruction but almost entirely saved—though saved for whom would be an open question. By 1974, the battle to stem the destruction of Victorian London had largely been won.

The decade of the 1960s was significant in other ways, too, most famously in the cultural revolution that saw London as a national, and for a time international, crucible. "London: The Swinging City" was how *Time* magazine in April 1966 described a phenomenon that had already been attracting European attention for at least two years before. With roots in café-based rock music, flavored by elements of the new culture imported from the West Indies, and with a host of brilliant talent most especially in the London fashion industry, "Swinging London" captured the world's imagination from about 1963 to 1972. Its centers were Carnaby Street and the rest of Soho, where London's sex industry had increasingly concentrated, and Chelsea, a riverside district west of the central area, where art and fashion had long felt at home. Newly gentrifying districts played their part too. In these years, some barriers were permanently broken down—sexual, political, racial (up to a point), and most notably class. Working-class footballers, rock singers, photographers, hairdressers, actors, and fashion models were iconic figures happily accepted into the worlds of the super-rich of old or new varieties. They would be so for the rest of the century and beyond.

The 1960s' wheels were greased by relative prosperity and full employment. Few at the time saw the troubles facing London that would work their way right through the troubled decades of the 1970s and 1980s. For the London economy entered a period of massive restructuring that World War II and its aftermath had begun. There was a collapse of manufacturing, especially in the well-established London metal trades. Some old connections between industry and locality—such as Fleet Street and the printing industry—disappeared altogether. There were 1.43 million manufacturing jobs in London in 1961, just 435,000 in 1989. From 1966 to 1981, the docks upriver from Tilbury closed one after another as large container ships, and roll-on roll-off truck freight, could no longer be accommodated in London's narrow waterway and congested roads. Fears of London's hypergrowth meant that office jobs were being relocated from the capital as a matter of official policy as late as 1978. In all, London lost some 30 percent of its jobs in the thirty years or so following 1962.

The 1970s and 1980s were bleak in other ways too. Some fierce trade union struggles, notably involving low-paid Asian migrants in west London in 1977 and high-paid print workers in the East End in 1986–1987, brought with them civil strife on a large scale. The Irish Republican Army, an old enemy of Londoners, waged two fierce bombing campaigns in 1973–1976 and 1978–1982, setting 252 bombs and killing fifty-six people; the civil war within Islam chose London as its battleground periodically during these years, too. Even more significantly, sore feelings between young black and Asian migrants and the Metropolitan Police, run by the home secretary and not by London government, erupted into fierce pitched battles. Whites joined in, but against the police and not against black Londoners. The worst civil unrest of the period was at Brixton, inner southwest London, 10–12 April 1981, and at Broadwater

London police use riot shields to advance on an angry crowd during the Brixton riots, April 1981. ©BETTMANN/CORBIS

Farm, a giant council estate in Tottenham, north London, where a popular community policeman, Keith Blakelock, was hacked to death in October 1985. Feelings between black people and a London police force unable to expunge racism from its ranks would be troubled again, but never as bad as they were in the early 1980s.

As if this were not enough, an oppositional tendency took root in much of London government, radical socialism allying itself with militant public sector trade unionism. Numerous battles within the GLC, led by a Labour Party left-winger called Ken Livingstone, led to the government of Margaret Thatcher abolishing that strategic arm of London government altogether in April 1986. This seemed to epitomize London's doldrums. Here was a city whose economy was in crisis, its people periodically at war with each other, now bereft of a voice to manage its own affairs. Unsurprisingly, Londoners voted with their feet. In 1983 it was estimated that London's population slumped to 6.77 million, nearly 2 million fewer than in 1939.

LONDON AND THE LONDONER REMADE: 1990–2004

Things could have gotten worse, but they did not. Embedded in the London economy's bad news were some green shoots of optimism. Heathrow Airport, long the busiest in the world, had to some extent made up for job losses caused by the closure of the port. Its huge employment area was based on tourism, an industry that had its ups and downs in London but that in the long term moved from strength to strength. New tourist attractions seemed to be added to the city every year, notably Sam Wanamaker's Globe Theatre and the Tate Modern Gallery, both on the south bank. Closely associated with tourism was London's great depth in cultural industries, especially all varieties of music, heritage, theater, art, animation, and to some extent film. London fashion, too, never suffered severe setbacks after the 1960s, and the garment industry was one element of metropolitan manufacturing that stood up well to restructuring. Most of all, London's financial services were so buoyant that they spilled out of the City eastward to fill a new "Manhattan on Thames" in the Isle of

Dogs, where Canary Wharf Tower added an elegant new spire to the skyline. This was all a much narrower base on which to build a city's economy than London had previously enjoyed, and several commentators highlighted the risks of an economy so heavily mortgaged to the stability of world finances. But by 2004, London had done well for almost a decade, certainly since 1997. It no longer lagged behind national unemployment figures and its people were in general more prosperous than at any time in history.

A consequence of prosperity was universally high property prices, a serious matter when owner-occupation had become the largest single form of housing tenure. The effects were seen all over London. Redevelopment opportunities in the City, on the south bank of the Thames, and in the docklands saw a self-confident resurrection of the skyscraper, many exploiting views of the river that had for so long been undervalued as a metropolitan asset. And London's residential areas changed character in a chameleon fashion that left older established Londoners breathless. Notting Hill, one of the worst districts of the 1950s, had become one of the "best" in the 1990s; and Hoxton, said to be the leading criminal quarter of London in 1914, had become a sought-after location for artists' lofts and smart bistros by 2004. There were numerous other examples. In all these places, the transformation was never quite complete. Each had a mixture, sometimes an uneasy one, of rich newcomers and poor locals and migrants.

Such a complex mix was typical of multicultural London. By 2004, it was perhaps the largest assemblage of diverse ethnicities anywhere in the world. Some significant parts, such as the boroughs of Brent (northwest London) and Newham (in the east), had nonwhite majority populations in 2001. In another, Hackney, schoolchildren spoke more than one hundred different home languages. Indeed, every part of the world's peoples found a home, to a greater or lesser extent, in London. It was also, many thought, the world's best instance of a harmonious multiculturalism, with flagship events such as the Notting Hill Carnival every August attracting one million visitors, and with miraculously little communal antagonism. Some old hatreds simmered beneath the surface, and

there were still isolated assaults, even killings, but in general peaceable mutual respect set the London tone; this was despite migration remaining highly mobile, with new groups in the 1990s and thereafter arriving in some numbers from the former Yugoslavia, from Poland and the former Soviet Union, from Somalia, from Iraq and Kurdistan.

There was more good news for Londoners when the first government of Tony Blair restored some elements of democratic control, providing for an elected mayor and a Greater London Assembly. These gained powers over transport, economic development, some planning, and—remarkably—the Metropolitan Police. The first mayor elected in May 2001 did not use all these new resources wisely. This was that same Livingstone whose struggle with Thatcher had led to the disabling of London government in the first place, now fallen out with his party and standing as an independent. But he bravely pushed through a traffic congestion charge for central London, the first on such a scale anywhere in the world. It was a qualified success and Livingstone, now reconciled with the Labour Party, was reelected for a second term in 2004.

A robust economy, a brighter city more tuned to the pursuit of pleasure than ever before, a smarter fabric constantly modernizing, a new governmental settlement more in tune with the needs of its people: all this was a more positive outcome for London than could reasonably have been forecast at any time since 1940. Not surprisingly, the population had risen again, to 7.19 million by 2001, possibly an undercount of the true figure. Not surprisingly, too, in 2004 old fears were resurrected of London's growth, seen once more as a negative force within the nation. That surely missed the point. All the evidence of the twentieth century indicated that when metropolitan consumption and innovation were powerful, the nation benefited too. And now there was more at stake than just the nation. London was, indeed, less British than at any time for a thousand years. For London, unique in Europe and only rivaled by New York, was a true world city. In fifty years it had become a multinational city-state. Of the world, it now belonged to the world and its people.

See also **Blitzkrieg; Housing; Immigration and Internal Migration; Thatcher, Margaret; United Kingdom.**

BIBLIOGRAPHY

Barker, T. C., and Michael Robbins. *A History of London Transport: Passenger Transport and the Development of the Metropolis*. Vol. 2: *The Twentieth Century to 1970*. Revised edition. London, 1975.

Bradley, Simon, and Nikolaus Pevsner. *London*. Vol. 1: *The City of London*. London, 1997.

Centre for Urban Studies, ed. *London: Aspects of Change*. London, 1964.

Clout, Hugh, ed. *Changing London*. Slough, U.K., 1978.

Donnison, David, and David Eversley, eds. *London: Urban Patterns, Problems, and Policies*. London, 1973.

Fainstein, Susan S. *The City Builders: Property, Politics, and Planning in London and New York*. Oxford, U.K., 1994.

Feldman, David, and Gareth Stedman Jones, eds. *Metropolis, London: Histories and Representations since 1800*. London, 1989.

Foley, Donald L. *Controlling London's Growth: Planning the Great Wen, 1940–1960*. Berkeley, Calif., 1963.

Hall, Peter Geoffrey. *London 2001*. London, 1989.

Hebbert, Michael. *London: More by Fortune Than Design*. Chichester, U.K., 1998.

Hoggart, Keith, and David Green, eds. *London: A New Metropolitan Geography*. London, 1991.

Howe, Darcus. *From Bobby to Babylon: Blacks and British Police*. London, 1988.

Jackson, Alan A. *Semi-Detached London: Suburban Development, Life, and Transport, 1900–1939*. London, 1973.

Kynaston, David. *The City of London, 1815–1945*. 3 Vols. London, 1994–99.

Marriott, Oliver. *The Property Boom*. London, 1967.

Martin, J. E. *Greater London: An Industrial Geography*. London, 1966.

Marwick, Arthur. *The Sixties: Cultural Revolution in Britain, France, Italy, and the United States, c. 1958–c. 1974*. Oxford, U.K., 1998.

Panayi, Panakos, ed. *Racial Violence in Britain in the Nineteenth and Twentieth Centuries*. Revised edition. London, 1996.

Phillips, Mike, and Trevor Phillips. *Windrush: The Irresistible Rise of Multi-racial Britain*. London, 1998.

Saint, Andrew, ed. *Politics and the People of London: The London County Council, 1889–1965*. London, 1989.

Storkey, Marian, J. Maguire, and R. Lewis. *Cosmopolitan London: Past, Present and Future*. London, 1997.

White, Jerry. *London in the Twentieth Century: A City and Its People*. London, 2001.

Ziegler, Philip. *London at War, 1939–1945*. London, 1995.

JERRY WHITE

LORENZ, KONRAD (1903–1989), primary founder of ethology.

Konrad Lorenz was the second son of Adolf Lorenz (1854–1946), a rich and internationally famous Viennese orthopedic surgeon. His family indulged him in his boyhood passion for raising animals, and later in his career he would claim that his mature scientific practices were continuous with the habits he developed in his youth as an animal lover. Urged by his father to become a physician, he enrolled as a medical student at the University of Vienna, where his teachers included the comparative anatomist Ferdinand Hochstetter (1861–1954), who taught him how to study evolution through the comparative method. Lorenz earned his doctorate in medicine in 1928 and then enrolled at the university's Zoological Institute, where he received a PhD in 1933.

Throughout his years as a student Lorenz continued his hobby of raising animals, especially birds. His observations of a hand-reared jackdaw initiated for him a series of researches and insights on bird behavior that soon brought him to the attention of Germany's leading ornithologists, most notably Oskar Heinroth (1871–1945) and Erwin Stresemann (1889–1972). Key to Lorenz's early ornithological work was the idea that the methods of comparative anatomy could be applied to innate animal behavior patterns just as effectively as they could be applied to animal structures. In other words, the comparative study of animal instincts could help zoologists reconstruct the evolutionary affinities of different animal species. Lorenz, however, was not content to study innate behavior patterns solely from the perspectives of evolutionary history and taxonomy. He also wanted to make sense of their physiological causation and their social and biological function. In an important monograph of 1935 he argued that birds are adapted to their environments not so much by acquired knowledge as by highly differentiated innate behavior patterns, built up over time by evolution. For these behavior patterns to be effective, they need to be "released" by stimuli emanating from appropriate objects in their environment, including other birds of the same species. Lorenz at this time also drew attention to the phenomenon of "imprinting." He went on to develop a theory of instinct featuring "releasers," "innate releasing mechanisms," "action-specific energies," and innate, fixed motor patterns. Distinguishing sharply between instinctive behavior patterns on the one hand and learned behavior on the other, he advocated studying the former first. He quickly became a leader in the newly established German Society for Animal Psychology.

Notwithstanding his rapid rise to prominence in the field of animal psychology, Lorenz found it difficult in the mid-1930s to gain a paid academic position. He attributed his lack of success to the Catholic educational establishment in Austria, which was unsympathetic to his idea of making sense of human, social psychology in terms of its continuities with the social instincts of lower animals. When Austria was incorporated into Germany in 1938, Lorenz welcomed the change. He believed that the National Socialist regime would welcome his general worldview and support his research. Claiming there to be a parallel between "domestication"-induced behavioral degeneration in animals and humans, he promoted his work as being consistent with the Third Reich's concerns about race purity. He also joined the Nazi Party. Scholars differ in their assessments of this part of his career. He was called to the chair of psychology at the Albertus University of Königsberg in 1940. The following year he was drafted for military service. Captured by Russian forces in 1944 while serving on the eastern front, he did not return to Austria until 1948.

Prior to the war Lorenz's greatest wish had been to have the Kaiser Wilhelm Society establish a research center for him in Altenberg, Austria, the site of his family home and his own private research station. Although this did not occur, after the war, in 1950, the Max Planck Society, the Kaiser Wilhelm Society's successor, established a research institute for him in Buldern, Westphalia. That operation was subsequently relocated in 1956 to Seewiesen, near Starnberg, in Bavaria, as a major institute for behavioral physiology, codirected by

Lorenz and the physiologist Erich von Holst (1908–1962). Lorenz settled at Seewiesen in 1957 and remained there until his retirement in 1973, when he returned home to Altenberg.

In the postwar period Lorenz continued to be a dominant figure in animal behavior studies, sharing the leadership of the new field of ethology with his friend, the Dutch-born naturalist Nikolaas Tinbergen (1907–1988), who established a major center for animal behavior studies at Oxford University. Lorenz attracted attention and controversy in the 1960s with his popularly written book, *On Aggression* (originally published in German as *Das sogenannte Böse: Zur Naturgeschichte der Aggression*). He also was a pioneer in the field of evolutionary epistemology, promoting the idea that the human brain apprehends the world in ways that reflect how that organ has been shaped by natural selection in the course of evolutionary history.

For his contributions to the study of animal behavior Lorenz was awarded the Nobel Prize in Physiology or Medicine in 1973. He shared this honor with Karl von Frisch (1886–1982) and Tinbergen.

See also **Austria; Science.**

BIBLIOGRAPHY

Burkhardt, Richard W., Jr. *Patterns of Behavior: Konrad Lorenz, Niko Tinbergen, and the Founding of Ethology.* Chicago, 2005.

Nisbett, Alec. *Konrad Lorenz.* New York, 1976.

Taschwer, Klaus, and Benedikt Föger. *Konrad Lorenz: Biographie.* Vienna, 2003.

RICHARD W. BURKHARDT JR.

LUDENDORFF, ERICH (1865–1937), German general and politician.

Erich Ludendorff never seemed comfortably integrated into any of the three German regimes his career in one way or another did so much to shape—the late Kaiserreich, the Weimar Republic, and the Nazi Third Reich. The problem seems not to have been lack of opportunity. Of not just common but unprosperous origins, Ludendorff had risen through German military schools, including the prestigious Kriegsakademie, to positions on the Imperial General Staff as early as 1904. A brigade commander in August 1914, he achieved instant fame by the storming of the Belgian city of Liège. With glory came appointment as Eighth Army chief of staff on the eastern front as the immediate subordinate of Paul von Hindenburg. Together the two won the greatest German victories of World War I, the battles of Tannenburg (August 1914) and Masurian Lakes (September 1914). Yet the elderly, aristocratic Hindenburg became the national hero rather than the commoner who had risen from the ranks.

Hindenburg and Ludendorff maintained a genuine partnership through most of the war, though many considered Ludendorff the real brains of the pair. Certainly, he thought more deeply about the complex consequences of mobilization for "total" war. Ludendorff masterminded the somewhat misnamed "Hindenburg Program," which aspired to the total mobilization of the German economy. More effectively than any other senior commander of the Great War, Ludendorff thought through a way to break through the stalemate of trench warfare. Rather than trying to rupture the enemy position through a massive artillery barrage that chewed up no-man's-land and gave the enemy plenty of time to bring up reinforcements, followed by an "over-the-top" assault of averagely trained infantry, Ludendorff laid the groundwork for the blitzkrieg tactics of the next war. A short but ferocious barrage would open up holes in the opposing lines large enough for specially trained *Sturmtruppen* (storm troopers) to race through. Their mission was not to gain ground but to sow confusion in enemy communications. Only after they had done so would the mass of infantry advance to complete the breakthrough.

Yet Ludendorff's greatest defeat proved the direct consequence of his greatest triumph. In planning for what became known as the "Ludendorff Offensive" beginning on 21 March 1918, Ludendorff forbade his subordinates to use the word *strategy*. Indeed, tactical breakthrough not further defined *became* strategy. "We will make a hole," Ludendorff famously posited, "and the rest will take care of itself." Prospects for success on the western front were further dimmed by the need to maintain some

one million German soldiers along the eastern front to guarantee the punitive Treaty of Brest-Litovsk of 3 March 1918. The result over the spring and summer of 1918 was a series of breakthroughs along the western front, none of which made the Germans effective masters of the strategic situation. By the summer, when the Allies counterattacked under the strategic direction of the French marshal Ferdinand Foch and were assured reinforcement by a seemingly unlimited supply of American soldiers, the fate of the entire German war effort seemed sealed. The common-born Ludendorff, whose origins no one in the disintegrating Kaiserreich had forgotten, proved easily expendable in the closing weeks of the war. He fled to Sweden and immediately began to write his exculpatory memoirs.

In the traumatic early years of the Weimar Republic, Ludendorff became the darling of the radical nationalists. He schemed behind the scenes to overthrow the republic in the Kapp Putsch of March 1920. At about this time, he befriended an aspiring extreme right-wing conspirator named Adolf Hitler. In November 1923 the pair and a band of like-minded plotters seized a *Bürgerbräukeller* (beer hall) in Munich where the Bavarian prime minister was addressing a meeting, in hopes that a Nazi seizure of power in Bavaria would swiftly extend to Germany as a whole. The plot failed, somewhat ludicrously, when German troops proved loyal to the regime. Having failed to overthrow the hated republic in the streets, Ludendorff decided to join it. He ran successfully for the Reichstag as a National Socialist deputy in 1924, and unsuccessfully for president against his former superior Hindenburg in 1925. Yet Ludendorff proved ill-suited to party politics. He divorced his wife in 1926 and married Mathilde von Kemnitz, who encouraged his increasingly confused mix of politics, military affairs, and German mythology. He wrote a steady stream of vituperative indictments of Jews and Freemasons as the perpetrators of Germany's woes.

Yet having done all he could do to undermine confidence in republican democracy, Ludendorff seemed no better suited to what followed it. He became increasingly critical of Hitler as a petty tyrant who pandered to the masses. Ludendorff rightly predicted national disaster when Hitler came to power in January 1933. He died a curiously marginal figure in 1937.

See also **Hindenburg, Paul von; Hitler, Adolf; World War I.**

BIBLIOGRAPHY

Asprey, Robert B. *The German High Command at War: Hindenburg and Ludendorff Conduct World War I.* New York, 1991.

Craig, Gordon A. *Germany, 1866–1945.* Oxford, U.K., 1978.

Ludendorff, Erich. *My War Memories, 1914–1918.* London, 1920.

LEONARD V. SMITH

LUKÁCS, GYÖRGY (1885–1971), Hungarian Marxist philosopher and literary critic.

György Lukács, who also published under the name Georg Lukácz, was born in Budapest, the son of a wealthy and recently ennobled Jewish banker. As a young man he had distinctly literary and aesthetic interests, but he discovered anarchism as a schoolboy and in 1909 went to Berlin and then Heidelberg to study philosophy. Here he came under the influence of neo-Kantians such as Heinrich Rickert, Wilhelm Windelband, and Emil Lask, who stressed the uniqueness of culture and its inaccessibility through the methods of natural science. Their influence can be seen in his first book, *Die Seele und die Formen* (1911; *Soul and Form*), which harks back to the late-nineteenth-century tradition of Friedrich Nietzsche, Wilhelm Dilthey, and the philosophy of life (*Lebensphilosophie*). His first book emphasized the necessity of giving one's life form and meaning in a world of alienation and absurdity. He was also influenced by Max Weber and Georg Simmel and their notion of the "tragedy of culture," in which man, in the modern "disenchanted" world, is necessarily alienated and transcendentally "homeless."

Lukács began to turn against this form of cultural pessimism after serious readings of Georg Wilhelm Friedrich Hegel and Fyodor Dostoyevsky. His next book, *Die Theorie des Romans* (1916; *The Theory of the Novel*), pointed the way to a possibility of redemption through history. In 1917 he returned to Budapest as one of the leaders of the Budapest Circle, an elite group of artists, writers, and thinkers including Karl Mannheim and Béla Bartók who met in Béla Balázs's elegant apartment or the Lukács country estate, discussing the fate of bourgeois civilization. In 1918 Lukács surprised his aesthete friends by throwing in his lot with the Soviet Communist Party. He served for a short time as People's Commissar for Public Education in the short-lived Hungarian Soviet Republic of Béla Kun. Although he presented himself as an orthodox communist, in fact he rejected the crude dialectical materialism that quickly became the established doctrine in the Soviet Union. In 1923 he published a series of essays under the title *Geschichte und Klassenbewusstein* (*History and Class Consciousness*). This book was attacked by Grigory Zinoviev and the leaders of the Communist Party. Lukács inflicted on himself the humiliation of self-critique and officially repudiated the work in a public confession in 1930. Although the book was banned in the Soviet Union and later in occupied Eastern Europe, it had an enormous influence on Marxist intellectuals in the West.

In this founding text of Western reform Marxism, Lukács argues that bourgeois life is false and superficial because it is based on formal rights that leave people as the passive object of economic, political, and legal forces. Authentic freedom, he argues, is a collective practice, or praxis. The most famous passages of this book deal with his discussion of *Verdinglichung* (reification, or "thingification" in English), which he took from his reading of Hegel and which mirrored the young Marx's own confrontation with Hegel. *Verdinglichung* means the rendering of something alive and dynamic into a lifeless object. Marx's most famous example was the way that capitalism took away the congealed labor of the proletariat, in the form of products, and created a "fetishized" world of commodities. Lukács argues that in bourgeois society human consciousness has become reified, and the alienated condition of subjects separated from objects has been taken as natural, as a "second nature." Once one recognizes that alienation can be overcome, by what would later be called consciousness-raising, capitalism could be abolished, the proletariat would cease to exist, and a classless society would ensue in which humans are both subject and object of history. This process would necessarily be led by revolutionary intellectuals who had to choose to be on the right side of history, no matter the consequences. This fatalist attitude explained Lukács's willingness to criticize his own work and submit to the dictates of the party.

The logic behind *History and Class Consciousness* explains why Lukács remained a devoted member of the party until the end. Unlike Marx, who believed that the dialectic of history would inevitably result in communism, Lukács understood that collective, voluntaristic action was necessary. The party was the indispensable motor of the revolution and had to ascribe class consciousness to the workers as an ideal type, even if the workers did not yet manifest the "correct" party solidarity. Lukács's book was seen as heretical to the party because he returned to a pre-Marxian notion of revolution as a hope, not as a certainty of the future, and because he openly avowed an elite dictatorship.

While many other communist and Jewish intellectuals fled westward from the Nazis, Lukács found refuge in the Soviet Union. From 1929 to 1944 he lived in Moscow and wrote about socialist realism. He remained committed to Stalin even through the show trials and purges of the late 1930s. Though his life was in danger and he was once arrested, he was saved by the intervention of Georgi Dimitrov, the general secretary of the Comintern. In 1944 Lukács returned to Budapest to teach philosophy at the university. He published a book called *Zerstörung der Vernunft* (1954; *The Destruction of Reason*), about the intellectual origins of fascism. It is generally considered his weakest work because of its sweeping condemnation of German culture, literature, and philosophy. Theodor Adorno called it the "destruction of Lukács's reason." He was appointed minister of culture under the reform prime minister Imre Nagy in 1956, but when the Hungarian uprising was crushed he was deported to Romania. He returned in 1957 but was banned from teaching because of his support for a more humane form of socialism. He was readmitted into the party in 1965 and seems to have then supported Nikita Khrushchev's reforms. His utopian spirits were rekindled in the heady days of 1968, when revolutions broke out in Prague, Paris, Berlin, Berkeley, and elsewhere. But when the German student leader Rudi Dutschke visited him in March 1968, Lukács continued to distance himself from the works he had written in his early years and that were having such a strong influence on the European student movements of the late 1960s. Lukács died in Budapest on 4 June 1971 and was buried with full party honors. Although his writings continue to have an influence on some leftist intellectuals in the West who wish to keep alive a post-Marxist critique of bourgeois society, the fall of the Berlin Wall in 1989 and the dwindling of attractive alternatives to liberal capitalism have rendered Lukács's work more of historical than vibrant theoretical interest.

See also **Bartók, Béla; Communism; Mannheim, Karl; 1968; 1989; Purges; Stalin, Joseph.**

BIBLIOGRAPHY

Arato, Andrew, and Paul Breines. *The Young Lukács and the Origins of Western Marxism.* New York, 1979.

Glück, Mary. *Georg Lukács and His Generation, 1900–1918.* Cambridge, Mass., 1985.

Heller, Agnes, ed. *Lukács Reappraised.* Oxford, U.K., 1983.

Jay, Martin. *Marxism and Totality: The Adventures of a Concept from Lukács to Habermas.* Berkeley, Calif., 1984.

Kadarkay, Arpad, ed. *The Lukács Reader.* Cambridge, Mass., 1995.

ELLIOT NEAMAN

LUMUMBA, PATRICE (1925–1961), Congolese leader.

The Congolese political leader Patrice Lumumba was born on 2 July 1925 in Onalua, Kasai province, a little village flanked by two large Christian missions, one Catholic, the other Protestant, both allied with the Belgian colonial authorities. At first called Isaïe Tasumbu, he was deeply affected by the rigidity of a system that made life so hard for the colonized. Taking advantage of wartime conditions, he migrated to Stanleyville (now Kisangani) in 1944 and there found employment first in the territorial administration and then in the post office. But it was membership in corporatist organizations that provided him with the loudspeaker he needed to get his voice heard. No one in the

Congolese elite was to achieve a political ascent comparable to his. By establishing himself in Léopoldville (now Kinshasa) at the end of 1957 and becoming the prime mover of his party, the Mouvement National Congolais, from its foundation in October 1958, Lumumba catapulted himself to the very center of the country's public life, and much of the Congolese political class was obliged to position itself relative to him.

From 1948 to 1956 Lumumba remained within the Catholic world, but in 1955 he aligned himself with the liberal minister Auguste Buisseret (1888–1965) and supported secular education in the Congo. He championed the values of western civilization, the principle of equality, and the rights and freedoms of all—this despite the fact that he had himself suffered the injustice and violence of a colonial system that flouted those very values while paying them lip service. He observed that the main Belgian opposition parties dissented from their country's colonialist agenda only on minor issues such as wages and schools and that they fell quiet as soon as such essential questions as the future status of the Congo arose. As he became aware both of the deepening crisis of the colonial order during the 1950s and of the unrelenting mistreatment of the colonized, he gradually abandoned the "corporatist" attitudes of most of the Congolese elite and instead called for the rights to progress, well-being, and dignity for all his "race brothers." This exigent and rebellious attitude, which became more radical in late 1958, naturally put Lumumba at odds with the colonial authorities; his belief in progress and modernity, coupled with his ambition to lead a mass movement, made him a threat to a variety of powerful figures. It was in this context that legal proceedings were brought against him and that he ended by spending more than a year incarcerated (from July 1956 to September 1957 and from November 1959 to January 1960) at a time when the independence of the Belgian Congo was clearly on the horizon and a change of leadership seemed inevitable.

After a meeting known as the "Political Round Table," held in Brussels in January and February, Belgium granted independence to the Congo but immediately decided to separate Lumumba from the process, even to eliminate him if need be. But as delays, hesitations, and contradictions continued to beset Belgian policy, Lumumba did not hesitate to display his self-confidence with respect to the authorities by openly defying them. He won the elections of May 1960, becoming prime minister upon the country's achievement of independence on 30 June 1960, but was obliged to share power with his rival Joseph Kasavubu (1917–1969), who was named head of state. The new regime inherited a precarious situation from the "colonial model," and things deteriorated rapidly when the army mutinied and the province of Katanga and part of Kasai seceded. Despite these realities, Lumumba held fast to attitudes he had maintained steadfastly since 1959: physical courage when confronted by violence and the threat of death and an unshakable commitment to his chosen cause—the total independence of a united Congo as a sovereign state ready to fight both outside pressures and internal corruption. He had no illusions about his destiny or the risks he was running, but he categorically rejected all compromise.

Some combination of western and Congolese forces (Belgium, the United States, the United Nations, and powerful groups in Léopoldville and Élisabethville) brought about Lumumba's assassination in Katanga on 17 January 1961. Lumumba had never espoused any revolutionary socialist or Marxist ideology. His personal development and his sad end are uniquely bound up with the history of the Congo, originally colonized as the personal enterprise of King Leopold II (r. 1865–1909) of Belgium. Lumumba's murky death was part and parcel of the Congo's bungled decolonization, the most rapid in history.

See also **Belgium; Colonialism; Decolonization.**

BIBLIOGRAPHY

Chambre des Représentants de Belgique. *Rapport de l'enquête parlementaire visant à déterminer les circonstances exactes de l'assassinat de Patrice Lumumba et l'implication éventuelle des responsables politiques belges dans celui-ci.* Vols. 1 and 2. 16 November 2001.

Omasombo, Jean, and Benoît Verhaegen. *Patrice Lumumba, jeunesse et apprentissage politique: 1925–1956.* Brussels and Paris, 1999.

———. *Patrice Lumumba, acteur politique: de la prison aux portes du pouvoir (juillet 1956–février 1960).* Tervuren and Paris, 2005.

JEAN OMASOMBO

LUXEMBOURG.

LUXEMBOURG. World War I affected Luxembourg at a time when the nation-building process was far from complete. The small grand duchy (2,586 square kilometers, about 260,000 inhabitants in 1914) opted for an ambiguous policy between 1914 and 1918. With the country occupied by German troops, the government, led by Paul Eyschen, chose to remain neutral. This strategy had been elaborated with the approval of Marie-Adélaïde, grand duchess of Luxembourg. Although continuity prevailed on the political level, the war caused social upheaval, which laid the foundation for the first trade union in Luxembourg.

The end of the occupation in November 1918 squared with a time of uncertainty on the international as well as the national level. The victorious Allies disapproved of the choices made by the local elites, and some Belgian politicians even demanded the integration of the country into a greater Belgium. Within Luxembourg a strong minority asked for the instauration of a republic. In the end, the grand duchy remained a monarchy but was led by a new head of state, Charlotte. In 1921 it entered into an economic and monetary union with Belgium, the Union Économique Belgo-Luxembourgeoise (UEBL). During most of the twentieth century, however, Germany remained its most important economic partner.

The introduction of universal suffrage for men and women favored the *Rechtspartei* (party of the Right), which played the dominant role in the government throughout the twentieth century, with the exception of 1925–1926 and 1974–1979, when the two other important parties, the Liberal and the Social Democratic, formed a coalition. The success of the resulting party was due partly to the support of the church—the population was more than 90 percent Catholic—and of its newspaper, the *Luxemburger Wort*.

On the international level, the interwar period was characterized by an attempt to put Luxembourg on the map. Especially under Joseph Bech, head of the Department of Foreign Affairs, the country participated more actively in several international organizations, in order to ensure its autonomy. On the economic level, the 1920s and the 1930s saw the decline of the agricultural sector in favor of industry, but above all of the service sector. The proportion of the active population in this last sector rose from 18 percent in 1907 to 31 percent in 1935.

The invasion of Luxembourg by German troops on 10 May 1940 was the beginning of a four-year period of occupation. Even though the country was not de jure integrated into the Reich, de facto the German *Zivilverwaltung* (civil administration) under the direction of Gustav Simon considered and treated Luxembourg as a part of the Third Reich. This policy reached a peak with the forced enlistment of 10,200 Luxembourgers in the Wehrmacht from September 1942 on. In Luxembourger historiography, World War II is generally perceived as the end of the nation-building process. The legitimacy of the state was indeed no longer questioned in 1944. On one hand, the government and Charlotte, grand duchess of Luxembourg, achieved important results from their lobbying activities during the four years they spent in exile (London and Montreal). On the other, the opposition to the German occupation found its expression within the country in several resistance movements. The power of the collaboration was not strong enough to make these two pillars tremble. World War II remains an important period in the legitimization of the nation, as illustrated by the many commemorations and the frequent references to it in official speeches.

Encouraged by the contacts established with the Dutch and Belgian governments in exile, Luxembourg pursued a policy of presence in international organizations. It was one of the six founding members of the European Coal and Steel Community in 1952 (ECSC) and of the European Economic Community (EEC) in 1957. In the context of the Cold War, Luxembourg clearly opted for the West by joining the North Atlantic Treaty Organization (NATO) in 1949, thus renouncing its traditional neutrality, which had determined its international policy since the founding of the state. Engagement in European construction was rarely questioned subsequently, either by politicians or by the greater population. Despite its small proportions, Luxembourg often played an intermediary role between larger countries. This role of mediator, especially between the two large and often bellicose nations of Germany and France, was considered one of the main characteristics of national identity, allowing the Luxembourger not to have to choose between one of these two neighbors. The country also hosted a large number of European institutions such as the European Court of Justice. Luxembourg's small size no longer seemed to be a challenge to the existence of the country, and the creation of the Banque Centrale du Luxembourg (1998) and of the University of Luxembourg (2003) was evidence of the continuing desire to become a "real" nation. The decision in 1985 to declare *Lëtzebuergesch* (Luxembourgian) the national language was also a step in the affirmation of the country's independence. In fact, the linguistic situation in Luxembourg was characterized by trilinguilism: *Lëtzebuergesch* was the spoken everyday language, German the written language, in which Luxembourgers were most fluent, and French the language of official letters and law.

In the early twenty-first century, the internal political situation was characterized by a great stability. The government was predominantly led by the Christian Democrats. They provided some important statesmen, such as Pierre Werner and Jean-Claude Juncker. Although the Communist Party, which obtained 11 percent of the vote in 1945, became insignificant, two other parties succeeded in imposing their presence beginning in the 1990s: Déi Greng, which sprang from the ecological movements, and the Committee for Democracy and Justice (ADR), a right-wing and populist party.

Between 1945 and 2005, the economic structure of Luxembourg changed significantly. The crisis of the metallurgy sector, which began in the mid-1970s and lasted till the late 1980s, nearly pushed the country into economic recession, given the monolithic dominance of that sector. The Tripartite Coordination Committee, consisting of members of the government, management representatives, and trade union leaders, succeeded in preventing major social unrest during those years, thus creating the myth of a "Luxembourg model" characterized by social peace. Although in the early years of the twenty-first century Luxembourg enjoyed one of the highest GNP per capita in the world, this was mainly due to the strength of its financial standing, which gained importance at the end of the 1960s. Thirty-five years later, one-third of the tax proceeds originated from that sector. The harmonization of the tax system across Europe could, however, seriously undermine the financial situation of the grand duchy.

In this small country, immigration played an important role in supporting economic development. Beginning in the 1930s, a large number of Italians worked in metallurgy. In the 1970s, the Portuguese became the most important group. The strong economic growth in the late 1990s and in the early years of the twenty-first century, and the presence of some important European institutions, explain why 38 percent of the total population of 450,000 was composed of foreigners in 2005; they even represented more than half the active population.

See also **Belgium.**

BIBLIOGRAPHY

Als, Georges. *Histoire quantitative du Luxembourg: 1839–1990.* Luxembourg, 1991.

Newcomer, James. *The Grand Duchy of Luxembourg: The Evolution of Nationhood, 963 A.D. to 1983.* Lanham Md., 1984.

Spizzo, Daniel. *La nation luxembourgeoise. Genèse et structure d'une identité.* Paris, 1995.

Trausch, Gilbert, ed. *Histoire du Luxembourg. Le destin européen d'un petit pays.* Toulouse, 2002.

BENOÎT MAJERUS

LUXEMBURG, ROSA (1870–1919), German socialist theorist and publicist.

Rosa Luxemburg was born Roszalia Luksenburg, the fifth child in a Jewish family in Russian Poland; her father was a merchant and her mother the daughter of a rabbi. The family moved to Warsaw in 1873, and there she attended the Russian Second Gymnasium for Girls (1880–1887) and was known to teachers and family for her intelligence, industry, independent spirit, and sharp tongue. Upon graduation she joined an illegal socialist group and also made plans to go to Zurich, Switzerland, where women could matriculate in the university. She arrived in Zurich early in 1889, adopted a German form (Rosa Luxemburg) of her name, and enrolled in the university.

Drawn to the milieu of radical émigré students there, in 1890 she met Leo Jogiches (1867–1919), already well known as a young revolutionary. From that time until their deaths (1919) their lives were closely intertwined: as lovers, as founders in 1892, along with Julian Marchlewski, of the Social Democracy of the Kingdom of Poland, and as revolutionary comrades. In the 1890s Luxemburg, with seemingly inexhaustible energy and despite her troublesome limp, combined increasing socialist involvement with her studies, which she completed in 1897 with a doctoral dissertation on the industrial development of Poland (*Die industrielle Entwicklung Polens,* published 1898). As editor of the Polish-language *Workers' Cause* (*Sprawa Robotnicza,* 1894–1896) she traveled frequently to Paris, where it was published, met with French socialists, and attended and spoke forcefully at the congresses of the Socialist International in Zurich (1893) and London (1896). At the London meeting she attempted unsuccessfully to persuade the delegates to oppose national self-determination on the ground that it distracted from the highest goal of socialism, the emancipation of the proletariat. Luxemburg desired fervently to be at the center of international socialism; ideally that meant participation in the German Social Democratic Party, something that would be difficult for a non-German. To obtain German citizenship, friends helped her arrange a legal but sham marriage to the son of German socialists in Zurich (April 1898), and less than a month later she arrived in Berlin as Dr. Rosalia Lübeck, a name she dropped forthwith.

Luxemburg's reputation rose rapidly in the socialist movement. Within weeks, party leaders sent her to Upper Silesia as a campaign speaker among the Polish population in the Reichstag election of 1898. She then plunged immediately into the revisionist debate with a biting critique of Eduard Bernstein in newspaper articles (September 1898) that then appeared as *Social Reform or Revolution?* (*Sozialreform oder Revolution?,* 1899). In trenchant speeches at the party congress (Stuttgart, October 1898) she sought to refute Bernstein point by point, exploiting her polemical skills and her knowledge of economics and Marxist theory to argue that although socialists could not stand against reforms, they first of all had to give priority to social revolution. Opponents of

Rosa Luxemburg with an unidentified man, 1919.
©BETTMANN/CORBIS

revisionism greeted her attack on Bernstein approvingly, but others were wary of a young Jewish woman, newly arrived in Germany, who seemed overly self-confident and used her high intelligence and rhetorical wit with such single-minded determination. Over the years Luxemburg fiercely assailed the party establishment, fought openly and sometimes harshly with many leaders, including August Bebel, and did not shy away from publicly humiliating her Marxist ally, Karl Kautsky, though she was at the same time a close friend of his wife. Although she and Vladimir Lenin had much in common, in "Organizational Questions of Russian Social Democracy" ("Organisationsfragen der russischen Sozialdemokraten," *Die Neue Zeit,* 1903/1904) she rigorously examined his conception of the vanguard party, arguing that centralized organizations were more likely to hinder than advance the cause of socialism because they would not privilege revolutionary spontaneity from below.

Luxemburg believed strongly that social revolution and proletarian emancipation took precedence over all other causes endorsed by socialists. Most socialists approved of national self-determination, but she downplayed it as irrelevant and denounced the Polish Socialist Party because it made self-determination a major objective. For the most part Luxemburg disregarded her Jewish heritage, contending that it would be misleading to stress the plight of the Jews because their condition was no worse than that of many other peoples. She also made no special plea for women. In the 1890s socialist feminists were establishing their own organization and identity within the labor movement, but she remained largely indifferent to their work. She wanted socialists to concentrate on broad class issues that would mobilize all revolutionary energies. For this purpose she believed that an important lesson could be learned from the 1905 revolution in Russia, namely, that mass strikes, generated by the spontaneous impulses of the masses, were a key weapon. She explicated this thesis in the pamphlet *Mass Strike, Party, and Trade Unions* (*Massenstreik, Partei und Gewerkschaften*, 1906), but the party never adopted her view of the mass strike.

Social Democratic leaders nonetheless showed their appreciation for Luxemburg's learning and mastery of Marxism in 1907 by appointing her to the Party School. Her courses in political economy, Marxist theory, and the history of trade unionism were among the most popular. For Luxemburg the appointment meant a steady income and the opportunity to use her lectures as the basis for two books. After working on *An Introduction to Political Economy* (*Einführung in die Nationalökonomie*, published posthumously, 1925) she put it aside to write *The Accumulation of Capital* (*Die Akkumulation des Kapitals*, 1913), clearly her most important contribution to Marxist theory. In it she offered an economic explanation both for the capacity of capitalism to survive and how that led necessarily to imperialism. Marx had postulated that capitalism would collapse of its own internal contradictions, but that had not yet happened. To realize the surplus value it needed to sustain itself, Luxemburg reasoned, capitalism constantly had to find the means to expand, first into lesser-developed areas of the market societies themselves and secondly into foreign noncapitalist regions, leading inevitably to imperialism. But at some point even imperialist expansion would no longer be possible; capitalism would exhaust the markets and resources of colonial territories and, without opportunities for growth, would collapse. Although *The Accumulation* won admirers, many others, including Kautsky and Lenin, responded with negative assessments.

The painful test for socialism came with the outbreak of World War I. The patriotic behavior of German and other European socialists dismayed and angered the radical wing. Luxemburg joined with other left-wing socialists in the International Group and began a close association with Karl Liebknecht (1871–1919). Sentenced in February 1915 to a three-year prison term for inciting public disobedience, she lashed out at the betrayal of the Social Democratic leaders in *The Crisis of the Social Democracy* (*Die Krise der Sozialdemokratie*, 1916—also popularly known as the Junius pamphlet after the pseudonym she used—and drafted a set of twelve "Guiding Principles" (*Leitsätze*), which the International Group adopted early in January 1916. Released from prison early in 1916 for five months, she was arrested again in July and remained incarcerated until 8 November 1918, during which time she managed to contribute to the antiwar *Spartacus Letters* (*Spartakusbriefen*), composed a lengthy answer to critics of *The Accumulation*, and translated the Russian writer Vladimir Korolenko's autobiography into German. She followed events in Russia and, in *The Russian Revolution* (*Die Russische Revolution*, published only in 1922 by Paul Levi), praised the revolutionary accomplishments of the Bolsheviks, but she also subjected several of their actions to stern criticism: the self-defeating land policy; their support of national self-determination; the dissolution of the Constituent Assembly; and the abolition of the right of association and freedom of the press, which, she contended, thwarted completely the possible rule of the masses or the building of socialism.

If Luxemburg's commentary in *The Russian Revolution* seems to suggest that she believed in liberal democracy, this conclusion is very misleading. It needs to be corrected by what she said when, after arriving back in Berlin (10 November 1918) she began to believe, in contrast to her earlier pessimism, that the German proletariat possessed the potential to overthrow the provisional government. If initially successful, the proletariat would have to secure its hold on power through the use of "the revolutionary violence of the proletariat" to destroy its enemies. She called for the abolition of all parliaments and local councils, to be replaced by workers' and soldiers' councils, and leaned toward the dictatorship of the proletariat, conceived of as democracy in a socialist sense. Also, Luxemburg declined to publish her critique of the Bolsheviks and publicly expressed no disagreement with them, leaving the impression that she implicitly accepted Leninism as a model for German communism. When the revolutionary executive of the Communists and Independent Socialists decided early in January 1919 to call for the overthrow of the provisional government, Luxemburg too overestimated the prospects for success and joined in support of the badly conceived uprising that troops crushed within days. Right-wing Freikorps soldiers hunted down and captured Luxemburg and Liebknecht and brutally murdered them on 15 January 1919.

Luxemburg left a highly contested legacy. In view of her sharp critique of the Bolsheviks, many Russian Communists viewed her with suspicion, but Lenin, despite long-standing differences, always honored her as a person and revolutionary. Communist denunciations of Luxemburg were at times strident. Ruth Fischer held "Luxemburgism" responsible for the German Communist Party's weaknesses and the term became a weapon used against anyone who resisted the bolshevization of the party. Nonetheless, most German Communists revered Luxemburg and Liebknecht as founders of the party and heroic martyrs who symbolized and inspired a revolutionary spirit. Luxemburg's writings, especially from late 1918, served as programmatic guidelines for the Communists. After World War II, leaders of the German Democratic Republic (East Germany), even when they continued officially to reject "Luxemburgism," exploited the heroic images of Luxemburg and Liebknecht to give their regime added legitimacy. In the late 1980s, however, Luxemburg's words were also used against the regime as protesters' banners carried one powerful sentence from *The Russian Revolution:* "Freedom is always the freedom of those who think differently." Luxemburg's life and ideas, it turned out, could be exploited to help legitimate and delegitimate the same regime.

See also **Liebknecht, Karl; Spartacists; Zetkin, Clara.**

BIBLIOGRAPHY

Primary Sources

Luxemburg, Rosa. *Gesammelte Werke.* Edited by G. Radczun. 5 vols. Berlin, 1970–1975.

———. *Selected Political Writings of Rosa Luxemburg.* Edited by Dick Howard. New York and London, 1971.

Secondary Sources

Abraham, Richard. *Rosa Luxemburg: A Life for the International.* Oxford, U.K., New York, and London, 1989. A balanced interpretive study of Luxemburg that also seeks to clear away misconceptions that are too favorable.

Ettinger, Elzbieta. *Rosa Luxemburg: A Life.* Boston, 1986. The emphasis is on Luxemburg's personal life, but with sufficient attention to politics and theory to provide an overall account.

Laschitza, Annelies. *Im Lebensrausch, trotz alledem: Rosa Luxemburg. Eine Biographie.* Berlin, 1996. A detailed and sympathetic personal and political biography by an author who was a Luxemburg specialist in the former German Democratic Republic.

Nettl, J. P. *Rosa Luxemburg.* 2 vols. London and New York, 1966. Still the most comprehensive, scholarly biography of Luxemburg, combining sympathy and criticism.

Scharrer, Manfred. *"Freiheit ist immer . . ." Die Legende von Rosa & Karl.* Berlin, 2002. Seeks to sort out the authentic factual substance from the myths that have grown up around Rosa Luxemburg and Karl Liebknecht.

VERNON L. LIDTKE

LYOTARD, JEAN-FRANÇOIS (1925–1998), philosopher of the postmodern.

Jean-François Lyotard was one of the most versatile of the so-called poststructuralist French philosophers. Lyotard's concept of "the figural" is important for aesthetics. His interpretations of Kantian idealism increased the importance of justice, judgment, rules, and rights in a late twentieth-century political and cultural environment.

Lyotard's first major work, *Discours, figure,* was published in 1971. Prior to that date, his principal public activity was dissident leftist political activism with the organization Socialisme ou Barbarie (1949–1965), for whose journal he wrote articles critical of France's colonization of Algeria, where he had taught high school. His later teaching experiences included posts at La Flèche military school, the Sorbonne, and Nanterre (now University of Paris X) and visiting professorships in many foreign universities. In the wake of the May 1968 uprising by students and workers, he was appointed to the "experimental" University of Vincennes (now Paris VIII, in Saint-Denis) where he taught in close association with Gilles Deleuze. He also served as the first president of the Collège International de Philosophie, founded in 1983.

An initially obscure "report on knowledge" to the provincial government of Quebec was to thrust Lyotard into the center of debates about postmodernism in the 1980s. Published under the title *The Postmodern Condition* (1979), the report enjoyed wide celebrity, but that could not prevent its claims and especially, its implications, from being widely misunderstood. "A work can become modern only if it is first postmodern," Lyotard explained. "Postmodernism thus understood is not modernism at its end but in the nascent state, and this state is constant" (p. 79). An explainer of the "postmodern condition," Lyotard was not necessarily a proponent of postmodernism.

Of greater importance for philosophy was Lyotard's revival of a reflection on "the sublime"—a notion with origins in Longinus (first century C.E.) and which had come to its modern culmination prior to Lyotard in the writings of Edmund Burke (1729–1797) and especially Immanuel Kant (1724–1804). *The Differend* (1983) is, from a philosophical perspective, Lyotard's most important work. At one level, the book is a massive and meticulous refutation of Holocaust revisionism. More fundamentally, Lyotard argues that in order to be believable, a witness need not necessarily have *seen* an event. Courts of law may well listen to such testimony, but they will not *hear* it because an intractable differend renders understanding impossible.

Lyotard's exploration of Judaism has inspired the claim that he went further than any other non-Jewish twentieth-century thinker in that engagement. His interest in painting was equally significant. In a vast array of books or major essays on Marcel Duchamp, Valerio Adami, Shusaku Arakawa, Daniel Buren, Ruth Francken, Sam Francis, Barnett Newman, Karel Appel, and many others, Lyotard tirelessly tested his own philosophical claims against the work of art.

Lyotard's interest in literature was equally wide-ranging, abiding, and important for literary studies in the late twentieth and early twenty-first century. His interpretations of Marcel Duchamp and Barnett Newman arguably deal as much with these painters' *writings* as they do with their contributions to visual art. What literary figures—whether Gertrude Stein (discussed in *The Differend*) or Pierre Klossowski (in *Libidinal Economy*, 1974)—have demonstrated stylistically or have asserted directly about the power of a phrase is frequently the crucible from which Lyotard deploys his highly original thought. Without examples borrowed from the poetry of Stéphane Mallarmé and Michel Butor, Lyotard's first major treatise, *Discours, figure,* would have been unable to display what the figural working within discourse looks like on the page. The problematic that Lyotard explores in his final works on André Malraux (1901–1976) and Saint Augustine (d. 604) could be characterized as philosophy's adoption of a literary style in order to speak or write itself.

Some were dismayed by Lyotard's late-life interest in André Malraux, the committed novelist whose subsequent espousal of Gaullism was never forgiven by the Left. Yet the works that most abidingly intrigue Lyotard are Malraux's writings on art: a few compact, obscure essays written early in his career and several massive studies published between the end of World War II and Malraux's death. Lyotard shared with Malraux an almost mystical belief in art's capacity to protect a space in which innovative politics and ethics can still be conceived and invented. In extremely different voices, employing disparate discursive modes, *Signed, Malraux* (1996) and *Soundproof Room* (1998) both significantly extend Lyotard's meditation on what remains intractable in the human, on what is inhuman in face of inhumanity. A similar intractability is legible in *Augustine's Confessions* (1998), Lyotard's last work, left unfinished but published posthumously.

See also **Malraux, André; Phenomenology; Postmodernism.**

BIBLIOGRAPHY

Harvey, Robert, and Lawrence R. Schehr, eds. *Jean-François: Time and Judgment.* New Haven, Conn., and London, 2001.

Malpas, Simon. *Jean-François Lyotard.* London, 2003.

Williams, James. *Lyotard: Towards a Modern Philosophy.* Cambridge, U.K., and Malden, Mass., 1998.

ROBERT HARVEY

LYSENKO AFFAIR.

Trofim Denisovich Lysenko's ideas about plant breeding and heredity contradicted the laws of Mendelian genetics, but promised great agricultural benefits for the Soviet Union. Lysenkoism refers to the process by which the Soviet state and Communist Party supported Lysenko's views and silenced his detractors. Lysenkoism became emblematic of all that was wrong with Soviet science policies and a cautionary tale about the detrimental effect political leaders can have on the development of science.

"THE BAREFOOT PROFESSOR"

Lysenko was born to a peasant family in Ukraine in 1898. Considerable ambition, determination, and a strong memory (which made up for poor reading and writing skills) led him from his village school to a regional vocational school. In 1922, benefiting from Soviet affirmative-action policies for workers and peasants, he became a correspondence student at the Kiev Agricultural Institute. Upon graduation in 1925, he moved to an experimental plant selection station in Azerbaijan. Lysenko's first brush with fame came with a 1927 article in *Pravda* that described his experiments with planting leguminous crops to enrich fields. The article contrasted his findings with the supposedly impractical theories of university-trained scientists who worked with the "hairy legs of flies." Lysenko's propaganda value as a "barefoot professor" outweighed the actual validity and originality of his claims. Before scientists could verify what he had done, Lysenko was on to his next major "discovery," a process he called "vernalization." By dampening or cooling winter varieties of wheat, Lysenko claimed that he could turn them into spring varieties capable of producing higher yields. He either did not know or simply ignored the fact

that other scientists had worked on and abandoned this idea. Soon, vernalization became Lysenko's recipe for solving a full range of agricultural problems and the foundation for a whole theory of heredity. Lysenko held that characteristics acquired through exposure to environmental factors could be inherited by subsequent generations. He rejected the existence of genes and dismissed the breakthroughs of Gregor Mendel, August Weismann, and Thomas Hunt Morgan that were at the core of modern genetics. That there was no experimental basis for Lysenko's assertions did not seem to deter him or his growing list of followers in the agricultural establishment. Revolutionary zeal, not measured caution, was the order of the day.

LYSENKO'S RISE

Initially such scientists as Nikolai Vavilov, the leading Soviet plant geneticist, nurtured Lysenko, perhaps because of Lysenko's popularity with the press and political leaders and perhaps because he promised precisely the kind of revolutionary agricultural advancements the state and Communist Party expected of Soviet science. But Lysenko did not return the favor. Instead, he took every opportunity to chastise geneticists for not recognizing the practical value of his experiments. He did not hesitate to use the language of class struggle, depicting himself as a representative of proletarian science and the geneticists as representatives of bourgeois science. With the aide of the Marxist-Leninist philosopher Isaak Prezent, Lysenko filled his speeches with references to Karl Marx, Friedrich Engels, and Vladimir Lenin. Prezent also helped Lysenko realize the benefits of describing his ideas as building on the work of the humble plant breeder and Soviet hero Ivan Michurin. Using the label *Michurinist* allowed Lysenko to place his theories within a Russian scientific tradition that was distinct from allegedly Western and capitalist genetics.

In 1935 Lysenko delivered a particularly divisive speech at a conference of agricultural shock workers in the Kremlin. Joseph Stalin, who was in attendance, responded by clapping and shouting, "Bravo, Comrade Lysenko, Bravo!" Even as it became increasingly clear to specialists that Lysenko's practical proposals did not bring about the results he had predicted and that his theories were untenable, challenging his views became increasingly risky. By the end of the 1930s Lysenko had managed to trade in

Trofim Lysenko examines a stalk of wheat on a collective farm near Odessa. ©HULTON-DEUTSCH COLLECTION/CORBIS

on his notoriety to secure key positions in the academy and government: between 1935 and 1940 he became an academician of the USSR Academy of Sciences, director of the Odessa Institute of Genetics and Breeding, director of the academy's Institute of Genetics (replacing Vavilov), president of the Lenin All-Union Agricultural Academy (VASKhNIL), and the deputy head of the USSR Supreme Soviet. Geneticists still managed to win some official support for their work, but Lysenko convinced agricultural ministers, philosophers, and party leaders that "Michurinism" was more practical, patriotic, and progressive than genetics. In 1940 Lysenko's vitriol contributed either directly or, at the very least, indirectly to Vavilov's arrest as a British spy. Vavilov died in prison in 1943.

THE DEFEAT OF SOVIET GENETICS

After World War II, some geneticists continued to challenge Lysenko's claims in scientific meetings and articles in scholarly journals. They even received some support in early 1948 from Yuri Zhdanov, head of the Science Section of the Central Committee and son of the party secretary, Andrei Zhdanov. But Stalin accepted the distinction Lysenko made between progressive Soviet biology and reactionary Weismannism-Morganism. In a private letter Stalin reassured Lysenko that "the future belongs to Michurin." In May 1948 Stalin chastised the younger Zhdanov for criticizing Lysenko. On July 31 Lysenko gave a speech to a session of VASKhNIL distinguishing his materialist, home-grown, practical work from the idealist, foreign, impractical theories of geneticists. Even though the speech was printed in *Pravda* (suggesting the party's approval), some scientists in the audience challenged Lysenko's authority to define Soviet biology. Lysenko responded at the end of the meeting by informing the audience that the Central Committee had approved his speech in advance. To challenge his scientific ideas was now tantamount to challenging the Communist Party itself. The Central Committee set about firing geneticists and appointing Lysenkoists to administrative posts in academic and teaching institutions.

Scientists in other fields used the situation in Soviet biology as a template for settling controversial issues, but with less success than Lysenko. By the end of Stalin's reign Lysenko's control of Soviet biology began to face challenges from within the party apparatus and from agricultural ministries that were consistently disappointed by the results of applying his ideas. But widespread criticism was possible only after Stalin's death in 1953. Nikita Khrushchev, apparently agreeing with scientists and administrators who complained about Lysenko's abuse of power, removed him from the presidency of VASKhNIL. But Lysenko soon managed to charm Khrushchev with promises of advances in corn breeding and dairy cow breeding at a time when the leader had staked much of his domestic and international reputation on the improvement of Soviet agriculture. Lysenko's final defeat came only with Khrushchev's ouster from power in 1964.

See also **Science; Soviet Union; Stalin, Joseph.**

BIBLIOGRAPHY

Graham, Loren R. *Science in Russia and the Soviet Union: A Short History.* Cambridge, U.K., 1993.

Joravsky, David. *The Lysenko Affair.* Cambridge, Mass., 1970. Reprint, Chicago, 1986.

Krementsov, Nikolai. *Stalinist Science.* Princeton, N.J., 1997.

Soyfer, Valery N. *Lysenko and the Tragedy of Soviet Science.* Translated by Leo Gruliow and Rebecca Gruliow. New Brunswick, N.J., 1994.

ETHAN POLLOCK

MAASTRICHT, TREATY OF. The Treaty of Maastricht, signed by the then twelve member states in 1991, is considered the symbol of the refoundation of the project of European integration, and for two reasons. First, it expanded the scope of European integration and thoroughly revised its institutional setting. Second, after it was signed, it gave rise in most member states, for the first time since the 1950s, to wide public debate on the future of European integration and the fate of nation-states.

THE REFOUNDATION OF EUROPEAN INTEGRATION

Created by the Treaty of Rome of 1957, the European Economic Communities progressed very slowly in the early decades. The 1960s saw the gradual formation of the customs union (the progressive reduction of protectionist measures) among the six founder states, but any attempt to extend the integration was thwarted by the French Gaullist governments. In the 1970s the governments launched broad discussions on further integration; they adopted new legislation in areas such as environmental protection, public health, and consumer policies, and initiated flexible mechanisms of cooperation in the fields of monetary policies and foreign affairs, but they proved unable to coordinate their economic policies to face the oil crises or to revise the EEC's institutional framework. The relaunching began in the mid-1980s, when the governments agreed to complete the "single market" objective set up by the Rome treaty. With the

exception of the rather technical 1965 treaty, the Single European Act of 1987 was the first new treaty signed since the establishment of the EEC. It set the objective of a single European market and adopted a clear deadline; extended qualified majority voting where this was deemed necessary to attain this objective; slightly enhanced the powers of the European parliament; and codified a mechanism of cooperation in the field of foreign affairs that had been practiced informally in the 1970s. Taken together, these revisions indicated the willingness of the member states to further European integration. Yet several governments, the European Commission, and the federalist movements within and around the European parliament found this treaty too modest. Many hoped that it would be but a first step toward a more ambitious project of economic and monetary union, on a par with deeper institutional changes.

The fall of the Berlin Wall in 1989 gave a new impetus to these ambitions. In the founding countries—France, Germany, Belgium, Luxembourg, the Netherlands, and Italy, as well as in Spain and Portugal, which joined the EEC in 1986—a majority of the political class argued that far from depriving the European project of its raison d'être, the disintegration of the Soviet bloc made European integration more necessary than ever. Although they had no clear idea at that time of what their relationship with central European countries and with Russia would be, the European leaders knew that a new era had opened and agreed that European institutions should be adapted to this

French citizens vote on the Maastricht Treaty in Paris, 1992. ©OWEN FRANKLIN/CORBIS

context. Moreover, the prospect of German reunification prompted widespread concerns in several capitals—first and foremost in Paris—where the diplomats and politicians feared the emergence of a hegemonic country with strong Eastern connections that would alter the European balance. In this climate, the governments agreed in the first months of 1990 to convene an "intergovernmental conference"—the political-diplomatic forum stipulated by the treaty to revise the treaty itself—endowed with a double task: on the one hand, to negotiate the mechanism of monetary unification that had been discussed in expert groups since 1988; on the other, to discuss the institutional reforms of the European Community and the decision-making rules of its foreign policy. The Treaty of Maastricht signed in 1991 was the outcome of this conference.

THE THREE PILLARS OF THE EUROPEAN UNION

The most innovative chapter of the treaty established a process leading toward an "economic and monetary Union" (EMU). The first plans for a single European currency were made in 1970, but in the 1970s and 1980s the member states managed only to coordinate their monetary policies within a "European monetary system" based on flexible and evolutive parity mechanisms between national currencies. The Treaty of Maastricht established a three-stage mechanism leading toward full monetary unification, inspired by a report written by a group of central bankers under the chairmanship of Jacques Delors (b. 1925): the countries that intended to adopt the euro had to respect the "Maastricht criteria"—regarding inflation and budget discipline—in order to make their economies converge. No country was forced to adopt the mechanism—this "opt-out" was required by the reluctant Britain and Denmark—but once they are part of the "eurozone" the member states transfer their monetary powers to an independent European central bank and have to abide by strict measures of budget discipline monitored through multilateral surveillance. This plan was the outcome of a major intergovernmental bargain spearheaded by France and Germany: France saw it as a condition for reanchoring a reunified Germany in the European Union, and the Federal Republic agreed to abandon the powerful deutsche mark if its own doctrine of monetary policy was codified by the treaty.

The second innovation of the Treaty of Maastricht was the creation of the European Union and its so-called intergovernmental pillars. Changing the name from European Economic Community was one of the symbolic measures aimed at highlighting the importance of this refoundation, but it was merely a compromise. The most pro-European governments—Germany, the Benelux countries, and Italy—had pleaded for the extension of the Community's tasks to foreign affairs and internal security policies, and for the preservation of a single institutional framework. The most reluctant countries—Britain, Denmark, Greece, and to a certain extent France—agreed to expand European integration in these new fields only on two conditions: first, these policies would remain intergovernmental affairs, governed by unanimity voting and granting a very limited role to the European institutions; second, they would be organized outside the framework of the existing Community. The Treaty of Maastricht combined these two views: it created "intergovernmental" pillars outside the Community in the areas of foreign security policies and justice and home affairs and also created a European Union that would incorporate both the Economic Community and the new cooperative security. This compromise was criticized because it complicated the European structures, but it symbolized the dual nature of the European project, based on fundamental integration in the original economic field and less extensive cooperation in the other areas.

A PERMANENT PROCESS OF TREATY CHANGE

The Treaty of Maastricht was also a turning point in institutional reform. Since the end of the 1970s, the European Community's institutional framework had been the object of two criticisms. On the one hand, the continued requirement for unanimity voting in many areas undermined its decision-making capacity. On the other, the Community was criticized for being insufficiently democratic. The governments endeavored to answer these two

concerns: they slightly expanded the use of qualified majority voting and made several reforms meant to curb the EU's alleged "democratic deficit." In this spirit, the treaty created a Committee of the Regions to give subnational entities a say in European processes; it set up an ombudsman and made the deliberations of the Council of Ministers public to address Denmark's concerns about the EU's "lack of transparency." Last but not least, it strengthened the European parliament by giving it a say in the appointment of the European Commission and a power of co-decision in many legislative areas. By so doing, the treaty furthered the parliamentarization of the EU and altered the original institutional balance of the "Community model."

In hindsight, the Treaty of Maastricht appears to have opened a new dynamic of European integration, characterized by gradual and constant revision of the founding treaties. Although they amounted to deep structural changes, these reforms were indeed deemed insufficient by several member states, which called for and obtained a clause stating that the treaty would be revised in five years. This paved the way for the process of quasi-uninterrupted treaty change that took place subsequently: the treaties of Amsterdam (1997), Nice (2000), and Rome (2004) were all meant to achieve the reforms initiated at Maastricht and to adapt the Union to its new dimensions after it was enlarged to include Eastern Europe. As of 2004, however, none had managed to produce a broad consensus on the "finality" of the European Union.

See also **Euro; European Constitution 2004–2005; European Union.**

BIBLIOGRAPHY

Craig, Paul, and Gráinne de Búrca, eds. *The Evolution of EU Law.* Oxford, U.K., 1999.

Magnette, Paul. *L'Europe, l'État et la démocratie: Le souverain apprivoisé.* Brussels, 2000.

Moravcsik, Andrew. *The Choice for Europe: Social Purpose and State Power from Messina to Maastricht.* Ithaca, N.Y., 1998.

Nicolaïdis, Kalypso, and Robert Howse, eds. *The Federal Vision: Legitimacy and Levels of Governance in the United States and the European Union.* Oxford, U.K., 2001.

Weiler, Joseph. *The Constitution of Europe: "Do the New Clothes Have an Emperor?" and Other Essays on European Integration.* Cambridge, U.K., 1999.

PAUL MAGNETTE

MACDONALD, RAMSAY (1866–1937),
prime minister of the first two British Labour governments of 1924 and 1929–1931.

Ramsay MacDonald is best remembered for his involvement in the financial crisis of 1931, which led to the formation of the National Government under his premiership, an event that resulted in his lasting denunciation by the Labour Party. Yet, despite the obloquy heaped upon him, his reputation has been revived since the 1970s by the political historian David Marquand.

MacDonald was born at Lossiemouth in Scotland on 12 October 1866, the illegitimate son of Anne Ramsay and, possibly, John MacDonald, a ploughman. Educated at a local school, he became a pupil teacher and was expected to become a teacher. However, in the 1880s he took up clerical posts in Bristol and London.

Throughout the 1880s and the early 1890s, MacDonald was active in many socialist and radical organizations. He joined the quasi-Marxist Social Democratic Federation while in Bristol and was active in radical and Liberal Party politics while in London. His attempt to become a Liberal candidate and member of Parliament for Southampton was thwarted in 1894, and so he moved to the new Independent Labour Party and became the ILP and Labour Electoral Association candidate for Southampton in 1895. By that time he had already developed other socialist credentials, becoming a Fabian Society lecturer in 1892. However, he was still toying with radical ideas when in 1896 he joined the Rainbow Circle, a body of radical liberals such as Herbert Samuel, who published the *Progressive Review.* At this point, in November 1896, MacDonald began to develop his political career as he married Margaret Gladstone (d. 1911), who brought with her a settlement of up to three hundred pounds per year. They moved into a flat at 3 Lincoln's Inn Fields, London, which became the headquarters of the Labour Representation

Prime minister Ramsay MacDonald leaves his residence to deliver his resignation to King George, November 1924. GETTY IMAGES

Committee (later Labour Party) in the early twentieth century.

MacDonald's political career blossomed. He was on the Executive Committee of the Fabian Society in 1894, sat on the National Administrative Council of the ILP in 1896, and was often its chairman or secretary until the First World War. However, MacDonald is mainly associated with the rise of the Labour Party. He was often secretary or chairman of the Labour Representation Committee/Labour Party from 1900 to 1914, chairman of the Parliamentary Labour Party between 1911 and 1914, and one of the architects of the "Lib-Lab" pact of 1903, which allowed Liberal and Labour candidates an unchallenged run against the Conservatives in a number of constituencies in the 1906 general election. MacDonald was himself a beneficiary of this arrangement, being returned for the two-member seat of Leicester in January 1906 and representing that constituency until 1918.

MacDonald's opposition to the First World War led him to lose his parliamentary seat in 1918, but that allowed him to become deeply involved in building up the Labour Party between 1918 and 1922, which partly paved the way for his return as M.P. for Aberavon in 1922. Almost immediately he was voted leader of the Labour Party, and it is in this capacity that he became Labour's first prime minister in January 1924, keeping a minority Labour government in power for about ten months, during which he, acting as foreign secretary, promoted conferences to secure lasting international peace. This government was defeated in the general election of 1924, which occurred in the climate of the infamous "Zinoviev letter," or "Red Letter scare," a fake letter indicating the intention of the Soviet Union to use the Labour Party to gain its revolutionary objectives. After being returned for Seaham, MacDonald was able to form a second minority Labour government in June 1929. However, the onset of the world recession, resulting from the Wall Street crash, raised unemployment in Britain from one to three million and effectively bankrupted the government. Forced to contemplate major cuts, including a 10 percent reduction in unemployment benefits, the Labour cabinet split in August 1931 and was replaced by a national coalition government, headed by MacDonald. L. MacNeill Weir, MacDonald's parliamentary private secretary from 1924 to 1931, along with the Labour critics, accused MacDonald of treachery, but more recently David Marquand has defended his actions as those of a man who put country before party.

After the general election of 1931, MacDonald headed a coalition government that was dominated overwhelmingly by Conservatives. He was little more than a figurehead but was allowed to indulge his interest in foreign policy and in 1931 was involved in the Geneva Disarmament Conference and the Lausanne Conference. Ill health forced him to resign on 7 June 1935. Although he lost his seat in the 1935 general election, he was found a safe seat for the Scottish Universities and remained a member of the House of Commons until his death on 9 November 1937, while cruising in the Caribbean. The fact that few of his old comrades attended his funeral indicates the enduring hatred the Labour Party felt for his actions in 1931.

Indeed, one might reflect that had it not been for the events of 1931, MacDonald would probably be one of the lionized figures in the party he helped to create.

See also **Labor Movements; United Kingdom.**

BIBLIOGRAPHY

Marquand, David. *Ramsay MacDonald.* 2nd ed. London, 1997.

Tanner, Duncan. "Ideological Debate in Edwardian Labour Politics: Radicalism, Revisionism, and Socialism." In *Currents of Radicalism,* edited by Eugenio F. Biagini and Alastair J. Reid, 271–293. Cambridge, U.K., 1991.

Weir, L. MacNeil. *The Tragedy of Ramsay MacDonald: A Political Biography.* London, 1938.

KEITH LAYBOURN

MACEDONIA. A milestone in the history of Macedonia came in 1913. In Bucharest on 10 August Greece, Montenegro, Romania, and Serbia, after a month of bloody warfare, settled their dispute with Bulgaria over the spoils of the war they had just fought together (1912–1913) against the Ottomans. The apple of discord was Macedonia, an ill-defined region, which in the late nineteenth century included most of the remaining European provinces of the Ottoman Empire to the West of the River Nestos (Mesta). The area had rich agricultural resources and a strategic position in Balkan communications. Macedonia's population consisted of Greek-, Slav-, Vlach-, Albanian-, and Turkish-speaking Muslims, and Christians (the latter divided since 1872 into the adherents of the Constantinople Patriarchate and the followers of the Bulgarian Exarchate). A considerable number of Jews resided in Thessaloniki and other urban centers. Through educational campaigns and irregular warfare against the Ottomans and each other, Bulgaria, Greece, and Serbia had managed to create national parties of varying loyalty out of the peasant Christian population.

Following the treaty of Bucharest victorious Greece annexed the southern littoral, mostly Greek-speaking and pro-Patriarchist, parts of Macedonia, roughly identified with the classical Kingdom of Macedonia. Serbia received the upper part of the

Vardar Valley, a region including the vilayet of Kosovo, partly identified as Old Serbia. Only Pirin—the upper part of the Mesta River—went to defeated Bulgaria. In 1915 the Bulgarians occupied large parts of Greek and Serbian Macedonia, but were driven out by the victorious Entente forces. In accordance with the Treaty of Neuilly (1919) a voluntary Greek-Bulgarian exchange of populations completed the population transfers that had started in 1912–1913, while the Treaty of Lausanne (1923) triggered a compulsory Greek-Turkish exchange that produced ethnic and religious homogeneity in Greek Macedonia, although Slav revisionism continued.

In the interwar period all three states faced the challenges of integration. In the Greek part—called Government General of Macedonia to stress its Hellenic character—Slav-speakers represented only 10 percent of the population. Yet their linguistic and social assimilation was difficult and their ethnic identity had only partially been crystallized. The governments of both Yugoslavia and Bulgaria were claiming a national minority in Greece, and the vision of a greater Bulgaria encompassing Macedonia was supported by both nationalists and communists. The former dispatched armed bands to Greece and Serbia. The latter proposed an "independent and united Macedonia": coined by Bulgarian federalists and socialists in the late nineteenth century, it was officially supported by the Balkan Communist Federation in the 1920s. The Yugoslav government had also suggested that Macedonians were a distinctive people destined, however, to be assimilated by Serbia. In 1929 the Serbs, unable to integrate Old Serbia, renamed it "Prefecture of Vardar" to neutralize Bulgarian and communist-inspired "Macedonianism." Financial and political instability; the shortcomings of land redistribution; clashes among locals, refugees, and "colonists"; and the rise of dictatorial regimes everywhere started to shape the ethnic character of Macedonian regionalism, especially in Yugoslavia.

With the war approaching, the Germans were aware of Bulgaria's and Yugoslavia's desires to secure a sea-outlet through Greek Macedonia. Indeed, Bulgarians were allowed to occupy large parts of both Greek and Yugoslav Macedonia (April 1941). But they could not hold them. Even in the Yugoslav territory, where the Bulgarian army was initially well received, the clash with the communist resistance neutralized their grips. Sabotage and reprisals stressed the lines dividing Yugoslav Macedonians from Bulgarians but also from the Albanians who tried to detach Kosovo. However, it was not until early 1943 that Tito's (Josip Broz, 1892–1980) resistance was able to exploit this cleavage by promising self-government to Macedonia, officially recognized at the Jajce Conference of the Anti-Fascist Council of National Liberation of Yugoslavia (November 1943). Soon, Yugoslav Macedonia acquired its own *irredenta:* the Greek Communist Party allowed the formation of Slav-Macedonian resistance units in Greece.

On 2 August 1944 the Anti-Fascist Assembly of the National Liberation of Macedonia met for the first time and proclaimed the formation of the People's Federative Republic of Macedonia. Liberation found its communist leadership in diplomatic negotiations for control of Bulgarian Macedonia and ready to invade Greek Macedonia to support their comrades, as a Greek civil war was escalating. By the Bled Accords (1947), Bulgaria acknowledged the inhabitants of Pirin as ethnic Macedonians but the Tito–Joseph Stalin (1879–1953) split (1948) reversed the situation. Moreover, it alienated Greek Stalinists from Yugoslavia. Their defeat in the civil war (1949) led to a mass exodus of Slav speakers who did not feel Greek and had supported the communist revolt.

Financially, the Socialist Republic of Macedonia did not catch up with the federation. Despite heavy investments after the 1963 earthquake in Skopje and the creation of institutions such as the Institute for Mining and Geological Research (1947), the Saints Cyril and Methodius University (1949), and the Macedonian Academy of Sciences and Arts (1967), financial progress was slow and emigration rapid. In the late 1980s there was one telephone for seven inhabitants, and one doctor for 454. An average family spent 44 percent of its income for food and 11 percent for clothing. At independence, in September 1991, the Republic of Macedonia was the least developed of all the Yugoslav republics and of the other two Macedonian parts.

Independence was not easy. The wars in Yugoslavia and United Nations sanctions dropped the GDP by more than 30 percent (1991–1995). The republic saw some economic growth in 1996 but unemployment was rife (more than 33 percent in 1995, 40 percent in 1998). The black-market economy also grew and in 1998 it accounted for one-half of the GDP. In 1998 a government program to create jobs began to reduce unemployment. Domestic politics were also complicated. Despite independence and the fall of communism, the republic is still dominated by the same political forces and troubled by the same issues. The Bulgarian government speedily recognized Macedonian independence but still considers its past as "the most romantic chapter of Bulgarian history." The Albanians (more than 20 percent of the population) press for equal participation and recognition as a founding nationality. In 2001 the country experienced a two-month armed clash with Albanian bands from Kosovo. This conflict was halted by the Ochrid agreement. The issue of the republic's formal name, however, is still open as of 2006. Skopje and Athens have not come to an agreement, the former unable to moderate its national history, based on the idea of a united Macedonia, the latter (especially Greek Macedonians) refusing to accept a monopoly of the classical Macedonian name by a Slavic people. In 2006 the official UN name of the republic is still Former Yugoslav Republic of Macedonia (FYROM).

See also **Albania; Bulgaria; Greece; Kosovo; Yugoslavia.**

BIBLIOGRAPHY

Barker, Elisabeth. *Macedonia: Its Place in Balkan Power Politics.* London and New York, 1950. A Cold War political analysis published by the Royal Institute of International Affairs.

Chiclet, Christophe, and Bernard Lory, eds. *La Republique de Macédoine. Nouvelle venue dans le concert européen.* Paris, 1998. Moderately pro-Macedonian collective work by international scholars, mostly on political and cultural identities.

Koliopoulos, Ioannis, and Ioannis Hassiotis, eds. *Modern and Contemporary Macedonia: History, Economy, Society, Culture.* 2 vols. Thessaloniki, 1993. Collective work by Greek scholars, mostly on developments in Greek Macedonia.

Kōphos, Euangelos. *Nationalism and Communism in Macedonia.* Thessaloniki, 1964. A masterpiece on the politics of the Macedonian Question by a Greek scholar.

Pettifer, James, ed. *The New Macedonian Question.* New York, 1999. Collective work by international scholars on the national question, ethnic minorities and international relations of FYROM.

Pribichevich, Stoyan. *Macedonia, Its People and History.* University Park, Pa., 1982. The Yugoslav view by a personal acquaintance of Marshal Tito.

Stoyanova-Boneva, Bonka, Sephan E. Nikolov, and Victor Roudometof. "In Search of 'Bigfoot': Competing Identities in Pirin Macedonia, Bulgaria." In *The Macedonian Question: Culture, Historiography, Politics,* edited by Victor Roudometof, 237–258. Boulder, Colo., 2000.

BASIL C. GOUNARIS

MACMILLAN, HAROLD (1897–1986),
British prime minister from 1957 to 1963.

Harold Macmillan was born on 10 February 1894 into the prosperous family of publishers. He gained a first-class degree at Oxford in 1914 and then served on the western front, where he was wounded three times. His marriage in 1920 to Lady Dorothy Cavendish, daughter of the duke of Devonshire, was a step up the social scale but led to much distress, as from 1929 until her death she conducted an affair with Macmillan's friend and fellow member of Parliament (MP) Robert Boothby. In 1924 Macmillan became Conservative MP for the industrial town of Stockton, where poverty and unemployment affected him deeply. An intellectual figure on the Conservative left wing, he began to publish books advocating planning and a mixed economy. He was defeated at Stockton in 1929, and during the opposition period his loyalty seemed doubtful, especially due to his links with the Liberal politician David Lloyd George. He recovered Stockton in 1931 but was out of favor with the Conservative leadership and was left on the backbenches. As the decade advanced, his criticism widened from economic policy to foreign affairs, and he became a vocal critic of the appeasement of Nazi Germany. However, in this period he was an awkward speaker who rapidly bored his listeners, and he had little impact.

Churchill gave him junior office in 1940, and from 1942 to 1945 he was minister resident in North Africa. Macmillan was skillful in dealing with the various French factions and in liaising with the newly arriving American forces, working effectively with the U.S. commander, General Eisenhower. In later years there was controversy about Macmillan's part in the return of anticommunist prisoners of war to the Soviet Union and Yugoslavia at the end of the war. After the Conservative defeat in 1945, Macmillan was a leading figure in the reappraisal of party policy, which was now moving in the direction he had previously advocated.

In 1951 Macmillan entered the cabinet as minister of housing, an important position as the pledge to build 300,000 new homes per year had been significant in the Conservative victory. Macmillan demonstrated drive and determination, and amid much publicity achieved the target in 1954. His success was rewarded by promotion to minister of defense in October 1954, although here his scope for initiative was restricted. When Anthony Eden became prime minister in April 1955 he appointed Macmillan to succeed him as foreign secretary, but again Macmillan found himself the subject of prime ministerial interventions. He was not as pliable as Eden wished, and in December 1955 he was moved aside to be chancellor of the exchequer. By this time Macmillan was clearly the third figure in the Conservative leadership, behind Eden and R. A. Butler. When Eden resigned after the disastrous Suez crisis, Macmillan's determined conduct led the rest of the cabinet to prefer him to Butler, and he became prime minister on 10 January 1957.

In the wake of Suez, the government was not expected to last, but Macmillan swiftly restored relations with the United States, and Conservative morale recovered under his firm leadership. Success and effort had transformed him into a confident and witty speaker, with a manner combining charm with calmness in a crisis. His cultivated and patrician style evoked the pre-1914 world, and this "Edwardian" image was an asset in the 1950s. With prosperity and living standards rising, the general election that Macmillan called in October 1959 saw the Conservative majority increased to a hundred. His visit to Moscow and presence at the Geneva conference in 1959 suggested that Britain still mattered in world affairs, while at the same time he increased the pace of decolonization. He seemed to have a golden touch, and a memorable cartoon depicting him as "Supermac" reflected his political dominance.

All this was to change after 1960, when economic stagnation, social changes, and political setbacks combined to make Macmillan seem elderly and outdated. His one success was the securing of the Polaris nuclear missile system from the United States at the Nassau conference in December 1962. However, the decision in 1961 to seek membership of the European Economic Community ended in the humiliation of the French president Charles de Gaulle's veto in January 1963. At home, the government's stock declined. A mishandled cabinet purge in July 1962 seemed to show that Macmillan was losing his grip, and his prestige was fatally damaged by errors of judgment in the Profumo scandal of 1963. His days already seemed numbered when sudden illness forced his resignation in October 1963; from his hospital bed, he maneuvered to ensure that Butler was not his successor. He accepted a peerage as earl of Stockton in 1984 and died on 29 December 1986.

See also **Appeasement; Suez Crisis.**

BIBLIOGRAPHY

Primary Sources

Catterall, Peter ed. *The Macmillan Diaries: The Cabinet Years, 1950–1957.* London, 2003.

Macmillan, Harold. *Memoirs.* 6 vols. London, 1966–1973. Lengthy account with extracts from Macmillan's private diary.

Secondary Sources

Aldous, Richard, and Sabine Lee, eds. *Harold Macmillan: Aspects of a Political Life.* Basingstoke, U.K., 1999.

Davenport-Hines, R. P. T. *The Macmillans.* London, 1992. Collective family biography.

Horne, Alistair. *Macmillan 1894–1956.* London, 1988. First volume of official life.

———. *Macmillan 1957–1986.* London, 1989. Second volume of official life.

Turner, John. *Macmillan.* London, 1994. Excellent medium-length biography.

STUART BALL

MAD COW DISEASE. Mad cow disease or bovine spongiform encephalopathy (BSE) was first identified in the United Kingdom in November 1986. The disease is one of a family of neurodegenerative diseases known as transmissible spongiform encephalopathies, which cause deterioration of cells in the brain and eventual death. By January 2005 more than 182,000 clinical cases of BSE had been confirmed in cattle in Great Britain, with epidemics also occurring on a smaller scale in other European countries including Northern Ireland, the Republic of Ireland, Switzerland, Portugal, and France. Worldwide cases have been confirmed as far away as Canada, the United States, and Japan. The economic impact of BSE in badly affected countries has been great, with the worldwide export ban imposed on the United Kingdom by the European Union between 1996 and 1999 having a long-lasting effect on the cattle industry in that country. In tandem, there has been a drop in consumer confidence, not only in beef products but also in the overall safety of food, triggered by other disease outbreaks caused by salmonella and other bacterial contamination. To combat this situation, the Food Standards Agency was formed as an independent food safety watchdog in 2000 to protect the public's health and consumer interests in relation to food.

BSE is thought to have originated in cattle from supplementary feed containing meat and bone meal (MBM) contaminated by a scrapie-like agent derived from sheep or cattle, although much debate continues over its origin. In the United Kingdom the disease was made notifiable in June 1988 and in July 1988 a ban on the use of ruminant-based MBM in cattle feed came into force in Great Britain. Although the ban did not prevent all infections and cases in animals born after 1988, the number of cases of BSE in Great Britain has continued to decline, demonstrating that MBM feeding practices had been the major route of transmission. However, even after stricter enforcement of the ban came into place in 1996, cases have still occurred in animals born after this time (known as Born After the Real Ban or BARBs) with more than one hundred such cases reported as of 2006. Extensive epidemiological investigations are under way for these BARB cases to identify remaining routes of transmission.

The appearance of BSE in cattle, while of veterinary, agricultural, and economic concern, was initially not thought to pose a threat to human health because of its similarity to scrapie, a disease in sheep that has been endemic in most parts of the world for more than two hundred years. This was demonstrated politically by the now-infamous picture of then–agriculture minister John Gummer feeding a hamburger to his young daughter. However this optimism was shattered in 1996 when the U.K. government announced a possible link between BSE and a new variant of Creutzfeldt-Jakob disease (vCJD) in humans. Since this time, scientific evidence in support of the hypothesis that vCJD is a direct consequence of exposure to BSE has been strengthened. In the United Kingdom alone it is estimated that more than two million infected cattle were slaughtered for human consumption, indicating widespread exposure of the population to the infectious agent. A variety of measures have been put in place to reduce exposure, including the ban on the use of high-risk materials (including the brain and spinal cord) and animals over thirty months of age in food production.

By 1 July 2005, 150 human deaths from vCJD had been reported in the United Kingdom with a further six patients with probable cases still alive. In addition cases have been reported in France, Italy, Republic of Ireland, the United States, Canada, Saudi Arabia, Portugal, and Japan. While the number of cases remains relatively small, concern has now shifted to the possibility of ongoing transmission through blood transfusions and surgical instruments given the potentially large number of people who could be harboring subclinical forms of the disease. A blood transfusion has been formally identified as the most probable source of infection for one vCJD case, and in addition signs of infection have been identified in the spleen of another patient who died from other causes but who was known to have received blood from a vCJD case. A number of measures to protect blood supplies both within the United Kingdom and elsewhere have been introduced over the past ten years, including leucodepletion of blood, which is thought to reduce the risk of transmitting infection by about 40 percent, and a ban on donors who have themselves received a blood transfusion. Transmission via surgical instruments has not been documented to date but remains a potential risk. Because of the many uncertainties about these secondary routes of transmission, the potential future scale of the outbreak is unclear. However the BSE and vCJD epidemics are likely to remain a cause for government and public concern for several years.

See also **Agriculture; Diet and Nutrition; Public Health.**

BIBLIOGRAPHY

Bruce, M. E., R. G. Will, J. W. Ironside, et al. "Transmissions to Mice Indicate that 'New Variant' CJD Is Caused by the BSE Agent." *Nature* 389 (1997): 498–501.

Hill, A. F., M. Desbruslais, S. Joiner, et al. "The Same Prion Strain Causes vCJD and BSE." *Nature* 389 (1997): 448–450.

Hilton, D. A., A. C. Ghani, L. Conyers, et al. "Prevalence of Lymphoreticular Prion Protein Accumulation in UK Tissue Samples." *Journal of Pathology* 203 (2004): 733–739.

Llewelyn, C. A., P. E. Hewitt, R. S. Knight, et al. "Possible Transmission of Variant Creutzfeldt-Jakob Disease by Blood Transfusion." *Lancet* 363 (2004): 417–421.

Peden, A., M. W. Head, D. L. Ritchie, et al. "Preclinical vCJD after Blood Transfusion in a PRNP Codon 129 Heterozygous Patient." *Lancet* 364 (2004): 527–529.

Statutory Instrument. "The Bovine Spongiform Encephalopathy Order 1988, no. 1039." HMSO London, 1988.

Wells, G. A., A. C. Scott, C. T. Johnson, et al. "A Novel Progressive Spongiform Encephalopathy in Cattle." *Veterinary Record* 121 (1987): 419–420.

Wilesmith, J. W., J. B. Ryan., and M. J. Atkinson. "Bovine Spongiform Encephalopathy: Epidemiological Studies on the Origin." *Veterinary Record* 128 (1991): 199–203.

AZRA GHANI

MAFIA. The origins of the Mafia remain mysterious. No two accounts agree. Some trace its existence back to medieval *mafie* or guerrilla bands. The De Mauro–Paravia dictionary says that it "arose in western Sicily in the nineteenth century." Most accounts explain the Mafia by citing the southern Italian great estate or *latifondo*. Absentee landlords hired an agent, the *gabellotto,* to manage their property. The agents used a paid armed force, called variously *campieri* or *caporali,* to discipline the landless peasants. This system operated across much of the Italian south, but *caporali* were hired guns, not mafiosi. Besides, the Mafia seems to have emerged only in western Sicily and only spread to the rest of the island after the Second World War. Why there? Again nobody really knows.

THE MAFIA AND THE UNIFICATION OF ITALY

The unification of Italy in 1861 brought organized government to the Italian south, and northern Italians discovered a new world. Giuseppe Rizzotto's "I Mafiusi della Vicaria," performed in 1863, turned the Mafia into a romantic conspiratorial organization complete with initiation rites. According to the *Oxford English Dictionary*, the earliest official use of the word in English comes from the same decade. *The Times* of London reported on 11 October 1866 that "the Maffia, a secret society, is said to include among its members many persons of an elevated class." Others denied that it was an organization at all. The scholar Pasquale Villari wrote in 1878 that the Mafia had "no established hierarchy, no set rules, no regular revenue. The Maffia has no written statutes; it is not a secret society, and hardly an association. It is formed by spontaneous generation" (p. 54). In the 1980s the so-called *pentiti* (repentant Mafia bosses who "talked" to the police and thus violated the notorious code of silence, *omertà*) described elaborate rites, annual meetings, and hierarchies. As in everything to do with the Mafia, there is no certainty here either. Villari could have been right in the nineteenth century and the Mafia then changed in the twentieth. Nobody knows.

MAFIA, CAMORRA, AND 'NDRANGHETA

By the middle of the nineteenth century observers had identified not just one system of organized crime but several. In Naples there was the Camorra, an urban version of the Mafia. Various branches of the Camorra continue to operate in Naples in the early twenty-first century. They dominate the building trades, control drugs and smuggling, and fight bloody battles for control of the city. A third version of the Mafia called the 'Ndrangheta operates in Calabria. The word is said to come from the Greek and to mean "honored society." All three criminal societies, the Mafia, Camorra, and 'Ndrangheta, maintain that their activities bring them "honor." Indeed, a traditional term for a mafioso is precisely that he is "a man of honor" (*uomo d'onore*).

The Mafia and 'Ndrangheta, unlike the Camorra, began in the countryside. The typical Mafia boss in the province of Palermo until the Second World War was the *macellaio,* who owned the local butcher shop, organized voting fraud, rustled cattle, and kept order. They acted as "middle men" and doffed their caps to the *gentiluomo* in his white suit who sat in cafés in the small towns. They supported the church, collected debts, and settled disputes. Pino Arlacchi, the leading Italian sociologist of the Mafia, sees this *comportamento mafioso* (Mafia behavior) as the distinctive characteristic of the phenomenon. The Mafia was not an organization but a way to behave: *farsi rispettare* (to make oneself respected), to acquire honor by *fatti provi* (proven facts or deeds), and, above all, to show courage by acts of violence. Killing a respected enemy gained the killer a huge quantum of honor. Because violence eliminated so many young men, the "family" or *cosca* extended itself by coparenthood (*comparaggio*) to young males not directly related by blood to the family. The *capo mafia* adopted them and became their *padrino* or godfather. All family members bound themselves by the oath of silence (*omertà*) to reveal nothing of the family's activities. In this sense, the Mafia is not simply a gang of crooks but represents what sociologists call a "total social fact," a highly complex, historic, social organism.

FASCISM ATTACKS THE MAFIA

The fascist regime of Benito Mussolini attacked the Mafia. Mussolini installed his "Iron Prefect," Cesare Mori, in the seat of government in Palermo in October 1925 with orders to smash the Mafia by any means. Mori used large forces of police and carabinieri to round up hundreds of rural mafiosi and small-time crooks. He put them in concentration camps, held them without trial, and drove many of the bigger figures to flee the country. By 1927 Mori declared that the Mafia had been eliminated. It survived, of course, because Mori stopped short at the so-called third level, the great landlords, aristocrats, and businessmen in Palermo and Torre del Greco whose funds supplied cash to the various Mafia families in return for violence by contract. The Mafia could not then and

cannot now be separated from Sicilian society, on which it lives in parasitic symbiosis.

Mussolini's war on the Mafia turned its victims into "antifascists." When the U.S. and British forces landed on Sicily in July 1943, they found hundreds of blameless antifascists all over the island who spoke English with Brooklyn or Philadelphia accents, knew the locals, and could tell the Allies where the Fascists and Nazis were to be found. The Allies named many friendly mafiosi mayors of their towns.

THE MAFIA IN POSTWAR ITALY

Between 1945 and the early 1970s, about eight million country dwellers left the land for better jobs in northern cities. The traditional Mafia lost its popular base. The Italian state intervened just in time to save the Mafia by creating a Sicilian autonomous region with substantial powers and beginning a massive investment in infrastructural improvements—roads, sewers, dams, hydroelectric power plants, swamp clearance, and disease control. Billions of lira flowed from north to south. The Mafia went into the construction business, the hotel and restaurant business, and set up travel agencies and casinos. A tertiary economy spread out. Universities turned the children of illiterate peasants into local bureaucrats, lawyers, and academics. Sicily, with its population of roughly seven million, was flooded with capital. Much of it financed "legitimate" businesses that banks knew perfectly well belonged to Mafia families.

In 1972 U.S. and French law enforcement agents broke the "French Connection," a Marseille-based heroin cartel controlled by Corsicans. The price of heroin in the United States went up sharply, and the Sicilian Mafia reacted. They hired the French chemists and set up labs for them in Palermo. The American Mafia families, after some hesitation—drugs were not "honorable"—took over the dispatch and marketing in the United States. The Mafia went from very profitable regional activities to international big business. Billions of "narco-lire" flowed through the Sicilian economy. The drug trade knew no boundaries. The sums at stake became astronomical, and waves of murders in the 1980s showed that jurisdictional disputes over territories and supply routes were now lethal. Between

Members of the mafia are held under guard while awaiting trial in Palermo, Sicily, February 1928. ©BETTMANN/CORBIS

1980 and the early 1990s, there were more than a hundred Mafia killings a year in Palermo alone.

The Italian state could not control the Mafia. The mafiosi had more money, better political connections than ever, and had outgrown their place as "middle men." Now they gave orders to the *gentiluomo* in the white suit, not the other way round. They killed policemen, they killed magistrates, and on 3 September 1982 they murdered General Alberto Dalla Chiesa, the commanding general of the carabinieri, in broad daylight. The following year, the Italian state got a break. Brazilian police arrested an Italian mafioso called Tommaso Buscetta, who decided to tell what he knew. He revealed that the Sicilian Mafia had a rigid organization ruled by a supreme commission of ten top bosses called the *cupola*. Using Buscetta's evidence, the state prosecutor Giovanni Falcone tried, and in December 1987 convicted, over three hundred leading Mafia figures in the so-called *maxi-processo*. The

American Mafia families were also weakened by waves of killings. In February 1985, after close cooperation between Italian and American police officers, nine of the top bosses of the main American clans—the Gambino, Lucchese, Bonanno, Colombo, and Genovese "families"—were arrested and successfully prosecuted.

THE FUTURE OF THE MAFIA

The Italian Mafia has been wounded but is not dead. It has lost its U.S. monopoly. Colombian drug syndicates offer a better product. The competition of cocaine and crack has reduced the demand for heroin, the main Mafia drug, but not eliminated it. Legal changes in Italy allow Italian magistrates to prosecute groups as well as individuals, but the connection between the "third level" and the Mafia still exists. In December 2004 Senator Marcello Dell'Utri, a founding member of Prime Minister Silvio Berlusconi's Forza Italia Party, was sentenced to nine years in prison for money laundering and serving as the link between the Mafia and the governing elites. Forty mafiosi testified against him. Nevertheless, as long as the Sicilian Mafia still lives as a parasite on the surrounding society and expresses some of its values, it will continue to exercise its malign influence on the community for years to come.

The word *mafia* has also been generalized. There are "Russian mafias," "Chinese mafias"; indeed, any number of criminal gangs or groups now bear the name. Few of them really fit the peculiarly tight social and cultural conditions that created and sustained the original Sicilian Mafia over the centuries of transformation from feudal agriculture to international business. The Sicilian Mafia survived these changes because its familial structure proved tight yet flexible enough to adapt to new conditions.

See also **Crime and Justice; Italy.**

BIBLIOGRAPHY

Arlacchi, Pino. *Mafia, Peasants, and Great Estates: Society in Traditional Calabria.* Translated by Jonathan Steinberg. Cambridge, U.K., 1983.

———. *Mafia Business: The Mafia Ethic and the Spirit of Capitalism.* London, 1986.

Duggan, Christopher. *Fascism and the Mafia.* New Haven, Conn., 1989.

Sciascia, Leonardo. *The Day of the Owl.* Translated by Archibald Colquhoun and Arthur Oliver. New York, 2003.

Stille, Alexander. *Excellent Cadavers: The Mafia and the Death of the First Italian Republic.* New York, 1995.

Villari, Pasquale. *Le lettere meridionali ed altri scritti sulla questione sociale in Italia.* Naples, 1979.

Walston, James. *The Mafia and Clientelism: The Roads to Rome in Post-War Calabria.* London, 1988.

JONATHAN STEINBERG

MAGINOT LINE. On 15 March 1935 the French war minister General Louis Maurin addressed the Chamber of Deputies in the following terms: "How could anyone imagine that we were still thinking in terms of offensive movements when we have spent billions building a fortified barrier? Why would we be so insane as to go beyond this barrier on who knows what adventure?" These few words summed up France's military thinking during the interwar years, and the implications were clear: though France had made a number of alliances in Europe, it would not come to the aid of its allies if the need arose because its army had no intention of emerging from behind its fortified lines.

The First World War had three phases: a war of movement based on an all-out offensive that was brought to an end by a true massacre of infantry; a stalemate period of trench warfare that was also very costly in human lives; and a resumption of mobile warfare in which tanks and aviation played a very large part. Good sense would have dictated the further development of these two kinds of armament, in the production of which France excelled in 1919, but psychological factors (the continuing spread of pacifism) combined with financial considerations brought any such course of action to a virtual halt. Military service was likewise reduced (to just one year in 1928). It is true that not all the politicians and military leaders—notably Marshal Ferdinand Foch—were in agreement on this issue; nor, a priori, was the idea of a line of fortifications necessarily incompatible with mobile warfare, once the mobilization and concentration of troops had been effected within the defended zone. But the views of Maréchal Philippe Pétain (1856–1951) prevailed, and the military option quickly chosen was all-out defense behind this line. Feasibility studies were made from 1925 to 1929 under the direction of war minister Paul Painlevé. The law of 13 July 1927 decreed that "the protection of the integrity of the national territory" should become "the essential objective of the military organization of the country." Construction was already under way by the time parliament, on 14 January 1930, passed the law that authorized the project and appropriated 2,900 million francs to support the work over a five-year period. The minister of war by that time was André Maginot, a parliamentary deputy for Bar-le-Duc since 1910, called up as a simple soldier in 1914, seriously wounded in action and hospitalized for almost a year, and now a significant political figure of the center-right who had held several ministerial posts since 1917. In reality, however, he had very little to do with the construction of the

Rows of posts mark the Maginot Line. ©HULTON-DEUTSCH COLLECTION/CORBIS

line of fortifications to which his name became attached.

The Maginot Line was not a Great Wall of China. It comprised very heavily fortified underground installations with less heavily protected positions spaced out between them. Deemed impregnable, it received a great deal of publicity in the 1930s and was glorified in all sorts of ways. In a sense it was France's military shop-window. Unfortunately, the widely believed claim that it protected the entire frontier of northern and northeastern France turned out to be false. The Maginot Line proper was the work of a "Commission for the Organization of Fortified Regions," and in fact it consisted of only two systems of fortifications, one covering the region around Metz and the other the Franco-German frontier along the left bank of the Rhine. Along the Rhine it was felt that relatively weaker positions would suffice to make the river impossible to cross. Farther west, in the Ardennes, whose forest terrain was considered impassable by a modern army, and along the Belgian border nothing was done. To

fortify the border with Belgium would have suggested that that country would be abandoned automatically in the event of war.

After Adolf Hitler came to power, when another war seemed possible, and when war indeed broke out in September 1939, it became apparent that the northern frontier needed fortifying, and a large number of structures of limited strength were built with military manpower (or *main d'oeuvre militaire,* whence the name "MOM Line"). The unquestionable strength of the Maginot Line inevitably led the German leadership to seek a way to flank it in the event of invasion—that is, to advance through Belgium. This eventuality was anticipated by the French, who threw their best troops into Belgium when the Germans moved; but the German plan had been modified—at the last minute, it is true—and the decision taken to pass through the almost undefended Ardennes. The resulting German offensive took the French troops from the rear while at the same time allowing the Germans to flow behind the Maginot Line. The Maginot positions still had the capacity to defend themselves but to no good purpose: the German armies were overrunning France, and once the armistice was signed the garrisons of the line had no choice but to surrender.

The building of the Maginot Line was thus a vain enterprise; it pointed up the French command's disastrous strategic notions and, worse still, swallowed immense amounts of money that would have been better spent on tanks and aircraft.

After the war, the Maginot Line was abandoned, and some of its physical structures were even sold off to private citizens.

See also **France; Pétain, Philippe; World War II.**

BIBLIOGRAPHY

Kaufman, Joseph, and Hanna Kaufman. *The Maginot Line: None Shall Pass.* Westport, Conn., and London, 1997.

Kemp, Anthony. *The Maginot Line: Myth and Reality.* New York, 1982.

Panouillé, Jean-Louis. "Autopsie de la ligne Maginot." In *L'Histoire* (April 1985), 3–18.

Vaïsse Maurice. "Ligne Maginot." In *Dictionnaire historique de la vie politique française au XXe siècle.* Paris, 1995.

JEAN-JACQUES BECKER

MALAPARTE, CURZIO (1898–1957),
Italian journalist and writer.

Curzio Malaparte was born Kurt Erick Suckert in Prato, Tuscany, into a petit-bourgeois family; his father was German, his mother Italian. As a politically committed journalist and writer who shifted from fascism to communism, his work and career were a fairly accurate reflection of the successive passions of not a few Italian intellectuals of his generation. He eventually came to be seen, at home and abroad, as one of Italy's most eminent writers. Piero Gobetti (1901–1926) called him "fascism's finest pen," but he had a complex and stormy relationship with Benito Mussolini's (1883–1945) regime.

In World War I, Kurt Suckert enlisted at the age of sixteen with the Garibaldi volunteers, alongside the French. He later wrote that the Garibaldi Legion, where he met many syndicalists and anarchists and discovered the Italian proletariat, was for him "the antechamber of fascism."

In December 1920 he published his first book, *Viva Caporetto!* The work was provocative, Caporetto being the site of a disastrous Italian defeat in 1917; the second edition (1921) was renamed *La rivolta dei santi maledetti* (*The Revolt of Damned Saints*). The work criticized the way the war had been managed by bourgeois elites, to the detriment of the masses, and suggested not a little admiration for the Russian Revolution. After a short diplomatic career, Suckert joined the Florence *fascio*, one of the most "radical" fascist groups in Italy. He went on to occupy a variety of positions in the Fascist Party and trade unions. His political friendships in the movement included leaders of the most intransigent tendencies (notably Roberto Farinacci [1892–1945]) and of "integral syndicalism" (Edmondo Rossoni [1884–1965]). According to him, the fascist revolution would complete the Italian Risorgimento and would be at once "anti-bourgeois" and "anti-proletarian," thus expressing the individualist aspirations of the Italian people. As a journalist, however, Suckert—who took the pen name Curzio Malaparte in 1925—was more eclectic: although he contributed to extremist fascist publications such as Mario Carli (1889–1935) and Emilio Settimelli's (1891–1954) *L'Impero,* he could also be read in Gobetti's antifascist review *La Rivoluzione liberale.*

When the decisive moment arrived, though, Malaparte was resolute in his support for fascism. He backed Mussolini during the Matteotti affair and the shift toward dictatorship that followed. In 1929 he became director of *La Stampa,* the prestigious Turin daily newspaper controlled by Fiat. In the spring of 1931 he was nevertheless dismissed by Giovanni Agnelli (1866–1945), head of the Fiat empire, who did not like Malaparte's way of running the paper. In 1931 Malaparte published a pamphlet against Mussolini in France, *Technique du coup d'Etat.* He was thoroughly disgraced in 1933 after trying to bring down Italo Balbo (1896–1940), the minister of the air force, by accusing him of corruption, and he spent more than a year in internal exile on the island of Lipari. When he returned to political activity, thanks to the intervention of Galeazzo Ciano (1903–1944), he resumed propaganda work for the regime, going so far as to urge Italian participation in the Spanish civil war at a time when some Italian intellectuals, among them Elio Vittorini (1908–1966), had begun to distance themselves from the government.

As a war correspondent for *Corriere della Sera*, Malaparte witnessed the atrocities of the Wehrmacht on the eastern front and abandoned fascism. As a liaison officer with the American army in the summer of 1944 Captain Malaparte accompanied the Allied advance up the Italian peninsula from Naples to Florence. He published a series of reports in *L'Unità* and incorporated his experiences into his novel *La Pelle* (The skin), which was published in 1949 and brought him celebrity. The work described a society riddled with corruption and threatened by disintegration in the wake of the war; the Mezzogiorno was portrayed as a land more desolate than ever. The lesson of the novel was that war obliterated ideological differences: "Today we suffer and we cause others to suffer, we kill and we die, we bring about marvels and we bring about horrors, not to save our souls but to save our skins. We believe we are struggling and suffering to save our own souls, but in reality we are struggling and suffering to save our own skins. Nothing else counts." Perhaps this cynical political stance accounted for the appeal of Malaparte's novel to a population whose dominant attitude had long been one of "wait and see."

After the war Malaparte went back to work as a reporter, visiting Joseph Stalin's (1879–1953) USSR and Mao's China. The People's Republic of China became one of his last political enthusiasms. He died in 1957.

See also **Agnelli, Giovanni; Fascism; Italy.**

BIBLIOGRAPHY

De Grand, A. J. "Curzio Malaparte: The Illusion of the Fascist Revolution." *Journal of Contemporary History* 7 (1972): 73–90.

Pardini, G. *Curzio Malaparte: Biografia politica.* Luni, Italy, 1998.

MARIE-ANNE MATARD-BONUCCI

MALEVICH, KAZIMIR (1879–1935), abstract painter.

Kazimir Malevich was born in Kiev on 11 February Old Style (23 February New Style) 1879 and died in Leningrad (now St. Petersburg) on 15 May 1935. Although he was of Polish extraction and was born and brought up in Ukraine, Malevich's artistic career was centered in Russia. Above all, he is associated with the innovative Russian artists of the 1910s and 1920s; he became one of the leaders of the avant-garde and emerged as an important pioneer of abstract painting with his invention of suprematism in 1915. After socialist realism was imposed in the Soviet Union during the 1930s, Malevich's work tended not to be shown or mentioned publicly in his homeland. In the West, however, from the 1950s onward, it provided inspiration for numerous artistic developments, including minimalism.

The only professional training Malevich seems to have received was at the private school run by Fedor Rerberg (1865–1938) in Moscow, which he attended intermittently from 1907 to 1910. Malevich's early output was eclectic, including impressionism (e.g., *Portrait of a Member of the Artist's Family,* 1906); postimpressionism (*The Church,* early 1900s); art nouveau (*Relaxation: Society in Top Hats,* 1908); and symbolism (*Self-Portrait,* 1907). In 1907 he showed his works at the fourteenth exhibition of the Moscow Society of Artists, where he may have met Natalya Goncharova (1881–1962) and Mikhail Larionov (1881–1964), who also contributed to the show.

Three years later, in 1910, Larionov invited Malevich to join the innovative Knave of Diamonds (also called "Jack of Diamonds") group. When Larionov rejected the group's Cézannist approach and developed a more stridently neoprimitivist idiom, Malevich followed suit. As shown at the *Donkey's Tail* exhibition in 1912, neoprimitivism sought to produce a distinctively Russian style by combining the inventions of Western painting, especially fauvism's emphasis on the plane and the use of arbitrary and expressive color, with the bold use of line and the naive quality of archaic Russian art forms such as the icon and the *lubok*, or popular print (e.g., *The Bather,* 1911, and *Chiropodist at the Baths,* 1912).

By 1913 Malevich's experiments with cubism and futurism had produced works such as *Harvest/ Bringing in the Rye* (1912); *Woman with Buckets II*

Suprematism. Painting by Kazimir Malevich c. 1917. ERICH LESSING/ART RESOURCE, NY

(1912); and the more dynamic and fragmented *Knife Grinder: Principle of Flickering* (1912–1913). From this time onward Malevich became more closely associated with the Union of Youth in St. Petersburg, through which he became acquainted with notions of the fourth dimension (as time, spatial construct, and elevated state of consciousness) and the literary theory of *zaum,* or the transrational, which proposed abandoning established linguistic structures based on logic and reason in pursuit of a universal language of irrational sounds. Such ideas became integrated with elements of cubism and futurism in Malevich's work, including the set and costumes he devised for the *zaum* opera *Victory over the Sun,* which opened in December 1913, and his alogist composition *Cow and Violin* (1914), in which he placed a figuratively painted, diminutive cow against a large violin, in the manner

of cubist collage, subverting logic and pictorial convention and seemingly defying gravity. Exploring synthetic cubism further, Malevich produced what have been called alogic compositions, such as *Lady at an Advertising Column* (1914; sometimes called *Woman at a Poster Column*), which incorporated collage, lettering, fragmented forms, and large quadrilaterals of color.

In early summer 1915, Malevich developed suprematism, which consisted of geometric forms painted in bright, primary colors on white grounds. Launched publicly that December at the *Last Exhibition of Futurist Painting 0.10,* suprematism was firmly associated with the fourth dimension through the titles given to some of the works. At the same time, the placement of *The Quadrilateral,* better known as *The Black Square* (1915), in the holy corner (where the icon would normally hang in a Russian Orthodox home) stressed the metaphysical content of the new style. After the *White on White* paintings of 1918, and in response to Russia's October Revolution of 1917, Malevich applied suprematism to designs for propaganda items, ceramics, and fabrics, as well as prototypes for architectural structures.

During the 1920s, he also devoted himself to his theoretical and art historical work. After his trip to Warsaw and Berlin in 1927, perhaps in an attempt to meet the government's demand for an art that was comprehensible to the masses, Malevich returned to painting. He produced figurative works that retained a strong spiritual and abstract flavor (e.g., *Sportsmen*, 1931), as well as realist paintings (*Portrait of Pavlov*, 1933) and portraits recalling the early Renaissance (*Self Portrait*, 1933).

See also **Painting, Avant-Garde.**

BIBLIOGRAPHY

Douglas, Charlotte. *Kazimir Malevich*. London, 1994.

Drutt, Matthew, ed. *Kazimir Malevich: Suprematism*. New York, 2003. A catalog for an exhibit at the Solomon R. Guggenheim Museum that traveled to Berlin and elsewhere.

Kazimir Malevich 1878–1935. Amsterdam, 1988.

Malevich, Kazimir. *Essays on Art*. Edited by Troels Andersen. Translated by Xenia Glowacki-Prus and Arnold McMillin. 2 vols. Copenhagen, 1968; London, 1969–1970.

———. *Unpublished Writings on Art*. 2 vols. Copenhagen, 1978–1979.

Milner, John. *Kazimir Malevich and the Art of Geometry*. London, 1996.

Petrova, Evgeniya, et al. *Malevich: Artist and Theoretician*. Translated by Sharon McKee. Paris, 1990.

Simmons, W. Sherwin. *Kazimir Malevich's "Black Square" and the Genesis of Suprematism 1907–1915*. New York, 1981.

CHRISTINA LODDER

MALRAUX, ANDRÉ (1901–1976), French novelist.

Born on 3 November 1901, André Malraux was successively, and often simultaneously, a risk-taker, a militant-activist, a writer, and both a witness to history and sometimes one of its actors—as a combatant in the Spanish civil war (1936–1939), then in the French Resistance, and finally as a government minister.

His novels were drenched in the atmosphere of the era in which he was born: "What distinguished us from our teachers," he once claimed, "was the presence of History. Nothing had happened to them. We were born in the thick of History itself, which barreled through our field like a tank" (Lacouture and Malraux, p. 15). The themes of Malraux's work were a continuation of their author's own actions, which he was forever measuring against the great events of his day, including the rise of fascism: in 1933 he presided over the National Committee against War and Fascism, and advocated "blood-for-blood" action against "Hitlerian terror"; in July 1936, just three days after the start of the putsch by the generals supporting the fascist leader Francisco Franco (1892–1975), he left for Spain to lead the "España" squadron fighting for the Republican cause; and finally in 1944 he joined the French Resistance. In his novels Malraux rendered homage to revolutionary action carried out under the aegis of the Communist International—in Europe in *Le temps du mépris* (1935; *Days of Contempt*), in China in both *Les conquérants* (1928; *The Conquerers*) and *La condition humaine* (1933; *Man's Fate*), and in Spain with *L'espoir* (1937; *Man's Hope*). However, even though Malraux was a communist sympathizer he never became a member of the Communist Party, and when he joined the Resistance it was on the side of the partisans of Charles de Gaulle (1890–1970).

His last novel, *Les noyers de l'Altenburg* (1943; The walnut trees of Altenburg), now seems like an unsettling meditation on European history. The text depicts a succession of temporally and spatially unconnected episodes: a French prisoner-of-war camp in Chartres in 1940; the activities of the Young Turks in the Middle East around 1910 (seeking to unite far-flung Turkish communities); and the First World War, via a depiction of the first German gas attacks against the Russians on the Vistula front in June 1915.

After the Second World War Malraux became information minister for de Gaulle (whom he met in 1945), and then minister for cultural affairs from 1959 to 1969. Always looking to make culture accessible to the greatest number, he created "Cultural Houses" charged with organizing artistic activities and demonstrations open to the public. Returning to a long-held fascination, he also devoted himself to writing copious essays on art (as early as 1923 Malraux had taken part in an expedition in search of the last vestiges of the Khmer Empire, which ruled from the ninth to fifteenth centuries in present-day Cambodia, and was sentenced to three years in prison for removing statues from the Temple of Banteay-Srey in the ancient capital of Angkor). These texts, *Les voix du silence* (1951; The voices of silence) in particular, led to a striking reappraisal of how we approach the work of art and our conception of the museum. By reinterrogating the idea of the radical separation between cultures, and refusing to view art as solely the product of a historically—or socially—determined reality, he united a series of spatially and temporally disconnected works. He also praised the photographic reproduction that made this union possible and demonstrated their unexpected shared lineage.

Malraux was a man of action—action that could take the form of sometimes whimsical personal adventures (as in 1934 when he took off with a pilot friend of his in search of the ruins of the land of the queen of Sheba), or that could be situated within a more institutional framework (as in 1925 upon his return from Indochina, when he founded a harshly anticolonialist journal, and during the Algerian War, when he publicly opposed the impounding of *La question,* Henri Alleg's 1958 book denouncing torture). Always a writer and thinker, he was more than just an intellectual. For him an act was never separate from a meditation on its meaning, a meditation that not infrequently took a lyrical or even oracular turn. In his work Malraux was forever exploring the same enigma of "Man's fate," an expression he took from the philosopher Blaise Pascal (1623–1662):

> Let's imagine we are a group of men in chains and all condemned to die, each day being made to watch another of its number have his throat cut in front of the others, such that the remaining men witness their own fate in that of their counterparts, and ... await it in their turn. This is the image of the fate of men [*la condition humaine*]. (p. 91; translated from the French)

Malraux trained his sights squarely on this fatalism, thought it and pushed it to its extreme, even as he remained forever defiant of it. Although for a long period of time he viewed armed conflicts, political battles, and struggles against subjection of all sorts as the main way for people to affirm their power and freedom, in the end it was art, in the way it transports us from a world we suffer through (the real) to one we master (the real shaped and reflected in a work that will endure over time), that he came to consider as a kind of antidestiny.

Fascinated by the figure of the man of genius, Malraux, a dazzling orator who was forever self-inventing, was himself the crafter of his own legend. After his death on 23 November 1976, his ashes were transferred to the Pantheon in Paris, the mausoleum for the great men of the French Republic, in 1996.

See also **France; Gaulle, Charles de; Resistance.**

BIBLIOGRAPHY

Cahiers de l'Herne. Edited by Michel Cazenave. Paris, 1982.

Godard, Henri. *L'autre face de la littérature: Essai sur André Malraux et la littérature.* Paris, 1990.

Lacouture, Jean, and André Malraux. *Une vie dans le siècle.* Paris, 1973.

Lyotard, Jean-François. *Signé Malraux.* Paris, 1996.

Pascal, Blaise. *Pensées.* 1670. Paris, 1927.

Picon, Gaëtan. *Malraux par lui-même.* Paris, 1953.

CARINE TREVISAN

MALTA. At the start of World War I in 1914, Malta was a Crown colony and the base for the British Mediterranean fleet. The islands were not directly involved in hostilities, but they supported actions against the Ottomans in Salonika, the Dardanelles, and the Near East. Malta had prisoner-of-war camps for captured Bulgarians and Turks, and the military hospitals treated the wounded. Employment at the naval dockyard expanded from four thousand workers in 1914 to twelve thousand by 1918. Labor was scarce, demand for goods high, and inflation appeared. Then the war ended. Workers were laid off, and the revenue of the Malta treasury, dependent upon import dues, declined. Food prices remained high. On 7 June 1919 there were riots in Valletta. Troops shot four Maltese dead.

A new governor arrived in the midst of the strife. Food subsidies were introduced and the wages of government workers raised. Leopold Stennett Amery, undersecretary of state for the colonies, working with the Maltese National Assembly, developed a new constitution. Amery introduced the concept of diarchy, with the governor conducting external affairs and an elected legislature running internal affairs. The National Assembly drafted a constitution, establishing an elected legislative assembly and a senate of elected and nominated members. The archbishop of Malta nominated the church representative.

Maltese members of earlier Councils of Government had formed alliances, but formal political parties had to be organized for the 1921 election. The Labour Party, the Constitutional Party, the Democratic Nationalist Party (PDN), and the Maltese Political Union (UPM) contested the election. The UPM won and Joseph Howard became the first prime minister of Malta. In the 1927 election the Constitutional Party, led by Lord Gerald Strickland, won the most seats but no overall majority. Cambridge educated, Anglo-Maltese, and a former colonial governor of wide experience, Strickland became prime minister and, with Labour Party help, got legislation through the lower house, but the senate blocked his budget. Strickland then came into conflict with the church, and in the 1930 election the archbishop of Malta and the bishop of Gozo told the Catholic population "You may not, without committing a grave sin, vote for Lord Strickland and his candidates." The colonial authorities suspended the election and the constitution.

In 1931 a Royal Commission reported on constitutional matters and the language question. Maltese is basically Arabic, incorporating words from European languages and written in a modified Roman script. Educated islanders spoke Italian in addition to Maltese, and many people of all ranks spoke English when doing business with the British services. Country folk spoke only Maltese. The 1931 commission recommended that Maltese be the language of the courts because several

Maltese tried in Italian had not understood the proceedings. The decision infuriated some, who thought it an attack on cultural ties with Italy. The situation was inflamed by Benito Mussolini, who promoted spying and insisted that Malta belonged to Fascist Italy. Today most Maltese speak Malti, are fluent in English and Italian, and watch TV channels in the three languages.

When Governor Charles Bonham-Carter arrived in 1936, the 1921 constitution was revoked, and he appointed an Executive Council consisting of senior Maltese civil servants and leading Maltese versed in public policy. Defense spending was expanding, and there was money to fund improved social services, public health, education, power generation, agriculture, and livestock production. In 1939, under a new constitution, ten members were elected to the council in addition to appointed members.

Then came World War II. Italy entered the war on 10 June 1940. Malta was bombed the next day. By the end of June only Britain, Malta, and their Commonwealth allies were contesting fascist control of Europe. From Malta Axis supply routes to North Africa were attacked. Malta was bombed and under siege from mid-1940 to mid-1943, when the invasion of Sicily was partially launched from the islands. During the siege rations were fifteen hundred calories a day, part of which came from "victory kitchens" fired with wood from bombed buildings, serving goat stew and other survival food. The British Crown awarded Malta the George Cross, the highest honor for civilian bravery. No other community has won the award collectively. The Maltese earned the medal. Had the islands fallen, the North African campaign would have been prolonged by a year, D-Day would have been postponed, and the Red Army could have occupied Europe to the Rhine.

After the war Britain provided a war damage fund to rebuild property. In 1947 internal self-government returned under a constitution creating a unicameral legislature. The Labour Party had a majority until it was split into the Malta Labour Party and the Malta Workers Party by a young politician, Dom Mintoff, a former Rhodes scholar. The split allowed the Nationalist Party to gain the most seats in 1950 and, under Dr. Giorgio Borg Olivier, win elections in 1951 and 1953.

The Labour Party won the 1955 election, and Prime Minister Mintoff proposed the integration of Malta with the United Kingdom. The leaders of political parties in Westminster viewed the proposal favorably, but the archbishop of Malta insisted that if Malta joined the United Kingdom, with its established Protestant churches, the status of the Catholic Church in Malta had to be safeguarded. British politicians accepted this. Prime Minister Mintoff called a referendum on integration before the church-state question was settled. He got a majority for integration, but turnout was low, with church leaders telling voters to avoid the referendum. Integration died. Relations between the Labour Party, the church, the governor, and Britain deteriorated. The constitution was suspended in 1959. Independence was the next step. In 1960 a new constitution provided for a fifty-seat legislature, elected by proportional representation.

In 1962 Dr. Borg Olivier led the Nationalist Party to victory. Malta became independent on 21 September 1964, signing a mutual defense and assistance agreement by which Britain continued to use its bases in return for economic aid. Mintoff and the Labour Party returned to power in 1971, and Malta became a republic in December 1974, with a president appointed by the House of Representatives for a five-year term. The bases closed in 1979.

The Nationalists won in 1987 and worked toward European Union (EU) membership, briefly losing office from 1996 to 1998, when a value-added tax was introduced. In 2003 a referendum was held in which 91 percent of the electorate voted, with 53 percent in favor of EU entry. In the April 2003 general election the Nationalists won thirty-five seats in the House of Representatives. Malta became an EU member in May 2004.

In 1960 nearly all jobs in Malta depended on British defense spending, but with independence funds were made available to open industrial parks and promote tourism. The naval dockyard converted to commercial work but is a drain on Malta's budget. Malta's prehistoric temples and the buildings of the Order of St. John attract visitors, with Britain being the major source. Financial services is a growing industry. The major problem for the islands since joining the EU is that of refugees and asylum seekers coming from Africa by boat to enter the European world.

See also **British Empire; British Empire, End of.**

BIBLIOGRAPHY

Austin, Dennis. *Malta and the End of Empire.* London, 1971.

Austin, Douglas. *Malta and British Strategic Policy, 1925–1943.* London, 2004.

Blouet, Brian W. *The Story of Malta.* Rev. ed. Valletta, Malta, 2004.

Dobie, Edith. *Malta's Road to Independence.* Norman, Okla., 1967.

Frendo, Henry. *Party Politics in a Fortress Colony: The Maltese Experience.* 2nd ed. Valletta, Malta, 1991.

BRIAN W. BLOUET

MAN, HENRI DE (1885–1953), Belgian socialist.

A native of Antwerp and a product of the prosperous Belgian bourgeoisie, Henri de Man became a major figure of European socialism. He was a leader among the many socialist theorists and activists of the early twentieth century who rejected orthodox Marxism and sought a new foundation for progressive politics.

According to de Man, Karl Marx's (1818–1883) theories, although perhaps well suited to the nineteenth century, were unhelpful in adequately addressing the realities of post–World War I capitalism. Bourgeois society had demonstrated, among other things, a kind of resilience that Marxist categories could not explain. The capitalist system of production and consumption had not produced a growing and increasingly immiserated proletariat. To the contrary, it had proven itself astonishingly effective in providing genuine material benefits to ever-wider segments of society. Moreover, Marxist class analysis could not account for the enormous success of American capitalism where, according to de Man's own firsthand observations, class consciousness, at least of the kind that had long characterized European societies, was largely absent.

In place of orthodox Marxism, de Man proposed a kind of humanism that was not limited to class analysis, that transcended purely economic notions of exploitation, and that sought to reestablish the importance of democratic culture and democratic politics for the socialist movement. The presumption of a purely utilitarian calculus of human wants, rooted in economic self-interest, was a serious defect that Marxism shared with bourgeois political economy. In response, de Man pursued larger notions of justice and human liberation involving, among other things, serious programs of worker education on the basis of which socialists might establish a truly democratic and responsible system of worker control over the industrial enterprise. He rejected what he regarded as abstract, mechanistic approaches to social analysis, Marxist and non-Marxist alike, and sought to emphasize instead the actual psychological features of modern social life.

De Man was a prolific and highly influential writer. But he is also one of those figures whose biography is perhaps as notable as his oeuvre. He was certainly the leading Belgian socialist of his time. He knew and worked with many of the great figures of the European Left, including Rosa Luxemburg (1870–1919), Karl Liebknecht (1871–1919), Karl Kautsky (1854–1938), and Leon Trotsky (1879–1940). Originally a radical Marxist roughly in the mold of Luxemburg and Liebknecht, de Man's views began to change with the advent of World War I. While socialists generally repudiated the war, de Man was deeply affected by the manifest victimization of Belgium. He enlisted in the Belgian army, fought in the trenches, and was decorated for valor.

After the war he visited Soviet Russia and witnessed the excesses of bolshevism; lived for a time in the Puget Sound area of Washington State, where he experienced the workings of American capitalism; and eventually moved to Germany, where he became a professor of social psychology at the University of Frankfurt, published his most important works—including *The Psychology of Socialism* (1926), *Joy in Work* (1927), and *The Socialist Idea* (1933)—and observed the rise of Nazism. After returning to Belgium in 1937 he authored the famous Plan du Travail, adopted by the Belgian Labor Party as a pragmatic economic strategy for dealing with the problems of the Great Depression. Eventually, he became a minister in the government.

Temperamentally ill suited to the give-and-take of official political life, de Man began to doubt the efficacy of democracy. In the face of the looming Nazi threat, he advocated a policy of appeasement, suggested that National Socialism could be a viable form of socialism, and was, in the end, nearly alone in supporting Leopold III's (r. 1934–1951) decision to surrender to, and even to embrace, the German invasion. De Man's notorious "Manifesto to the Members of the Belgian Labor Party" (1940) praised the Nazi regime as one that "has lessened class differences much more efficaciously than the self-styled democrats" and welcomed the prospect of an authoritarian type of socialism. For this, he earned the deep and enduring enmity of his countrymen. De Man fled Belgium in 1941 and after the war was convicted in absentia for treason as a collaborationist against the Belgian state—a symbol, to some, of the perils inherent in any attempt to adapt socialism to dictatorship.

See also **Belgium; Collaboration; Socialism.**

BIBLIOGRAPHY

Primary Sources

Man, Hendrik de. *A Documentary Study of Hendrik de Man, Socialist Critic of Marxism.* Compiled, edited, and largely translated by Peter Dodge. Princeton, N.J., 1979.

———. *The Psychology of Marxian Socialism.* Translated by Eden and Cedar Paul. New Brunswick, N.J., 1985. Translation of *Zur Psychologie des Socialismus.*

Secondary Sources

Dodge, Peter. *Beyond Marxism: The Faith and Works of Hendrik de Man.* The Hague, 1966.

PETER J. STEINBERGER

MANDELSTAM, OSIP (1891–1938), Russian poet.

Osip Emilevich Mandelstam, widely considered to be one of the greatest Russian poets of the twentieth century, was inspired in his art by diverse Western, Russian, and ancient Greek and Roman influences from the spheres of poetry, fiction, painting, music, architecture, philosophy, and mythology.

The word I meant to say has somehow slipped
   my mind.
A sightless swallow rejoins the shadows of the
   deep
On amputated wings, to frolic with its own
   invisible kind.
A nighttime song is sung in blissful sleep.

The birds are silent. The immortelles don't
   blossom.
Translucent are the manes of the nocturnal herd.
An empty bark floats on the dried-out riverbed
   like flotsam.
Among the droning crickets swoons the
   forgotten word. . . .
(translation by Alyssa Dinega Gillespie)

The result is a body of work that is saturated with references both direct and abstruse, intertextual and intratextual; his writing is powerfully moving in its music and imagery and brilliant in its scope and searing originality, yet not readily accessible to the casual reader. Two of Mandelstam's favorite themes are his "yearning for world culture" and the preservative mission of art in the face of state-sponsored terror.

Mandelstam was born in Warsaw into an assimilated Jewish family; his father was a leather merchant, his mother an accomplished pianist. When Osip was still very young the family moved to St. Petersburg; he would think of the city (later renamed Petrograd, then Leningrad) as his hometown all his life, despite the fact that he was often obliged to live far away from it. Between the years 1899 and 1907 Mandelstam studied in the elite, progressive Tenishev Commercial School. After graduation he lived for a time in Paris and Heidelberg before enrolling in the department of history and philology at the University of St. Petersburg in the fall of 1911. He preferred writing poems to pursuing his studies, however, and he never graduated.

Mandelstam's first poems were written while he was still a student at the Tenishev School; his first publication came in the journal *Apollon* (Apollo) in August 1910. He soon joined a group called Tsekh Poetov (Guild of Poets), which had formed in order to counteract the prevailing aesthetic of symbolism, with its obscure orientation toward mysticism and the transcendental. Tsekh Poetov led to the emergence of a new literary movement, acmeism, which emphasized craft, architecture, precision, and the details of physical existence. Mandelstam was one of the leaders of acmeism, and his theoretical essay "Utro akmeizma" (written 1913, published 1919; The morning of acmeism) was a manifesto for the movement.

Mandelstam's first volume of poetry, *Kamen* (Stone), appeared in 1913; it was republished subsequently in increasingly enlarged editions in 1916, 1923, and 1928 and brought him immediate fame as one of Russia's finest young poets. Mandelstam was exempted from military service during World War I due to poor health but worked for a Petrograd war relief organization; he also spent time in the Crimea during the war years. In 1916 he had a brief romance with the young poet Marina Tsvetaeva; both poets produced several fine poems commemorating their time together. In 1917 Mandelstam cautiously welcomed the February Revolution, but his response to the Bolshevik takeover in October was much more negative, though still complex and ambiguous. During the difficult civil war years (1918–1920) Mandelstam was itinerant, spending time in Petrograd, Moscow, Kiev, Georgia, and the Crimea. He met his future wife, Nadezhda Yakovlevna Khazina, in Kiev but was later arrested by both the Soviets and the Whites and was not reunited with her for two years. The couple married in 1922 and moved to Moscow, where they became acquainted with the communist functionary Nikolai Bukharin, who became Mandelstam's political benefactor for the next decade. The Mandelstams moved back to Leningrad in 1924, but Nadezhda often spent long periods in the south of Russia recuperating from tuberculosis.

Mandelstam's second poetry collection, *Tristia*, was published in 1922. During the 1920s he began writing more and more prose, ranging from his childhood memoir *Shum vremeni* (1923–1925; The noise of time) to the fictional work *Egipetskaya marka* (1927; The Egyptian stamp) to the bitter invective "Chetvertaya proza" (1929–1930; *Fourth Prose*). These works followed his penetrating philosophical and aesthetic essays of the 1910s, such as "O sobesednike" (1913; On the interlocutor), "Zametki o Shene" (1914; Notes on Chénier), and

"Pushkin i Skriabin" (1915; Pushkin and Scriabin). During the late 1920s Mandelstam unwillingly earned his living as a translator, and, claiming that the grind of translation sapped his creative energy, he gradually stopped writing poetry.

In 1928 Mandelstam's revision of an existing translation of Charles de Coster's novel *La Légende de Thyl Ulenspiegel et de Lamme Goedzak* (1867; *The Glorious Adventures of Thyl Ulenspiegel*) was erroneously published without credit being given to the original translators, who immediately charged Mandelstam with plagiarism. A political scandal ensued, and although Bukharin attempted to save the poet by sending him off on an extended sojourn to Armenia, the damage was irreversible. When Mandelstam returned to Russia he found he was unable to obtain a residence permit in Leningrad. He moved to Moscow but was arrested on 13 May 1934 and banished to Cherdyn, a small town in the Ural Mountains. The trigger for his arrest was his composition of a satirical epigram about Stalin. In Cherdyn he suffered an attack of apparent madness and attempted to commit suicide by jumping out of a hospital window. Thanks to Bukharin, his sentence was commuted to three years' exile in Voronezh, a small town in southern Russia.

Mandelstam's last years in Moscow and Voronezh were among his most creatively productive. He produced a cycle of poems on Armenia at the conclusion of his voyage there, along with the prose work *Puteshestvie v Armeniyu* (1931; *Journey to Armenia*). His great treatise on the nature of poetic art, *Razgovor o Dante* (1933; *Conversation about Dante*), followed soon after, in addition to the mature poetry of his two so-called *Moskovskie tetradi* (1930–1934; *Moscow Notebooks*) and three *Voronezhskie tetradi* (1935–1937; *Voronezh Notebooks*). These notebooks were heroically preserved by his wife Nadezhda and other close friends, and the works they contained were not published until decades after the poet's death. Nadezhda Mandelstam's two-volume memoir (published in English as *Hope against Hope*, 1970, and *Hope Abandoned*, 1974) chronicles the poet's final, desperate years in poignant detail. In May 1937 when Mandelstam's sentence was over, he was homeless, afflicted by extreme anxiety, ill, and unemployable. Despite his feeble attempt to restore his political fortune through composition of a tasteless "Ode to Stalin," he was denounced by the head of the Leningrad Writers' Union, rearrested on 1 May 1938, and sentenced to five years of hard labor in the Siberian gulag. He apparently died at a transit camp near Vladivostok on 27 December 1938. His wife Nadezhda survived him in exile for many years and was eventually rehabilitated, along with her husband; she died of old age in 1980. The first substantial edition of Mandelstam's work did not appear in the Soviet Union until 1973.

See also **Akhmatova, Anna; Bukharin, Nikolai; Dissidence; Gulag; Soviet Union; Tsvetaeva, Marina.**

BIBLIOGRAPHY

Primary Sources

Mandelstam, Osip. *Critical Prose and Letters.* Edited by Jane Gary Harris, translated by Harris and Constance Link. Ann Arbor, Mich., 1990. Contains Mandelstam's essays, reviews, and correspondence in addition to *Fourth Prose, Journey to Armenia,* and *Conversation about Dante.*

———. *The Moscow and Voronezh Notebooks: Poems 1930–37.* Translated by Richard and Elizabeth McKane. Tarset, U.K., 2003. Free-verse translations of the remarkable poetry from Mandelstam's last years, unpublished for several decades after his death.

———. *The Noise of Time: Selected Prose.* Translated by Clarence Brown. Evanston, Ill., 2002. Contains *The Noise of Time, The Egyptian Stamp, Fourth Prose, Theodosia,* and *Journey to Armenia.*

———. *The Selected Poems of Osip Mandelstam.* Translated by Clarence Brown and W. S. Merwin. New York, 2004. Readable free-verse translations of a broad selection of Mandelstam's poems (also includes *Conversation about Dante*).

Secondary Sources

Brown, Clarence. *Mandelstam.* Cambridge, U.K., 1973. A pioneering study on Mandelstam's life and work, containing excellent readings of his early poems.

Cavanagh, Clare. *Osip Mandelstam and the Modernist Creation of Tradition.* Princeton, N.J., 1995. Places Mandelstam's thought and writing in the context of the modernist movement, particularly the writings of T. S. Eliot and Ezra Pound.

Freidin, Gregory. *A Coat of Many Colors: Osip Mandelstam and His Mythologies of Self-Presentation.* Berkeley, Calif., 1987. An analysis of the various mythologies that Mandelstam develops in order to present himself as a poet endowed with charisma and symbolic authority.

Harris, Jane Gary. *Osip Mandelstam*. Boston, 1988. An informative basic survey of Mandelstam's biography and major writings in both poetry and prose.

Mandelstam, Nadezhda. *Hope against Hope*. Translated by Max Hayward. New York, 1999. The first volume of the compelling two-volume memoir by Mandelstam's wife, this chronicle of the Mandelstams' last four years together in the deathly environment of Stalinist Russia is a tribute to the saving powers of art.

ALYSSA DINEGA GILLESPIE

MANN, THOMAS (1875–1955), German writer and thinker.

Arguably the greatest writer in German of the twentieth century, Thomas Mann's life and work bear witness like no other to the deep intellectual and cultural history of his native country, its modern political upheavals, and its subsequent near self-destruction.

Mann, who was born in 1875 and died in 1955, lived through four different forms of government on German soil—not to speak of exile in various foreign lands—but until the outbreak of World War I when he was thirty-nine he remained remarkably, indeed willfully, unpolitical. His supreme achievement up to that point was his first novel, *Buddenbrooks*, which appeared in 1901 and ultimately won him the Nobel Prize in Literature, which he received in 1929. Although its plot coincides with much of the turbulent nineteenth century, it is, as its subtitle indicates, more of a description of the private "decline of a family" than a literary analysis of the waning bourgeoisie. Other, shorter works, such as *Tonio Kröger* (1902), *The Blood of the Wälsungs* (1905), and, most famously, *Death in Venice* (1912), are concerned predominantly with the complex interplay between art and life, focusing on the role and character of the artist and the dangers of decadence.

The year 1914 changed everything. Like many other writers, Thomas Mann initially greeted the war with enthusiasm, indeed he understood it as a kind of liberation from the debilitating decadence he had portrayed in his own works. In his notorious essay, "Thoughts During War," published in November 1914, he wrote: "How could the artist, the soldier in the artist, not praise God for the collapse of a peaceful world which he was so tired of, so thoroughly tired of! War! It was purification, liberation that we felt and an enormous hope" (Harpprecht, p. 380; author's translation). He amplified these ideas into a political-cultural manifesto, *Observations of an Unpolitical Man*, which he published in 1918. In its tone and tendency it is of a piece with the works of other nationalist, conservative, and vehemently antidemocratic German intellectuals of the time, notably Oswald Spengler, whose *Decline of the West* had just appeared and which Mann greatly admired at the time.

However, in the next several years, Mann changed his position and began, albeit somewhat hesitantly at first, to embrace democratic, or at least republican values. Initially outlined in detail in the essay "On the German Republic" (1922), his struggle with the opposing political ideals of democratic humanism and autocratic absolutism, together with his principled adherence to the former, finds its consummate novelistic expression in *The Magic Mountain* (1924). In some ways, the novel represents a renunciation not only of the political ideals Mann had articulated during the war but also of the aesthetic credo to which he had previously adhered: the novel's protagonist, Hans Castorp, in the end makes the decision to abandon the airy heights of the Swiss sanitorium where the novel takes place and to enter practical life, descending to the trenches of the Great War.

Combined with his newfound political allegiances, Mann's stature as a representative cultural figure—he received the Goethe Prize of the city of Frankfurt in 1932—made him an inevitable target of retribution when the Nazis came to power in 1933. His books, along with those of other political undesirables, were burned in public on 10 May. After five years in Switzerland, Mann went to the United States in 1938, where he remained until 1952, when he returned to Zurich, where he died and is buried. His last major novel, *Dr. Faustus* (1947), continues the vein of *The Magic Mountain* in that it again amounts to a vast, complex repudiation, only this time it symbolically forsakes Germany as a whole—represented in the life and art of the fictional composer Adrian Leverkühn, who relinquishes his soul to the devil in exchange for the ability to create an entirely new kind of music. As with Germany as a whole, the pact ends in madness and ruin.

One of the ironies of Mann's life and intellectual career is that, by renouncing Germany—or at least that version of Germany that physically ceased to exist in 1945 and committed moral suicide by implementing the Holocaust—he thereby managed to save some part of it for the future. It was with no small justification that, when Mann arrived in New York in 1938, a reporter asked him whether he found his exile difficult to bear, he replied with a mixture of defiance and pride: "Where I am, there is Germany"(Harpprecht, p. 978; author's translation). If there was a "good" or even "better" Germany, Thomas Mann did indeed embody it.

See also **Germany.**

BIBLIOGRAPHY

Harpprecht, Klaus. *Thomas Mann: Eine Biographie.* Rowohlt, Germany, 1995.

Kurzke, Hermann. *Thomas Mann: Life as a Work of Art. A Biography.* Translated by Leslie Willson. Princeton, N.J., 2002.

Prater, Donald. *Thomas Mann: A Life.* Oxford, U.K., and New York, 1995.

Winston, Richard. *Thomas Mann: The Making of an Artist, 1875–1911.* Afterword by Clara Winston. New York, 1981.

ROBERT E. NORTON

MANNHEIM, KARL (1893–1947), Hungarian Jewish sociologist.

Karl Mannheim, a Hungarian Jew, was a member of the Budapest intelligentsia and a great admirer of the Marxist philosopher György Lukács. After the failure of the revolutions of 1918–1919 he immigrated to Germany, settling in Heidelberg under the sponsorship of Max Weber's brother Alfred. He developed his earlier interest in cultural change in a series of long articles on topics including a theory of worldviews, the origins of conservatism, a theory of generations, and the sociology of knowledge. These interests took a more political form in *Ideology and Utopia* (*Ideologie und Utopie*, 1929), which earned him a chair in sociology at Frankfurt University in 1930. Three years later the Nazi seizure of power forced his immigration to Britain, where he held marginal academic positions until his death. While in Britain, his earlier theories were transformed into a theory of democratic planning.

Ideology and Utopia is generally acknowledged as Mannheim's most important work. The original version, which comprises the middle three chapters of the English translation, was an attempt to redefine the role of the German intellectual elite, especially those in academia, in light of the social and political changes that occurred at the end of World War I. It marked the completion of his transition from the historicism of an Ernst Troeltsch—which assumed the possibility of arriving at an organic unity of values for any epoch—to a view that recognized the primacy of conflict in the realms of society, politics, and culture. Like Marxism, his sociology of knowledge asserted that competing worldviews were "existentially connected" to specific sociopolitical groups, but it differed in two important ways. First, Mannheim defined the competing groups by their worldviews and not by their roles in the mode of economic production. Second, he noted that the Marxists' "unmasking" of their opponents' views as "existentially bound," as the perspective of a specific group not universal, could be turned back on them. The recognition that there was no privileged position from which to view others' worldviews comprised the essence of the sociology of knowledge.

Mannheim believed that history was propelled forward by the competition among groups to universalize their worldviews. Those groups who successfully disrupted the status quo were labeled "utopian" and distinguished from unsuccessful "ideological" ones. But while driving the dialectic onward, utopias could never realize their claims and achieve hegemony and would ultimately be unmasked by opponents and become ideologies. Mannheim feared that this mutual unmasking would replace all political will with administrative stasis.

As a hope for resolving this dilemma, he devised the concept of the socially "free-floating" intelligentsia and in doing so moved closer to the position of Max Weber's addresses on science and politics as vocations. Although the thought of individual intellectuals was connected to specific social groups, their marginality within those groups and ability to communicate with one another allowed them collectively to be free-floating, in other words, not bound to the perspective of any one of their groups. Their interaction served as a medium by which those groups could analytically assess their relation to one another and move toward the future not on the basis of utopian aspirations but on the basis of sociological insight. However, the intelligentsia could only assess the possible consequences of judgments made by political actors; they could not scientifically legitimize those judgments. This limitation resembled that of Max Weber's political scientists.

Mannheim's fear that the utopian will would disappear through mutual unmasking was likely a response to the apparent routinization of parliamentary politics and the loss of a truly progressive impulse in the middle 1920s. By 1930 he realized that the danger lay in the opposite direction—the triumph of the will in the form of National Socialism. In his final years in Frankfurt he deemphasized the sociology of knowledge as a vehicle for dialogue among political groups and their leaders and instead presented it as an academic discipline and the central component of the political education of individual citizens.

In *Man and Society in an Age of Reconstruction* (*Mensch und Gesellschaft im Zeitalter des Umbaus*, 1935), written in British exile, Mannheim melded his two previous versions of the sociology of knowledge in a theory of democratic planning. The discipline would aid the planning elite in structuring society to produce an informed and engaged democratic citizen. At the same time it would give that citizen the insight to participate in the selection of the planner, thus fostering reciprocity between the elite and ordinary citizens.

See also **Lukács, György.**

BIBLIOGRAPHY

Primary Sources

Mannheim, Karl. *Ideology and Utopia.* Translated by Louis Wirth and Edward Shils. London, 1936. Translation of *Ideologie und Utopie* (1929).

——. *Man and Society in an Age of Reconstruction.* Translated by Edward Shils. London, 1940. Translation of *Mensch und Gesellschaft im Zeitalter des Umbaus* (1935).

——. *From Karl Mannheim.* Edited by Kurt H. Wolff. 2nd exp. ed. New Brunswick, N.J., 1993.

——. *Sociology as Political Education.* Edited by David Kettler and Colin Loader. New Brunswick, N.J., 2001.

Secondary Sources

Kettler, David, and Volker Meja. *Karl Mannheim and the Crisis of Liberalism.* New Brunswick, N.J., 1995.

Loader, Colin. *The Intellectual Development of Karl Mannheim.* Cambridge, U.K., and New York, 1985.

Loader, Colin, and David Kettler. *Karl Mannheim's Sociology as Political Education.* New Brunswick, N.J., 2002.

Meja, Volker, and Nico Stehr, eds. *Knowledge and Politics: The Sociology of Knowledge Dispute.* London, 1990.

COLIN LOADER

MARCUSE, HERBERT (1898–1979), German-born American political philosopher.

Few scholars exemplified the fashionable late-twentieth-century notion of the "public intellectual" as clearly as the German-born critical theorist Herbert Marcuse. Born in Berlin at the turn of the century, Marcuse was a student of Martin Heidegger (1889–1976) and trained in classical German philosophy before breaking with his teacher on political grounds. Marcuse went on to become an eminent scholar of Georg Wilhelm Friedrich Hegel (1770–1831), and his *Reason and Revolution* (1941) helped revitalize interest in Hegelian Marxism and introduced the theory of alienation to North America. Marcuse played an important role in the intellectual cross-fertilization stimulated by German refugees in America during the Nazi era and was at the center of some of the most heated intellectual debates of the twentieth century.

A German philosopher and intellectual to the core, Marcuse lived in the United States for the most intellectually productive years of his life. Marcuse was a member of what came to be known as the "critical theory" group of the Frankfurt School, along with Max Horkheimer, Theodor Adorno, Leo Lowenthal, and Erich Fromm. A scholar and teacher at Brandeis University and the University of California at San Diego, Marcuse played a central role in the popularization of critical theory in America as well as being a major influence on the political movement of the New Left of the 1960s.

Marcuse was a controversial figure. For conservatives, Marcuse was one of the sources of the extremism and anti-Americanism that they argued characterized the New Left movement of the 1960s. As governor of California, the American conservative icon Ronald Reagan (1911–2004) spearheaded efforts to get Marcuse fired from his position at the University of California. In *The Closing of the American Mind* (1987), Allan Bloom captures the neoconservative critique of Marcuse with his bizarre attempt to link Marcuse, the Woodstock music festival of 1969, Heidegger's Nazism, and the alleged "Nietzscheanization of the American Left."

Marcuse also had his critics on the left. In a famous debate in the pages of the radical intellectual journal *Dissent* in the mid-1950s, the critical theorist Erich Fromm accused Marcuse of nihilism and of misreading Sigmund Freud (1856–1939). By the 1980s and 1990s, Marcuse's call for a revolution from the margins of the society was sometimes invoked as part of the problem for a Left that some believed had marginalized itself during the "days of rage" of the late 1960s.

Nonetheless, Marcuse was hardly the extremist radical portrayed by his most virulent critics, and some of his ideas do seem to capture some important contemporary trends. Surely there is something perverse about the cultural industries today, as we are exposed to "extreme makeovers," unreal "reality TV," and "shock and awe" televised war. And Marcuse was surely right that the old Freudian emphasis on sexual repression does not capture the extent to which contemporary societies are saturated with sexual images that create unrealistic and ultimately repressive expectations for what sexual freedom might look like. While Marcuse was wrong that the problems of scarcity and class inequality are essentially solved in modern Western societies, this error was one shared by some of the most thoughtful intellectuals of his time. And Marcuse was an early supporter of the political and cultural demands of gay and lesbian liberation movements, which achieved a degree of success in the late twentieth century.

Far from being someone who helped "close the American mind," Marcuse was an exceptional teacher of a critical version of the Western philosophical tradition and helped link these traditional humanist ideas to the social movements of the 1960s. He was mentor to a large number of political and intellectual radicals who themselves produced important intellectual work and engaged the world in radical and constructive ways. Marcuse's defense of gay rights, black liberation, feminism, and anticolonialism made important contributions to mid-twentieth-century intellectual life. And *Eros and Civilization* (1955) was an important influence in the development of feminist psychoanalysis, later developed by such scholars as Jessica Benjamin and Nancy Chodorow.

A brilliant philosopher and a controversial interpreter of Freud, Marcuse exhibited courage, principles, and imagination alongside questionable intellectual and political judgments. Marcuse's Hegelian-influenced recovery of the humanist principles and ideas of the early Marx pointed the way to the retrieval of certain elements of the Marxist tradition in the years after the debacle of Stalinism and Soviet communism. While Marcuse was ultimately more influential in his adopted home of the United States than in Germany itself, his cultural politics helped shape the emergence of German Green "postmaterialist" politics, his critique of positivism continues to be discussed, and his emphasis on the politics of the "margins" helped stimulate the "new social movements" literature of the 1970s and 1980s within European and then American sociology. The Frankfurt School focus on the culture industries and the politics of the irrational must be central to any serious contemporary radical intellectual agenda as well as retaining value for scholarship on politics and culture today. Thus Marcuse is likely to remain an important if contested resource for radical intellectuals well into the twenty-first century.

See also **Adorno, Theodor; Frankfurt School; Fromm, Erich.**

BIBLIOGRAPHY

Primary Sources

Marcuse, Herbert. *Reason and Revolution: Hegel and the Rise of Social Theory.* New York, 1941.

———. *Eros and Civilization: A Philosophical Inquiry into Freud.* Boston, 1955.

———. *One Dimensional Man: Studies in the Ideology of Advanced Industrial Society.* Boston, 1964.

Secondary Sources

Kellner, Douglas. *Herbert Marcuse and the Crisis of Marxism.* Berkeley, Calif., 1984.

Stirk, Peter M. R. *Critical Theory, Politics, and Society: An Introduction.* London, 2000.

Wiggershaus, Rolf. *The Frankfurt School: Its History, Theories, and Political Significance.* Cambridge, Mass., 1994.

NEIL MCLAUGHLIN

MARINETTI, F. T. (1876–1944), Italian writer and founder of Italian futurism.

Born in 1876 in Alexandria, Egypt, into a wealthy Italian family, Filippo Tommaso Marinetti was educated by Jesuits. A rebellious student, he was sent to study literature in Paris and then law in Italy. In 1898 he began publishing poetry and later novels and plays. These early writings, such as "The Old Sailors" (1898), *The Conquest of the Stars* (1902), *Destruction* (1904), *Le roi bombance* (1905; The feasting king), and *The Carnal City* (1908), reveal both his embrace of and revolt against symbolism. Characterized by extravagant and experimental language, anarchic tone, and violent and scandalous imagery, they owe a debt to thinkers as varied as Friedrich Nietzsche, Arthur Schopenhauer, François Rabelais, Alfred Jarry, and Walt Whitman. Marinetti also expressed both respect and distaste for the celebrated Italian, Gabriele D'Annunzio, whose melding of literature, politics, and public relations served as a model.

In 1905 in Milan, Marinetti started *Poesia,* an international review featuring modern radical writers. His 1909 "Founding and Manifesto of Futurism" brought him great notoriety. Part narrative, part list of prescriptions, it called for an art that embraced modernity, especially the sensations of speed, dynamism, and simultaneity produced by new technology, industry, and urbanism; expressed fascination with violence, revolution, and war; and rejected Italy's preoccupation with its glorious past. Because Italian unification had failed to effect genuine national rejuvenation, Marinetti aggressively called for a movement that would be a true *risorgimento,* or resurgence. Intending to put Italy back on the world's cultural map, Marinetti first published this manifesto in Paris, the center of the avant-garde. Its use, borrowed from politics, situated futurism within a lineage of movements stretching back to the mid-nineteenth century, in which art was integral to a broader social program. Dubbed "the caffeine of Europe" because he was so dynamic, Marinetti became part of a modernist line of artist-impresarios who intertwined aesthetics and public relations.

Futurism was ambitious and totalizing, as Marinetti and its practitioners theorized and worked in many areas, including painting, sculpture, assemblage, photography, poetry, architecture, design, music, theater, performance, politics, cinema, radio, television, and even lust and cuisine. Perhaps his greatest contribution was "words-in-freedom," announced in his 1912 "Technical Manifesto of Futurist Literature." Inspired by airplane flight, this new literary form liberated words from conventional contexts, arranging them expressively and imagistically on the page, substituted mathematical symbols for punctuation, exploited onomatopoeia to indicate noise, and tried to evoke smell, weight, and temperature. Marinetti even used this approach for battlefield reporting, an apt expression of war, which he called "the world's sole hygiene."

At futurist *serate* (evenings), which might include art, music, and performance, Marinetti declaimed politically charged manifestos that led to riots and arrests. The futurists vociferously advocated Italy's intervention into World War I, in which Marinetti and other futurists eventually served. In 1918 he launched the Futurist Political Party. A year later futurism became part of the Fascist combat groups, signaling the beginning of an oscillating futurist-Fascist relationship. Uncomfortable with fascism's obsession with order, authority, and tradition, Marinetti left the group in 1920, protesting Benito Mussolini's renouncing of anticlerical, antimonarchical, and pro-anarchist positions. Mussolini, in turn, distrusted futurism's formal correspondences with left-wing, vanguard developments elsewhere and felt that its modernist style

F. T. Marinetti (center) with (from left) Luigi Russolo, Carlo Carra, Umberto Boccioni, and Gino Severini. GETTY IMAGES

of fragmentation, simultaneity, and distortion was counter to Fascist values and too confusing as propaganda. Nonetheless, two years after Mussolini seized the reins of the Italian government in 1922, futurism and fascism forged an alliance, marked by Marinetti's 1924 pamphlet of compromise, titled *Futurism and Fascism*. The coupling provided the futurists with outlets for their work while making Mussolini appear to be the unifier of heterogeneous elements in Italian society.

This uneasy union was strongest in 1929, when Marinetti accepted appointment to the conservative Italian Royal Academy and founded the futurist submovement *aeropittura futurista* (futurist aerial painting), terming it "the daughter of Fascist aviation and Italian Futurism." The bond was most strained in 1938 when Marinetti objected to the enactment of racial laws in Italy as Mussolini's ties to Nazi Germany grew deeper. Still, Marinetti's audacious jingoism remained unflinching, and he volunteered to fight in Ethiopia in 1935 and, at age sixty-six, on the Russian front in 1942. Marinetti died in 1944.

His fervent engagement with avant-garde and progressive aesthetics, bellicose support of nationalism, and fluctuating ideological and official connections to fascism personify the complex and conflicting interactions of vanguard style and reactionary thought in the modern world.

See also **D'Annunzio, Gabriele; Fascism; Futurism; Mussolini, Benito.**

BIBLIOGRAPHY

Primary Sources

Marinetti, F. T. *Teoria e invenzione futurista.* Edited by Luciano De Maria. Verona, Italy, 1968.

———. *Let's Murder the Moonshine: Selected Writings.* Edited by R. W. Flint; translated by R. W. Flint and Arthur A. Coppotelli; preface by Marjorie Perloff. Los Angeles, 1991.

Secondary Sources

Blum, Cinzia Sartini. *The Other Modernism: F. T. Marinetti's Futurist Fiction of Power.* Berkeley, Calif., 1996.

Cammarota, Domenico. *Filippo Tommaso Marinetti: Bibliografia.* Milan, 2002.

Lista, Giovanni. *Marinetti*. Paris, 1976.

Salaris, Claudia. *Filippo Tommaso Marinetti*. Florence, 1988.

GERALD SILK

MARSHALL PLAN.

MARSHALL PLAN. The Marshall Plan—officially known as the European Recovery Program (ERP)—was an ambitious and far-reaching U.S. initiative to sponsor the recovery and reconstruction of western and southern Europe in the aftermath of World War II. The plan was named after one of its creators, George Marshall (1880–1959), the U.S. secretary of state. Marshall first announced this scheme for the rehabilitation of European economies at the Harvard University commencement on 5 June 1947. The Marshall Plan was formally launched on 2 April 1948, when the U.S. Congress passed the Economic Cooperation Act. Over the next four years, roughly $13 billion of aid was distributed to sixteen European recipient countries, who organized themselves into the Organisation for European Economic Cooperation (OEEC) for this purpose. Great Britain, France, Italy, the Federal Republic of Germany, and the Netherlands received the largest sums.

The Marshall Plan has received significant interest, both because of its far-reaching objectives and its pivotal role in the intensifying Cold War between the former wartime allies, the United States and the Soviet Union. Debate among historians and economists has revolved primarily around three issues. First, scholars have disagreed about what U.S. motivations had given rise to the program. A second point of debate concerns the way in which the ERP was assessed in Europe, particularly by the Soviet authorities. Finally, the economic and political effects and long-term implications of the Marshall Plan remain in dispute.

CONTEXT

When World War II finally came to a close, it had left behind a trail of destruction and devastation throughout Europe. It seemed clear to observers that the extent of damage was much more serious than it had been in 1918. Widespread destruction of factories together with shortages in raw materials and food, so it was argued, had not only psychological but also lasting economic effects. Restricted industrial production severely limited what could be achieved in national reconstruction programs. Stagnation and crisis seemed unavoidable.

Historians have since suggested that the extent of the postwar crisis was exaggerated. Physical destruction was less severe than it seemed at first, and in most countries infrastructures could be repaired relatively quickly. By 1947, overall European industrial production had already risen to 87 percent of what it had been in 1938. Nonetheless, there were of course real problems ahead. Recovery was driven by national spending on the repair and extension of industrial capacities. But European countries produced only a small amount of the capital goods they needed to keep this process going. Importing these goods from the United States was made unfeasible by the largely exhausted European dollar reserves. Governments needed money to pay for imports, but their capacity to earn dollars through exports was limited. It was a vicious circle, which gave rise to large trade and payments deficits. Moreover, classical free trade solutions were made impossible by governments' continued strict control of prices and trade. Political uncertainty produced further doom and gloom.

Several different priorities shaped policymaking on the U.S. side. On one hand, the administration sought to end its financial commitments in Europe. Already in August 1945 all lend-lease arrangements had been terminated, primarily to reassure Congress that the financial burdens of the war years were now finally over. Other funding programs, such as the United Nations Relief and Rehabilitation Administration, were canceled by 1947. On the other hand, these assessments were modified by growing political concerns. Already in February 1946, George Kennan at the U.S. embassy in Moscow expressed concern about the Soviet authorities' aggressive hostility toward the Western world. Just a month later, Winston Churchill warned that as a result of expansionist Soviet policies an Iron Curtain had descended across Europe, against which Western democracies had to stand firm. Concerns about Soviet expansion were further fueled by the electoral successes of the Italian and French Communist parties.

Tractors shipped from the United States to Turkey under the provisions of the Marshall Plan arrive in Istanbul, May 1949. ©BETTMANN/CORBIS

The 1946 midterm elections brought both the U.S. Senate and House under the control of the Republican Party, an influential wing of which argued that the reconstruction of Western Europe had to take priority, if only temporarily, over retreat into isolationism. Democratic President Harry S. Truman cooperated closely with Republicans in questions of foreign policy. In his speech to Congress on 12 March 1947, Truman argued (in what was later known as the Truman Doctrine) that the United States had to support actively countries struggling against communism, and he proposed military and economic aid to Greece and Turkey to this end.

Marshall developed these ideas further. He was concerned that communists in Western Europe would take advantage of popular discontent, stirred by plummeting living standards. As the State Department moved toward a policy of active intervention in Europe, the notion that without U.S.

support a European economic collapse was imminent and would, in turn, have serious consequences for the U.S. economy, proved useful to mobilizing political support. When Marshall announced the scheme to aid European recovery, this could thus be justified with established logic: it would not only salvage Europe but also protect the future of U.S. society and its economy.

SCOPE

While the Marshall Plan itself did not explicitly distinguish between Western and Eastern spheres, the logic behind it undoubtedly did. In fact, the plan developed a number of assumptions. First, the mistakes of World War I were not to be repeated. The inadequacy of the Treaty of Versailles was directly linked to the subsequent economic collapse, the rise of fascism and Nazism, and World War II. Second, the biggest threat to Western Europe came from the famished and disillusioned

Europeans who brought their Communist parties into power (through elections or revolt), which would then be subservient to Moscow. Third, Germany had to be rearmed and prevented from falling under Soviet rule. In the face of strong French opposition, the best way of achieving this was by transforming Germany into a prosperous democratic nation. Fourth, Marshall Plan aid would not only help to jump-start European economies and remove the material basis of discontent, but also restore self-confidence in capitalist democracy and thereby provide a strong alternative to communism.

The ERP was designed to enable Western European countries to buy American exports, which would both expand the market for U.S. products and reduce the cost of aid to Europe. ERP planners' goal was to achieve 30 percent growth in industrial production. The program also sought to integrate Western Europe into a single economic and political area. Apart from trade benefits, integration had the important function of reconciling France to a revived and rearmed Germany. French reconstruction plans had until then focused on shifting the center of European heavy industry from Germany to France, and thus prioritized access to German coal and steel resources. The Marshall Plan now assured France both that Germany was locked safely into Europe and that if it dropped its claims on German reparations it would be rewarded with Marshall Plan aid.

The ERP was directed by the Economic Cooperation Administration (ECA) in Washington, with an office in each receiving country. Because aid was made conditional on intra-European cooperation, a new body—the OEEC—was formed to coordinate the distribution of funds. Each country signed a bilateral treaty with the United States, committing itself to strong production, financial stability, and an expansion of foreign trade. Funds were provided in the form of dollar credits. European governments acted as purchasers of imports from the dollar area, which were then resold to consumers in their countries. Because consumers paid for these products in their national currencies, governments built up large balances of nondollar currencies—so-called counterpart funds—which could then be used for a range of purposes subject to the ECA's approval.

REACTIONS

Historians long assumed that the postwar division of Europe had been an inevitable result of expansionist Soviet policies, and that the Iron Curtain had been more or less in place by 1945. More recent assessments have suggested otherwise. Soviet policy in the immediate postwar period was more often reactive than proactively expansionist. Until 1947, the Soviet Union pursued a relatively moderate foreign policy. Popular Front–like coalition governments held power in most Eastern European states under Red Army control. In Germany, Soviet authorities maintained that the German problem could best be dealt with through multilateral Allied action. Scholars have argued that the Marshall Plan then changed Soviet calculations. The Soviet leadership identified the scheme as a U.S. attempt not just to consolidate the Western European bloc economically and politically, but also to intrude into its own sphere of influence, the buffer zone around the USSR, and thus to threaten Soviet security. As a result, Soviet policy shifted radically to contain and prevent American influence.

At any rate, the sincerity of the Western powers' offer for Soviet participation is questionable. Although Ernest Bevin and Georges Bidault, the foreign ministers of Britain and France, respectively, invited their Soviet counterpart Vyacheslav Molotov to discuss Marshall's scheme, this invitation was largely to preempt domestic criticism about excluding the Soviet Union. The Soviet leadership, in turn, hoped the scheme might be turned to their advantage. Molotov tried to gain agreement from other participants to forestall European integration and instead implement the recovery plan on a country-by-country basis. He failed, and the Soviet Union subsequently withdrew from the Paris Economic Conference and put pressure on the Eastern European countries that had been keen to benefit from the ERP. The Polish and Czechoslovak delegations soon gave in. Subsequently, the Soviet authorities developed more effective means of control over their Eastern European satellites. Joseph Stalin's reactions, in turn, persuaded the U.S. Congress that its assessment of the Soviet threat had been correct.

EFFECTS

The Marshall Plan's effects have been debated at length: to what degree did it contribute to the revival and reconstruction of Western Europe? At the height of the Cold War, scholars argued that the scheme was an act of U.S. benevolence in the face of the Soviet threat and the single most important cause of European economic recovery. Revisionist historians subsequently argued that the Marshall Plan was evidence of the imperialist policies of the United States in its efforts to turn Western European countries into economic and political satellites. Their assessment, however, did not actually revise earlier views of the plan's economic importance. For both orthodox and revisionist scholars, the ERP formed an indispensable starting point for Western European recovery from the brink of chaos and collapse.

Since the mid-1980s, several historians have argued that the ERP's direct impact on European developments has been overstated, as recovery was already well under way by the time ERP aid first arrived. Between 1948 and 1951, Marshall Plan aid amounted to only about 2 percent of the gross domestic product of recipient countries. As a result, the ERP did not give the United States sufficient leverage over the political reconstruction of Western Europe. Some historians also question the older emphasis on a homogenous impact of Marshall Plan aid and suggest instead that Western Europe was a patchwork of distinct national programs and ways of using Marshall funds. Different European governments found different strategies to neutralize or ignore specific U.S. requirements.

The Marshall Plan had several different results. Although its direct economic impact has been exaggerated, it seems clear that without this aid the speed of recovery would have been impeded. The Marshall Plan together with other U.S. aid programs reduced Europe's current account deficit with the United States, and allowed a much higher level of imports from the dollar area than would have been possible otherwise. The initial goal of 30 percent growth in industrial production was surpassed by a substantial margin. By 1951 the large dollar deficits had mostly disappeared, and projects for liberalizing trade could again be put on the agenda.

It also seems clear that the impact of the ERP cannot be understood in strictly quantitative terms. Even if the program was not as crucial to Americanization as had been claimed, it did appeal to forces within Europe who were eager to use U.S. aid as a lever to achieve their own objectives. The Marshall Plan also changed European attitudes toward production. Its "politics of productivity" (so called by Charles S. Maier) served as a new ideological yardstick for uniting a centrist political leadership and justifying a reliance on the private economy for growth. With the removal of communists from governing coalitions, the Marshall Plan helped to seal a division within the European labor movement between communist and noncommunist unions. The plan's psychological effects on the war-weary populations of Europe were perhaps most important of all. At a time of despair and uncertainty, it left no room for doubt about the commitment of the United States to the security of Western Europe.

See also **Organisation for European Economic Cooperation (OEEC).**

BIBLIOGRAPHY

Primary Sources

Acheson, Dean. *Present at the Creation: My Years in the State Department.* New York, 1969.

Hoffman, Paul G. *Peace Can Be Won.* Garden City, N.Y., 1951.

Kindleberger, Charles P. *Marshall Plan Days.* Boston, 1987.

Marshall, George. "Speech by the United States Secretary of State, General Marshall, at Harvard University: The Marshall Plan, 5 June 1947." *Foreign Relations of United States* 3 (1947): 237–239. Reprinted in *Department of State Bulletin* 16, no. 415 (15 June 1947): 1159–1160.

Secondary Sources

Cox, Michael, and Caroline Kennedy-Pipe. "The Tragedy of American Diplomacy? Rethinking the Marshall Plan." *Journal of Cold War Studies* 7, no. 1 (2005): 97–134.

Crafts, Nicholas, and Gianni Toniolo, eds. *Economic Growth in Europe since 1945.* Cambridge, U.K., 1996.

De Long, J. Bradford, and Barry Eichengreen. "The Marshall Plan: History's Most Successful Structural Adjustment Program." In *Postwar Economic Reconstruction and Lessons for the East Today,* edited by Rudiger Dornbusch, Wilhelm Nölling, and Richard Layard, 189–230. Cambridge, Mass., 1993.

Eichengreen, Barry, ed. *Europe's Post-war Recovery.* Cambridge, U.K., 1995.

Ellwood, David W. *Rebuilding Europe: Western Europe, America, and Postwar Reconstruction.* London, 1992.

Gaddis, John Lewis. *The Cold War: A New History.* New York, 2005.

Gimbel, John. *The Origins of the Marshall Plan*. Stanford, Calif., 1976.

Hoffmann, Stanley, and Charles Maier, eds. *The Marshall Plan: A Retrospective*. Boulder, Colo., 1984.

Hogan, Michael J. *The Marshall Plan: America, Britain, and the Reconstruction of Western Europe, 1947–1952*. Cambridge, U.K., 1987.

Maier, Charles S., ed. *The Cold War in Europe: Era of a Divided Continent*. 2nd ed. Princeton, N.J., 1996.

Milward, Alan S. *The Reconstruction of Western Europe, 1945–1951*. London, 1984.

Wexler, Imanuel. *The Marshall Plan Revisited: The European Recovery Program in Economic Perspective*. Westport, Conn., 1983.

JESSICA REINISCH

MASARYK, TOMÁŠ GARRIGUE

(1850–1937), first president of Czechoslovakia from 1918 to 1935.

Tomáš Masaryk was born on 7 March 1850 in the Moravian village of Hodonín. He had a varied education that included apprenticeships with both a locksmith and a blacksmith before ending at the University of Vienna, where he earned a doctorate in philosophy in 1876. After graduation, he traveled to Leipzig, where he spent a year writing and studying philosophy. During this sojourn, he met Charlotte Garrigue, an American who became his wife in 1878. As he often admitted, Charlotte had a profound influence on his thought, especially in the realm of women's equality. By the turn of the century, Tomáš Garrigue Masaryk (he took his wife's family name as his middle name) would be a major proponent of women's rights in the Czech lands.

Soon after his marriage, Masaryk accepted a professorship at the Czech university in Prague. From practically the moment of his arrival in Prague in 1882, Masaryk was a controversial figure in Czech society and he remained so for much of his life. He produced a constant stream of articles, books, and lectures that constantly challenged popular opinion. For example, in 1886–1887, he publicly challenged the authenticity of some supposedly ancient Czech manuscripts (which were eventually indeed exposed as forgeries), which earned him widespread public condemnation. In 1899, he loudly defended Leopold Hilsner, a Jew convicted of murdering a Christian girl. Masaryk insisted that Hilsner had been found guilty because of pervasive anti-Semitic prejudice and demanded a new trial. His unpopular stance called forth a wave of hateful attacks in the press, students demonstrated against him at the university and hecklers disrupted his lectures.

Masaryk's involvement in these kinds of public controversies would both shape and hinder his political career. His intense interest in public affairs moved him inexorably toward politics, but his intellectual independence and iconoclasm often brought him into conflict with established political parties. In 1889, Masaryk helped form a political group known as the Realists. The Realists published a political program advocating democratic freedoms like universal suffrage, social reform for the working class, and autonomy for all nations in the Habsburg Monarchy. The Realists did not, at that time, form an independent political party, but decided to join forces with an existing party, the Young Czechs. Masaryk was elected to the Reichsrat (the parliament of Habsburg Austria) in 1891 on the Young Czech ticket. However, his refusal to abstain from criticizing the Young Czech policies caused tension in the party, leading him to resign his parliamentary seat in 1893.

In 1900, Masaryk and some new followers finally did create their own political party, the People's (Realist) Party, which in 1906 merged with another group to become the Progressive Party. While the goals of the party changed over time, it consistently supported both democracy, in the form of universal suffrage, and Czech national autonomy. This was the kernel of Masaryk's often complicated political philosophy: the twinning of nationalism and what he called *humanita* or humanism, which encompassed notions of human equality and social justice. These twin goals, a more egalitarian, democratic society and the health of the Czech nation, were always among Masaryk's most cherished priorities.

Masaryk was elected to parliament again in 1907 and 1911. Although he was sometimes harshly critical of the Habsburg regime, he remained loyal to the Monarchy, believing that the Czech nation could peacefully exist within this multinational state. Slowly, however, he concluded that this was no longer possible. After the outbreak of the First World War in 1914, Masaryk fled abroad to work for Czech independence. Masaryk's efforts were rewarded when the Western Allies agreed to support an independent, democratic Czechoslovakia. The parliament of this new republic elected him president in 1918. Once the most polarizing figure in Czech politics, Masaryk now became beloved as the "President-Liberator" of his nation.

The post of president in Czechoslovakia was supposed to be mostly ceremonial, but Masaryk cannily used his position to obtain considerable political power in the new state. Although he did not have a political party, he established his own power center, known as the "Castle" (*Hrad*). Behind the scenes, Masaryk and his Castle group held enormous influence, keeping a tight grip, for example, on the ministry of foreign affairs. Ironically, in this way Masaryk, an eloquent proponent of democracy, helped to weaken Czechoslovakia's parliamentary system, encouraging politicians to turn to back-door deals instead of using the normal mechanisms of the legislature. Masaryk remained president of Czechoslovakia until he was eighty-five years old. He died in 1937, still revered as the father of his country.

See also **Czechoslovakia.**

BIBLIOGRAPHY

Hanak, Harry, Robert Pynsent, and Stanley Winters, eds. *T. G. Masaryk.* 3 vols. London, 1989–1990. Major essay collection dealing with all aspects of Masaryk's life and work.

Skilling, H. Gordon. *T. G. Masaryk: Against the Current, 1882–1914.* University Park, Pa., 1994. Very readable biography of Masaryk's life before 1914.

Szporluk, Roman. *The Political Thought of Thomas G. Masaryk.* New York, 1981. An essential introduction to Masaryk's political philosophy.

MELISSA FEINBERG

MATISSE, HENRI (1869–1954), French artist.

In his *Concerning the Spiritual in Art,* Wassily Kandinsky penned one of the clearest encapsulations of Matisse ever put to paper: "Matisse—color, Picasso—shape." Color and pattern are without a doubt the two primordial roads to understanding this painter's career. He was in turn a painter, a sculptor, an engraver (illustrating the poems of Baudelaire, Joyce, Mallarmé, and Montherlant), a fabric designer, and a stage designer for the ballets *Le chant du rossignol* (Song of the nightingale) in 1920 and *Le rouge et le noir* (The red and the black) in 1939.

The young Matisse first began a career in law, from 1887 to 1888, before fully committing himself to painting. He began his artistic training at the École des Arts Décoratifs de Paris and then at the Académie Julian, before completing his studies at the École des Beaux-Arts, in Gustave Moreau's studio. However, once he left these institutions, Matisse was constantly experimenting with methods and media. Ambroise Vollard coordinated his first one-man exposition in June 1904. His first pieces (dated 1897–1903) reflect the influences of Paul Cézanne, Paul Gauguin, Paul Signac, and Vincent van Gogh.

A few of his paintings, including the 1905 *Fenêtre à Collioure* (Window at Collioure), were so brightly colored they caused a sensation at the Salon d'Automne of 1905 and propelled him to the leadership position of the fauvist movement. The work effected a fusion between two distinct modes of painting: Georges Seurat's pointillism in conjunction with the tinted areas of color first innovated by Gauguin. *Luxe, calme et volupté*, also shown at the Salon, afforded Matisse the opportunity to return to the pointillist technique, but this time using more intense colors, whose loudness was increased by thick borders. Both these canvases convey Matisse's reflections on the sensory power of color. After them Matisse gave up pointillism and became more interested in lines and color, as in his *Femme au chapeau* (1905; Woman in a hat), where the patterns, facial colors, and tinting all compete to emphasize the power of each.

The years 1905–1908 were decisive for Matisse. In 1906 he showed *Le bonheur de vivre* (The pleasure of living), and then the following year *Nu bleu, souvenir de Biskra* (Blue nude, souvenir of Biskra), both at the Salon des Indépendants. These paintings were a fulcrum for compositions to come. Indeed their subjects, including dancing women, would

Henri Matisse draws a mural with a bamboo stick, 1931. ©THE BARNES FOUNDATION, MERION, PENNSYLVANIA, USA/THE BRIDGEMAN ART LIBRARY

reappear in numerous sculptures and paintings. In this way certain "Matissian" motifs forged lines of communication stretching beyond the specificity of the two mediums.

In his 1908 *La desserte*, Matisse transformed space through a decorative stylization of the elements on the canvas, thereby abolishing established rules of representation. The painting's elements were treated like decorative patterns melting into one another, including the objects in the room, the wallpaper, the rug, and the table, making it possible for color to become the element that held the painting together.

Matisse received a commission from a Russian collector named Sergei Shchukin for two panels of a mural, eventually titled *La danse* and *La musique*, which were completed in 1909–1910. Through these monumental murals Matisse radically altered his style and situated himself in the context of a

new modernism that distanced itself from the one being championed by cubism. Matisse in effect sought to mute the loudness of his colors and foreground the abstract background painted as large tinted areas whose borders delineated the corporeal space of the characters. The motif of dancing, already touched upon in *La joie de vivre*, would also appear several years later in two versions of the triptych commissioned by Albert Barnes in 1930–1933—still shown in the Barnes Foundation in Merion, Pennsylvania—and in his four sculptures entitled *Nu de dos* (1909–1930; Bare back). This triptych is a testament to the role of arabesque imagery in Matisse's work and his masterful execution of dynamism.

From 1912 to 1913 he traveled across Morocco, whose intensely colorful landscapes inspired him, and from 1914 to 1918—surprisingly ignoring the war—he began to work on the use of lines and arabesques, in search of a sufficiently supple idiom while at the same time reintroducing black to his color palette, as in *Porte-fenêtre à Collioure* (1914, French window at Collioure) and *Le violoniste à la fenêtre* (1918; The violinist at the window). In 1918 Matisse took up residence in Nice and brightened up his color palette once more, as he transcribed interiors and devoted himself to his favorite subjects: dance, nudes, and odalisques. In 1924 the first Matisse retrospective was opened to the public, in Copenhagen.

After a voyage to Tahiti in 1930, Matisse completed his first cutout gouaches in 1937 for the cover of *Verve,* which served as a launching pad for a series of works including *Les deux danseurs* (1937–1938; The two dancers), *La piscine* (1952; The pool), and *Jazz,* a book published in 1947. From 1948 to 1951 Matisse dedicated himself to designing the architecture, stained-glass windows, and frescos for the Chapelle du Rosaire in Vence, France, and for the Rockefeller chapel in New York state. These works represent the culmination of his explorations into the simplification of patterns and shapes. Matisse borrowed from compositions akin to his cutout gouaches, and his theories about painting as harmony and an aid to meditation were concretized in these devotional spaces. In 1950 Matisse was awarded a prize at the Twenty-fifth Biennial in Venice, and two years later he attended the opening of the Matisse Museum in his hometown, Le Cateau-Cambrésis.

See also **Expositions; Miró, Joan; Painting, Avant-Garde; Picasso, Pablo.**

BIBLIOGRAPHY

Aragon, Louis. *Henri Matisse, Roman.* Paris, 1971.

Benjamin, Roger. *Matisse's "Notes of a Painter": Criticism, Theory, and Context, 1891–1908.* Ann Arbor, Mich., 1987.

Bock-Weiss, Catherine C. *Henri Matisse: A Guide to Research.* New York and London, 1996.

Bois, Yve Alain. *Matisse et Picasso.* Paris, 1998.

Bonnard, Pierre. *Bonnard, Matisse: Correspondance, 1925–1946.* Paris, 1991.

Clement, Russell T. *Henri Matisse: A Bio-bibliography.* London, 1993.

Flam, Jack. *Matisse, the Dance.* Washington, D.C., 1993.

———. *Matisse and Picasso: The Story of Their Rivalry and Friendship.* Cambridge, Mass., 2003.

Golding, John. *Matisse and Cubism.* Glasgow, 1978.

Herrera, Hayden. *Matisse: A Portrait.* London, 1993.

Jacques-Marie, Sister. *Henri Matisse: The Vence Chapel.* Translated by Barbara F. Freed. Nice, 2001.

Matisse, Henri. *Henri Matisse: Écrits et propos sur l'art.* Edited by Dominique Fourcade. Paris, 1972.

———. *Matisse, Rouveyre: Correspondance.* Paris, 2001.

Robinson, Annette, Henri Matisse, and Isabelle Bréda. *Matisse at the Musée national d'art moderne.* Paris, 1999.

Schneider, Pierre. *Matisse.* Translated by Michael Taylor and Bridget Strevens Romer. Paris, 1984.

Spurling, Hilary. *The Unknown Matisse: A Life of Henri Matisse: The Early Years, 1869–1908.* New York, 1998.

CYRIL THOMAS

MAURRAS, CHARLES (1868–1952), French nationalist.

For more than five decades Charles Maurras attempted to delegitimize the French Revolution and the Third Republic (1875–1940). He was born on 20 April 1868 in Martigues in Provence, near Marseille. His father was a secular civil servant; his mother was an observant Catholic and royalist. Maurras's harsh view of life can be traced to childhood traumas—the death of his father when the boy was only six and a severe hearing loss at fourteen that eliminated the possibility of the naval career he had planned. In 1885 he moved to Paris to be a literary writer and journalist.

INTEGRAL NATIONALISM

Literature led Maurras to politics. He disliked Romanticism but admired the rationalism of ancient Greece and of French classicism. He blamed what he saw as nineteenth-century "barbarism" and "decadence" on the French Revolution, which had replaced hierarchy and authority with individual rights and democracy.

The Dreyfus affair was the driving force behind the rise of Maurras's organization, the Action Française. After Alfred Dreyfus, a Jewish captain on the General Staff of the French army, was falsely accused of providing French military secrets to Germany, France split into defenders of individual rights (Dreyfusards) and nationalists who placed the nation above the individual (anti-Dreyfusards). A leader of the anti-Dreyfusards,

Maurras argued that any means were justified in the defense of France and that "politics came first" ("*politique d'abord*"). Integral nationalism and monarchy would unite the country and eliminate Jews, Protestants, Freemasons, and *métèques* (a derogatory term for resident foreigners). While awaiting a coup d'état, he championed a reactionary political consciousness. Thus the Action Française established a newspaper, a league, and the Camelots du Roi, a group that disrupted universities, law courts, and theaters. By the outbreak of World War I, Maurras had already found a considerable following among students, royalists, nationalists, conservatives, and Catholics.

During the war he expressed limited support for the Union Sacrée (Sacred Union), and the Action Française's extreme nationalism raised the organization's prestige even further. But Maurras's vituperation against internationalists played a role in Raoul Villain's assassination of Jean Jaurès, the Socialist Party leader, on 31 July 1914, and allegations by Léon Daudet and Maurras against alleged foreign spies, based on little or no evidence, ruined many lives. Their partly unsubstantiated accusations against the Radical politicians Louis-Jean Malvy and Joseph Caillaux helped bring about the collapse of the Union Sacrée. They also contributed toward the climate of public opinion that brought the radical republican Georges Clemenceau to power in November 1917.

During the postwar period, the Action Française advocated a hard peace with Germany. Maurras praised Premier Raymond Poincaré's occupation of the Ruhr in January 1923 but castigated Aristide Briand's rapprochement with Germany at mid-decade.

The violence of the Action Française had a significant impact on domestic French politics in 1923. After the anarchist Germaine Berton assassinated Marius Plateau, head of the Camelots du Roi, in January, the Camelots destroyed opposition newspapers. In May, openly mimicking Italian Blackshirt methods, the Camelots physically assaulted four prominent liberal democratic and moderate socialist political figures (two of them deputies). In response, the Radical leader Édouard Herriot reoriented his party toward the Cartel des Gauches, a coalition with the Socialists, against "fascism." Premier Poincaré, who had

carried on a secret correspondence with Maurras, refused to break with the Action Française.

CHALLENGES FROM WITHIN AND WITHOUT

Maurras suffered a severe setback in 1926 when Pope Pius XI (r. 1922–1939) condemned the Action Française. An agnostic, Maurras nonetheless incorporated the Catholic Church of order, authority, hierarchy, and discipline into his integral nationalism. The pope wanted young Catholics to militate in the Catholic Action movement instead of the Action Française. The condemnation strictly forbade Catholics from belonging to the organization and from reading the Action Française's newspaper and Maurras's other writings.

The Action Française also faced a challenge from within its own ranks. Georges Valois wanted to fuse integral nationalism and syndicalism and to attract workers and veterans. For Maurras, Valois's creation of a newspaper and a fascist political party (the Faisceau) in 1925 opened an irreconcilable breach.

Some scholars regard the Action Française as an "early fascism," while others characterize it as reactionary but also as a link between earlier nationalism and 1930s fascism. Both the Action Française and fascism display a hostility toward liberal democracy, socialism, and communism; both embrace nationalism, call for violence, and eject groups from the national community, particularly Jews. Unlike fascist leaders, however, Maurras was an elitist, did not seek a mass following, lacked a will to action, and favored decentralization on the model of the ancien régime.

POLITICAL POLARIZATION

Maurras contributed to the intense political polarization of the mid-1930s in France. The Action Française served to publicize the Stavisky affair of 1934, yet the crisis showed once again that Maurras was more a polemicist than a man of action. On the night of 6 February 1934, as leaguers, most of them rightists and many inspired by Maurras's invectives, were seeking to storm the National Assembly, Maurras printed up the next morning's newspaper and wrote poetry. Subsequently, another secession/expulsion rocked the Action Française, as a group of dissident Camelots accused the "maison mère" (mother house) of inaction and formed the Comité Secrèt d'Action Révolutionnaire, or Organisation Secrète d'Action Révolutionnaire, which in 1936–1937 plotted to overthrow the Popular Front government and the Third Republic. In retaliation for their alleged betrayal, the Action Française nicknamed the secessionists "the Cagoule" ("the hooded ones," a derogatory comparison to the Ku Klux Klan). Maurras struggled for turf against other challengers on the extreme right as well, particularly Colonel François de la Rocque's large Croix de Feu/ Parti Social Français. Maurras hurled epithets at the Popular Front government, which dissolved the rightist leagues. His death threats against the Jewish and socialist premier Léon Blum and other parliamentarians earned Maurras a seven-month jail sentence in 1936–1937. In 1938, however, he was voted into the Académie Française, and in 1939 Pope Pius XII lifted the Catholic Church's interdict.

During the 1930s, ideology increasingly colored Maurras's assessments of foreign policy. He vehemently opposed sanctions against Benito Mussolini's invasion of Ethiopia and favored Francisco Franco's Nationalists during the Spanish civil war. Most significantly, Maurras fervently supported the Munich Treaty and appeasement, since he hated domestic enemies and Stalin's communism at least as much as Hitler's Germany.

SUPPORT OF VICHY

After the defeat of France and the advent of the Nazi occupation in 1940, Maurras enthusiastically characterized Marshal Philippe Pétain's policies as a "divine surprise." Although he did not support the ultracollaborationists in Paris, his unwavering defense of Pétain entailed support of Vichy's persistent collaboration with Germany. Maurras and his newspaper, published in Lyon, condemned Vichy's enemies, supported the paramilitary Milice against the Resistance, and continued his vicious rhetorical assaults against Jews. Until the end of his life, he blamed the Jews for the war and the German occupation. Sentenced to life in prison and stripped of his civil rights after the war, Maurras shouted, "This is the revenge of Dreyfus" (Weber, p. 475). He was freed from prison for health reasons shortly before his death on 16 November 1952.

Maurras's Action Française became perhaps the most influential mouthpiece for the reactionary Right in France. And Maurras shaped minds outside France, for example, in Belgium, Switzerland, the Iberian Peninsula, Quebec, and Latin America. His movement lay somewhere between reaction and fascism. He inculcated in his followers hostility to individual rights, to equality, democracy, and parliamentary government. He deepened French political divisions and inspired the Vichy regime and its war against the Jews, sharing in that regime's defeat.

See also **Action Française; Fascism; Stavisky Affair.**

BIBLIOGRAPHY

Arnal, Oscar L. *Ambivalent Alliance: The Catholic Church and the Action Française 1899–1939*. Pittsburgh, Pa., 1985.

Blatt, Joel. "Relatives and Rivals: The Responses of the Action Française to Italian Fascism, 1919–26." *European Studies Review* 11, no. 3 (July 1981): 263–292.

———. "Action Française and the Vatican." In *Encyclopedia of the Vatican and Papacy,* edited by Frank J. Coppa, 3–5. Westport, Conn., 1999.

———. "The Cagoule Plot, 1936–1937." In *Crisis and Renewal in France 1918–1962,* edited by Kenneth Mouré and Martin S. Alexander, 86–104. New York, 2002.

Goyet, Bruno. *Charles Maurras.* Paris, 2000.

Mazgaj, Paul. *The Action Française and Revolutionary Syndicalism.* Chapel Hill, N.C., 1979.

Nolte, Ernst. *Three Faces of Fascism: Action Française, Italian Fascism, National Socialism.* Translated by Leila Vennewitz. Munich, 1965.

Rémond, René. *The Right Wing in France from 1815 to De Gaulle.* Translated by James M. Laux. Philadelphia, 1966.

Soucy, Robert. *French Fascism: The First Wave, 1924–1933.* New Haven, Conn., 1986.

Tannenbaum, Edward R. *The Action Française.* New York, 1962.

Weber, Eugen. *Action Française.* Stanford, Calif., 1962.

Winock, Michel. "L'Action Française." In *Histoire de l'extreme droite en France,* edited by Michel Winock. Paris, 1993.

JOEL BLATT

MAYAKOVSKY, VLADIMIR (1893–1930), Russian poet.

One of the most influential poets and dramatists of his time, Vladimir Vladimirovich Mayakovsky was born in Georgia to parents of Russian descent. The family moved to Moscow in 1906, and Mayakovsky, who joined the Bolsheviks, was soon arrested for revolutionary activities. After his third incarceration, Mayakovsky enrolled in art school and came under the influence of the painter and poet David Burlyuk (1882–1967) and the burgeoning movement of futurism.

Mayakovsky allied himself with cubo-futurism, the most important of the four groups that made up Russian futurism. His first two published poems, "Day" and "Night," appeared in the futurist miscellany *A Slap in the Face of Public Taste* (1912), and he signed the famous manifesto of the same title. In so doing, he endorsed futurism's rejection of the past and its provocation of a bourgeois audience both in print and in person: Mayakovsky participated in the early futurist tours of Russia and in publicity stunts that in significant ways anticipated performance art. Even his first verse drama, entitled simply *Tragedy* (1913), was intended as an absolute break with the theatrical past. Despite Mayakovsky's intentions, the play, which alternated with *Victory over the Sun* (1913) by Alexei Kruchonykh (1886–1968), owes a significant debt to Alexander Blok's lyric dramas and to Nikolai Evreinov's monodramas.

Much of Mayakovsky's best poetry, the work that established and secured his reputation, is to be found in lyric poems such as "Lilichka!, Instead of a Letter," "Our March" (1917), and "Good Relations with Horses," and in his prerevolutionary narrative poems. In *Cloud in Pants* (1915), *The Backbone Flute* (1916), *War and the World* (1916), and *Man* (1918), Mayakovsky developed a style of startling originality. Mayakovsky employs accentual meters, liberal and creative rhymes, jarring dislocations of syntax, and an innovative visual presentation, together with an extravagance of hyperbole and metaphor, which often take on a life of their own.

Mayakovsky embraced the Russian Revolution of 1917 and laid his considerable talents at the feet of the fledgling Bolshevik state. His work, from the time of the Revolution until his death, proved uneven, ranging from the politically expedient narrative poem *Vladimir Ilyich Lenin* (1924) to such fine lyrics as "I Love" and "Letter to Tatyana Yakovleva," the narrative poem *About That* (1923), and the play *The Bedbug* (1929). The unevenness of Mayakovsky's work owes in no small part to a conscious and theoretically elaborated surrender of poetry's autonomy to the needs and demands of the state. Mayakovsky was swayed by his close friend, the critic Osip Brik, whose ideas about "sound repetition" helped to shape the poet's early work and whose conception of "social demand" helped to channel the later work. Not surprisingly, Mayakovsky devoted enormous energy to agitprop during this period and even created advertisements for state-owned stores.

To celebrate the first anniversary of the Revolution, Mayakovsky wrote *Mystery-Bouffe* (1918), which combines elements of mystery plays with low comedy to portray the triumph of the "unclean" proletariat over the "clean" bourgeoisie. Despite its defects and criticism from Bolshevik authorities, *Mystery-Bouffe* was important because it marked the first collaboration between Mayakovsky and the great director Vsevolod Meyerhold (1874–1940). Mayakovsky, who grew increasingly disenchanted with the Soviet state, again turned to Meyerhold with his next play, the biting satire *The Bedbug*, the production of which proved to be a theatrical landmark. The two again collaborated on Mayakovsky's last play, *The Bathhouse* (1930), which satirizes Soviet philistinism. The suppression of the play marked the end of an era not only for Mayakovsky and Meyerhold, but for Soviet culture as well.

Mayakovsky worked assiduously throughout the last years of his life to shape the aesthetic of the Revolution and the Soviet state. To that end, he joined and helped to found numerous cultural organizations, the most important of which was the Left Front of Art. As editor of the organization's journal *Lef* and its successor *New Lef,* Mayakovsky attempted to safeguard a revolutionary, avant-garde art for a revolutionary society. Despite the important work published in these journals, Mayakovsky's efforts to shape Soviet society ultimately ended in failure. He made one more, last-ditch effort when he founded Ref, the Revolutionary Front of Art, but soon had to abandon it. Under political pressure, Mayakovsky capitulated and joined the aesthetically conservative Russian Association of Proletarian Writers (RAPP) in the last year of his life. Together with the suppression of *The Bathhouse* and personal problems, this failure contributed to his eventual suicide. Mayakovsky's legacy includes not only great poems he wrote, but also a persona and style that fused politics and aesthetics into an influential model of the activist poet.

See also **Futurism; Russia; Socialist Realism; Soviet Union.**

BIBLIOGRAPHY

Briggs, A. D. P. *Vladimir Mayakovsky: A Tragedy*. Oxford, U.K., 1979.

Jangfeldt, Bengt. *Majakovskij and Futurism, 1917–1921*. Stockholm, 1976.

Shklovsky, Viktor. *Mayakovsky and His Circle*. Translated by Lily Feiler. New York, 1972.

Terras, Victor. *Vladimir Mayakovsky*. Boston, 1983.

Woroszylski, Wiktor. *The Life of Mayakovsky*. Translated by Boleslaw Taborski. New York, 1970.

TIMOTHY C. WESTPHALEN

MAY 1968. No other city in Europe is more synonymous with revolution than Paris, and the events of May 1968 are no exception. Just as in 1789, 1830, and 1848, students, young workers, and ordinary citizens built barricades in the Latin Quarter of Paris and took to the streets to fight the forces of public order. Like the previous revolts, the state's attempt at suppressing the *enragés* only widened the conflict throughout the entire country. However, unlike the previous revolutions, the governing regime remained intact after 1968. Most scholars agree that although the May events were the most spectacular west of the Iron Curtain during that eventful year, the French political system held and Charles DeGaulle's Fifth Republic did not go the way of the previous four. May 1968 proved to be the great rebellion in postwar Western Europe and represented the culmination of both international trends common to all West European countries and national forces unique to France.

By nearly any sociological, demographic, political, or financial measure, 1960s France was *not* ripe for revolution. Wages stood at relatively high levels, having grown 3.6 percent between 1963 and 1969, and automobile and television ownership had become more common. A growing middle class could afford to send its children to university, and public opinion polls showed that the French, like their European neighbors, cared little for politics. The postwar French seemed wary of political controversy and sought to delegate decisions to their great Resistance hero, de Gaulle. Furthermore, President de Gaulle remained enthroned in power under a constitution that he had written for France in 1958.

CAUSES

Despite these indicators of affluence and political complacency, a growing and potentially explosive cohort of young people had begun to voice their disapproval of French society. The spirit of anti-colonialism that spread through Western Europe and the United States had found a unique expression in France in the late 1950s. The French government had relinquished some of its former colonial holdings in North Africa and handed over its entanglements in Indochina to the United States, but still held onto its rule in Algeria. The civil war in Algeria lasted until 1962 and deeply divided the French people in much the same way that the Vietnam conflict would later divide Americans. Although de Gaulle had negotiated the French withdrawal from Algeria, many students and young workers felt that de Gaulle's time had passed and demanded new leadership.

Not only were the French baby boomers increasingly dissatisfied with politics, at the university they faced a new set of problems created by postwar prosperity. At the same time that enrollment numbers were mushrooming in West Germany and Italy, French universities had become perilously overcrowded by the mid-1960s. From 1958 to 1968, the number of university students in France had jumped from 170,000 to 514,000, and schools in Paris accounted for 130,000 of the total. Like their counterparts in West Berlin, Turin, and London, the universities of Paris could not expand

Students throw stones at police in the streets of Paris, May 1968. ©Hulton-Deutsch Collection/Corbis

fast enough to meet the needs of the growing student population. By the mid-1960s, the French government faced a crisis in higher education and chose to deal with the problem by simply limiting the number of students. The minister of education, Michel Fouchet, proposed a restructuring of university degrees in an attempt to limit those seeking the traditional four-year degree; his successor Alain Peyrefitte later suggested a plan to limit the number of students accepted to the universities. Students interpreted these political moves as an attempt to turn back the clock by limiting higher education to an elite few rather than expanding and reforming the entire university system. Such attempts to limit the French university, similar to proposed plans in West Germany and Italy, became part of a growing list of student grievances that included outdated curricula, authoritarian professors, ineffective pedagogy, overcrowded classrooms, and abysmal dormitories. Taken as a whole, the students' critique of university conditions, their professors, de Gaulle's politics, and later, the United States' war in Vietnam amounted to a potent mixture of dissent and anti-authoritarianism.

THE REVOLUTION BEGINS

The spark that was to ignite the students occurred in the unlikely place of Nanterre, a suburban campus of the University of Paris located far from the main university district in Paris's Latin Quarter. The university at Nanterre had been built in the early 1960s to accommodate more Parisian students and became a center for the social sciences. Paradoxically, at Nanterre there were hundreds of sociology students studying alienation at an institution located in the center of a community filled with thousands of poor foreign workers crammed into squalid urban housing. The students at

Nanterre also found themselves subjected to a greater number of restrictions on dormitory visitation privileges and social life than their peers at the Sorbonne and the main campus of the University of Paris. Beginning in January 1968, the students at Nanterre made their dissatisfaction known and would ultimately produce some of the key student leaders during the "events of May."

On 8 January 1968, a group of students at Nanterre jeered the minister for youth and sport, François Missoffe, who had come to Nanterre to dedicate a new swimming pool. Prior to his visit, some students had expressed anger over the university's strict regulation of visiting hours in female dormitories, prompting a feisty redhead named Daniel Cohn-Bendit (b. 1945) to mockingly ask the minister about his plans to study students' sexual behaviors. The minister replied that perhaps Cohn-Bendit ought to take a dip in the pool. To this answer, Cohn-Bendit accused the minister of acting like the head of the Hitler Youth. Seemingly insignificant, the exchange marked the emergence of Cohn-Bendit as the main leader of the student revolt. He later earned the nickname "Dany the Red" for his red hair and supposed political leanings.

In February 1968, a new round of student activity broke out throughout the world following the Tet Offensive. French students began a more concerted effort to oppose the U.S. war in Vietnam and staged demonstrations in Paris on 7 and 13 February. In both cases, the police responded with violence and university administrators condemned the student actions. Many students in both French universities and lycées (high schools) demanded their rights to free speech and assembly within the school campus, much as American students had done a few years before. Near the end of February, the minister of education publicly announced his intention to reform and improve access to the universities.

THE 22 MARCH MOVEMENT

On 22 March, Nanterre would lead the way in escalating the growing youth rebellion with the occupation of the administration building by 150 students. The students claimed to be anarchists and cited the numerous problems within the university and the French government as the cause for their actions. Once again "Dany the Red" figured prominently among the Nanterre rebels and was immediately subjected to disciplinary actions along with several others, a group that became known as the "22 March Movement."

The suspension of the 22 March group and closure of Nanterre only fanned the flames of the student movement at Nanterre. Cohn-Bendit, a child of German-Jewish parents who had fled to France during the war, was catapulted into the national spotlight. Although he claimed to be an anarchist during the 22 March occupation, his views were more akin to the Situationists who believed that one need only create revolutionary situations with outcomes that would be determined as they developed. Generally speaking, the students' politics fell within the spectrum of the New Left in their rejection of Soviet communism and disdain for hierarchical structures. Cohn-Bendit's prominent role in the demonstrations also ensured political controversy as he had claimed West German citizenship to avoid serving in compulsory French military service and the hard-nosed de Gaulle sought to have Cohn-Bendit deported. De Gaulle inflamed the students even more with his bigoted remark, "What's all this fuss over a German-Jew?" Throughout the month of April, the Nanterre activists moved their protests to the Sorbonne and other universities throughout Paris. On 27 April, "Dany the Red" was formally arrested. By the end of April, a growing youth rebellion had taken hold in the historic "Red Zone" of Paris, the Latin Quarter. Ominously, the prime minister Georges Pompidou (1911–1974), who sought a more conciliatory approach to the students, left town on a state visit to Iran and Afghanistan.

THE MAY EVENTS

The closure of Nanterre had shifted the focus of the movement to the Sorbonne and students from all over the city were converging upon the medieval university for meetings, demonstrations, and sit-ins. The suspicious President de Gaulle, fearing a socialist conspiracy, seized upon the minister's absence to call in a special police force known as the Companies for Republican Security (CRS) that had been trained to deal with labor strikes and demonstrations. On 3 May, the CRS swept into

Students participating in a strike at Goethe University in Frankfurt are sprayed with a fire hose by opponents of the strike, May 1968. ©Bettmann/Corbis

the courtyard of the Sorbonne, brutally clearing the campus of all protesters. In a scene that was to be repeated throughout the Western world in 1968, police would enter the hallowed grounds of university campuses. The CRS raid marked the first such intrusion in the Sorbonne's seven-hundred-year history. The 3 May incident resulted in 100 injuries and 596 arrests and began a process of escalation that would continue through the entire month. Each time the students demonstrated, the police would attack and the resulting violence and arrests only served to fan the rage of France's youth. The following day, the rector of the Sorbonne closed the university for an indeterminate time and the students took their protests to the heart of the city, often gathering near the Place de l'Etoile, Arc de Triomphe, and Boulevard Michel.

The closing of the Sorbonne prompted a meeting led by Jacques Sauvageot, the president of the National Union of French Students (UNEF), Alain Geismar, the head of the National Union of Teaching Assistants (SNESup), and Cohn-Bendit representing the 22 March Movement. The student leaders demanded the reopening of the universities, the withdrawal of the police, and the release of all those arrested. The state and the university responded on 5 May by convicting thirteen demonstrators and giving four of them jail sentences. Predictably, mushrooming crowds of young people, including many high school students, returned to the Sorbonne for another day of bloody street battles. This time, the students charged the CRS and fighting raged back and forth throughout the Latin Quarter; by day's end, around 600 students and 345 police had been injured and 422 were arrested. In the nineteenth century, French people joked that Paris sent the provinces revolution by telegram. In 1968, television had replaced the telegram and as news filtered out of the capital, many began to sympathize with the students. Throughout the entire May period, the local residents of the Latin Quarter would aid protesters and offer blankets and food to the chagrin of the police.

THE WIDENING REVOLT

On 10 May, a new round of protests and battles with police shook the Latin Quarter as students threw up barricades of paving stones and overturned cars. When the tear gas cleared, there were 367 people hospitalized and 468 people arrested. The street battles of 10 May initiated an unprecedented outpouring of sympathy from the workers of France as the major trade unions—the communist-led General Confederation of Labor-Workers (CGT), the Catholic workers' French Democratic Confederation of Labor, and the French schoolteachers' Federation of National Education (FEN)—called for a general strike on 13 May to protest the state's repression of the students. Prime Minister Pompidou, having returned to France to find its capitol on the verge of anarchy and realizing that the repressive measures taken during his absence had only swelled the numbers of the *enragés*, attempted to calm students by announcing the reopening of the Sorbonne for 13 May. Pompidou hoped that his conciliatory gesture to the students might also detach the workers' support from their allies in the university. Ultimately, French leaders correctly viewed the students' protests and workers' strikes as two separate struggles.

The offer to reopen the Sorbonne had no effect and on 13 May 1968, thousands of workers all over France downed their tools or refused to report for work. The country experienced its largest general strike since the mid-1930s, and hundreds of workers in and around Paris joined the students in the Latin Quarter. Nowhere else in 1968 had the workers risen up at the same time as the students and the resulting convergence of labor and university unrest effectively shutdown the French economy and created a national crisis at the highest levels. The following day, workers at the Sud-Aviation factory in Nantes, acting outside union directives, spontaneously occupied their factory; on 15 May, workers at the Renault plant in Cleon followed suit. By 18 May, two million French workers were on strike and about 120 factories

were closed down. Coal mining had ceased, dockworkers in Nantes had requisitioned cargoes, and city workers had proclaimed a "People's Republic." Electrical plants in France continued to function but workers limited their production to domestic users, and postal and rail services ceased by the 19 May. The following day, France's air traffic controllers came out on strike and the teachers' union (FEN) officially went on strike on 22 May.

By 20 May the strike had spread to an estimated ten million workers and France was literally closed for business. Left-wing politicians in the National Assembly narrowly failed in their motion to censure the president and prime minister and the Gaullists within the administration succeeded in withdrawing Cohn-Bendit's residency permit and threatened to deport him. Clearly, the events of May surpassed any of the students' or workers' expectations. The trade unions and the French Communist Party (PCF) began to fear that the revolution might slip from their hands and began to take steps to reassert their control over the workers.

The social theorist Raymond Aron (1905–1983) observed in late May that most people in Paris believed that government no longer existed and that anything was possible. France's renowned writer Jean-Paul Sartre (1905–1980) applauded the students' actions and frequently visited them at the Sorbonne. The perception of anarchy delighted some but frightened others and on 24 May, President de Gaulle addressed the nation by radio and noted that France needed reform but not violence and called for a national referendum on his presidency. De Gaulle's referendum idea was immediately ruled unconstitutional by the government and instead had the effect of bringing thousands more protesters out into the streets of Paris calling for de Gaulle's removal. The night of 24 May turned into the bloody culmination of weeks of street fighting in Paris, with 795 arrests and 456 people injured. At one point a group of protesters attempted to burn down the Bourse, or national stock exchange.

THE GRENELLE AGREEMENTS

Despite the uproar of 24 May, the government began to meet with major union leaders at the Ministry of Social Affairs in the Rue de Grenelle and hammered out labor agreements that gave

Riot police gather at a stone barricade erected by protesting students in Paris, May 1968. ©BETTMANN/CORBIS

significant concessions to French workers. The accords announced on 27 May included a minimum wage increase of 35 percent, a general 10 percent wage increase for industrial workers, a lower retirement age, and a forty-hour workweek. Clearly the unions had won a major deal for their workers, but many were still dissatisfied with the continued dominance and hierarchical structure of the unions. Renault workers refused to return to work and 30,000 students and workers held an antigovernment demonstration at Charlety stadium in Paris. The continued chaos and fact that the Grenelle agreements had not brought all of France back to work prompted President de Gaulle to secretly fly to Baden Baden on 29 May to meet with the French army's general staff. At the meeting, de Gaulle received assurances that the military would support him if the president needed troops to restore order.

Emboldened by the military's promise of support, President de Gaulle addressed the French nation on 30 May. De Gaulle again noted the need for reform and stated his decision to remain in office and keep Pompidou as prime minister until new elections for the National Assembly could be held at the end of June. De Gaulle also noted that force would be used to put down further threats to public order. The following day, thousands of French citizens, weary of the violence and eager to return to work, staged pro-government demonstrations. On the first of June, gas stations reopened for business, and in keeping with the Grenelle agreements, the minimum wage was raised to three francs per hour. After the holiday weekend, most workers returned to work on 3 June and the crisis beyond the universities had subsided. The quick resolution of the labor unrest shattered the illusion of a student-worker alliance.

In truth, the workers of France, like their counterparts in Europe and the United States, lived in a world apart from the students who came from the middle and upper classes, and the two groups that turned France upside down in 1968 were, in fact, parallel but nonintersecting movements. The government granted a general amnesty to participants in the May events and the electoral campaigns of June witnessed a few violent incidents but only the universities continued to experience disruptions.

The French election in June 1968 resulted in a swing to the right as Gaullists won large numbers of seats in the National Assembly and the Communists and Socialists lost support. The government authorized the police to begin checking identification cards of university students, a measure that lasted until December. The following year, French voters finally tired of the old General de Gaulle and elected Pompidou president. The French student movement continued into the early 1970s, until the end of the Vietnam War and a severe economic crisis precipitated by the oil embargo diverted student attentions away from "permanent revolution." The mass support among the students had already faded by the fall semester of 1968.

CONCLUSIONS

More important than the failed political rebellion of May 1968 was the victory recorded by labor allowing the working class of France to take its rightful share of the postwar prosperity, and French universities did liberalize access for lower-class students following the events of 1968. Culturally, the May events constituted a true revolution—many scholars have noted that people talked to each other as they had never done before, overturning traditions of deference and authority that had persisted since the last century. Creative new ideas and slogans entered the popular vocabulary and fired the imagination. Furthermore, in France as elsewhere, fashion changed and sexual attitudes became more open and tolerant. Art reflected the change as well. Italian historian Peppino Ortoleva wrote that 1968 blurred the line between fine art and Pop Art, between High Culture and low culture. Nowhere was this more apparent than at the Ecole des Beaux Arts in Paris during May 1968. Students at Paris's premier fine arts school established an *Atelier Populaire* or "people's workshop"

that produced hundred of posters supporting the students that were distributed and pasted all over Paris. Ultimately, the events of May 1968 proved to be a failed political rebellion that produced a true cultural revolution.

See also **Cohn-Bendit, Daniel; 1968; Student Movements.**

BIBLIOGRAPHY

Bureau of Public Secrets. "May 1968 Graffiti." Available from http://www.bopsecrets.org/CF/graffiti.htm. Berkeley, Calif., 1999. Includes a list of slogans from May 1968.

Caute, David. *The Year of the Barricades: A Journey Through 1968.* New York, 1988.

"The Chronology of 'May '68.'" Available from http://www.metropoleparis.com/1998/318/chron318.html. Paris, 1988. A good chronology of the May Events.

Ehrenreich, Barbara, and John Ehrenreich. *Long March, Short Spring: The Student Rising at Home and Abroad.* New York, 1969.

Fraser, Ronald. *1968: A Student Generation in Revolt.* London, 1988.

Institute National de l'Audiovisuel. "History and Society: May 1968." Available from http://www.ina.fr/voir_revoir/mai-68/video.en.html. Includes actual video footage of the May 1968 events.

Kurlansky, Mark. *1968: The Year that Rocked the World.* New York, 2004.

Marwick, Arthur. *The Sixties: Cultural Revolution in Britain, France, Italy, and the United States, c. 1958–c. 1974.* Oxford, U.K., 1998.

Victoria University in the University of Toronto. "Paris, May '68: Icons of Revolution." Available from http://library.vicu.utoronto.ca/exhibitions/posters/. Images from the Ecole des Beaux Arts' Atelier Populaire.

STUART J. HILWIG

MENDÈS-FRANCE, PIERRE (1907–1982), French politician.

Pierre Mendès-France was descended on his father's side from a Portuguese Jewish family that had settled in Bordeaux in the sixteenth century; his mother belonged to a Jewish family from Alsace. Although he was a victim of anti-Semitism virtually throughout his career and served as head of the French government only briefly, from 19 June 1954 to 4 February 1955, Mendès-France was one of the country's most esteemed politicians in modern times.

Some people of great ability never become prominent because circumstances do not permit it, but this was not the case with Mendès-France. Elected the youngest French deputy in 1932 after five years as a lawyer—he was barely twenty when he obtained his law degree—Mendès-France never compromised in terms of fairness and almost never on behalf of political realities. Perhaps the most significant example of his intransigence took place in 1945, when he was minister of the national economy in the government led by Charles de Gaulle. He resigned when his plan for a postwar economic reform was rejected by de Gaulle, who feared that its rigor might provoke discontent and disruption in a country already weakened by World War II.

Throughout his career, Mendès-France was particularly involved with national economic affairs, about which his competence was universally acknowledged. After World War II, he participated in a number of organizations concerned with international finance. Even after he abandoned the Radical Party, which he had joined when a young man, for the Socialists in 1960, he was skeptical regarding the Socialists' economic proposals, which he considered imprudent. But socialism for him was the beginning of political and economic democracy, and despite his own inclination for the economy, he became a pure politician.

Profoundly left-wing, secular, and republican, Mendès-France had intended to preserve the Radical Party—a centrist party originally "radical" due to its anticlericalism—along these lines. When in the late 1920s he felt the party moving to the right, he joined a group of "young turks" to return it to its leftward path. He was among those of the Radical Party most committed to the Popular Front in the mid-1930s and became undersecretary of state for the economy in the brief second government led by Léon Blum (13 March to 8 April 1938). When the Radicals deserted the Popular Front, Mendès-France found himself, not for the last time in his life, marginalized.

Mobilized in 1939, Mendès-France was one of the members of parliament who, after the French defeat, embarked on the vessel *Massilia*, hoping to pursue the war from North Africa. But the Vichy government had him arrested in Morocco, brought back to France, and imprisoned. He escaped in June 1941 and joined the Free French, serving as a pilot until 1943, when General de Gaulle appointed him finance commissioner of the French Committee for National Liberation.

After leaving the Gaullist government at war's end, Mendès-France once again found himself outside the centers of power. Although still faithful to the Radical Party, he criticized its policies and long remained isolated, until after the crucial French defeat in Indochina at Dien Bien Phu in 1954. Now he was appointed prime minister. Having refused to accept the Communists in government, he gained their lasting hostility. He succeeded in brokering the Geneva agreements with the Vietnamese in 1954, putting an end to the war in Indochina and to the French colonial presence there. Although he granted "internal autonomy" to Tunisia, he lost the case for the independence of Algiers, where an insurrection had started in November 1954. In fact, he was the victim of a heterogeneous coalition that included Communists, right-wing politicians, and pro-European members of the Mouvement Républicain Populaire (Popular Republican Movement), together with the Radicals who had not forgiven him for not supporting the Communauté Européenne de Defense (European Defense Community), a project rejected on 30 August 1954. In February 1955, at age forty-seven, Mendès-France was driven from power and would never return.

Nevertheless, he was highly popular among the general public and was vigorously supported by the new magazine *L'Express,* started by Jean-Jacques Servan-Schreiber and Françoise Giroud. Mendès-France was the symbol of the Front Républicain that won the elections in 1956. But René Coty, who had become president of the republic 1953, chose as prime minister the Socialist Guy Mollet. Mendès-France, who became Mollet's minister of state, resigned the post in disagreement on the Algerian question.

When de Gaulle returned to power in 1958 in the context of a political and constitutional crisis, Mendès-France disapproved. He viewed the general's return as undemocratic and remained a permanent and convinced opponent of the new Fifth Republic. In 1958 he lost his parliamentary seat—he represented the region of Eure—and only briefly returned to office in 1967, as a deputy from Grenoble. After playing an ambiguous role in the response to the demonstrations and civil unrest of May 1968, he again lost elected office. Mendès-France's last incursion into politics was to team up with Gaston Defferre during the presidential elections in 1969, after the resignation of de Gaulle in the wake of the events of May 1968. Winning just 5 percent of the vote demonstrated that, however eminent his public personality, he had no future in electoral politics.

Devoting himself to writing and traveling, he evinced sympathy with the renaissance of the left-wing coalition Union de la Gauche. Despite his mistrust of the Socialist François Mitterrand, who had served as his minister of the interior, Mendès-France was moved by his election to the presidency in 1981.

In all, Mendès-France's career was a singular one, and his persona and personality were unique to the era in which he lived. Perhaps just because he was a highbrow intellectual of impeccable morality, a Cassandra forever forecasting future perils, he could never find his true place in the political life of France.

See also **France; Gaulle, Charles de.**

BIBLIOGRAPHY

Bédarida, François, and Jean-Pierre Rioux, eds. *Pierre Mendès France et le mendésisme: L'expérience gouvernementale (1954–1955) et sa postérité.* Paris, 1985.

Gros, Simone. *Pierre Mendès France au quotidien.* Paris, 2004.

Lacouture, Jean. *Pierre Mendès France.* Paris, 1981.

Nicolet, Claude. *Pierre Mendès-France; ou, le métier de Cassandra.* Paris, 1959.

Rizzo, Jean-Louis. *Mendès France; ou, la rénovation en politique.* Paris, 1993.

JEAN-JACQUES BECKER

MENGELE, JOSEF (1911–1979), Nazi doctor and war criminal.

For twenty-one months Josef Mengele exercised the power of life and death over thousands of Auschwitz inmates. Nicknamed the "Angel of Death," he supervised a gas chamber at Auschwitz-Birkenau and conducted horrific pseudoscientific experiments that killed many and scarred the survivors. Testimony from Auschwitz commonly emphasizes his immaculate appearance, his whistling of arias, and his indifference to the pain of experimental subjects as well as the paradox of his occasionally apparent kindness toward Auschwitz children. With his professional ambition and commitment to National Socialist ideology, Mengele personified the evil of Auschwitz and the Third Reich.

Born 16 March 1911, Mengele lived comfortably with his wealthy, devoutly Roman Catholic, Bavarian family. Choosing an academic career, he began his studies at the University of Munich in 1930, where he also embraced National Socialist ideology. The politics of the age apparently influenced Mengele's interests; he chose to study anthropology and medicine, interested in how genetic and other manipulations might improve a race. He was awarded a PhD in 1935 and passed his state medical examination the following year. In 1937 Mengele joined a prestigious research team, headed by one of Europe's foremost geneticists, who was also a committed National Socialist, at the University of Frankfurt's Institute of Hereditary Biology and Race Research. This was his first step into elite National Socialist academic circles and toward Auschwitz. Mengele also joined the National Socialist Party in 1937 and the Schutzstaffel (SS) the next year. After a brief stint as a Wehrmacht medical officer in 1940 he transferred to the Waffen-SS, earning the Iron Cross First and Second Class on the eastern front.

In May 1943 Mengele became a camp doctor at Auschwitz, hoping to use this assignment as a stepping-stone to an academic career. He executed his duties with a flourish that impressed colleagues and terrified inmates. Shortly after his arrival he quelled a typhus epidemic by sending hundreds of inmates to the gas chambers with no apparent regard for their lives. Among their duties, the doctors selected which inmates went immediately to the gas chambers and which inmates were assigned to labor details. Unlike most of the other SS doctors, Mengele appeared to relish this responsibility, performing selections more frequently than required.

In a laboratory located in Crematorium 2, outfitted with modern equipment and staffed by inmate professionals, Mengele subjected prisoners to an array of injections and other caustic and toxic procedures in his quest to discover keys to the genetic manipulation of supposed Aryan features. Mengele particularly used twins, one serving as subject and the other the control. After the test, both twins might be fatally injected and immediately dissected to determine the impact of the test. Dyes were injected into eyes to see whether eye color could be altered. These tests, which had dubious scientific value, were conducted without any regard for the subjects themselves. Mengele also participated in the ongoing research on human sterilization, which was intended to find ways to prevent the reproduction of "undesirable" groups, thus guaranteeing the supposed racial purity of the Germans. Literally thousands of people suffered from the brutal treatments directed by Mengele; many perished.

By late 1944 Mengele's world began to collapse. The war was clearly lost, as were the doctor's hopes for a prestigious career in the Third Reich. Mengele left Auschwitz a few days before the Red Army liberated the camp in January 1945. As Germany disintegrated Mengele sought to evade capture. He was named a principal war criminal in April 1945 but successfully avoided detection in the chaos of postwar Germany by assuming the identity of another soldier.

Facing prosecution, he left Europe in 1949; family funds facilitated his escape to South America. Pursued sporadically and unsuccessfully by governments and by independent Nazi-hunters, he lived in Argentina, Paraguay, and Brazil, sometimes comfortable, sometimes fearful of capture, and sometimes in squalid circumstances. He resented the loss of the respect and recognition he thought his right as a man of science. As time passed, the circulation of stories about Auschwitz and Mengele's evasion of capture in spite of offers of substantial rewards made him seem a figure of almost mythical attributes. The actual story was mundane. Dependent upon an allowance from his family and shielded by sympathizers or hired caretakers, he was bitter, fearful, and largely isolated. Perhaps he eluded his day in court, but he lived in disgrace and exile. In 1979 Mengele suffered a stroke while swimming in the Atlantic Ocean, died, and was buried under a false name in Brazil. The mystery continued until 1985 when his body was exhumed and conclusively identified. However, some who had been subjects of his experiments refused to believe that body belonged to Mengele; he will likely always be "alive" to haunt them.

See also **Auschwitz-Birkenau; Concentration Camps; Eugenics; Nazism; SS (Schutzstaffel).**

BIBLIOGRAPHY

Aly, Götz, Peter Chroust, and Christian Pross. *Cleansing the Fatherland: Nazi Medicine and Racial Hygiene.* Translated by Belinda Cooper, foreword by Michael H. Kater. Baltimore, Md., 1994.

Astor, Gerald. *The "Last" Nazi: The Life and Times of Dr. Joseph Mengele.* New York, 1985.

Friedlander, Henry. *The Origins of Nazi Genocide: From Euthanasia to the Final Solution.* Chapel Hill, N.C., 1995.

Kater, Michael H. *Doctors under Hitler.* Chapel Hill, N.C., 1989.

Lagnado, Lucette Matalon, and Sheila Cohn Dekel. *Children of the Flames: Dr. Josef Mengele and the Untold Story of the Twins of Auschwitz.* New York, 1991.

Lifton, Robert Jay. *The Nazi Doctors: Medical Killing and the Psychology of Genocide.* New York, 1986.

Mitscherlich, Alexander, and Fred Mielke. *Doctors of Infamy: The Story of the Nazi Medical Crimes.* Translated by Heinz Norden. New York, 1949.

Posner, Gerald L., and John Ware. *Mengele: The Complete Story.* New York, 1986.

Proctor, Robert. *Racial Hygiene: Medicine under the Nazis.* Cambridge, Mass., 1988.

LARRY THORNTON

MENSHEVIKS. The Mensheviks emerged as a reluctant faction of the Russian Social Democratic Labor Party (RSDLP) after a clash between Yuli Martov and Vladimir Lenin at the party's second congress in Brussels and London in 1903. Lenin had argued that the party should be an elite, centralized band of professional revolutionaries, while Martov advocated a more open policy of membership to foster the kind of mass social democratic party found in western Europe. Martov and his supporters became known as Mensheviks ("minority group"), while Lenin and his group assumed the name Bolsheviks ("majority group"). In principle, Mensheviks argued that the RSDLP should pursue a Marxist model of an initial bourgeois revolution to be replaced at a later undefined point by a socialist revolution. The Bolsheviks argued that Russia should advance to a socialist revolution without tolerating a bourgeois, gradualist phase. Some Mensheviks, including Alexander Potresov and Peter Garvi, dedicated themselves to legal work in mass labor organizations in pursuit of the former, and were dubbed "liquidationists" by the Bolsheviks. Others, including Martov, Fyodor Dan, and Georgy Plekhanov, the "Father of Russian Marxism," advocated continuing both legal and illegal work during the especially difficult period of tsarist repression between 1907 and 1912 that forced many of them into the emigration.

Despite these differences, leading Mensheviks and Bolsheviks were political intimates, a product of the close political circles (*kruzhkovshchina*) and hothouse politics of their long periods in the emigration. Convinced of the fundamental unreadiness of Russia's working classes to take power, Martov and Dan worked to reconcile the two factions of Russian Social Democracy by appealing to more moderate Bolsheviks, notably at the party's "unification" congress in 1906. Over Lenin's objections, they managed to achieve a fragile unity in the RSDLP at the Paris plenum of January 1910. This brief unity lasted only until the divisive Prague conference in January 1912 at which Lenin in effect laid claim to the mantle of the RSDLP in the name of his own faction. Menshevik unification efforts nonetheless continued, culminating in the Brussels "unity" conference of July 1914, an attempt by the International Socialist Bureau, with the help of Martov, Plekhanov, Leon Trotsky, Pavel Axelrod, and others, to force Lenin to cooperate with the Mensheviks in a unified Russian Social Democracy.

World War I interrupted these unification efforts and exposed the fragilities of the Mensheviks. They constituted less a formal party than a loose group of like-minded individuals, who shared the belief that the workers had to be adequately prepared for revolution over a lengthy period of time. They splintered across the political spectrum over the issue of whether to support or oppose the tsarist government's prosecution of the war. The "defensists" ranged from Plekhanov's Unity (*Edinstvo*) group, which took a patriotic stance on the war, to Potresov's group of Menshevik practical workers (*praktiki*), who chose to work in mass organizations such as the war industries' committees that had been set up to help run the war. The "internationalists," including Martov and Axelrod, in Europe's émigré centers, wanted to end what they regarded as a war among capitalist powers. After the February Revolution of 1917, the Mensheviks split again over the issue of cooperation with the Provisional Government of Russia. Some, including Dan, Irakli Tsereteli, Vladimir Voitinsky, and Mikhail Skobelev, formed a separate influential group that worked together with members of the Socialist Revolutionary Party (PSR) in the network of soviets (councils) that sprang up all over Russia in the period of so-called dual power (the division of power between the Provisional Government and the Petrograd Soviet in 1917). In May, Tsereteli and Skobelev joined the newly re-formed Provisional Government, which also contained liberal members of the Constitutional Democratic (Kadet) Party. Martov's Menshevik internationalists rejected any such cooperation with nonsocialist groups inside or outside the Provisional Government, and preached an all-socialist coalition government throughout 1917.

The Mensheviks' reluctance to profile themselves as a distinct party per se exacerbated the historically weak identification of their supporters with them and perhaps the softness of their support among the broader masses in Russia. Martov and other Menshevik leaders were continually concerned about desertions and mass defections from their ranks to the Bolsheviks. Distinctions between the Bolsheviks and Mensheviks had not always been clear even to their own rank and file, for whom cooperation at the local level between Bolshevik and Menshevik organizations contrasted sharply with the intractable disagreements among their leaders who had returned from the emigration only in the course of 1917.

Curiously, the onset of Bolshevik power in October 1917, followed by the civil war, both destroyed the Mensheviks organizationally inside Soviet Russia and ensured their political survival outside it. Bolshevik repressions of their organizations began almost from the outset, and, notwithstanding a brief resurgence in their support in spring 1918 (and a short-lived Menshevik-run republic in Georgia from 1918 to 1921), Menshevik organizations were unable to mount a serious challenge to Bolshevik power. In early December 1917, the Extraordinary Congress of the RSDLP in Petrograd made Martov's internationalist group the official voice of the Mensheviks, and during the civil war Martov encouraged rank-and-file Mensheviks to fight in defense of the revolution alongside the Bolsheviks. The Mensheviks were always uncomfortable allies for the Bolsheviks, however, and Martov and Rafael Abramovich were permitted to leave Soviet Russia in late 1920, never to return. Dan, Potresov, Garvi, Grigory Aronson, Boris Nikolayevsky, and others followed them into the emigration in the early 1920s, although they would be stripped of their citizenship only in the early 1930s. In Berlin, Martov restructured the Mensheviks, setting up a Foreign Delegation of the RSDLP (Zagranichnaya delegatsiya RSDLP). When he died in 1923, Dan succeeded him as leader. The Menshevik internationalists fled the Nazis, first to Paris and later to the United States, where they continued their activities into the 1960s. They published a biweekly newspaper, *Socialist Courier* (*Sotsialistichesky vestnik*) throughout this period. As political "insiders" intimate with Russia's revolutionary origins, they mounted a sustained criticism of the Soviet Union for over forty years. They also influenced the ways in which the West conceived of the Soviet Union, helping to focus international attention on the gulag (the labor camp system), and to cement the term *totalitarian* in relation to the Soviet Union. In the heated context of the Cold War, their influence was felt in establishing the "discipline" of kremlinology, the intensely politicized and polarized approach to the study of the Soviet Union and its history.

See also **Bolshevism; Russian Revolutions of 1917.**

BIBLIOGRAPHY

Primary Sources

Shelokhaev, V. V., and S. V. Tiutiukin, eds. *Men'sheviki: Dokumenty i materialy, 1903–fevral' 1917 gg.* Moscow, 1996.

Secondary Sources

Ascher, Abraham. *Pavel Axelrod and the Development of Menshevism.* Cambridge, Mass., 1972.

Galili, Ziva. *The Menshevik Leaders in the Russian Revolution: Social Realities and Political Strategies.* Princeton, N.J., 1989.

Haimson, Leopold H., ed. *The Mensheviks: From the Revolution of 1917 to the Second World War.* Chicago, 1974.

Liebich, André. *From the Other Shore: Russian Social Democracy after 1921.* Cambridge, Mass., 1997.

FREDERICK C. CORNEY

MENTAL ILLNESS AND ASYLUMS.

By 1914 the new discipline of psychiatry was firmly established in Europe. The Continent was covered by a network of asylums and clinics that stretched from the west coast of Ireland to Russia's eastern provinces. Specialists in mental disease had formed professional organizations, publishing journals (such as Germany's *Archiv für Psychiatrie und Nervenkrankheiten*) that articulated a clear vision of the direction and purpose of the new science. Public policy and popular culture were informed by concepts such as degeneration, suggestion, and addiction that had been first articulated in psychiatric practice. It was a remarkable achievement, for the discipline of psychiatry had only emerged in the previous century as an ad hoc response to problems of legal process and welfare administration. Indeed, the subject matter of psychiatry had long been under dispute, and it was to be further confused by new political and economic demands and as novel therapies became available.

THE RISE OF THE ASYLUM

The changing subject and mission of psychiatry is demonstrated by the rise and decline of the great asylums of industrialized Europe. Upon their foundation in the early nineteenth century, they had been seen as curative institutions providing a therapeutic environment in which the deranged individual could recover his or her lost faculties. By the end of the century the massive growth in the asylums' population led many psychiatrists to reconceptualize their task. They no longer saw themselves curing individual patients; rather, they were working to preserve the health of the race and nation by isolating diseased individuals. This policy, which reflected a growing psychiatric pessimism, was underwritten by a new biological rationale: the theory of degeneration. Developed in the 1850s by the French alienists Benedict Augustin Morel (1809–1873) and Joseph Moreau de Tours (1808–1888), the theory was soon adopted by doctors and psychiatrists across Europe. Supporters such as Henry Maudsley (1835–1918) in England, Cesare Lombroso (1836–1909) in Italy, and Paul Mobius (1854–1907) and Max Nordau (1849–1923) in Germany argued that mental disorder resulted from the accumulation of inherited toxins that progressively weakened the diseased pedigrees of the race. Their position was reinforced by an increase in the asylum population, alarmist reports on the growth of crime and drunkenness in Europe's towns and cities, and new data on the failing health of potential military recruits. As the Edinburgh asylum keeper Thomas Coulston (1840–1915) argued, the threat of racial decay created a situation in which psychiatrists would have to become "the priests of the body and guardians of the physical and mental qualities of the race."

NEW CATEGORIES, NEW TREATMENTS

Given the therapeutic pessimism inherent in the doctrine of degeneration, it was unsurprising that much of the intellectual effort of European psychiatry was devoted to questions of "nosology," or the classification of disease rather than cure. The identification of different forms of mental and sexual abnormality, notably in the sexological work of Richard von Krafft-Ebing (1840–1902), created a set of intellectual categories that still inform the contemporary sense of identity. Yet this new emphasis on nosology created a plethora of competing diagnostic labels, which undermined the possibility of a unified psychiatric science. The Heidelberg psychiatrist Emil Kraepelin (1856–1926) tried to meet this confusion by arguing for a simplified model based on the long-term study of clinical outcomes rather than catalogs of mental symptoms or neurological anomalies. He reduced the nonorganic psychoses to two illnesses: manic-depressive insanity and dementia praecox. This latter category would in turn be redefined by Eugen Bleuler (1857–1939) as schizophrenia.

Kraepelin's work prioritized the patient's biography, rather than his or her pathological anatomy, as a source of clinical and diagnostic insight. And this turn to historical knowledge as the key to psychiatric practice was also reflected in contemporary developments in psychotherapy and psychodynamic psychiatry. In France, an active program of investigation into hypnosis and the generation of hysterical affects led Pierre Janet (1859–1947) to posit a dissociation (or splitting of consciousness) in response to psychological trauma. His approach was adopted and modified by psychotherapists and spiritual healers across Europe. In Vienna, Sigmund Freud (1856–1939) and Josef Breuer (1842–1945) experimented with the hypnotic recall of apparently repressed memories as a way of removing hysterical symptoms. This was to provide the foundation for Freud's later development of psychonalytic treatment. He abandoned hypnosis and instead developed the technique of free association to elicit unconscious material, arguing in *The Interpretation of Dreams* (1900) and *The Psychopathology of Everyday Life* (1901) that even the most capricious statement or action could be read as a meaningful symbol granting insight into the activities of the unconscious.

THERAPEUTIC ECLECTICISM

This mixture of clinical and literary approaches earned a wide, if sometimes critical, audience for psychoanalysis. The speculative nature of the structure imputed to the unconscious meant that Freud and his followers had to rigorously police the language and theories of the new psychotherapy. By 1914 conflicts over the sexual etiology of the neuroses had led pioneer psychoanalysts such as Alfred Adler (1870–1937) and Carl Gustav Jung (1875–1961) to break away from the Freudian movement and launch their own eclectic therapies. This flowering of new psychodynamic approaches was to continue throughout the twentieth century, although their impact on asylum psychiatry was marginal. Despite the claim that the epidemic of war neuroses in World War I helped to establish the legitimacy of psychoanalysis, it remained for the most part an elite preserve restricted to those who could enjoy the benefits of extended private consultation. When European asylum workers had the resources to deploy analytic methods, it was usually

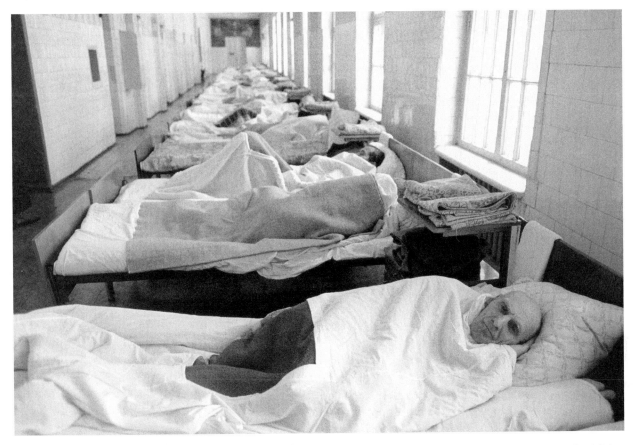

Patients in a psychiatric hospital near Moscow, 1992. Even after the fall of the Soviet Union, Eastern European hospitals lagged behind those in the West in modernizing their approach to the care and treatment of gravely ill psychiatric patients. ©PETER TURNLEY

accompanied by a mixture of physical and suggestive therapies.

Such therapeutic eclecticism was to remain characteristic of European psychiatry throughout the interwar years. The identification in 1913 of the syphilis spirochete as the infective agent in general paralysis of the insane led to a period of open-ended experimentation in which many new therapies and models of illness were developed. In 1917 the Austrian psychiatrist Julius Wagner-Jauregg (1857–1940) announced the successful treatment of neurosyphilis through the induction of malarial fever. In 1920 Jakob Klaesi (1883–1980) in Zurich used the newly developed barbiturate drugs to induce episodes of prolonged sleep to treat psychotic patients. The risks associated with this technique led the Polish neurophysiologist Manfred Sakel (1900–1957) to experiment with insulin comas, a practice that was widely imitated, particularly in Britain and Switzerland.

There was no shared theoretical basis underpinning these treatments. In 1935 the Portuguese neurologist Egas Moniz (1874–1955) claimed to have sucessfully treated obsessions and emotional disorders by surgically altering the brain's frontal lobes. In Hungary, Ladislaus Meduna (1896–1965) proposed that a biological antagonism existed between epilepsy and schizophrenia and that presence of one would lead to the elimination of the other. He used camphor (and later cardiac drugs) to induce therapeutic fits in schizophrenic patients. The apparent success of this approach was tempered by the high risk of injury experienced by the patient. In an attempt to control the severity of the fit, two Italian doctors, Ugo Cerletti (1877–1963) and Lucio Bini (1908–1964), experimented with a new technique of electrically induced convulsions (ECT). First trialed on humans in 1938, the technique has remained in use across Europe as a treatment for manic-depressive illness and depression.

PSYCHIATRIC POLITICS

The sheer variety of experimental treatments developed in interwar Europe was a reflection of some unhappy truths. Such open-ended experimentation was made possible by the lack of a widely accepted theoretical model of mental disorder and the absence of any clear agreement on the political status or rights of the patient. Indeed, illness models and patients' rights were inextricably linked. Hereditarian models of mental disorder arising out of the old doctrine of degeneration had encouraged the idea that the mentally ill were "a race apart" and as such could be subjected to new forms of control and intervention. In Germany in 1933, the Nazis passed a sterilization law, part-authored by Ernst Rudin (1874–1952), a Swiss expert in psychiatric genetics. By 1937 two hundred thousand had been sterilized. Similar laws were passed in Norway, Sweden, Denmark, Switzerland, Estonia, and Iceland and remained in place long after the end of World War II. This politicization of psychiatry and the implementation of racial employment laws encouraged a large-scale emigration of German and Austrian psychiatrists to western Europe and America. Supported, in part, by the Rockefeller Foundation, these émigrés helped to propagate new forms of phenomenological psychiatry, in which close attention was paid to the subjective experience of the patient.

During World War II, the Soviet security services (the NKVD) opened their own psychiatric hospital in Kazan, and after the war there was increased recourse to psychiatric diagnoses (in particular, "sluggish schizophrenia") as a means of controlling poltical dissent. These obvious examples of the political abuse of psychiatry raised large questions about the underlying rationale of the medical project. New forms of wartime treatment, such as the group therapies developed by British military psychiatrists, encouraged this debate. The idea that psychiatric diagnoses and treatments might help sustain mental illnesses was taken up by radical commentators across western Europe. In Italy, Francisco Basaglia (1924–1980) experimented with open communities as a means that would allow patients to escape the oppressive effects of labels and institutions. In Britain, R. D. Laing (1927–1989) and David Cooper (1931–1986) achieved considerable fame during the 1960s by arguing that mental illness was sustained by opressive social relations. This idea that society excluded the insight of the psychotic was taken up by the Dutch psychiatrist Jan Foudraine (b. 1929) and the French philosopher Michel Foucault (1926–1984), but its influence on contemporary policy and practice was limited.

Across western Europe, mental hospital populations began to fall in the early 1950s, due in part to the emergence of a new class of phenothiazine drugs and the right-wing critique of the financial costs of the welfare states. The discovery in 1952 of chlorpromazine, an antipsychotic developed by the French pharmaceutical company Rhone-Poulenc, encouraged a period of intense psychopharmocological experimentation. In 1958 the Swiss firm Geigy released imipramime, the first of the tricyclic antidepressants, onto the market. The antidepressants made possible new regimes of patient management, but they also encouraged a reconceptualization of mental illness. No longer seen as an intricate biographical problem requiring careful investigation, mental illness was presented as a chemical imbalance that could be corrected through pharmaceutical intervention. This simple model of psychopathology undermined much of the mental hospital's rationale. It was no longer needed, either as a therapeutic refuge or a eugenic solution, and mental health care began to be devolved to a number of frontline agencies: general practitioners, community psychiatrists, and psychiatric social workers. This system, pioneered in southern France during the interwar period, became dominant in Britain, France, and northern Europe during the 1960s and was taken up in Spain in the 1980s. In eastern Europe patterns of care remained more varied, with use of crib-beds and incarceration persisting long after the fall of the communist governments in Hungary, Slovakia, Estonia, and the Czech Republic.

THE END OF THE ASYLUM

The impetus for the ongoing transformation of mental health care services across Europe comes in part from the rationalizing demands of market economics, and countries such as England and Portugal have increasingly relied on the private sector in the provision of care. Yet a growing patient's advocacy movement, inspired by the examples of aid charities, has developed more global aspirations. Transnational institutions such as the European Union, media organizations, and pharmaceutical companies have created a new set of expectations that are changing the organization of European psychiatry. And these changes in psychiatric practice themselves encourage new theories and cultures of of mental health. Western Europe is beginning to emulate the American enthusiasm for antidepressant drugs, particularly the new generation of selective serotonin reuptake inhibitors—an enthusiasm that raises larger questions over the mission of psychiatry as it moves from being a remedial therapy to a technique for individual self-improvement.

See also **Psychiatry; Psychoanalysis; War Neuroses.**

BIBLIOGRAPHY

Angel, Katherine, Edgar Jones, and Michael Neve. *European Psychiatry on the Eve of War: Aubrey Lewis, the Maudsley Hospital, and the Rockefeller Foundation in the 1930s.* London, 2003. An edited version of the 1930s reports of the Anglo-Australian psychiatrist Aubrey Lewis on the state of European psychiatry.

Berrios, German E., and Roy Porter, eds. *A History of Clinical Psychiatry.* London, 1995. A useful collection on the history of individual mental illnesses.

Castel, Robert, Françoise Castel, and Anne Lovell. *The Psychiatric Society.* Translated by Arthur Goldhammer. New York, 1982. A political account of the rise of French psychiatry.

Finzsch, Norbert, and Robert Jütte. *Institutions of Confinement: Hospitals, Asylums, and Prisons in Western Europe and North America, 1500–1950.* Washington, D.C., 1996. A collection examining the disciplinary role of asylums.

Freeman, Hugh. *A Century of Psychiatry.* London, 1999. Useful collection of short essays on most aspects of twentieth-century psychiatry.

Healy, David. *The Antidepressant Era.* Cambridge, Mass., 1997. One of the best accounts of the rise of psychopharmocology.

Micale, Mark S. "The Psychiatric Body." In *Medicine in the Twentieth Century,* edited by Roger Cooter and John Pickstone, 323–346. Amsterdam, 2000. A good analysis of the main forces driving contemporary psychiatry.

Micale, Mark S., and Roy Porter, eds. *Discovering the History of Psychiatry.* Oxford, U.K., 1994. Includes useful essays on the historiography of psychiatry in Britain, France, Russia, and Germany.

Neve, Michael. "Medicine and the Mind." In *Western Medecine: An Illustrated History,* edited by Irvine Loudon, 232–263. Oxford, U.K., 1997. A fine introduction to the main themes.

Pressman, Jack. "Concepts of Mental Illness in the West." In *The Cambridge World History of Human Diseases,* edited by Kenneth F. Kiple, 59–84. Cambridge, U.K., 1993. A rich global history of the rise of psychiatry.

Shorter, Edward. *A History of Psychiatry: From the Age of the Asylum to the Age of Prozac.* New York, 1997. The most thorough historical overview available.

Weindling, Paul. *Health, Race, and German Politics between National Unification and Nazism, 1870–1945.* Cambridge, U.K., 1989.

RHODRI HAYWARD

MERLEAU-PONTY, MAURICE (1908–1961), French philosopher.

Maurice Merleau-Ponty (1908–1961) was, with Jean-Paul Sartre (1905–1980), one of the leading figures in French phenomenology and existentialism. He is best known for his account of the constitutive role of the body in perception in works such as *The Structure of Behavior* (1942) and *Phenomenology of Perception* (1945), but he also wrote and lectured on topics in biology, psychology, linguistics, anthropology, aesthetics, and politics. In 1945 he joined Simone de Beauvoir (1908–1986) and Raymond Aron (1905–1983) on the editorial staff of Sartre's journal, *Les Temps modernes.* He taught at Lyon and the Sorbonne before being elected to the Collège de France in 1952.

The most decisive influences on Merleau-Ponty's thought were the phenomenology of Edmund Husserl (1859–1938) and Martin Heidegger (1889–1976) and the Berlin school of Gestalt psychology. Like Husserl, Merleau-Ponty attempts to describe experience from a concrete first-person point of view, free of theoretical assumptions borrowed from the natural sciences. The *intentionality* (the *of*-ness or "aboutness") of perception, for instance, cannot be reduced to the causal effects of external stimuli on the inner states of an organism, for perception is always imbued with meaning for the percipient. With Heidegger, however, contrary to Husserl, Merleau-Ponty conceives of meaning and intentionality not in terms of cognition or mental representation but as modes of human existence. Experience and understanding are not private possessions of a worldless subject, but rather dimensions of what Heidegger called *being-in-the-world*. Finally, following Gestalt theorists such as Kurt Koffka (1886–1941) and Wolfgang Köhler (1887–1967), Merleau-Ponty argues that perceptual awareness consists in neither sensation nor judgment but in the skillful bodily exploration of an environment. Contemporary philosophers such as Hubert L. Dreyfus have consequently appealed to Merleau-Ponty in their critiques of cognitivism and artificial intelligence, which attempt to reduce intelligent behavior to purely formal computations performed on abstract symbols somehow represented in the mind or brain.

Merleau-Ponty was impressed and influenced by Sartre. Nevertheless, their ideas differed profoundly, both in phenomenology and in politics. Unlike Sartre, who in *Being and Nothingness* (1943) draws a sharp Cartesian distinction between the opacity of material reality and the transparency and frictionlessness of consciousness, Merleau-Ponty understands perceptual agents as *bodily subjects* fully enmeshed in the world, hence neither strictly determined nor radically free. Human perception of objects, for instance, is always essentially interwoven with the body's conditioned sense of its own position and orientation. Merleau-Ponty's last, unfinished work, *The Visible and the Invisible* (published in 1964), extends and elaborates his effort to supplant the subject-object dichotomy with an account of the "interlacing" of body and world.

Merleau-Ponty also wrote extensively about art and literature, especially the paintings of Paul Cézanne (1839–1906). In the essays "Cézanne's Doubt" and "Eye and Mind," for instance, he argues that by overcoming conventions of realism and linear perspective, and by resisting the futile and misguided effort of the impressionists to paint mere sensations, Cézanne managed to capture the concrete bodily character of vision, which is neither strictly geometrical nor brutely sensuous. People do not see data on a two-dimensional plane and then project or construct a sense of depth. Rather, because the body always already situates one in space, depth must be understood not as one

dimension among others but as the medium of all perceptual awareness, including vision.

Much of Merleau-Ponty's published writing deals with problems of theory and practice in history and politics. In what is probably his most controversial book, *Humanism and Terror* (1947), he criticizes anticommunists including Arthur Koestler (1905–1983) for ignoring the moral ambiguity of political action and state violence, in this case the Moscow Trials of the late 1930s. In the novel *Darkness at Noon* (1940), Rubashov, Koestler's fictionalized version of Nikolai Bukharin (1888–1938), cynically confesses to trumped-up charges of treason and espionage out of sheer nihilistic party discipline. According to Merleau-Ponty, the real Bukharin took the accusations seriously, pleading guilty to treason but denying the charge of espionage, thus acknowledging that at least some of his actions, whatever their motives, had indeed rendered him objectively guilty. (In fact, Koestler and Merleau-Ponty were both wrong: Bukharin's "confession" was neither voluntary nor sincere but brutally coerced, yet defiant.) Merleau-Ponty infers that communism cannot simply be condemned by appeal to liberal principles of justice, which serve to mask the systematic violence of Western capitalism and imperialism. In spite of the injustice and cruelty of Stalinism, Marxism remains the only hope, for it alone promises to make sense of history as tending rationally to the mutual recognition of a shared humanity.

Merleau-Ponty consequently became, with Sartre, one of the prime targets of Raymond Aron's anticommunist polemic *The Opium of the Intellectuals* (1955). By the 1950s, however, partly in response to the increasing obviousness of Soviet tyranny, Merleau-Ponty had grown more critical of the USSR and more skeptical of Marx's deterministic theory of history. Editorial disputes as well as disagreements with Sartre concerning Soviet aggression in Korea led to his resignation from the editorial board of *Les Temps modernes* in 1953. Whereas Sartre had become a resolute fellow traveler of the USSR, Merleau-Ponty recognized that communist oppression had robbed Marxism of its claim to historical destiny and rendered Marx's work itself one "classic" among others in the humanistic tradition. In *Adventures of the*

Dialectic (1955) Merleau-Ponty envisions a synthesis of Marxian egalitarianism and liberal skepticism, a kind of "Weberian Marxism," as an alternative to Sartre's "ultrabolshevism," which reduces the working class to an object over against the subjective will of the party.

Merleau-Ponty's contribution to contemporary thought lay as much in his efforts as an interpreter and advocate of the works of other thinkers as in his own original ideas. In *Adventures of the Dialectic,* for instance, he imbued the work of György Lukács (1885–1971) with new relevance under the now familiar rubric of "Western Marxism." He also played a key role in the emergence of structuralism by introducing the semiotic theories of Ferdinand de Saussure (1857–1913) to younger scholars including Jacques Lacan (1901–1981), Michel Foucault (1926–1984), and Jacques Derrida (1930–2004). More recently his influence has been felt among theorists of perception in analytic philosophy and in the cognitive and neurosciences.

See also **France; Sartre, Jean-Paul.**

BIBLIOGRAPHY

Primary Sources

Aron, Raymond. *The Opium of the Intellectuals.* 1957. Edited by D. J. Mahoney and H. C. Mansfield. New Brunswick, N.J., 2001.

Merleau-Ponty, Maurice. *Phenomenology of Perception.* Translated by Colin Smith. London, 1962.

———. *The Structure of Behavior.* Translated by Alden L. Fisher. Boston, 1963.

———. "Cézanne's Doubt." In *Sense and Non-Sense,* translated by Hubert L. Dreyfus and Patricia Allen Dreyfus. Evanston, Ill., 1964.

———. "Eye and Mind." In *The Primacy of Perception and Other Essays on Phenomenological Psychology, the Philosophy of Art, History and Politics,* edited by James M. Edie. Evanston, Ill., 1964.

———. *The Visible and the Invisible.* Translated by Alphonso Lingis. Evanston, Ill., 1968.

———. *Humanism and Terror: An Essay on the Communist Problem.* Translated by John O'Neill. Boston, 1969.

———. *Adventures of the Dialectic.* Translated by Joseph Bien. Evanston, Ill., 1973.

Koestler, Arthur. *Darkness at Noon.* Translated by Daphne Hardy. New York, 1941.

Sartre, Jean-Paul. *Being and Nothingness: An Essay on Phenomenological Ontology.* Translated by Hazel E. Barnes. New York, 1956.

Secondary Sources

Carman, Taylor. *Merleau-Ponty.* New York and London, forthcoming.

Carman, Taylor, and Mark B. N. Hansen, eds. *The Cambridge Companion to Merleau-Ponty.* Cambridge, U.K., and New York, 2005.

Dreyfus, Hubert L. *What Computers Still Can't Do: A Critique of Artificial Reason.* Cambridge, Mass., 1992.

Judt, Tony. *Past Imperfect: French Intellectuals, 1944–1956.* Berkeley, Calif., 1992.

Stewart, Jon, ed. *The Debate between Sartre and Merleau-Ponty.* Evanston, Ill., 1998.

TAYLOR CARMAN

MESSIAEN, OLIVIER (1908–1992), French composer.

Olivier Eugéne Prosper Charles Messiaen was born on 10 December 1908 in Avignon. From 1919 to 1930 he studied at the Conservatoire in Paris and graduated with first prize for piano accompaniment, organ, improvisation, counterpoint, and musical composition. In 1931 Messiaen was appointed organist at La Trinité in Paris, a position he retained for decades. In 1936, along with Jean Yves Daniel-Lésur, Yves Baudrier, and André Jolivet, Messiaen formed La Jeune France (Young France), a group of composers whose purpose was to reestablish humanism and sincerity in music (reacting to neoclassicism). He also composed poetry, and with a few exceptions, most of his vocal music for solo voice or chorus sets his own poetry, which strongly resembles the surrealist poetry of Paul Éluard (pen name of Eugène Grindel, 1895–1952). Messiaen saw colors whenever he heard music, a condition called synesthesia or chromaphonia. In 1932 he married the violinist and composer Claire Delbos, who died in 1959. In 1962 he married the pianist Yvonne Loriod, a former student. He was a member of the French Institute, the Academy of Beaux Arts Bavière of Berlin, Santa Cecilia of Rome, and the American Academy of Arts and Letters. Messiaen began his career as a professor of music in 1936, teaching sight-reading at the École Normale de

Musique and improvisation at the Schola Cantorum. In 1942 he became professor of harmony at the Conservatoire de Paris. In 1943 in the home of Guy-Bernard Delapierre he taught several students who would later become well-known: Serge Nigg, Maurice Le Roux, Pierre Boulez, and Yvonne Loriod. In 1947 a special class in music analysis was created for him at the Conservatoire. In 1966 he became professor of composition; his students included Pierre Henry (French), Karlheinz Stockhausen (German), Guy Reibel (Belgian), William Albright (American), Luigi Nono (Italian), and Iannis Xenakis (Greek/French). Authors of books, essays, and dissertations on Messiaen include former students: Harry Halbreich, Alain Périer, Larry Peterson, Pierrette Mari, and Michèle Reverdy. Composers attracted to his classes include Peter Maxwell Davies, Mikis Theodorakis, György Kurtág, and William Elden Bolcom.

After he was mobilized as a soldier in 1939, Messiaen was taken prisoner in 1940 and passed his captivity in Stalag VIIIA, at Görlitz in Silesia. While there, he composed the *Quatuor pour la fin du temps* for himself and three fellow prisoners: Henri Akoka, Étienne Pasquier, and Jean Le Boulaire. Messiaen commented later that when he was a prisoner his daily diet was water and one boiled egg per day and his dress in the bitter cold conditions consisted of a tattered green jacket and pants with wooden shoes. He said the lack of nourishment stimulated colored hallucinations. He saw halos and strange swirls of color.

His interesting and large variety of compositional techniques include his seven modes of limited transposition, his transcriptions of bird song for melodic material and his organization of parts into "three persons" (an idea taken from Shakespeare where one part remains static, and another progressively increases while a third progressively decreases in activity), communicable language (a technique of applying letters of the alphabet to particular pitches and rhythmic values), what he called his "Chord of Resonance" and "Chord of the Dominant," and totally serial music (in *Mode de valeurs et d'intensité* [1949] he created rows of pitches, rhythmic values, articulations, and dynamics). His totally serial technique, developed in 1948–1949, was the first attempt in Europe to serialize more than pitches.

His most significant contribution to music is found in his variety of rhythmic techniques. His vast array of rhythmic practices include "added values," rhythmic cells, fifteenth-century Hindu deci-tâlas (North Indian), Carnatic patterns (South Indian), Greek poetic feet, his interpretation of medieval ligatures and neumes, "rythmes non-retrogrades" (palindromic patterns), isorhythm, "interversion" and "permutation," "chromatic" rhythmic sequences, extremely slow tempi (*Le banquet celeste*, 1928, or *O Sacrum Convivium*, 1937). Early techniques appear in his treatise, *Technique de mon language musical* (1944; *Technique of My Musical Language*, 1971–1972). Messiaen's mammoth treatise on rhythm, on which he worked most of his life, is being published posthumously in a projected seven volumes as *Traité de rythme, de couleur, et d'ornithologie* (first volume published in 2004).

Messiaen often assigned titles that illustrate the mysteries of Christ or other aspects of Christian beliefs. In fact, his religious beliefs were central to his existence as a man and as a composer. His many commentaries about his beliefs, which appear as part of many of his published works as well as in several published interviews, reflect mysticism in the Roman Catholic tradition. Messiaen's spiritual and poetical outlook affected his choice of titles, his texts, and the form of his compositions. His vision of the world was governed by religious meditation, the sublimation of love, escape from the confines of time, and an intimate communion with nature. Messiaen's early concern for religion reflects the influence of his father, Pierre, who was a devout Catholic. In response to a reporter's question, Messiaen commented that his faith sustained him and that he was a Catholic composer. He stated that all of his works, whether religious or not, are documents of faith glorifying the mystery of Christ.

Messiaen's work is notable for his use of unusual numbers of movements: nine in *La nativité du Seigneur* (1935), ten in *Turangalîla-Symphonie* (1946–1948), eighteen in *Livre du Saint Sacrement* (1984), and twenty in *Vingt regards sur l'enfant-Jésus* (1944). His longest work is an opera that lasts more than four hours (*Saint-François d'Assise*, 1975–1983). His first published work—*Le banquet céleste*—was composed when he was seventeen. His last two works are *Éclairs sur l'au-delà* (1988–1992) and *Concert à quatre* (1990–1991); the latter was discovered incomplete by Loriod after his death.

See also **Boulez, Pierre; Catholicism; Modernism; Theodorakis, Mikis.**

BIBLIOGRAPHY

Primary Sources

Messiaen, Olivier. *Technique de mon langage musical.* Paris, Leduc, 1944. Also published as *The Technique of My Musical Language.* Translated by John Satterfield. Paris, 1956.

Secondary Sources

Buhn, Siglind, ed. *Messiaen's Language of Mystical Love.* New York, 1998.

Griffiths, Paul. *Olivier Messiaen and the Music of Time.* London and Boston, 1985.

Hill, Peter, ed. *The Messiaen Companion.* London and Boston, 1995.

Johnson, Robert Sherlaw. *Messiaen.* Berkeley, Calif., 1975.

Morris, David. *Olivier Messiaen: A Comparative Bibliography of Material in the English Language.* Belfast, 1991.

LARRY PETERSON

METAXAS, IOANNIS (1871–1941), Greek general and dictator.

Ioannis Metaxas (1871–1941) was a Greek general, statesman, and dictator. Born on the island of Ithaca on 12 April 1871, he graduated from the Military Academy in 1890. In the Greek-Turkish war of 1897 he served in the staff of the heir to the throne, Constantine. With the support of Constantine he went to Berlin to continue his military studies (1899–1903), and when he returned to Greece took part in the reorganization of the army. When World War I broke out in 1914, he was second in command in the general staff, and during the dispute between Prime Minister Eleutherios Venizelos (1864–1936) and King Constantine (r. 1913–1917 and 1920–1922), Metaxas, promoted to chief in 1915, sided with the latter and resigned. Following the flight of the king in 1917 Metaxas went to Italy (June 1917–November 1920). When the royalists came to power in 1920 he returned to Greece. A staunch royalist with close ties to King Constantine, he nevertheless voiced his opposition to the king's plans for a Greek military campaign in Asia Minor. He foresaw the danger of a disastrous defeat, which happened in August 1922 and resulted in the expulsion of 1.3 million Greeks from Turkey.

In 1922 Metaxas moved into politics and founded the Freethinkers' Party. In the 1926 election his party won fifty-four seats in the parliament but it did not repeat that success in the subsequent elections. In the 1936 election he polled only 4 percent and elected seven deputies. That election produced also a political stalemate because none of the two major political blocs (royalists and republicans) had the majority. In March 1936 King George II (r. 1922–1923 and 1935–1947) appointed Metaxas minister of war, and when the prime minister, Constantine Demertzis (1876–1936), died, the king appointed Metaxas as prime minister on 13 April 1936. On 4 August 1936 General Metaxas, using as a pretext a general strike that was scheduled for the next day, declared a state of emergency, dissolved the parliament, and suspended articles of the constitution that guaranteed fundamental civil liberties. Metaxas's dictatorship (1936–1941) was the result of long period of political instability, the tendency of the political establishment to accept authoritarian solutions, and a reaction to the emergency of a militant labor movement.

The "Fourth of August Regime," as the dictatorship was called, resembled other interwar authoritarian regimes, but it was very different from Italian fascism or German Nazism. There was no mass fascist movement or party despite the considerable efforts of Metaxas to create one through the foundation of the National Youth Organization (EON). With the EON the dictator sought to create a force loyal to the regime, and because its membership was low, the enrollment of the young became compulsory after 1939. At the same time the EON reflected Metaxas's idea about the Greek society of the future: disciplined, militant, nationalist, and non-individualist. Metaxas's dictatorship borrowed elements from the Fascist political culture, like the ideology of the "Third Hellenic Civilization" (Metaxas's rejuvenated Greece as a heir and a synthesis of ancient Greece and Byzantium), the systematic propaganda, the fascist salute, the short-lived Labor Battalions, and the cult of leadership (Metaxas presented himself as "First Worker," "First Peasant," "National Father").

Metaxas also shared with other interwar dictators antiparliamentarianism and anticommunism and a well-organized police force to repress his political opponents. Bourgeois political leaders who protested against the dictatorship were arrested and banished. The Communist Party in Greece eventually ceased to exist because most of its members were arrested, tortured, imprisoned, and forced to renounce their political ideas and their comrades. However, the regime was not based only on repression. The dictator, in an effort to gain the support of the lower classes, took important measures like the settlement of peasants' debts, the arbitration of labor disputes, and the establishment of the Social Security Administration (IKA).

The dictatorship was not very popular and the lack of political and social constituency that a fascist movement could have furnished made Metaxas dependent on King George II to remain in power. King George II was much more powerful than Metaxas because he enjoyed the support of the army and Great Britain. The fact that the king, although he could, did not try to reconstitute democracy and consented to the dictatorship, discredited monarchy and had a significant impact on Greek politics in the 1940s.

When World War II broke out Metaxas hoped to keep Greece out of the war without jeopardizing the relations with its traditional ally Great Britain. Benito Mussolini (1883–1945) wanted to show Adolf Hitler (1889–1945) that Italy was an equally victorious partner and decided to invade Greece. On 28 October 1940 Italy issued an ultimatum that Metaxas, reflecting the popular mood, rejected. The Italian campaign proved to be ill fated and by mid-November the Greek army had pushed back the Italians and had advanced into Albania. The Greek army, however, failed to deliver a decisive victory, and in December there was a military deadlock. Ioannis Metaxas died on 29 January 1941, and on 6 April 1941 the Germans began their offensive against Greece.

See also **Greece.**

BIBLIOGRAPHY

Primary Sources

Metaxas, Ioannis. *Logoi kai skepseis.* Athens, 1990.

Secondary Sources

Higham, Robin, and Veremis, Thanos, eds. *The Metaxas Dictatorship. Aspects of Greece, 1936–1940.* Athens, 1993.

Vatikiotis, P. J. *Popular Autocracy in Greece, 1936–41: A Political Biography of General Ioannis Metaxas.* London, 1998.

POLYMERIS VOGLIS

MICHNIK, ADAM (b. 1946), Polish historian, writer, and political thinker.

Adam Michnik became a leader of the March 1968 student movement for free speech in Warsaw—the beginning, as he put it, of his generation's road to freedom. Expelled from Warsaw University and sentenced to three years in prison, he was released after a year and a half as the result of an amnesty. Banned from the university, he worked for two years as a welder in the Rosa Luxemburg Bulb Factory before becoming a personal secretary to the distinguished writer Antoni Slonimski. In response to a massive government imprisonment of protesting workers from Ursus and Radom in 1976, Michnik co-founded the Committee for the Defense of Workers (KOR), the first successful attempt to institutionalize an initiative of the dissident initiative intelligentsia to assist imprisoned workers and their families. Michnik and the KOR benefited from fortuitous timing: the organization was established one year after the communist countries had signed the Helsinki Agreements on Security and Cooperation in Europe, which included a key chapter on rights and fundamental freedoms.

The language of rights empowered the thinking and activities of the democratic opposition (Michnik argued that people should behave as though they lived in a free country) and encouraged initiatives aimed at breaking the state monopoly on information, education, and the dissemination of prohibited literature. His classic 1976 essay, *The New Evolutionism,* articulates the strategies for creating and winning the spaces of freedom. The initial KOR activities led to the emergence of a clandestine system of printing and circulating independent periodicals and books. Michnik was an editor of and a frequent contributor to some of the most popular publications (*Biuletyn Informacyjny, Krytyka, Zapis*). One of the organizers of the Flying University, another clandestine structure independent of the state, he taught courses in private apartments on silenced aspects of Polish history. His 1977 book *The Church, the Left, and Dialogue* laid the groundwork for an alliance between the secular intelligentsia and the only autonomous institution in communist Poland, the Catholic Church. In 1980 Michnik became one of the key advisors to the trade union Solidarity, which emerged as a result of an agreement between the striking Gdansk shipyard workers and the communist authorities. Solidarity—with its principles of democratic self-governance, institutional pluralism, respect for the dignity of the individual, and citizens' agency—aimed at challenging the state's alleged monopoly on truth and was the ultimate expression of society's capacity for self-organization under communism. Solidarity was the alternative society that Michnik had called for and a model example of what was eventually labeled civil society.

The need for dialogue, negotiations, and—within limits—compromise, is a key theme in Michnik's writings, re-emerging with particular force after the imposition of martial law and the de-legalization of Solidarity in December 1981. Although hardly a pacifist, while imprisoned under martial law (altogether he spent over six years in communist prisons) he argued for a self-limiting revolution, renouncing revolutionary violence. His program, formed in response to the experience of totalitarianism, is that of a liberal, whose primary commitment is to freedom, to reducing coercion by an omnipotent state, to restoring individual initiatives on behalf of the public good, to creating conditions for the exercise of human rights, and to encouraging and cultivating pluralism.

His idea of achieving change through dialogue, through "replacing the logic of revolution by the logic of negotiation," turned into reality in April 1989, when the historic roundtable talks between the government (still holding dictatorial, although weakening, power), and Solidarity (still illegal but widely supported) were successfully completed. Michnik, one of the key actors in the negotiations, subsequently co-founded and became editor in chief of *Gazeta Wyborcza*, the largest daily in East and Central Europe, which he designed as a forum for major debates on the democratic transformation and a key site for general education about democracy. He introduced to the larger public his mentors: Hannah Arendt, Leszek Kolakowski, Czeslaw Miłosz, and Jacek Kuron, as well as such thinkers as Michel Foucault, Jürgen Habermas, and Jacques Derrida. His ardent writings—which sometimes divided his own admirers—have focused on the perils of de-communization, the dangers of nationalism, and the fundamentalist and populist temptations within new democracies. A passionate advocate of the region's accession to NATO and the European Union, he exposed Poland's major corruption scandal, known as Rywingate, involving an attempt to bribe *Gazeta Wyborcza* and a possible governmental cover-up, leading to parliamentary investigations that became a political watershed in post-1989 democratic Poland.

See also **Arendt, Hannah; Dissidence; Intelligentsia; Liberalism; Miłosz, Czesław; Poland; Solidarity.**

BIBLIOGRAPHY

Primary Sources

Michnik, Adam. *Letters from Prison and Other Essays.* Translated by Maya Latynski. Berkeley, Calif., 1985.

———. *Z dziejów honoru w Polsce: Wypisy wiezienne.* Paris, 1985.

———. *The Church and the Left.* Translated by David Ost. Chicago, 1993.

———. *Letters from Freedom: Post-Cold War Realities and Perspectives.* Translated by Jane Cave. Berkeley, Calif., 1998.

Michnik, Adam, Józef Tischner, and Jacek Zakowski. *Miedzy Panem a Plebanem.* Warsaw, 1995.

Secondary Sources

Katznelson, Ira. *Liberalism's Crooked Circle: Letters to Adam Michnik.* Princeton, N.J., 1998.

Schell, Jonathan. *The Unconquerable World: Power, Nonviolence, and the Will of the People.* New York, 2003.

Tismaneanu, Vladimir. *Reinventing Politics: Eastern Europe from Stalin to Havel.* New York, 1992.

ELZBIETA MATYNIA

MIES VAN DER ROHE, LUDWIG

(1886–1969), modernist architect.

Ludwig Mies van der Rohe is widely acknowledged as one of the founding fathers of a distinctive twentieth-century architecture, alongside such architects as Le Corbusier and Frank Lloyd Wright. The architect's extensive career covered more than six decades (1905–1969) in Germany and the United States, with approximately thirty years in Berlin and another thirty in Chicago. Mies van der Rohe commanded enormous respect for his rigorous approach to building problems, which he viewed as a series of interrelated material, structural, and spatial concerns. His avant-garde German projects introduced asymmetrical, dynamic compositions, shifting wall planes, and flowing, "universal" spaces that emphasized interior volume over exterior mass. In America his work achieved worldwide recognition in the 1950s and 1960s for its introduction of a monumental, dignified structural vocabulary for steel and glass high-rise architecture and a series of dramatic, open pavilions.

Born Ludwig Mies on 27 March 1886 in Aachen, Germany, the young Mies was educated in part by his father, a stonemason, and at a local high school and trade school. Mies augmented practical building experience in Aachen with drafting and design work for the architect Bruno Paul (1874–1968) in Berlin, for whom he worked between 1905 and 1907. After completing his first independent commission for a single-family house in 1907, Mies accepted a position in the prestigious office of the Berlin architect Peter Behrens (1868–1940) in 1908. Behrens, Germany's most celebrated architect before World War I, was at the height of his creative output as chief designer for Emil Rathenau's electrical conglomerate, the AEG. Mies's experiences with Paul and Behrens familiarized him with the Prussian classicism of the early-nineteenth-century architect Karl Friedrich Schinkel (1781–1841).

After marrying Ada Bruhn in 1913, the architect adopted the name "Rohe" from his mother's side of the family to become "Mies van der Rohe." Bruhn bore him three daughters between 1914 and 1917, and the couple separated in 1921. In Weimar-era Berlin the architect joined progressive architectural groups, helped edit the short-lived avant-garde journal *G*, and worked closely with the talented Berlin interior designer Lilly Reich. Inspired by such avant-garde movements as Russian constructivism and the Dutch neoplasticism of Theo van Doesburg, Mies van der Rohe attracted attention in the early 1920s by exhibiting a series of provocative, large-scale drawings (some as tall as eight feet) for five theoretical, unbuilt projects. The best-known of these, produced in 1921 and 1922, were for startlingly original conceptions of irregularly shaped high-rise buildings. Mies van der Rohe emphasized the soaring verticality of these high rises through dramatically rendered perspective views and transparent skins of glass. His unrealized 1921 proposal for a high rise on Berlin-Friedrichstrasse, with its crystalline facades and concrete floor plates, has been called the most influential unbuilt building in the history of twentieth-century modern architecture.

By the late 1920s, Mies van der Rohe had solidified his reputation as a leading architect of Germany's "Neues Bauen" (New Building) with three accomplishments: the Deutscher Werkbund appointed him to oversee the construction of the polemical international exhibition, "The Dwelling," in Stuttgart in 1927; the German government selected him to design what became his tour de force "Barcelona pavilion" in 1928–1929; and Walter Gropius backed his application to become the third director of the Bauhaus school between 1930 and 1933. After leaving Nazi Germany in 1938 for Chicago, Mies van der Rohe accepted the directorship of the Armour Institute (the Illinois Institute of Technology after 1940), which he held until 1958. From his base in Chicago the architect produced such paradigmatic designs as the twin apartment towers on Chicago's Lakeshore Drive (1951) and, with Philip Johnson, the Seagram Building on New York's Park Avenue (1958). His best-known open-span pavilion designs of this time are the jewel-like Farnsworth House in Plano, Illinois (1951); the S. R. Crown Hall architecture building on the campus he designed for IIT between 1939 and 1956; and the New National Gallery in Berlin (1967).

Understanding architecture as both a response to and a reflection of its epoch, Mies van der Rohe capitalized on the comparative availability of steel in the United States to perfect a building art of disciplined structural grids, modular steel frames, and elegant materials and detailing. His lifelong

The pavilion for the German exhibit at the International Art Exhibition in Barcelona, designed by Mies van der Rohe in 1929. ©FRANCESCO VENTURI/CORBIS

preference for opulent materials such as onyx, travertine, and chrome alienated him from some of the more socially minded European architects of the 1920s. By the 1960s in America, Mies van der Rohe's unwavering approach to building and his commissions from powerful corporate interests prompted disapproval from a younger generation of architects. This disapproval grew amid the profession's nascent postmodern reconsideration of historical form and its reawakening interest in architectural context. Mies van der Rohe was criticized somewhat unfairly for creating forms that inspired countless imitative yet far more cheaply built speculative corporate office buildings throughout the industrialized world. No other twentieth-century architect, in fact, so successfully dramatized the possibilities of pure modern form as an expression of meticulously handled structure and materials.

See also **Architecture; Bauhaus.**

BIBLIOGRAPHY

Lambert, Phyllis, ed. *Mies in America*. New York, 2001.

Neumeyer, Fritz. *The Artless Word: Mies van der Rohe on the Building Art*. Translated by Mark Jarzombek. Cambridge, Mass., 1991.

Riley, Terence, and Barry Bergdoll, eds. *Mies in Berlin*. New York, 2001.

Schulze, Franz. *Mies van der Rohe: A Critical Biography*. Chicago, 1985.

Tegethoff, Wolf. *Mies van der Rohe: The Villas and Country Houses*. Edited by William Dyckers. Translated by Russell M. Stockman. New York, 1985.

JOHN V. MACIUIKA

MIHAILOVIĆ, DRAGOLJUB (1893–1946), Serbian soldier.

Dragoljub (Draža) Mihailović was born on 27 March 1893 in Ivanjica, Serbia, and died 17 July 1946 in Belgrade, Yugoslavia. A veteran of the First World War, he served as a colonel in the Yugoslav army at the outbreak of the Second World War.

CHETNIKS

During the battle against the invading Nazis in April 1941, Mihailović avoided direct confrontation with the Germans, retreating instead to the west Serbian uplands, where he organized and became leader of a Serbian nationalist guerrilla resistance movement. With headquarters at Ravna Gora, the movement was officially known first as the Ravna Gora movement and later the Yugoslav Army in the Homeland. However, it was more popularly known as the Chetniks, a name derived from the Serbian and Macedonian guerrilla bands that had opposed Ottoman rule, and more recently from guerrillas of the First World War and local militias under King Alexander Karadjordjević's dictatorship.

Mihailović's Chetnik movement was built out of traditional Serbian nationalist forces, supporting the Karadjordjević dynasty and maintaining links with the Serbian Orthodox Church. The Chetniks' ultimate aim was to surface as the dominant power in a postwar Yugoslavia to bring about the restoration of the Karadjordjević dynasty and the creation of a Great Serbia within a Great Yugoslavia, once the occupying armies were defeated and the quisling governments fell. The primary obstacle to this goal was the communist resistance movement, the Partisans. The Chetnik forces, which initially numbered around ten thousand, fought primarily in Montenegro, Herzegovina, and areas of the Independent State of Croatia. The Chetniks initially attempted to coordinate resistance with the communist Partisans. However, the Partisans favored a far more aggressive strategy in fighting the occupiers, including the provocation of German reprisals to swell their own ranks, whereas Mihailović, whose forces were not numerous, not united, and not sufficiently armed, favored restraint and avoided large-scale fighting with the superior German forces. The differences in strategy, ideology, and ultimate postwar aims between the Chetniks and Partisans led to their split in September 1941, and the two resistance movements began to war with each other in addition to fighting the foreign occupiers. In

October 1941, Mihailović clandestinely turned to the German occupying powers to obtain the necessary military support he needed to fight the Partisans, only to be rebuffed by the Germans at a meeting with the chief German spokesman of the plenipotentiary commanding general in Serbia, who did not want Mihailović's cooperation, but his surrender. In fact, in December 1941, the Germans had launched the unsuccessful Operation Mihailović, aimed at capturing the Chetnik leader and breaking up his headquarters in Ravna Gora.

The Chetniks also allied themselves with the Italians against the communist forces, successfully driving them out of Montenegro in late 1941. In return for collaborating with the Italian forces, the Chetniks received arms, food, and pay. At this stage, the Chetniks were supported still by the British and American allies, as well as the Yugoslav government-in-exile in London, which named Mihailović minister of the army, navy, and air force in January 1942, and promoted the colonel to chief of the Supreme Command of the Yugoslav Army in the Homeland in June 1942, in order to officially reflect his status as the first successful resistance leader in Yugoslavia. British propaganda, which exaggerated the story of Mihailović's resistance to the Nazi occupiers, further contributed to Mihailović's heroic standing.

In June 1942, Mihailović relocated the Chetnik headquarters to Montenegro. The Chetniks continued to fight in Herzegovina and Montenegro under the Italian umbrella. During their battles, the Chetniks used mass terror against their enemies, which included counterterror against Croats in areas where the Ustaše had used terror against Serbs; retaliation against the Muslim population in Bosnia and Herzegovina and Sandjak for their cooperation with Austro-Hungarian forces during the First World War and the Ustaše in 1941; and terror against the Partisans, their principle enemy, which was often reciprocated. A series of military defeats to the Partisans in Herzegovina in March–April 1943 marked a turning point in Mihailović's fortunes, causing him to lose a number of followers to the Partisans and to return his headquarters and force of fifty thousand to Serbia in June 1943. Furthermore, in the months leading up to their capitulation in September 1943, the Italians ceased aid and protection to the Chetniks and even disarmed many units.

When the Germans replaced the Italians in Montenegro in the fall of 1943, the Chetniks did not enjoy the same status or privileges with the Axis Powers as they had under the Italians. The Germans had supported the quisling regime in Serbia, led by Milan Nedić, with whom the Chetniks generally did not have harmonious relations. Nedić disapproved of Mihailović's initial cooperation with the Partisans and resistance activities against the Germans. When the Chetniks broke with the Partisans, however, Nedić reached out to Mihailović. Their relations then passed through various phases throughout the war, remaining largely ambiguous. Some pro-Chetnik members of Nedić's regime supplied Mihailović with intelligence, money, and a small amount of arms received from the Germans. Central in the relations between Nedić and Mihailović were considerations of the posts they would hold in the postwar period. Although they agreed that the Partisans could not emerge as the dominant power at the end of the war, they could not agree among themselves who should rule. Nonetheless, in autumn 1943, Chetnik commanders concluded collaborationist agreements, or a so-called armistice, with the Nazis. Some Chetnik leaders had made contact with the Germans even prior to their arrival in Montenegro in 1943. This German recognition of the Chetniks, which undermined the Nedić regime and caused it to lose many members to the Chetniks, was an acknowledgement of Mihailović's strength and Nedić's weakness in influencing the Serbian population at that point in the war.

Mihailović also had the support of politicians from traditional political parties in Serbia, who shared his interest in counteracting the threat of the communist Partisans seizing power after the war. Mihailović and the Chetniks, together with members of these parties, met at a congress in January 1944 in a village in western Serbia and established the multinational Yugoslav Democratic Union and declared that the postwar Yugoslav state would be a federal state of Serbs, Croats, and Slovenes. However, at this point, having essentially lost the support of the Allied Powers, the members of the congress were not in a position to decide the fate of the postwar state. In May 1944, the Allied Powers fully switched their support from Mihailović to the Partisan leader, Tito (Josip Broz), primarily because they did not deem the Chetnik movement to be effective enough, and also because they had received reports of Chetnik collaboration with the Nazis. In fact, the British Special Operation Executive had established direct relations with the Partisan Supreme Headquarters already in May 1943. By June 1944 Mihailović lost both his posts as minister and chief of Supreme Command. At the end of the war, Mihailović retreated with about twelve thousand of his men. He was captured by the Partisans on 12 March 1946, and put on trial for treason and collaboration with the Nazis. Mihailović was found guilty and sentenced to death, and was executed in Belgrade on 17 July 1946.

See also **Bosnia-Herzegovina; Guerrilla Warfare; Montenegro; Partisan Warfare; Ustaše; Yugoslavia.**

BIBLIOGRAPHY

Committee for a Fair Trial for Gen. Draza Mihailovich, Commission of Inquiry. *Patriot or Traitor: The Case of General Mihailovich: Proceedings and Report of the Commission of Inquiry of the Committee for a Fair Trial for Draja Mihailovich.* Stanford, Calif., 1978.

Milazzo, Matteo J. *The Chetnik Movement and the Yugoslav Resistance.* Baltimore, Md., 1975.

Roberts, Walter. *Tito, Mihailović, and the Allies, 1941–1945.* New Brunswick, N.J., 1973.

Tomasevich, Jozo. *The Chetniks.* Stanford, Calif., 1975.

———. *War and Revolution in Yugoslavia, 1941–1945: Occupation and Collaboration.* Stanford, Calif., 2001.

Trew, Simon. *Britain, Mihailović, and the Chetniks, 1941–42.* New York, 1998.

Wheeler, Mark. *Britain and the War for Yugoslavia, 1940–1943.* Boulder, Colo., 1980.

JOVANA L. KNEŽEVIĆ

MILOŠEVIĆ, SLOBODAN (1941–2006), Serbian leader and accused war criminal.

Slobodan Milošević, the most prominent of the defendants at the International Criminal Tribunal for the Former Yugoslavia, was born in Požarevac, in Serbia, on 20 August 1941. He graduated from Belgrade's Faculty of Law (1964), and joined the League of Communists of Yugoslavia (LCY). Milošević made his early career as a technocrat, holding important posts in industry and banking in Serbia. He owed his advancement to Ivan Stambolić

(1936–2000), his political mentor and bosom friend from university days. Stambolić rose through the hierarchy of the League of Communists of Serbia (LCS) to become its president, and when he stepped down in 1986 he secured the election of Milošević as his successor in the top post. In 1987 Milošević destroyed the career of Stambolić in an act of personal and political betrayal. Milošević was sent to Priština, the capital of Kosovo, where the majority ethnic Albanian population had for years been simmering in revolt against Belgrade. The cause of his visit was a mass demonstration by Kosovo Serbs against alleged persecution aimed at forcing them to leave. Milošević was supposed to calm the situation. Instead, he stepped forward in an open show of support for the crowd, and from this moment on presented himself as the champion of Serb interests within the communist federation. Riding on a tide of nationalist populism, Milošević launched an "antibureaucratic revolution," mass meetings whipped up to intimidate opposition, supported by hysterical campaigns in the mass media and by a large police force. In 1989 Kosovo and Vojvodina, the two autonomous provinces within Serbia, were stripped of the constitutional powers conferred on them by Tito (Josip Broz, 1892–1980) in 1974 and subjected to direct rule from Belgrade.

Slovenia and Croatia reacted by paralyzing the workings of federal government, effectively killing off the LCY at its aborted Fourteenth Congress in January 1990. By April 1992 the disintegration of Yugoslavia was in full spate. Milošević now ruled the rump Federal Republic of Yugoslavia (Serbia and Montenegro), and Sarajevo was under siege by Serb forces that quickly acquired an evil reputation as they overran three-quarters of Bosnia. Milošević decimated Tito's professional, constitutionalist officer corps by means of repeated purges. The Yugoslav Army in Croatia, and its offshoot, the Bosnian Serb Army, were frequently involved in joint operations with infamous paramilitary units, gangsters greedy for booty and with an utter contempt for international law, and the rot spread to the regular units. The Western powers imposed drastic sanctions, bringing the economy to its knees—inflation hit 286 billion percent in 1993. Milošević was forced to withdraw his active support for the rebellious Serbs in Bosnia-Herzegovina and Croatia, and won limited relief from sanctions by

cooperating with international plans for peace in Bosnia, which came to fruition in the Dayton Agreements of December 1995. However, he then escalated the pressure on the ethnic Albanians in Kosovo, in a campaign of "pacification" that provoked massive NATO airstrikes in the name of humanitarian intervention. After seventy-eight days of continuous NATO bombing of targets in Kosovo and Serbia proper, all Serb forces were pulled out of Kosovo unconditionally (10 June 1999).

Milošević is commonly called a dictator, but the epithet does not explain the basis of his power. In 1990 Serbia moved to a multiparty system. Milošević had to submit himself to a number of elections, and there was never any shortage of opposition to his rule. The problem was that pluralist politics demand a pluralist society to make democracy work. The League of Communists of Serbia was rechristened the Socialist Party of Serbia (SPS), but the change was one of name only. The old communist bureaucracy was honeycombed with privilege and corruption, and the SPS simply took over its control of all major institutions, including state property, so that business continued as usual. Milošević's power was extra-institutional, based on interlocking networks of cronies at all formal levels of political representation. Votes were bought and sold, and where that did not work fraud, manipulation, and police harassment supplied the answer. The police apparatus became a kind of personal fiefdom of the SPS, and was increasingly enmeshed with organized crime, especially after Western sanctions made giant smuggling operations a normal arm of government. Last but not least, the domestic opposition to Milošević was divided, and Western intervention bolstered his appeal to many Serbs whose national pride was affronted.

Milošević was finally dislodged from office on 5 October 2000. His downfall came about as a result of a mass movement of citizens who found a way to take command of the streets of Belgrade. He was removed to The Hague the following June under controversial circumstances and charged with two counts of genocide and ten counts of crimes against humanity, to note only the most serious indictments. His trial raised complex questions of legal proof and international law not encountered since Nuremberg. Critics argue that the International Criminal Tribunal is dispensing biased justice. Most Serbs saw it this way and bitterly resented the sense of being tried as a nation in the person of Milošević. His trial also raised thorny questions about the complicity of the Western powers in the breakup of sovereign communist Yugoslavia; their failure to stop the killing once it had begun; and the international legality of the NATO bombing. After four years of dogged defense against all charges, Milošević was found dead in his cell on 11 March 2006.

See also **Bosnia-Herzegovina; Crime and Justice; Karadžić, Radovan; Mladić, Ratko; Sarajevo; Serbia; Yugoslavia.**

BIBLIOGRAPHY

Benson, Leslie. *Yugoslavia: A Concise History.* Revised and updated edition, Houndmills, Basingstoke, Hampshire, U.K., and New York, 2004. Chapters 8–10 give a succinct, analytical account of the background to the rise and fall of Milošević.

Cohen, Lenard J. *Serpent in the Bosom: The Rise and Fall of Slobodan Milošević.* Boulder, Colo., 2001.

Doder, Dusko, and Louise Branson. *Milošević: Portrait of a Tyrant.* New York, 1999.

LeBor, Adam. *Milošević: A Biography.* London, 2002.

Thomas, Raju G. C., ed. *Yugoslavia Unraveled: Sovereignty, Self-Determination, Intervention.* Lanham, Md., and Oxford, U.K., 2003. Chapters 7, 9, and 10 are recommended in the context of Milošević's responsibility for war crimes.

Thomas, Robert. *Serbia under Milošević: Politics in the 1990s.* London, 1998.

LESLIE BENSON

MIŁOSZ, CZESŁAW (1911–2004), Polish poet, essayist, translator, and man of letters.

Czesław Miłosz was born in 1911 to a Polish-speaking family of the gentry in the manorial village of Szetejnie on the Niewiaza River, an area that was then part of the tsarist Russian Empire and today belongs to Lithuania. He grew up multilingual and remained throughout his life deeply attached to the region of his birth and its rich intermingling of cultures. During World War I, Miłosz's father, an engineer, was mobilized to build roads and bridges for the Russian tsarist army. His family accompanied him, living a nomadic life.

After the war, Miłosz moved to Wilno (today Vilnius), which had become a part of newly independent Poland. There he attended Catholic schools. Between 1929 and 1934 he studied law at the Stefan Batory University (today Vilnius University), where he cofounded the Żagary literary circle and made his debut as a poet. The young Żagary poets felt acutely Poland's precarious position between rising Nazism to the west and rising Stalinism to the east. Their literary response was "catastrophism"—a foretelling of impending disasters on a cosmic scale—and an oscillation between Marxism and metaphysics.

Miłosz spent much of World War II in Nazi-occupied Warsaw, where he was involved in clandestine publishing and where he witnessed the Warsaw ghetto uprising of 1943 and the Warsaw uprising of 1944. Two of his best-known poems, "Campo dei Fiori" and "Biedny chrześcijanin patrzy na getto" ("A Poor Christian Looks at the Ghetto"), describe his experience of watching the Warsaw ghetto go up in flames. In January 1945, the Red Army drove the Wehrmacht from the Polish capital. Subsequently, Poland became a Soviet satellite state, and Miłosz served the Polish Communist regime as a foreign diplomat in the United States and France. In 1951, while serving as cultural attaché in Paris, he defected from Communist Poland. Shortly thereafter he wrote *The Captive Mind*, telling the story of four of his literary colleagues—Alpha (Jerzy Andrzejewski), Beta (Tadeusz Borowski), Gamma (Jerzy Putrament), and Delta (Konstanty Ildefons Gałczyński). It was a mixture, Miłosz argues, of conviction and psychological opportunism that induced his former colleagues to lend their talents to the Stalinist regime.

Following Miłosz's defection, his work was banned in Poland. In 1960 he left France for the United States, becoming Professor of Slavic Literature at the University of California at Berkeley. In the decades that followed, he became the most important representative of Polish literature in the West and one of the most articulate and widely heard dissident émigrés from Communist Europe.

In exile, Miłosz continued to write and translate prolifically. In the mid-1960s, he served as the émigré Polish poet Aleksander Wat's interlocutor for a recording of an extraordinary oral history (*My Century: The Odyssey of a Polish Intellectual*). He translated the Bible into Polish and much Polish poetry into English. Miłosz was also deeply involved in the Paris-based Polish émigré journal *Kultura*. He insisted on the existence of "Central Europe": "Central Europe is hardly a geographical notion. It is not easy to trace its boundaries on the map even if, while walking the streets of its cities, we do not doubt of its survival, whether that be in my baroque Wilno, or in the differently baroque Prague or the medieval-Renaissance Dubrovnik. The ways of feeling and thinking of its inhabitants must thus suffice for drawing mental lines which seem to be more durable than the borders of the states" (1990, p. 100).

A poet with a great sensitivity to nature and an early opponent of nationalism during his youth, Miłosz flirted with Marxism before breaking decisively with communism as it was practiced. He remained in his later years committed to tolerance and a universalist humanism. In 1980, just as the opposition movement Solidarity emerged in Poland, Miłosz won the Nobel Prize in Literature. His first wife, Janina, died in 1986. In the 1990s, after the fall of communism, he began to spend part of each year in Kraków. In 2003 he wrote the poem "Orfeusz i Eurydyka" (Orpheus and Eurydice), dedicated to the memory of his second wife, Carol, who had died suddenly that year. Miłosz himself died in Kraków in August 2004.

Other important works include *The Issa Valley* (1955); *The Seizure of Power* (1955); *Native Realm: A Search for Self-Definition* (1958); *The History of Polish Literature* (1969); *Emperor of the Earth: Modes of Eccentric Vision* (1976); *Miłosz's ABC's* (1997); and *New and Collected Poems 1931–2001* (2001).

See also **Dissidence; Poland.**

BIBLIOGRAPHY

Primary Sources

Miłosz, Czesław. *Trzy zimy*. Warsaw, 1936.

———. *Ocalenie*. Warsaw, 1945.

———. *Traktat poetycki*. Paris, 1957.

———. *Prywatne obowiązki*. Paris, 1972.

———. *Selected Poems*. New York, 1973, 1980.

———. "About Our Europe." In *Between East and West: Writings from Kultura*, edited by Robert Kostrzew, 99–108. New York, 1990.

———. *Wyprawa w dwudziestolecie*. Kraków, 1999.

Secondary Sources

Davie, Donald. *Czeslaw Milosz and the Insufficiency of Lyric*. Knoxville, Tenn., 1986.

Fiut, Aleksander. *The Eternal Moment: The Poetry of Czeslaw Milosz*. Berkeley, Calif., 1990.

Nathan, Leonard, and Arthur Quinn. *The Poet's Work: An Introduction to Czeslaw Milosz*. Cambridge, Mass., 1991.

MARCI SHORE

MINDSZENTY, JÓZSEF (1892–1975),

Hungarian prelate and opponent of communist rule in Hungary.

József Mindszenty, the future cardinal, was born into a peasant family as József Pehm in the little village of Csehimindszent in western Hungary. In 1941 he changed his name to Mindszenty to stress his identification with the Hungarian nation. He did not receive an education that would have prepared him to become a senior church official. After secondary education he attended a seminary but refused the offer of a scholarship to Catholic University in Vienna to study theology. Aside from Latin, he spoke no foreign languages. He was by no means an intellectual; he was strict, ascetic, and courageous but also narrow-minded, conservative, and extremely inflexible.

From the beginning of his career he took an active interest in politics. The bitterness of his opposition to the modern world was extreme even among senior churchmen, not only in Hungary but also in Europe. He was a man who never changed his ideas and remained a legitimist to the end of his days. As a young priest after the collapse of the Habsburg Monarchy in 1918, he wrote articles opposing land reform and the abolishment of the Monarchy. For his articles and organizational work against the republic he was briefly jailed in February 1919.

In the interwar period he continued his political activities in support of legitimist and conservative causes. In March 1944 he was named bishop of Veszprém. During Nazi rule in 1944 Mindszenty had organized some of the senior churchmen of western Hungary and delivered a letter in their name to the Nazi authorities advising them not to make western Hungary a battlefield. For this "disloyalty" he was promptly arrested and kept in prison until the Red Army freed him in April 1945. In August 1945, Pope Pius XII decided to name him the head of the Hungarian Church and in February 1946 gave him the cardinal's red hat. It was a surprising choice. The bishop of Veszprém was the most junior among the bishops and was not well known even within the church. The pope chose him because, unlike the heads of the Slovak and Croatian churches, he could not be accused of collaboration with the Nazis. Furthermore, in the course of the first few months following the end of the war Mindszenty had shown no interest in cooperating with the new authorities. It was characteristic of the foreign policy of Pope Pius XII that in 1945 he chose a man to be the head of the Hungarian Church who was known to be an opponent of accommodation with the victorious Soviet Union.

Between his appointment as head of the Hungarian Catholic Church and his arrest in December 1948 Mindszenty was the most determined opponent of the establishment of communist power in Hungary. Unlike many noncommunist politicians, he was never tempted to compromise. Under his leadership the Catholic Church was the most successful force in mobilizing the people against the coming communist dictatorship. Mindszenty voiced his opinion on all political matters, opposing land reform and the declaration of the republic, but he was most successful in organizing Catholics against making the study of religion voluntary in schools and the nationalization of religious schools. Once the communist regime was firmly established and the Cold War had already begun, in December 1948 the communists arrested the cardinal on ridiculously trumped-up charges. For spying and for illegal money transactions, among other "crimes," he was sentenced to life in prison.

He was freed by the Revolution of 1956, and in the course of Hungary's very few days of freedom he once again played a significant political role. In a speech on 3 November he demanded the return of Catholic institutions and the punishment of communist leaders, and he proudly announced that his political views had remained unchanged in the course of his imprisonment. After the suppression of the revolution by Soviet troops the cardinal received sanctuary in the American embassy, where he spent fifteen years.

In 1971, at a time when Washington, the Vatican, and the Hungarian reformist communist regime desired to reduce hostility, Mindszenty was allowed to leave the country for Rome. It was characteristic of the inflexibility of the cardinal that he refused the request of Pope Paul VI to resign and thereby enable him to name a new head of the Hungarian Church. The pope therefore had to remove him from his office in 1973. Instead of staying in the Vatican, Mindszenty moved to Vienna, where he spent his last days.

See also **Anticommunism; Catholicism; Eastern Bloc; Hungary.**

BIBLIOGRAPHY

Primary Sources

Mindszenty, József. *Emlékirataim.* Toronto, 1974.

———. *Memoirs.* Translated by Richard and Clara Winston. Documents translated by Jan van Jeurek. New York, 1974.

Secondary Sources

Gergely, Jenö. *A Katolikus Egyház Magyarországon, 1944–1971.* Budapest, 1985.

Mészáros, Msgr. Tibor. *Akit övei be nem Fogadtak. Mindszenty biboros Titkáranak Visszaemlékezései.* Pecs, Hungary, 1997.

PETER KENEZ

MINORITY RIGHTS. The fight for independence carried out by various religious and national minorities was a prominent factor in World War I, which from its start involved the rights of small nationalities (Serbia and Belgium). Nationality and self-determination were the basis of the postwar settlement advocated by President Woodrow Wilson in his Fourteen Points address to Congress on 8 January 1918, when he demanded at Point 9 "a readjustment of the frontiers of Italy ... along clearly recognized lines of nationality"; at Point 10 that "the peoples of Austria-Hungary ... should be accorded the freest opportunity of autonomous development"; at Point 11 the adjustment of Balkan relations "along historically established lines of nationality"; at Point 12 "an absolutely unmolested opportunity of autonomous development" for the minorities in Turkey; and at Point 13 the erection of an independent Polish state to include "the territories inhabited by indisputable Polish populations." In his address to Congress on 11 February 1918, the president declared that "all well-defined national aspirations shall be accorded the utmost satisfaction," under the condition that this would not have introduced new or perpetuated old elements of discord and antagonism likely to break the peace in Europe.

THE CHALLENGES OF WAR
AND ITS AFTERMATH

At the 1919 Paris Peace Conference that gave birth to the League of Nations the Allies were obliged to address the minority problem, given the twin impossibilities of giving birth to nation-states for all nationalities and of founding ethnically homogeneous nation-states in the territories of former multiethnic empires. International policy on the problem of minorities was developed in a twofold manner: firstly, in the drawing up of the Covenant of the League of Nations, based on President Wilson's Fourteen Points; and secondly, in the treaties on minorities, which for the first time established international regulation of this issue that included mechanisms of supervision and control. No provision for the protection of minorities was incorporated into the text of the Covenant of the League, although Wilson's second draft of 10 January 1919 contained an article according to which the League of Nations would have conditioned the recognition of new states on the promise to guarantee to all racial and national minorities the same legal status granted to the majority of the state population. Wilson's clauses would have required states to grant positive protection to minority groups, and there emerged a "general resistance to the formula of interposition of minorities as collectivities with special claims on the states" (Thornberry). More generally, the covenant shows a certain degree of ambiguity, and the concept of inferior and superior nations and peoples emerges in its provisions on mandates (Article 22: "peoples not yet able to stand by themselves"; "the tutelage of such peoples should be entrusted to advanced nations").

During the VIII Plenary Section President Wilson and French President Georges Clemenceau agreed on the need for special protection of minorities in certain states. A treaty was then signed at Versailles (28 June 1919) between the Allied and Associated Powers and Poland, which served as a model for similar "minorities treaties" signed with other nations, including Czechoslovakia and Yugoslavia (Saint-Germain, 10 September 1919), Romania (Paris, 9 December 1919), and Greece (Sèvres, 10 August 1920). Special chapters for the protection of minorities were also inserted into the peace treaties with Austria (Saint-Germain, 10 September 1919), Bulgaria (Neuilly, 27 November 1919), Hungary (Trianon, 4 June 1920), and Turkey (Lausanne, 24 July 1923). Later on, other treaties were signed with the aim of protecting minorities: the agreement between Sweden and Finland concerning the Swedish-speaking Åland Islands (approved by the Council on 27 June 1921); the German-Polish Convention on the protection of minorities in Upper Silesia (15 May 1922), the Graeco-Turkish agreement on the compulsory exchange of minority populations (30 January 1923), and the Convention on the Memel Territory of Lithuania (8 May 1924). Unilateral declarations regarding minorities were made before the Council of the League by five countries when admitted: Albania (2 October 1921), Lithuania (12 May 1922), Latvia (7 July 1923), Estonia (17 September 1923), and Iraq (30 May 1932).

The emphasis in these treaties was on the right to life and liberty; the free exercise of religion without discrimination on the grounds of race, religion, or language; equality before the law; the freedom to organize educational programs; and an obligation to ensure that elementary instruction of children was in their mother tongue. Such obligations were supervised by the League of Nations, and violations were subject to action by the League. Allegations of violations of the treaties were brought by the states to the Council of the League of Nations, and in many cases claims were taken to the Permanent Court of International Justice

(PCIJ). Individuals also had the right to present petitions that were examined by the so-called Three Persons Committee. Between 1926 and 1939, 585 petitions were registered, 360 of which were declared admissible. Some of the petitions were brought to the PCIJ. In the case law of the Permanent Court, the two principles that emerged as necessary and complementary in order to ensure the survival of minorities were equality and autonomy: "Equality in law precludes discrimination whereas equality in fact may involve the necessity of different treatment in order to attain a result which establishes an equilibrium between different situations" (Minority schools in Albania, Advisory Opinion, PCIJ Ser. A/B, no. 64, 1935). The Secretariat of the League of Nations established minority sections and had observers in the field.

The system was certainly a first important step toward the creation of international standards safeguarding minority rights. Compared with the Treaty of Berlin of 1878, the Versailles minorities treaties were innovative in the sense that they attempted to embrace a mechanism and procedure for enforced compliance. Nevertheless, they did not establish a general system with universal application: no minimum standard of protection was provided for all European minorities, because obligations were imposed only on the newly independent (expansionist and irredentist) states and not on Allied and Associated states or even on Germany. The new states were obliged to limit their newly awarded sovereignty by accepting minority clauses imposed by the Great Powers as a condition for recognizing their new frontiers. Minority protection represented therefore a limitation of self-determination for the new states and was connected with the rise of expansionist and irredentist nationalism: the "quest for international minority protection in Europe involved the fusing of two powerful opposites: the attainment and maintenance of full national independence versus the expansion of outside control" (Fink).

In spite of President Wilson's Point 9, Italy was granted new frontiers by the peace treaty that included German-speaking minorities (in South Tyrol and Trentino) and Slovene- and Croatian-speaking minorities (in Trieste and maritime provinces) that were not protected by any treaty. Although not obliged by international law, in the first postwar period the Italian liberal governments (1919–1922) granted administrative and legislative autonomy to the territories inhabited by minorities. The use of their languages in public life, courts, and schools was guaranteed and the Italian language was gradually introduced, alongside the languages of the minorities. After 1924, with the consolidation of the Fascist regime, a process of denationalization and persecution began.

In Spain the quest for autonomy by the Catalans was rejected by the dictator Miguel Primo de Rivera (r. 1923–1930), but the Republic then granted limited local autonomy to Catalonia in the constitution of 9 December 1931. The Catalan Charter of Autonomy of September 1932 granted Catalonia the right to its own flag, president, parliament, and cabinet and to its official language. The Basques received more limited autonomy on 8 October 1936. The establishment of the Francisco Franco dictatorship in 1939 put an end to autonomy during the civil war in Catalonia and in the Basque country, and persecution of all minorities began.

In Ireland, the Sinn Féin party, founded in 1905 by Arthur Griffith with the aim of separating from England, obtained an overwhelming success in the elections of 1918. The members of the party that called themselves Dáil Éireann (assembly of Ireland) proclaimed in January 1919 the independent Republic of Ireland under the presidency of Eamon De Valera. On 6 December 1921 a treaty was signed by Great Britain and the Irish representatives (Griffith and Michael Collins). Southern Ireland became the Free State (Saorstát Éireann) and obtained the status of a dominion, in which the king was represented by a governor. Despite its ratification by both parliaments, the treaty produced a civil war between the moderates (authors of the treaty) and extremists lead by De Valera, at the head of the National Party (Fianna Fáil). In Northern Ireland a quasi-federalist system (home rule) was applied with local political bodies. In practice, however, it resulted in a system of hegemonic control by the majority and in discrimination against the Catholic minority, "systematically pushed out of the skilled industrial occupations which increasingly became Protestant monopolies" (Hobsbawm).

The Russian Empire was inhabited by almost one hundred nationalities. Among them, the Germans in the Baltic provinces, along with the Poles and the Finns, enjoyed a high level of autonomy until the first half of the nineteenth century. Later, the policy of russification of all minorities began. All groups, and the Jews in particular, experienced oppression, especially the denial of equality and political rights. The situation of minorities began to improve with the revolution of 1905, and with the democratic revolution in March 1917 their complete equality was proclaimed. The Baltic states, the Finns, and the Poles proclaimed their independence, and the rest of the empire was reconstructed as the USSR (1924) in which European and Asian peoples were organized in "federal" republics (originally seven, then eleven, and finally sixteen in the early 1950s). The constitution of the Soviet Union even enshrined the right of secession, but recognition of this right, in Lenin's opinion, in no way led to the "formation of small States, but to the enlargement of the bigger ones, a phenomenon more advantageous for the masses and for the development of the economy" (V. I. Lenin, *Prosvestcenie* nos. 4, 5, 6, April–June 1914).

Equality was formally guaranteed to all persons belonging to all racial and linguistic minorities, and minority religions were held to be on the same footing as the Orthodox Church. From a political point of view, the USSR actively promoted the use of minority languages to implement many social goals, such as literacy, compulsory education, and equality between men and women. However, no effective cultural and political autonomy could exist in practice, because the public life of all citizens was uniformly molded in the pattern of the totalitarian dictatorship.

Movements for national independence on the part of the larger national groups (Ukrainians, Caucasians, and Muslims in Central Asia) were suppressed, and the totalitarian direction of all life and the administration by the strictly centralized Communist Party provided a framework for uniformity. The discontent of minorities emerged in World War II, in which it became clear that Soviet government represented Russian domination.

The need for a general discipline concerning minorities in Europe was urged by many states. In 1933, Poland, with the support of other states, presented a draft multilateral treaty to the League of Nations that was open to all states and contained rules on the protection of minorities. The draft was rejected, as many states (including France and Italy) were in favor of a reduction of the level of protection settled in the treaties and, as a consequence, of the external interference on states with minorities. As a consequence, Poland renounced the Polish treaty on minorities on 13 September 1934 and stated that from then on minorities would be protected only by Polish law. This renunciation by the most powerful minority state influenced the others and produced a loss of credibility in the whole supervisory system of the League. In 1939 only four petitions were brought to the Secretariat and three were rejected. The tendency from then on was to solve the minority problem through bilateral treaties, a system that lasted even after World War II.

The final blow to the system devised by the League was the deterioration of international relations due to the rise of Nazism. With the nationalistic propaganda in Germany, Austria, Italy, Hungary, and Bulgaria, the principle of the protection of minorities was definitely put aside.

The beginning of World War II produced a worsening of the repressive and assimilatory measures against minorities in all fascist regimes. In Italy on 6 October 1938 the Fascist Great Council approved a "declaration on the race" that contained discriminatory measures toward non-Italians and Jews in particular. Members of minorities were prevented from urbanization, and minority working-class families were transferred to the African colonies. An exception to this attitude was the annexation of the province of Ljubljana to Italy in 1941, which was accompanied by special legislation of the kind applied in the occupied Dalmation Slavic-speaking areas (Trau, Sebenico, Spalato, and Cattaro) and accorded to the local population a minimum standard of protection.

In Nazi Germany, there were two stages of genocide: the elimination of the national pattern of the oppressed peoples and the establishment of the national pattern of the oppressor. It included the prohibition of the use of local languages and compulsory education in the spirit of the official ideology ("cultural genocide"), various measures to favor a lower birthrate in non-German populations and a higher rate in German groups ("biological genocide"), racial discrimination, and mass killing of certain groups ("physical genocide").

POST–WORLD WAR II

The victorious powers decided with the Potsdam Declaration of 1945 to solve the German minority problem by compulsory transfer. As a result of the implementation of this decision 6,650,000 persons were sent to the four occupied zones. Between 1945 and 1947 a number of treaties were signed to allow voluntary repatriation of central and Eastern Europeans (for example, Poland signed such an agreement with the USSR, Czechoslovakia, Yugoslavia, and France).

The new multilateral and bilateral treaties Peace settlements after World War II led to the conclusion of several multilateral and bilateral instruments and measures forbidding discrimination or providing for special protective measures for ethnic, religious, and linguistic minorities. The agreement signed in 1946 between Austria and Italy related to the rights of the German-speaking minority in the Bolzano province. The 1947 peace treaty with Hungary and Romania and the 1955 Austrian State Treaty contained general provisions prohibiting discrimination. The latter also provided specific provisions concerning the Croats and Slovenes in the three Austrian provinces of Carinthia, Burgenland, and Styria. The 1954 agreement among Italy, Great Britain, the United States, and Yugoslavia concerning Trieste established the protection of the Yugoslav and Italian minorities in the respective parts of the region of Trieste. Also, agreed statements by Denmark and the Federal Republic of Germany in 1955 included special provisions to protect German and Danish minorities.

Such treaties, unlike the ones signed after World War I, did not provide a specific discipline for the protection of minorities. The reason is twofold: on one hand, the problem was significantly less consistent in practice thanks to the transfer of populations and the changing of the frontiers; on the other hand, the atmosphere in Europe had changed (mainly as a result of the use made by the Nazis of the alleged ill-treatment of German

minorities in central Europe). Minority rights fell into disfavor and were seen as a threat to peace.

International and supranational treaties protecting human rights After World War II a new universal and individualistic conception of human rights prevailed. For a long time the very idea of a specific, internationally recognized status for national minorities as collective subjects was put aside in the hope of solving the problem not through special group rights but by guaranteeing basic civic and political rights to all individuals regardless of group membership. However, the ongoing quest for rights by European minorities and their resistance to assimilation demonstrated the limits of such a conception—which resulted in rendering "minorities vulnerable to a significant injustice in the hands of the majority" (Kymlicka) and the importance of having an international discipline for the protection of minorities. Under the UN Charter of 1945 and the Universal Declaration on Human Rights (1948), persons that belonged to minority groups were protected only by the principles of equality before the law and the prohibition of discrimination on the grounds of race, language, and religion. Nevertheless, the Economic and Social Council authorized the Commission on Human Rights to make a recommendation on this subject and approved the establishment in 1947 of the Sub-Commission on the Prevention of Discrimination and Protection of Minorities. While nondiscrimination implies a formal guarantee of equal treatment before the law and a uniform treatment for all individuals, protection implies special measures or even affirmative action on the part of the state in order to protect the special features of the minority and prevent it from assimilation. Moreover, special rights may be conferred on individuals within minorities, but obviously they also have a collective dimension as they are aimed to protect the interests of the individual not only as an individual but also as a member of the group.

The first general convention to recognize and protect the fundamental collective rights of minorities was the Convention on the Prevention and Punishment of the Crime of Genocide (1948), which in Article 2 defines the objects of protection as a whole or part of "a national, ethnical, racial or religious group." Linguistic groups were not included because language was regarded as an element of national collective identity. This convention protects the right to the existence of a minority, which does not only coincide with the right to life of its members but also the right of the group to exist through the shared consciousness of its members, the prerequisite for the enjoyment of all other rights. Therefore Article 2 affirms that the acts that constitute genocide are: "(a) killing members of the group; (b) causing serious bodily or mental harm to members of the group; (c) deliberately inflicting on the group conditions of life calculated to bring about its physical destruction in whole or in part; (d) imposing measures intended to prevent births within the group; (e) forcibly transferring children of the group to another group."

Article 27 of the 1966 International Covenant on Civil and Political Rights declares that: "In those states in which ethnic, religious or linguistic minorities exist, persons belonging to such minorities shall not be denied the right, in community with the other members of their group, to enjoy their own culture, to profess and practise their own religion, or to use their own language." This implicitly confers on the states a precise duty that is likely to require, in order to be fulfilled, some form of positive action. In order to supervise the implementation of this article, three instruments can be used: state reports, state complaints, and individual petitions (Articles 40 and 41 and the Optional Protocol to the Covenant). Reports by states have developed dramatically since the first years, as most states have issued particular laws that protect minorities.

The same approach was taken by the 1960 UNESCO Convention against Discrimination in Education: "5(c) It is essential to recognize the right of members of national minorities to carry on their own educational activities, including the maintenance of schools and, depending on the educational policy of each State, the use or the teaching of their own language." More explicitly, the UN General Assembly's (non–legally binding) 1992 Declaration on the Rights of Persons Belonging to National, Ethnic, Religious, or Linguistic Minorities states the principle of both formal and substantial equality in order to preserve and develop the characteristics of the minorities.

The European Convention on Human Rights of 1950 refers to national minorities in Article 14, which states that "association with a national minority" constitutes one of the grounds on which discrimination is forbidden. Individuals belonging to national minorities are therefore protected, but minorities themselves do not enjoy any specific legal status. Despite this absence of specific attention to languages and minorities, there has been, as Geoff Gilbert puts it, a "burgeoning" minority rights jurisprudence of the European Court of Human Rights.

The Final Act of the Conference on Security and Co-operation (CSCE; since 1995 the OSCE) in Europe adopted in Helsinki in 1975 mentioned the right of persons belonging to minorities to equality before the law and the duty of the signatory states "on whose territory national minorities exist" to "afford them the full opportunity for the actual enjoyment of human rights and fundamental freedoms" in order to "protect their legitimate interests in this sphere" (Principle 7). Principle 7 also contains a guarantee for religious minorities: participating states will "recognize and respect the freedom of the individual to profess and practice, alone or in community with others, religion or belief." In the concluding documents produced by the follow-up meetings (Vienna, 1989; Copenhagen, 1990; Geneva, 1991; Helsinki, 1992), as well as the Oslo recommendations on linguistic rights (1998), the positive obligation of the states to preserve the collective rights of minorities was clearly stated, along with their duty to create conditions for the promotion of the ethnic, cultural, linguistic, and religious identity of national minorities in their territory. All decisions of the OSCE are not legally binding, although they have an important political significance.

In the framework of the Council of Europe, the European Charter for Regional or Minority Languages (1992) and the Framework Convention for the Protection of National Minorities (1994) form an important site for the gradual development of a minimum standard with regard to the legal position of regional and minority languages. The Framework Convention is self-executing, but only regarding the loose commitments that the states have undertaken toward the minorities. Beyond this point the execution of this convention requires special regulations in order to be effective at the domestic level. Both the Framework Convention and the Charter on Languages entered into force in 1998. By 2005 neither of the two was yet so universally accepted as the European Convention on Human Rights (1950), but the number of states parties was rising. Nineteen states had ratified the Charter on Regional and Minority Languages, including thirteen of the twenty-five member states of the European Union (United Kingdom, Sweden, Spain, Slovenia, Slovakia, Netherlands, Luxembourg, Hungary, Germany, Finland, Denmark, Germany, and Austria). The Framework Convention was much closer to becoming a genuine pan-European standard; by 2005 it had been ratified by thirty-seven states, and the only ones missing, apart from some mini-states, were Turkey and four European Union states: Belgium, France, Greece, and Luxembourg.

The provisions of these two treaties do not seem easily capable of directly affecting the national legal order of nation-states. Also, their international supervision mechanisms do not lead to binding judicial or quasi-judicial decisions. Periodic state reports on the application of the conventions must be submitted to the Committees of Experts that were set up under each of the two conventions. However, the dynamic approach adopted by these committees in fulfilling their monitoring tasks is quite remarkable, perhaps even unprecedented in international monitoring practice. They have established a dialogue with the governments concerned, visit the country and speak to minority groups, and do not hesitate to make statements as to whether the states have adequately complied with their obligations, expressing detailed views on how to improve the situation. These statements then lead to recommendations adopted by the Committee of Ministers of the Council of Europe and, in fact, the ministers have so far largely followed the views of the experts. Pressure is thus exerted on the states to adopt best practices as formulated by the expert bodies.

Within the European Union, the Treaties of Maastricht (1992), Amsterdam (1997), and Nice (2001) declare that the full development of the culture of the member state, respecting its national and regional differences, constitutes one of the objectives of the Community (Article 128 of the Treaty of Maastricht and Article 151 of the Treaty of Amsterdam). The Charter of Fundamental Rights of the European Union (2000) states, along with the principle of nondiscrimination on the grounds, inter alia, of ethnicity, language, and belonging to a national minority (Article 21), the respect by the EU of cultural, religious, and linguistic differences (Article 22). The project of the Constitutional Treaty of the EU (2004), which includes the Charter of Fundamental Rights, states, among the values that also have to be fulfilled by candidate member states, the respect for human rights, including the rights of persons belonging to a minority (Article I-2; Article I-57)

CONSTITUTIONAL PROTECTION

Not all European states protect minorities through positive measures. France is an example of a neutral, or agnostic, state, in the sense that it does not protect a (collective) "right to difference" or to cultural identity, the expressions of which should be left to the private sphere. Language, religion, and culture are grounds on which discrimination is forbidden but not on which a special status may be conferred. The only applicable principle is equality before the law: no one may suffer negative treatment because he or she belongs to a minority, but minorities are not protected as such. (With decision no. 99-412 DC of 15 June 1999, the French Constitutional Council ruled that Article 7 of the preamble of the European Charter of regional languages was unconstitutional as it confers "specific rights to those speaking regional or minority languages within the territories in which such languages are spoken.") Neutral states do not constitute the rule. Almost all European systems protect minorities also through domestic legislation. Most constitutions provide for the protection of linguistic or national minorities and/or minority or national languages: In the constitution of Italy, Article 6; Spain, Article 3, paragraphs 2 and 3; Switzerland, Articles 4 and 70; Belgium, Articles 2 and 30; Ireland, Article 8; Finland, Article 17; Sweden, Article 2, paragraph 4 and Article 15; Austria, Article 8; Slovakia, Articles 6 and 33; Poland, Articles 27 and 35; Croatia, Articles 12 and 15; Albania, Article 20, paragraph 1; Romania, Articles 6; 32, paragraph 2; 59, paragraph 2; and 127, paragraph 2; Slovenia, Articles 11 and 64; Lithuania, Article 45; and Estonia, Article 37.

The state representatives in the Meeting of Experts on National Minorities, held by the CSCE in Geneva in July 1991, took account of the diversity and the variations in constitutional systems and identified different positive approaches pursued by European democracies. These included advisory and decision-making bodies in which minorities are represented, in particular with regard to education, culture, and religion; elected bodies and assemblies of national minority affairs; local and autonomous administration as well as autonomy on a territorial basis, including the existence of consultative, legislative, and executive bodies chosen through free and periodic elections; self-administration by a national minority of aspects concerning its identity in situations where autonomy on a territorial basis does not apply; and decentralized or local forms of government.

In general terms there are two main constitutional models of protection. The first may be described as the "states of minorities," where all languages are co-official, despite the numeric consistence of the groups and in which the monopoly of each minority corresponds to the territorial dimension of the state sub-unit. This is typically the case of asymmetrical federations such as Belgium and Switzerland in which all languages enjoy an equal status at the federal level, whereas at the local level linguistic territoriality is strictly applied, resulting in monolingual sub-units. A second category is that of the states that recognize the existence of a linguistic majority/minority relationship and in which the protection of minority rights is a fundamental principle of the constitutional system. In such cases minorities enjoy a special degree of positive protection (that derogate to the principle of formal equality) on the basis of the classical principles of welfare states, in which the interests of social groups are legally relevant (for example, Article 6 of the Italian constitution: "The republic protects linguistic minorities by special laws"). Such states are typically those characterized by a large linguistic majority and by one or more linguistic minorities. If there are multiple minority groups, the level of protection of their linguistic rights may not be the same. Numerical, historical, political, and economic differences may constitute the grounds for choosing different models of protection, such as in Italy and Spain, in which the regions inhabited by the most consistent minorities enjoy a higher degree of autonomy, and such as Finland, in which political autonomy is conferred only to the Swedish-speaking Åland Islands.

If the protection is effective in "old" European democracies, younger ones have so far succeeded only to a limited extent in assuring a minimum standard of minority protection, in spite of the constitutional and legislative provisions that they have adopted with this aim. In most cases (e.g., the Balkan states) this is due to the foundation of the newly independent states on an ethnic and nationalistic basis, in which all citizens are equal before the law, regardless of their nationality, but the majority nation is the only subject that, having the right to statehood, is entitled to legitimize the newborn state. Consider the wording of the preamble to the Croatian constitution of 1990: "Proceeding from…the inalienable, indivisible, non-transferable and non-exhaustible right of the Croatian nation to self-determination and state sovereignty,…the Republic of Croatia is hereby established as the national state of the Croatian people and a state of members of other nations and minorities who are its citizens." Thus majority nations create states, and through their legitimacy, can recognize the rights of minorities to live there.

See also **Convention on Genocide; Genocide; Human Rights; Maastricht, Treaty of; Potsdam Conference; Refugees; Universal Declaration of Human Rights.**

BIBLIOGRAPHY

Azcárate y Flórez, Pablo de. *League of Nations and National Minorities: An Experiment.* Translated by Eileen E. Brooke. Washington, D.C., 1945.

Capotorti, Francesco. *Study on the Rights of Persons Belonging to Ethnic, Religious and Linguistic Minorities.* New York, 1979.

Fink, Carole. *Defending the Rights of Others: The Great Powers, the Jews, and International Minority Protection, 1878–1938.* Cambridge, U.K., and New York, 2004.

Gilbert, Geoff. "The Council of Europe and Minority Rights." *Human Rights Quarterly* 18, no. 1 (1996): 160–189.

———. "The Burgeoning Minority Rights Jurisprudence of the European Court of Human Rights." *Human Rights Quarterly* 24, no. 3 (2002): 736–780.

Heyking, Baron Alfons Alfonovich. *The International Protection of Minorities: The Achilles' Heel of the League of Nations.* London, 1928.

Hobsbawm, Erik J. *Nation and Nationalism since 1780: Programme, Myth, Reality.* Cambridge, U.K., and New York, 1990.

———. *Age of Extremes: The Short Twentieth Century, 1914–1991.* London, 1994.

Claude, Inis L. *National Minorities: An International Problem.* Cambridge, Mass., 1955.

Cumper, Peter, and Steven Wheatley, eds. *Minority Rights in the "New" Europe.* The Hague, London, and Boston, 1999.

Kymlicka Will, ed. *The Rights of Minority Cultures.* Oxford, U.K., and New York, 1995.

Lerner, Natan. "From Protection of Minorities to Group Rights." In *Israel Yearbook on Human Rights,* 101–120. Tel Aviv, 1990.

———. "The 1992 UN Declaration on Minorities." In *Israel Yearbook on Human Rights,* 111–128. Tel Aviv, 1993

Macartney, C. A. *National States and National Minorities.* London, 1934.

Mitic, M. "Protection of National Minorities in Europe." Rev. Int. Affairs, 1998.

Nimni, Ephraim. *Marxism and Nationalism: Theoretical Origins of a Political Crisis.* London, 1994.

Robinson, Jacob, et al. *Were the Minorities Treaties a Failure?* New York, 1943.

Ronzitti, Natolino. *Rescuing Nationals Abroad through Military Coercion and Intervention on Grounds of Humanity.* Dordrecht, Netherlands, 1985.

Roucek, J. S., ed. *A Challenge to Peacemakers: Conflicting National Aspirations in Central and Eastern Europe.* Philadelphia, 1944.

Ruiz Vieytez, Eduardo J. *The History of Legal Protection of Minorities in Europe.* Derby, U.K., 1999.

Schlager Erika. "The 1998 OSCE Implementation Meeting on Human Dimension Issues." *Helsinki Monitor* 10, no. 1 (1999): 43–47.

Seton-Watson, R. W. *The Problem of Small Nations and the European Anarchy.* London, 1939.

Shaw, M. N. "The Definition of Minorities in International Law." In *Israel Yearbook on Human Rights,* 13–43. Tel Aviv, 1991.

Simon, T. W. "Minorities in International Law." *Canadian Journal of Law and Jurisprudence* 10, no. 2 (July 1997): Appendix G, 512.

Thornberry, Patrick. *International Law and the Rights of Minorities.* Oxford, U.K., and New York, 1991.

Wippman, David. "The Evolution and Implementation of Minority Rights." *Fordham Law Review* 66 (1997): 597–626.

Wright, Jane. "The Protection of Minority Rights in Europe: From Conference to Implementation." *International Journal of Human Rights* 2, no. 1 (1998): 1–31.

SUSANNA MANCINI

MIRÓ, JOAN (1893–1983), Spanish painter, sculptor, and printmaker.

Joan Miró was born in Barcelona. Following secondary school, his father insisted that he attend business school apart from his art studies at La Escuela de la Lonja, where Modest Urgell was one of his teachers. In 1910–1911 his family purchased a farm in Montroig (Tarragona), which became one of his most important studios. In 1911 he fell ill with typhoid fever and recovered there. From 1912 to 1915 he studied with the innovative art instructor Francesc D'Assi Galí Fabra. In 1916 he met the dealer Josep Dalmau, who in February 1918 presented Miró's first solo exhibition in Barcelona.

1920S: PARIS AND SURREALISM

In early March 1920 Miró moved to Paris, where he met Pablo Picasso. He planned his first Paris exhibition with the help of Dalmau, scheduled for the next season. In June he returned to Spain, but in the autumn was represented with two paintings—*Self-Portrait* and *Montroig, Village and Church*—in a Paris group exhibition of Catalan artists in the Salon d'Automne.

In January 1921 he again traveled to Paris and in late February again met Picasso. The following month he worked in the studio of the Catalan sculptor Pablo Gargallo at 45 rue Blomet. Through March he painted new canvases and, with Dalmau, planned the opening of the exhibition. Miró now met several important writers—Max Jacob, Pierre Reverdy, and Tristan Tzara. Also in March he possibly met André Masson and discovered that the two artists' studios at 45 rue Blomet were adjacent. On 29 April his first solo show opened at the Galerie La Licorne, with a catalog preface by Maurice Raynal situating him as the heir of Cézanne and Picasso. In June he again

The Hunter: Catalan Landscape. Painting by Joan Miró, 1923–1924. MUSEUM OF MODERN ART

returned to Barcelona, remaining there for the rest of the year and beginning his most ambitious painting to date, *The Farm*. In early May 1922, again working at 45 rue Blomet, he finished *The Farm*, which was consigned to the art dealer Léonce Rosenberg and presented in the Salon d'Automne (1 November–17 December).

Through Masson, Miró met the writer and future ethnographer Michel Leiris in March 1923 and possibly also Antonin Artaud, Robert Desnos, Jean Dubuffet, Paul Éluard, Marcel Jouhandeau, Georges Limbour, Raymond Queneau, and Armand Salacrou. His painting *The Farm* was again exhibited at the Caméleon in boulevard Montparnasse in May before he returned to Spain in June. In July he began working on important transitional paintings that announced his move toward surrealism: *The Tilled Field, The Hunter,* and *Pastorale* (all July 1923–winter 1924).

Though André Breton had seen Masson's solo exhibition at Daniel-Henry Kahnweiler's Galerie

Simon in early 1924, the poet and painter would not meet until late September. Miró probably did not meet Breton until the following year, but Miró was already immersed in surrealist ideas. Evidence of this interest is his letter (10 August 1924) to Leiris: "I have done a series of small things on wood, in which I take off with some form in the wood. . . . I agree with Breton that there is something extremely disturbing about a page of writing" (Rowell, p. 86). Shortly after meeting Miró in early 1925, Breton purchased *The Hunter* and *The Gentleman*. Miró's June solo exhibition at the Galerie Pierre presented works in the surrealist idiom. By the autumn Miró's works appeared in the Galerie Pierre's group exhibition of surrealist painting. Breton's book *Le surréalisme et la peinture* (1928) represented Miró as one of the artists in the group.

Jacques Dupin has called Miró's works of the years 1925–1927 "dream paintings." The most famous and important of these is the 1925 *Birth of the World,* where highly schematic and transparent figures are set against a painterly field. These were complemented by landscapes, Dutch interiors, and imaginary portraits (1926–1929). Prompted by his success, Miró rejected the danger of facile repetition and proclaimed: "I want to assassinate painting." His works of the period 1928–1931 consisted of collages made out of deliberately crude materials (1928–1929), "anti-paintings" where he made an image and canceled it out (1930), and "object assemblages" made up of found objects and detritus (1931). These works reveal a sense of artistic crisis and capture the wider sense of cultural, economic, and political crisis that characterized the period.

1930S: POLITICAL AND ARTISTIC CRISIS

While Miró continued making collages and paintings in the early 1930s (especially 1933–1934), many of the canvases from 1934 onward are grotesquely distorted. Following Hitler's rise to power in 1933, in October 1934 a failed revolution in Miró's native Barcelona and in Asturias was brutally put down by the Spanish military, using the Moroccan army. This event was a prelude to the Spanish civil war. Things were no better in Paris, for on 6 February 1934 right-wing militants attempted to storm the French Assembly. The riot was only put down when the authorities fired on the crowd; within days there was a general strike (supported by the surrealists) and the government collapsed. Miró's unsettling 1930s "savage paintings" engage with the political crisis.

The city of Guernica in the Basque homeland was cynically destroyed in April 1937 when the German Condor Legion dropped incendiary bombs on it with General Francisco Franco's complicity. The bombings created a new sense of urgency on the part of the Republican government to seek international support, especially in the face of the nonaggression pact signed by France and England. The pact effectively isolated Spain from the matériel necessary to conduct the war, while Germany and Italy's support of the military rebellion was ignored by the international community. Plans were in preparation for the Spanish Pavilion at the Paris World's Fair, and the bombings introduced a new urgency. Miró's contribution was a large mural called *The Reaper (Catalan Peasant in Revolt)*. This now lost work was clearly a powerful political and artistic statement of identification with the Republic. Further, Miró made the stencil *Aidez l'Espagne* (Help Spain) with the intention of selling it as a stamp to raise money for the Republic.

The Spanish civil war was a prelude to World War II. In 1939, after the beginning of the world war, Miró fled from Paris to Varengeville, in Normandy, where he began a series of twenty-three gouaches known as the *Constellations* in January 1940. Following the German invasion of France in May 1940, Miró decided to go with his wife and daughter to Mallorca. En route, pausing in Perpignan, he continued working on the series of gouaches. The series was continued in Mallorca and completed in Montroig in September 1941. Executed during the darkest year of the war, when the outcome was by no means clear, this series condensed the artist's sense of spiritual resistance and humankind's capacity to triumph over adversity even in the face of insurmountable odds. When the *Constellations* were shown in New York in early 1945, they demonstrated that the Nazi assault had not extinguished culture in Europe.

POSTWAR

Miró declined to participate in the first Bienal Hispano-Americana de Arte (Madrid, 1951), an exhibition officially sanctioned by the Franco government. Miró's postwar years amounted to a form of internal exile within Franco's dictatorship (1 April 1939–20 November 1975). But Miró exhibited frequently in Paris and New York, thus avoiding the censorship that otherwise applied to works of art or literature in Spain.

Miró undertook numerous public commissions abroad. In 1947 he spent several months in New York, working in the studio of Carl Holty, where he prepared a large mural commission for the Cincinnati Terrace Plaza Hotel. Miró and Josep Lloréns Artigas's monumental ceramic works included commissions for UNESCO (1958), Harvard (1960), the Guggenheim (1967), Osaka (1970), and the Kunsthaus Zürich (1971–1972). In 1958 he began working on an ambitious commission to make the elaborate gardens for Aimé Maeght's foundation in Saint Paul de Vence. This project created an environment through the use of a variety of sculptural media; in this period Miró began intensively engaging with sculpture.

1960S AND BEYOND: A RENEWED REBELLION

During the 1960s Miró returned to painting, incorporating abstract expressionist and *informel* painting. The greater spontaneity of his methodology expressed solidarity with younger artists. His painted sculptures incorporated ideas from pop art. His 1968 retrospective, organized in France, was additionally presented in Barcelona (November 1968–January 1969), his only exhibition held in Spain during the dictatorship. Miró was concerned that such a retrospective would reduce his work to official culture. In a subversive action, working all night long, Miró worked with a team of architecture students to make a clandestine and ephemeral mural, called "Miró otro" (May 1969), executed on the glass windows of Col.legi de Architectes de Barcelona.

For his retrospective for the Grand Palais (Paris, May 1974), Miró executed a substantial body of work to assert the continued contemporary vitality of his art and aggressively to resist political oppression. Miró again rejected conventional painting and took up antiart. Among the found-object sculptures cast in bronze, tapestries, and ceramics, there was a striking series of burned canvases, where the center of the canvas was a void. One of the gestural paintings rendered the marks as the traces of an act of pictorial rebellion commensurate with the events in Paris: it was titled *May 1968* (1973).

Miró continued to make powerful paintings through the late 1970s. In 1976 he donated the majority of his drawings to the recently opened Fundació Joan Miró in Barcelona. For the first time, the little-known preparatory drawings, which underpinned most of his work, were published. His 1978–1979 retrospective, and donation of drawings, at the Centre Pompidou in Paris further made his drawings available. Miró continued working through the beginning of the 1980s on numerous projects, many now conserved in the Fundació Pilar i Joan Miró on Mallorca. His activity during the year 1983 was curtailed by ill health. On Christmas day of that year he died at age ninety.

See also **Picasso, Pablo; Spain; Surrealism; Tzara, Tristan.**

BIBLIOGRAPHY

Cabañas Bravo, Miguel. *Política artística del franquismo.* Madrid, 1996.

Dupin, Jacques. *Joan Miró: Life and Work.* New York, 1962.

Fitzsimmons, James. Introduction to *Miró: "Peintures sauvages" 1934 to 1953,* by Joan Miró. New York, 1958.

Jeffett, William. "Antitête: The Book as Object in the Collaboration of Tristan Tzara and Joan Miró (1946–47)." *Burlington Magazine,* 135, no. 1079 (February 1993): 81–92.

———. "The Shape of Color: Joan Miró's Painted Sculpture, Monumentality, Metaphor." In *The Shape of Color: Joan Miró's Painted Sculpture,* by Laura Coyle, William Jeffett, and Joan Punyet-Miró, 21–65. Washington, D.C., 2002.

———. "Miró's Unhappy Consciousness: Relief-Sculptures and Objects, 1930–1932." In *Joan Miró,* edited by Agnès de la Baumelle, 81–93. Paris and London, 2004.

Leymarie, Jean, and Jacques Dupin. *Joan Miró.* Paris, 1974.

Lubar, Robert S. "Paintings and Politics: Miró's *Still Life with Shoe* and the Spanish Republic." In *Surrealism, Politics, and Culture,* edited by Raymond Spiteri and Donald LaCoss, 127–161. Aldershot, U.K., 2003.

Malet, Rosa Maria, ed. *Obra de Miró.* Barcelona, 1979.

Raynal, Maurice. "Preface to the 1921 Miró Exhibition at the Galerie La Licorne, Paris." In *Miró: Biographical and Critical Study* by Jacques Lassaigne, 118–120. Geneva, 1963.

Rowell, Margit, ed. *Joan Miró: Selected Writings and Interviews.* Translated by Paul Auster and Patricia Mathews. Boston, 1986.

Umland, Anne. "Chronology." In *Joan Miró,* by Carolyn Lanchner, 317–361. New York, 1993.

WILLIAM JEFFETT

MITTERRAND, FRANÇOIS (1916–1996), French politician.

François Mitterrand, who lived to be seventy-nine years old, belonged to that special brand of French politician endowed with exceptional longevity. Once he entered into political life with the liberation of France from German occupation, he was destined not to leave it again until 1995, some fifty years later. But a long life such as this is not without its surprises, the most important being that he was "born" on the political right, but "died" on the left. Political evolutions are usually held to go in the other direction, but the reverse is often true. At any rate, François Mitterrand was born into a Catholic family in Jarnac, Charente, and "Catholic" at that time virtually always meant right wing. He went to a Catholic high school, and when he arrived in Paris at the end of the 1930s, as a student in law and literature, he lived in a religious dormitory. He was deeply Catholic, flirted with the Far Right at one point, and began to manifest his abilities as a leader.

At the start of World War II, during the 1939 campaign against Germany, Mitterrand was slightly wounded and then taken prisoner. Besides being fiercely anti-German, which was common at the time on both the right and the left, he could not bear being in a prisoner-of-war camp. He attempted escape several times and finally succeeded, at which point he offered his services at Vichy (the seat of the French government under the Nazi occupation), where, thanks to his political leanings and family connections, he had little trouble finding a position. He proved sufficiently supportive of Marshall Philippe Pétain's government to receive its highest honor, the Francisque; however, his anti-German sentiments drove him to simultaneously join the Resistance, where he soon occupied an important place in the underground activities carried out by former prisoners. This explains why he traveled to London and then Algiers to meet General Charles de Gaulle, the head of the Free French movement, with whom he maintained chilly relations from the outset.

EARLY POLITICAL CAREER
At the time of the Liberation in 1944, Mitterrand, twenty-eight years old and without a solid profession, turned to politics. He was elected deputy of Nièvre for the first time in 1946, a post he would be reelected to until 1958, but his personality quickly led him to become a minister. His first post was in the Socialist-led government of Paul Ramadier, one of many he held during the Fourth Republic, in which he played a unique role. Elected the first time as a more right-wing deputy (in a France that was leaning toward the left), he soon situated himself more on the left (in a France that was leaning to the right). He belonged to a splinter faction called the UDSR (Democratic and Socialist Union of the Resistance), a pivotal group buffeted between left and right wings, and which was above all a breeding ground for ministers because its vote

was often necessary to help one or another government win a majority. Mitterrand landed increasingly important posts. Pierre Mendès-France named him interior minister in 1954, and it was there that he was forced to confront the beginnings of the insurrection in Algeria, proclaiming forcefully that independence was impossible because France was one, from Dunkirk to the Congo. He had hopes of becoming cabinet chief when the collapse of the Fourth Republic, unable to handle the Algerian question, paved the way for the Fifth Republic, whose beginnings proved very painful for him. Not only did he lose his position as deputy in the 1958 elections, but he lost face in the 1959 "Affaire de l'Observatoire," a terrorist attack of which he would purportedly have been the victim, but which in fact he had more or less planned out himself.

However, this disgrace would turn out to his advantage. A determined opponent of General de Gaulle, Mitterrand ran for the presidency in 1965 and won the backing of the entire Left, as much because he stood almost no chance of winning as because he did not seem like a very formidable competitor to any of the other left-wing leaders of the time. Nonetheless his results, nearly 45 percent of the vote in the second round (whereas it had previously appeared that de Gaulle would win easily in the first round), catapulted him to the head of the ranks of the noncommunist left wing. From that moment forward he concentrated exclusively on becoming president of the republic.

Disgraced a second time when he vehemently announced his candidacy for president when the post was not vacant, he threw himself right back into the mix and, allied with a smaller faction called the Convention of Republican Institutions, displayed what it took to gain membership in the new Socialist Party and become its secretary all on the same day, at the Épinay-sur-Seine Congress in June 1971. His strategy then was simple: enter government by unifying the Left in alliance with the Communist Party, under the condition that the wing be reequilibrated, with the Socialist Party balancing out the Communists (an eventuality the Communists only took seriously when it was too late). The two parties agreed on a "Common Program for Government" in 1972 and fielded Mitterrand as the sole candidate from the left in

François Mitterrand shakes hands with supporters in Paris after his election to the French presidency, 14 May 1981. ©BETTMANN/CORBIS

the elections of 1974, following the unexpected death of Georges Pompidou. He got to within a hair's breadth of his goal, just barely losing in the second round to Valéry Giscard d'Estaing (49.19 percent versus 50.81 percent for his opponent).

Mitterrand's hopes seemed dashed when the Union of the Left fell apart in 1977 because the Communists realized it was not working to their advantage, and Giscard d'Estaing's party carried the legislative elections of 1978. Nevertheless, in the first round of presidential elections in 1981, Mitterrand easily beat the Communist candidate Georges Marchais (weakened by the growing discredit of the Soviet system), and in the second round he won out over d'Estaing with 52 percent of the vote, versus the latter's 48 percent. He would remain president of the republic for the next fourteen years, following his reelection in 1988. An

ardent adversary of the Fifth Republic's constitution because it accorded the president too many powers, he had no problem working with it when it played to his favor, but his two-term presidency was not without its pitfalls.

PRESIDENCY

Mitterrand's legislative agenda claimed to be socialist, and he announced early on he intended to complete the "changeover," meaning a break with capitalism. But after two years of major reforms, in particular the nationalization of a large portion of the industrial and financial sectors, the economic situation in 1983 forced him to change his policies. However, he had in the meantime become very unpopular as a result, and the Socialists lost the legislative elections in 1986. For the first time in its history, the Fifth Republic had a "cohabitation," in this case a president from the left and a parliamentary majority from the right. The same scenario was produced during his second presidency, when the Socialists lost the legislative elections in 1993, after having just barely regained their majority in 1988, and a new period of cohabitation ensued that lasted until the end of his second term in 1995. Under Mitterrand's presidencies, despite the presence of Communist ministers in the government from 1981 to 1984 (for the first time in thirty-four years), far from finally progressing down the path to socialism, France evolved toward liberalism.

Even though cohabitation deprived the president of a large part of his domestic political powers, it did make it possible for him to play a major role in foreign policy, and it was in this domain that Mitterrand truly made his lasting mark. At the beginning of his first seven-year term he had sought to implement a "leftist," "pro–third world" foreign policy, but as with domestic politics, he was forced to give it up because France lacked the means to pretend it could remake the world. Mitterrand played no specific role in the fall of European communism, except perhaps to try to slow it down. Although he had not been an especially passionate pro-Europe supporter during earlier periods of his career, he became one while president, and particularly during his second term he made great efforts to advance it. He worked actively to promote the passage of the Maastricht Treaty (1991–1992), the act that founded the European Union. When the United States began to take action against the Iraqi invasion of Kuwait in 1990, he brushed past a portion of both the Left and the Right and decided to associate France with the move, involving it in the Gulf War.

Mitterrand was without a doubt a forceful personality, but with a character that was perhaps too complex and contradictory to elicit consistent support. Tactically shrewd (his nickname during the Fourth Republic was "the Florentine," after Machiavelli, and he was forever breaking the everyday rules, in his private life in particular), highly cultured, a writer and a great orator, he incontestably dominated the twenty years of French political life before the end of his presidency, but he may not necessarily become one of its emblematic figures, on a par with Jean Jaurès, Georges Clemenceau, and de Gaulle.

Mitterrand carefully hid the fact that he suffered from cancer, which was diagnosed in the early years of his first term but also went into long periods of remission. He was gravely ill by the end of his second term and died less than one year after his official duties ended. In France, at least, an extraordinary days-long media frenzy ensued following his death.

See also **France; Gaulle, Charles de; Giscard d'Estaing, Valéry; Mendès-France, Pierre; Resistance.**

BIBLIOGRAPHY

Bell, David Scott. *François Mitterrand: A Political Biography.* Cambridge, U.K., 2005.

Berstein, Serge, Pierre Milza, and Jean-Louis Bianco. *Les années Mitterrand: Les années du changement (1981–1984).* Paris, 2001.

Duhamel, Eric. *François Mitterrand, L'unité d'un homme.* Paris, 1998.

Favier, Pierre, and Michel Martin-Roland. *La décennie Mitterrand.* 4 vols. Paris, 1990–.

Lacouture, Jean. *François Mitterrand: Une histoire de Français.* 2 vols. Paris, 1998.

Mitterrand, François. *Le coup d'état permanent.* Paris, 1964.

Nay, Catherine. *The Red and the Black, or the Story of a Dream.* Translated by Alan Sheridan. San Diego, 1987.

JEAN-JACQUES BECKER

MLADIĆ, RATKO (b. 1943), Bosnian Serb general and accused war criminal.

Ratko Mladić, a Bosnian Serb, is the son of a partisan fighter killed when Mladić was two. Then occupied by the Axis, Bosnia-Herzegovina was administered by a Nazi puppet regime, the Independent State of Croatia, which attempted the genocide of the Serbs; some three hundred thousand of them perished on its territory. Many fled to the ranks of Tito's (Josip Broz, 1892–1980) communist-led partisans, and Bosnian Serbs achieved a formidable postwar presence in the Communist Party of Yugoslavia, and in the Yugoslav People's Army (YPA), which Mladić chose to enter as a career soldier. Noted for his organizing skills, in 1991 he was chief of staff to the Army Corps based at Knin, in Croatia's Krajina, an area where Serb nationalist insurgency was waxing strong as Croatia moved toward independence. Mladić gave substantial material and moral support to the self-styled Serb Army of the Krajina, apparently without authorization from his military superiors.

In April 1992 the Federal Socialist Republic of Yugoslavia disappeared from the map. The Federal Republic of Yugoslavia (FRY) came into being, comprising only two of the six former communist republics, Serbia and Montenegro, with Slobodan Milošević (1941–2006) as president. One of his first acts was to promote Mladić to the rank of general in the Army of Yugoslavia, as the YPA was now restyled. Full-scale war broke out in Bosnia-Herzegovina, at which point the Army of Yugoslavia split to form the Army of Republika Srpska, more usually referred to as the Bosnian Serb Army (BSA). Mladić became military commander of the BSA at Milošević's insistence, but notionally he owed his appointment to a new political chief, Radovan Karadžić (b. 1945). On 27 March 1992, the Bosnian Serbs proclaimed an independent Republika Srpska (Serb Republic) within Bosnia-Herzegovina, and rejected the internationally recognized authority of the Sarajevo government. Karadžić was president of the new entity, with its representative assembly at Pale, twenty kilometers from Sarajevo. Milošević in this way represented the conflict in Bosnia as a civil war to which Belgrade was not party—the BSA was supposedly made up of fifty to eighty thousand troops of Bosnian origin, and therefore was not characterized as an invasion force. The United States and some European countries chose to swallow this nonsensical fiction for inglorious reasons of their own, with horrifying consequences.

The massive firepower of the BSA overwhelmed the Bosnian army loyal to Sarajevo, crippled by a Western embargo on the supply of arms. By 2 May 1992 Sarajevo was under close siege, and the Serbs controlled 70 percent of the territory of Bosnia-Herzegovina, a situation that remained unchanged until the last days of the war. Mladić's troops waged war against a people and a culture, in active collusion with paramilitaries from Serbia, in a sustained campaign of ethnic cleansing. The Muslim intelligentsia was targeted for elimination, and Serb forces carried out the wholesale destruction of all Islamic artifacts, from mosques to books. The Western media reported detention camps (some of them killing centers), mass rape, and the butchering of helpless civilians. Mladić was utterly contemptuous of international condemnation. As the war turned against him he revealed a streak of erratic wildness by threatening to bomb Western capitals, while his forces shot down NATO planes and took United Nations personnel as hostages, none of which advanced the Serbs' cause either militarily or politically. Mladić's worst crimes were committed in July 1995, when combined Croatian and Bosnian offensives were rolling the Serbs back. The Serbs retaliated by taking the UN "safe areas" of Žepa and Srebrenica, and at Srebrenica massacred seven thousand Muslims. For this atrocity, Mladić was indicted as a war criminal by the International Criminal Tribunal for the Former Yugoslavia.

Charged with two counts of genocide and thirteen other heinous crimes against international law, Mladić is still at large as of 2006. When the Dayton Agreements finally brought peace to Bosnia-Herzegovina in December 1995, he fled to Serbia, and lived openly in Belgrade under the protection of Milošević. Since the fall of Milošević he has remained in hiding, an important pawn in the endgame of the Balkan wars. The chief prosecutor at The Hague, Carla del Ponte (b. 1947), views the failure to capture Mladić as evidence of the bad faith of the government in Belgrade, although it is more likely he is being sheltered by elements of the military and security police operating outside the law. The threat of economic sanctions by the United States, which shares del Ponte's view that Mladić's capture is of the first importance in settling accounts with the Milošević regime, may partly explain why two of Mladić's military subordinates in Bosnia surrendered themselves in 2004. Mladić is very unlikely to follow them willingly, but in 2006 the net around him seemed to be slowly closing.

See also **Bosnia-Herzegovina; Crime and Justice; Karadžić, Radovan; Milošević, Slobodan; Sarajevo; Serbia; Srebrenica; Yugoslavia.**

BIBLIOGRAPHY

Bulatović, Ljiljana. *General Mladić*. Belgrade, Serbia, 1996.

O'Shea, Brendan. *Perception and Reality in the Modern Yugoslav Conflict: Myth, Falsehood, and Deceit 1991–1995*. New York, 2005. Has a great deal of interest to say about the character and conduct of Mladić, in the context of a survey of the war in Bosnia written by someone close to events.

LESLIE BENSON

MNOUCHKINE, ARIANE (b. 1939), French theater director and founder of the Théâtre de Soleil.

Ariane Mnouchkine was born in Paris in 1939 of a Russian father and English mother. Her career has been synonymous with the work of the outstanding modern French theater company Théâtre de Soleil, of which she is the founder and continuing artistic director. In 1959, while still a student at the Sorbonne, she formed with a group of fellow students a theater group that developed, in 1964, into the Soleil. Operating from the beginning as a collective, the group has continued to make decisions by majority vote, although Mnouchkine has always provided its central artistic vision. She has always been dedicated to the goal of popular theater and to the exploration of significant contemporary social and political concerns through highly theatrical productions drawing upon a very wide range of international performance sources, including commedia dell'arte, circus, and various Asian forms.

The company's first major success came in 1967 with Arnold Wesker's *The Kitchen*, which later, in the wake of the political upheavals in May 1968, toured to strikers in occupied factories. For both political and aesthetic reasons the Soleil then turned from the staging of literary texts toward "collective creations," building texts and performances out of the combined input and experience of the company. Their first such experiment was *The Clowns* in 1969, in which each company member developed his or her own personal "clown," reflecting their relationship with contemporary society.

In 1970 the company moved to their permanent quarters, the Cartoucherie, a former munitions storage center on the east edge of Paris. They divided the vast interior space of the Cartoucherie into two spaces, a large black-box theater and an adjoining immense lobby. In these spaces Mnouchkine and her company developed their unique performance aesthetic. Audiences gathered in the lobby before performances, often greeted by Mnouchkine herself, and could partake before or during the production of specially prepared food in some way connected with the current production. The entire lobby space would also be decorated to reflect the production, with books, maps, and charts to further immerse the spectator in that world. Inside the performance space actors were not hidden away but could be seen preparing for the production.

The opening productions at the Cartoucherie, *1789* (1970) and *1793* (1972) were among the most famous in the modern French theater. A number of individual platforms, some connected by walkways, others only by stairs from the floor, were scattered about the open space, and audience members were free to move about, surrounded by and sometimes engulfed by the events of the French Revolution. These productions placed Mnouchkine and her company at the forefront of modern French theatrical performance. Their next production, *L'age d'or* (1975; The golden age) moved their political concerns to contemporary France, dealing with the exploitation of immigrant laborers. *Mephisto* (1979), adapted by Mnouchkine from the novel by Klaus Mann, dealt with the problem of a theater artist's responsibility under a totalitarian regime.

This return to the literary text continued with one of Mnouchkine's most ambitious projects, a staging of three Shakespeare plays, *Richard II*, *Twelfth Night*, and *Henry IV, Part 1* (1982) in her own translations and utilizing costume and acting techniques from Asian traditions—Noh, Kabuki, and Kathakali. The dazzling resulting productions toured widely and established Mnouchkine's international reputation. The composer Jean-Jacques Lemêtre created musical accompaniment on instruments from around the world, and his work subsequently became an integral part of the ongoing Soleil aesthetic.

In 1984 Mnouchkine turned her attention to recent history, staging two modern epic dramas written by the feminist author Hélène Cixous: *L'histoire terrible mais inachevée de Norodom Sihanouk, roi de Cambodge* (1984; The terrible but unfinished history of Norodom Sihanouk, king of Cambodia) and *L'indiade ou L'Inde de leurs*

Ariane Mnouchkine with Paul Puaux, director of the Avignon Festival, July 1979. ©Pierre Vauthey/Corbis

rêves (1986; The Indiade, or the India of their dreams). Then in 1990 Mnouchkine returned again to the classics, with the monumental *Les Atrides,* a reworking of Euripides' *Iphigenia in Aulis* plus Aeschylus' *Oresteia,* with great visual spectacle including costumes based on the Indian Kathakali. In 1992 this production toured internationally.

Mnouchkine continued to be passionately devoted to social causes. In 1995 she went on a hunger strike to protest Europe's nonintervention in Bosnia and in 1995 welcomed illegal immigrants into her theater, an experience that inspired her production *Et soudain, des nuits d'éveil* (1997; And suddenly, sleepless nights). This social concern also grounded the Brechtian-like parable play *Tambours sur la digue* (2000; Drums on the dike), written by Cixous and staged in a style based upon Japanese Bunraku, and *Le dernier caravansérail* (2003; The last caravan), dealing with the search for sanctuary by displaced refugees in the contemporary world. In 2005 Mnouchkine received the UNESCO Picasso Medal for her work in the theater.

See also **Brecht, Bertolt; Cixous, Hélène; Theater.**

BIBLIOGRAPHY

Féral, Josette. *Trajectoires du Soleil: Autour d'Ariane Mnouchkine.* Paris, 1998.

Kiernander, Adrian. *Ariane Mnouchkine and the Théâtre de Soleil.* Cambridge, U.K., and New York, 1993.

Williams, David, ed. *Collaborative Theatre: The Théâtre de Soleil Sourcebook.* London, 1999.

Marvin Carlson

MODERNISM. The word *modernism* is used to characterize a wide range of aesthetic, political, and social movements in the twentieth century. Within the visual arts, architecture, and literature, modernism is most often recognized as demonstrating an intense engagement with a particular medium and the limits of its form. The larger constellation of social and political forces that bolster cultural production fall under the rubric of modernism as well. From the Bauhaus to surrealism to existentialism, all modernist works can be held to one overarching principle: the evaluation and expression of the governing parameters of an art form mobilized to critique and rediscover its proper essence. Indeed, the question "what is modernism?" is already anticipated by the very forms of modernist art. This self-critical tendency has given rise to a large, heterogeneous body of work, because each sociopolitical challenge to art and its role in modernity required a specifically devised aesthetic response.

EARLY EXPERIMENTS

Some of modernism's most important aesthetic experiments were conceived before 1914 but continued to exert influence on the arts throughout the rest of the century. In particular cubism—led by Pablo Picasso and Georges Braque—had a profound effect on painting, using the limits of two-dimensional representation as an analytical device for transforming everyday objects into drastically altered amalgams of lines and shapes. The cubists became a major touchstone for artists looking to radicalize a given medium, as well as for avant-gardes seeking to cut ties with the past; only the profound devastation and loss surrounding World War I would have as acute an impact on artistic production in the first half of the century.

WORLD WAR I: ALIENATION AND DISILLUSIONMENT

Between 1914 and 1918, scores of European intellectuals, artists, and writers fought in the trenches. The aesthetic and political sensibilities of those who survived were forever altered by the war. For many, the effects of the war and the impact of mechanization demanded a critical engagement based on the new relationships between self and community in light of emerging concerns about technology.

In Italy, the futurist artists and poets embraced the new machinery of war, creating works that attempted to embody the heightened sense of time and motion that accompanied the advance of technology. Founder Filippo Tommaso Marinetti drafted the group's "Founding and Manifesto of Futurism" (1909) shortly before the war began, arguing for the evisceration of Romantic-expressionistic concepts of the self under the new horizon of mechanical mediation and delineating the futurists' proto-fascist ambitions for art and politics to merge violently in the social sphere.

In other European nations, the avant-gardes were more critical of the political establishment. Dada, which was founded in Switzerland and later spread to Germany and France, used absurdist humor to ironize traditional art-world standards, the war, and the bourgeois values behind it. A diverse group of artists were associated with the movement, including Jean Arp, John Heartfield, Hannah Höch, Francis Picabia, and Hans Richter. The dadaists worked in nontraditional forms and employed innovative techniques such as photomontage to represent the vertiginous flow of visual information that typified the urban experience of the new postwar metropolis.

Surrealism was a direct outgrowth of the Dada movement and worked to reformulate its politically charged engagement with popular culture and the mass media. The French writer André Breton penned a manifesto for the group in 1924, but the movement had many distinct voices and expressions. The surrealists were fascinated with the operations of the unconscious and developed formal procedures for realizing its effects through automatism and chance procedures. Writers and artists alike worked to fuse a Marxist critique of capital with the newly popularized tenets of psychoanalysis developed by Sigmund Freud and later elaborated by Jacques Lacan, mining their unconscious desires to imagine pictorial and literary landscapes that were both liberating and derisive.

The combination of multiple endeavors in service of a singular aesthetic reached a pinnacle with the founding of the Bauhaus School of Art and Architecture. Formed in Germany in 1919, the Bauhaus's mission was nothing less than the amelioration of society on all fronts by combining the pedagogy and practice of craft and fine arts. The school preached the elimination of excessive ornamentation and superfluous design. Its affinity for clean, industrially inspired modeling was also championed by the Swiss architect Le Corbusier, whose treatise *Vers une architecture* (1923; *Towards*

Villa Savoie, Poissy, France. Designed by Le Corbusier, 1930. Le Corbusier's modernist designs transformed architecture in the twentieth century, emphasizing simplified geometric forms and innovative use of open space. ©EDIFICE/CORBIS

a New Architecture, 1927) helped to establish the international style in modernist architecture.

While the Bauhaus worked toward unification via the arts, writers throughout Europe attempted to capture and represent the alienation and fragmentation of the individual following the war, which resulted in an explosion of inventive narrative techniques. The Irish writer James Joyce radicalized the novel as a form, rejecting traditional structures such as plot in an attempt to represent the interior world of a character. Virginia Woolf, a British novelist and critic, developed a similarly innovative technique, writing in a stream-of-consciousness style that moved fleetingly through a range of characters' thoughts to produce connections between individuals that would not otherwise be evident. In the dark and surrealistic writings of the Czech writer Franz Kafka, the individual experience is again the focus; by placing an ordinary protagonist in an extreme and usually

unexplained circumstance, Kafka's works provided a worm's-eye view of one person's struggle against the dizzying and circuitous movement of an endlessly systematized bureaucracy.

The modernist torch was all but extinguished with the rise of National Socialism in Germany. Although many of the artists and intellectuals associated with these movements emigrated abroad, this critical phase of artistic engagement was all but eradicated by the Degenerate Art exhibition (1937), where Nazis confiscated some twenty thousand works that were deemed unsuitable to their social vision.

AFTER 1945: FINDING A PLACE FOR ART
In the wake of the Holocaust, artists in Europe worked to restore the potential for modernist art in a climate of tragedy and confusion. Some wished to revisit the legacy of the prewar avant-gardes, and others looked to the past with greater scrutiny. For

these artists, the avant-gardes' vision of mobilizing artistic movements for political ends helped define the ethos of prewar totalitarian regimes. The aesthetic movements that surfaced in the years immediately following World War II were thus largely characterized by an engagement with this contested past via a return to painting, specifically abstraction. The memory of the war and the legacy of both cubism and surrealism made an uneasy framework for painting. The multiplicity of artistic responses registered the inability of artists working in the wake of World War II to find a clear trajectory.

Several small, disparate movements that illustrate European artists' struggle to cope with the aftermath of the war and the ever-burgeoning influence of capitalism cropped up in the years between 1945 and 1960. One such movement in theater and literature aligned itself with the tenets of existentialist philosophy. These expressions were most thoroughly embodied in the work of Jean-Paul Sartre, whose plays, novels, and philosophical writings drew a portrait of the individual as an agent of responsibility set against the backdrop of a massive and hollow universe. In painting, a group of French abstractionists revisited the surrealists' notions of automatism and "informal" gestural practice under the appellation *art informel*. Artists such as Jean Fautrier and Hans Hartung employed disparate modes of representation that moved between heavily impastoed surfaces and lyrical, academic abstraction.

In the early 1950s, a collective of English artists and architects who called themselves the Independent Group began exhibiting works that turned away from art's past to engage directly with the new forms of advertising and consumerism. The Independent Group advocated a critical surrender to the philosophy of consumer capitalism by integrating art into innovation and leisure. In their signature 1956 exhibition, This Is Tomorrow, the group's members explored their growing fascination with the erotics of the artificial and the reproducible, blending the popularity of new styles of consumer advertising with the sensibility engendered by aesthetic encounters.

Beginning in the 1960s, artists across Europe began working outside of the traditional media of painting and sculpture. Groups such as the New

Realists in France and Arte Povera in Italy delved further (and sometimes fruitfully) into the cross-pollination of art and consumer culture. Opting for direct confrontations with the power structures of Europe, these movements proposed a more ambivalent relationship to the commodity form. They integrated into their canvases materials that were traditionally scorned by the practitioners of modernist painting. Paintings became fields in which the tensions between high and low culture, the aesthetic and the everyday, and the political and the social were mapped onto one another. The goal was to open the exclusionary boundaries of the picture frame to the contiguous social forms that were erupting in the changing political climate of the 1960s. Art's assumed place as an elite institution in the privileged realm of bourgeois society came under fire, and the search for its legitimacy in a culture of social revolution became a growing concern for modernists.

In Germany, the attempts to reckon with art's legacy in the aftershock of the war were especially fraught. Joseph Beuys, whose works and performances dealt with a return to the mythic structures of artistic practice, believed that everyone had the potential to be an artist. Under his tutelage, a new generation of young artists attempted to reconcile art-making with the broader community of student movements and social protests of the 1960s, most notably the fluxus and capitalist realist movements. The capitalist realists, lead by Konrad Lueg, Sigmar Polke, and Gerhard Richter, pursued painting as a necessary vehicle for critique of the commodity and of consumerism. For these artists, the longevity of modernist practice depended on pitting competing elements of popular culture against one another in an effort to reassert a place for art within the increasingly visualized forms of quotidian life.

With the 1970s came the rise of conceptualism, performance art, and other dematerialized artistic practices that stressed ideas over material production. This shift away from traditional modes of art-making is often considered the start of the so-called postmodern era. The legitimacy of this demarcation is a topic of serious debate within the study of modernist art, and has led some critics to argue that what has been hailed as postmodernism is merely the latest avatar of modernism itself. Advocates of postmodernism have maintained that the ambitions of modernism, which include its claims to authenticity and autonomy, were effectively exhausted or negated by the movements of the late 1960s and 1970s. In particular, turning away from the idea of originality and self-expression as elements essential to a work of art have been the key points of contention within these aesthetic movements.

This postmodern face of late-modernist art recodes the self-critical thrust of modernism as an investigation into the very groundwork of modernism itself. The material substrate of art as an object in the world is pulled apart and analyzed through language, performance, and institutional parameters. In the work of artists such as Marcel Broodthaers, Daniel Buren, and Hans Haacke, the museum itself took the place of traditional fine arts media, effectively becoming the nexus for modernism's reflexive explorations. These artists worked to expose the insidious social and commercial networks that support the production, exhibition, purchase, and sale of works of art, undermining the notion of the artist as a singular agent of creative expression in an effort to create awareness of the constructed division that art maintains between the social world and its own privileged spaces.

With the evolution of mass media, art has continually been forced to re-imagine its place in a globalizing market. As a result, the 1980s and 1990s saw a rise in concern with regionalism, nationally constructed identities, and nomadism through the work of artists caught between an inherited ethnicity and an adopted nationality. In England, the rise of cultural studies and postcolonial theory precipitated the emergence of the black British arts movement of the 1980s, which opened the formal questions of modernism to issues of race, gender, and sexuality. Young artists such as Sonia Boyce and Isaac Julien began working to destabilize these categories, employing a variety of media such as digital video and photography to investigate the construction of subjectivity under the influence of globalism.

Wherever art appears to be in crisis or the aesthetic is threatened by the demands of market capitalism or political censorship, one finds the circumstances vital to modernist practice. Predicated on the threat of its own obsolescence,

White Room. Installation by Marcel Broodthaers, 1975. Broodthaers continued the modernist exploration of the nature and meaning of art into the second half of the twentieth century, often juxtaposing text and images in the surrealist manner. CNAC/MNAM/Dist. Réunion des Musées Nationaux/Art Resource, NY

modernist art strikes out at itself in anticipation of the future conditions of its own compromised existence. Whether in feminist critique, performance, or photomontage, modernism is best understood as the need to envision new forms for art through intensive self-critical investigation. This is a peculiarly modern phenomenon, because art's place within the social sphere has become increasingly marginal since the dissolution of the state-controlled art academies of the nineteenth century. With the disappearance of this institutionalized reception, modernist art could look only to itself to replace its absent interlocutors. Both progenitor and critic, modernism will persist as long as the community that surrounds it continues to vanish.

See also **Avant-Garde; Cinema; Cubism; Dada; Existentialism; Futurism; Postmodernism; Surrealism; Theater.**

BIBLIOGRAPHY

Primary Sources

Breton, André. *Manifestoes of Surrealism.* Translated by Richard Seaver and Helen R. Lane. Ann Arbor, Mich., 1969.

Gropius, Walter. *The New Architecture and the Bauhaus.* Translated by P. Morton Shand. Cambridge, Mass., and London, 1965.

Secondary Sources

Curtis, William J. R. *Modern Architecture since 1900.* Englewood Cliffs, N.J., 1983.

Ellison, David R. *Ethics and Aesthetics in European Modernist Literature: From the Sublime to the Uncanny.* Cambridge, U.K., and New York, 2001.

Fer, Briony, David Batchelor, and Paul Wood. *Realism, Rationalism, Surrealism: Art between the Wars.* New Haven, Conn., 1993.

Foster, Hal, et al. *Art since 1900: Modernism, Anti-Modernism, Postmodernism.* London, 2004.

Travers, Martin. *An Introduction to Modern European Literature: From Romanticism to Postmodernism.* New York, 1998.

Wood, Paul, et al. *Modernism in Dispute: Art since the Forties.* New Haven, 1993.

COLIN LANG

MOHOLY-NAGY, LÁSZLÓ (1895–1946),

avant-garde painter, experimental sculptor and photographer, teacher, and philosopher of design education.

László Moholy-Nagy was born in Bácsborsod, Hungary, on 20 July 1895. Self-taught in the arts after abandoning the study of law in Budapest in 1913, Moholy-Nagy took up painting. After his military service in World War I, he held the first exhibit of his work in Budapest in 1918. Moholy-Nagy left Budapest for Vienna in 1919 and settled in Berlin in 1920. There he participated in the avant-garde artistic group *Gestaltung* (Form-giving), met constructivists such as El Lissitzky of Russia, and attended the Constructivist Congress in Dusseldorf. He met and married the photographer Lucia Schulz in 1921 and, in 1922, held his first solo exhibit in Berlin's Sturm Gallery.

Quick to adapt to new circumstances and absorb new artistic influences, Moholy-Nagy settled on a constructivist approach to art that emphasized the transformative potential of human engagement with machines and new modes of perception in a mechanized world. Recognized for his prodigious talent and natural teaching abilities by the visiting Walter Gropius (1883–1969) in 1923, Moholy-Nagy took a place as a Bauhaus "Master" the same year. At the Bauhaus in Weimar Moholy-Nagy inherited the celebrated "introductory course" from the recently departed Johannes Itten and directed the instructional workshop for metalwork. Moholy-Nagy cooperated closely with Walter Gropius as he reformed Bauhaus pedagogy to reflect his growing interest in forging a "new unity" between art and technology. Moholy-Nagy rejected Itten's emphasis on fostering the individual "artist-creator" in favor of a philosophy that emphasized the individual designer's contribution to reform in an industrial society. Of inestimable value to the experimental philosophical spirit and aesthetic adventurism of the Bauhaus was Moholy-Nagy's passionate interest in the way the fine arts and design interfaced with the latest, most advanced forms of industrial technology, modern communications, and manufacturing capabilities. Under his direction of the metals workshop, Bauhaus students engaged explicitly for the first time in industrial design rather than the crafts, developing prototypes of lamps and other metal objects for manufacture by industry. His creative projects for an array of utopian imaginary devices such as the "kinetic-constructive system" opened his students' minds further to the role that artists and designers could play in giving form to the material world amid burgeoning industrial growth and technological development. An innovator in sculpture as well as photography, Moholy-Nagy, with Gropius, also oversaw the design, layout, and typography for a series of fourteen influential *Bauhausbücher* (Bauhaus books) published by the school.

Moholy-Nagy resigned from the Bauhaus and separated from Lucia at the same time that Gropius stepped down as Bauhaus director in 1928. He opened a graphic design practice in Berlin and contributed stage set designs to the Kroll Opera House while continuing experiments in photography, film, and sculpture. His innovative construction of a "light-space modulator" broke new

AXXI. Painting by László Moholy-Nagy, 1925. Erich Lessing/ Art Resource, NY

ground in the realm of kinetic sculpture when it was exhibited in Paris in 1930. In this year he also met Sibyl Pietzsch, whom he married and with whom he had two daughters.

After emigrating to England with his family in 1934 and working there until 1937 as an industrial designer and graphic artist, Moholy-Nagy relocated to the United States to accept a position Gropius helped arrange for him at the school of the Association of Arts and Industries in Chicago. Moholy-Nagy renamed the school "The New Bauhaus" but was able to operate the school for only one year before financial difficulties caused it to be shut down. He opened his own school, the Institute of Design, the following year, and worked as a consultant and designer for numerous firms. The Chicago gallery owner Katharine Kuh exhibited his newest experiments with "light sculptures" in 1939.

The Institute of Design's efforts to expand the lessons of Gropius's Bauhaus faltered with Moholy-Nagy's early death in 1946. Nonetheless, working in proximity to Ludwig Mies van der Rohe's

Illinois Institute of Technology, Moholy-Nagy's school helped establish Chicago as a leading center for modern design and as an heir to the Bauhaus tradition in the mid-twentieth century. Moholy-Nagy's school and practice added a significant avant-garde layer to the city's proud tradition of architectural and design excellence. Moholy-Nagy's pedagogical ideas were summarized and disseminated in his posthumously published work, *Vision in Motion,* in 1947. The publication, like his teaching and practice, emphasized the development of the modern senses of all who lived in industrial society, so that a deeper design understanding and broader general appreciation of design would improve modern life as a whole.

See also **Bauhaus; Constructivism; Painting, Avant-Garde.**

BIBLIOGRAPHY

Hahn, Peter, and Lloyd C. Engelbrecht, eds. *50 Jahre New Bauhaus: Bauhausnachfolge in Chicago.* Translated by Lydia Buschan, Christian Wolsdorff, and Eva Heinemeyer. Berlin, 1987.

Moholy-Nagy, Sibyl. *Moholy-Nagy, Experiment in Totality.* Cambridge, Mass., 1950.

Schmitz, Norbert M. "László Moholy-Nagy." In *Bauhaus,* edited by Jeannine Fiedler and Peter Feierabend, 292–307. Translated by Translate-A-Book, Oxford, U.K. Cologne, Germany, 2000.

Wick, Rainer K. *Teaching at the Bauhaus.* Translated by Stephen Mason and Simon Lebe. Stuttgart, Germany, 2000.

JOHN V. MACIUIKA

MOLOTOV–VON RIBBENTROP PACT. On 23 August 1939 a nonaggression pact was signed between representatives of the Soviet Union and Germany committing both states to renounce violence against the other. A secret protocol was attached dividing parts of eastern Europe into spheres of interest for each of the two parties. The pact remained in force until 22 June 1941, when German armed forces attacked the Soviet Union without a formal declaration of war.

The background to the pact was closely linked with the collapse of the European balance of power in the second half of the 1930s. The revival of

German military and economic power in the 1930s with the appointment of Adolf Hitler (1889–1945) as chancellor in 1933 led to the redrawing of the political map of central Europe following German expansion into Austria (March 1938) and Czechoslovakia (October 1938, March 1939). By 1939 Britain and France were linked in a common cause to contain further German expansion. This presented the Soviet Union with a difficult choice, either to join the capitalist west to restrain Hitler and risk all-out European war, or to reach agreement with Germany and thus avoid war altogether. In May 1939 Soviet officials began exploratory discussion with German diplomats about the prospects for both economic and political agreements. While it is certain that Joseph Stalin (1879–1953) had not yet made up his mind which foreign policy option to take, the willingness of the German side to engage in negotiations began the process that resulted in the pact.

German interest in a pact with its chief ideological enemy stemmed from calculations of strategic interest. Hitler wanted to avoid any prospect of a major two-front war, and the German economy, facing heavy demands for the military buildup, needed additional raw materials and foodstuffs. Hitler's decision taken in April to launch war against Poland in late August 1939 made an agreement with the Soviet Union imperative. On 2 August the German foreign minister, Joachim von Ribbentrop (1893–1946), proposed a nonaggression pact and possible spheres of influence. On 19 August the first of a number of extensive trade agreements was signed. Hitler faced an ever tightening timetable for his war against Poland scheduled for a week later. On 21 August he wrote personally to Stalin asking him to accept an envoy to sign a political agreement. Stalin accepted and von Ribbentrop arrived in Moscow on 22 August. Terms were drawn up during the night: a formal commitment to nonaggression and a secret supplementary document assigning Finland, eastern Poland, Estonia, and Latvia to a possible Soviet sphere-of-interest. The pact was officially signed early in the morning of 23 August.

The consequences were profound. Hitler, on hearing the news, assumed that the western powers would now abandon Poland, or at the least make mere gestures of disapproval. Attack was postponed

from 26 August to 1 September, and a further agreement was made with the Soviet Union on 28 August clarifying the impending partition of Poland. Britain and France did not back down from their commitment to support Poland, arguing that the Soviet Union would have been a dangerous ally, and on 3 September declared war on Germany. The political outlook in Moscow was to accept the pact as part of a general revision of the European order and to hope that Germany, Britain, and France would fight a long slogging match leaving the two sides so weakened that the Soviet Union would be the political beneficiary. For communists outside the Soviet Union the pact came as a profound shock; some broke with Moscow, but most accepted that the real enemy was imperialist Britain. In the Soviet Union and Germany much of the party and public was unhappy and confused by the agreement but had to accept what was seen as the most expedient solution.

Further agreements followed on the pact and the joint occupation of Polish territory, completed when Soviet forces entered Poland on 17 September. A Treaty of Friendship and Borders was signed between von Ribbentrop and the Soviet foreign commissar Vyacheslav Molotov (1890–1986) on 28 September, which formalized the terms of the earlier secret protocol, with the important change that Lithuania was now assigned to the Soviet sphere while Germany was allowed more of central Poland. Between 29 September and 10 October the three Baltic states were forced to reach "mutual assistance" pacts with the Soviet Union and in June 1940 they were formally incorporated into the Soviet state. Finland, also assigned to the Soviet sphere, was attacked in November 1939 but succeeded in defending its borders sufficiently to reach an armistice with only minor territorial concessions.

Soviet-German collaboration suited Hitler while the war in the west was being fought, but he informed his close circle in late 1939 that this was only a breathing space before the great war of imperial conquest in the east. Soviet leaders thought that Germany would be mired in war for a long time, and even after French defeat in June 1940 assumed that Hitler would never attack the Soviet Union until the British Empire had been defeated as well. Molotov visited Berlin on 12 November 1940 in the hope that a second pact might be concluded giving the Soviet Union further concessions in eastern Europe. Hitler refused, and ordered final preparations for war. Stalin remained convinced, unlike many of his colleagues and the military leadership, that the nonaggression pact would remain intact in 1941, and made no extensive preparations against a possible German attack. On the morning of 22 June 1941 almost three million German and allied soldiers attacked the Soviet Union across a broad front and ended the pact. After the war the Soviet leadership never acknowledged the existence of the secret Soviet-German agreement.

See also **Germany; Soviet Union; World War II.**

BIBLIOGRAPHY

Bloch, Michael. *Ribbentrop.* London, 1992. Standard biography in English.

Gorodetsky, Gabriel. *Grand Delusion: Stalin and the German Invasion of Russia.* New Haven, Conn., 1999. Essential on aftermath of pact.

Nekrich, Alexander. *Pariahs, Partners, Predators: German-Soviet Relations, 1922–1941.* Edited and translated by Gregory L. Freeze; with a foreword by Adam B. Ulam. New York, 1997.

Pons, Silvio. *Stalin and the Inevitable War, 1936–1941.* London, 2002. Based on use of new Soviet sources.

Roberts, Geoffrey. "The Soviet Decision for a Pact with Nazi Germany." *Soviet Studies* 44 (1992): 67–87.

———. *The Soviet Union and the Origins of the Second World War.* London, 1995. Basic text on Soviet foreign policy in the 1930s.

RICHARD OVERY

MONDRIAN, PIET (1872–1944), abstract painter and modernist.

The Dutch artist Piet Mondrian was one of the great pioneers of abstract painting and an important figure in the advancement of modernism in the twentieth century. Generations of modern painters, architects, and designers were profoundly influenced by his distinctive geometric style of "neoplasticism." Mondrian's neoplastic paintings, composed of straight lines and rectangular planes of red, yellow, blue, white, black, and gray, were meant to render a new plasticity or space through abstract principles and primary colors. In his compositions, he pursued a balance and harmony intended to extend into the space of the built environment and stand as a model for the harmonious relationships he envisioned among people in a utopian future. Mondrian published his ideas in various avant-garde magazines, beginning in 1917 in *De Stijl* (The style), the journal of the eponymous group he cofounded that year with Theo van Doesburg and other painters and architects. The artists in this loose collective initially shared a vision of a better world through the integration and dissolution of the different arts in a complete, harmonious, and colored environment. Mondrian would always hold onto these ideas, though, like several of his peers before him, he left the group in 1925 over disagreements with its leader, Van Doesburg.

Pieter Cornelis Mondriaan was born in 1872 into a Reformed Protestant milieu. At age nineteen, he obtained a certificate to teach drawing and enrolled in classes at the State Academy of Fine Arts with the intent of becoming an artist. His earlier work up to 1908, which makes up the vast majority of his oeuvre, consists of rather traditional figurative paintings. Because international modernist movements were absorbed relatively late and in quick succession in Holland, Mondrian first experienced the influence of the postimpressionist painters Vincent van Gogh, Jan Toorop, Georges Seurat, and Paul Cézanne, and the cubism of Pablo Picasso between 1908 and 1911, resulting in a bolder technique, a brighter palette, and an increasingly systematic approach in his work. He changed his name to Mondrian when he lived in Paris between 1912 and 1914, assimilating the cubist vocabulary that would propel him toward complete abstraction in 1917. In *Composition in Line* of 1917, as in his later work, the emphasis is on the dynamic and purely relational interplay between verticals and horizontals. Through such ephemeral relations, Mondrian reinterpreted nature's spherical forms in terms of a dynamic play of interior and exterior forces, seeing deeper analogies with oppositions between energy and matter, and space and time, which recent science had also explained in relational terms. Mondrian's worldview was shaped by G. J. P. J. Bolland (1854–1922), the Dutch popularizer of the German idealist philosopher G. W. F. Hegel, and by Mathieu Schoenmaekers (1875–1944), a former Catholic priest and theosophist who invented the mystical theory of neoplasticism to explain the universe in terms of elementary cosmic forces.

Mondrian developed his own version of neoplasticism in painting during World War I while he was stranded in neutral Holland from 1914 to 1919, a time of restless searching and encounters with future De Stijl collaborators. He also returned to earlier motifs, such as ocean scenes and especially architecture. With its vertical-horizontal and interior-exterior oppositions, architecture became both motif and model for neoplastic painting, based on the elements they shared: the plane and rectangular relationships. When Mondrian returned to Paris in 1919 and arrived at his mature style, he also began to transform his studios into models of harmony by tacking rectangular colored pasteboards onto walls and furniture along neoplastic principles. The postwar Parisian avant-garde had mostly lost interest in abstraction, a "return to order" that demoralized Mondrian and almost made him give up painting. International recognition grew slowly, but by the early 1930s several avant-garde groups and journals devoted to abstraction included Mondrian in their exhibitions and publications (e.g., the movements Cercle et Carré and Abstraction-Création). By 1932 he had begun to multiply the lines in his compositions, creating a greater visual dynamism and compensating for the common misinterpretation of his "classic" compositions as static. In 1937 two of Mondrian's paintings were included in the Nazis' Degenerate Art exhibition. Fearing the threat of fascism, Mondrian moved to London in 1938, but the occupation of Holland, the fall of Paris, and the explosion of a V1 bomb in his street in 1940 made him flee to New York, where his reputation had preceded him. The septuagenarian artist celebrated the rhythms and sounds of the metropolis by reinvigorating his style with such late masterpieces as *Broadway Boogie Woogie* and *Victory Boogie Woogie*, which remained unfinished at the time of his death.

See also **De Stijl; Degenerate Art Exhibit; Modernism; Painting, Avant-Garde.**

BIBLIOGRAPHY

Blotkamp, Carel. *Mondrian: The Art of Destruction.* London, 1994.

Bois, Yve-Alain. "The Iconoclast." In *Piet Mondrian, 1872–1944*, edited by Yve-Alain Bois et al., 313–372. Boston, 1995. Published in conjunction with the exhibition at the Gemeentemuseum, The Hague; National Gallery of Art, Washington, D.C.; and the Museum of Modern Art, New York.

———. "Mondrian and the Theory of Architecture." *Assemblage* no. 4 (October 1987): 102–130.

Champa, Kermit Swiler. *Mondrian Studies.* Chicago, 1985.

Holtzman, Harry, and Martin S. James, eds. and trans. *The New Art—The New Life: The Collected Writings of Piet Mondrian.* Boston, 1986.

Jaffé, Hans L. C. *Mondrian.* New York, 1970.

Joosten, Joop M., and Robert P. Welsh. *Piet Mondrian: catalogue raisonné.* 2 vols. New York, 1998.

Mondrian: From Figuration to Abstraction. Tokyo, 1987. Published in conjunction with the exhibition in Tokyo, Miyagi, Shiga, Fukuoka, and The Hague.

Piet Mondrian, 1872–1944: Centennial Exhibition. New York, 1971. Published in conjunction with the exhibition at the Solomon Guggenheim Museum.

Seuphor, Michel. *Piet Mondrian, Life and Work.* New York, 1957.

Welsh, Robert P., and J. M. Joosten, eds. *Two Mondrian Sketchbooks 1912–1914.* Amsterdam, 1969.

MAREK WIECZOREK

MONNET, JEAN (1888–1979), French economist and diplomat.

Jean-Marie Omer Gabriel Monnet is, with Charles de Gaulle (1890–1970), one of the two giants of postwar French, European, and international affairs. Unlike de Gaulle, he was neither a politician nor a soldier. He never held elective office. Moreover, although his major contribution was in economic, administrative, and institutional reform and innovation, he was neither a trained economist nor a career civil servant. His originality and success are attributable to his unique combination of the virtues of French strategic vision and Anglo-Saxon tactical pragmatism.

EARLY CAREER

Born into a family of cooperative brandy merchants in Cognac on 9 November 1888, his early training was on the job. At sixteen, he was sent to London to learn English, his father having admonished him to not use books, but actively converse with people. In 1906, enrolling in the university of life, he set out as a salesman for the family firm tasked with challenging the major brands of cognac in key international markets. When war broke out, his international contacts and vision were mobilized in the cause of joint allied war-resource coordination, a scheme of intergovernmental collaboration unprecedented at that time, which helped, through the supply of wheat and shipping, to avert the worst dangers of submarine warfare. After the war, he was appointed deputy secretary general of the League of Nations, where he learned the hard way that states with veto powers can undermine the grandest of schemes. Disillusioned, he moved into investment banking, helping to refloat the Romanian and Polish currencies and to modernize China under Chiang Kai-shek (1887–1975).

In 1938, as World War II loomed, he was sent by the French government to lobby Franklin Delano Roosevelt (1882–1945) for the delivery of warplanes. He briefly headed the Anglo-French coordinating committee in London, where his May 1940 proposal for formal unification of the two nation-states was accepted by both Winston Churchill (1874–1965) and de Gaulle but aborted by the fall of France. He was then sent by Churchill to Washington, where he emerged as a major strategist behind Roosevelt's "Victory Program" of massive armaments production. After the Allied landings in North Africa, Monnet moved to Algiers and was instrumental in helping de Gaulle outmaneuver his rival General Henri Honoré Giraud (1879–1949). De Gaulle charged Monnet, within the National Liberation Committee, with armaments production.

POSTWAR DIPLOMACY

But Monnet's real influence was yet to come. After the Liberation of France, he persuaded de Gaulle to put him in charge of a brand new planning commission, the Commissariat Général du Plan, whose remit he saw as being not just to modernize and industrialize France but to change the mind-set of politicians, administrators, labor unions, and businessmen. "Modernization is not a material state, but a state of mind," he wrote. He saw his role as being "not to direct the regeneration of France, but rather to set the orientations, the methodologies and the

Jean Monnet, photographed at the first meeting of the ministers of the European Council in Paris, **15 January 1955.** GETTY IMAGES

rhythm." He identified six priorities: coal, electricity, transport, steel, cement, and agricultural equipment. Productivity was the key, indicative targets the objective, constant adaptation the methodology, and expansionism the mind-set. By 1950 the plan's targets were being exceeded, but more important, Monnet's method had achieved its objective of educating a new generation of French leaders to turn outward and embrace the economic and industrial world on its own terms. Investment in growth-oriented and sometimes even risky ventures became the new credo. France has never looked back.

Monnet's next vision was the European Coal and Steel Community (ECSC), whose objective was twofold: first, to maximize the joint ferro-carbon resources of France, West Germany, and neighboring countries (rejecting postwar French efforts to limit German coal and steel production); but second, and arguably more important, to merge the basic war-making capacities of Europe's two giants in such a way that conflict between them would be precluded. The 1951 ECSC, of whose federal "High Authority" Monnet became the first president, was the foundation stone for the European Community—later the European Union—of which he is universally considered to be the principal founding father. The project itself became known as the "Schuman Plan," because it was the foreign minister Robert Schuman (1886–1963) who sold it to the cabinet as the only way to square the circle between U.S. pressures for and French concerns about German rearmament. This was the first European institution with supranational authority. Konrad Adenauer (1876–1967), the German chancellor, confided to Monnet: "If this task succeeds, I will not have wasted my life."

The dilemma of how to build up German industrial and even military capacity as a bulwark against the Soviet Union had by 1950 (only five years after the war) become acute. Monnet was not content with devising the Coal and Steel Community. He also masterminded the proposal for a European Defence Community, the first of many subsequent schemes to pool Europe's security and defense capacity. Subsuming German armed force under a greater "European army" seemed the simplest way of squaring the rearmament circle. But the EDC ran up against two insuperable obstacles. The first was the obvious fact that, just as the German army would be subsumed in a European framework, so would the French army. This was too much for political opponents from right (Gaullists) and left (Communists) who effectively joined ranks in parliament to throw a (French) veto against this very French proposal. The other fatal flaw was the British refusal to be part of the project. Monnet's view that the pragmatic British would, with the EDC just as with the ECSC, eventually face up to "facts" proved correct in the long term but incorrect in the short term. The EDC was stillborn, paving the way for West Germany's accession to NATO in 1955.

But Monnet was already dreaming new dreams. His 1955 proposal for a European Atomic Energy Community (Euratom) was designed both to reduce European dependency on oil imports—a problem highlighted the following year by the Suez crisis—and to generate synergies between government, industry, and science in this key sector. Significantly, Euratom was founded on the principle that Europe's atomic program should have no military dimension, a proviso later overturned by de Gaulle. Concurrently, Monnet was heavily involved in the preparation of the Messina conference in June 1955, which not only endorsed the atomic energy proposal but also laid the groundwork for the more general European Economic Community (EEC), also known in the United Kingdom as the Common Market. Both projects were endorsed by the six founding member states, France, West Germany, Italy, Belgium, Netherlands, and Luxembourg, in the Rome Treaty of March 1957.

To ensure political support for the Rome Treaty, Monnet left the ECSC in October 1955 and launched his "Action Committee for the United States of Europe," geared, as he put it, not to "coalising states" but to "uniting peoples." He succeeded in attracting individual members from all the political parties and labor unions of the six founding states with the exception of Communists and Gaullists. His committee concentrated on overtures to both the United Kingdom (which Monnet urgently enjoined to embrace the European project) and the United States (which he invited to embrace a transatlantic "partnership of equals"). After some initial success in attracting Harold Macmillan (1894–1986) to the project, British membership was scuttled by de Gaulle's veto in January 1963. The U.S. president John Fitzgerald Kennedy (1917–1963), however, expressed enthusiasm for the Monnet vision of "two pillars" bridging the Atlantic. Monnet's influence seemed to be limitless.

DECLINING INFLUENCE

It was eventually cut short, however, by the return to power in 1958 of General de Gaulle. Although, paradoxically, de Gaulle accepted the EEC, and Monnet initially rallied to the general's parallel proposal for greater political cooperation between the Six (the Fouchet Plan), ultimately the objectives and methods of these two great Europeans proved incompatible. Monnet's penchant for supranational functionalism fell foul of de Gaulle's preference for a Europe of nation-states. De Gaulle's veto of British membership was a disavowal of Monnet's overtures toward the "Anglo-Saxon" world. Monnet himself was increasingly dismissed by the Gaullists as an agent of American influence in France and in Europe—the archetypal "Atlanticist." Although he continued with the work of the Action Committee for the United States of Europe until 1975, when it was disbanded his direct influence was over. It was left to a new generation trained in the committee, men such as President Valéry Giscard d'Estaing (b. 1926) and Chancellor Helmut Schmidt (b. 1918), to carry on his work.

Monnet's influence derives from three factors. First, his extraordinary capacity to launch visionary schemes of international cooperation often solved the right problems in the right place at the right time. Although he knew his fair share of failures (League of Nations, European Defence Community), he also enjoyed, as visionaries go, a much higher than average success rate. Second, although he himself was less interested in theory than in practice, his disciples carved out for him an undisputed legacy as the father of the "community method" a brand of neo-functionalism that believed that pragmatic success in one functional area would lead to "spillover" into other areas, with the result that "ever closer union" became an inexorable process, bypassing the political will of national leaders. Third, his fervent internationalism, while coexisting comfortably with the retention of national identity (he remained forever a native of France's southwest), has imposed itself across the globe as a model to be emulated wherever a group of nation-states embraces the political project of developing a whole that is greater than the sum of its parts.

Monnet retired to write his *Memoires* and when sympathizers called for advice invariably responded, "Keep going, keep going, there is no future for the people of Europe except in union." Monnet died in March 1979.

See also **European Coal and Steel Community (ECSC); European Union; League of Nations.**

BIBLIOGRAPHY

Primary Sources

Monnet, Jean. *Memoirs.* Translated by Richard Mayne. London, 1978

Secondary Sources

Brinkley, Douglas, and Clifford Hackett, eds. *Jean Monnet: The Path to European Unity.* Basingstoke, U.K., 1991.

Duchêne, François. *Jean Monnet: The First Statesman of Interdependence.* New York, 1994.

Roussel, Eric. *Jean Monnet, 1888–1979.* Paris, 1996.

JOLYON HOWORTH

MONTENEGRO. Historically Montenegro ("Black Mountain") represents one of the most turbulent spots in the Balkans; at first a semi-independent territory, it became a part of the Serbian medieval state in the twelfth century, and finally fell to the Ottomans in 1499. With a land-mass of only 5,333 square miles and a population of some 650,000, early-twenty-first-century Montenegro could soon become the smallest independent country yet to emerge from the ruins of what used to be Yugoslavia. This might come as part of the continuing political recomposition of southeastern Europe, following the unification of Germany and the collapse of the Soviet Union. However, the process would require the dissolution of Montenegro's union with Serbia, which may be difficult to accomplish because of the sharp division that splits the country into two equal political camps. This conflict echoes the dilemma that has plagued the Montenegrins since the beginning of the twentieth century: is their country a nation-state, a geographical territory, or a historical bastion of Serbdom? Meanwhile, the Montenegrin economy is largely dependent on foreign aid and the country is vulnerable to all kinds of outside pressures. These factors will probably decide Montenegro's political future in the same way they have shaped its past during the twentieth century.

As Serbia's staunch ally at the beginning of World War I, Montenegro fully coordinated its military operations with the Serbs in 1914 and 1915. However, when Nikola Petrović (1860–1918), the king of Montenegro—unable to hold out against superior Austrians—disbanded his army and left for France, his opponents, the pro-Serbian "Whites," pushed for the unification with Serbia. Despite some opposition by the king's supporters, the so-called Greens, the Great National Assembly voted in favor of the unification in November 1918, declaring that "the Serbian people in Montenegro are of one blood, one language, and one aspiration, one religion and custom with the people that live in Serbia and in other Serbian regions." After forty years of formal independence from the Ottoman Empire, Montenegro thus united with Serbia—soon to become a part of the Kingdom of Serbs, Croats, and Slovenes (renamed Yugoslavia in 1929) under the Serbian Karadjordjević dynasty.

After King Alexander Karadjordjević (1888–1934) introduced new internal borders in 1931 Montenegro became known as Zetska Banovina. A new player appeared on its political scene: Communists carried off 40 percent of the votes for the National Assembly in the election of 1920. The popularity of the new, "Russian" ideology was not entirely unexpected. From the first half of the eighteenth century to World War I Russia had supported Montenegro politically as well as financially, paying for its army, administration, infrastructure, and even food. Many Montenegrins traditionally claimed that they and the Russians were "one hundred million strong."

At the beginning of World War II, backed by the Italians who occupied Montenegro, the separatist Greens declared independence on 12 July 1941. The very next day, however, a popular uprising took place and most of Montenegro was temporarily liberated. Due to the disunity among the insurgents—the "internationalist" (communist) partisans were pitted against the "nationalist" Chetniks—the two-pronged, liberation/civil war was extremely bloody, and Montenegro lost almost 14 percent of its prewar population of four hundred thousand.

After 1945 Montenegro became one of Yugoslavia's six constituent republics. The victorious Communists supported the Greens' idea of the Montenegrin non-Serbian identity, and officially developed the concept of the Montenegrin nation. In economic terms, Montenegro remained poor, second only to the province of Kosovo, despite a number of Potemkin village projects, including two international airports built only sixty miles apart. In 1948—when the Yugoslav leadership split with Joseph Stalin—it again became clear how strong Soviet influence was in Montenegro: 20 percent of all pro-Soviet political prisoners in Yugoslavia were Montenegrins, although they made up less than 2.5 percent of the population.

After Yugoslavia's violent breakup in 1991 Montenegro joined Serbia in the "rump" Yugoslavia.

However, in 1997 President Milo Djukanović (b. 1962) distanced himself from his political mentor Slobodan Milošević (1941–2006) of Serbia and became a factor in the U.S. and European attempts to depose Milošević. After Milošević's fall in 2000 Serbia and Montenegro once again changed the nature of their relationship and formed a virtual confederation in 2002. Montenegro remains a sharply divided land: the traditional White/Green political conflict has multiplied in a number of various formal divisions (Serbian Orthodox Church versus noncanonical Montenegrin Orthodox Church; Montenegrin Academy of Arts and Sciences versus Doclean Academy).

See also **Milošević, Slobodan; Serbia; World War I; World War II; Yugoslavia.**

BIBLIOGRAPHY

Dedijer, Vladimir, et al. *History of Yugoslavia*. Translated by Kordja Kveder. New York, 1974.

Fleming, Thomas. *Montenegro: The Divided Land*. Rockford, Ill., 2002.

Lampe, John R. *Yugoslavia as History: Twice There Was a Country*. 2nd ed. Cambridge, U.K, and New York, 2000.

BOGDAN RAKIĆ

MORO, ALDO (1916–1978), Italian politician.

Aldo Moro was Italy's most powerful politician during the 1960s and 1970s. He was born to a devoutly Catholic professional family at Maglie, in the southern region of Apulia. A brilliant student at the University of Bari, he entered political life under Mussolini's regime by joining the Fascist youth movement, Gioventù Universitaria Fascista (Fascist University Youth). He accepted the dictatorship, whose corporate theory he viewed as compatible with Catholic social teachings and whose institutions he believed capable of creating a society based on religious principles. Making a rapid intellectual career at an unusually young age, he was appointed professor at Bari.

World War II alienated Moro from fascism. The war revealed the bankruptcy of a regime that brought Italy military defeat, economic collapse, and political crisis. The political system needed to be rebuilt, and Moro believed that Catholics had a vital role to play. To avoid the extremes of communism and fascism, Moro argued for social justice, toleration, and Christian charity. To achieve these ends, he entered the newly founded Christian Democratic Party (DC), where he took a position on the left of the party as a member of the progressive faction led by Giuseppe Dossetti and influenced by Jacques Maritain. Most distinctive was Moro's opinion that dialogue across the political spectrum had to include socialists and communists.

The DC, however, did not become the party of reform that Dossetti had envisaged. Faced with a powerful resistance movement led by the Left, fearing the possibility of revolution, and pressured by the Vatican, the DC under Alcide De Gasperi rapidly became the party of Italian capitalism, of the social status quo, and of the Cold War alliance with the United States. In 1951 Dossetti retired from politics in disillusionment and entered a religious community.

Ever subject to the allure of power, Moro remained with the party and assisted it in managing Italian politics. Moving to the center of DC politics, he retained the vocabulary of reform while shrewdly managing the interests of the political machine that dominated Italy. His great opportunity came in 1959, when the party chose him as its secretary. Serving variously as minister of foreign affairs, prime minister, and party leader, Moro dominated the period of social tensions that marked the 1960s and 1970s.

These tensions resulted from multiple causes: rapid economic growth, mass migration from the south to northern cities, deflationary policies that caused wages to lag far behind prices, environmental degradation, the failure of the state to carry out reforms, a long history of distrust on the part of Italians toward their political institutions, and the external pressures of the Cold War. The result was an upsurge in votes for the Italian Communist Party (PCI) and a series of protests by workers, students, the unemployed, and women, culminating in the student protests of 1968 and the workers' "hot autumn" of 1969. The extreme Right led a backlash that included violent police repression, fascist-inspired bombings, of which the most

notorious was at the Piazza Fontana, and plans for a coup d'état.

Unwilling to press for the social and economic reforms that he had urged in his early years, Moro sought to defuse the crisis by a political maneuver. His idea was that the stability of the state could be preserved by an "opening to the left"—first toward the Socialist Party in the 1960s and then the Communist Party in the 1970s. Moro believed that the Left could be outflanked by giving the opposition parties a share of power and a stake in the status quo. The first result of this strategy was a center-left coalition with the Socialist Party during the 1960s. Its dramatic culmination, however, was the government that was to be launched on 16 March 1978 and supported by Communist votes.

On that day, Moro's car was ambushed on its way to parliament. After killing his five bodyguards, the revolutionary and terrorist group the Red Brigades kidnapped Moro and held him in a "people's prison" for fifty-five days. After staging a trial, the brigades murdered him and left his body in the trunk of a car carefully parked halfway between the headquarters of the DC and those of the PCI.

The Red Brigades targeted Moro as the symbol of the Italian state and of the repressive political order they wanted to destroy. Because he was an advocate of the historic compromise with the PCI, they saw Moro as corrupting the revolutionary movement and leading it to betray the cause. By striking down Moro, they hoped to galvanize the masses into the uprising they believed to be imminent. This display of power was intended to foster a myth of the brigades' invincibility and the vulnerability of the authorities.

After a series of investigations and trials that resulted in numerous convictions of brigade members for murder, debate over ultimate responsibility for the assassination continues and conspiracy theories abound. The Moro family has insisted that the full truth never emerged and that the complicity of powerful interests was never exposed.

See also **Cold War; Communism; Fascism; New Left; Red Brigades; Socialism.**

BIBLIOGRAPHY

Curcio, Renato. *A viso aperto: intervista di Mario Scialoja.* Milan, 1993.

Drake, Richard. *The Aldo Moro Murder Case.* Cambridge, Mass., 1995.

Ginsborg, Paul. *History of Contemporary Italy: Society and Politics, 1943–1988.* London, 1990.

Lumley, Robert. *States of Emergency: Cultures of Revolt in Italy from 1968 to 1978.* London, 1990.

FRANK M. SNOWDEN

MOROCCO. Morocco has been in contact with its European neighbors (France, Spain, Portugal) since the sixteenth century. The Moroccan sultans captured European doctors, soldiers, and engineers in Mediterranean naval battles (maritime jihads) and brought them to the palace. These captives served the sultan as slaves or converted to Islam, married Moroccan women, took Muslim names, and assumed ranks in the sultan's administration. Such "renegades" included the Englishman Ismail Ingliz (English Ismael), who was tutor to the young sultan Mawlay Hasan (r. 1873–1894) and helped develop the Moroccan infantry. Morocco was also tied to Europe through trade, and the sultan's commercial dealings with Europeans were conducted mostly through Moroccan Jews. Jewish families maintained trade networks that linked London, Amsterdam, Livorno, and Morocco.

COLONIAL CONQUEST AND EUROPEAN RIVALRIES

The power balance between Morocco and Europe shifted dramatically after Morocco was defeated by France (1844) and Spain (1860) and with the colonial conquests of neighboring Algeria (1830) and Tunisia (1881). Sultan Mawlay Hasan was forced to institute large-scale, Ottoman-style state reforms and borrow money from European banks. In an effort to defend fragile Moroccan sovereignty, the sultan played French, Spanish, English, and German ambitions against one another. His young successor, Sultan Abd al-Aziz (r. 1894–1908), was no match for the Europeans, and Morocco fell deeply into debt between 1900 and 1904.

The European rivalry that erupted in 1914 was first expressed in a contest over Morocco. France consolidated its control over the Moroccan debt with a loan in June 1904 from the Banque de Paris et des Pays Bas; in exchange for 62.5 million francs, France acquired the right to the majority of Moroccan customs revenue. In the secret Franco-British Entente Cordiale (April 1904), Britain agreed to recognize French dominance in Morocco in exchange for a free hand in Egypt. Kaiser William II (r. 1888–1918) demanded an international conference to decide the Moroccan question in 1905. The Act of Algeciras (1906), signed by thirteen European countries, further opened Moroccan markets to foreign companies and sealed the fate of the Moroccan economy.

Popular Moroccan outrage at the sultan's concessions plunged Morocco into civil war in 1907. Tribal confederations waged jihad against the foreigners and proclaimed the sultan's brother, Mawlay Abd al-Hafid, the new sultan in 1907. In the southern Sus region, the religious reformer Ahmad Haybat Allah (Al-Hiba) led a jihad and proclaimed himself sultan in 1911. The French used this political chaos to justify occupying Oujda and the Chaouia region in 1907 and to force Sultan Mawlay Abd al-Hafid to accept French "protection" in the Treaty of Fès on 24 March 1912. The French had to share Morocco with the Spanish government, who negotiated the Treaty of Madrid on 27 November 1912. This created a Spanish Protectorate in Northern Morocco (capital Tétouan) and a 23,000 square kilometer territory in the Western Sahara. The city of Tangier became an "international zone," later home to American and British expatriates (Barbara Hutton), writers and artists (William S. Burroughs, Walter Harris, Henri Matisse) and an underworld of drugs and prostitution.

THE FRENCH AND SPANISH PROTECTORATES

Resident General Louis-Hubert Lyautey (1854–1934) conquered Morocco for France and became the architect of the French Protectorate (1912–1956). Troubled by the destructiveness of French colonialism in Algeria, Lyautey vowed to preserve the integrity of Moroccan society. The new regime would introduce "administrative, judicial, educational, economic, financial and military reforms," yet protect "the respect and traditional prestige of the Sultan, the practice of the Muslim religion and the religious institution" (Alaoui, pp. 247–248).

This respect for Islam did not preclude replacing Sultan Mawlay Abd al-Hafid with his more pliable relative Mawlay Yussuf (r. 1912–1927) or moving the Moroccan capital from Fès to Rabat. In practice, Lyautey left the sultan and his officials in place (they constituted what was known as the *Gouvernement Chérifien*) but created a French shadow government of "technical experts" who exercised the real authority over natural resources, cities, law, and commerce. The French Senate was skeptical about this new conquest, but Morocco proved immediately useful to France by providing 34,000 native troops in World War I and 114 million francs of agricultural exports in 1918.

French rule profoundly affected Moroccan society. First, as Lyautey intended, European colonists were never as powerful in Morocco as they were in Algeria. The French Protectorate remained military, and colonial agricultural development was conducted in part through industrial "agribusiness." Lyautey's policy protected Islamic life: medinas (traditional cities) were preserved, Moroccans controlled Islamic education and law, and there was minimal effort to Christianize Berbers. However, "protection" was also at times a policy of neglect. The traditional Islamic Qarawiyyin University fell into disrepair and Moroccans did not benefit from universal public education or modern urban planning. In 1931 there were only 1,618 Moroccan students in French secondary schools. To rule the countryside, the French encouraged local landlord intermediaries such as the rapacious Glaoua brothers, who grew immensely rich on the peasants of Marrakech. French rule also paradoxically laid the foundations for a postindependence Moroccan state by bringing remote tribal Berber regions (the Sus, the Sahara, High Atlas) under a new level of state surveillance and control.

Moroccan Jews were the population most transformed by the French presence. Under Muslim rule, Jews had inferior legal status and no access to political power. Forbidden by law to travel on horseback or carry weapons, Jews lived in self-governed, urban ghettos (*mellah*) near the palace. Some Jewish families who served the sultan became wealthy, but most were poor and their desperate state inspired European philanthropy and intervention. In Britain, Sir Moses Montefiore (1784–1885) lobbied the sultan to protect native Jews, and the French Alliance Israélite Universelle (AIU, founded 1860) created an extensive network of schools and medical clinics for Jews. The AIU schools provided French instruction in literature, science, hygiene, sewing, and administrative skills. Moroccan Jews assimilated quickly to French culture, found employment in European companies, and adopted French names and clothing. Jews did not leave Morocco in large numbers until after World War II, because the AIU was hostile to Zionism and the French Protectorate opposed Jewish emigration.

Spanish rule in Morocco had as much impact on Spain as on Morocco itself. The Spanish zone was disorganized and unproductive; it provided only 7 percent of total Moroccan exports in 1929. The Spanish army was also ill prepared to battle the fierce Rif Berbers, the wily bandit El Raisuni, and the nationalist Muhammad ibn Abd al-Karim al-Khattabi, who led a massive 1925 uprising and declared a republic in the Rif. Many Berbers joined the Spanish army as *regulares* and served under right-wing *Africanista* officers such as General Francisco Franco. The Spanish Left denounced these Moroccan troops as "stormtroopers of the Reaction," particularly after Franco imported Moroccan troops to crush a socialist uprising in Asturias in 1934. Franco launched his fascist revolution from Morocco in 1936 with his personal Moorish Guard and sixty to seventy thousand Moroccans fought for Franco in the Spanish civil war (1936–1939).

THE EFFECTS OF WORLD WAR II

World War II marked a transition between old and new Morocco. French prestige suffered a terrible blow with the 1940 defeat and the armistice. America appeared as Morocco's liberator and friend with the Allied landings in 1942, and the Morocco-American friendship continued after independence. Resident-General Charles Noguès implemented anti-Jewish legislation in Morocco but was prevented by Sultan Muhammad V (r. 1927–1961) from deporting Moroccan Jews. Still, Moroccan Jews left for Israel after 1946, first clandestinely with the help of the Haganah, a Jewish paramilitary organization in Palestine, then legally after 1949 through an Israeli organization, Cadima.

Moroccans brandish weapons during a demonstration against the French government, August 1955. The demonstrations in Khenifra were part of an uprising throughout French colonies in North Africa which resulted in violence and bloodshed. ©BETTMANN/CORBIS

World War II created unprecedented economic integration between France and Morocco; seventy thousand Moroccans served in the French army and more than one hundred thousand worked in the mines, factories, and fields of France during the war. Also, by 1946 the economy of Morocco had modernized. The use of motor power doubled between 1938 and 1949. New industries appeared (phosphate mining, citrus, viticulture, chemicals); older industries had been transformed (fishing, cereals, textiles, construction); and the French built transportation, communication, and irrigation infrastructure. A new Moroccan middle class invested in modern capital and a new Moroccan working class organized into (illegal) labor unions. In 1920 one tenth of the Moroccan population was urban, but by 1950 one quarter of the population lived in cities, giving rise to such social problems as shantytowns and tuberculosis.

THE NATIONALIST MOVEMENT AND THE LEGACY OF EUROPEAN RULE

The Moroccan nationalist movement was the intellectual product of Islamic modernism but developed in reaction to French rule. In 1921 Islamic scholars such as Allal al-Fassi and Muhammad al-Arabi al-Alawi opened "Free Schools" offering a modern Islamic Salafi-style curriculum. The Salafiyya, a branch of Islamic modernism, argued that the unified, pure Islam predating the "historical" divisions of Sufism and Shiism (Al-Salaf = the companions of the prophet Muhammad) was reconcilable with modernity. The future nationalists Muhammad Hassan al-Wazzani, Omar Abd al-Jalil, Muhammad Ahmad Belafrej, and Muhammad Lyazidi studied in France and became politicized. The traditional and modernist groups came together to oppose a French colonial law, the Dahir Berbère of 6 April 1930, which proposed to govern Berbers under customary law (*orf*) and Arabs under Islamic law (*sharia*). Nationalists across the country accused the French of trying to divide Arabs from Berbers and organized popular protests. The nationalists struggled first for a plan of reforms and later demanded formal independence (*Istiqlal*) in 1944. Sultan Muhammad V embraced the nationalists and became a symbol of the unified, independent Morocco that emerged in 1956.

European rule has a legacy in independent Morocco. The Susi Berbers have transformed their class status through migrant labor to France, saving their wages and investing in Moroccan land and industry. This new Berber bourgeoisie has come to rival the traditional Arab (*Fassi*) bourgeoisie. Moroccan Jews live mostly in Israel, France, and French-speaking Canada. A colonial contest between France and Spain over the Sahara has resulted in a military conflict between Morocco and Western Sahara. Yet France and Morocco have a unique relationship; the late King Hassan II (r. 1961–1999) stood beside President Jacques Chirac on Bastille Day, 14 July 1999, in honor of their fraternity and shared national histories.

See also **Algeria; Decolonization; French Empire.**

BIBLIOGRAPHY

Alaoui, Moulay Abdelhadi. *Le Maroc du traité de Fès à la libération, 1912–1956*. Rabat, Morocco, 1994.

Ayache, Albert. *Le mouvement syndical au Maroc*. 3 vols. Paris, 1982–1993.

Halstead, John P. *Rebirth of a Nation: The Origins and Rise of Moroccan Nationalism, 1912–1944*. Cambridge, Mass., 1967.

Laskier, Michael. *The Alliance Israélite Universelle and the Jewish Communities of Morocco, 1862–1962*. Albany, N.Y., 1983.

Pennell, C. R. *Morocco since 1830: A History*. New York, 2000.

Rivet, Daniel. *Lyautey et l'institution du Protectorat français au Maroc, 1912–1925*. 3 vols. Paris, 1988.

Waterbury, John. *Commander of the Faithful: The Moroccan Political Elite, A Study in Segmented Politics*. New York, 1970.

Wright, Gwendolyn. *The Politics of Design in French Colonial Urbanism*. Chicago, 1991.

ELLEN J. AMSTER

MOSCOW. Formerly the capital of the Union of Soviet Socialist Republics (USSR, 1922–1991), and in the early twenty-first century the capital of the Russian Federation, Moscow is Russia's principal megalopolis—an industrial, banking, scientific, and cultural center.

Between 1914 and 2004 the sociopolitical paradigm of Moscow's development changed twice: in 1917, when the Communist regime was established, and in 1991, when it collapsed. Accordingly, the forms of property ownership changed (from market to planned regulation, and then back to market), as well as the patterns of social life, local government, cultural development, and everyday life. From 1914 to 2004 the city's area grew fivefold, thanks to the incorporation of bordering settlements. In 1960 the oval Moscow Ring Road (MRR), 109 kilometers in length and encompassing an area of 886.5 square kilometers, became the city's border. In 1985, after a number of large tracts of land under housing construction beyond the MRR had been incorporated into the city, its area grew to 998 square kilometers.

POPULATION

With more than 1.6 million inhabitants, Moscow in 1914 ranked ninth among the world's largest cities (after London, New York City, Paris, Berlin, Chicago, Vienna, Philadelphia, and St. Petersburg). By 2002 it had grown to more than 10.3 million inhabitants. Throughout the twentieth century, population growth resulted mostly from in-migration. Twice the population fell dramatically as hundreds of thousands fled to safer regions: during the civil war (in 1918–1919 by 434 thousand) and World War II (in 1941 by 2.2 million). During the Soviet era, migration into Moscow was artificially restricted. On 27 December 1932, after the introduction of domestic passports and the *propiska* (residence registration) system in the USSR, settlement in Moscow was prohibited except in the event of marriage, enrollment in Moscow higher-educational institutions, or employment in certain specific jobs.

Stalinist policies imposed strict supervision over population movement. In 1934, for example, sixty thousand people left Moscow, fearing checks by the police and subsequent repression. The *propiska* was abolished only in 1993, replaced by a system of registration and permission to live and work in all regions. This change in legal norms resulted in a dramatic rise in migration into Moscow from the early 1990s onward (especially after the USSR's disintegration in 1991). By the mid-2000s, Moscow housed more than 7 percent of Russia's total population.

In the mid-2000s, Russian was the native language of 95 percent of Moscow residents. Despite a gradual rise in multiethnicity throughout the century, the majority of the population remained Russian: 87.8 percent in 1926, 89.2 percent in 1970, and 84.8 percent in 2002. Other major population groups included Ukrainians (2.2, 2.8, and 2.45 percent in 1939, 1989, and 2002, respectively) and Tatars (1.4, 2.1, and 1.6 percent in 1939, 1989, and 2002, respectively). After 1991 a decline in the number of Jews (0.76 percent in 2002) was caused by mass emigration to Israel, Germany, and the United States, and by the ethnic assimilation of new generations born in mixed marriages. By contrast, the proportion of Caucasians (Armenians, Azerbaijanis, Georgians, Chechens, and so forth) rose from 0.35 percent in 1939 to 0.95 percent in 1959 and to 4.5 percent in 2002.

The worst outbreaks of xenophobia occurred in 1915 (anti-German pogroms during World War 1, when Germany was Russia's major foe); in 1948–1953, during the campaigns against so-called cosmopolitanism, which targeted the Jewish intelligentsia; and in the late 1990s and early 2000s during anti-Caucasian pogroms at the markets, when traders from the Caucasus were targeted.

WORLD WAR I AND REVOLUTION

The twentieth-century history of Moscow, like that of other world megalopolises, was complicated and often dramatic. In 1914 Moscow was a picturesque city full of new, multistoried apartment blocks and old, prestigious detached houses. Twenty kilometers of central streets were illuminated by electricity. Thanks to efficient municipal authorities, the city had modern water-supply and sewage systems and a wide network of streetcar lines. Free medical service for the population was provided by eighteen hospitals with beds for seven thousand patients, eleven maternity homes, and thirty-two outpatient clinics. In 1915 all children had access to free primary education at 333 primary schools for seventy-five thousand pupils. The city had 15 higher-educational institutions and 160 libraries (including 76 public ones). In 1910 a telephone station for sixty thousand subscribers was built. Radio broadcasting started in 1914. Industry was represented by more than twelve hundred enterprises, of which twenty-five had a labor force ranging from one to six thousand workers. The dominant branches were the textile industry (43 percent of the general volume of production and 40 percent of the labor force) and the food industry.

This dynamic period of growth was interrupted by World War I, during which Moscow was inundated with refugees from the war-ravaged western provinces of the Russian Empire. More than 1,075 hospitals with 100,000 beds were established to treat wounded soldiers. The situation steadily deteriorated: wages could not keep up with inflation, and the supply of food and goods markedly declined. By 1916 there was a shortage of bread, the trams stopped, and the gas supply was repeatedly interrupted. The decline in the standard of living resulted in a rising wave of strikes, from 27 in 1914 to 235 in 1916. In January–March 1917 a fuel and food crisis erupted, followed by the onset of starvation.

Moscow was shaken by mass political demonstrations during the revolutionary year 1917. After the tsar abdicated in March, power passed into the hands of the provisional government. In June 650,000 persons (56 percent of all registered voters) took part in elections to the City Duma (municipal council) in which the Socialist Revolutionary Party (SR) won the overwhelming majority of votes. At the same time the Moscow Soviet (Mossovet), a rival political body of workers, steadily increased its influence on the population. After September the SR's chief rival, the Bolsheviks, dominated the Mossovet. By October the Soviet and the Duma were governing in parallel. On 25–26 October 1917 Bolsheviks seized power in Petrograd. During the next eight days Moscow was the scene of political confrontation between Reds (supporting the Bolshevik Soviet) and Whites (supporting the bourgeois Duma), which degenerated into armed clashes. Barricades were erected, fires started, and gradually, Red militias from the suburbs infiltrated the city center and started to gain the upper hand over the Whites. For four days Bolshevik detachments bombarded the Kremlin with artillery shells, until the Whites defending it capitulated. In November 1917 the City Duma was abolished, and power passed into the hands of the Mossovet.

During the civil war of 1918–1920 that followed the revolution, businesses were nationalized, and the Mossovet began to manage them in a centralized manner. Trying to solve the problem of insufficient housing, the Mossovet in April 1918 decided to pack more people into apartments (no more than one room per adult), and to settle the poor in the apartments of well-off residents. By the end of the civil war, the economy was in shambles. In 1920 industrial output in various enterprises was between 2 and 15 percent of the prewar level. Moscow streetcars stood idle, and water and electricity supplies were erratic. Bread rations were minimal even for children and hospital patients (133 grams per capita per diem, 400 grams per worker at major enterprises). In 1919–1921 a crime wave followed the release of criminals from prisons.

NEW ECONOMIC POLICY

After the introduction of the New Economic Policy (1921), which restored free trade and denationalized some small businesses, the economy revived. By the end of 1926 industrial production had risen to 93 percent of its 1913 level. But as early as 1926 the authorities already began to restrict the free market. In 1927 they introduced the centralized distribution of goods and the rationing of food and clothing. Two problems were especially acute: constantly rising unemployment due to the influx of newcomers from other regions (numbering about 270,000 new arrivals in 1927, for example), and thousands of homeless children who came to the city during the famine years right after the end of the civil war.

An authoritarian, one-party regime under the control of the All-Union Communist Party of Bolsheviks (later renamed the Communist Party of the Soviet Union) now controlled the country. In Moscow the Mossovet, despite its formally democratic principles, functioned under the vigilant supervision of the Moscow Committee of the Bolshevik Party.

The new regime had some indisputable achievements, such as the introduction of free medical care: between 1925 and 1929, for example, annual health screening for workers in state-owned enterprises and medical assistance to pregnant women were introduced. These measures led to a twofold decline in the rate of mortality. Another positive phenomenon was the increase in the literacy rate from 55 percent in 1914 to 85–87 percent in 1929. Relative political stability during the 1920s created favorable conditions for reviving the city's infrastructure. The years 1921–1925 saw the restoration and development of streetcar transport (eleven new lines connected the center with the suburbs); bus service, a public water supply, and road maintenance were all reintroduced; and electricity once again lit the streets. The shortage of housing was catastrophic, however. In 1928, for example, the average living space per person was just 5.5 square meters. Until the 1960s, communal apartments, where several families lodged together sharing one kitchen and one toilet, were the major type of housing.

Despite the primitive living conditions, Moscow in the 1920s had a thriving cultural life, with scores of theater and ballet schools and more than two hundred private and cooperative publishing houses. The quest for new solutions in architecture produced the innovative ideas of constructivism (pioneered by the Vesnin brothers Leonid, Victor, and Alexander, Moisei Ginzburg, and Konstantin Melnikov), which were reflected in the designs of office buildings, workers' clubs, and stadiums.

INDUSTRIAL RESTRUCTURING AND URBAN TRANSFORMATION IN THE 1930S

The campaign of the Soviet dictator Joseph Stalin (1879–1953) to develop heavy industry resulted in the restructuring of the whole system of Moscow enterprises. The textile industry ceded its leadership in the Moscow economy to heavy industry (especially the aircraft and automotive industries), whose share in the general volume of production rose to 34.7 percent (1931) and then to 61 percent (1940). The largest Soviet factories, such as the Likhachev Plant and the "Hammer and Sickle" Plant, were located in Moscow. In order to intensify production, workers were trained to operate the newest European and American machinery, and foreign engineers were invited to the USSR.

All existing resources were pumped into the development of heavy industry, which resulted in a sharp decline in the standard of living. In March 1929 the rationing of basic foodstuffs (bread, sugar, meat, butter, and tea) was again introduced in Moscow. For example, skilled workers received 800 grams of bread and 200 grams of meat per diem; and 3 kilograms of cereals, 50 grams of tea, 600 grams of butter, and 10 eggs per month; while the rest of the population received two to three times less. But even these meager rations could not be guaranteed. Free trade was replaced by closed retail establishments and public canteens at factories and offices, where approximately 80 percent of workers received their meals. Rationing was abolished only in 1935–1936, after the rural economy had begun to "overcome the shock of collectivization." The low standard of living gave rise to popular discontent. Social protest, both potential and actual, was crushed by repressions, which turned into the Great Terror of 1936–1938. Moscow prisons were overcrowded, and so-called enemies of the people were brutally tortured.

The 1930s were also years of unprecedented construction that radically changed Moscow's appearance. In 1931–1934, nearly 0.5 million city residents, out of the total of 3.6 million, received new "social" lodgings free-of-charge. In accordance with 1932 construction regulations, ceilings were to be at least 3.2 meters high, and bathrooms were obligatory in new apartments. Because of the acute shortage of housing, however, one family, no matter how large, was entitled to only one room in a new apartment, and thus the old system of communal apartments received a new lease on life. Bolshevik leaders saw great propaganda value in the 1935 General Plan for the Reconstruction of Moscow, a blueprint for converting the city into the "model capital of the Soviet State."

The transformation of Moscow into a model city proceeded at the expense of the most precious monuments of architecture, however. Churches were ruthlessly razed; in 1931 the colossal Cathedral of Christ the Savior was destroyed, along with most of the ecclesiastic valuables stored there. A chapel of white marble, which had somehow avoided destruction, was later purchased by Eleanor Roosevelt (1884–1962), the wife of the U.S. president Franklin Delano Roosevelt; she donated the chapel to the Vatican. In the center of the city, giant administrative and public buildings sprang up: the House of the Council of Labor and Defense (the present-day State Duma), the Hotel Moskva, the Lenin Library, and the Theater of the Red Army. Six radial streets cutting through the city from the center to the suburbs were widened from 16–18 meters to 40–60 meters at the expense of old buildings demolished in the process.

The acute transport crisis of the 1920s was resolved in the 1930s by the rapid development of the city's transportation system. In 1935–1939 the first three subway lines, 40 kilometers long, were put into operation. By 1941 other infrastructure problems had also generally been solved; the water supply network increased twofold, and the sewage system was also expanded.

WORLD WAR II AND THE POSTWAR DECADE
World War II was a difficult time for Moscow. German forces invaded the USSR on 22 June 1941 and rapidly advanced into the heart of the country. During the first year of the war the city endured the tragic battle for Moscow that raged from 30 September 1941 to 7 January 1942. By November 1941 the Germans were only 35–50 kilometers away from Moscow. On 15 October 1941 the government issued a resolution "On the evacuation of the capital of the USSR, the city of Moscow." Alarmed by rumors that top officials were fleeing the city, the inhabitants succumbed to panic, which raged for three days. Some people grabbed whatever belongings they could carry and left the city, on foot or by car, trying to reach the eastern regions of the country, while the rest decided to stay and resist the enemy. On the fourth day Stalin, who had remained in Moscow, was forced to change his strategy radically and issued a

new decree, "On the introduction of a state of emergency in Moscow," thereby, in effect, annulling the previous one. The decree imposed a curfew and around-the-clock street patrols.

After bitter fighting, by early January 1942 the frontlines were pushed westward and stabilized at 150–300 kilometers away from Moscow. Casualties were high on both sides: the Red Army lost 1 million servicemen killed in action, while the German army lost more than 0.5 million. Between July 1941 and June 1943, Moscow was also bombed repeatedly from the air.

The Moscow population conducted itself bravely during the war years. Between 1941 and 1945 more than 850,000 Muscovites went to the front. The remaining residents formed 3,600 voluntary self-defense units (81,600 strong) and about 13,000 fire brigades (205,200 persons). Volunteers built 211 kilometers of antitank barriers and dug 210 kilometers of trenches around Moscow. The Moscow subway functioned both as the most important means of transportation and as an excellent air-raid shelter. Between July and December 1941, 2.2 million Muscovites were evacuated east to Siberia and Central Asia, along with 498 industrial enterprises and numerous higher-educational institutions, museums, theaters, film studios, and so forth.

The remaining 654 enterprises were converted to military production under the slogan "Shells instead of buttons." Throughout the war they produced 126,000 aircraft, 3.5 million submachine guns, and 34 million artillery shells. The working day was eleven or twelve hours long. Sixty percent of workers were women and teenagers. In order to strengthen morale Stalin temporarily reduced the Communist doctrine's intolerance with respect to the Russian Orthodox Church. After Stalin met with church leaders in September 1943, a number of churches were reopened, and thousands of priests were released from the gulag (the abbreviation for Stalinist prison camps).

On 9 May 1945 Moscow joyfully celebrated the victory over Germany. The celebration of Moscow's eight hundredth anniversary (in September 1947) provided another occasion for an ideological demonstration of the regime's achievements: foreign delegations arrived (including from the wartime allies—the United Kingdom, France, and the United States), shows were held in the city's squares and stadiums, and temporary European-style cafés were installed in the streets. To the joy of the half-starved population, "gifts" from collective farmers arrived in the form of trucks loaded with agricultural produce.

New ideas in urban planning were embodied in a 1947 decision to construct eight high-rise buildings, modeled after those in New York City, in order to produce a single urban ensemble. (Seven were actually constructed.) Construction of eight-to ten-story residential buildings for the elite began in 1949 along the city's central avenues, such as Gorky Street and Kutuzov Prospekt. A tendency toward highly decorative classical splendor in building design replaced the ascetic style of worker housing on the city's outskirts.

The postwar decade was full of hardships for the Moscow population, however, with a housing crisis, food shortages, and increased street crime. Government concessions to popular hopes for more liberal policies alternated with "tightening the screws." Monetary reform was carried out in December 1947, accompanied by the abolition of the rationing of food and other basic necessities, and the introduction of a unified state system of retail prices. Factories were moved back to Moscow, and by 1948 industrial production reached prewar levels.

There was no liberalization in the sphere of politics, however. In order to inspire ideological consolidation of the population, in 1948 a campaign was initiated against "cosmopolitanism," mainly directed against the Jewish intelligentsia. It was followed in January 1953 by the fabricated "Doctors' Plot," when a number of physicians were accused of planning to murder some prominent Soviet bureaucrats and military commanders on the orders of foreign espionage services. A series of crowded meetings at factories and other enterprises were organized by the authorities to ignite hatred for the regime's "enemies." Only Stalin's death in March 1953 put a stop to such forms of "consolidating the people."

THE KHRUSHCHEV THAW

After six years as head of the Moscow Communist Party, Nikita Khrushchev (1894–1971) led the All-

USSR Communist Party from 1953 to 1964, and simultaneously served as premier of the USSR from 1958 to 1964. The period of his leadership became known as "the Thaw" because of the liberalization of the forms and methods of government. Khrushchev's address to the twentieth Communist Party Congress in 1956, for example, openly criticized the tyranny of Stalin. Khrushchev's policies were not well balanced, however; positive social measures alternated with negative ones, thus producing popular discontent.

On the one hand, 1956 saw the abolition of a 1940 law that had made it illegal for workers to quit their jobs. Between 1955 and 1959 the minimum wage at state enterprises was increased by 35 percent; the retirement age was lowered to 60 years for males and to 55 years for females; the average work week was reduced to 46 hours; and maternity leave was increased from 70 to 112 days. To address the housing crisis in Moscow, new districts were created with the construction of four- to five-story apartment blocks, stores, kindergartens, polyclinics, and schools. Almost one-third of Moscow's population moved into the new apartment blocks, popularly dubbed *khrushchebi* (a play on *trushchobi*, the Russian word for slums). With a ceiling height of 2.5 meters, all sanitary arrangements crammed into one small cubicle, and a tiny kitchenette, these dwellings were regarded by many architects as primitive; but the authorities viewed the social benefit of more housing as a higher priority than aesthetics. Simultaneously, in downtown areas, ten- to fourteen-story blocks of apartments of special design were erected, intended for the political elite who by now had become firmly established as a top stratum of the Moscow population, with privileges and access to closed stores. After Khrushchev's twelve-day visit to the United States in 1959, new features were added to the urban infrastructure, such as self-service stores, automatic laundries, and special machines for selling tickets on buses, streetcars, and subways.

On the other hand, in contrast to some successful social projects, the failure of Khrushchev's agrarian reforms led to shortages and irregular supplies of many foodstuffs in Moscow, especially meat. Housewives often stood in line from daybreak for five to seven hours to buy meat. In 1962 increases in the price of meat (by 30 percent)

and butter (by 25 percent) caused discontent among the population. Because of a crop failure, in 1963 more than twelve million tons of grain were imported at a cost of one billion dollars. From 1954 onward, the pendulum in the relations with the Russian Orthodox Church began to swing back in the opposite direction, and many churches and mosques were closed down or even destroyed.

After decades of "mutual suspicion" in private life under Stalin, social relations revived. One example of this is the "Moscow kitchen" phenomenon: frank late-night discussions and singing to the guitar in the tiny kitchens of private apartments. This phenomenon arose not only because restaurants and cafés were inaccessible to the Moscow intelligentsia (always short of money) but also because people feared that any open discussions in public places might be dangerous. Gradually, however, new communication spaces emerged, primarily in the sphere of the youth culture. Poetry recitals at the Polytechnic Museum drew thousands of people; fresh issues of the journal *Novy Mir* (New World) became the center of discussions; and a number of "jazz cafés" also opened in the late 1950s and early 1960s.

THE BREZHNEV ERA

Leonid Brezhnev (1906–1982), the leader of the USSR between 1964 and 1982, promoted the idea of turning Moscow into "a model communist city." Despite the propagandistic goals of this utopian slogan, the idea nevertheless led to the resolution of some of the most painful urban problems: moving environmentally dangerous industrial enterprises out of Moscow, implementing mass-housing construction projects and building new schools, and improving the public transport system. In the late 1960s and 1970s many inhabitants of downtown basements and 1930s-era barracks in working-class districts moved into more convenient lodgings with amenities in multistory apartment blocks. In twenty years the proportion of families inhabiting their own apartments grew from 35 percent to 85 percent. Thanks to the trend toward separate apartments, social communication changed among native Muscovites. Nuclear families now predominated, neighborhood ties were disrupted, and people lived more and more isolated private lives. The 1970s were also marked by the beginning of borrowing and copying

Western lifestyles and behaviors, especially by the younger generation, who idolized the Beatles and other Western pop-culture celebrities.

However, new construction could not satisfy all the housing needs because of the heavy influx of workers from other areas to fill vacant jobs in construction and heavy industry, which were unpopular with Muscovites because they involved hard working conditions and night shifts. The annual influx between 1967 and 1987 of fifty to eighty thousand *limitchiki*—that is, migrants granted Moscow residence permits in limited quotas for employment in high-demand jobs—changed the composition of Moscow's population and urban culture. In 1976, for example, they constituted 33 percent of the workforce in heavy industry and 75 percent in construction. Lacking even minimal experience of life in a megalopolis, the migrants stayed secluded in their dorms among similar strangers and adapted poorly to the cultural, hygienic, and social norms of Moscow urban life.

During the 1970s and 1980s Moscow's social atmosphere gradually lost some of its former severity and isolation. Muscovites increasingly sought entertainment in shows and movies. Soviet cinema and its film stars became very popular, along with Italian and French films, which managed to avoid the ideological ban on foreign films thanks to the prominence of Communist parties in those two countries. Among sports, figure skating and hockey were immensely popular: the successes of Soviet athletes on the international arena gave rise to the creation of numerous free-of-charge children's centers for winter sports. Simple skating-rinks for individual recreation sprang up in almost every yard. New buildings for entertainment and recreation were erected: a circus, a children's music theater, the Taganka Theater.

The new construction in Moscow downtown areas resulted in the brutal destruction of some unique historic architectural ensembles, however. The construction of Kalinin Prospekt was accomplished by leveling the early-nineteenth-century blocks in Arbat Street. Experts noted that the new projects, despite their technological achievements and professionalism, were planned "with no love for the Old Moscow." The issue of humanizing the urban environment gave rise to serious opposition between society and the authorities. The struggle

to save the city's historical legacy took the shape of a mass social movement, formalized as the All-Russian Voluntary Society for the Protection of Monuments of History and Art. The demolition of a block of sixteenth- and seventeenth-century buildings near the Kremlin in May 1972, shortly before the visit of U.S. president Richard Nixon (1913–1994) to Moscow, produced an outburst of protest from members of the artistic and scientific elites and from ordinary Muscovites, who wrote appeals to the Communist Party Central Committee and the Mossovet and sought meetings with top bureaucrats. The resulting compromise created nine preservation zones encompassing one-third of the city's central area, including pedestrian zones in the oldest streets (dating back to the fourteenth century), Stoleshniki Lane and the Arbat.

Preparations for the 1980 Moscow Olympic Games included radical improvements in the cleanliness and order of Moscow streets and squares and in the availability and quality of restaurants. Regrettably, this event failed to produce the expected effect, because the national teams of the United States, West Germany, Japan, the Netherlands, and other countries chose to boycott the games in protest against the Soviet invasion of Afghanistan.

THE COLLAPSE OF THE SOVIET UNION: 1985–1991

Mikhail Gorbachev's leadership of the USSR (1985–1991) was characterized by his restructuring policies known as perestroika. Gorbachev sought to preserve the Soviet Union by reforming its economy and culture. However, the collapse of the regime proceeded with unexpected rapidity, its disintegration accelerated by the Chernobyl nuclear power plant disaster in 1986, when the leaders of the environmental movement started to discuss not only the problems of the environment, but social issues as well.

Moscow became a focal point of open discussion and a free press, one example of which was the newspaper *Moskovskie Novosti* (Moscow News). Boris Yeltsin, the head of the Moscow Communist Party organization in 1986–1987, called Moscow a breeding ground for political stagnation and a haven for corrupt bureaucrats. He replaced 60 percent of Moscow officials, banned the admittance of new *limitchiki,* and tried to improve the food supply. Yeltsin's radicalism alienated the central authorities, and he was removed from office. Soon he became the leader of the democratic opposition, which comprised a number of political parties created in 1988–1989. In 1989 and 1990 Moscow streets were the scene of continual political demonstrations, including one with one hundred thousand participants in February 1990. In the spring of 1990 elections to the Mossovet brought the democrats more than 60 percent of votes, and for the first time since 1917 the Communists lost their monopoly on power. In 1991 Yeltsin was elected to the new position of president of the Russian Republic.

These political changes provoked a serious economic crisis, further aggravated by painful denationalization of the economy, inflation, and the 1991 monetary reform (which, in effect, wiped out the population's bank deposits). In Moscow the food supply completely collapsed; sugar, vodka, and tobacco were rationed; and transportation and central heating barely functioned.

In the summer of 1991 Yeltsin, as president of Russia, banned all Communist Party organizations at enterprises and institutions. The conflict between Yeltsin and Moscow democratic forces on the one hand, and the central Communist apparatus on the other, contributed to the revolutionary events of 19–22 August 1991. The radio station *Ekho Moskvy* (Echo of Moscow) reported that on the order of the self-proclaimed State Committee for the State of Emergency in the USSR—a group of high-ranking government officials and Communist Party leaders, which had already removed Gorbachev from power—the military was preparing to seize Yeltsin and the other Russian leaders barricaded inside the government headquarters known as the White House. The attempted coup failed when thousands of people encircled the building, ready to become its "human shield." On 22 August the Moscow police, acting on the orders of Vice-Mayor Yuri Luzhkov, sealed the building of the Central Committee of the Communist Party. The failed coup led to the final collapse of the Soviet Union, as one by one the Soviet republics declared independence. The political crisis ended when on 25 December 1991 Gorbachev resigned from the post of president and on 26 December the Supreme Soviet voted to end the treaty that formed the USSR. In 1992 Luzhkov became mayor of Moscow and subsequently was twice reelected.

ECONOMIC AND POLITICAL TRANSITION

The economic crisis that followed the collapse of the USSR hit Moscow's population hard, causing social polarization; in 1995, for example, 47 percent of Muscovites lived below subsistence level. During the following decade, however, the situation slowly began to improve. In Moscow, trade, gas stations, small and medium-size industrial enterprises, and freight transport began to be privatized. European investors now participated in projects for the creation of new confectioneries, bakeries, breweries, and sausage factories. As a result, the food crisis was overcome, and from the year 2000 Russian foodstuffs replaced imported goods, which had dominated the consumer market in the 1990s. For the first time since 1917 Muscovites were not faced with the problem of where to buy food, and a network of cafés, restaurants, and takeaway outlets also emerged. The municipal government subsidized free transportation for retired and disabled inhabitants and free meals for 40 percent of schoolchildren.

Three trends may be noted in the development of Moscow in the late twentieth century: (1) improvements to major Soviet-era buildings such as office buildings, stores, theaters, and stadiums; (2) the implementation of new unique architectural projects; and (3) the restoration of national historical monuments destroyed on Stalin's orders, such as the Cathedral of Christ the Savior, the Cathedral of the Kazan Mother of God, and the Iverian Gate. Since 1995, forty thousand to sixty thousand apartments per year have been built, while the tenements known as *khrushchebi* have been demolished and their inhabitants moved to new municipal housing. Another positive development is the revival of religious life: In 2002 there were approximately nine hundred officially registered religious associations (500 Russian Orthodox, 25 Moslem, 15 Jewish, 12 Catholic) in Moscow, along with 532 Russian Orthodox churches, 7 mosques, 5 synagogues, and 2 Catholic cathedrals.

Serious problems of the 1990s and early 2000s include air pollution and traffic. The number of automobiles grew from 1.2 million in 1993 to 4 million in 2004. Automobile exhaust, according to data of 2000–2004, was responsible for 80–93 percent of pollution. In May 2004 a municipal law concerning environmental control was enacted. The traffic problem was somewhat alleviated after the opening of the Third Ring Road, thirty-five kilometers long, through the city's peripheral districts at the distance of five to seven kilometers from the center. Terrorist attacks were another serious problem in Moscow. Between 1999 and 2004 explosions in residential buildings and trade centers, on the subway and on planes, and the taking of hostages claimed the lives of approximately six hundred people. Finally, the cost of living rose dramatically; as of early 2005 the *Economist* magazine ranked Moscow with New York City in twelfth place among the world's most expensive cities.

See also **Russia; Soviet Union.**

BIBLIOGRAPHY

Borrero, Mauricio. *Hungry Moscow: Scarcity and Urban Society in the Russian Civil War, 1917–1921.* New York, 2003.

Bradley, Joseph. *Muzhik and Muscovite: Urbanization in Late Imperial Russia.* Berkeley, Calif., 1985.

Brumfield, William Craft, and Blaire A. Ruble, eds. *Russian Housing in the Modern Age: Design and Social History.* Cambridge, U.K., 1993.

Chase, William J. *Workers, Society, and the Soviet State: Labor and Life in Moscow, 1918–1929.* Urbana, Ill., 1987.

Colton, Timothy J. *Moscow: Governing the Socialist Metropolis.* Cambridge, Mass., 1995.

Fitzpatrick, Sheila, Alexander Rabinowitch, and Richard Stites, eds. *Russia in the Era of NEP: Explorations in Soviet Society and Culture.* Bloomington, Ind., 1991.

Hamm, Michael F., ed. *The City in Russian History.* Lexington, Ky., 1976.

———. *The City in Late Imperial Russia.* Bloomington, Ind., 1986.

Koenker, Diane. *Moscow Workers and the 1917 Revolution.* Princeton, N.J., 1981.

Merridale, Catherine. *Moscow Politics and the Rise of Stalin: The Communist Party in the Capital, 1925–32.* Houndmills, U.K., 1990.

Murrell, Kathleen Berton. *Moscow: An Illustrated History.* New York, 2003.

Osokina, Elena. *Our Daily Bread: Socialist Distribution and the Art of Survival in Stalin's Russia, 1927–1941.* Translated and edited by Kate Transchel and Greta Bucher. Armonk, N.Y., 2001.

Pisarkova, L. F. *Moskovskaia Gorodskaia Duma, 1863–1917.* Moscow, 1998.

Porter, Cathy, and Mark Jones. *Moscow in World War II.* London, 1987.

Ruble, Blair A. *Second Metropolis: Pragmatic Pluralism in Gilded Age Chicago, Silver Age Moscow, and Meiji Osaka.* Washington, D.C., 2001.

Sakwa, Richard. *Soviet Communists in Power: A Study of Moscow during the Civil War, 1918–21.* Houndmills, U.K., 1988.

Schlögel, Karl. *Moscow.* Chicago, 2005.

Thurston, Robert W. *Liberal City, Conservative State: Moscow and Russia's Urban Crisis, 1906–1914.* New York, 1987.

Ulianova, G. N. *Blagotvoritel'nost' moskovskikh predprinimatelei, 1860–1914.* Moscow, 1999.

West, James L., and Iury Petrov, eds. *Merchant Moscow: Images of Russia's Vanished Bourgeoisie.* Princeton, N.J., 1997.

GALINA ULIANOVA

MOSLEY, OSWALD. *See* **British Union of Fascists.**

MOULIN, JEAN (1899–1943), French patriot and leader of the French Resistance.

In 1943, acting on the authority of General Charles de Gaulle, Jean Moulin organized and coordinated the various resistance groups inside France. After being arrested on 21 June 1943 he did not survive tortures inflicted on him on orders of Klaus Barbie, the head of the Gestapo in Lyon, France. As the head of the Resistance, the "chief of the people of the night," Moulin was honored by the French novelist André Malraux (1901–1976) upon the ceremonial transfer of his ashes to the Pantheon on 19 December 1964. He has become the key figure emblematic of the French Resistance during World War II.

POLITICS

Moulin was the son of a professor of history and geography, a republican of conviction who was active in regional politics. He studied law at the University of Montpellier while working in the office of the prefect, or regional chief administrator, of Hérault. Although he enlisted in the army when he came of age, he was mobilized too late to fight in World War I. Receiving his license to practice law, in 1922 he won an administrative appointment with the prefect in Savoy; three years later he became the youngest subprefect then, in 1937, the youngest prefect of the Aveyron region.

Moulin's political career began in the early 1930s with his appointment to the undersecretary of state Pierre Cot's office of foreign affairs. He followed Cot when the latter headed the Ministry of Air, initiating nationalization of the private airlines and establishing Air France.

In 1939, while prefect of the Eure-et-Loire region in Chartres, Moulin tried to enlist in the army but could not win release from his administrative duties. He remained at his post in the new government that formed under Philippe Pétain until 2 November 1940, when he was dismissed.

UNIFIER OF THE RESISTANCE

Moulin immediately joined the Resistance in the southern zone, then operating free of Nazi occupation but under Pétain's collaborationist government. At first he only distributed flyers and clandestine publications. But in September 1941 he left France, using the pseudonym Joseph Jean Mercier, and after a trip that took him to Lisbon, a month later he arrived in London. His objective was to obtain funds for the gathering French Resistance. General Charles de Gaulle (1890–1970), with whom he met several times, made him the representative of the French National Committee in the unoccupied zone.

Moulin returned to France with three missions. The first, codenamed "Rex," which would also be one of his noms de guerre (pseudonyms), was to develop a propaganda machine. Second, he was to initiate the creation of military cells in each of the resistance movements. Third, Moulin was to unite the action of the various, often conflicting independent resistance movements under the authority of General de Gaulle, leader of the Free French.

Provided with funds and protected by a double cover—as a farmer from Saint Andiol and as an employee of an art gallery in Nice—Moulin parachuted back into France near Avignon on the night of 1 January 1942. From Lyon, where he made his headquarters, he succeeded in rallying the major groups behind the Free French. He organized the distribution of funds, coordinated air operations, and set up a system of communications through various organizations such as Wireless Transmissions (WT), Service des Opérations Aériennes et Maritimes (Air and Naval Operations Service, SOAM), Bureau d'Information et de Presse (Press and Information Agency, BIP), and Comité Général des Études (General Study Committee, CGE).

In mid-May 1942 Moulin brought together the paramilitary units, creating the Armée Secrète (Secret Army, AS), placing it under the authority of General Charles Delestraint. In October 1942 Moulin set up a committee that coordinated the actions of the three major resistance movements in the southern zone—Combat, Libération, and Franc-Tireur—with himself at its head. Soon thereafter, in January 1943, this coordinating group was supplanted by a solid administrative arm, the Comité directeur des Mouvements Unis de la Résistance (United Resistance Movements, MUR), also with Moulin as leader; the development occurred separately from any decisions made by La France Combattante (Fighting France), as the movement led by de Gaulle was now called.

During a second visit to London in February and March 1943, Moulin was appointed the sole permanent representative of General de Gaulle and the French National Liberation Committee for the whole of occupied France. Back in Paris, after complex talks he established on 27 May 1943 the Conseil National de la Résistance (National Council of the Resistance, CNR). This brought together not only the representatives of the eight major paramilitary and civilian resistance movements but also representatives of the two major unions as well as six political parties. The CNR was the "embryo of national representation" according to André Philip, the representative of the Resistance in London, which recognized General de Gaulle's authority and reinforced his legitimacy with the allies.

All these achievements could not help but create tensions among the various protagonists. Moulin's authority—he was accused of being autocratic—was often contested by movement leaders. He was both the delegate of the National Liberation Committee in London and the most important figure in the central organization of the Resistance in occupied France. Criticisms made against him were often directed toward decisions that had been made in London and through him were intended to contest de Gaulle's authority.

THE CALUIRE AFFAIR

Starting in May 1943 came a succession of arrests. The imprisonment of General Delestraint left the Secret Army without its head, and Jean Multon, alias Lunel, cooperated with the German Sicherheitsdienst (Security Service, SD) after his arrest. Representatives of various resistance groups set up a summit meeting in Caluire. There agents of Klaus Barbie captured Moulin as well as seven other leaders on 21 June 1943. The Gestapo quickly identified Moulin as the famous "Max," as he was also known. He was severely tortured and survived just two weeks. The Germans failed to make him talk. The exact circumstances of his death, which probably occurred during his transfer to Germany, are not known.

Much has been written about the Caluire affair, and the issue of who was responsible for the arrests of 21 June was bitterly debated and discussed, fueling and in some cases reviving the political and personal hostilities that had contaminated the relationships among resistance leaders. René Hardy, close to Henri Frenay, the chief of Combat, was at the center of these polemics. Hardy himself had been arrested by the Gestapo on 7 June 1943 but succeeded in escaping. Two weeks later, though uninvited, he attended the meeting at Caluire and was again arrested—and once more he escaped. Some leaders denounced him as a traitor, while others defended him. Hardy was acquitted twice at trial, on 24 January 1947 and again on 8 May 1950. Although the details of his role remain uncertain, today it

seems established that he bears at least partial responsibility.

On the occasion of the ceremonial transfer of Moulin's ashes to the Panthéon in Paris, André Malraux, in a particularly moving speech, recalled that witnesses said Moulin had been savagely beaten about the face before his death. Malraux evoked "the poor face of the last day, the lips that did not speak," and added, "that day, there was the face of France."

See also **Barbie, Klaus; Gaulle, Charles de; Resistance; World War II.**

BIBLIOGRAPHY

Azéma, Jean-Pierre. *Jean Moulin: Le politique, le rebelle, le résistant.* Paris, 2003.

Azéme, Jean-Pierre, ed. *Jean Moulin.* Paris, 2004.

Cordier, Daniel. *Jean Moulin: La république des catacombes.* Paris, 1999.

RENÉE POZNANSKI

MÜLLER, HEINER (1929–1995), German playwright.

Heiner Müller emerged as Germany's most influential playwright during the second half of the twentieth century. No other German dramatist since Bertolt Brecht (1898–1956) achieved a comparable position in world theater. He reflected in his texts, more rigorously than any other writer, the violent trajectory of the last century's history. His writer's life began, one might say, when he was not quite four years old, the night after Adolf Hitler had become German chancellor. Heiner woke up upon hearing loud voices and books being thrown onto the floor in an adjacent room. The door to his bedroom opened and he saw his father, held by three SA men, softly calling his name. The terrified boy pretended to be asleep and so his father, a Socialist Party functionary, could not say goodbye to him before being taken away to a concentration camp. Later Müller described this event as his "first betrayal." And betrayal became a central topic in many of his texts, be they poetry, prose, or stage plays. His father was eventually released from the camp and the family led an impoverished life in a hostile Nazi society. After the war, his father became mayor of a small town in Saxony but soon defected with his wife to the West. Heiner decided to stay. He refused to betray the Marxism he had adopted, however much he would later criticize the iniquities that tainted the past and present of socialism.

Müller began to write after he returned from his brief military service, in 1945, and finished high school. For ten years he wrote mainly poetry while eking out a living as a librarian and, eventually, as a literary critic and occasional journalist. In 1955 he married the writer Inge Schwenker (1925–1966), who became his collaborator as he began writing for the stage. They jointly received a coveted literary award in 1959, for *The Scab* (1957) and *The Correction*, which had both premiered the previous year. The plays followed the model of Brecht's epic theater in portraying the difficulties of building the socialist industry of East Germany, a topic Brecht had tried and abandoned. Müller was determined to pursue it. His play *The Resettled Woman*, contemplating the consequences of East Germany's land reform, was in rehearsal when the Berlin Wall cemented the partition of Germany. It was banned after one preview performance at the end of September 1961. Müller himself was severely reprimanded and expelled from the Writers Association. For some years his texts could be neither published nor performed. The couple survived through the kindness of friends and occasional royalties from radio texts Müller submitted under an assumed name. His play *The Construction Site* was eventually published in 1965 but was harshly attacked for "ideological flaws." A year later, the deeply depressed Inge committed suicide.

Müller had begun to explore classical Greek drama for its relevance to the present and concentrated his efforts during the 1960s on adapting classic texts. Most of them received their premiere in the West, where his plays were mainly performed until the 1980s, when Müller became a dramaturge at East Berlin's Volksbühne.

During the 1970s, he dispensed with Brecht's model and developed a complex, multilinear dramaturgy which he called synthetic fragment, in texts such as *Germania Death in Berlin* (1971), *Gundling's Life Frederick of Prussia*

Lessing's Sleep Dream Scream (1976) and, foremost, *Hamletmachine*, which also attested to the influence of Antonin Artaud and Samuel Beckett. *Hamletmachine* (1977) is Müller's most recognized play, widely taught as a seminal text of postmodern literature. Like several other of his plays, it was performed all over the world, especially after Robert Wilson staged it in New York in 1985, thus beginning his close collaboration and friendship with Müller.

In 1975 Müller was invited to the University of Texas, Austin, as writer-in-residence, and traveled extensively in the United States, and later in Mexico and the Caribbean. The American experience profoundly changed his view of geography's impact on human history and reinforced his commitment to feminist positions he had taken in earlier texts.

During the 1980s Müller increasingly directed his own works, to great success, and received the highest literary awards of both former German states. His staging of *Hamlet/Machine*, combining Shakespeare's text (in his own translation) with *Hamletmachine*, began rehearsal before the Berlin Wall fell yet premiered after the collapse of the East German socialist state, in 1990. The eight-hour production reflected on German history since World War II and the fratricidal trends of the nation's past. In the final year of his life, Müller became the artistic director of the Berliner Ensemble where he staged Brecht's *Arturo Ui* (1995) in a highly acclaimed production. He had finally assumed the mantle of his erstwhile hero, Brecht, as Germany's foremost playwright/stage director. He also staged *Tristan and Isolde* at the 1993 Bayreuth Wagner Festival.

Throughout his career Müller has been blamed—from the Left and the Right—for promulgating an apocalyptic view of human history and society. He once quipped about such criticism: "I'm neither a hope- nor a dope-dealer" (1984, p. 140).

See also **Brecht, Bertolt; Theater.**

BIBLIOGRAPHY

Primary Sources

Müller, Heiner. *Hamletmachine and Other Texts for the Stage.* Edited and translated by Carl Weber. New York, 1984.

———. *The Battle: Plays, Prose, Poems.* Edited and translated by Carl Weber. New York, 1989.

———. *Explosion of a Memory. Writings.* Edited and translated by Carl Weber. New York, 1989.

———. *Krieg ohne Schlacht: Leben in Dikaturen.* Cologne, 1992.

———. *A Heiner Müller Reader. Plays, Poetry, Prose.* Edited and translated by Carl Weber. Baltimore, Md., 2001.

———. *Werke.* Edited by Frank Hörnigk. 7 vols. Frankfurt, 1998–2004.

Secondary Sources

Friedman, Dan, ed. *Müller in America: American Productions of Works by Heiner Müller.* New York, 2003.

Hauschild, Jan-Christoph. *Heiner Müller oder Das Prinzip Zweifel.* Berlin, 2001.

Kalb, Jonathan. *The Theater of Heiner Müller.* Cambridge, U.K., 1998.

Lehmann, Hans-Thies, and Patrick Primavesi, eds. *Heiner Müller Handbuch. Leben, Werk, Wirkung.* Stuttgart, 2003.

Teraoka, Arlene Akiko. *The Silence of Entropy or Universal Discourse: The Postmodernist Poetics of Heiner Müller.* New York, 1985.

CARL WEBER

MUNICH AGREEMENT. The Munich Agreement was the outcome of a four-power conference held in Munich, Germany, involving the prime ministers of Britain (Neville Chamberlain) and France (Édouard Daladier) and the dictators of Germany (Adolph Hitler) and Italy (Benito Mussolini) on 29–30 September 1938. It sought to resolve the international crisis that had arisen over the supposed mistreatment of the German minority population in the Sudetenland and the imminent threat of German troops being dispatched to their aid. The Czechs were not invited to the conference but were placed under intense pressure to cede the Sudetenland to Germany. For the Czechs to resist would have meant fighting Germany alone. Reluctantly and amid recriminations the Czech government complied.

Czechoslovakia became the center of diplomatic attention after Germany seized Austria in March 1938. It left the Czechs, as the British chiefs of staff observed, like a bone in the jaws of a dog. A vocal German minority in the Sudetenland, led by Konrad Henlein, was being actively stirred up by Nazi propaganda. As tension increased Hitler decided upon the need to destroy Czechoslovakia at the first opportunity. It forced the British to abandon their policy of "realistic isolationism" and directly intervene by dispatching Lord Runciman, a former cabinet member, to the region in August. While Runciman shuttled between Prague and Berlin seeking to resolve the crisis, Neville Chamberlain, the British prime minister, took the view that a personal appeal to Hitler would dissuade the dictator from any preemptive act of aggression. He secretly devised Plan Z on 28 August with Horace Wilson, a civil servant and confidant of the prime minister. Most foreign-office officials and senior British cabinet members were not informed of the plan until 8 September, with the rest of the world being kept in the dark until the day before Chamberlain flew to Germany for the first time to meet with Hitler at Berchtesgaden (15 September). During their meeting Hitler lay out his demands for an "instant solution" and a plebiscite of the Sudeten people. Chamberlain asked for time to discuss matters with the cabinet and the French government, although crucially he made no mention of the Czechs. When he returned to Bad Godesberg on 22 September, he found that Hitler had upped the ante, warning that German forces intended to occupy the Sudetenland on 28 September. Chamberlain returned to London expecting that Britain would have to go to war in defense of Czechoslovakia. War was postponed when an invitation was received from Mussolini, acting for Hitler, to attend a four-power conference to resolve the crisis.

The agreement reached at Munich was for the German occupation of the Sudetenland to take place between 1 and 10 October. Plebiscites would then be held to determine the new borders. The British and French would guarantee the remainder of Czechoslovakia. For the Czechs forced into accepting this arrangement, it meant that their natural and constructed defenses were lost to the Germans, as were vital industrial plants. Whether the defense of Czechoslovakia in 1938 would have been as desperate an undertaking as British and French military planners believed has been open to interpretation and has led to questions about whether appeasement was the only practicable policy for the democracies to follow. Chamberlain, anxious to further Anglo-German relations, also managed to have a private meeting with Hitler at which the pair signed the piece of paper, later waved at Heston Airport, promising that Britain and Germany would never to go to war again. It was this letter of accord that gave Chamberlain the confidence to declare "peace in our time."

While Munich was initially hailed as a triumph for the diplomacy of Chamberlain, Hitler took the view that it was a defeat, that he had been bluffed out of war. German troops had been primed to attack on 1 October. It meant that in 1939 Hitler was determined not to repeat what he had come to believe were the terrible mistakes that had led to the Munich Agreement. Any hopes that Chamberlain held of further diplomatic initiatives with Germany were dashed first by the *Kristallnacht* pogrom (9–10 November 1938) and finally in March 1939, when Hitler tore up the Munich settlement and sent troops into Prague.

The agreement has become synonymous with surrender. The stigma of the settlement still burdens the leadership of the modern British Conservative Party. In May 1992, John Major, the prime minister and party leader, signed an Anglo-Czech declaration formally nullifying the Munich Agreement. Two years previously his predecessor Margaret Thatcher had apologized for the "shame" of Munich while visiting Prague.

See also **Appeasement; Chamberlain, Neville; Sudetenland; World War II.**

BIBLIOGRAPHY

Aulach, Harinder. "Britain and the Sudeten Issue 1938." *Journal of Contemporary History* 18 (1983): 233–259.

Haslam, Jonathan. "The Soviet Union and the Czechoslovakian Crisis of 1938." *Journal of Contemporary History* 14 (1978): 441–461.

Hauner, Milan. "Czechoslovakia as a Military Factor in British Considerations of 1938." *Journal of Strategic Studies* 2 (1978): 194–222.

Jackson, Peter. "French Military Intelligence and Czechoslovakia, 1938." *Diplomacy and Statecraft* 5 (1994): 81–106.

Lacaze, Yvon. "Daladier, Bonnet, and the Decision-Making Process during the Munich Crisis, 1938." In *French Foreign and Defence Policy 1918–1940,* edited by Robert Boyce. London, 1998.

Lukes, Igor, and Erik Goldstein, eds. *The Munich Crisis, 1938.* London, 1999.

Robbins, Keith. *Munich 1938.* London, 1968.

NICK CROWSON

MURNAU, FRIEDRICH WILHELM
(1888–1931), German filmmaker.

Friedrich Wilhelm Murnau (1888–1931) created a "German style" of filmmaking that sought to evoke the spiritual and visual power of German Romanticism. His films explore phantoms and specters (*The Haunted Castle, Nosferatu, Phanton,* all 1922; *Faust,* 1926), but also probe existential questions (*Journey in to the Night,* 1921; *The Burning Soil,* 1922; *The Last Laugh,* 1924). He directed no fewer than sixteen silent films (of which half are lost) in Berlin between 1919 and 1926 before accepting an offer by the American motion picture executive William Fox to bring high-art film production to Hollywood. After only four films, Murnau's American career was cut short by a fatal automobile accident. He died at the age of forty-three.

Murnau's first masterpiece, *Nosferatu—Symphonie des Garuens* (Nosferatu the Vampire), reinterpreted Bram Stoker's 1897 novel *Dracula* and pushed the limits of what could be shown in the new medium. The film reconfigures the vampire legend in the tradition of expressionist art, whose credo was: "The world is there, why repeat it?" Like expressionist paintings and poetry, Murnau's filmic world appears distorted and stylized. His use of extreme camera angles and elongated shadows as well as such special effects as superimposition and time-lapse photography reveals his desire to experiment with the very language of film. Nosferatu, the vampire who cannot die, is shown as a phantom, an immaterial substance that, like a film image, dissolves when hit by a ray of sunlight. Murnau retells Bram Stoker's 1897 novel *Dracula* through the lens of World War I (1914–1918). Although his film is set in early nineteenth-century Germany and deals with the outbreak of the plague, it alludes to the encounter with mass death in the war, during which two million young Germans died. The film also expands the notion of dying for a higher good: only if the young woman sacrifices herself to the vampire can the town be saved. The hideous but strangely attractive monster as embodied by Max Schreck has become a stock figure in countless horror films. The surrealist Robert Desnos (1900–1945) treasured *Nosferatu* as an inspiration because

Max Schreck as the vampire in F. W. Murnau's *Nosferatu*, 1922. GETTY IMAGES

it mingled mystery and terror, while Werner Herzog (1942–) praised it as the quintessential German film in the Romantic tradition and as the film that helped him find his own style. He remade it with Klaus Kinski playing Nosferatu in 1979.

Murnau's social drama *Der letzte Mann* (*The Last Laugh*, 1924) was based on a script by Carl Mayer, the most brilliant German screenwriter of the 1920s. The film became famous because it succeeded in telling its story in purely visual terms. The film's melodrama of an old hotel porter who is humiliated by the loss of his job and his uniform moves inexorably to an ending in misery and death—but suddenly the film's sole title card pops up, declaring that the screenwriter took pity on him and offered an alternative ending: an American millionaire bequeaths the downtrodden old porter a fortune that allows him to have the "last laugh." This fairy tale ending resonated in 1924 with the

American Dawes Plan that miraculously rescued Germany from hyperinflation and ignominy. The stylistic importance of the film lies in its use of an "unchained" camera that travels down an elevator, moves through revolving doors, and even mimics the distorted movements of a drunkard. In this film expressionist distortion is no longer confined to abstract sets and stylized acting, as it is in the most famous expressionist film, Robert Wiene's *The Cabinet of Dr. Caligari* (1919). Rather, it extends to cinematography itself. The mobile camera becomes a character in the story; it does not just show things but makes them *visible*.

Murnau's first American film, *Sunrise–Song of Two Humans* (1927), continued the German tradition of studio productions, with its reliance on stylized sets and attention to lighting and mood. A psychological melodrama of adultery that contrasts country and big city, peasant and vamp, earth and water, good and evil, *Sunrise* has been hailed as one of the lasting achievements of silent cinema. The film displays narrative fluidity but also a pictorial density that charges each gesture with an excess of meaning. The meticulously staged scenarios and the slow movement give the film a rare melancholic mood. Murnau's last Hollywood film, *Tabu—a Story of the South Seas* (1931), narrates the tragic tale of a young fisherman who breaks the taboo on desiring an unattainable "holy" young woman. It is set in Bora-Bora and luxuriates in exotic location shots and documentary footage of natives' customs and dances. It is not a documentary, however, as the original collaboration with the documentarian Robert Flaherty (1884–1951) would suggest. Flaherty withdrew from the production once he became aware of Murnau's conviction that cinema was not there to record reality but to create a magic world of its own.

See also **Cinema.**

BIBLIOGRAPHY

Eisner, Lotte H. *The Haunted Screen: Expressionism in German Cinema and the Influence of Max Reinhardt.* Translated by Roger Greaves. Berkeley, Calif., 1969. An influential book that relates expressionist cinema to painting and the stage.

———. *Murnau.* Berkeley, Calif., 1973. A Weimar film critic in exile, Eisner published this biography in French in 1964.

Prinzler, Hans Helmut, Karin Messlinger, and Vera Thomas, eds. *Friedrich Wilhelm Murnau. Ein Melancholiker des Films.* Berlin, 2003. Collection of essays on the occasion of a Murnau retrospective at the 2003 Berlin Film Festival.

ANTON KAES

MUSIL, ROBERT (1880–1942), Austrian writer.

Robert Musil was born in Klagenfurt, Austria, into a bourgeois middle-class family. His parents envisioned an officer's career for their son, who was accordingly educated at a number of military boarding schools in Bohemia. The young man, however, rejected a lifelong future in the Austro-Hungarian army and instead opted for his father's profession of mechanical engineering. He received his diploma in Brünn in 1901 and was immediately offered a teaching position at the Technical University in Stuttgart, Germany. During the following two-year intermezzo the lecturer's profession was not fulfilling for Musil: he picked up earlier literary experiments and began to sketch his first novel, *Die Verwirrungen des Zöglings Törleß* (1906; The confusions of young Törless), the story of an adolescent boy exposed to an authoritarian educational system similar to the one the author had endured as a teenager.

By the end of his Stuttgart period in 1903 Musil decided to pursue a more academic path and moved to Berlin to study philosophy, logic, and experimental psychology. He entered a lively and productive intellectual milieu at the city's Friedrich-Wilhelms-Universität. Here he participated in the reshaping of Helmholtzian psychology into early Gestalt theory. He conducted experiments in the psychological laboratory of his academic advisor Carl Stumpf and in 1908 received his doctorate in philosophy, mathematics, and physics with a dissertation on Ernst Mach's doctrines, *Beitrag zur Beurteilung der Lehren Machs* (A contribution to the evaluation of Mach's doctrines). Parallel to his intellectual transformation from engineer to scientific philosopher, Musil kept up his literary activity, and the publication of *Törleß* in 1906 immediately earned him fame as a young, aspiring author. The psychologizing depiction of the protagonist's sexual experiences and his ambiguous sexual orientation caused some uproar; the book was a minor scandal and a public success. This convinced Musil to shift his professional goals once again. After the completion of his dissertation he parted with academia for good to become an independent author and critic.

In the following years Musil lived in Vienna and Berlin, coediting and publishing in a number of literary journals, most notably the *Neue Rundschau*. These first professional ventures were abruptly halted by the outbreak of World War I, during which Musil served as an officer in the Austro-Hungarian army at the Italian front. After the war Musil again took up his life between the German and Austrian capitals, writing prose and drama as well as essays, feuilletons, and literary and theater criticism: his *Drei Frauen* (Three women) was published in

1923, and the play *Die Schwärmer* (The enthusiasts) received the prestigious Kleist prize in 1924. His story "Die Amsel" (The blackbird), which appeard in the writer's 1935 collection *Nachlaß zu Lebzeiten,* attempts to find a literary form for the traumatic experience of war and is informed by Musil's immediate encounter with the overpowering impact of modern combat technology.

Musil's articles, essays, and literary texts are characterized by a radical openness toward the emerging culture of twentieth-century modernity. This openness also turned him into an ideological outsider and a maverick among German intellectuals: Musil never failed to emphasize the validity of scientific rationality, applied and theoretical, that was part of his heritage as a philosopher and engineer. Through his intellectual biography he was situated beyond the conventional antagonism of techno-rationality and classical German *Bildung* (education), and he never fell prey to the ideological temptations that were taking hold of the vanishing German bourgeoisie. For example, he rejected all distinctions between a traditional *Geist* (spirit), belonging to culture proper, and a merely instrumental, supposedly superficial modern *ratio* (reason). In contrast to cultural conservatives of all political colors, Musil also fully recognized the demise of nineteenth-century bourgeois culture in the face of a reality that embedded individual action in mass movements; that replaced the hollow concepts of fate or historical necessity by chance; and that became increasingly structured by technical media and their effects.

Throughout the 1920s Musil worked on his magnum opus, *Der Mann ohne Eigenschaften* (The man without qualities). The novel's first volume was published in 1930, marking a critical triumph for the author. The book portrays the Habsburg Monarchy's political disintegration and delineates more broadly the historical and epistemological ruptures that terminated the nineteenth century's order of knowledge and experience. *Der Mann ohne Eigenschaften* also offers a radical revision of literary storytelling and marks a qualitative break with Musil's earlier writings. Its critique of linear, anthropocentric narration leads to a mode of representation that no longer equates literary form with the depiction of narrative causality and character development. Rather, strands of contingencies produce narrative occurrences that are marked as possible but not necessary events. The book moves among a number of characters, thus producing a panorama of its time and locale. In addition, the novel consciously integrates essayistic passages that open zones of reflection in the midst of narration. The exploration of the probable and the possible—*das Mögliche*—is thus woven into the texture of a novel that is no longer classical.

In a sad irony, Musil's newly discovered art of charting the possible rather than the actual was echoed on a biographical level by his ongoing process of literary sketching and revision that only ended with the author's death. After the first part of the second volume of *Der Mann ohne Eigenschaften* appeared in 1932 Musil merely produced an enormous number of variations for potential chapters that did not make their way to publication until the mid-1950s. Musil did not live to see this moment when his oeuvre was rediscovered. His texts had been pushed into oblivion after the writer's political expulsion from the countries in which he lived and worked. When the National Socialists were elected in Germany, he left Berlin for Austria. In 1938 his native country joined the Third Reich, and *Der Mann ohne Eigenschaften* was banned. Musil emigrated to Switzerland, where he died in Geneva in 1942, in poverty.

See also **Germany.**

BIBLIOGRAPHY

Primary Sources

Musil, Robert. *Drei Frauen.* Reinbek bei Hamburg, Germany, 2001.

———. *Der Mann ohne Eigenschaften.* Reinbek bei Hamburg, Germany, 2001.

———. *Nachlaß zu Lebzeiten.* Reinbek bei Hamburg, Germany, 2001.

———. *Die Verwirrungen des Zöglings Törless.* Reinbek bei Hamburg, Germany, 2002.

Secondary Sources

Böhme, Hartmut. "Die 'Zeit ohne Eigenschaften' und die 'Neue Unübersichtlichkeit': Robert Musil und die Posthistoire." In *Kunst, Wissenschaft und Politik von Robert Musil bis Ingeborg Bachmann,* edited by Josef Strutz, 9–33. Munich, 1986. An overview that introduces the reader to the problem of contingency and the montage of various discourses in Musil's texts, as well as providing a comparison between Musil's works and postmodern philosophies.

Corino, Karl. *Robert Musil: Eine Biographie.* Reinbek bei Hamburg, Germany, 2003. The standard work by Musil's most important biographer.

Schöne, Albrecht. "Zum Gebrauch des Konjunktivs bei Robert Musil." In *Robert Musil,* edited by Renate von Heydebrand, 19–53. Darmstadt, Germany, 1982. A classical study of the use of the *potentialis*—the *Konjunktiv*—in Musil's texts and of the implications for the author's literary style.

Siegert, Bernhard. "Rauschfilterung als Hörspiel: Archäologie nachrichtentechnischen Wissens in Robert Musils 'Amsel.'" In *Robert Musil—Dichter, Essayist, Wissenschaftler,* edited by Hans-Georg Pott, 193–207. Munich, 1993. An exemplary reading of one of Musil's stories from the perspective of an archaeology of media and technology.

PHILIPP EKARDT

MUSSOLINI, BENITO (1883–1945), Fascist chief and head of the government in Italy from 1922 to 1945.

Benito Amilcare Andrea Mussolini was born at Dovia, an outlying settlement of the small town of Predappio, which lies on a spur of the Apennines not far from the city of Bologna. Mussolini's father, Alessandro, was prominent in local socialist politics and his mother, Rosa Maltoni, was a primary schoolteacher and pious Catholic. The young Mussolini began as a socialist but openly took a different line during the First World War when much of the purpose and behavior of what came to be called fascism was framed. In March 1919 the fascist movement was founded and it solidified into a party (the Partito Nazionale Fascista, PNF) during the second half of 1921. On 30 October 1922, at the age of thirty-nine, Mussolini became prime minister of Italy, the youngest in the country's history. On 3 January 1925 Mussolini announced his government had turned into a dictatorship. Thereafter he imposed tyrannical rule over his nation, boasting of framing the (first) "totalitarian state" and rejoicing in an unbounded personality cult that all but deified the *DUCE* (or Leader—the use of capitals became mandatory in the 1930s), as he was known.

After 1933 Mussolini had to measure himself against the Nazi dictatorship of Adolf Hitler, a man who frequently acknowledged his debt to the *Duce*

as a model in the führer's rise to power but who led a state that was more powerful and radical than was Mussolini's regime in Rome. By 1937 Fascist Italy and Nazi Germany were united in an unofficial alliance called the Axis, seemingly committed to overthrowing the "plutocratic" and parliamentary world order as well as to repelling the Soviet Union and international Marxism. In September 1939, however, Mussolini, in some embarrassment at his country's lack of military preparation, did not at first take Italy into the "War for Danzig." The sweeping German victories in the Low Countries and France in spring 1940 unleashed Mussolini, as the historian MacGregor Knox has put it. Italy entered the Second World War on 10 June and thereafter followed its German and Japanese allies into the wars against the Soviet Union and United States. Yet fascism's achievement at the various fronts scarcely matched regime rhetoric about a militarized nation that had finally become a genuine great power. Italian forces did win some short-term victories, but Italy was, by every index, no more than Nazi Germany's "ignoble second."

Public military humiliation and the inadequacy the dictatorship displayed in organizing its population and economy for modern war rapidly fretted the popular consent that the *Duce* had until then won from wide sections of Italian life. By the spring and early summer of 1943, Mussolini was willing to admit that he had become "the most hated man in Italy," and on 25 July, after a protracted meeting of the *Duce* and his longtime henchmen assembled in the Grand Council, the Fascist regime fell. King Victor Emmanuel III, who had remained constitutional head of state throughout the dictatorship, arrested Mussolini and replaced him as prime minister with Marshal Pietro Badoglio, the former chief of general staff.

The Mussolini story had a coda. On 8 September 1943, Badoglio bungled Italy's withdrawal from the war. As a result the country was occupied by the competing armies (the Germans coming from the north to Naples and beyond, the Allies moving forward from Salerno). Mussolini was rescued by an intrepid SS glider pilot from imprisonment at a mountain resort east of Rome. Taken to Germany, he was reunited with his family and soon agreed to being restored as leader of what was left of fascism. His new regime called itself the

Benito Mussolini addresses a huge crowd in Pistoia, Italy, during a tour of provincial cities, May 1930. ©BETTMANN/ CORBIS

Italian Social Republic (Repubblica Sociale Italiana, RSI). Mussolini based himself at the small town of Salò on Lago di Garda, between Milan and Verona and patently near the German world.

Now northern Italy became the site of a civil war while the Allied armies slowly pushed back the Germans. The RSI added its own brutality to the tally of previous Fascist killing fields where, especially as the result of aggressive war, the *Duce* bore responsibility for the deaths of at least one million people. At Salò, given formal respect but little else by his German masters, Mussolini swung from one rhetorical option to the next, but in practice he now had the bathetic fate of being a puppet dictator. The end came in April 1945, when the German forces dissolved. Mussolini moved from

his villa at Gargnano to Milan and thence to Como and an uncertain destination farther north. On 27 April he was recognized by partisans who had stopped a German military convoy fleeing toward the mountains. The next afternoon Mussolini, in the company of his last mistress, Claretta Petacci, was shot at the orders of the Anti-Fascist Committee of National Liberation. His body was thrown onto a truck and taken, along with those of Petacci and a number of executed Fascist chiefs, to a suburban square in Milan, the Piazzale Loreto. There the corpse was abused by the populace and eventually hung upside down outside some gas pumps as a traditional demonstration of the disdain the tyrant by now inspired in the people. The U.S. military authorities gave the body an autopsy and took away some brain matter, claiming they wanted to investigate whether the dictator had syphilis (with the imminent Cold War, they soon dropped the matter from their priorities). The rest of the *Duce* was buried secretly in Milan.

Still the story was not quite over. On 22 April 1946, Mussolini's corpse was kidnapped from its anonymous resting place by a squad of Fascist nostalgics, headed by Domenico Leccisi. They successfully hid the *Duce*'s remains until 11 August (and so through the political campaign during which Italians opted to replace the Savoy monarchy with a democratic republic). Again the dictator's remains were interred in Milan, now with a modest note of his name. It was not until 31 August 1957 that Mussolini finally returned to Predappio and was belatedly laid in the family tomb there. In the twenty-first century the place retains some ambiguity since it is a place of neo-Fascist pilgrimage. Such surviving remembrance suggests that Italians have not been fully successful in absorbing their recent history. Much reticence remains in comprehending the tragedies and disasters of the generation of Mussolinian and Fascist dictatorship.

So much is the basic detail of the Mussolini story. But what was Benito Mussolini like and what were his essential historical achievements? Or, rather, what effect did he as an individual have on Italian and world history?

FAMILY MAN

The first point to be made about Mussolini as a person is that he was not mad but rather displayed throughout his life many of the assumptions and much of the behavior of ambitious Italians of his era. Unlike Hitler, Mussolini was a "family man." In 1910 he had begun living with Rachele Guidi, seven years his junior and the daughter of his father's mistress from a family further down the village social scale than were the Mussolinis. By the end of that year their first child, Edda, had been born. At that stage the relationship between Benito Mussolini and Rachele Guidi was a socialist one, but in 1915 they were married in a state ceremony and their union received church sanctification in December 1925. Eventually the marriage produced four more offspring, three sons and another daughter. There were other complications.

It seems now established that, in some ceremony or other, Mussolini had earlier married Ida Dalser, a woman he had met while working as a socialist journalist in Trento. Dalser certainly produced a son, Benito Albino, in November 1915, acknowledged by the future dictator. Although Mussolini continued to contribute to their upkeep, neither mother nor son was destined for a happy life. Each died after being confined to a lunatic asylum, Dalser in 1937 and Benito Albino in 1942.

This blot on the family escutcheon, not to be mentioned once Mussolini was dictator, was dealt with by Mussolini's younger brother, Arnaldo (1885–1931). Arnaldo was somewhat better educated than Benito and, following conscription, served as a lieutenant in the First World War. Family hierarchy, however, was more powerful than that suggested by the state or by class. After 1919, while Benito rose to dominate the Fascist movement, Arnaldo was always somewhere near in the background, providing sensible advice, good contacts, and an open purse. When Mussolini became prime minister, he at once promoted his brother to the key position of editor of *Il Popolo d'Italia* (The people of Italy), his personal newspaper, founded in November 1914 when Mussolini had opted to back Italian intervention in the First World War and so broke with orthodox socialism. After 1922, still edited from Mussolini's first citadel in Milan, *Il Popolo d'Italia* became the official organ of the Fascist ideology and of the regime. Its financing, management, and line were crucial matters, details that could only be handed to Arnaldo—the one man, Mussolini would later remark regretfully after his brother's early death, he had ever trusted. Until 1931 the dictator and Arnaldo were accustomed to speaking on the phone each night.

Mussolini's private life remained bohemian, with his mistresses including Margherita Sarfatti, a wealthy Jewish Venetian who moved from socialism to fascism along with her younger lover. Sarfatti was also self-consciously intellectual. Under the dictatorship she was a major figure in the cultural world until overborne by the deepening anti-Semitism of the 1930s (then, Mussolini, no longer her lover, assisted her emigration to the United States). Mussolini had many other sexual partners, with whom any relationship was nasty,

Mussolini and Hitler watch a parade staged for the former's visit to Germany, October 1937. ©BETTMANN/CORBIS

brutish, and short. By the 1930s, as a sign of his own deteriorating health, Claretta Petacci, a starstruck and avaricious member of the Roman upper bourgeoisie, younger than Edda Mussolini, became the *Duce*'s semiofficial mistress, a tie that signaled his cynicism and misanthropy (and deepening depression).

INTELLECTUAL

In his halcyon days Mussolini had himself aspired to be a man of ideas. The forty-four volumes of his

"complete works" include a novel, a history of the Reformation preacher Jan Hus, and an autobiography, penned when he was not yet thirty years old (but exclude plays about Napoleon and Julius Caesar on which he collaborated once installed as dictator). Mussolini was first trained as an elementary and then middle school teacher of French and, unlike quite a few politicians between the wars, he retained some knowledge of French, German, and English. His potential as a pedagogue of the young, however, soon surrendered to his career as a political journalist. From editing such news sheets as the painfully Marxist *La Lotta di Classe* (The class struggle) in Forlì, in 1912 Mussolini took control of *Avanti!*, the national paper of the Italian socialist movement. Over the next two years he proved able in the job, quadrupling the paper's circulation through his trenchant writing and ruthless downsizing of staff. As a further sign of intellectual interest or aspiration, in 1913 he began editing a monthly, optimistically entitled *Utopia*.

This writing has led some commentators, notably the political scientist A. J. Gregor, to argue that Mussolini was a genuine man of ideas, an important and independent thinker whose eventual fascism was forged from the mixture of socialist, syndicalist, and nationalist theories that eddied around his mind and those of his contemporaries. For Gregor, as well for neo-Fascists and their friends in early-twenty-first-century Italy, Mussolini was one of the greatest political philosophers of the twentieth century.

More skeptical historians remained unconvinced. A review of Mussolini's numerous speeches and articles before his break with socialism over the war in October 1914 discloses many contradictions. They are scarcely surprising in an ambitious young man from the provinces who was blessed with some education and quite a bit of curiosity but scarcely possessed of a trained mind, while also always busy with political schemes, active sexuality, and family demands. The prewar Mussolini was able to mouth the phrases of more and less orthodox socialism, while never altogether renouncing his national identity as an Italian. But he was always more a Mussolinian than anything else.

Two points are fundamental here. Unlike Hitler, Mussolini was not entirely "made by the First World War." In 1914, although there was still much that was brittle about his achievement, he was doing well as a radical socialist. Fascism, by contrast, was forged in the war. After 1922, to a major degree Fascist rule was that of the nation's idiosyncratic First World War prolonged into peacetime. Mussolini and almost all of his henchmen were returned soldiers, bearers of a conflict they could not forget and so, as the historian Omer Bartov has put it with greater regard to Germany, men with "murder in their midst."

POLITICIAN AND FASCIST

During the campaign for Italian intervention in 1914–1915, Mussolini won some prominence because of the dramatic nature of his break with mainstream socialism and the aggression and activism of the first issues of *Il Popolo d'Italia*. In September 1915, however, he was in his turn conscripted. Although he retained a political profile, wrote a war diary (to become a much cherished text after 1922) and in 1917 was wounded, thereafter to resume his life as a journalist, in early 1919 Mussolini was scarcely the most prominent man in the Right's political firmament. There the basic medley of fascist ideas was coalescing: a defense of the war and its history; nationalism; a soldierly concept of welfare to the deserving; a fusion, replicating that in the army between hierarchy and individual opportunity and activity, united with a profound hostility to the antiwar orthodox socialists. In March 1919, a meeting at a building in the Piazza di San Sepolcro in Milan hailed the formation of bodies to be called *fasci di combattimento* (returned soldiers' leagues), with great local autonomy but with an announced national purpose of defending and expanding the territorial gains in the war and simultaneously fostering and enforcing the social unity then decreed mandatory.

In the succeeding months Mussolini emerged as the *Duce* of this still inchoate movement. His position with regard to the Fascists retained some ambiguity until the open proclamation of dictatorship in 1925. Before that, fascism rose to power and installed its leader as prime minister through a combination of brutally antisocialist (and sometimes anti-Catholic) social action in the provinces (especially in northern and central Italy) and adroit political negotiation, above and below the table, in Rome. Mussolini, the owner-editor of *Il Popolo d'Italia*, was the Fascist with national recognition; the *ras*, or local Fascist bosses of the provinces, were the men who imposed their version of order on their towns and their hinterlands.

After 1925 the dictatorship continued to possess what some have seen as a double face. There was plenty of accommodation with the existing elites. The Lateran Pacts of February 1929, resolving the "Roman question," that is, the relationship between church and state in a modern Italy, are the classic example, but so too is the way Mussolini, at

Italian premier Benito Mussolini shakes hands with British prime minister Neville Chamberlain after the signing of the Munich Agreement, September 1938. ©Hulton-Deutsch Collection/Corbis

least until 1943, accepted that King Victor Emmanuel III was head of state and that the army officer corps remained more monarchist than Fascist. Neither large landowners nor industrialists found that Mussolini's rule required much more sacrifice than that they don a Fascist black shirt on official occasions. Similarly, the personality cult (fascism was very much a "propaganda state") and Mussolini's personal rule (he was a hardworking executive) were countered by the talk about a Fascist Party revolution and the totalitarian intrusion of Fascist forms, practice, and mentality into all Italians' lives.

Although never officially clashing with the legal system inherited from the liberal regime before 1922 (many leading Fascists were lawyers by training and profession), Mussolini relied heavily on

his secret police and took very seriously his daily meetings with the police chief, Arturo Bocchini (d. 1940). After Arnaldo Mussolini, Bocchini was the figure whose advice the *Duce* followed most readily. Again the implications are ambiguous since Bocchini was a career official, a man who joked that his fascism did not extend below his waist, a lover of the good life and anything other than a true-believing Italian Himmler. Mussolini's secret police was designed to quiet the population, not to muster it into political or racial revolution.

Deciding whether Mussolini was a "weak" or "strong" dictator is thus a complex matter. It is clear that from time to time Mussolini made decisions and imposed them willy-nilly on his party colleagues and Italy (the high valuation of the lira in 1927 and the war against Ethiopia in 1935 are examples). Yet Mussolini also often told his listeners what they wanted to hear and was as likely to "work towards the Italians" as charismatically demand that they "worked towards him." He was, somewhere beneath the rhetoric about Fascist revolution, a more nervous figure than Hitler, and a politician who feared that a week was a long time in politics, more a tactician than a strategist. He was also, in almost every way, a disastrous failure in both his domestic and foreign policies. His version of fascism brought death and destruction to Italians and to those painted with rapid and peremptory strokes (Mussolini always rejoiced in his own "savagery") as their enemies.

See also **Fascism; Hitler, Adolf; Italy; Stalin, Joseph; Totalitarianism.**

BIBLIOGRAPHY

Primary Sources

Ciano, Galeazzo. *Diario 1937–1943*. Milan, 1980.

Mussolini, Benito. *Opera omnia*. Edited by Edoardo and Duilio Susmel. 36 vols. Florence, 1951–1962; *Appendici I–VIII* (vols. 37–44), Florence, 1978–1980.

Secondary Sources

Bosworth, Richard J. B. *The Italian Dictatorship: Problems and Perspectives in the Interpretation of Mussolini and Fascism*. London and New York, 1998.

———. *Mussolini*. London and New York, 2002.

———. *Mussolini's Italy: Life under the Fascist Dictatorship. 1915–1945*. London and New York, 2005.

Cannistraro, Philip, and Brian R. Sullivan. *Il Duce's Other Woman*. New York, 1993.

Clark, Martin. *Mussolini*. Harlow, U.K., 2005.

De Felice, Renzo. *Mussolini*. 7 vols. Turin, Italy, 1965–1997.

De Grazia, Victoria. *How Fascism Ruled Women: Italy 1922–1945*. Berkeley, Calif., 1992.

Knox, MacGregor. *Common Destiny: Dictatorship, Foreign Policy, and War in Fascist Italy and Nazi Germany*. Cambridge, U.K., and New York, 2000.

———. *Hitler's Italian Allies: Royal Armed Forces, Fascist Regime, and the War of 1940–1943*. Cambridge, U.K., and New York, 2000.

Passerini, Luisa. *Mussolini immaginario: Storia di una biografia 1915–1939*. Bari, Italy, 1991.

R. J. B. BOSWORTH

MYRDAL, GUNNAR (1898–1987), Nobel Prize–winning Swedish economist, politician, social scientist, and internationalist.

Gunner Myrdal early in his career established himself as one of the foremost proponents of the Stockholm school of thought in economics. In his thesis from 1927, *Prisbildningsproblemet och föränderligheten* (The price formation problem of variability), he emphasized the role of expectations in economic life, criticizing the static character of neoclassical equilibrium-oriented economics. In *Monetary Equilibrium* (1933) he introduced the *ex ante/ex post* distinction to overcome the deficiency in neoclassical economics. Another fundamental line of argument was his critique of conceptions of neutrality of social science: in *Vetenskap och politik i nationalekonomien* (1930) he criticized open and concealed value premises in prevailing economic theory. He further developed this critique in *The Political Element in the Development of Economic Theory* (1953).

ECONOMIST

As an economist Myrdal presented a very early theoretical underpinning for a counter-cyclical-oriented economic policy in *Konjunkturer och offentlig hushållning* (1933; Business cycles and public finance) and published an appendix to the Swedish government's budget proposition, emphasizing the need for state powers to counteract economic depression through increased public expenditure. Later, as chairman of Sweden's Postwar Economic Planning Commission (1944–1945) he further developed his analysis of financial policies, taking into account the larger possibilities opened up by an economic policy consciously geared toward macroeconomic growth. He was the main architect behind the formulation of full employment as an overarching goal of Swedish economic policy after World War II. Contemporary with but distinct from John Maynard Keynes, he argued for the role of investment levels as the key element of economic policy.

SOCIAL SCIENTIST

Myrdal's scientific and political work were to be intertwined from the 1930s on when he and his wife, Alva Myrdal, joined the Swedish Social Democracy. Together they gained considerable political influence, both as writers and as part of a larger network of modernizers. During the 1930s they were central to the reformulation of Swedish social policy. Starting with their *Kris i befolknings-frågan* (1934; The population problem in crisis), which challenged contemporary attitudes about racial biology, they advocated a "prophylactic social policy" focused on better housing, child allocations, and free school meals. Their ideas came to be the tenets of Swedish postwar welfare policies.

In 1938 Myrdal was chosen to be the director of an extensive research project on "Negro relations" sponsored by the Carnegie Foundation. It resulted in the publication of *An American Dilemma: The Negro Problem and Modern Democracy* (1944), a landmark study in U.S. sociology. Arguing that the problem did not concern the "other" but was central to the self-conception of U.S. society, a true dilemma for the "American creed" on which its constitution was based. Myrdal further developed these ideas in works on welfare problems including *Challenge to Affluence* (1963).

INTERNATIONALIST

During World War II, Myrdal developed close contacts with U.S. New Deal economists, and as chairman of the Commission for Economic Postwar Planning of the Swedish Commission he largely pursued their ideas in the economic planning for Sweden after the war. Internationalist in attitude, Myrdal worked with exiled Social Democrats in Sweden such as Willy Brandt and Bruno Kreisky on postwar reconstruction plans. He argued for a common all-European reconstruction effort and promoted the planning of vast Swedish government credits to support reconstruction efforts in neighboring countries.

In 1945 Myrdal became Sweden's minister of trade and promoted a broad trade policy, including agreements with Poland and the Soviet Union to open up world trade. With the onslaught of Cold War tensions these agreements—although ratified—became subject to heated domestic debate, and Myrdal personally came under fire. Partly because of this—but also because of tensions within the government—Myrdal resigned in 1947 to become executive secretary of the United Nations Economic Commission for Europe (ECE), a position he would hold for ten years. Myrdal developed the ECE into a first-rate analysis agency while at the same time facilitating East-West trade relations on a practical level.

Myrdal's later works concentrated on international development, trade, and cooperation issues (*Economic Theory and Development*, 1957; *Asian Drama*, 1968; *Challenge of World Poverty*, 1970), developing an institutional economic analysis and criticizing classic free-trade theory. In 1974 he was awarded the Nobel Prize in economics for his groundbreaking work in monetary and market theory and for his studies of the relationship between economic, social, and institutional conditions. Egalitarian in social politics and intellectually provocative, Myrdal was a heterodox Swedish social democrat, a radically liberal American, and a world citizen.

See also **Keynes, J. M.; Reconstruction; Sweden; United Nations and Europe.**

BIBLIOGRAPHY

Andersson, Stellan, and Örjan Appelqvist, eds. *The Essential Gunnar Myrdal*. Translated by Richard Litell, Sonia Wichmann, et al. New York, 2005.

ÖRJAN APPELQVIST

For Reference

Not to be taken from this room